UK Accounting Stand
and Company Law 2

CU00868999

**Permitted text for ICAEW 2017
Financial Accounting and Reporting
UK GAAP examinations**

UK Accounting Standards and Company Law 2016

Permitted text for ICAEW 2017
Financial Accounting and Reporting
UK GAAP examinations

 Wolters Kluwer

Disclaimer

This publication is sold with the understanding that neither the publisher nor ICAEW nor the authors are engaged in rendering legal or professional services. The material contained in this publication neither purports, nor is intended to be, advice on any particular matter.

Although this publication incorporates a considerable degree of standardisation, subjective judgment by the user, based on individual circumstances, is indispensable. This publication is an 'aid' and cannot be expected to replace such judgment.

Neither the publisher nor ICAEW nor the authors can accept any responsibility or liability to any person, whether a purchaser of this publication or not, in respect of anything done or omitted to be done by any such person in reliance, whether sole or partial, upon the whole or any part of the contents of this publication.

© 2016 Wolters Kluwer (UK) Ltd

Wolters Kluwer
145 London Road
Kingston upon Thames
KT2 6SR

ISBN 978-1-78540-349-1

British Library Cataloguing-in-Publication Data.

A catalogue record for this book is available from the British Library.

Typeset by Innodata Inc., India.

Printed in Spain by Rotabook, S.L.

UK Accounting Standards and Company Law 2016

Permitted text for ICAEW 2017 Financial Accounting and Reporting UK GAAP examinations

This publication is recommended for students sitting the Financial Accounting and Reporting – UK GAAP examinations in 2017.

The text may be annotated ONLY to the extent of underlining, sidelining and highlighting. Page tabs may be used, but must not be written on.

For more information on suggested texts and exam regulations, please visit icaew.com/exams.

Preface
Welcome to ICAEW

I am delighted that you have chosen ICAEW to progress your journey towards joining the chartered accountancy profession. It is one of the best decisions I also made.

The role of the accountancy profession in the world's economies has never been more important. People making financial decisions need knowledge and guidance based on the highest technical and ethical standards. ICAEW Chartered Accountants provide this better than anyone. They challenge people and organisations to think and act differently, to provide clarity and rigour, and so help create and sustain prosperity all over the world.

As a world leader of the accountancy and finance profession, we are proud to promote, develop and support over 146,000 chartered accountants worldwide. Our members have the knowledge, skills and commitment to maintain the highest professional standards and integrity. They are part of something special, and now, so are you. It's with our support and dedication that our members, and hopefully you, will realise career ambitions, maintain a professional edge and contribute to the profession.

You are in good company, with a network of over 28,000 students around the world made up of like-minded people. You are all supported by ICAEW. We are here to support you as you progress through your studies and career; we will be with you every step of the way. Visit icaew.com/dashboard to review the key resources available as you study.

I wish you the best of luck with your studies and look forward to welcoming you to the profession in the future.

Michael Izza
Chief Executive
ICAEW

Contents

Page

Preface   **vii**

Part One Accounting Standards (versions effective from 1/1/16)
Foreword to Accounting Standards   3
Overview of the financial reporting framework   7
FRS 100 Application of Financial Reporting Requirements   17
FRS 101 Reduced Disclosure Framework – Disclosure exemptions
     from EU-adopted IFRS for qualifying entities   51
Amendments to FRS 101 Reduced Disclosure Framework 2015/16 cycle   99
FRS 102 The Financial Reporting Standard applicable in the UK and
     Republic of Ireland   107
FRS 103 Insurance Contracts – Consolidated accounting and reporting
     requirements for entities in the UK and Republic of Ireland issuing
     insurance contracts   447
Amendments to FRS 103: Insurance Contracts – Solvency II   507
FRS 104 Interim Financial Reporting   525
FRS 105 The Financial Reporting Standard applicable to the
     Micro-entities Regime   567
Amendments to FRS 105: The Financial Reporting Standard applicable
     to the Micro-entities Regime – Limited Liability Partnerships and
     Qualifying Partnerships   677

Part Two Company Law
Large and Medium-sized Companies and Groups (Accounts and Reports)
     Regulations 2008 (SI 2008/410)   689
     Part 1 Introduction   690
     Part 2 Form and content of accounts   690
     Part 3 Directors' report   693
     Part 4 Directors' remuneration report   694
     Part 5 Interpretation   695
     Schedule 1 – Companies Act individual accounts: companies which
         are not banking or insurance companies   696
     Schedule 2 – Banking companies: Companies Act individual accounts   731
     Schedule 3 – Insurance companies: Companies Act individual accounts   773
     Schedule 4 – Information on related undertakings required whether
         preparing Companies Act or IAS accounts   820
     Schedule 5 – Information about benefits of directors   832
     Schedule 6 – Companies Act group accounts   839
     Schedule 7 – Matters to be dealt with in Directors' Report   853
     Schedule 8 – Quoted companies: Directors' Remuneration Report   862
     Schedule 9 – Interpretation of term "provisions"   891
     Schedule 10 – General interpretation   893
Companies Act 2006 – Extracts from Part 15 Accounts and Reports   897
     Chapter 1 – Introduction (Sections 380–385)   901
     Chapter 2 – Accounting Records (Sections 386–389)   908
     Chapter 3 – A Company's Financial Year (Sections 390–392)   911
     Chapter 4 – Annual Accounts (Sections 393–414)   913

Contents

Chapter 4A – Strategic report (Sections 414A–414D)   937

Chapter 5 – Directors' Report (Sections 415–419A)   939

Chapter 6 – Quoted Companies: Directors' Remuneration Report
(Sections 420–422A)   945

Chapter 7 – Publication of Accounts and Reports (Sections 423–436)   947

Chapter 8 – Public Companies: Laying of Accounts and Reports
Before General Meeting (Sections 437–438)   958

Chapter 9 – Quoted Companies: Members' Approval of Directors'
Remuneration Report (Sections 439–440)   959

Chapter 10 – Filing of Accounts and Reports (Sections 441–453)   961

Chapter 11 – Revision of Defective Accounts and Reports (Sections 454–462)   978

Chapter 12 – Supplementary Provisions (Sections 463–474)   989

Part One

Accounting Standards
(versions effective from 1/1/16)

Foreword to Accounting Standards

(March 2015)

Contents

Paragraphs

Foreword to Accounting Standards

Introduction 1–2
Scope of accounting standards 3–6
Authority for issuing accounting standards 7–8
Identification of accounting standards 9–12
Early adoption of Financial Reporting Exposure Drafts 13–15
Withdrawal of Foreword to Accounting Standards (issued November 2012) 16

Foreword to Accounting Standards

Introduction

1   This foreword explains the scope, authority and identification of accounting standards, issued by the Financial Reporting Council (FRC), for the purposes of the *Companies Act 2006* (the Act) and Regulations made thereunder.

2   This foreword relates to financial statements prepared in accordance with UK and Republic of Ireland legislation and accounting standards (for companies these are referred to in the Act as 'Companies Act accounts'). It does not apply to financial statements prepared in accordance with EU-adopted IFRS (for companies these are referred to in the Act as 'IAS accounts').

Scope of accounting standards

3   Directors of companies incorporated under the Act are required by the Act to prepare financial statements that give a true and fair view of:

(a)   the assets, liabilities and financial position of the company and, where relevant, the group at the end of the reporting period; and

(b)   the profit or loss of the company and, where relevant, the group for the reporting period.

In the case of a micro-entity, financial statements drawn up in accordance with the micro-entity provisions of company law are presumed to give a true and fair view.

4   Accounting standards are applicable to the financial statements of a reporting entity[1] that are required to give a true and fair view of its financial position at the reporting date[2] and of its profit or loss (or income and expenditure) for the reporting period.

5   The whole essence of accounting standards is to provide for recognition, measurement, presentation and disclosure for specific aspects of financial reporting in a way that reflects economic reality and hence provides a true and fair view.

6   More information about the 'true and fair' concept can be found on the FRC's website at   http://frc.org.uk/Our-Work/Codes-Standards/Accounting-and-Reporting-Policy/True-and-Fair.aspx.

Authority for issuing accounting standards

7   The FRC, in accordance with the *Statutory Auditors (Amendment of Companies Act 2006 and Delegation of Functions etc) Order 2012* (SI 2012/1741), is a prescribed body for issuing accounting standards in the UK. In the Republic of Ireland the accounting standards issued by the FRC are promulgated by the Institute of Chartered Accountants in Ireland (ICAI). The objective of the FRC and ICAI is a regime of accounting standards common to both the United Kingdom and the Republic of Ireland.

---

[1] *This includes entities incorporated under the Act and preparing Companies Act accounts, and also entities that are not constituted as companies, but are otherwise required to prepare financial statements that give a true and fair view.*

[2] *For companies this is the accounting reference date.*

In relation to the setting of accounting standards the FRC has identified that its objective **8** is to enable users of accounts to receive high-quality, understandable financial reporting proportionate to the size and complexity of the entity and users' information needs.

Identification of accounting standards

Accounting standards developed by the FRC will be designated Financial Reporting **9** Standards (FRSs)[3].

The FRC may issue FRSs that relate to other aspects of financial reporting, but which are **10** not accounting standards.

Each FRS will indicate its status, ie that it is an accounting standard or, if not, the **11** circumstances in which it may be applied. For the avoidance of doubt, those FRSs issued prior to the issue of this edition of the *Foreword to Accounting Standards* are accounting standards.

The FRC may issue other material with, or alongside, an FRS. This material is only part **12** of an accounting standard where it is identified as an integral part of an FRS that is an accounting standard.

Early adoption of Financial Reporting Exposure Drafts

An exposure draft is issued for comment and is subject to revision. Until it is finalised as **13** an accounting standard the requirements of any existing accounting standards that would be affected by proposals in the exposure draft remain in force.

Some reporting entities may wish to provide additional information reflecting proposals in **14** an exposure draft. In the FRC's view there are two ways that this can be achieved:

(a) Insofar as the information does not conflict with existing accounting standards, it could be incorporated into the financial statements. It should be remembered, however, that the proposals may change before forming part of an accounting standard and the consequences of a change to the proposals should be considered.
(b) The information could be provided in supplementary form.

Similar considerations apply to consultation documents or discussion documents issued by **15** the FRC, and to proposals to amend FRSs that are not accounting standards.

Withdrawal of Foreword to Accounting Standards (issued November 2012)

The *Foreword to Accounting Standards* issued by the FRC in November 2012 is superseded **16** by this Foreword and is accordingly withdrawn.

---

[3] *For accounting periods beginning on or after 1 January 2015, as set out in FRS 100 Application of Financial Reporting Requirements, a number of accounting standards were withdrawn. Some of these accounting standards did not have the designation FRS, but were nevertheless accounting standards and continue to be applicable to accounting periods beginning prior to 1 January 2015.*

Overview of the financial reporting framework

(July 2015)

Contents

	Paragraphs
1 Introduction	1.1–1.3
2 The financial reporting framework	2.1–2.10
UK and Ireland GAAP	2.4–2.6
The core UK GAAP and Ireland regimes	2.7–2.10
3 Key features of the core UK and Ireland GAAP regimes	3.1–3.12
FRS 102	3.1–3.2
The micro-entities regime (FRS 105)	3.3–3.6
Comparison to the FRSSE	3.7
The small entities regime (Section 1A *Small Entities* of FRS 102)	3.8–3.11
Comparison to the FRSSE	3.12
4 Additional options for entities that are part of a group	4.1–4.4

Appendix 1: Key differences between FRS 105 and the FRSSE

Appendix 2: Key differences between Section 1A *Small Entities* of FRS 102 and the FRSSE

1 Introduction

1.1   As a consequence of the changes to company law arising from the implementation of the EU Accounting Directive, it has been necessary to make amendments to UK and Republic of Ireland (RoI) accounting standards to ensure continued consistency between the revised legal frameworks and the financial reporting framework. This has also given the FRC the opportunity to reconsider the most appropriate way that accounting standards can support the new micro-entities regime.

1.2   The changes to company law predominantly affect the small companies regime, however other more minor amendments affect other aspects of UK and Republic of Ireland accounting standards.

1.3   This overview describes the financial reporting framework that will be applicable for accounting periods beginning on or after 1 January 2016 (early application is permitted subject to the provisions in each standard).

2 The financial reporting framework

2.1   Company law recognises two financial reporting frameworks – IFRS and UK and Ireland GAAP (generally accepted accounting practice).

2.2   Publicly listed companies are required to apply IFRS in the preparation of their group accounts but may choose between IFRS and UK and Ireland GAAP for the preparation of their individual parent accounts. Other entities have a free choice between the two frameworks.

2.3   FRS 100 *Application of Financial Reporting Requirements* sets out the overall framework, which can be illustrated as follows:

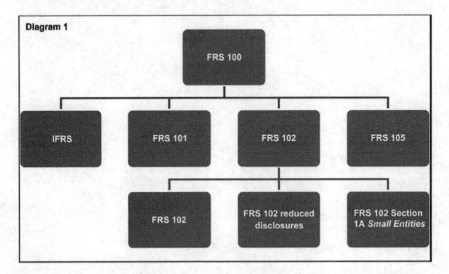

UK and Ireland GAAP

2.4   The UK and Ireland GAAP reporting framework is made up of five regimes, three of which are available within FRS 102 *The Financial Reporting Standard applicable in the UK and Republic of Ireland*. The other two are FRS 101 *Reduced Disclosure*

Framework and FRS 105 *The Financial Reporting Standard applicable to the Micro-entities Regime.*

Table 1: UK and Ireland GAAP					
Framework	**Micro-entities regime**	**Small entities regime**	**FRS 102**	**Reduced disclosure framework (FRS 101)**	**Reduced disclosures for subsidiaries and ultimate parents (FRS 102)**
Related accounting standard(s)	FRS 105	Section 1A *Small Entities* of FRS 102	FRS 102	FRS 101	Paragraphs 1.8 to 1.13 of FRS 102

Smaller entities have a choice between three core UK GAAP regimes subject to meeting relevant criteria: **2.5**

- the micro-entities regime (FRS 105);
- the small entities regime (Section 1A *Small Entities* of FRS 102); and
- FRS 102.

Entities that are part of a group may apply either of the reduced disclosure regimes. These additional options are discussed in more detail in Section 4 *Additional options for entities that are part of a group.*   **2.6**

The core UK GAAP and Ireland regimes

The financial reporting requirements of each standard get progressively more complex and comprehensive the further up the suite of standards you go. The increase in complexity correlates to the increasing size and complexity of the entities that are most likely to apply a given standard. In all cases, an entity may choose to opt up to a more comprehensive regime.   **2.7**

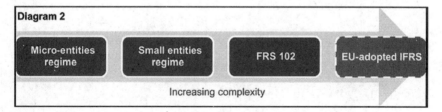

Diagram 2

Micro-entities regime   Small entities regime   FRS 102   EU-adopted IFRS

Increasing complexity

The selection of which regime to apply will depend on a number of factors including the following: **2.8**

- Whether an entity is eligible to apply that particular regime. Eligibility criteria may include the type of financial statements (ie individual or group) being prepared, size thresholds and entity type.
- Where a choice of regime exists, entities should consider which of the regimes is the most appropriate to the individual circumstances of the entity. Factors to consider will differ from entity to entity and may relate to certain characteristics or restrictions of a particular regime, the resources available and the information needs of users of the accounts, amongst many others.

2.9   The following table outlines the key eligibility criteria for the micro-entities and small entities regimes. Entities should refer to the detailed eligibility criteria in the relevant legislation in order to determine if they are eligible or not.

Table 2: UK Eligibility criteria		
Regime	**Micro-entities regime[1]**	**Small entities regime[2]**
Source of eligibility criteria	Sections 384A to 384B of the Companies Act 2006.	Sections 382 to 384 of the Companies Act 2006.
Eligible entities	• Companies only (Note: Whilst the legislation and consequently FRS 105 uses the term micro-entities regime, it is only currently available in law to companies.)	• Companies • Limited liability partnerships[3] • Any other type of entity that would have met the criteria of the small companies regime had it been a company incorporated under company law (for example charities)
Size thresholds	A company qualifies if it does not exceed two or more of the following criteria: • Turnover £632,000 • Balance sheet total £312,000 • No. of employees 10	A company[3] qualifies if it does not exceed two or more of the following criteria: • Turnover £10.2m • Balance sheet total £5.1m • No. of employees 50

[1] *For Irish entities, if legislation is enacted, the equivalent thresholds are: Turnover €700,000, Balance sheet total €350,000 and Number of employees 10.*

[2] *For Irish entities, qualification as a small company is set out in section 350 of The Companies Act 2014. The current equivalent size criteria are: Turnover not exceeding €8.8m, Balance Sheet total not exceeding €4.4m, and number of employees not exceeding 50. The equivalent thresholds after implementation of the EU Accounting Directive have not yet been set, however the limits in the Directive are: Turnover at or above €8m and not exceeding €12m; Balance sheet total at or above €4m and not exceeding €6m.*

[3] *As set out in the The Limited Liability Partnerships (Accounts and Audit) (Application of Companies Act 2006) Regulations 2008 (SI 2008/1911). The thresholds differ from those applicable to companies.*

Table 2: UK Eligibility criteria		
Regime	**Micro-entities regime[1]**	**Small entities regime[2]**
Ineligible entities	<ul><li>Any companies excluded from the small companies regime</li><li>Financial institutions including credit and insurance institutions</li><li>Charities</li><li>Small parent companies that choose to prepare group accounts</li><li>Companies that are not parent companies but their accounts are included in group accounts</li></ul>	<ul><li>Public companies</li><li>Financial institutions including insurance companies and banking companies</li></ul>

The following decision tree will help an entity identify the options that may be open to it in selecting its reporting regime: **2.10**

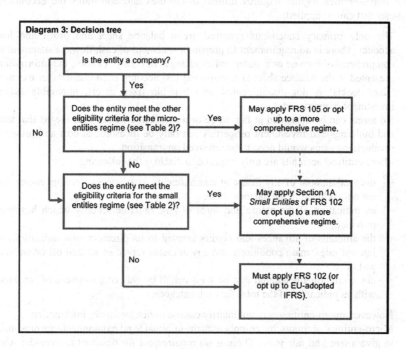

Diagram 3: Decision tree

3 Key features of the core UK and Ireland GAAP regimes

FRS 102

FRS 102 was first issued in March 2013 and is effective for accounting periods beginning on or after 1 January 2015. Subsequent amendments have revised it responding to both issues raised by stakeholders and changes in company law, with the most recent revision being in July 2015. For convenience, a revised edition of FRS 102 will be published periodically to   **3.1** incorporate any recent amendments, usually after any significant amendments have been issued.

3.2   FRS 102 replaced over 70 accounting standards and UITF Abstracts spanning more than 2,400 pages, with one succinct standard of a little over 300 pages. It reflects developments in the way businesses operate and uses up-to-date accounting treatment and language. One of the key improvements in financial reporting is that FRS 102 requires the recognition of financial instruments and disclosure of the risks associated with those instruments. It also improves intellectual mobility and reduces the costs of education and training.

The micro-entities regime (FRS 105)

3.3   Micro-entities are the smallest of entities (with turnover of up to £632,000) and a subset of small entities. The accounting standard for micro-entities, FRS 105, has been developed around the legal framework and simplified the requirements of FRS 102 for this group of entities.

3.4   Although FRS 105 is the least complex standard, every entity that is eligible to apply it should consider whether the regime meets its individual needs. It is important to remember that the micro-entities regime is optional even if an entity meets the eligibility criteria.

3.5   The micro-entities regime requires limited disclosures and constrains the accounting policies that can be applied:

- The only primary statements required are a balance sheet and profit and loss account. There is no requirement to prepare a statement of cash flows, a statement of comprehensive income or a statement of changes in equity. Further, the information presented in the balance sheet and profit and loss account is condensed (for example 'fixed assets' is not disaggregated into tangible fixed assets, intangible assets, investment properties etc).
- No assets can be measured at fair value or a revalued amount. This means that land and buildings and investment properties can only be measured at cost and previous revaluations gains would need to be removed on transition.
- Micro-entities' accounts are **only** required to disclose the following:

  − the total amount of any financial commitments, guarantees or contingencies that are not included in the balance sheet;
  − an indication of the nature and form of any valuable security which has been provided;
  − the amounts of advances and credits granted to its directors with indications of interest rates, main conditions and any amounts repaid or written off or waived; and
  − any commitments entered into on their behalf by way of guarantees of any kind, with an indication of the total for each category.

- However, micro-entities may voluntarily choose to disclose more information.
- Micro-entities' accounts that comply with the minimal legal requirements are presumed to give a true and fair view. There is no requirement for directors to consider what additional information may be needed in order for the accounts to give a true and fair view.

3.6   In addition to these legal constraints, FRS 105 is simplified further, for example:

- deferred tax and equity-settled share-based payments shall not be recognised; and
- all accounting policy choices have been removed, including the options to capitalise development costs and borrowing costs.

More detailed discussion of the additional simplifications can be found in FRS 105.

Comparison to the FRSSE

For entities previously applying the FRSSE, Appendix 1 to this document sets out the key **3.7**
differences between that standard and FRS 105. In the majority of instances, the accounting
treatment of FRS 105 is either simpler or the same as that of the FRSSE.

The small entities regime (Section 1A *Small Entities* of FRS 102)

The thresholds for the small entities regime have increased resulting in more entities **3.8**
qualifying as small.

Similarly to FRS 105, Section 1A *Small Entities* of FRS 102 has been developed around **3.9**
the legal framework from the requirements of FRS 102.

The requirements of the small entities regime are more comprehensive than the micro- **3.10**
entities regime and the recognition and measurement requirements of Section 1A are the
same as those set out in the rest of FRS 102. In relation to recognition and measurement,
key differences between the small entities regime and the micro-entities regime include the
use of fair value and revaluation accounting and the additional accounting requirements in
respect of derivatives, deferred tax and equity-settled share-based payments.

The law only mandates a limited number of specified disclosures. However, unlike the **3.11**
micro-entities regime, directors of small entities are legally obligated to prepare accounts
that give a true and fair view whereas micro-entity accounts are automatically presumed
to give a true and fair view if the legal minimum is adhered to. In practical terms this
will require more judgement of directors of small entities in considering what additional
information (if any) is needed to ensure the accounts give a true and fair view. Section 1A
of FRS 102 provides additional guidance to assist directors.

Comparison to the FRSSE

For entities previously applying the FRSSE, Appendix 2 to this document sets out the **3.12**
key differences between that standard and Section 1A of FRS 102. In the main, the
requirements of Section 1A and the FRSSE are the same. However, there are a handful of
key differences in accounting treatment between the two standards worth noting, including
the recognition of additional financial instruments such as derivatives like interest rate
swaps and foreign exchange contracts.

4 Additional options for entities that are part of a group

For entities that are part of a group and included in the consolidated financial statements **4.1**
(known as qualifying entities), UK and Ireland GAAP provides an additional two further
reporting regimes. Both regimes aim to make group reporting more efficient and cost-
effective by permitting consistent accounting policies to be applied across a group, but
with reduced disclosures.

Table 3: Eligibility criteria		
Regime	Reduced disclosure framework (FRS 101)	Reduced disclosures for subsidiaries and ultimate parents (FRS 102)
Source of eligibility criteria	Definition of a qualifying entity as set out in the glossary to FRS 101.	Definition of a qualifying entity as set out in the glossary to FRS 102.
Eligible entities	A member of a group: • where the parent prepares publicly available consolidated financial statements which are intended to give a true and fair view; and • that is included in the consolidation	A member of a group: • where the parent prepares publicly available consolidated financial statements which are intended to give a true and fair view; and • that is included in the consolidation
Size thresholds	None	None
Ineligible entities	Charities	None

4.2   Each regime is based on a different underlying reporting framework:

- FRS 101 *Reduced Disclosure Framework* is based on EU-adopted IFRS; whereas
- the reduced disclosures for subsidiaries and ultimate parents in FRS 102 are based on FRS 102.

4.3   In essence, entities applying either reduced disclosure regime are required to otherwise apply the underlying requirements of the related standard (ie EU-adopted IFRS or FRS 102) but are permitted to take advantage of certain disclosure exemptions.

4.4   Both reduced disclosure regimes are optional.

Appendix 1
Key differences between FRS 105 and the FRSSE

Table 4: Key differences between FRS 105 and the FRSSE	
Key features of FRS 105:	
Presumed true and fair view	Financial statements prepared in accordance with the legal requirements of the micro-entities regime are presumed to give a true and fair view, therefore directors are not required to consider what additional information is required for the financial statements of the entity to give a true and fair view. This is in contrast to the FRSSE where directors were legally obligated to ensure the financial statements provided a true and fair view.
Preparation of only two primary statements required	Micro-entities are only required to prepare a balance sheet and profit and loss account and not a statement of recognised gains and losses (STRGL) or a cash flow statement.
Significantly condensed formats of statements	The statutory formats for the balance sheet and profit and loss accounts are significantly condensed, for example 'current assets' is not disaggregated into stocks, debtors, investments and cash.
Significantly reduced number of disclosures	Micro-entities are only legally required to provide two disclosures, and are not required to provide any more. However, micro-entities can voluntarily provide more disclosures. This is in contrast to the FRSSE which mandates significantly more disclosures.
Simplified accounting treatment	FRS 105 has simplified the accounting treatment for some transactions. For example, micro-entities shall not account for deferred tax.
Fair value and revaluation accounting not permitted	Micro-entities are not permitted to fair value or revalue any assets or liabilities, therefore all assets and liabilities (such as land and buildings and investment properties) must be held at cost. This is in contrast to the FRSSE which permitted or required certain assets to be revalued.
No accounting policy choices	All accounting policy options have been removed. In general, the mandatory treatments result in earlier recognition of income / expenses in the profit and loss account rather than deferring on the balance sheet.
More helpful guidance included	In many instances, the requirements of FRS 105 do not differ from those of the FRSSE, but more guidance is provided in FRS 105 to help preparers apply and interpret the treatment required.
Not all company law requirements are reproduced	FRS 105 does not reproduce all the reporting requirements from company law applicable to micro-entities unlike the FRSSE, but does incorporate those relating to the financial statements. Micro-entities will need to satisfy themselves that they have met all their legal requirements.
Terminology used consistent with FRS 102	FRS 105 uses terminology consistent with FRS 102 such as 'statement of financial position' rather than 'balance sheet'. A table of equivalence is included in Appendix II to FRS 105 for convenience.

Appendix 2
Key differences between Section 1A
Small Entities of FRS 102 and the FRSSE

Table 5: Key differences between Section 1A of FRS 102 and the FRSSE	
Key features of Section 1A of FRS 102:	
Preparation of only two primary statements required	Small entities are only required to prepare a balance sheet and profit and loss account and not a statement of recognised gains and losses (STRGL) or a cash flow statement.
Reduced number of mandatory disclosures	Small entities are only legally required to provide a limited number of specified disclosures. However, directors of small entities are still required to ensure the financial statements provide a true and fair view and therefore must consider what additional information may be needed to achieve this and provide that information.
More helpful guidance included	In many instances, the requirements of Section 1A of FRS 102 do not differ from those of the FRSSE, however more guidance is provided in FRS 102 to help preparers apply and interpret the treatment required.
Improved reporting for financial instruments	FRS 102 will require recognition of some financial instruments that the FRSSE did not. In particular, small entities will need to recognise derivatives such as options, swaps and forward contracts at fair value.
Removal of contract rate accounting for foreign currency transactions	FRS 102 does not permit the use of contract rate accounting in relation to foreign currency transactions and a small entity must apply the hedge accounting requirements of FRS 102 instead if they wish to achieve similar accounting results.
Deferred tax arising on revaluations	FRS 102 requires small entities to recognise deferred tax arising on revaluations of fixed assets.
Addition of the performance method of accounting for government grants	FRS 102 permits an accounting policy choice between the accruals method (the method mandated in the FRSSE) and the performance method in relation to government grants. The performance method is simpler to apply and may lead to earlier recognition of income in the profit and loss account in some circumstances.
Gains / losses on investment properties recognised in profit or loss	FRS 102 requires that gains and losses on investment properties must be recognised in profit or loss, rather than in reserves as previously required by the FRSSE.
Not all company law requirements are reproduced	Section 1A of FRS 102 does not reproduce all the reporting requirements from company law applicable to small entities unlike the FRSSE, but does include those relating to the financial statements. Small entities will need to satisfy themselves that they have met all their legal requirements.
Terminology used consistent with FRS 102	Section 1A of FRS 102 uses terminology consistent with the rest of FRS 102 such as 'statement of financial position' rather than 'balance sheet'. A table of equivalence is included in Appendix III to FRS 102 for convenience.

FRS 100
Application of Financial Reporting Requirements

(September 2015)

Contents

	Paragraphs
Summary	
FRS 100 Application of Financial Reporting Requirements	
Objective	1
Scope	2
Abbreviations and definitions	3
Basis of preparation of financial statements	4
Application of statements of recommended practice (SORPs)	5–8
Statement of compliance	9
Date from which effective and transitional arrangements	10–13
Withdrawal of current accounting standards	14–15A
Application Guidance: The Interpretation of Equivalence	
Introduction	AG1–AG3
Section 401 of the Companies Act 2006	AG4–AG7
Equivalent disclosures are included in the consolidated financial statements of the group	AG8–AG10
Approval by the FRC	
The Accounting Council's Advice to the FRC to issue FRS 100	
Introduction	1–3
Advice	4–5
Background	6–9
A differential financial reporting system and the elimination of 'public accountability'	10–13
FRS 101 *Reduced disclosure framework*	14–15
FRS 102 *The Financial Reporting Standard applicable in the UK and Republic of Ireland*	16
The Financial Reporting Standard for Smaller Entities (FRSSE)	17–20
Statements of Recommended Practice (SORPs)	21–23
Clarification of equivalence	24
Withdrawn publications	25
Effective date and early application	26–27
Approval of this advice	28
The Accounting Council's Advice to the FRC to issue Amendments to FRS 100	
Introduction	1–4
Advice	5–7
Background	8–9
Objective	10–11

Small entities regime   12
Other minor amendments   13–14
Effective date   15
Approval of this Advice   16

Appendices
I   Glossary
II   Note on legal requirements
III   Previous consultations
IV   Republic of Ireland (RoI) legal references

FRS 100 *Application of Financial Reporting Requirements* is an accounting standard. It is issued by the Financial Reporting Council in respect of its application in the United Kingdom and promulgated by the Institute of Chartered Accountants in Ireland in respect of its application in the Republic of Ireland.

Summary

With effect from 1 January 2015 the Financial Reporting Council (FRC) revised financial **(i)** reporting standards for the United Kingdom and Republic of Ireland. The revision fundamentally reformed financial reporting, replacing the extant standards with five Financial Reporting Standards:

(a)   FRS 100 *Application of Financial Reporting Requirements*;
(b)   FRS 101 *Reduced Disclosure Framework*;
(c)   FRS 102 *The Financial Reporting Standard applicable in the UK and Republic of Ireland*;
(d)   FRS 103 *Insurance Contracts*; and
(e)   FRS 104 *Interim Financial Reporting*.

The FRC has also issued FRS 105 The *Financial Reporting Standard applicable to the Micro-entities Regime* to support the implementation of the new micro-entities regime.

The FRC's overriding objective in setting accounting standards is to enable users of **(ii)** accounts to receive high-quality understandable financial reporting proportionate to the size and complexity of the entity and users' information needs.

In meeting this objective, the FRC aims to provide succinct financial reporting standards **(iii)** that:

(a)   have consistency with international accounting standards through the application of an IFRS-based solution unless an alternative clearly better meets the overriding objective;
(b)   reflect up-to-date thinking and developments in the way entities operate and the transactions they undertake;
(c)   balance consistent principles for accounting by all UK and Republic of Ireland entities with practical solutions, based on size, complexity, public interest and users' information needs;
(d)   promote efficiency within groups; and
(e)   are cost-effective to apply.

The requirements in this Financial Reporting Standard (FRS) take into consideration the **(iv)** findings from all relevant consultations.

This FRS sets out the financial reporting requirements for UK and Republic of Ireland **(v)** entities. Financial statements (whether consolidated financial statements or individual financial statements) that are within the scope of this FRS must be prepared in accordance with the following requirements:

(a)   If the financial statements are those of an entity that is eligible to apply FRS 105, they may be prepared in accordance with that standard.
(b)   If the financial statements are those of an entity that is not eligible to apply FRS 105, or of an entity that is eligible to apply FRS 105 but chooses not to do so, they must be prepared in accordance with FRS 102, EU-adopted IFRS or, if the financial statements are the individual financial statements of a qualifying entity, FRS 101[1].

FRS 101 sets out a reduced disclosure framework which addresses the financial reporting **(vi)** requirements and disclosure exemptions for the individual financial statements of subsidiaries and ultimate parents that otherwise apply the recognition, measurement and disclosure requirements of EU-adopted IFRS.

---

[1] *Under company law in the Republic of Ireland, certain entities are permitted to prepare 'Companies Act accounts' using a financial reporting framework based on accounting standards other than those issued by the FRC.*

(vii)   FRS 102 is a single financial reporting standard that applies to the financial statements of entities that are not applying EU-adopted IFRS, FRS 101 or the FRSSE.

(viii)   FRS 105 sets out the financial reporting requirements for micro-entities, as defined by company law, choosing to apply the micro-entities regime.

(ix)   This edition of FRS 100 issued in September 2015 updates the edition of FRS 100 issued in November 2012 for the following:

   (a)   the withdrawal of FRS 27 *Life Assurance* (as set out in FRS 103 *Insurance Contracts* issued in March 2014);

   (b)   consequential amendments to FRS 102 included in FRS 104 *Interim Financial Reporting* issued in March 2015;

   (c)   *Amendments to FRS 100* issued in July 2015;

   (d)   an editorial amendment to paragraph A2.19 to include a reference to the Strategic Report; and

   (e)   some minor typographical or presentational corrections.

FRS 100
Application of Financial Reporting Requirements

Objective

The objective of this Financial Reporting Standard (FRS) is to set out the applicable 1
financial reporting framework for entities preparing financial statements in accordance
with legislation, regulations or accounting standards applicable in the United Kingdom
and Republic of Ireland.

Scope

This FRS applies to financial statements that are intended to give a true and fair view of 2
the assets, liabilities, financial position and profit or loss for a period.

Abbreviations and definitions

The terms **Accounting Directive, Act, date of transition, EU-adopted IFRS, financial** 3
institution, FRS 100, FRS 101, FRS 102, FRS 105, IAS Regulation, IFRS, individual
financial statements, public benefit entity, qualifying entity, small entity and **SORP**
are defined in the glossary included as Appendix I to this FRS.

Basis of preparation of financial statements

Financial statements (whether consolidated financial statements or individual financial 4
statements) that are within the scope of this FRS, and that are not required by the IAS
Regulation or other legislation or regulation to be prepared in accordance with EU-adopted
IFRS, must be prepared in accordance with the following requirements:

(a) If the financial statements are those of an entity that is eligible to apply FRS 105[2],
    they may be prepared in accordance with that standard;
(b) If the financial statements are those of an entity that is not eligible to apply FRS 105,
    or of an entity that is eligible to apply FRS 105 but chooses not to do so, they must[3]
    be prepared in accordance with FRS 102, EU-adopted IFRS[4] or, if the financial
    statements are the individual financial statements of a qualifying entity, FRS 101.[5]

Application of statements of recommended practice (SORPs)

If an entity's financial statements are prepared in accordance with FRS 102 SORPs will 5
apply in the circumstances set out in that FRS.

---

[2] *The eligibility criteria for applying FRS 105 are set out in legislation and FRS 105. In establishing whether the
eligibility criteria have been met turnover and balance sheet total shall be measured in accordance with FRS 105;
the measurement of turnover and balance sheet total in accordance with FRS 101 or FRS 102 need not be considered.*

[3] *Under company law in the Republic of Ireland, certain entities are permitted to prepare 'Companies Act accounts'
using a financial reporting framework based on accounting standards other than those issued by the FRC.*

[4] *Some entities are prohibited from applying EU-adopted IFRS, for example section 395(2) of the Act states that 'the
individual accounts of a company that is a charity must be Companies Act individual accounts', and section 403(3)
of the Act mirrors this for the group accounts of a parent company that is a charity.*

[5] *Individual accounts that are prepared by a company in accordance with FRS 101, FRS 102 or FRS 105 are
Companies Act individual accounts (section 395(1)(a) of the Act), whereas individual accounts that are prepared by
a company in accordance with EU-adopted IFRS are IAS individual accounts (section 395(1)(b) of the Act).*

6   When a SORP applies, an entity, other than a small entity applying the small entities regime in FRS 102, shall state in its financial statements the title of the SORP and whether its financial statements have been prepared in accordance with the SORP's provisions that are currently in effect[6]. In the event of a departure from those provisions, the entity shall give a brief description of how the financial statements depart from the recommended practice set out in the SORP, which shall include:

    (a)   for any treatment that is not in accordance with the SORP, the reasons why the treatment adopted is judged more appropriate to the entity's particular circumstances; and

    (b)   brief details of any disclosures recommended by the SORP that have not been provided, and the reasons why they have not been provided.

A small entity applying the small entities regime in FRS 102 is encouraged to provide these disclosures.

7   SORPs recommend particular accounting treatments and disclosures with the aim of narrowing areas of difference and variety between comparable entities. Compliance with a SORP that has been generally accepted by an industry or sector leads to enhanced comparability between the financial statements of entities in that industry or sector. Comparability is further enhanced if users are made aware of the extent to which an entity complies with a SORP, and the reasons for any departures. The effect of a departure from a SORP need not be quantified, except in those rare cases where such quantification is necessary for the entity's financial statements to give a true and fair view.

8   Entities whose financial statements do not fall within the scope of a SORP may, if the SORP is otherwise relevant to them, nevertheless choose to comply with the SORP's recommendations when preparing financial statements, provided that the SORP does not conflict with the requirements of the framework adopted. Where this is the case, entities are encouraged to disclose that fact.

Statement of compliance

9   Where an entity prepares its financial statements in accordance with FRS 101 or FRS 102, it shall include a statement of compliance in the notes to the financial statements in accordance with the requirements set out in the relevant standard unless it is a small entity applying the small entities regime in FRS 102, in which case it is encouraged to include a statement of compliance in the notes to the financial statements.

Date from which effective and transitional arrangements

10   An entity shall apply this FRS for accounting periods beginning on or after 1 January 2016. Early application of this FRS is permitted, providing an entity also applies the edition of FRS 101, FRS 102 and FRS 105 effective for accounting periods beginning on or after 1 January 2016 and is subject to the early application provisions set out in those standards. An entity choosing not to apply these amendments to accounting periods beginning before 1 January 2016 shall not adopt the associated amendments made to FRS 101, FRS 102 nor FRS 105 to accounting periods beginning before 1 January 2016. If an entity applies this FRS before 1 January 2016 it shall disclose that fact, unless the entity is a micro-entity or a small entity. A small entity is encouraged to provide this disclosure.

---

[6] *The provisions of a SORP will cease to have effect, for example, to the extent that they conflict with a more recent financial reporting standard.*

On first-time application of this FRS, or when an entity changes the basis of preparation of **11** its financial statements within the requirements of this FRS, it shall apply the transitional arrangements relevant to its circumstances as follows:

(a) An entity transitioning to EU-adopted IFRS shall apply the transitional arrangements set out in IFRS 1 *First-time Adoption of International Financial Reporting Standards* as adopted by the EU.

(b) A qualifying entity transitioning to FRS 101 shall, unless it is applying EU-adopted IFRS prior to the date of transition (see paragraph 12), apply the requirements of paragraphs 6 to 33 of IFRS 1 as adopted by the EU including the relevant appendices except for the requirement of paragraphs 6 and 21 to present an opening statement of financial position at the date of transition; references to IFRSs in IFRS 1 are interpreted to mean EU-adopted IFRS as amended in accordance with paragraph 5(b) of FRS 101.

(c) An entity transitioning to FRS 102 shall apply the transitional arrangements set out in that standard.

(d) An entity transitioning to FRS 105 shall apply the transitional arrangements set out in FRS 105.

A qualifying entity applying EU-adopted IFRS prior to the date of transition to FRS 101 will **12** then be preparing Companies Act individual accounts in accordance with section 395(1)(a) of the Act and thus will no longer be preparing IAS individual accounts in accordance with section 395(1)(b) of the Act.[7] It shall consider whether amendments are required to comply with paragraph 5(b) of FRS 101, but it does not reapply the provisions of IFRS 1. Where amendments to the recognition, measurement and disclosure requirements of EU-adopted IFRS in accordance with paragraph 5(b) of FRS 101 are required, the entity shall determine whether the amendments have a material effect on the first financial statements presented. Where there is:

(a) no material effect, the qualifying entity shall disclose that it has undergone transition to FRS 101 and a brief narrative of the disclosure exemptions adopted, for all periods presented; or

(b) a material effect, the qualifying entity's first financial statements shall include:

(i) a description of the nature of each material change in accounting policy;

(ii) reconciliations of its equity determined in accordance with EU-adopted IFRS to its equity determined in accordance with FRS 101 for both the date of transition to FRS 101 and for the end of the latest period presented in the entity's most recent annual financial statements prepared in accordance with EU-adopted IFRS; and

(iii) a reconciliation of the profit or loss determined in accordance with EU-adopted IFRS to its profit or loss determined in accordance with FRS 101 for the latest period presented in the entity's most recent annual financial statements prepared in accordance with EU-adopted IFRS.

Where paragraph 12(b) applies but it is impracticable to apply the amendments **13** retrospectively, a qualifying entity shall apply the amendments to the earliest period for which it is practicable to do so, and it shall identify the data presented for prior periods that are not comparable with data for the period in which it prepares its first financial statements that conform with the reduced disclosure framework set out in FRS 101.

---

[7] *Further relevant information can be found at paragraph A2.14 of Appendix II.*

Withdrawal of current accounting standards

14 The following SSAPs, FRSs and UITF Abstracts are superseded on the early application of this FRS. These SSAPs, FRSs and UITF Abstracts will be withdrawn for accounting periods beginning on or after 1 January 2015.

SSAP 4	*Accounting for government grants;*
SSAP 5	*Accounting for value added tax;*
SSAP 9	*Stocks and long-term contracts;*
SSAP 13	*Accounting for research and development;*
SSAP 19	*Accounting for investment properties;*
SSAP 20	*Foreign currency translation;*
SSAP 21	*Accounting for leases and hire purchase contracts; including the Guidance Notes on SSAP 21;*
SSAP 25	*Segmental reporting;*
FRS 1	*Cash flow statements (revised 1996);*
FRS 2	*Accounting for subsidiary undertakings;*
FRS 3	*Reporting financial performance;*
FRS 4	*Capital instruments;*
FRS 5	*Reporting the substance of transactions;*
FRS 6	*Acquisitions and mergers;*
FRS 7	*Fair values in acquisition accounting;*
FRS 8	*Related party disclosures;*
FRS 9	*Associates and joint ventures;*
FRS 10	*Goodwill and intangible assets;*
FRS 11	*Impairment of fixed assets and goodwill;*
FRS 12	*Provisions, contingent liabilities and contingent assets;*
FRS 13	*Derivatives and other financial instruments: disclosures;*
FRS 15	*Tangible fixed assets;*
FRS 16	*Current tax;*
FRS 17	*Retirement benefits;*
FRS 18	*Accounting policies;*
FRS 19	*Deferred tax;*
FRS 20 (IFRS 2)	*Share-based payment;*
FRS 21 (IAS 10)	*Events after the balance sheet date;*
FRS 22 (IAS 33)	*Earnings per share;*
FRS 23 (IAS 21)	*The effects of changes in foreign exchange rates;*
FRS 24 (IAS 29)	*Financial reporting in hyperinflationary economies;*
FRS 25 (IAS 32)	*Financial instruments: Presentation;*
FRS 26 (IAS 39)	*Financial instruments: Recognition and Measurement;*
FRS 27	*Life Assurance;*
FRS 28	*Corresponding amounts;*
FRS 29 (IFRS 7)	*Financial instruments: Disclosures;*
FRS 30	*Heritage assets;*

UITF Abstract 4:   *Presentation of long-term debtors in current assets;*

UITF Abstract 5:   *Transfers from current assets to fixed assets;*

UITF Abstract 9:   *Accounting for operations in hyper-inflationary economies;*

UITF Abstract 11:   *Capital instruments: Issuer call options;*

UITF Abstract 15:   *Disclosure of substantial acquisitions (Revised 1999);*

UITF Abstract 19:   *Tax on gains and losses on foreign currency borrowings that hedge an investment in a foreign enterprise;*

UITF Abstract 21:   *Accounting issues arising from the proposed introduction of the euro;*

UITF Abstract 22:   *The acquisition of a Lloyd's business;*

UITF Abstract 23:   *Application of the transitional rules in FRS 15;*

UITF Abstract 24:   *Accounting for start-up costs;*

UITF Abstract 25:   *National Insurance contributions on share option gains;*

UITF Abstract 26:   *Barter transactions for advertising;*

UITF Abstract 27:   *Revision to estimates of the useful economic life of goodwill and intangible assets;*

UITF Abstract 28:   *Operating lease incentives;*

UITF Abstract 29:   *Website development costs;*

UITF Abstract 31:   *Exchanges of businesses or other non-monetary assets for an interest in a subsidiary, joint venture or associate;*

UITF Abstract 32:   *Employee benefit trusts and other intermediate payment arrangements;*

UITF Abstract 34:   *Pre-contract costs;*

UITF Abstract 35:   *Death-in-service and incapacity benefits;*

UITF Abstract 36:   *Contracts for sales of capacity;*

UITF Abstract 38:   *Accounting for ESOP trusts;*

UITF Abstract 39:   *(IFRIC Interpretation 2) Members' shares in co-operative entities and similar instruments;*

UITF Abstract 40:   *Revenue recognition and service contracts;*

UITF Abstract 41:   *(IFRIC Interpretation 8) Scope of FRS 20 (IFRS 2);*

UITF Abstract 42:   *(IFRIC Interpretation 9) Reassessment of embedded derivatives;*

UITF Abstract 43:   *The interpretation of equivalence for the purposes of section 228A of the Companies Act 1985;*

UITF Abstract 44:   *(IFRIC Interpretation 11) FRS 20 (IFRS 2) Group and Treasury Share Transactions;*

UITF Abstract 45:   *(IFRIC Interpretation 6) Liabilities arising from participating in a specific market – Waste electrical and electronic equipment;*

UITF Abstract 46:   *(IFRIC Interpretation 16) Hedges of a net investment in a foreign operation;*

UITF Abstract 47:   *(IFRIC Interpretation 19) Extinguishing financial liabilities with equity instruments;* and

UITF Abstract 48:   *Accounting implications of the replacement of the retail prices index with the consumer prices index for retirement benefits.*

15   The following statements are also withdrawn:

Statement of Principles for Financial Reporting;
Statement of Principles for Financial Reporting – Interpretation for public benefit entities;
Reporting Statement: Retirement Benefits – Disclosures;
Reporting Statement: Preliminary announcements; and
Reporting Statement: Half-yearly financial reports.

15A   The *Financial Reporting Standard for Smaller Entities* (effective January 2015) (FRSSE) is superseded on the early application of the amendments set out in *Amendments to FRS 100* (and the related amendments to other accounting standards, particularly FRS 102 and FRS 105) issued in July 2015 and the early application of *The Companies, Partnerships and Groups (Accounts and Reports) Regulations 2015* (SI 2015/980) and is withdrawn for accounting periods beginning on or after 1 January 2016.

Application Guidance: The Interpretation of Equivalence

This application guidance forms an integral part of FRS 100

Introduction

Section 401 of the Act exempts, subject to certain conditions, an intermediate parent AG1
from the requirement to prepare consolidated financial statements where its parent is not
established under the law of an EEA state. The exemption is conditional on the company
and all of its subsidiaries being included in consolidated financial statements for a larger
group drawn up to the same date, or an earlier date in the same financial year, and those
financial statements must be drawn up:

(a)   in accordance with, or in a manner that is equivalent to, the Accounting Directive
      (Section 401(2)(b)(i) and (ii));
(b)   in accordance with EU-adopted IFRS (Section 401(2)(b)(iii)); or
(c)   in accordance with accounting standards which are equivalent to EU-adopted
      IFRS, as determined in accordance with the EU mechanism (see paragraph AG7)
      (Section 401(2)(b)(iv)).

FRS 101 and FRS 102 permit certain exemptions from disclosures, but those exemptions AG2
are in some cases subject to **equivalent** disclosures being included in the consolidated
financial statements of the group in which the entity is consolidated.

This Application Guidance provides guidance on interpreting the meaning of equivalence AG3
in the two circumstances set out above.

Section 401 of the Companies Act 2006

Use of the exemption in section 401(2)(b)(ii) requires an analysis of a particular set of AG4
consolidated financial statements to determine whether they are drawn up in a manner
equivalent to consolidated financial statements that are drawn up in accordance with the
Accounting Directive. This Application Guidance aims to assist entities in adopting a
consistent approach to this issue. In the absence of this guidance, companies and their
auditors might feel obliged to take an overly cautious approach in response to uncertainty
about whether the exemptions can be used.

It is generally accepted that the reference to equivalence in section 401(2)(b)(ii) of the Act AG5
does not mean compliance with every detail of the Accounting Directive. When assessing
whether consolidated financial statements of a higher non-EEA parent are drawn up in a
manner equivalent to consolidated financial statements drawn up in accordance with the
Accounting Directive, it is necessary to consider whether they meet the basic requirements
of the Accounting Directive; in particular the requirement to give a true and fair view,
without implying strict conformity with each and every provision. A qualitative approach
is more in keeping with the deregulatory nature of the exemption than a requirement to
consider the detailed requirements on a checklist basis.

The consequences of the exemptions in section 401(2)(b) and adopting the principle in AG6
paragraph AG5 in relation to section 401(2)(b)(ii) are that consolidated financial statements
of the higher parent will meet the exemption or the test of equivalence in the Accounting
Directive if they are intended to give a true and fair view and:

(a)   are prepared in accordance with FRS 102;
(b)   are prepared in accordance with EU-adopted IFRS;

(c)   are prepared in accordance with IFRS, subject to the consideration of the reasons for any failure by the European Commission to adopt a standard or interpretation; or

(d)   are prepared using other GAAPs which are closely related to IFRS, subject to consideration of the effect of any differences from EU-adopted IFRS.

Consolidated financial statements of the higher parent prepared using other GAAPs or the IFRS for SMEs should be assessed for equivalence with the Accounting Directive based on the particular facts, including the similarities to and differences from the Accounting Directive.

AG7   A mechanism to determine the equivalence of the Generally Accepted Accounting Principles (GAAP) from third countries was established in 2007. Subsequently, the European Commission has identified as equivalent to IFRS the following:

GAAP	Applicable from
GAAP of Japan	1 January 2009
GAAP of the United States of America	1 January 2009
GAAP of the People's Republic of China	1 January 2012
GAAP of Canada	1 January 2012
GAAP of the Republic of Korea	1 January 2012

Further, third country issuers shall be permitted to prepare their annual consolidated financial statements and half-yearly consolidated financial statements in accordance with the Generally Accepted Accounting Principles of the Republic of India for financial years starting before 1 January 2015. For reporting periods beginning on or after 1 January 2015, in relation to GAAP of the Republic of India, equivalence should be assessed on the basis of the particular facts.

Equivalent disclosures are included in the consolidated financial statements of the group

AG8   In deciding whether the consolidated financial statements of the parent provide disclosures which are equivalent to the requirements of EU-adopted IFRS or FRS 102, from which relief is provided in paragraphs 8 to 9 of FRS 101 and paragraphs 1.12 to 1.13 of FRS 102 respectively, it is necessary to consider whether the consolidated financial statements of the parent provide disclosures that meet the basic disclosure requirements of the relevant standard or interpretation issued (or adopted) by the relevant standard setter, without requiring strict conformity with each and every disclosure. This assessment should be based on the particular facts, including the similarities to and differences from the requirements of the relevant standard from which relief is provided.

AG9   The concept of 'equivalence' described in paragraph AG8 is intended to be aligned to that described for section 401 of the Act.

AG10   Disclosure exemptions for subsidiaries are permitted where the relevant disclosure requirements are met in the consolidated financial statements, even where the disclosures are made in aggregate or in an abbreviated form, or in relation to intra-group balances, those intra-group balances have been eliminated on consolidation. If, however, no disclosure is made in the consolidated financial statements on the grounds of materiality, the relevant disclosures should be made at the subsidiary level if material in those financial statements.

Approval by the FRC

Financial Reporting Standard 100 *Application of Financial Reporting Requirements* was approved for issue by the Board of the Financial Reporting Council on 1 November 2012, following its consideration of the Accounting Council's advice for this FRS.

Amendments to FRS 100 Application of Financial Reporting Requirements was approved for issue by the Board of the Financial Reporting Council on 1 July 2015, following its consideration of the Accounting Council's Advice.

The Accounting Council's Advice to the FRC to issue FRS 100

Introduction

1   This report provides an overview of the main issues which have been considered by the Accounting Council in advising the Financial Reporting Council (FRC) to issue FRS 100 *Application of Financial Reporting Requirements*. The FRC, in accordance with the *Statutory Instrument Statutory Auditors (Amendment of Companies Act 2006 and Delegation of Functions etc) Order 2012* (SI 2012/1741), is the prescribed body for issuing accounting standards in the UK. *The Foreword to Accounting Standards* sets out the application of accounting standards in the Republic of Ireland.

2   In accordance with *FRC Codes and Standards: procedures*, any proposal to issue, amend or withdraw a code or standard is put to the FRC with the full advice of the relevant Councils and/or the Codes & Standards Committee. Ordinarily, the FRC will only reject the advice put to it where:

- it is apparent that a significant group of stakeholders has not been adequately consulted;
- the necessary assessment of the impact of the proposal has not been completed, including an analysis of costs and benefits;
- insufficient consideration has been given to the timing or cost of implementation; or
- the cumulative impact of a number of proposals would make the adoption of an otherwise satisfactory proposal inappropriate.

3   The FRC has established the Accounting Council as the relevant Council to assist it in the setting of accounting standards.

Advice

4   The Accounting Council is advising the FRC to issue:

FRS 100 *Application of Financial Reporting Requirements*; and
FRS 101 *Reduced Disclosure Framework*.

5   FRS 102 *The Financial Reporting Standard Applicable in the UK and Republic of Ireland* completes the new suite of financial reporting standards. The Accounting Council will provide its advice to the FRC on FRS 102 in that standard.

Background

6   Accounting standards were formerly developed by the Accounting Standards Board (ASB). The ASB commenced its project to update accounting standards in 2002; Appendix III provides a history of the previous consultations and a summary of how the overall proposals have developed.[8]

7   The ASB (and subsequently the Accounting Council) gave careful consideration to the project's objective and intended effects during its consultations on updating accounting standards. In developing the requirements in this FRS, FRS 101 and FRS 102, the overriding objective is:

> To enable users of accounts to receive high-quality understandable financial reporting proportionate to the size and complexity of the entity and users' information needs.

[8] *References in this section and Appendix III are made to the FRC, ASB or Accounting Council, as appropriate in terms of the time period and context of the reference.*

In achieving this objective, the ASB decided (and the Accounting Council subsequently **8** agreed) that it should provide succinct financial reporting standards that:

- have consistency with global accounting standards through the application of an IFRS-based solution unless an alternative clearly better meets the overriding objective;
- reflect up-to-date thinking and developments in the way businesses operate and the transactions they undertake;
- balance consistent principles for accounting by all UK and Republic of Ireland entities with practical solutions, based on size, complexity, public interest and users' information needs;
- promote efficiency within groups; and
- are cost-effective to apply.

The requirements in this FRS were principally consulted on in two exposure drafts; **9** FRED 43 *Application of Financial Reporting Requirements* issued in October 2010, and FRED 46 *Application of Financial Reporting Requirements* (revised) issued in January 2012.

A differential financial reporting system and the elimination of 'public accountability'

In the early stages of developing this FRS, the ASB consulted on whether to introduce a **10** differential financial reporting system. A differential system requires an entity to apply specified accounting standards as prescribed based on the size, nature or other differentiating feature of the entity. FRED 43 set out proposals for a differential financial reporting system based on three tiers of entities using public accountability and size as differentiators. The proposals in FRED 43 would have extended the application of EU-adopted IFRS to those entities with public accountability[9]. Whilst there was some support for a differential financial reporting system, entities that would be required to apply EU-adopted IFRS did not support the proposal, principally on the basis of costs and benefits.

The ASB gave careful consideration to the concerns raised and concluded that public **11** accountability (and therefore the differential financial reporting system) could be eliminated if it were to extend the proposals by including additional requirements in FRED 44 *Financial Reporting Standard for Medium-sized Entities* for entities with publicly traded debt or equity, and for financial institutions, so that the proposals in that FRED applied to a broader group of entities. FRED 44 proposed to replace the majority of extant financial reporting standards with a single standard based on the International Financial Reporting Standard for Small and Medium-sized Entities (IFRS for SMEs). As a consequence, FRED 44 was revised and FRED 48 issued, which addressed a broader group of entities including those previously considered to have public accountability, single entities listed on a regulated market, entities listed on a non-regulated market and additional disclosure requirements for financial instruments held by financial institutions.

Respondents to FRED 46 supported the removal of the public accountability criteria **12** and the Accounting Council agreed to advise the FRC not to extend the application of EU-adopted IFRS beyond that already required by company law or other legislation or regulation.

---

[9] *FRED 43 defined an entity as having public accountability if:*
(a) *as at the reporting date, its debt or equity instruments are traded in a public market or it is in the process of issuing such instruments for trading in a public market (a domestic or foreign stock exchange or an over-the-counter market, including local and regional markets); or*
(b) *as one of its primary businesses, it holds assets in a fiduciary capacity for a broad group of outsiders and/or it is a deposit taking entity for a broad group of outsiders. This is typically the case for banks, credit unions, insurance companies, securities brokers/dealers, mutual funds or investment banks.*

13   Once this FRS becomes effective, there will be five FRSs applicable in the UK and Republic of Ireland:

- FRS 100 *Application of Financial Reporting Requirements;*
- FRS 101 *Reduced Disclosure Framework;*
- FRS 102 *The Financial Reporting Standard applicable in the UK and Republic of Ireland;*
- *Financial Reporting Standard for Smaller Entities* (effective January 2015) (the FRSSE); and
- FRS 27 *Life assurance.*[10]

FRS 101 *Reduced disclosure framework*

14   FRS 101 was developed in response to concerns that arose from earlier consultations (see Appendix III). Respondents to those consultations (and particularly the 2009 Policy Proposal) noted that a move to the IFRS for SMEs for subsidiaries of entities that apply EU-adopted IFRS would require recognition and measurement differences to be monitored and maintained at group level, and yet the alternative of a move to EU-adopted IFRS would increase disclosure in comparison to current accounting standards. The ASB therefore developed a reduced disclosure framework to address these concerns.

15   Further details regarding the development of FRS 101 are located in the Accounting Council's Advice to the FRC accompanying that FRS.

FRS 102 *The Financial Reporting Standard applicable in the UK and Republic of Ireland*

16   FRS 102 will replace the majority of current accounting standards applicable in the UK and Republic of Ireland with a single FRS based on the IFRS for SMEs. Details of the development of FRS 102 will be set out in the Accounting Council's Advice to the FRC accompanying that FRS. One member of the Accounting Council considers that the level of input from users does not constitute adequate consultation, despite extensive efforts at outreach, and holds an alternative view on aspects of the Accounting Council's expected advice on FRS 102.

The Financial Reporting Standard for Smaller Entities (FRSSE)

17   The Accounting Council advises the FRC (consistent with FREDs 43 and 46) to retain the FRSSE for a period following the application of FRS 102, with a view to consulting again on the FRSSE's future in the short to medium term.

18   The eligibility criteria for applying the FRSSE are set out in paragraph 8 of the FRSSE. One of the criteria is that the entity must be 'small' as defined in company law. Turnover and balance sheet total should be measured in accordance with the FRSSE for the purposes of establishing whether the entity is 'small'; the measurement of turnover and balance sheet total in accordance with FRS 101 or FRS 102 need not be considered.

19   The Accounting Council also advises the FRC to undertake further consultation to address the implications for the FRSSE of:

(a)   the European Commission proposals arising from its review of the EU Accounting Directives (an initial proposed Directive was issued in October 2011); and

---

[10] *At the time of approving this advice consideration is being given to updating FRS 27.*

(b) the Directive on annual accounts of micro-entities that was approved by the European Council in February 2012.

The amendments to the FRSSE set out in this FRS arise as a consequence of withdrawing current accounting standards.   **20**

Statements of Recommended Practice (SORPs)

In its 2009 Policy Proposal, the ASB's recommendation was to remove almost all of the   **21**
SORPs. Respondents to the Policy Proposal questioned this and many noted that SORPs contribute to improving the quality of financial reporting in the UK. Instead FRED 43 proposed to streamline the number of SORPs in existence. Respondents to FRED 43 were supportive of this revised proposal. The decision, however, to eliminate the definition of public accountability and thereby broaden the scope of entities eligible to apply FRS 102 had a consequential impact on the SORPs (for example, pension funds would no longer be required to apply EU-adopted IFRS), so the ASB amended its proposals again in FRED 48.

The proposals in FRED 48 received support and the Accounting Council is now advising   **22**
the FRC that they be taken forward, as follows:

SORP	Accounting Council Advice
Accounting for insurance business	A separate consultation will be undertaken on accounting for insurance
Accounting for oil & gas	The SORP-making body has indicated that they do not believe that it would make sense to update the 2001 SORP
Authorised funds	Update to be based on FRS 102
Banking segments	Withdraw
Charities	Update to be based on FRS 102
Financial reports of pension funds	Update for consistency with FRS 102 to supplement Section 34 of FRS 102
Further and higher education	Update to be based on FRS 102
Investment companies	Update to be based on FRS 102
Leasing	Withdraw
Limited liability partnerships	Update to be based on FRS 102
Registered social housing providers	Update to be based on FRS 102

In response to a request for clarification as to the role of the SORPs, the Accounting   **23**
Council is advising the FRC that a reference to the application of SORPs be included in this FRS and in Section 10 *Accounting policies, estimates and errors* of FRS 102, to note that they are a source of guidance on accounting policies.

Clarification of equivalence

FRS 101 and FRS 102 permit certain exemptions from disclosures, which are in some cases   **24**
subject to equivalent disclosures being included in the consolidated financial statements of the group in which the entity is consolidated. Clarification on interpreting the meaning of the term equivalence is included in Application Guidance I of this FRS.

Withdrawn publications

25   Paragraph 14 of this FRS sets out the withdrawal of current accounting standards. For the avoidance of doubt, the Accounting Council (and FRC) will also not proceed with developing the following superseded Financial Reporting Exposure Drafts (FREDs):

> Leases: Implementation of a new approach
> IASB Exposure draft of a proposed IFRS for small and medium-sized entities (Issued April 2007)
> FRED 22 *Revision of FRS 3 Reporting financial performance*
> FRED 28 *Inventories: Construction and service contracts*
> FRED 29 *Property, plant and equipment: Borrowing costs*
> FRED 32 *Disposal of non-current assets and presentation of discontinued operations*
> FRED 36 *Business combinations*
> FRED 37 *Intangible assets (IAS 38) and FRED 38 Impairment of assets (IAS 36)*
> FRED 39 *Amendments to FRS 12 Provisions, contingent liabilities and contingent assets and FRS 17 Retirement benefits*
> FRED 43 *Application of Financial Reporting Requirements*
> FRED 44 *The Financial Reporting Standards for Medium-sized Entities*
> FRED 45 *The Financial Reporting Standard for Public Benefit Entities*

Effective date and early application

26   In reassessing the effective date as proposed in FREDs 46 to 48, the Accounting Council supports the previous view of the ASB that application should be deferred to January 2015 for the following reasons:

(a)   although the revisions to the ASB's original proposals should ease the transition, an 18 month period between the publication of the final standard and effective date should be retained as there are significant changes to the accounting requirements for financial instruments; and

(b)   the effective date should take into consideration the process of updating the SORPs.

27   This decision was reassessed by the Accounting Council when it considered the responses to FREDs 46 to 48. It decided that it was not necessary to have the same early application provisions for FRS 101, FRS 102 and the FRSSE (effective January 2015) and that specific requirements relating to early application should be set out separately in each standard.

Approval of this advice

28   This advice to the FRC was approved by the nine members of the Accounting Council on 25 October 2012. The Accounting Council is comprised of the following members:

Roger Marshall   (Chair of the Accounting Council)
Nick Anderson
Dr Richard Barker
Edward Beale
Peter Elwin
Ken Lever
Robert Overend
Andy Simmonds
Pauline Wallace

The Accounting Council's Advice to the FRC to issue Amendments to FRS 100

Introduction

This report provides an overview of the main issues that have been considered by the   1
Accounting Council in advising the Financial Reporting Council (FRC) to issue
Amendments to FRS 100 Application of Financial Reporting Requirements incorporating
the Council's advice following the Consultation Document *Accounting standards for small
entities – Implementation of the EU Accounting Directive* and FRED 60 *Draft amendments
to FRS 100 and FRS 101.*

The FRC, in accordance with the *Statutory Auditors (Amendment of Companies Act 2006*   2
and Delegation of Functions etc) Order 2012 (SI 2012/1741), is a prescribed body for
issuing accounting standards in the UK. The *Foreword to Accounting Standards* sets out
the application of accounting standards in the Republic of Ireland.

In accordance with the *FRC Codes and Standards: procedures*, any proposal to issue,   3
amend or withdraw a code or standard is put to the FRC Board with the full advice of the
relevant Councils and/or the Codes & Standards Committee. Ordinarily, the FRC Board
will only reject the advice put to it where:

(a)   it is apparent that a significant group of stakeholders has not been adequately
      consulted;
(b)   the necessary assessment of the impact of the proposal has not been completed,
      including an analysis of costs and benefits;
(c)   insufficient consideration has been given to the timing or cost of implementation; or
(d)   the cumulative impact of a number of proposals would make the adoption of an
      otherwise satisfactory proposal inappropriate.

The FRC has established the Accounting Council as the relevant Council to assist it in the   4
setting of accounting standards.

Advice

The Accounting Council is advising the FRC to issue *Amendments to FRS 100 Application*   5
of Financial Reporting Requirements.

The Accounting Council advises that these proposals will update the framework of   6
accounting standards and maintain consistency of accounting standards with company law.

The Accounting Council's Advice to the FRC to issue FRS 100 *Application of Financial*   7
Reporting Requirements was set out in the standard. The Accounting Council's Advice to
the FRC in respect of these amendments will be included in the revised FRS 100.

Background

The new EU Accounting Directive (Directive 2013/34/EU of the European Parliament and   8
of the Council of 26 June 2013) is being implemented in the UK and Republic of Ireland.
In doing so there are changes to company law to reflect new requirements and, where
considered appropriate, to take advantage of new options that are available. Accounting
standards are developed within the context of company law and amendments are also
required to accounting standards.

9   In September 2014, the FRC issued a Consultation Document *Accounting standards for small entities – Implementation of the EU Accounting Directive*[11] (the Consultation Document), outlining its proposal that the *Financial Reporting Standard for Smaller Entities* (FRSSE) would be withdrawn. A small number of amendments to FRS 100 would also be necessary to maintain consistency with company law. The Accounting Council considered the responses to the Consultation Document in developing FRED 60 *Draft amendments to FRS 100 and FRS 101*. It has also considered the responses to FRED 60, which was issued in February 2015, in developing its advice on these amendments.

Objective

10   In developing its advice to the FRC, the Accounting Council was guided by the overriding objective to enable users of accounts to receive high-quality understandable financial reporting proportionate to the size and complexity of the entity and users' information needs.

11   In meeting this objective, the FRC aims to provide succinct financial reporting standards that:

   (a)   have consistency with international accounting standards through the application of an IFRS-based solution unless an alternative clearly better meets the overriding objective;

   (b)   reflect up-to-date thinking and developments in the way entities operate and the transactions they undertake;

   (c)   balance consistent principles for accounting by all UK and Republic of Ireland entities with practical solutions, based on size, complexity, public interest and users' information needs;

   (d)   promote efficiency within groups; and

   (e)   are cost-effective to apply.

Small entities regime

12   In the Consultation Document and FRED 60 the FRC proposed that the FRSSE should be withdrawn and that it should be replaced with:

   (a)   a new standard for micro-entities, FRS 105 *The Financial Reporting Standard applicable to the Micro-entities Regime*; and

   (b)   for small entities ineligible for or choosing not to apply the micro-entities regime, it should be replaced with a new Section 1A *Small Entities* within FRS 102.

This proposal was supported by respondents and the Accounting Council advises that the FRSSE is withdrawn, with consequential amendments made to FRS 100 *Application of Financial Reporting Requirements* to set out the revised framework.

Other minor amendments

13   The Accounting Council advises that other minor amendments are made to FRS 100 for compliance with company law. This principally relates to the *Application Guidance: The Interpretation of Equivalence*.

14   One respondent to FRED 60 requested clarification relating to the meaning of equivalent disclosures included in the consolidated financial statements in relation to intra-group balances eliminated on consolidation. The Accounting Council agreed that this could

[11] *Available on the FRC website (www.frc.org.uk).*

usefully be clarified whilst amendments were being made to the *Application Guidance: The Interpretation of Equivalence* and advises that it is made clear that, provided relevant disclosures have been made in the consolidated financial statements, the exemption is permitted when intra-group balances have been eliminated on consolidation. This is, of course, subject to any disclosures that are required by law.

Effective date

The Accounting Council advises that the amendments to FRS 100 arising from the **15** implementation of the new Accounting Directive are effective for accounting periods beginning on or after 1 January 2016, with early application available providing an entity also applies the edition of FRS 101, FRS 102 or FRS 105 effective for accounting periods beginning on or after 1 January 2016 and subject to the early application provisions set out in those standards.

Approval of this Advice

This advice to the FRC was approved by the Accounting Council on 4 June 2015.   **16**

Appendix I: Glossary

Accounting Directive	**Directive 2013/34/EU of the European Parliament and of the Council of 26 June 2013**
Act	The Companies Act 2006
date of transition	The beginning of the earliest period for which an entity presents full comparative information under a given standard in its first financial statements that comply with that standard.
EU-adopted IFRS	IFRS that have been adopted in the European Union in accordance with EU Regulation 1606/2002.

financial institution	Any of the following:
	(a) a bank which is:
	    (i) a firm with a Part IV permission[12] which includes accepting deposits and:
	        (a) which is a credit institution; or
	        (b) whose Part IV permission includes a requirement that it complies with the rules in the General Prudential sourcebook and the Prudential sourcebook for Banks, Building Societies and Investment Firms relating to banks, but which is not a building society, a friendly society or a credit union;
	    (ii) an EEA bank which is a full credit institution;
	(b) a building society which is defined in section 119(1) of the Building Societies Act 1986 as a building society incorporated (or deemed to be incorporated) under that act;
	(c) a credit union, being a body corporate registered under the Industrial and Provident Societies Act 1965 as a credit union in accordance with the Credit Unions Act 1979, which is an authorised person;
	(d) custodian bank, broker-dealer or stockbroker;
	(e) an entity that undertakes the business of effecting or carrying out insurance contracts, including general and life assurance entities;
	(f) an incorporated friendly society incorporated under the Friendly Societies Act 1992 or a registered friendly society registered under section 7(1)(a) of the Friendly Societies Act 1974 or any enactment which it replaced, including any registered branches;
	(g) an investment trust, Irish investment company, venture capital trust, mutual fund, exchange traded fund, unit trust, open-ended investment company (OEIC);
	(h) a retirement benefit plan; or
	(i) any other entity whose principal activity is to generate wealth or manage risk through financial instruments. This is intended to cover entities that have business activities similar to those listed above but are not specifically included in the list above.
	
	A parent entity whose sole activity is to hold investments in other group entities is not a financial institution.

[12] *As defined in section 40(4) of the Financial Services and Markets Act 2000 or references to equivalent provisions of any successor legislation.*

FRS 100	FRS 100 *Application of Financial Reporting Requirements*
FRS 101	FRS 101 *Reduced Disclosure Framework*
FRS 102	FRS 102 *The Financial Reporting Standard applicable in the UK and Republic of Ireland*
FRS 105	FRS 105 *The Financial Reporting Standard applicable to the Micro-entities Regime*
IAS Regulation	EU Regulation 1606/2002
IFRS	Standards and interpretations issued (or adopted) by the International Accounting Standards Board (IASB). They comprise: (a) International Financial Reporting Standards; (b) International Accounting Standards; and (c) Interpretations developed by the IFRS Interpretations Committee (the Interpretations Committee) or the former Standing Interpretations Committee (SIC).
individual financial statements	The accounts that are required to be prepared by an entity in accordance with the **Act** or relevant legislation, for example: (a) 'individual accounts', as set out in section 394 of the Act; (b) 'statement of accounts', as set out in section 132 of the Charities Act 2011; or (c) 'individual accounts', as set out in section 72A of the Building Societies Act 1986. Separate financial statements are included in the meaning of this term.
public benefit entity	An entity whose primary objective is to provide goods or services for the general public, community or social benefit and where any equity is provided with a view to supporting the entity's primary objectives rather than with a view to providing a financial return to equity providers, shareholders or members.
qualifying entity (for the purposes of FRS 100 and FRS 101)	A member of a group where the parent of that group prepares publicly available consolidated financial statements which are intended to give a true and fair view (of the assets, liabilities, financial position and profit or loss) and that member is included in the consolidation[13]. A charity may not be a qualifying entity.
small entity	(a) A company meeting the definition of a small company as set out in section 382 or 383 of the **Act** and not excluded from the small companies regime by section 384; (b) an LLP qualifying as small and not excluded from the small LLPs regime, as set out in LLP Regulations; or (c) any other entity that would have met the criteria in (a) had it been a company incorporated under company law.
Statement of Recommended Practice (SORP)	An extant Statement of Recommended Practice developed in accordance with *SORPs: Policy and Code of Practice*. SORPs recommend accounting practices for specialised industries or sectors. They supplement accounting standards and other legal and regulatory requirements in the light of the special factors prevailing or transactions undertaken in a particular industry or sector.

[13] *As set out in section 474(1) of the Act.*

Appendix II: Note on legal requirements

INTRODUCTION

A2.1 This appendix provides an overview of how the requirements in FRS 100 address United Kingdom company law requirements. It is therefore written from the perspective of a company to which the Companies Act 2006 applies[14]. Appendix IV discusses the Republic of Ireland legal references.

A2.2 Many entities that are not constituted as companies apply accounting standards promulgated by the FRC for the purposes of preparing financial statements that present a true and fair view. A brief consideration of the legal framework for some other entities can be found at A2.20 and A2.21. For those entities that are within the scope of a SORP, the relevant SORP may provide more details on the legal framework.

A2.3 References to the Act in this appendix are to the *Companies Act 2006*. References to the Regulations are to *The Large and Medium-sized Companies and Groups (Accounts and Reports) Regulations 2008* (SI 2008/410).

Applicable accounting framework

A2.4 Group accounts of certain parent entities (those with securities admitted for trading on a regulated market in an EU Member State) are required by Article 4 of EU Regulation 1606/2002 (IAS Regulation) to be prepared in accordance with EU-adopted IFRS.

A2.5 All other entities, except those that are eligible and choose to apply FRS 105 *The Financial Reporting Standard applicable to the Micro-entities Regime*, must apply either FRS 102 *The Financial Reporting Standard applicable in the UK and Republic of Ireland*, EU-adopted IFRS or, for financial statements that are the individual financial statements of a qualifying entity, FRS 101 *Reduced Disclosure Framework*[15].

A2.6 Section 395(1) of the Act states:
A company's individual accounts may be prepared–

(a) in accordance with section 396 ('Companies Act individual accounts'), or

(b) in accordance with international accounting standards ('IAS individual accounts').

Section 403(2) of the Act states:
The group accounts of other companies may be prepared–

(a) in accordance with section 404 ('Companies Act group accounts'), or

(b) in accordance with international accounting standards ('IAS group accounts').

A2.7 Accounts prepared in accordance with EU-adopted IFRS are therefore within the scope of the IAS Regulation. All other accounts are classified as either 'Companies Act individual accounts', including those of qualifying entities applying FRS 101, or 'Companies Act group accounts' and are therefore required to comply with the applicable provisions of Parts 15 and 16 of the Act and with the Regulations.

---

[14] *Some charities are also companies, and are therefore required to apply the requirements of both the Companies Act 2006 and the Charities Act 2011.*

[15] *Under company law in the Republic of Ireland, certain companies are permitted to prepare Companies Act accounts using a financial reporting framework based on accounting standards other than those issued by the FRC.*

Financial reporting by small entities

The Small Companies and Groups (Accounts and Directors' Report) Regulations 2008 **A2.8**
(SI 2008/409) set out the legal framework for both the micro-entities regime and the
small companies regime, with the eligibility criteria for both set out in Part 15 of the Act.
FRS 105 and FRS 102 contain notes on legal requirements applicable to these regimes.

[Deleted]   **A2.9**

[Deleted]   **A2.10**

[Deleted]   **A2.11**

[Deleted]   **A2.12**

Financial reporting by charitable companies

Section 395(2) of the Act states that 'the individual accounts of a company that is a charity **A2.13**
must be Companies Act individual accounts', and section 403(3) of the Act mirrors this for
a parent company that is a charity.

Moving between IAS accounts and Companies Act accounts

Sections 395 and 403 of the Act restrict an entity's ability to move from preparing IAS **A2.14**
individual accounts to preparing Companies Act individual accounts and from preparing
IAS group accounts to preparing Companies Act group accounts respectively. A company
or group is permitted to switch from IAS accounts to Companies Act accounts preparation:

(a)   if there is a 'relevant change in circumstance' (as defined in the Act); or
(b)   for financial years ending on or after 1 October 2012, for a reason other than a
      relevant change of circumstance, once in a five year period.[16]

For example, provided the condition in section 395(4A) is met, a subsidiary company **A2.15**
which previously prepared IAS individual accounts is permitted to move to preparing
Companies Act individual accounts in applying FRS 101 or FRS 102, providing it is also
complying with other requirements of the Act, such as those relating to consistency of
financial reporting within groups

Consistency of financial reporting within groups

Section 407 of the Act requires that the directors of the parent company secure that **A2.16**
individual accounts of a parent company and each of its subsidiaries[17] are prepared using
the same financial reporting framework, except to the extent that in the directors' opinion
there are good reasons for not doing so.

In addition, consistency is not required in the following situations:

(a)   when the parent company does not prepare consolidated accounts; or
(b)   when some subsidiaries are charities (consistency is not needed between the
      framework used for these and for other subsidiaries).

---

[16] *The Companies and Limited Liability Partnership (Accounts and Audit Exemptions and Change of Accounting
Framework) Regulations 2012 (SI 2012/2301).*

[17] *This only applies to accounts of subsidiaries that are required to be prepared under Part 15 of the Act.*

Where the directors of a parent company prepare IAS group accounts and IAS individual accounts, there only has to be consistency across the individual financial statements of the subsidiaries.

A2.17   All companies, other than those which elect or are required to prepare IAS individual accounts in accordance with law, prepare Companies Act individual accounts.

Applicability of UK company law to entities preparing IAS accounts

A2.18   Entities that prepare IAS accounts, either voluntarily or because they are required to do so by law, only need apply certain sections of the Act as it relates to financial reporting. They are not required to comply with Schedules 1 and 6 to the Regulations (for companies and groups), nor with Schedules 2 or 3 (for banks and insurance companies). Schedules 4, 5, 7 and 8 to the Regulations are, however, still applicable.

A2.19   The sections of parts 15 and 16 of the Act that contain financial reporting requirements applying to IAS accounts, as well as to Companies Act accounts, are as follows (in some cases the requirements only apply to companies meeting certain criteria):

Section 410A	*Off-balance sheet arrangements*;
Section 411	*Employee numbers and costs*;
Section 412	*Directors' benefits: Remuneration*;
Section 413	*Directors' benefits: Advances, credit and guarantees*;
Sections 414A to 414D	*Strategic Report*;
Sections 415 to 419	*Directors' Report*;
Sections 420 to 421	*Directors' Remuneration Report*; and
Section 494	*Services provided by auditor and associates and related remuneration.*

Entities not subject to company law

A2.20   Many entities that may apply FRS 102 are not companies, but are nevertheless required by their governing legislation or other regulation or requirement, to prepare financial statements that present a true and fair view of the financial performance and financial position of the reporting entity. However, the FRC sets accounting standards within the framework of the Act and therefore it is the company law requirements that the FRC primarily considered when developing FRS 102. Entities preparing financial statements within other legal frameworks will need to satisfy themselves that FRS 102 does not conflict with any relevant legal obligations.

A2.21   However, the FRC notes the following:

Legislation	Overview of requirements
Building Societies Act 1986	The annual accounts of a building society shall give a true and fair view of the income and expenditure for the year and the balance sheet shall give a true and fair view of the state of affairs of the society at the end of the financial year. Regulations make further requirements about the form and content of building society accounts, which do not appear inconsistent with the requirement of FRS 102.
Charity law in England and Wales: Charities Act 2011 and regulations made thereunder	All charities are required to prepare accounts. The regulations require financial statements (other than cash-based receipts and payments accounts prepared by smaller charities) to present a true and fair view of the incoming resources, application of resources and the balance sheet, and to be prepared in accordance with the SORP. However company charities prepare their accounts in accordance with UK company law to give a 'true and fair view'. The Charities SORP (FRS 102) is compatible with the legal requirements, clarifying how they apply to accounting by charities applying FRS 102. UK Company law prohibits charities from preparing IAS accounts.
Charity law in Scotland: Charities and Trustee Investments Act (Scotland) 2005 and regulations made thereunder	All charities are required to prepare accounts. The regulations require financial statements (other than cash-based receipts and payments accounts prepared by smaller charities) to present a true and fair view of the incoming resources, application of resources and the balance sheet, and to be prepared in accordance with the SORP. These regulations apply equally to company charities.
Charity law in Northern Ireland: Charities Act (Northern Ireland) 2008	The Charities Act 2008 has yet to come fully into effect. The Act provides for all charities to prepare accounts. The Act provides for regulations concerning the financial statements. The financial statements other than cash-based receipts and payments accounts prepared by smaller charities are to present a true and fair view of the incoming resources, application of resources and the balance sheet. However company charities prepare their accounts in accordance with UK company law to give a 'true and fair view'.
Friendly and Industrial and Provident Societies Act 1968	Every Society shall prepare a revenue account and a balance sheet giving a true and fair view of the income and expenditure and state of affairs of the Society. FRS 102 does not appear to give rise to any legal conflicts for Societies. However, Societies often carry out activities that are regulated and may be required to comply with additional regulations on top of the legal requirements and accounting standards. Some Societies fall within the scope of SORPs, which reflect the requirements of FRS 102.

Legislation	Overview of requirements
Friendly Societies Act 1992	Every society shall prepare a balance sheet and an income and expenditure account for each financial year giving a true and fair view of the affairs of the society and its income and expenditure for the year. The Regulations[18] make further requirements about the form and content of friendly society accounts, which do not appear inconsistent with the requirements of FRS 102.
The Occupational Pension Schemes (Requirement to obtain Audited Accounts and a Statement from the Auditor) Regulations 1996	The accounts of pension funds within the scope of the regulations should show a true and fair view of the transactions during the year, assets held at the end of the year and liabilities of the scheme, other than those to pay pensions and benefits. FRS 102 includes retirement benefit plans as a specialised activity.

---

[18] *The Friendly Societies (Accounts and Related Provisions) Regulations 1994 (as amended).*

Appendix III: Previous consultations

HISTORY OF PREVIOUS CONSULTATIONS

The requirements in FRSs 100 to 102 are the outcome of a lengthy and extensive   **A3.1**
consultation. The FRC (and formerly the ASB) together with the Department for Business,
Innovation and Skills have consulted on the future of accounting standards in the UK and
Republic of Ireland (RoI) over a ten-year period.

Table 1 – Consultations conducted

Year	Consultation
2002	DTI[19] consults on adoption of IAS Regulation
2004	Discussion Paper – Strategy for Convergence with IFRS
2005	Exposure Draft – Policy Statement: The Role of the ASB
2006	Public Meeting and Proposals for Comment
2006	Press Notice seeking views
2007	Consultation Paper – Proposed IFRS for SMEs
2009	Consultation Paper – Policy Proposal: The future of UK GAAP
2010	Request for Responses – Development of the Impact Assessment
2010	Financial Reporting Exposure Drafts 43 and 44
2011	Financial Reporting Exposure Draft 45
2012	Financial Reporting Exposure Drafts 46, 47 and 48

2004

In 2004 the Discussion Paper contained two key elements underpinning the proposals: **A3.2**
firstly that UK and Republic of Ireland (RoI) accounting standards should be based on
IFRS and secondly that a phased approach to the introduction of the standards should be
adopted.

The ASB embarked on the phased approach and issued a number of standards based on   **A3.3**
IFRS. The majority of respondents agreed with a framework based on IFRS, and although
supportive overall, the response to the phased approach was mixed.

2005

In its 2005 Exposure Draft (2005 ED) of a Policy Statement *Accounting standard-setting in a*   **A3.4**
changing environment: The role of the Accounting Standards Board, amongst other aspects
of its role, the ASB identified its intention to converge with IFRS by implementing new
IFRS in the UK as soon as possible. It also proposed to continue the phased approach to
adopting UK accounting standards based on older IFRSs, but recognised there was little
case for being more prescriptive than IFRS.

---

[19] *The Department of Trade and Industry (DTI) was a United Kingdom government department which was replaced
with the announcement of the creation of the Department for Business, Enterprise and Regulatory Reform and
the Department for Innovation, Universities and Skills on 28 June 2007, which were themselves merged into the
Department for Business, Innovation and Skills (BIS) on 6 June 2009.*

A3.5   Although the ASB had, in the 2005 ED, wanted to move the debate on to how it would seek to influence the IASB's agenda, respondents' main concern remained about convergence. In 2005, the ASB issued an exposure draft proposing the IASB's standard on Business Combinations be adopted in the UK and RoI. This exposure draft highlighted the complexity of a mixed set of UK accounting standards, with some based on IFRSs and others developed independently by the ASB. The majority of respondents continued to agree with the aim of basing UK accounting standards on IFRS, but a broader set of views on how to achieve this was emerging.

A3.6   As time progressed the ASB formed the view that convergence by adopting certain IFRSs was not meeting the needs of its constituents, which no longer included quoted groups. The ASB was concerned about the complexity of certain IFRSs, and it noted that introducing them piecemeal created complications and anomalies within the body of current FRSs. This arose because IFRS-based standards were not an exact replacement for current FRSs and many consequential amendments were required to 'fit' each replacement IFRS-based standard into the existing body of UK FRS. The ASB agreed to continue with its convergence programme, but decided to re-examine how to achieve this.

2006

A3.7   The ASB published revised proposals to be discussed at the 2006 public meeting. By this time the IASB had started its IFRS for SMEs project, and the ASB decided this might have a role as one of the tiers in the UK financial reporting framework. The ASB proposed a 'big bang' with new IFRS-based UK accounting standards mandatory from a single date, 1 January 2009. The ASB's proposal was for a three-tier system, with Tier 1 being EU-adopted IFRS, and the other two tiers being developed as the IASB progressed with its project on the IFRS for SMEs.

A3.8   Those attending the public meeting supported the aim of basing UK and RoI accounting standards on IFRS and adapting them to ensure they were appropriate for the entities applying them.

A3.9   Taking this feedback into account, later in 2006 the ASB issued a Press Notice (PN 289) seeking views on its current thinking:

(a)   All quoted and publicly accountable companies should apply EU-adopted IFRS.

(b)   The FRSSE should be retained and extended to include medium-sized entities.

(c)   UK subsidiaries of groups applying full IFRS should apply EU-adopted IFRS, but with reduced disclosure requirements.

(d)   No firm decision on the remainder (Tier 2), but options included extending the FRSSE, extending full IFRS, maintaining separate UK accounting standards or some combination of these.

A3.10   The responses were mixed, but there was agreement that whatever the solution, it should be based on IFRS and there should be different reporting tiers to ensure proportionality.

2007

A3.11   The IASB published an exposure draft of its IFRS for SMEs in early 2007; shortly afterwards the ASB published its own consultation paper. This sought views on how the IFRS for SMEs might fit into the future UK financial reporting framework, for example whether it might be appropriate for Tier 2, with the FRSSE continuing for those eligible for the small companies' regime.

Feedback on the IFRS for SMEs was largely positive: it would be suitable for Tier 2, it was   **A3.12**
international, it was compatible with IFRS, and it represented a significant simplification.
Overall, it was seen as a workable alternative to IFRS. In addition, respondents wanted
to retain the FRSSE (because it reduces the regulatory burden on smaller entities) and to
give subsidiaries the option of applying the IFRS for SMEs as well as a reduced disclosure
regime if applying full IFRS.

2009

The IFRS for SMEs was published in 2009, allowing the ASB to further develop its proposals   **A3.13**
in the Consultation Paper *Policy Proposal: The future of UK GAAP*. The proposals were
largely consistent with the cumulative results of the preceding consultations and included:

(a)   a move to an IFRS-based framework;
(b)   a three-tier approach;
(c)   publicly accountable entities would be Tier 1 and would apply EU-adopted IFRS;
(d)   small companies would be Tier 3 and continue to apply the FRSSE; and
(e)   other entities would be Tier 2 and should apply a UK and RoI accounting standard
       based on the IFRS for SMEs.

The only significant proposal that was inconsistent with respondents' previous comments   **A3.14**
was that subsidiaries should simply apply the requirement of the tier they individually
met – respondents had wanted subsidiaries to be able to take advantage of disclosure
exemptions, and at that time the ASB had yet to be convinced that significant cost savings
were available from a reduced disclosure framework. Taking into account the feedback
received, this proposal was subsequently reversed and the reduced disclosure framework
was incorporated into FREDs 43 and then 46, and it is now set out in FRS 101.

In addition to the many useful and detailed points made, some common themes included   **A3.15**
general agreement that change was needed to UK accounting standards and that there was
support for many of the changes proposed in the consultation paper.

2010 onwards

The request for responses to aid development of the Impact Assessment focused on   **A3.16**
obtaining feedback on the expected costs, benefits and impact of the proposals subsequently
set out in FREDs 43 and 44, rather than on the accounting principles. As the focus was
on costs and benefits no specific question was asked about the principle of the proposed
introduction of an IFRS-based framework, but nevertheless respondents commented on
this: of the 32 responses received only 12.5% did not agree with the introduction of an
IFRSbased framework.

FRED 43 and 44 issued in October 2010 set out the draft suggested text for two new   **A3.17**
accounting standards that would replace the majority of extant Financial Reporting
Standards (current FRS) in the UK and RoI. The ASB issued a supplementary FRED
addressing specific needs of public benefit entities (FRED 45) in March 2011. The ASB
then updated FREDs 43, 44 and 45, replacing them with the revised FREDs 46, 47 and 48
in January 2012, by eliminating the concept of public accountability and by introducing
a number of accounting treatment options that are available in EU-adopted IFRS. The
Accounting Council's advice to the FRC to issue FRSs 100 to 102 includes more discussion
of the feedback received on FREDs 43 to 48 and how the proposals have been refined and
developed into the standards.

How have the proposals been developed?

A3.18   As set out above, the FRC, the Accounting Council (and previously the ASB) have consulted regularly on the future of financial reporting in the UK and RoI. Over the consultations the ASB's (and the Accounting Council's) thinking has evolved based on careful consideration of the feedback at each stage. Whilst responses were sometimes mixed, there has been agreement that:

(a)   current FRS, which are a mixture of Statements of Standard Accounting Practice (SSAPs) issued by the Consultative Committee of Accounting Bodies, FRSs developed and issued by the ASB and IFRS-based standards issued by the ASB to converge with international standards, are an uncomfortable mismatch that lack strong underlying principles or cohesion; and

(b)   whatever the solution, it should be based on IFRS and there should be different reporting tiers to ensure proportionality.

A3.19   During the consultation process to date, the Accounting Council and formerly the ASB have been guided by the following principles:

(a)   The framework must be fit for purpose, so that each entity required to produce true and fair financial statements under UK and RoI law will deliver financial statements that are suited to the needs of its primary users. The Accounting Council has kept in close contact with constituent users on this point, including investors, creditor institutions and the tax authorities.

(b)   The framework must be proportionate, so that preparing entities are not unduly burdened by costs that outweigh the benefit to them and to the primary users of information in their financial statements. The FRC believes that the proposals will produce a lower cost regime, while enhancing user benefits. It has carried out a consultation stage impact assessment with input from interested parties, and will continue to assess cost-benefit issues.

(c)   The framework must be in line with UK company law. This determines which entities must produce true and fair financial statements. Exemptions within the law have generally been retained. The detailed requirements of the Companies Act 2006 are driven to a great extent by the European Accounting Directives, which are being revised[20].

(d)   The framework must be future-proofed, where possible. The FRC will continue to monitor the situation and has sovereignty over UK accounting standards (subject to the law). Changes to the Accounting Directives may lead to further developments, for example the European Council and European Parliament decision to permit Member States an option to treat micro-entities as a separate category of Company and exempt them from certain accounting requirements.

Summary of outreach

A3.20   During the development and throughout the consultation period of FREDs 43 to 48, the ASB undertook an extensive programme of outreach aimed at raising awareness of the proposals and to address the view (held by some) that previous consultations had not gathered sufficient evidence to support and test the assumptions made.

A3.21   As part of the outreach programme to obtain both formal and informal feedback, a series of meetings and events took place with users, including with lenders to small and medium-sized entities. Lenders noted that financial statements are an important part of

---

[20]   *The EU's consultation process on review of the Accounting Directives is summarised at http://ec.europa.eu/ internal_market/accounting/sme_accounting/review_directives_en.htm*

their decision-making process when considering whether to provide finance and, whilst a decision to provide finance is not based on financial statements alone, they provide useful information and verification to the lender.

Although the ASB and the Accounting Council employed their best efforts to obtain **A3.22** feedback from users (a constituent group historically difficult to engage with formally) it is disappointing that limited formal responses were received and the Accounting Council has not been more successful in obtaining input from users.

In addition, a review was made of academic research that addressed the users of the **A3.23** financial statements of small and medium-sized entities. The conclusion drawn from the research was that many entities requested financial statements from Companies House when considering whether to trade with another entity. The European Federation of Accountants and Auditors (EFAA) issued, in May 2011, a statement that identified the users of financial statements, noting who the users of SMEs' financial statements are and that information on the public record assists all users of financial statements of SMEs by providing, in an efficient manner, basic information that protects their rights.

The ASB considered that the outreach programme had gleaned information from people **A3.24** who would not normally submit formal responses to a consultation and provided very useful information that could be used in developing the next stage of the project. The ASB noted that whilst this information was not part of the public record, as are formal consultation responses, it could use the information to assist in developing the revised FREDs 46 to 48, supplementing information contained in responses, and would seek further comment in the next stage of its deliberations.

The Accounting Council continued the work of the ASB in finalising FRSs 100 to 102. **A3.25** The responses to FREDs 46 to 48 were analysed and discussed, and engagements were conducted to take into account the views and suggestions of all relevant associations and contacts. Respondents and outreach contacts were satisfied with FREDs 46 to 48, and many of the response letters were forthcoming in their overall praise for the proposals. A significant number of constituents anticipated cost savings arising from the application of FRS 101. Many respondents considered that FRS 102 would improve UK accounting standards, in particular by introducing requirements for accounting for financial instruments. Further they considered that the improvements will be achieved in a way that will be proportionate to the needs of users, and that once the transition phase has been overcome, it will have the effect of reducing the reporting burden on those UK companies that adopt it.

Appendix IV: Republic of Ireland (RoI) legal references

A4.1   Appendix IV: *Republic of Ireland (RoI) legal references* will be updated as appropriate for both the Companies Act 2014 and the Irish legislation implementing the EU Accounting Directive once the latter has been made. This will be made available on the FRC website and included in the next edition of FRS 100.

FRS 101
Reduced Disclosure Framework – Disclosure exemptions from EU-adopted IFRS for qualifying entities

(September 2015)

Contents

Paragraphs

Summary

FRS 101 Reduced Disclosure Framework
Disclosure exemptions from EU-adopted IFRS for qualifying entities   1–12

Application Guidance

Approval by the FRC

The Accounting Council's Advice to the FRC to issue FRS 101
Introduction   1–3
Advice   4–5
Background   6–7
The reduced disclosure framework principles   8–9
The scope of the reduced disclosure framework   10–11
Application of the reduced disclosure framework to financial institutions   12–16
Related party exemption for the reduced disclosure framework   17
Extension of the reduced disclosure framework to recently issued
    International Financial Reporting Standards and amendments   18–20
The precedence of the Companies Act   21
Approval of this advice   22

**The Accounting Council's Advice to the FRC to issue Amendments
to FRS 101 Reduced Disclosure Framework (2013/14 Cycle)**
Introduction   1–4
Advice   5–6
Background   7–9
IASB projects completed since those considered in
    the development of FRS 101   10–24
Editorial amendment to paragraph 6 of FRS 101   25–35
Date from which effective and transitional arrangements   36–38
Approval of this Advice   39

**The Accounting Council's Advice to the FRC to issue Amendments to
FRS 101 – 2014/15 cycle and other minor amendments**

Appendices
    I   Glossary
    II   Note on legal requirements
    III   Previous consultations
    IV   Republic of Ireland (RoI) legal references

Editor's note: Limited amendments to FRS 101 relating to IFRS 15 and to the order in which notes are presented, effective from 1 January 2016, are included in the next section of this book.

FRS 101 *Reduced Disclosure Framework* is an accounting standard. It is issued by the Financial Reporting Council in respect of its application in the United Kingdom and promulgated by the Institute of Chartered Accountants in Ireland in respect of its application in the Republic of Ireland.

Summary

With effect from 1 January 2015 the Financial Reporting Council (FRC) revised financial **(i)** reporting standards in the United Kingdom and Republic of Ireland. The revisions fundamentally reformed financial reporting, replacing the extant standards with five Financial Reporting Standards:

(a) FRS 100 *Application of Financial Reporting Requirements*;
(b) FRS 101 *Reduced Disclosure Framework*;
(c) FRS 102 *The Financial Reporting Standard applicable in the UK and Republic of Ireland*;
(d) FRS 103 *Insurance Contracts*; and
(e) FRS 104 *Interim Financial Reporting*.

The FRC has also issued FRS 105 *The Financial Reporting Standard applicable to the Micro-entities Regime* to support the implementation of the new micro-entities regime.

The FRC's overriding objective in setting accounting standards is to enable users of **(ii)** accounts to receive high-quality understandable financial reporting proportionate to the size and complexity of the entity and users' information needs.

In meeting this objective, the FRC aims to provide succinct financial reporting standards **(iii)** that:

(a) have consistency with international accounting standards through the application of an IFRS-based solution unless an alternative clearly better meets the overriding objective;
(b) reflect up-to-date thinking and developments in the way entities operate and the transactions they undertake;
(c) balance consistent principles for accounting by all UK and Republic of Ireland entities with practical solutions, based on size, complexity, public interest and users' information needs;
(d) promote efficiency within groups; and
(e) are cost-effective to apply.

The requirements in this Financial Reporting Standard (FRS) take into consideration the **(iv)** findings from all relevant consultations.

This FRS sets out a reduced disclosure framework which addresses the financial reporting **(v)** requirements and disclosure exemptions for the individual financial statements of subsidiaries and ultimate parents that otherwise apply the recognition, measurement and disclosure requirements of EU-adopted IFRS. It is envisaged that the provision of these disclosure exemptions could result in cost savings in the preparation of financial statements of subsidiaries and ultimate parents, without reducing the quality of financial reporting.

Disclosure exemptions are available to a qualifying entity, as defined in the glossary to this **(vi)** FRS, in its individual financial statements (but not in consolidated financial statements which it is required or voluntarily chooses to prepare). However, a qualifying entity which is a financial institution is not exempt from the disclosure requirements of IFRS 7 *Financial Instruments: Disclosures*, IFRS 13 *Fair Value Measurement* to the extent that they apply to financial instruments, and paragraphs 134 to 136 of IAS 1 *Presentation of Financial Statements*.

A qualifying entity may apply the reduced disclosure framework regardless of whether **(vii)** the financial reporting framework applied in the consolidated financial statements of the group is based on standards and interpretations issued (or adopted) by the International Accounting Standards Board.

(viii)   Financial statements prepared by a qualifying entity in accordance with this FRS are not accounts prepared in accordance with EU-adopted IFRS. A qualifying entity must ensure it complies with any relevant legal requirements applicable to it. For example, individual financial statements prepared by companies in accordance with this FRS are Companies Act accounts and not IAS accounts as set out in section 395(1) of the Act, and therefore such accounts must comply with the requirements of the Act and any relevant regulations such as the *Large and Medium-Sized Companies and Groups (Accounts and Reports) Regulations 2008* (SI 2008/410).

(ix)   Disclosure exemptions are also available to qualifying entities applying the recognition and measurement principles of FRS 102; the relevant financial reporting requirements and disclosure exemptions are set out in that FRS.

(x)   This edition of FRS 101 issued in September 2015 updates the edition of FRS 101 issued in August 2014 for the following amendments:

   (a)   *Amendments to FRS 101 Reduced Disclosure Framework – 2014/15 cycle and other minor amendments* issued in July 2015; and

   (b)   some minor typographical or presentational corrections.

FRS 101 Reduced Disclosure Framework

Disclosure exemptions from EU-adopted IFRS for qualifying entities

Objective

The objective of this Financial Reporting Standard (FRS) is to set out the disclosure   1
exemptions (a reduced disclosure framework) for the individual financial statements of
subsidiaries, including intermediate parents, and ultimate parents that otherwise apply the
recognition, measurement and disclosure requirements of EU-adopted IFRS.

Scope

This FRS may be applied to the individual financial statements of a qualifying entity,   2
as defined in the glossary, that are intended to give a true and fair view of the assets,
liabilities, financial position and profit or loss for a period.

A qualifying entity which is required to prepare consolidated financial statements (for   3
example, if the entity is required by section 399 of the Act to prepare group accounts, and is
not entitled to any of the exemptions in sections 400 to 402 of the Act), or which voluntarily
chooses to do so, may not apply this FRS in its consolidated financial statements.

Abbreviations and definitions

The terms **Act, date of transition, EU-adopted IFRS, financial institution, FRS 100,**   4
FRS 101, FRS 102, IAS Regulation, IFRS, individual financial statements, public
benefit entity, qualifying entity and **Regulations** are defined in the glossary included as
Appendix I to this FRS.

Financial statements prepared by qualifying entities in accordance with this FRS are not   4A
accounts prepared in accordance with EU-adopted IFRS. A qualifying entity must ensure
it complies with any relevant legal requirements applicable to it. For example, individual
financial statements prepared by companies in accordance with this FRS are Companies
Act accounts and not IAS accounts as set out in section 395(1) of the Act, and therefore
such accounts must comply with the requirements of the Act and any relevant regulations
such as the *Large and Medium-Sized Companies and Groups (Accounts and Reports)*
Regulations 2008 (SI 2008/410).

Reduced disclosures for subsidiaries and ultimate parents

A qualifying entity applying this FRS to its individual financial statements may take   5
advantage of the disclosure exemptions in paragraphs 7A to 9, subject to paragraph 7,
provided that:

(a)   Its shareholders have been notified in writing about, and do not object to, the use of
the disclosure exemptions. Objections to the use of the disclosure exemptions may be
served on the qualifying entity, in accordance with reasonable specified timeframes
and format requirements, by a shareholder that is the immediate parent of the entity,
or by a shareholder or shareholders holding in aggregate 5% or more of the total
allotted shares in the entity or more than half of the allotted shares in the entity that
are not held by the immediate parent.

(b)   It otherwise applies as its financial reporting framework the recognition, measurement
and disclosure requirements of EU-adopted IFRS, but makes amendments to
EU-adopted IFRS requirements where necessary in order to comply with the Act

and the Regulations. This is to ensure that the financial statements prepared by companies in accordance with this FRS, comply with the requirements of the Act and Regulations. The Application Guidance to this FRS sets out the amendments necessary to remove conflicts between EU-adopted IFRS and the Act and Regulations. For the avoidance of doubt, the Application Guidance is an integral part of this FRS and is applicable to any qualifying entity applying this FRS, including those that are not companies.

(c)   It discloses in the notes to its financial statements:

    (i)   a brief narrative summary of the disclosure exemptions adopted; and

    (ii)   the name of the parent[1] of the group in whose consolidated financial statements its financial statements are consolidated, and from where those financial statements may be obtained.

6   [Deleted]

7   A qualifying entity which is a financial institution may take advantage in its individual financial statements of the disclosure exemptions set out in paragraphs 8 to 9 of this FRS, except for:

(a)   the disclosure exemptions from IFRS 7 *Financial Instruments: Disclosures* (see paragraph 8(d));

(b)   the disclosure exemptions from IFRS 13 *Fair Value Measurement* (see paragraph 8(e)) to the extent that they apply to financial instruments[2]; and

(c)   the disclosure exemptions from paragraphs 134 to 136 of IAS 1 *Presentation of Financial Statements* (see paragraph 8(g)).

7A   On first-time adoption of this standard, a qualifying entity shall apply the requirements of paragraphs 6 to 33 of IFRS 1 *First-time adoption of International Financial Reporting Standards* except for the requirement of paragraphs 6 and 21 to present an opening statement of financial position at the date of transition. References to IFRS in IFRS 1 shall be interpreted as references to EU-adopted IFRS as amended in accordance with paragraph 5(b) of this FRS.

8   A qualifying entity may take advantage of the following disclosure exemptions, from when the relevant standard is applied[3]:

(a)   The requirements of paragraphs 45(b) and 46 to 52 of IFRS 2 *Share-based Payment*, provided that for a qualifying entity that is:

    (i)   a subsidiary, the share-based payment arrangement concerns equity instruments of another group entity;

    (ii)   an ultimate parent, the share-based payment arrangement concerns its own equity instruments and its separate financial statements are presented alongside the consolidated financial statements of the group;

and, in both cases, provided that equivalent disclosures are included in the consolidated financial statements of the group in which the entity is consolidated.

---

[1] *The parent identified in the definition of the term 'qualifying entity' (see the glossary included as Appendix I to this FRS).*

[2] *A qualifying entity that is a financial institution may take advantage in its individual financial statements of the disclosure exemptions from IFRS 13 (see paragraph 8(e)) to the extent that they apply to assets and liabilities other than financial instruments.*

[3] *Where a paragraph within a given standard cross-refers to an exempted paragraph listed above, the qualifying entity is permitted to still take the exemption.*

(b)   The requirements of paragraphs 62, B64(d), B64(e), B64(g), B64(h), B64(j) to B64(m), B64(n)(ii), B64(o)(ii), B64(p), B64(q)(ii), B66 and B67 of IFRS 3 *Business Combinations* provided that equivalent disclosures are included in the consolidated financial statements of the group in which the entity is consolidated.

(c)   The requirements of paragraph 33(c) of IFRS 5 *Non-current Assets Held for Sale and Discontinued Operations* provided that equivalent disclosures are included in the consolidated financial statements of the group in which the entity is consolidated.

(d)   The requirements of IFRS 7 *Financial Instruments: Disclosures*, provided that equivalent disclosures are included in the consolidated financial statements of the group in which the entity is consolidated[4].

(e)   The requirement in paragraph 38 of IAS 1 *Presentation of Financial Statements* to present comparative information in respect of:

   (i)   paragraph 79(a)(iv) of IAS 1;
   (ii)   paragraph 73(e) of IAS 16 *Property, Plant and Equipment*;
   (iii)   paragraph 118(e) of IAS 38 *Intangible Assets*;
   (iv)   paragraphs 76 and 79(d) of IAS 40 *Investment Property*; and
   (v)   paragraph 50 of IAS 41 *Agriculture*.

(f)   The requirements of paragraphs 10(d), 10(f), 16, 38A, 38B, 38C, 38D, 40A, 40B, 40C, 40D, 111 and 134 to 136 of IAS 1 *Presentation of Financial Statements*.
   For accounting periods beginning before 1 January 2013, paragraphs 38A, 38B, 38C, 38D, 40A, 40B, 40C and 40D of IAS 1 (effective 1 January 2013) should be replaced with paragraphs 39 and 40 of IAS 1 (effective 1 January 2009).

(g)   The requirements of IAS 7 *Statement of Cash Flows*.

(h)   The requirements of paragraphs 30 and 31 of IAS 8 *Accounting Policies, Changes in Accounting Estimates and Errors*.

(i)   The requirements of paragraphs 17 and 18A of IAS 24 *Related Party Disclosures*.

(j)   The requirements in IAS 24 *Related Party Disclosures* to disclose related party transactions entered into between two or more members of a group, provided that any subsidiary which is a party to the transaction is wholly owned by such a member.

(k)   The requirements of paragraphs 130(f)(ii), 130(f)(iii), 134(d) to 134(f) and 135(c) to 135(e) of IAS 36 *Impairment of Assets*, provided that equivalent disclosures are included in the consolidated financial statements of the group in which the entity is consolidated.

Prospective amendments: FRED 63 (December 2015) proposes amendments to this paragraph with effect for annual periods beginning on or after [date].

Reference should be made to the Application Guidance to FRS 100 in deciding whether the   9
consolidated financial statements of the group provide disclosures which are equivalent to the requirements of EU-adopted IFRS, from which relief is provided in paragraph 8 of this FRS.

Statement of compliance

Where a qualifying entity prepares its financial statements in accordance with FRS 101,   10
it shall state in the notes to the financial statements: '*These financial statements were prepared in accordance with Financial Reporting Standard 101 Reduced Disclosure Framework.*'. The financial statements of such an entity do not comply with all of the requirements of EU-adopted IFRS and shall not therefore contain the unreserved statement

---

[4] *It should be noted that companies which are subject to the requirements of the Act and Regulations are legally required to provide disclosures related to financial instruments, including those measured at fair value. Further guidance in relation to financial instruments measured at fair value is provided in Appendix II Note on legal requirements.*

of compliance referred to in paragraph 3 of IFRS 1 and otherwise required by paragraph 16 of IAS 1 *Presentation of Financial Statements.*

Date from which effective and transitional arrangements

11   A qualifying entity may apply this FRS for accounting periods beginning on or after 1 January 2015. Early application of this FRS is permitted. If an entity applies this FRS before 1 January 2015 it shall disclose that fact.

12   In July 2015 amendments were made to this FRS as a consequence of changes made to EU-adopted IFRS and to maintain consistency with company law. In relation to the amendments set out in *Amendments to FRS 101 – 2014/15 cycle and other minor amendments* a qualifying entity shall apply:

(a)   the amendments to paragraphs 5, 7A and 8(j) arising from the 2014/15 cycle for accounting periods beginning on or after 1 January 2015 (subject also to the effective date of the relevant EU-adopted IFRS). Early application is permitted; and

(b)   the amendments arising for consistency with company law for accounting periods beginning on or after 1 January 2016. Early application is:

(i)   permitted for accounting periods beginning on or after 1 January 2015 provided that *The Companies, Partnerships, and Groups (Accounts and Reports) Regulations 2015* (SI 2015/980) are applied from the same date;

(ii)   required if a qualifying entity applies *The Companies, Partnerships, and Groups (Accounts and Reports) Regulations 2015* (SI 2015/980) to a reporting period beginning before 1 January 2016.

If an entity applies these amendments early it shall disclose that fact.

Application Guidance: Amendments to International Financial Reporting Standards as adopted in the European Union for compliance with the Act and the Regulations

This application guidance forms an integral part of FRS 101

In accordance with the Act, an entity may prepare Companies Act accounts or IAS **AG1** accounts. A qualifying entity which applies FRS 101 prepares Companies Act accounts. This Application Guidance to FRS 101 sets out amendments to EUadopted IFRS that are necessary to achieve compliance with the Act and related Regulations (deleted text is struck through and inserted text is underlined):

(a) Paragraph D16 of IFRS 1 *First-time Adoption of International Financial Reporting Standards* is amended as follows:

If a subsidiary becomes a first-time adopter later than its parent, the subsidiary shall, in its financial statements, measure its assets and liabilities at either:

(a) the carrying amounts that would be included in the parent's consolidated financial statements, based on the parent's date of transition to IFRSs, if no adjustments were made for consolidation procedures and for the effects of the business combination in which the parent acquired the subsidiary; or

(b) the carrying amounts required by the rest of this IFRS, based on the subsidiary's date of transition to IFRSs. These carrying amounts could differ from those described in (a):

(i) when the exemptions in this IFRS result in measurements that depend on the date of transition to IFRSs;

(ii) when the accounting policies used in the subsidiary's financial statements differ from those in the consolidated financial statements. For example, the subsidiary may use as its accounting policy the cost model in IAS 16 *Property, Plant and Equipment*, whereas the group may use the revaluation model.

A similar election is available to an associate or joint venture that becomes a first-time adopter later than an entity that has significant influence or joint control over it.

A qualifying entity that applies this provision must ensure that its assets and liabilities are measured in compliance with FRS 101.

(b) Paragraph D17 of IFRS 1 *First-time Adoption of International Financial Reporting Standards* is amended as follows:

However, if an entity becomes a first-time adopter later than its subsidiary (or associate or joint venture) the entity shall, in its consolidated financial statements, measure the assets and liabilities of the subsidiary (or associate or joint venture) at the same carrying amounts as in the financial statements of the subsidiary (or associate or joint venture), after adjusting for consolidation and equity accounting adjustments and for the effects of the business combination in which the entity acquired the subsidiary. Similarly, if a parent becomes a first-time adopter for its separate financial statements earlier or later than for its consolidated financial statements, it shall measure its assets and liabilities at the same amounts in both financial statements, except for consolidation adjustments.

A qualifying entity that applies this provision must ensure that its assets and liabilities are measured in compliance with FRS 101.

(c) Paragraph 34 of IFRS 3 *Business Combinations* is amended as follows:

Occasionally, an acquirer will make a bargain purchase, which is a business combination in which the amount in paragraph 32(b) exceeds the aggregate of the amounts specified in paragraph 32(a). If that excess remains after applying the requirements in paragraph 36, the acquirer shall recognise and separately disclose the resulting ~~gain in profit or loss~~ excess on the face of the statement of financial position on the acquisition date, immediately below goodwill, and followed by a subtotal of the net amount of goodwill and the excess. The ~~gain~~ excess shall be attributed to the acquirer. Subsequently, the excess up to the fair value of the non-monetary assets acquired shall be recognised in profit or loss in the periods in which the non-monetary assets are recovered. Any excess exceeding the fair value of non-monetary assets acquired shall be recognised in profit or loss in the periods expected to be benefited.

(d)   Contingent consideration balances arising from business combinations whose acquisition dates preceded the date when an entity first applied the amendments to company law set out in *The Companies, Partnerships and Groups (Accounts and Reports) Regulations 2015* (SI 2015/980) shall not be adjusted as a result of the change in company law (ie generally the start of accounting periods beginning on or after 1 January 2016). Instead the entity's previous accounting policies for contingent consideration shall continue to apply. Contingent consideration balances arising from business combinations whose acquisition dates are on or after the date an entity first applied the amendments to company law set out in *The Companies, Partnerships and Groups (Accounts and Reports) Regulations 2015* (SI 2015/980) shall be accounted for in accordance with IFRS 3 *Business Combinations* (Revised 2008).

(e)   [Deleted]

(f)   Without amending paragraph B63(a) of IFRS 3 *Business Combinations*, its requirement shall be read in conjunction with paragraph A2.8 of this standard.

(fA)   Paragraph 14(a) of IFRS 4 *Insurance Contracts* is amended as follows:

(a)   unless otherwise required by the regulatory framework that applies to the entity, shall not recognise as a liability any provisions for possible future claims, if those claims arise under insurance contracts that are not in existence at the end of the reporting period (such as catastrophe provisions and equalisation provisions). The presentation of any such liabilities shall follow the requirements of the Regulations (or other legal framework that applies to that entity).

(g)   Paragraph 33 of IFRS 5 *Non-current Assets Held for Sale and Discontinued Operations* is amended as follows:

An entity shall disclose:

(a)   a single amount in the statement of comprehensive income comprising the total of:

(i)   the post-tax profit or loss of discontinued operations and

(ii)   the post-tax gain or loss recognised on the measurement to fair value less costs to sell or on the disposal of the assets or disposal group(s) constituting the discontinued operation.

(b)   an analysis of the single amount in (a) into:

(i)   the revenue, expenses and pre-tax profit or loss of discontinued operations;

(ii)   the related income tax expense as required by paragraph 81(h) of IAS 12;

(iii)   the gain or loss recognised on the measurement to fair value less costs to sell or on the disposal of the assets or disposal group(s) constituting the discontinued operation; and

(iv)   the related income tax expense as required by paragraph 81(h) of IAS 12.

The analysis ~~may be~~ shall be presented in ~~the notes or in the statement of comprehensive income. If it is presented In~~ the statement of comprehensive income ~~it shall be presented~~ in a ~~section~~ column identified as relating to discontinued operations, ie separately from continuing operations; a total column shall also be presented. The analysis is not required for disposal groups that are newly acquired subsidiaries that meet the criteria to be classified as held for sale on acquisition (see paragraph 11).

(c) the net cash flows attributable to the operating, investing and financing activities of discontinued operations. These disclosures may be presented either in the notes or in the financial statements. These disclosures are not required for disposal groups that are newly acquired subsidiaries that meet the criteria to be classified as held for sale on acquisition (see paragraph 11).

(d) the amount of income from continuing operations and from discontinued operations attributable to owners of the parent. These disclosures ~~may be~~ are presented ~~either in the notes or~~ in the statement of comprehensive income.

(h) Paragraph 53A and corresponding footnote are inserted into IAS 1 *Presentation of Financial Statements* as follows:

Statement of financial position

Information to be presented in the statement of financial position

53A A qualifying entity choosing to apply paragraph 1A(1) of Schedule 1 to the Regulations and adapt one of the balance sheet formats shall apply the relevant presentation requirements of IAS 1 *Presentation of Financial Statements*. A qualifying entity not permitted or not choosing to apply paragraph 1A(1) of Schedule 1 to the Regulations shall comply with the balance sheet format requirements of the Act* instead of paragraphs 54 to 76 of IAS 1.

[Footnote text]

* An entity shall apply, as required by company law, either Part 1 *General Rules and Formats* of Schedule 1 to the Regulations; Part 1 *General Rules and Formats* of Schedule 2 to the Regulations; Part 1 *General Rules and Formats* of Schedule 3 to the Regulations; or Part 1 *General Rules and Formats* of Schedule 1 to the LLP Regulations.

(i) Paragraph 81C and corresponding footnote are inserted into IAS 1 *Presentation of Financial Statements* as follows:

Information to be presented in profit or loss

81C A qualifying entity choosing to apply paragraph 1A(2) of Schedule 1 to the Regulations and adapt one of the profit and loss account formats shall apply the relevant presentation requirements of IAS 1 *Presentation of Financial Statements*, and in addition shall disclose 'profit or loss before taxation'. A qualifying entity not permitted or not choosing to apply paragraph 1A(2) of Schedule 1 to the Regulations shall present the components of profit or loss in the statement of comprehensive income (in either the single statement or two statement approach) in accordance with the profit and loss account format requirements of the Act* instead of paragraphs 82 and 85 to 86 of IAS 1.

[Footnote text]

* An entity shall apply, as required by company law, either Part 1 *General Rules and Formats* of Schedule 1 to the Regulations; Part 1 *General Rules and Formats* of Schedule 2 to the Regulations; Part 1 *General Rules and Formats* of Schedule 3 to the Regulations; or Part 1 *General Rules and Formats* of Schedule 1 to the LLP Regulations.

(j) Paragraph 87 of IAS 1 *Presentation of Financial Statements* is amended and paragraphs 87A and 87B are inserted into IAS 1 as follows:

87 ~~An~~ qualifying entity applying Schedule 1 to the Regulations shall not present or describe any items of income and expense as 'extraordinary items' in the statement of comprehensive income (or in the income statement, if presented) or in the notes.

A qualifying entity applying Schedule 2 or Schedule 3 to the Regulations or Schedule 1 to the LLP Regulations shall apply paragraphs 87A and 87B.

87A Ordinary activities are any activities which are undertaken by a reporting entity as part of its business and such related activities in which the reporting entity engages in furtherance of, incidental to, or arising from, these activities. Ordinary activities include any effects on the reporting entity of any event in the various environments in which it operates, including the political, regulatory, economic and geographical environments, irrespective of the frequency or unusual nature of the events.

87B Extraordinary items are material items possessing a high degree of abnormality which arise from events or transactions that fall outside the ordinary activities of the reporting entity and which are not expected to recur. They do not include items occurring within the entity's ordinary activities that are required to be disclosed by IAS 1.97, nor do they include prior period items merely because they relate to a prior period.

(k)   Paragraph 88 of IAS 1 *Presentation of Financial Statements* is amended as follows:

An entity shall recognise all items of income and expense arising in a period in profit or loss unless an IFRS requires or permits otherwise, or unless prohibited by the Act.

(l)   Paragraph 28 of IAS 16 *Property, Plant and Equipment* is deleted.

(m)   Paragraph 24 of IAS 20 *Accounting for Government Grants and Disclosure of Government Assistance* is amended as follows:

Government grants related to assets, including non-monetary grants at fair value, shall be presented in the statement of financial position ~~either~~ by setting up the grant as deferred income ~~or by deducting the grant in arriving at the carrying amount of the asset~~.

(n)   Paragraph 25 of IAS 20 *Accounting for Government Grants and Disclosure of Government Assistance* is deleted.

(o)   Paragraph 26 of IAS 20 *Accounting for Government Grants and Disclosure of Government Assistance* is amended as follows:

~~One method recognises the~~ The grant is recognised as deferred income that is recognised in profit or loss on a systematic basis over the useful life of the asset.

(p)   Paragraph 27 of IAS 20 *Accounting for Government Grants and Disclosure of Government Assistance* is deleted.

(q)   Paragraph 28 of IAS 20 *Accounting for Government Grants and Disclosure of Government Assistance* is amended as follows:

The purchase of assets and the receipt of related grants can cause major movements in the cash flow of an entity. For this reason and in order to show the gross investment in assets, such movements are ~~often~~ disclosed as separate items in the statement of cash flows ~~regardless of whether or not the grant is deducted from the related asset for presentation purposes in the statement of financial position~~.

(r)   Paragraph 29 of IAS 20 *Accounting for Government Grants and Disclosure of Government Assistance* is amended as follows:

Grants related to income are presented as part of profit or loss, either separately or under a general heading such as 'Other income'; ~~alternatively,~~ they are not deducted in reporting the related expense.

(s)   Paragraph 92 of IAS 37 *Provisions, Contingent Liabilities and Contingent Assets* is amended as follows:

92 In extremely rare cases, disclosure of some or all of the information required by paragraphs 84–89 can be expected to prejudice seriously the position of the entity in a dispute with other parties on the subject matter of the provision, contingent liability or contingent asset. In such cases, an entity need not disclose all of the information required by those paragraphs insofar as it relates to the dispute, but shall disclose at least the following ~~general nature of the dispute, together with the fact that, and reason why, the information has not been disclosed~~.

In relation to provisions, the following information shall be given:

(a)   a table showing the reconciliation required by paragraph 84 in aggregate, including the source and application of any amounts transferred to or from provisions during the reporting period;

(b)   particulars of each provision in any case where the amount of the provision is material; and

(c)   the fact that, and reason why, the information required by paragraphs 84 and 85 has not been disclosed.

In relation to contingent liabilities, the following information shall be given:

(a)   particulars and the total amount of any contingent liabilities (excluding those which arise out of insurance contracts) that are not included in the statement of financial position;

(b)   the total amount of contingent liabilities which are undertaken on behalf of or for the benefit of:

(i)   any parent or fellow subsidiary of the entity;

(ii)   any subsidiary of the entity; or

(iii)   any entity in which the reporting entity has a participating interest,

shall each be stated separately; and

(c)   the fact that, and reason why, the information required by paragraph 86 has not been disclosed.

In relation to contingent assets, the entity shall disclose the general nature of the dispute, together with the fact that, and reason why, the information required by paragraph 89 has not been disclosed.

Approval by the FRC

Financial Reporting Standard 101 *Reduced Disclosure Framework* was approved for issue by the Board of the Financial Reporting Council on 1 November 2012, following its consideration of the Accounting Council's Advice for this FRS.

Amendments to FRS 101 Reduced Disclosure Framework (2013/14 Cycle) was approved for issue by the Board of the Financial Reporting Council on 2 July 2014, following its consideration of the Accounting Council's Advice.

Amendments to FRS 101 Reduced Disclosure Framework – 2014/15 cycle and other minor amendments was approved for issue by the Board of the Financial Reporting Council on 1 July 2015, following its consideration of the Accounting Council's Advice.

The Accounting Council's Advice to the FRC to issue FRS 101

Introduction

This report provides an overview of the main issues which have been considered by the   **1**
Accounting Council in advising the Financial Reporting Council (FRC) to issue FRS 101
Reduced Disclosure Framework. The FRC, in accordance with the Statutory Instrument
*Statutory Auditors (Amendment of Companies Act 2006 and Delegation of Functions etc)
Order 2012* (SI 2012/1741), is the prescribed body for issuing accounting standards in
the UK. *The Foreword to Accounting Standards* sets out the application of accounting
standards in the Republic of Ireland.

In accordance with FRC *Codes and Standards: procedures*, any proposal to issue, amend   **2**
or withdraw a code or standard is put to the FRC with the full advice of the relevant
Councils and/or the Codes & Standards Committee. Ordinarily, the FRC will only reject
the advice put to it where:

- it is apparent that a significant group of stakeholders has not been adequately consulted;
- the necessary assessment of the impact of the proposal has not been completed,
  including an analysis of costs and benefits;
- insufficient consideration has been given to the timing or cost of implementation; or
- the cumulative impact of a number of proposals would make the adoption of an
  otherwise satisfactory proposal inappropriate.

The FRC has established the Accounting Council as the relevant Council to assist it in the   **3**
setting of accounting standards.

Advice

The Accounting Council is advising the FRC to issue: **4**

FRS 100 *Application of Financial Reporting Requirements*; and
FRS 101 *Reduced Disclosure Framework*.

FRS 102 *The Financial Reporting Standard Applicable in the UK and Republic of Ireland*   **5**
completes the new suite of financial reporting standards. The Accounting Council will
provide its advice to the FRC on FRS 102 in that standard.

Background

Accounting standards were formerly developed by the Accounting Standards Board   **6**
(ASB). The ASB commenced its project to update accounting standards in 2002; Appendix
III provides a history of the previous consultations and a summary of how the overall
proposals have developed[5].

FRS 101 was developed in response to concerns that arose from earlier consultations   **7**
(see Appendix III). Respondents to those consultations (and particularly the 2009 Policy
Proposal) noted that a move to the IFRS for SMEs for subsidiaries of entities that apply
EU-adopted IFRS would require recognition and measurement differences to be monitored
and maintained at group level, and yet the alternative of a move to EU-adopted IFRS would
increase disclosure in comparison to current accounting standards. The ASB therefore
developed a reduced disclosure framework to address these concerns.

---

[5] *References in this section and Appendix III are made to the FRC, ASB or Accounting Council, as appropriate in
terms of the time period and context of the reference.*

The reduced disclosure framework principles

8   In developing the reduced disclosure framework, the ASB set principles for determining which of the disclosure requirements in EU-adopted IFRS should be applied by qualifying entities. Setting principles provides a structure for future amendments to the reduced disclosure framework as new and revised IFRSs are adopted in the EU. The principles are specific to qualifying entities, so the impact on preparers and users of qualifying entity individual financial statements is a common theme to be considered in applying the principles. The agreed principles, which were first introduced when FRED 47 *Reduced Disclosure Framework* was issued, are as follows:

(a)   Relevance:
       Does the disclosure requirement provide information that is capable of making a difference to the decisions made by the users of the financial statements of a qualifying entity?

(b)   Cost constraint on useful financial reporting:
       Does the disclosure requirement impose costs on the preparers of the financial statements of a qualifying entity that are not justified by the benefits to the users of those financial statements?

(c)   Avoid gold plating:

       Does the disclosure requirement override an existing exemption provided by company law in the UK?

9   The Accounting Council is advising the FRC to adopt these principles.

The scope of the reduced disclosure framework

10   The reduced disclosure framework was first proposed in FRED 43 *Application of Financial Reporting Requirements*, and revised proposals were issued in FRED 47. FRED 43 proposed that qualifying subsidiaries could apply the reduced disclosure framework. The scope of the framework was extended beyond subsidiaries in FRED 47, so that the ultimate parent of a group may take advantage of the disclosure framework in its individual financial statements. Intermediate parents are subsidiaries and so were already included within the scope of the reduced disclosure framework.

11   The ASB decided, in clarifying the scope of the reduced disclosure framework in FRED 47, that a qualifying entity which is required to prepare consolidated financial statements (for example, if the entity is required by section 399 of the Act to prepare group accounts, and is not entitled to any of the exemptions in sections 400 to 402 of the Act), or a qualifying entity which voluntarily chooses to prepare consolidated financial statements, should not be permitted to apply the reduced disclosure framework in its consolidated financial statements. The ASB recognised that entities which are required or voluntarily choose to prepare consolidated financial statements generally have users with greater information requirements than the users of entities which only prepare individual financial statements. The ASB's decision not to extend the reduced disclosure framework to consolidated financial statements was questioned by a few respondents to FRED 47. The Accounting Council noted that the concerns raised were industry-specific and held the view previously identified that users of these financial statements had greater information requirements. The Accounting Council is therefore advising the FRC that the scope of the FRS remains unchanged from that proposed in FRED 47.

Application of the reduced disclosure framework to financial institutions

FRED 43 proposed that a subsidiary with public accountability should not be permitted **12**
to apply the reduced disclosure framework (see the Accounting Council's Advice to the
FRC for FRS 100). With the elimination of 'public accountability' as a differentiator for a
financial reporting system in FRED 46 (which replaced FRED 43), the ASB reconsidered
which entities should be eligible to apply the reduced disclosure framework.

FRED 47 proposed consistent disclosure requirements for financial institutions, between **13**
those financial institutions that would be required to provide additional disclosures in
accordance with FRED 48 and those financial institutions that are a qualifying entity
taking advantage of the reduced disclosure framework. The ASB sought views on whether
qualifying entities which are financial institutions should:

(a)   provide disclosures required by IFRS 7 *Financial Instrument: Disclosures* and the
disclosure requirements of IFRS 13 *Fair Value Measurement*; or

(b)   provide disclosures required by IFRS 7 except for paragraphs 6, 7, 9(b), 16, 27A,
31, 33, 36, 37, 38, 39, 40 and 41 (this would provide consistency with disclosures
required by FRED 48), and from paragraphs 92 to 99 of IFRS 13 (all disclosure
requirements except the disclosure objectives).

Respondents had mixed views. Some held the view that a qualifying entity that is a **14**
financial institution should be permitted some exemptions from financial instrument
disclosures in line with those in FRED 48, but others constituents disagreed on the basis
that financial instruments are a significant part of the business for financial institutions
and that those entities should provide an appropriate level of disclosure. The Accounting
Council is advising the FRC that there should be no exemptions from IFRS 7 for financial
institutions. This is also simple to apply and ensures financial institutions provide
appropriate disclosure about their financial instruments.

Some respondents noted that there was an inconsistency in the application of the disclosure **15**
requirements in IFRS 13 between financial institutions and other entities. The inconsistency
arose because financial institutions were required to provide disclosures for assets and
liabilities held at fair value that are not financial instruments whereas other entities were
exempt. The Accounting Council therefore considers that FRS 101 should clarify that a
qualifying entity which is a financial institution is restricted from taking advantage of
the disclosure exemptions from IFRS 13 only to the extent that they apply to financial
instruments.

The Accounting Council is also advising the FRC that financial institutions should not **16**
be permitted to take advantage of the exemption from applying the capital disclosure
requirements in IAS 1 *Presentation of Financial Statements*. Responses to FRED 47 had
noted that capital disclosures provide relevant information for financial institutions.

Related party exemption for the reduced disclosure framework

In issuing FRED 47 the ASB decided to include an exemption in the reduced disclosure **17**
framework from disclosing a related party transaction in accordance with IAS 24 *Related
Party Disclosures* where the related party transaction was entered into between two or
more members of a group, provided that any subsidiary which is a party to a transaction
is wholly owned by such a member. This exemption is consistent with company law and
was well-received by constituents; the Accounting Council advises the FRC to carry the
exemption forward into FRS 101. The exemption set out in paragraph 8(k) of FRS 101
should only be applied where all subsidiaries which are a party to the transaction are
wholly owned by a member of the group. The provision of this exemption is in line with
principle 3 in paragraph 8 of this report.

Extension of the reduced disclosure framework to recently issued International Financial Reporting Standards and amendments

18   The reduced disclosure framework principles (see paragraph 7) were applied in FRED 47 to those IFRSs issued or amended in 2011, including:

(a)   IFRS 9 *Financial Instruments* (as revised in 2011);
(b)   IFRS 10 *Consolidated Financial Statements*;
(c)   IFRS 11 *Joint Arrangements*;
(d)   IFRS 12 *Disclosure of Interests in Other Entities;*
(e)   IFRS 13 *Fair Value Measurement*;
(f)   IAS 1 *Presentation of Financial Statements* (as revised in 2011);
(g)   IAS 19 *Employee Benefits* (as revised in 2011);
(h)   IAS 27 *Separate Financial Statements* (as revised in 2011); and
(i)   IAS 28 *Investments in Associates and Joint Ventures* (as revised in 2011).

19   The Accounting Council subsequently considered the application of the reduced disclosure framework principles to *Annual Improvements to IFRSs 2009–2011 Cycle* which was issued by the IASB in May 2012. The application of the reduced disclosure framework principles leads the Accounting Council to advise the FRC (paragraph 8(g) of FRS 101) to provide disclosure exemptions from paragraphs 38A, 38B, 38C, 38D, 40A, 40B, 40C and 40D of IAS 1 *Presentation of Financial Statements*. Paragraphs 38A, 38B, 38C and 38D are concerned with comparative information in respect of the preceding period, and paragraphs 40A, 40B, 40C and 40D are concerned with a statement of financial position as at the beginning of the preceding period.

20   The Accounting Council advises the FRC to update FRS 101 at regular intervals, to ensure that the disclosure framework maintains consistency with EU-adopted IFRS.

The precedence of the Companies Act

21   The presentation requirements applicable to the statement of financial position and the statement of comprehensive income in IAS 1 have been amended in the Application Guidance of FRS 101 to clarify that a qualifying entity must comply with the company law format requirements. The Accounting Council advises the FRC to reconsider the format requirements of FRS 101 should the Government decide to amend company law at a future date.

Approval of this advice

22   This advice to the FRC was approved by the nine members of the Accounting Council on 25 October 2012. The Accounting Council is comprised of the following members:

Roger Marshall   (Chair of the Accounting Council)
Nick Anderson
Dr Richard Barker
Edward Beale
Peter Elwin
Ken Lever
Robert Overend
Andy Simmonds
Pauline Wallace

The Accounting Council's Advice to the FRC to issue Amendments to FRS 101 Reduced Disclosure Framework (2013/14 Cycle)

Introduction

This section provides an overview of the main issues that have been considered by the Accounting Council in advising the Financial Reporting Council (FRC) to issue *Amendments to FRS 101 Reduced Disclosure Framework (2013/14 Cycle)*. 1

The FRC, in accordance with the *Statutory Auditors (Amendment of Companies Act 2006 and Delegation of Functions etc) Order 2012* (SI 2012/1741), is a prescribed body for issuing accounting standards in the UK. The *Foreword to Accounting Standards* sets out the application of accounting standards in the Republic of Ireland. 2

In accordance with the *FRC Codes and Standards: procedures*, any proposal to issue, amend or withdraw a code or standard is put to the FRC Board with the full advice of the relevant Councils and/or the Codes & Standards Committee. Ordinarily, the FRC Board will only reject the advice put to it where: 3

(a) it is apparent that a significant group of stakeholders has not been adequately consulted;

(b) the necessary assessment of the impact of the proposal has not been completed, including an analysis of costs and benefits;

(c) insufficient consideration has been given to the timing or cost of implementation; or

(d) the cumulative impact of a number of proposals would make the adoption of an otherwise satisfactory proposal inappropriate.

The FRC has established the Accounting Council as the relevant Council to assist it in the setting of accounting standards. 4

Advice

The Accounting Council is advising the FRC to issue *Amendments to FRS 101 Reduced Disclosure Framework (2013/14 Cycle)* to ensure that FRS 101 continues to maintain consistency with EU-adopted IFRS and continues to promote efficiencies in reporting for groups. 5

The Accounting Council's Advice to the FRC to issue FRS 101 *Reduced Disclosure Framework* was set out in that standard. When these amendments are finalised, the Accounting Council's Advice to the FRC on these amendments will be included in the revised FRS 101. 6

Background

The Accounting Council advised the FRC to update FRS 101 at regular intervals to ensure that the disclosure framework maintains consistency with EU-adopted IFRS[6] so that it remains effective as EU-adopted IFRS develops. 7

The Accounting Council also advised the FRC that the following principles should be applied when determining which of the disclosure requirements in EU-adopted IFRS should be applied by qualifying entities: 8

---

[6] *Paragraph 20 of the Accounting Council's Advice to the FRC to issue FRS 101.*

(1)   Relevance:
Does the disclosure requirement provide information that is capable of making a difference to the decisions made by the users of the financial statements of a qualifying entity?

(2)   Cost constraint on useful financial reporting:
Does the disclosure requirement impose costs on the preparers of the financial statements of a qualifying entity that are not justified by the benefits to the users of those financial statements?

(3)   Avoid gold plating:
Does the disclosure requirement override an existing exemption provided by company law in the UK?

9   The Accounting Council considered the responses to the consultation *Financial Reporting Exposure Draft 53: Amendments to FRS 101 Reduced Disclosure Framework (2013/14)* (FRED 53) which was issued in December 2013, in developing its advice.

IASB projects completed since those considered in the development of FRS 101

10   The IASB has completed six projects since those considered in the development of FRS 101:

	IFRS	Date issued by IASB	Endorsed by EU
1	IAS 32 *Financial Instruments: Presentation* – Offsetting Financial Assets And Financial Liabilities (amendment)	Dec 2011	Dec 2012
2	Disclosures – Offsetting Financial Assets and Financial Liabilities (Amendments to IFRS 7)	Dec 2011	Dec 2012
3	Government loans (amendments to IFRS 1)	Mar 2012	Mar 2013
4	Consolidated Financial Statements, Joint Arrangements and Disclosure of Interests in Other Entities: Transition Guidance (Amendments to IFRS 10, IFRS 11 and IFRS 12)	Jun 2012	Apr 2013
5	Investment Entities (Amendments to IFRS 10, IFRS 12 and IAS 27)	Oct 2012	Nov 2013
6	Recoverable Amount Disclosures for Non-Financial Assets (Amendment to IAS 36)	May 2013	Dec 2013

11   The amendments[7] resulting from these projects were reviewed in the context of the reduced disclosure framework for any amendments that:

(a)   alter disclosure requirements, as consideration will need to be given as to whether changes should be made to the disclosure exemptions permitted in FRS 101; and/or

(b)   are inconsistent with current UK legal requirements, as consideration will need to be given to whether changes should be made to the Application Guidance: *Amendments to International Financial Reporting Standards as Adopted in the European Union for Compliance with the Act and the Regulations* to FRS 101.

---

[7] *The full IASB documents setting out the amendments for each project are available on the IASB website (www.ifrs.org).*

Investment Entities (Amendments to IFRS 10, IFRS 12 and IAS 27)

The amendments resulting from this IASB project introduced into IFRS 10 *Consolidated*   **12**
Financial Statements an exception from consolidation of subsidiaries for parents that are
investment entities. These amendments require an investment entity to measure those
subsidiaries at fair value through profit or loss in accordance with IFRS 9 *Financial
Instruments* in its consolidated and separate financial statements. The amendments also
introduce new disclosure requirements for investment entities into IFRS 12 *Disclosure of
Interests in Other Entities* and IAS 27 *Separate Financial Statements*.

Compliance with UK company law

Several respondents questioned whether the proposed amendment to the Application   **13**
Guidance of FRS 101 in relation to IFRS 10 was necessary given that IFRS 10 is only
applicable to the preparation of consolidated financial statements, and FRS 101 is only
applicable to the preparation of the individual financial statements of a qualifying entity.

Although FRS 101 is not applicable to the preparation of consolidated financial statements,   **14**
the amendments to IFRS 10 in respect of investment entities will have a knock-on effect on
the preparation of individual financial statements as paragraph 11A of IAS 27 states that 'if
a parent is required, in accordance with paragraph 31 of IFRS 10, to measure its investment
in a subsidiary at fair value through profit or loss in accordance with IFRS 9, it shall also
account for those investments in the same way in its separate financial statements'[8].

However, the Accounting Council noted the respondents' concerns and advises that the   **15**
proposed amendment to the Application Guidance set out in FRED 53 is not made but
additional guidance is inserted into Appendix II *Note on legal requirements*, in particular
to clarify that a qualifying entity that meets the definition of an investment entity under
IFRS 10 must measure its investments in subsidiaries at fair value through profit or loss in
its individual financial statements.

Disclosure exemptions

The Accounting Council considers that the new disclosure requirements in IFRS 12   **16**
and IAS 27 in respect of qualifying entities that are investment entities are relevant to
a user's understanding of the qualifying entity's financial statements, particularly as no
consolidated financial statements would have been prepared in respect of the exempt
subsidiaries. Further, the qualifying entity would also be a financial institution and these
disclosures relate to its financial instruments. The Accounting Council advises that no
exemption should be given for these new disclosure requirements.

A respondent to the consultation questioned whether the Accounting Council had   **17**
considered paragraphs 24 to 31 of IFRS 12 in relation to unconsolidated structured entities
as paragraph 6(b) of IFRS 12 states that 'this IFRS does not apply to ... an entity's separate
financial statements to which IAS 27 Separate Financial Statements applies. However,
if an entity has interests in unconsolidated structured entities and prepares separate
financial statements as its only financial statements, it shall apply the requirements in
paragraph 24–31 when preparing those financial statements.'

The Accounting Council had not specifically considered paragraph 6(b) of IFRS 12   **18**
in developing the proposals in FRED 53, but on further consideration advises that the
disclosures required by that paragraph provide relevant information and no exemption

---

[8] *As set out in the Appendix I Glossary, separate financial statements are included in the meaning of individual
financial statements.*

should be given in FRS 101. For the avoidance of doubt, the other requirements of IFRS 12 do not apply to the preparation of individual financial statements and therefore are not relevant to financial statements prepared by qualifying entities applying FRS 101.

Recoverable Amount Disclosures for Non-Financial Assets (Amendment to IAS 36)

19   The Accounting Council noted that FRS 101 already allows disclosure exemptions for qualifying entities against paragraphs 134(d) to 134(f) and 135(c) to 135(e) of IAS 36. These disclosures relate to cash-generating units that, either individually or in combination, have a significant amount of goodwill or intangible assets with indefinite useful lives allocated to them. These exemptions are only permitted if equivalent disclosures are included in the consolidated financial statements of the group.

20   The IASB has made amendments to the disclosure requirements of paragraph 130(f) of IAS 36 in relation to fair value, where fair value less costs of disposal is the recoverable amount of an individual asset or cash-generating unit.

21   The Accounting Council considered that, on balance, the additional detailed disclosure requirements of paragraph 130(f) of IAS 36 are unlikely to provide relevant information to users of the financial statements of qualifying entities, given that general information on impairments will be disclosed through the requirements of paragraphs 130(a) to (e).

22   In addition, this detailed information would be available in the consolidated financial statements, and if no disclosure is made in the consolidated financial statements on the grounds of materiality, the relevant disclosures would need to be made at subsidiary level[9].

23   The Accounting Council noted, however, that should an exemption be permitted for paragraph 130(f) in its entirety, basic information about the basis of measurement of the fair value would be lost, and an imbalance between the disclosure requirements relating to fair value less costs of disposal and value in use would exist. Therefore the Accounting Council advises that:

   (a)   an exemption should not be permitted against the requirements of paragraph 130(f)(i) and entities should provide disclosure of the level of the fair value hierarchy used in measuring fair value; and

   (b)   an exemption should be permitted against subparagraphs 130(f)(ii) and 130(f)(iii), provided that equivalent disclosures are included the consolidated financial statements of the group.

24   This proposed disclosure exemption was supported by all respondents and the Accounting Council advises that paragraph 8(l) of FRS 101 is amended to include this exemption.

Editorial amendment to paragraph 6 of FRS 101

25   It has been brought to the attention of the Accounting Council that the drafting of paragraph 6 of FRS 101 does not accurately reflect the requirements of paragraph 36(4) of Schedule 1 to the *Large and Medium-sized Companies and Groups (Accounts and Reports) Regulations 2008* (SI 2008/410) (the Regulations) and is potentially confusing.

26   The Accounting Council proposed in FRED 53 that paragraph 6 should be amended and paragraph 4A be inserted to remind entities that financial statements prepared under

---

[9] *As required by paragraph AG10 of the Application Guidance to FRS 100 Application of Financial Reporting Requirements.*

FRS 101 are not IAS Accounts but Companies Act Accounts, and therefore qualifying entities must comply with the Act and the Regulations.

In general, respondents welcomed the insertion of paragraph 4A and the proposed simplification of paragraph 6. However, some noted that entities which are not companies can apply FRS 101 and therefore the drafting of paragraphs 4A and 6 needed to be revisited. The Accounting Council acknowledged this point and advises that the drafting of paragraph 4A is further improved to reflect this fact, and consequential amendments to the paragraphs (ix) of the Summary and A2.3 of Appendix II are made for consistency.   **27**

In light of the proposed insertion of paragraph 4A, some respondents commented that further consideration of the drafting of paragraph 5(b) is needed to clarify whether the Application Guidance to FRS 101 is applicable to all qualifying entities or to companies only. The Accounting Council noted that its intention was that all entities applying FRS 101 (regardless of whether they are a company or otherwise) should use the same recognition and measurement bases, in line with the principle adopted in developing FRS 102. Although direct comparability across entities applying FRS 101 is not critical, given that the standard only applies to the individual financial statements of group entities where the most common user is likely to be the parent entity, the Accounting Council nonetheless noted that in general, users will have an expectation that all financial statements prepared in accordance with FRS 101 will be applying a consistent recognition and measurement framework.   **28**

The Accounting Council acknowledged that the standard as originally drafted was not clear on this point and therefore it advises that paragraph 5(b) is amended to clarify for any avoidance of doubt that the Application Guidance (which amends EU-adopted IFRS to remove conflicts with company law) is an integral part of the FRS and is applicable to all entities, not just companies, applying FRS 101.   **29**

In reconsidering paragraph 6 of FRS 101, the Accounting Council considered whether the same underlying principle should be applied to disclosure requirements, and it drew a distinction between the recognition and measurement framework and the availability of reduced disclosures. It noted that the key objective of FRS 101 is to promote more efficient group reporting by permitting qualifying entities exemptions from certain disclosure requirements set out in EU-adopted IFRS. However, in some circumstances, the level of exemptions that can be taken by a qualifying entity may be restricted by legal requirements applicable to the entity.   **30**

This is the case for companies (and limited liability partnerships (LLPs)) that measure financial instruments at fair value subject to the requirements of paragraph 36(4) of Schedule 1 to the relevant regulations. FRS 101 provides an exemption against the disclosure requirements of IFRS 7 *Financial Instruments: Disclosures* and IFRS 13 *Fair Value Measurement*; however companies (and LLPs) with financial instruments of this nature are required by law to provide certain disclosures.   **31**

In relation to paragraph 6 of FRS 101 (which was intended to help companies to identify the disclosure requirements necessary to comply with paragraph 36(4) of Schedule 1 to the Regulations), the Accounting Council concluded that this paragraph should not be mandatory for all qualifying entities (despite footnote 2 of FRS 101 which states otherwise) given that entities that are not subject to the Regulations would otherwise have been permitted to take advantage of the exemptions from the disclosure requirements of IFRS 7 and IFRS 13.   **32**

The Accounting Council noted that the equivalent requirement in FRS 102 does not specifically state that it is applicable to all qualifying entities but rather it is only applicable   **33** to qualifying entities that have '*financial instruments held at fair value subject to the requirements of paragraph 36(4) of Schedule 1 to the Regulations*'[10]; this infers that it is only applicable to companies, indicating that there is inconsistency between the two standards.

34   In light of this, the Accounting Council concluded that paragraph 6 of FRS 101 should not be applicable to all qualifying entities and is simply an interpretation of a company law disclosure requirement which restricts the level of exemptions that a company can take. It therefore advises that paragraph 6 of FRS 101 is deleted and further explanatory guidance is inserted into Appendix II *Note on legal requirements*.

35   In inserting further guidance into Appendix II, the Accounting Council noted that a company will comply with the requirements of paragraph 36(4) of Schedule 1 to the Regulations if it provides the disclosures required by IAS 32 or IFRS 7 as at 5 September 2006. However, the most practical solution would be for a qualifying entity to provide the disclosures required by IFRS 7 as entities may find it difficult to obtain a copy of IAS 32 as at that date. IFRS 7 has been amended since September 2006 but the Accounting Council advises that if an entity applies the current version of IFRS 7 (extant at the date of this Advice), it will still be complying with the requirements of the Regulations.

Date from which effective and transitional arrangements

36   The effective date of FRS 101 is for accounting periods beginning on or after 1 January 2015 with early application permitted.

37   The amendments resulting from both the *Investment Entities (Amendments to IFRS 10, IFRS 12 and IAS 27)* project and the *Recoverable Amount Disclosures for Non-Financial Assets (Amendments to IAS 36)* project have an effective date for accounting periods beginning on or after 1 January 2014 with early application permitted as set out in IFRS 10 and IAS 36.

38   The Accounting Council advises that the amendments to FRS 101 have the same effective date as currently stated in FRS 101 and early adoption is permitted to the extent that a qualifying entity can apply the amendments of the underlying IFRSs (ie IFRS 10 and IAS 36).

Approval of this Advice

39   This advice to the FRC was approved by the Accounting Council on 19 June 2014.

[10] *See paragraph 1.8 of FRS 102.*

The Accounting Council's Advice to the FRC to issue Amendments to FRS 101 – 2014/15 cycle and other minor amendments

Introduction

This section provides an overview of the main issues that have been considered by the Accounting Council in advising the Financial Reporting Council (FRC) to issue *Amendments to FRS 101 Reduced Disclosure Framework – 2014/15 cycle and other minor amendments*.   1

The FRC, in accordance with the *Statutory Auditors (Amendment of Companies Act 2006 and Delegation of Functions etc) Order 2012* (SI 2012/1741), is a prescribed body for issuing accounting standards in the UK. The *Foreword to Accounting Standards* sets out the application of accounting standards in the Republic of Ireland.   2

In accordance with the *FRC Codes and Standards: procedures*, any proposal to issue, amend or withdraw a code or standard is put to the FRC Board with the full advice of the relevant Councils and/or the Codes & Standards Committee. Ordinarily, the FRC Board will only reject the advice put to it where: 3

(a) it is apparent that a significant group of stakeholders has not been adequately consulted;

(b) the necessary assessment of the impact of the proposal has not been completed, including an analysis of costs and benefits;

(c) insufficient consideration has been given to the timing or cost of implementation; or

(d) the cumulative impact of a number of proposals would make the adoption of an otherwise satisfactory proposal inappropriate.

The FRC has established the Accounting Council as the relevant Council to assist it in the setting of accounting standards.   4

Advice

The Accounting Council is advising the FRC to issue *Amendments to FRS 101 Reduced Disclosure Framework – 2014/15 cycle and other minor amendments* to ensure FRS 101 maintains consistency with IFRS and company law and continues to be effective.   5

The Accounting Council's Advice to the FRC to issue FRS 101 *Reduced Disclosure Framework* was set out in the standard. The Accounting Council's Advice to the FRC in respect of these amendments will be included in the revised FRS 101.   6

Background

The Accounting Council advised the FRC to update FRS 101 at regular intervals to ensure that the reduced disclosure framework maintains consistency with EUadopted IFRS.   7

The Accounting Council also advised the FRC that the following principles should be applied when determining which of the disclosure requirements in EU-adopted IFRS should be applied by qualifying entities: 8

(1)   Relevance:
      Does the disclosure requirement provide information that is capable of making
      a difference to the decisions made by the users of the financial statements of a
      qualifying entity?

(2)   Cost constraint on useful financial reporting:
      Does the disclosure requirement impose costs on the preparers of the financial
      statements of a qualifying entity that are not justified by the benefits to the users of
      those financial statements?

(3)   Avoid gold plating:
      Does the disclosure requirement override an existing exemption provided by
      company law in the UK?

9   FRS 101 also requires limited other amendments for compliance with company law
    following the implementation of the new Accounting Directive.

10 The Accounting Council considered the responses to:

    (a)   FRED 57 *Draft amendments to FRS 101 Reduced Disclosure Framework (2014/15
          Cycle)*, which was issued in December 2014; and

    (b)   FRED 60 *Draft amendments to FRS 100 Application of Financial Reporting
          Requirements and FRS 101 Reduced Disclosure Framework*, which was issued in
          February 2015,

    in developing its advice.

IASB projects completed since the 2013/14 cycle

11 The IASB has completed 13 projects since those considered in the review for the 2013/14
    cycle performed in August 2013:

	IFRS	IFRS Date issued by IASB	Effective date	Endorsed by EU
1	IFRIC 21 *Levies*	May 2013	1 Jan 2014	Jun 2014
2	Novation of Derivatives and Continuation of Hedge Accounting – Amendments to IAS 39	Jun 2013	1 Jan 2014	Dec 2013
3	IFRS 9 *Financial Instruments* – Hedge Accounting and amendments to IFRS 9, IFRS 7 and IAS 39	Nov 2013	1 Jan 2018	Expected H2 2015
4	Defined Benefit Plans: Employee Contributions – Amendments to IAS 19	Nov 2013	1 Jul 2014	Dec 2014
5	Annual Improvements to IFRSs 2010–2012 Cycle	Dec 2013	1 Jul 2014	Dec 2014
6	Annual Improvements to IFRSs 2011–2013 Cycle	Dec 2013	1 Jul 2014	Dec 2014
7	IFRS 14 *Regulatory Deferral Accounts*	Jan 2014	1 Jan 2016	Not endorsed

	IFRS	IFRS Date issued by IASB	Effective date	Endorsed by EU
8	IFRS 15 *Revenue from Contracts with Customers*	May 2014	1 Jan 2017	To be decided
9	Accounting for Acquisitions of Interests in Joint Operations	May 2014	1 Jan 2016	Expected Q4 2015
10	Clarification of Acceptable Methods of Depreciation and Amortisation	May 2014	1 Jan 2016	Expected Q4 2015
11	Agriculture: Bearer Plants – Amendments to IAS 16 and IAS 41	Jun 2014	1 Jan 2016	Expected Q4 2015
12	IFRS 9 Financial Instruments – Classification and Measurement, Impairments	Jun 2014	1 Jan 2018	Expected H2 2015
13	Equity Method in Separate Financial Statements (Amendments to IAS 27)	Aug 2014	1 Jan 2016	Expected Q4 2015

The Accounting Council advises that consideration of the final project listed above (*Equity* **12** *Method in Separate Financial Statements (Amendments to IAS 27)*) should be deferred until the 2015/16 cycle as its application in the UK was not permitted at the time of the review, but changes to company law made as part of the implementation of the EU Accounting Directive mean that it will be permitted for accounting periods beginning on or after 1 January 2015 (if an entity adopts the changes to company law early).

The amendments[11] resulting from the remaining 12 projects were reviewed in the context **13** of the reduced disclosure framework for any amendments that:

(a)   alter disclosure requirements, as consideration will need to be given to whether changes should be made to the disclosure exemptions permitted in FRS 101; and/or
(b)   are inconsistent with current UK legal requirements, as consideration will need to be given to whether changes should be made to the Application Guidance: *Amendments to International Financial Reporting Standards as Adopted in the European Union for Compliance with the Act and the Regulations* to FRS 101.

The most significant amendments / standards are considered below. **14**

IAS 24 Related Party Disclosures – Key management services from management entities

The *Annual Improvements to IFRSs (2010–2012 Cycle)* introduces three main changes to **15** IAS 24 *Related Party Disclosures*:

(a)   Insertion of paragraph 9(b)(viii) changing the definition of a related party to clarify that a management entity that provides key management personnel services to the reporting entity is a related party.
(b)   Insertion of paragraph 17A which states that where an entity obtains key management personnel services from a management entity, it is not required to apply paragraph 17 which requires disclosure of key management personnel compensation.

---

[11] *The full IASB documents setting out the amendments for each project are available on the IASB website (www.ifrs.org).*

(c)   Insertion of paragraph 18A which requires an entity that obtains key management personnel services from a management entity to disclose amounts incurred for the provision of those services.

16   The Council noted that FRS 101 currently allows an exemption against paragraph 17 of IAS 24 (which requires disclosure of key management personnel compensation) on the basis that company law requires disclosure of directors' emoluments and further information about key management personnel compensation is unlikely to be relevant to the users of a qualifying entity's financial statements.

17   The majority of the respondents to FRED 57 supported this proposal.

18   The Council advises that on the basis that FRS 101 already allows an exemption against paragraph 17 it considers that FRS 101 should also allow an exemption against paragraph 18A.

IFRS 15 Revenue from Contracts with Customers

19   The disclosure requirements of IFRS 15 *Revenue from Contracts with Customers* are significantly more detailed than those currently required by IAS 18 *Revenue* and IAS 11 *Construction Contracts*, and the Council notes that the majority of the additional requirements are qualitative in nature, around judgements exercised in the recognition and measurement of revenue.

20   The Council also notes that paragraph 111 of IFRS 15 calls for entities to consider the level of detail necessary to satisfy the disclosure objective to provide sufficient information to enable users of financial statements to understand the nature, amount, timing and uncertainty of revenue and cash flows arising from contracts with customers, and how much emphasis to place on each of the various requirements, requiring that entities aggregate/disaggregate as appropriate. So although the disclosure requirements are extensive, there is scope for entities to apply judgement in their preparation.

21   IFRS 15 is effective for accounting periods beginning on or after 1 January 2017 (albeit early adoption is permitted), although the IASB is currently consulting on deferring the effective date by one year to 1 January 2018. At this stage, with the effective date some way off and the European Union endorsement process not yet complete, the Council advises that no exemptions from the disclosure requirements of IFRS 15 should be added to FRS 101. The majority of respondents to FRED 57 supported this proposal.

22   IFRS 15 will be applicable from the same date for both entities applying IFRS and those qualifying entities applying FRS 101. The Council advises that IFRS 15 should be revisited as part of the 2015/16 cycle in order to consider whether any disclosure exemptions are appropriate in FRS 101; two respondents to FRED 57 commented that in their view exemptions would be appropriate.

IFRS 9 Financial Instruments

23   IFRS 9 *Financial Instruments* issued in July 2014 combines the outputs from the classification and measurement, hedge accounting and impairment projects to date, and amends the requirements of IFRS 7 *Financial Instruments: Disclosures*. EFRAG indicates that endorsement may be expected in H2 2015.

24   The Accounting Council advises that the existing position of FRS 101 (ie that financial institutions are not permitted any exemptions against the disclosure requirements of

IFRS 7 or the financial instruments disclosures in IFRS 13 *Fair Value Measurement* and that non-financial institutions are permitted exemptions) should remain even after IFRS 9 is endorsed.

2013/14 cycle: IFRS 1 *First-time Adoption of International Financial Reporting Standards* – Presentation of an opening statement of financial position on transition

The Council noted its earlier advice to revisit a query raised by a respondent to the   25
2013/14 cycle highlighting that although FRS 101 provides an explicit exemption from paragraph 10(f) of IAS 1 *Presentation of Financial Statements* there is no explicit exemption from a similar requirement set out in paragraph 21 (and paragraph 6) of IFRS 1 *First-time Adoption of International Financial Reporting Standards* to present a third statement of financial position:

(a)   Paragraph 10(f) of IAS 1 requires the presentation of a statement of financial position as at the beginning of the preceding period when an entity applies an accounting policy retrospectively or makes a retrospective restatement of its financial statements.

(b)   Paragraph 6 of IFRS 1 requires an entity to prepare and present an opening statement of financial position at the date of transition, and paragraph 21 of IFRS 1 requires that an entity's first IFRS financial statements should include at least three statements of financial position.

The Council advises in addition to the apparent inconsistency within FRS 101 as noted   26
above, paragraph 35.7 of the IFRS for SMEs was amended in developing FRS 102 *The Financial Reporting Standard applicable in the UK and Republic of Ireland* to require the preparation of, but not the presentation of, an opening statement of financial position in the first set of financial statements prepared under FRS 102. Therefore the Council advises that an exemption from the requirement in IFRS 1 to present an opening statement of financial position on transition to FRS 101 should be permitted.

All the respondents to FRED 57 agreed with this proposal, and some respondents noted   27
that a consequential amendment would be necessary to paragraph 11(b) of FRS 100 *Application of Financial Reporting Requirements*. The Accounting Council agrees with this comment and advises that paragraph 11(b) of FRS 100 is amended for consistency. This amendment is set out in *Amendments to FRS 100 Application of Financial Reporting Requirements* issued in July 2015.

Editorial amendments to the Application Guidance to FRS 101

IFRS 3 Business Combinations – Contingent consideration

The *Annual Improvements to IFRSs (2010–2012 Cycle)* amended the requirements in   28
relation to contingent consideration set out in paragraphs 40 and 58 of IFRS 3 *Business Combinations*.

The Application Guidance to FRS 101 already amends paragraphs 39 and 40, and deletes   29
paragraph 58 of IFRS 3 for compliance with company law which prior to the implementation of the new Accounting Directive did not permit contingent consideration to be measured at fair value. Therefore, FRED 57 proposed an amendment to the Application Guidance to ensure the underlying text from IFRS 3 is correct. However, as these requirements of IFRS 3 are no longer inconsistent with company law, FRED 60 proposed deleting this paragraph. As a result, the Council advises paragraph AG1(d) is deleted and replaced with a new paragraph AG1(d) that sets out transitional provisions arising from the change in company law.

IFRS 5 Discontinued Operations and Assets Held for Sale

30   The IASB issued a set of editorial amendments in July 2012 which included the deletion of paragraph 33(b)(iv) of IFRS 5 *Discontinued Operations and Assets Held for Sale*. Therefore FRED 57 proposed that the underlying text included in paragraph AG1(g) of the Application Guidance to FRS 101 was amended to reflect this editorial amendment. However, in September 2014 (after the cut-off period for this review cycle) the IASB retracted this editorial amendment and therefore the proposed amendment of paragraph AG1(g) of the Application Guidance to FRS 101 is no longer necessary and has not been made.

Implementation of the new Accounting Directive

31   The new EU Accounting Directive (Directive 2013/34/EU of the European Parliament and of the Council of 26 June 2013) is being implemented in the UK and Republic of Ireland. In doing so there are changes to company law to reflect new requirements and, where considered appropriate, to take advantage of new options that are available. Accounting standards are developed within the context of company law and amendments will also be required to accounting standards.

32   In September 2014, the FRC issued a Consultation Document *Accounting standards for small entities – Implementation of the EU Accounting Directive*[12] (the Consultation Document), outlining its proposal that a small number of amendments to FRS 101 *Reduced Disclosure Framework* would be necessary to maintain consistency with company law. The Accounting Council considered the responses to the Consultation Document in developing FRED 60 *Draft amendments to FRS 100 and FRS 101*. It has also considered the responses to FRED 60, which was issued in February 2015, in developing its advice on these amendments.

Amendments to FRS 101

33   A small number of amendments, principally to the Application Guidance to FRS 101, are necessary to maintain consistency between FRS 101 and company law.

34   The amendments proposed include:

(a)   Greater flexibility in relation to the format of the profit and loss account and balance sheet, which will allow entities choosing this option to adopt a presentation that is closer to that applied by entities preparing 'IAS accounts'.

(b)   Revisions to certain requirements relating to financial instruments that are, or may be, measured at fair value. The new Accounting Directive permits measurement of certain financial instruments at fair value where it is in accordance with EU-adopted IFRS; previously this was restricted to IFRS endorsed by 5 September 2006. The consequences of this change have been considered. As a result, there is no longer a prohibition on measuring contingent consideration at fair value[13] and the Accounting Council advises that the relevant amendment to IFRS can be deleted.

(c)   Prohibiting the reversal of impairment losses for goodwill.

---

[12] *Available on the FRC website (www.frc.org.uk).*

[13] *Although paragraph 36(3) of the Regulations will continue to prohibit the measurement of contingent consideration at fair value through profit or loss (as required by IFRS 3* Business Combinations*), this measurement will now be permitted through paragraph 36(4) of the Regulations.*

The Accounting Council noted that, following amendments proposed to the 'seriously **35** prejudicial' disclosure exemption in FRS 102 *The Financial Reporting Standard applicable in the UK and Republic of Ireland* some respondents to FRED 60 suggested that FRS 101 should include an amendment to paragraph 92 of IAS 37 *Provisions, Contingent Liabilities and Contingent Assets* to note that the exemption does not apply to disclosures that are required by company law (for example by paragraphs 59 and 63 of the Regulations). Although this was already covered by paragraph 4A of FRS 101, which notes that the requirements of the Regulations must be complied with, the Accounting Council advises that this constraint on the exemption in IAS 37 should be specifically highlighted in FRS 101 and it is set out in new paragraph AG1(s) of the Application Guidance to FRS 101.

Future amendments to FRS 101

The Accounting Council notes that IFRS 9 *Financial Instruments* has not yet been **36** endorsed for use in the EU, and therefore is not yet applicable to an entity applying FRS 101. However, the Accounting Council notes that one aspect of its recognition and measurement requirements is inconsistent with company law. This relates to where changes in fair value shall be presented. Once IFRS 9 has been endorsed the Accounting Council intends to advise that, for entities applying FRS 101, recording fair value gains and losses attributable to changes in credit risk in other comprehensive income in accordance with IFRS 9 will usually be a departure from the requirement of paragraph 40 of Schedule 1 to the Regulations, for the overriding purpose of giving a true and fair view.

The Accounting Council notes that company law will permit the use of the equity method **37** in an entity's individual financial statements for accounting periods beginning on or after 1 January 2016 (or with early application from 1 January 2015) and therefore when it considers the recent amendment to IAS 27 *Separate Financial Statements* as part of the next annual review of FRS 101, it expects to advise that amendments are not necessary to FRS 101 for compliance with company law.

Date from which effective and transitional arrangements

The effective date of FRS 101 is for accounting periods beginning on or after 1 January 2015 **38** with early application permitted. A qualifying entity is permitted to apply EU-adopted IFRS extant at the time of preparing its financial statements.

The Accounting Council advises that the amendments to FRS 101 arising from FRED 57 **39** have the same effective date as currently stated in FRS 101 and early adoption is permitted to the extent that a qualifying entity can apply the amendments of the underlying IFRSs.

The Accounting Council advises that the amendments to FRS 101 arising from the **40** implementation of the new Accounting Directive are effective for accounting periods beginning on or after 1 January 2016, with early application:

(a) permitted for accounting periods beginning on or after 1 January 2015 provided that *The Companies, Partnerships and Groups (Accounts and Reports) Regulations 2015* (SI 2015/980) are applied from the same date; and

(b) required if an entity applies *The Companies, Partnerships and Groups (Accounts and Reports) Regulations 2015* (SI 2015/980) to a reporting period beginning before 1 January 2016.

Approval of this Advice

This advice to the FRC was approved by the Accounting Council on 4 June 2015. **41**

Appendix I: Glossary

Act	The Companies Act 2006
date of transition	The beginning of the earliest period for which an entity presents full comparative information under a given standard in its first financial statements that comply with that standard.
EU-adopted IFRS	IFRS that have been adopted in the European Union in accordance with EU Regulation 1606/2002

financial institution	Any of the following:
	(a) a bank which is:
	    (i) a firm with a Part IV permission[14] which includes accepting deposits and:
	        (a) which is a credit institution; or
	        (b) whose Part IV permission includes a requirement that it complies with the rules in the General Prudential sourcebook and the Prudential sourcebook for Banks, Building Societies and Investment Firms relating to banks, but which is not a building society, a friendly society or a credit union;
	    (ii) an EEA bank which is a full credit institution;
	(b) a building society which is defined in section 119(1) of the Building Societies Act 1986 as a building society incorporated (or deemed to be incorporated) under that act;
	(c) a credit union, being a body corporate registered under the Industrial and Provident Societies Act 1965 as a credit union in accordance with the Credit Unions Act 1979, which is an authorised person;
	(d) custodian bank, broker-dealer or stockbroker;
	(e) an entity that undertakes the business of effecting or carrying out insurance contracts, including general and life assurance entities;
	(f) an incorporated friendly society incorporated under the Friendly Societies Act 1992 or a registered friendly society registered under section 7(1)(a) of the Friendly Societies Act 1974 or any enactment which it replaced, including any registered branches;
	(g) an investment trust, Irish investment company, venture capital trust, mutual fund, exchange traded fund, unit trust, open-ended investment company (OEIC);
	(h) a retirement benefit plan; or
	(i) any other entity whose principal activity is to generate wealth or manage risk through financial instruments. This is intended to cover entities that have business activities similar to those listed above but are not specifically included in the list above.

[14] *As defined in section 40(4) of the Financial Services and Markets Act 2000 or references to equivalent provisions of any successor legislation.*

	A parent entity whose sole activity is to hold investments in other group entities is not a financial institution.
FRS 100	FRS 100 *Application of Financial Reporting Requirements*
FRS 101	FRS 101 *Reduced Disclosure Framework*
FRS 102	FRS 102 *The Financial Reporting Standard applicable in the UK and Republic of Ireland*
IAS Regulation	EU Regulation 1606/2002
IFRS	Standards and interpretations issued (or adopted) by the International Accounting Standards Board (IASB). They comprise: (a) International Financial Reporting Standards; (b) International Accounting Standards; and (c) Interpretations developed by the IFRS Interpretations Committee (the Interpretations Committee) or the former Standing Interpretations Committee (SIC).
individual financial statements	The accounts that are required to be prepared by an entity in accordance with the Act or relevant legislation, for example:
	(a) 'individual accounts', as set out in section 394 of the Act;' (b) 'statement of accounts', as set out in section 132 of the Charities Act 2011; or (c) 'individual accounts', as set out in section 72A of the Building Societies Act 1986. Separate financial statements are included in the meaning of this term.
public benefit entity	An entity whose primary objective is to provide goods or services for the general public, community or social benefit and where any equity is provided with a view to supporting the entity's primary objectives rather than with a view to providing a financial return to equity providers, shareholders or members.
qualifying entity	A member of a group where the parent of that group prepares publicly available consolidated financial statements which are intended to give a true and fair view (of the assets, liabilities, financial position and profit or loss) and that member is included in the consolidation[15]. A charity may not be a qualifying entity.
Regulations	The Large and Medium-sized Companies and Groups (Accounts and Reports) Regulations 2008 (SI 2008/410)

---

[15] *As set out in section 474(1) of the Act*

Appendix II: Note on legal requirements

INTRODUCTION

A2.1   This appendix provides an overview of how the requirements in FRS 101 address United Kingdom company law requirements. It is therefore written from the perspective of a company to which the Companies Act 2006 applies. Limited liability partnerships (LLPs) are subject to similar legal requirements and therefore may find this appendix useful (see paragraph A2.21). Appendix IV discusses Republic of Ireland legal references.

A2.2   References to the Act in this appendix are to the *Companies Act 2006*. References to the Regulations are to *The Large and Medium-sized Companies and Groups (Accounts and Reports) Regulations 2008* (SI 2008/410) as amended by *The Companies, Partnerships and Groups (Accounts and Reports) Regulations 2015* (SI 2015/980). References to specific provisions are to Schedule 1 to the Regulations; entities applying Schedules 2 or 3 should read them as referring to the equivalent paragraph in those schedules.

Companies Act accounts

A2.3   For companies, accounts prepared in accordance with EU-adopted IFRS are 'IAS accounts', and are within the scope of EU Regulation 1606/2002 (IAS Regulation). As stated in paragraph 4A of FRS 101, where a company prepares accounts in accordance with FRS 101, those accounts are Companies Act accounts and not IAS accounts as set out in section 395 of the Act. Therefore those accounts must comply with the applicable provisions of Parts 15 and 16 of the Act and with the Regulations.

Applicable accounting framework

Consistency of financial reporting within groups

A2.4   Section 407 of the Act requires that the directors of the parent company secure that individual accounts of a parent company and each of its subsidiaries are prepared using the same financial reporting framework, except to the extent that in the directors' opinion there are good reasons for not doing so.

In addition, consistency is not required in the following situations:

(a)   when the parent company does not prepare consolidated accounts; or
(b)   when some subsidiaries are charities (consistency is not needed between the framework used for these and for other subsidiaries).

Where the directors of a parent company prepare IAS group accounts and IAS individual accounts, there only has to be consistency across the individual financial statements of the subsidiaries.

A2.5   All companies, other than those which elect or are required to prepare IAS individual accounts in accordance with the Act, prepare Companies Act individual accounts.

Financial instruments measured at fair value

A2.5A   Paragraph 8 of FRS 101 permits qualifying entities that are not financial institutions to take advantage of exemptions from the disclosure requirements of IFRS 7 *Financial*

Instruments: Disclosures and IFRS 13 *Fair Value Measurement*. However, as noted in paragraph 4A of FRS 101 a qualifying entity must comply with any relevant legal requirements that are applicable to it.

Paragraph 36 of Schedule 1 to the Regulations states that: A2.6

1   *Subject to sub-paragraphs (2) to (5), financial instruments (including derivatives) may be included at fair value.*

2   *Sub-paragraph (1) does not apply to financial instruments that constitute liabilities unless—*

    (a)   *they are held as part of a trading portfolio,*

    (b)   *they are derivatives, or*

    (c)   *they are financial instruments falling within sub-paragraph (4).*

3   *Unless they are financial instruments falling within sub-paragraph (4), sub-paragraph (1) does not apply to—*

    (a)   *financial instruments (other than derivatives) held to maturity,*

    (b)   *loans and receivables originated by the company and not held for trading purposes,*

    (c)   *interests in subsidiary undertakings, associated undertakings and joint ventures,*

    (d)   *equity instruments issued by the company,*

    (e)   *contracts for contingent consideration in a business combination, or*

    (f)   *other financial instruments with such special characteristics that the instruments, according to generally accepted accounting principles or practice, should be accounted for differently from other financial instruments.*

4   *Financial instruments which under international accounting standards may be included in accounts at fair value, may be so included, provided that the disclosures required by such accounting standards are made.*

    [...]

A qualifying entity that has financial instruments measured at fair value in accordance with   A2.7
the requirements of paragraph 36(4) of Schedule 1 to the Regulations (or equivalent[16]), is legally required to provide the relevant disclosures set out in international accounting standards adopted by the European Commission. Such disclosures should be based on extant standards.

[Not used]   A2.7A

[Not used]   A2.7B

[Not used]   A2.7C

In addition, qualifying entities that are preparing Companies Act accounts must provide   A2.7D
the disclosures required by paragraph 55 of Schedule 1 to the Regulations which sets out requirements relating to financial instruments measured at fair value.

Non-amortisation of goodwill

A qualifying entity preparing accounts in accordance with FRS 101 may have recognised   A2.8
goodwill which, in accordance with IFRS 3 *Business Combinations*, is not amortised. The

---

[16] *The Small Companies and Groups (Accounts and Directors' Report) Regulations 2008 (SI 2008/409) contain an identical provision for companies subject to the small companies regime,* The Large and Medium-sized Limited Liability Partnerships (Accounts) Regulations 2008 *(SI 2008/1913) and* The Small Limited Liability Partnerships (Accounts) Regulations 2008 *(SI 2008/1912) contain similar requirements for limited liability partnerships (see paragraph A2.21).*

non-amortisation of goodwill conflicts with paragraph 22 of Schedule 1 to the Regulations, which requires acquired goodwill to be written off over its useful economic life. As such, the non-amortisation of goodwill will usually be a departure, for the overriding purpose of giving a true and fair view, from the requirement of paragraph 22 of Schedule 1 to the Regulations. In this circumstance there will need to be given in the notes to the accounts 'particulars of the departure, the reasons for it and its effect' (paragraph 10(2) of Schedule 1 to the Regulations). This is not a new instance of the use of the 'true and fair override' as paragraph 18 of FRS 10 *Goodwill and intangible* assets noted that it would have been required by companies applying paragraph 17 of FRS 10 which states 'Where goodwill and intangible assets are regarded as having indefinite useful economic lives, they should not be amortised.'

A2.8A   In addition, similar considerations may apply to intangible assets that are not amortised because they have an indefinite life and intangible assets that have a residual value that is not zero.

Presentation and formats

A2.9   A qualifying entity preparing accounts in accordance with FRS 101 must comply with the company law format requirements applicable to the statement of financial position and the statement of comprehensive income.

A2.9A   A qualifying entity choosing to apply paragraphs 1A(1) and 1A(2) of Schedule 1 to the Regulations, which permit a company to adapt the formats providing that the information given is at least equivalent to that which would have been required by the formats set out in the Regulations, shall apply the relevant presentation requirements of IAS 1, subject to:

(a)   the disclosure of profit or loss before taxation and the amendment to IFRS 5 *Non-current Assets Held for Sale and Discontinued Operations* set out in paragraph AG1(g) of this FRS; and

(b)   any further disaggregation of the statement of financial position, for example in relation to trade and other receivables and trade and other payables, (which may be provided in the notes to the financial statements) that is necessary to meet the requirement to give equivalent information.

This option is not available to a qualifying entity applying Schedule 2 or Schedule 3 to the Regulations or Schedule 1 to the LLP Regulations.

A2.9B   For a qualifying entity not permitted or not choosing to apply paragraphs 1A(1) and 1A(2) of Schedule 1 to the Regulations the format and presentation requirements of IAS 1 *Presentation of Financial Statements* may conflict with those in company law because of the following:

(a)   Differences in the definition of 'fixed assets'[17] (the term used in the Regulations) and 'non-current assets' (the term used in EU-adopted IFRS).

(b)   Differences in the definition of 'current assets' as the term is used in the Regulations and EU-adopted IFRS.

(c)   Differences in the definition of 'creditors falling due within or after one year' (the terms used in the Regulations) and 'current and non-current liabilities' (the term used in EU-adopted IFRS). Under the Act a loan is treated as due for repayment on the earliest date on which a lender could require repayment, whilst under EU-adopted IFRS the due date is based on when the entity expects to settle the liability or has no unconditional right to defer payment.

---

[17] *Assets of an entity which are intended for use on a continuing basis in the entity's activities.*

(d)   The Act requires presentation of debtors falling due after more than one year within current assets. Under EU-adopted IFRS those items would be presented in non-current assets. UITF Abstract 4 *Presentation of long-term debtors in current assets* (the UITF's consensus is reproduced below in paragraph A2.10) addressed the inclusion of debtors due after more than one year within 'current assets'.

In relation to paragraph A2.9(d), in most cases it will be satisfactory to disclose the size   **A2.10** of debtors due after more than one year in the notes to the accounts. There will be some instances, however, where the amount is so material in the context of the total net current assets that in the absence of disclosure of the debtors due after more than one year on the face of the balance sheet readers may misinterpret the accounts. In such circumstances, the amount should be disclosed on the face of the balance sheet within current assets.

Schedule 2 and Schedule 3 to the Regulations and the LLP Regulations require the separate   **A2.11** disclosure of extraordinary items in the profit and loss account. A qualifying entity preparing financial statements in accordance with FRS 101 must therefore disclose items that are deemed to be extraordinary items separately in the statement of comprehensive income. Entities should note that extraordinary items are extremely rare as they relate to highly abnormal events or transactions.

Prospective amendments: FRED 63 (December 2015) proposes insertion of paragraph A2.11A and the sub-heading preceding it with effect for annual periods beginning on or after [date].

Realised profits

Paragraph 13(a) of Schedule 1 to the Regulations requires that only profits realised at the   **A2.12** balance sheet date are included in the profit and loss account, a requirement modified from that in Article 3.1(c)(aa) of the Fourth Directive[18] which refers to profits 'made' at the balance sheet date.

Paragraph 39 of Schedule 1 to the Regulations allows stocks, investment property and   **A2.13** living animals and plants to be held at fair value in Companies Act accounts.

Paragraph 40(2) of Schedule 1 to the Regulations then requires that, in general, movements   **A2.14** in the value of financial instruments, stocks, investment properties or living animals or plants are recognised in the profit and loss account, notwithstanding the usual restrictions allowing only realised profits and losses to be included in the profit and loss account. Paragraph 40 of Schedule 1 to the Regulations thereby overrides the requirements of Paragraph 13(a) of Schedule 1.

Entities measuring investment properties, living animals or plants, or financial instruments   **A2.15** at fair value should note that they may transfer such amounts to a separate non-distributable reserve instead of carrying them forward in retained earnings but are not required to do so. Presenting fair value movements that are not distributable profits in a separate reserve may assist with the identification of profits available for that purpose.

Entities should also continue to note that whether profits are available for distribution must   **A2.16** be determined in accordance with applicable law. Entities may also refer to the Technical Release 02/10 *Guidance on Realised and Distributable Profits under the Companies Act 2006* issued by the Institute of Chartered Accountants in England and Wales and the Institute of Chartered Accountants of Scotland or any successor document, to determine profits available for distribution.

---

[18] *European Commission, Council Directive 78/660/EEC.*

Accounting for investment entities

A2.17   FRS 101 is not applicable to the preparation of consolidated financial statements as it is only applicable to the individual financial statements of a qualifying entity. However, the requirement set out in paragraph 11A of IAS 27 *Separate Financial Statements* which states:

> *If a parent is required, in accordance with paragraph 31 of IFRS 10 to measure its investment in a subsidiary at fair value through profit or loss in accordance with IFRS 9, it shall also account for its investment in a subsidiary in the same way in its separate financial statements.*

will be applicable to the treatment of investments in subsidiaries in the individual financial statements of a qualifying entity applying FRS 101, if the entity meets the definition of an investment entity in IFRS 10 *Consolidated Financial Statements*. In other words, a qualifying entity that meets the definition of an investment entity under IFRS 10 must measure its investment in subsidiaries at fair value through profit or loss in its individual financial statements.

A2.18   The Regulations permit investments in subsidiaries to be measured on three different bases as follows:

(a)   at historical cost using the historical cost accounting rules;
(b)   at fair value with fair value movements recognised in reserves using the alternative accounting rules; or
(c)   at fair value with fair value movements recognised in profit or loss using the fair value accounting rules.

A2.19   The requirement to measure investments in subsidiaries at fair value through profit or loss under paragraph 11A of IAS 27 does not conflict with these requirements but merely restricts the measurement bases that an investment entity may apply to such investments.

A2.20   Paragraph 36(4) of Schedule 1 to the Regulations permits investments in subsidiaries to be measured at fair value provided that international accounting standards adopted in the EU allow such measurement, and that an entity makes the disclosures required by such standards. IAS 39 *Financial Instruments: Recognition and Measurement* which was endorsed by the EU in November 2004 and was applicable to accounting periods beginning on or after 1 January 2005, permits the designation of financial instruments at fair value through profit or loss on initial recognition. As noted in paragraph A2.7 such disclosures should be based on extant standards.

LLPs

A2.21   Limited liability partnerships (LLPs) applying FRS 101 will be doing so in conjunction with the LLP Regulations. In many cases these Regulations are similar to the Regulations, limiting the situations in which legal matters relevant to the financial statements of LLPs are not addressed in this Appendix. However, amendments made to the Regulations by *The Companies, Partnerships and Groups (Accounts and Reports) Regulations 2015* (SI 2015/980) have not been reflected in the LLP Regulations. This gives rise to some differences for LLPs. Areas where this may have an impact include:

(a)   the flexibility available in relation to the format of the balance sheet and of the profit and loss account;
(b)   the scope of financial instruments that can be measured at fair value through profit or loss;
(c)   the reversal of impairment losses in relation to goodwill; and
(d)   the application of merger accounting.

If following the requirements of FRS 101 would lead to a conflict with applicable legislation, an LLP shall instead apply its own legal requirements and consider whether disclosure of a departure from FRS 101 is required.

Table I Areas for consideration by a qualifying entity preparing accounts in accordance with FRS 101 *Reduced Disclosure Framework*, in order to ensure compliance with the Act

IFRS	Explanation/potential issues	Amendment to EU-adopted IFRS
IFRS 1	*Assets and liabilities of a parent or subsidiaries*	
	IFRS 1 provides an option for a subsidiary which becomes a first-time adopter later than its parent, which allows the subsidiary to measure its assets and liabilities at the carrying amounts that would be included in the parent's consolidated financial statements, based on the parent's date of transition to IFRS (D16).	Restricted the application of the first-time adoption options in IFRS 1 D16 and D17 to situations where the measurement of assets and liabilities in the subsidiary's or parent's individual financial statements based on the consolidated financial statements would comply with FRS 101.
	Under IFRS 1, if a parent becomes a first-time adopter later than in its consolidated financial statements, it shall measure its assets and liabilities at the same carrying amounts as in the consolidated financial statements (D17).	
	Entities preparing their financial statements in accordance with FRS 101 must comply with the measurement requirements of the Act, which may be inconsistent with those of EU-adopted IFRS applied in the consolidated financial statements.	
IFRS 3	*Negative goodwill*	
	IFRS 3 requires that negative goodwill is recognised as a gain in profit or loss at the acquisition date (IFRS 3.34). The Act does not contain accounting requirements for a negative consolidation difference subsequent to recognition. Nevertheless, the Seventh Directive 19 sets out conditions under which a negative consolidation difference may be transferred to the profit and loss account. The conditions under the Seventh Accounting Directive may be inconsistent with the recognition requirements for negative goodwill under EU-adopted IFRS.	Amended IFRS 3.34 to align with FRS 102, Section 19 *Business Combinations and Goodwill*, paragraph 19.24.

IFRS	Explanation/potential issues	Amendment to EU-adopted IFRS
IFRS 5	*Analysis of results of discontinued operation*	
	IFRS 5 allows the analysis of post-tax results of discontinued operations to be presented on the face of the statement of comprehensive income or in the notes (IFRS 5.33). The Regulations require an entity to show totals for turnover, profit or loss before taxation and tax arising from ordinary activities on the face of the profit and loss account.	Removed the option in IFRS 5.33 to present the analysis in the notes to the accounts. The information must be presented on the face of the statement of comprehensive income in a columnar format.
IAS 1	*Formats*	
	The format requirements applicable under IAS 1 and those under the Regulations may be incompatible.	IAS 1.53A and IAS 1.81C are inserted to disapply IAS 1.54 to IAS 1.76, IAS 1.82 and IAS 1.84 to IAS 1.86, unless certain options in Schedule 1 to the Regulations are chosen.
	Extraordinary items	
	IAS 1 does not permit the presentation of extraordinary items (IAS 1.87) however, for some companies and LLPs the Regulations (and LLP Regulations) require it.	Amended IAS 1.87 and inserted IAS 1.87A and IAS 1.87B to include the definition of extraordinary items consistent with that in FRS 102, Section 5 *Statement of comprehensive income and income statement*, paragraphs 5.10A and 5.10B.
	Realised profits	
	IAS 1 requires the recognition of all income and expenses in profit or loss, unless otherwise required or permitted by an IFRS (IAS 1.88). The Regulations require that only profits realised at the balance sheet date are included in the profit and loss account (see paragraphs A2.12 to A2.15 above).	Amended IAS 1.88 to clarify the precedence of the Act.
IAS 16	*Government grants*	

IFRS	Explanation/potential issues	Amendment to EU-adopted IFRS
	IAS 16.28 permits the carrying amount of property, plant and equipment to be reduced by government grants in accordance with IAS 20. Off-setting of items that represent assets against items that represent liabilities is prohibited under the Regulations, unless specifically permitted or required. This option in EU-adopted IFRS is not compliant with the Regulations.	Deleted IAS 16.28.
IAS 20	*Balance sheet off-setting*	
	IAS 20.24 contains an option which permits government grants related to assets to be deducted in arriving at the carrying amount of the asset. Off-setting of items that represent assets against items that represent liabilities is prohibited under the Regulations, unless specifically permitted or required. This option in EU-adopted IFRS is not compliant with the Regulations.	Amended IAS 20.24, IAS 20.26, IAS 20.28 and deleted IAS 20.25 and IAS 20.27 to remove the off-set option.
	Profit and loss account off-setting	
	IAS 20.29 contains an option which permits grants related to income to be deducted in reporting the related expense. Off-setting of items that represent income against items that represent expenditure is prohibited under the Regulations, unless specifically permitted or required. This option in EU-adopted IFRS is not compliant with the Regulations.	Amended IAS 20.29 to remove the off-set option.

[19] *European Commission, Council Directive 83/349/EEC.*

Appendix III: Previous consultations

HISTORY OF PREVIOUS CONSULTATIONS

The requirements in FRSs 100 to 102 are the outcome of a lengthy and extensive **A3.1**
consultation. The FRC (and formerly the ASB) together with the Department for Business,
Innovation and Skills have consulted on the future of accounting standards in the UK and
Republic of Ireland (RoI) over a ten year period.

Table 1 – Consultations conducted

Year	Consultation
2002	DTI[20] consults on adoption of IAS Regulation
2004	Discussion Paper – Strategy for Convergence with IFRS
2005	Exposure Draft – Policy Statement: The Role of the ASB
2006	Public Meeting and Proposals for Comment
2006	Press Notice seeking views
2007	Consultation Paper – Proposed IFRS for SMEs
2009	Consultation Paper – Policy Proposal: The future of UK GAAP
2010	Request for Responses – Development of the Impact Assessment
2010	Financial Reporting Exposure Drafts 43 and 44
2011	Financial Reporting Exposure Draft 45
2012	Financial Reporting Exposure Drafts 46, 47 and 48

2004

In 2004 the Discussion Paper contained two key elements underpinning the proposals: **A3.2**
firstly that UK and Republic of Ireland (RoI) accounting standards should be based on
IFRS and secondly that a phased approach to the introduction of the standards should be
adopted.

The ASB embarked on the phased approach and issued a number of standards based on **A3.3**
IFRS. The majority of respondents agreed with a framework based on IFRS, and although
supportive overall, the response to the phased approach was mixed.

2005

In its 2005 Exposure Draft (2005 ED) of a Policy Statement *Accounting standard-setting in a* **A3.4**
changing environment: The role of the Accounting Standards Board, amongst other aspects
of its role, the ASB identified its intention to converge with IFRS by implementing new
IFRS in the UK as soon as possible. It also proposed to continue the phased approach to
adopting UK accounting standards based on older IFRSs, but recognised there was little
case for being more prescriptive than IFRS.

---

[20] *The Department of Trade and Industry (DTI) was a United Kingdom government department which was replaced
with the announcement of the creation of the Department for Business, Enterprise and Regulatory Reform and
the Department for Innovation, Universities and Skills on 28 June 2007, which were themselves merged into the
Department for Business, Innovation and Skills (BIS) on 6 June 2009.*

A3.5   Although the ASB had, in the 2005 ED, wanted to move the debate on to how it would seek to influence the IASB's agenda, respondents' main concern remained about convergence. In 2005, the ASB issued an exposure draft proposing the IASB's standard on Business Combinations be adopted in the UK and RoI. This exposure draft highlighted the complexity of a mixed set of UK accounting standards, with some based on IFRSs and others developed independently by the ASB. The majority of respondents continued to agree with the aim of basing UK accounting standards on IFRS, but a broader set of views on how to achieve this was emerging.

A3.6   As time progressed the ASB formed the view that convergence by adopting certain IFRSs was not meeting the needs of its constituents, which no longer included quoted groups. The ASB was concerned about the complexity of certain IFRSs, and it noted that introducing them piecemeal created complications and anomalies within the body of current FRSs. This arose because IFRS-based standards were not an exact replacement for current FRSs and many consequential amendments were required to 'fit' each replacement IFRS-based standard into the existing body of UK FRS. The ASB agreed to continue with its convergence programme, but decided to re-examine how to achieve this.

2006

A3.7   The ASB published revised proposals to be discussed at the 2006 public meeting. By this time the IASB had started its IFRS for SMEs project, and the ASB decided this might have a role as one of the tiers in the UK financial reporting framework. The ASB proposed a 'big bang' with new IFRS-based UK accounting standards mandatory from a single date, 1 January 2009. The ASB's proposal was for a three-tier system, with Tier 1 being EU-adopted IFRS, and the other two tiers being developed as the IASB progressed with its project on the IFRS for SMEs.

A3.8   Those attending the public meeting supported the aim of basing UK and RoI accounting standards on IFRS and adapting them to ensure they were appropriate for the entities applying them.

A3.9   Taking this feedback into account, later in 2006 the ASB issued a Press Notice (PN 289) seeking views on its current thinking:

(a)   All quoted and publicly accountable companies should apply EU-adopted IFRS.

(b)   The FRSSE should be retained and extended to include medium-sized entities.

(c)   UK subsidiaries of groups applying full IFRS should apply EU-adopted IFRS, but with reduced disclosure requirements.

(d)   No firm decision on the remainder (Tier 2), but options included extending the FRSSE, extending full IFRS, maintaining separate UK accounting standards or some combination of these.

A3.10   The responses were mixed, but there was agreement that whatever the solution, it should be based on IFRS and there should be different reporting tiers to ensure proportionality.

2007

A3.11   The IASB published an exposure draft of its IFRS for SMEs in early 2007; shortly afterwards the ASB published its own consultation paper. This sought views on how the IFRS for SMEs might fit into the future UK financial reporting framework, for example whether it might be appropriate for Tier 2, with the FRSSE continuing for those eligible for the small companies' regime.

Feedback on the IFRS for SMEs was largely positive: it would be suitable for Tier 2, it was **A3.12** international, it was compatible with IFRSs, and it represented a significant simplification. Overall, it was seen as a workable alternative to IFRS. In addition, respondents wanted to retain the FRSSE (because it reduces the regulatory burden on smaller entities) and to give subsidiaries the option of applying the IFRS for SMEs as well as a reduced disclosure regime if applying full IFRS.

2009

The IFRS for SMEs was published in 2009, allowing the ASB to further develop its proposals **A3.13** in the Consultation Paper *Policy Proposal: The future of UK GAAP*. The proposals were largely consistent with the cumulative results of the preceding consultations and included:

(a)   a move to an IFRS-based framework;
(b)   a three-tier approach;
(c)   publicly accountable entities would be Tier 1 and would apply EU-adopted IFRS;
(d)   small companies would be Tier 3 and continue to apply the FRSSE; and
(e)   other entities would be Tier 2 and should apply a UK and RoI accounting standard based on the IFRS for SMEs.

The only significant proposal that was inconsistent with respondents' previous comments **A3.14** was that subsidiaries should simply apply the requirement of the tier they individually met – respondents had wanted subsidiaries to be able to take advantage of disclosure exemptions, and at that time the ASB had yet to be convinced that significant cost savings were available from a reduced disclosure framework. Taking into account the feedback received, this proposal was subsequently reversed and the reduced disclosure framework was incorporated into FREDs 43 and then 46, and it is now set out in FRS 101.

In addition to the many useful and detailed points made, some common themes included **A3.15** general agreement that change was needed to UK accounting standards and that there was support for many of the changes proposed in the consultation paper.

2010 onwards

The request for responses to aid development of the Impact Assessment focused on **A3.16** obtaining feedback on the expected costs, benefits and impact of the proposals subsequently set out in FREDs 43 and 44, rather than on the accounting principles. As the focus was on costs and benefits no specific question was asked about the principle of the proposed introduction of an IFRS-based framework, but nevertheless respondents commented on this: of the 32 responses received only 12.5% did not agree with the introduction of an IFRS-based framework.

FREDs 43 and 44 issued in October 2010 set out the draft suggested text for two new **A3.17** accounting standards that would replace the majority of extant Financial Reporting Standards (current FRS) in the UK and RoI. The ASB issued a supplementary FRED addressing specific needs of public benefit entities (FRED 45) in March 2011. The ASB then updated FREDs 43, 44 and 45, replacing them with the revised FREDs 46, 47 and 48 in January 2012, by eliminating the concept of public accountability and by introducing a number of accounting treatment options that are available in EU-adopted IFRS. The Accounting Council's advice to the FRC to issue FRSs 100 to 102 includes more discussion of the feedback received on FREDs 43 to 48 and how the proposals have been refined and developed into the standards.

How have the proposals been developed?

A3.18   As set out above, the FRC, the Accounting Council (and previously the ASB) have consulted regularly on the future of financial reporting in the UK and RoI. Over the consultations the ASB's (and the Accounting Council's) thinking has evolved based on careful consideration of the feedback at each stage. Whilst responses were sometimes mixed, there has been agreement that:

(a)   current FRS, which are a mixture of Statements of Standard Accounting Practice (SSAPs) issued by the Consultative Committee of Accounting Bodies, FRSs developed and issued by the ASB and IFRS-based standards issued by the ASB to converge with international standards, are an uncomfortable mismatch that lack strong underlying principles or cohesion; and

(b)   whatever the solution, it should be based on IFRS and there should be different reporting tiers to ensure proportionality.

A3.19   During the consultation process to date, the Accounting Council and formerly the ASB have been guided by the following principles:

(a)   The framework must be fit for purpose, so that each entity required to produce true and fair financial statements under UK and RoI law will deliver financial statements that are suited to the needs of its primary users. The Accounting Council has kept in close contact with constituent users on this point, including investors, creditor institutions and the tax authorities.

(b)   The framework must be proportionate, so that preparing entities are not unduly burdened by costs that outweigh the benefit to them and to the primary users of information in their financial statements. The FRC believes that the proposals will produce a lower cost regime, while enhancing user benefits. It has carried out a consultation stage impact assessment with input from interested parties, and will continue to assess cost-benefit issues.

(c)   The framework must be in line with UK company law. This determines which entities must produce true and fair financial statements. Exemptions within the law have generally been retained. The detailed requirements of the Companies Act 2006 are driven to a great extent by the European Accounting Directives, which are being revised[14].

(d)   The framework must be future-proofed, where possible. The FRC will continue to monitor the situation and has sovereignty over UK accounting standards (subject to the law). Changes to the Accounting Directives may lead to further developments, for example the European Council and European Parliament decision to permit Member States an option to treat micro-entities as a separate category of Company and exempt them from certain accounting requirements.

Summary of outreach

A3.20   During the development and throughout the consultation period of FREDs 43 to 48, the ASB undertook an extensive programme of outreach aimed at raising awareness of the proposals and to address the view (held by some) that previous consultations had not gathered sufficient evidence to support and test the assumptions made.

A3.21   As part of the outreach programme to obtain both formal and informal feedback, a series of meetings and events took place with users, including with lenders to small and medium-sized entities. Lenders noted that financial statements are an important part of

---

[14] *The EU's consultation process on review of the Accounting Directives is summarised at http://ec.europa.eu/ internal_market/accounting/sme_accounting/review_directives_en.htm*

their decision-making process when considering whether to provide finance and, whilst a decision to provide finance is not based on financial statements alone, they provide useful information and verification to the lender.

Although the ASB and the Accounting Council employed their best efforts to obtain feedback from users (a constituent group historically difficult to engage with formally) it is disappointing that limited formal responses were received and the Accounting Council has not been more successful in obtaining input from users.   **A3.22**

In addition, a review was made of academic research that addressed the users of the financial statements of small and medium-sized entities. The conclusion drawn from the research was that many entities requested financial statements from Companies House when considering whether to trade with another entity. The European Federation of Accountants and Auditors (EFAA) issued, in May 2011, a statement that identified the users of financial statements, noting who the users of SMEs' financial statements are and that information on the public record assists all users of financial statements of SMEs' by providing, in an efficient manner, basic information that protects their rights.   **A3.23**

The ASB considered that the outreach programme had gleaned information from people who would not normally submit formal responses to a consultation and provided very useful information that could be used in developing the next stage of the project. The ASB noted that whilst this information was not part of the public record, as are formal consultation responses, it could use the information to assist in developing the revised FREDs 46 to 48, supplementing information contained in responses, and would seek further comment in the next stage of its deliberations.   **A3.24**

The Accounting Council continued the work of the ASB in finalising FRSs 100 to 102. The responses to FREDs 46 to 48 were analysed and discussed, and engagements were conducted to take into account the views and suggestions of all relevant associations and contacts. Respondents and outreach contacts were satisfied with FREDs 46 to 48, and many of the response letters were forthcoming in their overall praise for the proposals. A significant number of constituents anticipated cost savings arising from the application of FRS 101. Many respondents considered that FRS 102 would improve UK accounting standards, in particular by introducing requirements for accounting for financial instruments. Further they considered that the improvements will be achieved in a way that will be proportionate to the needs of users, and that once the transition phase has been overcome, it will have the effect of reducing the reporting burden on those UK companies that adopt it.   **A3.25**

Appendix IV: Republic of Ireland (RoI) legal references

A4.1   Appendix IV: *Republic of Ireland (RoI) legal references* will be updated as appropriate for both the Companies Act 2014 and the Irish legislation implementing the EU Accounting Directive once the latter has been made. This will be made available on the FRC website and included in the next edition of FRS 101.

Amendments to FRS 101 Reduced Disclosure Framework 2015/16 cycle

(July 2016)

Contents

Paragraphs

Summary

Amendments to FRS 101 Reduced Disclosure Framework
Amendments to FRS 101   1–2

Amendments to Appendix II: Note on legal requirements   3–5

Approval by the FRC

The Corporate Reporting Council's Advice to the FRC to issue Amendments to FRS 101 – 2015/16 cycle
Introduction   1–4
Advice   5–7
Background   8–10
Amendments to FRS 101   11–15
Equity method in separate financial statements   16
Disclosure initiative   17–23
Approval of this advice   24

Amendments to FRS 101 Reduced Disclosure Framework – 2015/16 cycle amends an accounting standard. It is issued by the Financial Reporting Council in respect of its application in the United Kingdom and promulgated by the Institute of Chartered Accountants in Ireland in respect of its application in the Republic of Ireland.

Summary

(i)   With effect from 1 January 2015, the Financial Reporting Council (FRC) revised financial reporting standards in the United Kingdom and Republic of Ireland. The revisions fundamentally reformed financial reporting, replacing the extant standards with five Financial Reporting Standards:

   (a)   FRS 100 *Application of Financial Reporting Requirements*;
   (b)   FRS 101 *Reduced Disclosure Framework*;
   (c)   FRS 102 *The Financial Reporting Standard applicable in the UK and Republic of Ireland*;
   (d)   FRS 103 *Insurance Contracts*; and
   (e)   FRS 104 *Interim Financial Reporting*.

   The FRC has also issued FRS 105 *The Financial Reporting Standard applicable to the Micro-entities Regime* to support the implementation of the new micro-entities regime. It is effective from 1 January 2016 with early application permitted.

   These limited amendments to FRS 101 arise as a result of the 2015/16 annual review and provide additional disclosure exemptions.

(ii)   The FRC's overriding objective in setting accounting standards is to enable users of accounts to receive high-quality understandable financial reporting proportionate to the size and complexity of the entity and users' information needs.

(iii)   In meeting this objective, the FRC aims to provide succinct financial reporting standards that:

   (a)   have consistency with international accounting standards through the application of an IFRS-based solution unless an alternative clearly better meets the overriding objective;
   (b)   reflect up-to-date thinking and developments in the way entities operate and the transactions they undertake;
   (c)   balance consistent principles for accounting by all UK and Republic of Ireland entities with practical solutions, based on size, complexity, public interest and users' information needs;
   (d)   promote efficiency within groups; and
   (e)   are cost-effective to apply.

Amendments to FRS 101

(iv)   After considering the 2015/16 annual review of FRS 101 these amendments principally provide certain disclosure exemptions in relation to IFRS 15 *Revenue from Contracts with Customers* and clarify a legal requirement relating to the order in which the notes to the financial statements are presented.

Amendments to FRS 101 Reduced Disclosure Framework

Amendments to FRS 101

The following paragraphs set out the amendments to FRS 101 *Reduced Disclosure* 1
Framework (inserted text is underlined).

Paragraph 8(eA) is inserted as follows: 2

8(eA) The requirements of the second sentence of paragraph 110 and paragraphs 113(a),
114, 115, 118, 119(a) to (c), 120 to 127 and 129 of IFRS 15 *Revenue from Contracts
with Customers*.

Amendments to Appendix II: Note on legal requirements

The following paragraphs set out the amendments to Appendix II: *Note on legal* 3
requirements (inserted text is underlined).

Paragraph A2.7E and the sub-heading preceding it are inserted as follows: 4

Equity method in separate financial statements

A2.7E Paragraph 29A of Schedule 1 to the Regulations permits participating interests
to be accounted for using the equity method. However, Schedules 2 and 3 to the
Regulations do not include an equivalent paragraph. Therefore entities applying either
Schedule 2 or Schedule 3 to the Regulations may not take advantage of the option in
paragraph 10(c) of IAS 27 *Separate Financial Statements* to account for investments
in subsidiaries, joint ventures and associates using the equity method.

Paragraphs A2.11A and A2.11B and the sub-heading preceding them are inserted as 5
follows:

Notes to the financial statements

A2.11A Paragraph 42(2) of Schedule 1 to the Regulations requires the notes to the
financial statements to be presented in the order in which, where relevant, the items
to which they relate are presented in the statement of financial position and the
income statement. A qualifying entity preparing financial statements in accordance
with FRS 101 shall have regard to this requirement when determining a systematic
manner for the presentation of its notes to the financial statements in accordance with
paragraphs 113 and 114 of IAS 1.

A2.11B Paragraph 68 of Schedule 1 to the Regulations requires particulars of
turnover to be disclosed, including the amount of turnover attributable to each class
of business carried on by the company. When relevant, turnover attributable to
different geographical markets must also be disclosed. Although this FRS provides an
exemption from paragraph 114 of IFRS 15 *Revenue from Contracts with Customers*,
the requirements of the Regulations shall still be complied with.

Approval by the FRC

Amendments to FRS 101 *Reduced Disclosure Framework – 2015/16 cycle* was approved for issue by the Board of the Financial Reporting Council on 28 June 2016, following its consideration of the Corporate Reporting Council's Advice.

The Corporate Reporting Council's Advice to the FRC to issue Amendments to FRS 101 – 2015/16 cycle

Introduction

1   This report provides an overview of the main issues that have been considered by the Corporate Reporting Council in advising the Financial Reporting Council (FRC) to issue *Amendments to FRS 101 Reduced Disclosure Framework – 2015/16 cycle*.

2   The FRC, in accordance with the *Statutory Auditors (Amendment of Companies Act 2006 and Delegation of Functions etc) Order 2012* (SI 2012/1741), is a prescribed body for issuing accounting standards in the UK. The *Foreword to Accounting Standards* sets out the application of accounting standards in the Republic of Ireland.

3   In accordance with the *FRC Codes and Standards: procedures*, any proposal to issue, amend or withdraw a code or standard is put to the FRC Board with the full advice of the relevant Councils and/or the Codes & Standards Committee. Ordinarily, the FRC Board will only reject the advice put to it where:

   (a)   it is apparent that a significant group of stakeholders has not been adequately consulted;
   (b)   the necessary assessment of the impact of the proposal has not been completed, including an analysis of costs and benefits;
   (c)   insufficient consideration has been given to the timing or cost of implementation; or
   (d)   the cumulative impact of a number of proposals would make the adoption of an otherwise satisfactory proposal inappropriate.

4   The FRC has established the Corporate Reporting Council as the relevant Council to assist it in the setting of accounting standards.

Advice

5   The Corporate Reporting Council is advising the FRC to issue *Amendments to FRS 101 Reduced Disclosure Framework – 2015/16 cycle*.

6   The Corporate Reporting Council advises that these proposals will ensure that FRS 101 *Reduced Disclosure Framework* continues to be effective in providing disclosure reductions when compared with EU-adopted IFRS and maintains consistency with company law.

7   The Accounting Council's Advice[1] to the FRC to issue FRS 101 was set out in that standard. The Corporate Reporting Council's Advice to the FRC in respect of these amendments will be included in the revised FRS 101.

---

[1] *From 1 April 2016 the Accounting Council was renamed as the Corporate Reporting Council.*

Background

In October 2012, as part of its advice relating to the first edition of FRS 101, the Accounting **8** Council advised the FRC to update FRS 101 at regular intervals to ensure that the reduced disclosure framework continues to be effective in providing disclosure reductions when compared with EU-adopted IFRS. An annual review is carried out to consider changes in IFRS and their potential impact on FRS 101.

The 2015/16 annual review considered: **9**

(a)   IASB projects completed since the 2014/15 cycle; and
(b)   IFRS 15 *Revenue from Contracts with Customers*, which was carried forward from the previous review.

The FRC consulted on proposals for amendments to FRS 101 in FRED 63 *Draft* **10** *amendments to FRS 101 – 2015/16 cycle*. The responses to FRED 63 have been considered in developing this advice.

Amendments to FRS 101

The Accounting Council advised the FRC that the following principles should be applied **11** when determining which of the disclosure requirements in EU-adopted IFRS should be applied by qualifying entities:

1   Relevance:
     Does the disclosure requirement provide information that is capable of making a difference to the decisions made by the users of the financial statements of a qualifying entity?
2   Cost constraint on useful financial reporting:
     Does the disclosure requirement impose costs on the preparers of the financial statements of a qualifying entity that are not justified by the benefits to the users of those financial statements?
3   Avoid gold plating:
     Does the disclosure requirement override an existing exemption provided by company law in the UK?

The Corporate Reporting Council notes that respondents to FRED 63 continue to support **12** these principles. It also notes that when applying FRS 101, and deciding which disclosure exemptions to take advantage of, entities shall bear in mind the need to ensure that disclosures are relevant and targeted to meet the needs of users.

IASB projects completed since the 2014/15 cycle

The IASB has completed four projects since those considered in the review for the 2014/15 **13** cycle, which was performed in August 2014. In addition, one project was brought forward for consideration as part of this review.

	IASB project	Date issued	Date effective	Date endorsed in the EU
1	Equity Method in Separate Financial Statements (Amendments to IAS 27)	Aug 2014	1 Jan 2016	Dec 2015
2	Sale or Contribution of Assets between an Investor and its Associate or Joint Venture (Amendments to IFRS 10 and IAS 28)	Sept 2014	1 Jan 2016	Postponed

IASB project	Date issued	Date effective	Date endorsed in the EU
3 Annual Improvements to IFRSs (2012–2014 Cycle)	Sept 2014	1 Jan 2016	Dec 2015
4 Investment Entities: Applying the Consolidation Exception (Amendments to IFRS 10, IFRS 12 and IAS 28)	Dec 2014	1 Jan 2016	Expected Q3 2016
5 Disclosure Initiative (Amendments to IAS 1)	Dec 2014	1 Jan 2016	Dec 2015

14   The amendments[2] resulting from these five projects were reviewed in the context of the reduced disclosure framework for any amendments that:

(a)   alter disclosure requirements, as consideration will need to be given to whether changes should be made to the disclosure exemptions permitted in FRS 101; and/or

(b)   are inconsistent with current UK legal requirements, as consideration will need to be given to whether changes should be made to the Application Guidance: *Amendments to International Financial Reporting Standards as Adopted in the European Union for Compliance with the Act and the Regulations* to FRS 101.

15   The Corporate Reporting Council advises that only limited amendment to FRS 101 are necessary in relation to these amendments to IFRS. These are discussed below.

Equity method in separate financial statements

16   Following changes that implemented the EU Accounting Directive, company law now permits the use of the equity method in an entity's individual financial statements for entities applying Schedule 1 to the Regulations. This is not the case for entities applying Schedule 2 or Schedule 3 to the Regulations. As a result, the Corporate Reporting Council advises that no amendments to FRS 101 itself are necessary in relation to the recent amendment to IAS 27 *Separate Financial Statements*. However, an additional paragraph (paragraph A2.7E) has been included in Appendix II: Note on legal requirements to discuss this issue as the requirements are not universal.

Disclosure initiative

17   The Corporate Reporting Council notes that this project was intended to clarify existing requirements and give greater guidance, particularly on the application of materiality to disclosures, the levels of aggregation (or disaggregation) permitted and the order in which notes might be presented. As a result, it did not change disclosure requirements.

18   However, one area where additional guidance was included relates to the systematic manner in which the notes to the financial statements are presented. Company law contains a requirement about the order in which the notes to the financial statements shall be presented. The amendments to IAS 1 *Presentation of Financial Statements* paragraphs 113 and 114 do not require entities to present notes to the financial statements in an order that would conflict with this legal requirement. However, some of the examples of how to present notes in a systematic manner are unlikely to comply with company law. Therefore the Corporate Reporting Council advises including an additional paragraph (paragraph A2.11A) in Appendix II to discuss this issue.

---

[2] *The full IASB documents setting out the amendments for each project are available on the IASB website (www.ifrs.org).*

IFRS 15 Revenue from Contracts with Customers

The disclosure requirements of IFRS 15 have been compared to the principles set out in **19** paragraph 11. In doing so, the Corporate Reporting Council considered further how the principle of 'relevance' should be applied in the context of disclosure by qualifying entities. It noted that qualifying entities usually have few users of their financial statements, and particularly few users that would be external to the group that the qualifying entity is part of. Any external users are likely to be providers of credit to the qualifying entity.

The Corporate Reporting Council considered that the interest which a provider of credit **20** has in the financial statements of a qualifying entity is generally likely to be focused on information about the liquidity and solvency of the qualifying entity. This is because that information might be relevant to the ability of the qualifying entity to pay (or repay) any credit advanced. As a result, in relation to the detailed disclosures required by IFRS 15, there would be greater interest in information supporting the statement of financial position, rather than information supporting the income statement.

As a result, the Corporate Reporting Council advises that significant disclosure exemptions **21** from IFRS 15 should be available to qualifying entities. The Corporate Reporting Council noted the following related requirements:

(a) company law requirements relating to disaggregation of turnover (which are reflected in paragraph A2.11B); and
(b) IAS 1 contains requirements relating to judgements having a significant effect on the amounts recognised in an entity's financial statements.

Having taken into account user's information needs and existing disclosure requirements, the **22** Corporate Reporting Council advises that disclosure exemptions from paragraphs 113(a), 114, 115, 118, 119(a) to (c), 120 to 127 and 129 should be available. In order to clarify the remaining requirements:

(a) an exemption from the second sentence of paragraph 110 should be provided to remove the cross-references to these later paragraphs; and
(b) it should be noted that although paragraph 117 (from which a qualifying entity is not exempt) cross-refers to paragraph 119, it is not necessary to comply with paragraph 119 in order to meet the requirements of paragraph 117.

Effective date

Paragraph 8 of FRS 101 notes that the exemptions are available from when the relevant **23** standard is applied. Therefore there is no need to amend the effective date for these proposed amendments. However, it should be noted that the change in company law to permit the equity method in individual financial statements is effective from 1 January 2016 (or 1 January 2015 if it is applied early), which is the same date as the amendment to IAS 27.

Approval of this advice

This advice to the FRC was approved by the Corporate Reporting Council on 18 May 2016. **24**

FRS 102
The Financial Reporting Standard applicable in the UK and Republic of Ireland

(September 2015)

Contents

Paragraphs

Summary

FRS 102 The Financial Reporting Standard applicable in the UK and Republic of Ireland

Section 1	Scope	1.1–1.13
Section 1A	Small Entities	1A.1–1A.22
Appendix A:	Guidance on adapting the balance sheet formats	1AA.1–1AA.6
Appendix B:	Guidance on adapting the profit and loss account formats	1AB.1–1AB.4
Appendix C:	Disclosure requirements for small entities	1AC.1–1AC.39
Appendix D:	Additional disclosures encouraged for small entities	1AD.1
Section 2	Concepts and Pervasive Principles	2.1–2.52
Section 3	Financial Statement Presentation	3.1–3.25
Section 4	Statement of Financial Position	4.1–4.14
Section 5	Statement of Comprehensive Income and Income Statement	5.1–5.11
Section 6	Statement of Changes in Equity and Statement of Income and Retained Earnings	6.1–6.5
Section 7	Statement of Cash Flows	7.1–7.21
Section 8	Notes to the Financial Statements	8.1–8.7
Section 9	Consolidated and Separate Financial Statements	9.1–9.38
Section 10	Accounting Policies, Estimates and Errors	10.1–10.23
Section 11	Basic Financial Instruments	11.1–11.48C
Section 12	Other Financial Instruments Issues	12.1–12.29A
Section 13	Inventories	13.1–13.22
Section 14	Investments in Associates	14.1–14.15A
Section 15	Investments in Joint Ventures	15.1–15.21A
Section 16	Investment Property	16.1–16.11
Section 17	Property, Plant and Equipment	17.1–17.32A
Section 18	Intangible Assets other than Goodwill	18.1–18.29A
Section 19	Business Combinations and Goodwill	19.1–19.33
Section 20	Leases	20.1–20.35
Section 21	Provisions and Contingencies	21.1–21.17A
Section 22	Liabilities and Equity	22.1–22.19
Section 23	Revenue	23.1–23.32
Section 24	Government Grants	24.1–24.7
Section 25	Borrowing Costs	25.1–25.3A
Section 26	Share-based Payment	26.1–26.23

Section 27   Impairment of Assets   27.1–27.33A
Section 28   Employee Benefits   28.1–28.44
Section 29   Income Tax   29.1–29.27
Section 30   Foreign Currency Translation   30.1–30.27
Section 31   Hyperinflation   31.1–31.15
Section 32   Events after the End of the Reporting Period   32.1–32.11
Section 33   Related Party Disclosures   33.1–33.14
Section 34   Specialised Activities   34.1–PBE34.97
Section 35   Transition to this FRS   35.1–35.15

Approval by the FRC

The Accounting Council's Advice to the FRC to issue FRS 102

Introduction   1–3
Advice   4–6
Background   7–8
Objective   9–11
Consultation with stakeholders   12–20
Using the IFRS for SMEs as a basis   21–25
Amendments made to the IFRS for SMEs in developing FRS 102   26
Scope of FRS 102   27–30
Consequences of the scope of FRS 102   31–40
Presentation   41–45
Consolidated financial statements   46–53
Distribution of non-cash assets to owners   54
Financial instruments   55–63
Group reconstructions   64
Leases   65–66
Grants   67–71
Share-based payment   72
Employee benefits   73–81
Income tax   82–91
Related party disclosures   92–93
Specialised activities   94–111
Other options available in EU-adopted IFRS   112–116
Providing clarifications in FRS 102   117
Other matters   118–124
Public benefit entities (PBEs)   125–160
Transition to FRS 102   161
Effective date   162–166
Approval of this advice   167

Appendices

I   Glossary
II   Significant differences between FRS 102 and the IFRS for SMEs
III   Table of equivalence for UK Companies Act terminology
IV   Note on legal requirements
V   Previous consultations
VI   Republic of Ireland (RoI) legal references

FRS 102 *The Financial Reporting Standard applicable in the UK and Republic of Ireland* is an accounting standard. It is issued by the Financial Reporting Council in respect of its application in the United Kingdom and promulgated by the Institute of Chartered Accountants in Ireland in respect of its application in the Republic of Ireland.

Summary

(i)   With effect from 1 January 2015 the Financial Reporting Council (FRC) revised financial reporting standards in the United Kingdom and Republic of Ireland. The revisions fundamentally reformed financial reporting, replacing the extant standards with five Financial Reporting Standards:

    (a)   FRS 100 *Application of Financial Reporting Requirements*;

    (b)   FRS 101 *Reduced Disclosure Framework*;

    (c)   FRS 102 *The Financial Reporting Standard applicable in the UK and Republic of Ireland*;

    (d)   FRS 103 *Insurance Contracts*; and

    (e)   FRS 104 *Interim Financial Reporting*.

The FRC has also issued FRS 105 *The Financial Reporting Standard applicable to the Micro-entities Regime* to support the implementation of the new micro-entities regime.

(ii)   The FRC's overriding objective in setting accounting standards is to enable users of accounts to receive high-quality understandable financial reporting proportionate to the size and complexity of the entity and users' information needs.

(iii)   In meeting this objective, the FRC aims to provide succinct financial reporting standards that:

    (a)   have consistency with international accounting standards through the application of an IFRS-based solution unless an alternative clearly better meets the overriding objective;

    (b)   reflect up-to-date thinking and developments in the way entities operate and the transactions they undertake;

    (c)   balance consistent principles for accounting by all UK and Republic of Ireland entities with practical solutions, based on size, complexity, public interest and users' information needs;

    (d)   promote efficiency within groups; and

    (e)   are cost-effective to apply.

(iv)   The requirements in this Financial Reporting Standard (FRS) take into consideration the findings from all relevant consultations.

(v)   This FRS is a single financial reporting standard that applies to the financial statements of entities that are not applying EU-adopted IFRS, FRS 101 or FRS 105[1].

The Financial Reporting Standard applicable in the UK and Republic of Ireland and the IFRS for SMEs

(vi)   This FRS aims to provide entities with succinct financial reporting requirements. The requirements in this FRS are based on the International Accounting Standards Board's (IASB) International Financial Reporting Standard for Small and Medium-sized Entities (IFRS for SMEs) issued in 2009. The IFRS for SMEs is intended to apply to the general purpose financial statements of, and other financial reporting by, entities that in many countries are referred to by a variety of terms including 'small and medium-sized', 'private' and 'non-publicly accountable'.

---

[1] *This FRS does not, however apply to the preparation of 'Companies Act accounts' of certain companies under company law in the Republic of Ireland.*

The FRC has modified the IFRS for SMEs substantially, both in terms of the scope of entities eligible to apply it and in terms of the accounting treatments provided. To reflect this wider scope the proposed name of the standard was revised to FRS 102 *Financial Reporting Standard applicable in the UK and Republic of Ireland.* **(vii)**

FRS 102 is designed to apply to the general purpose financial statements and financial reporting of entities including those that are not constituted as companies and those that are not profit-oriented. General purpose financial statements are intended to focus on the common information needs of a wide range of users; shareholders, lenders, other creditors, employees and members of the public, for example. **(viii)**

Organisation of FRS 102

FRS 102 is organised by topic with each topic presented in a separate numbered section. Cross-references to paragraphs are identified by section followed by paragraph number. Paragraph numbers are in the form of xx.yy, where xx is the section number and yy is the sequential paragraph number within that section. Those paragraphs that apply solely to public benefit entities are identified by the prefix 'PBE'[2]. In order to maintain consistency with the paragraph numbering of the IFRS for SMEs, when a paragraph from the IFRS for SMEs has been deleted and not replaced with an alternative paragraph, the phrase [not used] is given. In examples that include monetary amounts, the measuring unit is Currency Unit (abbreviated as CU). **(ix)**

All the paragraphs of FRS 102 have equal authority. Some sections include appendices of implementation guidance or examples. Some of these are an integral part of the FRS while others provide guidance concerning its application; each specifies its status. **(x)**

This FRS is set out in Sections 1 to 35 and the Glossary (Appendix I). Terms defined in the Glossary are in **bold type** the first time they appear in each section and sub-section within Section 34. **(xi)**

This edition of FRS 102 issued in September 2015 updates the edition of FRS 102 issued in August 2014 for the following: **(xii)**

(a) an editorial amendment to Section 12 *Other Financial Instruments Issues* in relation to the examples of hedge accounting issued on 17 September 2014;

(b) *Amendments to FRS 102 – Pension obligations* issued in February 2015;

(c) consequential amendments to FRS 102 included in FRS 104 *Interim Financial Reporting* issued in March 2015;

(d) *Amendments to FRS 102 – Small entities and other minor amendments* issued in July 2015; and

(e) some minor typographical or presentational corrections.

---

[2] *In some cases 'PBE' prefixed paragraphs also apply to other entities in a public benefit entity group.*

FRS 102 The Financial Reporting Standard applicable in the UK and Republic of Ireland

Section 1 *Scope*

Scope of this Financial Reporting Standard

1.1   This FRS applies to **financial statements** that are intended to give a true and fair view of a reporting entity's **financial position** and **profit or loss** (or **income and expenditure**) for a period.

1.2   The requirements of this FRS are applicable to **public benefit entities** and other entities, not just to companies. However, those paragraph numbers prefixed with 'PBE' shall only be applied by public benefit entities, and shall not be applied directly, or by analogy, by entities that are not public benefit entities, other than, where specifically directed, entities within a **public benefit entity group**.

1.2A   An entity applying this FRS must ensure it complies with any relevant legal requirements applicable to it. This FRS does not necessarily contain all legal disclosure requirements. In relation to small companies (see Section 1A *Small Entities*) most legal disclosure requirements are included, but, for example, those only relevant when the financial statements have been audited are not included.

Basis of preparation of financial statements

1.3   As stated in **FRS 100**, an entity that is required by the **IAS Regulation** (or other legislation or regulation) to prepare **consolidated financial statements** in accordance with **EU-adopted IFRS** must do so. The **individual financial statements** of such an entity, or the individual financial statements or consolidated financial statements of any other entity within the scope of FRS 100, must be prepared in accordance with the following requirements:

(a)   If the financial statements are the individual financial statements of an entity that is eligible to apply **FRS 105**[3], they may be prepared in accordance with that standard.

(b)   If the financial statements are those of an entity that is not eligible to apply FRS 105, or of an entity that is eligible to apply FRS 105 but chooses not to do so, they must[4] be prepared in accordance with this FRS, EU-adopted IFRS or **FRS 101**[5].

1.4   An entity whose **ordinary shares** or **potential ordinary shares** are **publicly traded**, or that files, or is in the process of filing, its financial statements with a securities commission or other regulatory organisation for the purpose of issuing ordinary shares in a public market, or an entity that chooses to disclose earnings per share, shall apply IAS 33 *Earnings per Share* (as adopted in the EU).

---

[3] *The eligibility criteria for applying FRS 105 are set out in legislation and FRS 105. In establishing whether the eligibility criteria have been met turnover and balance sheet total shall be measured in accordance with FRS 105; the measurement of turnover and balance sheet total in accordance with FRS 101 or FRS 102 need not be considered.*

[4] *Under company law in the Republic of Ireland, certain companies are permitted to prepare 'Companies Act accounts' using accounting standards other than those issued by the FRC.*

[5] *Individual financial statements that are prepared by a company in accordance with FRS 101 or FRS 102 are Companies Act individual accounts (section 395(1)(a) of the Act), whereas those prepared in accordance with EU-adopted IFRS are IAS individual accounts (section 395(1)(b) of the Act).*

An entity whose debt or equity instruments are publicly traded, or that files, or is in the **1.5** process of filing, its financial statements with a securities commission or other regulatory organisation for the purpose of issuing any class of instruments in a public market, or an entity that chooses to provide information described as segment information, shall apply IFRS 8 *Operating Segments* (as adopted in the EU). If an entity discloses disaggregated information, but the information does not comply with the requirements of IFRS 8, it shall not describe the information as segment information.

An entity shall apply FRS 103 *Insurance Contracts* to: **1.6**

(a) **insurance contracts** (including **reinsurance contracts**) that it issues and reinsurance contracts that it holds; and

(b) **financial instruments** with a **discretionary participation feature** that it issues.

When applying IAS 33, IFRS 8 and IFRS 6 *Exploration for and Evaluation of Mineral* **1.7** *Resources* (see paragraph 34.11), references made to other IFRSs within those standards shall be taken to be references to the relevant section or paragraph in this FRS.

Reduced disclosures for subsidiaries (and ultimate parents)

A **qualifying entity** (for the purposes of this FRS) which is not a **financial institution** **1.8** may take advantage in its individual financial statements of the disclosure exemptions set out in paragraph 1.12. In relation to paragraph 1.12(c) for **financial liabilities** that are held at **fair value** that are either part of a trading portfolio or are **derivatives**, the qualifying entity can take advantage of those exemptions. Where the qualifying entity has financial instruments held at fair value subject to the requirements of paragraph 36(4) of Schedule 1 to the **Regulations**, it must apply the disclosure requirements of Section 11 *Basic Financial Instruments* to those financial instruments held at fair value.

A qualifying entity (for the purposes of this FRS) which is a financial institution may **1.9** take advantage in its individual financial statements of the disclosure exemptions set out in paragraph 1.12, except for the disclosure exemptions from Section 11 and Section 12 *Other Financial Instruments Issues.*

A qualifying entity (for the purposes of this FRS) which is required to prepare consolidated **1.10** financial statements (for example, if the entity is required by section 399 of the **Act** to prepare consolidated financial statements, and is not entitled to any of the exemptions in sections 400 to 402 of the Act), or which voluntarily chooses to do so, may not take advantage of the disclosure exemptions set out in paragraph 1.12 in its consolidated financial statements.

A qualifying entity (for the purposes of this FRS) may take advantage of the disclosure **1.11** exemptions in paragraph 1.12, in accordance with paragraphs 1.8 to 1.10, provided that:

(a) Its shareholders have been notified in writing about, and do not object to, the use of the disclosure exemptions. Objections to the use of the disclosure exemptions may be served on the qualifying entity, in accordance with reasonable specified timeframes and format requirements, by a shareholder that is the immediate **parent** of the entity, or by a shareholder or shareholders holding in aggregate 5 per cent or more of the total allotted shares in the entity or more than half of the allotted shares in the entity that are not held by the immediate parent.

(b) It otherwise applies the **recognition, measurement** and disclosure requirements of this FRS.

(c)   It discloses in the **notes** to its financial statements:

(i)   a brief narrative summary of the disclosure exemptions adopted; and

(ii)   the name of the parent[6] of the **group** in whose consolidated financial statements its financial statements are consolidated, and from where those financial statements may be obtained.

1.12   A qualifying entity (for the purposes of this FRS) may take advantage of the following disclosure exemptions:

(a)   The requirements of Section 4 *Statement of Financial Position* paragraph 4.12(a)(iv).

(b)   The requirements of Section 7 *Statement of Cash Flows* and Section 3 *Financial Statement Presentation* paragraph 3.17(d).

(c)   The requirements of Section 11 paragraphs 11.41(b), 11.41(c), 11.41(e), 11.41(f), 11.42, 11.44, 11.45, 11.47, 11.48(a)(iii), 11.48(a)(iv), 11.48(b) and 11.48(c) and Section 12 paragraphs 12.26 (in relation to those cross-referenced paragraphs from which a disclosure exemption is available), 12.27, 12.29(a), 12.29(b), and 12.29A providing disclosures equivalent to those required by this FRS are included in the consolidated financial statements of the group in which the entity is consolidated.

(d)   The requirements of Section 26 *Share-based Payment* paragraphs 26.18(b), 26.19 to 26.21 and 26.23, provided that for a qualifying entity that is:

(i)   a **subsidiary**, the share-based payment arrangement concerns equity instruments of another group entity;

(ii)   an ultimate parent, the share-based payment arrangement concerns its own equity instruments and its **separate financial statements** are presented alongside the consolidated financial statements of the group;

and, in both cases, provided that the equivalent disclosures required by this FRS are included in the consolidated financial statements of the group in which the entity is consolidated.

(e)   The requirement of Section 33 *Related Party Disclosures* paragraph 33.7.

1.13   Reference shall be made to the Application Guidance to FRS 100 in deciding whether the consolidated financial statements of the parent provide disclosures which are equivalent to the requirements of this FRS (ie the full requirements of this FRS when not applying the disclosure exemptions) from which relief is provided in paragraph 1.12.

Date from which effective and transitional arrangements

1.14   An entity shall apply this FRS for accounting periods beginning on or after 1 January 2015. Early application is permitted for accounting periods ending on or after 31 December 2012. For entities that are within the scope of a SORP, early application is permitted for accounting periods ending on or after 31 December 2012 providing it does not conflict with the requirements of a current SORP or legal requirements for the preparation of financial statements. If an entity applies this FRS before 1 January 2015 it shall disclose that fact.

1.14A   This FRS permits a financial instrument (provided it meets certain criteria) to be designated on initial recognition as a **financial asset** or financial liability at fair value through profit or loss. Entities that have applied this FRS in financial statements authorised for issue prior to 1 August 2014 are permitted in their first financial statements authorised for issue on or after 1 August 2014 to designate, as at the date of transition to this FRS, any financial asset or financial liability at fair value through profit or loss provided the asset or liability meets the criteria in paragraph 11.14(b) at that date. Entities that have applied this FRS in financial statements authorised for issue prior to 1 August 2014 are permitted in their

---

[6] *The parent identified in the definition of the term 'qualifying entity'.*

first financial statements authorised for issue on or after 1 August 2014 to de-designate any financial asset or financial liability previously designated at fair value through profit or loss and classify and measure the financial instrument in accordance with Section 11.

This FRS permits entities to apply hedge accounting, provided certain qualifying conditions are met. Entities that have applied this FRS in financial statements authorised for issue prior to 1 August 2014 are permitted to apply hedge accounting to a hedging relationship existing on or before 31 July 2014 as set out in Section 12 of this FRS from a date no earlier than the conditions of paragraphs 12.18(a) to (c) are met, provided the conditions of paragraphs 12.18(d) and (e) are met no later than the date the first financial statements issued on or after 1 August 2014 are authorised for issue. This choice applies to each hedging relationship existing on or before 31 July 2014. This choice only applies in respect of the first financial statements that comply with this FRS that are authorised for issue on or after 1 August 2014.   **1.14B**

In a fair value hedge the cumulative **hedging gain or loss** on the hedged item from the date hedge accounting commenced, shall be recorded in retained earnings (or if appropriate, another category of **equity**). In a cash flow hedge and net investment hedge, the lower of the following (in absolute amounts) shall be recorded in equity (in respect of cash flow hedges in the cash flow hedge reserve):

(a)   the cumulative gain or loss on the hedging instrument from the date hedge accounting commenced to the reporting date of the last financial statements authorised for issue prior to 1 August 2014; and

(b)   the cumulative change in fair value (ie the present value of the cumulative change of expected future cash flows) on the hedged item from the date hedge accounting commenced to the reporting date of the last financial statements authorised for issue prior to 1 August 2014.

In July 2015 amendments were made to this FRS to incorporate the new small entities regime and make other amendments necessary to maintain consistency with company law. An entity shall apply the amendments set out in *Amendments to FRS 102 – Small entities and other minor amendments* (the July 2015 amendments) other than the replacement of paragraph 26.15 with new paragraphs 26.15 to 26.15B for accounting periods beginning on or after 1 January 2016. Early application is: **1.15**

(a)   permitted for accounting periods beginning on or after 1 January 2015 provided that *The Companies, Partnerships and Groups (Accounts and Reports) Regulations 2015* (SI 2015/980) are applied from the same date; and

(b)   required if an entity applies *The Companies, Partnerships and Groups (Accounts and Reports) Regulations 2015* (SI 2015/980) to a reporting period beginning before 1 January 2016.

For entities not subject to company law, early application is permitted from 1 January 2015.

If an entity applies the July 2015 amendments before 1 January 2016 it shall disclose that fact, unless it is a **small entity**, in which case it is encouraged to disclose that fact.

Prospective amendments: Amendments to FRS 102 The Financial Reporting Standard applicable in the UK and Republic of Ireland – Fair value hierarchy disclosures (March 2016) inserts paragraph 1.16 with effect for annual periods beginning on or after 1 January 2017.

Section 1A *Small Entities*

Scope of this section

1A.1   This section sets out the information that shall be presented and disclosed in the **financial statements** of a **small entity** that chooses to apply the small entities regime. Unless excluded below, all of the requirements of this FRS apply to a small entity, including the **recognition** and **measurement** requirements.

1A.2   Unless a small entity chooses to apply EU-adopted IFRS, or if eligible, FRS 101, a small entity that chooses not to apply the small entities regime shall apply FRS 102 excluding Section 1A.

1A.3   References to a small entity in paragraphs 1A.4 to 1A.22 and the Appendices to Section 1A are to a small entity that chooses to apply the small entities regime.

1A.4   This section applies to all small entities applying the small entities regime, whether or not they report under the **Act**. Small entities that do not report under the Act shall comply with the requirements of this section, and with the **Small Companies Regulations** (or, where applicable, the **Small LLP Regulations**) where referred to in this section, except to the extent that these requirements are not permitted by any statutory framework under which such entities report.

True and fair view

1A.5   The financial statements of a small entity shall give a true and fair view of the **assets**, **liabilities**, **financial position** and **profit or loss** of the small entity for the **reporting period** (Section 393 of the Act).

1A.6   A small entity may need to provide disclosures in addition to those set out in this section in order to comply with the requirement of paragraph 1A.5 (see also paragraphs 1A.16 and 1A.17).

Complete set of financial statements of a small entity

1A.7   A small entity is not required to comply with the requirements of paragraphs 3.3, PBE3.3A, 3.9, 3.17, 3.18, 3.19 and 3.24(b) which relate to presentation and disclosure requirements that are not required of small companies in company law, Section 4 *Statement of Financial Position*, Section 5 *Statement of Comprehensive Income and Income Statement*, Section 6 *Statement of Changes in Equity and Statement of Income and Retained Earnings* and Section 7 *Statement of Cash Flows*.

1A.8   Instead a complete set of financial statements of a small entity shall include all of the following:

(a)   a **statement of financial position** as at the **reporting date** in accordance with paragraph 1A.12;

(b)   an **income statement** for the reporting period in accordance with paragraph 1A.14; and

(c)   **notes** in accordance with paragraphs 1A.16 to 1A.20.

In addition to the statements required by company law and set out in paragraph 1A.8: **1A.9**

(a) when a small entity recognises **gains** or losses in **other comprehensive income** it is encouraged to present a statement of total comprehensive income (see Section 5); and

(b) when a small entity has transactions with equity holders it is encouraged to present a statement of changes in equity, or a **statement of income and retained earnings**, (see Section 6),

in order to meet the requirements of paragraph 1A.5.

In accordance with paragraph 3.14 a small entity shall present comparative information in **1A.10** respect of the preceding period for all amounts presented in the current period's financial statements, except when this FRS permits or requires otherwise.

In accordance with paragraph 3.22 a small entity may use titles for the financial statements **1A.11** other than those used in this FRS as long as they are not misleading.

Information to be presented in the statement of financial position

A small entity shall present a statement of financial position in accordance with the **1A.12** requirements for a balance sheet set out in either Part 1 *General Rules and Formats* of Schedule 1 to the Small Companies Regulations or Part 1 *General Rules and Formats* of Schedule 1 to the Small LLP Regulations.

Guidance on applying these requirements is set out in Appendix A to this section, which **1A.13** shall be applied by a small entity.

Information to be presented in the income statement

A small entity shall present its profit or loss for a period in an income statement in **1A.14** accordance with the requirements for a profit and loss account set out in either Part 1 *General Rules and Formats* of Schedule 1 to the Small Companies Regulations or Part 1 *General Rules and Formats* of Schedule 1 to the Small LLP Regulations.

Guidance on applying these requirements is set out in in Appendix B to this section, which **1A.15** shall be applied by a small entity.

Information to be presented in the notes to the financial statements

A small entity shall present sufficient information in the notes to the financial statements **1A.16** to meet the requirement for the financial statements to give a true and fair view of the assets, liabilities, financial position and profit or loss of the small entity for the reporting period.

A small entity is not required to comply with the disclosure requirements of Section 3 (to the **1A.17** extent set out in paragraph 1A.7) and Sections 8 to 35 of this FRS. However, because those disclosures are usually considered relevant to giving a true and fair view, a small entity is encouraged to consider and provide any of those disclosures that are relevant to **material** transactions, other events or conditions of the small entity in order to meet the requirement set out in paragraphs 1A.5 and 1A.16. In accordance with paragraph 3.16A a small entity need not provide a specific disclosure (including those set out in paragraph 1A.18 and Appendix C to this section) if the information is not material.

As a minimum, where relevant to its transactions, other events and conditions, a small **1A.18** entity shall provide the disclosures set out in Appendix C to this section.

1A.19   The paragraphs of this FRS that are cross-referenced in Appendix C are also highlighted in those sections by including an * in the left-hand margin.

1A.20   In addition, a small entity is encouraged to make the disclosures set out in Appendix D to this section, which may nevertheless be necessary to give a true and fair view.

Voluntary preparation of consolidated financial statements

1A.21   A small entity that is a **parent** entity is not required to prepare **consolidated financial statements**.

1A.22   If a small entity that is a parent voluntarily chooses to prepare consolidated financial statements it:

    (a)   shall apply the consolidation procedures set out in Section 9 *Consolidated and Separate Financial Statements*;

    (b)   is encouraged to provide the disclosures set out in paragraph 9.23;

    (c)   shall comply so far as practicable with the requirements of Section 1A as if it were a single entity (Schedule 6 of the Small Companies Regulations, paragraph 1(1)), subject to any restrictions or exemptions set out in legislation; and

    (d)   shall provide any disclosures required by Schedule 6 of the Small Companies Regulations.

Appendix A to Section 1A

Guidance on adapting the balance sheet formats

This appendix is an integral part of the Standard.

1AA.1   As set out in paragraph 1A.12 a small entity shall present a statement of financial position in accordance with the requirements for a balance sheet set out in either Part 1 *General Rules and Formats* of Schedule 1 to the Small Companies Regulations or Part 1 *General Rules and Formats* of Schedule 1 to the Small LLP Regulations. This results in three alternatives:

    (a)   apply the required balance sheet formats as set out in legislation (subject to any permitted flexibility);

    (b)   draw up an abridged balance sheet (see paragraph 1AA.2); or

    (c)   adapt one of the balance sheet formats (see paragraphs 1AA.3 to 1AA.6).

Abridged balance sheet

1AA.2   A small entity choosing to apply paragraph 1A(1) of Schedule 1 to the Small Companies Regulations and draw up an abridged balance sheet must still meet the requirement for the financial statements to give a true and fair view. A small entity shall therefore also consider the requirements of paragraph 1A.16, and provide any additional disclosure that is necessary in the notes to the financial statements, for example in relation to disaggregating the information in the balance sheet.

Adapted balance sheet

1AA.3   A small entity choosing to apply paragraph 1B(1) of Schedule 1 to the Small Companies Regulations and adapt one of the balance sheet formats shall, as a minimum, include in its statement of financial position line items that present the following, distinguishing between those items that are **current** and those that are **non-current**:

(a) **property, plant and equipment**;
(b) **investment property** carried at **fair value** through profit or loss;
(c) **intangible assets**;
(d) **financial assets** (excluding amounts shown under (e), (f), (j) and (k));
(e) investments in **associates**;
(f) investments in **jointly controlled entities**;
(g) **biological assets** carried at cost less accumulated **depreciation** and impairment;
(h) biological assets carried at fair value through profit or loss;
(i) **inventories**;
(j) trade and other receivables;
(k) **cash** and **cash equivalents**;
(l) trade and other payables;
(m) **provisions**;
(n) financial liabilities (excluding amounts shown under (l) and (m));
(o) liabilities and assets for **current tax**;
(p) **deferred tax liabilities** and **deferred tax assets** (classified as non-current);
(q) **non-controlling interest**, presented within equity separately from the equity attributable to the owners of the parent; and
(r) equity attributable to the owners of the parent.

A small entity choosing to apply paragraph 1B(1) of Schedule 1 to the Small Companies Regulations and adapt one of the balance sheet formats shall also disclose, either in the statement of financial position or in the notes, the following sub-classifications of the line items presented: **1AA.4**

(a) property, plant and equipment in classifications appropriate to the small entity;
(b) **goodwill** and other intangible assets;
(c) investments, showing separately shares and loans;
(d) trade and other receivables, showing separately amounts due from **related parties** and amounts due from other parties;
(e) trade and other payables, showing separately amounts payable to trade suppliers and amounts payable to related parties; and
(f) classes of equity, such as called up share capital, share premium, retained earnings, revaluation reserve, fair value reserve and other reserves.

The descriptions used in paragraphs 1AA.3 and 1AA.4, and the ordering of items or aggregation of similar items, may be amended according to the nature of the small entity and its transactions, to provide information that is relevant to an understanding of the small entity's financial position, providing the information given is at least equivalent to that required by the balance sheet format had it not been adapted.   **1AA.5**

In order to comply with the requirement to distinguish between those items that are current and those that are non-current a small entity shall present current and non-current assets, and current and non-current liabilities, as separate classifications in its statement of financial position.   **1AA.6**

Appendix B to Section 1A

Guidance on adapting the profit and loss account formats

This appendix is an integral part of the Standard.

1AB.1   As set out in paragraph 1A.14 a small entity shall present its profit or loss for a period in an income statement in accordance with the requirements for a profit and loss account set out in either Part 1 *General Rules and Formats* of Schedule 1 to the Small Companies Regulations or Part 1 *General Rules and Formats* of Schedule 1 to the Small LLP Regulations. This results in three alternatives:

   (a)   apply the required profit and loss account formats as set out in legislation (subject to any permitted flexibility);
   (b)   draw up an abridged profit and loss account (see paragraph 1AB.2); or
   (c)   adapt one of the profit and loss account formats (see paragraphs 1AB.3 and 1AB.4).

Abridged profit and loss account

1AB.2   A small entity choosing to apply paragraph 1A(2) of Schedule 1 to the Small Companies Regulations and draw up an abridged profit and loss account must still meet the requirement for the financial statements to give a true and fair view. A small entity shall therefore also consider the requirements of paragraph 1A.16 and provide any additional disclosure that is necessary in the notes to the financial statements, for example in relation to disaggregating gross profit or loss and disclosing turnover.

Adapted profit and loss account

1AB.3   A small entity choosing to apply paragraph 1B(2) of Schedule 1 to the Small Companies Regulations and adapt one of the profit and loss account formats shall, as a minimum, include in its income statement line items that present the following amounts for the period:

   (a)   **revenue**;
   (b)   finance costs;
   (c)   share of the profit or loss of investments in associates (see Section 14 *Investments in Associates*) and jointly controlled entities (see Section 15 *Investments in Joint Ventures*) accounted for using the equity method;
   (d)   profit or loss before taxation;
   (e)   **tax expense** excluding tax allocated to other comprehensive income or equity; and
   (f)   profit or loss.

1AB.4   A small entity may include additional line items in the income statement and it amends the descriptions used in paragraph 1AB.3, and the ordering of items, when this is necessary to explain the elements of financial performance, providing the information given is at least equivalent to that required by the profit and loss account format had it not been adapted.

Appendix C to Section 1A

Disclosure requirements for small entities

This appendix is an integral part of the Standard.

This appendix sets out the disclosure requirements for small entities based on the requirements of company law. These are shown in italic font in the paragraphs below. Other than substituting company law terminology with the equivalent terminology used in FRS 102 (see Appendix III) the drafting is as close as possible to that set out in company law. References to Schedule 1 are to Schedule 1 of the Small Companies Regulations.

Where there is a similar disclosure requirement in FRS 102 this has been indicated and those paragraphs of FRS 102 that have been cross-referenced are also highlighted *by including an * in the left-hand margin. In many cases compliance with the similar requirement of FRS 102 will result in compliance with the requirements below.*

As a minimum, where relevant to its transactions, other events and conditions, a small entity shall provide the disclosures set out in this Appendix.   **1AC.1**

The notes must be presented in the order in which, where relevant, the items to which they relate are presented in the statement of financial position and in the income statement. (Schedule 1, paragraph 42(2))   **1AC.2**

Paragraphs 8.3 and 8.4 address similar requirements.

Accounting policies

The accounting policies adopted by the small entity in determining the amounts to be included in respect of items shown in the statement of financial position and in determining the profit or loss of the small entity must be stated (including such policies with respect to the depreciation and impairment of assets). (Schedule 1, paragraph 44)   **1AC.3**

Paragraph 8.5 addresses similar requirements. Including information about the judgements made in applying the small entity's accounting policies, as set out in paragraph 8.6, may be useful to users of the small entity's financial statements.

If any amount is included in a small entity's statement of financial position in respect of development costs, the note on accounting policies must include the following information: **1AC.4**

(a)   *the period over which the amount of those costs originally capitalised is being or is to be written off; and*

(b)   *the reasons for capitalising the development costs in question. (Schedule 1, paragraph 21(2))*

Paragraph 18.27(a) addresses similar requirements to paragraph 1AC.4(a).

Where development costs are shown or included as an asset in the small entity's financial statements and the amount is not treated as a realised loss because there are special circumstances justifying this, a note to the financial statements must state the reasons for showing development costs as an asset and that it is not a realised loss. (Section 844 of the Act)   **1AC.5**

Where in exceptional cases the useful life of intangible assets cannot be reliably estimated, there must be disclosed in a note to the financial statements the period over which those intangible assets are being written off and the reasons for choosing that period. (Schedule 1, paragraph 22(4))   **1AC.6**

Intangible assets include goodwill. Paragraphs 18.27(a) and 19.25(g) address similar requirements.

Changes in presentation and accounting policies and corrections of prior period errors

Where there is a change in the presentation of a small entity's statement of financial position or income statement, particulars of any such change must be given in a note to the financial statements in which the new presentation is first used, and the reasons for the change must be explained. (Schedule 1, paragraph 2(2))   **1AC.7**

Paragraphs 3.12 and 3.13 address similar requirements.

1AC.8   *Where the corresponding amount for the immediately preceding financial year is not comparable with the amount to be shown for the item in question in respect of the reporting period, and the corresponding amount is adjusted, the particulars of the non-comparability and of any adjustment must be disclosed in a note to the financial statements. (Schedule 1, paragraph 7(2))*

This is likely to be relevant where there has either been a change in accounting policy or the correction of a material prior period error. Paragraphs 10.13, 10.14 and 10.23 address similar requirements.

1AC.9   *Where any amount relating to a preceding reporting period is included in any item in the income statement, the effect must be stated. (Schedule 1, paragraph 61(1))*

True and fair override

1AC.10   *If it appears to the small entity that there are special reasons for departing from any of the principles set out in company law in preparing the small entity's financial statements in respect of any reporting period, it may do so, in which case particulars of the departure, the reasons for it, and its effects must be given in the notes to the financial statements. (Schedule 1, paragraph 10(2))*

This is only expected to occur in special circumstances. Paragraphs 3.4 and 3.5 address similar requirements.

Notes supporting the statement of financial position

1AC.11   *Where an asset or liability relates to more than one item in the statement of financial position, the relationship of such asset or liability to the relevant items must be disclosed either under those items or in the notes to the financial statements. (Schedule 1, paragraph 9A)*

Fixed assets

1AC.12   *In respect of each item which is shown under the general item 'fixed assets' in the small entity's statement of financial position the following information must be given:*

(a)   *the aggregate amounts (on the basis of cost or revaluation) in respect of that item as at the date of the beginning of the reporting period and as at the reporting date respectively;*

(b)   *the effect on any amount shown in the statement of financial position in respect of that item of:*

(i)   *any revision of the amount in respect of any assets included under that item made during the reporting period as a result of revaluation;*

(ii)   *acquisitions during the reporting period of any assets;*

(iii)   *disposals during the reporting period of any assets; and*

(iv)   *any transfers of assets of the small entity to and from that item during the reporting period. (Schedule 1, paragraphs 48(1) and 48(2))*

1AC.13   *In respect of each item within paragraph 1AC.12 there must also be stated:*

(a)   *the cumulative amount of provisions for depreciation and impairment of assets included under that item as at the date of the beginning of the reporting period and as at the reporting date respectively;*

(b)   *the amount of any such provisions made in respect of the reporting period;*

(c)   *the amount of any adjustments made in respect of any such provisions during the reporting period in consequence of the disposal of any assets; and*

(d)   *the amount of any other adjustments made in respect of any such provisions during the reporting period. (Schedule 1, paragraph 48(3))*

These two paragraphs apply to all fixed assets, including investment property, property, plant and equipment, intangible assets (including goodwill), fixed asset investments, biological assets and heritage assets recognised in the statement of financial position.

Each item refers to a class of fixed assets shown separately either in the statement of financial position, or in the notes to the financial statements.

These reconciliations need not be presented for prior periods.

Paragraph 16.10(e) addresses similar requirements for investment property. Paragraphs 17.31(d) and (e) address similar requirements for property, plant and equipment. Paragraphs 18.27(c) and (e) address similar requirements for intangible assets other than goodwill. Paragraph 19.26 addresses similar requirements for goodwill. Paragraphs 34.7(c) and 34.10(e) address similar requirements for biological assets. Paragraphs 34.55(e) and (f) address similar requirements for heritage assets recognised in the statement of financial position.

Fixed assets measured at revalued amounts

When fixed assets are measured at revalued amounts the items affected and the basis   **1AC.14** *of valuation adopted in determining the amounts of the assets in question in the case of each such item must be disclosed in the note on accounting policies. (Schedule 1, paragraph 34(2))*

These requirements apply when:

- investments in subsidiaries, associates and joint ventures are measured at fair value with changes in fair value recognised in other comprehensive income. Paragraph 9.27(b) addresses a similar disclosure requirement;
- property, plant and equipment are revalued using the revaluation model set out in paragraphs 17.15B to 17.15F. Paragraph 17.31(a) addresses a similar disclosure requirement; and
- intangible assets other than goodwill are revalued using the revaluation model set out in paragraphs 18.18B to 18.18H.

These requirements do not apply to investment property and biological assets measured at fair value through profit or loss.

Where any fixed assets of the small entity (other than listed investments) are included   **1AC.15** *under any item shown in the small entity's statement of financial position at a revalued amount, the following information must be given:*

(a)   *the years (so far as they are known to the directors) in which the assets were severally valued and the several values;*

(b)   *in the case of assets that have been valued during the reporting period, the names of the persons who valued them or particulars of their qualifications for doing so and (whichever is stated) the bases of valuation used by them. (Schedule 1, paragraph 49)*

Paragraphs 17.32A(a) and (c), 18.29A(a) and (c) and 34.55(e)(ii) address similar requirements. These paragraphs do not require the names or qualifications of the persons who valued the fixed assets to be disclosed; paragraphs 17.32A(b) and 18.29A(b) address only whether or not the valuer was independent.

These requirements apply in the same circumstances as those set out in paragraph 1AC.14.

1AC.16   *In the case of each item in the statement of financial position measured at a revalued amount, the comparable amounts determined according to the historical cost accounting rules must be shown in a note to the financial statements. (Schedule 1, paragraph 34(3))*

The comparable amounts refers to the aggregate amount of cost and the aggregate of accumulated depreciation and accumulated impairment losses that would have been required according to the historical cost accounting rules (Schedule 1, paragraph 34(4)).

Paragraphs 17.32A(d) and 18.29A(d) address similar requirements.

These requirements apply in the same circumstances as those set out in paragraph 1AC.14.

1AC.17   *Where fixed assets are measured at revalued amounts the following information must be given in tabular form:*

(a)   *movements in the revaluation reserve in the reporting period, with an explanation of the tax treatment of items therein; and*
(b)   *the carrying amount in the statement of financial position that would have been recognised had the fixed assets not been revalued. (Schedule 1, paragraph 54(2))*

Paragraphs 6.3A, 17.32A(d), 18.29A(d) and 29.27(a) address similar requirements.

These requirements apply in the same circumstances as those set out in paragraph 1AC.14.

1AC.18   *The treatment for taxation purposes of amounts credited or debited to the revaluation reserve must be disclosed in a note to the financial statements. (Schedule 1, paragraph 35(6))*

Paragraph 29.27(a) addresses similar requirements.

These requirements apply in the same circumstances as those set out in paragraph 1AC.14.

Capitalisation of borrowing costs

1AC.19   *When a small entity adopts a policy of capitalising borrowing costs, the inclusion of interest in determining the cost of the asset and the amount of the interest so included is disclosed in a note to the financial statements. (Schedule 1, paragraph 27(3))*

Paragraph 25.3A(a) addresses a similar requirement to the second part of this.

Impairment of assets

1AC.20   *Provisions for impairment of fixed assets (including fixed asset investments) must be disclosed separately in a note to the financial statements if not shown separately in the income statement. (Schedule 1, paragraph 19(3))*

Paragraph 27.32(a) addresses similar requirements.

Any provisions for impairment of fixed assets that are reversed because the reasons for **1AC.21**
which they were made have ceased to apply must be disclosed (either separately or in
aggregate) in a note to the financial statements if not shown separately in the income
statement. (Schedule 1, paragraph 20(2))

Paragraph 27.32(b) addresses similar requirements.

Fair value measurement

Where financial instruments or other assets have been measured at fair value through **1AC.22**
profit or loss there must be stated:

(a)   *the significant assumptions underlying the valuation models and techniques used to*
      determine the fair values;
(b)   *for each category of financial instrument or other asset, the fair value of the assets*
      in that category and the change in value:

    (i)   *included directly in the income statement; or*
    (ii) *credited to or (as the case may be) debited from the fair value reserve,*

in respect of those assets. (Schedule 1, paragraphs 51(2)(a) and (b))

This does not apply where financial instruments or other assets are measured at fair value
only on initial recognition.

This applies where financial instruments, certain inventories, investment property and
biological assets are subsequently measured at fair value through profit or loss, which is
permitted or required by paragraphs 9.26(c), 11.14(b), 11.14(d)(i), 12.8, 13.4A, 14.4(d),
15.9(d), 16.7 and 34.4.

Paragraphs 11.41(a), 11.41(d), 11.43, 11.48(a)(i), 11.48(a)(ii), 12.28, 12.29(c), and 12.29(e)
address similar disclosure requirements for financial instruments. Paragraphs 16.10(a)
and 16.10(e)(ii) address similar disclosure requirements for investment property.
Paragraphs 34.7(b) and 34.7(c)(i) address similar disclosure requirements for biological
assets.

Where financial instruments or other assets have been measured at fair value through **1AC.23**
profit or loss there must be stated for each class of derivatives, the extent and nature of the
instruments, including significant terms and conditions that may affect the amount, timing
and certainty of future cash flows. (Schedule 1, paragraph 51(2)(c))

Where any amount is transferred to or from the fair value reserve during the reporting **1AC.24**
period, there must be stated in tabular form:

(a)   *the amount of the reserve as at the beginning of the reporting period and as at the*
      reporting date respectively; and
(b)   *the amount transferred to or from the reserve during that year. (Schedule 1,*
      paragraph 51(3))

Paragraphs 6.3A, 12.29(c) and 12.29(d) address similar requirements.

The treatment for taxation purposes of amounts credited or debited to the fair value reserve **1AC.25**
must be disclosed in a note to the financial statements. (Schedule 1, paragraph 41(2))

Paragraph 29.27(a) addresses similar requirements.

Financial instruments measured at fair value

1AC.26   *Financial instruments which under international accounting standards may be included in accounts at fair value, may be so included, provided that the disclosures required by such accounting standards are made. (Schedule 1, paragraph 36(4))*

This only applies in certain circumstances; for example, it does not apply to derivatives. It applies where investments in subsidiaries, associates and joint ventures are measured at fair value through profit or loss. When it applies, the disclosures required by Section 11 that relate to financial assets and financial liabilities measured at fair value, including paragraph 11.48A, shall be given.

Indebtedness, guarantees and financial commitments

1AC.27   *For the aggregate of all items shown under 'creditors' in the small entity's statement of financial position there must be stated the aggregate of the following amounts:*

(a)   *the amount of any debts included under 'creditors' which are payable or repayable otherwise than by instalments and fall due for payment or repayment after the end of the period of five years beginning with the day next following the reporting date; and*

(b)   *in the case of any debts so included which are payable or repayable by instalments, the amount of any instalments which fall due for payment after the end of that period. (Schedule 1, paragraph 55(1))*

1AC.28   *In respect of each item shown under 'creditors' in the small entity's statement of financial position there must be stated the aggregate amount of any debts included under that item in respect of which any security has been given by the small entity with an indication of the nature and form of any such security. (Schedule 1, paragraph 55(2))*

Paragraphs 11.46, 13.22(e), 16.10(c), 17.32(a) and 18.28(c) address similar requirements.

1AC.29   *The total amount of any financial commitments, guarantees and contingencies that are not included in the balance sheet must be stated. (Schedule 1, paragraph 57(1))*

The total amount of any commitments concerning pensions must be separately disclosed. (Schedule 1, paragraph 57(3))

The total amount of any commitments which are undertaken on behalf of or for the benefit of:

(a)   *any parent, fellow subsidiary or any subsidiary of the small entity; or*

(b)   *any undertaking in which the small entity has a participating interest,*

must be separately stated and those within (a) must also be stated separately from those within (b). (Schedule 1, paragraph 57(4))

Such commitments can arise in a variety of situations, including in relation to group entities, investments, property, plant and equipment, leases and pension obligations. Paragraphs 15.19(d), 16.10(d), 17.32(b), 18.28(d), 20.16, 21.15, 28.40A(a), 28.40A(b), 28.41A(d), 33.9(b)(ii) and 34.62 address similar requirements.

1AC.30   *An indication of the nature and form of any valuable security given by the small entity in respect of commitments, guarantees and contingencies within paragraph 1AC.29 must be given. (Schedule 1, paragraph 57(2))*

Paragraphs 11.46, 13.22(e), 16.10(c), 17.32(a) and 18.28(c) address similar requirements.

If in any reporting period a small entity is or has been party to arrangements that are not reflected in its statement of financial position and at the reporting date the risks or benefits arising from those arrangements are material the nature and business purpose of the arrangements must be given in the notes to the financial statements to the extent necessary for enabling the financial position of the small entity to be assessed. (Section 410A of the Act) **1AC.31**

Examples of off-balance sheet arrangements include risk and benefit-sharing arrangements or obligations arising from a contract such as debt factoring, combined sale and repurchase arrangements, consignment stock arrangements, take or pay arrangements, securitisation arranged through separate entities, pledged assets, operating lease arrangements, outsourcing and the like. In many cases the disclosures about financial commitments and contingencies required by paragraphs 1AC.29 and 1AC.30 will also address such arrangements.

Notes supporting the income statement

The amount and nature of any individual items of income or expenses of exceptional size or incidence must be stated. (Schedule 1, paragraph 61(2)) **1AC.32**

Paragraph 5.9A addresses a similar requirement in relation to material items.

The notes to a small entity's financial statements must disclose the average number of persons employed by the small entity in the reporting period. (Section 411 of the Act) **1AC.33**

Related party disclosures

Where the small entity is a subsidiary, the following information must be given in respect of the parent of the smallest group for which consolidated financial statements are drawn up of which the small entity is a member: **1AC.34**

(a)   *the name of the parent which draws up the consolidated financial statements;*
(b)   *the address of the parent's registered office (whether in or outside the UK); or*
(c)   *if it is unincorporated, the address of its principal place of business. (Schedule 1, paragraph 65)*

Paragraph 33.5 addresses a similar requirement to paragraph (a).

Particulars must be given of material transactions the small entity has entered into that have not been concluded under normal market conditions with: **1AC.35**

(a)   *owners holding a participating interest in the small entity;*
(b)   *companies in which the small entity itself has a participating interest; and*
(c)   *the small entity's directors [or members of its governing body].*

Particulars must include:

(a)   *the amount of such transactions;*
(b)   *the nature of the related party relationship; and*
(c)   *other information about the transactions necessary for an understanding of the financial position of the small entity.*

Information about individual transactions may be aggregated according to their nature, except where separate information is necessary for an understanding of the effects of the related party transactions on the financial position of the small entity.

Particulars need not be given of transactions entered into between two or more members of a group, provided that any subsidiary which is a party to the transaction is wholly-owned by such a member. (Schedule 1, paragraph 66)

Although disclosure is only required of material transactions with the specified related parties that have not been concluded under normal market conditions, small entities disclosing all transactions with such related parties would still be compliant with company law.

Transactions with directors, or members of an entity's governing body, include directors' remuneration and dividends paid to directors.

Paragraphs 33.9 and 33.14 address similar requirements for all related parties.

1AC.36   *Details of advances and credits granted by the small entity to its directors and guarantees of any kind entered into by the small entity on behalf of its directors must be shown in the notes to the financial statements.*

The details required of an advance or credit are:

(a)   *its amount;*
(b)   *an indication of the interest rate;*
(c)   *its main conditions;*
(d)   *any amounts repaid;*
(e)   *any amounts written off; and*
(f)   *any amounts waived.*

There must also be stated in the notes to the financial statements the totals of amounts stated under (a), (d), (e) and (f).

The details required of a guarantee are:

(a)   *its main terms;*
(b)   *the amount of the maximum liability that may be incurred by the small entity; and*
(c)   *any amount paid and any liability incurred by the small entity for the purpose of fulfilling the guarantee (including any loss incurred by reason of enforcement of the guarantee).*

There must also be stated in the notes to the financial statements the totals of amounts stated under (b) and (c). (Section 413 of the Act)

Paragraph 33.9 addresses similar requirements for all related parties.

A small entity that is not a company shall provide this disclosure in relation to members of its governing body.

Other

1AC.37   *The financial statements must state:*

(a)   *the part of the UK in which the small entity is registered;*
(b)   *the small entity's registered number;*
(c)   *whether the small entity is a public or a private company and whether the small entity is limited by shares or by guarantee;*
(d)   *the address of the small entity's registered office; and*
(e)   *where appropriate, the fact that the entity is being wound up. (Section 396 of the Act)*

Paragraph 3.24(a) addresses similar requirements.

Where items to which Arabic numbers are given in any of the formats have been combined,   **1AC.38**
unless they are not material, the individual amounts of any items which have been combined
must be disclosed in a note to the financial statements. (Schedule 1, paragraph 4(3))

The nature and financial effect of material events arising after the reporting date which   **1AC.39**
are not reflected in the income statement or statement of financial position must be stated.
(Schedule 1, paragraph 64)

Paragraphs 32.10 and 32.11 address similar requirements.

Appendix D to Section 1A

Additional disclosures encouraged for small entities

This appendix is an integral part of the Standard.

Where relevant to its transactions, other events and conditions, a small entity is encouraged   **1AD.1**
to provide the following disclosures:

(a)   a statement of compliance with this FRS as set out in paragraph 3.3, adapted to refer
      to Section 1A;
(b)   a statement that it is a public benefit entity as set out in paragraph PBE3.3A;
(c)   the disclosures relating to going concern set out in paragraph 3.9;
(d)   dividends declared and paid or payable during the period (for example, as set out in
      paragraph 6.5(b)); and
(e)   on first-time adoption of this FRS an explanation of how the transition has affected
      its financial position and financial performance as set out in paragraph 35.13.

Section 2 *Concepts and Pervasive Principles*

Scope of this section

This section describes the **objective of financial statements** of entities within the scope of   **2.1**
this FRS and the qualities that make the information in the **financial statements** of entities
within the scope of this FRS useful. It also sets out the concepts and basic principles
underlying the financial statements of entities within the scope of this FRS.

Although this section sets out the concepts and pervasive principles underlying financial   **2.1A**
statements, in some circumstances there may be inconsistencies between the concepts and
principles in this section of the FRS and the specific requirements of another section. In
these circumstances the specific requirements of the other section within the FRS take
precedence over this section.

Objective of financial statements

The objective of financial statements is to provide information about the **financial**   **2.2**
position, **performance** and **cash flows** of an entity that is useful for economic decision-
making by a broad range of users who are not in a position to demand reports tailored to
meet their particular information needs.

Financial statements also show the results of the stewardship of management—the   **2.3**
accountability of management for the resources entrusted to it.

Qualitative characteristics of information in financial statements

Understandability

2.4   The information provided in financial statements should be presented in a way that makes it comprehensible by users who have a reasonable knowledge of **business** and economic activities and accounting and a willingness to study the information with reasonable diligence. However, the need for **understandability** does not allow relevant information to be omitted on the grounds that it may be too difficult for some users to understand.

Relevance

2.5   The information provided in financial statements must be relevant to the decision-making needs of users. Information has the quality of **relevance** when it is capable of influencing the economic decisions of users by helping them evaluate past, present or future events or confirming, or correcting, their past evaluations.

Materiality

2.6   Information is **material**—and therefore has relevance—if its omission or misstatement, individually or collectively, could influence the economic decisions of users taken on the basis of the financial statements. Materiality depends on the size and nature of the omission or misstatement judged in the surrounding circumstances. The size or nature of the item, or a combination of both, could be the determining factor. However, it is inappropriate to make, or leave uncorrected, immaterial departures from this FRS to achieve a particular presentation of an entity's financial position, financial performance or cash flows.

Reliability

2.7   The information provided in financial statements must be reliable. Information is reliable when it is free from material **error** and bias and represents faithfully that which it either purports to represent or could reasonably be expected to represent. Financial statements are not free from bias (ie not neutral) if, by the selection or presentation of information, they are intended to influence the making of a decision or judgement in order to achieve a predetermined result or outcome.

Substance over form

2.8   Transactions and other events and conditions should be accounted for and presented in accordance with their substance and not merely their legal form. This enhances the **reliability** of financial statements.

Prudence

2.9   The uncertainties that inevitably surround many events and circumstances are acknowledged by the disclosure of their nature and extent and by the exercise of **prudence** in the preparation of the financial statements. Prudence is the inclusion of a degree of caution in the exercise of the judgements needed in making the estimates required under conditions of uncertainty, such that **assets** or **income** are not overstated and **liabilities** or **expenses** are not understated. However, the exercise of prudence does not allow the deliberate understatement of assets or income, or the deliberate overstatement of liabilities or expenses. In short, prudence does not permit bias.

Completeness

To be reliable, the information in financial statements must be complete within the bounds of materiality and cost. An omission can cause information to be false or misleading and thus unreliable and deficient in terms of its relevance. **2.10**

Comparability

Users must be able to compare the financial statements of an entity through time to identify trends in its financial position and performance. Users must also be able to compare the financial statements of different entities to evaluate their relative financial position, performance and cash flows. Hence, the **measurement** and display of the financial effects of like transactions and other events and conditions must be carried out in a consistent way throughout an entity and over time for that entity, and in a consistent way across entities. In addition, users must be informed of the **accounting policies** employed in the preparation of the financial statements, and of any changes in those policies and the effects of such changes. **2.11**

Timeliness

To be relevant, financial information must be able to influence the economic decisions of users. **Timeliness** involves providing the information within the decision time frame. If there is undue delay in the reporting of information it may lose its relevance. Management may need to balance the relative merits of timely reporting and the provision of reliable information. In achieving a balance between relevance and reliability, the overriding consideration is how best to satisfy the needs of users in making economic decisions. **2.12**

Balance between benefit and cost

The benefits derived from information should exceed the cost of providing it. The evaluation of benefits and costs is substantially a judgemental process. Furthermore, the costs are not necessarily borne by those users who enjoy the benefits, and often the benefits of the information are enjoyed by a broad range of external users. **2.13**

Financial reporting information helps capital providers make better decisions, which results in more efficient functioning of capital markets and a lower cost of capital for the economy as a whole. Individual entities also enjoy benefits, including improved access to capital markets, favourable effect on public relations, and perhaps lower costs of capital. The benefits may also include better management decisions because financial information used internally is often based at least partly on information prepared for general purpose financial reporting purposes. **2.14**

Financial position

The financial position of an entity is the relationship of its assets, liabilities and **equity** as of a specific date as presented in the **statement of financial position**. These are defined as follows: **2.15**

(a) An asset is a resource controlled by the entity as a result of past events and from which future economic benefits are expected to flow to the entity.

(b)   A liability is a present obligation of the entity arising from past events, the settlement of which is expected to result in an outflow from the entity of resources embodying economic benefits.

(c)   Equity is the residual interest in the assets of the entity after deducting all its liabilities.

2.16   Some items that meet the definition of an asset or a liability may not be recognised as assets or liabilities in the statement of financial position because they do not satisfy the criteria for **recognition** in paragraphs 2.27 to 2.32. In particular, the expectation that future economic benefits will flow to or from an entity must be sufficiently certain to meet the probability criterion before an asset or liability is recognised.

Assets

2.17   The future economic benefit of an asset is its potential to contribute, directly or indirectly, to the flow of **cash** and **cash equivalents** to the entity. Those cash flows may come from using the asset or from disposing of it.

2.18   Many assets, for example **property, plant and equipment**, have a physical form. However, physical form is not essential to the existence of an asset. Some assets are intangible.

2.19   In determining the existence of an asset, the right of ownership is not essential. Thus, for example, property held on a **lease** is an asset if the entity controls the benefits that are expected to flow from the property.

Liabilities

2.20   An essential characteristic of a liability is that the entity has a present obligation to act or perform in a particular way. The obligation may be either a legal obligation or a **constructive obligation**. A legal obligation is legally enforceable as a consequence of a binding contract or statutory requirement. A constructive obligation is an obligation that derives from an entity's actions when:

(a)   by an established pattern of past practice, published policies or a sufficiently specific current statement, the entity has indicated to other parties that it will accept certain responsibilities; and

(b)   as a result, the entity has created a valid expectation on the part of those other parties that it will discharge those responsibilities.

2.21   The settlement of a present obligation usually involves the payment of cash, transfer of other assets, provision of services, the replacement of that obligation with another obligation, or conversion of the obligation to equity. An obligation may also be extinguished by other means, such as a creditor waiving or forfeiting its rights.

Equity

2.22   Equity is the residual interest in the assets of the entity after deducting all its liabilities. It may be sub-classified in the statement of financial position. For example, in a corporate entity, sub-classifications may include funds contributed by shareholders, retained earnings and **gains** or losses recognised in **other comprehensive income**.

Performance

2.23   Performance is the relationship of the income and expenses of an entity during a **reporting period**. This FRS permits entities to present performance in a single financial statement (a **statement of comprehensive income**) or in two financial statements (an **income statement** and a statement of comprehensive income). **Total comprehensive income** and **profit or loss** are frequently used as measures of performance or as the basis for other measures, such as return on investment or earnings per share. Income and expenses are defined as follows:

(a)   Income is increases in economic benefits during the reporting period in the form of inflows or enhancements of assets or decreases of liabilities that result in increases in equity, other than those relating to contributions from equity investors.

(b)   Expenses are decreases in economic benefits during the reporting period in the form of outflows or depletions of assets or incurrences of liabilities that result in decreases in equity, other than those relating to distributions to equity investors.

The recognition of income and expenses results directly from the recognition and   **2.24** measurement of assets and liabilities. Criteria for the recognition of income and expenses are discussed in paragraphs 2.27 to 2.32.

Income

The definition of income encompasses both **revenue** and gains.   **2.25**

(a)   Revenue is income that arises in the course of the ordinary activities of an entity and is referred to by a variety of names including sales, fees, interest, dividends, royalties and rent.

(b)   Gains are other items that meet the definition of income but are not revenue. When gains are recognised in the statement of comprehensive income, they are usually displayed separately because knowledge of them is useful for making economic decisions.

Expenses

The definition of expenses encompasses losses as well as those expenses that arise in the   **2.26** course of the ordinary activities of the entity.

(a)   Expenses that arise in the course of the ordinary activities of the entity include, for example, cost of sales, wages and **depreciation**. They usually take the form of an outflow or depletion of assets such as cash and cash equivalents, **inventory**, or property, plant and equipment.

(b)   Losses are other items that meet the definition of expenses and may arise in the course of the ordinary activities of the entity. When losses are recognised in the statement of comprehensive income, they are usually presented separately because knowledge of them is useful for making economic decisions.

Recognition of assets, liabilities, income and expenses

Recognition is the process of incorporating in the statement of financial position or   **2.27** statement of comprehensive income an item that meets the definition of an asset, liability, equity, income or expense and satisfies the following criteria:

(a)   it is **probable** that any future economic benefit associated with the item will flow to or from the entity; and

(b)   the item has a cost or value that can be measured reliably.

The failure to recognise an item that satisfies those criteria is not rectified by disclosure of   **2.28** the accounting policies used or by **notes** or explanatory material.

The probability of future economic benefit

2.29   The concept of probability is used in the first recognition criterion to refer to the degree of uncertainty that the future economic benefits associated with the item will flow to or from the entity. Assessments of the degree of uncertainty attaching to the flow of future economic benefits are made on the basis of the evidence relating to conditions at the end of the reporting period available when the financial statements are prepared. Those assessments are made individually for individually significant items, and for a group for a large population of individually insignificant items.

Reliability of measurement

2.30   The second criterion for the recognition of an item is that it possesses a cost or value that can be measured with reliability. In many cases, the cost or value of an item is known. In other cases it must be estimated. The use of reasonable estimates is an essential part of the preparation of financial statements and does not undermine their reliability. When a reasonable estimate cannot be made, the item is not recognised in the financial statements.

2.31   An item that fails to meet the recognition criteria may qualify for recognition at a later date as a result of subsequent circumstances or events.

2.32   An item that fails to meet the criteria for recognition may nonetheless warrant disclosure in the notes or explanatory material or in supplementary schedules. This is appropriate when knowledge of the item is relevant to the evaluation of the financial position, performance and changes in financial position of an entity by the users of financial statements.

Measurement of assets, liabilities, income and expenses

2.33   Measurement is the process of determining the monetary amounts at which an entity measures assets, liabilities, income and expenses in its financial statements. Measurement involves the selection of a basis of measurement. This FRS specifies which measurement basis an entity shall use for many types of assets, liabilities, income and expenses.

2.34   Two common measurement bases are historical cost and **fair value**:

(a)   For assets, historical cost is the amount of cash or cash equivalents paid or the fair value of the consideration given to acquire the asset at the time of its acquisition. For liabilities, historical cost is the amount of proceeds of cash or cash equivalents received or the fair value of non-cash assets received in exchange for the obligation at the time the obligation is incurred, or in some circumstances (for example, **income tax**) the amounts of cash or cash equivalents expected to be paid to settle the liability in the normal course of business. Amortised historical cost is the historical cost of an asset or liability plus or minus that portion of its historical cost previously recognised as an expense or income.

(b)   Fair value is the amount for which an asset could be exchanged, a liability settled, or an equity instrument granted could be exchanged, between knowledgeable, willing parties in an arm's length transaction. In the absence of any specific guidance provided in the relevant section of this FRS, where fair value measurement is permitted or required the guidance in paragraphs 11.27 to 11.32 shall be applied.

Pervasive recognition and measurement principles

2.35   The requirements for recognising and measuring assets, liabilities, income and expenses in this FRS are based on pervasive principles that are derived from the IASB *Framework for the Preparation and Presentation of Financial Statements*[7] and from **EU-adopted IFRS**. In the absence of a requirement in this FRS that applies specifically to a transaction or other event or condition, paragraph 10.4 provides guidance for making a judgement and paragraph 10.5 establishes a hierarchy for an entity to follow in deciding on the appropriate accounting policy in the circumstances. The second level of that hierarchy requires an entity to look to the definitions, recognition criteria and measurement concepts for assets, liabilities, income and expenses and the pervasive principles set out in this section.

Accrual basis

An entity shall prepare its financial statements, except for cash flow information, using the **accrual basis** of accounting. On the accrual basis, items are recognised as assets, liabilities, equity, income or expenses when they satisfy the definitions and recognition criteria for those items.   **2.36**

Recognition in financial statements

Assets

An entity shall recognise an asset in the statement of financial position when it is probable that the future economic benefits will flow to the entity and the asset has a cost or value that can be measured reliably. An asset is not recognised in the statement of financial position when expenditure has been incurred for which it is considered not probable that economic benefits will flow to the entity beyond the current reporting period. Instead such a transaction results in the recognition of an expense in the statement of comprehensive income (or in the income statement, if presented).   **2.37**

An entity shall not recognise a **contingent asset** as an asset. However, when the flow of future economic benefits to the entity is virtually certain, then the related asset is not a contingent asset, and its recognition is appropriate.   **2.38**

Liabilities

An entity shall recognise a liability in the statement of financial position when: **2.39**

(a)   the entity has an obligation at the end of the reporting period as a result of a past event;

(b)   it is probable that the entity will be required to transfer resources embodying economic benefits in settlement; and

(c)   the settlement amount can be measured reliably.

A **contingent liability** is either a possible but uncertain obligation or a present obligation that is not recognised because it fails to meet one or both of the conditions (b) and (c) in paragraph 2.39. An entity shall not recognise a contingent liability as a liability, except for contingent liabilities of an acquiree in a **business combination** (see Section 19 *Business Combinations and Goodwill*).   **2.40**

Income

The recognition of income results directly from the recognition and measurement of assets and liabilities. An entity shall recognise income in the statement of comprehensive income (or in the income statement, if presented) when an increase in future economic benefits   **2.41**

---

[7] *In 2010 the IASB issued the* Conceptual Framework for Financial Reporting, *which superseded the* Framework for the Preparation and Presentation of Financial Statements.

related to an increase in an asset or a decrease of a liability has arisen that can be measured reliably.

Expenses

2.42   The recognition of expenses results directly from the recognition and measurement of assets and liabilities. An entity shall recognise expenses in the statement of comprehensive income (or in the income statement, if presented) when a decrease in future economic benefits related to a decrease in an asset or an increase of a liability has arisen that can be measured reliably.

Total comprehensive income and profit or loss

2.43   Total comprehensive income is the arithmetical difference between income and expenses. It is not a separate element of financial statements, and a separate recognition principle is not needed for it.

2.44   Profit or loss is the arithmetical difference between income and expenses other than those items of income and expense that this FRS classifies as items of other comprehensive income. It is not a separate element of financial statements, and a separate recognition principle is not needed for it.

2.45   Generally this FRS does not allow the recognition of items in the statement of financial position that do not meet the definition of assets or of liabilities regardless of whether they result from applying the notion commonly referred to as the 'matching concept' for measuring profit or loss.

Measurement at initial recognition

2.46   At initial recognition, an entity shall measure assets and liabilities at historical cost unless this FRS requires initial measurement on another basis such as fair value.

Subsequent measurement

Financial assets and financial liabilities

2.47   An entity measures basic **financial assets** and basic **financial liabilities** at **amortised cost** less impairment except for:

(a)   investments in non-convertible preference shares and non-puttable ordinary and preference shares that are **publicly traded** or whose fair value can otherwise be measured reliably, which are measured at fair value with changes in fair value recognised in profit or loss; and

(b)   any financial instruments that upon their initial recognition were designated by the entity as at fair value through profit or loss.

2.48   An entity generally measures all other financial assets and financial liabilities at fair value, with changes in fair value recognised in profit or loss, unless this FRS requires or permits measurement on another basis such as cost or amortised cost.

Non-financial assets

2.49   Most non-financial assets that an entity initially recognised at historical cost are subsequently measured on other measurement bases. For example:

(a) An entity measures property, plant and equipment using either the cost model or the revaluation model.
(b) An entity measures inventories at the lower of cost and selling price less costs to complete and sell.

Measurement of assets at amounts lower than initial historical cost is intended to ensure that an asset is not measured at an amount greater than the entity expects to recover from the sale or use of that asset.

For certain types of non-financial assets, this FRS permits or requires measurement at fair value. For example: **2.50**

(a) Investments in **associates** and **joint ventures** that an entity measures at fair value (see paragraphs 14.4(b) and 14.4B, and 15.9(b) and 15.9B respectively).
(b) **Investment property** that an entity measures at fair value (see paragraph 16.7).
(c) **Biological assets** that an entity measures at fair value less estimated costs to sell in accordance with the fair value model (see paragraph 34.3A(a)) and **agricultural produce** that an entity measures, at the point of harvest, at fair value less estimated costs to sell in accordance with either the fair value model (see paragraph 34.3A(a)) or cost model (see paragraph 34.9).
(d) Property, plant and equipment that an entity measures in accordance with the revaluation model (see paragraph 17.15B).
(e) **Intangible assets** that an entity measures in accordance with the revaluation model (see paragraph 18.18B).

Liabilities other than financial liabilities

Most liabilities other than financial liabilities are measured at the best estimate of the amount that would be required to settle the obligation at the **reporting date**. **2.51**

Offsetting

An entity shall not offset assets and liabilities, or income and expenses, unless required or permitted by an FRS. **2.52**

(a) Measuring assets net of valuation allowances (for example, allowances for inventory obsolescence and allowances for uncollectible receivables) is not offsetting.
(b) If an entity's normal **operating activities** do not include buying and selling **fixed assets**, including investments and operating assets, then the entity reports gains and losses on disposal of such assets by deducting from the proceeds on disposal the **carrying amount** of the asset and related selling expenses.

Section 3 *Financial Statement Presentation*

Scope of this section

This section explains that the **financial statements** of an entity shall give a true and fair view, what compliance with this FRS requires, and what is a complete set of financial statements. **3.1**

A **small entity** applying Section 1A *Small Entities* is not required to comply with paragraphs 3.3, PBE3.3A, 3.9, 3.17, 3.18, 3.19 and 3.24(b). **3.1A**

True and fair view

3.2   The financial statements shall give a true and fair view of the **assets, liabilities, financial position**, financial **performance** and, when required to be presented, **cash flows** of an entity.

(a)   The application of this FRS, with additional disclosure when necessary, is presumed to result in financial statements that give a true and fair view of the financial position, financial performance and, when required to be presented, cash flows of entities within the scope of this FRS.

(b)   [Not used]

The additional disclosures referred to in (a) are necessary when compliance with the specific requirements in this FRS is insufficient to enable users to understand the effect of particular transactions, other events and conditions on the entity's financial position and financial performance.

Compliance with this FRS

3.3   An entity whose financial statements comply with this FRS shall make an explicit and unreserved statement of such compliance in the **notes**. Financial statements shall not be described as complying with this FRS unless they comply with all the requirements of this FRS.

PBE3.3A   A **public benefit entity** that applies the 'PBE' prefixed paragraphs shall make an explicit and unreserved statement that it is a public benefit entity.

*3.4   In special circumstances when management concludes that compliance with any requirement of this FRS or applicable legislation (only when it allows for a true and fair override) is inconsistent with the requirement to give a true and fair view, the entity shall depart from that requirement in the manner set out in paragraph 3.5.

*3.5   When an entity departs from a requirement of this FRS in accordance with paragraph 3.4, or from a requirement of applicable legislation, it shall disclose the following:

(a)   that management has concluded that the financial statements give a true and fair view of the entity's financial position, financial performance and, when required to be presented, cash flows;

(b)   that it has complied with this FRS or applicable legislation, except that it has departed from a particular requirement of this FRS or applicable legislation to the extent necessary to give a true and fair view; and

(c)   the nature and effect of the departure, including the treatment that this FRS or applicable legislation would require, the reason why that treatment would be so misleading in the circumstances that it would conflict with the objective of financial statements set out in Section 2, and the treatment adopted.

3.6   When an entity has departed from a requirement of this FRS or applicable legislation in a prior period, and that departure affects the amounts recognised in the financial statements for the current period, it shall make the disclosures set out in paragraph 3.5(c).

3.7   [Not used]

Going concern

When preparing financial statements, the management of an entity using this FRS shall **3.8** make an assessment of the entity's ability to continue as a **going concern**. An entity is a going concern unless management either intends to liquidate the entity or to cease trading, or has no realistic alternative but to do so. In assessing whether the going concern assumption is appropriate, management takes into account all available information about the future, which is at least, but is not limited to, twelve months from the date when the financial statements are authorised for issue.

When management is aware, in making its assessment, of **material** uncertainties related **3.9** to events or conditions that cast significant doubt upon the entity's ability to continue as a going concern, the entity shall disclose those uncertainties. When an entity does not prepare financial statements on a going concern basis, it shall disclose that fact, together with the basis on which it prepared the financial statements and the reason why the entity is not regarded as a going concern.

Frequency of reporting

An entity shall present a complete set of financial statements (including comparative **3.10** information as set out in paragraph 3.14) at least annually. When the end of an entity's **reporting period** changes and the annual financial statements are presented for a period longer or shorter than one year, the entity shall disclose the following:

(a)   that fact;
(b)   the reason for using a longer or shorter period; and
(c)   the fact that comparative amounts presented in the financial statements (including the related notes) are not entirely comparable.

Consistency of presentation

An entity shall retain the presentation and classification of items in the financial statements **3.11** from one period to the next unless:

(a)   it is apparent, following a significant change in the nature of the entity's operations or a review of its financial statements, that another presentation or classification would be more appropriate having regard to the criteria for the selection and application of **accounting policies** in Section 10 *Accounting Policies, Estimates and Errors*; or
(b)   this FRS, or another applicable FRS or FRC Abstract, requires a change in presentation.

When the presentation or classification of items in the financial statements is changed, an ***3.12** entity shall reclassify comparative amounts unless the reclassification is **impracticable**. When comparative amounts are reclassified, an entity shall disclose the following:

(a)   the nature of the reclassification;
(b)   the amount of each item or class of items that is reclassified; and
(c)   the reason for the reclassification.

If it is impracticable to reclassify comparative amounts, an entity shall disclose why ***3.13** reclassification was not practicable.

Comparative information

3.14 Except when this FRS permits or requires otherwise, an entity shall present comparative information in respect of the preceding period for all amounts presented in the current period's financial statements. An entity shall include comparative information for narrative and descriptive information when it is relevant to an understanding of the current period's financial statements.

Materiality and aggregation

3.15 An entity shall present separately each material class of similar items. An entity shall present separately items of a dissimilar nature or function unless they are immaterial.

3.16 Financial statements result from processing large numbers of transactions or other events that are aggregated into classes according to their nature or function. The final stage in the process of aggregation and classification is the presentation of condensed and classified data, which form line items in the financial statements. If a line item is not individually material, it is aggregated with other items either in those statements or in the notes. An item that may not warrant separate presentation in those statements may warrant separate presentation in the notes.

3.16A An entity need not provide a specific disclosure required by this FRS if the information is not material.

Complete set of financial statements

3.17 A complete set of financial statements of an entity shall include all of the following:

(a) a **statement of financial position** as at the **reporting date**;

(b) either:

    (i) a single **statement of comprehensive income** for the reporting period displaying all items of income and expense recognised during the period including those items recognised in determining **profit or loss** (which is a subtotal in the statement of comprehensive income) and items of **other comprehensive income**; or

    (ii) a separate **income statement** and a separate statement of comprehensive income. If an entity chooses to present both an income statement and a statement of comprehensive income, the statement of comprehensive income begins with profit or loss and then displays the items of other comprehensive income;

(c) a **statement of changes in equity** for the reporting period;

(d) a **statement of cash flows** for the reporting period; and

(e) notes, comprising a summary of significant accounting policies and other explanatory information.

3.18 If the only changes to **equity** during the periods for which financial statements are presented arise from profit or loss, payment of dividends, corrections of prior period **errors**, and changes in accounting policy, the entity may present a single **statement of income and retained earnings** in place of the statement of comprehensive income and statement of changes in equity (see paragraph 6.4).

3.19 If an entity has no items of other comprehensive income in any of the periods for which financial statements are presented, it may present only an income statement, or it may present a statement of comprehensive income in which the 'bottom line' is labelled 'profit or loss'.

Because paragraph 3.14 requires comparative amounts in respect of the previous period for all amounts presented in the financial statements, a complete set of financial statements means that an entity shall present, as a minimum, two of each of the required financial statements and related notes. **3.20**

In a complete set of financial statements, an entity shall present each financial statement with equal prominence. **3.21**

An entity may use titles for the financial statements other than those used in this FRS as long as they are not misleading. **3.22**

Identification of the financial statements

An entity shall clearly identify each of the financial statements and the notes and distinguish them from other information in the same document. In addition, an entity shall display the following information prominently, and repeat it when necessary for an understanding of the information presented: **3.23**

(a)   the name of the reporting entity and any change in its name since the end of the preceding reporting period;

(b)   whether the financial statements cover the individual entity or a group of entities;

(c)   the date of the end of the reporting period and the period covered by the financial statements;

(d)   the **presentation currency**, as defined in Section 30 *Foreign Currency Translation*; and

(e)   the level of rounding, if any, used in presenting amounts in the financial statements.

An entity shall disclose the following in the notes: **3.24**

*(a)   the legal form of the entity, its country of incorporation and the address of its registered office (or principal place of business, if different from the registered office); and

(b)   a description of the nature of the entity's operations and its principal activities, unless this is disclosed in the business review (or similar statement) accompanying the financial statements.

Presentation of information not required by this FRS

This FRS does not address presentation of **interim financial reports**. An entity that prepares such reports shall describe the basis for preparing and presenting the information. **FRS 104** sets out a basis for the preparation and presentation of interim financial reports that an entity may apply. **3.25**

Section 4 *Statement of Financial Position*

Scope of this section

This section sets out the information that is to be presented in a **statement of financial position** and how to present it. The statement of financial position (which is referred to as the balance sheet in the **Act**) presents an entity's **assets, liabilities** and **equity** as of a specific date—the end of the **reporting period**. This section applies to all entities, whether **4.1** or not they report under the Act. Entities that do not report under the Act should comply with the requirements of this section, and with the **Regulations** (or, where applicable, the **LLP Regulations**) where referred to in this section, except to the extent that these requirements are not permitted by any statutory framework under which such entities report.

4.1A   A **small entity** applying Section 1A *Small Entities* is not required to comply with this section.

Information to be presented in the statement of financial position

4.2   An entity shall present a statement of financial position in accordance with one of the following requirements for a balance sheet:

(a)   Part 1 *General Rules and Formats* of Schedule 1 to the Regulations.
(b)   Part 1 *General Rules and Formats* of Schedule 2 to the Regulations.
(c)   Part 1 *General Rules and Formats* of Schedule 3 to the Regulations.
(d)   Part 1 *General Rules and Formats* of Schedule 1 to the LLP Regulations.

The consolidated statement of financial position of a **group** shall be presented in accordance with the requirements for a consolidated balance sheet in Schedule 6 to the Regulations or Schedule 3 to the LLP Regulations.

4.2A   An entity choosing to apply paragraph 1A(1) of Schedule 1 to the Regulations and adapt one of the balance sheet formats shall, as a minimum, include in its statement of financial position line items that present the following, distinguishing between those items that are **current** and those that are **non-current**:

(a)   **property, plant and equipment**;
(b)   **investment property** carried at **fair value** through profit or loss;
(c)   **intangible assets**;
(d)   **financial assets** (excluding amounts shown under (e), (f), (j) and (k));
(e)   investments in **associates**;
(f)   investments in **jointly controlled entities**;
(g)   **biological assets** carried at cost less accumulated **depreciation** and impairment;
(h)   biological assets carried at fair value through profit or loss;
(i)   **inventories**;
(j)   trade and other receivables;
(k)   **cash** and **cash equivalents**;
(l)   trade and other payables;
(m)   **provisions**;
(n)   financial liabilities (excluding amounts shown under (l) and (m));
(o)   liabilities and assets for **current tax**;
(p)   **deferred tax liabilities** and **deferred tax assets** (classified as non-current);
(q)   **non-controlling interest**, presented within equity separately from the equity attributable to the owners of the **parent**; and
(r)   equity attributable to the owners of the parent.

4.2B   An entity choosing to apply paragraph 1A(1) of Schedule 1 to the Regulations shall also disclose, either in the statement of financial position or in the **notes**, the following sub-classifications of the line items presented:

(a)   property, plant and equipment in classifications appropriate to the entity;
(b)   intangible assets and **goodwill** in classifications appropriate to the entity;
(c)   investments, showing separately shares and loans;

(d)   trade and other receivables showing separately amounts due from **related parties**, amounts due from other parties, prepayments and receivables arising from accrued income not yet billed;

(e)   inventories, showing separately amounts of inventories:

   (i)   held for sale in the ordinary course of business;
   (ii)   in the process of production for such sale; and
   (iii)   in the form of materials or supplies to be consumed in the production process or in the rendering of services.

(f)   trade and other payables, showing separately amounts payable to trade suppliers, payable to related parties, deferred income and accruals; and

(g)   classes of equity, such as share capital, share premium, retained earnings, revaluation reserve, fair value reserve and other reserves.

The descriptions used in paragraphs 4.2A and 4.2B, and the ordering of items or aggregation of similar items, may be amended according to the nature of the entity and its transactions, to provide information that is relevant to an understanding of the entity's financial position, providing the information given is at least equivalent to that required by the balance sheet format had it not been adapted. **4.2C**

In order to comply with the requirement to distinguish between those items that are current and those that are non-current an entity shall present current and non-current assets, and current and non-current liabilities, as separate classifications in its statement of financial position. **4.2D**

An entity shall present additional line items, headings and subtotals in the statement of financial position when such presentation is relevant to an understanding of the entity's **financial position**. **4.3**

Debtors due after more than one year

[Not used] **4.4**

Unless an entity chooses to apply paragraph 1A(1) of Schedule 1 to the Regulations, in instances where the amount of debtors due after more than one year is so **material** in the context of the total net current assets that in the absence of disclosure of the debtors due after more than one year on the face of the statement of financial position readers may misinterpret the **financial statements**, the amount should be disclosed on the face of the statement of financial position within **current assets**. In most cases it will be satisfactory to disclose the amount due after more than one year in the **notes** to the financial statements. **4.4A**

[Not used] **4.5**

[Not used] **4.6**

Creditors: amounts falling due within one year

Unless an entity chooses to apply paragraph 1A(1) of Schedule 1 to the Regulations, an entity shall classify a creditor as due within one year when the entity does not have an unconditional right, at the end of the reporting period, to defer settlement of the creditor for at least 12 months after the **reporting date**. For example, this would be the case if the earliest date on which the lender, exercising all available options and rights, could require repayment or (as the case may be) payment was within 12 months after the reporting date. **4.7**

[Not used] **4.8**

Information to be presented either in the statement of financial position or in the notes

4.9   [Not used]

4.10   [Not used]

4.11   [Not used]

4.12   An entity with share capital shall disclose the following, either in the statement of financial position or in the notes:

(a)   For each class of share capital:

    (i)   [Not used]

    (ii)   The number of shares issued and fully paid, and issued but not fully paid.

    (iii)   Par value per share, or that the shares have no par value.

    (iv)   A reconciliation of the number of shares outstanding at the beginning and at the end of the period. This reconciliation need not be presented for prior periods.

    (v)   The rights, preferences and restrictions attaching to that class including restrictions on the distribution of dividends and the repayment of capital.

    (vi)   Shares in the entity held by the entity or by its **subsidiaries**, **associates**, or **joint ventures**.

    (vii)   Shares reserved for issue under options and contracts for the sale of shares, including the terms and amounts.

(b)   A description of each reserve within equity.

4.13   An entity without share capital, such as a partnership or trust, shall disclose information equivalent to that required by paragraph 4.12(a), showing changes during the period in each category of equity, and the rights, preferences and restrictions attaching to each category of equity.

Information to be presented in the notes

4.14   If, at the reporting date, an entity has a binding sale agreement for a major disposal of assets, or a **disposal group**, the entity shall disclose the following information:

(a)   a description of the asset(s) or the disposal group;

(b)   a description of the facts and circumstances of the sale; and

(c)   the **carrying amount** of the assets or, for a disposal group, the carrying amounts of the underlying assets and liabilities.

Section 5 *Statement of Comprehensive Income and Income Statement*

Scope of this section

5.1   This section requires an entity to present its **total comprehensive income** for a period— ie its financial **performance** for the period—in one or two statements. It sets out the information that is to be presented in those statements and how to present it. This section applies to all entities, whether or not they report under the **Act**. Entities that do not report under the Act should comply with the requirements of this section, and with the **Regulations** (or, where applicable, the **LLP Regulations**) where referred to in this section, except to the extent that these requirements are not permitted by any statutory framework under which such entities report. If an entity meets specified conditions and chooses to do so, it may present a **statement of income and retained earnings** as set out in Section 6 *Statement of Change in Equity and Statement of Income and Retained Earnings*.

A **small entity** applying Section 1A *Small Entities* is not required to comply with this section.   **5.1A**

Presentation of total comprehensive income

An entity shall present its total comprehensive income for a period either: **5.2**

(a)   in a single **statement of comprehensive income**, in which case the statement of comprehensive income presents all items of **income** and **expense** recognised in the period; or

(b)   in two statements—an **income statement** (which is referred to as the profit and loss account in the Act) and a statement of comprehensive income—in which case the income statement presents all items of income and expense recognised in the period except those that are recognised in total comprehensive income outside of **profit or loss** as permitted or required by this FRS.

A change from the single-statement approach to the two-statement approach, or vice versa, is a change in **accounting policy** to which Section 10 *Accounting Policies, Estimates and Errors* applies.   **5.3**

Single-statement approach

[Not used]   **5.4**

An entity shall present, in the statement of comprehensive income, the items to be included in a profit and loss account in accordance with one of the following requirements: **5.5**

(a)   Part 1 *General Rules and Formats* of Schedule 1 to the Regulations;
(b)   Part 1 *General Rules and Formats* of Schedule 2 to the Regulations;
(c)   Part 1 *General Rules and Formats* of Schedule 3 to the Regulations; or
(d)   Part 1 *General Rules and Formats* of Schedule 1 to the LLP Regulations.

The consolidated statement of comprehensive income of a **group** shall be presented in accordance with the requirements for a consolidated profit and loss account of Schedule 6 to the Regulations or Schedule 3 to the LLP Regulations.

In addition an entity shall include, in the statement of comprehensive income, line items that present the following amounts for the period: **5.5A**

(a)   Classified by nature (excluding amounts in (b)), the components of **other comprehensive income** recognised as part of total comprehensive income outside profit or loss as permitted or required by this FRS. An entity may present the components of other comprehensive income either:

   (i)   net of related tax effects; or
   (ii)   before the related tax effects with one amount shown for the aggregate amount of **income tax** relating to those components.

(b)   Its share of the other comprehensive income of **associates** and **jointly controlled entities** accounted for by the equity method.

(c)   Total comprehensive income.

An entity choosing to apply paragraph 1A(2) of Schedule 1 to the Regulations and adapt one of the profit and loss account formats shall, as a minimum, include in its statement of comprehensive income line items that present the following amounts for the period: **5.5B**

(a)   **revenue**;
(b)   finance costs;
(c)   share of the profit or loss of investments in **associates** (see Section 14 *Investments in Associates*) and **jointly controlled entities** (see Section 15 *Investments in Joint Ventures*) accounted for using the equity method;
(d)   profit or loss before taxation;
(e)   **tax expense** excluding tax allocated to items (h) and (i) below or to **equity** (see paragraph 29.27);
(f)   as set out in paragraph 5.7E (including a column identified as **discontinued operations**) a single amount comprising the total of:

    (i)   the post-tax profit or loss of a discontinued operation, and
    (ii)   the post-tax gain or loss recognised on the remeasurement of the impairment or on the disposal of the **assets** or **disposal group(s)** constituting discontinued operations.

(g)   profit or loss;
(h)   each item of other comprehensive income classified by nature (excluding amounts in (i));
(i)   share of other comprehensive income of associates and jointly controlled entities accounted for by the equity method; and
(j)   total comprehensive income.

5.5C   An entity may include additional line items in the income statement and amend the descriptions used in paragraph 5.5B, and the ordering of items, when this is necessary to explain the elements of financial performance, providing the information given is at least equivalent to that required by the profit and loss account format had it not been adapted.

5.6   An entity shall present the following items as allocations of profit or loss and other comprehensive income in the statement of comprehensive income for the period:

(a)   Profit or loss for the period attributable to:

    (i)   **non-controlling interest**; and
    (ii)   **owners** of the **parent**.

(b)   Total comprehensive income for the period attributable to:

    (i)   non-controlling interest; and
    (ii)   owners of the parent.

Two-statement approach

5.7   Under the two-statement approach, an entity shall present in an income statement, the items to be included in a profit and loss account in accordance with one of the following requirements:

(a)   Part 1 *General Rules and Formats* of Schedule 1 to the Regulations;
(b)   Part 1 *General Rules and Formats* of Schedule 2 to the Regulations;
(c)   Part 1 *General Rules and Formats* of Schedule 3 to the Regulations; or
(d)   Part 1 *General Rules and Formats* of Schedule 1 to the LLP Regulations.

The consolidated income statement of a group shall be presented in accordance with the requirements for a consolidated profit and loss account of Schedule 6 to the Regulations or Schedule 3 to the LLP Regulations.

5.7A   An entity choosing to apply paragraph 1A(2) of Schedule 1 to the Regulations and adapt one of the profit and loss account formats shall, as a minimum, include in its income statement line items that present the amounts in paragraphs 5.5B(a) to 5.5B(g), with profit or loss as the last line. The statement of comprehensive income shall begin with profit or loss as its first line and shall display, as a minimum, line items that present the amounts in paragraphs 5.5B(h) to 5.5B(j) and paragraph 5.6(b) for the period, with total comprehensive income as the last line.

If an entity presents profit or loss in an income statement, it shall present the information required in paragraph 5.6(a) in that statement. **5.7B**

The statement of comprehensive income shall begin with profit or loss as its first line and shall display, as a minimum, line items that present the amounts in paragraphs 5.5A and 5.6(b) for the period. **5.7C**

Requirements applicable to both approaches

In addition to the requirements of paragraphs 5.5 or 5.7, as a minimum, **turnover** must be presented on the face of the income statement (or statement of comprehensive income if presented). **5.7D**

An entity shall also disclose on the face of the income statement (or statement of comprehensive income if presented) an amount comprising the total of: **5.7E**

(a) the post-tax profit or loss of discontinued operations; and
(b) the post-tax gain or loss attributable to the impairment or on the disposal of the assets or disposal group(s) constituting discontinued operations.

A line-by-line analysis shall be presented in the income statement (or statement of comprehensive income if presented), in a column identified as relating to discontinued operations, ie separately from continuing operations; a total column shall also be presented.

An entity shall re-present the disclosures in paragraph 5.7D for prior periods presented in the **financial statements** so that the disclosures relate to all operations that have been discontinued by the end of the **reporting period** for the latest period presented. **5.7F**

Under this FRS, the effects of corrections of **material errors** and changes in accounting policies are presented as retrospective adjustments of prior periods rather than as part of profit or loss in the period in which they arise (see Section 10). **5.8**

An entity shall present additional line items, headings and subtotals in the statement of comprehensive income (and in the income statement, if presented), when such presentation is relevant to an understanding of the entity's financial performance. **5.9**

When items included in total comprehensive income are material, an entity shall disclose their nature and amount separately, in the statement of comprehensive income (and in the income statement, if presented) or in the **notes**. ***5.9A**

This FRS does not require disclosure of 'operating profit'. However, if an entity elects to disclose the results of **operating activities** the entity should ensure that the amount disclosed is representative of activities that would normally be regarded as 'operating'. For example, it would be inappropriate to exclude items clearly related to operations (such as inventory write-downs and restructuring and relocation expenses) because they occur irregularly or infrequently or are unusual in amount. Similarly, it would be inappropriate to exclude items on the grounds that they do not involve **cash flows**, such as **depreciation** and **amortisation** expenses. **5.9B**

Ordinary activities and extraordinary items

5.10   An entity applying paragraph 5.5(a) or 5.7(a) shall not present or describe any items of income or expense as 'extraordinary items' in the statement of comprehensive income (or in the income statement, if presented) or in the notes.

Paragraphs 5.10A and 5.10B apply to entities applying paragraphs 5.5(b), 5.5(c), 5.5(d), 5.7(b), 5.7(c) or 5.7(d).

5.10A   Ordinary activities are any activities which are undertaken by a reporting entity as part of its business and such related activities in which the reporting entity engages in furtherance of, incidental to, or arising from, these activities. Ordinary activities include any effects on the reporting entity of any event in the various environments in which it operates, including the political, regulatory, economic and geographical environments, irrespective of the frequency or unusual nature of the events.

5.10B   Extraordinary items are material items possessing a high degree of abnormality which arise from events or transactions that fall outside the ordinary activities of the reporting entity and which are not expected to recur. The additional line items required to be presented by paragraph 5.9 and material items required to be disclosed by paragraph 5.9A, are not extraordinary items when they arise from the ordinary activities of the entity. Extraordinary items do not include prior period items merely because they relate to a prior period.

Analysis of expenses

5.11   Unless otherwise required under the Regulations, an entity shall present an analysis of expenses using a classification based on either the nature of expenses or the function of expenses within the entity, whichever provides information that is reliable and more relevant.

Analysis by nature of expense

(a)   Under this method of classification, expenses are aggregated in the statement of comprehensive income (or in the income statement, under the two-statement approach) according to their nature (eg depreciation, raw materials and consumables and staff costs), and are not reallocated among various functions within the entity.

Analysis by function of expense

(b)   Under this method of classification, expenses are aggregated according to their function as part of cost of sales or, for example, the costs of distribution or administrative activities.

Appendix to Section 5

Example showing presentation of discontinued operations

This appendix accompanies, but is not part of, Section 5. It provides guidance on applying the requirements of Section 5 paragraph 5.7E for presenting discontinued operations. The example illustrates the presentation of comprehensive income in a single statement and the classification of expenses within profit by function. A columnar format is used in order to present a single line item as required by paragraph 5.7E, while still complying with the requirements of the Act to show totals for ordinary activities of items such as turnover, profit or loss before taxation and tax.

Statement of comprehensive income

For the year ended 31 December 20X1

	20X1 Continuing operations	20X1 Discontinued operations	20X1 Total	20X0 Continuing operations (as restated)	20X0 Discontinued operations (as restated)	20X0 Total
	CU	CU	CU	CU	CU	CU
Turnover	4,200	1,232	5,432	3,201	1,500	4,701
Cost of Sales	(2,591)	(1,104)	(3,695)	(2,281)	(1,430)	(3,711)
Gross profit	1,609	128	1,737	920	70	990
Administrative expenses	(452)	(110)	(562)	(418)	(120)	(538)
Other operating income	212	–	212	198	–	198
Profit on disposal of operations	–	301	301	–	–	–
Operating profit	1,369	319	1,688	700	(50)	650
Interest receivable and similar income	14	–	14	16	–	16
Interest payable and similar charges	(208)	–	(208)	(208)	–	(208)
Profit on ordinary activities before tax	1,175	319	1,494	508	(50)	458
Taxation	(390)	(4)	(394)	(261)	3	(258)
Profit on ordinary activities after taxation and profit for the financial year	785	315	1,100	247	(47)	200
Other comprehensive income						
Actuarial losses on defined benefit pension plans			(108)			(68)
Deferred tax movement relating to actuarial losses			28			18
Total comprehensive income for the year			1,020			150

Section 6 *Statement of Changes in Equity and Statement of Income and Retained Earnings*

Scope of this section

This section sets out requirements for presenting the changes in an entity's **equity** for a period, either in a statement of changes in equity or, if specified conditions are met and an entity chooses, in a **statement of income and retained earnings**.   **6.1**

A **small entity** applying Section 1A *Small Entities* is not required to comply with this section. However, paragraph 1A.9 encourages a small entity to present a statement of changes in equity or a statement of income and retained earnings.   **6.1A**

Statement of changes in equity

Purpose

6.2   The statement of changes in equity presents an entity's **profit or loss** for a **reporting period**, **other comprehensive income** for the period, the effects of changes in **accounting policies** and corrections of **material errors** recognised in the period, and the amounts of investments by, and dividends and other distributions to, equity investors during the period.

Information to be presented in the statement of changes in equity

6.3   An entity shall present a statement of changes in equity showing in the statement:

(a)   **total comprehensive income** for the period, showing separately the total amounts attributable to **owners** of the **parent** and to **non-controlling interests**;

(b)   for each component of equity, the effects of **retrospective application** or retrospective restatement recognised in accordance with Section 10 *Accounting Policies, Estimates and Errors*; and

(c)   for each component of equity, a reconciliation between the **carrying amount** at the beginning and the end of the period, separately disclosing changes resulting from:

(i)   profit or loss;

(ii)   other comprehensive income; and

(iii)   the amounts of investments by, and dividends and other distributions to, owners, showing separately issues of shares, purchase of own share transactions, dividends and other distributions to owners, and changes in ownership interests in **subsidiaries** that do not result in a loss of **control**.

Information to be presented in the statement of changes in equity or in the notes

*6.3A   For each component of equity, an entity shall present, either in the statement of changes in equity or in the **notes**, an analysis of other comprehensive income by item (see paragraph 6.3(c)(ii)).

Statement of income and retained earnings

Purpose

6.4   The statement of income and retained earnings presents an entity's profit or loss and changes in retained earnings for a reporting period. Paragraph 3.18 permits an entity to present a statement of income and retained earnings in place of a **statement of comprehensive income** and a statement of changes in equity if the only changes to its equity during the periods for which **financial statements** are presented arise from profit or loss, payment of dividends, corrections of prior period material errors, and changes in accounting policy.

Information to be presented in the statement of income and retained earnings

6.5   An entity shall present, in the statement of income and retained earnings, the following items in addition to the information required by Section 5 *Statement of Comprehensive Income and Income Statement*:

(a)   retained earnings at the beginning of the reporting period;

(b)   dividends declared and paid or payable during the period;

(c)   restatements of retained earnings for corrections of prior period material errors;

(d)   restatements of retained earnings for changes in accounting policy; and

(e)   retained earnings at the end of the reporting period.

Section 7 *Statement of Cash Flows*

Scope of this section

This section sets out the information that is to be presented in a **statement of cash flows** and how to present it. The statement of cash flows provides information about the changes in **cash** and **cash equivalents** of an entity for a **reporting period**, showing separately changes from **operating activities**, **investing activities** and **financing activities**.   **7.1**

This section and paragraph 3.17(d) do not apply to: **7.1A**

(a)   mutual life assurance companies;

(b)   **retirement benefit plans**; or

(c)   investment funds that meet all the following conditions:

    (i)   substantially all of the entity's investments are highly liquid;

    (ii)   substantially all of the entity's investments are carried at market value; and

    (iii)   the entity provides a statement of changes in net assets.

A **small entity** is not required to comply with this section.   **7.1B**

Cash equivalents

Cash equivalents are short-term, highly liquid investments that are readily convertible to known amounts of cash and that are subject to an insignificant risk of changes in value. Therefore, an investment normally qualifies as a cash equivalent only when it has a short maturity of, say, three months or less from the date of acquisition. Bank overdrafts are normally considered financing activities similar to borrowings. However, if they are repayable on demand and form an integral part of an entity's cash management, bank overdrafts are a component of cash and cash equivalents.   **7.2**

Information to be presented in the statement of cash flows

An entity shall present a statement of **cash flows** that presents cash flows for a reporting period classified by operating activities, investing activities and financing activities.   **7.3**

Operating activities

Operating activities are the principal revenue-producing activities of the entity. Therefore, cash flows from operating activities generally result from the transactions and other events and conditions that enter into the determination of **profit or loss**. Examples of cash flows from operating activities are: **7.4**

(a)   cash receipts from the sale of goods and the rendering of services;

(b)   cash receipts from royalties, fees, commissions and other revenue;

(c)   cash payments to suppliers for goods and services;

(d)   cash payments to and on behalf of employees;

(e)   cash payments or refunds of **income tax**, unless they can be specifically identified with financing and investing activities;

(f)   cash receipts and payments from investments, loans and other contracts held for dealing or trading purposes, which are similar to **inventory** acquired specifically for resale; and

(g)   cash advances and loans made to other parties by **financial institutions**.

Some transactions, such as the sale of an item of plant by a manufacturing entity, may give rise to a **gain** or loss that is included in profit or loss. However, the cash flows relating to such transactions are cash flows from investing activities.

Investing activities

7.5   Investing activities are the acquisition and disposal of long-term assets and other investments not included in cash equivalents. Examples of cash flows arising from investing activities are:

(a)   cash payments to acquire **property, plant and equipment** (including self-constructed property, plant and equipment), **intangible assets** and other long-term assets. These payments include those relating to capitalised development costs and self-constructed property, plant and equipment;

(b)   cash receipts from sales of property, plant and equipment, intangibles and other long-term assets;

(c)   cash payments to acquire **equity** or debt instruments of other entities and interests in **joint ventures** (other than payments for those instruments classified as cash equivalents or held for dealing or trading);

(d)   cash receipts from sales of equity or debt instruments of other entities and interests in joint ventures (other than receipts for those instruments classified as cash equivalents or held for dealing or trading);

(e)   cash advances and loans made to other parties (except those made by financial institutions – see paragraph 7.4(g));

(f)   cash receipts from the repayment of advances and loans made to other parties;

(g)   cash payments for futures contracts, forward contracts, option contracts and swap contracts, except when the contracts are held for dealing or trading, or the payments are classified as financing activities; and

(h)   cash receipts from futures contracts, forward contracts, option contracts and swap contracts, except when the contracts are held for dealing or trading, or the receipts are classified as financing activities.

When a contract is accounted for as a hedge (see Section 12 *Other Financial Instruments Issues*), an entity shall classify the cash flows of the contract in the same manner as the cash flows of the item being hedged.

Financing activities

7.6   Financing activities are activities that result in changes in the size and composition of the contributed equity and borrowings of an entity. Examples of cash flows arising from financing activities are:

(a)   cash proceeds from issuing shares or other equity instruments;

(b)   cash payments to **owners** to acquire or redeem the entity's shares;

(c)   cash proceeds from issuing debentures, loans, notes, bonds, mortgages and other short-term or long-term borrowings;

(d)   cash repayments of amounts borrowed; and

(e)   cash payments by a lessee for the reduction of the outstanding **liability** relating to a **finance lease**.

Reporting cash flows from operating activities

An entity shall present cash flows from operating activities using either: **7.7**

(a)   the indirect method, whereby profit or loss is adjusted for the effects of non-cash transactions, any deferrals or accruals of past or future operating cash receipts or payments, and items of **income** or **expense** associated with investing or financing cash flows; or

(b)   the direct method, whereby major classes of gross cash receipts and gross cash payments are disclosed.

Indirect method

Under the indirect method, the net cash flow from operating activities is determined by   **7.8**
adjusting profit or loss for the effects of:

(a)   changes during the period in inventories and operating receivables and payables;

(b)   non-cash items such as **depreciation, provisions, deferred tax**, accrued income (expenses) not yet received (paid) in cash, unrealised foreign currency gains and losses, undistributed profits of **associates**, and **non-controlling interests**; and

(c)   all other items for which the cash effects relate to investing or financing.

Direct method

Under the direct method, net cash flow from operating activities is presented by disclosing   **7.9**
information about major classes of gross cash receipts and gross cash payments. Such
information may be obtained either:

(a)   from the accounting records of the entity; or

(b)   by adjusting sales, cost of sales and other items in the **statement of comprehensive income** (or the **income statement**, if presented) for:

(i)   changes during the period in inventories and operating receivables and payables;

(ii)   other non-cash items; and

(iii)   other items for which the cash effects are investing or financing cash flows.

Reporting cash flows from investing and financing activities

An entity shall present separately major classes of gross cash receipts and gross cash   **7.10**
payments arising from investing and financing activities, except to the extent that net
presentation is permitted by paragraphs 7.10A to 7.10E. The aggregate cash flows arising
from acquisitions and from disposals of **subsidiaries** or other business units shall be
presented separately and classified as investing activities.

Reporting cash flows on a net basis

Cash flows arising from the following operating, investing or financing activities may be   **7.10A**
reported on a net basis:

(a)   cash receipts and payments on behalf of customers when the cash flows reflect the activities of the customer rather than those of the entity; and

(b)   cash receipts and payments for items in which the turnover is quick, the amounts are large, and the maturities are short.

7.10B   Examples of cash receipts and payments referred to in paragraph 7.10A(a) are:

    (a)   the acceptance and repayment of demand deposits of a bank;

    (b)   funds held for customers by an investment entity; and

    (c)   rents collected on behalf of, and paid over to, the owners of properties.

7.10C   Examples of cash receipts and payments referred to in paragraph 7.10A(b) are advances made for, and the repayment of:

    (a)   principal amounts relating to credit card customers;

    (b)   the purchase and sale of investments; and

    (c)   other short-term borrowings, for example, those which have a maturity period of three months or less.

7.10D   Financial institutions may report cash flows described in paragraph 34.33 on a net basis.

7.10E   A financial institution that undertakes the business of effecting or carrying out **insurance contracts**, other than mutual life assurance companies scoped out of this section in paragraph 7.1A(a), should include the cash flows of their long-term business only to the extent of cash transferred and available to meet the obligations of the company or group as a whole.

Foreign currency cash flows

7.11   An entity shall record cash flows arising from transactions in a foreign currency in the entity's **functional currency** by applying to the foreign currency amount the exchange rate between the functional currency and the foreign currency at the date of the cash flow or an exchange rate that approximates the actual rate (for example, a weighted average exchange rate for the period).

7.12   An entity shall translate cash flows of a foreign subsidiary at the exchange rate between the entity's functional currency and the foreign currency at the date of the cash flow or at an exchange rate that approximates the actual rate (for example, a weighted average exchange rate for the period).

7.13   Unrealised gains and losses arising from changes in foreign currency exchange rates are not cash flows. However, to reconcile cash and cash equivalents at the beginning and the end of the period, the effect of exchange rate changes on cash and cash equivalents held or due in a foreign currency must be presented in the statement of cash flows. Therefore, the entity shall remeasure cash and cash equivalents held during the reporting period (such as amounts of foreign currency held and foreign currency bank accounts) at period-end exchange rates. The entity shall present the resulting unrealised gain or loss separately from cash flows from operating, investing and financing activities.

Interest and dividends

7.14   An entity shall present separately cash flows from interest and dividends received and paid. The entity shall classify these cash flows consistently from period to period as operating, investing or financing activities.

7.15   An entity may classify interest paid and interest and dividends received as operating cash flows because they are included in profit or loss. Alternatively, the entity may classify interest paid and interest and dividends received as financing cash flows and investing cash flows respectively, because they are costs of obtaining financial resources or returns on investments.

An entity may classify dividends paid as a financing cash flow because they are a cost of obtaining financial resources. Alternatively, the entity may classify dividends paid as a component of cash flows from operating activities because they are paid out of operating cash flows.   **7.16**

Income tax

An entity shall present separately cash flows arising from income tax and shall classify them as cash flows from operating activities unless they can be specifically identified with financing and investing activities. When tax cash flows are allocated over more than one class of activity, the entity shall disclose the total amount of taxes paid.   **7.17**

Non-cash transactions

An entity shall exclude from the statement of cash flows investing and financing transactions that do not require the use of cash or cash equivalents. An entity shall disclose such transactions elsewhere in the **financial statements** in a way that provides all the relevant information about those investing and financing activities.   **7.18**

Many investing and financing activities do not have a direct impact on current cash flows even though they affect the capital and asset structure of an entity. The exclusion of non-cash transactions from the statement of cash flows is consistent with the objective of a statement of cash flows because these items do not involve cash flows in the current period. Examples of non-cash transactions are: **7.19**

(a)   the acquisition of assets either by assuming directly related liabilities or by means of a finance lease;
(b)   the acquisition of an entity by means of an equity issue; and
(c)   the conversion of debt to equity.

Components of cash and cash equivalents

An entity shall present the components of cash and cash equivalents and shall present a reconciliation of the amounts presented in the statement of cash flows to the equivalent items presented in the **statement of financial position**. However, an entity is not required to present this reconciliation if the amount of cash and cash equivalents presented in the statement of cash flows is identical to the amount similarly described in the statement of financial position.   **7.20**

Entities applying Part 1 *General Rules and Formats* of Schedule 2 to the **Regulations** should include as cash, only cash and balances at central banks and loans and advances to banks repayable on demand.   **7.20A**

Other disclosures

An entity shall disclose, together with a commentary by management, the amount of significant cash and cash equivalent balances held by the entity that are not available for use by the entity. Cash and cash equivalents held by an entity may not be available for use by the entity because of, among other reasons, foreign exchange controls or legal restrictions.   **7.21**

Section 8 *Notes to the Financial Statements*

Scope of this section

8.1 This section sets out the principles underlying information that is to be presented in the **notes** to the **financial statements** and how to present it. Notes contain information in addition to that presented in the **statement of financial position, statement of comprehensive income** (if presented), **income statement** (if presented), combined **statement of income and retained earnings** (if presented), **statement of changes in equity** (if presented), and **statement of cash flows**. Notes provide narrative descriptions or disaggregations of items presented in those statements and information about items that do not qualify for **recognition** in those statements. In addition to the requirements of this section, nearly every other section of this FRS requires disclosures that are normally presented in the notes.

Structure of the notes

8.2 The notes shall:

(a) present information about the basis of preparation of the financial statements and the specific **accounting policies** used, in accordance with paragraphs 8.5 to 8.7;

(b) disclose the information required by this FRS that is not presented elsewhere in the financial statements; and

(c) provide information that is not presented elsewhere in the financial statements but is relevant to an understanding of any of them.

*8.3 An entity shall, as far as practicable, present the notes in a systematic manner. An entity shall cross-reference each item in the financial statements to any related information in the notes.

*8.4 An entity normally[8] presents the notes in the following order:

(a) a statement that the financial statements have been prepared in compliance with this FRS (see paragraph 3.3);

(b) a summary of significant accounting policies applied (see paragraph 8.5);

(c) supporting information for items presented in the financial statements, in the sequence in which each statement and each line item is presented; and

(d) any other disclosures.

Disclosure of accounting policies

*8.5 An entity shall disclose the following in the summary of significant accounting policies:

(a) the measurement basis (or bases) used in preparing the financial statements; and

(b) the other accounting policies used that are relevant to an understanding of the financial statements.

Information about judgements

*8.6 An entity shall disclose, in the summary of significant accounting policies or other notes, the judgements, apart from those involving estimations (see paragraph 8.7), that management has made in the process of applying the entity's accounting policies and that have the most significant effect on the amounts recognised in the financial statements.

---

[8] *Company law requires the notes to be presented in the order in which, where relevant, the items to which they relate are presented in the statement of financial position and in the income statement.*

Information about key sources of estimation uncertainty

An entity shall disclose in the notes information about the key assumptions concerning the **8.7** future, and other key sources of estimation uncertainty at the reporting date, that have a significant risk of causing a **material** adjustment to the **carrying amounts** of **assets** and **liabilities** within the next financial year. In respect of those assets and liabilities, the notes shall include details of:

(a)　their nature; and
(b)　their carrying amount as at the end of the **reporting period**.

Section 9 *Consolidated and Separate Financial Statements*

Scope of this section

This section applies to all **parents** that present **consolidated financial statements** (which **9.1** are referred to as group accounts in the **Act**) intended to give a true and fair view of the **financial position** and **profit or loss** (or **income and expenditure**) of their **group**, whether or not they report under the Act. Parents that do not report under the Act should comply with the requirements of this section, and of the Act where referred to in this section, except to the extent that these requirements are not permitted by any statutory framework under which such entities report. This section also includes guidance on **individual financial statements** and **separate financial statements**.

Requirement to present consolidated financial statements

Except as permitted or required by paragraph 9.3, a parent entity shall present consolidated **9.2** financial statements in which it consolidates all its investments in **subsidiaries** in accordance with this FRS. A parent entity need only prepare consolidated accounts under the Act if it is a parent at the year end.

A parent is exempt from the requirement to prepare consolidated financial statements on **9.3** any one of the following grounds:

When its immediate parent is established under the law of an EEA State (Section 400 of the Act):

(a)　The parent is a wholly-owned subsidiary. Exemption is conditional on compliance with certain further conditions set out in section 400(2) of the Act.
(b)　The immediate parent holds 90% or more of the allotted shares in the entity and the remaining shareholders have approved the exemption. Exemption is conditional on compliance with certain further conditions set out in section 400(2) of the Act.
(bA)　The immediate parent holds more than 50% (but less than 90%) of the allotted shares in the entity, and notice requesting the preparation of consolidated financial statements has not been served on the entity by shareholders holding in aggregate at least 5% of the allotted shares in the entity. Exemption is conditional on compliance with certain further conditions set out in section 400(2) of the Act.

When its parent is not established under the law of an EEA State (Section 401 of the Act):

(c)　The parent is a wholly-owned subsidiary. Exemption is conditional on compliance with certain further conditions set out in section 401(2) of the Act.
(d)　The parent holds 90% or more of the allotted shares in the entity and the remaining shareholders have approved the exemption. Exemption is conditional on compliance with certain further conditions set out in section 401(2) of the Act.

(dA) The parent holds more than 50% (but less than 90%) of the allotted shares in the entity, and notice requesting the preparation of consolidated financial statements has not been served on the entity by shareholders holding in aggregate at least 5% of the allotted shares in the entity. Exemption is conditional on compliance with certain further conditions set out in section 401(2) of the Act.

Other situations

(e)   The parent, and the group headed by it, qualify as small as set out in section 383 of the Act and the parent and the group are considered eligible for the exemption as determined by reference to sections 384 and 399(2A) of the Act.

(f)   All of the parent's subsidiaries are required to be excluded from consolidation by paragraph 9.9 (Section 402 of the Act).

(g)   For a parent not reporting under the Act, if its statutory framework does not require the preparation of consolidated financial statements.

In sub-paragraphs (a) to (dA), the parent is not exempt if any of its transferable securities are admitted to trading on a regulated market of any EEA State within the meaning of Directive 2004/39/EC.

9.4   A subsidiary is an entity that is controlled by the parent. **Control** is the power to govern the financial and operating policies of an entity so as to obtain benefits from its activities.

9.5   Control is presumed to exist when the parent owns, directly or indirectly through subsidiaries, more than half of the voting power of an entity. That presumption may be overcome in exceptional circumstances if it can be clearly demonstrated that such ownership does not constitute control. Control also exists when the parent owns half or less of the voting power of an entity but it has:

(a)   power over more than half of the voting rights by virtue of an agreement with other investors;

(b)   power to govern the financial and operating policies of the entity under a statute or an agreement;

(c)   power to appoint or remove the majority of the members of the board of directors or equivalent governing body and control of the entity is by that board or body; or

(d)   power to cast the majority of votes at meetings of the board of directors or equivalent governing body and control of the entity is by that board or body.

9.6   Control can also be achieved by having options or convertible instruments that are currently exercisable or by having an agent with the ability to direct the activities for the benefit of the controlling entity.

9.6A   Control can also exist when the parent has the power to exercise, or actually exercises, dominant influence or control over the undertaking or it and the undertaking are managed on a unified basis.

9.7   [Not used]

9.8   A subsidiary is not excluded from consolidation because its business activities are dissimilar to those of the other entities within the consolidation. Relevant information is provided by consolidating such subsidiaries and disclosing additional information in the consolidated financial statements about the different business activities of subsidiaries.

9.8A   A subsidiary is not excluded from consolidation because the information necessary for the preparation of consolidated financial statements cannot be obtained without disproportionate **expense** or undue delay, unless its inclusion is not **material** (individually or collectively for more than one subsidiary) for the purposes of giving a true and fair view in the context of the group.

A subsidiary shall be excluded from consolidation where: **9.9**

(a) severe long-term restrictions substantially hinder the exercise of the rights of the parent over the **assets** or management of the subsidiary; or

(b) the interest in the subsidiary is **held exclusively with a view to subsequent resale**; and the subsidiary has not previously been consolidated in the consolidated financial statements prepared in accordance with this FRS.

A subsidiary excluded from consolidation on the grounds set out in paragraph 9.9(a) **9.9A** shall be measured using an accounting policy selected by the parent in accordance with paragraph 9.26, except where the parent still exercises a significant influence over the subsidiary. If this is the case, the parent should treat the subsidiary as an associate using the equity method set out in paragraph 14.8.

A subsidiary excluded from consolidation on the grounds set out in paragraph 9.9(b) **9.9B** which is:

(a) **held as part of an investment portfolio** shall be measured at **fair value** with changes in fair value recognised in profit or loss;[9] or

(b) not held as part of an investment portfolio shall be measured using an **accounting policy** selected by the parent in accordance with paragraph 9.26.

Special purpose entities

An entity may be created to accomplish a narrow objective (eg to effect a **lease**, undertake **9.10** **research** and **development** activities, securitise **financial assets** or facilitate employee shareholdings under remuneration schemes, such as Employee Share Ownership Plans (ESOPs)). Such a special purpose entity (SPE) may take the form of a corporation, trust, partnership or unincorporated entity. Often, SPEs are created with legal arrangements that impose strict requirements over the operations of the SPE.

Except as permitted or required by paragraph 9.3, a parent entity shall prepare consolidated **9.11** financial statements that include the entity and any SPEs that are controlled by that entity. In addition to the circumstances described in paragraph 9.5, the following circumstances may indicate that an entity controls a SPE (this is not an exhaustive list):

(a) the activities of the SPE are being conducted on behalf of the entity according to its specific business needs;

(b) the entity has the ultimate decision-making powers over the activities of the SPE even if the day-to-day decisions have been delegated;

(c) the entity has rights to obtain the majority of the benefits of the SPE and therefore may be exposed to risks incidental to the activities of the SPE; and

(d) the entity retains the majority of the residual or ownership risks related to the SPE or its assets.

Paragraphs 9.10 and 9.11 do not apply to **post-employment benefit plans** or other long- **9.12** term employee benefit plans to which Section 28 *Employee Benefits* applies. A special purpose entity that is an intermediate payment arrangement shall be accounted for in accordance with paragraphs 9.33 to 9.38.

---

[9] *Additional disclosures may need to be provided in accordance with company law (see Appendix IV, paragraph A4.17).*

Consolidation procedures

9.13　The consolidated financial statements present financial information about the group as a single economic entity. In preparing consolidated financial statements, an entity shall:

(a)　combine the **financial statements** of the parent and its subsidiaries line by line by adding together like items of assets, **liabilities, equity, income** and expenses;

(b)　eliminate the **carrying amount** of the parent's investment in each subsidiary and the parent's portion of equity of each subsidiary;

(c)　measure and present **non-controlling interest** in the profit or loss of consolidated subsidiaries for the **reporting period** separately from the interest of the **owners** of the parent; and

(d)　measure and present non-controlling interest in the net assets of consolidated subsidiaries separately from the parent shareholders' equity in them. Non-controlling interest in the net assets consists of:

(i)　the amount of the non-controlling interest's share in the net amount of the identifiable assets, liabilities and contingent liabilities recognised and measured in accordance with Section 19 *Business Combinations and Goodwill* at the date of the original combination; and

(ii)　the non-controlling interest's share of changes in equity since the date of the combination.

9.14　The proportions of profit or loss and changes in equity allocated to the owners of the parent and to the non-controlling interest are determined on the basis of existing ownership interests and do not reflect the possible exercise or conversion of options or convertible instruments.

Intragroup balances and transactions

9.15　Intragroup balances and transactions, including income, expenses and dividends, are eliminated in full. Profits and losses resulting from intragroup transactions that are recognised in assets, such as **inventory** and **property, plant and equipment**, are eliminated in full. Intragroup losses may indicate an impairment that requires **recognition** in the consolidated financial statements (see Section 27 *Impairment of Assets*). Section 29 *Income Tax* applies to **timing differences** that arise from the elimination of profits and losses resulting from intragroup transactions.

Uniform reporting date and reporting period

9.16　The financial statements of the parent and its subsidiaries used in the preparation of the consolidated financial statements shall be prepared as of the same **reporting date**, and for the same reporting period, unless it is **impracticable** to do so. Where the reporting date and reporting period of a subsidiary are not the same as the parent's reporting date and reporting period, the consolidated financial statements must be made up:

(a)　from the financial statements of the subsidiary as of its last reporting date before the parent's reporting date, adjusted for the effects of significant transactions or events that occur between the date of those financial statements and the date of the consolidated financial statements, provided that reporting date is no more than three months before that of the parent; or

(b)　from interim financial statements prepared by the subsidiary as at the parent's reporting date.

Uniform accounting policies

Consolidated financial statements shall be prepared using uniform accounting policies for **9.17** like transactions and other events and conditions in similar circumstances. If a member of the group uses accounting policies other than those adopted in the consolidated financial statements for like transactions and events in similar circumstances, appropriate adjustments are made to its financial statements in preparing the consolidated financial statements.

Acquisition and disposal of subsidiaries

The income and expenses of a subsidiary are included in the consolidated financial **9.18** statements from the **acquisition date**, except when a **business combination** is accounted for by using the merger accounting method under Section 19 or, for certain public benefit entity combinations, Section 34 *Specialised Activities*. The income and expenses of a subsidiary are included in the consolidated financial statements until the date on which the parent ceases to control the subsidiary. A parent may cease to control a subsidiary with or without a change in absolute or relative ownership levels. This could occur, for example, when a subsidiary becomes subject to the control of a government, court, administrator or regulator.

Disposal – where control is lost

Where a parent ceases to control a subsidiary, a **gain** or loss is recognised in the consolidated **9.18A** statement of comprehensive income (or in the **income statement**, if presented) calculated as the difference between:

(a)   the proceeds from the disposal (or the event that resulted in the loss of control); and

(b)   the proportion of the carrying amount of the subsidiary's net assets, including any related **goodwill**, disposed of (or lost) as at the date of disposal (or date control is lost).

The cumulative amount of any exchange differences that relate to a foreign subsidiary recognised in equity in accordance with Section 30 *Foreign Currency Translation* is not recognised in profit or loss as part of the gain or loss on disposal of the subsidiary and shall be transferred directly to retained earnings.

The gain or loss arising on the disposal shall also include those amounts that have been **9.18B** recognised in **other comprehensive income** in relation to that subsidiary, where those amounts are required to be reclassified to profit or loss upon disposal in accordance with other sections of this FRS. Amounts that are not required to be reclassified to profit or loss upon disposal of the related assets or liabilities in accordance with other sections of this FRS shall be transferred directly to retained earnings.

If an entity ceases to be a subsidiary but the investor (former parent) continues to hold: **9.19**

(a)   an investment that is not an **associate** (see paragraph 9.19(b)) or a **jointly controlled entity** (see paragraph 9.19(c)), that investment shall be accounted for as a financial asset in accordance with Section 11 *Basic Financial Instruments* or Section 12 *Other Financial Instruments Issues* from the date the entity ceases to be a subsidiary;

(b)   an associate, that associate shall be accounted for in accordance with Section 14 *Investments in Associates*; or

(c)   a jointly controlled entity, that jointly controlled entity shall be accounted for in accordance with Section 15 *Investments in Joint Ventures*.

The carrying amount of the net assets (and goodwill) attributable to the investment at the date that the entity ceases to be a subsidiary shall be regarded as the cost on initial **measurement** of the financial asset, investment in associate or jointly controlled entity, as appropriate. In applying the equity method to investments in associate or jointly controlled entities as required in sub-paragraphs (b) and (c) above, paragraph 14.8(c) shall not be applied.

Disposal – where control is retained

9.19A   Where a parent reduces its holding in a subsidiary and control is retained, it shall be accounted for as a transaction between equity holders and the resulting change in non-controlling interest shall be accounted for in accordance with paragraph 22.19. No gain or loss shall be recognised at the date of disposal.

Acquisition – Control achieved in stages

9.19B   Where a parent acquires control of a subsidiary in stages, the transaction shall be accounted for in accordance with paragraphs 19.11A and 19.14 applied at the date control is achieved.

Acquisition – Increasing a controlling interest in a subsidiary

9.19C   Where a parent increases its controlling interest in a subsidiary, the identifiable assets and liabilities and a **provision** for **contingent liabilities** of the subsidiary shall not be revalued to fair value and no additional goodwill shall be recognised at the date the controlling interest is increased.

9.19D   The transaction shall be accounted for as a transaction between equity holders and the resulting change in non-controlling interest shall be accounted for in accordance with paragraph 22.19.

Non-controlling interest in subsidiaries

9.20   An entity shall present non-controlling interest in the consolidated statement of financial position within equity, separately from the equity of the owners of the parent.

9.21   An entity shall disclose non-controlling interest in the profit or loss of the group separately in the **statement of comprehensive income** (or income statement, if presented).

9.22   Profit or loss and each component of other comprehensive income shall be attributed to the owners of the parent and to non-controlling interest. **Total comprehensive income** shall be attributed to the owners of the parent and to non-controlling interest even if this results in non-controlling interest having a deficit balance.

Disclosures in consolidated financial statements

9.23   The following disclosures shall be made in consolidated financial statements:

(a)   the fact that the statements are consolidated financial statements;

(b)   the basis for concluding that control exists when the parent does not own, directly or indirectly through subsidiaries, more than half of the voting power;

(c)   any difference in the reporting date of the financial statements of the parent and its subsidiaries used in the preparation of the consolidated financial statements;

(d)   the nature and extent of any significant restrictions (eg resulting from borrowing arrangements or regulatory requirements) on the ability of subsidiaries to transfer funds to the parent in the form of cash dividends or to repay loans; and

(e)   the name of any subsidiary excluded from consolidation and the reason for exclusion.

Individual and separate financial statements

Preparation of individual and separate financial statements

The requirements for the preparation of individual financial statements are set out in the Act or other statutory framework.   **9.23A**

Separate financial statements are those prepared by a parent in which the investments in subsidiaries, associates or jointly controlled entities are accounted for either at cost or fair value rather than on the basis of the reported results and net assets of the investees. Separate financial statements are included within the meaning of individual financial statements.   **9.24**

An entity that is not a parent shall account for any investments in associates and any interests in jointly controlled entities in accordance with paragraph 14.4 or 15.9, as appropriate in its individual financial statements.   **9.25**

Accounting policy election in separate financial statements

When an entity that is a parent prepares separate financial statements and describes them as conforming to this FRS, those financial statements shall comply with all of the requirements of this FRS. The parent shall select and adopt a policy of accounting for its investments in subsidiaries, associates and jointly controlled entities either: **9.26**

(a)   at cost less impairment;

(b)   at fair value with changes in fair value recognised in other comprehensive income in accordance with paragraphs 17.15E and 17.15F; or

(c)   at fair value with changes in fair value recognised in profit or loss (paragraphs 11.27 to 11.32 provide guidance on fair value).

The entity shall apply the same accounting policy for all investments in a single class (subsidiaries, associates or jointly controlled entities), but it can elect different policies for different classes.

A parent that is exempt in accordance with paragraph 9.3 from the requirement to present consolidated financial statements, and presents separate financial statements as its only financial statements, shall account for its investments in subsidiaries, associates and jointly controlled entities in accordance with paragraph 9.26.   **9.26A**

Disclosures in separate financial statements

When a parent prepares separate financial statements, those separate financial statements shall disclose: **9.27**

(a)   that the statements are separate financial statements; and

*(b)   a description of the methods used to account for the investments in subsidiaries, jointly controlled entities and associates.

A parent that uses one of the exemptions from presenting consolidated financial statements (described in paragraph 9.3) shall disclose the grounds on which the parent is exempt.   **9.27A**

9.27B   When a parent adopts a policy of accounting for its investments in subsidiaries, associates or jointly controlled entities at fair value with changes in fair value recognised in profit or loss, it must comply with the requirements of paragraph 36(4) of Schedule 1 to the **Regulations** by applying the disclosure requirements of Section 11 *Basic Financial Instruments* to those investments.

9.28   [Not used]

9.29   [Not used]

9.30   [Not used]

Exchanges of businesses or other non-monetary assets for an interest in a subsidiary, jointly controlled entity or associate

9.31   Where a reporting entity exchanges a **business**, or other non-monetary assets, for an interest in another entity, and that other entity thereby becomes a subsidiary, jointly controlled entity or associate of the reporting entity, the following accounting treatment shall apply in the consolidated financial statements of the reporting entity:

(a)   To the extent that the reporting entity retains an ownership interest in the business, or other non-monetary assets, exchanged, even if that interest is then held through the other entity, that retained interest, including any related goodwill, is treated as having been owned by the reporting entity throughout the transaction and should be included at its pre-transaction carrying amount.

(b)   Goodwill should be recognised as the difference between:

(i)   the fair value of the consideration given; and

(ii)   the fair value of the reporting entity's share of the pre-transaction identifiable net assets of the other entity.

The consideration given for the interest acquired in the other entity will include that part of the business, or other non-monetary assets, exchanged and no longer owned by the reporting entity. The consideration may also include **cash** or monetary assets to achieve equalisation of values. Where it is difficult to value the consideration given, the best estimate of its value may be given by valuing what is acquired.

(c)   To the extent that the fair value of the consideration received by the reporting entity exceeds the carrying value of the part of the business, or other non-monetary assets exchanged and no longer owned by the reporting entity, and any related goodwill together with any cash given up, the reporting entity should recognise a gain. Any unrealised gain arising on the exchange shall be recognised in other comprehensive income.

(d)   To the extent that the fair value of the consideration received by the reporting entity is less than the carrying value of the part of the business, or other non-monetary assets no longer owned by the reporting entity, and any related goodwill, together with any cash given up, the reporting entity should recognise a loss. This loss should be recognised either as an impairment in accordance with Section 27 *Impairment of Assets* or, for any loss remaining after an impairment review of the relevant assets, in profit or loss.

9.32   No gain or loss should be recognised in those rare cases where the artificiality or lack of substance of the transaction is such that a gain or loss on the exchange could not be justified. Where a gain or loss on the exchange is not taken into account because the transaction is artificial or has no substance, the circumstances should be explained.

Intermediate payment arrangements

Intermediate payment arrangements may take a variety of forms: **9.33**

(a)   The intermediary is usually established by a sponsoring entity and constituted as a trust, although other arrangements are possible.

(b)   The relationship between the sponsoring entity and the intermediary may take different forms. For example, when the intermediary is constituted as a trust, the sponsoring entity will not have a right to direct the intermediary's activities. However, in these and other cases the sponsoring entity may give advice to the intermediary or may be relied on by the intermediary to provide the information it needs to carry out its activities. Sometimes, the way the intermediary has been set up gives it little discretion in the broad nature of its activities.

(c)   The arrangements are most commonly used to pay employees, although they are sometimes used to compensate suppliers of goods and services other than employee services. Sometimes the sponsoring entity's employees and other suppliers are not the only beneficiaries of the arrangement. Other beneficiaries may include past employees and their dependants, and the intermediary may be entitled to make charitable donations.

(d)   The precise identity of the persons or entities that will receive payments from the intermediary, and the amounts that they will receive, are not usually agreed at the outset.

(e)   The sponsoring entity often has the right to appoint or veto the appointment of the intermediary's trustees (or its directors or the equivalent).

(f)   The payments made to the intermediary and the payments made by the intermediary are often cash payments but may involve other transfers of value.

Examples of intermediate payment arrangements are employee share ownership plans (ESOPs) and employee benefit trusts that are used to facilitate employee shareholdings under remuneration schemes. In a typical employee benefit trust arrangement for share-based payments, an entity makes payments to a trust or guarantees borrowing by the trust, and the trust uses its funds to accumulate assets to pay the entity's employees for services the employees have rendered to the entity.

Although the trustees of an intermediary must act at all times in accordance with the interests of the beneficiaries of the intermediary, most intermediaries (particularly those established as a means of remunerating employees) are specifically designed so as to serve the purposes of the sponsoring entity, and to ensure that there will be minimal risk of any conflict arising between the duties of the trustees of the intermediary and the interest of the sponsoring entity, such that there is nothing to encumber implementation of the wishes of the sponsoring entity in practice. Where this is the case, the sponsoring entity has de facto control.

Accounting for intermediate payment arrangements

When a sponsoring entity makes payments (or transfers assets) to an intermediary, there is   **9.34**
a rebuttable presumption that the entity has exchanged one asset for another and that the payment itself does not represent an immediate expense. To rebut this presumption at the time the payment is made to the intermediary, the entity must demonstrate:

(a)   it will not obtain future economic benefit from the amounts transferred; or

(b)   it does not have control of the right or other access to the future economic benefit it is expected to receive.

Where a payment to an intermediary is an exchange by the sponsoring entity of one asset   **9.35**
for another, any assets that the intermediary acquires in a subsequent exchange transaction

will also be under the control of the entity. Accordingly, assets and liabilities of the intermediary shall be accounted for by the sponsoring entity as an extension of its own business and recognised in its own individual financial statements. An asset will cease to be recognised as an asset of the sponsoring entity when, for example, the asset of the intermediary vests unconditionally with identified beneficiaries.

9.36   A sponsoring entity may distribute its own equity instruments, or other equity instruments, to an intermediary in order to facilitate employee shareholdings under a remuneration scheme. Where this is the case and the sponsoring entity has control, or de facto control, of the assets and liabilities of the intermediary, the commercial effect is that the sponsoring entity is, for all practical purposes, in the same position as if it had purchased the shares directly.

9.37   Where an intermediary holds the sponsoring entity's equity instruments, the sponsoring entity shall account for the equity instruments as if it had purchased them directly. The sponsoring entity shall account for the assets and liabilities of the intermediary in its individual financial statements as follows:

(a)   The consideration paid for the equity instruments of the sponsoring entity shall be deducted from equity until such time that the equity instruments **vest** unconditionally with employees.

(b)   Consideration paid or received for the purchase or sale of the sponsoring entity's own equity instruments shall be shown as separate amounts in the **statement of changes in equity**.

(c)   Other assets and liabilities of the intermediary shall be recognised as assets and liabilities of the sponsoring entity.

(d)   No gain or loss shall be recognised in profit or loss or other comprehensive income on the purchase, sale, issue or cancellation of the entity's own equity instruments.

(e)   Finance costs and any administration expenses shall be recognised on an accruals basis rather than as funding payments are made to the intermediary.

(f)   Any dividend income arising on the sponsoring entity's own equity instruments shall be excluded from profit or loss and deducted from the aggregate of dividends paid.

Disclosures in individual and separate financial statements

9.38   When a sponsoring entity recognises the assets and liabilities held by an intermediary, it should disclose sufficient information in the **notes** to its financial statements to enable users to understand the significance of the intermediary and the arrangement in the context of the sponsoring entity's financial statements. This should include:

(a)   a description of the main features of the intermediary including the arrangements for making payments and for distributing equity instruments;

(b)   any restrictions relating to the assets and liabilities of the intermediary;

(c)   the amount and nature of the assets and liabilities held by the intermediary, which have not yet vested unconditionally with the beneficiaries of the arrangement;

(d)   the amount that has been deducted from equity and the number of equity instruments held by the intermediary, which have not yet vested unconditionally with the beneficiaries of the arrangement;

(e)   for entities that have their equity instruments listed or **publicly traded** on a stock exchange or market, the market value of the equity instruments held by the intermediary which have not yet vested unconditionally with employees;

(f)   the extent to which the equity instruments are under option to employees, or have been conditionally gifted to them; and

(g)   the amount that has been deducted from the aggregate dividends paid by the sponsoring entity.

Section 10 *Accounting Policies, Estimates and Errors*

Scope of this section

This section provides guidance for selecting and applying the **accounting policies** used in preparing **financial statements**. It also covers **changes in accounting estimates** and corrections of **errors** in prior period financial statements.
   10.1

Selection and application of accounting policies

Accounting policies are the specific principles, bases, conventions, rules and practices applied by an entity in preparing and presenting financial statements.
   10.2

If an FRS or FRC Abstract specifically addresses a transaction, other event or condition, an entity shall apply that FRS or FRC Abstract. However, the entity need not follow a requirement in an FRS or FRC Abstract if the effect of doing so would not be **material**.
   10.3

If an FRS or FRC Abstract does not specifically address a transaction, other event or condition, an entity's management shall use its judgement in developing and applying an accounting policy that results in information that is:
   10.4

(a)   relevant to the economic decision-making needs of users; and
(b)   reliable, in that the financial statements:

    (i)   represent faithfully the **financial position**, financial **performance** and **cash flows** of the entity;
    (ii)   reflect the economic substance of transactions, other events and conditions, and not merely the legal form;
    (iii)   are neutral, ie free from bias;
    (iv)   are prudent; and
    (v)   are complete in all material respects.

In making the judgement described in paragraph 10.4, management shall refer to and consider the applicability of the following sources in descending order:
   10.5

(a)   the requirements and guidance in an FRS or FRC Abstract dealing with similar and related issues;
(b)   where an entity's financial statements are within the scope of a **Statement of Recommended Practice (SORP)** the requirements and guidance in that SORP dealing with similar and related issues; and
(c)   the definitions, **recognition** criteria and measurement concepts for **assets**, **liabilities**, **income** and **expenses** and the pervasive principles in Section 2 *Concepts and Pervasive Principles*.

In making the judgement described in paragraph 10.4, management may also consider the requirements and guidance in **EU-adopted IFRS** dealing with similar and related issues. Paragraphs 1.4 to 1.7 require certain entities to apply IAS 33 *Earnings per Share* (as adopted in the EU) , IFRS 8 *Operating Segments* (as adopted in the EU) or IFRS 6 *Exploration for and Evaluation of Mineral Resources*.
   10.6

Consistency of accounting policies

An entity shall select and apply its accounting policies consistently for similar transactions, other events and conditions, unless an FRS or FRC Abstract specifically requires or permits categorisation of items for which different policies may be appropriate. If an FRS or FRC
   10.7

Abstract requires or permits such categorisation, an appropriate accounting policy shall be selected and applied consistently to each category.

Changes in accounting policies

10.8   An entity shall change an accounting policy only if the change:

(a)   is required by an FRS or FRC Abstract; or

(b)   results in the financial statements providing reliable and more relevant information about the effects of transactions, other events or conditions on the entity's financial position, financial performance or cash flows.

10.9   The following are not changes in accounting policies:

(a)   the application of an accounting policy for transactions, other events or conditions that differ in substance from those previously occurring;

(b)   the application of a new accounting policy for transactions, other events or conditions that did not occur previously or were not material; and

(c)   a change to the cost model when a reliable measure of **fair value** is no longer available (or vice versa) for an asset that an FRS or FRC Abstract would otherwise require or permit to be measured at fair value.

10.10   If an FRS or FRC Abstract allows a choice of accounting treatment (including the measurement basis) for a specified transaction or other event or condition and an entity changes its previous choice, that is a change in accounting policy.

10.10A   The initial application of a policy to revalue assets in accordance with Section 17 *Property, Plant and Equipment* or Section 18 *Intangible Assets other than Goodwill* is a change in accounting policy to be dealt with as a revaluation in accordance with those sections, rather than in accordance with paragraphs 10.11 and 10.12.

Applying changes in accounting policies

10.11   An entity shall account for changes in accounting policy as follows:

(a)   an entity shall account for a change in accounting policy resulting from a change in the requirements of an FRS or FRC Abstract in accordance with the transitional provisions, if any, specified in that amendment;

(b)   when an entity has elected to follow IAS 39 *Financial Instruments: Recognition and Measurement* and/or IFRS 9 *Financial Instruments* instead of following Section 11 *Basic Financial Instruments* and Section 12 *Other Financial Instruments Issues* as permitted by paragraph 11.2, and the requirements of IAS 39 and/or IFRS 9 change, the entity shall account for that change in accounting policy in accordance with the transitional provisions, if any, specified in the revised IAS 39 and/or IFRS 9; and

(c)   when an entity is required or has elected to follow IAS 33, IFRS 8 or IFRS 6 and the requirements of those standards change, the entity shall account for that change in accounting policy in accordance with the transitional provisions, if any, specified in those standards as amended; and

(d)   an entity shall account for all other changes in accounting policy retrospectively (see paragraph 10.12).

Retrospective application

10.12   When a change in accounting policy is applied retrospectively in accordance with paragraph 10.11, the entity shall apply the new accounting policy to comparative information for prior periods to the earliest date for which it is practicable, as if the new accounting policy had always been applied. When it is **impracticable** to determine the individual-period effects of a change in accounting policy on comparative information for one or more prior periods presented, the entity shall apply the new accounting policy to the **carrying amounts** of assets and liabilities as at the beginning of the earliest period for which **retrospective application** is practicable, which may be the current period, and shall make a corresponding adjustment to the opening balance of each affected component of **equity** for that period.

Disclosure of a change in accounting policy

When an amendment to an FRS or FRC Abstract has an effect on the current period or any prior period, or might have an effect on future periods, an entity shall disclose the following:　　***10.13**

(a)　the nature of the change in accounting policy;
(b)　for the current period and each prior period presented, to the extent practicable, the amount of the adjustment for each financial statement line item affected;
(c)　the amount of the adjustment relating to periods before those presented, to the extent practicable; and
(d)　an explanation if it is impracticable to determine the amounts to be disclosed in (b) or (c) above.

Financial statements of subsequent periods need not repeat these disclosures.

When a voluntary change in accounting policy has an effect on the current period or any prior period, an entity shall disclose the following:　　***10.14**

(a)　the nature of the change in accounting policy;
(b)　the reasons why applying the new accounting policy provides reliable and more relevant information;
(c)　to the extent practicable, the amount of the adjustment for each financial statement line item affected, shown separately:

    (i)　for the current period;
    (ii)　for each prior period presented; and
    (iii)　in the aggregate for periods before those presented; and

(d)　an explanation if it is impracticable to determine the amounts to be disclosed in (c) above.

Financial statements of subsequent periods need not repeat these disclosures.

Changes in accounting estimates

A **change in accounting estimate** is an adjustment of the carrying amount of an asset or a liability, or the amount of the periodic consumption of an asset, that results from the assessment of the present status of, and expected future benefits and obligations associated with, assets and liabilities. Changes in accounting estimates result from new information or new developments and, accordingly, are not corrections of errors. When it is difficult to distinguish a change in an accounting policy from a change in an accounting estimate, the change is treated as a change in an accounting estimate.　　**10.15**

An entity shall recognise the effect of a change in an accounting estimate, other than a change to which paragraph 10.17 applies, **prospectively** by including it in **profit or loss** in:　　**10.16**

(a)　the period of the change, if the change affects that period only; or
(b)　the period of the change and future periods, if the change affects both.

10.17   To the extent that a change in an accounting estimate gives rise to changes in assets and liabilities, or relates to an item of equity, the entity shall recognise it by adjusting the carrying amount of the related asset, liability or equity item in the period of the change.

Disclosure of a change in estimate

10.18   An entity shall disclose the nature of any change in an accounting estimate and the effect of the change on assets, liabilities, income and expense for the current period. If it is practicable for the entity to estimate the effect of the change in one or more future periods, the entity shall disclose those estimates.

Corrections of prior period errors

10.19   Prior period errors are omissions from, and misstatements in, an entity's financial statements for one or more prior periods arising from a failure to use, or misuse of, reliable information that:

(a)   was available when financial statements for those periods were authorised for issue; and

(b)   could reasonably be expected to have been obtained and taken into account in the preparation and presentation of those financial statements.

10.20   Such errors include the effects of mathematical mistakes, mistakes in applying accounting policies, oversights or misinterpretations of facts, and fraud.

10.21   To the extent practicable, an entity shall correct a material prior period error retrospectively in the first financial statements authorised for issue after its discovery by:

(a)   restating the comparative amounts for the prior period(s) presented in which the error occurred; or

(b)   if the error occurred before the earliest prior period presented, restating the opening balances of assets, liabilities and equity for the earliest prior period presented.

10.22   When it is impracticable to determine the period-specific effects of a material error on comparative information for one or more prior periods presented, the entity shall restate the opening balances of assets, liabilities and equity for the earliest period for which retrospective restatement is practicable (which may be the current period).

Disclosure of prior period errors

*10.23   An entity shall disclose the following about material prior period errors:

(a)   the nature of the prior period error;

(b)   for each prior period presented, to the extent practicable, the amount of the correction for each financial statement line item affected;

(c)   to the extent practicable, the amount of the correction at the beginning of the earliest prior period presented; and

(d)   an explanation if it is not practicable to determine the amounts to be disclosed in (b) or (c) above.

Financial statements of subsequent periods need not repeat these disclosures.

Section 11 *Basic Financial Instruments*

Scope of Sections 11 and 12

Section 11 *Basic Financial Instruments* and Section 12 *Other Financial Instruments* **11.1**
Issues together deal with recognising, derecognising, measuring and disclosing **financial instruments (financial assets** and **financial liabilities)**. Section 11 applies to basic financial instruments and is relevant to all entities. Section 12 applies to other, more complex financial instruments and transactions. If an entity enters into only basic financial instrument transactions then Section 12 is not applicable. However, even entities with only basic financial instruments shall consider the scope of Section 12 to ensure they are exempt.

Public benefit entities and other members of a **public benefit entity group** that make or **PBE11.1A**
receive **public benefit entity concessionary loans** shall refer to the relevant paragraphs of
Section 34 *Specialised Activities* for the accounting requirements for such loans.

Accounting policy choice

An entity shall choose to apply either: **11.2**

(a) the provisions of both Section 11 and Section 12 in full; or
(b) the **recognition** and **measurement** provisions of IAS 39 *Financial Instruments: Recognition and Measurement* (as adopted for use in the EU), the disclosure requirements of Sections 11 and 12 and the presentation requirements of paragraphs 11.38A or 12.25B; or
(c) the recognition and measurement provisions of IFRS 9 *Financial Instruments* and/or IAS 39 (as amended following the publication of IFRS 9) subject to the restriction in paragraph 11.2A, the disclosure requirements of Sections 11 and 12 and the presentation requirements of paragraphs 11.38A or 12.25B;

to account for all of its financial instruments. Where an entity chooses (b) or (c) it applies the scope of the relevant standard to its financial instruments. An entity's choice of (a), (b) or (c) is an **accounting policy** choice. Paragraphs 10.8 to 10.14 contain requirements for determining when a change in accounting policy is appropriate, how such a change should be accounted for and what information should be disclosed about the change.

An entity, including an entity that is not a company, that has made the accounting policy **11.2A**
choice in paragraph 11.2(c) to apply the recognition and measurement provisions of IFRS 9
shall depart from the provisions of IFRS 9 as follows:

A financial asset that is not permitted by the **Small Companies Regulations**, the **Regulations, the Small LLP Regulations** or the **LLP Regulations** to be measured at **fair value** through **profit or loss** shall be measured at **amortised cost** in accordance with paragraphs 5.4.1 to 5.4.4 of IFRS 9.

Introduction to Section 11

A financial instrument is a contract that gives rise to a financial asset of one entity and a **11.3**
financial liability or equity instrument of another entity.

11.4
[Not used]

11.5   Basic financial instruments within the scope of Section 11 are those that satisfy the conditions in paragraph 11.8. Examples of financial instruments that normally satisfy those conditions include:

(a)   **cash**;

(b)   demand and fixed-term deposits when the entity is the depositor, eg bank accounts;

(c)   commercial paper and commercial bills held;

(d)   accounts, notes and loans receivable and payable;

(e)   bonds and similar debt instruments;

(f)   investments in non-convertible preference shares and non-puttable ordinary and preference shares; and

(g)   commitments to receive a loan and commitments to make a loan to another entity that meet the conditions of paragraph 11.8(c).

11.6   Examples of financial instruments that do not normally satisfy the conditions in paragraph 11.8, and are therefore within the scope of Section 12, include:

(a)   asset-backed securities, such as collateralised mortgage obligations, repurchase agreements and securitised packages of receivables;

(b)   options, rights, warrants, futures contracts, forward contracts and interest rate swaps that can be settled in cash or by exchanging another financial instrument;

(c)   financial instruments that qualify and are designated as hedging instruments in accordance with the requirements in Section 12; and

(d)   commitments to make a loan to another entity and commitments to receive a loan, if the commitment can be settled net in cash.

(e)   [not used]

Scope of Section 11

11.7   Section 11 applies to all financial instruments meeting the conditions of paragraph 11.8 except for the following:

(a)   Investments in **subsidiaries, associates** and **joint ventures** that are accounted for in accordance with Section 9 *Consolidated and Separate Financial Statements*, Section 14 *Investments in Associates* or Section 15 *Investments in Joint Ventures*.

(b)   Financial instruments that meet the definition of an entity's own equity and the equity component of **compound financial instruments** issued by the reporting entity that contain both a **liability** and an equity component (see Section 22 *Liabilities and Equity*).

(c)   **Leases**, to which Section 20 *Leases* applies. However, the **derecognition** requirements in paragraphs 11.33 to 11.35 and impairment accounting requirements in paragraphs 11.21 to 11.26 apply to derecognition and impairment of receivables recognised by a lessor and the derecognition requirements in paragraphs 11.36 to 11.38 apply to payables recognised by a lessee arising under a **finance lease**. Section 12 applies to leases with characteristics specified in paragraph 12.3(f).

(d)   Employers' rights and obligations under employee benefit plans, to which Section 28 *Employee Benefits* applies, although paragraphs 11.27 to 11.32 do apply in determining the fair value of **plan assets**.

(e)   Financial instruments, contracts and obligations to which Section 26 *Share-based Payment* applies, and contracts within the scope of paragraph 12.5.

(f)   **Insurance contracts** (including **reinsurance contracts**) that the entity issues and reinsurance contracts that the entity holds (see FRS 103 *Insurance Contracts*).

(g)   Financial instruments issued by an entity with a **discretionary participation feature** (see FRS 103 *Insurance Contracts*).

(h)   Reimbursement assets accounted for in accordance with Section 21 *Provisions and Contingencies*.

(i)   **Financial guarantee contracts** (see Section 21).

A reporting entity that issues the financial instruments set out in (f) or (g) or holds the financial instruments in (f) is required by paragraph 1.6 of this FRS to apply FRS 103 to those financial instruments.

Basic financial instruments

An entity shall account for the following financial instruments as basic financial instruments in accordance with Section 11:   **11.8**

(a)   cash;

(b)   a debt instrument (such as an account, note, or loan receivable or payable) that meets the conditions in paragraph 11.9 and is not a financial instrument described in paragraph 11.6(b);

(c)   commitments to receive or make a loan to another entity that:

(i)   cannot be settled net in cash; and

(ii)   when the commitment is executed, are expected to meet the conditions in paragraph 11.9; and

(d)   an investment in non-convertible preference shares and non-puttable **ordinary shares** or preference shares.

The conditions a debt instrument shall satisfy in accordance with paragraph 11.8(b) are: **11.9**

(a)   The contractual return to the holder (the lender), assessed in the currency in which the debt instrument is denominated, is:

(i)   a fixed amount;

(ii)   a positive fixed rate or a positive variable rate[10]; or

(iii)   [not used]

(iv)   a combination of a positive or a negative fixed rate and a positive variable rate (eg LIBOR plus 200 basis points or LIBOR less 50 basis points, but not 500 basis points less LIBOR).

(aA)   The contract may provide for repayments of the principal or the return to the holder (but not both) to be linked to a single relevant observable index of general price inflation of the currency in which the debt instrument is denominated, provided such links are not leveraged.

(aB)   The contract may provide for a determinable variation of the return to the holder during the life of the instrument, provided that:

(i)   the new rate satisfies condition (a) and the variation is not contingent on future events other than:

(1)   a change of a contractual variable rate;

(2)   to protect the holder against credit deterioration of the issuer;

(3)   changes in levies applied by a central bank or arising from changes in relevant taxation or law; or

(ii)   the new rate is a market rate of interest and satisfies condition (a).

Contractual terms that give the lender the unilateral option to change the terms of the contract are not determinable for this purpose.

(b)   There is no contractual provision that could, by its terms, result in the holder losing the principal amount or any interest attributable to the current period or prior periods. The fact that a debt instrument is subordinated to other debt instruments is not an example of such a contractual provision.

---

[10] *A variable rate for this purpose is a rate which varies over time and is linked to a single observable interest rate or to a single relevant observable index of general price inflation of the currency in which the instrument is denominated, provided such links are not leveraged.*

(c) Contractual provisions that permit the issuer (the borrower) to prepay a debt instrument or permit the holder (the lender) to put it back to the issuer before maturity are not contingent on future events other than to protect:

(i)   the holder against the credit deterioration of the issuer (eg defaults, credit downgrades or loan covenant violations), or a change in control of the issuer; or

(ii) the holder or issuer against changes in levies applied by a central bank or arising from changes in relevant taxation or law.

The inclusion of contractual terms that, as a result of the early termination, require the issuer to compensate the holder for the early termination does not, in itself, constitute a breach of this condition.

(d) [Not used]

(e) Contractual provisions may permit the extension of the term of the debt instrument, provided that the return to the holder and any other contractual provisions applicable during the extended term satisfy the conditions of paragraphs (a) to (c).

Examples – Debt instruments

1   A zero-coupon loan

For a zero-coupon loan, the holder's return is the difference between the nominal value of the loan and the issue price. The holder (lender) receives a fixed amount when the loan matures and the issuer (borrower) repays the loan. The return to the holder meets the condition of paragraph 11.9(a)(i).

2   A fixed interest rate loan with an initial tie-in period which reverts to the bank's standard variable interest rate after the tie-in period

The initial fixed rate is a return permitted by paragraph 11.9(a)(ii). A bank's standard variable interest rate is an observable interest rate and, in accordance with the definition of a variable rate, is a permissible link. In accordance with paragraph 11.9(a)(ii) the variable rate should be a positive rate.

The variation of the interest rate after the tie-in period is non-contingent and since the new rate (ie the bank's standard variable rate) meets the condition of paragraph 11.9(a), paragraph 11.9(aB)(i) is met.

3   A loan with interest payable at the bank's standard variable rate plus 1 per cent throughout the life of the loan

As discussed under Example 2 above, a bank's standard variable rate is a permitted variable rate in accordance with the definition of variable rate. The combination of a positive fixed rate (ie plus 1 per cent) and a positive variable rate is a permitted return under paragraph 11.9(a)(iv). The combination of a bank's standard variable rate plus a fixed interest rate of 1 per cent therefore meets the condition in paragraph 11.9(a)(iv).

4   A loan with interest payable at the bank's standard variable rate less 1 per cent throughout the life of the loan, with the condition that the interest rate can never fall below 2 per cent

Paragraph 11.9(aB)(i)(1) permits variation of a return to a holder (lender) that is contingent on a change of a contractual variable rate. In this example the contractual variable rate is the bank's standard variable rate. The variation of the return to the holder is between the bank's standard variable rate less 1 and 2 per cent, depending on the bank's standard variable rate. For example, if the bank's standard variable rate is less than 3 per cent, the return to the holder is

Examples – Debt instruments

fixed at 2 per cent; if the bank's standard variable rate is higher than 3 per cent, the return to the holder is the bank's standard variable rate less 1 per cent. The contractual variation meets the condition of paragraph 11.9(aB)(i)(1).

The holder is protected against the risk of losing the principal amount of the loan via the interest rate floor of 2 per cent. The requirement of paragraph 11.9(b) is therefore also met.

5   **Interest on a loan is referenced to 2 times the bank's standard variable rate**

In accordance with the definition of a variable rate, the contractual interest rate payable can be linked to a single observable interest rate. A bank's standard variable rate is an observable rate and meets the definition of a variable rate, but the rate in this example is 2 times the bank's standard variable rate and the link to the observable interest rate is leveraged. Therefore, the rate in this example is not a variable rate as described in paragraph 11.9(a). The instrument is measured at fair value in accordance with Section 12.

6   **Interest on a loan is charged at 10 per cent less 6-month LIBOR over the life of the loan**

The effect of combining a negative variable rate with a positive fixed rate is that the interest on the loan increases as and when the variable rate decreases and vice versa (so called inverse floating interest).

Under paragraph 11.9(a)(iv) the combination of positive or negative fixed rate and positive variable rate is a permitted return. The variable rate (6-month LIBOR) meets the definition of a variable rate, as the rate is a quoted interest rate. However, since the variable rate is negative (minus 6-month LIBOR), the rate is in breach of paragraph 11.9(a)(iv). The instrument is measured at fair value in accordance with Section 12.

7   **Interest on a GBP denominated mortgage is linked to the UK Land Registry House Price Index (HPI) plus 3 per cent**

In accordance with paragraph 11.9(aA) the holder's return may be linked to an index of general price inflation of the currency of the debt instrument. The mortgage is denominated in GBP and a permitted inflation index would be an index that measures general price inflation of goods and services denominated in GBP.

The HPI measures inflation for residential properties in the UK and is not a measure of general price inflation. The return to the holder therefore fails to meet the condition in paragraph 11.9(aA). The instrument is measured at fair value in accordance with Section 12.

Examples of financial instruments that would normally satisfy the conditions in paragraph 11.9 are: **11.10**

(a)   trade accounts and notes receivable and payable, and loans from banks or other third parties;

(b)   accounts payable in a foreign currency. However, any change in the account payable because of a change in the exchange rate is recognised in profit or loss as required by paragraph 30.10;

(c)   loans to or from subsidiaries or associates that are due on demand; and

(d)   a debt instrument that would become immediately receivable if the issuer defaults on an interest or principal payment (such a provision does not violate the conditions in paragraph 11.9).

11.11   Examples of financial instruments that do not satisfy the conditions in paragraph 11.9 (and are therefore within the scope of Section 12) include:

(a)   an investment in another entity's equity instruments other than non-convertible preference shares and non-puttable ordinary and preference shares (see paragraph 11.8(d)); and

(b)   [not used]

(c)   [not used]

(d)   investments in convertible debt, because the return to the holder can vary with the price of the issuer's equity shares rather than just with market interest rates.

(e)   [not used]

Initial recognition of financial assets and liabilities

11.12   An entity shall recognise a financial asset or a financial liability only when the entity becomes a party to the contractual provisions of the instrument.

Initial measurement

11.13   When a financial asset or financial liability is recognised initially, an entity shall measure it at the transaction price (including **transaction costs** except in the initial measurement of financial assets and liabilities that are measured at fair value through profit or loss) unless the arrangement constitutes, in effect, a financing transaction. A financing transaction may take place in connection with the sale of goods or services, for example, if payment is deferred beyond normal business terms or is financed at a rate of interest that is not a market rate. If the arrangement constitutes a financing transaction, the entity shall measure the financial asset or financial liability at the **present value** of the future payments discounted at a market rate of interest for a similar debt instrument.

Examples – financial assets
1   For a long-term loan at a market rate of interest made to another entity, a receivable is recognised at the amount of the cash advanced to that entity plus transaction costs incurred by the entity (see the example following paragraph 11.20).
2   For goods sold to a customer on short-term credit, a receivable is recognised at the undiscounted amount of cash receivable from that entity, which is normally the invoice price.
3   For an item sold to a customer on two-years interest-free credit, a receivable is recognised at the current cash sale price for that item (in financing transactions conducted on an arm's length basis the cash sales price would normally approximate to the present value). If the current cash sale price is not known, it may be estimated as the present value of the cash receivable discounted using the **prevailing market rate(s)** of interest for a similar receivable.
4   For a cash purchase of another entity's ordinary shares, the investment is recognised at the amount of cash paid to acquire the shares.

Examples – financial liabilities
1 For a loan received from a bank at a market rate of interest, a payable is recognised initially at the amount of the cash received from the bank less separately incurred transaction costs.
2 For goods purchased from a supplier on short-term credit, a payable is recognised at the undiscounted amount owed to the supplier, which is normally the invoice price.

Subsequent measurement

At the end of each **reporting period**, an entity shall measure financial instruments as follows, without any deduction for transaction costs the entity may incur on sale or other disposal: **11.14**

(a) Debt instruments that meet the conditions in paragraph 11.8(b) shall be measured at amortised cost using the **effective interest method**. Paragraphs 11.15 to 11.20 provide guidance on determining amortised cost using the effective interest method. Debt instruments that are payable or receivable within one year shall be measured at the undiscounted amount of the cash or other consideration expected to be paid or received (ie net of impairment—see paragraphs 11.21 to 11.26) unless the arrangement constitutes, in effect, a financing transaction (see paragraph 11.13). If the arrangement constitutes a financing transaction, the entity shall measure the debt instrument at the present value of the future payments discounted at a market rate of interest for a similar debt instrument.

(b) Debt instruments that meet the conditions in paragraph 11.8(b) and commitments to receive a loan and to make a loan to another entity that meet the conditions in paragraph 11.8(c) may upon their initial recognition be designated by the entity as at fair value through profit or loss (paragraphs 11.27 to 11.32 provide guidance on fair value) provided doing so results in more relevant information, because either:

  (i) it eliminates or significantly reduces a measurement or recognition inconsistency (sometimes referred to as 'an accounting mismatch') that would otherwise arise from measuring assets or debt instruments or recognising the **gains** and losses on them on different bases; or

  (ii) a group of debt instruments or financial assets and debt instruments is managed and its performance is evaluated on a fair value basis, in accordance with a documented risk management or investment strategy, and information about the group is provided internally on that basis to the entity's **key management personnel** (as defined in Section 33 *Related Party Disclosures*, paragraph 33.6), for example members of the entity's board of directors and its chief executive officer.

(c) Commitments to receive a loan and to make a loan to another entity that meet the conditions in paragraph 11.8(c) shall be measured at cost (which sometimes is nil) less impairment.

(d) Investments in non-convertible preference shares and non-puttable ordinary shares or preference shares shall be measured as follows (paragraphs 11.27 to 11.32 provide guidance on fair value):

  (i) if the shares are **publicly traded** or their fair value can otherwise be measured reliably, the investment shall be measured at fair value with changes in fair value recognised in profit or loss; and

  (ii) all other such investments shall be measured at cost less impairment.

Impairment or uncollectability must be assessed for financial assets in (a), (c) and (d)(ii) above. Paragraphs 11.21 to 11.26 provide guidance.

Amortised cost and effective interest method

11.15   The amortised cost of a financial asset or financial liability at each **reporting date** is the net of the following amounts:

(a)   the amount at which the financial asset or financial liability is measured at initial recognition;

(b)   minus any repayments of the principal;

(c)   plus or minus the cumulative amortisation using the effective interest method of any difference between the amount at initial recognition and the maturity amount;

(d)   minus, in the case of a financial asset, any reduction (directly or through the use of an allowance account) for impairment or uncollectability.

Financial assets and financial liabilities that have no stated interest rate (and do not constitute a financing transaction) and are classified as payable or receivable within one year are initially measured at an undiscounted amount in accordance with paragraph 11.14(a). Therefore, (c) above does not apply to them.

11.16   The effective interest method is a method of calculating the amortised cost of a financial asset or a financial liability (or a group of financial assets or financial liabilities) and of allocating the interest income or interest expense over the relevant period. The **effective interest rate** is the rate that exactly discounts estimated future cash payments or receipts through the expected life of the financial instrument or, when appropriate, a shorter period, to the **carrying amount** of the financial asset or financial liability. The effective interest rate is determined on the basis of the carrying amount of the financial asset or liability at initial recognition. Under the effective interest method:

(a)   the amortised cost of a financial asset (liability) is the present value of future cash receipts (payments) discounted at the effective interest rate; and

(b)   the interest expense (income) in a period equals the carrying amount of the financial liability (asset) at the beginning of a period multiplied by the effective interest rate for the period.

11.17   When calculating the effective interest rate, an entity shall estimate cash flows considering all contractual terms of the financial instrument (eg prepayment, call and similar options) and known credit losses that have been incurred, but it shall not consider possible future credit losses not yet incurred.

11.18   When calculating the effective interest rate, an entity shall amortise any related fees, finance charges paid or received (such as 'points'), transaction costs and other premiums or discounts over the expected life of the instrument, except as follows. The entity shall use a shorter period if that is the period to which the fees, finance charges paid or received, transaction costs, premiums or discounts relate. This will be the case when the variable to which the fees, finance charges paid or received, transaction costs, premiums or discounts relate is repriced to market rates before the expected maturity of the instrument. In such a case, the appropriate amortisation period is the period to the next such repricing date.

11.19   For variable rate financial assets and variable rate financial liabilities, periodic re-estimation of cash flows to reflect changes in market rates of interest alters the effective interest rate. If a variable rate financial asset or variable rate financial liability is recognised initially at an amount equal to the principal receivable or payable at maturity, re-estimating the future interest payments normally has no significant effect on the carrying amount of the asset or liability.

11.20   If an entity revises its estimates of payments or receipts, the entity shall adjust the carrying amount of the financial asset or financial liability (or group of financial instruments) to reflect actual and revised estimated cash flows. The entity shall recalculate the carrying amount by computing the present value of estimated future cash flows at the financial instrument's original effective interest rate. The entity shall recognise the adjustment as **income** or **expense** in profit or loss at the date of the revision.

Example of determining amortised cost for a five-year loan using the effective interest method

On 1 January 20X0, an entity acquires a bond for Currency Units (CU)900, incurring transaction costs of CU50. Interest of CU40 is receivable annually, in arrears, over the next five years (31 December 20X0 to 31 December 20X4). The bond has a mandatory redemption of CU1100 on 31 December 20X4.

Year	Carrying amount at beginning of period	Interest income at 6.9583%*	Cash inflow	Carrying amount at end of period
	CU	CU	CU	CU
20X0	950.00	66.11	(40.00)	976.11
20X1	976.11	67.92	(40.00)	1,004.03
20X2	1,004.03	69.86	(40.00)	1,033.89
20X3	1,033.89	71.94	(40.00)	1,065.83
20X4	1,065.83	74.16	(40.00)	1,100.00
			(1,100.00)	0

* The effective interest rate of 6.9583 per cent is the rate that discounts the expected cash flows on the bond to the initial carrying amount:
$40/(1.069583)^1 + 40/(1.069583)^2 + 40/(1.069583)^3 + 40/(1.069583)^4 + 1,140/(1.069583)^5 = 950$

Impairment of financial instruments measured at cost or amortised cost

Recognition

At the end of each reporting period, an entity shall assess whether there is objective evidence of impairment of any financial assets that are measured at cost or amortised cost. If there is objective evidence of impairment, the entity shall recognise an **impairment loss** in profit or loss immediately. **11.21**

Objective evidence that a financial asset or group of assets is impaired includes observable data that come to the attention of the holder of the asset about the following loss events: **11.22**

(a) significant financial difficulty of the issuer or obligor;
(b) a breach of contract, such as a default or delinquency in interest or principal payments;
(c) the creditor, for economic or legal reasons relating to the debtor's financial difficulty, granting to the debtor a concession that the creditor would not otherwise consider;
(d) it has become **probable** that the debtor will enter bankruptcy or other financial reorganisation; and
(e) observable data indicating that there has been a measurable decrease in the estimated future cash flows from a group of financial assets since the initial recognition of those assets, even though the decrease cannot yet be identified with the individual financial assets in the group, such as adverse national or local economic conditions or adverse changes in industry conditions.

11.23   Other factors may also be evidence of impairment, including significant changes with an adverse effect that have taken place in the technological, market, economic or legal environment in which the issuer operates.

11.24   An entity shall assess the following financial assets individually for impairment:

(a)   all equity instruments regardless of significance; and
(b)   other financial assets that are individually significant.

An entity shall assess other financial assets for impairment either individually or grouped on the basis of similar **credit risk** characteristics.

Measurement

11.25   An entity shall measure an impairment loss on the following instruments measured at cost or amortised cost as follows:

(a)   For an instrument measured at amortised cost in accordance with paragraph 11.14(a), the impairment loss is the difference between the asset's carrying amount and the present value of estimated cash flows discounted at the asset's original effective interest rate. If such a financial instrument has a variable interest rate, the discount rate for measuring any impairment loss is the current effective interest rate determined under the contract.
(b)   For an instrument measured at cost less impairment in accordance with paragraph 11.14(c) and (d)(ii) the impairment loss is the difference between the asset's carrying amount and the best estimate (which will necessarily be an approximation) of the amount (which might be zero) that the entity would receive for the asset if it were to be sold at the reporting date.

Reversal

11.26   If, in a subsequent period, the amount of an impairment loss decreases and the decrease can be related objectively to an event occurring after the impairment was recognised (such as an improvement in the debtor's credit rating), the entity shall reverse the previously recognised impairment loss either directly or by adjusting an allowance account. The reversal shall not result in a carrying amount of the financial asset (net of any allowance account) that exceeds what the carrying amount would have been had the impairment not previously been recognised. The entity shall recognise the amount of the reversal in profit or loss immediately.

Fair value

11.27   Paragraph 11.14(b) and other sections of this FRS make reference to the fair value guidance in paragraphs 11.27 to 11.32, including Section 9 *Consolidated and Separate Financial Statements*, Section 12 *Other Financial Instruments Issues*, Section 13 *Inventories*, Section 14 *Investments in Associates*, Section 15 *Investments in Joint Ventures*, Section 16 *Investment Property*, Section 17 *Property, Plant and Equipment*, Section 18 *Intangible Assets other than Goodwill*, Section 27 *Impairment of Assets*, Section 28 *Employee Benefits* (in relation to plan assets) and Section 34 *Specialised Activities*. In applying the fair value guidance to assets or liabilities accounted for in accordance with those sections, the reference to ordinary shares or preference shares in these paragraphs should be read to include the types of assets and liabilities addressed in those sections.

Paragraph 11.14(d)(i) requires an investment in non-convertible preference shares and non-puttable ordinary shares or preference shares to be measured at fair value if the shares are publicly traded or if their fair value can otherwise be measured reliably. An entity shall use the following hierarchy to estimate the fair value of the shares:

(a)   The best evidence of fair value is a quoted price for an identical asset in an **active market**. Quoted in an active market in this context means quoted prices are readily and regularly available and those prices represent actual and regularly occurring market transactions on an arm's length basis. The quoted price is usually the current bid price.

(b)   When quoted prices are unavailable, the price of a recent transaction for an identical asset provides evidence of fair value as long as there has not been a significant change in economic circumstances or a significant lapse of time since the transaction took place. If the entity can demonstrate that the last transaction price is not a good estimate of fair value (eg because it reflects the amount that an entity would receive or pay in a forced transaction, involuntary liquidation or distress sale), that price is adjusted.

(c)   If the market for the asset is not active and recent transactions of an identical asset on their own are not a good estimate of fair value, an entity estimates the fair value by using a valuation technique. The objective of using a valuation technique is to estimate what the transaction price would have been on the measurement date in an arm's length exchange motivated by normal business considerations.

Valuation technique

Valuation techniques include using recent arm's length market transactions for an identical asset between knowledgeable, willing parties, if available, reference to the current fair value of another asset that is substantially the same as the asset being measured, discounted cash flow analysis and option pricing models. If there is a valuation technique commonly used by market participants to price the asset and that technique has been demonstrated to provide reliable estimates of prices obtained in actual market transactions, the entity uses that technique.   **11.28**

The objective of using a valuation technique is to establish what the transaction price would have been on the measurement date in an arm's length exchange motivated by normal business considerations. Fair value is estimated on the basis of the results of a valuation technique that makes maximum use of market inputs, and relies as little as possible on entity-determined inputs. A valuation technique would be expected to arrive at a reliable estimate of the fair value if: **11.29**

(a)   it reasonably reflects how the market could be expected to price the asset; and

(b)   the inputs to the valuation technique reasonably represent market expectations and measures of the risk return factors inherent in the asset.

No active market

The fair value of ordinary shares or preference shares that do not have a quoted market price in an active market is reliably measurable if: **11.30**

(a)   the variability in the range of reasonable fair value estimates is not significant for that asset; or

(b)   the probabilitics of the various estimates within the range can be reasonably assessed and used in estimating fair value.

There are many situations in which the variability in the range of reasonable fair value estimates of assets that do not have a quoted market price is likely not to be significant. Normally it is possible to estimate the fair value of ordinary shares or preference shares   **11.31** that an entity has acquired from an outside party. However, if the range of reasonable fair value estimates is significant and the probabilities of the various estimates cannot be reasonably assessed, an entity is precluded from measuring the ordinary shares or preference shares at fair value.

11.32   If a reliable measure of fair value is no longer available for an asset measured at fair value (eg ordinary shares or preference shares measured at fair value through profit or loss), its carrying amount at the last date the asset was reliably measurable becomes its new cost. The entity shall measure the ordinary shares or preference shares at this cost amount less impairment until a reliable measure of fair value becomes available.

Derecognition of a financial asset

11.33   An entity shall derecognise a financial asset only when:

(a)   the contractual rights to the cash flows from the financial asset expire or are settled; or

(b)   the entity transfers to another party substantially all of the risks and rewards of ownership of the financial asset; or

(c)   the entity, despite having retained some significant risks and rewards of ownership, has transferred control of the asset to another party and the other party has the practical ability to sell the asset in its entirety to an unrelated third party and is able to exercise that ability unilaterally and without needing to impose additional restrictions on the transfer. In this case, the entity shall:

     (i)   derecognise the asset; and

     (ii)   recognise separately any rights and obligations retained or created in the transfer.

The carrying amount of the transferred asset shall be allocated between the rights or obligations retained and those transferred on the basis of their relative fair values at the transfer date. Newly created rights and obligations shall be measured at their fair values at that date. Any difference between the consideration received and the amounts recognised and derecognised in accordance with this paragraph shall be recognised in profit or loss in the period of the transfer.

11.34   If a transfer does not result in derecognition because the entity has retained significant risks and rewards of ownership of the transferred asset, the entity shall continue to recognise the transferred asset in its entirety and shall recognise a financial liability for the consideration received. The asset and liability shall not be offset. In subsequent periods, the entity shall recognise any income on the transferred asset and any expense incurred on the financial liability.

11.35   If a transferor provides non-cash collateral (such as debt or equity instruments) to the transferee, the accounting for the collateral by the transferor and the transferee depends on whether the transferee has the right to sell or repledge the collateral and on whether the transferor has defaulted. The transferor and transferee shall account for the collateral as follows:

(a)   If the transferee has the right by contract or custom to sell or repledge the collateral, the transferor shall reclassify that asset in its **statement of financial position** (eg as a loaned asset, pledged equity instruments or repurchase receivable) separately from other assets.

(b)   If the transferee sells collateral pledged to it, it shall recognise the proceeds from the sale and a liability measured at fair value for its obligation to return the collateral.

(c) If the transferor defaults under the terms of the contract and is no longer entitled to redeem the collateral, it shall derecognise the collateral, and the transferee shall recognise the collateral as its asset initially measured at fair value or, if it has already sold the collateral, derecognise its obligation to return the collateral.

(d) Except as provided in (c), the transferor shall continue to carry the collateral as its asset, and the transferee shall not recognise the collateral as an asset.

Example: Transfer that qualifies for derecognition

An entity sells a group of its accounts receivable to a bank at less than their face amount. The entity continues to handle collections from the debtors on behalf of the bank, including sending monthly statements, and the bank pays the entity a market-rate fee for servicing the receivables. The entity is obliged to remit promptly to the bank any and all amounts collected, but it has no obligation to the bank for slow payment or non-payment by the debtors. In this case, the entity has transferred to the bank substantially all of the risks and rewards of ownership of the receivables. Accordingly, it removes the receivables from its statement of financial position (ie derecognises them), and it shows no liability in respect of the proceeds received from the bank. The entity recognises a loss calculated as the difference between the carrying amount of the receivables at the time of sale and the proceeds received from the bank. The entity recognises a liability to the extent that it has collected funds from the debtors but has not yet remitted them to the bank.

Example: Transfer that does not qualify for derecognition

The facts are the same as the preceding example except that the entity has agreed to buy back from the bank any receivables for which the debtor is in arrears as to principal or interest for more than 120 days.

In this case, the entity has retained the risk of slow payment or non-payment by the debtors—a significant risk with respect to receivables. Accordingly, the entity does not treat the receivables as having been sold to the bank, and it does not derecognise them. Instead, it treats the proceeds from the bank as a loan secured by the receivables. The entity continues to recognise the receivables as an asset until they are collected or written off as uncollectible.

Derecognition of a financial liability

An entity shall derecognise a financial liability (or a part of a financial liability) only when it is extinguished—ie when the obligation specified in the contract is discharged, is cancelled or expires. **11.36**

If an existing borrower and lender exchange financial instruments with substantially different terms, the entities shall account for the transaction as an extinguishment of the original financial liability and the recognition of a new financial liability. Similarly, an entity shall account for a substantial modification of the terms of an existing financial liability or a part of it (whether or not attributable to the financial difficulty of the debtor) as an extinguishment of the original financial liability and the recognition of a new financial liability. **11.37**

The entity shall recognise in profit or loss any difference between the carrying amount of the financial liability (or part of a financial liability) extinguished or transferred to **11.38** another party and the consideration paid, including any non-cash assets transferred or liabilities assumed.

Presentation

11.38A   A financial asset and a financial liability shall be offset and the net amount presented in the statement of financial position when, and only when, an entity:

(a)   currently has a legally enforceable right to set off the recognised amounts; and

(b)   intends either to settle on a net basis, or to realise the asset and settle the liability simultaneously.

Disclosures

11.39   The disclosures below make reference to disclosures for certain financial instruments measured at fair value through profit or loss. Entities that have only basic financial instruments (and therefore do not apply Section 12), and have not chosen to designate financial instruments as at fair value through profit or loss (in accordance with paragraph 11.14(b)) will not have any financial instruments measured at fair value through profit or loss and hence will not need to provide such disclosures.

Disclosure of accounting policies for financial instruments

11.40   In accordance with paragraph 8.5, an entity shall disclose, in the summary of significant accounting policies, the measurement basis (or bases) used for financial instruments and the other accounting policies used for financial instruments that are relevant to an understanding of the **financial statements**.

Statement of financial position – categories of financial assets and financial liabilities

11.41   An entity shall disclose the carrying amounts of each of the following categories of financial assets and financial liabilities at the reporting date, in total, either in the statement of financial position or in the **notes**:

*(a)   financial assets measured at fair value through profit or loss (paragraphs 11.14(b), 11.14(d)(i), 12.8 and 12.9);

(b)   financial assets that are debt instruments measured at amortised cost (paragraph 11.14(a));

(c)   financial assets that are equity instruments measured at cost less impairment (paragraphs 11.14(d)(ii), 12.8 and 12.9);

*(d)   financial liabilities measured at fair value through profit or loss (paragraphs 11.14(b), 12.8 and 12.9). Financial liabilities that are not held as part of a trading portfolio and are not **derivatives** shall be shown separately;

(e)   financial liabilities measured at amortised cost (paragraph 11.14(a)); and

(f)   loan commitments measured at cost less impairment (paragraph 11.14(c)).

11.42   An entity shall disclose information that enables users of its financial statements to evaluate the significance of financial instruments for its **financial position** and **performance**. For example, for long-term debt such information would normally include the terms and conditions of the debt instrument (such as interest rate, maturity, repayment schedule, and restrictions that the debt instrument imposes on the entity).

*11.43**   For all financial assets and financial liabilities measured at fair value, the entity shall disclose the basis for determining fair value, eg quoted market price in an active market or a valuation technique. When a valuation technique is used, the entity shall disclose the assumptions applied in determining fair value for each class of financial assets or financial liabilities. For example, if applicable, an entity discloses information about the assumptions relating to prepayment rates, rates of estimated credit losses, and interest rates or discount rates.

If a reliable measure of fair value is no longer available for ordinary or preference shares measured at fair value through profit or loss, the entity shall disclose that fact.   **11.44**

Derecognition

If an entity has transferred financial assets to another party in a transaction that does not qualify for derecognition (see paragraphs 11.33 to 11.35), the entity shall disclose the following for each class of such financial assets: **11.45**

(a)   the nature of the assets;

(b)   the nature of the risks and rewards of ownership to which the entity remains exposed; and

(c)   the carrying amounts of the assets and of any associated liabilities that the entity continues to recognise.

Collateral

When an entity has pledged financial assets as collateral for liabilities or **contingent liabilities**, it shall disclose the following: ***11.46**

(a)   the carrying amount of the financial assets pledged as collateral; and

(b)   the terms and conditions relating to its pledge.

Defaults and breaches on loans payable

For **loans payable** recognised at the reporting date for which there is a breach of terms or default of principal, interest, sinking fund, or redemption terms that has not been remedied by the reporting date, an entity shall disclose the following: **11.47**

(a)   details of that breach or default;

(b)   the carrying amount of the related loans payable at the reporting date; and

(c)   whether the breach or default was remedied, or the terms of the loans payable were renegotiated, before the financial statements were authorised for issue.

Items of income, expense, gains or losses

An entity shall disclose the following items of income, expense, gains or losses: **11.48**

(a)   income, expense, net gains or net losses, including changes in fair value, recognised on:

    *(i)   financial assets measured at fair value through profit or loss;

    *(ii)   financial liabilities measured at fair value through profit or loss (with separate disclosure of movements on those which are not held as part of a trading portfolio and are not derivatives);

    (iii) financial assets measured at amortised cost; and

    (iv)   financial liabilities measured at amortised cost;

(b)   total interest income and total interest expense (calculated using the effective interest method) for financial assets or financial liabilities that are not measured at fair value through profit or loss; and

(c)   the amount of any impairment loss for each class of financial asset. A class of financial asset is a grouping that is appropriate to the nature of the information disclosed and that takes into account the characteristics of the financial assets.

Financial instruments at fair value through profit or loss

*11.48A   An entity, including an entity that is not a company, shall provide the following disclosures only for financial instruments measured at fair value through profit or loss in accordance with paragraph 36(4) of Schedule 1 to the Regulations[11]. This does not include financial liabilities held as part of a trading portfolio nor derivatives. The required disclosures are:

(a)   The amount of change, during the period and cumulatively, in the fair value of the financial instrument that is attributable to changes in the credit risk of that instrument, determined either:

(i)   as the amount of change in its fair value that is not attributable to changes in market conditions that give rise to **market risk**; or

(ii)   using an alternative method the entity believes more faithfully represents the amount of change in its fair value that is attributable to changes in the credit risk of the instrument.

(b)   The method used to establish the amount of change attributable to changes in own credit risk, or, if the change cannot be measured reliably or is not **material**, that fact.

(c)   For a financial liability, the difference between the financial liability's carrying amount and the amount the entity would be contractually required to pay at maturity to the holder of the obligation.

(d)   If an instrument contains both a liability and an equity feature, and the instrument has multiple features that substantially modify the cash flows and the values of those features are interdependent (such as a callable convertible debt instrument), the existence of those features.

(e)   If there is a difference between the fair value of a financial instrument at initial recognition and the amount determined at that date using a valuation technique, the aggregate difference yet to be recognised in profit or loss at the beginning and end of the period and a reconciliation of the changes in the balance of this difference.

(f)   Information that enables users of the entity's financial statements to evaluate the nature and extent of relevant risks arising from financial instruments to which the entity is exposed at the end of the reporting period. These risks typically include, but are not limited to, credit risk, **liquidity risk** and market risk. The disclosure should include both the entity's exposure to each type of risk and how it manages those risks.

Financial institutions

11.48B   A **financial institution** (other than a **retirement benefit plan**) shall, in addition, apply the requirements of paragraph 34.17.

11.48C   A retirement benefit plan shall, in addition, apply the requirements of paragraphs 34.39 to 34.48.

Section 12 *Other Financial Instruments Issues*

Scope of Sections 11 and 12

12.1   Section 11 *Basic Financial Instruments* and Section 12 *Other Financial Instruments Issues* together deal with recognising, derecognising, measuring, and disclosing **financial instruments** (**financial assets** and **financial liabilities**). Section 11 applies to basic financial instruments and is relevant to all entities. Section 12 applies to other, more complex financial instruments and transactions. If an entity enters into only basic financial

[11] *And the equivalent requirements of the Small Companies Regulations, the Small LLP Regulations and the LLP Regulations.*

instrument transactions then Section 12 is not applicable. However, even entities with only basic financial instruments shall consider the scope of Section 12 to ensure they are exempt.

Public benefit entities or other members of a **public benefit entity group** that make or receive **public benefit entity concessionary loans** shall refer to the relevant paragraphs of Section 34 *Specialised Activities* for the accounting requirements for such loans.   **PBE12.1A**

Accounting policy choice

An entity shall choose to apply either: **12.2**

(a)   the provisions of both Section 11 and Section 12 in full; or

(b)   the **recognition** and **measurement** provisions of IAS 39 *Financial Instruments: Recognition and Measurement* (as adopted for use in the EU), the disclosure requirements of Sections 11 and 12 and the presentation requirements of paragraphs 11.38A or 12.25B; or

(c)   the recognition and measurement provisions of IFRS 9 *Financial Instruments* and/or IAS 39 (as amended following the publication of IFRS 9) subject to the restriction in paragraph 12.2A, the disclosure requirements of Sections 11 and 12 and the presentation requirements of paragraph 11.38A or 12.25B;

to account for all of its financial instruments. Where an entity chooses (b) or (c) it applies the scope of the relevant standard to its financial instruments. An entity's choice of (a), (b) or (c) is an **accounting policy** choice. Paragraphs 10.8 to 10.14 contain requirements for determining when a change in accounting policy is appropriate, how such a change should be accounted for and what information should be disclosed about the change in accounting policy.

An entity, including an entity that is not a company, that has made the accounting policy choice in paragraph 12.2(c) to apply the recognition and measurement provisions of IFRS 9 shall depart from those provisions of IFRS 9 as follows: **12.2A**

A financial asset that is not permitted by the **Small Companies Regulations**, the **Regulations, the Small LLP Regulations** or the **LLP Regulations** to be measured at **fair value** through **profit or loss** shall be measured at **amortised cost** in accordance with paragraphs 5.4.1 to 5.4.4 of IFRS 9.

Scope of Section 12

Section 12 applies to all financial instruments except the following: **12.3**

(a)   Those covered by Section 11.

(b)   Investments in **subsidiaries** (see Section 9 *Consolidated and Separate Financial Statements*), **associates** (see Section 14 *Investments in Associates*) and **joint ventures** (see Section 15 *Investments in Joint Ventures*).

(c)   Employers' rights and obligations under employee benefit plans (see Section 28 *Employee Benefits*).

(d)   **Insurance contracts** (including **reinsurance contracts**) that the entity issues and reinsurance contracts that the entity holds (see FRS 103 *Insurance Contracts*).

(e)   Financial instruments that meet the definition of an entity's own **equity** and the equity component of **compound financial instruments** issued by the reporting entity that contain both a **liability** and an equity component (see Section 22 *Liabilities and Equity*).

(f)   **Leases** (see Section 20 *Leases*) unless the lease could, as a result of non-typical contractual terms, result in a loss to the lessor or the lessee.

(g)   Contracts for contingent consideration in a **business combination** (see Section 19 *Business Combinations and Goodwill*). This exemption applies only to the acquirer.

(h)   Any forward contract between an acquirer and a selling shareholder to buy or sell an acquiree that will result in a business combination at a future **acquisition date**. The term of the forward contract should not exceed a reasonable period normally necessary to obtain any required approvals and to complete the transaction.

(i)   Financial instruments, contracts and obligations to which Section 26 *Share-based Payment* applies, except for contracts within the scope of paragraph 12.5.

(j)   Financial instruments issued by an entity with a **discretionary participation feature** (see FRS 103).

(k)   Reimbursement assets accounted for in accordance with Section 21 *Provisions and Contingencies*.

(l)   **Financial guarantee contracts** (see Section 21).

A reporting entity that issues the financial instruments set out in (d) or (j) or holds the financial instruments set out in (d) is required by paragraph 1.6 to apply FRS 103 to those financial instruments.

12.4   Most contracts to buy or sell a non-financial item such as a commodity, **inventory**, or **property, plant and equipment** are excluded from this section because they are not financial instruments. However, this section applies to all contracts that impose risks on the buyer or seller that are not typical of contracts to buy or sell non-financial items. For example, this section applies to contracts that, as a result of its contractual terms, could result in a loss to the buyer or seller that is unrelated to changes in the price of the non-financial item, changes in foreign exchange rates, or a default by one of the counterparties.

12.5   In addition to the contracts described in paragraph 12.4, this section applies to contracts to buy or sell non-financial items if the contract can be settled net in **cash** or another financial instrument, or by exchanging financial instruments as if the contracts were financial instruments, with the following exception: contracts that were entered into and continue to be held for the purpose of the receipt or delivery of a non-financial item in accordance with the entity's expected purchase, sale or usage requirements are not financial instruments for the purposes of this section.

Initial recognition of financial assets and liabilities

12.6   An entity shall recognise a financial asset or a financial liability only when the entity becomes a party to the contractual provisions of the instrument.

Initial measurement

12.7   When a financial asset or financial liability is recognised initially, an entity shall measure it at its fair value, which is normally the transaction price (including **transaction costs** except in the initial measurement of financial assets and liabilities that are measured at fair value through profit or loss). If payment for an asset is deferred beyond normal business terms or is financed at a rate of interest that is not a market rate, the entity shall initially measure the asset at the **present value** of the future payments discounted at a market rate of interest for a similar debt instrument.

Subsequent measurement

At the end of each **reporting period**, an entity shall measure all financial instruments **12.8** within the scope of Section 12 at fair value and recognise changes in fair value in profit or loss, except as follows:

(a) investments in equity instruments that are not **publicly traded** and whose fair value cannot otherwise be measured reliably and contracts linked to such instruments that, if exercised, will result in delivery of such instruments, shall be measured at cost less impairment;

(b) hedging instruments in a designated hedging relationship accounted for in accordance with paragraph 12.23; and

(c) financial instruments that are not permitted by the Small Company Regulations, the Regulations, the Small LLP Regulations or the LLP Regulations to be measured at fair value through profit or loss shall be measured at amortised cost in accordance with paragraphs 11.15 to 11.20.

If a reliable measure of fair value is no longer available for an equity instrument (or a **12.9** contract linked to such an instrument) that is not publicly traded but is measured at fair value through profit or loss, its fair value at the last date the instrument was reliably measurable is treated as the cost of the instrument. The entity shall measure the instrument at this cost amount less impairment until a reliable measure of fair value becomes available.

Fair value

An entity shall apply the guidance on fair value in paragraphs 11.27 to 11.32 to fair value **12.10** measurements in accordance with this section as well as for fair value measurements in accordance with Section 11.

The fair value of a financial liability that is due on demand is not less than the amount **12.11** payable on demand, discounted from the first date that the amount could be required to be paid.

An entity shall not include transaction costs in the initial measurement of financial assets **12.12** and liabilities that will be measured subsequently at fair value through profit or loss.

Impairment of financial instruments measured at cost or amortised cost

An entity shall apply the guidance on impairment of a financial instrument measured at **12.13** cost in paragraphs 11.21 to 11.26 to financial instruments measured at cost less impairment in accordance with this section.

Derecognition of a financial asset or financial liability

An entity shall apply the **derecognition** requirements in paragraphs 11.33 to 11.38 to **12.14** financial assets and financial liabilities to which this section applies.

Hedge accounting

A hedging relationship consists of a hedging instrument and a hedged item. Provided the **12.15** qualifying conditions in paragraph 12.18 are met, an entity may apply hedge accounting.

Hedged items

12.16   A hedged item can be a recognised **asset** or liability, an unrecognised **firm commitment**, a **highly probable forecast transaction** or a **net investment in a foreign operation**, or a component of any such item, provided the item is reliably measurable.

12.16A   For hedge accounting purposes, only assets, liabilities, firm commitments or a highly probable forecast transaction with a party external to the reporting entity can be a hedged item. Hedge accounting can be applied to transactions between entities in the same **group** only in the **individual financial statements** of those entities, except for:

(a)   transactions with subsidiaries, where the subsidiaries are not consolidated in the **consolidated financial statements**;

(b)   the foreign currency risk of intragroup **monetary items** that result in an exposure to foreign exchange **gains** or losses that are not fully eliminated on consolidation in accordance with Section 30 *Foreign Currency Translation*; and

(c)   the foreign currency risk of highly probable forecast intragroup transactions, provided the transactions are denominated in a currency other than the **functional currency** of the entity entering into the transactions and the foreign currency risk affects consolidated profit or loss.

12.16B   A group of items, including components of items, can be an eligible hedged item provided that all of the following conditions are met:

(a)   it consists of items that are individually eligible hedged items;

(b)   the items in the group share the same risk;

(c)   the items in the group are managed together on a group basis for risk management purposes; and

(d)   it does not include items with offsetting risk positions.

12.16C   A component of an item comprises less than the entire fair value change or **cash flow** variability of an item. The following components of an item (including combinations thereof) may be a hedged item:

(a)   changes in the cash flows or fair value attributable to a separately identifiable and reliably measureable specific risk or risks, including cash flow and fair value changes above or below a specified price or other variable;

(b)   one or more selected contractual cash flows; or

(c)   a specified part of the nominal amount of an item.

Hedging instruments

12.17   An instrument may be a hedging instrument provided all of the following conditions are met:

(a)   it is a financial instrument measured at fair value through profit or loss;

(b)   it is a contract with a party external to the reporting entity (ie external to the group or individual entity that is being reported on); and

(c)   it is not a written option, except as described in paragraph 12.17C.

12.17A   An instrument (or a combination of such instruments) meeting the conditions of paragraph 12.17, may only be a hedging instrument:

(a)   in its entirety; or

(b)   a proportion of such an instrument or a proportion of a combination of such instruments, eg 50 per cent of the nominal amount of the instrument.

For a hedge of foreign currency risk, the foreign currency risk component of a financial **12.17B** instrument, provided that it is not a financial instrument as described in paragraph 11.6(b), may be a hedging instrument.

A written option is not a hedging instrument unless the written option is an offset to or is **12.17C** combined with a purchased option and the effect of the offset or combination is not a net written option. An example of a combination of a written and a purchased option that is not a net written option is a zero cost interest rate collar.

Conditions for hedge accounting

An entity may apply hedge accounting to a hedging relationship from the date all of the **12.18** following conditions are met:

(a)   the hedging relationship consists only of a hedging instrument and a hedged item as described in paragraphs 12.16 to 12.17C;
(b)   the hedging relationship is consistent with the entity's risk management objectives for undertaking hedges;
(c)   there is an economic relationship between the hedged item and the hedging instrument;
(d)   the entity has documented the hedging relationship so that the risk being hedged, the hedged item and the hedging instrument are clearly identified; and
(e)   the entity has determined and documented causes of hedge ineffectiveness.

An economic relationship between a hedged item and hedging instrument exists when the **12.18A** entity expects that the values of the hedged item and hedging instrument will typically move in opposite directions in response to movements in the same risk, which is the hedged risk.

Accounting for qualifying hedging relationships

There are three types of hedging relationships: **12.19**

(a)   fair value hedge: a hedge of the exposure to changes in fair value of a recognised asset or liability or an unrecognised firm commitment, or a component of any such item, that are attributable to a particular risk and could affect profit or loss;
(b)   cash flow hedge: a hedge of the exposure to variability in cash flows that is attributable to a particular risk associated with all, or a component of, a recognised asset or liability (such as all or some future interest payments on variable rate debt) or a highly probable forecast transaction, and could affect profit or loss; and
(c)   hedge of a net investment in a foreign operation.

A hedge of the foreign currency risk of an unrecognised firm commitment may be **12.19A** accounted for as a fair value hedge or as a cash flow hedge.

Fair value hedges

A fair value hedge shall be accounted for as follows from the date the conditions in **12.20** paragraph 12.18 are met:

(a)   the gain or loss on the hedging instrument shall be recognised in profit or loss; and
(b)   the **hedging gain or loss** on the hedged item shall adjust the carrying amount of the hedged item (if applicable) and be recognised in profit or loss. When a hedged item is an unrecognised firm commitment, the cumulative hedging gain or loss on the hedged item is recognised as an asset or liability with a corresponding gain or loss recognised in profit or loss.

12.21   When an unrecognised firm commitment to acquire an asset or assume a liability is the hedged item, the initial carrying amount of the asset or liability that results from the entity meeting the firm commitment is adjusted to include the cumulative hedging gain or loss of the hedged item that was recognised in the statement of financial position.

12.22   Any adjustment arising from paragraph 12.20(b) shall be amortised to profit or loss if the hedged item is a financial instrument measured at amortised cost. Amortisation may begin as soon as an adjustment exists and shall begin no later than when the hedged item ceases to be adjusted for hedging gains and losses. The amortisation is based on a recalculated effective interest rate at the date amortisation begins.

Cash flow hedges

12.23   A cash flow hedge shall be accounted for as follows from the date the conditions in paragraph 12.18 are met:

    (a)   the separate component of equity associated with the hedged item (cash flow hedge reserve) is adjusted to the lower of the following (in absolute amounts):

        (i)   the cumulative gain or loss on the hedging instrument from the date the conditions of paragraph 12.18 are met; and

        (ii)   the cumulative change in fair value on the hedged item (ie the present value of the cumulative change of expected future cash flows) from the date the conditions of paragraph 12.18 are met;

    (b)   the portion of the gain or loss on the hedging instrument that is determined to be an effective hedge (ie the portion that is offset by the change in the cash flow hedge reserve calculated in accordance with (a)) shall be recognised in **other comprehensive income**;

    (c)   any remaining gain or loss on the hedging instrument (or any gain or loss required to balance the change in the cash flow hedge reserve calculated in accordance with (a)), is hedge ineffectiveness that shall be recognised in profit or loss; and

    (d)   the amount that has been accumulated in the cash flow hedge reserve in accordance with (a) shall be accounted for as follows:

        (i)   if a hedged forecast transaction subsequently results in the recognition of a non-financial asset or non-financial liability, or a hedged forecast transaction for a non-financial asset or non-financial liability becomes a firm commitment for which fair value hedge accounting is applied, the entity shall remove that amount from the cash flow hedge reserve and include it directly in the initial cost or other carrying amount of the asset or liability;

        (ii)   for cash flow hedges other than those covered by (i), that amount shall be reclassified from the cash flow hedge reserve to profit or loss in the same period or periods during which the hedged expected future cash flows affect profit or loss (for example, in the periods that interest income or interest expense is recognised or when a forecast sale occurs); and

        (iii)   if the amount is a loss, and all or part of that loss is not expected to be recovered, the amount of the loss not expected to be recovered shall be reclassified to profit or loss immediately.

Hedges of a net investment in a foreign operation

12.24   Hedges of a net investment in a foreign operation, including a hedge of a monetary item that is accounted for as part of the net investment (see Section 30), shall be accounted for similarly to cash flow hedges from the date the conditions of paragraph 12.18 are met:

    (a)   the portion of the gain or loss on the hedging instrument that is determined to be an effective hedge shall be recognised in other comprehensive income (see paragraphs 12.23(a) and (b)); and

    (b)   the ineffective portion shall be recognised in profit or loss.

The cumulative gain or loss on the hedging instrument relating to the effective portion of the hedge that has been accumulated in equity shall not be reclassified from equity to profit or loss on disposal or partial disposal of the foreign operation.

Discontinuing hedge accounting

The entity may discontinue hedge accounting provided the entity has documented its election.   **12.25**

The entity shall discontinue hedge accounting when:

(a)   the hedging instrument has expired, is sold, terminated or exercised; or
(b)   the conditions for hedge accounting in paragraph 12.18 are no longer met.

In all cases, hedge accounting shall be discontinued prospectively.

In a fair value hedge, any adjustment arising from paragraph 12.20(b) is dealt with in accordance with paragraph 12.22.   **12.25A**

In a cash flow hedge, if the hedged future cash flows are no longer expected to occur, the amount that has been accumulated in the cash flow hedge reserve in accordance with paragraph 12.23(a) shall be reclassified from the cash flow hedge reserve to profit or loss immediately. If the hedged future cash flows are still expected to occur (for example a future cash flow that is no longer highly probable may still be expected to occur), the cumulative gain or loss in the cash flow hedge reserve is dealt with in accordance with paragraph 12.23(d).

In a net investment hedge, in accordance with paragraph 12.24, the amount that has been accumulated in equity is not reclassified to profit or loss.

Presentation

A financial asset and a financial liability shall be offset and the net amount presented in the **statement of financial position** when, and only when, an entity: **12.25B**

(a)   currently has a legally enforceable right to set off the recognised amounts; and
(b)   intends either to settle on a net basis, or to realise the asset and settle the liability simultaneously.

Disclosures

An entity applying this section shall make all of the disclosures required in Section 11 incorporating in those disclosures, financial instruments that are within the scope of this section as well as those within the scope of Section 11. For financial instruments in the scope of this section that are not held as part of a trading portfolio and are not **derivative** instruments, an entity shall provide additional disclosures as set out in paragraph 11.48A. In addition, if the entity uses hedge accounting, it shall make the additional disclosures in paragraphs 12.27 to 12.29A.   **12.26**

An entity shall disclose the following separately for each type of hedging relationship described in paragraph 12.19:   **12.27**

(a)   a description of the hedge;
(b)   a description of the financial instruments designated as hedging instruments and their fair values at the **reporting date**; and
(c)   the nature of the risks being hedged, including a description of the hedged item.

*12.28 If an entity uses hedge accounting for a fair value hedge it shall disclose the following:

(a) the amount of the change in fair value of the hedging instrument recognised in profit or loss for the period; and

(b) the amount of the change in fair value of the hedged item recognised in profit or loss for the period.

12.29 If an entity uses hedge accounting for a cash flow hedge it shall disclose the following:

(a) the periods when the cash flows are expected to occur and when they are expected to affect profit or loss;

(b) a description of any forecast transaction for which hedge accounting had previously been used, but which is no longer expected to occur;

*(c) the amount of the change in fair value of the hedging instrument that was recognised in other comprehensive income during the period;

*(d) the amount, if any, that was reclassified from equity to profit or loss for the period; and

*(e) the amount, if any, of any excess of the fair value of the hedging instrument over the change in the fair value of the expected cash flows that was recognised in profit or loss for the period.

12.29A If an entity uses hedge accounting for a net investment in a foreign operation it shall disclose separately the amounts recognised in other comprehensive income in accordance with paragraph 12.24(a) and the amounts recognised in profit or loss in accordance with paragraph 12.24(b).

Appendix to Section 12

Examples of hedge accounting

This appendix accompanies, but is not part of, Section 12. It provides guidance for applying the requirements of paragraphs 12.15 to 12.25A.

Example 1

Fair value hedge accounting – Hedge of forward foreign currency risk of an unrecognised firm commitment

In accordance with paragraph 12.19A, a hedge of the foreign currency risk of an unrecognised firm commitment may be accounted for as a cash flow or fair value hedge. This example illustrates fair value hedge accounting.

12A.1 On 9 June 20X5 an entity enters into a purchase agreement with a third party over a non-financial asset in a foreign currency (FC) for FC515,000. On the same day, the entity enters into a forward currency contract to buy FC500,000 for CU1,000,000. Under the purchase agreement, the non-financial asset will be delivered and paid for on 30 March 20X6, the same day the forward currency contract is required to be settled.

In this example the hedged item is the total of the commitment of FC515,000 and the hedging instrument is the forward contract to buy FC500,000. Since the nominal amounts of the two contracts do not match, hedge ineffectiveness arises. It should be noted that in practice an entity could avoid ineffectiveness arising for this reason by identifying an amount of FC500,000 of the total commitment as the hedged item in accordance with paragraph 12.16C.

For simplification, this example disregards other sources of ineffectiveness, eg counter party credit risk associated with the forward currency contract.

The entity's financial year ends on 31 December.

This example assumes that the qualifying conditions for hedge accounting in paragraph 12.18 are met from 9 June 20X5.

The table below sets out the applicable forward exchange rates, the fair value of the forward currency contract (the hedging instrument) and the hedging gains/losses on the purchase commitment (the hedged item) on the relevant dates. This example ignores the effects of discounting.

	9 Jun 20X5	31 Dec 20X5	30 Mar 20X6
Forward exchange rate (CU:FC)	2:1	2.2:1	2.16:1
Forward currency contract (hedging instrument)			
Fair value	nil	FC500,000 × CU0.2:FC = CU100,000	FC500,000 × CU0.16:FC = CU80,000†
Fair value change	nil	CU100,000 − 0 = CU100,000	CU80,000 − CU100,000 = (CU20,000)
Purchase commitment (hedged item)			
Cumulative hedging (loss)‡	nil	(FC515,000) × CU0.2:FC = (CU103,000)	(FC515,000) × CU0.16:FC = (CU82,400)
Hedging (loss)/ gain	nil	(CU103,000) − 0 = (CU103,000)	(CU82,400) − (CU103,000) = CU20,600

Key to table:
† *This is the fair value of the contract prior to settlement.*
‡ *In accordance with paragraph 12.20(b), the commitment is fair valued only for the hedged risk, which in this example is the forward exchange rate risk.*

Hedge accounting: 12A.2

Note that there are no hedge accounting entries on 9 June 20X5.

31 December 20X5

(1)   In accordance with paragraph 12.20(a) the fair value gain of CU100,000 on the forward currency contract is recognised in profit or loss.

(2)   In accordance with paragraph 12.20(b) the cumulative hedging loss of CU103,000 on the commitment is recorded as a liability with a corresponding loss recognised in profit or loss.

Accounting entries:

Ref		Debit	Credit
(1)	Forward currency contract	CU100,000	
	Profit or loss		CU100,000
(2)	Profit or loss	CU103,000	
	Hedged item (commitment)		CU103,000

30 March 20X6

(1)   In accordance with paragraph 12.20(a) the fair value loss of CU20,000 on the forward currency contract is recognised in profit or loss.

(2)   In accordance with paragraph 12.20(b) the hedging gain on the commitment of CU20,600 is recognised in profit or loss with a corresponding adjustment to the recognised liability from CU103,000 to CU82,400.

(3)   In accordance with paragraph 12.21 the non-financial asset's carrying amount is adjusted to include the cumulative hedging loss on the hedged item of CU82,400.

Note A: For illustrative purposes the accounting entry in respect of the settlement of the forward currency contract in cash for CU80,000 is shown below.

Note B: For illustrative purposes the accounting entry for the purchase of the non-financial asset at the applicable spot rate of FC2.16:CU for CU1,112,400 (settled in cash) is shown below.

Accounting entries:

Ref		Debit	Credit
(1)	Profit or loss	CU20,000	
	Forward currency contract		CU20,000
(2)	Hedged item (commitment)	CU20,600	
	Profit or loss		CU20,600
(3)	Hedged item (commitment)	CU82,400	
	Property, plant and equipment (PP&E)		CU82,400
(A)	Cash	CU80,000	
	Forward currency contract		CU80,000
(B)	Property, plant and equipment (PP&E)	CU1,112,400	
	Cash		CU1,112,400

Example 2

Cash flow hedge accounting – Hedge of variability in cash flows in a floating rate loan due to interest rate risk

This example illustrates the accounting for a cash flow hedge of interest rate risk associated with a floating rate loan. The entity borrows money at a floating rate and enters into an interest rate swap with the effect of paying a fixed rate overall.

12A.3   On 1 January 20X5, an entity borrows CU10,000,000 from a bank at a floating rate of 3-month LIBOR plus 2.5 per cent. The interest is payable annually in arrears on 31 December. The loan is repayable on 31 December 20X7.

On 1 January 20X5 the entity also enters into an interest rate swap with a third party, under which it receives 6-month LIBOR and pays a fixed rate of interest of 4.5 per cent. The notional amount of the swap is CU10,000,000. The swap is settled annually in arrears on 31 December and expires on 31 December 20X7.

The LIBOR rates on the loan and the interest rate swap are reset and fixed annually in advance on 31 December based on the expected LIBOR rates applicable at that time. Note that in practice the loan and swap interest rates would be reset more frequently than assumed for the purpose of simplification in this example.

The entity hedges the variability of the interest rate payments on the bank loan based on 3-month LIBOR. It should be noted that because the entity receives interest based on 6-month LIBOR under the interest rate swap, ineffectiveness will arise because the expected cash flows of the hedged item and the hedging instrument differ. The fair value of the interest rate swap may be affected by other factors that cause ineffectiveness, for example counter party credit risk, but these have been disregarded in this example.

There are no transaction costs.

The entity's financial year ends on 31 December.

This example assumes that the qualifying conditions for hedge accounting in paragraph 12.18 are met from 1 January 20X5.

The table in paragraph 12A.5 summarises the impact of hedge accounting on the interest rate swap, profit or loss and other comprehensive income.

The table below sets out the applicable LIBOR rates, interest payments and swap settlements. The fair values of the interest rate swap and the hedged item shown in the table are shown for illustrative purposes only.

Note that in practice, when forecasted variable interest rate payments are the hedged item, the fair value of a hypothetical swap, that would be expected to perfectly offset the hedged cash flows, is used as a proxy of the fair value of the hedged item. The hypothetical derivative in this scenario is a fixed to floating interest rate swap with terms that match those of the loan and a fixed rate of 4.3 per cent, which for the purpose of this example, is the interest rate where the fair value of the hypothetical swap is nil at the inception of the hedging relationship.

	1 Jan 20X5	31 Dec 20X5	31 Dec 20X6	31 Dec 20X7
Actual 3-month LIBOR	4.3%	5%	3%	n/a
Actual 6-month LIBOR	4.5%	4.9%	3.2%	n/a
Interest payments based on 3-month LIBOR	n/a	CU10m × (4.3% + 2.5%) = CU680,000	CU10m × (5% + 2.5%) = CU750,000	CU10m × (3% + 2.5%) = CU550,000
Interest rate swap (hedging instrument)				
Fair value	nil	CU78,000	(CU89,000)[†]	(CU130,000)[‡]
Fair value change	nil	CU78,000 − 0 = CU78,000	(CU89,000) − CU78,000 = (CU167,000)	(CU130,000) − (CU40,000)[§] − (CU89,000) = (CU1,000)

	1 Jan 20X5	31 Dec 20X5	31 Dec 20X6	31 Dec 20X7
Swap settlement receipts/(payments) based on 6-month LIBOR	n/a	CU10m × (4.5% – 4.5%) = nil	CU10m × (4.9% – 4.5%) = CU40,000	CU10m* (3.2% – 4.5%) = (CU130,000)
Hedged item				
Fair value	nil	(CU137,000)	CU59,000	CU130,000

Key to table:
† This valuation is determined before the receipt of the cash settlement of CU40,000 due on 31 December 20X6.
‡ This valuation is determined before the payment of the cash settlement of CU130,000 due on 31 December 20X7.
§ CU40,000 is the settlement of the interest rate swap as at 31 December 20X6 which affects the fair value of the swap, but is not included in the fair value of the swap at 31 December 20X6 of CU89,000.

12A.4   Hedge accounting:

31 December 20X5

(1)   In accordance with paragraph 12.23(a), the cash flow hedge reserve is adjusted to the lower of (in absolute amounts) the cumulative gain on the hedging instrument (ie the interest rate swap), which equals its fair value, of CU78,000 and the cumulative change in fair value of the hedged item, which equals its fair value of (CU137,000).

In accordance with paragraph 12.23(b), the gain of CU78,000 on the interest rate swap is recognised in other comprehensive income.

(2)   The fixed interest element on the hypothetical swap is CU430,000, the same amount as the variable rate component. The variability of the 3-month LIBOR did therefore not affect profit or loss during the period. The reclassification adjustment in accordance with paragraph 12.23(d)(ii) is nil. (Note that no accounting entry is shown below.)

Note A: For illustrative purposes the accounting entry for interest payments is shown below. Note that in practice the accrual and payment of interest may be recorded in separate accounting entries.

Accounting entries:

Note that the accounting entries shown are only those relevant to demonstrate the effects of hedge accounting. In practice other accounting entries would be required, eg an entry to recognise the loan liability.

Ref		Debit	Credit
(1)	Interest rate swap	CU78,000	
	Other comprehensive income		CU78,000
(A)	Profit or loss	CU680,000	
	Cash		CU680,000

31 December 20X6

(1)   In accordance with paragraph 12.23(a), the cash flow hedge reserve is adjusted to the lower of (in absolute amounts) the cumulative loss on the hedging instrument (ie the interest rate swap) which equals its fair value of (CU89,000) and the cumulative change in fair value of the hedged item, which equals its fair value of CU59,000.

The cash flow hedge reserve moves from CU78,000 to (CU59,000), a change of (CU137,000).

In accordance with paragraph 12.23(b), a loss of CU137,000 on the interest rate swap is recognised in other comprehensive income, as this part of the loss is fully off-set by the change in the cash flow hedge reserve. The remainder of the loss on the interest rate swap of CU30,000 is recognised in profit or loss, as required by paragraph 12.23(c).

(2) The fixed interest element on the hypothetical swap is CU430,000, whilst the variable rate component is CU500,000. The variability of the 3-month LIBOR affects profit or loss during the period by CU70,000. Accordingly, the reclassification adjustment in accordance with paragraph 12.23(d)(ii) is CU70,000.

Note A: For illustrative purposes the accounting entry for interest payments is shown below. Note that in practice the accrual and payment of interest may be recorded in separate accounting entries.

Note B: For illustrative purposes the accounting entry for the settlement of the swap is shown below.

Accounting entries:

Ref		Debit	Credit
(1)	Other comprehensive income	CU137,000	
	Profit or loss	CU30,000	
	Interest rate swap		CU167,000
(2)	Other comprehensive income	CU70,000	
	Profit or loss		CU70,000
(A)	Profit or loss	CU750,000	
(B)	Cash		CU750,000
	Cash	CU40,000	
	Interest rate swap		CU40,000

31 December 20X7

(1) In accordance with paragraph 12.23(a), the cash flow hedge reserve is adjusted to the lower of (in absolute amounts) the cumulative loss on the hedging instrument (ie the interest rate swap) which equals the fair value of (CU130,000) and the cumulative change in fair value of the hedged item, which equals its fair value of CU130,000. The cash flow hedge reserve moves from (CU129,000) to (CU130,000), a change of (CU1,000). In accordance with paragraph 12.23(b), the loss of CU1,000 on the interest rate swap is recognised in other comprehensive income.

(2) The fixed interest element on the hypothetical swap is CU430,000, whilst the variable rate component is CU300,000. The variability of the 3-month LIBOR affects profit or loss during the period by (CU130,000). Accordingly, the reclassification adjustment in accordance with paragraph 12.23(d)(ii) is (CU130,000).

Note A: For illustrative purposes the accounting entry for interest payments is shown below. Note that in practice the accrual and payment of interest may be recorded in separate accounting entries.

Note B: For illustrative purposes the accounting entry for the settlement of the swap is shown below.

Accounting entries:

Ref		Debit	Credit
(1)	Other comprehensive income	CU1,000	
	Interest rate swap		CU1,000
(2)	Profit or loss	CU130,000	
	Other comprehensive income		CU130,000
(A)	Profit or loss	CU550,000	
	Cash		CU550,000
(B)	Interest rate swap	CU130,000	
	Cash		CU130,000

12A.5 The table below summarises the effects of the accounting entries shown in paragraph 12A.4 on the interest rate swap, profit or loss and other comprehensive income.

Description	Interest rate swap	Other comprehensive income	Profit or loss
31 December 20X5			
Opening balance	nil	nil[†]	–
Interest on the loan			CU680,000
Interest rate swap fair value movement	CU78,000	(CU78,000)	–
Closing balance	**CU78,000**	**(CU78,000)[†]**	–
31 December 20X6			
Opening balance	**CU78,000**	**(CU78,000)[†]**	–
Interest on the loan			CU750,000
Interest rate swap fair value movement	(CU167,000)	CU137,000	CU30,000
Settlement receipt interest rate swap	(40,000)	–	
Reclassification from cash flow hedge reserve	–	CU70,000	(CU70,000)
Closing balance	**(CU129,000)**	**CU129,000[†]**	–
31 December 20X7			
Opening balance	**(CU129,000)**	**CU129,000[†]**	–
Interest on the loan			CU550,000
Interest rate swap movement	(1,000)	1,000	–
Settlement payment interest rate swap	CU130,000	–	–
Reclassification from cash flow hedge reserve	–	(CU130,000)	CU130,000
Closing balance	**nil**	**nil[†]**	–

Key to table:
[†] *This is the balance of the cash flow hedge reserve.*

Example 3

Hedge accounting: Net investment in a foreign operation

This example illustrates the accounting for a net investment hedge in the consolidated financial statements. The entity has a foreign operation and hedges its exposure to foreign currency risk in the foreign operation by the use of a foreign currency loan.

On 1 April 20X5 an entity with functional currency CU acquires an investment in an overseas subsidiary (with functional currency FC) at a cost of FC1,200,000. On the same day the entity takes out a loan with a third party of FC1,200,000 to finance the investment. This example disregards the effects of interest or other transaction costs associated with the loan.

12A.6

This example assumes that the carrying amount of the investment denominated in FC is impaired below FC1,200,000 as presented in the table below, which causes ineffectiveness.

The entity's financial year ends on 31 December.

This example assumes that the qualifying conditions for hedge accounting in paragraph 12.18 are met from 1 April 20X5.

The table below sets out the applicable exchange rates, the carrying amount of the loan and the foreign exchange gains and losses on the loan as determined in accordance with Section 30, as well as the retranslation differences on the foreign investment recognised in other comprehensive income in accordance with Section 30.

	1 Apr 20X5	**31 Dec 20X5**	**31 Dec 20X6**
Spot exchange rate CU:FC	0.35:1	0.3:1	0.45:1
Loan (hedging instrument)			
Carrying amount under Section 30	(FC1,200,000) × CU0.35:FC = (CU420,000)	(FC1,200,000) × CU0.3:FC = (CU360,000)	(FC1,200,000) × CU0.45:FC = (CU540,000)
Cumulative gain/(loss)	nil	(CU360,000) – (CU420,000) = CU60,000	(CU540,000) – (CU420,000) = (CU120,000)
Gain/(loss)	nil	(CU360,000) – (CU420,000) = CU60,000	(CU540,000) – (CU360,000) = (CU180,000)
Investment in foreign operation (hedged item)			
Retranslation difference in accordance with Section 30	nil	(CU55,000)[†]	CU157,500[‡]
Cumulative retranslation differences	nil	(CU55,000) – 0 = (CU55,000)	CU157,500 + (CU55,000) = CU102,500

Key to table:

[†] *This is the exchange difference referred to in paragraph 30.20 which is recognised in other comprehensive income. The amount under paragraph 30.20(a) is CU5,000 and under paragraph 30.20(b) (CU60,000). The calculation is based on the translation of the FC200,000 loss at the average rate of 0.325CU:FC.*

[‡] *This is the exchange difference referred to in paragraph 30.20 which is recognised in other comprehensive income. The amount under paragraph 30.20(a) is CU7,500 and under paragraph 30.20(b) CU150,000. The calculation is based on the translation of the FC100,000 profit at the average rate of 0.375CU:FC.*

12A.7   Hedge accounting:

31 December 20X5

A component of equity is adjusted to the lower of (in absolute amounts) the cumulative exchange gain on the loan of CU60,000 and the cumulative retranslation difference on the net investment of (CU55,000).

In accordance with paragraph 12.24(a), a gain of CU55,000 on the loan is recognised in other comprehensive income. The remainder of the gain of CU5,000 is recognised in profit or loss, as required by paragraph 12.24(b).

Accounting entry:

Note that only the accounting entry in relation to hedge accounting as described in paragraph 12.24 is shown. Other accounting entries in relation to the loan and the investment in the foreign operation would be required in practice.

	Debit	Credit
Loan	CU60,000	
Other comprehensive income		CU55,000
Profit or loss		CU5,000

31 December 20X6

A component of equity is adjusted to the lower of (in absolute amounts) the cumulative exchange loss on the loan of CU120,000 and the cumulative exchange difference on the net investment of CU102,500.

The amount recorded in equity changes from CU55,000 to (CU102,500), a change of (CU157,500). In accordance with paragraph 12.24(a) a loss of CU157,500 on the loan is recognised in other comprehensive income. The remainder of the loss of CU22,500 is recorded in profit or loss, as required by paragraph 12.24(b).

Accounting entry:

	Debit	Credit
Other comprehensive income	CU157,500	
Profit or loss	CU22,500	
Loan		CU180,000

Section 13 *Inventories*

Scope of this section

13.1   This section sets out the principles for recognising and measuring **inventories**. Inventories are **assets**:

    (a)   held for sale in the ordinary course of business;

    (b)   in the process of production for such sale; or

    (c)   in the form of materials or supplies to be consumed in the production process or in the rendering of services.

This section applies to all inventories, except: **13.2**

(a) work in progress arising under **construction contracts**, including directly related service contracts (see Section 23 *Revenue*);

(b) **financial instruments** (see Section 11 *Basic Financial Instruments* and Section 12 *Other Financial Instruments Issues*); and

(c) **biological assets** related to **agricultural activity** and **agricultural produce** at the point of harvest (see Section 34 *Specialised Activities*).

Other than the disclosure requirements in paragraph 13.22, this section does not apply to **13.3** the **measurement** of inventories at **fair value less costs to sell** through **profit or loss** at each **reporting date**. Inventories shall not be measured at fair value less costs to sell unless it is a more relevant measure of the entity's **performance** because the entity operates in an **active market** where sale can be achieved at published prices, and inventory is a store of readily realisable value.

Measurement of inventories

An entity shall measure inventories at the lower of **cost** and estimated selling price less **13.4** costs to complete and sell.

Inventories held for distribution at no or nominal consideration shall be measured **13.4A** at the lower of cost adjusted, when applicable, for any loss of **service potential** and replacement cost.

Cost of inventories

An entity shall include in the cost of inventories all costs of purchase, costs of conversion **13.5** and other costs incurred in bringing the inventories to their present location and condition.

Where inventories are acquired through a **non-exchange transaction**, their cost shall be **13.5A** measured at their **fair value** as at the date of acquisition. For **public benefit entities** and entities within a **public benefit entity group**, this requirement only applies to inventories that are recognised as a result of the requirements for incoming resources from non-exchange transactions as prescribed in Section 34 *Specialised Activities*.

Costs of purchase

The costs of purchase of inventories comprise the purchase price, import duties and **13.6** other taxes (other than those subsequently recoverable by the entity from the taxing authorities), and transport, handling and other costs directly attributable to the acquisition of finished goods, materials and services. Trade discounts, rebates and other similar items are deducted in determining the costs of purchase.

An entity may purchase inventories on deferred settlement terms. In some cases, the **13.7** arrangement effectively contains an unstated financing element, for example, a difference between the purchase price for normal credit terms and the deferred settlement amount. In these cases, the difference is recognised as interest expense over the period of the financing and is not added to the cost of the inventories unless the inventory is a **qualifying asset** (see Section 25 *Borrowing Costs*) and the entity adopts a policy of capitalisation of borrowing costs.

Costs of conversion

13.8   The costs of conversion of inventories include costs directly related to the units of production, such as direct labour. They also include a systematic allocation of fixed and variable production overheads that are incurred in converting materials into finished goods. Fixed production overheads are those indirect costs of production that remain relatively constant regardless of the volume of production, such as **depreciation** and maintenance of factory buildings and equipment, and the cost of factory management and administration. Variable production overheads are those indirect costs of production that vary directly, or nearly directly, with the volume of production, such as indirect materials and indirect labour.

13.8A   Production overheads include the costs for obligations (recognised and measured in accordance with Section 21 *Provisions and Contingencies*) for dismantling, removing and restoring a site on which an item of **property, plant and equipment** is located that are incurred during the **reporting period** as a consequence of having used that item of property, plant and equipment to produce inventory during that period.

Allocation of production overheads

13.9   An entity shall allocate fixed production overheads to the costs of conversion on the basis of the normal capacity of the production facilities. Normal capacity is the production expected to be achieved on average over a number of periods or seasons under normal circumstances, taking into account the loss of capacity resulting from planned maintenance. The actual level of production may be used if it approximates normal capacity. The amount of fixed overhead allocated to each unit of production is not increased as a consequence of low production or idle plant. Unallocated overheads are recognised as an **expense** in the period in which they are incurred. In periods of abnormally high production, the amount of fixed overhead allocated to each unit of production is decreased so that inventories are not measured above cost. Variable production overheads are allocated to each unit of production on the basis of the actual use of the production facilities.

Joint products and by-products

13.10   A production process may result in more than one product being produced simultaneously. This is the case, for example, when joint products are produced or when there is a main product and a by-product. When the costs of raw materials or conversion of each product are not separately identifiable, an entity shall allocate them between the products on a rational and consistent basis. The allocation may be based, for example, on the relative sales value of each product either at the stage in the production process when the products become separately identifiable, or at the completion of production. Most by-products, by their nature, are immaterial. When this is the case, the entity shall measure them at selling price less costs to complete and sell and deduct this amount from the cost of the main product. As a result, the **carrying amount** of the main product is not materially different from its cost.

Other costs included in inventories

13.11   An entity shall include other costs in the cost of inventories only to the extent that they are incurred in bringing the inventories to their present location and condition.

13.12   [Not used]

Costs excluded from inventories

Examples of costs excluded from the cost of inventories and recognised as expenses in the   **13.13**
period in which they are incurred are:

(a)   abnormal amounts of wasted materials, labour or other production costs;
(b)   storage costs, unless those costs are necessary during the production process before
       a further production stage;
(c)   administrative overheads that do not contribute to bringing inventories to their
       present location and condition; and
(d)   selling costs.

Cost of inventories of a service provider

To the extent that service providers have inventories, they measure them at the costs of   **13.14**
their production. These costs consist primarily of the labour and other costs of personnel
directly engaged in providing the service, including supervisory personnel, and attributable
overheads. Labour and other costs relating to sales and general administrative personnel are
not included but are recognised as expenses in the period in which they are incurred. The
cost of inventories of a service provider does not include profit margins or non-attributable
overheads that are often factored into prices charged by service providers.

Cost of agricultural produce harvested from biological assets

Section 34 requires that inventories comprising agricultural produce that an entity has   **13.15**
harvested from its biological assets should be measured on initial **recognition**, at the
point of harvest, at either their fair value less estimated costs to sell or the lower of cost
and estimated selling price less costs to complete and sell. This becomes the cost of the
inventories at that date for application of this section.

Techniques for measuring cost, such as standard costing, retail method and most recent purchase price

An entity may use techniques such as the standard cost method, the retail method or most   **13.16**
recent purchase price for measuring the cost of inventories if the result approximates cost.
Standard costs take into account normal levels of materials and supplies, labour, efficiency
and capacity utilisation. They are regularly reviewed and, if necessary, revised in the light
of current conditions. The retail method measures cost by reducing the sales value of the
inventory by the appropriate percentage gross margin.

Cost formulas

An entity shall measure the cost of inventories of items that are not ordinarily interchangeable   **13.17**
and goods or services produced and segregated for specific projects by using specific
identification of their individual costs.

An entity shall measure the cost of inventories, other than those dealt with in paragraph 13.17,   **13.18**
by using the first-in, first-out (FIFO) or weighted average cost formula. An entity shall use
the same cost formula for all inventories having a similar nature and use to the entity. For
inventories with a different nature or use, different cost formulas may be justified. The
last-in, first-out method (LIFO) is not permitted by this FRS.

Impairment of inventories

13.19   Paragraphs 27.2 to 27.4 require an entity to assess at the end of each reporting period whether any inventories are impaired, ie the carrying amount is not fully recoverable (eg because of damage, obsolescence or declining selling prices). If an item (or group of items) of inventory is impaired, those paragraphs require the entity to measure the inventory at its selling price less costs to complete and sell, and to recognise an **impairment loss**. Those paragraphs also require a reversal of a prior impairment in some circumstances.

Recognition as an expense

13.20   When inventories are sold, the entity shall recognise the carrying amount of those inventories as an expense in the period in which the related **revenue** is recognised.

13.20A   When inventories held for distribution at no or nominal consideration are distributed, the carrying amount of those inventories shall be recognised as an expense.

13.21   Some inventories may be allocated to other asset accounts, for example, inventory used as a component of self-constructed property, plant or equipment. Inventories allocated to another asset in this way are accounted for subsequently in accordance with the section of this FRS relevant to that type of asset.

Disclosures

13.22   An entity shall disclose the following:

    (a)   the **accounting policies** adopted in measuring inventories, including the cost formula used;

    (b)   the total carrying amount of inventories and the carrying amount in classifications appropriate to the entity;

    (c)   the amount of inventories recognised as an expense during the period;

    (d)   impairment losses recognised or reversed in profit or loss in accordance with Section 27; and

    *(e)   the total carrying amount of inventories pledged as security for **liabilities**.

Section 14 *Investments in Associates*

Scope of this section

14.1   This section applies to accounting for **associates** in **consolidated financial statements**. This section also applies to accounting for investments in associates in the **individual financial statements** of an investor that is not a **parent**. An entity that is a parent shall account for its investments in associates in its **separate financial statements** in accordance with paragraphs 9.26 and 9.26A, as appropriate.

Associates defined

14.2   An associate is an entity, including an unincorporated entity such as a partnership, over which the investor has **significant influence** and that is neither a **subsidiary** nor an interest in a **joint venture**.

14.3   Significant influence is the power to participate in the financial and operating policy decisions of the associate but is not **control** or **joint control** over those policies.

(a)   If an investor holds, directly or indirectly (eg through subsidiaries), 20 per cent or more of the voting power of the associate, it is presumed that the investor has significant influence, unless it can be clearly demonstrated that this is not the case.
(b)   Conversely, if the investor holds, directly or indirectly (eg through subsidiaries), less than 20 per cent of the voting power of the associate, it is presumed that the investor does not have significant influence, unless such influence can be clearly demonstrated.
(c)   A substantial or majority ownership by another investor does not preclude an investor from having significant influence.

Measurement—accounting policy election

An investor that is not a parent but that has an investment in one or more associates shall, in its individual financial statements, account for all of its investments in associates using either: **14.4**

(a)   the cost model in accordance with paragraphs 14.5 to 14.6;
(b)   [not used]
(c)   the fair value model in accordance with paragraphs 14.9 to 14.10A; or
(d)   at fair value with changes in fair value recognised in profit or loss (paragraphs 11.27 to 11.32 provide guidance on fair value).

An investor that is a parent shall, in its consolidated financial statements, account for all of its investments in associates using the equity method in accordance with paragraph 14.8, except as required by paragraph 14.4B.   **14.4A**

Where an investor is a parent and has an associate that is **held as part of an investment portfolio**, the associate shall be measured at **fair value** with changes in fair value recognised in **profit or loss** in the consolidated financial statements.   **14.4B**

Cost model

An investor that is not a parent, that chooses to adopt the cost model, shall measure its investments in associates at cost less any accumulated **impairment losses** recognised in accordance with Section 27 *Impairment of Assets*.   **14.5**

The investor shall recognise dividends and other distributions received from the investment as **income** without regard to whether the distributions are from accumulated profits of the associate arising before or after the date of acquisition.   **14.6**

[Not used]   **14.7**

Equity method

Under the equity method of accounting, an equity investment is initially recognised at the transaction price (including **transaction costs**) and is subsequently adjusted to reflect the investor's share of the profit or loss, **other comprehensive income** and **equity** of the associate.   **14.8**

(a)   *Distributions and other adjustments to carrying amount.* Distributions received from the associate reduce the **carrying amount** of the investment. Adjustments to the carrying amount may also be required as a consequence of changes in the associate's equity arising from items of other comprehensive income.
(b)   *Potential voting rights.* Although potential voting rights are considered in deciding whether significant influence exists, an investor shall measure its share of profit or loss and other comprehensive income of the associate and its share of changes in the associate's equity on the basis of present ownership interests. Those measurements shall not reflect the possible exercise or conversion of potential voting rights.

(c)   *Implicit goodwill and fair value adjustments.* On acquisition of the investment in an associate, an investor shall account for any difference (whether positive or negative) between the cost of acquisition and the investor's share of the fair values of the net identifiable assets of the associate in accordance with paragraphs 19.22 to 19.24. An investor shall adjust its share of the associate's profits or losses after acquisition to account for additional **depreciation** or **amortisation** of the associate's depreciable or amortisable assets (including **goodwill**) on the basis of the excess of their fair values over their carrying amounts at the time the investment was acquired.

(d)   *Impairment.* If there is an indication that an investment in an associate may be impaired, an investor shall test the entire carrying amount of the investment for impairment in accordance with Section 27 as a single **asset**. Any goodwill included as part of the carrying amount of the investment in the associate is not tested separately for impairment but, rather, as part of the test for impairment of the investment as a whole.

(e)   *Investor's transactions with associates.* The investor shall eliminate unrealised profits and losses resulting from upstream (associate to investor) and downstream (investor to associate) transactions to the extent of the investor's interest in the associate. Unrealised losses on such transactions may provide evidence of an impairment of the asset transferred.

(f)   *Date of associate's financial statements.* In applying the equity method, the investor shall use the **financial statements** of the associate as of the same date as the financial statements of the investor unless it is **impracticable** to do so. If it is impracticable, the investor shall use the most recent available financial statements of the associate, with adjustments made for the effects of any significant transactions or events occurring between the accounting period ends.

(g)   *Associate's accounting policies.* If the associate uses **accounting policies** that differ from those of the investor, the investor shall adjust the associate's financial statements to reflect the investor's accounting policies for the purpose of applying the equity method unless it is impracticable to do so.

(h)   *Losses in excess of investment.* If an investor's share of losses of an associate equals or exceeds the carrying amount of its investment in the associate, the investor shall discontinue recognising its share of further losses. After the investor's interest is reduced to zero, the investor shall recognise additional losses by a **provision** (see Section 21 *Provisions and Contingencies*) only to the extent that the investor has incurred legal or **constructive obligations** or has made payments on behalf of the associate. If the associate subsequently reports profits, the investor shall resume recognising its share of those profits only after its share of the profits equals the share of losses not recognised.

(i)   *Discontinuing the equity method.* An investor shall cease using the equity method from the date that significant influence ceases and, provided the associate does not become a subsidiary in accordance with *Section 19 Business Combinations and Goodwill* or a joint venture in accordance with Section 15 *Investments in Joint Ventures*, shall account for the investment as follows:

   (i)   If the investor loses significant influence over an associate as a result of a full or partial disposal, it shall derecognise that associate and recognise in profit or loss the difference between the proceeds from the disposal and the carrying amount of the investment in the associate relating to the proportion disposed of or lost at the date significant influence is lost. The investor shall account for any retained interest using Section 11 *Basic Financial Instruments* or Section 12 *Other Financial Instruments Issues*, as appropriate. The carrying amount of the investment at the date that it ceases to be an associate shall be regarded as its cost on initial **measurement** as a **financial asset**; and

   (ii)   If an investor loses significant influence for reasons other than a partial disposal of its investment, the investor shall regard the carrying amount of the investment at that date as a new cost basis and shall account for the investment using Sections 11 or 12, as appropriate.

The gain or loss arising on the disposal shall also include those amounts that have been recognised in **other comprehensive income** in relation to that associate, where those amounts are required to be reclassified to profit or loss upon disposal in accordance with other sections of this FRS. Amounts that are not required to be reclassified to profit or loss upon disposal of the related assets or liabilities in accordance with other sections of this FRS shall be transferred directly to retained earnings.

Fair value model

When an investment in an associate is recognised initially, an investor that is not a parent, that chooses to adopt the fair value model, shall measure it at the transaction price. **14.9**

At each reporting date, an investor that is not a parent, that chooses to adopt the fair value model, shall measure its investments in associates at fair value, with changes in fair value recognised in other comprehensive income in accordance with paragraphs 17.15E and 17.15F, using the fair value guidance in paragraphs 11.27 to 11.32. An investor using the fair value model shall use the cost model for any investment in an associate for which it is impracticable to measure fair value reliably without undue cost or effort. **14.10**

The investor shall recognise dividends and other distributions received from the investment as income without regard to whether the distributions are from accumulated profits of the associate arising before or after the date of acquisition. **14.10A**

Presentation in individual and consolidated financial statements

Unless otherwise required under the Regulations, an investor shall classify investments in associates as **fixed assets**. **14.11**

Disclosures in individual and consolidated financial statements

The financial statements shall disclose: **14.12**

(a)   the accounting policy for investments in associates;
(b)   the carrying amount of investments in associates; and
(c)   the fair value of investments in associates accounted for using the equity method for which there are published price quotations.

For investments in associates accounted for in accordance with the cost model, an investor shall disclose the amount of dividends and other distributions recognised as income. **14.13**

For investments in associates accounted for in accordance with the equity method, an investor shall disclose separately its share of the profit or loss of such associates and its share of any **discontinued operations** of such associates. **14.14**

For investments in associates accounted for in accordance with the fair value model, an investor shall make the disclosures required by paragraphs 11.43 and 11.44. **14.15**

The individual financial statements of an investor that is not a parent shall disclose summarised financial information about the investments in the associates, along with the effect of including those investments as if they had been accounted for using the equity method. Investing entities that are exempt from preparing consolidated financial statements, or would be exempt if they had subsidiaries, are exempt from this requirement. **14.15A**

Section 15 *Investments in Joint Ventures*

Scope of this section

15.1   This section applies to accounting for **joint ventures** in **consolidated financial statements**, for investments in joint ventures in the **individual financial statements** of a **venturer** that is not a **parent**, and for investment in **jointly controlled operations** and **jointly controlled assets** in the **separate financial statements** of a venturer that is a parent. A venturer that is a parent shall account for interests in **jointly controlled entities** in its **separate financial statements** in accordance with paragraphs 9.26 and 9.26A, as appropriate.

Joint ventures defined

15.2   **Joint control** is the contractually agreed sharing of **control** over an economic activity, and exists only when the strategic financial and operating decisions relating to the activity require the unanimous consent of the parties sharing control (the venturers).

15.3   A joint venture is a contractual arrangement whereby two or more parties undertake an economic activity that is subject to joint control. Joint ventures can take the form of jointly controlled operations, jointly controlled assets, or jointly controlled entities.

Jointly controlled operations

15.4   The operation of some joint ventures involves the use of the **assets** and other resources of the venturers rather than the establishment of a corporation, partnership or other entity, or a financial structure that is separate from the venturers themselves. Each venturer uses its own **property, plant and equipment** and carries its own **inventories**. It also incurs its own **expenses** and **liabilities** and raises its own finance, which represent its own obligations. The joint venture activities may be carried out by the venturer's employees alongside the venturer's similar activities. The joint venture agreement usually provides a means by which the **revenue** from the sale of the joint product and any expenses incurred in common are shared among the venturers.

15.5   In respect of its interests in jointly controlled operations, a venturer shall recognise in its **financial statements**:

(a)   the assets that it controls and the liabilities that it incurs; and

(b)   the expenses that it incurs and its share of the **income** that it earns from the sale of goods or services by the joint venture.

Jointly controlled assets

15.6   Some joint ventures involve the joint control, and often the joint ownership, by the venturers of one or more assets contributed to, or acquired for the purpose of, the joint venture and dedicated to the purposes of the joint venture.

15.7   In respect of its interest in a jointly controlled asset, a venturer shall recognise in its financial statements:

(a)   its share of the jointly controlled assets, classified according to the nature of the assets;

(b)   any liabilities that it has incurred;

(c)   its share of any liabilities incurred jointly with the other venturers in relation to the joint venture;

(d)   any income from the sale or use of its share of the output of the joint venture, together with its share of any expenses incurred by the joint venture; and

(e)   any expenses that it has incurred in respect of its interest in the joint venture.

Jointly controlled entities

A jointly controlled entity is a joint venture that involves the establishment of a corporation, partnership or other entity in which each venturer has an interest. The entity operates in the same way as other entities, except that a contractual arrangement between the venturers establishes joint control over the economic activity of the entity.   **15.8**

Measurement—accounting policy election

A venturer that is not a parent but has one or more interests in jointly controlled entities shall, in its individual financial statements, account for all of its interests in jointly controlled entities using either: **15.9**

(a)   the cost model in accordance with paragraphs 15.10 to 15.11;

(b)   [not used]

(c)   the fair value model in accordance with paragraphs 15.14 to 15.15A; or

(d)   at fair value with changes in fair value recognised in profit or loss (paragraphs 11.27 to 11.32 provide guidance on fair value).

A venturer that is a parent shall, in its consolidated financial statements, account for all of its investments in jointly controlled entities using the equity method in accordance with paragraph 15.13, except as required by paragraph 15.9B.   **15.9A**

A venture that is a parent, shall measure its investments in jointly controlled entities **held as part of an investment portfolio** at **fair value** with changes in fair value recognised in **profit or loss** in the consolidated financial statements.   **15.9B**

Cost model

A venturer that is not a parent, that chooses to adopt the cost model, shall measure its investments in jointly controlled entities, at cost less any accumulated **impairment losses** recognised in accordance with Section 27 *Impairment of Assets.*   **15.10**

The venturer shall recognise distributions received from the investment as income without regard to whether the distributions are from accumulated profits of the jointly controlled entity arising before or after the date of acquisition.   **15.11**

[Not used]   **15.12**

Equity method

A venturer shall measure its investments in jointly controlled entities by the equity method using the procedures in accordance with paragraph 14.8 (substituting 'joint control' where that paragraph refers to 'significant influence', and 'jointly controlled entity' where that paragraph refers to 'associate').   **15.13**

Fair value model

When an investment in a jointly controlled entity is recognised initially, a venturer that is not a parent, that chooses to adopt the fair value model, shall measure it at the transaction price.   **15.14**

15.15   At each reporting date, a venturer that is not a parent, that chooses to adopt the fair value model, shall measure its investments in jointly controlled entities at fair value using the fair value guidance in paragraphs 11.27 to 11.32. Changes in fair value shall be recognised in accordance with paragraphs 17.15E and 17.15F. A venturer using the fair value model shall use the cost model for any investment in a jointly controlled entity for which it is **impracticable** to measure fair value reliably without undue cost or effort.

15.15A   The venturer shall recognise dividends and other distributions received from the investment as income without regard to whether the distributions are from accumulated profits of the jointly controlled entity arising before or after the date of acquisition.

Transactions between a venturer and a joint venture

15.16   When a venturer contributes or sells assets to a joint venture, **recognition** of any portion of a **gain** or loss from the transaction shall reflect the substance of the transaction. While the assets are retained by the joint venture, and provided the venturer has transferred the significant risks and rewards of ownership, the venturer shall recognise only that portion of the gain or loss that is attributable to the interests of the other venturers. The venturer shall recognise the full amount of any loss when the contribution or sale provides evidence of an impairment loss.

15.17   When a venturer purchases assets from a joint venture, the venturer shall not recognise its share of the profits of the joint venture from the transaction until it resells the assets to an independent party. A venturer shall recognise its share of the losses resulting from these transactions in the same way as profits except that losses shall be recognised immediately when they represent an impairment loss.

If investor does not have joint control

15.18   An investor in a joint venture that does not have joint control shall account for that investment in accordance with Section 11 *Basic Financial Instruments* or Section 12 *Other Financial Instruments Issues* or, if it has **significant influence** in the joint venture, in accordance with Section 14 *Investments in Associates*.

Disclosures in individual and consolidated financial statements

15.19   The financial statements shall disclose the following:

    (a)   the **accounting policy** for recognising investments in jointly controlled entities;

    (b)   the **carrying amount** of investments in jointly controlled entities;

    (c)   the fair value of investments in jointly controlled entities accounted for using the equity method for which there are published price quotations; and

  *(d)   the aggregate amount of its commitments relating to joint ventures, including its share in the capital commitments that have been incurred jointly with other venturers, as well as its share of the capital commitments of the joint ventures themselves.

15.20   For jointly controlled entities accounted for in accordance with the equity method, the venturer shall disclose separately its share of the profit or loss of such investments and its share of any **discontinued operations** of such jointly controlled entities.

15.21   For jointly controlled entities accounted for in accordance with the fair value model, the venturer shall make the disclosures required by paragraphs 11.43 and 11.44.

The individual financial statements of a venturer that is not a parent shall disclose summarised financial information about the investments in the jointly controlled entities, along with the effect of including those investments as if they had been accounted for using the equity method. Investing entities that are exempt from preparing consolidated financial statements, or would be exempt if they had subsidiaries, are exempt from this requirement.   **15.21A**

Section 16 *Investment Property*

Scope of this section

This section applies to accounting for investments in land or buildings that meet the definition of **investment property** in paragraph 16.2 and some property interests held by a lessee under an **operating lease** (see paragraph 16.3) that are treated like investment property. Only investment property whose **fair value** can be measured reliably without undue cost or effort on an on-going basis is accounted for in accordance with this section at fair value through **profit or loss**. All other investment property is accounted for as **property, plant and equipment** using the cost model in Section 17 *Property, Plant and Equipment* and remains within the scope of Section 17 unless a reliable measure of fair value becomes available and it is expected that fair value will be reliably measurable on an on-going basis.   **16.1**

Definition and initial recognition of investment property

Investment property is property (land or a building, or part of a building, or both) held by the owner or by the lessee under a **finance lease** to earn rentals or for capital appreciation or both, rather than for: **16.2**

(a)   use in the production or supply of goods or services or for administrative purposes; or

(b)   sale in the ordinary course of business.

A property interest that is held by a lessee under an operating lease may be classified and accounted for as investment property using this section if, and only if, the property would otherwise meet the definition of an investment property and the lessee can measure the fair value of the property interest without undue cost or effort on an on-going basis. This classification alternative is available on a property-by-property basis.   **16.3**

Property held primarily for the provision of social benefits, eg social housing held by a **public benefit entity**, shall not be classified as investment property and shall be accounted for as property, plant and equipment in accordance with Section 17.   **16.3A**

Mixed use property shall be separated between investment property and property, plant and equipment. However, if the fair value of the investment property component cannot be measured reliably without undue cost or effort, the entire property shall be accounted for as property, plant and equipment in accordance with Section 17.   **16.4**

Measurement at initial recognition

An entity shall measure investment property at its cost at initial **recognition**. The cost of a purchased investment property comprises its purchase price and any directly attributable expenditure such as legal and brokerage fees, property transfer taxes and other transaction costs. If payment is deferred beyond normal credit terms, the cost is the **present value** of all future payments. An entity shall determine the cost of a self-constructed investment property in accordance with paragraphs 17.10 to 17.14.   **16.5**

16.6 The initial cost of a property interest held under a **lease** and classified as an investment property shall be as prescribed for a finance lease by paragraphs 20.9 and 20.10, even if the lease would otherwise be classified as an operating lease if it was in the scope of Section 20 *Leases*. In other words, the **asset** is recognised at the lower of the fair value of the property and the present value of the **minimum lease payments**. An equivalent amount is recognised as a **liability** in accordance with paragraphs 20.9 and 20.10. Any premium paid for a lease is treated as part of the minimum lease payments for this purpose, and is therefore included in the cost of the asset, but is excluded from the liability.

Measurement after recognition

16.7 Investment property whose fair value can be measured reliably without undue cost or effort shall be measured at fair value at each **reporting date** with changes in fair value recognised in profit or loss. If a property interest held under a lease is classified as investment property, the item accounted for at fair value is that interest and not the underlying property. Paragraphs 11.27 to 11.32 provide guidance on determining fair value. An entity shall account for all other investment property as property, plant and equipment using the cost model in Section 17.

Transfers

16.8 If a reliable measure of fair value is no longer available without undue cost or effort for an item of investment property measured using the fair value model, the entity shall thereafter account for that item as property, plant and equipment in accordance with Section 17 until a reliable measure of fair value becomes available. The **carrying amount** of the investment property on that date becomes its cost under Section 17. Paragraph 16.10(e) (iii) requires disclosure of this change. It is a change of circumstances and not a change in **accounting policy**.

16.9 Other than as required by paragraph 16.8, an entity shall transfer a property to, or from, investment property only when the property first meets, or ceases to meet, the definition of investment property.

Disclosures

16.10 An entity shall disclose the following for all investment property accounted for at fair value through profit or loss (paragraph 16.7):

*(a) the methods and significant assumptions applied in determining the fair value of investment property;

(b) the extent to which the fair value of investment property (as measured or disclosed in the **financial statements**) is based on a valuation by an independent valuer who holds a recognised and relevant professional qualification and has recent experience in the location and class of the investment property being valued. If there has been no such valuation, that fact shall be disclosed;

*(c) the existence and amounts of restrictions on the realisability of investment property or the remittance of **income** and proceeds of disposal;

*(d) contractual obligations to purchase, construct or develop investment property or for repairs, maintenance or enhancements; and

*(e) a reconciliation between the carrying amounts of investment property at the beginning and end of the period, showing separately:

(i) additions, disclosing separately those additions resulting from acquisitions through **business combinations**;

*(ii) net gains or losses from fair value adjustments;

  (iii) transfers to property, plant and equipment when a reliable measure of fair value is no longer available without undue cost or effort (see paragraph 16.8);
  (iv) transfers to and from **inventories** and owner-occupied property; and
  (v) other changes.

This reconciliation need not be presented for prior periods.

In accordance with Section 20 *Leases*, an entity shall provide all relevant disclosures **16.11**
required in that section about leases into which it has entered.

Section 17 *Property, Plant and Equipment*

Scope

This section applies to the accounting for **property, plant and equipment** and to **17.1**
investment property whose **fair value** cannot be measured reliably without undue cost or
effort. Section 16 *Investment Property* applies to investment property whose fair value can
be measured reliably without undue cost or effort.

Property, plant and equipment are tangible assets that: **17.2**

(a) are held for use in the production or supply of goods or services, for rental to others,
  or for administrative purposes; and
(b) are expected to be used during more than one period;

Property, plant and equipment does not include: **17.3**

(a) **biological assets** related to **agricultural activity** (see Section 34 *Specialised
  Activities*) or **heritage assets** (see Section 34); or
(b) mineral rights and mineral reserves, such as oil, natural gas and similar non-
  regenerative resources (see Section 34).

Recognition

An entity shall apply the **recognition** criteria in paragraph 2.27 in determining whether to **17.4**
recognise an item of property, plant or equipment. Therefore, the entity shall recognise the
cost of an item of property, plant and equipment as an **asset** if, and only if:

(a) it is **probable** that future economic benefits associated with the item will flow to the
  entity; and
(b) the cost of the item can be measured reliably.

Spare parts and servicing equipment are usually carried as **inventory** and recognised **17.5**
in **profit or loss** as consumed. However, major spare parts and stand-by equipment are
property, plant and equipment when an entity expects to use them during more than one
period. Similarly, if the spare parts and servicing equipment can be used only in connection
with an item of property, plant and equipment, they are considered property, plant and
equipment.

Parts of some items of property, plant and equipment may require replacement at regular **17.6**
intervals (eg the roof of a building). An entity shall add to the **carrying amount** of an item
of property, plant and equipment the cost of replacing part of such an item when that cost
is incurred if the replacement part is expected to provide incremental future benefits to the
entity. The carrying amount of those parts that are replaced is derecognised in accordance
with paragraphs 17.27 to 17.30. Paragraph 17.16 provides that if the major components
of an item of property, plant and equipment have significantly different patterns of

consumption of economic benefits, an entity shall allocate the initial cost of the asset to its major components and depreciate each such component separately over its **useful life**.

17.7   A condition of continuing to operate an item of property, plant and equipment (eg a bus) may be performing regular major inspections for faults regardless of whether parts of the item are replaced. When each major inspection is performed, its cost is recognised in the carrying amount of the item of property, plant and equipment as a replacement if the recognition criteria are satisfied. Any remaining carrying amount of the cost of the previous major inspection (as distinct from physical parts) is derecognised. This is done regardless of whether the cost of the previous major inspection was identified in the transaction in which the item was acquired or constructed. If necessary, the estimated cost of a future similar inspection may be used as an indication of what the cost of the existing inspection component was when the item was acquired or constructed.

17.8   Land and buildings are separable assets, and an entity shall account for them separately, even when they are acquired together.

Measurement at initial recognition

17.9   An entity shall measure an item of property, plant and equipment at initial recognition at its cost.

Elements of cost

17.10   The cost of an item of property, plant and equipment comprises all of the following:

(a)   Its purchase price, including legal and brokerage fees, import duties and non-refundable purchase taxes, after deducting trade discounts and rebates.

(b)   Any costs directly attributable to bringing the asset to the location and condition necessary for it to be capable of operating in the manner intended by management. These can include the costs of site preparation, initial delivery and handling, installation and assembly, and testing of functionality.

(c)   The initial estimate of the costs, recognised and measured in accordance with Section 21 *Provisions and Contingencies*, of dismantling and removing the item and restoring the site on which it is located, the obligation for which an entity incurs either when the item is acquired or as a consequence of having used the item during a particular period for purposes other than to produce inventories during that period.

(d)   Any **borrowing costs** capitalised in accordance with paragraph 25.2.

17.11   The following costs are not costs of an item of property, plant and equipment, and an entity shall recognise them as an **expense** when they are incurred:

(a)   costs of opening a new facility;

(b)   costs of introducing a new product or service (including costs of advertising and promotional activities);

(c)   costs of conducting business in a new location or with a new class of customer (including costs of staff training); and

(d)   administration and other general overhead costs.

17.12   The **income** and related expenses of incidental operations during construction or development of an item of property, plant and equipment are recognised in profit or loss if those operations are not necessary to bring the item to its intended location and operating condition.

Measurement of cost

The cost of an item of property, plant and equipment is the cash price equivalent at the recognition date. If payment is deferred beyond normal credit terms, the cost is the **present value** of all future payments.

17.13

Exchanges of assets

An item of property, plant or equipment may be acquired in exchange for a non-monetary asset or assets, or a combination of monetary and non-monetary assets. An entity shall measure the cost of the acquired asset at fair value unless:

17.14

(a)   the exchange transaction lacks commercial substance; or

(b)   the fair value of neither the asset received nor the asset given up is reliably measurable. In that case, the asset's cost is measured at the carrying amount of the asset given up.

Measurement after initial recognition

An entity shall measure all items of property, plant and equipment after initial recognition using the cost model (in accordance with paragraph 17.15A) or the revaluation model (in accordance with paragraphs 17.15B to 17.15F). Where the revaluation model is selected, this shall be applied to all items of property, plant and equipment in the same class (ie having a similar nature, function or use in the business). An entity shall recognise the costs of day-to-day servicing of an item of property, plant and equipment in profit or loss in the period in which the costs are incurred.

17.15

Cost model

Under the cost model, an entity shall measure an item of property, plant and equipment at cost less any accumulated **depreciation** and any accumulated **impairment losses**.

17.15A

Revaluation model

Under the revaluation model, an item of property, plant and equipment whose fair value can be measured reliably shall be carried at a revalued amount, being its fair value at the date of revaluation less any subsequent accumulated depreciation and subsequent accumulated impairment losses. Revaluations shall be made with sufficient regularity to ensure that the carrying amount does not differ materially from that which would be determined using fair value at the end of the **reporting period**.

17.15B

The fair value of land and buildings is usually determined from market-based evidence by appraisal that is normally undertaken by professionally qualified valuers. The fair value of items of plant and equipment is usually their market value determined by appraisal. Paragraphs 11.27 to 11.32 provide further guidance on determining fair value.

17.15C

If there is no market-based evidence of fair value because of the specialised nature of the item of property, plant and equipment and the item is rarely sold, except as part of a continuing business, an entity may need to estimate fair value using an income or a **depreciated replacement cost** approach.

17.15D

Reporting gains and losses on revaluations

If an asset's carrying amount is increased as a result of a revaluation, the increase shall be recognised in **other comprehensive income** and accumulated in **equity**. However, the increase shall be recognised in profit or loss to the extent that it reverses a revaluation decrease of the same asset previously recognised in profit or loss.

17.15E

17.15F   The decrease of an asset's carrying amount as a result of a revaluation shall be recognised in other comprehensive income to the extent of any previously recognised revaluation increase accumulated in equity, in respect of that asset. If a revaluation decrease exceeds the accumulated revaluation gains accumulated in equity in respect of that asset, the excess shall be recognised in **profit or loss**.

Depreciation

17.16   If the major components of an item of property, plant and equipment have significantly different patterns of consumption of economic benefits, an entity shall allocate the initial cost of the asset to its major components and depreciate each such component separately over its useful life. Other assets shall be depreciated over their useful lives as a single asset. There are some exceptions, such as land which generally has an unlimited useful life and therefore is not usually depreciated.

17.17   The depreciation charge for each period shall be recognised in profit or loss unless another section of this FRS requires the cost to be recognised as part of the cost of an asset. For example, the depreciation of manufacturing property, plant and equipment is included in the costs of inventories (see Section 13 *Inventories*).

Depreciable amount and depreciation period

17.18   An entity shall allocate the **depreciable amount** of an asset on a systematic basis over its useful life.

17.19   Factors such as a change in how an asset is used, significant unexpected wear and tear, technological advancement, and changes in market prices may indicate that the **residual value** or useful life of an asset has changed since the most recent annual **reporting date**. If such indicators are present, an entity shall review its previous estimates and, if current expectations differ, amend the residual value, depreciation method or useful life. The entity shall account for the change in residual value, depreciation method or useful life as a change in an accounting estimate in accordance with paragraphs 10.15 to 10.18.

17.20   Depreciation of an asset begins when it is available for use, ie when it is in the location and condition necessary for it to be capable of operating in the manner intended by management. Depreciation of an asset ceases when the asset is derecognised. Depreciation does not cease when the asset becomes idle or is retired from active use unless the asset is fully depreciated. However, under usage methods of depreciation the depreciation charge can be zero while there is no production.

17.21   An entity shall consider all the following factors in determining the useful life of an asset:

(a)   The expected usage of the asset. Usage is assessed by reference to the asset's expected capacity or physical output.

(b)   Expected physical wear and tear, which depends on operational factors such as the number of shifts for which the asset is to be used and the repair and maintenance programme, and the care and maintenance of the asset while idle.

(c)   Technical or commercial obsolescence arising from changes or improvements in production, or from a change in the market demand for the product or service output of the asset.

(d)   Legal or similar limits on the use of the asset, such as the expiry dates of related **leases**.

Depreciation method

An entity shall select a depreciation method that reflects the pattern in which it expects to **17.22** consume the asset's future economic benefits. The possible depreciation methods include the straight-line method, the diminishing balance method and a method based on usage such as the units of production method.

If there is an indication that there has been a significant change since the last annual **17.23** reporting date in the pattern by which an entity expects to consume an asset's future economic benefits, the entity shall review its present depreciation method and, if current expectations differ, change the depreciation method to reflect the new pattern. The entity shall account for the change as a change in an accounting estimate in accordance with paragraphs 10.15 to 10.18.

Impairment

Recognition and measurement of impairment

At each reporting date, an entity shall apply Section 27 *Impairment of Assets* to determine **17.24** whether an item or group of items of property, plant and equipment is impaired and, if so, how to recognise and measure the impairment loss. That section explains when and how an entity reviews the carrying amount of its assets, how it determines the **recoverable amount** of an asset, and when it recognises or reverses an impairment loss.

Compensation for impairment

An entity shall include in profit or loss, compensation from third parties for items **17.25** of property, plant and equipment that were impaired, lost or given up only when the compensation is virtually certain.

Property, plant and equipment held for sale

Paragraph 27.9(f) states that a plan to dispose of an asset before the previously expected **17.26** date is an indicator of impairment that triggers the calculation of the asset's recoverable amount for the purpose of determining whether the asset is impaired.

Derecognition

An entity shall derecognise an item of property, plant and equipment: **17.27**

(a) on disposal; or
(b) when no future economic benefits are expected from its use or disposal.

An entity shall recognise the **gain** or loss on the **derecognition** of an item of property, **17.28** plant and equipment in profit or loss when the item is derecognised (unless Section 20 *Leases* requires otherwise on a sale and leaseback). The entity shall not classify such gains as **revenue**.

In determining the date of disposal of an item, an entity shall apply the criteria in Section 23 **17.29** *Revenue* for recognising revenue from the sale of goods. Section 20 applies to disposal by a sale and leaseback.

An entity shall determine the gain or loss arising from the derecognition of an item of **17.30** property, plant and equipment as the difference between the net disposal proceeds, if any, and the carrying amount of the item.

Disclosures

17.31   An entity shall disclose the following for each class of property, plant and equipment:

*(a)   the measurement bases used for determining the gross carrying amount;

(b)   the depreciation methods used;

(c)   the useful lives or the depreciation rates used;

*(d)   the gross carrying amount and the accumulated depreciation (aggregated with accumulated impairment losses) at the beginning and end of the reporting period;

*(e)   a reconciliation of the carrying amount at the beginning and end of the reporting period showing separately:

(i)   additions;

(ii)   disposals;

(iii) acquisitions through **business combinations**;

(iv)   revaluations;

(v)   transfers to or from investment property if a reliable measure of fair value becomes available or unavailable (see paragraph 16.8);

(vi)   impairment losses recognised or reversed in profit or loss in accordance with Section 27 *Impairment of Assets*;

(vii) depreciation; and

(viii) other changes.

This reconciliation need not be presented for prior periods.

17.32   The entity shall also disclose the following:

*(a)   the existence and carrying amounts of property, plant and equipment to which the entity has restricted title or that is pledged as security for **liabilities**; and

*(b)   the amount of contractual commitments for the acquisition of property, plant and equipment.

17.32A   If items of property, plant and equipment are stated at revalued amounts, the following shall be disclosed:

*(a)   the effective date of the revaluation;

(b)   whether an independent valuer was involved;

*(c)   the methods and significant assumptions applied in estimating the items' fair values; and

*(d)   for each revalued class of property, plant and equipment, the carrying amount that would have been recognised had the assets been carried under the cost model.

Section 18 *Intangible Assets other than Goodwill*

Scope of this section

18.1   This section applies to accounting for all **intangible assets** other than **goodwill** (see Section 19 *Business Combinations and Goodwill*) and intangible assets held by an entity for sale in the ordinary course of business (see Section 13 *Inventories* and Section 23 *Revenue*).

18.1A   This section does not apply to the accounting for **deferred acquisition costs** and intangible assets arising from contracts in the scope of FRS 103 *Insurance Contracts*, except for the disclosure requirements in this section which apply to intangible assets arising from contracts in the scope of FRS 103.

An intangible asset is an identifiable non-monetary asset without physical substance. Such an **asset** is identifiable when: **18.2**

(a)   it is separable, ie capable of being separated or divided from the entity and sold, transferred, licensed, rented or exchanged, either individually or together with a related contract, asset or **liability**; or

(b)   it arises from contractual or other legal rights, regardless of whether those rights are transferable or separable from the entity or from other rights and obligations.

This section does not apply to the following: **18.3**

(a)   **financial assets** (see Section 11 *Basic Financial Instruments* and Section 12 *Other Financial Instruments Issues*);

(b)   **heritage assets** (see Section 34 *Specialised Activities*); or

(c)   mineral rights and mineral reserves, such as oil, natural gas and similar non-regenerative resources (see Section 34).

Recognition

General principle for recognising intangible assets

An entity shall apply the **recognition** criteria in paragraph 2.27 in determining whether to recognise an intangible asset. Therefore, the entity shall recognise an intangible asset as an asset if, and only if: **18.4**

(a)   it is **probable** that the expected future economic benefits that are attributable to the asset will flow to the entity; and

(b)   the cost or value of the asset can be measured reliably.

An entity shall assess the probability of expected future economic benefits using reasonable and supportable assumptions that represent management's best estimate of the economic conditions that will exist over the **useful life** of the asset.   **18.5**

An entity uses judgement to assess the degree of certainty attached to the flow of future economic benefits that are attributable to the use of the asset on the basis of the evidence available at the time of initial recognition, giving greater weight to external evidence.   **18.6**

The probability recognition criterion in paragraph 18.4(a) is always considered satisfied for intangible assets that are separately acquired.   **18.7**

Acquisition as part of a business combination

An intangible asset acquired in a **business combination** is normally recognised as an asset because its **fair value** can be measured with sufficient **reliability**. However, an intangible asset acquired in a business combination is not recognised when it arises from legal or other contractual rights and there is no history or evidence of exchange transactions for the same or similar assets, and otherwise estimating fair value would be dependent on immeasurable variables.   **18.8**

Internally generated intangible assets

To assess whether an internally generated intangible asset meets the criteria for recognition, an entity classifies the generation of the asset into: **18.8A**

(a)   a **research** phase; and

(b)   a **development** phase.

18.8B   If an entity cannot distinguish the research phase from the development phase of an internal project to create an intangible asset, the entity treats the expenditure on that project as if it were incurred in the research phase only.

18.8C   An entity shall recognise expenditure on the following items as an **expense** and shall not recognise such expenditure as intangible assets:

(a)   Internally generated brands, logos, publishing titles, customer lists and items similar in substance.

(b)   Start-up activities (ie start-up costs), which include establishment costs such as legal and secretarial costs incurred in establishing a legal entity, expenditure to open a new facility or business (ie pre-opening costs) and expenditure for starting new operations or launching new products or processes (ie pre-operating costs).

(c)   Training activities.

(d)   Advertising and promotional activities (unless it meets the definition of **inventories held for distribution at no or nominal consideration** (see paragraph 13.4A)).

(e)   Relocating or reorganising part or all of an entity.

(f)   Internally generated goodwill.

18.8D   Paragraph 18.8C does not preclude recognising a prepayment as an asset when payment for goods or services has been made in advance of the delivery of the goods or the rendering of the services.

Research phase

18.8E   No intangible asset arising from research (or from the research phase of an internal project) shall be recognised. Expenditure on research (or on the research phase of an internal project) shall be recognised as an expense when it is incurred.

18.8F   In the research phase of an internal project, an entity cannot demonstrate that an intangible asset exists that will generate probable future economic benefits.

18.8G   Examples of research activities are:

(a)   Activities aimed at obtaining new knowledge.

(b)   The search for, evaluation and final selection of, applications of research findings and other knowledge.

(c)   The search for alternatives for materials, devices, products, processes, systems or services.

(d)   The formulation, design, evaluation and final selection of possible alternatives for new or improved material, devices, projects, processes, systems or services.

Development phase

18.8H   An entity may recognise an intangible asset arising from development (or from the development phase of an internal project) if, and only if, an entity can demonstrate all of the following:

(a)   The technical feasibility of completing the intangible asset so that it will be available for use or sale.

(b)   Its intention to complete the intangible asset and use or sell it.

(c)   Its ability to use or sell the intangible asset.

(d)   How the intangible asset will generate probable future economic benefits. Among other things, the entity can demonstrate the existence of a market for the output of the intangible asset or the intangible asset itself or, if it is to be used internally, the usefulness of the intangible asset.

(e) The availability of adequate technical, financial and other resources to complete the development and to use or sell the intangible asset.

(f) Its ability to measure reliably the expenditure attributable to the intangible asset during its development.

In the development phase of an internal project, an entity can, in some instances, identify an intangible asset and demonstrate that the asset will generate probable future economic benefits. This is because the development phase of a project is further advanced than the research phase. **18.8I**

Examples of development activities are: **18.8J**

(a) The design, construction and testing of pre-production or pre-use prototypes and models.

(b) The design of tools, jigs, moulds and dies involving new technology.

(c) The design, construction and operation of a pilot plant that is not of a scale economically feasible for commercial production.

(d) The design, construction and testing of a chosen alternative for new or improved materials, devices, products, processes, systems or services.

Where an entity adopts a policy of capitalising expenditure in the development phase that meets the conditions of paragraph 18.8H, that policy shall be applied consistently to all expenditure that meets the requirements of paragraph 18.8H. Expenditure that does not meet the conditions of paragraph 18.8H is expensed as incurred. **18.8K**

Initial measurement

An entity shall measure an intangible asset initially at cost. **18.9**

Separate acquisition

The cost of a separately acquired intangible asset comprises: **18.10**

(a) its purchase price, including import duties and non-refundable purchase taxes, after deducting trade discounts and rebates; and

(b) any directly attributable cost of preparing the asset for its intended use.

Internally generated intangible assets

The cost of an internally generated intangible asset for the purpose of paragraph 18.9 is the sum of expenditure incurred from the date when the intangible asset first meets the recognition criteria in paragraphs 18.4 and 18.8H. **18.10A**

The cost of an internally generated intangible asset comprises all directly attributable costs necessary to create, produce and prepare the asset to be capable of operating in the manner intended by management. Examples of directly attributable costs are: **18.10B**

(a) costs of materials and services used or consumed in generating the intangible asset;

(b) costs of **employee benefits** (as defined in Section 28 *Employee Benefits*) arising from the generation of the intangible asset;

(c) fees to register a legal right; and

(d) **amortisation** of patents and licences that are used to generate the intangible asset.

Section 25 *Borrowing Costs* specifies criteria for the recognition of interest as an element of the cost of an internally generated intangible asset.

Acquisition as part of a business combination

18.11   If an intangible asset is acquired in a business combination, the cost of that intangible asset is its fair value at the **acquisition date**.

Acquisition by way of a grant

18.12   If an intangible asset is acquired by way of a grant, the cost of that intangible asset is its fair value at the date the grant is received or receivable in accordance with Section 24 *Government Grants*.

Exchanges of assets

18.13   An intangible asset may be acquired in exchange for a non-monetary asset or assets, or a combination of monetary and non-monetary assets. An entity shall measure the cost of such an intangible asset at fair value unless:

(a)   the exchange transaction lacks commercial substance; or

(b)   the fair value of neither the asset received nor the asset given up is reliably measurable. In that case, the asset's cost is measured at the **carrying amount** of the asset given up.

18.14   [Replaced by paragraph 18.8A]

18.15   [Moved to paragraph 18.8C]

18.16   [Moved to paragraph 18.8D]

Past expenses not to be recognised as an asset

18.17   Expenditure on an intangible item that was initially recognised as an expense shall not be recognised at a later date as part of the cost of an asset.

Measurement after initial recognition

18.18   An entity shall measure intangible assets after initial recognition using the cost model (in accordance with paragraph 18.18A) or the revaluation model (in accordance with paragraphs 18.18B to 18.18H). Where the revaluation model is selected, this shall be applied to all intangible assets in the same class. If an intangible asset in a class of revalued intangible assets cannot be revalued because there is no **active market** for this asset, the asset shall be carried at its cost less any accumulated amortisation and impairment losses.

Cost model

18.18A   Under the cost model, an entity shall measure its assets at cost less any accumulated amortisation and any accumulated **impairment losses**. The requirements for amortisation are set out in paragraphs 18.19 to 18.24.

Revaluation model

18.18B   Under the revaluation model, an intangible asset shall be carried at a revalued amount, being its fair value at the date of revaluation less any subsequent accumulated amortisation and subsequent accumulated impairment losses, provided that the fair value can be determined by reference to an active market. The requirements for amortisation are set out in paragraphs 18.19 to 18.24.

The revaluation model does not allow: **18.18C**

(a) the revaluation of intangible assets that have not previously been recognised as
     assets; or
(b) the initial recognition of intangible assets at amounts other than cost.

Revaluations shall be made with sufficient regularity to ensure that the carrying amount   **18.18D**
does not differ materially from that which would be determined using fair value at the end
of the **reporting period**.

If the fair value of a revalued intangible asset can no longer be determined by reference to   **18.18E**
an active market in accordance with the requirements of paragraph 18.18B, the carrying
amount of the asset shall be its revalued amount at the date of the last revaluation by
reference to the active market, less any subsequent accumulated amortisation and any
subsequent accumulated impairment losses.

The revaluation model is applied after an asset has been initially recognised at cost.   **18.18F**
However, if only part of the cost of an intangible asset is recognised as an asset because
the asset did not meet the criteria for recognition until part of the way through the process
(see paragraph 18.10A), the revaluation model may be applied to the whole of that asset.

Reporting gains and losses on revaluations

If an asset's carrying amount is increased as a result of a revaluation, the increase shall   **18.18G**
be recognised in **other comprehensive income** and accumulated in **equity**. However, the
increase shall be recognised in **profit or loss** to the extent that it reverses a revaluation
decrease of the same asset previously recognised in profit or loss.

The decrease of an asset's carrying amount as a result of a revaluation shall be recognised   **18.18H**
in other comprehensive income to the extent of any previously recognised revaluation
increase accumulated in equity, in respect of that asset. If a revaluation decrease exceeds
the accumulated revaluation gains recognised in equity in respect of that asset, the excess
shall be recognised in profit or loss.

Amortisation over useful life

For the purpose of this FRS, all intangible assets shall be considered to have a finite useful   **18.19**
life. The useful life of an intangible asset that arises from contractual or other legal rights
shall not exceed the period of the contractual or other legal rights, but may be shorter
depending on the period over which the entity expects to use the asset. If the contractual
or other legal rights are conveyed for a limited term that can be renewed, the useful life of
the intangible asset shall include the renewal period(s) only if there is evidence to support
renewal by the entity without significant cost.

If, in exceptional cases, an entity is unable to make a reliable estimate of the useful life of   **18.20**
an intangible asset, the life shall not exceed 10 years.

Amortisation period and amortisation method

An entity shall allocate the **depreciable amount** of an intangible asset on a systematic   **18.21**
basis over its useful life. The amortisation charge for each period shall be recognised in
profit or loss, unless another section of this FRS requires the cost to be recognised as part
of the cost of an asset. For example, the amortisation of an intangible asset may be included
in the costs of **inventories** or **property, plant and equipment**.

18.22   Amortisation begins when the intangible asset is available for use, ie when it is in the location and condition necessary for it to be usable in the manner intended by management. Amortisation ceases when the asset is derecognised. The entity shall choose an amortisation method that reflects the pattern in which it expects to consume the asset's future economic benefits. If the entity cannot determine that pattern reliably, it shall use the straight-line method.

Residual value

18.23   An entity shall assume that the **residual value** of an intangible asset is zero unless:

   (a)   there is a commitment by a third party to purchase the asset at the end of its useful life; or
   (b)   there is an active market for the asset and:

       (i)   residual value can be determined by reference to that market; and
       (ii)   it is probable that such a market will exist at the end of the asset's useful life.

Review of amortisation period and amortisation method

18.24   Factors such as a change in how an intangible asset is used, technological advancement, and changes in market prices may indicate that the residual value or useful life of an intangible asset has changed since the most recent annual **reporting date**. If such indicators are present, an entity shall review its previous estimates and, if current expectations differ, amend the residual value, amortisation method or useful life. The entity shall account for the change in residual value, amortisation method or useful life as a change in an accounting estimate in accordance with paragraphs 10.15 to 10.18.

Recoverability of the carrying amount—impairment losses

18.25   To determine whether an intangible asset is impaired, an entity shall apply Section 27 *Impairment of Assets*. That section explains when and how an entity reviews the carrying amount of its assets, how it determines the **recoverable amount** of an asset, and when it recognises or reverses an impairment loss.

Retirements and disposals

18.26   An entity shall derecognise an intangible asset, and shall recognise a **gain** or loss in profit or loss:

   (a)   on disposal; or
   (b)   when no future economic benefits are expected from its use or disposal.

Disclosures

18.27   An entity shall disclose the following for each class of intangible assets:

   *(a)   the useful lives or the amortisation rates used and the reasons for choosing those periods;
   (b)   the amortisation methods used;
   *(c)   the gross carrying amount and any accumulated amortisation (aggregated with accumulated impairment losses) at the beginning and end of the reporting period;
   (d)   the line item(s) in the **statement of comprehensive income** (or in the **income statement**, if presented) in which any amortisation of intangible assets is included; and

*(e) a reconciliation of the carrying amount at the beginning and end of the reporting period showing separately:

(i) additions, indicating separately those from internal development and those acquired separately;

(ii) disposals;

(iii) acquisitions through business combinations;

(iv) revaluations;

(v) amortisation;

(vi) impairment losses; and

(vii) other changes.

This reconciliation need not be presented for prior periods.

An entity shall also disclose: **18.28**

(a) a description, the carrying amount and remaining amortisation period of any individual intangible asset that is **material** to the entity's **financial statements**;

(b) for intangible assets acquired by way of a grant and initially recognised at fair value (see paragraph 18.12):

(i) the fair value initially recognised for these assets; and

(ii) their carrying amounts.

*(c) the existence and carrying amounts of intangible assets to which the entity has restricted title or that are pledged as security for liabilities; and

*(d) the amount of contractual commitments for the acquisition of intangible assets.

An entity shall disclose the aggregate amount of research and development expenditure   **18.29**
recognised as an expense during the period (ie the amount of expenditure incurred internally on research and development that has not been capitalised as an intangible asset or as part of the cost of another asset that meets the recognition criteria in this FRS).

If intangible assets are accounted for at revalued amounts, an entity shall disclose the   **18.29A**
following:

*(a) the effective date of the revaluation;

(b) whether an independent valuer was involved;

*(c) the methods and significant assumptions applied in estimating the assets' fair values; and

*(d) for each revalued class of intangible assets, the carrying amount that would have been recognised had the assets been carried under the cost model.

Section 19 *Business Combinations and Goodwill*

Scope of this section

This section applies to accounting for **business combinations**. It provides guidance on   **19.1**
identifying the acquirer, measuring the cost of the business combination, and allocating that cost to the **assets** acquired and **liabilities** and **provisions** for **contingent liabilities** assumed. It also addresses accounting for **goodwill** both at the time of a business combination and subsequently.

This section specifies the accounting for all business combinations except: **19.2**

(a) the formation of a **joint venture**; and

(b) acquisition of a group of assets that does not constitute a **business**.

PBE19.2A   In addition, **public benefit entities** shall consider the requirements of Section 34 *Specialised Activities* in accounting for **public benefit entity combinations**.

Business combinations defined

19.3   A business combination is the bringing together of separate entities or businesses into one reporting entity. The result of nearly all business combinations is that one entity, the acquirer, obtains **control** of one or more other businesses, the acquiree. The **acquisition date** is the date on which the acquirer obtains control of the acquiree.

19.4   A business combination may be structured in a variety of ways for legal, taxation or other reasons. It may involve the purchase by an entity of the **equity** of another entity, the purchase of all the net assets of another entity, the assumption of the liabilities of another entity, or the purchase of some of the net assets of another entity that together form one or more businesses.

19.5   A business combination may be effected by the issue of equity instruments, the transfer of **cash**, **cash equivalents** or other assets, or a mixture of these. The transaction may be between the shareholders of the combining entities or between one entity and the shareholders of another entity. It may involve the establishment of a new entity to control the combining entities or net assets transferred, or the restructuring of one or more of the combining entities.

Purchase method

19.6   All business combinations shall be accounted for by applying the purchase method, except for:

    (a)   **group reconstructions** which may be accounted for by using the merger accounting method (see paragraphs 19.27 to 19.33); and

    (b)   public benefit entity **combinations that are in substance a gift** or that are a **merger** which shall be accounted for in accordance with Section 34 *Specialised Activities*.

19.7   Applying the purchase method involves the following steps:

    (a)   identifying an acquirer;

    (b)   measuring the cost of the business combination; and

    (c)   allocating, at the acquisition date, the cost of the business combination to the assets acquired and liabilities and provisions for contingent liabilities assumed.

Identifying the acquirer

19.8   An acquirer shall be identified for all business combinations accounted for by applying the purchase method. The acquirer is the combining entity that obtains control of the other combining entities or businesses.

19.9   Control is the power to govern the financial and operating policies of an entity or business so as to obtain benefits from its activities. Control of one entity by another is described in Section 9 *Consolidated and Separate Financial Statements*.

19.10   Although it may sometimes be difficult to identify an acquirer, there are usually indications that one exists. For example:

    (a)   If the **fair value** of one of the combining entities is significantly greater than that of the other combining entity, the entity with the greater fair value is likely to be the acquirer.

(b) If the business combination is effected through an exchange of voting ordinary equity instruments for cash or other assets, the entity giving up cash or other assets is likely to be the acquirer.

(c) If the business combination results in the management of one of the combining entities being able to dominate the selection of the management team of the resulting combined entity, the entity whose management is able so to dominate is likely to be the acquirer.

Cost of a business combination

The acquirer shall measure the cost of a business combination as the aggregate of: **19.11**

(a) the fair values, at the acquisition date, of assets given, liabilities incurred or assumed, and equity instruments issued by the acquirer, in exchange for control of the acquiree; plus

(b) any costs directly attributable to the business combination.

Where control is achieved following a series of transactions, the cost of the business   **19.11A** combination is the aggregate of the fair values of the assets given, liabilities assumed and equity instruments issued by the acquirer at the date of each transaction in the series.

Adjustments to the cost of a business combination contingent on future events

When a business combination agreement provides for an adjustment to the cost of the   **19.12** combination contingent on future events, the acquirer shall include the estimated amount of that adjustment in the cost of the combination at the acquisition date if the adjustment is **probable** and can be measured reliably.

However, if the potential adjustment is not recognised at the acquisition date but   **19.13** subsequently becomes probable and can be measured reliably, the additional consideration shall be treated as an adjustment to the cost of the combination.

Allocating the cost of a business combination to the assets acquired and liabilities and contingent liabilities assumed

The acquirer shall, at the acquisition date, allocate the cost of a business combination   **19.14** by recognising the acquiree's identifiable assets and liabilities and a provision for those contingent liabilities (that satisfy the **recognition** criteria in paragraph 19.20) at their fair values at that date, except for the items specified in paragraphs 19.15A to 19.15C. Any difference between the cost of the business combination and the acquirer's interest in the net amount of the identifiable assets, liabilities and provisions for contingent liabilities so recognised shall be accounted for in accordance with paragraphs 19.22 to 19.24.

Except for the items specified in paragraphs 19.15A to 19.15C, the acquirer shall recognise   **19.15** separately the acquiree's identifiable assets, liabilities and contingent liabilities at the acquisition date only if they satisfy the following criteria at that date:

(a) In the case of an asset other than an **intangible asset**, it is probable that any associated future economic benefits will flow to the acquirer, and its fair value can be measured reliably.

(b) In the case of a liability other than a contingent liability, it is probable that an outflow of resources will be required to settle the obligation, and its fair value can be measured reliably.

(c) In the case of an intangible asset or a contingent liability, its fair value can be measured reliably.

19.15A   The acquirer shall recognise and measure a **deferred tax asset** or **liability** arising from the assets acquired and liabilities assumed in accordance with Section 29 *Income Tax*.

19.15B   The acquirer shall recognise and measure a liability (or asset, if any) related to the acquiree's employee benefit arrangements in accordance with Section 28 *Employee Benefits*.

19.15C   The acquirer shall recognise and measure a share-based payment in accordance with Section 26 *Share-based Payment*.

19.16   The acquirer's **statement of comprehensive income** shall incorporate the acquiree's profits or losses after the acquisition date by including the acquiree's **income** and **expenses** based on the cost of the business combination to the acquirer. For example, depreciation expense included after the acquisition date in the acquirer's statement of comprehensive income that relates to the acquiree's depreciable assets shall be based on the fair values of those depreciable assets at the acquisition date, ie their cost to the acquirer.

19.17   Application of the purchase method starts from the acquisition date, which is the date on which the acquirer obtains control of the acquiree. Because control is the power to govern the financial and operating policies of an entity or business so as to obtain benefits from its activities, it is not necessary for a transaction to be closed or finalised at law before the acquirer obtains control. All pertinent facts and circumstances surrounding a business combination shall be considered in assessing when the acquirer has obtained control.

19.18   In accordance with paragraph 19.14, the acquirer recognises separately only the identifiable assets, liabilities and contingent liabilities of the acquiree that existed at the acquisition date and satisfy the recognition criteria in paragraph 19.15 (except for the items specified in paragraphs 19.15A to 19.15C). Therefore:

(a)   the acquirer shall recognise liabilities for terminating or reducing the activities of the acquiree as part of allocating the cost of the combination only to the extent that the acquiree has, at the acquisition date, an existing liability for restructuring recognised in accordance with Section 21 *Provisions and Contingencies*; and

(b)   the acquirer, when allocating the cost of the combination, shall not recognise liabilities for future losses or other costs expected to be incurred as a result of the business combination.

19.19   If the initial accounting for a business combination is incomplete by the end of the **reporting period** in which the combination occurs, the acquirer shall recognise in its **financial statements** provisional amounts for the items for which the accounting is incomplete. Within twelve months after the acquisition date, the acquirer shall retrospectively adjust the provisional amounts recognised as assets and liabilities at the acquisition date (ie account for them as if they were made at the acquisition date) to reflect new information obtained. Beyond twelve months after the acquisition date, adjustments to the initial accounting for a business combination shall be recognised only to correct a **material error** in accordance with Section 10 *Accounting Policies, Estimates and Errors*.

Contingent liabilities

19.20   Paragraph 19.15(c) specifies that the acquirer recognises separately a provision for a contingent liability of the acquiree only if its fair value can be measured reliably. If its fair value cannot be measured reliably:

(a)   there is a resulting effect on the amount recognised as goodwill or the amount accounted for in accordance with paragraph 19.24; and

(b)   the acquirer shall disclose the information about that contingent liability as required by Section 21.

After their initial recognition, the acquirer shall measure contingent liabilities that are recognised separately in accordance with paragraph 19.15(c) at the higher of: **19.21**

(a) the amount that would be recognised in accordance with Section 21; and
(b) the amount initially recognised less amounts previously recognised as **revenue** in accordance with Section 23 *Revenue*.

Goodwill

The acquirer shall, at the acquisition date: **19.22**

(a) recognise goodwill acquired in a business combination as an asset; and
(b) initially measure that goodwill at its cost, being the excess of the cost of the business combination over the acquirer's interest in the net amount of the identifiable assets, liabilities and contingent liabilities recognised and measured in accordance with paragraphs 19.15, 19.15A to 19.15C.

After initial recognition, the acquirer shall measure goodwill acquired in a business combination at cost less accumulated **amortisation** and accumulated **impairment losses**: **19.23**

(a) An entity shall follow the principles in paragraphs 18.19 to 18.24 for amortisation of goodwill. Goodwill shall be considered to have a finite **useful life**, and shall be amortised on a systematic basis over its life. If, in exceptional cases, an entity is unable to make a reliable estimate of the useful life of goodwill, the life shall not exceed 10 years.
(b) An entity shall follow Section 27 *Impairment of Assets* for recognising and measuring the impairment of goodwill.

Excess over cost of acquirer's interest in the net fair value of acquiree's identifiable assets, liabilities and contingent liabilities

If the acquirer's interest in the net amount of the identifiable assets, liabilities and provisions for contingent liabilities recognised in accordance with paragraph 19.14 exceeds the cost of the business combination (also referred to as 'negative goodwill'), the acquirer shall: **19.24**

(a) Reassess the identification and **measurement** of the acquiree's assets, liabilities and provisions for contingent liabilities and the measurement of the cost of the combination.
(b) Recognise and separately disclose the resulting excess on the face of the **statement of financial position** on the acquisition date, immediately below goodwill, and followed by a subtotal of the net amount of goodwill and the excess.
(c) Recognise subsequently the excess up to the fair value of non-monetary assets acquired in profit or loss in the periods in which the non-monetary assets are recovered. Any excess exceeding the fair value of non-monetary assets acquired shall be recognised in profit or loss in the periods expected to be benefited.

Disclosures

For business combinations effected during the reporting period

For each business combination, excluding any group reconstructions, that was effected during the period, the acquirer shall disclose the following: **19.25**

(a) the names and descriptions of the combining entities or businesses;
(b) the acquisition date;
(c) the percentage of voting equity instruments acquired;

(d)   the cost of the combination and a description of the components of that cost (such as cash, equity instruments and debt instruments);

(e)   the amounts recognised at the acquisition date for each class of the acquiree's assets, liabilities and contingent liabilities, including goodwill;

(f)   [not used]

*(g)   the useful life of goodwill, and if this cannot be reliably estimated, supporting reasons for the period chosen; and

(h)   the periods in which the excess recognised in accordance with paragraph 19.24 will be recognised in profit or loss.

19.25A   The acquirer shall disclose, separately for each material business combination that occurred during the reporting period, the amounts of revenue and profit or loss of the acquiree since the acquisition date included in the consolidated statement of comprehensive income for the reporting period. The disclosure may be provided in aggregate for business combinations that occurred during the reporting period which, individually, are not material.

For all business combinations

*19.26   An acquirer shall disclose a reconciliation of the **carrying amount** of goodwill at the beginning and end of the reporting period, showing separately:

(a)   changes arising from new business combinations;

(b)   amortisation;

(c)   impairment losses;

(d)   disposals of previously acquired businesses; and

(e)   other changes.

This reconciliation need not be presented for prior periods.

19.26A   An acquirer shall disclose a reconciliation of the carrying amount of the excess recognised in accordance with paragraph 19.24 at the beginning and end of the reporting period, showing separately:

(a)   changes arising from new business combinations;

(b)   amounts recognised in profit or loss in accordance with paragraph 19.24(c);

(c)   disposals of previously acquired businesses; and

(d)   other changes.

This reconciliation need not be presented for prior periods.

Group reconstructions

19.27   Group reconstructions may be accounted for by using the merger accounting method provided:

(a)   the use of the merger accounting method is not prohibited by company law or other relevant legislation;

(b)   the ultimate equity holders remain the same, and the rights of each equity holder, relative to the others, are unchanged; and

(c)   no **non-controlling interest** in the net assets of the **group** is altered by the transfer.

Applicability to various structures of business combinations

19.28   The provisions of paragraphs 19.29 to 19.33, which are explained by reference to an acquirer or issuing entity that issues shares as consideration for the transfer to it of shares in the other parties to the combination, should also be read so as to apply to other arrangements that achieve similar results.

Merger accounting method

With the merger accounting method the carrying values of the assets and liabilities of **19.29** the parties to the combination are not required to be adjusted to fair value, although appropriate adjustments shall be made to achieve uniformity of **accounting policies** in the combining entities.

The results and cash flows of all the combining entities shall be brought into the financial **19.30** statements of the combined entity from the beginning of the financial year in which the combination occurred, adjusted so as to achieve uniformity of accounting policies. The comparative information shall be restated by including the **total comprehensive income** for all the combining entities for the previous reporting period and their statement of financial position for the previous **reporting date**, adjusted as necessary to achieve uniformity of accounting policies.

The difference, if any, between the nominal value of the shares issued plus the fair value **19.31** of any other consideration given, and the nominal value of the shares received in exchange shall be shown as a movement on other reserves in the **consolidated financial statements**. Any existing balances on the share premium account or capital redemption reserve of the new subsidiary shall be brought in by being shown as a movement on other reserves. These movements shall be shown in the **statement of changes in equity**.

Merger expenses are not to be included as part of this adjustment, but shall be charged to **19.32** the statement of comprehensive income as part of profit or loss of the combined entity at the effective date of the group reconstruction.

Disclosures

For each group reconstruction, that was effected during the period, the combined entity **19.33** shall disclose the following:

(a) the names of the combining entities (other than the reporting entity);
(b) whether the combination has been accounted for as an acquisition or a merger; and
(c) the date of the combination.

Section 20 *Leases*

Scope of this section

This section covers accounting for all **leases** other than: **20.1**

(a) leases to explore for or use minerals, oil, natural gas and similar non-regenerative resources (see Section 34 *Specialised Activities*);
(b) licensing agreements for such items as motion picture films, video recordings, plays, manuscripts, patents and copyrights (see Section 18 *Intangible Assets other than Goodwill*);
(c) **measurement** of property held by lessees that is accounted for as **investment property** and measurement of investment property provided by lessors under **operating leases** (see Section 16 *Investment Property*);
(d) measurement of **biological assets** held by lessees under **finance leases** and biological assets provided by lessors under operating leases (see Section 34); and
(e) leases that could lead to a loss to the lessor or the lessee as a result of non-typical contractual terms (see paragraph 12.3(f)).
(f) [not used]

20.2   This section applies to agreements that transfer the right to use **assets** even though substantial services by the lessor may be called for in connection with the operation or maintenance of such assets. This section does not apply to agreements that are contracts for services that do not transfer the right to use assets from one contracting party to the other.

20.3   Some arrangements do not take the legal form of a lease but convey rights to use assets in return for payments. Examples of arrangements in which one entity (the supplier) may convey a right to use an asset to another entity (the purchaser), often together with related services, may include outsourcing arrangements, telecommunication contracts that provide rights to capacity and take-or-pay contracts.

20.3A Determining whether an arrangement is, or contains, a lease shall be based on the substance of the arrangement and requires an assessment of whether:

(a)   fulfilment of the arrangement is dependent on the use of a specific asset or assets. Although a specific asset may be explicitly identified in an arrangement, it is not the subject of a lease if fulfilment of the arrangement is not dependent on the use of the specified asset. An asset is implicitly specified if, for example, the supplier owns or leases only one asset with which to fulfil the obligation and it is not economically feasible or practicable for the supplier to perform its obligation through the use of alternative assets; and

(b)   the arrangement conveys a right to use the asset. This will be the case where the arrangement conveys to the purchaser the right to control the use of the underlying asset.

Classification of leases

20.4   A lease is classified as a finance lease if it transfers substantially all the risks and rewards incidental to ownership. A lease is classified as an operating lease if it does not transfer substantially all the risks and rewards incidental to ownership.

20.5   Whether a lease is a finance lease or an operating lease depends on the substance of the transaction rather than the form of the contract. Examples of situations that individually or in combination would normally lead to a lease being classified as a finance lease are:

(a)   the lease transfers ownership of the asset to the lessee by the end of the **lease term**;

(b)   the lessee has the option to purchase the asset at a price that is expected to be sufficiently lower than the **fair value** at the date the option becomes exercisable for it to be reasonably certain, at the **inception of the lease**, that the option will be exercised;

(c)   the lease term is for the major part of the economic life of the asset even if title is not transferred;

(d)   at the inception of the lease the **present value** of the **minimum lease payments** amounts to at least substantially all of the fair value of the leased asset; and

(e)   the leased assets are of such a specialised nature that only the lessee can use them without major modifications.

20.6   Indicators of situations that individually or in combination could also lead to a lease being classified as a finance lease are:

(a)   if the lessee can cancel the lease, the lessor's losses associated with the cancellation are borne by the lessee;

(b)   **gains** or losses from the fluctuation in the **residual value** of the leased asset accrue to the lessee (eg in the form of a rent rebate equalling most of the sales proceeds at the end of the lease); and

(c)   the lessee has the ability to continue the lease for a secondary period at a rent that is substantially lower than market rent.

The examples and indicators in paragraphs 20.5 and 20.6 are not always conclusive. If it is clear from other features that the lease does not transfer substantially all risks and rewards incidental to ownership, the lease is classified as an operating lease. For example, this may be the case if ownership of the asset is transferred to the lessee at the end of the lease for a variable payment equal to the asset's then fair value, or if there are **contingent rents**, as a result of which the lessee does not have substantially all risks and rewards incidental to ownership.

20.7

Lease classification is made at the inception of the lease and is not changed during the term of the lease unless the lessee and the lessor agree to change the provisions of the lease (other than simply by renewing the lease), in which case the lease classification shall be re-evaluated.

20.8

Financial statements of lessees: finance leases

Initial recognition

At the **commencement of the lease term**, a lessee shall recognise its rights of use and obligations under finance leases as assets and **liabilities** in its **statement of financial position** at amounts equal to the fair value of the leased asset or, if lower, the present value of the minimum lease payments, determined at the inception of the lease. Any initial direct costs of the lessee (incremental costs that are directly attributable to negotiating and arranging a lease) are added to the amount recognised as an asset.

20.9

The present value of the minimum lease payments shall be calculated using the **interest rate implicit in the lease**. If this cannot be determined, the **lessee's incremental borrowing rate** shall be used.

20.10

Subsequent measurement

A lessee shall apportion minimum lease payments between the finance charge and the reduction of the outstanding liability using the **effective interest method** (see paragraphs 11.15 to 11.20). The lessee shall allocate the finance charge to each period during the lease term so as to produce a constant periodic rate of interest on the remaining balance of the liability. A lessee shall charge contingent rents as **expenses** in the periods in which they are incurred.

20.11

A lessee shall depreciate an asset leased under a finance lease in accordance with Section 17 *Property, Plant and Equipment*. If there is no reasonable certainty that the lessee will obtain ownership by the end of the lease term, the asset shall be fully depreciated over the shorter of the lease term and its **useful life**. A lessee shall also assess at each **reporting date** whether an asset leased under a finance lease is impaired (see Section 27 *Impairment of Assets*).

20.12

Disclosures

A lessee shall make the following disclosures for finance leases:

20.13

(a) for each **class of asset**, the net **carrying amount** at the end of the **reporting period**;
(b) the total of future minimum lease payments at the end of the reporting period, for each of the following periods:

    (i) not later than one year;
    (ii) later than one year and not later than five years; and
    (iii) later than five years; and

(c)   a general description of the lessee's significant leasing arrangements including, for example, information about contingent rent, renewal or purchase options and escalation clauses, subleases, and restrictions imposed by lease arrangements.

20.14   In addition, the requirements for disclosure about assets in accordance with Sections 17 and 27 apply to lessees for assets leased under finance leases.

Financial statements of lessees: operating leases

Recognition and measurement

20.15   A lessee shall recognise lease payments under operating leases (excluding costs for services such as insurance and maintenance) as an expense over the lease term on a straight-line basis unless either:

(a)   another systematic basis is representative of the time pattern of the user's benefit, even if the payments are not on that basis; or

(b)   the payments to the lessor are structured to increase in line with expected general inflation (based on published indexes or statistics) to compensate for the lessor's expected inflationary cost increases. If payments to the lessor vary because of factors other than general inflation, then this condition (b) is not met.

Example of applying paragraph 20.15(b):
X operates in a jurisdiction in which the consensus forecast by local banks is that the general price level index, as published by the government, will increase by an average of 10 per cent annually over the next five years. X leases some office space from Y for five years under an operating lease. The lease payments are structured to reflect the expected 10 per cent annual general inflation over the five-year term of the lease as follows:

Year 1	CU100,000
Year 2	CU110,000
Year 3	CU121,000
Year 4	CU133,000
Year 5	CU146,000

X recognises annual rent expense equal to the amounts owed to the lessor as shown above. If the escalating payments are not clearly structured to compensate the lessor for expected inflationary cost increases based on published indexes or statistics, then X recognises annual rent expense on a straight-line basis: CU122,000 each year (sum of the amounts payable under the lease divided by five years).

20.15A   A lessee shall recognise the aggregate benefit of **lease incentives** as a reduction to the expense recognised in accordance with paragraph 20.15 over the lease term, on a straight-line basis unless another systematic basis is representative of the time pattern of the lessee's benefit from the use of the leased asset. Any costs incurred by the lessee (for example costs for termination of a pre-existing lease, relocation or leasehold improvements) shall be accounted for in accordance with the applicable section of this FRS.

20.15B   Where an operating lease becomes an **onerous contract** an entity shall also apply Section 21 *Provisions and Contingencies.*

Disclosures

A lessee shall make the following disclosures for operating leases: *20.16

(a) the total of future minimum lease payments under non-cancellable operating leases for each of the following periods:

    (i) not later than one year;

    (ii) later than one year and not later than five years; and

    (iii) later than five years; and

(b) lease payments recognised as an expense.

(c) [not used]

Financial statements of lessors: finance leases

Initial recognition and measurement

A lessor shall recognise assets held under a finance lease in its statement of financial 20.17
position and present them as a receivable at an amount equal to the net investment in
the lease. The **net investment in a lease** is the lessor's **gross investment in the lease**
discounted at the interest rate implicit in the lease. The gross investment in the lease is the
aggregate of:

(a) the minimum lease payments receivable by the lessor under a finance lease; and

(b) any unguaranteed residual value accruing to the lessor.

For finance leases other than those involving manufacturer or dealer lessors, initial direct 20.18
costs (costs that are incremental and directly attributable to negotiating and arranging a
lease) are included in the initial measurement of the finance lease receivable and reduce
the amount of **income** recognised over the lease term.

Subsequent measurement

The **recognition** of finance income shall be based on a pattern reflecting a constant 20.19
periodic rate of return on the lessor's net investment in the finance lease. Lease payments
relating to the period, excluding costs for services, are applied against the gross investment
in the lease to reduce both the principal and the unearned finance income. If there is an
indication that the estimated unguaranteed residual value used in computing the lessor's
gross investment in the lease has changed significantly, the income allocation over the
lease term is revised, and any reduction in respect of amounts accrued is recognised
immediately in **profit or loss**.

Manufacturer or dealer lessors

Manufacturers or dealers often offer to customers the choice of either buying or leasing 20.20
an asset. A finance lease of an asset by a manufacturer or dealer lessor gives rise to two
types of income:

(a) profit or loss equivalent to the profit or loss resulting from an outright sale of the
asset being leased, at normal selling prices, reflecting any applicable volume or trade
discounts; and

(b) finance income over the lease term.

The sales **revenue** recognised at the commencement of the lease term by a manufacturer 20.21
or dealer lessor is the fair value of the asset or, if lower, the present value of the minimum
lease payments accruing to the lessor, computed at a market rate of interest. The cost of

sale recognised at the commencement of the lease term is the cost, or carrying amount if different, of the leased asset less the present value of the unguaranteed residual value. The difference between the sales revenue and the cost of sale is the selling profit, which is recognised in accordance with the entity's policy for outright sales.

20.22   If artificially low rates of interest are quoted, selling profit shall be restricted to that which would apply if a market rate of interest were charged. Costs incurred by manufacturer or dealer lessors in connection with negotiating and arranging a lease shall be recognised as an expense when the selling profit is recognised.

Disclosures

20.23   A lessor shall make the following disclosures for finance leases:

(a)   a reconciliation between the gross investment in the lease at the end of the reporting period, and the present value of minimum lease payments receivable at the end of the reporting period. In addition, a lessor shall disclose the gross investment in the lease and the present value of minimum lease payments receivable at the end of the reporting period, for each of the following periods:

(i)   not later than one year;
(ii)   later than one year and not later than five years; and
(iii)   later than five years;

(b)   unearned finance income;
(c)   the unguaranteed residual values accruing to the benefit of the lessor;
(d)   the accumulated allowance for uncollectible minimum lease payments receivable;
(e)   contingent rents recognised as income in the period; and
(f)   a general description of the lessor's significant leasing arrangements, including, for example, information about contingent rent, renewal or purchase options and escalation clauses, subleases, and restrictions imposed by lease arrangements.

Financial statements of lessors: operating leases

Recognition and measurement

20.24   A lessor shall present assets subject to operating leases in its statement of financial position according to the nature of the asset.

20.25   A lessor shall recognise lease income from operating leases (excluding amounts for services such as insurance and maintenance) in profit or loss on a straight-line basis over the lease term, unless either:

(a)   another systematic basis is representative of the time pattern of the lessee's benefit from the leased asset, even if the receipt of payments is not on that basis; or
(b)   the payments to the lessor are structured to increase in line with expected general inflation (based on published indexes or statistics) to compensate for the lessor's expected inflationary cost increases. If payments to the lessor vary according to factors other than inflation, then condition (b) is not met.

20.25A   A lessor shall recognise the aggregate cost of lease incentives as a reduction to the income recognised in accordance with paragraph 20.25 over the lease term on a straight-line basis, unless another systematic basis is representative of the time pattern over which the lessor's benefit from the leased asset is diminished.

A lessor shall recognise as an expense, costs, including **depreciation**, incurred in earning the lease income. The depreciation policy for depreciable leased assets shall be consistent with the lessor's normal depreciation policy for similar assets. **20.26**

A lessor shall add to the carrying amount of the leased asset any initial direct costs it incurs in negotiating and arranging an operating lease and shall recognise such costs as an expense over the lease term on the same basis as the lease income. **20.27**

To determine whether a leased asset has become impaired, a lessor shall apply Section 27. **20.28**

A manufacturer or dealer lessor does not recognise any selling profit on entering into an operating lease because it is not the equivalent of a sale. **20.29**

Disclosures

A lessor shall disclose the following for operating leases: **20.30**

(a) the future minimum lease payments under non-cancellable operating leases for each of the following periods:

(i) not later than one year;
(ii) later than one year and not later than five years; and
(iii) later than five years;

(b) total contingent rents recognised as income; and
(c) a general description of the lessor's significant leasing arrangements, including, for example, information about contingent rent, renewal or purchase options and escalation clauses, and restrictions imposed by lease arrangements.

In addition, the requirements for disclosure about assets in accordance with Sections 17 and 27 apply to lessors for assets provided under operating leases. **20.31**

Sale and leaseback transactions

A sale and leaseback transaction involves the sale of an asset and the leasing back of the same asset. The lease payment and the sale price are usually interdependent because they are negotiated as a package. The accounting treatment of a sale and leaseback transaction depends on the type of lease. **20.32**

Sale and leaseback transaction results in a finance lease

If a sale and leaseback transaction results in a finance lease, the seller-lessee shall not recognise immediately, as income, any excess of sales proceeds over the carrying amount. Instead, the seller-lessee shall defer such excess and amortise it over the lease term. **20.33**

Sale and leaseback transaction results in an operating lease

If a sale and leaseback transaction results in an operating lease, and it is clear that the transaction is established at fair value, the seller-lessee shall recognise any profit or loss immediately. If the sale price is below fair value, the seller-lessee shall recognise any profit or loss immediately unless the loss is compensated for by future lease payments at below market price. In that case the seller-lessee shall defer and amortise such loss in proportion to the lease payments over the period for which the asset is expected to be used. If the sale price is above fair value, the seller-lessee shall defer the excess over fair value and amortise it over the period for which the asset is expected to be used. **20.34**

Disclosures

20.35   Disclosure requirements for lessees and lessors apply equally to sale and leaseback transactions. The required description of significant leasing arrangements includes description of unique or unusual provisions of the agreement or terms of the sale and leaseback transactions.

Section 21 *Provisions and Contingencies*

Scope of this section

21.1   This section applies to all **provisions** (ie **liabilities** of uncertain timing or amount), **contingent liabilities** and **contingent assets** except those provisions covered by other sections of this FRS. Where those other sections contain no specific requirements to deal with contracts that have become onerous, this section applies to those contracts.

21.1A   This section applies to **financial guarantee contracts** unless:

(a)   an entity has chosen to apply IAS 39 *Financial Instruments: Recognition and Measurement* and/or IFRS 9 *Financial Instruments* to its **financial instruments** (see paragraphs 11.2 and 12.2); or

(b)   an entity has elected under FRS 103 *Insurance Contracts* to continue the application of insurance contract accounting.

21.1B   This section does not apply to financial instruments (including loan commitments) that are within the scope of Section 11 *Basic Financial Instruments* and 12 *Other Financial Instruments Issues*. This section does not apply to **insurance contracts** (including **reinsurance contracts**) that an entity issues and reinsurance contracts that the entity holds, or financial instruments issued by an entity with a **discretionary participation feature** that are within the scope of FRS 103 *Insurance Contracts*.

21.2   The requirements in this section do not apply to executory contracts unless they are **onerous contracts**. Executory contracts are contracts under which neither party has performed any of its obligations or both parties have partially performed their obligations to an equal extent.

21.3   The word 'provision' is sometimes used in the context of such items as **depreciation**, impairment of **assets**, and uncollectible receivables. Those are adjustments of the **carrying amounts** of assets, rather than **recognition** of liabilities, and therefore are not covered by this section.

Initial recognition

21.4   An entity shall recognise a provision only when:

(a)   the entity has an obligation at the **reporting date** as a result of a past event;

(b)   it is **probable** (ie more likely than not) that the entity will be required to transfer economic benefits in settlement; and

(c)   the amount of the obligation can be estimated reliably.

21.5   The entity shall recognise the provision as a liability in the **statement of financial position** and shall recognise the amount of the provision as an **expense**, unless another section of this FRS requires the cost to be recognised as part of the cost of an asset such as **inventories** or **property, plant and equipment**.

The condition in paragraph 21.4(a) means that the entity has no realistic alternative to settling the obligation. This can happen when the entity has a legal obligation that can be enforced by law or when the entity has a **constructive obligation** because the past event (which may be an action of the entity) has created valid expectations in other parties that the entity will discharge the obligation. Obligations that will arise from the entity's future actions (ie the future conduct of its business) do not satisfy the condition in paragraph 21.4(a), no matter how likely they are to occur and even if they are contractual. To illustrate, because of commercial pressures or legal requirements, an entity may intend or need to carry out expenditure to operate in a particular way in the future (for example, by fitting smoke filters in a particular type of factory). Because the entity can avoid the future expenditure by its future actions, for example by changing its method of operation or selling the factory, it has no present obligation for that future expenditure and no provision is recognised.

21.6

Initial measurement

An entity shall measure a provision at the best estimate of the amount required to settle the obligation at the reporting date. The best estimate is the amount an entity would rationally pay to settle the obligation at the end of the **reporting period** or to transfer it to a third party at that time.

21.7

(a)   When the provision involves a large population of items, the estimate of the amount reflects the weighting of all possible outcomes by their associated probabilities. The provision will therefore be different depending on whether the probability of a loss of a given amount is, for example, 60 per cent or 90 per cent. Where there is a continuous range of possible outcomes, and each point in that range is as likely as any other, the mid-point of the range is used.

(b)   When the provision arises from a single obligation, the individual most likely outcome may be the best estimate of the amount required to settle the obligation. However, even in such a case, the entity considers other possible outcomes. When other possible outcomes are either mostly higher or mostly lower than the most likely outcome, the best estimate will be a higher or lower amount.

When the effect of the time value of money is **material**, the amount of a provision shall be the **present value** of the amount expected to be required to settle the obligation. The discount rate (or rates) shall be a pre-tax rate (or rates) that reflect(s) current market assessments of the time value of money and risks specific to the liability. The risks specific to the liability shall be reflected either in the discount rate or in the estimation of the amounts required to settle the obligation, but not both.

An entity shall exclude **gains** from the expected disposal of assets from the **measurement** of a provision.

21.8

When some or all of the amount required to settle a provision may be reimbursed by another party (eg through an insurance claim), the entity shall recognise the reimbursement as a separate asset only when it is virtually certain that the entity will receive the reimbursement on settlement of the obligation. The amount recognised for the reimbursement shall not exceed the amount of the provision. The reimbursement receivable shall be presented in the statement of financial position as an asset and shall not be offset against the provision. In the **statement of comprehensive income** (or in the **income statement**, if presented) the expense relating to a provision may be presented net of the amount recognised for a reimbursement.

21.9

Subsequent measurement

21.10   An entity shall charge against a provision only those expenditures for which the provision was originally recognised.

21.11   An entity shall review provisions at each reporting date and adjust them to reflect the current best estimate of the amount that would be required to settle the obligation at that reporting date. Any adjustments to the amounts previously recognised shall be recognised in **profit or loss** unless the provision was originally recognised as part of the cost of an asset (see paragraph 21.5). When a provision is measured at the present value of the amount expected to be required to settle the obligation, the unwinding of the discount shall be recognised as a finance cost in profit or loss in the period it arises.

Onerous contracts

21.11A   If an entity has an **onerous contract**, the present obligation under the contract shall be recognised and measured as a provision (see Example 2 of the Appendix to this section).

Future operating losses

21.11B   Provisions shall not be recognised for future operating losses (see Example 1 of the Appendix to this section).

Restructuring

21.11C   A **restructuring** gives rise to a constructive obligation only when an entity:

(a)   has a detailed formal plan for the restructuring identifying at least:

(i)   the business or part of a business concerned;

(ii)   the principal locations affected;

(iii) the location, function, and approximate number of employees who will be compensated for terminating their services;

(iv)   the expenditures that will be undertaken; and

(v)   when the plan will be implemented; and

(b)   has raised a valid expectation in those affected that it will carry out the restructuring by starting to implement that plan or announcing its main features to those affected by it.

21.11D   An entity recognises a provision for restructuring costs only when it has a legal or constructive obligation at the reporting date to carry out the restructuring.

Contingent liabilities

21.12   A contingent liability is either a possible but uncertain obligation or a present obligation that is not recognised because it fails to meet one or both of the conditions (b) and (c) in paragraph 21.4. An entity shall not recognise a contingent liability as a liability, except for provisions for contingent liabilities of an acquiree in a **business combination** (see paragraphs 19.20 and 19.21). Disclosure of a contingent liability is required by paragraph 21.15 unless the possibility of an outflow of resources is remote. When an entity is jointly and severally liable for an obligation, the part of the obligation that is expected to be met by other parties is treated as a contingent liability.

Contingent assets

An entity shall not recognise a contingent asset as an asset. Disclosure of a contingent asset is required by paragraph 21.16 when an inflow of economic benefits is probable. However, when the flow of future economic benefits to the entity is virtually certain, then the related asset is not a contingent asset, and its recognition is appropriate.   **21.13**

Disclosures

Disclosures about provisions

For each class of provision, an entity shall disclose the following: **21.14**

(a)   a reconciliation showing:

    (i)   the carrying amount at the beginning and end of the period;

    (ii)   additions during the period, including adjustments that result from changes in measuring the discounted amount;

    (iii)   amounts charged against the provision during the period; and

    (iv)   unused amounts reversed during the period;

(b)   a brief description of the nature of the obligation and the expected amount and timing of any resulting payments;

(c)   an indication of the uncertainties about the amount or timing of those outflows; and

(d)   the amount of any expected reimbursement, stating the amount of any asset that has been recognised for that expected reimbursement.

Comparative information for prior periods is not required.

Disclosures about contingent liabilities

Unless the possibility of any outflow of resources in settlement is remote, an entity shall disclose, for each class of contingent liability at the reporting date, a brief description of the nature of the contingent liability and, when practicable: ***21.15**

(a)   an estimate of its financial effect, measured in accordance with paragraphs 21.7 to 21.11;

(b)   an indication of the uncertainties relating to the amount or timing of any outflow; and

(c)   the possibility of any reimbursement.

If it is **impracticable** to make one or more of these disclosures, that fact shall be stated.

Disclosures about contingent assets

If an inflow of economic benefits is probable (more likely than not) but not virtually certain, an entity shall disclose a description of the nature of the contingent assets at the end of the reporting period, and, when practicable, an estimate of their financial effect, measured using the principles set out in paragraphs 21.7 to 21.11. If it is impracticable to make this disclosure, that fact shall be stated.   **21.16**

Prejudicial disclosures

In extremely rare cases, disclosure of some or all of the information required by paragraphs 21.14 to 21.16 can be expected to prejudice seriously the position of the entity in a dispute with other parties on the subject matter of the provision, contingent liability or contingent asset. In such cases, an entity need not disclose all of the information required by those paragraphs insofar as it relates to the dispute, but shall disclose at least the following.   **21.17**

In relation to provisions, the following information shall be given:

(a) a table showing the reconciliation required by paragraph 21.14(a) in aggregate, including the source and application of any amounts transferred to or from provisions during the reporting period;

(b) particulars of each provision in any case where the amount of the provision is material; and

(c) the fact that, and reason why, the information required by paragraph 21.14 has not been disclosed.

In relation to contingent liabilities, the following information shall be given:

(a) particulars and the total amount of any contingent liabilities (excluding those which arise out of insurance contracts) that are not included in the statement of financial position;

(b) the total amount of contingent liabilities which are undertaken on behalf of or for the benefit of:

   (i)   any **parent** or fellow **subsidiary** of the entity;

   (ii)   any subsidiary of the entity; or

   (iii) any entity in which the reporting entity has a participating interest,

   shall each be stated separately; and

(c) the fact that, and reason why, the information required by paragraph 21.15 has not been disclosed.

In relation to contingent assets, the entity shall disclose the general nature of the dispute, together with the fact that, and reason why, the information required by paragraph 21.16 has not been disclosed.

Disclosure about financial guarantee contracts

21.17A An entity shall disclose the nature and business purpose of the financial guarantee contracts it has issued. If applicable, an entity shall also provide the disclosures required by paragraphs 21.14 and 21.15.

Appendix to Section 21

Examples of recognising and measuring provisions

This appendix accompanies, but is not part of, Section 21. It provides guidance for applying the requirements of Section 21 in recognising and measuring provisions.

All of the entities in the examples in this appendix have 31 December as their reporting date. In all cases, it is assumed that a reliable estimate can be made of any outflows expected. In some examples the circumstances described may have resulted in impairment of the assets; this aspect is not dealt with in the examples. References to 'best estimate' are to the present value amount, when the effect of the time value of money is material.

Example 1 Future operating losses

21A.1 An entity determines that it is probable that a segment of its operations will incur future operating losses for several years.

Present obligation as a result of a past obligating event: There is no past event that obliges the entity to pay out resources.

Conclusion: The entity does not recognise a provision for future operating losses. Expected future losses do not meet the definition of a liability. The expectation of future operating losses may be an indicator that one or more assets are impaired (see Section 27 *Impairment of Assets*).

Example 2 Onerous contracts

An onerous contract is one in which the unavoidable costs of meeting the obligations under the contract exceed the economic benefits expected to be received under it. The unavoidable costs under a contract reflect the least net cost of exiting from the contract, which is the lower of the cost of fulfilling it and any compensation or penalties arising from failure to fulfil it. For example, an entity may be contractually required under an operating lease to make payments to lease an asset for which it no longer has any use. **21A.2**

Present obligation as a result of a past obligating event: The entity is contractually required to pay out resources for which it will not receive commensurate benefits.

Conclusion: If an entity has a contract that is onerous, the entity recognises and measures the present obligation under the contract as a provision.

Example 3 Restructurings

[Moved to paragraph 21.11C] **21A.3**

Example 4 Warranties

A manufacturer gives warranties at the time of sale to purchasers of its product. Under the terms of the contract for sale, the manufacturer undertakes to make good, by repair or replacement, manufacturing defects that become apparent within three years from the date of sale. On the basis of experience, it is probable (ie more likely than not) that there will be some claims under the warranties. **21A.4**

Present obligation as a result of a past obligating event: The obligating event is the sale of the product with a warranty, which gives rise to a legal obligation.

An outflow of resources embodying economic benefits in settlement: Probable for the warranties as a whole.

Conclusion: The entity recognises a provision for the best estimate of the costs of making good under the warranty products sold before the reporting date.

Illustration of calculations:

In 20X0, goods are sold for CU1,000,000. Experience indicates that 90 per cent of products sold require no warranty repairs; 6 per cent of products sold require minor repairs costing 30 per cent of the sale price; and 4 per cent of products sold require major repairs or replacement costing 70 per cent of sale price. Therefore estimated warranty costs are:

CU1,000,000 × 90% × 0 =	CU0
CU1,000,000 × 6% × 30% =	CU18,000
CU1,000,000 × 4% × 70% =	CU28,000
Total	CU46,000

The expenditures for warranty repairs and replacements for products sold in 20X0 are expected to be made 60 per cent in 20X1, 30 per cent in 20X2, and 10 per cent in 20X3, in each case at the end of the period. Because the estimated cash flows already reflect the probabilities of the cash outflows, and assuming there are no other risks or uncertainties that must be reflected, to determine the present value of those cash flows the entity uses a 'risk-free' discount rate based on government bonds with the same term as the expected cash outflows (6 per cent for one-year bonds and 7 per cent for two-year and three-year bonds). Calculation of the present value, at the end of 20X0, of the estimated cash flows related to the warranties for products sold in 20X0 is as follows:

Year		Expected cash payments (CU)	Discount rate	Discount factor	Present value (CU)
1	60% × CU46,000	27,600	6%	0.9434 (at 6% for 1 year)	26,038
2	30% × CU46,000	13,800	7%	0.8734 (at 7% for 2 years)	12,053
3	10% × CU46,000	4,600	7%	0.8163 (at 7% for 3 years)	3,755
Total					41,846

The entity will recognise a warranty obligation of CU41,846 at the end of 20X0 for products sold in 20X0.

Example 5 Refunds policy

21A.5   A retail store has a policy of refunding purchases by dissatisfied customers, even though it is under no legal obligation to do so. Its policy of making refunds is generally known.

Present obligation as a result of a past obligating event: The obligating event is the sale of the product, which gives rise to a constructive obligation because the conduct of the store has created a valid expectation on the part of its customers that the store will refund purchases.

An outflow of resources embodying economic benefits in settlement: Probable that a proportion of goods will be returned for refund.

Conclusion: The entity recognises a provision for the best estimate of the amount required to settle the refunds.

Example 6 Closure of a division: no implementation before end of reporting period

21A.6   On 12 December 20X0 the board of an entity decided to close down a division. Before the end of the reporting period (31 December 20X0) the decision was not communicated to any of those affected and no other steps were taken to implement the decision.

Present obligation as a result of a past obligating event: There has been no obligating event, and so there is no obligation.

Conclusion: The entity does not recognise a provision.

Example 7 Closure of a division: communication and implementation before end of reporting period

On 12 December 20X0 the board of an entity decided to close a division making a particular product. On 20 December 20X0 a detailed plan for closing the division was agreed by the board, letters were sent to customers warning them to seek an alternative source of supply, and redundancy notices were sent to the staff of the division.

21A.7

Present obligation as a result of a past obligating event: The obligating event is the communication of the decision to the customers and employees, which gives rise to a constructive obligation from that date, because it creates a valid expectation that the division will be closed.

An outflow of resources embodying economic benefits in settlement: Probable.

Conclusion: The entity recognises a provision at 31 December 20X0 for the best estimate of the costs that would be incurred to close the division at the reporting date.

Example 8 Staff retraining as a result of changes in the income tax system

The government introduces changes to the income tax system. As a result of those changes, an entity in the financial services sector will need to retrain a large proportion of its administrative and sales workforce in order to ensure continued compliance with tax regulations. At the end of the reporting period, no retraining of staff has taken place.

21A.8

Present obligation as a result of a past obligating event: The tax law change does not impose an obligation on an entity to do any retraining. An obligating event for recognising a provision (the retraining itself) has not taken place.

Conclusion: The entity does not recognise a provision.

Example 9 A court case

A customer has sued Entity X, seeking damages for injury the customer allegedly sustained from using a product sold by Entity X. Entity X disputes liability on grounds that the customer did not follow directions in using the product. Up to the date the board authorised the financial statements for the year to 31 December 20X1 for issue, the entity's lawyers advise that it is probable that the entity will not be found liable. However, when the entity prepares the financial statements for the year to 31 December 20X2, its lawyers advise that, owing to developments in the case, it is now probable that the entity will be found liable.

21A.9

(a)   At 31 December 20X1
Present obligation as a result of a past obligating event: On the basis of the evidence available when the financial statements were approved, there is no obligation as a result of past events.
Conclusion: No provision is recognised. The matter is disclosed as a contingent liability unless the probability of any outflow is regarded as remote.

(b)   At 31 December 20X2
Present obligation as a result of a past obligating event: On the basis of the evidence available, there is a present obligation. The obligating event is the sale of the product to the customer.

An outflow of resources embodying economic benefits in settlement: Probable.

Conclusion: A provision is recognised at the best estimate of the amount to settle the obligation at 31 December 20X2, and the expense is recognised in profit or loss. It is not a correction of an error in 20X1 because, on the basis of the evidence available when the 20X1 financial statements were approved, a provision should not have been recognised at that time.

Section 22 *Liabilities and Equity*

Scope of this section

22.1   This section establishes principles for classifying **financial instruments** as either **liabilities** or **equity** and deals with the accounting for **compound financial instruments**. It also addresses the issue of equity instruments and distributions to individuals or other parties acting in their capacity as investors in equity instruments (ie in their capacity as **owners**) and the accounting for purchases of own equity. This section also deals with the accounting for **non-controlling interests** in **consolidated financial statements**. Section 26 *Share-based Payment* addresses accounting for a transaction in which the entity receives goods or services (including employee services) as consideration for its equity instruments (including shares or **share options**) from employees and other vendors acting in their capacity as vendors of goods and services.

22.2   This section shall be applied to all types of financial instruments except:

(a)   Investments in **subsidiaries, associates** and **joint ventures** that are accounted for in accordance with Section 9 *Consolidated and Separate Financial Statements*, Section 14 *Investments in Associates* or Section 15 *Investments in Joint Ventures*.

(b)   Employers' rights and obligations under employee benefit plans, to which Section 28 *Employee Benefits* applies.

(c)   Contracts for contingent consideration in a **business combination** (see Section 19 *Business Combinations and Goodwill*). This exemption applies only to the acquirer.

(d)   Financial instruments, contracts and obligations under **share-based payment transactions** to which Section 26 applies, except that paragraphs 22.3 to 22.6 shall be applied to **treasury shares** issued, purchased, sold, transferred or cancelled in connection with employee share option plans, employee share purchase plans, and all other share-based payment arrangements.

(e)   **Insurance contracts** (including **reinsurance contracts**) that an entity issues and reinsurance contracts that it holds (see FRS 103 *Insurance Contracts*).

(f)   Financial instruments with a **discretionary participation feature** that an entity issues (see FRS 103).

(g)   **Financial guarantee contracts** (see Section 21 *Provisions and Contingencies*).

A reporting entity that issues the financial instruments set out in (e) and (f) or holds the financial instruments set out (e) is required by paragraph 1.6 to apply FRS 103 to those financial instruments.

Classification of an instrument as liability or equity

22.3   Equity is the residual interest in the **assets** of an entity after deducting all its liabilities. Equity includes investments by the owners of the entity, plus additions to those investments earned through profitable operations and retained for use in the entity's operations, minus reductions to owners' investments as a result of unprofitable operations and distributions to owners.

A **financial liability** is any liability that is:

(a)   a contractual obligation:

      (i)   to deliver **cash** or another **financial asset** to another entity; or

      (ii)   to exchange financial assets or financial liabilities with another entity under conditions that are potentially unfavourable to the entity; or

(b)   a contract that will or may be settled in the entity's own equity instruments and:

      (i)   under which the entity is or may be obliged to deliver a variable number of the entity's own equity instruments; or

      (ii)   which will or may be settled other than by the exchange of a fixed amount of cash or another financial asset for a fixed number of the entity's own equity instruments. For this purpose the entity's own equity instruments do not include instruments that are themselves contracts for the future receipt or delivery of the entity's own equity instruments.

A financial instrument, where the issuer does not have the unconditional right to avoid settling in cash or by delivery of another financial asset (or otherwise to settle it in such a way that it would be a financial liability) and where settlement is dependent on the occurrence or non-occurrence of uncertain future events beyond the control of the issuer and the holder, is a financial liability of the issuer unless: **22.3A**

(a)   the part of the contingent settlement provision that could require settlement in cash or another financial asset (or otherwise in such a way that it would be a financial liability) is not genuine;

(b)   the issuer can be required to settle the obligation in cash or another financial asset (or otherwise to settle it in such a way that it would be a financial liability) only in the event of liquidation of the issuer; or

(c)   the instrument has all the features and meets the conditions in paragraph 22.4.

Some financial instruments that meet the definition of a liability are classified as equity because they represent the residual interest in the net assets of the entity: **22.4**

(a)   A puttable instrument is a financial instrument that gives the holder the right to sell that instrument back to the issuer for cash or another financial asset or is automatically redeemed or repurchased by the issuer on the occurrence of an uncertain future event or the death or retirement of the instrument holder. A puttable instrument that has all of the following features is classified as an equity instrument:

      (i)   It entitles the holder to a pro rata share of the entity's net assets in the event of the entity's liquidation. The entity's net assets are those assets that remain after deducting all other claims on its assets.

      (ii)   The instrument is in the class of instruments that is subordinate to all other classes of instruments.

      (iii)   All financial instruments in the class of instruments that is subordinate to all other classes of instruments have identical features.

      (iv)   Apart from the contractual obligation for the issuer to repurchase or redeem the instrument for cash or another financial asset, the instrument does not include any contractual obligation to deliver cash or another financial asset to another entity, or to exchange financial assets or financial liabilities with another entity under conditions that are potentially unfavourable to the entity, and it is not a contract that will or may be settled in the entity's own equity instruments as set out in paragraph 22.3(b) of the definition of a financial liability.

      (v)   The total expected **cash flows** attributable to the instrument over the life of the instrument are based substantially on the **profit or loss**, the change in the recognised net assets or the change in the **fair value** of the recognised and unrecognised net assets of the entity over the life of the instrument (excluding any effects of the instrument).

(b)   Instruments, or components of instruments, that are subordinate to all other classes of instruments are classified as equity if they impose on the entity an obligation to deliver to another party a pro rata share of the net assets of the entity only on liquidation.

22.5   The following are examples of instruments that are either classified as liabilities or equity:

(a)   An instrument of the type described in paragraph 22.4(b) is classified as a liability if the distribution of net assets on liquidation is subject to a maximum amount (a ceiling). For example, if on liquidation the holders of the instrument receive a pro rata share of the net assets, but this amount is limited to a ceiling and the excess net assets are distributed to a charity organisation or the government, the instrument is not classified as equity.

(b)   A puttable instrument is classified as equity if, when the put option is exercised, the holder receives a pro rata share of the net assets of the entity determined by:

(i)   dividing the entity's net assets on liquidation into units of equal amounts; and

(ii)   multiplying that amount by the number of the units held by the financial instrument holder.

However, if the holder is entitled to an amount measured on some other basis the instrument is classified as a liability.

(c)   An instrument is classified as a liability if it obliges the entity to make payments to the holder before liquidation, such as a mandatory dividend.

(d)   A puttable instrument that is classified as equity in a subsidiary's **financial statements** is classified as a liability in the consolidated financial statements.

(e)   A preference share that provides for mandatory redemption by the issuer for a fixed or determinable amount at a fixed or determinable future date, or gives the holder the right to require the issuer to redeem the instrument at or after a particular date for a fixed or determinable amount, is a financial liability.

22.6   Members' shares in co-operative entities and similar instruments are equity if:

(a)   the entity has an unconditional right to refuse redemption of the members' shares; or

(b)   redemption is unconditionally prohibited by local law, regulation or the entity's governing charter.

Original issue of shares or other equity instruments

22.7   An entity shall recognise the issue of shares or other equity instruments as equity when it issues those instruments and another party is obliged to provide cash or other resources to the entity in exchange for the instruments.

(a)   [Not used]

(b)   If the entity receives the cash or other resources before the equity instruments are issued, and the entity cannot be required to repay the cash or other resources received, the entity shall recognise the corresponding increase in equity to the extent of consideration received.

(c)   To the extent that the equity instruments have been subscribed for but not issued (or called up), and the entity has not yet received the cash or other resources, the entity shall not recognise an increase in equity.

22.8   An entity shall measure the equity instruments at the fair value of the cash or other resources received or receivable, net of direct costs of issuing the equity instruments. If payment is deferred and the time value of money is **material**, the initial **measurement** shall be on a **present value** basis.

An entity shall account for the **transaction costs** of an equity transaction as a deduction **22.9** from equity, net of any related income tax benefit.

How the increase in equity arising on the issue of shares or other equity instruments is **22.10** presented in the **statement of financial position** is determined by applicable laws. For example, the par value (or other nominal value) of shares and the amount paid in excess of par value may be presented separately.

Exercise of options, rights and warrants

An entity shall apply the principles in paragraphs 22.7 to 22.10 to equity issued by means **22.11** of exercise of options, rights, warrants and similar equity instruments.

Capitalisation or bonus issues of shares and share splits

A capitalisation or bonus issue (sometimes referred to as a stock dividend) is the issue **22.12** of new shares to shareholders in proportion to their existing holdings. For example, an entity may give its shareholders one dividend or bonus share for every five shares held. A share split (sometimes referred to as a stock split) is the dividing of an entity's existing shares into multiple shares. For example, in a share split, each shareholder may receive one additional share for each share held. In some cases, the previously outstanding shares are cancelled and replaced by new shares. Capitalisation and bonus issues and share splits do not change total equity. An entity shall reclassify amounts within equity as required by applicable laws.

Convertible debt or similar compound financial instruments

On issuing convertible debt or similar compound financial instruments that contain both **22.13** a liability and an equity component, an entity shall allocate the proceeds between the liability component and the equity component. To make the allocation, the entity shall first determine the amount of the liability component as the fair value of a similar liability that does not have a conversion feature or similar associated equity component. The entity shall allocate the residual amount as the equity component. Transaction costs shall be allocated between the debt component and the equity component on the basis of their relative fair values.

The entity shall not revise the allocation in a subsequent period. **22.14**

In periods after the instruments were issued, the entity shall account for the liability **22.15** component as a financial instrument in accordance with Section 11 *Basic Financial Instruments* or Section 12 *Other Financial Instruments Issues* as appropriate. The appendix to this section illustrates the issuer's accounting for convertible debt where the liability component is a basic financial instrument.

Treasury shares

Treasury shares are the equity instruments of an entity that have been issued and **22.16** subsequently reacquired by the entity. An entity shall deduct from equity the fair value of the consideration given for the treasury shares. The entity shall not recognise a **gain** or loss in profit or loss on the purchase, sale, transfer or cancellation of treasury shares.

Distributions to owners

22.17   An entity shall reduce equity for the amount of distributions to its owners (holders of its equity instruments).

22.18   An entity shall disclose the fair value of any non-cash assets that have been distributed to its owners during the **reporting period**, except when the non-cash assets are ultimately controlled by the same parties both before and after the distribution.

Non-controlling interest and transactions in shares of a consolidated subsidiary

22.19   In the consolidated financial statements, a non-controlling interest in the net assets of a subsidiary is included in equity. An entity shall treat changes in a parent's controlling interest in a subsidiary that do not result in a loss of **control** as transactions with equity holders in their capacity as equity holders. Accordingly, the **carrying amount** of the non-controlling interest shall be adjusted to reflect the change in the parent's interest in the subsidiary's net assets. Any difference between the amount by which the non-controlling interest is so adjusted and the fair value of the consideration paid or received, if any, shall be recognised directly in equity and attributed to equity holders of the parent. An entity shall not recognise a gain or loss on these changes. Also, an entity shall not recognise any change in the carrying amounts of assets (including goodwill) or liabilities as a result of such transactions.

Appendix to Section 22

Example of the issuer's accounting for convertible debt

The appendix accompanies, but is not part of, Section 22. It provides guidance for applying the requirements of paragraphs 22.13 to 22.15.

On 1 January 20X5 an entity issues 500 convertible bonds. The bonds are issued at par with a face value of CU100 per bond and are for a five-year term, with no transaction costs. The total proceeds from the issue are CU50,000. Interest is payable annually in arrears at an annual interest rate of 4 per cent. Each bond is convertible, at the holder's discretion, into 25 ordinary shares at any time up to maturity. At the time the bonds are issued, the market interest rate for similar debt that does not have the conversion option is 6 per cent.

When the instrument is issued, the liability component must be valued first, and the difference between the total proceeds on issue (which is the fair value of the instrument in its entirety) and the fair value of the liability component is assigned to the equity component. The fair value of the liability component is calculated by determining its present value using the discount rate of 6 per cent. The calculations and journal entries are illustrated below:

	CU
Proceeds from the bond issue (A)	50,000
Present value of principal at the end of five years (see calculations below)	37,363
Present value of interest payable annually in arrears for five years	8,425
Present value of liability, which is the fair value of liability component (B)	45,788
Residual, which is the fair value of the equity component (A) – (B)	4,212

The issuer of the bonds makes the following journal entry at issue on 1 January 20X5:

Dr Cash	CU50,000
Cr Financial Liability – Convertible bond	CU45,788
Cr Equity	CU4,212

The CU4,212 represents a discount on issue of the bonds, so the entry could also be shown 'gross':

Dr Cash	CU50,000
Dr Financial Liability – Convertible bond discount	CU4,212
Cr Financial Liability – Convertible bond	CU50,000
Cr Equity	CU4,212

After issue, the issuer will amortise the bond discount according to the following table:

	(a) Interest payment	(b) Total interest expense = 6% × (e)	(c) Amortisation of bond discount = (b) – (a)	(d) Bond discount = (d) – (c)	(e) Net liability = 50,000 – (d)
	CU	CU	CU	CU	CU
1/1/20X5				4,212	45,788
31/12/20X5	2,000	2,747	747	3,465	46,535
31/12/20X6	2,000	2,792	792	2,673	47,327
31/12/20X7	2,000	2,840	840	1,833	48,167
31/12/20X8	2,000	2,890	890	943	49,057
31/12/20X9	2,000	2,943	943	0	50,000
Totals	10,000	14,212	4,212		

At the end of 20X5, the issuer would make the following journal entry:

Dr Interest expense	CU2,747
Cr Bond discount	CU747
Cr Cash	CU2,000

Calculations

Present value of principal of CU50,000 at 6 per cent

$CU50,000/(1.06)^5 = 37,363$

Present value of the interest annuity of CU2,000 (= CU50,000 × 4 per cent) payable at the end of each of five years

The CU2,000 annual interest payments are an annuity: a cash flow stream with a limited number (n) of periodic payments (C), receivable at dates 1 to n. To calculate the present value of this annuity, future payments are discounted by the periodic rate of interest (i) using the following formula:

$$PV = C/i \times [1 - 1/(1 + i)^n]$$

Therefore, the present value of the CU2,000 interest payments is $(2,000/.06) \times [1 - [(1/1.06)^5] = 8,425$

This is equivalent to the sum of the present values of the five individual CU2,000 payments, as follows:

	CU
Present value of interest payment at 31 December 20X5 = 2,000/1.06	1,887
Present value of interest payment at 31 December 20X6 = $2,000/1.06^2$	1,780
Present value of interest payment at 31 December 20X7 = $2,000/1.06^3$	1,679
Present value of interest payment at 31 December 20X8 = $2,000/1.06^4$	1,584
Present value of interest payment at 31 December 20X9 = $2,000/1.06^5$	1,495
Total	8,425

Yet another way to calculate this is to use a table of present value of an ordinary annuity in arrears, five periods, interest rate of 6 per cent per period. (Such tables are easily found on the Internet.) The present value factor is 4.2124. Multiplying this by the annuity payment of CU2,000 determines the present value of CU8,425.

Section 23 *Revenue*

Scope of this section

23.1   This section shall be applied in accounting for **revenue** arising from the following transactions and events:

(a)   the sale of goods (whether produced by the entity for the purpose of sale or purchased for resale);

(b)   the rendering of services;

(c)   **construction contracts** in which the entity is the contractor; and

(d)   the use by others of entity assets yielding interest, royalties or dividends.

23.2   Revenue or other income arising from some transactions and events is dealt with in other sections of this FRS:

(a)   lease agreements (see Section 20 *Leases*);

(b)   dividends and other income arising from investments that are accounted for using the equity method (see Section 14 *Investments in Associates* and Section 15 *Investments in Joint Ventures*);

(c)   changes in the **fair value** of **financial assets** and **financial liabilities** or their disposal (see Section 11 *Basic Financial Instruments* and Section 12 *Other Financial Instruments Issues*);

(d)   changes in the fair value of **investment property** (see Section 16 *Investment Property*);

(e)   initial **recognition** and changes in the fair value of **biological assets** related to **agricultural activity** (see Section 34 *Specialised Activities*); and

(f)   initial recognition of **agricultural produce** (see Section 34).

23.2A   This section excludes revenue or other income arising from transactions and events dealt with in FRS 103 *Insurance Contracts*.

Measurement of revenue

An entity shall measure revenue at the fair value of the consideration received or receivable. The fair value of the consideration received or receivable takes into account the amount of any trade discounts, prompt settlement discounts and volume rebates allowed by the entity.   **23.3**

An entity shall include in revenue only the gross inflows of economic benefits received and receivable by the entity on its own account. An entity shall exclude from revenue all amounts collected on behalf of third parties such as sales taxes, goods and services taxes and value added taxes. In an agency relationship, an entity (the **agent**) shall include in revenue only the amount of its commission. The amounts collected on behalf of the **principal** are not revenue of the entity.   **23.4**

Deferred payment

When the inflow of **cash** or **cash equivalents** is deferred, and the arrangement constitutes in effect a financing transaction, the fair value of the consideration is the **present value** of all future receipts determined using an **imputed rate of interest**. A financing transaction arises when, for example, an entity provides interest-free credit to the buyer or accepts a note receivable bearing a below-market interest rate from the buyer as consideration for the sale of goods. The imputed rate of interest is the more clearly determinable of either: **23.5**

(a)   the prevailing rate for a similar instrument of an issuer with a similar credit rating; or
(b)   a rate of interest that discounts the nominal amount of the instrument to the current cash sales price of the goods or services.

An entity shall recognise the difference between the present value of all future receipts and the nominal amount of the consideration as interest revenue in accordance with paragraphs 23.28 and 23.29 and Section 11.

Exchanges of goods or services

An entity shall not recognise revenue: **23.6**

(a)   when goods or services are exchanged for goods or services that are of a similar nature and value; or
(b)   when goods or services are exchanged for dissimilar goods or services but the transaction lacks commercial substance.

An entity shall recognise revenue when goods are sold or services are exchanged for dissimilar goods or services in a transaction that has commercial substance. In that case, the entity shall measure the transaction: **23.7**

(a)   at the fair value of the goods or services received adjusted by the amount of any cash or cash equivalents transferred;
(b)   if the amount under (a) cannot be measured reliably, then at the fair value of the goods or services given up adjusted by the amount of any cash or cash equivalents transferred; or
(c)   if the fair value of neither the goods or services received nor the goods or services given up can be measured reliably, then at the **carrying amount** of the goods or services given up adjusted by the amount of any cash or cash equivalents transferred.

Identification of the revenue transaction

An entity usually applies the revenue recognition criteria in this section separately to each transaction. However, an entity applies the recognition criteria to the separately   **23.8** identifiable components of a single transaction when necessary to reflect the substance of the transaction. For example, an entity applies the recognition criteria to the separately identifiable components of a single transaction when the selling price of a product includes an identifiable amount for subsequent servicing. Conversely, an entity applies the recognition criteria to two or more transactions together when they are linked in such a way that the commercial effect cannot be understood without reference to the series of transactions as a whole. For example, an entity applies the recognition criteria to two or more transactions together when it sells goods and, at the same time, enters into a separate agreement to repurchase the goods at a later date, thus negating the substantive effect of the transaction.

23.9   Sometimes, as part of a sales transaction, an entity grants its customer a loyalty award that the customer may redeem in the future for free or discounted goods or services. In this case, in accordance with paragraph 23.8, the entity shall account for the award credits as a separately identifiable component of the initial sales transaction. The entity shall allocate the fair value of the consideration received or receivable in respect of the initial sale between the award credits and the other components of the sale. The consideration allocated to the award credits shall be measured by reference to their fair value, ie the amount for which the award credits could be sold separately.

Sale of goods

23.10   An entity shall recognise revenue from the sale of goods when all the following conditions are satisfied:

(a)   the entity has transferred to the buyer the significant risks and rewards of ownership of the goods;

(b)   the entity retains neither continuing managerial involvement to the degree usually associated with ownership nor effective control over the goods sold;

(c)   the amount of revenue can be measured reliably;

(d)   it is **probable** that the economic benefits associated with the transaction will flow to the entity; and

(e)   the costs incurred or to be incurred in respect of the transaction can be measured reliably.

23.11   The assessment of when an entity has transferred the significant risks and rewards of ownership to the buyer requires an examination of the circumstances of the transaction. In most cases, the transfer of the risks and rewards of ownership coincides with the transfer of the legal title or the passing of possession to the buyer. This is the case for most retail sales. In other cases, the transfer of risks and rewards of ownership occurs at a time different from the transfer of legal title or the passing of possession.

23.12   An entity does not recognise revenue if it retains significant risks and rewards of ownership. Examples of situations in which the entity may retain the significant risks and rewards of ownership are:

(a)   when the entity retains an obligation for unsatisfactory performance not covered by normal warranties;

(b)   when the receipt of the revenue from a particular sale is contingent on the buyer selling the goods;

(c)   when the goods are shipped subject to installation and the installation is a significant part of the contract that has not yet been completed; and

(d)   when the buyer has the right to rescind the purchase for a reason specified in the sales contract, or at the buyer's sole discretion without any reason, and the entity is uncertain about the probability of return.

If an entity retains only an insignificant risk of ownership, the transaction is a sale and the   **23.13**
entity recognises the revenue. For example, a seller recognises revenue when it retains the
legal title to the goods solely to protect the collectability of the amount due. Similarly an
entity recognises revenue when it offers a refund if the customer finds the goods faulty
or is not satisfied for other reasons, and the entity can estimate the returns reliably. In
such cases, the entity recognises a **provision** for returns in accordance with Section 21
Provisions and Contingencies.

Rendering of services

When the outcome of a transaction involving the rendering of services can be estimated   **23.14**
reliably, an entity shall recognise revenue associated with the transaction by reference to
the stage of completion of the transaction at the end of the **reporting period** (sometimes
referred to as the percentage of completion method). The outcome of a transaction can be
estimated reliably when all the following conditions are satisfied:

(a)   the amount of revenue can be measured reliably;
(b)   it is probable that the economic benefits associated with the transaction will flow to
      the entity;
(c)   the stage of completion of the transaction at the end of the reporting period can be
      measured reliably; and
(d)   the costs incurred for the transaction and the costs to complete the transaction can be
      measured reliably.

Paragraphs 23.21 to 23.27 provide guidance for applying the percentage of completion
method.

When services are performed by an indeterminate number of acts over a specified period   **23.15**
of time, an entity recognises revenue on a straight-line basis over the specified period
unless there is evidence that some other method better represents the stage of completion.
When a specific act is much more significant than any other act, the entity postpones
recognition of revenue until the significant act is executed.

When the outcome of the transaction involving the rendering of services cannot be   **23.16**
estimated reliably, an entity shall recognise revenue only to the extent of the **expenses**
recognised that are recoverable.

Construction contracts

When the outcome of a construction contract can be estimated reliably, an entity shall   **23.17**
recognise contract revenue and contract costs associated with the construction contract as
revenue and expenses respectively by reference to the stage of completion of the contract
activity at the end of the reporting period (often referred to as the percentage of completion
method). Reliable estimation of the outcome requires reliable estimates of the stage of
completion, future costs and collectability of billings. Paragraphs 23.21 to 23.27 provide
guidance for applying the percentage of completion method.

The requirements of this section are usually applied separately to each construction   **23.18**
contract. However, in some circumstances, it is necessary to apply this section to the
separately identifiable components of a single contract or to a group of contracts together
in order to reflect the substance of a contract or a group of contracts.

When a contract covers a number of **assets**, the construction of each asset shall be treated   **23.19**
as a separate construction contract when:

(a)   separate proposals have been submitted for each asset;

(b)   each asset has been subject to separate negotiation, and the contractor and customer are able to accept or reject that part of the contract relating to each asset; and

(c)   the costs and revenues of each asset can be identified.

23.20   A group of contracts, whether with a single customer or with several customers, shall be treated as a single construction contract when:

(a)   the group of contracts is negotiated as a single package;

(b)   the contracts are so closely interrelated that they are, in effect, part of a single project with an overall profit margin; and

(c)   the contracts are performed concurrently or in a continuous sequence.

Percentage of completion method

23.21   This method is used to recognise revenue from rendering services (see paragraphs 23.14 to 23.16) and from construction contracts (see paragraphs 23.17 to 23.20). An entity shall review and, when necessary, revise the estimates of revenue and costs as the service transaction or construction contract progresses.

23.22   An entity shall determine the stage of completion of a transaction or contract using the method that measures most reliably the work performed. Possible methods include:

(a)   the proportion that costs incurred for work performed to date bear to the estimated total costs. Costs incurred for work performed to date do not include costs relating to future activity, such as for materials or prepayments;

(b)   surveys of work performed; and

(c)   completion of a physical proportion of the contract work or the completion of a proportion of the service contract.

Progress payments and advances received from customers often do not reflect the work performed.

23.23   An entity shall recognise costs that relate to future activity on the transaction or contract, such as for materials or prepayments, as an asset if it is probable that the costs will be recovered.

23.24   An entity shall recognise as an expense immediately any costs whose recovery is not probable.

23.25   When the outcome of a construction contract cannot be estimated reliably:

(a)   an entity shall recognise revenue only to the extent of contract costs incurred that it is probable will be recoverable; and

(b)   the entity shall recognise contract costs as an expense in the period in which they are incurred.

23.26   When it is probable that total contract costs will exceed total contract revenue on a construction contract, the expected loss shall be recognised as an expense immediately, with a corresponding provision for an **onerous contract** (see Section 21).

23.27   If the collectability of an amount already recognised as contract revenue is no longer probable, the entity shall recognise the uncollectible amount as an expense rather than as an adjustment of the amount of contract revenue.

Interest, royalties and dividends

An entity shall recognise revenue arising from the use by others of entity assets yielding **23.28** interest, royalties and dividends on the bases set out in paragraph 23.29 when:

(a)   it is probable that the economic benefits associated with the transaction will flow to the entity; and

(b)   the amount of the revenue can be measured reliably.

An entity shall recognise revenue on the following bases: **23.29**

(a)   Interest shall be recognised using the **effective interest method** as described in paragraphs 11.15 to 11.20. When calculating the **effective interest rate**, an entity shall include any related fees, finance charges paid or received (such as 'points'), **transaction costs** and other premiums or discounts.

(b)   Royalties shall be recognised on an **accrual basis** in accordance with the substance of the relevant agreement.

(c)   Dividends shall be recognised when the shareholder's right to receive payment is established.

Disclosures

General disclosures about revenue

An entity shall disclose: **23.30**

(a)   the **accounting policies** adopted for the recognition of revenue, including the methods adopted to determine the stage of completion of transactions involving the rendering of services; and

(b)   the amount of each category of revenue recognised during the period, showing separately, at a minimum, revenue arising from:

   (i)   the sale of goods;
   (ii)   the rendering of services;
   (iii) interest;
   (iv)   royalties;
   (v)   dividends;
   (vi)   commissions;
   (vii) grants; and
   (viii) any other significant types of revenue.

Disclosures relating to revenue from construction contracts

An entity shall disclose the following: **23.31**

(a)   the amount of contract revenue recognised as revenue in the period;

(b)   the methods used to determine the contract revenue recognised in the period; and

(c)   the methods used to determine the stage of completion of contracts in progress.

An entity shall present: **23.32**

(a)   the gross amount due from customers for contract work, as an asset; and

(b)   the gross amount due to customers for contract work, as a **liability**.

Appendix to Section 23

Examples of revenue recognition under the principles in Section 23

This appendix accompanies, but is not part of, Section 23. It provides guidance for applying the requirements of Section 23 in recognising revenue.

23A.1   The following examples focus on particular aspects of a transaction and are not a comprehensive discussion of all the relevant factors that might influence the recognition of revenue. The examples generally assume that the amount of revenue can be measured reliably, it is probable that the economic benefits will flow to the entity and the costs incurred or to be incurred can be measured reliably.

Sale of goods

23A.2   The law in different countries may cause the recognition criteria in Section 23 to be met at different times. In particular, the law may determine the point in time at which the entity transfers the significant risks and rewards of ownership. Therefore, the examples in this appendix need to be read in the context of the laws relating to the sale of goods in the country in which the transaction takes place.

Example 1 'Bill and hold' sales, in which delivery is delayed at the buyer's request but the buyer takes title and accepts billing

23A.3   The seller recognises revenue when the buyer takes title, provided:

    (a)   it is probable that delivery will be made;

    (b)   the item is on hand, identified and ready for delivery to the buyer at the time the sale is recognised;

    (c)   the buyer specifically acknowledges the deferred delivery instructions; and

    (d)   the usual payment terms apply.

Revenue is not recognised when there is simply an intention to acquire or manufacture the goods in time for delivery.

Example 2 Goods shipped subject to conditions: installation and inspection

23A.4   The seller normally recognises revenue when the buyer accepts delivery, and installation and inspection are complete. However, revenue is recognised immediately upon the buyer's acceptance of delivery when:

    (a)   the installation process is simple, for example the installation of a factory-tested television receiver that requires only unpacking and connection of power and antennae; or

    (b)   the inspection is performed only for the purposes of final determination of contract prices, for example, shipments of iron ore, sugar or soya beans.

Example 3 Goods shipped subject to conditions: on approval when the buyer has negotiated a limited right of return

23A.5   If there is uncertainty about the possibility of return, the seller recognises revenue when the shipment has been formally accepted by the buyer or the goods have been delivered and the time period for rejection has elapsed.

Example 4 Goods shipped subject to conditions: consignment sales under which the recipient (buyer) undertakes to sell the goods on behalf of the shipper (seller)

The shipper recognises revenue when the goods are sold by the recipient to a third party. **23A.6**

Example 5 Goods shipped subject to conditions: cash on delivery sales

The seller recognises revenue when delivery is made and cash is received by the seller or **23A.7** its agent.

Example 6 Layaway sales under which the goods are delivered only when the buyer makes the final payment in a series of instalments

The seller recognises revenue from such sales when the goods are delivered. However, when **23A.8** experience indicates that most such sales are consummated, revenue may be recognised when a significant deposit is received, provided the goods are on hand, identified and ready for delivery to the buyer.

Example 7 Orders when payment (or partial payment) is received in advance of delivery for goods not currently held in inventory, for example, the goods are still to be manufactured or will be delivered direct to the buyer from a third party

The seller recognises revenue when the goods are delivered to the buyer. **23A.9**

Example 8 Sale and repurchase agreements (other than swap transactions) under which the seller concurrently agrees to repurchase the same goods at a later date, or when the seller has a call option to repurchase, or the buyer has a put option to require the repurchase, by the seller, of the goods

For a sale and repurchase agreement on an asset other than a financial asset, the seller **23A.10** must analyse the terms of the agreement to ascertain whether, in substance, the risks and rewards of ownership have been transferred to the buyer. If they have been transferred, the seller recognises revenue. When the seller has retained the risks and rewards of ownership, even though legal title has been transferred, the transaction is a financing arrangement and does not give rise to revenue. For a sale and repurchase agreement on a financial asset, the derecognition provisions of Section 11 apply.

Example 9 Sales to intermediate parties, such as distributors, dealers or others for resale

The seller generally recognises revenue from such sales when the risks and rewards of **23A.11** ownership have been transferred. However, when the buyer is acting, in substance, as an agent, the sale is treated as a consignment sale.

Example 10 Subscriptions to publications and similar items

When the items involved are of similar value in each time period, the seller recognises **23A.12** revenue on a straight-line basis over the period in which the items are dispatched. When the items vary in value from period to period, the seller recognises revenue on the basis of the sales value of the item dispatched in relation to the total estimated sales value of all items covered by the subscription.

Example 11 Instalment sales, under which the consideration is receivable in instalments

23A.13   The seller recognises revenue attributable to the sales price, exclusive of interest, at the date of sale. The sale price is the present value of the consideration, determined by discounting the instalments receivable at the imputed rate of interest. The seller recognises the interest element as revenue using the effective interest method.

Example 12 Agreements for the construction of real estate

23A.14   An entity that undertakes the construction of real estate, directly or through subcontractors, and enters into an agreement with one or more buyers before construction is complete, shall account for the agreement using the percentage of completion method, only if:

(a)   the buyer is able to specify the major structural elements of the design of the real estate before construction begins and/or specify major structural changes once construction is in progress (whether it exercises that ability or not); or

(b)   the buyer acquires and supplies construction materials and the entity provides only construction services.

23A.15   If the entity is required to provide services together with construction materials in order to perform its contractual obligation to deliver real estate to the buyer, the agreement shall be accounted for as the sale of goods. In this case, the buyer does not obtain control or the significant risks and rewards of ownership of the work in progress in its current state as construction progresses. Rather, the transfer occurs only on delivery of the completed real estate to the buyer.

Example 13 Sale with customer loyalty award

23A.16   An entity sells product A for CU100. Purchasers of product A get an award credit enabling them to buy product B for CU10. The normal selling price of product B is CU18. The entity estimates that 40 per cent of the purchasers of product A will use their award to buy product B at CU10. The normal selling price of product A, after taking into account discounts that are usually offered but that are not available during this promotion, is CU95.

23A.17   The fair value of the award credit is 40 per cent × [CU18 – CU10] = CU3.20. The entity allocates the total revenue of CU100 between product A and the award credit by reference to their relative fair values of CU95 and CU3.20 respectively. Therefore:

(a)   Revenue for product A is CU100 × [CU95 / (CU95 + CU3.20)] = CU96.74

(b)   Revenue for product B is CU100 × [CU3.20 / (CU95 + CU3.20)] = CU3.26

Rendering of services

Example 14 Installation fees

23A.18   The seller recognises installation fees as revenue by reference to the stage of completion of the installation, unless they are incidental to the sale of a product, in which case they are recognised when the goods are sold.

Example 15 Servicing fees included in the price of the product

23A.19   When the selling price of a product includes an identifiable amount for subsequent servicing (eg after sales support and product enhancement on the sale of software), the seller defers that amount and recognises it as revenue over the period during which the service is performed. The amount deferred is that which will cover the expected costs of the services under the agreement, together with a reasonable profit on those services.

Example 16 Advertising commissions

Media commissions are recognised when the related advertisement or commercial appears before the public. Production commissions are recognised by reference to the stage of completion of the project.   23A.20

Example 17 Insurance agency commissions

Insurance agency commissions received or receivable that do not require the agent to render further service are recognised as revenue by the agent on the effective commencement or renewal dates of the related policies. However, when it is probable that the agent will be required to render further services during the life of the policy, the agent defers the commission, or part of it, and recognises it as revenue over the period during which the policy is in force.   23A.21

Example 17A Financial services fees

The recognition of revenue for financial service fees depends on the purposes for which the fees are assessed and the basis of accounting for any associated financial instrument. The description of fees for financial services may not be indicative of the nature and substance of the services provided. Therefore it is necessary to distinguish between fees that are an integral part of the effective interest rate of a financial instrument, fees that are earned as services are provided, and fees that are earned on the execution of a significant act.   23A.21A

Example 18 Admission fees

The seller recognises revenue from artistic performances, banquets and other special events when the event takes place. When a subscription to a number of events is sold, the seller allocates the fee to each event on a basis that reflects the extent to which services are performed at each event.   23A.22

Example 19 Tuition fees

The seller recognises revenue over the period of instruction.   23A.23

Example 20 Initiation, entrance and membership fees

Revenue recognition depends on the nature of the services provided. If the fee permits only membership, and all other services or products are paid for separately, or if there is a separate annual subscription, the fee is recognised as revenue when no significant uncertainty about its collectability exists. If the fee entitles the member to services or publications to be provided during the membership period, or to purchase goods or services at prices lower than those charged to non-members, it is recognised on a basis that reflects the timing, nature and value of the benefits provided.   23A.24

Franchise fees

Franchise fees may cover the supply of initial and subsequent services, equipment and other tangible assets, and know-how. Accordingly, franchise fees are recognised as revenue on a basis that reflects the purpose for which the fees were charged. The following methods of franchise fee recognition are appropriate.   23A.25

Example 21 Franchise fees: Supplies of equipment and other tangible assets

23A.26   The franchisor recognises the fair value of the assets sold as revenue when the items are delivered or title passes.

Example 22 Franchise fees: Supplies of initial and subsequent services

23A.27   The franchisor recognises fees for the provision of continuing services, whether part of the initial fee or a separate fee, as revenue as the services are rendered. When the separate fee does not cover the cost of continuing services together with a reasonable profit, part of the initial fee, sufficient to cover the costs of continuing services and to provide a reasonable profit on those services, is deferred and recognised as revenue as the services are rendered.

23A.28   The franchise agreement may provide for the franchisor to supply equipment, inventories, or other tangible assets at a price lower than that charged to others or a price that does not provide a reasonable profit on those sales. In these circumstances, part of the initial fee, sufficient to cover estimated costs in excess of that price and to provide a reasonable profit on those sales, is deferred and recognised over the period the goods are likely to be sold to the franchisee. The balance of an initial fee is recognised as revenue when performance of all the initial services and other obligations required of the franchisor (such as assistance with site selection, staff training, financing and advertising) has been substantially accomplished.

23A.29   The initial services and other obligations under an area franchise agreement may depend on the number of individual outlets established in the area. In this case, the fees attributable to the initial services are recognised as revenue in proportion to the number of outlets for which the initial services have been substantially completed.

23A.30   If the initial fee is collectible over an extended period and there is a significant uncertainty that it will be collected in full, the fee is recognised as cash instalments are received.

Example 23 Franchise fees: Continuing franchise fees

23A.31   Fees charged for the use of continuing rights granted by the agreement, or for other services provided during the period of the agreement, are recognised as revenue as the services are provided or the rights used.

Example 24 Franchise fees: Agency transactions

23A.32   Transactions may take place between the franchisor and the franchisee that, in substance, involve the franchisor acting as agent for the franchisee. For example, the franchisor may order supplies and arrange for their delivery to the franchisee at no profit. Such transactions do not give rise to revenue.

Example 25 Fees from the development of customised software

23A.33   The software developer recognises fees from the development of customised software as revenue by reference to the stage of completion of the development, including completion of services provided for post-delivery service support.

Interest, royalties and dividends

Example 26 Licence fees and royalties

The licensor recognises fees and royalties paid for the use of an entity's assets (such as trademarks, patents, software, music copyright, record masters and motion picture films) in accordance with the substance of the agreement. As a practical matter, this may be on a straight-line basis over the life of the agreement, for example, when a licensee has the right to use specified technology for a specified period of time.   **23A.34**

An assignment of rights for a fixed fee or non-refundable guarantee under a non-cancellable contract that permits the licensee to exploit those rights freely and the licensor has no remaining obligations to perform is, in substance, a sale. An example is a licensing agreement for the use of software when the licensor has no obligations after delivery. Another example is the granting of rights to exhibit a motion picture film in markets in which the licensor has no control over the distributor and expects to receive no further revenues from the box office receipts. In such cases, revenue is recognised at the time of sale.   **23A.35**

In some cases, whether or not a licence fee or royalty will be received is contingent on the occurrence of a future event. In such cases, revenue is recognised only when it is probable that the fee or royalty will be received, which is normally when the event has occurred.   **23A.36**

Section 24 *Government Grants*

Scope of this section

This section specifies the accounting for all **government grants**. A government grant is assistance by government in the form of a transfer of resources to an entity in return for past or future compliance with specified conditions relating to the **operating activities** of the entity.   **24.1**

Government grants exclude those forms of government assistance that cannot reasonably have a value placed upon them and transactions with government that cannot be distinguished from the normal trading transactions of the entity.   **24.2**

This section does not cover government assistance that is provided for an entity in the form of benefits that are available in determining **taxable profit (tax loss)**, or are determined or limited on the basis of income tax liability. Examples of such benefits are income tax holidays, investment tax credits, accelerated depreciation allowances and reduced income tax rates. Section 29 *Income Tax* covers accounting for taxes based on **income**.   **24.3**

Recognition and measurement

Government grants, including non-monetary grants shall not be recognised until there is reasonable assurance that: **24.3A**

(a)   the entity will comply with the conditions attaching to them; and
(b)   the grants will be received.

An entity shall recognise grants either based on the performance model or the accrual model. This policy choice shall be applied on a class-by-class basis.   **24.4**

An entity shall measure grants at the **fair value** of the **asset** received or receivable.   **24.5**

24.5A   Where a grant becomes repayable it shall be recognised as a **liability** when the repayment meets the definition of a liability.

Performance model

24.5B   An entity applying the performance model shall recognise grants as follows:

(a)   A grant that does not impose specified future **performance-related conditions** on the recipient is recognised in income when the grant proceeds are received or receivable.

(b)   A grant that imposes specified future performance-related conditions on the recipient is recognised in income only when the performance-related conditions are met.

(c)   Grants received before the **revenue recognition** criteria are satisfied are recognised as a liability.

Accrual model

24.5C   An entity applying the accrual model shall classify grants either as a grant relating to revenue or a grant relating to assets.

24.5D   Grants relating to revenue shall be recognised in income on a systematic basis over the periods in which the entity recognises the related costs for which the grant is intended to compensate.

24.5E   A grant that becomes receivable as compensation for **expenses** or losses already incurred or for the purpose of giving immediate financial support to the entity with no future related costs shall be recognised in income in the period in which it becomes receivable.

24.5F   Grants relating to assets shall be recognised in income on a systematic basis over the expected **useful life** of the asset.

24.5G   Where part of a grant relating to an asset is deferred it shall be recognised as deferred income and not deducted from the **carrying amount** of the asset.

Disclosures

24.6   An entity shall disclose the following:

(a)   the **accounting policy** adopted for grants in accordance with paragraph 24.4;

(b)   the nature and amounts of grants recognised in the **financial statements**;

(c)   unfulfilled conditions and other contingencies attaching to grants that have been recognised in income; and

(d)   an indication of other forms of government assistance from which the entity has directly benefited.

24.7   For the purpose of the disclosure required by paragraph 24.6(d), government assistance is action by government designed to provide an economic benefit specific to an entity or range of entities qualifying under specified criteria. Examples include free technical or marketing advice, the provision of guarantees, and loans at nil or low interest rates.

Section 25 *Borrowing Costs*

Scope of this section

This section specifies the accounting for **borrowing costs**. Borrowing costs are interest   **25.1**
and other costs that an entity incurs in connection with the borrowing of funds. Borrowing
costs include:

(a) interest expense calculated using the **effective interest method** as described in
Section 11 *Basic Financial Instruments*;

(b) finance charges in respect of **finance leases** recognised in accordance with Section 20
Leases; and

(c) exchange differences arising from foreign currency borrowings to the extent that
they are regarded as an adjustment to interest costs.

Recognition

An entity may adopt a policy of capitalising borrowing costs that are directly attributable   **25.2**
to the acquisition, construction or production of a **qualifying asset** as part of the cost of
that **asset**. Where an entity adopts a policy of capitalisation of borrowing costs, it shall be
applied consistently to a class of qualifying assets. Where an entity does not adopt a policy
of capitalising borrowing costs, all borrowing costs shall be recognised as an **expense** in
profit or loss in the period in which they are incurred.

The borrowing costs that are directly attributable to the acquisition, construction or   **25.2A**
production of a qualifying asset are those borrowing costs that would have been avoided if
the expenditure on the qualifying asset had not been made.

To the extent that an entity borrows funds specifically for the purpose of obtaining a   **25.2B**
qualifying asset, the entity shall determine the amount of borrowing costs eligible for
capitalisation as the actual borrowing costs incurred on that borrowing during the period
less any investment income on the temporary investment of those borrowings.

To the extent that funds applied to obtain a qualifying asset form part of the entity's general   **25.2C**
borrowings, the amount of borrowing costs eligible for capitalisation are determined
by applying a capitalisation rate to the expenditure on that asset. For this purpose the
expenditure on the asset is the average **carrying amount** of the asset during the period,
including borrowing costs previously capitalised. The capitalisation rate used in an
accounting period shall be the weighted average of rates applicable to the entity's general
borrowings that are outstanding during the period. This excludes borrowings by the entity
that are specifically for the purpose of obtaining other qualifying assets. The amount of
borrowing costs that an entity capitalises during a period shall not exceed the amount of
borrowing costs it incurred during that period.

An entity shall: **25.2D**

(a) capitalise borrowing costs as part of the cost of a qualifying asset from the point when
it first incurs both expenditure on the asset and borrowing costs, and undertakes
activities necessary to prepare the asset for its intended use or sale;

(b) suspend capitalisation during extended periods where active development of the
asset has paused; and

(c) cease capitalisation when substantially all the activities necessary to prepare the
qualifying asset for its intended use or sale are complete.

Disclosures

25.3   Paragraph 5.5 sets out the presentation requirements for items of profit or loss, including interest payable. Paragraph 11.48(b) requires disclosure of total interest expense (using the effective interest method) for **financial liabilities** that are not at fair value through profit or loss. When a policy of capitalising borrowing costs is not adopted, this section does not require any additional disclosure.

25.3A   Where a policy of capitalisation is adopted, an entity shall disclose:

*(a)   the amount of borrowing costs capitalised in the period; and

(b)   the capitalisation rate used.

Section 26 *Share-based Payment*

Scope of this section

26.1   This section specifies the accounting for all **share-based payment transactions** including:

(a)   **equity-settled share-based payment transactions**, in which the entity:

(i)   receives goods or services as consideration for its own equity instruments (including shares or **share options**); or

(ii)   receives goods or services but has no obligation to settle the transaction with supplier;

(b)   **cash-settled share-based payment transactions**, in which the entity acquires goods or services by incurring a **liability** to transfer **cash** or other assets to the supplier of those goods or services for amounts that are based on the price (or value) of the entity's shares or other equity instruments of the entity or another group entity; and

(c)   transactions in which the entity receives or acquires goods or services and the terms of the arrangement provide either the entity or the supplier of those goods or services with a choice of whether the entity settles the transaction in cash (or other assets) or by issuing equity instruments.

26.1A   A share-based payment transaction may be settled by another group entity (or a shareholder of any group entity) on behalf of the entity receiving or acquiring the goods or services. Paragraph 26.1 also applies to an entity that:

(a)   receives goods or services when another entity in the same group (or shareholder of any group entity) has the obligation to settle the share-based payment transaction; or

(b)   has an obligation to settle a share-based payment transaction when another entity in the same group receives the goods or services

unless the transaction is clearly for a purpose other than payment for goods or services supplied to the entity receiving them.

26.2   Cash-settled share-based payment transactions include share appreciation rights. For example, an entity might grant share appreciation rights to employees as part of their remuneration package, whereby the employees will become entitled to a future cash payment (rather than an equity instrument), based on the increase in the entity's share price from a specified level over a specified period of time. Or an entity might grant to its employees a right to receive a future cash payment by granting to them a right to shares (including shares to be issued upon the exercise of share options) that are redeemable, either mandatorily (eg upon cessation of employment) or at the employee's option.

Recognition

An entity shall recognise the goods or services received or acquired in a share-based payment transaction when it obtains the goods or as the services are received. The entity shall recognise a corresponding increase in **equity** if the goods or services were received in an equity-settled share-based payment transaction, or a liability if the goods or services were acquired in a cash-settled share-based payment transaction. **26.3**

When the goods or services received or acquired in a share-based payment transaction do not qualify for **recognition** as assets, the entity shall recognise them as **expenses**. **26.4**

Recognition when there are vesting conditions

If the share-based payments granted to employees **vest** immediately, the employee is not required to complete a specified period of service before becoming unconditionally entitled to those share-based payments. In the absence of evidence to the contrary, the entity shall presume that services rendered by the employee as consideration for the share-based payments have been received. In this case, on **grant date** the entity shall recognise the services received in full, with a corresponding increase in equity or liabilities. **26.5**

If the share-based payments do not vest until the employee completes a specified period of service, the entity shall presume that the services to be rendered by the counterparty as consideration for those share-based payments will be received in the future, during the vesting period. The entity shall account for those services as they are rendered by the employee during the vesting period, with a corresponding increase in equity or liabilities. **26.6**

Measurement of equity-settled share-based payment transactions

Measurement principle

For equity-settled share-based payment transactions, an entity shall measure the goods or services received, and the corresponding increase in equity, at the **fair value** of the goods or services received, unless that fair value cannot be estimated reliably. If the entity cannot estimate reliably the fair value of the goods or services received, the entity shall measure their value, and the corresponding increase in equity, by reference to the fair value of the equity instruments granted measured in accordance with paragraphs 26.10 and 26.11. To apply this requirement to transactions with employees and others providing similar services, the entity shall measure the fair value of the services received by reference to the fair value of the equity instruments granted, because typically it is not possible to estimate reliably the fair value of the services received. **26.7**

For transactions with employees (including others providing similar services), the fair value of the equity instruments shall be measured at grant date. For transactions with parties other than employees, the measurement date is the date when the entity obtains the goods or the counterparty renders service. **26.8**

A grant of equity instruments might be conditional on employees satisfying specified vesting conditions related to service or performance. An example of a vesting condition relating to service is where a grant of shares or share options is conditional on the employee remaining in the entity's employ for a specified period of time. Examples of vesting conditions relating to performance are where a grant of shares or share options is conditional on the entity achieving a specified growth in profit (an example of a non-market condition) or a specified increase in the entity's share price (an example of a **market condition**). All vesting conditions related solely to employee service or to a non- **26.9** market performance condition shall be taken into account when estimating the number of equity instruments expected to vest. Subsequently, the entity shall revise that estimate, if necessary, if new information indicates that the number of equity instruments expected to vest differs from previous estimates. On the vesting date, the entity shall revise the estimate to equal the number of equity instruments that ultimately vested. All market conditions and non-vesting conditions shall be taken into account when estimating the fair value of the shares or share options at the measurement date, with no subsequent adjustment irrespective of the outcome of the market or non-vesting condition, provided that all other vesting conditions are satisfied.

Shares

26.10   An entity shall measure the fair value of shares (and the related goods or services received) using the following three-tier measurement hierarchy:

(a)   If an observable market price is available for the equity instruments granted, use that price.

(b)   If an observable market price is not available, measure the fair value of equity instruments granted using entity-specific observable market data such as:

(i)   a recent transaction in the entity's shares; or

(ii)   a recent independent fair valuation of the entity or its principal assets.

(c)   If an observable market price is not available and obtaining a reliable **measurement** of fair value under (b) is **impracticable**, indirectly measure the fair value of the shares using a valuation method that uses market data to the greatest extent practicable to estimate what the price of those equity instruments would be on the grant date in an arm's length transaction between knowledgeable, willing parties. The entity's directors shall use their judgement to apply a generally accepted valuation methodology for valuing equity instruments that is appropriate to the circumstances of the entity.

Share options and equity-settled share appreciation rights

26.11   An entity shall measure the fair value of share options and equity-settled share appreciation rights (and the related goods or services received) using the following three-tier measurement hierarchy:

(a)   If an observable market price is available for the equity instruments granted, use that price.

(b)   If an observable market price is not available, measure the fair value of share options and share appreciation rights granted using entity-specific observable market data such as for a recent transaction in the share options.

(c)   If an observable market price is not available and obtaining a reliable measurement of fair value under (b) is impracticable, indirectly measure the fair value of share options or share appreciation rights using an alternative valuation methodology such as an option pricing model. The inputs for an option pricing model (such as the weighted average share price, exercise price, expected volatility, option life, expected dividends and the risk-free interest rate) shall use market data to the greatest extent possible. Paragraph 26.10 provides guidance on determining the fair value of the shares used in determining the weighted average share price. The entity shall derive an estimate of expected volatility consistent with the valuation methodology used to determine the fair value of the shares.

26.12   **Modifications to the terms and conditions on which equity instruments were granted**

If an entity modifies the vesting conditions in a manner that is beneficial to the employee, for example, by reducing the exercise price of an option or reducing the vesting period or by modifying or eliminating a performance condition, the entity shall take the modified vesting conditions into account in accounting for the share-based payment transaction, as follows:

(a) If the modification increases the fair value of the equity instruments granted (or increases the number of equity instruments granted) measured immediately before and after the modification, the entity shall include the incremental fair value granted in the measurement of the amount recognised for services received as consideration for the equity instruments granted. The incremental fair value granted is the difference between the fair value of the modified equity instrument and that of the original equity instrument, both estimated as at the date of the modification. If the modification occurs during the vesting period, the incremental fair value granted is included in the measurement of the amount recognised for services received over the period from the modification date until the date when the modified equity instruments vest, in addition to the amount based on the grant date fair value of the original equity instruments, which is recognised over the remainder of the original vesting period.

(b) If the modification reduces the total fair value of the share-based payment arrangement, or apparently is not otherwise beneficial to the employee, the entity shall nevertheless continue to account for the services received as consideration for the equity instruments granted as if that modification had not occurred.

Cancellations and settlements

An entity shall account for a cancellation or settlement of an equity-settled share-based payment award as an acceleration of vesting, and therefore shall recognise immediately the amount that otherwise would have been recognised for services received over the remainder of the vesting period. **26.13**

Cash-settled share-based payment transactions

For cash-settled share-based payment transactions, an entity shall measure the goods or services acquired and the liability incurred at the fair value of the liability. Until the liability is settled, the entity shall remeasure the fair value of the liability at each **reporting date** and at the date of settlement, with any changes in fair value recognised in **profit or loss** for the period. **26.14**

Share-based payment transactions with cash alternatives

Some share-based payment transactions give either the entity or the counterparty a choice of settling the transaction in cash (or other assets) or by the transfer of equity instruments. **26.15**

When the entity has a choice of settlement of the transaction in cash (or other assets) or by the transfer of equity instruments, the entity shall account for the transaction as a wholly equity-settled share-based payment transaction in accordance with paragraphs 26.7 to 26.13 unless: **26.15A**

(a) the choice of settlement in equity instruments has no commercial substance (eg because the entity is legally prohibited from issuing shares); or

(b) the entity has a past practice or a stated policy of settling in cash, or generally settles in cash whenever the counterparty asks for cash settlement.

In circumstances (a) and (b) the entity shall account for the transaction as a wholly cash-settled transaction in accordance with paragraph 26.14.

26.15B   When the counterparty has a choice of settlement of the transaction in cash (or other assets) or by the transfer of equity instruments, the entity shall account for the transaction as a wholly cash-settled share-based payment transaction in accordance with paragraph 26.14 unless:

(a)   the choice of settlement in cash (or other assets) has no commercial substance because the cash settlement amount (or value of the other assets) bears no relationship to, and is likely to be lower in value than, the fair value of the equity instruments.

In circumstance (a) the entity shall account for the transaction as a wholly equity-settled transaction in accordance with paragraphs 26.7 to 26.13.

Group plans

26.16   If a share-based payment award is granted by an entity to the employees of one or more members in the **group**, the members are permitted, as an alternative to the treatment set out in paragraphs 26.3 to 26.15, to recognise and measure the sharebased payment expense on the basis of a reasonable allocation of the expense for the group.

Government-mandated plans

26.17   Some jurisdictions have programmes established under law by which equity investors (such as employees) are able to acquire equity without providing goods or services that can be specifically identified (or by providing goods or services that are clearly less than the fair value of the equity instruments granted). This indicates that other consideration has been or will be received (such as past or future employee services). These are equity-settled share-based payment transactions within the scope of this section. The entity shall measure the unidentifiable goods or services received (or to be received) as the difference between the fair value of the share-based payment and the fair value of any identifiable goods or services received (or to be received) measured at the grant date.

Disclosures

26.18   An entity shall disclose the following information about the nature and extent of share-based payment arrangements that existed during the period:

(a)   A description of each type of share-based payment arrangement that existed at any time during the period, including the general terms and conditions of each arrangement, such as vesting requirements, the maximum term of options granted, and the method of settlement (eg whether in cash or equity). An entity with substantially similar types of share-based payment arrangements may aggregate this information.

(b)   The number and weighted average exercise prices of share options for each of the following groups of options:

(i)   outstanding at the beginning of the period;

(ii)   granted during the period;

(iii)   forfeited during the period;

(iv)   exercised during the period;

(v)   expired during the period;

(vi)   outstanding at the end of the period; and

(vii)   exercisable at the end of the period.

26.19   For equity-settled share-based payment arrangements, an entity shall disclose information about how it measured the fair value of goods or services received or the value of the equity instruments granted. If a valuation methodology was used, the entity shall disclose the method and its reason for choosing it.

For cash-settled share-based payment arrangements, an entity shall disclose information about how the liability was measured.   **26.20**

For share-based payment arrangements that were modified during the period, an entity shall disclose an explanation of those modifications.   **26.21**

If the entity is part of a group share-based payment plan, and it recognises and measures its share-based payment expense on the basis of a reasonable allocation of the expense recognised for the group, it shall disclose that fact and the basis for the allocation (see paragraph 26.16).   **26.22**

An entity shall disclose the following information about the effect of share-based payment transactions on the entity's profit or loss for the period and on its **financial position**:   **26.23**

(a)   the total expense recognised in profit or loss for the period; and
(b)   the total **carrying amount** at the end of the period for liabilities arising from share-based payment transactions.

Section 27 *Impairment of Assets*

Objective and scope

An **impairment loss** occurs when the **carrying amount** of an **asset** exceeds its **recoverable amount**. This section shall be applied in accounting for the impairment of all assets other than the following, for which other sections of this FRS establish impairment requirements: **27.1**

(a)   assets arising from **construction contracts** (see Section 23 *Revenue*);
(b)   **deferred tax assets** (see Section 29 *Income Tax*);
(c)   assets arising from **employee benefits** (see Section 28 *Employee Benefits*);
(d)   **financial assets** within the scope of Section 11 *Basic Financial Instruments* or Section 12 *Other Financial Instruments Issues*;
(e)   **investment property** measured at **fair value** (see Section 16 *Investment Property*); and
(f)   **biological assets** related to **agricultural activity** measured at fair value less estimated costs to sell (see Section 34 *Specialised Activities*).

This section shall not apply in accounting for the impairment of **deferred acquisition costs** and **intangible assets** arising from contracts within the scope of FRS 103 *Insurance Contracts*.   **27.1A**

Impairment of inventories

Selling price less costs to complete and sell

An entity shall assess at each **reporting date** whether any **inventories** are impaired. The entity shall make the assessment by comparing the carrying amount of each item of inventory (or group of similar items – see paragraph 27.3) with its selling price less costs to complete and sell. If an item of inventory (or group of similar items) is impaired, the entity shall reduce the carrying amount of the inventory (or the group) to its selling price less costs to complete and sell. That reduction is an impairment loss and it is recognised immediately in **profit or loss**.   **27.2**

27.3 If it is **impracticable** to determine the selling price less costs to complete and sell for inventories item by item, the entity may group items of inventory relating to the same product line that have similar purposes or end uses and are produced and marketed in the same geographical area for the purpose of assessing impairment.

Reversal of impairment

27.4 An entity shall make a new assessment of selling price less costs to complete and sell at each subsequent reporting date. When the circumstances that previously caused inventories to be impaired no longer exist or when there is clear evidence of an increase in selling price less costs to complete and sell because of changed economic circumstances, the entity shall reverse the amount of the impairment (ie the reversal is limited to the amount of the original impairment loss) so that the new carrying amount is the lower of the cost and the revised selling price less costs to complete and sell.

Impairment of assets other than inventories

General principles

27.5 If, and only if, the recoverable amount of an asset is less than its carrying amount, the entity shall reduce the carrying amount of the asset to its recoverable amount. That reduction is an impairment loss. Paragraphs 27.11 to 27.20A provide guidance on measuring recoverable amount.

27.6 An entity shall recognise an impairment loss immediately in profit or loss, unless the asset is carried at a revalued amount in accordance with another section of this FRS (for example, in accordance with the revaluation model in Section 17 *Property, Plant and Equipment*). Any impairment loss of a revalued asset shall be treated as a revaluation decrease in accordance with that other section.

Indicators of impairment

27.7 An entity shall assess at each reporting date whether there is any indication that an asset may be impaired. If any such indication exists, the entity shall estimate the recoverable amount of the asset. If there is no indication of impairment, it is not necessary to estimate the recoverable amount.

27.8 If it is not possible to estimate the recoverable amount of the individual asset, an entity shall estimate the recoverable amount of the **cash-generating unit** to which the asset belongs. This may be the case because measuring recoverable amount requires forecasting **cash flows**, and sometimes individual assets do not generate cash flows by themselves. An asset's cash-generating unit is the smallest identifiable group of assets that includes the asset and generates cash inflows that are largely independent of the cash inflows from other assets or groups of assets.

27.9 In assessing whether there is any indication that an asset may be impaired, an entity shall consider, as a minimum, the following indications:

External sources of information

(a) During the period, an asset's market value has declined significantly more than would be expected as a result of the passage of time or normal use.

(b) Significant changes with an adverse effect on the entity have taken place during the period, or will take place in the near future, in the technological, market, economic or legal environment in which the entity operates or in the market to which an asset is dedicated.

(c)   Market interest rates or other market rates of return on investments have increased during the period, and those increases are likely to affect materially the discount rate used in calculating an asset's **value in use** and decrease the asset's **fair value less costs to sell**.

(d)   The carrying amount of the net assets of the entity is more than the estimated fair value of the entity as a whole (such an estimate may have been made, for example, in relation to the potential sale of part or all of the entity).
Internal sources of information

(e)   Evidence is available of obsolescence or physical damage of an asset.

(f)   Significant changes with an adverse effect on the entity have taken place during the period, or are expected to take place in the near future, in the extent to which, or manner in which, an asset is used or is expected to be used. These changes include the asset becoming idle, plans to discontinue or restructure the operation to which an asset belongs, plans to dispose of an asset before the previously expected date, and reassessing the **useful life** of an asset as finite rather than indefinite.

(g)   Evidence is available from internal reporting that indicates that the economic performance of an asset is, or will be, worse than expected. In this context economic performance includes operating results and cash flows.

If there is an indication that an asset may be impaired, this may indicate that the entity should review the remaining useful life, the **depreciation (amortisation)** method or the **residual value** for the asset and adjust it in accordance with the section of this FRS applicable to the asset (eg Section 17 *Property, Plant and Equipment* and Section 18 *Intangible Assets other than Goodwill*), even if no impairment loss is recognised for the asset.   **27.10**

Measuring recoverable amount

The recoverable amount of an asset or a cash-generating unit is the higher of its fair value less costs to sell and its value in use. If it is not possible to estimate the recoverable amount of an individual asset, references to an asset in paragraphs 27.12 to 27.20A should be read as references also to an asset's cash-generating unit.   **27.11**

It is not always necessary to determine both an asset's fair value less costs to sell and its value in use. If either of these amounts exceeds the asset's carrying amount, the asset is not impaired and it is not necessary to estimate the other amount.   **27.12**

If there is no reason to believe that an asset's value in use materially exceeds its fair value less costs to sell, the asset's fair value less costs to sell may be used as its recoverable amount. This will often be the case for an asset that is held for disposal.   **27.13**

Fair value less costs to sell

Fair value less costs to sell is the amount obtainable from the sale of an asset in an arm's length transaction between knowledgeable, willing parties, less the costs of disposal. The best evidence of the fair value less costs to sell of an asset is a price in a binding sale agreement in an arm's length transaction or a market price in an **active market**. If there is no binding sale agreement or active market for an asset, fair value less costs to sell is based on the best information available to reflect the amount that an entity could obtain, at the reporting date, from the disposal of the asset in an arm's length transaction between knowledgeable, willing parties, after deducting the costs of disposal. In determining this amount, an entity considers the outcome of recent transactions for similar assets within the same industry.   **27.14**

When determining an asset's fair value less costs to sell, consideration shall be given to any restrictions imposed on that asset. Costs to sell shall also include the cost of obtaining   **27.14A** relaxation of a restriction where necessary in order to enable the asset to be sold. If a restriction would also apply to any potential purchaser of an asset, the fair value of the asset may be lower than that of an asset whose use is not restricted.

Value in use

27.15   Value in use is the **present value** of the future cash flows expected to be derived from an asset. This present value calculation involves the following steps:

(a)   estimating the future cash inflows and outflows to be derived from continuing use of the asset and from its ultimate disposal; and

(b)   applying the appropriate discount rate to those future cash flows.

27.16   The following elements shall be reflected in the calculation of an asset's value in use:

(a)   an estimate of the future cash flows the entity expects to derive from the asset;

(b)   expectations about possible variations in the amount or timing of those future cash flows;

(c)   the time value of money, represented by the current market risk-free rate of interest;

(d)   the price for bearing the uncertainty inherent in the asset; and

(e)   other factors, such as illiquidity, that market participants would reflect in pricing the future cash flows the entity expects to derive from the asset.

27.17   In measuring value in use, estimates of future cash flows shall include:

(a)   projections of cash inflows from the continuing use of the asset;

(b)   projections of cash outflows that are necessarily incurred to generate the cash inflows from continuing use of the asset (including cash outflows to prepare the asset for use) and can be directly attributed, or allocated on a reasonable and consistent basis, to the asset; and

(c)   net cash flows, if any, expected to be received (or paid) for the disposal of the asset at the end of its useful life in an arm's length transaction between knowledgeable, willing parties.

The entity may wish to use any recent financial budgets or forecasts to estimate the cash flows, if available. To estimate cash flow projections beyond the period covered by the most recent budgets or forecasts an entity may wish to extrapolate the projections based on the budgets or forecasts using a steady or declining growth rate for subsequent years, unless an increasing rate can be justified.

27.18   Estimates of future cash flows shall not include:

(a)   cash inflows or outflows from **financing activities**; or

(b)   income tax receipts or payments.

27.19   Future cash flows shall be estimated for the asset in its current condition. Estimates of future cash flows shall not include estimated future cash inflows or outflows that are expected to arise from:

(a)   a future restructuring to which an entity is not yet committed; or

(b)   improving or enhancing the asset's performance.

27.20   The discount rate (rates) used in the present value calculation shall be a pre-tax rate (rates) that reflect(s) current market assessments of:

(a)   the time value of money; and

(b)   the risks specific to the asset for which the future cash flow estimates have not been adjusted.

The discount rate (rates) used to measure an asset's value in use shall not reflect risks for which the future cash flow estimates have been adjusted, to avoid double-counting.

For assets held for their **service potential**, a cash flow driven valuation (such as value in use) may not be appropriate. In these circumstances **value in use (in respect of assets held for their service potential)** is determined by the present value of the asset's remaining service potential plus the net amount the entity will receive from its disposal. In some cases this may be taken to be costs avoided by possession of the asset. Therefore, **depreciated replacement cost**, may be a suitable measurement model but other approaches may be used where more appropriate. **27.20A**

Recognising and measuring an impairment loss for a cash-generating unit

An impairment loss shall be recognised for a cash-generating unit if, and only if, the recoverable amount of the unit is less than the carrying amount of the unit. The impairment loss shall be allocated to reduce the carrying amount of the assets of the unit in the following order: **27.21**

(a) first, to reduce the carrying amount of any **goodwill** allocated to the cash-generating unit; and

(b) then, to the other assets of the unit pro rata on the basis of the carrying amount of each asset in the cash-generating unit.

However, an entity shall not reduce the carrying amount of any asset in the cash-generating unit below the highest of: **27.22**

(a) its fair value less costs to sell (if determinable);

(b) its value in use (if determinable); and

(c) zero.

Any excess amount of the impairment loss that cannot be allocated to an asset because of the restriction in paragraph 27.22 shall be allocated to the other assets of the unit pro rata on the basis of the carrying amount of those other assets. **27.23**

Additional requirements for impairment of goodwill

Goodwill, by itself, cannot be sold. Nor does it generate cash flows to an entity that are independent of the cash flows of other assets. As a consequence, the fair value of goodwill cannot be measured directly. Therefore, the fair value of goodwill must be derived from **measurement** of the fair value of the cash-generating unit(s) of which the goodwill is a part. **27.24**

For the purpose of impairment testing, goodwill acquired in a **business combination** shall, from the **acquisition date**, be allocated to each of the acquirer's cash-generating units that are expected to benefit from the synergies of the combination, irrespective of whether other assets or **liabilities** of the acquiree are assigned to those units. **27.25**

Part of the recoverable amount of a cash-generating unit is attributable to the **non-controlling interest** in goodwill. For the purpose of impairment testing of a non-wholly-owned cash-generating unit with goodwill, the carrying amount of that unit is notionally adjusted, before being compared with its recoverable amount, by grossing up the carrying amount of goodwill allocated to the unit to include the goodwill attributable to the non-controlling interest. This notionally adjusted carrying amount is then compared with the recoverable amount of the unit to determine whether the cash-generating unit is impaired. **27.26**

27.27   If goodwill cannot be allocated to individual cash-generating units (or groups of cash-generating units) on a non-arbitrary basis, then for the purposes of testing goodwill the entity shall test the impairment of goodwill by determining the recoverable amount of either:

(a)   the acquired entity in its entirety, if the goodwill relates to an acquired entity that has not been integrated. Integrated means the acquired **business** has been restructured or dissolved into the reporting entity or other **subsidiaries**; or

(b)   the entire group of entities, excluding any entities that have not been integrated, if the goodwill relates to an entity that has been integrated.

In applying this paragraph, an entity will need to separate goodwill into goodwill relating to entities that have been integrated and goodwill relating to entities that have not been integrated. Also the entity shall follow the requirements for cash-generating units in this section when calculating the recoverable amount of, and allocating impairment losses and reversals to assets belonging to, the acquired entity or group of entities.

Reversal of an impairment loss

27.28   An impairment loss recognised for goodwill shall not be reversed in a subsequent period.

27.29   For all assets other than goodwill, if and only if the reasons for the impairment loss have ceased to apply, an impairment loss shall be reversed in a subsequent period. An entity shall assess at each reporting date whether there is any indication that an impairment loss recognised in prior periods may no longer exist or may have decreased. Indications that an impairment loss may have decreased or may no longer exist are generally the opposite of those set out in paragraph 27.9. If any such indication exists, the entity shall determine whether all or part of the prior impairment loss should be reversed. The procedure for making that determination will depend on whether the prior impairment loss on the asset was based on:

(a)   the recoverable amount of that individual asset (see paragraph 27.30); or

(b)   the recoverable amount of the cash-generating unit to which the asset belongs (see paragraph 27.31).

Reversal where recoverable amount was estimated for an individual impaired asset

27.30   When the prior impairment loss was based on the recoverable amount of the individual impaired asset, the following requirements apply:

(a)   The entity shall estimate the recoverable amount of the asset at the current reporting date.

(b)   If the estimated recoverable amount of the asset exceeds its carrying amount, the entity shall increase the carrying amount to recoverable amount, subject to the limitation described in (c) below. That increase is a reversal of an impairment loss. The entity shall recognise the reversal immediately in profit or loss unless the asset is carried at revalued amount in accordance with another section of this FRS (for example, the revaluation model in Section 17 *Property, plant and equipment*). Any reversal of an impairment loss of a revalued asset shall be treated as a revaluation increase in accordance with the relevant section of this FRS.

(c)   The reversal of an impairment loss shall not increase the carrying amount of the asset above the carrying amount that would have been determined (net of amortisation or depreciation) had no impairment loss been recognised for the asset in prior years.

(d)   After a reversal of an impairment loss is recognised, the entity shall adjust the depreciation (amortisation) charge for the asset in future periods to allocate the asset's revised carrying amount, less its residual value (if any), on a systematic basis over its remaining useful life.

Reversal when recoverable amount was estimated for a cash-generating unit

When the original impairment loss was based on the recoverable amount of the cash-generating unit to which the asset, including goodwill belongs, the following requirements apply:

27.31

(a)   The entity shall estimate the recoverable amount of that cash-generating unit at the current reporting date.

(b)   If the estimated recoverable amount of the cash-generating unit exceeds its carrying amount, that excess is a reversal of an impairment loss. The entity shall allocate the amount of that reversal to the assets of the unit, except for goodwill, pro rata with the carrying amounts of those assets, subject to the limitation described in (c) below. Those increases in carrying amounts shall be treated as reversals of impairment losses and recognised immediately in profit or loss unless an asset is carried at revalued amount in accordance with another section of this FRS (for example, the revaluation model in Section 17 *Property, plant and equipment*). Any reversal of an impairment loss of a revalued asset shall be treated as a revaluation increase in accordance with the relevant section of this FRS.

(c)   In allocating a reversal of an impairment loss for a cash-generating unit, the reversal shall not increase the carrying amount of any asset above the lower of:

   (i)   its recoverable amount; and

   (ii)   the carrying amount that would have been determined (net of amortisation or depreciation) had no impairment loss been recognised for the asset in prior periods.

(d)   Any excess amount of the reversal of the impairment loss that cannot be allocated to an asset because of the restriction in (c) above shall be allocated pro rata to the other assets of the cash-generating unit, except for goodwill.

(e)   After a reversal of an impairment loss is recognised, if applicable, the entity shall adjust the depreciation (amortisation) charge for each asset in the cash-generating unit in future periods to allocate the asset's revised carrying amount, less its residual value (if any), on a systematic basis over its remaining useful life.

Disclosures

An entity shall disclose the following for each **class of assets** indicated in paragraph 27.33:

27.32

*(a)   the amount of impairment losses recognised in profit or loss during the period and the line item(s) in the **statement of comprehensive income** (or in the **income statement**, if presented) in which those impairment losses are included; and

*(b)   the amount of reversals of impairment losses recognised in profit or loss during the period and the line item(s) in the statement of comprehensive income (or in the income statement, if presented) in which those impairment losses are reversed.

An entity shall disclose the information required by paragraph 27.32 for each of the following classes of asset:

27.33

(a)   inventories;

(b)   **property, plant and equipment** (including investment property accounted for by the cost method);

(c)   goodwill;

(d)   **intangible assets** other than goodwill;

(e)   investments in **associates**; and

(f)   investments in **joint ventures**.

An entity shall disclose a description of the events and circumstances that led to the **recognition** or reversal of the impairment loss.

27.33A

Section 28 *Employee Benefits*

Scope of this section

28.1   **Employee benefits** are all forms of consideration given by an entity in exchange for service rendered by employees, including directors and management. This section applies to all employee benefits, except for **share-based payment transactions**, which are covered by Section 26 *Share-based Payment*. Employee benefits covered by this section will be one of the following four types:

  (a)   short-term employee benefits, which are employee benefits (other than **termination benefits**) that are expected to be settled wholly before twelve months after the end of the **reporting period** in which the employees render the related service;

  (b)   **post-employment benefits**, which are employee benefits (other than termination benefits and short-term employee benefits) that are payable after the completion of employment;

  (c)   other long-term employee benefits, which are all employee benefits, other than short-term employee benefits, post-employment benefits and termination benefits; or

  (d)   termination benefits, which are employee benefits provided in exchange for the termination of an employee's employment as a result of either:

   (i)   an entity's decision to terminate an employee's employment before the normal retirement date; or

   (ii)   an employee's decision to accept voluntary redundancy in exchange for those benefits.

28.2   [Not used]

General recognition principle for all employee benefits

28.3   An entity shall recognise the cost of all employee benefits to which its employees have become entitled as a result of service rendered to the entity during the reporting period:

  (a)   As a **liability**, after deducting amounts that have been paid either directly to the employees or as a contribution to an employee benefit fund[12]. If the amount paid exceeds the obligation arising from service before the **reporting date**, an entity shall recognise that excess as an asset to the extent that the prepayment will lead to a reduction in future payments or a cash refund.

  (b)   As an **expense**, unless another section of this FRS requires the cost to be recognised as part of the cost of an asset such as **inventories** (for example in accordance with paragraph 13.8) or **property, plant and equipment** (in accordance with paragraph 17.10).

Short-term employee benefits

Examples

28.4   Short-term employee benefits include items such as the following, if expected to be settled wholly before 12 months after the end of the annual reporting period in which the employees render the related service:

---

[12] *Contributions to an employee benefit fund that is an intermediate payment arrangement shall be accounted for in accordance with paragraphs 9.33 to 9.38, and as a result if the employer is a sponsoring entity the assets and liabilities of the intermediary will be accounted for by the sponsoring entity as an extension of its own business. In which case the payment to the employee benefit fund does not extinguish the liability of the employer.*

(a) wages, salaries and social security contributions;
(b) paid annual leave and paid sick leave;
(c) profit-sharing and bonuses; and
(d) non-monetary benefits (such as medical care, housing, cars and free or subsidised goods or services) for current employees.

Measurement of short-term benefits generally

When an employee has rendered service to an entity during the reporting period, the entity shall measure the amounts recognised in accordance with paragraph 28.3 at the undiscounted amount of short-term employee benefits expected to be paid in exchange for that service. **28.5**

Recognition and measurement: Short-term compensated absences

An entity may compensate employees for absence for various reasons including annual leave and sick leave. Some short-term compensated absences accumulate—they can be carried forward and used in future periods if the employee does not use the current period's entitlement in full. Examples include annual leave and sick leave. An entity shall recognise the expected cost of **accumulating compensated absences** when the employees render service that increases their entitlement to future compensated absences. The entity shall measure the expected cost of accumulating compensated absences at the undiscounted additional amount that the entity expects to pay as a result of the unused entitlement that has accumulated at the end of the reporting period. The entity shall present this amount as falling due within one year at the reporting date. **28.6**

An entity shall recognise the cost of other (non-accumulating) compensated absences when the absences occur. The entity shall measure the cost of non-accumulating compensated absences at the undiscounted amount of salaries and wages paid or payable for the period of absence. **28.7**

Recognition: Profit-sharing and bonus plans

An entity shall recognise the expected cost of profit-sharing and bonus payments only when: **28.8**

(a) the entity has a present legal or **constructive obligation** to make such payments as a result of past events (this means that the entity has no realistic alternative but to make the payments); and
(b) a reliable estimate of the obligation can be made.

Post-employment benefits: Distinction between defined contribution plans and defined benefit plans

Post-employment benefits include, for example: **28.9**

(a) retirement benefits, such as pensions; and
(b) other post-employment benefits, such as post-employment life insurance and post-employment medical care.

Arrangements whereby an entity provides post-employment benefits are **post-employment benefit plans**. An entity shall apply this section to all such arrangements whether or not they involve the establishment of a separate entity to receive contributions and to pay benefits. In some cases, these arrangements are imposed by law rather than by action of the entity. In some cases, these arrangements arise from actions of the entity even in the absence of a formal, documented plan.

28.10   Post-employment benefit plans are classified as either **defined contribution plans** or **defined benefit plans**, depending on their principal terms and conditions:

(a)   Defined contribution plans are post-employment benefit plans under which an entity pays fixed contributions into a separate entity (a fund) and has no legal or constructive obligation to pay further contributions or to make direct benefit payments to employees if the fund does not hold sufficient assets to pay all employee benefits relating to employee service in the current and prior periods. Thus, the amount of the post-employment benefits received by the employee is determined by the amount of contributions paid by an entity (and perhaps also the employee) to a post-employment benefit plan or to an insurer, together with investment returns arising from the contributions.

(b)   Defined benefit plans are post-employment benefit plans other than defined contribution plans. Under defined benefit plans, the entity's obligation is to provide the agreed benefits to current and former employees, and actuarial risk (that benefits will cost more or less than expected) and investment risk (that returns on assets set aside to fund the benefits will differ from expectations) are borne, in substance, by the entity. If actuarial or investment experience is worse than expected, the entity's obligation may be increased, and vice versa if actuarial or investment experience is better than expected.

Multi-employer plans and state plans

28.11   **Multi-employer plans** and **state plans** are classified as defined contribution plans or defined benefit plans on the basis of the terms of the plan, including any constructive obligation that goes beyond the formal terms. However, if sufficient information is not available to use defined benefit accounting for a multi-employer plan that is a defined benefit plan, an entity shall account for the plan in accordance with paragraphs 28.13 and 28.13A as if it was a defined contribution plan and make the disclosures required by paragraphs 28.40 and 28.40A. An entity shall account for a state plan in the same way as for a multi-employer plan.

28.11A   Where an entity participates in a defined benefit plan, which is a multi-employer plan that in accordance with paragraph 28.11 is accounted for as if the plan were a defined contribution plan, and the entity has entered into an agreement with the multi-employer plan that determines how the entity will fund a deficit, the entity shall recognise a liability for the contributions payable that arise from the agreement (to the extent that they relate to the deficit) and the resulting expense in **profit or loss** in accordance with paragraphs 28.13 and 28.13A.

Insured benefits

28.12   An entity may pay insurance premiums to fund a post-employment benefit plan. The entity shall treat such a plan as a defined contribution plan unless the entity has a legal or constructive obligation either:

(a)   to pay the employee benefits directly when they become due; or

(b)   to pay further amounts if the insurer does not pay all future employee benefits relating to employee service in the current and prior periods.

A constructive obligation could arise indirectly through the plan, through the mechanism for setting future premiums, or through a **related party** relationship with the insurer. If the entity retains such a legal or constructive obligation, the entity shall treat the plan as a defined benefit plan.

Post-employment benefits: Defined contribution plans

Recognition and measurement

An entity shall recognise the contribution payable for a period: **28.13**

(a)   As a liability, after deducting any amount already paid. If contribution payments exceed the contribution due for service before the reporting date, an entity shall recognise that excess as an asset to the extent that the prepayment will lead to a reduction in future payments or a cash refund.

(b)   As an expense, unless another section of this FRS requires the cost to be recognised as part of the cost of an asset such as inventories or property, plant and equipment.

When contributions to a defined contribution plan (or a defined benefit plan which, in   **28.13A** accordance with paragraph 28.11, is accounted for as a defined contribution plan) are not expected to be settled wholly within 12 months after the end of the reporting period in which the employees render the related service, the liability shall be measured at the **present value** of the contributions payable using the methodology for selecting a discount rate specified in paragraph 28.17. The unwinding of the discount shall be recognised as a finance cost in profit or loss in the period in which it arises.

Post-employment benefits: Defined benefit plans

Recognition

In applying the general **recognition** principle in paragraph 28.3 to defined benefit plans,   **28.14** an entity shall recognise:

(a)   a liability for its obligations under defined benefit plans net of **plan assets**—its '**net defined benefit liability**' (see paragraphs 28.15 to 28.22); and

(b)   the net change in that liability during the period as the cost of its defined benefit plans during the period (see paragraphs 28.23 to 28.27).

Measurement of the net defined benefit liability

An entity shall measure the net defined benefit liability for its obligations under defined   **28.15** benefit plans at the net total of the following amounts:

(a)   the present value of its obligations under defined benefit plans (its **defined benefit obligation**) at the reporting date (paragraphs 28.16 to 28.21A provide guidance for measuring this obligation); minus

(b)   the **fair value** at the reporting date of plan assets (if any) out of which the obligations are to be settled. Paragraphs 11.27 to 11.32 establish requirements for determining the fair values of those plan assets, except that, if the asset is an insurance policy that exactly matches the amount and timing of some or all of the benefits payable under the plan, the fair value of the asset is deemed to be the present value of the related obligation.

Where an entity has measured its defined benefit obligation using the **projected unit**   **28.15A** **credit method** (including the use of appropriate **actuarial assumptions**), as set out in paragraph 28.18, it shall not recognise any additional liabilities to reflect differences between these assumptions and those used for the most recent actuarial valuation of the plan for funding purposes. For the avoidance of doubt, no additional liabilities shall be recognised in respect of an agreement with the defined benefit plan to fund a deficit (such as a schedule of contributions).

Inclusion of both vested and unvested benefits

28.16   The present value of an entity's obligations under defined benefit plans at the reporting date shall reflect the estimated amount of benefit that employees have earned in return for their service in the current and prior periods, including benefits that are not yet **vested** (see paragraph 28.26) and including the effects of benefit formulas that give employees greater benefits for later years of service. This requires the entity to determine how much benefit is attributable to the current and prior periods on the basis of the plan's benefit formula and to make estimates (actuarial assumptions) about demographic variables (such as employee turnover and mortality) and financial variables (such as future increases in salaries and medical costs) that influence the cost of the benefit. The actuarial assumptions shall be unbiased (neither imprudent nor excessively conservative), mutually compatible, and selected to lead to the best estimate of the future **cash flows** that will arise under the plan.

Discounting

28.17   An entity shall measure its defined benefit obligation on a discounted present value basis. The entity shall determine the rate used to discount the future payments by reference to market yields at the reporting date on high quality corporate bonds. In countries with no deep market in such bonds, the entity shall use the market yields (at the reporting date) on government bonds. The currency and term of the corporate bonds or government bonds shall be consistent with the currency and estimated period of the future payments.

Actuarial valuation method

28.18   An entity shall use the projected unit credit method to measure its defined benefit obligation and the related expense. If defined benefits are based on future salaries, the projected unit credit method requires an entity to measure its defined benefit obligations on a basis that reflects estimated future salary increases. Additionally, the projected unit credit method requires an entity to make various actuarial assumptions in measuring the defined benefit obligation, including discount rates, employee turnover, mortality, and (for defined benefit medical plans) medical cost trend rates.

28.19   [Not used]

28.20   This FRS does not require an entity to engage an independent actuary to perform the comprehensive actuarial valuation needed to calculate its defined benefit obligation. Nor does it require that a comprehensive actuarial valuation must be done annually. In the periods between comprehensive actuarial valuations, if the principal actuarial assumptions have not changed significantly the defined benefit obligation can be measured by adjusting the prior period measurement for changes in employee demographics such as number of employees and salary levels.

Plan introductions, changes, curtailments and settlements

28.21   If a defined benefit plan has been introduced or the benefits have changed in the current period, the entity shall increase or decrease its net defined benefit liability to reflect the change, and shall recognise the increase (decrease) as an expense (**income**) in measuring **profit or loss** in the current reporting period.

28.21A   If a defined benefit plan has been curtailed (ie benefits or group of covered employees are reduced) or settled (the relevant part of the employer's obligation is completely discharged) in the current period, the defined benefit obligation shall be decreased or eliminated, and the entity shall recognise the resulting **gain** or loss in profit or loss in the current period.

Defined benefit plan asset

If the present value of the defined benefit obligation at the reporting date is less than the **28.22** fair value of plan assets at that date, the plan has a surplus. An entity shall recognise a plan surplus as a defined benefit plan asset only to the extent that it is able to recover the surplus either through reduced contributions in the future or through refunds from the plan.

Cost of a defined benefit plan

An entity shall recognise the cost of a defined benefit plan, except to the extent that **28.23** another section of this FRS requires part or all of the cost to be recognised as part of the cost of an asset, as follows:

(a)   the change in the net defined benefit liability arising from employee service rendered during the reporting period in profit or loss;

(b)   net interest on the net defined benefit liability during the reporting period in profit or loss;

(c)   the cost of plan introductions, benefit changes, curtailments and settlements in profit or loss (see paragraphs 28.21 and 28.21A); and

(d)   remeasurement of the net defined benefit liability in **other comprehensive income**.

Some defined benefit plans require employees or third parties to contribute to the cost of the plan. Contributions by employees reduce the cost of the benefits to the entity.

The net interest on the net defined benefit liability shall be determined by multiplying the **28.24** net defined benefit liability by the discount rate in paragraph 28.17, both as determined at the start of the annual reporting period, taking account of any changes in the net defined benefit liability during the period as a result of contribution and benefit payments.

The net interest on the net defined benefit liability can be viewed as comprising interest **28.24A** cost on the defined benefit obligation and interest income on plan assets excluding the effect of any surplus that is not recoverable in accordance with paragraph 28.22.

Interest income on plan assets, excluding the effect of any surplus that is not recoverable **28.24B** in accordance with paragraph 28.22, is a component of the return on plan assets, and is determined by multiplying the fair value of the plan assets by the discount rate specified in paragraph 28.17 both as determined at the start of the annual reporting period, taking account of any changes in the plan assets held during the period as a result of contribution and benefit payments. The difference between the interest income on plan assets and the return on plan assets is included in the remeasurement of the net defined benefit liability.

Remeasurement of the net defined benefit liability comprises: **28.25**

(a)   **actuarial gains and losses**;

(b)   the return on plan assets, excluding amounts included in net interest on the net defined benefit liability; and

(c)   any change in the amount of a defined benefit plan surplus that is not recoverable (see paragraph 28.22), excluding amounts included in net interest on the net defined benefit liability.

Remeasurement of the net defined benefit liability recognised in other comprehensive **28.25A** income shall not be reclassified to profit or loss in a subsequent period.

Employee service gives rise to an obligation under a defined benefit plan even if the **28.26** benefits are conditional on future employment (in other words, they are not yet vested). Employee service before the vesting date gives rise to a constructive obligation because, at each successive reporting date, the amount of future service that an employee will have to render before becoming entitled to the benefit is reduced. In measuring its defined benefit obligation, an entity considers the probability that some employees may not satisfy vesting requirements. Similarly, although some post-employment benefits (such as post-employment medical benefits) become payable only if a specified event occurs when an employee is no longer employed (such as an illness), an obligation is created when the employee renders service that will provide entitlement to the benefit if the specified event occurs. The probability that the specified event will occur affects the **measurement** of the obligation, but does not determine whether the obligation exists.

28.27   If defined benefits are reduced for amounts that will be paid to employees under government-sponsored plans, an entity shall measure its defined benefit obligations on a basis that reflects the benefits payable under the government plans, but only if:

(a)   those plans were enacted before the reporting date; or

(b)   past history, or other reliable evidence, indicates that those state benefits will change in some predictable manner, for example, in line with future changes in general price levels or general salary levels.

Reimbursements

28.28   If an entity is virtually certain that another party will reimburse some or all of the expenditure required to settle a defined benefit obligation, the entity shall recognise its right to reimbursement as a separate asset. An entity shall treat that asset in the same way as plan assets.

Other long-term employee benefits

28.29   Other long-term employee benefits include items such as the following, if not expected to be settled wholly before 12 months after the end of the annual reporting period in which the employees render the related service:

(a)   long-term paid absences such as long-service or sabbatical leave;

(b)   other long-service benefits;

(c)   long-term disability benefits;

(d)   profit-sharing and bonuses; and

(e)   deferred remuneration.

28.30   An entity shall recognise a liability for other long-term employee benefits measured at the net total of the following amounts:

(a)   the present value of the benefit obligation at the reporting date (calculated using the methodology for selecting a discount rate in paragraph 28.17); minus

(b)   the fair value at the reporting date of plan assets (if any) out of which the obligations are to be settled directly.

An entity shall recognise the change in the liability in profit or loss, except to the extent that this FRS requires or permits their inclusion in the cost of an asset.

Termination benefits

28.31   An entity may be committed, by legislation, by contractual or other agreements with employees or their representatives or by a constructive obligation based on business practice, custom or a desire to act equitably, to make payments (or provide other benefits) to employees when it terminates their employment. Such payments are termination benefits.

Recognition

Because termination benefits do not provide an entity with future economic benefits, an entity shall recognise them as an expense in profit or loss immediately.　**28.32**

When an entity recognises termination benefits, the entity may also have to account for a curtailment of retirement benefits or other employee benefits.　**28.33**

An entity shall recognise termination benefits as a liability and an expense only when the entity is demonstrably committed either:　**28.34**

(a)　to terminate the employment of an employee or group of employees before the normal retirement date; or

(b)　to provide termination benefits as a result of an offer made in order to encourage voluntary redundancy.

An entity is demonstrably committed to a termination only when the entity has a detailed formal plan for the termination[13] and is without realistic possibility of withdrawal from the plan.　**28.35**

Measurement

An entity shall measure termination benefits at the best estimate of the expenditure that would be required to settle the obligation at the reporting date. In the case of an offer made to encourage voluntary redundancy, the measurement of termination benefits shall be based on the number of employees expected to accept the offer.　**28.36**

When termination benefits are due more than 12 months after the end of the reporting period, they shall be measured at their discounted present value using the methodology for selecting a discount rate specified in paragraph 28.17.　**28.37**

Group plans

Where an entity participates in a defined benefit plan that shares risks between entities under common control it shall obtain information about the plan as a whole measured in accordance with this FRS on the basis of assumptions that apply to the plan as a whole. If there is a contractual agreement or stated policy for charging the net defined benefit cost of a defined benefit plan as a whole measured in accordance with this FRS to individual group entities, the entity shall, in its individual financial statements, recognise the net defined benefit cost of a defined benefit plan so charged. If there is no such agreement or policy, the net defined benefit cost of a defined benefit plan shall be recognised in the individual financial statements of the group entity which is legally responsible for the plan. The other group entities shall, in their **individual financial statements**, recognise a cost equal to their contribution payable for the period.　**28.38**

Disclosures

Disclosures about short-term employee benefits

This section does not require specific disclosures about short-term employee benefits.　**28.39**

---

[13] *An example of the features of a detailed formal plan for restructuring, which may include termination benefits, is given in paragraph 21.11C.*

Disclosures about defined contribution plans

28.40   An entity shall disclose the amount recognised in profit or loss as an expense for defined contribution plans.

28.40A   If an entity treats a defined benefit multi-employer plan as a defined contribution plan because sufficient information is not available to use defined benefit accounting (see paragraph 28.11) it shall:

*(a)   disclose the fact that it is a defined benefit plan and the reason why it is being accounted for as a defined contribution plan, along with any available information about the plan's surplus or deficit and the implications, if any, for the entity;

*(b)   include a description of the extent to which the entity can be liable to the plan for other entities' obligations under the terms and conditions of the multi-employer plan; and

(c)   disclose how any liability recognised in accordance with paragraph 28.11A has been determined.

Disclosures about defined benefit plans

28.41   An entity shall disclose the following information about defined benefit plans (except for any defined multi-employer benefit plans that are accounted for as a defined contribution plan in accordance with paragraphs 28.11 and 28.11A, for which the disclosures in paragraphs 28.40 and 28.40A apply instead). If an entity has more than one defined benefit plan, these disclosures may be made in aggregate, separately for each plan, or in such groupings as are considered to be the most useful:

(a)   A general description of the type of plan, including **funding** policy. This includes the amount and timing of the future payments to be made by the entity under any agreement with the defined benefit plan to fund a deficit (such as a schedule of contributions).

(b)   [Not used]

(c)   [Not used]

(d)   The date of the most recent comprehensive actuarial valuation and, if it was not as of the reporting date, a description of the adjustments that were made to measure the defined benefit obligation at the reporting date.

(e)   A reconciliation of opening and closing balances for each of the following:

(i)   the defined benefit obligation;

(ii)   the fair value of plan assets; and

(iii)   any reimbursement right recognised as an asset.

(f)   Each of the reconciliations in paragraph 28.41(e) shall show each of the following, if applicable:

(i)   the change in the defined benefit liability arising from employee service rendered during the reporting period in profit or loss;

(ii)   interest income or expense;

(iii)   remeasurement of the defined benefit liability, showing separately actuarial gains and losses and the return on plan assets less amounts included in (ii) above; and

(iv)   plan introductions, changes, curtailments and settlements.

(g)   The total cost relating to defined benefit plans for the period, disclosing separately the amounts:

(i)   recognised in profit or loss as an expense; and

(ii)   included in the cost of an asset.

(h) For each major class of plan assets, which shall include, but is not limited to, equity instruments, debt instruments, property, and all other assets, the percentage or amount that each major class constitutes of the fair value of the total plan assets at the reporting date.

(i) The amounts included in the fair value of plan assets for:

  (i) each class of the entity's own **financial instruments**; and
  (ii) any property occupied by, or other assets used by, the entity.

(j) The return on plan assets.

(k) The principal actuarial assumptions used, including, when applicable:

  (i) the discount rates;
  (ii) [not used]
  (iii) the expected rates of salary increases;
  (iv) medical cost trend rates; and
  (v) any other **material** actuarial assumptions used.

The reconciliations in (e) and (f) above need not be presented for prior periods.

If an entity participates in a defined benefit plan that shares risks between entities under common control (see paragraph 28.38) it shall disclose the following information: **28.41A**

(a) The contractual agreement or stated policy for charging the cost of a defined benefit plan or the fact that there is no policy.

(b) The policy for determining the contribution to be paid by the entity.

(c) If the entity accounts for an allocation of the net defined benefit cost, all the information required in paragraph 28.41.

*(d) If the entity accounts for the contributions payable for the period, the information about the plan as a whole required by paragraph 28.41(a), (d), (h) and (i).

This information can be disclosed by cross-reference to disclosures in another group entity's **financial statements** if:

(i) that group entity's financial statements separately identify and disclose the information required about the plan; and

(ii) that group entity's financial statements are available to users of the financial statements on the same terms as the financial statements of the entity and at the same time as, or earlier than, the financial statements of the entity.

Disclosures about other long-term benefits

For each category of other long-term benefits that an entity provides to its employees, the entity shall disclose the nature of the benefit, the amount of its obligation and the extent of funding at the reporting date. **28.42**

Disclosures about termination benefits

For each category of termination benefits that an entity provides to its employees, the entity shall disclose the nature of the benefit, its **accounting policy**, and the amount of its obligation and the extent of funding at the reporting date. **28.43**

When there is uncertainty about the number of employees who will accept an offer of termination benefits, a **contingent liability** exists. Section 21 *Provisions and Contingencies* requires an entity to disclose information about its contingent liabilities unless the possibility of an outflow in settlement is remote. **28.44**

Section 29 *Income Tax*

Scope of this section

29.1   For the purpose of this FRS, **income tax** includes all domestic and foreign taxes that are based on **taxable profit**. Income tax also includes taxes, such as withholding taxes, that are payable by a **subsidiary**, **associate** or **joint venture** on distributions to the reporting entity.

29.2   This section covers accounting for income tax. It requires an entity to recognise the current and future tax consequences of transactions and other events that have been recognised in the **financial statements**. These recognised tax amounts comprise **current tax** and **deferred tax**. Current tax is tax payable (refundable) in respect of the taxable profit (tax loss) for the current period or past **reporting periods**. Deferred tax represents the future tax consequences of transactions and events recognised in the financial statements of the current and previous periods. This section also requires that deferred tax is recognised in respect of **assets** (other than **goodwill**) and **liabilities** recognised as a result of a **business combination**.

29.2A This section also covers accounting for value added tax (VAT) and other similar sales taxes, which are not income taxes.

Recognition and measurement of current tax

29.3   An entity shall recognise a current tax liability for tax payable on taxable profit for the current and past periods. If the amount of tax paid for the current and past periods exceeds the amount of tax payable for those periods, the entity shall recognise the excess as a current tax asset.

29.4   An entity shall recognise a current tax asset for the benefit of a tax loss that can be carried back to recover tax paid in a previous period.

29.5   An entity shall measure a current tax liability (asset) at the amount of tax it expects to pay (recover) using the tax rates and laws that have been enacted or **substantively enacted** by the **reporting date**.

Recognition of deferred tax

Timing differences

29.6   Deferred tax shall be recognised in respect of all **timing differences** at the reporting date, except as otherwise required by paragraphs 29.7 to 29.9 and 29.11 below. Timing differences are differences between taxable profits and **total comprehensive income** as stated in the financial statements that arise from the inclusion of **income** and **expenses** in tax assessments in periods different from those in which they are recognised in financial statements.

29.7   Unrelieved tax losses and other **deferred tax assets** shall be recognised only to the extent that it is **probable** that they will be recovered against the reversal of **deferred tax liabilities** or other future taxable profits (the very existence of unrelieved tax losses is strong evidence that there may not be other future taxable profits against which the losses will be relieved).

29.8   Deferred tax shall be recognised when the tax allowances for the cost of a **fixed asset** are received before or after the **depreciation** of the fixed asset is recognised in **profit or loss**.

If and when all conditions for retaining the tax allowances have been met, the deferred tax shall be reversed.

Deferred tax shall be recognised when income or expenses from a subsidiary, associate, branch, or interest in joint venture have been recognised in the financial statements, and will be assessed to or allowed for tax in a future period, except where:

29.9

(a)   the reporting entity is able to control the reversal of the timing difference; and

(b)   it is probable that the timing difference will not reverse in the foreseeable future.

Such timing differences may arise, for example, where there are undistributed profits in a subsidiary, associate, branch or interest in a joint venture.

Permanent differences

Permanent differences arise because certain types of **income** and expenses are non-taxable or disallowable, or because certain tax charges or allowances are greater or smaller than the corresponding income or expense in the financial statements. Deferred tax shall not be recognised on permanent differences except for circumstances set out in paragraph 29.11.

29.10

Business combinations

When the amount that can be deducted for tax for an asset (other than goodwill) that is recognised in a business combination is less (more) than the value at which it is recognised, a deferred tax liability (asset) shall be recognised for the additional tax that will be paid (avoided) in respect of that difference. Similarly, a deferred tax asset (liability) shall be recognised for the additional tax that will be avoided (paid) because of a difference between the value at which a liability is recognised and the amount that will be assessed for tax. The amount attributed to goodwill shall be adjusted by the amount of deferred tax recognised.

29.11

Measurement of deferred tax

An entity shall measure a deferred tax liability (asset) using the tax rates and laws that have been enacted or substantively enacted by the reporting date that are expected to apply to the reversal of the timing difference except for the cases dealt with in paragraphs 29.15 and 29.16 below.

29.12

When different tax rates apply to different levels of taxable profit, an entity shall measure deferred tax expense (income) and related deferred tax liabilities (assets) using the average enacted or substantively enacted rates that it expects to be applicable to the taxable profit (tax loss) of the periods in which it expects the deferred tax asset to be realised or the deferred tax liability to be settled.

29.13

In some jurisdictions, income taxes are payable at a higher or lower rate if part or all of the profit or retained earnings is paid out as a dividend to shareholders of the entity. In other jurisdictions, income taxes may be refundable or payable if part or all of the profit or retained earnings is paid out as a dividend to shareholders of the entity. In both of those circumstances, an entity shall measure current and deferred taxes at the tax rate applicable to undistributed profits until the entity recognises a liability to pay a dividend. When the entity recognises a liability to pay a dividend, it shall recognise the resulting current or deferred tax liability (asset), and the related **tax expense** (income).

29.14

Deferred tax relating to a non-depreciable asset that is measured using the revaluation model in Section 17 *Property, Plant and Equipment* shall be measured using the tax rates and allowances that apply to the sale of the asset.

29.15

29.16   Deferred tax relating to **investment property** that is measured at **fair value** in accordance with Section 16 *Investment Property* shall be measured using the tax rates and allowances that apply to sale of the asset, except for investment property that has a limited **useful life** and is held within a business model whose objective is to consume substantially all of the economic benefits embodied in the property over time.

Measurement of both current and deferred tax

29.17   An entity shall not discount current or deferred tax assets and liabilities.

Withholding tax on dividends

29.18   When an entity pays dividends to its shareholders, it may be required to pay a portion of the dividends to taxation authorities on behalf of shareholders. Outgoing dividends and similar amounts payable shall be recognised at an amount that includes any withholding tax but excludes other taxes, such as attributable tax credits.

29.19   Incoming dividends and similar income receivable shall be recognised at an amount that includes any withholding tax but excludes other taxes, such as attributable tax credits. Any withholding tax suffered shall be shown as part of the tax charge.

Value Added Tax ('VAT') and other similar sales taxes

29.20   **Turnover** shown in profit or loss shall exclude VAT and other similar sales taxes on taxable outputs and VAT imputed under the flat rate VAT scheme. Expenses shall exclude recoverable VAT and other similar recoverable sales taxes. Irrecoverable VAT allocable to fixed assets and to other items disclosed separately in the financial statements shall be included in their cost where practicable and **material**.

Presentation

Allocation in comprehensive income and equity

29.21   An entity shall present changes in a current tax liability (asset) and changes in a deferred tax liability (asset) as tax expense (income) with the exception of those changes arising on the initial **recognition** of a business combination which shall be dealt with in accordance with paragraph 29.11.

29.22   An entity shall present tax expense (income) in the same component of **total comprehensive income** (ie continuing or **discontinued operations**, and profit or loss or **other comprehensive income**) or **equity** as the transaction or other event that resulted in the tax expense (income).

Presentation in the statement of financial position

29.23   An entity shall present deferred tax liabilities within provisions for liabilities and deferred tax assets within debtors.

Offsetting

29.24   An entity shall offset current tax assets and current tax liabilities, if and only if, it has a legally enforceable right to set off the amounts and it intends either to settle on a net basis or to realise the asset and settle the liability simultaneously.

An entity shall offset deferred tax assets and deferred tax liabilities if, and only if: **29.24A**

(a)   the entity has a legally enforceable right to set off current tax assets against current tax liabilities; and

(b)   the deferred tax assets and deferred tax liabilities relate to income taxes levied by the same taxation authority on either the same taxable entity or different taxable entities which intend either to settle current tax liabilities and assets on a net basis, or to realise the assets and settle the liabilities simultaneously, in each future period in which significant amounts of deferred tax liabilities or assets are expected to be settled or recovered.

Disclosures

An entity shall disclose information that enables users of its financial statements to evaluate   **29.25**
the nature and financial effect of the current and deferred tax consequences of recognised transactions and other events.

An entity shall disclose separately the major components of tax expense (income). Such   **29.26**
components of tax expense (income) may include:

(a)   current tax expense (income);

(b)   any adjustments recognised in the period for current tax of prior periods;

(c)   the amount of deferred tax expense (income) relating to the origination and reversal of timing differences;

(d)   the amount of deferred tax expense (income) relating to changes in tax rates or the imposition of new taxes;

(e)   adjustments to deferred tax expense (income) arising from a change in the tax status of the entity or its shareholders; and

(f)   the amount of tax expense (income) relating to changes in **accounting policies** and **material errors** (see Section 10 *Accounting Policies, Estimates and Errors*).

An entity shall disclose the following separately: **29.27**

*(a)   the aggregate current and deferred tax relating to items that are recognised as items of other comprehensive income or equity;

(b)   a reconciliation between:

(i)   the tax expense (income) included in profit or loss; and

(ii)   the profit or loss on ordinary activities before tax multiplied by the applicable tax rate;

(c)   the amount of the net reversal of deferred tax assets and deferred tax liabilities expected to occur during the year beginning after the **reporting period** together with a brief explanation for the expected reversal;

(d)   an explanation of changes in the applicable tax rate(s) compared with the previous reporting period;

(e)   the amount of deferred tax liabilities and deferred tax assets at the end of the reporting period for each type of timing difference and the amount of unused tax losses and tax credits;

(f)   the expiry date, if any, of timing differences, unused tax losses and unused tax credits; and

(g)   in the circumstances described in paragraph 29.14, an explanation of the nature of the potential income tax consequences that would result from the payment of dividends to its shareholders.

Section 30 *Foreign Currency Translation*

Scope of this section

30.1 An entity can conduct foreign activities in two ways. It may have transactions in foreign currencies or it may have **foreign operations**. In addition, an entity may present its **financial statements** in a foreign currency. This section prescribes how to include foreign currency transactions and foreign operations in the financial statements of an entity and how to translate financial statements into a **presentation currency**. Hedge accounting of foreign currency items is dealt with in Section 12 *Other Financial Instruments Issues*.

Functional currency

30.2 Each entity shall identify its **functional currency**. An entity's functional currency is the currency of the primary economic environment in which the entity operates.

30.3 The primary economic environment in which an entity operates is normally the one in which it primarily generates and expends **cash**. Therefore, the following are the most important factors an entity considers in determining its functional currency:

(a) the currency:

   (i)   that mainly influences sales prices for goods and services (this will often be the currency in which sales prices for its goods and services are denominated and settled); and

   (ii) of the country whose competitive forces and regulations mainly determine the sales prices of its goods and services; and

(b) the currency that mainly influences labour, material and other costs of providing goods or services (this will often be the currency in which such costs are denominated and settled).

30.4 The following factors may also provide evidence of an entity's functional currency:

(a) the currency in which funds from **financing activities** (issuing debt and equity instruments) are generated; and

(b) the currency in which receipts from **operating activities** are usually retained.

30.5 The following additional factors are considered in determining the functional currency of a foreign operation, and whether its functional currency is the same as that of the reporting entity (the reporting entity, in this context, being the entity that has the foreign operation as its **subsidiary**, branch, **associate** or **joint venture**):

(a) Whether the activities of the foreign operation are carried out as an extension of the reporting entity, rather than being carried out with a significant degree of autonomy. An example of the former is when the foreign operation only sells goods imported from the reporting entity and remits the proceeds to it. An example of the latter is when the operation accumulates cash and other **monetary items**, incurs **expenses**, generates **income** and arranges borrowings, all substantially in its local currency.

(b) Whether transactions with the reporting entity are a high or a low proportion of the foreign operation's activities.

(c) Whether **cash flows** from the activities of the foreign operation directly affect the cash flows of the reporting entity and are readily available for remittance to it.

(d) Whether cash flows from the activities of the foreign operation are sufficient to service existing and normally expected debt obligations without funds being made available by the reporting entity.

Reporting foreign currency transactions in the functional currency

Initial recognition

A foreign currency transaction is a transaction that is denominated or requires settlement **30.6** in a foreign currency, including transactions arising when an entity:

(a) buys or sells goods or services whose price is denominated in a foreign currency;
(b) borrows or lends funds when the amounts payable or receivable are denominated in a foreign currency; or
(c) otherwise acquires or disposes of **assets**, or incurs or settles **liabilities**, denominated in a foreign currency.

An entity shall record a foreign currency transaction, on initial **recognition** in the functional **30.7** currency, by applying to the foreign currency amount the spot exchange rate between the functional currency and the foreign currency at the date of the transaction.

The date of a transaction is the date on which the transaction first qualifies for recognition **30.8** in accordance with this FRS. For practical reasons, a rate that approximates the actual rate at the date of the transaction is often used, for example, an average rate for a week or a month might be used for all transactions in each foreign currency occurring during that period. However, if exchange rates fluctuate significantly, the use of the average rate for a period is inappropriate.

Reporting at the end of the subsequent reporting periods

At the end of each **reporting period**, an entity shall: **30.9**

(a) translate foreign currency monetary items using the **closing rate**;
(b) translate non-monetary items that are measured in terms of historical cost in a foreign currency using the exchange rate at the date of the transaction; and
(c) translate non-monetary items that are measured at **fair value** in a foreign currency using the exchange rates at the date when the fair value was determined.

An entity shall recognise, in **profit or loss** in the period in which they arise, exchange **30.10** differences arising on the settlement of monetary items or on translating monetary items at rates different from those at which they were translated on initial recognition during the period or in previous periods, except as described in paragraph 30.13.

When another section of this FRS requires a **gain** or loss on a non-monetary item to be **30.11** recognised in **other comprehensive income**, an entity shall recognise any exchange component of that gain or loss in other comprehensive income. Conversely, when a gain or loss on a non-monetary item is recognised in profit or loss, an entity shall recognise any exchange component of that gain or loss in profit or loss.

Net investment in a foreign operation

An entity may have a monetary item that is receivable from or payable to a foreign operation. **30.12** An item for which settlement is neither planned nor likely to occur in the foreseeable future is, in substance, a part of the entity's net investment in that foreign operation, and is accounted for in accordance with paragraph 30.13. Such monetary items may include long-term receivables or loans. They do not include trade receivables or trade payables.

Exchange differences arising on a monetary item that forms part of a reporting entity's **net** **30.13** **investment in a foreign operation** shall be recognised in profit or loss in the **separate** **financial statements** of the reporting entity or the **individual financial statements** of the foreign operation, as appropriate. In the financial statements that include the foreign operation and the reporting entity (eg **consolidated financial statements** when the foreign operation is a subsidiary), such exchange differences shall be recognised in other comprehensive income and accumulated in **equity**. They shall not be recognised in profit or loss on disposal of the net investment.

Change in functional currency

30.14   When there is a change in an entity's functional currency, the entity shall apply the translation procedures applicable to the new functional currency prospectively from the date of the change.

30.15   As noted in paragraphs 30.2 to 30.5, the functional currency of an entity reflects the underlying transactions, events and conditions that are relevant to the entity. Accordingly, once the functional currency is determined, it can be changed only if there is a change to those underlying transactions, events and conditions. For example, a change in the currency that mainly influences the sales prices of goods and services may lead to a change in an entity's functional currency.

30.16   The effect of a change in functional currency is accounted for prospectively. In other words, an entity translates all items into the new functional currency using the exchange rate at the date of the change. The resulting translated amounts for non-monetary items are treated as their historical cost.

Use of a presentation currency other than the functional currency

Translation to the presentation currency

30.17   An entity may present its financial statements in any currency (or currencies). If the presentation currency differs from the entity's functional currency, the entity shall translate its items of income and expense and **financial position** into the presentation currency. For example, when a **group** contains individual entities with different functional currencies, the items of income and expense and financial position of each entity are expressed in a common currency so that consolidated financial statements may be presented.

30.18   An entity whose functional currency is not the currency of a hyperinflationary economy shall translate its results and financial position into a different presentation currency using the following procedures:

(a)   assets and liabilities for each **statement of financial position** presented (ie including comparatives) shall be translated at the closing rate at the date of that statement of financial position;

(b)   income and expenses for each **statement of comprehensive income** (ie including comparatives) shall be translated at exchange rates at the dates of the transactions; and

(c)   all resulting exchange differences shall be recognised in other comprehensive income.

30.19   For practical reasons, an entity may use a rate that approximates the exchange rates at the dates of the transactions, for example an average rate for the period to translate income and expense items. However, if exchange rates fluctuate significantly, the use of the average rate for a period is inappropriate.

The exchange differences referred to in paragraph 30.18(c) result from: **30.20**

(a) translating income and expenses at the exchange rates at the dates of the transactions and assets and liabilities at the closing rate; and

(b) translating the opening net assets at a closing rate that differs from the previous closing rate.

When the exchange differences relate to a foreign operation that is consolidated but not wholly-owned, accumulated exchange differences arising from translation and attributable to the **non-controlling interest** are allocated to, and recognised as part of, non-controlling interest in the consolidated statement of financial position.

An entity whose functional currency is the currency of a hyperinflationary economy shall adjust its results and financial position using the procedures specified in Section 31 *Hyperinflation* before applying the requirements of this section. **30.21**

Translation of a foreign operation into the investor's presentation currency

In incorporating the assets, liabilities, income and expenses of a foreign operation with those of the reporting entity, the entity shall follow normal consolidation procedures, such as the elimination of intragroup balances and intragroup transactions of a subsidiary (see Section 9 *Consolidated and Separate Financial Statements*) and the translation procedures set out in paragraphs 30.17 to 30.21. An intragroup monetary asset (or liability), whether short-term or long-term, cannot be eliminated against the corresponding intragroup liability (or asset) without showing the results of currency fluctuations in the consolidated financial statements. This is because the monetary item represents a commitment to convert one currency into another and exposes the reporting entity to a gain or loss through currency fluctuations. Accordingly, in the consolidated financial statements, a reporting entity continues to recognise such an exchange difference in profit or loss or, if it arises from the circumstances described in paragraph 30.13, the entity shall recognise it in other comprehensive income. **30.22**

Any **goodwill** arising on the acquisition of a foreign operation and any fair value adjustments to the **carrying amounts** of assets and liabilities arising on the acquisition of that foreign operation shall be treated as assets and liabilities of the foreign operation. Thus, they shall be expressed in the functional currency of the foreign operation and shall be translated at the closing rate in accordance with paragraph 30.18. **30.23**

Disclosures

In paragraphs 30.26 and 30.27, references to functional currency apply, in the case of a group, to the functional currency of the **parent**. **30.24**

An entity shall disclose the following: **30.25**

(a) the amount of exchange differences recognised in profit or loss during the period, except for those arising on **financial instruments** measured at fair value through profit or loss in accordance with Sections 11 *Basic Financial Instruments* and Section 12.

(b) the amount of exchange differences arising during the period and classified in equity at the end of the period.

An entity shall disclose the currency in which the financial statements are presented. When the presentation currency is different from the functional currency, an entity shall state that fact and shall disclose the functional currency and the reason for using a different presentation currency. **30.26**

30.27 When there is a change in the functional currency of either the reporting entity or a significant foreign operation, the entity shall disclose that fact and the reason for the change in functional currency.

Section 31 *Hyperinflation*

Scope of this section

31.1 This section applies to an entity whose **functional currency** is the currency of a hyperinflationary economy. It requires such an entity to prepare **financial statements** that have been adjusted for the effects of hyperinflation.

Hyperinflationary economy

31.2 This section does not establish an absolute rate at which an economy is deemed hyperinflationary. An entity shall make that judgement by considering all available information including, but not limited to, the following possible indicators of hyperinflation:

(a) The general population prefers to keep its wealth in non-monetary assets or in a relatively stable foreign currency. Amounts of local currency held are immediately invested to maintain purchasing power.

(b) The general population regards monetary amounts not in terms of the local currency but in terms of a relatively stable foreign currency. Prices may be quoted in that currency.

(c) Sales and purchases on credit take place at prices that compensate for the expected loss of purchasing power during the credit period, even if the period is short.

(d) Interest rates, wages and prices are linked to a price index.

(e) The cumulative inflation rate over three years is approaching, or exceeds, 100 per cent.

Measuring unit in the financial statements

31.3 All amounts in the financial statements of an entity whose functional currency is the currency of a hyperinflationary economy shall be stated in terms of the measuring unit current at the end of the **reporting period**. The comparative information for the previous period required by paragraph 3.14, and any information presented in respect of earlier periods, shall also be stated in terms of the measuring unit current at the **reporting date**.

31.4 The restatement of financial statements in accordance with this section requires the use of a general price index that reflects changes in general purchasing power. In most economies there is a recognised general price index, normally produced by the government, that entities will follow.

Procedures for restating historical cost financial statements

Statement of financial position

31.5 **Statement of financial position** amounts not expressed in terms of the measuring unit current at the end of the reporting period are restated by applying a general price index.

31.6 **Monetary items** are not restated because they are expressed in terms of the measuring unit current at the end of the reporting period. Monetary items are money held and items to be received or paid in money.

Assets and **liabilities** linked by agreement to changes in prices, such as index-linked bonds   **31.7**
and loans, are adjusted in accordance with the agreement and presented at this adjusted
amount in the restated statement of financial position.

All other assets and liabilities are non-monetary: **31.8**

(a)   Some non-monetary items are carried at amounts current at the end of the reporting
period, such as net realisable value and **fair value**, so they are not restated. All
other non-monetary assets and liabilities are restated.

(b)   Most non-monetary items are carried at cost or cost less **depreciation**; hence they
are expressed at amounts current at their date of acquisition. The restated cost, or
cost less depreciation, of each item is determined by applying to its historical cost
and accumulated depreciation the change in a general price index from the date of
acquisition to the end of the reporting period.

(c)   The restated amount of a non-monetary item is reduced, in accordance with
Section 27 *Impairment of Assets*, when it exceeds its **recoverable amount**.

At the beginning of the first period of application of this section, the components of **equity**,   **31.9**
except retained earnings, are restated by applying a general price index from the dates the
components were contributed or otherwise arose. Restated retained earnings are derived
from all the other amounts in the restated statement of financial position.

At the end of the first period and in subsequent periods, all components of owners' equity   **31.10**
are restated by applying a general price index from the beginning of the period or the
date of contribution, if later. The changes for the period in owners' equity are disclosed in
accordance with Section 6 *Statement of Changes in Equity and Statement of Income and
Retained Earnings*.

Statement of comprehensive income and income statement

All items in the **statement of comprehensive income** (and in the **income statement**, if   **31.11**
presented) shall be expressed in terms of the measuring unit current at the end of the
reporting period. Therefore, all amounts need to be restated by applying the change in
the general price index from the dates when the items of **income** and **expenses** were
initially recognised in the financial statements. If general inflation is approximately even
throughout the period, and the items of income and expense arose approximately evenly
throughout the period, an average rate of inflation may be appropriate.

Statement of cash flows

An entity shall express all items in the **statement of cash flows** in terms of the measuring   **31.12**
unit current at the end of the reporting period.

Gain or loss on net monetary position

In a period of inflation, an entity holding an excess of monetary assets over monetary   **31.13**
liabilities loses purchasing power, and an entity with an excess of monetary liabilities
over monetary assets gains purchasing power, to the extent the assets and liabilities are
not linked to a price level. An entity shall include in **profit or loss** the **gain** or loss on the
net monetary position. An entity shall offset the adjustment to those assets and liabilities
linked by agreement to changes in prices made in accordance with paragraph 31.7 against
the gain or loss on net monetary position.

Economies ceasing to be hyperinflationary

When an economy ceases to be hyperinflationary and an entity discontinues the   **31.14**
preparation and presentation of financial statements prepared in accordance with this

section, it shall treat the amounts expressed in the **presentation currency** at the end of the previous reporting period as the basis for the **carrying amounts** in its subsequent financial statements.

Disclosures

31.15   An entity to which this section applies shall disclose the following:

(a)   the fact that financial statements and other prior period data have been restated for changes in the general purchasing power of the functional currency;

(b)   the identity and level of the price index at the reporting date and changes during the current reporting period and the previous reporting period; and

(c)   amount of gain or loss on monetary items.

Section 32 *Events after the End of the Reporting Period*

Scope of this section

32.1   This section defines events after the end of the **reporting period** and sets out principles for recognising, measuring and disclosing those events.

Events after the end of the reporting period defined

32.2   Events after the end of the reporting period are those events, favourable and unfavourable, that occur between the end of the reporting period and the date when the **financial statements** are authorised for issue. There are two types of events:

(a)   those that provide evidence of conditions that existed at the end of the reporting period (adjusting events after the end of the reporting period); and

(b)   those that are indicative of conditions that arose after the end of the reporting period (non-adjusting events after the end of the reporting period).

32.3   Events after the end of the reporting period include all events up to the date when the financial statements are authorised for issue, even if those events occur after the public announcement of **profit or loss** or other selected financial information.

Recognition and measurement

Adjusting events after the end of the reporting period

32.4   An entity shall adjust the amounts recognised in its financial statements, including related disclosures, to reflect adjusting events after the end of the reporting period.

32.5   The following are examples of adjusting events after the end of the reporting period that require an entity to adjust the amounts recognised in its financial statements, or to recognise items that were not previously recognised:

(a)   The settlement after the end of the reporting period of a court case that confirms that the entity had a present obligation at the end of the reporting period. The entity adjusts any previously recognised **provision** related to this court case in accordance with Section 21 *Provisions and Contingencies* or recognises a new provision. The entity does not merely disclose a **contingent liability**. Rather, the settlement provides additional evidence to be considered in determining the provision that should be recognised at the end of the reporting period in accordance with Section 21.

(b)   The receipt of information after the end of the reporting period indicating that an **asset** was impaired at the end of the reporting period, or that the amount of a previously recognised **impairment loss** for that asset needs to be adjusted. For example:

   (i)   the bankruptcy of a customer that occurs after the end of the reporting period usually confirms that a loss existed at the end of the reporting period on a trade receivable and that the entity needs to adjust the **carrying amount** of the trade receivable; and

   (ii)   the sale of **inventories** after the end of the reporting period may give evidence about their selling price at the end of the reporting period for the purpose of assessing impairment at that date.

(c)   The determination after the end of the reporting period of the cost of assets purchased, or the proceeds from assets sold, before the end of the reporting period.

(d)   The determination after the end of the reporting period of the amount of profit-sharing or bonus payments, if the entity had a legal or **constructive obligation** at the end of the reporting period to make such payments as a result of events before that date (see Section 28 *Employee Benefits*).

(e)   The discovery of fraud or **errors** that show that the financial statements are incorrect.

Non-adjusting events after the end of the reporting period

An entity shall not adjust the amounts recognised in its financial statements to reflect non-adjusting events after the end of the reporting period.   **32.6**

Examples of non-adjusting events after the end of the reporting period include: **32.7**

(a)   A decline in market value of investments between the end of the reporting period and the date when the financial statements are authorised for issue. The decline in market value does not normally relate to the condition of the investments at the end of the reporting period, but reflects circumstances that have arisen subsequently. Therefore, an entity does not adjust the amounts recognised in its financial statements for the investments. Similarly, the entity does not update the amounts disclosed for the investments as at the end of the reporting period, although it may need to give additional disclosure in accordance with paragraph 32.10.

(b)   An amount that becomes receivable as a result of a favourable judgement or settlement of a court case after the **reporting date** but before the financial statements are authorised for issued. This would be a **contingent asset** at the reporting date (see paragraph 21.13), and disclosure may be required by paragraph 21.16. However, agreement on the amount of damages for a judgement that was reached before the reporting date, but was not previously recognised because the amount could not be measured reliably, may constitute an adjusting event.

Further examples of non-adjusting events are set out in paragraph 32.11.

Going concern

An entity shall not prepare its financial statements on a **going concern** basis if management determines after the reporting period either that it intends to liquidate the entity or to cease trading, or that it has no realistic alternative but to do so.   **32.7A**

Deterioration in operating results and **financial position** after the reporting period may indicate a need to consider whether the going concern assumption is still appropriate. If the going concern assumption is no longer appropriate, the effect is so pervasive that this section requires a fundamental change in the basis of accounting, rather than an adjustment to the amounts recognised within the original basis of accounting and therefore the disclosure requirements of paragraph 3.9 apply.   **32.7B**

Dividends

32.8   If an entity declares dividends to holders of its equity instruments after the end of the reporting period, the entity shall not recognise those dividends as a **liability** at the end of the reporting period because no obligation exists at that time. The amount of the dividend may be presented as a segregated component of retained earnings at the end of the reporting period.

Disclosure

Date of authorisation for issue

32.9   An entity shall disclose the date when the financial statements were authorised for issue and who gave that authorisation. If the entity's **owners** or others have the power to amend the financial statements after issue, the entity shall disclose that fact.

Non-adjusting events after the end of the reporting period

*32.10   An entity shall disclose the following for each category of non-adjusting event after the end of the reporting period:

(a)   the nature of the event; and
(b)   an estimate of its financial effect or a statement that such an estimate cannot be made.

*32.11   The following are examples of non-adjusting events after the end of the reporting period that would generally result in disclosure. The disclosures will reflect information that becomes known after the end of the reporting period but before the financial statements are authorised for issue:

(a)   a major **business combination** or disposal of a major **subsidiary**;
(b)   announcement of a plan to discontinue an operation;
(c)   major purchases of assets, disposals or plans to dispose of assets, or expropriation of major assets by government;
(d)   the destruction of a major production plant by a fire;
(e)   announcement, or commencement of the implementation, of a major restructuring;
(f)   issues or repurchases of an entity's debt or equity instruments;
(g)   abnormally large changes in asset prices or foreign exchange rates;
(h)   changes in tax rates or tax laws enacted or announced that have a significant effect on current and **deferred tax assets and liabilities**;
(i)   entering into significant commitments or contingent liabilities, for example, by issuing significant guarantees; and
(j)   commencement of major litigation arising solely out of events that occurred after the end of the reporting period.

Section 33 *Related Party Disclosures*

Scope of this section

33.1   This section requires an entity to include in its **financial statements** the disclosures necessary to draw attention to the possibility that its **financial position** and **profit or loss** have been affected by the existence of **related parties** and by transactions and outstanding balances with such parties.

Disclosures need not be given of transactions entered into between two or more members of a **group**, provided that any **subsidiary** which is a party to the transaction is wholly owned by such a member. **33.1A**

Related party defined

A related party is a person or entity that is related to the entity that is preparing its financial statements (the reporting entity). **33.2**

(a) A person or a **close member of that person's family** is related to a reporting entity if that person:

    (i)   has **control** or **joint control** over the reporting entity;

    (ii) has **significant influence** over the reporting entity; or

    (iii) is a member of the **key management personnel** of the reporting entity or of a **parent** of the reporting entity.

(b) An entity is related to a reporting entity if any of the following conditions apply:

    (i)   the entity and the reporting entity are members of the same group (which means that each parent, subsidiary and fellow subsidiary is related to the others).

    (ii) one entity is an **associate** or **joint venture** of the other entity (or an associate or joint venture of a member of a group of which the other entity is a member).

    (iii) both entities are joint ventures of the same third party.

    (iv) one entity is a joint venture of a third entity and the other entity is an associate of the third entity.

    (v) the entity is a **post-employment benefit plan** for the benefit of employees of either the reporting entity or an entity related to the reporting entity. If the reporting entity is itself such a plan, the sponsoring employers are also related to the reporting entity.

    (vi) the entity is controlled or jointly controlled by a person identified in (a).

    (vii) a person identified in (a)(i) has significant influence over the entity or is a member of the key management personnel of the entity (or of a parent of the entity).

    (viii) the entity, or any member of a group of which it is a part, provides key management personnel services to the reporting entity or to the parent of the reporting entity.

In considering each possible related party relationship, an entity shall assess the substance of the relationship and not merely the legal form. **33.3**

In the context of this FRS, the following are not related parties: **33.4**

(a) Two entities simply because they have a director or other member of key management personnel in common or because a member of key management personnel of one entity has significant influence over the other entity.

(b) Two **venturers** simply because they share joint control over a joint venture.

(c) Any of the following simply by virtue of their normal dealings with an entity (even though they may affect the freedom of action of an entity or participate in its decision-making process):

    (i)   providers of finance;

    (ii) trade unions;

    (iii) public utilities; and

    (iv) government departments and agencies.

(d) A customer, supplier, franchisor, distributor or general agent with whom an entity transacts a significant volume of business, merely by virtue of the resulting economic dependence.

33.4A   In the definition of a related party, an associate includes subsidiaries of the associate and a joint venture includes subsidiaries of the joint venture. Therefore, for example, an associate's subsidiary and the investor that has significant influence over the associate are related to each other.

Disclosures

Disclosure of parent-subsidiary relationships

*33.5   Relationships between a parent and its subsidiaries shall be disclosed irrespective of whether there have been **related party transactions**. An entity shall disclose the name of its parent and, if different, the ultimate controlling party. If neither the entity's parent nor the ultimate controlling party produces financial statements available for public use, the name of the next most senior parent that does so (if any) shall also be disclosed.

Disclosure of key management personnel compensation

33.6   Key management personnel are those persons having authority and responsibility for planning, directing and controlling the activities of the entity, directly or indirectly, including any director (whether executive or otherwise) of that entity. Compensation includes all **employee benefits** (as defined in Section 28 *Employee Benefits*) including those in the form of share-based payments (see Section 26 *Share-based Payment*). Employee benefits include all forms of consideration paid, payable or provided by the entity, or on behalf of the entity (eg by its parent or by a shareholder), in exchange for services rendered to the entity. It also includes such consideration paid on behalf of a parent of the entity in respect of goods or services provided to the entity.

33.7   An entity shall disclose key management personnel compensation in total.

Disclosure of related party transactions

33.8   A related party transaction is a transfer of resources, services or obligations between a reporting entity and a related party, regardless of whether a price is charged. Examples of related party transactions that are common to entities within the scope of this FRS include, but are not limited to:

(a)   transactions between an entity and its principal **owner(s)**;

(b)   transactions between an entity and another entity when both entities are under the common control of a single entity or person; and

(c)   transactions in which an entity or person that controls the reporting entity incurs **expenses** directly that otherwise would have been borne by the reporting entity.

*33.9   If an entity has related party transactions, it shall disclose the nature of the related party relationship as well as information about the transactions, outstanding balances and commitments necessary for an understanding of the potential effect of the relationship on the financial statements. Those disclosure requirements are in addition to the requirements in paragraph 33.7 to disclose key management personnel compensation. At a minimum, disclosures shall include:

(a)   The amount of the transactions.

(b)   The amount of outstanding balances and:

   (i)   their terms and conditions, including whether they are secured, and the nature of the consideration to be provided in settlement; and

   **(ii)   details of any guarantees given or received.

(c)   Provisions for uncollectible receivables related to the amount of outstanding balances.

(d)   The expense recognised during the period in respect of bad or doubtful debts due

Such transactions could include purchases, sales, or transfers of goods or services, **leases**, guarantees and settlements by the entity on behalf of the related party or vice versa.

An entity shall make the disclosures required by paragraph 33.9 separately for each of the following categories:　　**33.10**

(a)　entities with control, joint control or significant influence over the entity;
(b)　entities over which the entity has control, joint control or significant influence;
(c)　key management personnel of the entity or its parent (in the aggregate);
(d)　entities that provide key management personnel services to the entity; and
(e)　other related parties.

An entity is exempt from the disclosure requirements of paragraph 33.9 in relation to:　　**33.11**

(a)　a **state** (a national, regional or local government) that has control, joint control or significant influence over the reporting entity; and
(b)　another entity that is a related party because the same state has control, joint control or significant influence over both the reporting entity and the other entity.

However, the entity must still disclose a parent-subsidiary relationship as required by paragraph 33.5.

The following are examples of transactions that shall be disclosed if they are with a related party:　　**33.12**

(a)　purchases or sales of goods (finished or unfinished);
(b)　purchases or sales of property and other **assets**;
(c)　rendering or receiving of services;
(d)　leases;
(e)　transfers of **research** and **development**;
(f)　transfers under licence agreements;
(g)　transfers under finance arrangements (including loans and equity contributions in **cash** or in kind);
(h)　provision of guarantees or collateral;
(i)　settlement of **liabilities** on behalf of the entity or by the entity on behalf of another party; and
(j)　participation by a parent or subsidiary in a **defined benefit plan** that shares risks between group entities.

An entity shall not state that related party transactions were made on terms equivalent to those that prevail in arm's length transactions unless such terms can be substantiated.　　**33.13**

An entity may disclose items of a similar nature in the aggregate except when separate disclosure is necessary for an understanding of the effects of related party transactions on the financial statements of the entity.　　**33.14**

Section 34 *Specialised Activities*

Scope of this section

This section sets out the financial reporting requirements for entities applying this FRS involved in the following types of specialised activities:　　**34.1**

(a)　Agriculture (see paragraphs 34.2 to 34.10A);
(b)　Extractive Activities (see paragraphs 34.11 to 34.11C);
(c)　Service Concession Arrangements (see paragraphs 34.12 to 34.16A);
(d)　Financial Institutions (see paragraphs 34.17 to 34.33);
(e)　Retirement Benefit Plans: Financial Statements (see paragraphs 34.34 to 34.48);

(f)   Heritage Assets (see paragraphs 34.49 to 34.56);

(g)   Funding Commitments (see paragraphs 34.57 to 34.63);

(h)   Incoming Resources from Non-Exchange Transactions (see paragraphs 34.64 to 34.74);

(i)   Public Benefit Entity Combinations (see paragraphs 34.75 to 34.86); and

(j)   Public Benefit Entity Concessionary Loans (see paragraphs 34.87 to 34.97).

Agriculture

34.2   An entity using this FRS that is engaged in **agricultural activity** shall determine an **accounting policy** for each class of **biological asset** and its related **agricultural produce**.

Recognition

34.3   An entity shall recognise a biological asset or an item of agricultural produce when, and only when:

(a)   the entity controls the **asset** as a result of past events;

(b)   it is **probable** that future economic benefits associated with the asset will flow to the entity; and

(c)   the **fair value** or cost of the asset can be measured reliably.

Measurement

34.3A   For each class of biological asset and its related agricultural produce an entity shall choose as its accounting policy either:

(a)   the fair value model set out in paragraphs 34.4 to 34.7A; or

(b)   the cost model set out in paragraphs 34.8 to 34.10A.

34.3B   If an entity has chosen the fair value model for a class of biological asset and its related agricultural produce, it shall not subsequently change its accounting policy to the cost model.

Measurement – fair value model

34.4   An entity applying the fair value model shall measure a biological asset on initial **recognition** and at each **reporting date** at its **fair value less costs to sell**. Changes in fair value less costs to sell shall be recognised in **profit or loss**.

34.5   Agricultural produce harvested from an entity's biological assets shall be measured at the point of harvest at its fair value less costs to sell. Such **measurement** is the cost at that date when applying Section 13 *Inventories* or another applicable section of this FRS.

34.6   In determining fair value, an entity shall consider the following:

(a)   If an **active market** exists for a biological asset or agricultural produce in its present location and condition, the quoted price in that market is the appropriate basis for determining the fair value of that asset. If an entity has access to different active markets, the entity shall use the price existing in the market that it expects to use.

(b)   If an active market does not exist, an entity uses one or more of the following, when available, in determining fair value:

(i)   the most recent market transaction price, provided that there has not been a significant change in economic circumstances between the date of that transaction and the end of the **reporting period**;

(ii)   market prices for similar assets with adjustment to reflect differences; and

(iii) sector benchmarks such as the value of an orchard expressed per export tray, bushel, or hectare, and the value of cattle expressed per kilogram of meat.

(c) In some cases, the information sources listed in (b) may suggest different conclusions as to the fair value of a biological asset or an item of agricultural produce. An entity considers the reasons for those differences, to arrive at the most reliable estimate of fair value within a relatively narrow range of reasonable estimates.

(d) In some circumstances, fair value may be readily determinable even though market determined prices or values are not available for a biological asset in its present condition. An entity shall consider whether the present value of expected net cash flows from the asset discounted at a current market determined rate results in a reliable measure of fair value.

If the fair value of a biological asset cannot be measured reliably, the entity shall apply the cost model to that biological asset in accordance with paragraphs 34.8 and 34.10A until such time that the fair value can be reliably measured. | **34.6A**

Disclosures – fair value model

An entity shall disclose the following for each class of biological asset measured using the fair value model: | **34.7**

(a) A description of each class of biological asset.

*(b) The methods and significant assumptions applied in determining the fair value of each class of biological asset.

*(c) A reconciliation of changes in the **carrying amount** of each class of biological asset between the beginning and the end of the current period. The reconciliation shall include:

*(i) the **gain** or loss arising from changes in fair value less costs to sell;
(ii) increases resulting from purchases;
(iii) decreases attributable to sales;
(iv) decreases resulting from harvest;
(v) increases resulting from **business combinations**; and
(vi) other changes.

This reconciliation need not be presented for prior periods.

If an entity measures any individual biological assets at cost in accordance with paragraph 34.6A, it shall explain why fair value cannot be reliably measured. If the fair value of such a biological asset becomes reliably measurable during the current period an entity shall explain why fair value has become reliably measurable and the effect of the change. | **34.7A**

An entity shall disclose the methods and significant assumptions applied in determining the fair value at the point of harvest of each class of agricultural produce. | **34.7B**

Measurement – cost model

An entity applying the cost model shall measure biological assets at cost less any accumulated **depreciation** and any accumulated **impairment losses**. | **34.8**

In applying the cost model, agricultural produce harvested from an entity's biological assets shall be measured at the point of harvest at either: | **34.9**

(a) the lower of cost and estimated selling price less costs to complete and sell; or

(b) its fair value less costs to sell. Any gain or loss arising on initial recognition of agricultural produce at fair value less costs to sell shall be included in profit or loss for the period in which it arises.

Such measurement is the cost at that date when applying Section 13 or another applicable section of this FRS.

Disclosures – cost model

34.10   An entity shall disclose the following for each class of biological asset measured using the cost model:

(a)   a description of each class of biological asset;

(b)   [not used]

(c)   the depreciation method used;

(d)   the useful lives or the depreciation rates used; and

*(e)   a reconciliation of changes in the carrying amount of each class of biological asset between the beginning and the end of the current period. The reconciliation shall include:

(i)   increases resulting from purchases;

(ii)   decreases attributable to sales;

(iii)   decreases resulting from harvest;

(iv)   increases resulting from business combinations;

(v)   impairment losses recognised or reversed in profit or loss in accordance with Section 27 *Impairment of Assets*; and

(vi)   other changes.

This reconciliation need not be presented for prior periods.

34.10A   An entity shall disclose, for any agricultural produce measured at fair value less costs to sell, the methods and significant assumptions applied in determining the fair value at the point of harvest of each class of agricultural produce.

Extractive Activities

34.11   An entity using this FRS that is engaged in the exploration for and/or evaluation of mineral resources (extractive activities) shall apply the requirements of IFRS 6 *Exploration for and Evaluation of Mineral Resources*.

34.11A   When applying the requirements of IFRS 6, references made to other IFRSs within that standard shall be taken to be references to the relevant section or paragraph within this FRS.

34.11B   Notwithstanding the requirements of paragraph 34.11A, when applying paragraph 21 of IFRS 6, a **cash-generating unit** or group of cash-generating units shall be no larger than an **operating segment** and the reference to IFRS 8 *Operating Segments* shall be ignored.

34.11C   On first-time adoption of this FRS if it is not practical to apply a particular requirement of paragraph 18 of IFRS 6 to previous comparative amounts, an entity shall disclose that fact.

Service Concession Arrangements

34.12   A **service concession arrangement** is an arrangement whereby a public sector body, or a **public benefit entity** (the grantor) contracts with a private sector entity (the operator) to construct (or upgrade), operate and maintain **infrastructure assets** for a specified period of time (concession period). The operator is paid for its services over the period of the arrangement. A common feature of a service concession arrangement is the public service nature of the obligation undertaken by the operator, whereby the arrangement contractually obliges the operator to provide services to, or on behalf of, the grantor for the benefit of the public.

Specifically an arrangement is a service concession arrangement when the following conditions apply: **34.12A**

(a)   the grantor controls or regulates what services the operator must provide using the infrastructure assets, to whom, and at what price; and

(b)   the grantor controls, through ownership, beneficial entitlement or otherwise, any significant **residual interest** in the assets at the end of the term of the arrangement.

Where the infrastructure assets have no significant **residual value** at the end of the term of the arrangement (ie the arrangement is for its entire useful life), then the arrangement shall be accounted for as a service concession if the conditions in (a) are met.

For the purpose of condition (b), the grantor's control over any significant residual interest should both restrict the operator's practical ability to sell or pledge the infrastructure assets and give the grantor a continuing right of use throughout the concession period.

A service concession arrangement shall be accounted for in accordance with the requirements of paragraphs 34.12E to 34.16A.   **34.12B**

A service concession arrangement may contain a group of contracts and sub-arrangements as elements of the service concession arrangement as a whole. Such an arrangement shall be treated as a whole when the group of contracts and sub-arrangements are linked in such a way that the commercial effect cannot be understood without reference to them as a whole. Accordingly, the contractual terms of certain contracts or arrangements may meet both the scope requirements of paragraphs 34.12 and 34.12A, and Section 20 *Leases*. Where this is the case, the requirements of this section shall prevail.   **34.12C**

Where an arrangement does not meet the requirements of paragraphs 34.12 and 34.12A, it shall be accounted for in accordance with Section 17 *Property, Plant and Equipment*, Section 18 *Intangible Assets other than Goodwill*, Section 20 or Section 23 *Revenue*, based on the nature of the arrangement.   **34.12D**

Accounting by grantors – Finance lease liability model

The infrastructure assets shall be recognised as **assets** of the grantor together with a **liability** for its obligations under the service concession arrangement.   **34.12E**

The grantor shall initially recognise the infrastructure assets and associated liability in accordance with paragraphs 20.9 and 20.10. If as a result of applying paragraphs 20.9 and 20.10 the grantor has not recognised a liability to make payments to the operator, it shall not recognise the infrastructure assets.   **34.12F**

The liability shall be recognised as a finance lease liability and subsequently accounted for in accordance with paragraph 20.11.   **34.12G**

The infrastructure assets shall be recognised as **property, plant and equipment** or as **intangible assets**, as appropriate, and subsequently accounted for in accordance with Section 17 or Section 18.   **34.12H**

Accounting by operators

Treatment of the operator's rights over the infrastructure

34.12I   Infrastructure assets shall not be recognised as property, plant and equipment by the operator because the contractual service arrangement does not convey the right to control the use of the public service assets to the operator. The operator has access to operate the infrastructure to provide the public service on behalf of the grantor in accordance with the terms specified in the arrangement.

Recognition and measurement of consideration

34.13   There are two principal categories of service concession arrangements:

(a)   In one, the operator receives a **financial asset** – an unconditional contractual right to receive a specified or determinable amount of **cash** or another financial asset from, or at the direction of, the grantor in return for constructing (or upgrading) the infrastructure assets, and then operating and maintaining the asset for a specified period of time. This category includes guarantees by the grantor to pay for any shortfall between amounts received from users of the public service and specified or determinable amounts.

(b)   In the other, the operator receives an **intangible asset** – a right to charge for use of the infrastructure assets that it constructs (or upgrades) and then operates and maintains for a specified period of time. A right to charge users is not an unconditional right to receive cash because the amounts are contingent on the extent to which the public uses the service.

Sometimes, a single arrangement may contain both types: to the extent that the grantor has given an unconditional guarantee of payment for the construction (or upgrade) of the infrastructure assets, the operator has a financial asset; to the extent that the operator receives a right to charge the public for using the service the operator has an intangible asset.

Accounting – financial asset model

34.14   The operator shall recognise a financial asset to the extent that it has an unconditional contractual right to receive cash or another financial asset from, or at the direction of, the grantor for the construction (or upgrade) services. The operator shall initially recognise the financial asset at fair value for the consideration received or receivable, based on the fair value of the construction (or upgrade) services provided. Thereafter, it shall account for the financial asset in accordance with Section 11 *Basic Financial Instruments* and Section 12 *Other Financial Instruments Issues*.

Accounting – intangible asset model

34.15   The operator shall recognise an intangible asset to the extent that it receives a right (a licence) to charge users of the public service. The operator shall initially recognise the intangible asset at fair value for the consideration received or receivable, based on the fair value of the construction (or upgrade) services provided. Thereafter, it shall account for the intangible asset in accordance with Section 18.

Operating services

34.16   The operator shall account for **revenue** in accordance with Section 23 for the operating services it performs.

Borrowing costs

Borrowing costs attributable to the arrangement shall be recognised as an **expense**, in accordance with Section 25 *Borrowing Costs*, in the period in which they are incurred unless the operator has an intangible asset. In this case borrowing costs attributable to the arrangement may be capitalised in accordance with Section 25 where a policy of capitalisation has been adopted in accordance with that section. **34.16A**

Financial Institutions

A **financial institution** (other than a **retirement benefit plan**) applying this FRS shall, in addition to the disclosure requirements in Section 11 *Basic Financial Instruments* and Section 12 *Other Financial Instruments Issues*, provide the disclosures in paragraphs 34.19 to 34.33. The disclosures in paragraphs 34.19 to 34.33 are required to be provided in: **34.17**

(a) the **individual financial statements** of a financial institution (other than a retirement benefit plan); and

(b) the **consolidated financial statements** of a **group** containing a financial institution (other than a retirement benefit plan) when the **financial instruments** held by the financial institution are **material** to the group. Where this is the case, the disclosures apply regardless of whether the principal activity of the group is being a financial institution or not. The disclosures in paragraphs 34.19 to 34.33 only need to be given in respect of financial instruments held by entities within the group that are financial institutions (other than retirement benefit plans).

A retirement benefit plan shall provide the disclosures in paragraphs 34.35 to 34.48 of this FRS. **34.18**

Disclosures

Significance of financial instruments for financial position and performance

A financial institution shall disclose information that enables users of its **financial statements** to evaluate the significance of financial instruments for its **financial position** and **performance**. **34.19**

A financial institution shall disclose a disaggregation of the **statement of financial position** line item by class of financial instrument. A class is a grouping of financial instruments that is appropriate to the nature of the information disclosed and that takes into account the characteristics of those financial instruments. **34.20**

Impairment

Where a financial institution uses a separate allowance account to record impairments, it shall disclose a reconciliation of changes in that account during the period for each class of **financial asset**. **34.21**

Fair value

For financial instruments held at **fair value** in the statement of financial position, a financial institution shall disclose for each class of financial instrument, an analysis of the level in the fair value hierarchy (as set out in paragraph 11.27) into which the fair value measurements are categorised. **34.22**

Prospective amendments: Amendments to FRS 102 The Financial Reporting Standard applicable in the UK and Republic of Ireland – Fair value hierarchy disclosures (March 2016) amends paragraph 34.22 with effect for annual periods beginning on or after 1 January 2017.

Nature and extent of risks arising from financial instruments

34.23   A financial institution shall disclose information that enables users of its financial statements to evaluate the nature and extent of **credit risk**, **liquidity risk** and **market risk** arising from financial instruments to which the financial institution is exposed at the end of the **reporting period**.

34.24   For each type of risk arising from financial instruments, a financial institution shall disclose:

   (a)   the exposures to risk and how they arise;
   (b)   its objectives, policies and processes for managing the risk and the methods used to measure the risk; and
   (c)   any changes in (a) or (b) from the previous period.

Credit risk

34.25   A financial institution shall disclose by class of financial instrument:

   (a)   The amount that best represents its maximum exposure to credit risk at the end of the reporting period. This disclosure is not required for financial instruments whose **carrying amount** best represents the maximum exposure to credit risk.
   (b)   A description of collateral held as security and of other credit enhancements, and the extent to which these mitigate credit risk.
   (c)   The amount by which any related credit **derivatives** or similar instruments mitigate that maximum exposure to credit risk.
   (d)   Information about the credit quality of **financial assets** that are neither past due nor impaired.

34.26   A financial institution shall provide, by class of financial asset, an analysis of:

   (a)   the age of financial assets that are past due as at the end of the reporting period but not impaired; and
   (b)   the financial assets that are individually determined to be impaired as at the end of the reporting period, including the factors the financial institution considered in determining that they are impaired.

34.27   When a financial institution obtains financial or non-financial assets during the period by taking possession of collateral it holds as security or calling on other credit enhancements (eg guarantees), and such **assets** meet the **recognition** criteria in other sections, a financial institution shall disclose:

   (a)   the nature and carrying amount of the assets obtained; and
   (b)   when the assets are not readily convertible into **cash**, its policies for disposing of such assets or for using them in its operations.

Prospective amendments: Amendments to FRS 102 The Financial Reporting Standard applicable in the UK and Republic of Ireland – Fair value hierarchy disclosures (March 2016) amends paragraph 34.27 with effect for annual periods beginning on or after 1 January 2017.

Liquidity risk

A financial institution shall provide a maturity analysis for **financial liabilities** that shows the remaining contractual maturities at undiscounted amounts separated between derivative and non-derivative financial liabilities. **34.28**

Market risk

A financial institution shall provide a sensitivity analysis for each type of market risk (eg interest rate risk, currency risk, other price risk) it is exposed to, showing the impact on **profit or loss** and **equity**. Details of the methods and assumptions used should be provided. **34.29**

If a financial institution prepares a sensitivity analysis, such as value-at-risk, that reflects interdependencies between risk variables (eg interest rates and exchange rates) and uses it to manage **financial risks**, it may use that sensitivity analysis instead. **34.30**

Capital

A financial institution shall disclose information that enables users of its financial statements to evaluate the entity's objectives, policies and processes for managing capital. A financial institution shall disclose the following: **34.31**

(a) Qualitative information about its objectives, policies and processes for managing capital, including:

    (i) a description of what it manages as capital;

    (ii) when an entity is subject to externally imposed capital requirements, the nature of those requirements and how those requirements are incorporated into the management of capital; and

    (iii) how it is meeting its objectives for managing capital.

(b) Summary quantitative data about what it manages as capital. Some entities regard some financial liabilities (eg some forms of subordinated debt) as part of capital. Other entities regard capital as excluding some components of equity (eg components arising from cash flow hedges).

(c) Any changes in (a) and (b) from the previous period.

(d) Whether during the period it complied with any externally imposed capital requirements to which it is subject.

(e) When the entity has not complied with such externally imposed capital requirements, the consequences of such non-compliance.

A financial institution bases these disclosures on the information provided internally to **key management personnel**.

A financial institution may manage capital in a number of ways and be subject to a number of different capital requirements. For example, a conglomerate may include entities that undertake insurance activities and banking activities and those entities may operate in several jurisdictions. When an aggregate disclosure of capital requirements and how capital is managed would not provide useful information or would distort a financial statement user's understanding of the financial institution's capital resources, the financial institution shall disclose separate information for each capital requirement to which the entity is subject. **34.32**

Reporting cash flows on a net basis

34.33   A financial institution that presents a statement of cash flow in accordance with Section 7 *Statement of Cash Flows* may report cash flows arising from each of the following activities on a net basis:

(a)   cash receipts and payments for the acceptance and repayment of deposits with a fixed maturity date;

(b)   the placement of deposits with and withdrawal of deposits from other financial institutions; and

(c)   cash advances and loans made to customers and the repayment of those advances and loans.

This paragraph does not impose a requirement to produce a cash flow statement.

Retirement Benefit Plans: Financial Statements

34.34   An entity applying this FRS that is a **retirement benefit plan** shall also apply the requirements of paragraphs 34.35 to 34.48. A retirement benefit plan may be a **defined benefit plan**, a **defined contribution plan**, or have both defined benefit and defined contribution elements. The **financial statements** shall distinguish between defined benefit and defined contribution elements, where **material**.

Requirements applicable to both defined benefit plans and defined contribution plans

34.35   A retirement benefit plan need not comply with the requirements of paragraph 3.17. The financial statements of a retirement benefit plan shall contain as part of the financial statements:

(a)   a statement of changes in **net assets available for benefits** (which can also be called a Fund Account) (see paragraph 34.37);

(b)   a statement of net assets available for benefits (see paragraph 34.38); and

(c)   **notes**, comprising a summary of significant **accounting policies** and other explanatory information.

34.36   At each **reporting date**, the net assets available for benefits shall be measured in accordance with paragraph 28.15(b). Changes in fair value shall be recognised in the statements of changes in net assets available for benefits.

Statement of changes in net assets available for benefits (Fund Account)

34.37   The financial statements of a retirement benefit plan, whether defined contribution or defined benefit, shall present the following in the statement of changes in net assets available for benefits:

(a)   employer contributions;

(b)   employee contributions;

(c)   investment income such as interest and dividends;

(d)   other income;

(e)   benefits paid or payable (analysed, for example, as retirement, death and disability benefits, and lump sum payments);

(f)   administrative expenses;

(g)   other expenses;

(h)   taxes on income;

(i)   profits and losses on disposal of investments and changes in value of investments; and

(j)   transfers from and to other plans.

Statement of net assets available for benefits

The financial statements of a retirement benefit plan, whether defined contribution or defined benefit, shall present the following in the statement of net assets available for benefits: **34.38**

(a) **assets** at the end of the period suitably classified; and

(b) **liabilities** other than the actuarial **present value** of promised retirement benefits.

The basis of valuation of assets shall be presented in the notes to the financial statements.

Disclosures

Assets other than financial instruments held at fair value

Where a retirement benefit plan holds assets other than financial instruments at fair value in accordance with paragraph 34.36, it shall apply the disclosure requirements of the relevant section of this FRS, for example in relation to **investment property** it shall provide the disclosures required by paragraph 16.10. **34.39**

Significance of financial instruments for financial position and performance

A retirement benefit plan shall disclose information that enables users of its financial statements to evaluate the significance of financial instruments for its **financial position** and **performance**. **34.40**

A retirement benefit plan shall disclose a disaggregation of the statement of net assets available for benefits by class of financial instrument. A class is a grouping of financial instruments that is appropriate to the nature of the information disclosed and that takes into account the characteristics of those financial instruments. **34.41**

Fair value

For financial instruments held at fair value in the statement of net assets available for benefits, a retirement benefit plan shall disclose for each class of financial instrument, an analysis of the level in the fair value hierarchy (as set out in paragraph 11.27) into which the fair value measurements are categorised. **34.42**

Prospective amendments: Amendments to FRS 102 The Financial Reporting Standard applicable in the UK and Republic of Ireland – Fair value hierarchy disclosures (March 2016) amends paragraph 34.42 with effect for annual periods beginning on or after 1 January 2017.

Nature and extent of risks arising from financial instruments

A retirement benefit plan shall disclose information that enables users of its financial statements to evaluate the nature and extent of **credit risk** and **market risk** arising from financial instruments to which the retirement benefit plan is exposed at the end of the **reporting period**. **34.43**

For each type of credit and market risk arising from financial instruments, a retirement benefit plan shall disclose: **34.44**

(a) the exposures to risk and how they arise;

(b) its objectives, policies and processes for managing the risk and the methods used to measure the risk; and

(c) any changes in (a) or (b) from the previous period.

In relation to credit risk, a retirement benefit plan shall, in addition, provide the disclosures set out in paragraphs 34.45 and 34.46.

Credit risk

34.45   A retirement benefit plan shall disclose by class of financial instrument:

(a)   The amount that best represents its maximum exposure to credit risk at the end of the reporting period. This disclosure is not required for financial instruments whose **carrying amount** best represents the maximum exposure to credit risk.

(b)   A description of collateral held as security and of other credit enhancements, and the extent to which these mitigate credit risk.

(c)   The amount by which any related credit **derivatives** or similar instruments mitigate that maximum exposure to credit risk.

(d)   Information about the credit quality of financial assets that are neither past due nor impaired.

34.46   When a retirement benefit plan obtains financial or non-financial assets during the period by taking possession of collateral it holds as security or calling on other credit enhancements (eg guarantees), and such assets meet the **recognition** criteria in other sections, a retirement benefit plan shall disclose:

(a)   the nature and carrying amount of the assets obtained; and

(b)   when the assets are not readily convertible into **cash**, its policies for disposing of such assets or for retaining them.

Defined benefit plans – actuarial liabilities

34.47   A defined benefit plan is not required to recognise a liability in relation to the promised retirement benefits.

34.48   A defined benefit plan shall disclose, in a report alongside the financial statements, information regarding the actuarial present value of promised retirement benefits including:

(a)   a statement of the actuarial present value of promised retirement benefits, based on the most recent valuation of the scheme;

(b)   the date of the most recent valuation of the scheme; and

(c)   the significant actuarial assumptions made and the method used to calculate the actuarial present value of promised retirement benefits.

Heritage Assets

34.49   All **heritage assets** shall be accounted for in accordance with the requirements of paragraphs 34.50 to 34.56. These paragraphs do not apply to **investment property**, **property, plant and equipment** or **intangible assets** which fall within the scope of Section 16 *Investment Properties*, Section 17 *Property, Plant and Equipment* and Section 18 *Intangible Assets other than Goodwill*.

34.50   Works of art and similar objects are sometimes held by commercial entities but are not heritage assets because they are not maintained principally for their contribution to knowledge and culture. These assets shall therefore be accounted for in accordance with Section 17. Heritage assets used by the entity itself, for example historic buildings used for teaching by education establishments, shall also be accounted for in accordance with Section 17. This is based on the view that an operational perspective is likely to be most relevant for most users of **financial statements**. However, entities that use historic buildings and similar assets may wish to consider whether it is appropriate to apply the disclosures required by paragraphs 34.55 and 34.56.

Recognition and measurement

An entity shall recognise and measure heritage assets in accordance with Section 17 (ie using the cost model or revaluation model), subject to the requirements set out in paragraphs 34.52 to 34.53 below.   **34.51**

Heritage assets shall be recognised in the **statement of financial position** separately from other assets.   **34.52**

Where heritage assets have previously been capitalised or are recently purchased, information on the cost or value of the asset will be available. Where this information is not available, and cannot be obtained at a cost which is commensurate with the benefits to users of the financial statements, the assets shall not be recognised in the statement of financial position, but must be disclosed in accordance with the requirements below.   **34.53**

At each **reporting date**, an entity shall apply Section 27 *Impairment of Assets* to determine whether a heritage asset is impaired and, if so, how to recognise and measure the **impairment loss**. A heritage asset may be impaired, for example where it has suffered physical deterioration, breakage or doubts arise as to its authenticity.   **34.54**

Disclosure

An entity shall disclose the following for all heritage assets it holds: **34.55**

(a)   An indication of the nature and scale of heritage assets held by the entity.
(b)   The policy for the acquisition, preservation, management and disposal of heritage assets (including a description of the records maintained by the entity of its collection of heritage assets and information on the extent to which access to the assets is permitted).
(c)   The **accounting policies** adopted for heritage assets, including details of the measurement bases used.
(d)   For heritage assets that have not been recognised in the statement of financial position, the **notes** to the financial statements shall:

   (i)   explain the reasons why;
   (ii)   describe the significance and nature of those assets; and
   (iii)   disclose information that is helpful in assessing the value of those heritage assets.

*(e)   Where heritage assets are recognised in the statement of financial position the following disclosure is required:

   (i)   the **carrying amount** of heritage assets at the beginning of the **reporting period** and the reporting date, including an analysis between classes or groups of heritage assets recognised at cost and those recognised at valuation; and
   *(ii)   where assets are recognised at valuation, sufficient information to assist in understanding the valuation being recognised (date of valuation, method used, whether carried out by external valuer and if so their qualification and any significant limitations on the valuation).

*(f)   A summary of transactions relating to heritage assets for the reporting period and each of the previous four reporting periods disclosing:

   (i)   the cost of acquisitions of heritage assets;
   (ii)   the value of heritage assets acquired by donations;

(iii)   the carrying amount of heritage assets disposed of in the period and proceeds received; and

(iv)   any impairment recognised in the period.

The summary shall show separately those transactions included in the statement of financial position and those that are not.

(g)   In exceptional circumstances where it is **impracticable** to obtain a valuation of heritage assets acquired by donation the reason shall be stated.

Disclosures can be aggregated for groups or classes of heritage assets, provided this does not obscure significant information.

34.56   Where it is impracticable to do so, the disclosures required by paragraph 34.55(f) need not be given for any accounting period earlier than the previous comparable period, and a statement to the effect that it is impracticable shall be made.

Funding Commitments

34.57   An entity that commits to provide resources to other entities shall apply the requirements of paragraphs 34.58 to 34.63 and the accompanying guidance at Appendix A to this section, except for commitments to make a loan to which entities shall apply Section 11 *Basic Financial Instruments* or Section 12 *Other Financial Instruments Issues*, as applicable.

34.58   When applying these paragraphs, the requirements of Section 2 *Concepts and Pervasive Principles* and Section 21 *Provisions and Contingencies* shall also be taken into consideration.

Recognition

34.59   An entity shall recognise a **liability** and, usually, a corresponding **expense**, when it has made a commitment that it will provide resources to another party, if, and only if:

(a)   the definition and **recognition** criteria for a liability have been satisfied;

(b)   the obligation (which may be a **constructive obligation**) is such that the entity cannot realistically withdraw from it; and

(c)   the entitlement of the other party to the resources does not depend on the satisfaction of **performance-related conditions**.

34.60   Commitments that are performance-related will be recognised when those performance-related conditions are met.

Measurement

34.61   An entity shall measure any recognised liability at the **present value** of the resources committed.

Disclosure

*34.62   An entity that has made a commitment shall disclose the following:

(a)   the commitment made;

(b)   the time-frame of that commitment;

(c)   any performance-related conditions attached to that commitment; and

(d)   details of how that commitment will be funded.

The above disclosures may be made in aggregate, providing that such aggregation does not obscure significant information. However, separate disclosure shall be made for recognised and unrecognised commitments. **34.63**

Incoming Resources from Non-Exchange Transactions

The accounting for **government grants** is addressed in Section 24 *Government Grants*. **PBE34.64**

Paragraphs PBE34.67 to PBE34.74 and the accompanying guidance at Appendix B to this section apply to other resources received from **non-exchange transactions** by **public benefit entities** or entities within a **public benefit entity group**. A non-exchange transaction is a transaction whereby an entity receives value from another entity without directly giving approximately equal value in exchange or gives value to another entity without directly receiving approximately equal value in exchange. **PBE34.65**

Non-exchange transactions include, but are not limited to, donations (of **cash**, goods, and services) and legacies. **PBE34.66**

Recognition and measurement

An entity shall recognise receipts of resources from non-exchange transactions as follows: **PBE34.67**

(a) Transactions that do not impose specified future performance-related conditions on the recipient are recognised in **income** when the resources are received or receivable.
(b) Transactions that do impose specified future performance-related conditions on the recipient are recognised in income only when the performance-related conditions are met.
(c) Where resources are received before the **revenue recognition** criteria are satisfied, a **liability** is recognised.

The existence of a **restriction** does not prohibit a resource from being recognised in income when receivable. **PBE34.68**

When applying the requirements of paragraph PBE34.67, an entity must take into consideration whether the resource can be measured reliably and whether the benefits of recognising the resource outweigh the costs. **PBE34.69**

Therefore, where it is not practicable to estimate the value of the resource with sufficient **reliability**, the income shall be included in the financial period when the resource is sold. **PBE34.70**

An entity shall recognise a liability for any resource that has previously been received and recognised in income when, as a result of a subsequent failure to meet restrictions or performance-related conditions attached to it, repayment becomes **probable**. **PBE34.71**

Donations of services that can be reasonably quantified will usually result in the recognition of income and an **expense**. An **asset** will be recognised only when those services are used for the production of an asset and the services received will be capitalised as part of the cost of that asset. **PBE34.72**

An entity shall measure incoming resources from non-exchange transactions as follows: **PBE34.73**

(a) Donated services and facilities, that would otherwise have been purchased, shall be measured at the value to the entity.
(b) All other incoming resources from non-exchange transactions shall be measured at the **fair value** of the resources received or receivable.

Disclosure

PBE34.74   An entity shall disclose the following:

(a)   the nature and amounts of resources receivable from non-exchange transactions recognised in the **financial statements**;

(b)   any unfulfilled conditions or other contingencies attaching to resources from non-exchange transactions that have not been recognised in income; and

(c)   an indication of other forms of resources from non-exchange transactions from which the entity has benefited.

Public Benefit Entity Combinations

PBE34.75   Paragraphs PBE34.76 to PBE34.86 apply only to **public benefit entities** for the following categories of **entity combinations** which involve a whole entity or parts of an entity combining with another entity:

(a)   combinations at nil or nominal consideration which are in substance a gift; and

(b)   combinations which meet the definition and criteria of a **merger**.

PBE34.76   Combinations which are determined to be acquisitions shall be accounted for in accordance with Section 19 *Business Combinations and Goodwill*.

Combinations that are in substance a gift

Accounting treatment and disclosure

PBE34.77   A **combination that is in substance a gift** shall be accounted for in accordance with Section 19 except for the matters addressed in paragraphs PBE34.78 and PBE34.79 below.

PBE34.78   Any excess of the **fair value** of the **assets** received over the fair value of the **liabilities** assumed is recognised as a **gain** in **income and expenditure**. This gain represents the gift of the value of one entity to another and shall be recognised as income.

PBE34.79   Any excess of the fair value of the liabilities assumed over the fair value of the assets received is recognised as a loss in income and expenditure. This loss represents the net obligations assumed, for which the receiving entity has not received a financial reward and shall be recognised as an **expense**.

Combinations that are a merger

PBE34.80   Unless it is not permitted by the statutory framework under which a public benefit entity reports, an entity combination that is a merger shall apply merger accounting as prescribed below. If merger accounting is not permitted, an entity combination shall be accounted for as an acquisition in accordance with Section 19.

PBE34.81   Any entity combination:

(a)   which is neither a combination that is in substance a gift nor a merger; or

(b)   for which merger accounting is not permitted by the statutory framework under which the public benefit entity reports

shall be accounted for as an acquisition in accordance with Section 19.

Accounting treatment

Under merger accounting the carrying value of the assets and liabilities of the parties to the combination are not adjusted to fair value, although adjustments shall be made to achieve uniformity of **accounting policies** across the combining entities. **PBE34.82**

The results and **cash flows** of all the combining entities shall be brought into the **financial statements** of the newly formed entity from the beginning of the financial period in which the merger occurs. **PBE34.83**

The comparative amounts shall be restated by including the results for all the combining entities for the previous accounting period and their **statement of financial positions** for the previous **reporting date**. The comparative figures shall be marked as 'combined' figures. **PBE34.84**

All costs associated with the merger shall be charged as an expense in the period incurred. **PBE34.85**

Disclosure

For each entity combination accounted for as a merger in the **reporting period** the following shall be disclosed in the newly formed entity's financial statements: **PBE34.86**

(a)   the names and descriptions of the combining entities or businesses;
(b)   the date of the merger;
(c)   an analysis of the principal components of the current year's **total comprehensive income** to indicate:

    (i)   the amounts relating to the newly formed merged entity for the period after the date of the merger; and

    (ii)   the amounts relating to each party to the merger up to the date of the merger.

(d)   an analysis of the previous year's total comprehensive income between each party to the merger;
(e)   the aggregate carrying value of the net assets of each party to the merger at the date of the merger; and
(f)   the nature and amount of any significant adjustments required to align accounting policies and an explanation of any further adjustments made to net assets as a result of the merger.

Public Benefit Entity Concessionary Loans

Paragraphs PBE34.89 to PBE34.97 address the **recognition, measurement** and disclosure of **public benefit entity concessionary loan** arrangements within the **financial statements** of **public benefit entities** or entities within a **public benefit entity group** making or receiving public benefit entity concessionary loans. These paragraphs apply to public benefit entity concessionary loan arrangements only and are not applicable to loans which are at a market rate or to other commercial arrangements. **PBE34.87**

Public benefit entity concessionary loans are loans made or received between a public benefit entity or an entity within the public benefit entity group, and another party at below the **prevailing market rate** of interest that are not repayable on demand and are for the purposes of furthering the objectives of the public benefit entity or public benefit entity **parent**. **PBE34.88**

Accounting treatment

PBE34.89   Entities making or receiving public benefit entity concessionary loans shall use either:

(a)   the recognition, measurement and disclosure requirements in Section 11 *Basic Financial Instruments* or Section 12 *Other Financial Instruments Issues* (for example, Section 11 requires initial measurement at **fair value** and subsequent measurement at **amortised cost** using the **effective interest method**); or

(b)   the accounting treatment set out in paragraphs PBE34.90 to PBE34.97 below.

A public benefit entity or an entity within a public benefit entity group shall apply the same **accounting policy** to concessionary loans both made and received.

Initial measurement

PBE34.90   A public benefit entity or an entity within a public benefit entity group making or receiving concessionary loans shall initially measure these arrangements at the amount received or paid and recognise them in the **statement of financial position**.

Subsequent measurement

PBE34.91   In subsequent years, the **carrying amount** of concessionary loans in the financial statements shall be adjusted to reflect any accrued interest payable or receivable.

PBE34.92   To the extent that a loan that has been made is irrecoverable, an **impairment loss** shall be recognised in **income and expenditure**.

Presentation and disclosure

PBE34.93   The entity shall present concessionary loans made and concessionary loans received either as a separate line items on the face of the statement of financial position or in the **notes** to the financial statements.

PBE34.94   Concessionary loans shall be presented separately between amounts repayable or receivable within one year and amounts repayable or receivable after more than one year.

PBE34.95   The entity shall disclose in the summary of significant accounting policies the measurement basis used for concessionary loans and any other accounting policies which are relevant to the understanding of these transactions within the financial statements.

PBE34.96   The entity shall disclose the following:

(a)   the terms and conditions of concessionary loan arrangements, for example the interest rate, any security provided and the terms of the repayment; and

(b)   the value of concessionary loans which have been committed but not taken up at the year end.

PBE34.97   Concessionary loans made or received shall be disclosed separately. However multiple loans made or received may be disclosed in aggregate, providing that such aggregation does not obscure significant information.

Appendix A to Section 34

Guidance on funding commitments (paragraphs 34.57 to 34.63)

This guidance is an integral part of the Standard.

Entities often make commitments to provide cash or other resources to other entities. In such a case, it is necessary to determine whether the commitment should be recognised as a liability. The definition of a liability requires that there be a present obligation, and not merely an expectation of a future outflow.

34A.1

A general statement that the entity intends to provide resources to certain classes of potential beneficiaries in accordance with its objectives does not in itself give rise to a liability, as the entity may amend or withdraw its policy, and potential beneficiaries do not have the ability to insist on their fulfilment. Similarly, a promise to provide cash conditional on the receipt of future income in itself may not give rise to a liability where the entity cannot be required to fulfil it if the future income is not received and it is probable that the economic benefits will not be transferred.

34A.2

A liability is recognised only for a commitment that gives the recipient a valid expectation that payment will be made and from which the grantor cannot realistically withdraw. One of the implications of this is that a liability only exists where the commitment has been communicated to the recipient.

34A.3

Commitments are not recognised if they are subject to performance-related conditions. In such a case, the entity is required to fulfil its commitment only when the performance-related conditions are met and no liability exists until that time.

34A.4

A commitment may contain conditions that are not performance-related conditions. For example, a requirement to provide an annual financial report to the grantor may serve mainly as an administrative tool because failure to comply would not release the grantor from its commitment. This may be distinguished from a requirement to submit a detailed report for review and consideration by the grantor of how funds will be utilised in order to secure payment. A mere restriction on the specific purpose for which funds are to be used does not in itself constitute a performance-related condition.

34A.5

For funding commitments that are not recognised, it is important that full and informative disclosures are made of their existence and of the sources of funding for these unrecognised commitments.

34A.6

Appendix B to Section 34

Guidance on incoming resources from non-exchange transactions (paragraphs 34.64 to 34.74)

This guidance is an integral part of the Standard.

Recognition

The receipt of resources will usually result in an entity recognising an asset and corresponding income for the fair value of resources when those resources become received or receivable. Instances when this may differ include where:

PBE34B.1

(a)   an entity received those resources in the form of services (see paragraphs PBE34B.8 to PBE34B.12); or

(b)   there are performance-related conditions attached to the resources, which have yet to be fulfilled (see paragraphs PBE34B.13 to PBE34B.14).

PBE34B.2   Resources shall only be recognised when the fair value of the incoming resources can be measured reliably.

PBE34B.3   The concepts of materiality (see paragraph 2.6), and balance between benefit and cost (see paragraph 2.13) should be considered when deciding which resources received shall be recognised in the financial statements.

PBE34B.4   When it is impracticable to recognise resources from non-exchange transactions, the income is recognised in the period in which the resources are sold or distributed. The most common example is that of high volume, low value second-hand goods donated for resale.

Legacies

PBE34B.5   Donations in the form of legacies are recognised when it is probable that the legacy will be received and its value can be measured reliably. These criteria will normally be met following probate once the executor(s) of the estate has established that there are sufficient assets in the estate, after settling liabilities, to pay the legacy.

PBE34B.6   Evidence that the executor(s) has determined that a payment can be made, may arise on the agreement of the estate's accounts or notification that payment will be made. Where notification is received after the year-end but it is clear that the executor(s) has agreed prior to the year-end that the legacy can be paid, the legacy is accrued in the financial statements. The certainty and measurability of the receipt may be affected by subsequent events such as valuations and disputes.

PBE34B.7   Entities that are in receipt of numerous immaterial legacies for which individual identification would be burdensome may take a portfolio approach.

Services

PBE34B.8   Donated services that can be reasonably quantified shall be recognised in the financial statements when they are received.

PBE34B.9   Donated services that are consumed immediately are usually recognised as an expense. However, there may be circumstances when a service is used in the production of an asset, for example erecting a building. In these cases, the associated donated service (eg plumbing and electrical services) would be recognised as a part of the cost of that asset.

PBE34B.10   Donated services that can be reasonably quantified include donated facilities, such as office accommodation, services that would otherwise have been purchased and services usually provided by an individual or an entity as part of their trade or profession for a fee.

PBE34B.11   It is expected that contributions made by volunteers cannot be reasonably quantified and therefore these services shall not be recognised.

PBE34B.12   Paragraph PBE34.74(c) requires an entity to disclose other forms of resources from non-exchange transactions from which the entity has benefited. This will include the disclosure of unrecognised volunteer services.

Performance-related conditions

Some resources are given with performance-related conditions attached which require the recipient to use the resources to provide a specified level of service in order to be entitled to retain the resources. An entity will not recognise income from those resources until these performance-related conditions have been met.

PBE34B.13

However, some requirements are stated so broadly that they do not actually impose a performance-related condition on the recipient. In these cases the recipient will recognise income on receipt of the transfer of resources.

PBE34B.14

Measurement

Paragraph PBE34.73(a) requires donated services and facilities to be measured at the value to the entity. This requirement only applies to those services and facilities that would otherwise have been purchased by the entity. The value placed on these services and facilities should be the estimated value to the entity of the service or facility received, this will be the price the entity estimates it would pay in the open market for a service or facility of equivalent utility to the entity.

PBE34B.15

Paragraph PBE34.73(b) requires resources received or receivable, that are not services or facilities, to be measured at their fair value. These fair values are usually the price that the entity would have to pay on the open market for an equivalent resource.

PBE34B.16

When there is no direct evidence of an open market value for an equivalent item a value may be derived from sources such as:

PBE34B.17

(a)   the cost of the item to the donor; or

(b)   in the case of goods that are expected to be sold, the estimated resale value (which may reflect the amount actually realised) after deducting the cost to sell the goods.

Donated services are recognised as income and an equivalent amount shall be recognised as an expense in income and expenditure, unless the expense can be capitalised as part of the cost of an asset.

PBE34B.18

Section 35 *Transition to this FRS*

Scope of this section

This section applies to a **first-time adopter of this FRS**, regardless of whether its previous accounting framework was **EU-adopted IFRS** or another set of generally accepted accounting principles (GAAP) such as its national accounting standards, or another framework such as the local income tax basis.

35.1

Notwithstanding the requirements in paragraphs 35.3 and 35.4, an entity that has applied **FRS 102** in a previous **reporting period**, but whose most recent previous annual **financial statements** did not contain an explicit and unreserved statement of compliance with this FRS, must either apply this section or else apply FRS 102 retrospectively in accordance with Section 10 *Accounting Policies, Changes in Estimates and Errors* as if the entity had never stopped applying this FRS.

35.2

First-time adoption

A first-time adopter of this FRS shall apply this section in its first financial statements that conform to this FRS.

35.3

35.4 An entity's first financial statements that conform to this FRS are the first financial statements[14] in which the entity makes an explicit and unreserved statement in those financial statements of compliance with this FRS. Financial statements prepared in accordance with this FRS are an entity's first such financial statements if, for example, the entity:

(a) did not present financial statements for previous periods;

(b) presented its most recent previous financial statements under previous UK and Republic of Ireland requirements that are therefore not consistent with this FRS in all respects; or

(c) presented its most recent previous financial statements in conformity with EU-adopted IFRS.

35.5 Paragraph 3.17 defines a complete set of financial statements.

35.6 Paragraph 3.14 requires an entity to disclose, in a complete set of financial statements, comparative information in respect of the preceding period for all amounts presented in the financial statements, as well as specified comparative narrative and descriptive information. An entity may present comparative information in respect of more than one preceding period. Therefore, an entity's **date of transition** to this FRS is the beginning of the earliest period for which the entity presents full comparative information in accordance with this FRS in its first financial statements that comply with this FRS.

Procedures for preparing financial statements at the date of transition

35.7 Except as provided in paragraphs 35.9 to 35.11B, an entity shall, in its opening **statement of financial position** as of its date of transition to this FRS (ie the beginning of the earliest period presented):

(a) recognise all **assets** and **liabilities** whose **recognition** is required by this FRS;

(b) not recognise items as assets or liabilities if this FRS does not permit such recognition;

(c) reclassify items that it recognised under its previous financial reporting framework as one type of asset, liability or component of equity, but are a different type of asset, liability or component of equity under this FRS; and

(d) apply this FRS in measuring all recognised assets and liabilities.

This section does not require the opening statement of financial position to be presented.

35.8 The **accounting policies** that an entity uses in its opening statement of financial position under this FRS may differ from those that it used for the same date using its previous financial reporting framework. The resulting adjustments arise from transactions, other events or conditions before the date of transition to this FRS. Therefore, an entity shall recognise those adjustments directly in retained earnings (or, if appropriate, another category of equity) at the date of transition to this FRS.

35.9 On first-time adoption of this FRS, an entity shall not retrospectively change the accounting that it followed under its previous financial reporting framework for any of the following transactions:

(a) *Derecognition of financial assets and financial liabilities:*
Financial assets and liabilities derecognised under an entity's previous accounting framework before the date of transition shall not be recognised upon adoption of this FRS. Conversely, for financial assets and liabilities that would have been derecognised under this FRS in a transaction that took place before the date of

---

[14] *This excludes interim financial statements.*

transition, but that were not derecognised under an entity's previous accounting framework, an entity may choose:

    (i)   to derecognise them on adoption of this FRS; or

    (ii)   to continue to recognise them until disposed of or settled.

(b)   [Not used]

(c)   *Accounting estimates.*

(d)   **Discontinued operations***.*

(e)   *Measuring **non-controlling interests***:

    The requirements:

    (i)   to allocate **profit or loss** and **total comprehensive income** between non-controlling interest and **owners** of the **parent**;

    (ii)   for accounting for changes in the parent's ownership interest in a subsidiary that do not result in a loss of control; and

    (iii) for accounting for a loss of control over a subsidiary

    shall be applied prospectively from the date of transition to this FRS (or from such earlier date as this FRS is applied to restate **business combinations**— see paragraph 35.10(a)).

An entity may use one or more of the following exemptions in preparing its first financial statements that conform to this FRS: **35.10**

(a)   **Business combinations, including group reconstructions**

    A first-time adopter may elect not to apply Section 19 *Business Combinations and Goodwill* to business combinations that were effected before the date of transition to this FRS. However, if a first-time adopter restates any business combination to comply with Section 19, it shall restate all later business combinations. If a first-time adopter does not apply Section 19 retrospectively, the first-time adopter shall recognise and measure all its assets and liabilities acquired or assumed in a past business combination at the date of transition to this FRS in accordance with paragraphs 35.7 to 35.9 or if applicable, with paragraphs 35.10(b) to (r) except for:

    (i)   **intangible assets** other than **goodwill** – intangible assets subsumed within goodwill shall not be separately recognised; and

    (ii)   goodwill – no adjustment shall be made to the carrying value of goodwill.

(b)   **Share-based payment transactions**

    A first-time adopter is not required to apply Section 26 *Share-based Payment* to equity instruments (including the equity component of share-based payment transactions previously treated as compound instruments) that were granted before the date of transition to this FRS, or to liabilities arising from share-based payment transactions that were settled before the date of transition to this FRS. Except that a first-time adopter previously applying FRS 20 *(IFRS 2) Share-based Payment* or IFRS 2 *Share-based Payment* shall, in relation to equity instruments (including the equity component of share-based payment transactions previously treated as compound instruments) that were granted before the date of transition to this FRS, apply either FRS 20/IFRS 2 (as applicable) or Section 26 of this FRS at the date of transition.

    In addition, for a small entity that first adopts this FRS for an accounting period that commences before 1 January 2017, this exemption is extended to equity instruments that were granted before the start of the first reporting period that complies with this FRS, provided that the small entity did not previously apply FRS 20 or IFRS 2. A small entity that chooses to apply this exemption shall provide disclosures in accordance with paragraph 1AC.31.

(c)   *Fair value as deemed cost*

A first-time adopter may elect to measure an:

(i)   item of **property, plant and equipment**;

(ii)   **investment property**; or

(iii) intangible asset which meets the recognition criteria and the criteria for revaluation in Section 18 *Intangible Assets other than Goodwill*

on the date of transition to this FRS at its fair value and use that **fair value** as its **deemed cost** at that date.

(d)   *Revaluation as deemed cost*

A first-time adopter may elect to use a previous GAAP revaluation of an:

(i)   item of property, plant and equipment;

(ii)   investment property; or

(iii) intangible asset which meets the recognition criteria and the criteria for revaluation in Section 18

at, or before, the date of transition to this FRS as its deemed cost at the revaluation date.

(e)   [Not used]

(f)   *Individual and separate financial statements*

When an entity prepares individual or **separate financial statements**, paragraphs 9.26, 14.4 and 15.9 require the entity to account for its investments in **subsidiaries**, **associates**, and **jointly controlled entities** either at cost less impairment or at fair value.

If a first-time adopter measures such an investment at cost, it shall measure that investment at one of the following amounts in its individual or separate opening statement of financial position, as appropriate, prepared in accordance with this FRS:

(i)   cost determined in accordance with Section 9 *Consolidated and Separate Financial Statements*, Section 14 *Investments in Associates* or Section 15 *Investments in Joint Ventures*; or

(ii)   deemed cost, which shall be the **carrying amount** at the date of transition as determined under the entity's previous GAAP.

(g)   *Compound financial instruments*

Paragraph 22.13 requires an entity to split a **compound financial instrument** into its liability and equity components at the date of issue. A first-time adopter need not separate those two components if the liability component is not outstanding at the date of transition to this FRS.

(h)   [Not used]

(i)   *Service concession arrangements – Accounting by operators*

A first-time adopter is not required to apply paragraphs 34.12I to 34.16A to **service concession arrangements** that were entered into before the date of transition to this FRS. Such service concession arrangements shall continue to be accounted for using the same accounting policies being applied at the date of transition to this FRS.

(j)   *Extractive activities*

A first-time adopter that under a previous GAAP accounted for exploration and development costs for oil and gas properties in the development or production phases, in cost centres that included all properties in a large geographical area may elect to measure oil and gas assets at the date of transition to this FRS on the following basis:

(i)   Exploration and evaluation assets at the amount determined under the entity's previous GAAP.

(ii)   Assets in the development or production phases at the amount determined for the cost centre under the entity's previous GAAP. The entity shall allocate this amount to the cost centre's underlying assets pro rata using reserve volumes or reserve values as of that date.

The entity shall test exploration and evaluation assets and assets in the development and production phases for impairment at the date of transition to this FRS in accordance with Section 34 *Specialised Activities* or Section 27 *Impairment of Assets* of this FRS respectively, and if necessary, reduce the amount determined in accordance with (i) or (ii) above. For the purposes of this paragraph, oil and gas assets comprise only those assets used in the exploration, evaluation, development or production of oil and gas.

(k) *Arrangements containing a lease*
A first-time adopter may elect to determine whether an arrangement existing at the date of transition to this FRS contains a **lease** (see paragraph 20.3A) on the basis of facts and circumstances existing at that date, rather than when the arrangement was entered into.

(l) *Decommissioning liabilities included in the cost of property, plant and equipment*
Paragraph 17.10(c) states that the cost of an item of property, plant and equipment includes the initial estimate of the costs of dismantling and removing the item and restoring the site on which it is located, the obligation for which an entity incurs either when the item is acquired or as a consequence of having used the item during a particular period for purposes other than to produce **inventories** during that period. A first-time adopter may elect to measure this component of the cost of an item of property, plant and equipment at the date of transition to this FRS, rather than on the date(s) when the obligation initially arose.

(m) *Dormant companies*
A company within the Companies Act definition of a dormant company may elect to retain its accounting policies for reported assets, liabilities and equity at the date of transition to this FRS until there is any change to those balances or the company undertakes any new transactions.

(n) *Deferred development costs as a deemed cost*
A first-time adopter may elect to measure the carrying amount at the date of transition to this FRS for development costs deferred in accordance with SSAP 13 *Accounting for research and development* as its deemed cost at that date.

(o) *Borrowing costs*
An entity electing to adopt an accounting policy of capitalising **borrowing costs** as part of the cost of a **qualifying asset** may elect to treat the date of transition to this FRS as the date on which capitalisation commences.

(p) *Lease incentives*
A first-time adopter is not required to apply paragraphs 20.15A and 20.25A to **lease incentives** provided the term of the lease commenced before the date of transition to this FRS. The first-time adopter shall continue to recognise any residual benefit or cost associated with these lease incentives on the same basis as that applied at the date of transition to this FRS.

(q) *Public benefit entity combinations*
A first-time adopter may elect not to apply paragraphs PBE34.75 to PBE34.86 relating to **public benefit entity combinations** to combinations that were effected before the date of transition to this FRS. However, if on first-time adoption a **public benefit entity** restates any entity combination to comply with this section, it shall restate all later entity combinations.

(r) *Assets and liabilities of subsidiaries, associates and joint ventures*
If a subsidiary becomes a first-time adopter later than its parent, the subsidiary shall in its financial statements measure its assets and liabilities at either:

(i) the carrying amounts that would be included in the parent's **consolidated financial statements**, based on the parent's date of transition to this FRS, if no adjustments were made for consolidation procedures and for the effects of the business combination in which the parent acquired the subsidiary; or

(ii)   the carrying amounts required by the rest of this FRS, based on the subsidiary's date of transition to this FRS. These carrying amounts could differ from those described in (i) when:

(a)   the exemptions in this FRS result in measurements that depend on the date of transition to this FRS; or

(b)   the accounting policies used in the subsidiary's financial statements differ from those in the consolidated financial statements. For example, the subsidiary may use as its accounting policy the cost model in Section 17 *Property, Plant and Equipment*, whereas the **group** may use the revaluation model.

A similar election is available to an associate or **joint venture** that becomes a first-time adopter later than an entity that has **significant influence** or **joint control** over it.

However, if an entity becomes a first-time adopter later than its subsidiary (or associate or joint venture) the entity shall, in its consolidated financial statements, measure the assets and liabilities of the subsidiary (or associate or joint venture) at the same carrying amounts as in the financial statements of the subsidiary (or associate or joint venture), after adjusting for consolidation (and equity accounting) adjustments and for the effects of the business combination in which the entity acquired the subsidiary (or transaction in which it acquired the associate or joint venture). Similarly, if a parent becomes a first-time adopter for its separate financial statements earlier or later than for its consolidated financial statements, it shall measure its assets and liabilities at the same amounts in both financial statements, except for consolidation adjustments.

(s)   *Designation of previously recognised financial instruments*

This FRS permits a financial instrument (provided it meets certain criteria) to be designated on initial recognition as a financial asset or financial liability at fair value through profit or loss. Despite this an entity is permitted to designate, as at the date of transition to this FRS, any financial asset or financial liability at fair value through profit or loss provided the asset or liability meets the criteria in paragraph 11.14(b) at that date.

(t)   *Hedge accounting*

(i)   *A hedging relationship existing on the date of transition*

A first-time adopter may choose to apply hedge accounting to a hedging relationship of a type described in paragraph 12.19 which exists on the date of transition between a **hedging instrument** and a **hedged item**, provided the conditions of paragraphs 12.18(a) to (c) are met on the date of transition to this FRS and the conditions of paragraphs 12.18(d) and (e) are met no later than the date the first financial statements that comply with this FRS are authorised for issue. This choice applies to each hedging relationship existing on the date of transition.

Hedge accounting as set out in Section 12 *Other Financial Instruments Issues* of this FRS may commence from a date no earlier than the conditions of paragraphs 12.18(a) to (c) are met. In a fair value hedge the cumulative **hedging gain or loss** on the hedged item from the date hedge accounting commenced to the date of transition, shall be recorded in retained earnings (or if appropriate, another category of equity). In a cash flow hedge and net investment hedge, the lower of the following (in absolute amounts) shall be recorded in equity (in respect of cash flow hedges in the cash flow hedge reserve):

(a)   the cumulative gain or loss on the hedging instrument from the date hedge accounting commenced to the date of transition; and

(b)   the cumulative change in fair value (ie the present value of the cumulative change of expected future cash flows) on the hedged item from the date hedge accounting commenced to the date of transition.

(ii) ***A hedging relationship that ceased to exist before the date of transition because the hedging instrument has expired, was sold, terminated or exercised prior to the date of transition***

A first-time adopter may elect not to adjust the carrying amount of an asset or liability for previous GAAP accounting effects of a hedging relationship that has ceased to exist.

A first-time adopter may elect to account for amounts deferred in equity in a cash flow hedge under a previous GAAP, as described in paragraph 12.23(d) from the date of transition. Any amounts deferred in equity in relation to a hedge of a **net investment in a foreign operation** under a previous GAAP shall not be reclassified to profit or loss on disposal or partial disposal of the foreign operation.

(iii) ***A hedging relationship that commenced after the date of transition***

A first-time adopter may elect to apply hedge accounting to a hedging relationship of a type described in paragraph 12.19 that commenced after the date of transition between a hedging instrument and a hedged item, starting from the date the conditions of paragraphs 12.18(a) to (c) are met, provided that the conditions of paragraphs 12.18(d) and (e) are met no later than the date the first financial statements that comply with this FRS are authorised for issue.

The choice applies to each hedging relationship that commenced after the date of transition.

(iv) ***Entities taking the accounting policy choice under paragraphs 11.2(b) or (c) or paragraphs 12.2(b) or (c) to apply IAS 39 Financial Instruments: Recognition and Measurement or IFRS 9 Financial Instruments***

A first-time adopter adopting an accounting policy set out in paragraphs 11.2(b) or (c) or paragraphs 12.2(b) or (c) shall not apply the transitional provisions of paragraphs (i) to (iii) above. Such a first-time adopter shall apply the transitional requirements applicable to hedge accounting in IFRS 1 *First–time adoption of International Financial Reporting Standards*, paragraphs B4 to B6, except that the designation and documentation of a hedging relationship may be completed after the date of transition, and no later than the date the first financial statements that comply with this FRS are authorised for issue, if the hedging relationship is to qualify for hedge accounting from the date of transition.

A first-time adopter adopting an accounting policy set out in paragraphs 11.2(b) or (c) or paragraphs 12.2(b) or (c) that has entered into a hedging relationship as described in IAS 39 or IFRS 9 in the period between the date of transition and the **reporting date** for the first financial statements that comply with this FRS may elect to apply hedge accounting prospectively from the date all qualifying conditions for hedge accounting in IAS 39 or IFRS 9 are met, except that an entity shall complete the formal designation and documentation of a hedging relationship no later than the date the first financial statements that comply with this FRS are authorised for issue.

(u) ***Small entities – fair value measurement of financial instruments***

A small entity that first adopts this FRS for an accounting period that commences before 1 January 2017 need not restate comparative information to comply with the fair value measurement requirements of Section 11 *Basic Financial Instruments* or Section 12, unless those financial instruments were measured at fair value in accordance with the small entity's previous accounting framework.

A small entity that chooses to present comparative information that does not comply with the fair value measurement requirements of Sections 11 and 12 in its first year of adoption:

(a) shall apply its existing accounting policies to the relevant financial instruments in the comparative information and is encouraged to disclose this fact;

(b) shall disclose the accounting policies applied (in accordance with paragraph 1AC.3); and

(c) shall treat any adjustment between the statement of financial position at the comparative period's reporting date and the statement of financial position at the start of the first reporting period that complies with Sections 11 and 12 as an adjustment, in the current reporting period, to opening equity.

(v) **Small entities – financing transactions involving related parties**
A small entity that first adopts this FRS for an accounting period that commences before 1 January 2017 need not restate comparative information to comply with the requirements of paragraph 11.13 only insofar as they related to financing transactions involving **related parties**.

A small entity that chooses to present comparative information that does not comply with the financing transaction requirements of Section 11 in its first year of adoption:

(a) shall apply its existing accounting policies to the relevant financial instruments in the comparative information and is encouraged to disclose this fact;

(b) shall disclose the accounting policies applied (in accordance with paragraph 1AC.3); and

(c) shall treat any adjustment between the statement of financial position at the comparative period's reporting date and the statement of financial position at the start of the first reporting period that complies with paragraph 11.13 as an adjustment, in the current reporting period, to opening equity. The **present value** of the financial asset or financial liability at the start of the first reporting period that complies with this FRS may be determined on the basis of the facts and circumstances existing at that date, rather than when the arrangement was entered into.

35.11 If it is **impracticable** for an entity to restate the opening statement of financial position at the date of transition for one or more of the adjustments required by paragraph 35.7, the entity shall apply paragraphs 35.7 to 35.10 for such adjustments in the earliest period for which it is practicable to do so, and shall identify the data presented for prior periods that are not comparable with data for the period in which it prepares its first financial statements that conform to this FRS. If it is impracticable for an entity to provide any disclosures required by this FRS for any period before the period in which it prepares its first financial statements that conform to this FRS, the omission shall be disclosed.

35.11A Where applicable to the transactions, events or arrangements affected by applying these exemptions, an entity may continue to use the exemptions that are applied at the date of transition to this FRS when preparing subsequent financial statements, until such time when the assets and liabilities associated with those transactions, events or arrangements are derecognised.

35.11B Where there is subsequently a significant change in the circumstances or conditions associated with transactions, events or arrangements that existed at the date of transition, to which an exemption has been applied, an entity shall reassess the appropriateness of applying that exemption in preparing subsequent financial statements in order to maintain **fair presentation** in accordance with Section 3 *Financial Statement Presentation*.

Disclosures

Explanation of transition to this FRS

35.12 An entity shall explain how the transition from its previous financial reporting framework to this FRS affected its reported **financial position** and financial **performance**.

Reconciliations

To comply with paragraph 35.12, an entity's first financial statements prepared using this FRS shall include: **35.13**

(a)   A description of the nature of each change in accounting policy.

(b)   Reconciliations of its equity determined in accordance with its previous financial reporting framework to its equity determined in accordance with this FRS for both of the following dates:

    (i)   the date of transition to this FRS; and

    (ii)   the end of the latest period presented in the entity's most recent annual financial statements determined in accordance with its previous financial reporting framework.

(c)   A reconciliation of the profit or loss determined in accordance with its previous financial reporting framework for the latest period in the entity's most recent annual financial statements to its profit or loss determined in accordance with this FRS for the same period.

If an entity becomes aware of **errors** made under its previous financial reporting framework, the reconciliations required by paragraphs 35.13(b) and (c) shall, to the extent practicable, distinguish the correction of those errors from changes in accounting policies.   **35.14**

If an entity did not present financial statements for previous periods, it shall disclose that fact in its first financial statements that conform to this FRS.   **35.15**

Approval by the FRC

Financial Reporting Standard 102 *The Financial Reporting Standard applicable in the UK and Republic of Ireland* was approved for issue by the Financial Reporting Council on 5 March 2013, following its consideration of the Accounting Council's Advice for this FRS.

Amendments to FRS 102 The Financial Reporting Standard applicable in the UK and Republic of Ireland – Basic financial instruments and Hedge accounting was approved for issue by the Financial Reporting Council on 2 July 2014, following its consideration of the Accounting Council's Advice.

Amendments to FRS 102 The Financial Reporting Standard applicable in the UK and Republic of Ireland – Pension obligations was approved for issue by the Board of the Financial Reporting Council on 25 February 2015, following its consideration of the Accounting Council's Advice.

Amendments to FRS 102 The Financial Reporting Standard applicable in the UK and Republic of Ireland – Small entities and other minor amendments was approved for issue by the Board of the Financial Reporting Council on 1 July 2015, following its consideration of the Accounting Council's Advice.

The Accounting Council's Advice to the FRC to issue FRS 102

Introduction

This report provides an overview of the main issues that have been considered by the Accounting Council in advising the Financial Reporting Council (FRC) to issue FRS 102 *The Financial Reporting Standard applicable in the UK and Republic of Ireland*. The FRC, in accordance with the Statutory Auditors (Amendment of Companies Act 2006 and Delegation of Functions etc) Order 2012 (SI 2012/1741), is the prescribed body for issuing accounting standards in the UK. The Foreword to Accounting Standards sets out the application of accounting standards in the Republic of Ireland. **1**

In accordance with the *FRC Codes and Standards: procedures*, any proposal to issue, amend or withdraw a code or standard is put to the FRC Board with the full advice of the relevant Councils and/or the Codes & Standards Committee. Ordinarily, the FRC Board will only reject the advice put to it where: **2**

- it is apparent that a significant group of stakeholders has not been adequately consulted;
- the necessary assessment of the impact of the proposal has not been completed, including an analysis of costs and benefits;
- insufficient consideration has been given to the timing or cost of implementation; or
- the cumulative impact of a number of proposals would make the adoption of an otherwise satisfactory proposal inappropriate.

The FRC has established the Accounting Council as the relevant Council to assist it in the setting of accounting standards. **3**

Advice

All but one member of the Accounting Council is advising the FRC to issue FRS 102 *The Financial Reporting Standard Applicable in the UK and Republic of Ireland*. **4**

One member of the Accounting Council, Edward Beale, does not agree with some aspects of the Accounting Council's advice and his dissenting view is set out in the appendix to the Accounting Council's Advice. **5**

FRS 100 *Application of Financial Reporting Requirements* and FRS 101 *Reduced Disclosure Framework* which are also part of this suite of financial reporting standards were issued by the FRC in November 2012. The Accounting Council's advice to the FRC on those standards is contained in those standards. **6**

Background

Accounting standards were formerly developed by the Accounting Standards Board (ASB). The ASB commenced its project to update accounting standards in 2002; Appendix V provides a history of the previous consultations and a summary of how the overall proposals have developed.[15] **7**

FRS 102 was developed from the IASB's IFRS for SMEs to replace the majority of UK accounting standards in a single volume. **8**

---

[15] *References in this section and Appendix V are made to the FRC, ASB or Accounting Council, as appropriate in terms of the time period and context of the reference.*

Objective

9   During its consultations on updating accounting standards, the ASB (and subsequently the FRC) gave careful consideration to its objective and the intended effects. In developing the requirements in this FRS, FRS 100 and FRS 101, the overriding objective is:

> To enable users of accounts to receive high-quality understandable financial reporting proportionate to the size and complexity of the entity and users' information needs.

10   In achieving this objective, the Accounting Council decided (and the FRC subsequently adopted this decision) that it should provide succinct financial reporting standards that:

- have consistency with global accounting standards through the application of an IFRS-based solution unless an alternative clearly better meets the overriding objective;
- reflect up-to-date thinking and developments in the way businesses operate and the transactions they undertake;
- balance consistent principles for accounting by all UK and Republic of Ireland entities with practical solutions, based on size, complexity, public interest and users' information needs;
- promote efficiency within groups; and
- are cost-effective to apply.

11   The requirements in this FRS were principally consulted on in four exposure drafts:

- FRED 44 *Financial Reporting Standard for Medium-sized Entitles* issued in October 2010;
- FRED 45 *Financial Reporting Standard for Public Benefit Entities* issued in March 2011;
- FRED 48 *Financial Reporting Standard applicable in the UK and Republic of Ireland* issued in January 2012; and
- Amendment to FRED 48 issued in October 2012.

Consultation with stakeholders

12   The Accounting Council has obtained feedback from stakeholders throughout the project in a variety of ways. Appendix V sets out a history of the consultation on this project. In addition to formal consultation through exposure drafts, and previous consultation papers, feedback has been obtained through an extensive programme of outreach aimed at raising awareness of the proposals and to address the view (held by some) that earlier consultations had not gathered sufficient evidence to support and test its assumptions.

13   The Accounting Council recognised that sometimes stakeholders who will be affected by the outcome of a proposal can be difficult to engage in formal, written consultation. As a result, and in accordance with the principles of Better Regulation it developed an outreach programme that would reach beyond those stakeholders that typically respond to Exposure Drafts.

14   As part of the outreach programme a series of meetings and events took place with lenders to small and medium-sized entities. Lenders noted that financial statements are an important part of their decision-making process when considering providing finance and whilst a decision to provide finance is not based on financial statements alone, they provide useful information and verification to the lender.

15   In addition, a review was made of academic research that addressed the users of small and medium-sized entities' financial statements. The conclusion drawn from the research

was that many entities requested financial statements from Companies House when considering whether to trade with another entity. The European Federation of Accountants and Auditors (EFAA) issued in May 2011 a statement that identified the users of financial statements noting who the users of SMEs financial statements are and that information on the public record assists all users of financial statements of SMEs by providing, in an efficient manner, basic information that protects their rights.

The Accounting Council considers that the outreach programme, across the project as a whole, has gleaned information from stakeholders who would not normally submit formal responses to a consultation and provided very useful information. The Accounting Council noted that whilst this information was not part of the public record, as formal consultation responses are, it could use the information to assist in finalising the standards, which supplemented the information contained in formal responses. **16**

Consultation with stakeholders carried out by others

In addition to the consultation and outreach work carried out by the Accounting Council itself, the Accounting Council notes that some respondents, notably the accountancy institutes, conducted their own outreach amongst their members in determining their responses to the exposure drafts. **17**

Classification of respondents

When analysing responses to consultations it has been the Accounting Council's practice to classify respondents into a number of standard categories in order to determine whether similar views are consistently held by a particular category of respondents. This classification is set out in the Feedback Statement that accompanies this FRS. **18**

The classification of respondents only allows respondents to be classified to a single category and is based on the main perspective articulated in the response. However, the Accounting Council notes that many people that are interested in financial reporting and respond to consultations have a number of different perspectives, for example those that prepare financial statements often also use the financial statements of customers, suppliers and competitors in making decisions about running their business. **19**

Therefore, there is an inherent limitation in the classification of respondents, which tends to underestimate the number of users of financial statements that have responded. **20**

Using the IFRS for SMEs as a basis

Set out in Appendix V is a history of previous consultations. The ASB first started to consider the future of UK and Republic of Ireland accounting standards following the EU decision to require consolidated accounts of listed companies to comply with IFRS. The long held view is that there can be no justification for two different sets of accounting standards in the UK. Consequently, throughout the various consultations it has been proposed that the new accounting standards should have consistency with global accounting standards; this has continually been supported by the majority of respondents. Therefore the Accounting Council has proceeded with the project on this basis. The Impact Assessment accompanying this standard sets out alternative strategic options that the Accounting Council considered in framing the project (including UK accounting standards not based on IFRS), but taking into account consultation responses these were rejected. Therefore the Accounting Council developed the standard within the strategic context of an IFRS-based solution. **21**

22   The Accounting Council noted that the IFRS for SMEs:

- is a way of achieving a consistent accounting framework, as it is a simplification of IFRS;
- was developed by the IASB and published in 2009, reflecting more up-to-date thinking and developments than current FRS, especially for financial instruments;
- is a single book setting out clear accounting requirements; and
- is a cost effective way of updating current FRS.

23   The Accounting Council noted that one of the most significant changes being introduced in this standard is the changes to the recognition, measurement and disclosures related to financial instruments. Current FRSs contain limited requirements on accounting for financial instruments for unlisted entities or those that do not apply the fair value accounting rules. Entities use derivatives to manage risk and it is important that financial statements recognise and provide disclosures about the effect of those instruments on the entity's performance and position. The Accounting Council believes that the approach under current FRSs, where derivatives are not recognised, does not adequately reflect the risks arising from financial instruments. FRS 102 will lead to an improvement in accounting for financial instruments.

24   The Accounting Council adopted guidelines for developing this standard from the IFRS for SMEs, and noted that some pragmatism was required in determining when it would be appropriate to diverge from the IFRS for SMEs. The objective is high-quality understandable financial reporting, and the standard needs to work within the legal framework in the UK and Republic of Ireland, including enabling the provisions of company law to be adhered to. The guidelines also balance high-quality understandable financial reporting and cost effective application. The high degree of support from respondents for the strategic thrust of the approach to developing the new standards suggested that respondents were prepared to balance high-quality financial reporting and costs/benefits. The Accounting Council therefore concluded that its objective and guidelines for making changes to the IFRS for SMEs should be:

In amending the IFRS for SMEs for application in the UK and Republic of Ireland (RoI) the FRC maintains its commitment to:

(a)   ensuring high-quality financial reporting by UK and RoI entities applying FRS 102;

(b)   operate under an international accounting framework; and

(c)   acknowledge that users' preference for consistent financial reporting must be balanced with costs to preparers.

The guidelines when considering amendments to the IFRS for SMEs are:

(a)   changes should be made to permit accounting treatments that exist in FRSs at the transition date that align with EU-adopted IFRS;

(b)   changes should be consistent with EU-adopted IFRS unless a non-IFRS-based solution clearly better meets the objective of providing high-quality understandable financial reporting proportionate to the size and complexity of the entity and the users' information needs. In these cases elements of an IFRS-based solution may nevertheless be retained;

(c)   use should be made, where possible, of existing exemptions in company law to avoid gold-plating; and

(d)   changes should be made to provide clarification, by reference to EU-adopted IFRS, that will avoid unnecessary diversity in practice.

The Accounting Council noted that by providing clarifications within FRS 102 when   25
compared with the IFRS for SMEs it could avoid unnecessary diversity in practice.
Similarly, whilst maintaining its commitment to high-quality financial reporting and a
global framework, the Accounting Council determined that it should amend the IFRS for
SMEs by reference to EU-adopted IFRS.

Amendments made to the IFRS for SMEs in developing FRS 102

In developing FRS 102 from the IFRS for SMEs, the Accounting Council advises that   26
a number of amendments should be made to the IFRS for SMEs. The following table
identifies the more significant amendments and which of the guidelines were applied
in making those amendments. Where an amendment is marked ✓✓ it indicates that the
amendment is as a consequence of the decision that the scope of FRS 102 is different from
that of the IFRS for SMEs.

Amendment	Guideline				Law
	a)	b)	c)	d)	
Scope					
Elimination of public accountability		✓			
Cross-references to IFRS 8 and IAS 33 for listed entities.			✓✓		
Definition of a financial institution			✓		
Inclusion of public benefit entities		✓			
Presentation					
True and fair override					✓
Statement of financial position					✓
Statement of comprehensive income, including discontinued operations					✓
Statement of changes in equity	✓				
Consolidated financial statements					
Consistency with the Act					✓
ESOPs		✓			
Subsidiaries held exclusively for resale, including in an investment portfolio	✓				
Changes in stake and gains or losses on disposals	✓			✓	✓
Exchanges of businesses for interests in another business (was UITF Abstract 31)			✓		
Accounting policies					
Clarification of when to refer to a SORP in developing accounting policies		✓			
Financial instruments					
Disclosures required by financial institutions (might be considered an expansion of paragraph 11.42 for those entities)				✓✓	
Treatment of loan covenants for determining whether an instrument is basic	✓				

Amendment	Guideline	Law
Disclosures for certain financial instruments required by law		✓
Hedge accounting is permitted for a net investment in a foreign operation and in respect of foreign exchange risks in a debt instrument measured at amortised cost	✓ ✓	
Borrowing costs may be capitalised in certain circumstances	✓	
Public benefit entities can account for concessionary loans at transaction amount	✓✓	
Fair value option	✓	
Option to apply IAS 39 or IFRS 9 recognition and measurement requirements	✓	
Financial guarantee contracts scoped out of financial instrument accounting	✓	
Property, plant and equipment		
Revaluation	✓	
Intangible assets		
Capitalisation of development costs	✓	
Revaluation after initial recognition	✓	
Where unable to make a reliable estimate of useful life, it should not exceed 5 years.		✓
Business combinations and goodwill		
Permit merger accounting for group reconstructions	✓	
Permit merger accounting by public benefit entities	✓✓	
Where unable to make a reliable estimate of useful life of goodwill, it should not exceed 5 years.		✓
Leases		
Clarification of definitions		✓
Clarification of scope for 'arrangements that contain a lease'		✓
Liabilities and equity		
Clarification of whether an instrument is a financial liability or equity in certain circumstances		✓
Only disclosure required for non-cash distributions to owners	✓	
Grants		
Introduction of accrual method as an option for accounting for government grants	✓	
Share-based payment		
Clarification that option pricing models are not required particularly for unquoted shares		✓

Amendment	Guideline				Law
Share-based payments granted by another group entity					✓
Employee benefits					
Presentation of the cost of a defined benefit pension is consistent with IAS 19's 2011 amendments.	✓				
Recognition of liability by entities in multi-employer schemes with a schedule of funding for a deficit					✓
Income tax					
Timing differences plus approach	✓				
Revised disclosure requirements	✓				
Guidance on accounting for VAT				✓	
Related party disclosures					
Disclosure exemption for wholly-owned entities			✓		
Specialised activities					
Agriculture – permit historical cost model for biological assets.	✓				
Extractive industries – refer to IFRS 6	✓				
Service concession arrangements – grantors				✓ ✓	
Service concession arrangements – operators				✓	
Retirement benefit plans	✓				
Heritage assets	✓				
Funding commitments			✓ ✓		
PBE – incoming resources from non-exchange transactions (including performance-related conditions and restrictions)	✓ ✓				

Scope of FRS 102

In an earlier consultation the Accounting Council proposed a differential financial reporting system based on three tiers of entities using public accountability as a differentiator, which would have required some entities to apply EU-adopted IFRS that would not otherwise have been required to do so. Several concerns were noted about this; the more significant include: **27**

(a) the costs for those entities that would be required to apply EU-adopted IFRS could not be justified in relation to the benefit to users of those entities financial statements;

(b) inconsistencies in the recognition and measurement requirements between EU-adopted IFRS and the proposals at the time for FRS 102 would reduce comparability between entities; and

(c) the application guidance addressing the definition of public accountability remained unclear despite the guidance being developed further from the Policy Proposal.

The Accounting Council wanted to address the concerns from respondents that the costs for those entities that would be required to apply EU-adopted IFRS could not be justified in relation to the benefit to users of those entities' financial statements. As a result it proposed eliminating public accountability as a differentiator and determined that FRS 102 **28** should be applied by entities that were not required to apply EU-adopted IFRS, nor were eligible and chose to apply the FRSSE. Respondents agreed with this approach.

29   As a consequence various entities that are outside the scope of the IFRS for SMEs are within the scope of FRS 102, typically these are financial institutions.

30   The Accounting Council noted that a significant number of public benefit entities apply UK accounting standards, and would be within the scope of FRS 102.

Consequences of the scope of FRS 102

31   As the scope of FRS 102 is wider than the scope of the IFRS for SMEs, there are areas not addressed in the IFRS for SMEs that might be relevant to the broader group of entities applying FRS 102.

32   In considering these areas the Accounting Council reflected on users' needs for additional information relevant to entities that are listed but not on a regulated market, ie those entities that were in part (a) of the definition of public accountability but were not required by EU Regulation to apply EU-adopted IFRS. This identified that earnings per share, operating segments and accounting for insurance contracts were not addressed in the IFRS for SMEs and accounting requirements would need to be set in these areas.

33   The Accounting Council, however, noted that in addressing the needs of this broader group of entities it should not lose sight of its objective to provide succinct financial reporting standards. Consequently, consideration was given to whether entities listed on a non-regulated market could apply EU-adopted IFRS for the areas identified by including cross references to EU-adopted IFRS in FRS 102 rather than setting out the requirements in the FRS itself.

34   The Accounting Council broadly termed as financial institutions those entities that, in accordance with FRED 43 were within the scope of part (b) of the definition of public accountability, (ie entities that hold assets in a fiduciary capacity or take deposits, including credit unions, building societies and investment entities). In considering the users' needs for financial information on financial institutions the Accounting Council noted that FRS 102 set out improvements, from current FRS, for the recognition and measurement of financial instruments, however, it had limited specific disclosure requirements for financial instruments. The Accounting Council decided that if it were to eliminate the definition of public accountability it would need to address the disclosure requirements for financial institutions, noting that financial instruments are central to the business model of these entities and how such entities generate wealth and manage risk.

35   Having identified that it would need to improve the disclosure requirements for financial institutions if it were to remove the definition of public accountability, the Accounting Council sought to find a clear definition of a financial institution. Various options were considered including whether to retain part (b) of the definition of publicly accountable, however this approach was rejected because it did not address the application difficulties raised by respondents to FRED 43.

36   The second option considered was to use the definition in section 467(1) of the Companies Act 2006; one advantage was that this was in part basing the definition on whether the entity was regulated or not.

37   The third option was simply to list the types of entity which should provide additional disclosures for financial instruments. In this regard the Accounting Council gave consideration to its previous accounting standard FRS 13 *Derivatives and Financial*

Instrument: Disclosures, which applied a differential disclosure regime depending on the category of entity. On balance the Accounting Council decided that a list of entities provided the clearest approach to determine which entities should be defined as financial institutions. However, the Accounting Council also agreed with some respondents to FRED 48 that a principle behind entities selected for inclusion on the list should be articulated. As a result the Accounting Council added a final item to the list, intended to capture any entities similar to those listed above, which would also add an element of future-proofing to the definition. The Accounting Council advises that a parent entity whose sole activity is to hold investments in other group entities is not a financial institution, but notes that a subsidiary entity engaged solely in treasury activities for the group as a whole is likely to meet the definition of a financial institution.

Having undertaken the analysis above, it was concluded that public accountability could   **38** be eliminated and FRS 102 could apply to a broader group of entities than the IFRS for SMEs. To address the users' information needs for entities listed on a non-regulated market, FRS 102 includes cross-referencing to EU-adopted IFRS and additional disclosure requirements have been inserted for financial instruments held by financial institutions.

The Accounting Council observed that if it were to require a financial institution applying   **39** FRS 102 to disclose additional information regarding its financial instruments, it also needed to consider its proposals for reduced disclosures. It decided that financial institutions applying reduced disclosures would not be permitted exemptions from the additional disclosures for financial institutions.

The Accounting Council considered whether broadening the scope of FRS 102 would   **40** increase the pressure to update the standard (in line with changes being made to full IFRS) more frequently than on a three-year cycle. The Accounting Council agreed that there may be circumstances where FRS 102 would require updating in an interim period between the three-year cycles, but where this occurred the amendments proposed should be limited.

Presentation

The Accounting Council considered feedback to FRED 44 and to the draft case studies   **41** prepared by its staff that were posted on its website that addressed the interaction between FRED 44 and the presentation formats required by company law. The Accounting Council noted that there were specific conflicts between the IFRS for SMEs and the formats, specifically the definition of current assets differed between the two sets of requirements.

The Accounting Council considered whether to replicate the requirements set out in   **42** company law for the information to be presented in the statement of financial position and the income statement, but was concerned that this would add clutter to FRS 102 which was not consistent with its objectives. However, it needed to work within company law and whilst it had encouraged changes to simplify the Accounting Directives it was unlikely such change would take place in the near future. The Accounting Council decided that it should promote only formats already determined in company law. This would have the consequence of all entities being required to comply with the company law formats, promoting consistency amongst all those preparing financial statements intended to give a true and fair view.

In amending the IFRS for SMEs to include the Companies Act formats, it was noted that   **43** the ASB had had a long-standing policy that company law formats on their own were not sufficient and should be supplemented to highlight a range of important components of financial performance to aid users' understanding of the performance of the entity. Therefore some requirements from FRS 3 *Reporting Financial Performance*, notably covering acquisitions, exceptional items and discontinued operations need to be factored in. The IFRS for SMEs was amended so that FRS 102 includes:

(a)   the disclosure of post-acquisition revenue and profit or loss of an acquiree in a business combination in the notes to the financial statements;

(b)   no mandatory requirement to disclose an operating profit line but guidance, based on IAS 1 *Presentation of Financial Statements*, on matters to consider where entities choose to present operating profit; and

(c)   the inclusion of an explicit requirement to disclose material items.

44   The existing FRS 3 requirement to show separately on the face of the profit and loss account: profits or losses on sale or termination of an operation; costs of a fundamental reorganisation materially affecting the operation and profits; and losses on disposal of fixed assets (all of which would still have to be disclosed where material) has not been included.

45   The Accounting Council advises that, in view of the company law requirement that turnover includes the turnover from discontinued operations, a practical way of presenting this and the post-tax profit or loss on discontinued operations would be for the information about discontinued operations to be presented via a columnar approach. An example illustrating this is set out in FRS 102.

Consolidated financial statements

Definitions of control, parent and subsidiary

46   The Accounting Council notes that the definitions of control, parent and subsidiary included in FRS 102 are consistent with the IFRS for SMEs (and based on EU adopted IFRS prior to the issuing of IFRS 10 *Consolidated Financial Statements*), but differ from those used in current FRS. Some respondents queried whether the definitions should be based on company law. The Accounting Council rejected this suggestion, but noted that by using the IFRS for SMEs definitions (consistently with its objective and guidelines), it was widening the application of control to include certain special purpose entities within the definition of a group. However, as noted below, the Accounting Council advises that this should not include employee benefit trusts and ESOPs (which should continue to be accounted for as if they are assets and liabilities of the sponsoring entity).

Employee benefit trusts, ESOPs and similar arrangements

47   In clarifying the requirements for consolidation, including considering consistency with company law requirements, the Accounting Council noted that the accounting treatment for employee benefit trusts, ESOPs or similar arrangements would give rise to a change in accounting from current FRS. The removal of UITF Abstract 38 *Accounting for ESOP trusts* would mean that such arrangements would no longer be included in individual financial statements but only in consolidated financial statements. Further, for an entity with such an arrangement, which is not a parent entity, a change in accounting requirements would lead to the preparation of 'group' financial statements where they would otherwise not have been required. Therefore the Accounting Council decided to retain the accounting treatment from UITF Abstract 32 *Employee benefit trusts and other intermediate payment arrangements* which are included in Section 9 *Consolidated and Separate Financial Statements* of FRS 102.

Investment entities exemption from consolidation

In September 2011 the IASB issued an exposure draft proposing to exempt qualifying investment entities from consolidating their investments. The accounting requirements were finalised and published as an amendment to IFRS 10 *Consolidated Financial Statements*, IFRS 12 *Disclosure of Interests in Other Entities* and IAS 27 *Separate Financial Statements* in October 2012. The Accounting Council noted that without a similar exemption in FRS 102, investment entities eligible to apply FRS 102, would need to elect to prepare EU-adopted IFRS in order to take advantage of the exemption. The Accounting Council did not consider this to be a logical or meaningful outcome and therefore sought to find a solution.   **48**

Section 405(3) of the Companies Act sets out the circumstances in which a subsidiary may be excluded from consolidation and the Accounting Council must work within these requirements. Section 405(3) permits a subsidiary to be excluded from consolidation on the following grounds: **49**

(a)   severe long-term restrictions substantially hinder the exercise of the rights of the parent company over the assets or management of that subsidiary;

(b)   the information necessary for the preparation of group accounts cannot be obtained without disproportion expense or undue delay; or

(c)   the interest of the parent company is held exclusively with a view to subsequent resale.

Taking into account the IASB's publication of *Investment Entities* (Amendments to IFRS 10, IFRS 12 and IAS 27) in October 2012, the Accounting Council advises that the definition of an interest held exclusively with a view to subsequent resale should include interests held as part of an investment portfolio.   **50**

FRS 102 permits that subsidiaries excluded from consolidation may be measured at fair value through profit or loss. This is a departure from the requirements of the Companies Act for the overriding purpose of giving a true and fair view in the consolidated financial statements.   **51**

Changes in stake and gains or losses on disposals

The Accounting Council noted that the requirements of the IFRS for SMEs in relation to changes in stake and gains and losses on disposals were not entirely coherent being based partly on IFRS 3 *Business combinations* (issued 2004) and partly on IFRS 3 *Business combinations* (revised 2008), and further some of the requirements are not consistent with company law provisions on the recognition of unrealised gains.   **52**

The Accounting Council considered that a coherent model for increases and decreases in stakes held in another entity was required, and that it must be consistent with company law. As a result the requirements of Section 9 *Consolidated and Separate Financial Statements* and Section 19 *Business Combinations and Goodwill* are now based on IFRS 3 (issued 2004), providing an IFRS-based solution that is consistent with company law.   **53**

Distribution of non-cash assets to owners

The Accounting Council had also been asked to clarify that the distribution of non-cash assets to owners did not apply to distributions within groups. In considering this requirement, the Accounting Council noted a distinction between the disposal of an asset at fair value followed by a distribution to shareholders of the profit, and making a distribution of the asset to shareholders. In its view, a distribution to shareholders does not   **54** generate a profit, whereas a disposal does generate a profit that may then be distributed to shareholders. The Accounting Council decided, given it did not support the accounting requirement, to remove the requirement in the IFRS for SMEs to recognise a liability to pay a dividend for a non-cash asset at fair value and to require disclosure of the fair value of the assets distributed to shareholders.

Financial instruments

55   In FREDs 43 and 44 the ASB noted that current FRSs were in need of updating and that they permitted certain transactions not to be recorded. Sections 11 *Basic Financial Instruments* and 12 *Other Financial Instruments Issues* of FRED 44 proposed to address these weaknesses in current FRS. The Accounting Council noted that the IFRS for SMEs has simplified the accounting for financial instruments when compared with IAS 39 *Financial Instruments: Recognition and Measurement*, whilst generally achieving similar accounting. However, there will be areas where those familiar with IAS 39 will need to take care to ensure compliance with FRS 102, for example the hierarchy to be used in determining the fair value of an asset set out in paragraph 11.27 is not the same as the 'fair value hierarchy' set out in IAS 39.

56   The Accounting Council carefully considered the views of respondents to FRED 44 concerning the proposed accounting for financial instruments set out in the FRED.

57   The Accounting Council noted the concern, primarily from the social housing sector, that recognition of derivatives used for hedging purposes at fair value may result in volatility in profit or loss. It considered carefully the requirement to recognise derivatives at fair value but noted that any changes to the financial instrument proposals should be consistent with the guidelines for amending the IFRS for SMEs. The Accounting Council concluded that it would not be consistent with the objective of providing high-quality information, or the guidelines for amending the IFRS for SMEs, to change the recognition requirements for derivatives. Recognition of derivatives, and associated disclosure, will provide relevant information to users about the risks an entity has in relation to its financial instruments.

Impact of the IASB hedge accounting and impairment projects

58   The requirements for hedge accounting and impairment of financial assets in FRS 102 are based on the requirements of IAS 39. The IASB is currently reviewing hedge accounting and impairment requirements (including developing an 'expected loss' model for the recognition of impairments of financial assets) and the Accounting Council is reluctant to propose new accounting requirements in respect of these areas before the IASB's projects are finalised in IFRS 9 *Financial Instruments*. The Accounting Council is concerned that doing so would risk financial instruments requirements in FRS 102 being out of line with both IFRS 9 and IAS 39. Simultaneously, the Accounting Council believes that the next scheduled amendment date for FRS 102 is too far in the future and consequential amendments to FRS 102 may therefore be untimely for entities that would like to apply the new IFRS 9 accounting requirements without undue delay. For that reason the Accounting Council agreed that a proposed amendment to FRS 102 would be issued for public consultation once the IASB has completed the hedge accounting and impairment projects and IFRS 9 has been updated; it is likely that there will be two separate exposure drafts, one addressing each topic. The Accounting Council intends to make amendments to FRS 102 (should the consultation determine this is appropriate) prior its effective date, although the exact timetable of any possible amendment is dependent upon when the IASB completes the impairment and hedge accounting requirements in IFRS 9.

Financial instruments accounting policy choices

In order to allow entities applying FRS 102 maximum flexibility, entities have a choice of either: **59**

(a)   applying the requirements of Sections 11 and 12 of FRS 102;

(b)   applying the recognition and measurement requirements in IAS 39 (as adopted for use in the EU) as the standard applies prior to the application of IFRS 9; or

(c)   applying IFRS 9 (as far as it has replaced the requirements in IAS 39) and IAS 39 (as far it remains applicable if IFRS 9 is applied).

By providing these accounting policy choices entities have the flexibility to apply the accounting requirements of IFRS 9 without delay should they wish to do so[16]. Entities that elect to account for financial instruments by applying the requirements of Sections 11 and 12, especially those entities that choose to apply FRS 102 before its effective date, may be required to change their accounting for financial instruments should some of the requirements in Sections 11 and 12 be amended for consistency with the principles of IFRS 9 in respect of hedge and impairment accounting, once those have been determined.

Disclosures by financial institutions

Having defined financial institutions, the Accounting Council advises that additional disclosures should be provided for the financial instruments held by these entities. It developed a proportionate set of disclosures for financial institutions, using IFRS 7 *Financial Instruments: Disclosures* as the basis. **60**

Fair value option

A number of respondents to FRED 48 noted that bonds within the scope of Section 11 must be measured at amortised cost, even if they are managed on a fair value basis or their measurement at amortised cost introduces measurement differences, and suggested that an option to measure such items at fair value should be permitted in FRS 102. The Accounting Council agreed that, consistently with EU-adopted IFRS, an option should be available to designate financial assets and liabilities to be measured at fair value through profit or loss. **61**

Hedge accounting

In light of the comments received in response to FREDs 44 and 48, and in order to reduce inconsistencies with EU-adopted IFRS, the Accounting Council advises that hedge accounting of a net investment in a foreign operation in consolidated financial statements be permitted and that entities are permitted to hedge foreign exchange risk arising in a debt instrument measured at amortised cost. Consistently with EU-adopted IFRS the Accounting Council also advises that hedge accounting of a net investment in a foreign operation should not be permitted in the separate financial statements of a parent. **62**

Financial guarantee contracts

Respondents to FRED 48 asked for clarification of the accounting requirements for financial guarantee contracts. The accounting for financial guarantee contracts is within the scope of Section 21 *Provisions and Contingencies* unless an entity has chosen to apply IAS 39 and/or IFRS 9, or has an existing accounting policy of insurance contract **63**

---

[16] *As FRS 102 is a UK and Republic of Ireland accounting standard, IFRS 9 can be applied through FRS 102 in advance of EU endorsement.*

accounting for financial guarantee contracts and chooses to continue to apply that policy under FRS 103 *Insurance Contracts*.

Group reconstructions

64   The Accounting Council advises that FRS 102 should retain the current accounting permitted by FRS 6 *Acquisitions and mergers* for group reconstructions. The Accounting Council noted that whilst EU-adopted IFRS does not provide accounting requirements for the accounting for business combinations under common control the accounting provided by FRS 6 is well understood and provides useful requirements. It therefore decided to carry forward these requirements into FRS 102. In practice, the Accounting Council does not expect the introduction of FRS 102 to change the accounting for group reconstructions. For example, where a combination is effected by using a newly formed parent company to hold the shares of each of the parties to a combination, the accounting treatment depends on the substance of the business combination being effected.

Leases

65   Leases are accounted for in accordance with the requirements of Section 20 *Leases*, except for those leases falling within the scope of Section 12, which are those that could result in a loss to the lessor or the lessee as a result of non-typical contractual terms, for example those that are unrelated to:

(a)   changes in the price of the leased asset;

(b)   changes in foreign exchange rates; or

(c)   a default by one of the counterparties.

66   The Accounting Council notes that the reference to 'changes in the price of the leased asset' is framed widely and in practice it does not expect many leases to fall within the scope of Section 12.

Grants

67   A number of respondents, particularly from the public benefit entity sector, raised concerns about the proposed changes to the recognition requirements for grants received from government and other bodies. The proposals in FRED 44 based the recognition of income from grants on when an entity fulfilled the performance criteria stipulated in the grant. This would have been a change from both current FRS and EU-adopted IFRS which attempt to match grant income with the related expenditure. The Accounting Council observed that the IFRS for SMEs used an approach not in current EU-adopted IFRSs.

68   The Accounting Council reviewed the concerns of entities noting that it could amend the performance criterion approach to provide application guidance on performance outcome. This approach would require a research project to be undertaken and cause delay to the finalisation of FRS 102. An alternative was to amend the requirements in the IFRS for SMEs so that they were consistent with EU-adopted IFRS and defer a research project on the accounting for grants until after the publication of FRS 102. However, respondents also noted that some entities, mainly in the public benefit entity sector, currently recognised income from grants on the basis of performance criteria and that reverting to the requirements of EU-adopted IFRS (which is similar to current FRS) would introduce a change for these entities. The Accounting Council did not wish to implement a change for entities that might be reversed when it subsequently undertook a research project on grant accounting. It therefore concluded it should allow entities a choice between the accounting requirements of the IFRS for SMEs and those in EU-adopted IFRS.

The Accounting Council recognises that the respondents to FRED 44 highlighted an inconsistency in current practice and that the solution in FRS 102 is therefore, an interim solution until completion on a research project is undertaken. **69**

Respondents have further commented that as Section 24 *Government Grants* is restricted to government grants, grants received by public benefit entities from other sources will be accounted for in accordance with Section 34 *Specialised Activities: Incoming Resources from Non-Exchange Transactions*, and there is now the possibility that the accounting for grants depends on the source of the grant, rather than whether or not the underlying terms and conditions of the grants differ. Whilst this is not ideal, the Accounting Council advises permitting the accrual model for government grants in accordance with its guidelines for amending the IFRS for SMEs as an interim solution to avoid changes in accounting that might be reversed in the future. **70**

For those entities that apply the performance model to capital grants, either as an accounting policy choice for government grants, or through applying Section 34 to grants from other sources, the Accounting Council notes that there may be a change from current accounting practice, which may lead to greater volatility in the income statement. The effect of this volatility can be explained in the notes to the financial statements. **71**

Share-based payment

The Accounting Council noted that at present entities in the UK and Republic of Ireland[17] that enter into share-based payment transactions are required to apply FRS 20 *(IFRS 2) Share-based Payment*. However, for unlisted entities it can be difficult to apply option pricing models and therefore the benefits outweigh the costs. As a result the Accounting Council advises that directors apply judgement by using models that are appropriate to the entity's circumstance. The Accounting Council considers that this provides a cost effective way of recognising the cost of share-based payments. **72**

Employee benefits

The Accounting Council noted that the requirements of FRS 17 *Retirement benefits* are broadly consistent with the equivalent requirements of IAS 19 *Employee Benefits*, which form the basis of the IFRS for SMEs in this area, including the principles for the measurement of the net defined benefit liability and the recognition of plan deficits and surpluses. The disclosure requirements of FRS 102 for defined benefit pension plans are reduced when compared with those in FRS 17. **73**

Cost of a defined benefit plan

Respondents noted that the presentation requirements for post-employment benefit plans were not clear in FRED 44. Specifically a request was made to clarify where the difference between the actual return on plan assets and expected return on plan assets should be presented. The Accounting Council, in considering this request, noted that the presentation requirements in IAS 19 had been amended in 2011. The amendments to IAS 19 were consistent with the ASB's recommendations in its report following the consultation document *The Financial Reporting of Pensions*. In view of this, the Accounting Council decided to update FRS 102 to be consistent with the revised IAS 19, which requires an entity to recognise the net change in the defined benefit liability as follows: **74**

---

[17] *Other than those applying the FRSSE.*

(a)   the change in the defined benefit liability arising from employee service rendered during the reporting period in profit or loss;

(b)   net interest on the net defined benefit liability in profit or loss; and

(c)   remeasurement of the net defined benefit liability in other comprehensive income.

75   In advising this amendment, the Accounting Council also noted that the accounting requirements in the IFRS for SMEs for group pension plan arrangements were more stringent than those set out in IAS 19 (revised 2011). The Accounting Council therefore decided to update these requirements to be consistent with the IAS 19 (revised 2011).

Group defined benefit pension plans

76   Consistently with IAS 19 (revised 2011), paragraph 28.38 of FRS 102 requires entities participating in a group defined benefit pension plan to recognise the net defined benefit cost in their individual financial statements where a relevant agreement or policy exists. Otherwise the entity that is legally responsible for the group pension plan will recognise the entire net defined benefit cost in its individual financial statements. The Accounting Council noted that although this paragraph only refers explicitly to the cost of the pension plan, the net defined benefit cost is calculated by reference to both the defined benefit obligation and the fair value of plan assets. Therefore paragraph 28.38 does require the recognition of the relevant net defined benefit liability in the individual financial statements of any group entities recognising a net defined benefit cost.

Multi-employer defined benefit plans

77   In October 2012 the FRC issued an exposure draft of proposed amendments to FRED 48, including amendments to Section 28 *Employee Benefits*. These amendments related to multi-employer defined benefit plans that are accounted for as defined contribution plans. The Accounting Council is aware that diversity in accounting practice had arisen in relation to entities who participate in a defined benefit multi-employer plan, who account for that plan as a defined contribution plan and who have entered into a funding agreement for future payments relating to past service liabilities, to recognise a liability in relation to the deficit in the plan in their financial statements.

78   Consistently with the guidelines for amending the IFRS for SMEs, the Accounting Council advises incorporating the relevant requirement from IAS 19 and notes that the IASB's basis for conclusions said that 'In relation to the funding of a deficit, […] this principle [is] consistent with the recognition of a provision in accordance with IAS 37.'

79   The Accounting Council also advises clarifying the measurement requirements for such a liability. In the circumstances that the entity has entered into a funding agreement for future payments relating to past service it shall recognise those future payments as a liability, discounted using the methodology for selecting a discount rate for post-employment benefit liabilities. The Accounting Council debated whether the discount rate should alternatively be based on the entity's cost of capital, but decided to advise the use of a rate consistent with the methodology used for accounting for other pension liabilities.

80   The Accounting Council noted that some respondents to the exposure draft disagreed with the proposed amendment or requested a delay in implementation, but the Accounting Council believes that where participants in a multi-employer defined benefit pension plan have entered into an agreement to fund a deficit, and have applied defined contribution accounting, a liability exists and its recognition provides useful information to users.

Some respondents suggested that FRS 102 should also address situations where a multi-employer pension plan was in surplus, and entered into an agreement to distribute that surplus to the participating employers. Although the Accounting Council noted that this is addressed in IAS 19, it expected that the situation would arise rarely in practice, and considered that entities would be able to determine the appropriate accounting using the principles set out in FRS 102. Therefore it does not advise making an amendment for this. **81**

Income tax

In FRED 44 the ASB proposed using the text of IAS 12 *Income Taxes* in place of the IFRS for SMEs section on income tax. The ASB had amended the tax section of the IFRS for SMEs because it had been based on proposals subsequently abandoned by the IASB and therefore the IFRS for SMEs was not consistent with full IFRS. Respondents to the Policy Proposal had not supported retaining the IFRS for SMEs requirements in this area. Respondents to FRED 44 had accepted that the IFRS for SMEs treatment could not be used, but did not support the ASB's proposal to replace the tax section with IAS 12. **82**

In developing FRED 48 the ASB considered what would be the most suitable alternative, and took into account the findings of its research work with EFRAG in developing the Discussion Paper *Improving the Financial Reporting of Income Tax* (issued in December 2011), as well as its commitment to an IFRS-based solution and the requirements of FRS 19 *Deferred Tax* from which entities would be transitioning. It set out an alternative approach that based the recognition requirements on timing differences, with additional recognition requirements for certain temporary differences that are not timing differences, which was referred to as a 'timing differences plus' approach. The advantages of this approach seemed to be that it would: **83**

(a) provide useful information to users of financial statements; and
(b) provide the simple solution preparers were looking for that was close to current FRS and that would give the same answers as IFRSs in most cases.

Most respondents supported the 'timing differences plus' approach, which has therefore been retained in FRS 102. **84**

The most significant change to the requirements in current FRS is that the proposed approach requires the recognition of the deferred tax implications of the revaluation of assets. Gains and losses recognised on a revaluation are timing differences and the tax effects should be recognised. Such a requirement is consistent with IAS 12 and the IFRS for SMEs. **85**

Another significant change from current FRS is that discounting of current and deferred tax is not allowed which is consistent with the IFRS for SMEs. **86**

Under IAS 12 deferred tax is not generally recognised on the initial recognition of an asset, except that of assets and liabilities arising from a business combination. No specific exception for this is necessary under the 'timing differences plus' approach as no timing difference arises. The proposed treatment is therefore consistent in this respect with IAS 12. **87**

A pure timing difference approach does not provide complete consistency with the requirements of IAS 12. In particular, IAS 12 requires that deferred tax is recognised in respect of the difference between the amount recognised on a business combination for assets and liabilities (other than goodwill) and the amount that will be allowed for or assessed to tax in respect of such assets and liabilities. These differences are not timing differences. In order to maintain consistency with IFRS on this major issue, the Accounting **88**

Council agreed to supplement the timing difference approach with a requirement to recognise deferred tax on business combinations.

89   However, the 'timing differences plus' approach adopted in FRS 102 does not ensure complete consistency with the requirements of IAS 12. For example FRS 102 does not permit the recognition of deferred tax:

(a)   where the tax deduction (or estimated future deduction) for share-based payment exceeds the cumulative amount of the related remuneration expense; and

(b)   in some cases, where the tax basis of an asset is changed, for example where legislation changes the amount of future tax relief relating to the asset.

90   The Accounting Council considered, however, that the differences from IAS 12 were likely to be relatively rare and that in such cases the relevance of the information produced in accordance with IAS 12 was unclear.

91   The proposed disclosure requirements have been reviewed in the light of comments on FRED 48. In particular the requirement to disclose differences between the current tax charge and a standard rate of tax for the next three years has been replaced by a requirement to disclose expected net reversals of timing differences for the next year. The requirement to disclose is on a net basis, which takes account of both the reversal of existing timing differences and the origination of new ones. The net basis provides information that is relevant to the entity's future cash flows, and hence is more relevant than disclosure on a gross basis. The Accounting Council considers that the additional benefit of disclosure on a net basis outweighed the cost to preparers of forecasting future new timing differences.

Related party disclosures

92   In response to feedback from respondents, the Accounting Council advises that the company law exemption from disclosing intra-group related party transactions should be included in FRS 102.

93   Some respondents raised the issue of a possible exemption from the disclosure of outstanding balances as well as transactions. However, the Accounting Council noted that there is a separate legal requirement, in relation to the format of the balance sheet which requires disclosure of outstanding balances in aggregate for group undertakings and, separately, for undertakings in which the company has a participating interest. As Section 33 *Related Party Disclosures* requires disclosure in aggregate for a category of related parties, one of which is 'entities over which the entity has control, joint control or significant influence' this should be met by compliance with the requirements of Section 4 *Statement of Financial Position.* As a result it is not possible to provide an effective exemption from the disclosure of outstanding balances with group undertakings.

Specialised activities

Agriculture

94   The IFRS for SMEs includes guidance for specialised activities including agriculture. The proposed requirements for agriculture are a predominately fair value model and are based on IAS 41 *Agriculture.* Respondents questioned the proposed requirements noting that current FRSs do not set out accounting requirements and although the proposals included an exemption from applying fair value where there is undue cost or effort, the fair value information is inconsistent with the way most agricultural businesses are managed and would not benefit the users of financial statements.

The Accounting Council evaluated the comments raised and advises that entities engaged in **95** agricultural activities should be permitted an accounting policy choice for their biological assets, between the cost model and fair value model set out in the IFRS for SMEs.

The Accounting Council noted that both the cost model and the fair value model, as set out **96** in the IFRS for SMEs, require agricultural produce to be measured at the point of harvest at fair value less costs to sell. However, it considered that respondents in favour of the cost model would have expected the cost model to mean that both biological assets and agricultural produce would be measured at cost.

The Accounting Council noted that agricultural produce should be capable of measurement **97** at fair value without undue cost or effort, and should provide more relevant information to users. However, it noted that respondents argued that agricultural businesses often manage their business on the basis of cost information and advises that agricultural produce should be permitted to be measured at cost. The Accounting Council advises limiting the use of the cost model for agricultural produce to those entities that have chosen the cost model for biological assets; however these entities should also have the option of using the fair value model for agricultural produce.

Extractive activities

Respondents noted that the requirements of the IFRS for SMEs in relation to extractive **98** activities were not consistent with IFRS 6 *Exploration for and Evaluation of Mineral Resources*, and the application of the IFRS for SMEs requirements, in conjunction with other elements of FRS 102 would significantly change accounting practices for entities engaged in extractive activities. It would be likely that no assets could be recognised from the costs of exploration activities, yet entities applying EUadopted IFRS would be permitted to recognise such assets.

The Accounting Council agreed that entities applying FRS 102 should not be prohibited **99** from applying accounting policies that are available to those entities applying EU-adopted IFRS, and advises that the requirements of IFRS 6 are incorporated into FRS 102 by cross reference.

Service concession arrangements

Respondents raised two main issues relating to the accounting for service concession **100** arrangements. The first was that the requirements of the IFRS for SMEs in relation to the accounting by operators had been over-simplified when compared with IFRIC 12 *Service Concession Arrangements*. The Accounting Council agreed and FRS 102 includes additional clarification of the principles of accounting by operators for service concession arrangements, which were developed from IFRIC 12.

The second issue related to grantors, with some respondents noting that grantors might be **101** within the scope of FRS 102. This was addressed in the October 2012 exposure draft of proposed amendments to FRED 48 issued by the FRC.

EU-adopted IFRS does not address accounting by grantors of service concession **102** arrangements; grantors are expected to be outside the scope of EU-adopted IFRS. As a result, and consistently with the guidelines for amending the IFRS for SMEs, the Accounting Council sought to develop accounting for grantors that is consistent with the principles underpinning the accounting by operators of service concession arrangements, which is set out in IFRIC 12. The scope of IFRIC 12 is such that the grantor controls the residual interest in the infrastructure asset, and therefore for service concession arrangements meeting the definition in FRS 102, the Accounting Council advises that the grantor recognises its interest in the infrastructure asset usually as property, plant and equipment, with a corresponding liability measured using a finance lease model.

103   The Accounting Council noted that the International Public Sector Accounting Standards Board (IPSASB) has issued a standard IPSAS 32 *Service Concession Arrangements: Grantor*, which includes two models for accounting by the grantor, depending on the terms of the arrangement with the operator. In addition to the finance lease model advised by the Accounting Council, IPSAS 32 includes a 'grant of right to the operator model' which applies to 'user-pays' arrangements. The Accounting Council does not advise the application of this model because it appears to result in the recognition as liabilities of amounts that may not meet the definition of a liability. However, some respondents to the exposure draft suggested that this model should be permitted. The Accounting Council advises that further research should be carried out on the most appropriate accounting for user-pays service concession arrangements, but that this should not delay the issue of FRS 102.

104   The Accounting Council considered whether transitional provisions should be available for grantors. It noted that for some grantors, the proposals would result in recognising assets and liabilities for the infrastructure assets that are not presently recognised. It considered that this provides more relevant information to users, and therefore advises the FRC that transitional provisions should not be available. As a result grantors will not be permitted to apply the transitional exemptions that are available to operators, as set out in FRS 102 paragraph 35.10(i), by analogy.

Retirement benefit plans

105   FRED 43 proposed that retirement benefit plans were publicly accountable and therefore should apply EU-adopted IFRS, but having decided to eliminate the definition of publicly accountable, retirement benefit plans are now within the scope of FRS 102, yet the IFRS for SMEs contains no specific provisions for retirement benefit plans.

106   The Accounting Council considered whether to direct retirement benefit plans to IAS 26 *Accounting and Reporting by Retirement Benefit Plans* and request that the Statement of Recommended Practice (SORP) *Financial Reports of Pension Schemes* be updated to be consistent with IAS 26. This option was, however, rejected based on feedback which suggested that the application of IAS 26 would be difficult for two reasons:

(a)   legal accounting and reporting requirements in the UK are different to those in IAS 26; and

(b)   IAS 26 itself makes references to other IFRSs and the interaction between these references and FRS 102 would be complicated.

A further complication would arise as the SORP would also provide application guidance for retirement benefit plans.

107   Following this feedback the Accounting Council decided to develop, as part of the specialised activities section, accounting requirements for retirement benefit plans financial statements that could be supplemented by the SORP.

108   In developing the proposals, the Accounting Council considered the issue of whether the financial statements of retirement benefit plans need to provide disclosure regarding the pension liabilities and the related funding of the plan. Following feedback from respondents, the Accounting Council decided that such information should not be recognised in the financial statements, but provided alongside it, as is currently the case.

The Accounting Council advises that because of the way in which retirement benefit   **109**
plans use financial instruments they should be considered to be financial institutions.
However, not all of the disclosure requirements for financial institutions are relevant to
retirement benefit plans and it will be more user-friendly to have all requirements in one
place. Therefore Section 34 sets out all the requirements for retirement benefit plans in
one sub-section.

Insurance contracts

FRED 48 proposed that entities with insurance contracts should apply IFRS 4 *Insurance*   **110**
Contracts to those contracts. In addition, insurance-related contracts not meeting the
definition of an insurance contract shall usually be accounted for as financial instruments
in accordance with Sections 11 and 12.

The FRC also has FRS 27 *Life Assurance* in issue. The Accounting Council debated the   **111**
various options for setting out the requirements for entities engaged in insurance business,
and decided that it should advise the FRC to issue a separate accounting standard on
insurance contracts, FRS 103 *Insurance Contracts*. An exposure draft of this standard will
be available after FRS 102 has been issued, but FRS 102 cross-refers to it. The Accounting
Council's Advice to the FRC to issue FRS 103 will be set out in that standard.

Other options available in EU-adopted IFRS

Respondents to FRED 44, in general, supported the use of the IFRS for SMEs as a base   **112**
for a future financial reporting standard in the UK and Republic of Ireland. There were,
however, concerns raised that would require careful consideration, most notably the
removal of certain accounting treatments (options) that are available in current FRSs and
EU-adopted IFRS but were not proposed in FRED 44.

Responses from the housing associations particularly focused on how the removal of   **113**
options might have behavioural implications that the Accounting Council should take into
consideration. The housing associations noted that:

(a)   the removal of the options would reduce comparability between entities that apply
      EU-adopted IFRS and those applying FRED 44 for entities operating in the same
      market, for example entities applying FRED 44 would not be permitted to revalue
      property, plant and equipment whereas entities applying EU-adopted IFRS could;
      and
(b)   the inability to include borrowing costs as part of the costs of property, plant and
      equipment may cause some housing associations to breach terms and conditions of
      current financing arrangements; this gave potential for banks and other lenders to
      renegotiate existing financing arrangements but at a higher cost of capital.

Other respondents noted that removal of the accounting options was potentially an   **114**
oversimplification for the UK and Republic of Ireland. These respondents noted the
IFRS for SMEs had been developed by the IASB for countries that had a less developed
financial reporting framework than the UK and Republic of Ireland. They considered
that as options existed in current FRSs the simplification had not been justified by the
Accounting Council.

A further view put forward by respondents was that retaining the options that existed   **115**
in current FRS would reduce transition costs and ease transition between the different
standards and also with EU-adopted IFRS.

356   UK Accounting Standards and Company Law 2016

116   Application of the guidelines permitted the introduction of accounting options that exist in current FRS and EU-adopted IFRS that respondents had highlighted as reducing comparability. FRS 102 therefore includes accounting options for:

(a)   capitalisation of borrowing costs;

(b)   revaluation of property, plant and equipment and intangible assets; and

(c)   capitalisation of development costs, in certain circumstances.

Providing clarifications in FRS 102

117   Having agreed guidelines that include making amendments to the IFRS for SMEs to provide clarifications, the Accounting Council considered relevant requests from respondents. Some clarifications were made by reference to EU-adopted IFRS (see column (d) of the table at paragraph 26 of the Accounting Council's Advice), others were made by reference to current FRS, for example whether there is an interaction with company law. As a result a number of clarifications have been made, examples include:

(a)   disclosure requirements for discontinued operations;

(b)   treatment of loan covenants, so that the treatment is consistent with IFRS 9 *Financial Instruments*;

(c)   financial instruments that would be equity under IAS 32 *Financial Instruments: Presentation* are not liabilities, when an entity is required to prepare consolidated financial statements;

(d)   when an investor that is not a parent but has an investment in one or more associates and/or jointly controlled entities shall account for its investments and/or jointly controlled entities using either cost or fair value;

(e)   the presumed life for goodwill, in particular when an entity is otherwise unable to make a reliable estimate shall not be in excess of five years and thereby consistent with company law. The same also applies to intangible assets;

(f)   accounting treatment for group share-based payments where the award is granted by the parent or another group entity; and

(g)   that option pricing models are not required for the value of shared-based payments, particularly for unquoted shares or share options.

Other matters

118   The Accounting Council considered whether to provide guidance for the term 'undue cost or effort' where respondents had sought clarification. The Accounting Council noted that Section 2 *Concepts and Pervasive Principles* discussed the balance between benefit and cost and that no further clarification was required.

The retention of Urgent Issue Task Force (UITF) Abstracts

119   FREDs 43 and 44 proposed to withdraw all UITF Abstracts except UITF Abstract 43 *The Interpretation of equivalence for the purposes of section 228A of the Companies Act*. Respondents to the FRED proposed that in addition to UITF Abstract 43, other UITF Abstracts should be retained. The Accounting Council gave consideration to this request and noted that rather than retain UITF Abstracts, consistent with its objective to provide succinct financial reporting standards, it should incorporate any guidance into FRS 102.

120   Based on feedback the Accounting Council advises that the following accounting requirements of UITF Abstracts are retained by incorporation, as follows:

UITF Abstract		Action
4	*Presentation of long-term debtors in current assets*	Incorporated into the legal appendix.
31	*Exchange of businesses or other non-monetary assets for an interest in a subsidiary, joint venture or associate*	Additional paragraphs 9.31 and 9.32 are inserted.
32	*Employee benefit trusts and other intermediate payment arrangements*	Additional paragraphs are inserted into Section 9.
43	*The interpretation of equivalence for the purposes of section 228A of the Companies Act 1985*	The guidance has been updated and included as Application Guidance to FRS 100.

The Accounting Council decided to advise the withdrawal of UITF Abstract 48 *Accounting*   **121**
implications of the replacement of the retail prices index with the consumer prices index for retirement benefits as the circumstance it addressed were related to a one time period which has now expired.

Interaction with company law

The Accounting Council gave careful consideration to the comments received to its   **122**
draft legal appendix set out in FREDs 44 and 48. The Accounting Council agreed with respondents' views that the appendix should address entities that are not companies.

The Accounting Council also considered whether it should retain, as proposed in FRED   **123**
44, accounting options that had been removed because the option conflicted with company law, where an entity that is not a company would not be restricted in the same way as a company. For example, SSAP 4 *Accounting for government grants* contained an option that was not permitted by the company law.

The Accounting Council confirmed the position it had taken in developing FRED 44 that   **124**
options that existed in the IFRS for SMEs, but not permitted by company law, should be removed. This would promote consistency between reporting entities regardless of the legal framework under which they operate.

Public benefit entities (PBEs)

The Consultation Paper *Policy Proposal: The Future of UK GAAP* (issued in 2009) set   **125**
out 10 issues that could be included in a Public Benefit Entities (PBEs) specific standard. However, these 10 issues were refined to six which were deemed to be those most significant and relevant to the PBE sectors that were not satisfactorily addressed by the IFRS for SMEs. These six issues were:

(a)   Concessionary loans;
(b)   Property held for the provision of social benefits;
(c)   Entity combinations;
(d)   Impairment of assets: public benefit considerations;
(e)   Funding commitments; and
(f)   Incoming resources from non-exchange transactions.

Concessionary loans

126   Paragraphs have been inserted into Section 34 *Specialised Activities* to address the accounting requirements for PBEs making and receiving concessionary loans.

127   There are two main accounting treatments to consider when determining the basis for the measurement of concessionary loans; the amount paid or received, and fair value. This has been the subject of significant discussion and debate by the Accounting Council, taking into account the information that users of PBE accounts may consider useful and the difficulties that may arise for smaller organisations in measuring concessionary loans at fair value.

128   Accounting for concessionary loans at the amount paid or received rather than fair value is not consistent with the accounting requirements set out in either Section 11 of FRS 102, EU-adopted IFRS or IPSAS 29 *Financial Instruments: Recognition and Measurement* (which require that such arrangements are measured and recognised in the financial statements at their fair value).

129   Nevertheless the Accounting Council advises that due to the difficulties that smaller PBEs may face with using fair value, PBEs that make or receive concessionary loans may have the option of measuring such loans at either the amount paid or received or at fair value. However, PBEs that make and receive concessionary loans must apply the same measurement method to both. Further the Accounting Council proposes that the same accounting may be applied by other wholly-owned entities in a public benefit entity group, to eliminate the need to restate concessionary loans made or received for the purposes of furthering the PBEs objectives on consolidation.

130   Presentation and disclosure of concessionary loan arrangements are an important part of the proposals for concessionary loans and the Accounting Council concluded that the disclosure requirements in FRS 102 will provide sufficient information to understand and interpret the impact of this type of transaction on the financial statements.

Property held for the provision of social benefits

131   Subsequent to FRED 45, the Accounting Council decided that the requirements for property held for the provision of social benefits should apply to all entities applying FRS 102 and should not be restricted to PBEs.

132   Consideration was given as to whether properties that are held for the provision of social benefits meet the definition of an investment property. The definition of investment property in paragraph 16.2 of FRS 102, excludes properties held for use in the production or supply of goods and services or for administrative purposes. A property held to earn rentals and/or for capital appreciation, but not used in the production or supply of goods or services, meets this definition. The Accounting Council noted that although many PBEs that engage in the provision of social housing receive rental income, their primary purpose is to provide social benefits.

133   Provision of social housing is akin to supplying a service and therefore, property held for the primary purpose of providing social benefits should be excluded from the scope of investment property and be accounted for as property, plant and equipment.

134   The Accounting Council acknowledges that PBEs may hold 'investment properties' which are not held primarily to provide social benefits and will return market value rentals and/or are held for their capital appreciation. FRS 102 requires those properties to be accounted for as investment properties.

Public benefit entity combinations

In considering the issue of entity combinations involving two or more public benefit **135** entities, the Accounting Council noted that there is some debate over whether the use of acquisition accounting for all combinations would be appropriate. In particular whether acquisition accounting reflects the substance of a transaction if there is a gift of one entity to another in a combination at nil or nominal consideration, or where two or more organisations genuinely merge to form a new entity.

Where there is a combination of entities at nil or nominal consideration which is in **136** substance a gift, it is appropriate to follow the same accounting principles as donations of assets (as set out in Section 34 *Specialised Activities: Incoming Resources from Non-Exchange Transactions*) by recognising the fair value of the assets received and liabilities assumed as a gain or loss in income and expenditure.

Accounting for combinations that meet the definition of a merger requires a different **137** methodology to acquisition accounting in order to reflect the true substance of the transaction. Whilst it is not anticipated that all combinations involving two or more public benefit entities are mergers or that merger accounting will generally be applicable to such combinations it is considered appropriate to retain merger accounting in certain circumstances. In considering this matter it was noted that the accounting requirements for PBEs in some jurisdictions, for example, the US and Australia have recently been reviewed and noted that merger accounting has been retained for the public and not-for-profit sectors.

In retaining merger accounting, the Accounting Council considered the criteria to be met **138** for a merger. The criteria set out in FRS 6 *Acquisitions and Mergers* provided a starting point, but are framed in the context of the commercial sector and therefore the criteria have been adapted to make them more appropriate for public benefit entities. In particular, a criterion has been added to include consideration of the impact of the combination on beneficiaries and the benefits to which they are entitled.

One specific concern highlighted in relation to the requirements of FRS 6, is the need to **139** restate comparatives by adding together the previous periods' reported figures of each of the combining entities. This does not reflect the substance of the transaction as the historical parties which formed the entity did not exist in the previous accounting period and therefore FRS 102 requires that comparatives are marked as 'combined' to make it clear that they are a combination of previously reported figures for the combining entities.

Impairment of assets

FRS 102 requires impaired assets to be measured at the lower of their fair value less **140** costs to sell and their value in use. In a for-profit context, value in use is determined by measuring the present value of the cash flows derived from the asset. However, often PBE assets are held for their service potential rather than their ability to generate cash flows. In such a case it is sometimes impossible to determine value in use by reference to cash flows and it is more appropriate to regard value in use as the present value of future service potential rather than cash flows.

International Public Sector Accounting Standard (IPSAS) 21 *Impairment of Non-Cash* **141** *Generating Assets* permits value in use to be determined by any of three approaches:

(a) depreciated replacement cost (DRC);
(b) restoration cost; and
(c) the service units approach.

Restoration cost and the service units approach are applications of DRC as DRC is used as the starting point. DRC reflects the cash outflows that are saved through ownership of an asset and is likely to be widely applicable and appropriate for PBEs. Therefore FRS 102 permits a service potential driven valuation to be used for assets held for their service potential.

142   The use of DRC is not mandated; other methods that value service potential rather than cash flows may be used if those methods are more appropriate in those particular circumstances.

143   FRED 45 only allowed this alternative valuation method for PBEs, however subsequent to that consultation, the Accounting Council advises that any entity that holds an asset for service potential can use a service potential valuation method. It is not expected that, for example, headquarters buildings that do not generate cash flows independently of other assets or groups of assets but nevertheless contribute to the cash-generating activities of the entity, will usually be measured on the basis of their service potential.

144   The Accounting Council also discussed whether a restriction on the use of an asset would affect its fair value. As an asset's fair value is based on the amount that an entity could obtain, restrictions might impact on the fair value where they prevent a purchaser from using the asset for another purpose that would be more valuable than that required by the restriction. In addition, the costs to sell should include the costs of breaking the restriction.

145   Another issue for discussion was indicators of impairment. Although the indicators provided in FRS 102 are mainly linked to the expected cash flow of an asset and as such may not necessarily be relevant to some PBE assets, the Accounting Council considered that they must, as a minimum, be considered by PBEs as possible indicators of impairment.

146   In addition, the Accounting Council noted that other accounting literature (eg IPSAS 21 and SORPs) identified other indicators of impairment including:

(a)   cessation, or near cessation of the demand or need for services provided by the asset;
(b)   social, demographic or environmental changes resulting in a reduction of beneficiaries; and
(c)   a major loss of key employees associated with particular activities.

147   The Accounting Council concluded that it would not be appropriate to include these indicators in FRS 102, as they are not exclusively relevant to PBEs and because the indicators given in FRS 102 will continue to apply to PBEs. Therefore, their inclusion would make such entities subject to a confusing list of overlapping indicators. The indicators given in FRS 102 are merely minimum requirements, and recognition of an impairment loss is required irrespective of whether any of the given indicators are met.

148   The Accounting Council also considered whether to specify that an indicator of impairment was present where an asset's service potential was not fully utilised and noted that an entity may require standby or surplus capacity to ensure that it has adequate capacity to provide services at all times. For example, a building that provides accommodation for the homeless may not be used to full capacity during the summer months but is utilised fully during winter. In this circumstance, the surplus capacity is part of the required service potential of the asset and the asset is not impaired. For this reason, it was concluded that it would be inappropriate to specify that the unutilised capacity should be treated as an indicator of impairment.

Funding commitments

The Accounting Council also discussed when to recognise a commitment to provide 149
funding in a non-exchange transaction. The *Statement of Principles: Interpretation for
Public Benefit Entities* previously addressed this issue, and it was considered necessary to
incorporate these details into FRS 102 to be used in conjunction with Sections 2 *Concepts
and Pervasive Principles* and 21 *Provisions and Contingencies*.

The issue was identified as being particularly important because many PBEs provide 150
funding on an on-going basis and there is little guidance on how such multi-year
commitments should be recognised.

The Accounting Council considered when a liability for such a commitment should be 151
recognised and determined that an entity would only recognise a liability if the commitment
to provide funding was made unconditionally, and the grantor could not realistically
withdraw from the commitment. In this situation, an entity would recognise a liability for
the present value of the total funding promised.

As this is an application of the principles in Sections 2 and 21, the Accounting Council 152
advises that the requirements for funding commitments should apply to all entities and not
just PBEs.

Incoming resources from non-exchange transactions

The receipt of resources from non-exchange transactions is an inflow of resources that is 153
highly significant for many PBEs: the receipt of donations, grants and legacies from non-
exchange transactions are a major source of their funding and this issue is not addressed in
the IFRS for SMEs apart from in Section 24 *Government Grants*.

The Accounting Council considered that for PBE financial statements to be complete, 154
they should reflect the benefit that the inflow of these resources had to the entity.
FRS 102 requires, in principle, PBEs to value the resources they receive from non-exchange
transactions at their fair value. The Accounting Council discussed whether using fair value
would overstate the value of a donation where the entity is unable to exploit fully an asset,
and the equivalent service potential could be derived from a lower value asset. Being able
to achieve the same service potential from a lower value asset might suggest that the value
of the donated asset should be at the lower value. However, FRS 102 requires donated
assets to be valued at their fair value. This reflects that the circumstances described above
would rarely occur. In many cases, an entity would be able to sell the donated asset and if
appropriate, purchase a cheaper asset with the equivalent service potential.

Incorporating an exception for donated assets which may not be fully exploited would 155
make the application of FRS 102 more onerous, as it would require all entities in receipt of
donated assets (except those intended for resale) to consider whether they would be able to
exploit the asset fully. This would be subjective and may incur the risk of understatement
of the value of donated assets.

The Accounting Council noted that where goods are donated for subsequent sale (for 156
example donations to charity shops), it could be argued that the donated goods should
be valued only when they are sold. This is not consistent with the accruals concept which
requires the financial statements to recognise goods when they are received. However, the
Accounting Council advises, on pragmatic grounds, that donated goods should only be
recognised as income on receipt when the item is material, can be measured reliably and
if the benefits of recognising the item outweigh the costs. Further the Accounting Council
proposes that the same accounting may be applied by other wholly-owned entities in a

public benefit entity group, to eliminate the need to restate goods donated for subsequent sale on consolidation (for example where a charity operates it shops through a subsidiary that is a non-charitable company).

157   FRS 102 requires donated services that would otherwise have been purchased to be accounted for at their estimated value to the recipient. This is a pragmatic solution recognising that there are potential issues in determining a value for volunteer services and their contribution to the organisation and notes that quantifying this type of service may not be practicable. There is an argument to suggest that valuing volunteer services could be measured by reference to a metric such as the minimum wage, however this measure does not take into consideration an organisation's requirements for volunteers. In addition, this would be attributing an arbitrary value onto a volunteer's time which may not be reflective of their skills, experience or role and to determine a different method of valuation would be very subjective.

158   However, when a service is provided voluntarily for which the entity would otherwise have to pay (eg legal or financial advice) the value of that service should be recognised in the financial statements where, as will usually be the case, its value can be reasonably quantified.

Other PBE issues

159   The Accounting Council discussed the issue of reporting entity control and the indicators of control that may be specific to the PBE sectors. The indicators of control set out in Section 9 *Consolidated and Separate Financial Statements* of FRS 102 focus on benefits, and in the PBE sectors benefit can be in the form of indirect benefit through a PBE's beneficiaries or benefit which furthers a PBE's activities. Following discussion of these issues the Accounting Council advises that FRS 102 can be interpreted and applied to PBEs and therefore no separate guidance for PBEs is considered necessary.

160   A number of additional topics were identified through the development of FRS 102, which may be considered in the future and as possible updates to FRS 102. The following table summarises these subjects:

Narrative Reporting	To consider narrative reporting requirements for public benefit entities and any specific matters.
Fresh Start Accounting	To consider the concept of fresh start accounting as an alternative accounting treatment for entity combinations where the effect of a combination is to create a new entity that cannot be reasonably portrayed as the enlargement of a pre-existing party.
Social Benefit Obligations	To consider if and how social benefit obligations should be recognised and measured in the financial statements. The International Public Sector Accounting Standards Board currently have a project addressing this issue and it is likely to be most productive to await the outcome of that work.
Fund Accounting	To consider how fund accounting would be applied in accordance with the requirements of FRS 102 for segmental reporting.

Transition to FRS 102

161   The Accounting Council noted that FRS 102 does not permit goodwill to have an indefinite useful life, unlike current FRS. On transition to FRS 102 entities that previously determined

that goodwill had an indefinite useful life will need to reassess goodwill to determine its remaining useful life, and subsequently amortise the goodwill over that period.

Effective date

FREDs 43 and 44 proposed an effective date for accounting periods beginning on or after 1 July 2013, with early application being permitted. Respondents' views regarding the proposals were very mixed with some calling for earlier adoption and others for deferral of the proposals. **162**

The Accounting Council took into consideration its decision that FRS 102 would apply to a broader scope of entities and its revised guidelines for amending the IFRS for SMEs in relation to the effective date. The Accounting Council noted that: **163**

(a)   Although the revisions to its original proposals should ease the transition, an 18 month period between the publication of the final standard and effective date should be retained as there are significant changes to the accounting requirements for financial instruments.

(b)   The IASB's decision to revise the effective date of IFRS 9 *Financial Instruments* to 2015. The ASB noted that entities that apply current FRS without FRS 26, who wished to move to the proposed reduced disclosure framework would not be able to apply IFRS 9 until it was adopted by the EU. Consequently such entities would need to apply IAS 39 *Financial Instruments: Recognition and Measurement* for an interim period. The costs associated with these changes were not justifiable.

(c)   The effective date needed to take into consideration the updating of the SORPs that is required.

The Accounting Council advises that the effective date of FRS 102 should be accounting periods beginning on or after 1 January 2015. **164**

The Accounting Council also considered whether to permit early application of FRS 102. It noted that as FRS 102 represents an improvement in financial reporting it would not be appropriate to prevent early application of its requirements. However, the Accounting Council advises that early application of FRS 102 should not be permitted for accounting periods before those ending on or after 31 December 2012, which is consistent with the first date at which it is likely to be practical for entities applying FRS 101 to apply that standard. **165**

The Accounting Council also considered the early application of FRS 102 by entities that are within the scope of a SORP. It noted that most of the SORPs require updating for consistency with FRS 102, and for charities there are legal requirements relating to the application of the SORP. The Accounting Council therefore advises that early application should be permitted for entities applying a SORP provided that FRS 102 does not conflict with the requirements of a current SORP or legal requirements for the preparation of financial statements. **166**

Approval of this advice

This advice to the FRC was approved by eight of the nine members of the Accounting Council on 17 January 2013. Mr Beale dissented from the approval of the advice and his dissenting view is set out in the Appendix to the Accounting Council's advice. The Accounting Council is comprised of the following members: **167**

Roger Marshall   (Chair of the Accounting Council)

Nick Anderson

Dr Richard Barker

Edward Beale

Peter Elwin

Ken Lever

Robert Overend

Andy Simmonds

Pauline Wallace

Appendix to the Accounting Council's Advice to the FRC to issue FRS 102

Dissenting view of Mr Beale

Mr Beale agrees that it is fundamental that financial statements should provide useful **1** information to users, who are defined as being: investors not involved in management, customers and suppliers, including suppliers of capital and of non-equity finance. He agrees with the Accounting Council that it is disappointing that despite extensive outreach activities, the Accounting Council has not received more feedback from users, both formal and informal, on whether or not financial statements prepared in accordance with FRS 102 will meet their information needs.

Mr Beale does not believe that the consultation responses from industry representative **2** bodies[18], and from organisations which are both preparers and users, can be considered to be input from users since these responses are from a preparer perspective.

The informal input received by the FRC staff supports FRS 102 as drafted, and is generally **3** consistent with the input from preparers and industry representative bodies. However, this informal input is inconsistent with the five[19] formal consultation responses received from users and the informal input received personally by Mr Beale. This inconsistency in the content of informal input may be due to the informal input received by FRC staff being from providers of non-equity finance whereas the informal input received by Mr Beale has been from directors (who are both users and preparers) and investors.

This informal input received by FRC staff in relation to FRS 102 differs from comments **4** that FRC staff have recently received on other projects:

(a)   from credit analysts and bond fund managers in relation to the financial statements of listed entities[20] (that there is not sufficient forward looking information on cash flows and challenging the usefulness of fair value); and

(b)   as part of the Financial Reporting Laboratory's work on a single figure for remuneration[21] (regarding valuation of equity incentives and pension costs).

In Mr Beale's experience users are concerned with issues identified by the FRC in *Louder* **5** *than Words*[22], which they believe have not been adequately addressed in FRS 102. In his analysis, the common thread behind these user concerns is a desire for clearer, more understandable, information, from which they can derive better predictions about future cash flows on a going concern basis, even at the expense of further divergence from IFRS. Understandability is crucial to confidence in the integrity of financial reporting, and thus maximising the benefits from accounts. Despite the importance of maintaining consistency with IFRS, Mr Beale believes that the FRC should not be issuing new accounting standards perpetuating problems identified in existing standards.

---

[18] *Some of which have been classified in the Feedback Statements as 'user representative bodies'.*

[19] *Four of these formal consultation responses are from users connected to Mr Beale and include three responses to FREDs 43 and 44, of which two were formally classified as being from preparers and one from an academic.*

[20] *http://www.frc.org.uk/getattachment/b0eff085-b542-4eaf-bc36-d52e26eb3833/How-credit-analysts-view-and-use-the-financial-statements.aspx*

[21] *http://frc.org.uk/getattachment/5310093d-c092-45e1-8106-278ae7ac1a4b/A-single-figure-for-remuneration.aspx*

[22] *http://www.frc.org.uk/getattachment/7d952925-74ea-4deb-b659-e9242b09f2fa/Louder-than-words.aspx*

6   In particular Mr Beale believes that there are significant further opportunities to improve the balance between costs and benefits in the sections of FRS 102 dealing with: Financial Instruments, Deferred Tax, Defined Benefit Pension Schemes, and Equity Settled Share-based Payments. This is discussed further below. In his view FRS 102 could have achieved clearer reporting in the above areas by departing further from the IFRS for SMEs, thus better meeting users' needs for high-quality financial information in line with the overriding objective.

7   The FRC needs to consider whether the extensive outreach activities undertaken constitute 'adequate consultation'. In Mr Beale's opinion the determination of 'adequate consultation' should be based on the outcome from the consultation process and, regrettably, there has been virtually no formal input from the people who will be using accounts prepared under FRS 102. Based on the consultation responses from users and the informal input from users that he has received, Mr Beale is advising that the FRC defer approval of FRS 102 until it has a better understanding of the degree of support from users, and in the meantime to work on improving the balance between costs and benefits in the areas outlined above.

8   In Mr Beale's experience, users do not consider UK GAAP to be in need of urgent replacement, and will not be concerned about any delays to FRS 102 necessary to determine the degree of user support and resolve any outstanding issues.

Further opportunities to improve the balance between costs and benefits

9   There are two issues of principle underpinning the areas of FRS 102 that, in Mr Beale's opinion, can be significantly improved:

(a)   Since the purpose of accounts is to supply useful information to users, the most important concepts underpinning accounting standards should be 'relevance' (include information that is useful to users) and its converse, 'materiality' (exclude information that is not useful). All other accounting concepts should clearly be subsidiary to these. Such an emphasis on the priority attributable to 'relevance' and 'materiality' will promote measurement of assets and liabilities in a manner that conveys useful information to users, and will normally exclude mark to model valuations, and limit application of fair value elsewhere.

(b)   At present some assets and liabilities are revalued, and some unrealised profits are taken to earnings. To ensure a principled base for accounting standards the FRC needs to determine general principles covering (i) when it is appropriate for assets and liabilities to be revalued, and (ii) whether unrealised profits arising from revaluations should be recognised in earnings or as a movement in reserves. A consistent approach to revaluation of items such as fixed assets and financial instruments, and a consistent approach to profit recognition, cannot be achieved without such principles. In his opinion, for the purposes of FRS 102: assets should be revalued when there is a sufficiently liquid market for their market value to be determined reliably, or when an impairment provision is necessary; liabilities should only be revalued when there are changes to the amount required to settle them when they fall due; and unrealised profits should not be included within earnings, except for profits on liquid investments.

In Mr Beale's opinion, opportunities to significantly improve the balance of costs and benefits within FRS 102 exist in four areas, two of general application: financial instruments, and deferred tax; and two of more limited application: equity settled share based payments and defined benefit pension schemes. These are summarised below.

Financial instruments

Current FRSs have been criticised in that they allow certain financial instruments not to   **10**
be recorded. Such criticism is incorrect in that the existence of, and details about, these
financial instruments should (where 'material') be recorded in the notes to the accounts.
This criticism has been used by some to justify moving to an IFRS based approach to
accounting for financial instruments, which has been widely criticised, and which is not
the most cost effective approach to providing users of accounts with the information that
they desire.

Many different assets and liabilities fall within the definition of financial instruments and   **11**
attempting to deal with all of these in the same manner introduces unnecessary complexity.
The two sections on financial instruments include three to four pages of rules on which
section should be applied, and are written in a language which is in places very difficult
for people not accustomed to IFRS to understand. These sections have also been drafted
to cater for financial institutions as well as ordinary businesses, and this exacerbates the
difficulty that non-experts will have in applying them. Preparers of accounts will generally
only refer to accounting standards once a year in the lead up to preparation of their annual
accounts. FRS 102 needs to be readily understandable for such preparers, and there is a risk
that if accounting standards are not sufficiently accessible they will be applied in a manner
that generates unnecessary complexity and clutter.

The two sections on financial instruments should be redrafted in language that is   **12**
understandable to the normal businessperson and is not the preserve of experts. Redrafting
of these sections should focus on the information that users need relating to ordinary
businesses, with additional requirements for financial institutions dealt with in the section
for specialised activities, by expanding the part relating to financial institutions, and which
can in turn refer to IAS 39 *Financial Instruments: Recognition and Measurement*, IFRS 7
Financial Instruments: Disclosure and IFRS 9 *Financial Instruments* where appropriate.

Users need different 'information sets' on financial instruments that are: fixed assets,   **13**
current assets and liabilities; and FRS 102 should consider financial instruments in these
three categories, rather than trying to cover all three categories with one set of rules.
Prudence should be incorporated where necessary so that the treatment of assets is not
necessarily the mirror of the treatment of liabilities.

Financial assets

For normal businesses, financial assets should be carried at fair value when the principles   **14**
for revaluation set out above are met, and failing that at cost less any necessary impairment
provision. Income should be recognised in a prudent manner: as it is earned (eg interest on
a daily basis), or when it can be reliably measured (eg dividends).

Circumstances may arise which cause the valuation basis of financial assets to change, but   **15**
such situations are unlikely to occur frequently outside financial institutions. Where they
do occur, the consequences of reclassifications can be made obvious to users of accounts
through note disclosures. Strict anti-abuse rules are not necessary. A clear analysis in the
notes can highlight where reclassification is potentially being abused to manage earnings,
so that users can discuss their concerns with management, auditors or regulators as
appropriate. Any additional requirements considered necessary for financial institutions
can be dealt with in the section for specialised activities.

Financial liabilities

16   When a financial liability is included in the balance sheet at a value which is different from the amount required to settle the liability when it falls due, disclosure of amount of principal repayable is necessary, so that users can understand the underlying cash flow. The notes then show two different values for the same liability. This duplication of valuation bases creates extra cost to both preparers and users of accounts and risks causing confusion. Confusion can be minimised by using the settlement value in the statement of financial position, rather than fair values or amortised cost, recognising deferred financing costs where necessary, and providing information in the notes about financing costs and settlement dates. Interested users will then have the information necessary to perform their own comparisons with other businesses, as well as clearer information on the business's funding requirements.

17   The above approach to liabilities could lead to extensive disclosures for financial institutions and others where there are a large number of different types of financial liability. The section on specialised activities should set out an approach for the aggregation of necessary disclosures and allow an opt into IFRS 9/IAS 39.

Impairment of financial assets

18   Impairment provisions are only allowed in FRS 102 where there is 'objective evidence' of impairment. Businesses are not allowed to make provision for expected losses, even where there is past experience supporting the likelihood of such losses. Expected loss provisions should be allowed now, before IFRS 9 has been updated, to avoid assets being overvalued. A clear analysis in the notes will highlight where impairment provisions are potentially being abused to manage earnings, so that users can discuss their concerns with management, auditors or regulators as appropriate. Additional requirements may be imposed on financial institutions through the section on specialised activities.

Hedging

19   Hedge accounting is only permitted in FRS 102 if 'specified criteria' are met. In the past similar restrictions have led to businesses not hedge accounting for financial instruments acquired, or entered into, for hedging purposes. The purpose of accounting standards is not to promote good management but good reporting. Accounting standards are not the appropriate way to attempt to stop the miss-selling, or miss-buying, of derivatives. There needs to be transparency over hedges entered into so that the effect of hedges in managing risk can be understood by users of accounts. This can be achieved by linked accounting for hedges and items being hedged, so that accounting faithfully represents the underlying commercial activity.

20   Concerns over earnings management can be alleviated by disclosure of the impact on earnings of hedges closed out in a different period to the risk that they purported to hedge. Businesses other than financial institutions should be able to allay concerns over the effectiveness of hedges by explaining how their limited number of material risks are being hedged. Financial institutions may have too many hedges to be able to provide this information in a meaningful manner and an alternative approach for such businesses should be set out in the section on specialised activities.

Deferred tax

21   As the recent ASB/EFRAG discussion paper on tax identified, users want to know how future tax payments will differ from the amount calculated by applying the standard tax

rate to future profits. This difference will be in part due to future actions and in part due to past actions.

The section of FRS 102 on deferred tax is not predicated on a going concern basis, and in effect identifies the impact on future tax payments if the business ceases trading. As such, except for the disclosure of amounts expected to reverse in the next period, the approach in FRS 102 is of little relevance to most users and will create disclosures which will generally be ignored by users.   22

The disclosure required by FRS 102 of the amount of the deferred tax provision which will be released in the next period is of limited usefulness. This is only part of the difference between expected tax cost and standard tax rate. Prediction of the element due to future actions is not currently required.   23

The information that users need can best be provided by way of disclosure of the expected future tax rate and any other material information that may influence future tax payments, eg losses carried forward. A deferred tax provision should not be made because this does not provide useful information in a cost effective manner. The exception to this is that the logic behind revaluing certain items dictates that, for consistency, the tax impact of such revaluations needs to be recognised too.   24

Equity settled share-based payments

As identified by the recent financial reporting laboratory work on valuation of remuneration, users do not understand the complex models used to value equity settled share based payments. The cost of creating these values is therefore wasted.   25

These valuation models also generate a substantial amount of clutter when trying to explain how the valuation is arrived at.   26

It should also be noted that the standard valuation models assume liquid markets and negligible spreads. These assumptions are not appropriate for the types of businesses that will be applying FRS 102. Given the lack of guidance in FRS 102, and the complexity of the valuation models, in Mr Beale's opinion it is highly likely that preparers will use inappropriate valuation models, or use valuation models in inappropriate ways, and that users will not have enough knowledge to identify this.   27

Unless there is a liquid market to provide a relevant value for equity settled share based payments, their existence should be disclosed in the notes to the accounts, and there should be no notional cost in the income statement.   28

Defined benefit pension schemes

The information relating to defined benefit pension schemes that users need is: the current cost of providing the benefit, the expected additional payments required to make good any funding deficit (or payment holiday because of funding surpluses) and an explanation of the contingent liability in respect of potential future funding shortfalls.   29

At present there is a requirement to prepare a fund valuation solely for accounting purposes and then to consolidate the net assets or, more usually, liabilities of the fund. Changes in the net assets/liabilities are then split into three parts and recognised in operating costs, financing costs and other comprehensive income. This is supplemented by extensive disclosures. However, the disclosures do not require information about the uncertainties or   30 sensitivities attached to the valuation inputs eg the time periods over which payments out of the fund will be made, discount and inflation rates, and other risks inherent in the fund.

31 Most users do not understand pension scheme valuations. They see fund valuations which are massively volatile, and perceive most current requirements as adding to clutter and generating additional preparation costs for no benefit.

32 Clutter could be reduced by not consolidating the pension fund, but instead disclosing the level of normal contributions being made and providing for contributions required to make good any funding shortfall. Changes in this liability to make good any funding shortfall should be expensed and explained. In addition disclosures should be made describing the contingent liability to fund any future increases in fund deficits. Those users who do understand pension scheme valuations can obtain the more detailed information that they are likely to want about pension scheme funding from the fund valuation prepared for that purpose, which should be made available on demand or on a web site. Such an approach would save the costs associated with preparing a valuation solely for accounting purposes as well as reducing clutter in the accounts.

Training costs

33 Maintaining limited UK GAAP differences from IFRS will marginally increase the cost of training accountants, but should improve their employability, and will increase the challenge on the IASB to further improve IFRS, thereby improving the balance between benefits and costs overall.

The Accounting Council's Advice to the FRC to issue Amendments to FRS 102 – Basic financial instruments and Hedge accounting

Introduction

This report provides an overview of the main issues that have been considered by the Accounting Council in advising the Financial Reporting Council (FRC) to issue *Amendments to FRS 102 The Financial Reporting Standard applicable in the UK and Republic of Ireland – Basic financial instruments and Hedge accounting.* **1**

The FRC, in accordance with the *Statutory Auditors (Amendment of Companies Act 2006 and Delegation of Functions etc) Order 2012* (SI 2012/1741), is a prescribed body for issuing accounting standards in the UK. The *Foreword to Accounting Standards* sets out the application of accounting standards in the Republic of Ireland. **2**

In accordance with the *FRC Codes and Standards: procedures*, any proposal to issue, amend or withdraw a code or standard is put to the FRC Board with the full advice of the relevant Councils and/or the Codes & Standards Committee. Ordinarily, the FRC Board will only reject the advice put to it where: **3**

(a) it is apparent that a significant group of stakeholders has not been adequately consulted;

(b) the necessary assessment of the impact of the proposal has not been completed, including an analysis of costs and benefits;

(c) insufficient consideration has been given to the timing or cost of implementation; or

(d) the cumulative impact of a number of proposals would make the adoption of an otherwise satisfactory proposal inappropriate.

The FRC has established the Accounting Council as the relevant Council to assist it in the setting of accounting standards. **4**

Advice

The Accounting Council is advising the FRC to issue *Amendments to FRS 102 The Financial Reporting Standard applicable in the UK and Republic of Ireland – Basic financial instruments and Hedge accounting* to: **5**

(a) remove the unintended accounting consequences arising for the classification of certain financial instruments. It believes these changes will result in a reduction in the cost of compliance for entities within the scope of the standard; and

(b) to make the application of the hedge accounting requirements easier and more cost effective to apply for entities that choose to take advantage of this option.

The Accounting Council's Advice to the FRC in FRS 102 *The Financial Reporting Standard applicable in the UK and Republic of Ireland* is supplemented by the inclusion of its advice on these amendments. **6**

Background

The FRC issued FRS 102 in March 2013, which is effective for accounting periods beginning on or after 1 January 2015. **7**

8   After the publication of FRS 102, feedback from constituents indicated that the implementation of the accounting requirements of FRS 102 for loans with common contractual features could have unintended consequences for many entities. The amendments to Section 11 *Basic Financial Instruments* address the issues identified and take into account responses to FRED 54 *Draft Amendments to FRS 102 Financial Reporting Standard applicable in the UK and Ireland – Basic financial instruments.*

9   At the time of issue of FRS 102, the Accounting Council and the FRC were of the view that the standard should reflect up-to-date thinking on hedge accounting, but the IASB had not yet finalised the hedge accounting requirements in IFRS 9 *Financial Instruments*. The Accounting Council advised the FRC at that time that amending the hedge accounting requirements in FRS 102 prior to the IASB finalising the hedge accounting requirements in IFRS 9, would risk implementing hedge accounting requirements in FRS 102 that were inconsistent with IFRS.

10   The hedge accounting amendments to FRS 102 were developed based on the hedge accounting requirements in IFRS 9 and take into account the responses to FRED 51 *Draft Amendments to FRS 102 Financial Reporting Standard applicable in the UK and Ireland – Hedge Accounting.*

Objective

11   The FRC gives careful consideration to its objective and the intended effects when developing new accounting standards or requirements for the UK and Republic of Ireland. In developing accounting standards, including FRS 102, the overriding objective of the FRC is:

> To enable users of accounts to receive high-quality understandable financial reporting proportionate to the size and complexity of the entity and users' information needs.

12   In meeting this objective, the FRC aims to provide succinct financial reporting standards that:

(a)   have consistency with global accounting standards through the application of an IFRS-based solution unless an alternative clearly better meets the overriding objective;

(b)   reflect up-to-date thinking and developments in the way businesses operate and the transactions they undertake;

(c)   balance consistent principles for accounting by all UK and Republic of Ireland entities with practical solutions, based on size, complexity, public interest and users' information needs;

(d)   promote efficiency within groups; and

(e)   are cost-effective to apply.

Basic financial instruments

Rules vs principles-based solution

13   The classification of financial instruments as 'basic' or 'other' in FRS 102 is dependent on a list of prescriptive conditions. The Accounting Council considered whether a principles-based solution to relaxing the conditions, based on the principle articulated in IFRS 9 in respect of the classification of financial assets, would be more effective, but advises retaining the rules-based conditions of FRS 102 instead, for the following reasons:

(a) the IFRS 9 principle is yet untested in practice and, at the time of giving the advice, the IASB is currently debating possible amendments to IFRS 9; and

(b) the IFRS 9 principle in relation to the classification of financial instruments only applies to financial assets. The classification conditions in FRS 102, however, apply equally to debt instruments that are assets or liabilities.

Interaction with Regulations or LLP Regulations on measurement of certain financial instruments

Subsequent to receiving the responses to FRED 54, the Accounting Council was made **14** aware of an additional issue in relation to a conflict between the Regulations and LLP Regulations and the requirements in FRS 102, as originally issued, on measurement of some financial liabilities. The original text of FRS 102 could have resulted in the standard requiring certain financial liabilities to be measured at fair value where such measurement may be prohibited by the Regulations. The Regulations prohibit the measurement of financial liabilities at fair value, except for those held as part of a trading portfolio, that are derivatives or where permitted by EU-adopted IFRS.

For example, the original text of FRS 102 would have required certain financial liabilities, **15** where the cash outflows are linked to non-financial variables specific to one party to the contract, to be classified as non-basic and measured at fair value. Fair value measurement is not permitted for such liabilities under EU-adopted IFRS and so would be prohibited by the Regulations.

Such liabilities commonly arise in insurance contracts where the amount an insurer is **16** liable to pay depends on the occurrence of insured events specific to the insured party and its activities.

The Accounting Council is aware that there are divergent views on what constitutes a 'non- **17** financial variable' in other cases. For example, there is no clear consensus as to whether measures of performance such as turnover, profits or EBITDA are 'non-financial variables … specific to a party to the contract'. The Accounting Council is unable to resolve this divergence as to do so would involve interpreting EU-adopted IFRS on an issue that the IFRS Interpretations Committee has so far not reached a definitive conclusion.

Similarly, FRS 102 would have required that financial assets which are similarly linked to **18** non-financial variables specific to one party to the contract, be classified as non-basic and measured at fair value through profit or loss. Although Regulations permit financial assets to be classified at fair value, this classification is only available as permitted by EU-adopted IFRS, which in some cases is restricted to fair value through other comprehensive income.

The Accounting Council also notes that there may be other non-basic financial assets **19** and liabilities that EU-adopted IFRS, and hence the Regulations, would not permit to be measured at fair value through profit or loss although it expected that such instruments would be rare in practice.

As a result, the Accounting Council advises the inclusion of an exception in Section 12 **20** in respect of non-basic financial instruments where the Regulations would not permit the use of fair value through profit or loss, instead requiring them to be measured at amortised cost. In advising this, the Accounting Council is conscious that this exception would be applicable to a small number of entities under a narrow set of circumstances.

Loans in the social housing sector

21   In response to FRED 54, a number of respondents from the social housing sector raised concerns about the classification of certain lending arrangements common within that sector. It was noted that a number of these arrangements were structured in different ways but often to achieve the same economic outcome. After detailed consideration the Accounting Council advises that a loan cannot be classified as basic if it includes contractual terms giving the lender the unilateral option to change the terms of that loan, for example from a pre-determined fixed rate to a variable rate or to a different fixed rate chosen by the lender, even if the holder can avoid it by repaying the loan.

Structured financial instruments

22   In response to FRED 54, a number of respondents raised questions about the classification of certain financial instruments that were structured in a complex way and requested that the final amendment clarify their classification in accordance with FRS 102. The Accounting Council noted that such structured financial instruments are not based on contracts that are standardised across an industry. As a result, the repayment of principal and interest on such loans can be impacted in a complex way by a number of different variables defined in the contractual terms. The Accounting Council noted that it was not possible to conclude on the classification of such financial instruments without a close reading of the individual contracts and an understanding of the detailed clauses. Therefore, the Accounting Council advises that the reporting entity's directors should apply their judgement to determine whether the contractual terms enable a financial instrument to be classified as basic in accordance with the requirements in FRS 102.

Classification subsequent to initial recognition

23   The Accounting Council noted that the initial classification assessment of a financial instrument should take into account the relevant clauses dealing with the returns and any subsequent contractual variations relating to returns, prepayments and extensions of terms etc. Once the classification of a financial instrument is determined at initial recognition, no re-assessment is required at subsequent dates unless there is a modification of contractual terms.

Hedge accounting

24   The previous hedge accounting requirements in FRS 102 narrowly defined the types of permitted arrangements that may qualify for hedge accounting, which was not necessarily representative of an entity's risk management objectives and hedging practices.

25   The Accounting Council's aim was to develop new hedge accounting requirements that allow for a reflection of an entity's hedging activities in the financial statements that is consistent with the entity's risk management objectives and are, as far as appropriate for constituents of FRS 102, consistent with IFRS.

26   These amendments to FRS 102 have been developed on the basis of IFRS, and substantively adopt the terminology and hedge accounting requirements in IFRS 9, with notable exceptions described in more detail below. The Accounting Council has been mindful that the requirements in IFRS 9 deal with hedging transactions that can be far more complex than those typically entered into by entities applying FRS 102. The departures from the requirements in IFRS 9 are therefore intended to simplify the application of hedge accounting.

Eligible hedged items

The Accounting Council was requested to reconsider the exclusion of explicit macrohedging   **27**
provisions in FRS 102, similar to those in IAS 39 *Financial Instruments: Recognition and Measurement*. After consideration of the specific concerns of entities that raised this as an issue, the Accounting Council concluded that in the interest of developing straight-forward hedge accounting requirements that are relevant for a majority of entities, it retains its previous advice stated in FRED 51. Entities wishing to apply the IFRS macrohedging provisions are able to apply the accounting policy choice in FRS 102 to apply IAS 39 and/ or IFRS 9 instead.

Qualifying hedge accounting conditions

The qualifying hedge accounting conditions in FRS 102 have been simplified compared   **28**
to the criteria set out in IFRS 9, with the aim of making hedge accounting easier to apply.

Under the amended hedge accounting requirements it is not necessary to achieve a   **29**
prescribed level of effectiveness in a hedging relationship in order to qualify for hedge accounting, but an economic relationship between the hedged item and the hedging instrument has to exist. In response to feedback on FRED 51, an explanation has been added of when an economic relationship between a hedged item and a hedging instrument exists, which is in line with IFRS 9.

The Accounting Council notes that although a quantitative assessment of hedge effectiveness   **30**
is not required, it is nevertheless important for entities to identify the different factors that affect the valuation of the hedging instrument and hedged item, including factors that may be a source of hedge ineffectiveness. Entities are therefore required to identify and document causes of hedge ineffectiveness before they commence hedge accounting, to ensure that ineffectiveness is properly captured in profit or loss.

Entities are required to document a hedging relationship, to avoid hedge accounting being   **31**
misused. The hedge documentation requirements are, however, relatively informal and undemanding and should not be an administrative burden for entities in practice.

Discontinuing hedge accounting

These amendments permit entities to discontinue hedge accounting voluntarily. This is a   **32**
departure from IFRS 9. The Accounting Council considered that the restrictions in IFRS 9 on discontinuance are unnecessarily onerous, and instead has retained the existing option of voluntary discontinuation. An entity must document the election to discontinue hedge accounting, which is consistent with the requirement for documentation at the start of hedge accounting.

Disclosure

These amendments retain substantially the disclosure requirements of FRS 102. The   **33**
disclosure requirements in relation to the hedge accounting requirements in IFRS 9, contained in IFRS 7 *Financial Instruments: Disclosure* focus on risks and risk mitigation through hedging. The Accounting Council notes that risk disclosures are not generally required in FRS 102, except for financial institutions.

Transitional provisions for first-time adopters of FRS 102

34   The Accounting Council's aim was to develop transitional provisions that are consistent with the permissive hedge accounting regime of FRS 102 and give entities a choice over whether to commence, continue or end hedge accounting on transition to FRS 102. Some respondents to FRED 51 were concerned that this flexibility may be abused, as it allows entities to apply a degree of hindsight. The Accounting Council is mindful of this possible exploitation of the transitional provisions. Nevertheless, on balance it believes that in the interests of the majority of entities, especially entities that have not applied hedge accounting before, flexibility should take precedence over restrictions aimed at preventing abuse.

35   The Accounting Council is conscious that entities may have applied diverse hedge accounting practices before the adoption of FRS 102. Entities may have applied the hedge accounting requirements in accordance with FRS 26 (IAS 39) *Financial Instruments: Recognition and Measurement* or may have applied synthetic accounting practices permitted under SSAP 20 *Foreign currency translation*. Accommodating these different accounting practices introduces complexity that the transitional provisions need to address. Under the transitional provisions, regardless of what accounting practices were applied previously, entities have the choice to continue hedge accounting in accordance with FRS 102, provided the conditions for hedge accounting are met. Entities that elect not to apply the FRS 102 hedge accounting requirements, have to comply with the applicable measurement requirements for assets and liabilities set out elsewhere in FRS 102 from the date of transition.

36   The amendments are issued after the date of transition to FRS 102 for many entities. The transitional provisions take this into account by providing an extended deadline for hedge documentation on first-time adoption.

Alternative reporting of economic hedges

37   The Accounting Council advises modifying the provision in Section 11 to allow the designation of loan commitments at fair value through profit or loss (in addition to the designation of debt instruments at fair value through profit or loss). This will have the effect of allowing economic hedge accounting where an entity balances the risks from a first instrument by taking out a second which is measured at fair value: it will be able to choose to measure the first at fair value too, thus matching the movements in profit and reflecting, in financial reporting, the combined economic effect of the instruments.

Impairment provisions

38   Originally it was planned to amend FRS 102 prior to its effective date in respect of the requirements relating to hedge accounting and the impairment of financial assets. The IASB's project on the new IFRS impairment model is delayed and the FRC's consultation on introducing equivalent requirements in FRS 102 has therefore been deferred. Respondents to FRED 51 requested the exemption of certain entities from the requirement to adopt the impairment accounting requirements in FRS 102 until the new impairment requirements in FRS 102 are finalised.

39   The Accounting Council deliberated on the likely impact of the adoption of the impairment accounting requirements in FRS 102. It concluded that the incurred loss impairment model in FRS 102 is consistent with UK GAAP, as applicable prior to the introduction of FRS 102. The Accounting Council considers that it is therefore unnecessary to provide a temporary relief from the impairment accounting requirements in FRS 102.

Effective date

The Accounting Council advises that the amendments should be effective from the **40** effective date of FRS 102 (ie accounting periods beginning on or after 1 January 2015), and therefore no amendment to the effective date is required.

Approval of this advice

This advice to the FRC was approved by the Accounting Council on 19 June 2014.   **41**

The Accounting Council's Advice to the FRC to issue Amendments to FRS 102 – Pension obligations

Introduction

1   This report provides an overview of the main issues that have been considered by the Accounting Council in advising the Financial Reporting Council (FRC) to issue *Amendments to FRS 102 The Financial Reporting Standard applicable in the UK and Republic of Ireland – Pension obligations*.

2   The FRC, in accordance with the *Statutory Auditors (Amendment of Companies Act 2006 and Delegation of Functions etc) Order 2012* (SI 2012/1741), is a prescribed body for issuing accounting standards in the UK. The *Foreword to Accounting Standards* sets out the application of accounting standards in the Republic of Ireland.

3   In accordance with the *FRC Codes and Standards: procedures*, any proposal to issue, amend or withdraw a code or standard is put to the FRC Board with the full advice of the relevant Councils and/or the Codes & Standards Committee. Ordinarily, the FRC Board will only reject the advice put to it where:

(a)   it is apparent that a significant group of stakeholders has not been adequately consulted;

(b)   the necessary assessment of the impact of the proposal has not been completed, including an analysis of costs and benefits;

(c)   insufficient consideration has been given to the timing or cost of implementation; or

(d)   the cumulative impact of a number of proposals would make the adoption of an otherwise satisfactory proposal inappropriate.

4   The FRC has established the Accounting Council as the relevant Council to assist it in the setting of accounting standards.

Advice

5   The Accounting Council is advising the FRC to issue *Amendments to FRS 102 The Financial Reporting Standard applicable in the UK and Republic of Ireland – Pension obligations*.

6   The amendments will resolve an issue of uncertainty over the requirements of FRS 102 in relation to a commitment to make payments under a 'schedule of contributions' to a defined benefit pension plan which the entity accounts for on a defined benefit basis, and therefore reduce potential diversity in practice and the cost of compliance with FRS 102.

7   The Accounting Council's Advice to the FRC to issue FRS 102 *The Financial Reporting Standard applicable in the UK and Republic of Ireland* was set out in that standard. The Accounting Council's Advice to the FRC on these amendments will be included in the revised FRS 102.

Background

8   After the publication of FRS 102 in March 2013 the FRC issued, in October 2013, a Press Notice[23] addressing the accounting in accordance with EU-adopted IFRS for a 'schedule of contributions' payable by an entity to a defined benefit pension plan. Subsequently

---

[23] *FRC PN 089* Findings of the FRC in respect of the accounts of WH Smith Plc for the year ended 31 August 2012.

the FRC received enquiries about the accounting for similar circumstances by entities applying FRS 102.

The issue concerns whether or not an entity applying FRS 102 should have regard to the **9** principles of IFRIC 14 *IAS 19 – The Limit on a Defined Benefit Asset, Minimum Funding Requirements and their Interaction* where it might be relevant to its circumstances. There appeared to be a diversity of views on the matter, and because the potential implications for an entity's financial statements could be significant the FRC decided to address the matter outside the intended three-yearly review cycle for FRS 102.

The Accounting Council considered the responses to the consultation FRED 55 *Draft* **10** *Amendments to FRS 102 – Pension obligations*, which was issued in August 2014, in developing its advice.

Objective

In developing its advice to the FRC, the Accounting Council was guided by the overriding **11** objective to enable users of accounts to receive high-quality understandable financial reporting proportionate to the size and complexity of the entity and users' information needs.

In meeting this objective, the FRC aims to provide succinct financial reporting standards **12** that:

(a) have consistency with international accounting standards through the application of an IFRS-based solution unless an alternative clearly better meets the overriding objective;

(b) reflect up-to-date thinking and developments in the way entities operate and the transactions they undertake;

(c) balance consistent principles for accounting by all UK and Republic of Ireland entities with practical solutions, based on size, complexity, public interest and users' information needs;

(d) promote efficiency within groups; and

(e) are cost-effective to apply.

Proportionate measurement of the net defined benefit liability for a defined benefit plan

The Accounting Council considered whether FRS 102 required an entity with a defined **13** benefit plan to consider the principles of IFRIC 14 in interpreting its requirements to measure the net defined benefit liability. The Accounting Council noted that there appeared to be uncertainty over this issue and that there was the possibility of significant diversity arising in accounting practice, particularly because the amounts that might be recognised (or not) could be very significant.

The Accounting Council considers that for entities applying FRS 102, the recognition **14** of the net defined benefit liability or asset (which may be limited by paragraph 28.22) for a defined benefit pension plan as the net total of the present value of the obligations under the plan and the fair value of the plan assets is a proportionate way to measure the present obligation to employees as a result of service rendered. It noted that in some circumstances IFRIC 14 would result in an additional liability being recognised in relation to a schedule of contributions that had been agreed with the defined benefit plan in order to address a deficit that had arisen on the basis of the funding assumptions. It further noted that the measurement of the present value of the obligations under the plan for funding purposes differs from the measurement for accounting purposes, but they are different measurements of the same obligation, not separate obligations.

15   Therefore the Accounting Council advises that, as a practical and proportionate solution, in measuring its defined benefit obligation an entity need not include the present value of contributions payable that arise from an agreement with the defined benefit plan to fund a deficit. The Accounting Council also advises that Section 28 *Employee Benefits* explicitly states that, in applying FRS 102, no additional liabilities shall be recognised in respect of an agreement with the defined benefit plan to fund a deficit (such as a schedule of contributions). This should ensure there are no divergent interpretations of the scope of Section 21 *Provisions and Contingencies* in relation to a schedule of contributions, because they are clearly within the scope of Section 28, and therefore outside the scope of Section 21.

16   The Accounting Council considered another potential solution to determining whether or not an additional obligation should be recognised in certain circumstances. It noted the interaction with the recognition of a defined benefit plan asset, and considered whether removing the restriction on recognising a defined benefit plan asset in some circumstances might be an alternative solution. However, the Accounting Council rejected this because it could have the unintended consequence of permitting an asset to be recognised where other factors would indicate the reporting entity was not able to recover the surplus.

17   These amendments to FRS 102 do not affect the accounting for a schedule of contributions or other funding agreement between a reporting entity and a multi-employer plan, which is set out in paragraph 28.11A of FRS 102. Where an entity participates in a defined benefit plan that is a multi-employer plan accounted for as if it were a defined contribution plan, it shall recognise a liability for the contributions payable that arise from the agreement (to the extent that they relate to a deficit) because this is the most cost-effective way of recognising the entity's obligation to employees as a result of service rendered. This contrasts with the approach for defined benefit plans because the obligation has already been recognised as the net defined benefit liability.

18   The majority of respondents to FRED 55 supported the proposal.

Effect of a restriction on the recoverability of a plan surplus

19   The Accounting Council also noted that FRS 102 does not specify where an entity shall recognise the effects of a restriction on the recoverability of a plan surplus, and therefore FRS 102 would require it to be recognised in profit or loss. A plan surplus may be irrecoverable because the entity is not able to recover the surplus through reduced contributions in the future or through refunds from the plan (see paragraph 28.22 of FRS 102). The Accounting Council considers that, except for any amount included in net interest on the net defined benefit liability, the effect of any such restriction should be recognised in other comprehensive income and advises that paragraph 28.25 is amended so that any such amounts are part of remeasurements, and therefore recognised in other comprehensive income. This is consistent with IAS 19 *Employee Benefits*.

Disclosure

20   Four respondents to FRED 55 commented on the benefits of an entity disclosing the amounts it had committed to pay under a schedule of contributions, and some requested clarification that the requirement in paragraph 28.41(a) of FRS 102 to disclose the funding policy was intended to include such disclosure.

The Accounting Council agreed that the disclosure of information about the amount and timing of payments intended to fund a deficit in a defined benefit plan would be useful information for users of financial statements. Although this should already be covered by the requirement to describe the funding policy, the Accounting Council advises that paragraph 28.41(a) is amended to clarify this. **21**

Effective date

The Accounting Council advises that these amendments should be effective from the effective date of FRS 102 (ie accounting periods beginning on or after 1 January 2015), and therefore no amendment to the effective date of FRS 102 is required. **22**

Approval of this Advice

This advice to the FRC was approved by the Accounting Council on 15 January 2015. **23**

The Accounting Council's Advice to the FRC to issue Amendments to FRS 102 – Small entities and other minor amendments

Introduction

1   This report provides an overview of the main issues that have been considered by the Accounting Council in advising the Financial Reporting Council (FRC) to issue *Amendments to FRS 102 The Financial Reporting Standard applicable in the UK and Republic of Ireland – Small entities and other minor amendments* incorporating the Council's advice following the Consultation Document *Accounting standards for small entities – Implementation of the EU Accounting Directive*, FRED 59 *Draft Amendments to FRS 102 The Financial Reporting Standard applicable in the UK and Republic of Ireland – Small entities and other minor amendments* and FRED 61 *Draft amendments to FRS 102 – Share-based payment arrangements with cash alternatives.*

2   The FRC, in accordance with the *Statutory Auditors (Amendment of Companies Act 2006 and Delegation of Functions etc) Order 2012* (SI 2012/1741), is a prescribed body for issuing accounting standards in the UK. The *Foreword to Accounting Standards* sets out the application of accounting standards in the Republic of Ireland.

3   In accordance with the *FRC Codes and Standards: procedures*, any proposal to issue, amend or withdraw a code or standard is put to the FRC Board with the full advice of the relevant Councils and/or the Codes & Standards Committee. Ordinarily, the FRC Board will only reject the advice put to it where:

(a)   it is apparent that a significant group of stakeholders has not been adequately consulted;

(b)   the necessary assessment of the impact of the proposal has not been completed, including an analysis of costs and benefits;

(c)   insufficient consideration has been given to the timing or cost of implementation; or

(d)   the cumulative impact of a number of proposals would make the adoption of an otherwise satisfactory proposal inappropriate.

4   The FRC has established the Accounting Council as the relevant Council to assist it in the setting of accounting standards.

Advice

5   The Accounting Council is advising the FRC to issue *Amendments to FRS 102 The Financial Reporting Standard applicable in the UK and Republic of Ireland – Small entities and other minor amendments.*

6   The Accounting Council advises that these proposals will maintain consistency of accounting standards with company law and will improve the financial reporting by small entities by, for example, requiring the recognition of various financial instruments that the *Financial Reporting Standard for Smaller Entities (effective January 2015)* (FRSSE) does not currently require.

7   The Accounting Council's Advice to the FRC to issue FRS 102 *The Financial Reporting Standard applicable in the UK and Republic of Ireland* was set out in the standard. The Accounting Council's Advice to the FRC in respect of these amendments will be included in the revised FRS 102.

Background

The new EU Accounting Directive (Directive 2013/34/EU of the European Parliament and   **8**
of the Council of 26 June 2013) is being implemented in the UK and Republic of Ireland.
In doing so there are changes to company law to reflect new requirements and, where
considered appropriate, to take advantage of new options that are available. Accounting
standards are developed within the context set by company law; when company law
changes, amendments may also be required to accounting standards.

In September 2014, the FRC issued a Consultation Document *Accounting standards*   **9**
for small entities – Implementation of the EU Accounting Directive[24] (the Consultation
Document), outlining its proposal that small entities will apply FRS 102 *The Financial*
Reporting Standard applicable in the UK and Republic of Ireland. It was proposed
that a new section would be inserted into FRS 102 setting out the presentation and
disclosure requirements applicable to small entities, which would be based on the new
legal provisions, and as a consequence the FRSSE would be withdrawn. A small number
of other amendments to FRS 102 would also be necessary to maintain consistency with
company law. The Accounting Council considered the responses to the Consultation
Document in developing FRED 59. It has also considered the responses to FRED 59,
which was issued in February 2015, in developing its advice on these amendments.

In addition, in April 2015 the FRC issued FRED 61 to address an implementation issue in   **10**
relation to FRS 102. The responses to FRED 61 have also been considered in developing
this advice.

Objective

In developing its advice to the FRC, the Accounting Council was guided by the overriding   **11**
objective to enable users of accounts to receive high-quality understandable financial
reporting proportionate to the size and complexity of the entity and users' information
needs.

In meeting this objective, the FRC aims to provide succinct financial reporting standards   **12**
that:

(a)   have consistency with international accounting standards through the application
       of an IFRS-based solution unless an alternative clearly better meets the overriding
       objective;
(b)   reflect up-to-date thinking and developments in the way entities operate and the
       transactions they undertake;
(c)   balance consistent principles for accounting by all UK and Republic of Ireland
       entities with practical solutions, based on size, complexity, public interest and users'
       information needs;
(d)   promote efficiency within groups; and
(e)   are cost-effective to apply.

Small entities regime

In the Consultation Document, the FRC proposed that the FRSSE should be withdrawn and   **13**
that, for small entities ineligible for the micro-entities regime, it should be replaced with
a new Section 1A *Small Entities* within FRS 102. It was proposed that Section 1A would
set out the presentation and disclosure requirements applicable to small entities, whilst
the recognition and measurement requirements of the remainder of FRS 102 would apply.

---

[24] *Available on the FRC website (www.frc.org.uk).*

This proposal was supported by the majority of respondents. In particular, respondents supported the proposals that:

(a)   the FRSSE should be withdrawn (see FRED 60 *Draft amendments to FRS 100 and FRS 101*);

(b)   Section 1A should apply to all entities (that are required to prepare financial statements that present a true and fair view) meeting the relevant criteria and not just companies; and

(c)   small entities should apply the same recognition and measurement criteria as other entities applying FRS 102.

14   FRED 59 set out these proposals in more detail.

15   The Accounting Council notes that, whilst the financial statements of a small company must give a true and fair view, the new legal framework for small companies restricts the specific disclosures that may be required of small companies. As these restrictions do not apply to entities that are not companies, the Accounting Council considered whether to have two small entities regimes, one applying to companies and one to other entities. As set out in the Consultation Document and FRED 59, the Accounting Council advises that it may be confusing to have two different sets of presentation and disclosure requirements for small entities, depending on legal form, particularly when the overall objective of the financial statements is the same (that they give a true and fair view), and therefore Section 1A should apply to all entities meeting the relevant criteria.

16   Eligibility for the small companies regime is set out in company law. The Accounting Council advises that Section 1A should apply to companies eligible for the small companies regime, LLPs eligible for the small LLPs regime and any other entity that would have met the criteria for the small companies regime had they been companies. This is broadly the same as the scope of the FRSSE. At the time of giving this advice the Accounting Council notes that different thresholds apply to the small companies regime and the small LLPs regime and entities will need to take care to ensure they are eligible to apply Section 1A.

Presentation and disclosure

17   A key feature of the new small companies regime set out in the new Accounting Directive is that it specifies the maximum mandatory disclosures to be included in a small company's financial statements, which may not be added to. However, the financial statements of a small company must still give a true and fair view of the financial performance and financial position of the entity; this has been emphasised in Section 1A. The directors of a company will need to consider whether additional disclosures are necessary to give a true and fair view and, if so, provide those additional disclosures.

18   The Accounting Council advises that, as the disclosures required by FRS 102 of larger entities are those that are usually considered necessary (but not necessarily sufficient) to give a true and fair view, a small entity should be encouraged to consider all of these disclosures in order to determine the additional disclosures necessary in its own circumstances.

19   In addition, the Accounting Council considers that it will be helpful to small entities applying FRS 102 for the disclosures required by law to be included and cross-referenced to the same or similar disclosures elsewhere in FRS 102. This has been set out in Appendix C to Section 1A, where the drafting of the disclosures is as close as possible to the company law requirements, with a note of the source of the legal requirement, and an indication of which paragraphs of FRS 102 address similar requirements.

There are a small number of specific disclosures that the Accounting Council considers will be particularly useful to users of the financial statements of a small entity, including a statement of compliance with FRS 102 and a note of dividends declared and paid or payable. The Accounting Council advises specifically encouraging small entities to provide these disclosures. 20

Another feature of the small companies regime is that additional 'statements' may not be required of small companies. This includes a statement of comprehensive income, a statement of changes in equity and the cash flow statement. Section 1A makes it clear that such statements are not required of small entities, but the Accounting Council considers that a statement of comprehensive income and a statement of changes in equity (or statement of income and retained earnings) will be useful to users of the financial statements of a small entity in explaining the financial performance for the reporting period and the effect that this has had on financial position. Therefore the Accounting Council advises that a small entity is encouraged to provide these statements. 21

The Accounting Council notes that, although the FRSSE encouraged the presentation of a cash flow statement by small entities, FRS 1 (Revised 1996) *Cash flow statements* simply exempted small entities from presenting a cash flow statement on the basis that it was not required by company law for a small company. The Accounting Council advises retaining the exemption from FRS 1. As a result, a small entity choosing to apply 'full' FRS 102 is not required to present a cash flow statement. 22

Recognition and measurement

The Accounting Council advises that small entities should follow the recognition and measurement requirements of FRS 102. This will improve financial reporting by small entities by, for example, requiring the recognition of various financial instruments that the FRSSE does not currently require, such as derivatives like interest rate swaps and forward foreign currency contracts. Almost all respondents to FRED 59 agreed with this; those that did not generally suggested that changes should be made to FRS 102 that would apply to all entities. These suggestions will be considered as part of the triennial review of FRS 102. 23

In FRS 105 *The Financial Reporting Standard applicable to the Micro-entities Regime* the Accounting Council has considered and applied a set of principles for simplifying the recognition and measurement requirements for micro-entities. For the larger small entities within the scope of FRS 102 the Accounting Council advises that the principle it has applied is that there should not be recognition and measurement differences from the requirements applicable to larger entities. This reinstates the principle of consistency in accounting policies between those entities that are smaller and those that are larger that applied when the FRSSE was originally developed. 24

A small number of additional transitional provisions have been provided for small entities applying FRS 102 for the first time for an accounting period that commences before 1 January 2017 (see paragraphs 42 to 44). 25

Other matters relating to the small entities regime

Some respondents to FRED 59 noted that Section 1A did not address situations where a small entity voluntarily chooses to prepare consolidated financial statements. The Accounting Council advises that this is addressed in Section 1A. 26

Company law and the new Accounting Directive restrict the disclosures that can be required of small companies in relation to related party transactions. In particular, disclosure 27 can only be required of transactions not conducted under normal market conditions. Respondents noted that it could be burdensome for a small entity to identify those related party transactions that were not conducted under normal market conditions, because a significant degree of judgement would be involved. Instead, disclosure of all transactions with the specified related parties would meet the legal disclosure requirement. The Accounting Council notes that the Accounting Regulatory Committee reached a conclusion in 2007 that disclosing all related party transactions would comply with the requirement to disclose those not conducted under normal market conditions (as previously set out in paragraph 36 of Appendix IV to FRS 8 *Related Party Disclosures*). Therefore it advises including guidance in Appendix C to Section 1A that notes that although disclosure is only required of material transactions with the specified related parties that have not been concluded under normal market conditions, small entities disclosing all transactions with such related parties would still be compliant with company law.

True and fair view

28   In Section 1A the drafting of various requirements is as close as possible to the company law requirements, reflecting the need for the financial statements of a small entity to give a true and fair view. The Accounting Council noted that Section 3 *Financial Statement Presentation* expressed some of the same requirements in a different way, and advises that Section 3 is amended to more closely reflect the requirements of company law. These changes are not considered to have any substantive effect as 'true and fair' and 'presents fairly' are synonymous, being different articulations of the same concept, as confirmed by legal opinion.

Other minor amendments

29   A small number of other amendments were also necessary to maintain consistency between FRS 102 and company law. This was not a comprehensive review of the requirements of FRS 102.

30   The amendments include:

(a)   Greater flexibility in relation to the format of the profit and loss account and balance sheet, which will allow entities choosing this option to adopt a presentation that is closer to that applied by entities preparing 'IAS accounts'. The Accounting Council advises that these new options available in company law should be available to entities applying FRS 102, but that a framework should be provided in FRS 102 to assist entities applying it.

(b)   Revisions to certain requirements relating to financial instruments that are, or may be, measured at fair value. The new Accounting Directive permits measurement of certain financial instruments at fair value where it is in accordance with EU-adopted IFRS; previously this was restricted to IFRS endorsed by 5 September 2006. The consequences of this change, as well as any interaction with IFRS 9 *Financial Instruments* that was issued in July 2014 and which an entity may make an accounting policy choice to apply under paragraphs 11.2(c) and 12.2(c), have been considered. As a result, the Accounting Council advises that some amendments are made for compliance with company law, although these are only likely to affect a minority of entities applying FRS 102. In addition, Appendix IV: *Note on legal requirements* advises that entities applying IFRS 9 will need to consider an override of the Regulations for the purposes of giving a true and fair view, in order to recognise certain fair value gains or losses in other comprehensive income.

(c)   Revising the 'seriously prejudicial' exemption that applies, in extremely rare circumstances, to disclosure of provisions and contingencies. The Accounting Council notes that company law requires certain disclosures in relation to provisions and contingencies, and that it advises consistency of disclosure by entities that are companies and those that are not. Therefore the 'seriously prejudicial' exemption has been redrafted to remind companies of the legal disclosure requirements and ensure that equivalent disclosures are provided by all entities.

(d)   Revising the maximum period over which goodwill and other intangible assets may be amortised to 10 years, in those exceptional cases where an entity is unable to make a reliable estimate of the asset's useful economic life. The Accounting Council advises that, as this only applies in exceptional cases, the change in the maximum period so soon after it was introduced in the first edition of FRS 102 should have a limited impact in practice.

(e)   Prohibiting the reversal of impairment losses for goodwill.

(f)   Clarifying that a public benefit entity may apply merger accounting to an entity combination that is a merger provided that it is permitted by the statutory framework under which it reports. The new Accounting Directive only permits companies to apply merger accounting for group reconstructions and the Accounting Council advises that this amendment is made to ensure merger accounting is not applied by public benefit entities that are companies where not permitted in law. Some respondents to FRED 59 suggested that FRS 102 should continue to require the use of merger accounting by all public benefit entity combinations meeting the definition and criteria of a merger, through requiring the use of the true and fair override. The Accounting Council noted that 'true mergers' (other than those that might be considered group reconstructions) are not likely to be common. However, Appendix IV: *Note on legal requirements* notes that an individual public benefit entity may apply the true and fair override if it considers it appropriate to its circumstances, and provides the corresponding disclosures.

(g)   Amending the definitions of a 'related party' and 'turnover' in accordance with changes in company law.

(h)   Clarifying in paragraph 1.12(c) that, because company law requires certain disclosures relating to financial instruments, a qualifying entity choosing to provide reduced disclosures will not be exempt from all the disclosure requirements of Sections 11 and 12. This was previously addressed in paragraph A4.10, which notes that preparers need to have regard to the requirements of company law in addition to accounting standards.

The Accounting Council noted that in relation to small entities, Section 1A of FRS 102   **31** will include all the disclosure requirements set out in company law, but that FRS 102 does not presently include all the equivalent disclosures for larger entities. The majority of respondents to the Consultation Document agreed that the current approach for larger entities should not be amended because this would increase the length of FRS 102 and make it potentially less user-friendly, especially as a significant number of larger entities applying FRS 102 are not companies and the additional disclosure requirements would not be applicable to them. Some respondents suggested including any additional disclosures as an appendix, but noted that this could be considered as part of the triennial review of FRS 102. The Accounting Council advises not amending FRS 102 for additional disclosures for larger entities at present, but notes that the suggestion of an appendix could be reconsidered at a later date.

The Accounting Council noted that in some areas the amendments made to the Regulations   **32** and the Small Companies Regulations make new accounting options available alongside existing requirements. In these areas it is not necessary to amend FRS 102, as it already complies with the existing requirements. The Accounting Council considered the following two areas:

(a)   Equity method in individual accounts – paragraph 29A of the Regulations and the Small Companies Regulations permits participating interests to be accounted for in the financial statements of an investor using the equity method. FRS 102 already includes a number of options for accounting for such investments (see paragraph 9.26) and the Accounting Council does not advise introducing this option at present.

(b)   Contingent consideration in a business combination – an amendment to paragraph 36 of the Regulations and the Small Companies Regulations would permit contingent consideration in a business combination to be measured and remeasured at fair value, which would be consistent with EU-adopted IFRS (IFRS 3 *Business Combinations* (revised 2008)). The Accounting Council notes that the requirements of FRS 102 are based on IFRS 3 (issued 2004) and does not advise amending the accounting for contingent consideration outside the context of a wider review of the accounting for business combinations. Therefore an amendment to accounting for contingent consideration in a business combination is not proposed at present.

33   In addition, the following amendments are advised:

(a)   Two of the examples following paragraph 11.13 are being amended for clarity.
(b)   The reduced disclosures for subsidiaries, set out in paragraphs 1.8 to 1.13, have been amended in relation to financial instruments measured at fair value through profit or loss to ensure they are consistent with company law disclosure requirements.

Residents' Management Companies

34   In considering the feedback received from the FRC's previous consultations, the Accounting Council noted that no clear consensus existed amongst respondents on the appropriate basis of accounting in the statutory financial statements of residents' management companies[25] where service charge monies are held on trust in accordance with section 42 of the Landlord and Tenant Act 1987. However, there was general agreement that no change should be made to FRS 102, or any other relevant financial reporting standard (including FRS 105), to address such a narrow and sector-specific issue.

35   The Accounting Council considered this issue carefully. It assessed the case for further intervention by reference to the FRC's published *Principles for the development of Codes, Standards and Guidance*[26] and, in particular, the extent to which the anticipated benefits from any changes to current practices would outweigh the costs incurred by the entities involved. It agreed with respondents that this matter does not merit a change in accounting standards, and therefore advises that no changes are made to FRS 102 (or FRS 105) that are specific to residents' management companies.

Share-based payment arrangements with cash alternatives

36   After the introduction of FRS 102, it was brought to the FRC's attention that the accounting it required for share-based payment transactions that give the reporting entity an option to settle in cash or equity could result in the recognition of a liability even though the conditions for the recognition of a liability under the standard were not clearly met. The Accounting Council notes that the requirement to account for such transactions as cash-settled is more onerous than the requirements under EU-adopted IFRS, under which they would generally be treated as equity-settled, since it requires the measurement of the obligation at fair value at each reporting date.

---

[25] *An organisation which may be referred to in the lease, which is responsible for the provision of services, and manages and arranges maintenance of the property, but which does not necessarily have any legal interest in the property.*

[26] *This can be found on the FRC's website at www.frc.org.uk/FRC-Documents/FRC/About-the-FRC/Principles-for-the-development-of-Codes.pdf.*

The Accounting Council therefore advises that FRS 102 should be amended with the result that such transactions are accounted for as equity-settled share-based payment arrangements unless the option to settle in equity has no commercial substance or the entity has created a valid expectation that it would settle in cash.

37

In some schemes the recipient may have an option to request settlement in cash or equity instruments. If an entity cannot avoid settling in cash should the recipient request it, FRS 102 requires the entity to account for the transaction as cash-settled by measuring the goods or services acquired at the fair value of the liability unless the cash settlement option has no commercial substance. The Accounting Council notes that this requirement is different to EU-adopted IFRS which requires the separate recognition of debt and equity components. The Accounting Council continues to believe that the simpler requirements of FRS 102 provide a practical and proportionate solution for those applying the standard and notes that this is generally consistent with the requirements in the IFRS for SMEs. In FRED 61 the exemption from cash-settlement accounting when the option to settle in cash has no commercial substance was omitted and the Accounting Council advises that this be retained in FRS 102.

38

The FRC had consulted on additional amendments that would have resulted in cash-settlement treatment for all share-based payment arrangements with terms that could result in the transfer of cash on the occurrence of an event outside the control of either party to the transaction. Some respondents commented that this could result in the recognition of a liability in situations when the probability of settlement in cash is remote. They also noted that the accounting for such transactions is under consideration by the IASB and its Interpretation Committee who have so far been unable to reach a conclusion. For the reasons noted by these respondents, the Accounting Council advises that FRS 102 should not be amended in this regard, but the need for further amendment be re-considered as part of the next review of the standard.

39

The FRC did not propose any additional transitional exemptions for entities that had chosen to early adopt FRS 102 and had granted awards under share-based payment arrangements that would be affected by the changes in FRED 61. The majority of respondents agreed that there was no need for additional transitional exemptions as such instances would be very rare and early adopters would have had the benefit of the transitional exemption for awards granted before the date of transition.

40

However, some respondents did identify an issue with the transitional exemption where greater clarity is needed. The transitional exemption in paragraph 35.10(b) of FRS 102 refers only to equity instruments granted before the date of transition. Some respondents noted that it was not clear if this reference also applies to the equity components of instruments that had been treated as compound instruments under FRS 20 or IFRS 2. The Accounting Council notes that the transitional exemption was intended to alleviate the costs of transition in respect of equity-settled share-based payment arrangements for companies that had previously applied the FRSSE, where such arrangements were not recognised, and for companies that had previously applied FRS 20 / IFRS 2 should FRS 102 require different accounting. As FRS 20 / IFRS 2 can result in compound instruments being partly accounted for as equity-settled and partly as cash-settled, the Accounting Council agrees it should be clarified that the reference to equity instruments includes the equity component of compound instruments accounted for in accordance with FRS 20 / IFRS 2. The Accounting Council also notes that there is no need for transitional exemptions to be added for liabilities not settled at the transition date, including those arising from arrangements previously treated as compound instruments, because the liability will not continue to be measured in the same way under FRS 102, being the fair value of the liability.

41

Transitional provisions for small entities

42 The Accounting Council considered whether transitional provisions should be provided for small entities applying FRS 102 for the first time. The Accounting Council noted that FRS 102 already includes Section 35 *Transition to this FRS*, which applies to any first-time adopter of FRS 102, which has a significant number of optional exemptions from full retrospective application of FRS 102 that are designed to reduce the burden of first-time adoption. This is particularly where it may be difficult to restate historical transactions on the basis otherwise required by FRS 102 because the relevant data would not have been obtained at the time the transaction occurred.

43 The Accounting Council advised in FRED 59 that no further transitional provisions were necessary for small entities that are not already provided for. Although the majority of respondents to FRED 59 agreed with this assessment, a small number of respondents suggested that additional transitional provisions should be made available. These suggestions related to areas where additional burdens may be incurred in applying FRS 102 for the first time because an entity's transition date to FRS 102 occurred before these amendments were finalised.

44 The Accounting Council considered these suggestions carefully and agreed to provide additional transitional exemptions for all small entities applying FRS 102 for the first time for an accounting period that commences before 1 January 2017. These relate to equity-settled share-based payment arrangements, financial instruments measured at fair value and financing transactions with related parties. On first-time application they provide relief from the full application of FRS 102 in the comparative period.

Effective date

45 The Accounting Council advises that, other than the replacement of paragraph 26.15 with new paragraphs 26.15 to 26.15B, these amendments should be effective for accounting periods beginning on or after 1 January 2016, with early application:

(a) permitted for accounting periods beginning on or after 1 January 2015 provided that *The Companies, Partnerships and Groups (Accounts and Reports) Regulations 2015* (SI 2015/980) are applied from the same date; and

(b) required if an entity applies *The Companies, Partnerships and Groups (Accounts and Reports) Regulations 2015* (SI 2015/980) to a reporting period beginning before 1 January 2016.

46 The Accounting Council advises that the replacement of paragraph 26.15 with new paragraphs 26.15 to 26.15B shall be effective for accounting periods beginning on or after 1 January 2015, with early application permitted in line with FRS 102 generally.

Approval of this Advice

47 This advice to the FRC was approved by the Accounting Council on 16 June 2015.

Appendix I:
Glossary

This glossary is an integral part of the Standard.

accounting policies	The specific principles, bases, conventions, rules and practices applied by an entity in preparing and presenting **financial statements**.
accrual basis (of accounting)	The effects of transactions and other events are recognised when they occur (and not as **cash** or its equivalent is received or paid) and they are recorded in the accounting records and reported in the **financial statements** of the periods to which they relate.
accumulating compensated absences	Compensated absences that are carried forward and can be used in future periods if the current period's entitlement is not used in full.
acquisition date	The date on which the acquirer obtains **control** of the acquiree.
Act	The Companies Act 2006
active market	A market in which all the following conditions exist: (a) the items traded in the market are homogeneous; (b) willing buyers and sellers can normally be found at any time; and (c) prices are available to the public.
actuarial assumptions	An entity's unbiased and mutually compatible best estimates of the demographic and financial variables that will determine the ultimate cost of providing post-employment benefits.
actuarial gains and losses	Changes in the **present value** of the **defined benefit obligation** resulting from: (a) experience adjustments (the effects of differences between the previous **actuarial assumptions** and what has actually occurred); and (b) the effects of changes in actuarial assumptions.
agent	An entity is acting as an agent when it does not have exposure to the significant risks and rewards associated with the sale of goods or the rendering of services. One feature indicating that an entity is acting as an agent is that the amount the entity earns is predetermined, being either a fixed fee per transaction or a stated percentage of the amount billed to the customer.
agricultural activity	The management by an entity of the biological transformation of **biological assets** for sale, into agricultural produce or into additional biological assets.
agricultural produce	The harvested product of the entity's **biological assets**.
amortisation	The systematic allocation of the **depreciable amount** of an **asset** over its **useful life**.

amortised cost (of a financial asset or financial liability)	The amount at which the **financial asset** or **financial liability** is measured at initial **recognition** minus principal repayments, plus or minus the cumulative **amortisation** using the **effective interest method** of any difference between that initial amount and the maturity amount, and minus any reduction (directly or through the use of an allowance account) for impairment or uncollectability.
asset	A resource controlled by the entity as a result of past events and from which future economic benefits are expected to flow to the entity.

asset held by a long-term employee benefit fund	An **asset** (other than non-transferable financial instruments issued by the reporting entity) that:
	 (a) is held by an entity (a fund) that is legally separate from the reporting entity and exists solely to pay or fund **employee benefits**; and
	 (b) is available to be used only to pay or fund employee benefits, is not available to the reporting entity's own creditors (even in bankruptcy), and cannot be returned to the reporting entity, unless either:
	    (i) the remaining assets of the fund are sufficient to meet all the related employee benefit obligations of the plan or the reporting entity; or
	    (ii) the assets are returned to the reporting entity to reimburse it for employee benefits already paid.

associate	An entity, including an unincorporated entity such as a partnership, over which the investor has **significant influence** and that is neither a **subsidiary** nor an interest in a **joint venture**.
biological asset	A living animal or plant.
borrowing costs	Interest and other costs incurred by an entity in connection with the borrowing of funds.
business	An integrated set of activities and **assets** conducted and managed for the purpose of providing: (a) a return to investors; or (b) lower costs or other economic benefits directly and proportionately to policyholders or participants. A business generally consists of inputs, processes applied to those inputs, and resulting outputs that are, or will be, used to generate **revenues**. If **goodwill** is present in a transferred set of activities and assets, the transferred set shall be presumed to be a business.
business combination	The bringing together of separate entities or **businesses** into one reporting entity.
carrying amount	The amount at which an **asset** or **liability** is recognised in the **statement of financial position**.
cash	Cash on hand and demand deposits.
cash equivalents	Short-term, highly liquid investments that are readily convertible to known amounts of **cash** and that are subject to an insignificant risk of changes in value.
cash flows	Inflows and outflows of **cash** and **cash equivalents**.

cash-generating unit	The smallest identifiable group of **assets** that generates cash inflows that are largely independent of the cash inflows from other assets or groups of assets.
cash-settled share-based payment transaction	A **share-based payment transaction** in which the entity acquires goods or services by incurring a **liability** to transfer **cash** or other **assets** to the supplier of those goods or services for amounts that are based on the price (or value) of the entity's shares or other equity instruments of the entity or another group entity.
change in accounting estimate	An adjustment of the **carrying amount** of an **asset** or a **liability**, or the amount of the periodic consumption of an asset, that results from the assessment of the present status of, and expected future benefits and obligations associated with, assets and liabilities. Changes in accounting estimates result from new information or new developments and, accordingly, are not corrections of **errors**.
class of assets	A grouping of **assets** of a similar nature and use in an entity's operations.
close members of the family of a person	Those family members who may be expected to influence, or be influenced by, that person in their dealings with the entity including: (a) that person's children and spouse or domestic partner; (b) children of that person's spouse or domestic partner; and (c) dependants of that person or that person's spouse or domestic partner.
closing rate	The spot exchange rate at the end of the **reporting period**
combination that is in substance is a gift	A combination carried out at nil or nominal consideration that is not a fair value exchange but in substance the gift of one entity to another.
commencement of lease term	The date from which the lessee is entitled to exercise its right to use the leased asset. It is the date of initial **recognition** of the **lease** (ie the recognition of the **assets**, **liabilities**, **income** or **expenses** resulting from the lease, as appropriate).
component of an entity	Operations and **cash flows** that can be clearly distinguished, operationally and for financial reporting purposes, from the rest of the entity.
compound financial instrument	A financial instrument that, from the issuer's perspective, contains both a **liability** and an **equity** element.
consolidated financial statements	The financial statements of a **parent** and its **subsidiaries** presented as those of a single economic entity.
construction contract	A contract specifically negotiated for the construction of an **asset** or a combination of assets that are closely interrelated or interdependent in terms of their design, technology and function or their ultimate purpose or use.

constructive obligation	An obligation that derives from an entity's actions where: (a) by an established pattern of past practice, published policies or a sufficiently specific current statement, the entity has indicated to other parties that it will accept certain responsibilities; and (b) as a result, the entity has created a valid expectation on the part of those other parties that it will discharge those responsibilities.
contingent asset	A possible **asset** that arises from past events and whose existence will be confirmed only by the occurrence or non-occurrence of one or more uncertain future events not wholly within the control of the entity.
contingent liability	(a) a possible obligation that arises from past events and whose existence will be confirmed only by the occurrence or non-occurrence of one or more uncertain future events not wholly within the control of the entity; or (b) a present obligation that arises from past events but is not recognised because: (i) it is not **probable** that an outflow of resources embodying economic benefits will be required to settle the obligation; or (ii) the amount of the obligation cannot be measured with sufficient **reliability**.
contingent rent	That portion of the lease payments that is not fixed in amount but is based on the future amount of a factor that changes other than with the passage of time (eg percentage of future sales, amount of future use, future price indices, and future market rates of interest).
control (of an entity)	The power to govern the financial and operating policies of an entity so as to obtain benefits from its activities.
credit risk	The risk that one party to a financial instrument will cause a financial loss for the other party by failing to discharge an obligation.
current assets	**Assets** of an entity which: (a) for an entity choosing to apply paragraph 1A(1) of Schedule 1 to the Regulations, are not non-current assets; or (b) for all other entities, are not fixed assets.
current liabilities (for the purposes of an entity applying paragraph 1A(1) of Schedule 1 to the Regulations)	**Liabilities** of the entity which: (a) it expects to settle in its normal operating cycle; (b) it holds primarily for the purpose of trading; (c) are due to be settled within 12 months after the reporting period; or (d) it does not have an unconditional right to defer settlement for at least 12 months after the reporting period.
current tax	The amount of income tax payable (refundable) in respect of the taxable profit (tax loss) for the current period or past **reporting periods**.

date of transition	The beginning of the earliest period for which an entity presents full comparative information in a given standard in its first **financial statements** that comply with that standard.
deemed cost	An amount used as a surrogate for cost or depreciated cost at a given date. Subsequent **depreciation** or **amortisation** assumes that the entity had initially recognised the **asset** or **liability** at the given date and that its cost was equal to the deemed cost.
deferred acquisition costs	Costs arising from the conclusion of **insurance contracts** that are incurred during a **reporting period** but which relate to a subsequent reporting period.
deferred tax	Income tax payable (recoverable) in respect of the **taxable profit (tax loss)** for future **reporting periods** as a result of past transactions or events.
deferred tax assets	Income tax recoverable in future **reporting periods** in respect of: (a) future tax consequences of transactions and events recognised in the financial statements of the current and previous periods; (b) the carry forward of unused tax losses; and (c) the carry forward of unused tax credits.
deferred tax liabilities	Income tax payable in future **reporting periods** in respect of future tax consequences of transactions and events recognised in the **financial statements** of the current and previous periods.
defined benefit obligation (present value of)	The **present value**, without deducting any **plan assets**, of expected future payments required to settle the obligation resulting from employee service in the current and prior periods.
defined benefit plans	**Post-employment benefit plans** other than **defined contribution plans**.
defined contribution plans	**Post-employment benefit plans** under which an entity pays fixed contributions into a separate entity (a fund) and has no legal or **constructive obligation** to pay further contributions or to make direct benefit payments to employees if the fund does not hold sufficient **assets** to pay all **employee benefits** relating to employee service in the current and prior periods.
depreciable amount	The cost of an **asset**, or other amount substituted for cost (in the **financial statements**), less its residual value.
depreciated replacement cost	The most economic cost required for the entity to replace the **service potential** of an **asset** (including the amount that the entity will receive from its disposal at the end of its **useful life**) at the **reporting date**.
depreciation	The systematic allocation of the **depreciable amount** of an **asset** over its **useful life**.
derecognition	The removal of a previously recognised **asset** or **liability** from an entity's **statement of financial position**.

derivative	A financial instrument or other contract with all three of the following characteristics: (a) its value changes in response to the change in a specified interest rate, financial instrument price, commodity price, foreign exchange rate, index of prices or rates, credit rating or credit index, or other variable (sometimes called the 'underlying'), provided in the case of a non-financial variable that the variable is not specific to a party to the contract; (b) it requires no initial net investment or an initial net investment that is smaller than would be required for other types of contracts that would be expected to have a similar response to changes in market factors; and (c) it is settled at a future date.
development	The application of **research** findings or other knowledge to a plan or design for the production of new or substantially improved materials, devices, products, processes, systems or services before the start of commercial production or use.
discontinued operation	A **component of an entity** that has been disposed of and: (a) represented a separate major line of business or geographical area of operations; (b) was part of a single co-ordinated plan to dispose of a separate major line of business or geographical area of operations; or (c) was a subsidiary acquired exclusively with a view to resale.
discretionary participation feature	A contractual right to receive, as a supplement to guaranteed benefits, additional benefits: (a) that are likely to be a significant portion of the total contractual benefits; (b) whose amount or timing is contractually at the discretion of the issuer; and (c) that are contractually based on: (i) the performance of a specified pool of contracts or a specified type of contract; (ii) realised and/or unrealised investment returns on a specified pool of **assets** held by the issuer; or (iii) the **profit or loss** of the company, fund or other entity that issues the contract.
disposal group	A group of **assets** to be disposed of, by sale or otherwise, together as a group in a single transaction, and **liabilities** directly associated with those assets that will be transferred in the transaction. The group includes **goodwill** acquired in a **business combination** if the group is a **cash-generating unit** to which goodwill has been allocated in accordance with the requirements of paragraphs 27.24 to 27.27 of this FRS.
effective interest method	A method of calculating the **amortised cost** of a **financial asset** or a **financial liability** (or a group of financial assets or financial liabilities) and of allocating the interest income or interest expense over the relevant period.

effective interest rate	The rate that exactly discounts estimated future cash payments or receipts through the expected life of the financial instrument or, when appropriate, a shorter period to the **carrying amount** of the **financial asset** or **financial liability**.
employee benefits	All forms of consideration given by an entity in exchange for service rendered by employees.
entity combination	See **business combination**.
equity	The residual interest in the **assets** of the entity after deducting all its **liabilities**.
equity-settled share-based payment transaction	A **share-based payment transaction** in which the entity: (a) receives goods or services as consideration for its own equity instruments (including shares or share options); or (b) receives goods or services but has no obligation to settle the transaction with the supplier.
errors	Omissions from, and misstatements in, the entity's **financial statements** for one or more prior periods arising from a failure to use, or misuse of, reliable information that: (a) was available when financial statements for those periods were authorised for issue; and (b) could reasonably be expected to have been obtained and taken into account in the preparation and presentation of those financial statements.
expenses	Decreases in economic benefits during the **reporting period** in the form of outflows or depletions of **assets** or incurrences of **liabilities** that result in decreases in **equity**, other than those relating to distributions to equity investors.
EU-adopted IFRS	IFRS that have been adopted in the European Union in accordance with EU Regulation 1606/2002.
fair value	The amount for which an **asset** could be exchanged, a **liability** settled, or an equity instrument granted could be exchanged, between knowledgeable, willing parties in an arm's length transaction. In the absence of any specific guidance provided in the relevant section of this FRS, the guidance in paragraphs 11.27 to 11.32 shall be used in determining fair value.
fair value less costs to sell	The amount obtainable from the sale of an **asset** or **cash-generating unit** in an arm's length transaction between knowledgeable, willing parties, less the costs of disposal.
finance lease	A **lease** that transfers substantially all the risks and rewards incidental to ownership of an **asset**. Title may or may not eventually be transferred. A lease that is not a finance lease is an operating lease.

financial asset	Any **asset** that is:
	(a) **cash**;
	(b) an equity instrument of another entity;
	(c) a contractual right:
	   (i) to receive cash or another financial asset from another entity, or
	   (ii) to exchange financial assets or **financial liabilities** with another entity under conditions that are potentially favourable to the entity; or
	(d) a contract that will or may be settled in the entity's own equity instruments and:
	   (i) under which the entity is or may be obliged to receive a variable number of the entity's own equity instruments; or
	   (ii) that will or may be settled other than by the exchange of a fixed amount of cash or another financial asset for a fixed number of the entity's own equity instruments. For this purpose the entity's own equity instruments do not include instruments that are themselves contracts for the future receipt or delivery of the entity's own equity instruments.

financial guarantee contract	A contract that requires the issuer to make specified payments to reimburse the holder for a loss it incurs because a specified debtor fails to make payments when due in accordance with the original or modified terms of a debt instrument.

financial institution	Any of the following:
	(a) a bank which is:
	   (i) a firm with a Part IV permission[27] which includes accepting deposits and:
	     (a) which is a credit institution; or
	     (b) whose Part IV permission includes a requirement that it complies with the rules in the General Prudential sourcebook and the Prudential sourcebook for Banks, Building Societies and Investment Firms relating to banks, but which is not a building society, a friendly society or a credit union;
	   (ii) an EEA bank which is a full credit institution;
	(b) a building society which is defined in section 119(1) of the Building Societies Act 1986 as a building society incorporated (or deemed to be incorporated) under that act;
	(c) a credit union, being a body corporate registered under the Industrial and Provident Societies Act 1965 as a credit union in accordance with the Credit Unions Act 1979, which is an authorised person;
	(d) custodian bank, broker-dealer or stockbroker;
	(e) an entity that undertakes the business of effecting or carrying out insurance contracts, including general and life assurance entities;

[27] *As defined in section 40(4) of the Financial Services and Markets Act 2000 or references to equivalent provisions of any successor legislation.*

	(f) an incorporated friendly society incorporated under the Friendly Societies Act 1992 or a registered friendly society registered under section 7(1)(a) of the Friendly Societies Act 1974 or any enactment which it replaced, including any registered branches; (g) an investment trust, Irish investment company, venture capital trust, mutual fund, exchange traded fund, unit trust, open-ended investment company (OEIC); (h) a **retirement benefit plan**; or (i) any other entity whose principal activity is to generate wealth or manage risk through financial instruments. This is intended to cover entities that have business activities similar to those listed above but are not specifically included in the list above. A **parent** entity whose sole activity is to hold investments in other group entities is not a financial institution.
financial instrument	A contract that gives rise to a **financial asset** of one entity and a **financial liability** or equity instrument of another entity.

financial liability	Any **liability** that is:
	 (a) a contractual obligation:
	    (i) to deliver **cash** or another **financial asset** to another entity; or
	    (ii) to exchange financial assets or financial liabilities with another entity under conditions that are potentially unfavourable to the entity, or
	 (b) a contract that will or may be settled in the entity's own equity instruments and:
	    (i) under which the entity is or may be obliged to deliver a variable number of the entity's own equity instruments; or
	    (ii) will or may be settled other than by the exchange of a fixed amount of cash or another financial asset for a fixed number of the entity's own equity instruments. For this purpose the entity's own equity instruments do not include instruments that are themselves contracts for the future receipt or delivery of the entity's own equity instruments.

financial position	The relationship of the **assets**, **liabilities** and **equity** of an entity as reported in the **statement of financial position**.
financial statements	Structured representation of the **financial position**, financial **performance** and **cash flows** of an entity.
financial risk	The risk of a possible future change in one or more of a specified interest rate, financial instrument price, commodity price, foreign exchange rate, index of prices or rates, credit rating or credit index or other variable, provided in the case of a non-financial variable that the variable is not specific to a party to the contract.
financing activities	Activities that result in changes in the size and composition of the contributed **equity** and borrowings of the entity.

firm commitment	A binding agreement for the exchange of a specified quantity of resources at a specified price on a specified future date or dates.
first-time adopter of this FRS	An entity that presents its first annual **financial statements** that conform to this FRS, regardless of whether its previous accounting framework was **EU-adopted IFRS** or another set of accounting standards.
fixed assets	**Assets** of an entity which are intended for use on a continuing basis in the entity's activities.
forecast transaction	An uncommitted but anticipated future transaction.
foreign operation	An entity that is a **subsidiary**, **associate**, **joint venture** or branch of a reporting entity, the activities of which are based or conducted in a country or currency other than those of the reporting entity.
FRS 100	FRS 100 *Application of Financial Reporting Requirements*
FRS 101	FRS 101 *Reduced Disclosure Framework*
FRS 102	FRS 102 *The Financial Reporting Standard applicable in the UK and Republic of Ireland*
FRS 103	FRS 103 *Insurance Contracts*
FRS 104	FRS 104 *Interim Financial Reporting*
FRS 105	FRS 105 *The Financial Reporting Standard applicable to the Micro-entities Regime*
functional currency	The currency of the primary economic environment in which the entity operates.
funding (of post-employment benefits)	Contributions by an entity, and sometimes its employees, into an entity, or fund, that is legally separate from the reporting entity and from which the **employee benefits** are paid.
gains	Increases in economic benefits that meet the definition of **income** but are not **revenue**.
general purpose financial statements (generally referred to simply as financial statements)	**Financial statements** directed to the general financial information needs of a wide range of users who are not in a position to demand reports tailored to meet their particular information needs.
going concern	An entity is a going concern unless management either intends to liquidate the entity or to cease trading, or has no realistic alternative but to do so.
goodwill	Future economic benefits arising from **assets** that are not capable of being individually identified and separately recognised.
government grant	Assistance by government in the form of a transfer of resources to an entity in return for past or future compliance with specified conditions relating to the **operating activities** of the entity. Government refers to government, government agencies and similar bodies whether local, national or international.

grant date	The date at which the entity and another party (including an employee) agree to a share-based payment arrangement, being when the entity and the counterparty have a shared understanding of the terms and conditions of the arrangement. At grant date the entity confers on the counterparty the right to **cash**, other **assets**, or equity instruments of the entity, provided the specified vesting conditions, if any, are met. If that agreement is subject to an approval process (for example, by shareholders), grant date is the date when that approval is obtained.
gross investment in a lease	The aggregate of: (a) the **minimum lease payments** receivable by the lessor under a **finance lease**; and (b) any unguaranteed **residual value** accruing to the lessor.
group	A **parent** and all its **subsidiaries**.
group reconstruction	Any one of the following arrangements: (a) the transfer of an equity holding in a subsidiary from one group entity to another; (b) the addition of a new parent entity to a group; (c) the transfer of equity holdings in one or more subsidiaries of a group to a new entity that is not a group entity but whose equity holders are the same as those of the group's parent; or (d) the combination into a group of two or more entities that before the combination had the same equity holders.
hedging gain or loss	The change in fair value of a hedged item that is attributable to the hedged risk.
held exclusively with a view to subsequent resale	An interest: (a) for which a purchaser has been identified or is being sought, and which is reasonably expected to be disposed of within approximately one year of its date of acquisition; or (b) that was acquired as a result of the enforcement of a security, unless the interest has become part of the continuing activities of the **group** or the holder acts as if it intends the interest to become so; or (c) which is **held as part of an investment portfolio**.
held as part of an investment portfolio	An interest is held as part of an investment portfolio if its value to the investor is through **fair value** as part of a directly or indirectly held basket of investments rather than as media through which the investor carries out **business**. A basket of investments is indirectly held if an investment fund holds a single investment in a second investment fund which, in turn, holds a basket of investments.
heritage assets	Tangible and **intangible assets** with historic, artistic, scientific, technological, geophysical, or environmental qualities that are held and maintained principally for their contribution to knowledge and culture.

highly probable	Significantly more likely than **probable**.
IAS Regulation	EU Regulation 1606/2002
IFRS (International Financial Reporting Standards)	Standards and interpretations issued (or adopted) by the International Accounting Standards Board (IASB). They comprise: (a) International Financial Reporting Standards; (b) International Accounting Standards; and (c) Interpretations developed by the IFRS Interpretations Committee (IFRIC) or the former Standing Interpretations Committee (SIC).
impairment loss	The amount by which the **carrying amount** of an **asset** exceeds: (a) in the case of **inventories**, its selling price less costs to complete and sell; or (b) in the case of other assets, its **recoverable amount**.
impracticable	Applying a requirement is impracticable when the entity cannot apply it after making every reasonable effort to do so.
imputed rate of interest	The more clearly determinable of either: (a) the prevailing rate for a similar instrument of an issuer with a similar credit rating; or (b) a rate of interest that discounts the nominal amount of the instrument to the current cash sales price of the goods or services.
inception of the lease	The earlier of the date of the lease agreement and the date of commitment by the parties to the principal provisions of the **lease**.
income	Increases in economic benefits during the **reporting period** in the form of inflows or enhancements of **assets** or decreases of **liabilities** that result in increases in **equity**, other than those relating to contributions from equity investors.
income and expenditure	The total of **income** less **expenses**, excluding the components of **other comprehensive income**. In the for-profit sector this is known as **profit or loss**.
income statement	**Financial statement** that presents all items of **income** and **expense** recognised in a **reporting period**, excluding the items of **other comprehensive income** (referred to as the profit and loss account in the **Act**).
income tax	All domestic and foreign taxes that are based on **taxable profits**. Income tax also includes taxes, such as withholding taxes, that are payable by a **subsidiary**, **associate** or **joint venture** on distributions to the reporting entity.

individual financial statements	The accounts that are required to be prepared by an entity in accordance with the Act or relevant legislation, for example: (a) 'individual accounts', as set out in section 394 of the Act; (b) 'statement of accounts', as set out in section 132 of the Charities Act 2011; or (c) 'individual accounts', as set out in section 72A of the Building Societies Act 1986. **Separate financial statements** are included in the meaning of this term.
infrastructure assets	Infrastructure for public services, such as roads, bridges, tunnels, prisons, hospitals, airports, water distribution facilities, energy supply and telecommunications networks.
insurance contract	A contract under which one party (the insurer) accepts significant insurance risk from another party (the policyholder) by agreeing to compensate the policyholder if a specified uncertain future event (the insured event) adversely affects the policyholder.
intangible asset	An identifiable non-monetary asset without physical substance. Such an **asset** is identifiable when: (a) it is separable, ie capable of being separated or divided from the entity and sold, transferred, licensed, rented or exchanged, either individually or together with a related contract, asset or **liability**; or (b) it arises from contractual or other legal rights, regardless of whether those rights are transferable or separable from the entity or from other rights and obligations.
interest rate implicit in the lease	The discount rate that, at the **inception of the lease**, causes the aggregate **present value** of: (a) the **minimum lease payments**; and (b) the unguaranteed **residual value** to be equal to the sum of: (i) the **fair value** of the leased asset; and (ii) any initial direct costs of the lessor.
interim financial report	A financial report containing either a complete set of **financial statements** or a set of condensed financial statements for an **interim period**.
interim period	A financial **reporting period** shorter than a full financial year.
intrinsic value	The difference between the fair value of the shares to which the counterparty has the (conditional or unconditional) right to subscribe or which it has the right to receive, and the price (if any) the counterparty is (or will be) required to pay for those shares. For example, a share option with an exercise price of CU15, on a share with a fair value of CU20, has an intrinsic value of CU5.

inventories	**Assets**:
	(a) held for sale in the ordinary course of business;
	(b) in the process of production for such sale; or
	(c) in the form of materials or supplies to be consumed in the production process or in the rendering of services.
inventories held for distribution at no or nominal consideration	**Assets** that are:
	(a) held for distribution at no or nominal consideration in the ordinary course of operations;
	(b) in the process of production for distribution at no or nominal consideration in the ordinary course of operations; or
	(c) in the form of material or supplies to be consumed in the production process or in the rendering of services at no or nominal consideration.
investing activities	The acquisition and disposal of long-term assets and other investments not included in **cash equivalents**.
investment property	Property (land or a building, or part of a building, or both) held by the owner or by the lessee under a **finance lease** to earn rentals or for capital appreciation or both, rather than for:
	(a) use in the production or supply of goods or services or for administrative purposes, or
	(b) sale in the ordinary course of **business**.
joint control	The contractually agreed sharing of **control** over an economic activity. It exists only when the strategic financial and operating decisions relating to the activity require the unanimous consent of the parties sharing control (the **venturers**).
joint venture	A contractual arrangement whereby two or more parties undertake an economic activity that is subject to **joint control**. Joint ventures can take the form of jointly controlled operations, jointly controlled assets, or **jointly controlled entities**.
jointly controlled entity	A **joint venture** that involves the establishment of a corporation, partnership or other entity in which each **venturer** has an interest. The entity operates in the same way as other entities, except that a contractual arrangement between the venturers establishes **joint control** over the economic activity of the entity.
key management personnel	Those persons having authority and responsibility for planning, directing and controlling the activities of the entity, directly or indirectly, including any director (whether executive or otherwise) of that entity.
lease	An agreement whereby the lessor conveys to the lessee in return for a payment or series of payments the right to use an **asset** for an agreed period of time.
lease incentives	Incentives provided by the lessor to the lessee to enter into a new or renew an operating lease. Examples of such incentives include up-front cash payments to the lessee, the reimbursement or assumption by the lessor of costs of the lessee (such as relocation costs, leasehold improvements and costs associated with pre-existing lease commitments of the lessee), or initial periods of the **lease** provided by the lessor rent-free or at a reduced rent.

lease term	The non-cancellable period for which the lessee has contracted to **lease** the **asset** together with any further terms for which the lessee has the option to continue to lease the asset, with or without further payment, when at the **inception of the lease** it is reasonably certain that the lessee will exercise the option.
lessee's incremental borrowing rate (of interest)	The rate of interest the lessee would have to pay on a similar **lease** or, if that is not determinable, the rate that, at the **inception of the lease**, the lessee would incur to borrow over a similar term, and with a similar security, the funds necessary to purchase the **asset**.
liability	A present obligation of the entity arising from past events, the settlement of which is expected to result in an outflow from the entity of resources embodying economic benefits.
liquidity risk	The risk that an entity will encounter difficulty in meeting obligations associated with **financial liabilities** that are settled by delivering **cash** or another **financial asset**.
LLP Regulations	The Large and Medium-sized Limited Liability Partnerships (Accounts) Regulations 2008 (SI 2008/1913)
loans payable	**Financial liabilities** other than short-term trade payables on normal credit terms.
market condition	A condition upon which the exercise price, vesting or exercisability of an equity instrument depends that is related to the market price of the entity's equity instruments, such as attaining a specified share price or a specified amount of **intrinsic value** of a **share option**, or achieving a specified target that is based on the market price of the entity's equity instruments relative to an index of market prices of equity instruments of other entities.
market risk	The risk that the **fair value** or future **cash flows** of a financial instrument will fluctuate because of changes in market prices. Market risk comprises three types of risk: currency risk, interest rate risk and other price risk.
	Interest rate risk – the risk that the fair value or future cash flows of a financial instrument will fluctuate because of changes in market interest rates.
	Currency risk – the risk that the fair value or future cash flows of a financial instrument will fluctuate because of changes in foreign exchange rates.
	Other price risk – the risk that the fair value or future cash flows of a financial instrument will fluctuate because of changes in market prices (other than those arising from interest rate risk or currency risk), whether those changes are caused by factors specific to the financial instrument or its issuer, or factors affecting all similar financial instruments traded in the market.
material	Omissions or misstatements of items are material if they could, individually or collectively, influence the economic decisions of users taken on the basis of the **financial statements**. Materiality depends on the size and nature of the omission or misstatement judged in the surrounding circumstances. The size or nature of the item, or a combination of both, could be the determining factor.

measurement	The process of determining the monetary amounts at which the elements of the **financial statements** are to be recognised and carried in the **statement of financial position** and **statement of comprehensive income**.
merger	An **entity combination** that results in the creation of a new reporting entity formed from the combining parties, in which the controlling parties of the combining entities come together in a partnership for the mutual sharing of risks and benefits of the newly formed entity and in which no party to the combination in substance obtains **control** over any other, or is otherwise seen to be dominant.
	All of the following criteria must be met for an entity combination to meet the definition of a merger:
	(a) no party to the combination is portrayed as either acquirer or acquiree, either by its own board or management or by that of another party to the combination;
	(b) there is no significant change to the classes of beneficiaries of the combining entities or the purpose of the benefits provided as a result of the combination; and
	(c) all parties to the combination, as represented by the members of the board, participate in establishing the management structure of the combined entity and in selecting the management personnel, and such decisions are made on the basis of a consensus between the parties to the combination rather than purely by exercise of voting rights.
minimum lease payments	The payments over the **lease term** that the lessee is or can be required to make, excluding **contingent rent**, costs for services and taxes to be paid by and reimbursed to the lessor, together with:
	(a) for a lessee, any amounts guaranteed by the lessee or by a party related to the lessee; or
	(b) for a lessor, any **residual value** guaranteed to the lessor by:
	(i) the lessee;
	(ii) a party related to the lessee; or
	(iii) a third party unrelated to the lessor that is financially capable of discharging the obligations under the guarantee.
	However, if the lessee has an option to purchase the **asset** at a price that is expected to be sufficiently lower than **fair value** at the date the option becomes exercisable for it to be reasonably certain, at the **inception of the lease**, that the option will be exercised, the minimum lease payments comprise the minimum payments payable over the lease term to the expected date of exercise of this purchase option and the payment required to exercise it.
monetary items	Units of currency held and **assets** and **liabilities** to be received or paid in a fixed or determinable number of units of currency.

multi-employer (benefit) plans	**Defined contribution plans** (other than **state plans**) or **defined benefit plans** (other than state plans) that: (a) pool the **assets** contributed by various entities that are not under common control, and (b) use those assets to provide benefits to employees of more than one entity, on the basis that contribution and benefit levels are determined without regard to the identity of the entity that employs the employees concerned.
net assets available for benefits	The **assets** of a plan less **liabilities** other than the actuarial **present value** of promised retirement benefits
net defined benefit liability	The **present value** of the **defined benefit obligation** at the **reporting date** minus the **fair value** at the reporting date of **plan assets** (if any) out of which the obligations are to be settled.
net investment in a foreign operation	The amount of the reporting entity's interest in the net assets of that operation.
net investment in a lease	The **gross investment in a lease** discounted at the **interest rate implicit in the lease**.
non-controlling interest	The **equity** in a **subsidiary** not attributable, directly or indirectly, to a **parent**.
non-current assets	**Assets** of the entity which: (a) it does not expect to realise, or intend to sell or consume, in its normal operating cycle; (b) it does not hold primarily for the purpose of trading; (c) it does not expect to realise within 12 months after the **reporting period**; or (d) are **cash** or **cash equivalents** restricted from being exchanged or used to settle a **liability** for at least 12 months after the reporting period.
non-current liabilities	**Liabilities** of the entity which are not **current liabilities**.
non-exchange transaction	A transaction whereby an entity receives value from another entity without directly giving approximately equal value in exchange, or gives value to another entity without directly receiving approximately equal value in exchange.
notes (to financial statements)	Notes contain information in addition to that presented in the **statement of financial position, statement of comprehensive income, income statement** (if presented), combined **statement of income and retained earnings** (if presented), **statement of changes in equity** and **statement of cash flows**. Notes provide narrative descriptions or disaggregations of items presented in those statements and information about items that do not qualify for **recognition** in those statements.
notional amount	The quantity of currency units, shares, bushels, pounds or other units specified in a financial instrument contract.

objective of financial statements	To provide information about the **financial position, performance** and, when required to be presented, **cash flows** of an entity that is useful for economic decision-making by a broad range of users who are not in a position to demand reports tailored to meet their particular information needs.
onerous contract	A contract in which the unavoidable costs of meeting the obligations under the contract exceed the economic benefits expected to be received under it.
operating activities	The principal revenue-producing activities of the entity and other activities that are not investing or **financing activities**.
operating lease	A **lease** that does not transfer substantially all the risks and rewards incidental to ownership. A lease that is not an operating lease is a **finance lease**.
operating segment	An operating segment is a **component of an entity**: (a) that engages in business activities from which it may earn **revenues** and incur **expenses** (including revenues and expenses relating to transactions with other components of the same entity); (b) whose operating results are regularly reviewed by the entity's chief operating decision maker to make decisions about resources to be allocated to the segment and assess its **performance**; and (c) for which discrete financial information is available.
ordinary share	An equity instrument that is subordinate to all other classes of equity instrument.
other comprehensive income	Items of **income** and **expense** (including reclassification adjustments) that are not recognised in **profit or loss** as required or permitted by this FRS.
owners	Holders of instruments classified as **equity**.
parent	An entity that has one or more **subsidiaries**.
performance	The relationship of the **income** and **expenses** of an entity, as reported in the **statement of comprehensive income**.
performance-related condition	A condition that requires the performance of a particular level of service or units of output to be delivered, with payment of, or entitlement to, the resources conditional on that performance.
permanent differences	Differences between an entity's **taxable profits** and its **total comprehensive income** as stated in the **financial statements**, other than **timing differences**.
plan assets (of an employee benefit plan)	(a) **assets held by a long-term employee benefit fund**; and (b) **qualifying insurance policies**.
post-employment benefits	**Employee benefits** (other than **termination benefits** and short-term employee benefits) that are payable after the completion of employment.

post-employment benefit plans	Formal or informal arrangements under which an entity provides **post-employment benefits** for one or more employees.
potential ordinary share	A financial instrument or other contract that may entitle its holder to **ordinary shares**.
present value	A current estimate of the present discounted value of the future net **cash flows** in the normal course of **business**.
presentation currency	The currency in which the **financial statements** are presented.
prevailing market rate	The rate of interest that would apply to the entity in an open market for a similar financial instrument.
principal	An entity is acting as a principal when it has exposure to the significant risks and rewards associated with the sale of goods or the rendering of services. Features that indicate that an entity is acting as a principal include: (a) the entity has the primary responsibility for providing the goods or services to the customer or for fulfilling the order, for example by being responsible for the acceptability of the products or services ordered or purchased by the customer; (b) the entity has inventory risk before or after the customer order, during shipping or on return; (c) the entity has latitude in establishing prices, either directly or indirectly, for example by providing additional goods or services; and (d) the entity bears the customer's credit risk for the amount receivable from the customer.
probable	More likely than not.
profit or loss	The total of **income** less **expenses**, excluding the components of **other comprehensive income**.
projected unit credit method	An actuarial valuation method that sees each period of service as giving rise to an additional unit of benefit entitlement and measures each unit separately to build up the final obligation (sometimes known as the accrued benefit method pro-rated on service or as the benefit/years of service method).
property, plant and equipment	Tangible assets that: (a) are held for use in the production or supply of goods or services, for rental to others, or for administrative purposes, and (b) are expected to be used during more than one period.
prospectively (applying a change in accounting policy)	Applying the new **accounting policy** to transactions, other events and conditions occurring after the date as at which the policy is changed.
provision	A **liability** of uncertain timing or amount.
prudence	The inclusion of a degree of caution in the exercise of the judgements needed in making the estimates required under conditions of uncertainty, such that **assets** or **income** are not overstated and **liabilities** or **expenses** are not understated.

public benefit entity	An entity whose primary objective is to provide goods or services for the general public, community or social benefit and where any **equity** is provided with a view to supporting the entity's primary objectives rather than with a view to providing a financial return to equity providers, shareholders or members.[28]
public benefit entity concessionary loan	A loan made or received between a **public benefit entity** or an entity within a **public benefit entity group** and another party: (a) at below the **prevailing market rate** of interest; (b) that is not repayable on demand; and (c) is for the purposes of furthering the objectives of the public benefit entity or public benefit entity **parent**.
public benefit entity group	A **public benefit entity parent** and all of its wholly-owned **subsidiaries**.
publicly traded (debt or equity instruments)	Traded, or in process of being issued for trading, in a public market (a domestic or foreign stock exchange or an over-the-counter market, including local and regional markets).
qualifying asset	An **asset** that necessarily takes a substantial period of time to get ready for its intended use or sale. Depending on the circumstances any of the following may be qualifying assets: (a) **inventories**; (b) manufacturing plants; (c) power generation facilities; (d) **intangible assets**; and (e) **investment properties**. **Financial assets**, and inventories that are produced over a short period of time, are not qualifying assets. Assets that are ready for their intended use or sale when acquired are not qualifying assets.

[28] *The term public benefit entity does not necessarily imply that the purpose of the entity is for the benefit of the public as a whole. For example, many PBEs exist for the direct benefit of a particular group of people, although it is possible that society as a whole also benefits indirectly. The important factor is what the primary purpose of such an entity is, and that it does not exist primarily to provide economic benefit to its investors. Organisations such as mutual insurance companies, other mutual co-operative entities and clubs that provide dividends or other economic benefits directly and proportionately to their owners, members or participants are not PBEs.*

Some PBEs undertake certain activities that are intended to make a surplus in order to fund their primary activities. Consideration should be given to the primary purpose of an entity's (or group's) activities in assessing whether it meets the definition of a PBE.

PBEs may have received contributions in the form of equity, even though the entity does not have a primary profit motive. However, because of the fundamental nature of public benefit entities, any such contributions are made by the equity holders of the entity primarily to enable the provision of goods or services to beneficiaries rather than with a view to a financial return for themselves. This is different from the position of lenders; loans do not fall into the category of equity.

qualifying entity (for the purposes of this FRS)	A member of a **group** where the **parent** of that group prepares publicly available **consolidated financial statements** which are intended to give a true and fair view (of the **assets, liabilities, financial position** and **profit or loss**) and that member is included in the consolidation[29].

qualifying insurance policies	An insurance policy[30] issued by an insurer that is not a **related party** of the reporting entity, if the proceeds of the policy:
	(a) can be used only to pay or fund **employee benefits** under a **defined benefit plan**; and
	(b) are not available to the reporting entity's own creditors (even in bankruptcy) and cannot be paid to the reporting entity, unless either:
	  (i) the proceeds represent surplus **assets** that are not needed for the policy to meet all the related employee benefit obligations; or
	  (ii) the proceeds are returned to the reporting entity to reimburse it for employee benefits already paid.

recognition	The process of incorporating in the **statement of financial position** or **statement of comprehensive income** an item that meets the definition of an asset, liability, equity, income or expense and satisfies the following criteria: (a) it is **probable** that any future economic benefit associated with the item will flow to or from the entity; and (b) the item has a cost or value that can be measured with **reliability**.
recoverable amount	The higher of an **asset's** (or **cash-generating unit's**) **fair value less costs to sell** and its value in use.
Regulations	The Large and Medium-sized Companies and Groups (Accounts and Reports) Regulations 2008 (SI 2008/410)
reinsurance contract	An **insurance contract** issued by one insurer (the reinsurer) to compensate another insurer (the cedant) for losses on one or more contracts issued by the cedant.

---

[29] *As set out in section 474(1) of the Act.*
[30] *A qualifying insurance policy is not necessarily an insurance contract.*

related party	A related party is a person or entity that is related to the entity that is preparing its **financial statements** (the reporting entity).
	
	(a) A person or a close member of that person's family is related to a reporting entity if that person:
	    (i) has **control** or **joint control** over the reporting entity;
	    (ii) has **significant influence** over the reporting entity; or
	    (iii) is a member of the **key management personnel** of the reporting entity or of a **parent** of the reporting entity.
	
	(b) An entity is related to a reporting entity if any of the following conditions apply:
	    (i) the entity and the reporting entity are members of the same **group** (which means that each parent, **subsidiary** and fellow subsidiary is related to the others).
	    (ii) one entity is an **associate** or **joint venture** of the other entity (or of a member of a group of which the other entity is a member).
	    (iii) both entities are joint ventures of the same third entity.
	    (iv) one entity is a joint venture of a third entity and the other entity is an associate of the third entity.
	    (v) the entity is a **post-employment benefit plan** for the benefit of employees of either the reporting entity or an entity related to the reporting entity. If the reporting entity is itself such a plan, the sponsoring employers are also related to the reporting entity.
	    (vi) the entity is controlled or jointly controlled by a person identified in (a).
	    (vii) a person identified in (a)(i) has significant influence over the entity or is a member of the key management personnel of the entity (or of a parent of the entity).
	    (viii) the entity, or any member of a group of which it is a part, provides key management personnel services to the reporting entity or to the parent of the reporting entity.

related party transaction	A transfer of resources, services or obligations between a reporting entity and a **related party**, regardless of whether a price is charged.
relevance	The quality of information that allows it to influence the economic decisions of users by helping them evaluate past, present or future events or confirming, or correcting, their past evaluations.
reliability	The quality of information that makes it free from **material error** and bias and represents faithfully that which it either purports to represent or could reasonably be expected to represent.

reporting date	The end of the latest period covered by **financial statements** or by an **interim financial report**.
reporting period	The period covered by **financial statements** or by an **interim financial report**.
research	Original and planned investigation undertaken with the prospect of gaining new scientific or technical knowledge and understanding.
residual value (of an asset)	The estimated amount that an entity would currently obtain from disposal of an **asset**, after deducting the estimated costs of disposal, if the asset were already of the age and in the condition expected at the end of its **useful life**.
restriction	A requirement that limits or directs the purposes for which a resource may be used that does not meet the definition of a **performance-related condition**.
restructuring	A restructuring is a programme that is planned and controlled by management and materially changes either: (a) the scope of a business undertaken by an entity; or (b) the manner in which that business is conducted.
retirement benefit plan	Arrangements whereby an entity provides benefits for employees on or after termination of service (either in the form of an annual **income** or as a lump sum) when such benefits, or the contributions towards them, can be determined or estimated in advance of retirement from the provisions of a document or from the entity's practice.
retrospective application (of an accounting policy)	Applying a new **accounting policy** to transactions, other events and conditions as if that policy had always been applied.
revenue	The gross inflow of economic benefits during the period arising in the course of the ordinary activities of an entity when those inflows result in increases in **equity**, other than increases relating to contributions from equity participants.
separate financial statements	Those presented by a **parent** in which the investments in **subsidiaries**, **associates** or **jointly controlled entities** are accounted for either at cost or **fair value** rather than on the basis of the reported results and net assets of the investees. Separate financial statements are included within the meaning of **individual financial statements**.
service concession arrangement	An arrangement whereby a public sector body or a **public benefit entity** (the grantor) contracts with a private sector entity (the operator) to construct (or upgrade), operate and maintain **infrastructure assets** for a specified period of time (the concession period).
service potential	The economic utility of an **asset**, based on the total benefit expected to be derived by the entity from use (and/or through sale) of the asset.

share-based payment transaction	A transaction in which the entity: (a) receives goods or services (including employee services) as consideration for its own equity instruments (including shares or **share options**); or (b) receives goods or services but has no obligation to settle the transaction with supplier; or (c) acquires goods or services by incurring **liabilities** to the supplier of those goods or services for amounts that are based on the price (or value) of the entity's shares or other equity instruments of the entity or another group entity.
share option	A contract that gives the holder the right, but not the obligation, to subscribe to the entity's shares at a fixed or determinable price for a specific period of time.
significant influence	Significant influence is the power to participate in the financial and operating policy decisions of the **associate** but is not **control** or **joint control** over those policies.
Small Companies Regulations	The Small Companies and Groups (Accounts and Directors' Report) Regulations 2008 (SI 2008/409)
small entity	(a) A company meeting the definition of a small company as set out in section 382 or 383 of the **Act** and not excluded from the small companies regime by section 384; (b) an LLP qualifying as small and not excluded from the small LLPs regime, as set out in LLP Regulations; or (c) any other entity that would have met the criteria in (a) had it been a company incorporated under company law.
Small LLP Regulations	The Small Limited Liability Partnership (Accounts) Regulations 2008 (SI 2008/1912)
Statement of Recommended Practice (SORP)	An extant Statement of Recommended Practice developed in accordance with *SORPs: Policy and Code of Practice*. SORPs recommend accounting practices for specialised industries or sectors. They supplement accounting standards and other legal and regulatory requirements in the light of the special factors prevailing or transactions undertaken in a particular industry or sector.
state	A national, regional, or local government.
state (employee benefit) plan	Employee benefit plans established by legislation to cover all entities (or all entities in a particular category, for example a specific industry) and operated by national or local government or by another body (for example an autonomous agency created specifically for this purpose) which is not subject to control or influence by the reporting entity.
statement of cash flows	**Financial statement** that provides information about the changes in **cash** and **cash equivalents** of an entity for a period, showing separately changes during the period from operating, investing and **financing activities**.

statement of comprehensive income	**Financial statement** that presents all items of **income** and **expense** recognised in a period, including those items recognised in determining **profit or loss** (which is a subtotal in the statement of comprehensive income) and items of **other comprehensive income**. If an entity chooses to present both an **income statement** and a statement of comprehensive income, the statement of comprehensive income begins with profit or loss and then displays the items of other comprehensive income.
statement of financial position	**Financial statement** that presents the relationship of an entity's **assets**, **liabilities** and **equity** as of a specific date (referred to as the balance sheet in the **Act**).
statement of income and retained earnings	**Financial statement** that presents the **profit or loss** and changes in retained earnings for a **reporting period**.
subsidiary	An entity, including an unincorporated entity such as a partnership, that is **controlled** by another entity (known as the **parent**).
substantively enacted	Tax rates shall be regarded as substantively enacted when the remaining stages of the enactment process historically have not affected the outcome and are unlikely to do so.
	A UK tax rate shall be regarded as having been substantively enacted if it is included in either:
	(a) a Bill that has been passed by the House of Commons and is awaiting only passage through the House of Lords and Royal Assent; or
	(b) a resolution having statutory effect that has been passed under the Provisional Collection of Taxes Act 1968. (Such a resolution could be used to collect taxes at a new rate before that rate has been enacted. In practice, corporation tax rates are now set a year ahead to avoid having to invoke the Provisional Collection of Taxes Act for the quarterly payment system.)
	A Republic of Ireland tax rate can be regarded as having been substantively enacted if it is included in a Bill that has been passed by the Dail.
tax expense	The aggregate amount included in **total comprehensive income** or **equity** for the **reporting period** in respect of **current tax** and **deferred tax**.
taxable profit (tax loss)	The profit (loss) for a **reporting period** upon which income taxes are payable or recoverable, determined in accordance with the rules established by the taxation authorities. Taxable profit equals taxable income less amounts deductible from taxable income.
termination benefits	**Employee benefits** provided in exchange for the termination of an employee's employment as a result of either:
	(a) an entity's decision to terminate an employee's employment before the normal retirement date; or
	(b) an employee's decision to accept voluntary redundancy in exchange for those benefits.

timing differences	Differences between **taxable profits** and **total comprehensive income** as stated in the **financial statements** that arise from the inclusion of **income** and **expenses** in tax assessments in periods different from those in which they are recognised in financial statements.
timeliness	Providing the information in **financial statements** within the decision time frame.
total comprehensive income	The change in **equity** during a period resulting from transactions and other events, other than those changes resulting from transactions from equity participants (equal to the sum of **profit or loss** and **other comprehensive income**).
transaction costs (financial instruments)	Incremental costs that are directly attributable to the acquisition, issue or disposal of a **financial asset** or **financial liability**, or the issue or reacquisition of an entity's **own equity instrument**. An incremental cost is one that would not have been incurred if the entity had not acquired, issued or disposed of the financial asset or financial liability, or had not issued or reacquired its own equity instrument.
treasury shares	An entity's own equity instruments, held by that entity or other members of the consolidated group.
turnover	The amounts derived from the provision of goods and services after deduction of: (a) trade discounts; (b) value added tax; and (c) any other taxes based on the amounts so derived.
understandability	The presentation of information in a way that makes it comprehensible by users who have a reasonable knowledge of business and economic activities and accounting and a willingness to study the information with reasonable diligence.
useful life	The period over which an **asset** is expected to be available for use by an entity or the number of production or similar units expected to be obtained from the asset by an entity.
value in use	The **present value** of the future **cash flows** expected to be derived from an **asset** or **cash-generating unit**.
value in use (in respect of assets held for their service potential)	When the future economic benefits of an **asset** are not primarily dependent on the asset's ability to generate net cash inflows, **value in use** (in respect of assets held for their **service potential**) is the **present value** to the entity of the asset's remaining service potential if it continues to be used, plus the net amount that the entity will receive from its disposal at the end of its **useful life**.
venturer	A party to a **joint venture** that has **joint control** over that joint venture.
vest	Become an entitlement. Under a share-based payment arrangement, a counterparty's right to receive **cash**, other **assets** or equity instruments of the entity vests when the counterparty's entitlement is no longer conditional on the satisfaction of any vesting conditions.
vested benefits	Benefits, the rights to which, under the conditions of a **retirement benefit plan**, are not conditional on continued employment.

Appendix II:
Significant differences between FRS 102 and the IFRS for SMEs

Section		Changes to the IFRS for SMEs (July 2009)
1	Scope of this FRS	This section of the IFRS for SMEs has been replaced. The IFRS for SMEs applies to small and medium sized entities that do not have public accountability and publish general purpose financial statements. FRS 100 *Application of Financial Reporting Requirements* sets out the scope of entities applying this FRS. Paragraphs 1.14A and 1.14B are added to provide transitional provisions in respect of the designation of financial instruments at fair value and hedge accounting which are available to entities that have authorised for issue financial statements compliant with this FRS prior to 1 August 2014.
1A	Small Entities	This section has been inserted to set out the information that is to be presented and disclosed in the financial statements of a small entity, based on the legal framework for small companies.
2	Concepts and Pervasive Principles	No significant changes.
3	Financial Statement Presentation	The drafting of the requirements has been more closely aligned with the drafting of company law. The requirements in paragraph 3.7 are deleted. Paragraph 3.16 is amended to clarify the role of materiality in the preparation of financial statements. Paragraph 3.16A is inserted to specify that disclosures are not required if the information is not material.
4	Statement of Financial Position	The requirements of this section have predominantly been removed and replaced by the requirements set out in the Act. Entities that do not report under the Act comply with the requirements of this section, and of the Regulations, except to the extent that these requirements are not permitted by any statutory framework under which such entities report.
5	Statement of Comprehensive Income and Income Statement	The requirements of this section have predominantly been removed and replaced by the requirements set out in the Act. Entities that do not report under the Act comply with the requirements of this section and of the Regulations except to the extent that these requirements are not permitted by any statutory framework under which such entities report.

Section		Changes to the IFRS for SMEs (July 2009)
		Paragraph 5.10 has been amended and paragraphs 5.10A and 5.10B are inserted to comply with the Regulations and include the definition of an extraordinary item.
6	Statement of Changes in Equity and Statement of Income and Retained Earnings	Paragraph 6.3A is inserted to require presentation for each component of equity an analysis of other comprehensive income by item, either in the notes, or in the statement of changes in equity.
7	Statement of Cash Flows	The scope of this section is amended to exclude mutual life assurance companies, pension funds and certain investment funds.
		Paragraphs 7.10A to 7.10E are inserted to require the reporting of cash flows on a net basis in some circumstances.
		Paragraphs 7.11 and 7.12 are amended to provide some relaxation of the exchange rates permitted to be used.
8	Notes to the Financial Statements	No significant changes.
9	Consolidated and Separate Financial Statements	The scope of this section is amended to clarify that it applies to all parent entities that present consolidated financial statements intended to give a true and fair view.
		The requirements to present consolidated financial statements are amended to comply with the Act.
		Paragraph 9.9 requires a subsidiary that is held exclusively with a view to subsequent resale because it is held as part of an investment portfolio, to be excluded from consolidation. Such subsidiaries are required to be measured at fair value with changes recognised in profit or loss. This exemption is required irrespective of whether the subsidiary was previously consolidated under previous GAAP, prior to transition to FRS 102. In addition paragraphs 14.4B and 15.9B are inserted to require an investor that has investments in associates or jointly controlled entities that are held as part of an investment portfolio to measure those investments at fair value with the changes recognised in profit or loss in their consolidated financial statements.
		Clarification is added to paragraph 9.10 that Employee Share Ownership Plans and similar arrangements are Special Purpose Entities.

Section		Changes to the IFRS for SMEs (July 2009)
		Paragraph 9.16 is amended to comply with paragraph 2(2) of Schedule 6 to the Regulations in order to require a subsidiary's financial statements, which are included in the consolidated financial statements, to be for the same reporting period (financial year) and as at the same reporting date (year-end). Where it is not practicable to align the subsidiary's reporting date (year-end) with the parent's, paragraph 9.16 has been amended to specify which financial statements of the subsidiary are permitted to be used in the consolidation.
		Paragraphs 9.18A and 9.18B are inserted to clarify the treatment of a disposal where control is lost.
		Paragraph 9.19A is inserted to clarify the treatment of the disposal where control is retained.
		Paragraph 9.19B is inserted to clarify the treatment of an acquisition made in stages.
		Paragraphs 9.19C and 9.19D are inserted to clarify the treatment of non-controlling interest when a parent changes its holding in a subsidiary but control is retained.
		Paragraphs 9.23A to 9.25 are amended to clarify the distinction between the individual financial statements and separate financial statements and that the Act specifies when individual financial statements are required to be prepared.
		Paragraphs 9.28 to 9.30 relating to combined financial statements are deleted.
		Paragraphs 9.31 and 9.32 provide guidance on exchanges of businesses or other non-monetary assets for an interest in a subsidiary, joint venture or associate. This guidance was previously contained in UITF Abstract 31 *Exchanges of businesses or other non-monetary assets for an interest in a subsidiary, joint venture or associate.*
		Paragraphs 9.33 to 9.38 are inserted to provide guidance on the accounting treatment for intermediate payment arrangements. These were previously contained in UITF Abstract 32 *Employee benefit trusts and other intermediate payment arrangements.*
10	Accounting Policies, Estimates and Errors	Paragraph 10.5 clarifies when an entity is required to refer to SORPs in developing an accounting policy. Paragraph 10.10A is inserted to bring the accounting treatment for changes in accounting policy relating to property, plant and equipment (Section 17) and intangible assets (Section 18) in line with IAS 10 *Accounting Policies, Estimate and Errors.*

Section		Changes to the IFRS for SMEs (July 2009)
11	Basic Financial Instruments	The scope of Section 11 is amended to clarify that certain financial instruments are not within its scope.
		Paragraph 11.2A is inserted to ensure that an entity choosing to apply the recognition and measurement requirements of IFRS 9 complies with the Regulations.
		Paragraph 11.8(b) is amended to clarify that instruments as described in paragraph 11.6(b) are not debt instruments accounted for under Section 11.
		Paragraph 11.9(a) is amended to clarify the permissible contractual returns to the lender.
		Paragraph 11.9(aA) is added to include some contractual provisions that provide for a linkage of repayments and/or returns to the lender based on inflation.
		Paragraph 11.9(aB) is added to permit certain variations of the return to the holder during the life of the instrument.
		Paragraph 11.9(c) is amended to clarify that contractual prepayment provisions which are contingent future events exclude those which protect the holder from credit deterioration, changes in central bank levies or tax changes and to clarify when compensation payments do not breach the condition.
		The text of paragraph 11.9(d) is deleted as it is no longer needed.
		Paragraph 11.9(e) is added to permit certain contractual extension options.
		Examples are inserted after paragraph 11.9 to illustrate the application of paragraph 11.9.
		Paragraphs 11.11(b) and (c) are deleted as the instruments shown as examples are excluded from debt instruments within the scope of Section 11 under paragraph 11.8(b).
		Paragraph 11.14(b) is inserted to clarify that entities may choose to designate debt instruments and loan commitments as fair value through profit or loss under certain circumstances.
		Paragraph 11.38A is inserted to allow offsetting of certain financial assets and financial liabilities in the statement of financial position.
		Paragraph 11.48A is inserted to provide disclosures required in accordance with the Regulations for certain financial instruments held at fair value.
		Paragraphs 11.48B and 11.48C require additional disclosures for financial institutions.

Section		Changes to the IFRS for SMEs (July 2009)
12	Other Financial Instruments Issues	The scope of Section 12 is amended to exclude financial instruments issued by an entity with a discretionary participation feature, reimbursement assets and financial guarantee contracts.
		Paragraph 12.2A is inserted to ensure that an entity choosing to apply the recognition and measurement requirements of IFRS 9 complies with the Regulations.
		Paragraph 12.8(c) is added to clarify when financial instruments within the scope of Section 12 should be measured at amortised cost.
		Paragraphs 12.15 to 12.29 are deleted and replaced with paragraphs 12.15 to 12.29A to include revised hedge accounting requirements which have the following effect:
		(a) the scope of permissible hedged items and hedging instruments is expanded;
		(b) the hedge accounting conditions are revised and simplified;
		(c) it determines three hedge accounting models, ie cash flow, fair value and net investment hedges;
		(d) it clarifies that the cumulative amount of foreign exchange differences relating to a hedge of a net investment in a foreign operation is not reclassified to profit or loss on disposal or partial disposal; and
		(e) it introduces a documentation requirement in cases of voluntary hedge accounting discontinuation.
		Paragraph 12.25B is inserted to allow offsetting of certain financial assets and financial liabilities in the statement of financial position.
		Paragraph 12.26 is amended to comply with requirements set out in the Act.
		The Appendix to Section 12 is inserted to illustrate by way of example the application of the hedge accounting requirements.
13	Inventories	Paragraph 13.3 is amended to permit inventory to be measured at fair value less costs to sell through profit or loss in certain circumstances.
		Paragraphs 13.4A and 13.20A are inserted to provide guidance on inventories held for distribution at no or nominal consideration.
		Paragraph 13.5A is inserted to provide guidance on inventory acquired through non-exchange transactions.

Section		Changes to the IFRS for SMEs (July 2009)
		Paragraph 13.8A is inserted to clarify the treatment for provisions made against dismantling and restoration costs (of PPE) in the cost of inventory.
		Paragraph 13.12 is deleted because of the revisions to the hedge accounting requirements.
		Paragraph 13.15 is amended to allow for the inclusion of a cost model for agricultural produce in Section 34 *Specialised Activities*.
14	Investments in Associates	The scope of this section is amended to clarify its application to consolidated financial statements and to the financial statements of an entity that is not a parent but which holds investments in associates.
		Paragraph 14.4(b) of the IFRS for SMEs is deleted as the equity method of accounting for investments in associates in individual financial statements is not compliant with company law. Paragraph 14.4(d) is inserted to allow non-parent investors to account for investments in associates at fair value with changes recognised in profit or loss.
		Paragraphs 14.4B is inserted to require an investor that is a parent which has investments in associates that are held as part of an investment portfolio to measure those investments at fair value with the changes recognised in profit or loss in their consolidated financial statements.
		Paragraph 14.9 is amended to require transaction costs to be included as part of the transaction price on initial recognition.
		Paragraph 14.10 is amended to require changes in fair value to be recognised through other comprehensive income, in accordance with paragraphs 17.15E and 17.15F, when the fair value model is applied, rather than through profit or loss.
		Paragraph 14.15A is inserted to provide information about associates held by entities that are not parents.
15	Investments in Joint Ventures	The scope of this section is amended to clarify its application to consolidated financial statements and to the financial statements of a venture that is not a parent.
		Paragraph 15.9(b) of the IFRS for SMEs is deleted as the equity method of accounting for interests in jointly controlled entities in individual financial statements is not compliant with company law. Paragraph 15.9(d) is inserted to allow non-parent investors to account for investments in jointly controlled entities at fair value with the changes recognised in profit or loss.

Section		Changes to the IFRS for SMEs (July 2009)
		Paragraph 15.9B is inserted to require an investor that is a parent which has investments in jointly controlled entities that are held as part of an investment portfolio to measure those investments at fair value with the changes recognised in profit or loss in their consolidated financial statements.
		Paragraph 15.14 is amended to require transaction costs to be included as part of the transaction price on initial recognition.
		Paragraph 15.15 is amended to require changes in fair value to be recognised through other comprehensive income, in accordance with paragraphs 17.15E and 17.15F, when the fair value model is applied, rather than through profit or loss.
		Paragraph 15.21A is inserted to provide information about associates held by entities that are not parents.
16	Investment Property	No significant changes.
17	Property, Plant and Equipment	Section 17 is amended to provide, after initial recognition, that an entity may use the cost model or revaluation model.
18	Intangible Assets other than Goodwill	Section 18 is amended to permit entities to recognise intangible assets that result from expenditure incurred on the internal development of an intangible item (subject to certain criteria). The section provides guidance on what comprises the cost of an internally generated intangible asset and the criteria for initial recognition.
		The section is also amended to provide, after initial recognition, that an entity may use the cost model or revaluation model.
19	Business Combinations and Goodwill	Section 19 is amended to permit the use of the merger accounting method for group reconstructions. The merger method is set out in paragraphs 19.29 to 19.33.
		Paragraphs 19.15A to 19.15C are inserted to provide guidance on the treatment of deferred tax assets or liabilities, employee benefit arrangements and share-based payments of a subsidiary on acquisition.
		Paragraph 19.24 is amended and paragraph 19.26A is inserted to comply with the requirements of the Act for bargain purchases (negative goodwill).
20	Leases	The scope of Section 20 is amended to include operating leases that are onerous within its scope.
		Paragraphs 20.15A and 20.25A are inserted to clarify the treatment of operating lease incentives for lessees and lessors respectively.

Section		Changes to the IFRS for SMEs (July 2009)
		Paragraph 20.15B is inserted to provide guidance on the treatment of onerous operating lease contracts.
21	Provisions and Contingencies	The scope of Section 21 is amended to include financial guarantee contracts. Paragraph 21.17A is inserted to provide guidance on the accounting treatment of financial guarantee contracts.
		Paragraph 21.17 is amended to comply with disclosure requirements set out in the Regulations.
22	Liabilities and Equity	Paragraph 22.3A is inserted to clarify that a financial instrument where the issuer does not have the unconditional right to avoid settling in cash or by delivery of another financial asset (or otherwise to settle it in such a way that it would be a financial liability); and where settlement is dependent on the occurrence or non-occurrence of uncertain future events beyond the control of the issuer and the holder, is a financial liability of the issuer unless specific circumstances apply.
		The requirement for an entity to recognise a liability at fair value when non-cash assets are distributed to owners is removed and only disclosure is required in paragraph 22.18.
23	Revenue	No significant changes.
24	Government Grants	Paragraphs 24.5C to 24.5G are inserted to allow an additional model of accounting for grants (the accrual model). The model permits entities to recognise grant income on a systematic basis over the period in which the entity recognises the related costs for which the grant is intended to compensate.
25	Borrowing Costs	Section 25 is amended to allow an option that permits entities to capitalise borrowing costs that are directly attributable to the acquisition, construction or production of a qualifying asset.
26	Share-based Payment	The definition of equity-settled share based payments has been amended to align with the revised IFRS 2 definition. It is clarified that option pricing models do not have to be applied in all circumstances.
		Paragraph 26.15 has been replaced with new paragraphs 26.15 to 26.15B to bring the accounting for share-based payment arrangements with cash alternatives closer to that required by IFRS 2 when the entity has the settlement choice.
27	Impairment of Assets	Paragraph 27.20A is inserted to provide guidance on the treatment of impairments on assets held for their service potential.

Section		Changes to the IFRS for SMEs (July 2009)
		Paragraph 27.33A is inserted to include a descriptive disclosure requirement of the events and circumstances that led to the recognition or reversal of the impairment loss.
28	Employee Benefits	The presentation of the cost of a defined benefit plan and the accounting for group plans have been amended to be consistent with the requirements of IAS 19 *Employee Benefits* as amended in 2011.
		Paragraph 28.11A is inserted to require the recognition of a liability on a defined benefit multi-employer plan, which is accounted as defined contribution scheme, where funding of a deficit has been agreed.
		Paragraph 28.19 is deleted to remove the option to use a simplified valuation method in measuring the liability.
29	Income Tax	Section 29 of the IFRS for SMEs has been entirely replaced with revised requirements.
30	Foreign Currency Translation	No significant changes.
31	Hyperinflation	No significant changes.
32	Events after the End of the Reporting Period	Paragraphs 32.7A and 32.7B are inserted to provide guidance on the impact of changes in an entity's going concern status.
33	Related Party Disclosures	Paragraph 33.1A is inserted to include the exemption from disclosure of related party transactions for wholly-owned entities available in the Act.
		The definition of a related party in paragraph 33.2 is amended for consistency with company law.
34	Specialised Activities	Agriculture – this sub-section is amended to allow the option to hold biological assets and agricultural produce at cost.
		Extractives – this sub-section has been amended to require application of IFRS 6.
		Service concession arrangements – this sub-section is amended to clarify the accounting by operators and provide guidance to grantors.
		The following additional sub-sections are inserted: • Financial Institutions; • Retirement Benefit Plans: Financial Statements; • Heritage Assets; • Funding Commitments; • Incoming Resources from Non-Exchange Transactions; • Public Benefit Entity Combinations; and • Public Benefit Entity Concessionary Loans.
35	Transition to this FRS	Amendments to this section reflect the changes in preceding sections and the different effective date for small entities.

Appendix III:
Table of equivalence for UK Companies Act terminology

The following table compares company law terminology with broadly equivalent terminology used in FRS 102. In some cases there are minor differences between the broadly equivalent definitions, which are also summarised below.

Company law terminology	FRS 102 terminology
Accounting reference date	Reporting date
Accounts	Financial statements
Associated undertaking	Associate
Balance sheet	Statement of financial position
Capital and reserves	Equity
Cash at bank and in hand	Cash[31]
Debtors	Trade receivables
Diminution in value [of assets]	Impairment
Financial year	Reporting period
Group [accounts]	Consolidated [financial statements]
IAS	EU-adopted IFRS
Individual [accounts]	Individual [financial statements]
Interest payable and similar charges	Finance costs
Interest receivable and similar income	Finance income/Investment income
Minority interests	Non-controlling interest
Net realisable value [of any current asset]	Estimated selling price less costs to complete and sell
Parent undertaking	Parent
Profit and loss account	Income statement (under the two-statement approach)
	Part of the statement of comprehensive income (under the single-statement approach)
Related undertakings[32]	Subsidiaries, associates and joint ventures
Stocks	Inventories
Subsidiary undertaking	Subsidiary
Tangible assets	Includes: Property, plant equipment; Investment property
Trade creditors	Trade payables

---

[31] *FRS 102 requires the cash flow statement to reconcile the movement in cash and cash equivalents. Disclosure is required of reconciliation between amounts presented in the statement of financial position (ie cash) and cash and cash equivalents.*

[32] *This would also include entities in which a company has at least a 20 per cent holding, but which are not a subsidiary, joint venture or an associate. A shareholding of 20 per cent is presumed to give significant influence to the holder, such that the investment would be classified as an associate, therefore in practice there are unlikely to be many related undertakings that are not subsidiaries, joint ventures or associates.*

Appendix IV:
Note on legal requirements

INTRODUCTION

This appendix provides an overview of how the requirements in FRS 102 address United   **A4.1**
Kingdom company law requirements. It is therefore written from the perspective of a
company to which the Companies Act 2006 applies[27]. Appendix VI discusses the Republic
of Ireland legal references.

Many entities that are not constituted as companies apply accounting standards promulgated   **A4.2**
by the FRC for the purposes of preparing financial statements that present a true and
fair view[28]. A brief consideration of the legal framework for some other entities can be
found at A4.41 and A4.42. For those entities that are within the scope of a Statement of
Recommended Practice (SORP), the relevant SORP will provide more details on the legal
framework.

References to the Act in this appendix are to the *Companies Act 2006*. References to the   **A4.3**
Regulations are to *The Large and Medium-sized Companies and Groups (Accounts and
Reports) Regulations 2008* (SI 2008/410) as amended by *The Companies, Partnerships
and Groups (Accounts and Reports) Regulations 2015* (SI 2015/980) following the
implementation of the EU Accounting Directive. References to specific provisions are to
Schedule 1 to the Regulations; entities applying Schedules 2, 3 or 6 should read them as
referring to the equivalent paragraph in those schedules; and small entities applying the
Small Companies Regulations should read them as referring to the equivalent paragraph in
Schedule 1 to the Small Companies Regulations. Similar provisions generally also apply to
limited liability partnerships applying the Small LLP Regulations or the LLP Regulations
although some differences do exist (see paragraphs A4.43 to A4.47).

Applicable accounting framework

Group accounts of certain parent entities (those with securities admitted to trading   **A4.4**
on a regulated market in an EU Member State) are required by Article 4 of EU
Regulation 1606/2002 (IAS Regulation) to be prepared in accordance with EU-adopted
IFRS.

All other entities, except those that are eligible to apply FRS 105 *The Financial Reporting*   **A4.5**
Standard applicable to the Micro-entities Regime, must apply[29] either FRS 102 *The
Financial Reporting Standard applicable in the UK and Republic of Ireland*, EU-adopted
IFRS or FRS 101 *Reduced Disclosure Framework* (if the financial statements are the
individual financial statements of a qualifying entity eligible to apply FRS 101).

---

[27] *Some charities are also companies, and are therefore required to apply the requirements of both the* Companies
Act 2006 *and the* Charities Act 2011.

[28] *More information about the 'true and fair' concept can be found on the FRC's website at http://www.frc.org.uk/
Our-Work/Codes-Standards/Accounting-and-Reporting-Policy/True-and-Fair.aspx.*

[29] *Under company law in the Republic of Ireland, certain entities are permitted to prepare Companies Act accounts
using accounting standards other than those issued by the FRC.*

A4.6   Section 395(1) of the Act states:

A company's individual accounts may be prepared—

(a)   in accordance with section 396 ('Companies Act individual accounts'), or

(b)   in accordance with international accounting standards ('IAS individual accounts').

Section 403(2) of the Act states:

The group accounts of other companies may be prepared—

(a)   in accordance with section 404 ('Companies Act group accounts'), or

(b)   in accordance with international accounting standards ('IAS group accounts').

A4.7   Accounts prepared in accordance with FRS 102 are classified as either 'Companies Act individual accounts', including those of qualifying entities applying FRS 102, or 'Companies Act group accounts' and are therefore required to comply with the applicable provisions of Parts 15 and 16 of the Act and with the Regulations.

Consistency of financial reporting within groups

A4.8   Section 407 of the Act requires that the directors of the parent company secure that individual accounts of a parent company and each of its subsidiaries are prepared using the same financial reporting framework, except to the extent that in the directors' opinion there are good reasons for not doing so.

In addition, consistency is not required in the following situations:

(a)   when the parent company does not prepare consolidated financial statements; or

(b)   when some subsidiaries are charities (consistency is not needed between the framework used for these and for other subsidiaries).

Where the directors of a parent company prepare IAS group accounts and IAS individual accounts, there only has to be consistency across the individual financial statements of the subsidiaries.

A4.9   All companies, other than those which elect or are required to prepare IAS individual accounts in accordance with the Act, prepare Companies Act individual accounts.

Application of FRS 102

Compliance with company law

The FRS has been developed for application in the UK and Republic of Ireland, using the IFRS for SMEs as a basis. Part of that development process included making amendments to the IFRS for SMEs to ensure compliance with the Act and the Regulations. For example, changes were made to eliminate options that are not permitted by company law. However, FRS 102 is not intended to be a one-stop-shop for all accounting and legal requirements, and although the FRC believes FRS 102 is not inconsistent with company law, compliance with FRS 102 alone will often be insufficient to ensure compliance with all the disclosure requirements set out in the Act and the Regulations. As a result preparers will continue to be required to have regard to the requirements of company law in addition to accounting standards. | **A4.10**

This appendix does not list every legal requirement, but instead focuses on those areas where greater judgement might be required in determining compliance with the law. | **A4.11**

Small companies

The definition of a small company is contained in sections 382 and 383 of the Act; certain companies are excluded from the small companies regime by section 384. Subject to certain conditions and exclusions, the qualifying conditions are met by a company in a year in which it does not exceed two or more of the following criteria: | **A4.11A**

(a) Turnover   £10.2 million
(b) Balance sheet total   £5.1 million
(c) Average number of employees   50

A parent company qualifies as a small company in relation to a financial year only if the group that it heads qualifies as small (as set out in section 383 of the Act). | **A4.11B**

The Small Companies Regulations set out the small companies regime. Although FRS 102 was developed on the basis of the Regulations (which apply to large and medium-sized companies) the recognition and measurement requirements of FRS 102 should also be consistent with the Small Companies Regulations. | **A4.11C**

In accordance with section 393 of the Act the directors of any company, including a small company, must not approve accounts unless they are satisfied that they give a true and fair view of the assets, liabilities, financial position and profit or loss of the company. In order to achieve this, a company, including a small company, may need to provide disclosures additional to those required by company law. In relation to small companies, paragraph 1A.16 of FRS 102 reflects this requirement and paragraph 1A.17 encourages a small company to consider all other disclosures in FRS 102 to determine any additional disclosures to provide. | **A4.11D**

The Small Companies Regulations include options for small companies to prepare an abridged balance sheet and an abridged profit and loss account. In order to take this option small companies must comply with the additional legal requirement that all members of the company have consented to the drawing up of abridged financial statements (which may only be given in respect of the preceding financial year). In accordance with paragraph 1A(4) of Schedule 1 to the Small Companies Regulations this option is not available to small entities that are charities. When a small entity that is not a company chooses to prepare abridged financial statements it should ensure that: | **A4.11E**

(a)   similar consent is obtained from the members of its governing body, taking into account its legal form; and

(b)   abridged financial statements would not be prohibited by relevant laws or regulation.

Financial instruments measured at fair value

A4.12   All preparers of Companies Act accounts must comply with the requirements of paragraph 36 of Schedule 1 to the Regulations, which provides that:

(1)   Subject to sub-paragraphs (2) to (5), financial instruments (including derivatives) may be included at fair value.

(2)   Sub-paragraph (1) does not apply to financial instruments that constitute liabilities unless—

(a)   they are held as part of a trading portfolio,

(b)   they are derivatives, or

(c)   they are financial instruments falling within sub-paragraph (4).

(3)   Unless they are financial instruments falling within sub-paragraph (4), sub-paragraph (1) does not apply to –

(a)   financial instruments (other than derivatives) held to maturity,

(b)   loans and receivables originated by the company and not held for trading purposes,

(c)   interests in subsidiary undertakings, associated undertakings and joint ventures,

(d)   equity instruments issued by the company,

(e)   contracts for contingent consideration in a business combination, or

(f)   other financial instruments with such special characteristics that the instruments, according to generally accepted accounting principles or practice, should be accounted for differently from other financial instruments.

(4)   Financial instruments which under international accounting standards may be included in accounts at fair value, may be so included, provided that the disclosures required by such accounting standards are made.

(4)   [...]

A4.12A   In limited circumstances, an entity applying this FRS to its financial instruments that are classified as non-basic in accordance with Section 11 *Basic Financial Instruments* may be prohibited, by paragraph 36 of Schedule 1 to the Regulations, to measure those financial instruments at fair value through profit or loss in accordance with the requirements of this FRS. The Regulations prohibit the measurement of certain financial instruments at fair value through profit or loss, unless the instruments could be designated for such measurement under EU-adopted IFRS. EU-adopted IFRS permits designation at fair value through profit or loss upon initial recognition for financial instruments where: doing so eliminates or reduces a measurement or recognition inconsistency; or a group of financial instruments is managed and their performance evaluated on a fair value basis; or for a hybrid financial instruments which contains a component that, if recognised separately, would meet the definition of a derivative. Paragraph 12.8(c) of this FRS is applicable to the measurement of financial instruments prohibited under the Regulations to be measured at fair value through profit or loss and requires them to be measured at amortised cost.

A4.12B   Further, an entity that has made the accounting policy choice in paragraph 11.2(c) or paragraph 12.2(c) to apply the recognition and measurement provisions of IFRS 9 *Financial Instruments* shall depart from those provisions of IFRS 9 where the measurement of financial assets at fair value through profit or loss is not permitted by paragraph 36 of Schedule 1 to the Regulations. This can occur in relation to financial assets because the classification and measurement requirements of IFRS 9 are not identical to the equivalent requirements of IAS 39 *Financial Instruments: Recognition and Measurement*, which is the standard presently adopted by the EU and is therefore the reference point for paragraph 36(4) of Schedule 1 to the Regulations.

Paragraph 40 of Schedule 1 to the Regulations requires companies to include fair value gains and losses on financial instruments measured at fair value in the profit and loss account, except when the financial instrument is a hedging instrument or an available for sale security. Therefore, for those companies making the accounting policy choice, in accordance with paragraph 11.2(c) and 12.2(c) of FRS 102, to apply the recognition and measurement requirements of IFRS 9 *Financial Instruments*, recording fair value gains and losses attributable to changes in credit risk in other comprehensive income in accordance with IFRS 9 will usually be a departure from the requirement of paragraph 40 of Schedule 1 to the Regulations, for the overriding purpose of giving a true and fair view.   **A4.12C**

Entities that are preparing Companies Act accounts must provide the disclosures required by paragraph 55 of Schedule 1 to the Regulations, which sets out requirements relating to financial instruments measured at fair value through profit or loss. Most of these disclosures will be satisfied by equivalent requirements of FRS 102, but entities will need to take care to ensure appropriate disclosure of derivatives is provided.   **A4.12D**

An entity applying this FRS and holding financial instruments measured at fair value may be required to provide the disclosures required by paragraph 36(4) of Schedule 1 to the Regulations. The disclosures required by paragraph 36(4) have been incorporated into Section 11. Some of the Section 11 disclosure requirements apply to all financial instruments measured at fair value, whilst others (see paragraph 11.48A of FRS 102) apply only to certain financial instruments (this does not include financial liabilities held as part of a trading portfolio nor derivatives). The disclosure requirements of paragraph 11.48A will predominantly apply to certain financial liabilities, however, there may be instances where paragraph 36(3) of Schedule 1 to the Regulations requires that the disclosures must also be provided in relation to financial assets, for example investments in subsidiaries, associates or jointly controlled entities measured at fair value (see paragraph 9.27B of FRS 102).   **A4.13**

Requirement to present financial statements

FRS 102 does not prescribe which entities prepare financial statements and preparers should apply the requirements of the Act in determining whether financial statements (either individual or consolidated) are required. FRS 102 sets out the requirements for a complete set of financial statements that give a true and fair view of the financial position, financial performance and, where required to be presented, cash flows of an entity, where these are required by law, or other regulation or requirement.   **A4.14**

A parent company preparing consolidated financial statements under section 434(2) of the Act must publish its company financial statements together with the consolidated financial statements, although section 408 of the Act provides an exemption from including the company's individual profit and loss account.   **A4.15**

Subsidiaries excluded from consolidation

Paragraph 9.9(b) of Section 9 *Consolidated and Separate Financial Statements* requires a group to exclude subsidiaries from consolidation on the grounds that they are held exclusively with a view to subsequent resale. By defining 'held exclusively with a view to subsequent resale' in FRS 102 to include those interests that are held as part of an investment portfolio, subsidiaries held as part of such an investment portfolio are excluded   **A4.16** from consolidation in accordance with section 405(3) of the Act and an entity will not need to apply the true and fair override in this circumstance.

A4.17   Paragraph 9.9B(a) requires a group to measure subsidiaries excluded from consolidation by virtue of paragraph 9.9(b) and held as part of an investment portfolio, at fair value through profit or loss. The measurement at fair value through profit and loss, in circumstances where it would not be required by IFRS 10 *Consolidated Financial Statements*, is a departure from the requirements of paragraph 36 of Schedule 1 to the Regulations, for the overriding purpose of giving a true and fair view in the consolidated financial statements. In this circumstance entities must provide, in the notes to the financial statements, the 'particulars of the departure, the reasons for it and its effect' (paragraph 10(2) of Schedule 1 to the Regulations).

Calculation of goodwill where a business combination is achieved in stages

A4.18   Paragraph 9 of Schedule 6 to the Regulations sets out the requirements for the acquisition method of accounting, which results in goodwill (or negative goodwill) being calculated as the difference between:

(a)   the fair value of the group's share of identifiable assets and liabilities of the subsidiary at the date control is achieved; and

(b)   the total acquisition cost of the interests held by the group in that subsidiary.

This applies even where part of the acquisition cost arises from purchases at earlier dates.

A4.19   In most cases, this method provides a practical means of applying acquisition accounting because it does not require retrospective assessments of the fair value of the identifiable assets and liabilities of the subsidiary. In certain circumstances, however, not using fair values at the dates of earlier purchases while using acquisition costs which in part relate to earlier purchases may result in accounting that is inconsistent with the way the investment has been treated previously and, for that reason, may fail to give a true and fair view.

A4.20   For example, an undertaking that has been treated as an associate may then be acquired by that group as a subsidiary. Using the method required by the Regulations and paragraph 9.19B of FRS 102 to calculate goodwill on such an acquisition has the effect that the group's share of profits or losses and reserve movements of its associate becomes reclassified as goodwill (usually negative goodwill). A similar problem may arise where the group has substantially restated its investment in an undertaking that subsequently becomes its subsidiary. For example, where such an investment has been written down because it is impaired, the effect of applying the Regulations' method of acquisition accounting would be to increase reserves and create an asset (goodwill).

A4.21   In the rare cases where the method for calculating goodwill set out in the Regulations and in paragraph 9.19B of FRS 102 would be misleading, the goodwill should be calculated as the sum of goodwill arising from each purchase of an interest in the relevant undertaking adjusted as necessary for any subsequent impairment. Goodwill arising on each purchase should be calculated as the difference between the cost of that purchase and the fair value at the date of that purchase of the identifiable assets and liabilities attributable to the interest purchased. The difference between the goodwill calculated using this method and that calculated using the method provided by the Regulations and FRS 102 is shown in reserves. Section 404(5) of the Act sets out the disclosures required in cases where the statutory requirement is not applied. Paragraph 3.5 of FRS 102 sets out the disclosures when an entity departs from a requirement of FRS 102 or from a requirement of applicable legislation.

Netting

FRS 102 permits an expense relating to a provision to be presented net of the amount recognised for a reimbursement (which may only be recognised if it is virtually certain it will be received) (see paragraph 21.9 of FRS 102). Paragraph 8 of Schedule 1 to the Regulations requires that 'Amounts in respect of items representing assets or income may not be set off against amounts in respect of items representing liabilities or expenditure (as the case may be), or vice versa.' The reimbursement asset is recognised separately from the underlying obligation to reflect the fact that the entity often will continue to be liable if the third party from which the reimbursement is due fails to pay. On the other hand, the net presentation in the income statement reflects the cost to the entity and net presentation therefore does not conflict with the Regulations.

A4.22

FRS 102 requires that a financial asset and financial liability are offset and the net amount presented in the statement of financial position, if certain criteria are met (see paragraph 11.38A of FRS 102). The net presentation does not conflict with paragraph 8 of Schedule 1 to the Regulations, because provided the criteria for the net presentation are met, the presentation reflects the expected net cash flows from settling two or more separate financial instruments.

A4.23

Recording investments at cost

Paragraph 9.26 of FRS 102 requires that in an investor's separate financial statements its investments in subsidiaries are accounted for at cost less impairment, or at fair value. Where the cost model is applied, sections 611 to 615 of the Act set out the treatment where 'merger relief' or 'group reconstruction relief' are available. These reliefs reduce the amount required to be included in share premium; they also (in section 615) allow the initial carrying amount to be adjusted downwards so it is equal to either the previous carrying amount of the investment in the transferor's books or the nominal value of the shares issued, depending on which relief applies. If the fair value model in paragraph 9.26 is used, then the relief in section 615 is not available, so the investment's carrying value may not be reduced, although the provisions in sections 611 and 612 remain relevant in respect of amounts required to be recorded in share premium.

A4.24

Realised profits

Paragraph 13(a) of Schedule 1 to the Regulations requires that only profits realised at the reporting date are included in profit or loss, a requirement modified from that in Article 31.1(c)(aa) of the Fourth Directive which refers to profits 'made' at the balance sheet date.

A4.25

Paragraph 36 and paragraph 39 of Schedule 1 to the Regulations allow financial instruments, stocks, investment property, and living animals and plants to be held at fair value in Companies Act accounts.

A4.26

Paragraph 40(2) of Schedule 1 to the Regulations then requires that movements in the value of financial instruments, investment properties and living animals and plants are recognised in the profit and loss account, notwithstanding the usual restrictions allowing only realised profits and losses to be included in the profit and loss account. Paragraph 40 of Schedule 1 to the Regulations thereby overrides the requirements of paragraph 13(a) of Schedule 1.

A4.27

Entities measuring financial instruments, investment properties, and living animals and plants at fair value should note that they may transfer such amounts to a separate non-distributable reserve, instead of a transfer to retained earnings, but are not required to

A4.28

do so. Presenting fair value movements, that are not distributable profits, in the separate reserve may assist with the identification of profits available for that purpose.

A4.29   The determination of profits available for distribution is a complex area where accounting and company law interface. In determining profits available for distribution an entity may refer to Technical Release 02/10 *Guidance on realised and distributable profits under the Companies Act 2006* issued by the Institute of Chartered Accountants in England and Wales and the Institute of Chartered Accountants of Scotland, or any successor document, to determine profits available for distribution.

Merger accounting

A4.30   Paragraph 10 of Schedule 6 to the Regulations states:
>   The conditions for accounting for an acquisition as a merger are—
>
>   (a)   that the undertaking whose shares are acquired is ultimately controlled by the same party both before and after the acquisition,
>   (b)   that the control referred to in paragraph (a) is not transitory, and
>   (c)   that adoption of the merger method accords with generally accepted accounting principles or practice.

Therefore, paragraph 10 of Schedule 6 to the Regulations permits the use of merger accounting in certain limited circumstances, which is generally consistent with paragraph 19.27 of FRS 102 (group reconstructions). If an entity considers that, for the overriding purpose of giving a true and fair view, merger accounting should be applied in circumstances other than those set out in paragraph 10 of Schedule 6 to the Regulations, it may do so providing the relevant disclosures are made in the notes to the financial statements.

A4.30A   Section 34 *Specialised Activities* requires that combinations by public benefit entities meeting certain criteria are accounted for as a merger, unless this is not permitted by the relevant statutory framework. FRS 102 therefore does not extend the use of merger accounting beyond its applicability in company law, or other relevant statutory framework. If a public benefit entity that is a company considers that, for the overriding purpose of giving a true and fair view, merger accounting should be applied in circumstances other than those set out in paragraph 10 of Schedule 6 to the Regulations, it may do so providing the relevant disclosures are made in the notes to the financial statements.

Treasury shares

A4.31   Paragraph 22.16 of FRS 102 sets out the accounting requirements when an entity purchases its own equity instruments (ie treasury shares).

A4.32   Companies subject to the Act, need to comply with the accounting requirements of paragraph 22.16 as well as with the requirements of the Act when they purchase their own equity and hold it in treasury (Sections 690 to 708 and 724 to 732, respectively).

Measurement of investments in associates and jointly controlled entities for an investor, which is not a parent

A4.33   Paragraph 36 of Schedule 1 to the Regulations sets out the fair value accounting rules and permits investments in associates and joint ventures to be measured at fair value through profit or loss only where they are permitted to be treated as financial instruments in accordance with IAS Regulation. EU-adopted IFRS does allow investments in subsidiaries, associates and jointly controlled entities to be measured in accordance with IAS 39 *Financial Instruments Recognition and Measurement* within separate financial statements (as set out in IAS 27 *Consolidated and Separate Financial Statements*).

Therefore, where the fair value model is applied by an investor, changes in fair value may be recognised through profit or loss, or other comprehensive income. Under the alternative accounting rules set out in Section C of Schedule 1 to the Regulations, the initial recognition of the investment must include any expenses that are incidental to the acquisition of the investment. **A4.34**

Measurement of inventories held for distribution at no or nominal value

Paragraph 24(1) of Schedule 1 to the Regulations requires that if the net realisable value of any current asset is lower than its purchase price or production cost, the amount to be included in respect of that asset must be the net realisable value. However, paragraph 39 permits stocks to be included at their fair value, when applying fair value accounting. **A4.35**

Inventories held for distribution at no or nominal value include items that might be distributed to beneficiaries by public benefit entities and items such as advertising and promotional material. As the items will be distributed at no or nominal cost, the net realisable value will usually be lower than the purchase price. **A4.36**

Paragraph 13.4A of FRS 102 requires inventories held for distribution at no or nominal cost to be measured at the lower of cost (adjusted for any loss in service potential) and replacement cost. This is an application of fair value accounting. For inventories, including those held for distribution at no or nominal value (particularly items distributed to beneficiaries by public benefit entities), there is unlikely to be a significant difference between replacement cost and fair value. **A4.37**

Amortisation of intangible assets

Paragraph 22 of Schedule 1 to the Regulations requires intangible assets to be written off over their useful economic lives. This is broadly consistent with paragraph 18.21 of FRS 102, except that FRS 102 allows for the possibility that an intangible asset will have a residual value, in which case it is the depreciable amount that shall be amortised, not the cost (or revalued amount) of the intangible asset. In practice it will be uncommon for an intangible asset to have a residual value (paragraph 18.23 requires an entity to assume that the residual value is zero other than in specific circumstances). In those cases where an intangible asset has a residual value that is not zero, the amortisation of the depreciable amount of an intangible asset over its useful economic life is a departure from the requirements of paragraph 22 of Schedule 1 to the Regulations for the overriding purpose of giving a true and fair view. In these circumstances entities must provide, in the notes to the financial statements, the 'particulars of the departure, the reasons for it and its effect' (paragraph 10(2) of Schedule 1 to the Regulations). **A4.37A**

Accounts formats

Sections 1A, 4 and 5 of FRS 102 require entities to apply one of the profit and loss account and balance sheet formats set out in the Small Companies Regulations, the Regulations, the Small LLP Regulations and the LLP Regulations, when preparing their statement of comprehensive income (single-statement approach) or income statement (two-statement approach) and statement of financial position, respectively. The *General Rules* preceding *The Required Formats for Accounts* include certain flexibilities for companies (but not LLPs at present), this includes permitting adaptation of the formats, providing the adapted **A4.38** presentation is equivalent to that set out in the formats and that it is consistent with generally accepted accounting practice. For entities within its scope FRS 102 sets out a framework for the information to be presented by those entities choosing to adapt the formats.

Discontinued operations

A4.39   FRS 102 requires an entity with discontinued operations, to provide an analysis between continuing operations and discontinued operations of each of the line items on the face of the statement of comprehensive income, or income statement, up to and including post-tax profit or loss for the period and illustrates this presentation in a columnar format. This is in order to present the post-tax results of those operations, combined with the profit or loss on their disposal, as a single line item while still complying with the requirement of company law to show totals for ordinary activities of items such as turnover, profit or loss before taxation and tax.

Long-term debtors

A4.40   UITF Abstract 4 *Presentation of long-term debtors in current assets* addressed the inclusion of debtors due after more than one year within 'current assets'; that UITF consensus has been withdrawn, but its conclusions remain valid and have been included in paragraph 4.4A of FRS 102.

Entities not subject to company law

A4.41   Many entities that apply FRS 102 are not companies, but are nevertheless required by their governing legislation, or other regulation or requirement to prepare financial statements that present a true and fair view of the financial performance and financial position of the reporting entity. However, the FRC sets accounting standards within the framework of the Act and therefore it is the company law requirements that the FRC primarily considered when developing FRS 102. Entities preparing financial statements within other legal frameworks will need to satisfy themselves that FRS 102 does not conflict with any relevant legal obligations.

A4.42   However, the FRC notes the following:

Legislation	Overview of requirements
Building Societies Act 1986	The annual accounts of a building society shall give a true and fair view of the income and expenditure for the year and the balance sheet shall give a true and fair view of the state of affairs of the society at the end of the financial year.
	Regulations make further requirements about the form and content of building society accounts, which do not appear inconsistent with the requirement of FRS 102.
Charity law in England and Wales: Charities Act 2011 and regulations made thereunder	All charities are required to prepare accounts. The regulations require financial statements (other than cash-based receipts and payments accounts prepared by smaller charities) to present a true and fair view of the incoming resources, application of resources and the balance sheet, and to be prepared in accordance with the SORP. However company charities prepare their accounts in accordance with UK company law to give a 'true and fair view'.

Legislation	Overview of requirements
	The Charities SORP (FRS 102) is compatible with the legal requirements, clarifying how they apply to accounting by charities applying FRS 102.
	UK company law prohibits charities from preparing IAS accounts.
Charity law in Scotland: Charities and Trustee Investments Act (Scotland) 2005 and regulations made thereunder	All charities are required to prepare accounts. The regulations require financial statements (other than cash-based receipts and payments accounts prepared by smaller charities) to present a true and fair view of the incoming resources, application of resources and the balance sheet, and to be prepared in accordance with the SORP. These regulations apply equally to company charities.
Charity law in Northern Ireland: Charities Act (Northern Ireland) 2008	The Charities Act 2008 has yet to come fully into effect. The Act provides for all charities to prepare accounts. The Act provides for regulations concerning the financial statements. The financial statements other than cash-based receipts and payments accounts prepared by smaller charities are to present a true and fair view of the incoming resources, application of resources and the balance sheet.
	However company charities prepare their accounts in accordance with UK company law to give a 'true and fair view'.
Friendly and Industrial and Provident Societies Act 1968	Every Society shall prepare a revenue account and a balance sheet giving a true and fair view of the income and expenditure and state of affairs of the Society.
	FRS 102 does not appear to give rise to any legal conflicts for Societies. However, Societies often carry out activities that are regulated and may be required to comply with additional regulations on top of the legal requirements and accounting standards. Some Societies fall within the scope of SORPs, which reflect the requirements of FRS 102.
Friendly Societies Act 1992	Every society shall prepare a balance sheet and an income and expenditure account for each financial year giving a true and fair view of the affairs of the society and its income and expenditure for the year.
	The Regulations[36] make further requirements about the form and content of friendly society accounts, which do not appear inconsistent with the requirements of FRS 102.
The Occupational Pension Schemes (Requirement to obtain Audited Accounts and a Statement from the Auditor) Regulations 1996	The accounts of pension funds within the scope of the regulations should show a true and fair view of the transactions during the year, assets held at the end of the year and liabilities of the scheme, other than those to pay pensions and benefits.
	FRS 102 includes retirement benefit plans as a specialised activity.

[36] *The Friendly Societies (Accounts and Related Provisions) Regulations 1994* (as amended).

A4.43   Limited liability partnerships (LLPs) will be applying FRS 102 in conjunction with the LLP Regulations or the Small LLP Regulations. In many cases these regulations are similar to the Regulations or the Small Companies Regulations, which reduces the situations in which legal matters relevant to the financial statements of LLPs are not addressed in this Appendix. However, the amendments made to the Regulations and the Small Companies Regulations by *The Companies, Partnerships and Groups (Accounts and Reports) Regulations 2015* (SI 2015/980) have not been reflected in the LLP Regulations or the Small LLP Regulations. This gives rise to some differences for LLPs.

Small LLPs

A4.44   The thresholds that are part of the qualifying conditions of a small company and a small LLP have diverged, with the thresholds for a small LLP being lower than those for a small company. Of LLPs, only those qualifying as small (and not otherwise excluded) in accordance with the LLP Regulations, will be able to apply Section 1A *Small Entities*.

A4.45   A small LLP choosing to apply Section 1A shall provide the following disclosures:

   (a)   those set out in Appendix C to Section 1A;
   (b)   those required by the Small LLP Regulations that are additional to those set out in Appendix C to Section 1A; and
   (c)   any additional disclosures necessary to meet the requirement to give a true and fair view, as set out in paragraph 1A.17.

In accordance with paragraph 1A.20 a small LLP is also encouraged to provide the disclosures set out in Appendix D to Section 1A.

All LLPs

A4.46   In a relatively small number of areas *The Companies, Partnerships and Groups (Accounts and Reports) Regulations 2015* (SI 2015/980) made changes to the recognition and measurement requirements applicable to companies. These changes have not been made to the LLP Regulations or the Small LLP Regulations and therefore, in a small number of cases, the requirements of FRS 102 will be inconsistent with the LLP Regulations and the Small LLP Regulations. Areas where this may have an impact include:

   (a)   the flexibility available in relation to the format of the balance sheet and of the profit and loss account;
   (b)   the scope of financial instruments that can be measured at fair value through profit or loss;
   (c)   the reversal of impairment losses in relation to goodwill; and
   (d)   the application of merger accounting.

If following the requirements of FRS 102 would lead to a conflict with applicable legislation, an LLP shall instead apply its own legal requirements and consider whether disclosure of a departure from FRS 102 is required.

LLP consolidated financial statements

A4.47   When LLPs prepare consolidated financial statements, whether mandatorily or voluntarily, there will also be differences between company law and the similar requirements applicable to LLPs. If following the requirements of FRS 102 would lead to a conflict with applicable legislation, an LLP shall instead apply its own legal requirements and consider whether disclosure of a departure from FRS 102 is required.

Appendix V:
Previous consultations

The requirements in FRSs 100 to 102 are the outcome of a lengthy and extensive **A5.1**
consultation. The FRC (and formerly the ASB) together with the Department for Business,
Innovation and Skills have consulted on the future of accounting standards in the UK and
Republic of Ireland (RoI) over a ten-year period.

Year	Consultation
2002	DTI[37] consults on adoption of IAS Regulation
2004	Discussion Paper – Strategy for Convergence with IFRS
2005	Exposure Draft – Policy Statement: The Role of the ASB
2006	Public Meeting and Proposals for Comment
2006	Press Notice seeking views
2007	Consultation Paper – Proposed IFRS for SMEs
2009	Consultation Paper – Policy Proposal: The future of UK GAAP
2010	Request for Responses – Development of the Impact Assessment
2010	Financial Reporting Exposure Drafts 43 and 44
2011	Financial Reporting Exposure Draft 45
2012	Financial Reporting Exposure Drafts 46, 47 and 48
2012	Financial Reporting Exposure Draft: Amendment to FRED 48

---

[37] *The Department of Trade and Industry (DTI) was a United Kingdom government department which was replaced
with the announcement of the creation of the Department for Business, Enterprise and Regulatory Reform and
the Department for Innovation, Universities and Skills on 28 June 2007, which were themselves merged into the
Department for Business, Innovation and Skills (BIS) on 6 June 2009.*

2004

A5.2   In 2004 the Discussion Paper contained two key elements underpinning the proposals: firstly that UK and Republic of Ireland (RoI) accounting standards should be based on IFRS and secondly that a phased approach to the introduction of the standards should be adopted.

A5.3   The ASB embarked on the phased approach and issued a number of standards based on IFRS. The majority of respondents agreed with a framework based on IFRS, and although supportive overall, the response to the phased approach was mixed.

2005

A5.4   In its 2005 Exposure Draft (2005 ED) of a Policy Statement *Accounting standard-setting in a changing environment: The role of the Accounting Standards Board*, amongst other aspects of its role, the ASB identified its intention to converge with IFRS by implementing new IFRS in the UK as soon as possible. It also proposed to continue the phased approach to adopting UK accounting standards based on older IFRSs, but recognised there was little case for being more prescriptive than IFRS.

A5.5   Although the ASB had, in the 2005 ED, wanted to move the debate on to how it would seek to influence the IASB's agenda, respondents' main concern remained about convergence. In 2005, the ASB issued an exposure draft proposing the IASB's standard on Business Combinations be adopted in the UK and RoI. This exposure draft highlighted the complexity of a mixed set of UK accounting standards, with some based on IFRSs and others developed independently by the ASB. The majority of respondents continued to agree with the aim of basing UK accounting standards on IFRS, but a broader set of views on how to achieve this was emerging.

A5.6   As time progressed the ASB formed the view that convergence by adopting certain IFRSs was not meeting the needs of its constituents, which no longer included quoted groups. The ASB was concerned about the complexity of certain IFRSs, and it noted that introducing them piecemeal created complications and anomalies within the body of current FRSs. This arose because IFRS-based standards were not an exact replacement for current FRSs and many consequential amendments were required to 'fit' each replacement IFRS-based standard into the existing body of UK FRS. The ASB agreed to continue with its convergence programme, but decided to re-examine how to achieve this.

2006

A5.7   The ASB published revised proposals to be discussed at the 2006 public meeting. By this time the IASB had started its IFRS for SMEs project, and the ASB decided this might have a role as one of the tiers in the UK financial reporting framework. The ASB proposed a 'big bang' with new IFRS-based UK accounting standards mandatory from a single date, 1 January 2009. The ASB's proposal was for a three-tier system, with Tier 1 being EU-adopted IFRS, and the other two tiers being developed as the IASB progressed with its project on the IFRS for SMEs.

A5.8   Those attending the public meeting supported the aim of basing UK and RoI accounting standards on IFRS and adapting them to ensure they were appropriate for the entities applying them.

A5.9   Taking this feedback into account, later in 2006 the ASB issued a Press Notice (PN 289) seeking views on its current thinking:

(a) All quoted and publicly accountable companies should apply EU-adopted IFRS.

(b) The FRSSE should be retained and extended to include medium-sized entities.

(c) UK subsidiaries of groups applying full IFRS should apply EU-adopted IFRS, but with reduced disclosure requirements.

(d) No firm decision on the remainder (Tier 2), but options included extending the FRSSE, extending full IFRS, maintaining separate UK accounting standards or some combination of these.

The responses were mixed, but there was agreement that whatever the solution, it should be based on IFRS and there should be different reporting tiers to ensure proportionality.   **A5.10**

2007

The IASB published an exposure draft of its IFRS for SMEs in early 2007; shortly afterwards the ASB published its own consultation paper. This sought views on how the IFRS for SMEs might fit into the future UK financial reporting framework, for example whether it might be appropriate for Tier 2, with the FRSSE continuing for those eligible for the small companies' regime.   **A5.11**

Feedback on the IFRS for SMEs was largely positive: it would be suitable for Tier 2, it was international, it was compatible with IFRS, and it represented a significant simplification. Overall, it was seen as a workable alternative to IFRS. In addition, respondents wanted to retain the FRSSE (because it reduces the regulatory burden on smaller entities) and to give subsidiaries the option of applying the IFRS for SMEs as well as a reduced disclosure regime if applying full IFRS.   **A5.12**

2009

The IFRS for SMEs was published in 2009, allowing the ASB to further develop its proposals in the Consultation Paper *Policy Proposal: The future of UK GAAP*. The proposals were largely consistent with the cumulative results of the preceding consultations and included: **A5.13**

(a) a move to an IFRS-based framework;

(b) a three-tier approach;

(c) publicly accountable entities would be Tier 1 and would apply EU-adopted IFRS;

(d) small companies would be Tier 3 and continue to apply the FRSSE; and

(e) other entities would be Tier 2 and should apply a UK and RoI accounting standard based on the IFRS for SMEs.

The only significant proposal that was inconsistent with respondents' previous comments was that subsidiaries should simply apply the requirement of the tier they individually met – respondents had wanted subsidiaries to be able to take advantage of disclosure exemptions, and at that time the ASB had yet to be convinced that significant cost savings were available from a reduced disclosure framework. Taking into account the feedback received, this proposal was subsequently reversed and the reduced disclosure framework was incorporated into FREDs 43 and then 46, and it is now set out in FRS 101.   **A5.14**

In addition to the many useful and detailed points made, some common themes included general agreement that change was needed to UK accounting standards and that there was support for many of the changes proposed in the consultation paper.   **A5.15**

2010 onwards

A5.16   The request for responses to aid development of the Impact Assessment focused on obtaining feedback on the expected costs, benefits and impact of the proposals subsequently set out in FREDs 43 and 44, rather than on the accounting principles. As the focus was on costs and benefits no specific question was asked about the principle of the proposed introduction of an IFRS-based framework, but nevertheless respondents commented on this: of the 32 responses received only 12.5 per cent did not agree with the introduction of an IFRS-based framework.

A5.17   FRED 43 and 44 issued in October 2010 set out the draft suggested text for two new accounting standards that would replace the majority of extant Financial Reporting Standards (current FRS) in the UK and RoI. The ASB issued a supplementary FRED addressing specific needs of public benefit entities (FRED 45) in March 2011. The ASB then updated FREDs 43, 44 and 45, replacing them with the revised FREDs 46, 47 and 48 in January 2012, by eliminating the concept of public accountability and by introducing a number of accounting treatment options that are available in EU-adopted IFRS. The Accounting Council's advice to the FRC to issue FRSs 100 to 102 includes more discussion of the feedback received on FREDs 43 to 48 and how the proposals have been refined and developed into the standards.

How have the proposals been developed?

A5.18   As set out above, the FRC, the Accounting Council (and previously the ASB) have consulted regularly on the future of financial reporting in the UK and RoI. Over the consultations the ASB's (and the Accounting Council's) thinking has evolved based on careful consideration of the feedback at each stage. Whilst responses were sometimes mixed, there has been agreement that:

(a)   current FRS, which are a mixture of Statements of Standard Accounting Practice (SSAPs) issued by the Consultative Committee of Accounting Bodies, FRSs developed and issued by the ASB and IFRS-based standards issued by the ASB to converge with international standards, are an uncomfortable mismatch that lack strong underlying principles or cohesion; and

(b)   whatever the solution, it should be based on IFRS and there should be different reporting tiers to ensure proportionality.

A5.19   During the consultation process to date, the Accounting Council and formerly the ASB have been guided by the following principles:

(a)   The framework must be fit for purpose, so that each entity required to produce true and fair financial statements under UK and RoI law will deliver financial statements that are suited to the needs of its primary users. The Accounting Council has kept in close contact with constituent users on this point, including investors, creditor institutions and the tax authorities.

(b)   The framework must be proportionate, so that preparing entities are not unduly burdened by costs that outweigh the benefit to them and to the primary users of information in their financial statements. The FRC believes that the proposals will produce a lower cost regime, while enhancing user benefits. It has carried out a consultation stage impact assessment with input from interested parties, and will continue to assess cost-benefit issues.

(c)   The framework must be in line with UK company law. This determines which entities must produce true and fair financial statements. Exemptions within the law have generally been retained. The detailed requirements of the Companies Act 2006 are driven to a great extent by the European Accounting Directives, which are being revised[38].

(d) The framework must be future-proofed, where possible. The FRC will continue to monitor the situation and has sovereignty over UK accounting standards (subject to the law). Changes to the Accounting Directives may lead to further developments, for example the European Council and European Parliament decision to permit Member States an option to treat micro-entities as a separate category of Company and exempt them from certain accounting requirements.

Summary of outreach

During the development and throughout the consultation period of FREDs 43 to 48, the ASB undertook an extensive programme of outreach aimed at raising awareness of the proposals and to address the view (held by some) that previous consultations had not gathered sufficient evidence to support and test the assumptions made.   **A5.20**

As part of the outreach programme to obtain both formal and informal feedback, a series of meetings and events took place with users, including with lenders to small and medium-sized entities. Lenders noted that financial statements are an important part of their decision-making process when considering whether to provide finance and, whilst a decision to provide finance is not based on financial statements alone, they provide useful information and verification to the lender.   **A5.21**

Although the ASB and the Accounting Council employed their best efforts to obtain feedback from users (a constituent group historically difficult to engage with formally) it is disappointing that limited formal responses were received and the Accounting Council has not been more successful in obtaining input from users.   **A5.22**

In addition, a review was made of academic research that addressed the users of the financial statements of small and medium-sized entities. The conclusion drawn from the research was that many entities requested financial statements from Companies House when considering whether to trade with another entity. The European Federation of Accountants and Auditors (EFAA) issued, in May 2011, a statement that identified the users of financial statements, noting who the users of SMEs' financial statements are and that information on the public record assists all users of financial statements of SMEs by providing, in an efficient manner, basic information that protects their rights.   **A5.23**

The ASB considered that the outreach programme had gleaned information from people who would not normally submit formal responses to a consultation and provided very useful information that could be used in developing the next stage of the project. The ASB noted that whilst this information was not part of the public record, as are formal consultation responses, it could use the information to assist in developing the revised FREDs 46 to 48, supplementing information contained in responses, and would seek further comment in the next stage of its deliberations.   **A5.24**

The Accounting Council continued the work of the ASB in finalising FRSs 100 to 102. The responses to FREDs 46 to 48 were analysed and discussed, and engagements were conducted to take into account the views and suggestions of all relevant associations and contacts. Respondents and outreach contacts were satisfied with FREDs 46 to 48, and many of the response letters were forthcoming in their overall praise for the proposals. A significant number of constituents anticipated cost savings arising from the application of FRS 101.   **A5.25**

---

[38] *The EU's consultation process on review of the Accounting Directives is summarised at http://ec.europa.eu/ internal_market/ accounting/sme_accounting/review_directives_en.htm*

Many respondents considered that FRS 102 would improve UK accounting standards, in particular by introducing requirements for accounting for financial instruments. Further they considered that the improvements will be achieved in a way that will be proportionate to the needs of users, and that once the transition phase has been overcome, it will have the effect of reducing the reporting burden on those UK companies that adopt it.

Appendix VI:
Republic of Ireland (RoI) legal references

Appendix VI: *Republic of Ireland (RoI) legal references* will be updated as appropriate for both the Companies Act 2014 and the Irish legislation implementing the EU Accounting Directive once the latter has been made. This will be made available on the FRC website and included in the next edition of FRS 102.

A6.1

FRS 103
Insurance Contracts – Consolidated accounting and reporting requirements for entities in the UK and Republic of Ireland issuing insurance contracts

(March 2014)

Contents

Paragraphs

Summary

FRS 103 Insurance Contracts – Consolidated accounting and reporting requirements for entities in the UK and Republic of Ireland issuing insurance contracts

Section 1	Scope	1.1–1.14
Section 2	Accounting Policies, Recognition and Measurement	2.1–2.34
Section 3	Recognition and Measurement: Requirements for entities with long-term insurance business	3.1–3.18
Section 4	Disclosure	4.1–4.10
Section 5	Disclosure: Additional requirements for with-profits business	5.1–5.5
Section 6	Transition to this FRS	6.1–6.4

Approval by the FRC

The Accounting Council's Advice to the FRC to issue FRS 103

Introduction	1–3
Advice	4–7
Background	8–10
Objective	11–12
Using IFRS 4 *Insurance Contracts* as a basis for FRS 103	13–22
Supplementing IFRS 4 from FRS 27 and the ABI SORP	23–25
Definition of an insurance contract	26–27
Continuation of existing accounting policies	28–34
Embedded derivatives	35
Insurance contracts denominated in foreign currencies	36–37
Compliance with company law	38
Applicability to insurance contracts and to insurance companies	39–40
Disclosure	41–45
Disclosure: Capital	46–49
Implementation Guidance accompanying draft FRS 103	50–51
Memorandum of Understanding concerning FRS 27 *Life Assurance*	52–53
Approval of this advice	54

Appendices

I	Glossary
II	Definition of an insurance contract
III	Tables of concordance between FRS 103, FRS 27 and the ABI SORP
IV	Note on Legal Requirements: Introduction
V	Republic of Ireland (RoI) Legal References

Editor's note: Limited amendments to FRS 103 update it to reflect the implementation, from 1 January 2016, of the Solvency II Directive and are included in the next section of this book.

Summary

(i)   In 2012 and 2013 the Financial Reporting Council (FRC) revised financial reporting standards in the United Kingdom and Republic of Ireland. The revisions fundamentally reformed financial reporting, replacing almost all extant standards with three Financial Reporting Standards:

FRS 100   *Application of Financial Reporting Requirements;*

FRS 101   *Reduced Disclosure Framework;* and

FRS 102   *The Financial Reporting Standard applicable in the UK and Republic of Ireland.*

FRS 103   *Insurance Contracts* is a fourth standard added to the suite of accounting standards, which is relevant to entities applying FRS 102 that have insurance contracts.

(ii)   The FRC's overriding objective in setting accounting standards is to enable users of accounts to receive high-quality understandable financial reporting proportionate to the size and complexity of the entity and users' information needs.

(iii)   In meeting this objective, the FRC aims to provide succinct financial reporting standards that:

(a)   have consistency with international accounting standards through the application of an IFRS-based solution unless an alternative clearly better meets the overriding objective;

(b)   reflect up-to-date thinking and developments in the way entities operate and the transactions they undertake;

(c)   balance consistent principles for accounting by all UK and Republic of Ireland entities with practical solutions, based on size, complexity, public interest and users' information needs;

(d)   promote efficiency within groups; and

(e)   are cost-effective to apply.

(iv)   The requirements in this Financial Reporting Standard (FRS) take into consideration:

(a)   the findings from the previous consultations on the future of financial reporting in the UK and Republic of Ireland that took place between 2002 and 2012, which includes responses to the Discussion Paper *Insurance Accounting – Mind the UK GAAP* issued in 2012; and

(b)   the responses to FRED 49: Draft FRS 103 *Insurance Contracts* issued in July 2013.

(v)   Entities that are applying FRS 102, whether or not they are 'insurance companies', shall also apply this FRS to insurance contracts (including reinsurance contracts) that the entity issues and reinsurance contracts that the entity holds, and to other financial instruments that the entity issues with a discretionary participation feature.

FRS 103 *Insurance Contracts*

(vi)   This FRS (and the accompanying non-mandatory Implementation Guidance) consolidates existing financial reporting requirements and guidance for insurance contracts. The requirements in this FRS (and the guidance in the accompanying non-mandatory Implementation Guidance) are based on the International Accounting Standards Board's (IASB) IFRS 4 *Insurance Contracts* extant in 2013 (except to the extent that it was amended by IFRS 13 *Fair Value Measurement*), the requirements of FRS 27 *Life Assurance* (prior to it being withdrawn by this standard) and elements of the Association of British Insurers' *Statement of Recommended Practice on*

Accounting for Insurance Business (the ABI SORP) (published in December 2005 and amended in December 2006).

In particular, this FRS:

(a) allows entities, generally, to continue with their existing accounting policies for insurance contracts including the appropriate measurement of long-term insurance business, whilst permitting limited improvements to accounting by insurers; and

(b) requires disclosure that:

    (i) identifies and explains the amounts in an insurer's financial statements arising from the insurance contracts (including reinsurance contracts) it issues and reinsurance contracts that it holds;

    (ii) relate to the financial strength of entities carrying on long-term insurance business; and

    (iii) helps users of those financial statements understand the amount, timing and uncertainty of future cash flows from those insurance contracts.

(vii) This FRS allows entities, generally, to continue with their current accounting practices for insurance contracts, but permits entities the same flexibility to make improvements (subject to legal and regulatory requirements) as entities in the UK and Republic of Ireland applying IFRS 4 have, because the FRC does not want the standard to be more onerous to apply than IFRS 4. Nevertheless, this FRS is part of a suite of new accounting standards, including FRS 102, that improve financial reporting for financial instruments (other than insurance contracts); some of the requirements of FRS 102 and of this FRS in relation to financial instruments will lead to changes for insurers.

(viii) One of the reasons that this FRS permits entities to, generally, continue with their current accounting practice is that the FRC expects this FRS to have a limited life. The FRC expects to review this standard once the IASB has issued its updated standard on insurance contracts. The most appropriate timing for this review cannot be determined at the present time. The FRC may make interim amendments to FRS 103 once changes in the regulatory regime for insurers have been finalised.

Entities that are not legally constituted as insurance providers

(ix) Some entities that are not legally constituted as insurance providers may be issuing contracts meeting the definition of an insurance contract in this FRS. Examples include appliance servicing agreements and some product warranty arrangements (when issued by another party for the manufacturer, dealer or retailer). Although such contracts are within the scope of this FRS an entity should generally be able to continue to apply its previous accounting policies to such contracts, as noted above, although additional considerations may be relevant, for example the liability adequacy test and additional disclosures to those provided in the past.

Organisation of FRS 103

(x) All the paragraphs of FRS 103 have equal authority. Some appendices are an integral part of the FRS while others provide guidance concerning its application; each specifies its status. FRS 103 is accompanied by non-mandatory Implementation Guidance providing guidance on applying:

(a) the requirements of FRS 103;

(b) the requirements and principles of FRS 102 by entities with general insurance business or long-term insurance business; and

(c) the requirements of Schedule 3 to the Regulations.

(xi) The elements of the ABI SORP that have been included are largely set out in Section 2 *Guidance for entities with general insurance business or long-term insurance business* of the Implementation Guidance.

(xii) This FRS is set out in Sections 1 to 6, the Glossary (Appendix I) and the Definition of an Insurance Contract (Appendix II). Terms defined in the Glossary are in **bold type** the first time they appear in each section in the FRS.

FRS 103 Insurance Contracts – Consolidated accounting and reporting requirements for entities in the UK and Republic of Ireland issuing insurance contracts

Section 1 *Scope*

Scope of this Financial Reporting Standard

1.1 This FRS applies to **financial statements** prepared by an entity that applies **FRS 102** and that are intended to give a true and fair view of a reporting entity's **financial position** and **profit or loss** (or income and expenditure) for a period.

1.2 An entity that applies FRS 102 shall apply this FRS to:

   (a) **insurance contracts** (including **reinsurance contracts**) that it issues and reinsurance contracts that it holds; and

   (b) **financial instruments** (other than insurance contracts) that it issues with a **discretionary participation feature** (see paragraph 2.30).

1.3 This FRS applies to entities with insurance contracts and financial instruments with discretionary participation features within the scope of paragraph 1.2 as follows:

   (a) Section 1 Scope, Section 2 *Accounting Policies, Recognition and Measurement*, Section 4 *Disclosure* and Section 6 *Transition to this FRS* apply to all entities applying this FRS.

   (b) Section 3 *Recognition and Measurement: Requirements for entities with long-term insurance business* and Section 5 *Disclosure: Additional requirements for with-profits business* only apply to entities with **long-term insurance business**.

   (c) Appendix II: *Definition of an insurance contract* applies to all entities.

   The **Regulations** (or other legal framework that applies to the entity) may set out requirements in addition to those within this FRS.

1.4 The Implementation Guidance accompanying this FRS provides additional guidance for applying:

   (a) the requirements of this FRS;

   (b) the requirements or principles of FRS 102 by entities with **general insurance business** or long-term insurance business; and

   (c) the requirements of Schedule 3 to the Regulations.

   In particular the Implementation Guidance may be relevant as follows:

   (a) Section 1: *Guidance for entities with long-term business* provides guidance on applying Section 3 of FRS 103.

   (b) Section 2: *Guidance for entities with general insurance business or long-term business* provides guidance for all entities applying FRS 103.

   (c) Section 3: *Guidance on capital disclosures for entities with long-term insurance business* applies to entities with long-term insurance business.

1.5 Paragraph 2.3 permits entities to change their **accounting policies**, either on adoption of this FRS or subsequently, providing the new accounting policies meet certain criteria. Entities that are setting accounting policies in relation to insurance contracts, or other financial instruments with discretionary participation features, for the first time, shall for long-term insurance business either:

(a)   first consider the requirements of Section 3, the Regulations and any relevant parts of FRS 102 as a benchmark before assessing whether to set accounting policies that differ from those benchmark policies in accordance with paragraph 2.3; or

(b)   establish accounting policies that are based on the rules under the **Solvency II Directive** for the recognition and measurement of technical provisions, and any relevant requirements of this FRS, the Regulations and FRS 102. In doing so an entity shall make appropriate adjustments to the Solvency II rules to ensure that the accounting policies result in information that is relevant and reliable.

The Implementation Guidance accompanying this FRS also provides guidance.

This FRS does not address other aspects of accounting by **insurers**, such as accounting for **financial assets** held by insurers and **financial liabilities** issued by insurers (see Sections 11 *Basic Financial Instruments*, 12 *Other Financial Instruments Issues* and 34 *Specialised Activities* of FRS 102), except in paragraph 1.8 and in the transitional provisions in paragraph 6.4.   1.6

An entity shall not apply this FRS to: 1.7

(a)   product warranties issued directly by a manufacturer, dealer or retailer (see Sections 21 *Provisions and Contingencies* and 23 *Revenue* of FRS 102);

(b)   employers' assets and **liabilities** under employee benefit plans (see Sections 26 *Share-based Payment* and 28 *Employee Benefits* of FRS 102) and retirement benefit obligations reported by defined benefit retirement plans (see Section 34 of FRS 102);

(c)   contractual rights or contractual obligations that are contingent on the future use of, or right to use, a non-financial item (for example, some licence fees, royalties, contingent lease payments and similar items), as well as a lessee's residual value guarantee embedded in a finance lease (see Sections 18 *Intangible Assets other than Goodwill*, 20 *Leases* and 23 of FRS 102);

(d)   **financial guarantee contracts** unless the issuer has previously asserted explicitly that it regards such contracts as insurance contracts and has used accounting applicable to insurance contracts, in which case the issuer may elect to apply either Section 21 of FRS 102 or this FRS to such financial guarantee contracts. The issuer may make that election contract by contract, but the election for each contract is irrevocable;

(e)   contingent consideration payable or receivable in a **business combination** (see Section 19 *Business Combinations and Goodwill* of FRS 102); or

(f)   **direct insurance contracts** that the entity holds (ie direct insurance contracts in which the entity is the **policyholder**) (for which an accounting policy shall be selected in accordance with the principles of FRS 102). However, a **cedant** shall apply this FRS to reinsurance contracts that it holds.

Some contracts that have the legal form of an insurance contract do not meet the definition of an insurance contract in this FRS. Paragraph A2.19 provides examples of items that are not insurance contracts, and paragraphs A2.20 to A2.24 provide further information on accounting for contracts that are not insurance contracts.   1.8

For ease of reference, this FRS describes any entity that issues an insurance contract as an **insurer**, whether or not the issuer is regarded as an insurer for legal or supervisory purposes.   1.9

A reinsurance contract is a type of insurance contract. Accordingly, all references in this FRS to insurance contracts also apply to reinsurance contracts.   1.10

Date from which effective and transitional arrangements

1.11   An entity shall apply this FRS for accounting periods beginning on or after 1 January 2015. Early application is permitted provided that if an entity applies this FRS before 1 January 2015 it shall:

(a)   also apply FRS 102 from the same date and is not subject to the transitional arrangements in paragraph 1.14 of FRS 102 relating to entities within the scope of a SORP; and

(b)   disclose the fact that it has applied FRS 103 before 1 January 2015.

1.11A   In May 2016 amendments were made to this FRS, to update it for changes in the regulatory framework. An entity shall apply these amendments for accounting periods ending on or after 1 January 2016.

Compliance with this FRS

1.12   An entity whose financial statements comply with this FRS shall, in addition to its statement of compliance with FRS 102 (made in accordance with paragraphs 3.3 to 3.6 of FRS 102), make an explicit and unreserved statement of compliance with this FRS in the **notes to the financial statements**.

Withdrawal of FRS 27

1.13   FRS 27 *Life Assurance* is superseded on the early application of this FRS. FRS 27 will be withdrawn for accounting periods beginning on or after 1 January 2015.

Consequential amendment to FRS 101 *Reduced Disclosure Framework*

1.14   **The following consequential amendment is made to FRS 101 (inserted text is underlined):**

Paragraph (fA) of the Application Guidance: *Amendments to International Financial Reporting Standards as Adopted in the European Union for Compliance with the Act and Regulations* **is inserted as follows:**

fA   Paragraph 14(a) of IFRS 4 *Insurance Contracts* is amended as follows:

(a)   unless otherwise required by the regulatory framework that applies to the entity, shall not recognise as a liability any provisions for possible future claims, if those claims arise under insurance contracts that are not in existence at the end of the reporting period (such as catastrophe provisions and equalisation provisions). The presentation of any such liabilities shall follow the requirements of the Regulations (or other legal framework that applies to the entity).

Section 2 *Accounting Policies, Recognition and Measurement*

Scope of this section

2.1   This section provides guidance for selecting and applying the **accounting policies** used in the **recognition** and measurement of **insurance contracts** when preparing **financial statements**. Entities with **long-term insurance business** shall also apply the requirements of Section 3 *Recognition and Measurement: Requirements for entities with long-term insurance business* in selecting accounting policies for long-term insurance business.

Changes in accounting policy

Paragraphs 2.3 to 2.11 apply both to changes made by an **insurer** that already applies this FRS and to changes made by an insurer adopting this FRS for the first time. **2.2**

As an exception to paragraph 10.8 of **FRS 102** an insurer may change its accounting policies for insurance contracts if, and only if, the change makes the financial statements more relevant to the economic decision-making needs of users and no less reliable, or more reliable and no less relevant to those needs. An insurer shall judge relevance and reliability by the criteria in paragraph 10.4 of FRS 102 and the qualitative characteristics of information in financial statements set out in Section 2 *Concepts and Pervasive Principles* of FRS 102. **2.3**

One basis for changing accounting policies might be to enable them to be more consistent with the rules under the **Solvency II Directive** for the recognition and measurement of technical provisions. In doing so an entity shall make appropriate adjustments to the Solvency II rules to meet the requirements of paragraph 2.3. **2.3A**

To justify changing its accounting policies for insurance contracts, an insurer shall show that the change brings its financial statements closer to meeting the criteria in paragraph 10.4 of FRS 102, but the change need not achieve full compliance with those criteria. The following specific issues are discussed below: **2.4**

(a)   current interest rates (paragraph 2.5);
(b)   continuation of existing practices (paragraph 2.6);
(c)   prudence (paragraph 2.7);
(d)   future investment margins (paragraphs 2.8 to 2.10); and
(e)   shadow accounting (paragraph 2.11).

Current market interest rates

An insurer is permitted, but not required, to change its accounting policies so that it remeasures designated **insurance liabilities**[1] to reflect current market interest rates and recognises changes in those **liabilities** in **profit or loss**. At that time, it may also introduce accounting policies that require other current estimates and assumptions for the designated liabilities. The election in this paragraph permits an insurer to change its accounting policies for designated liabilities, without applying those policies consistently to all similar liabilities as Section 10 *Accounting Policies, Estimates and Errors* of FRS 102 would otherwise require. If an insurer designates liabilities for this election, it shall continue to apply current market interest rates (and, if applicable, the other current estimates and assumptions) consistently in all periods to all these liabilities until they are extinguished. **2.5**

Continuation of existing practices

An insurer may continue the following practices, but the introduction of any of them does not satisfy paragraph 10.8(b) of FRS 102: **2.6**

(a)   unless otherwise required by the **Regulations** (or other legal framework that applies to the entity), measuring insurance liabilities on an undiscounted basis.
(b)   measuring contractual rights to future investment management fees at an amount that exceeds their **fair value** as implied by a comparison with current fees charged by other market participants for similar services. It is likely that the fair value at inception of those contractual rights equals the origination costs paid, unless future investment management fees and related costs are out of line with market comparables.

---

[1] *In this paragraph, insurance liabilities include related deferred acquisition costs and related intangible assets, such as those discussed in paragraphs 2.27 and 2.28.*

(c)   as an exception to paragraph 9.17 of FRS 102, using non-uniform accounting policies for the insurance contracts (and related **deferred acquisition costs** and related **intangible assets**, if any) of subsidiaries, except as permitted by paragraph 2.5. If those accounting policies are not uniform, an insurer may change them if the change does not make the accounting policies more diverse and also satisfies the other requirements in this FRS.

Prudence

2.7   An insurer need not change its accounting policies for insurance contracts to eliminate excessive prudence. However, if an insurer already measures its insurance contracts with sufficient prudence, it shall not introduce additional prudence.

Future investment margins

2.8   An insurer need not change its accounting policies for insurance contracts to eliminate future investment margins. However, there is a rebuttable presumption that an insurer's financial statements will become less relevant and reliable if it introduces an accounting policy that reflects future investment margins in the measurement of insurance contracts, unless those margins affect the contractual payments. Two examples of accounting policies that reflect those margins are:

(a)   using a discount rate that reflects the estimated return on the insurer's assets; or

(b)   projecting the returns on those assets at an estimated rate of return, **discounting** those projected returns at a different rate and including the result in the measurement of the liability.

2.9   Provided it is permitted by the Regulations an insurer may overcome the rebuttable presumption described in paragraph 2.8 if, and only if, the other components of a change in accounting policies increase the relevance and reliability of its financial statements sufficiently to outweigh the decrease in relevance and reliability caused by the inclusion of future investment margins. For example, suppose that an insurer's **existing accounting policies** for insurance contracts involve excessively prudent assumptions set at inception and a discount rate prescribed by a regulator without direct reference to market conditions, and ignore some embedded **options and guarantees**. The insurer might make its financial statements more relevant and no less reliable by switching to a comprehensive investor-oriented basis of accounting that is widely used and involves:

(a)   current estimates and assumptions;

(b)   a reasonable (but not excessively prudent) adjustment to reflect risk and uncertainty;

(c)   measurements that reflect both the intrinsic value and time value of embedded options and guarantees; and

(d)   a current market discount rate, even if that discount rate reflects the estimated return on the insurer's assets.

2.10   In some measurement approaches, the discount rate is used to determine the **present value** of a future profit margin. That profit margin is then attributed to different periods using a formula. In those approaches, the discount rate affects the measurement of the liability only indirectly. In particular, the use of a less appropriate discount rate has a limited or no effect on the measurement of the liability at inception. However, in other approaches, the discount rate determines the measurement of the liability directly. In the latter case, because the introduction of an asset-based discount rate has a more significant effect, it is highly unlikely that an insurer could overcome the rebuttable presumption described in paragraph 2.8.

Shadow accounting

In some accounting models, realised gains or losses on an insurer's assets have a direct **2.11** effect on the measurement of some or all of (a) its insurance liabilities, (b) related deferred acquisition costs and (c) related intangible assets, such as those described in paragraphs 2.27 and 2.28. An insurer is permitted, but not required, to change its accounting policies so that a recognised but unrealised gain or loss on an asset affects those measurements in the same way that a realised gain or loss does. The related adjustment to the insurance liability (or deferred acquisition costs or intangible assets) shall be recognised in other comprehensive income if, and only if, the unrealised gains or losses are recognised in other comprehensive income. This practice is sometimes described as 'shadow accounting'.

Exemption from some requirements of FRS 102

Paragraphs 10.4 to 10.6 of FRS 102 set out how an entity's management shall use its **2.12** judgement in developing and applying an accounting policy if no FRS or FRC Abstract applies specifically to a transaction, other event or condition. However, this FRS exempts an insurer from the considerations in paragraphs 10.4 to 10.6 of FRS 102 in relation to its accounting policies for:

(a)   insurance contracts that it issues (including related **acquisition costs** and related intangible assets, such as those described in paragraphs 2.27 and 2.28, and paragraphs 3.16 to 3.18); and

(b)   **reinsurance contracts** that it holds.

Nevertheless, this FRS does not exempt an insurer from some implications of the **2.13** considerations in paragraphs 10.4 to 10.6 of FRS 102. Specifically, an insurer:

(a)   unless otherwise required by the regulatory framework that applies to the entity, shall not recognise as a liability any provisions for possible future **claims**, if those claims arise under insurance contracts that are not in existence at the end of the **reporting period** (such as **catastrophe provisions** and **equalisation provisions**). The presentation of any such liabilities shall follow the requirements of the Regulations (or other legal framework that applies to the entity);

(b)   shall carry out the **liability adequacy test** described in paragraphs 2.14 to 2.18;

(c)   shall remove an insurance liability (or a part of an insurance liability) from its **statement of financial position** when, and only when, it is extinguished—ie when the obligation specified in the contract is discharged or cancelled or expires;

(d)   shall not offset:

(i)   **reinsurance assets** against the related insurance liabilities; or

(ii)   income or expense from reinsurance contracts against the expense or income from the related insurance contracts; and

(e)   shall consider whether its reinsurance assets are impaired (see paragraph 2.19).

Liability adequacy test

An insurer shall assess at the end of each reporting period whether its recognised insurance **2.14** liabilities are adequate, using current estimates of future cash flows under its insurance contracts. If that assessment shows that the carrying amount of its insurance liabilities (less related deferred acquisition costs and related intangible assets, such as those discussed in paragraphs 2.27 and 2.28) is inadequate in the light of the estimated future cash flows, the entire deficiency shall be recognised in profit or loss.

2.15   If an insurer applies a liability adequacy test that meets specified minimum requirements, this FRS imposes no further requirements. The minimum requirements are the following:

(a)   The test considers current estimates of all contractual cash flows, and of related cash flows such as claims handling costs, as well as cash flows resulting from embedded options and guarantees.

(b)   If the test shows that the liability is inadequate, the entire deficiency is recognised in profit or loss.

2.16   If an insurer's accounting policies do not require a liability adequacy test that meets the minimum requirements of paragraph 2.15, the insurer shall:

(a)   determine the carrying amount of the relevant insurance liabilities[2] less the carrying amount of:

(i)   any related deferred acquisition costs; and

(ii)   any related intangible assets, such as those acquired in a **business combination** or **portfolio transfer** (see paragraphs 2.27 and 2.28). However, related reinsurance assets are not considered because an insurer accounts for them separately (see paragraph 2.19); and

(b)   determine whether the amount described in (a) is less than the carrying amount that would be required if the relevant insurance liabilities were within the scope of Section 21 *Provisions and Contingencies* of FRS 102. If it is less, the insurer shall recognise the entire difference in profit or loss and decrease the carrying amount of the related deferred acquisition costs or related intangible assets or increase the carrying amount of the relevant insurance liabilities.

2.17   If an insurer's liability adequacy test meets the minimum requirements of paragraph 2.15, the test is applied at the level of aggregation specified in that test. If its liability adequacy test does not meet those minimum requirements, the comparison described in paragraph 2.16 shall be made at the level of a portfolio of contracts that are subject to broadly similar risks and managed together as a single portfolio.

2.18   The amount described in paragraph 2.16(b) (ie the result of applying Section 21 of FRS 102) shall reflect future investment margins (see paragraphs 2.8 to 2.10) if, and only if, the amount described in paragraph 2.16(a) also reflects those margins.

Impairment of reinsurance assets

2.19   If a **cedant**'s reinsurance asset is impaired, the cedant shall reduce its carrying amount accordingly and recognise that impairment loss in profit or loss. A reinsurance asset is impaired if, and only if:

(a)   there is objective evidence, as a result of an event that occurred after initial recognition of the reinsurance asset, that the cedant may not receive all amounts due to it under the terms of the contract; and

(b)   that event has a reliably measurable impact on the amounts that the cedant will receive from the **reinsurer**.

Embedded derivatives

2.20   An entity applying this FRS shall determine whether it has any **separable embedded derivatives**. Subject to paragraphs 2.21 and 2.22, if the separable embedded derivative is not itself an insurance contract, the entity shall separate the **embedded derivative** from the host contract and account for it in accordance with Sections 11 *Basic Financial Instruments*

---

[2] *The relevant insurance liabilities are those insurance liabilities (and related deferred acquisition costs and related intangible assets) for which the insurer's accounting policies do not require a liability adequacy test that meets the minimum requirements of paragraph 2.15*

and 12 *Other Financial Instruments Issues* of FRS 102 (or, if the entity has made the accounting policy choice under paragraphs 11.2(b) or (c), or paragraphs 12.2(b) or (c) of FRS 102 to apply the recognition and measurement provisions of either IAS 39 *Financial Instruments: Recognition and Measurement* or IFRS 9 *Financial Instruments*, the disclosure requirements of Section 11 of FRS 102 and the recognition and measurement requirements of IAS 39 or IFRS 9, as applicable) as if it is a **financial instrument**. For an entity that is a **financial institution** the disclosure requirements of paragraphs 34.17 to 34.33 of FRS 102 also apply to any separable embedded derivatives.

As an exception to the requirements in paragraph 2.20, an insurer need not separate, and measure at fair value, a **policyholder's** option to **surrender** an insurance contract for a fixed amount (or for an amount based on a fixed amount and an interest rate), even if the exercise price differs from the carrying amount of the host insurance liability. However, the requirements in paragraph 2.20 do apply to a put option or cash **surrender option** embedded in an insurance contract if the surrender value varies in response to the change in a financial variable (such as an **equity** or commodity price or index), or a non-financial variable that is not specific to a party to the contract. Furthermore, those requirements also apply if the holder's ability to exercise a put option or cash surrender option is triggered by a change in such a variable (for example, a put option that can be exercised if a stock market index reaches a specified level). **2.21**

Paragraph 2.21 applies equally to options to surrender a financial instrument containing a **discretionary participation feature**. **2.22**

Unbundling of deposit components

Some insurance contracts contain both an insurance component and a **deposit component**. In some cases, an insurer is required or permitted to **unbundle** those components: **2.23**

(a)   Unbundling is required if both the following conditions are met:

    (i)   the insurer can measure the deposit component (including any embedded surrender options) separately (ie without considering the insurance component); and

    (ii)   the insurer's accounting policies do not otherwise require it to recognise all obligations and rights arising from the deposit component.

(b)   Unbundling is permitted, but not required, if the insurer can measure the deposit component separately as in (a)(i) but its accounting policies require it to recognise all obligations and rights arising from the deposit component, regardless of the basis used to measure those rights and obligations.

(c)   Unbundling is prohibited if an insurer cannot measure the deposit component separately as in (a)(i).

The following is an example of a case when an insurer's accounting policies do not require it to recognise all obligations arising from a deposit component. A cedant receives compensation for losses from a reinsurer, but the contract obliges the cedant to repay the compensation in future years. That obligation arises from a deposit component. If the cedant's accounting policies would otherwise permit it to recognise the compensation as income without recognising the resulting obligation, unbundling is required. **2.24**

To unbundle a contract, an insurer shall: **2.25**

(a)   apply this FRS to the insurance component; and

(b)   apply Section 11 or 12 of FRS 102 (or, if the entity has made the accounting policy choice under paragraphs 11.2(b) or (c), or paragraphs 12.2(b) or (c) of FRS 102 to apply the recognition and measurement provisions of either IAS 39 or IFRS 9, the disclosure requirements of Section 11 of FRS 102 and the recognition and measurement requirements of IAS 39 or IFRS 9, as applicable) to the deposit component.

Reporting foreign currency transactions in the functional currency

2.26   Paragraph 30.9 of FRS 102 requires an entity, at the end of each reporting period, to translate foreign currency monetary items using the closing rate and non-monetary items using the exchange rate at the date of the transaction or the date when fair value was determined (for non-monetary items measured at fair value). For the purposes of applying the requirements of Section 30 *Foreign Currency Translation* of FRS 102 an entity shall treat all assets and liabilities arising from an insurance contract as monetary items.

Insurance contracts acquired in a business combination or portfolio transfer

2.27   To comply with Section 19 *Business Combinations and Goodwill* of FRS 102, an insurer shall, at the acquisition date, measure at fair value the insurance liabilities assumed and **insurance assets** acquired in a business combination. However, an insurer is permitted, but not required, to use an expanded presentation that splits the fair value of acquired insurance contracts into two components:

(a)   a liability measured in accordance with the insurer's accounting policies for insurance contracts that it issues; and

(b)   an intangible asset, representing the difference between (i) the fair value of the contractual insurance rights acquired and insurance obligations assumed and (ii) the amount described in (a). As an exception to Section 18 *Intangible Assets other than Goodwill* of FRS 102, the subsequent measurement of this asset shall be consistent with the measurement of the related insurance liability.

2.28   An insurer acquiring a portfolio of insurance contracts may use the expanded presentation described in paragraph 2.27.

2.29   The intangible assets described in paragraphs 2.27 and 2.28 are excluded from the scope of Sections 18 and 27 *Impairment of Assets* of FRS 102. However, Sections 18 and 27 of FRS 102 apply to customer lists and customer relationships reflecting the expectation of future contracts that are not part of the contractual insurance rights and contractual insurance obligations that existed at the date of a business combination or portfolio transfer.

Discretionary participation features

Discretionary participation features in insurance contracts

2.30   Some insurance contracts contain a discretionary participation feature as well as a **guaranteed element**. The issuer of such a contract:

(a)   may, but need not, recognise the guaranteed element separately from the discretionary participation feature. If the issuer does not recognise them separately, it shall classify the whole contract as a liability. If the issuer classifies them separately, it shall classify the guaranteed element as a liability;

(b)   shall, if it recognises the discretionary participation feature separately from the guaranteed element, classify that feature as either a liability or a separate component of equity (where this is permitted by the Regulations). The issuer may split that feature into liability and equity components and shall use a consistent accounting policy for that split. The issuer shall not classify that feature as an intermediate category that is neither liability nor equity;

(c)   may recognise all premiums received as revenue without separating any portion that relates to the equity component. The resulting changes in the guaranteed element and in the portion of the discretionary participation feature classified as a liability shall be recognised in profit or loss. If part or all of the discretionary participation feature is classified in equity, a portion of profit or loss may be attributable to that feature (in the same way that a portion may be attributable to **non-controlling interests**). Where legislation permits the discretionary participation feature to be classified as a component of equity, the issuer shall recognise the portion of profit or loss attributable to any equity component as an allocation of profit or loss, not as expense or income (see Section 5 *Statement of Comprehensive Income and Income Statement* of FRS 102);

(d) shall, if it has made an accounting policy choice in accordance with paragraphs 11.2(b) or (c), or paragraphs 12.2(b) or (c) of FRS 102 to apply the recognition and measurement provisions of either IAS 39 or IFRS 9, and the contract contains an embedded derivative within the scope of IAS 39 or IFRS 9, apply IAS 39 or IFRS 9 to that embedded derivative; and

(e) shall, in all respects not described in paragraphs 2.13 to 2.19 and 2.30(a) to (d), continue its existing accounting policies for such contracts, unless it changes those accounting policies in a way that complies with paragraphs 2.2 to 2.11.

Discretionary participation features in financial instruments other than insurance contracts

The requirements in paragraph 2.30 also apply to a financial instrument other than an insurance contract that contains a discretionary participation feature. In addition: **2.31**

(a) If the issuer classifies the entire discretionary participation feature as a liability, it shall apply the liability adequacy test in paragraphs 2.14 to 2.18 to the whole contract (ie both the guaranteed element and the discretionary participation feature). The issuer need not determine the amount that would result from applying IAS 39, IFRS 9 or Sections 11 and 12 of FRS 102 (depending on the entity's accounting policy choice) to the guaranteed element.

(b) If the issuer classifies part or all of that feature as a separate component of equity, the liability recognised for the whole contract shall not be less than the amount that would result from applying IAS 39, IFRS 9 or Sections 11 and 12 of FRS 102 (depending on the entity's accounting policy choice) to the guaranteed element. That amount shall include the intrinsic value of an option to surrender the contract, but need not include its time value if paragraph 2.22 exempts that option from measurement at fair value. The issuer need not disclose the amount that would result from applying IAS 39, IFRS 9 or Sections 11 and 12 of FRS 102 (depending on the entity's accounting policy choice) to the guaranteed element, nor need it present that amount separately. Furthermore, the issuer need not determine that amount if the total liability recognised is clearly higher.

(c) Although these contracts are financial instruments, the issuer may continue to recognise the premiums for those contracts as revenue and recognise as an expense the resulting increase in the carrying amount of the liability.

(d) Although these contracts are financial instruments, an issuer shall disclose the total interest expense recognised in profit or loss, but need not calculate such interest expense using the **effective interest method**.

Recognition in the Income Statement for entities required to maintain a non-technical account

Exchange gains and losses

Where Section 30 of FRS 102 requires entities to include exchange differences within profit or loss, these differences shall be dealt with through the **non-technical account** except for long-term insurance business where exchange differences shall be recognised in the **technical account** for long-term business. In respect of paragraph 30.18(c) of FRS 102 in the case of the long-term insurance business, where appropriate, entities may recognise the resulting exchange differences in the **fund for future appropriations (FFA)**.   **2.32**

Employee benefits

2.33   In applying paragraph 28.23(b) of FRS 102 the net interest on the net defined benefit liability during the reporting period shall be recognised, as appropriate, in the technical account for long-term insurance business or the non-technical account.

2.34   As an exception to paragraph 28.23(d) of FRS 102 the remeasurement of the net defined benefit liability which is not attributable to **owners** shall be treated as an amount, the allocation of which, either to policyholders or to owners, has not been determined by the **reporting date**. It shall be included as a separate line in the technical account for long-term insurance business immediately above the line for transfer to or from the fund for future appropriations, and reflected in that transfer. The impact shall be disclosed separately in the **notes to the financial statements**.

Section 3 *Recognition and Measurement: Requirements for entities with long-term insurance business*

Scope of this section

3.1   This section sets out requirements for entities applying this FRS that are carrying out **long-term insurance business**:

(a)   Paragraphs 3.3 to 3.9 and 3.16 to 3.18 apply to all long-term insurance business.

(b)   Paragraphs 3.10 to 3.15 apply to **with-profits business** and with-profits funds, to which the **Prudential Regulatory Authority (PRA)** realistic capital regime (as set out in section 1.3 of **INSPRU** as at 31 December 2015) was being applied, either voluntarily or compulsorily , prior to 1 January 2016.

3.1A   This section sets out the benchmark for setting **accounting policies** for long-term insurance business as at 1 January 2015. Entities are permitted to change their accounting policies in accordance with paragraph 2.3. Entities that are setting accounting policies for the first time may apply this benchmark in accordance with paragraph 1.5(a) or are permitted to set alternative policies in accordance with paragraph 1.5(b).

3.2   Where an entity has changed its **accounting policies** in accordance with paragraph 2.3 or adopted accounting policies in accordance with paragraph 1.5(b), and its accounting policies are not consistent with this section, the requirements of this section that are not consistent with the entity's accounting policies need not be applied.

Gross premiums written

3.3   Premiums, including those for inwards reinsurance business, shall be recognised when due for payment. Where the amount due is not known, for example with certain pensions business, estimates should be used. For **linked business** the due date for payment may be taken as the date when the **liability** is established.

3.4   Reinsurance outwards premiums shall be recognised when paid or payable.

Claims recognition

3.5   **Claims** payable on maturity shall be recognised when the claims become due for payment and claims payable on death shall be recognised on notification. Where a claim is payable and the policy or contract remains in force, the relevant instalments shall be recognised when due for payment. There should be consistent treatment between the **recognition** of the claim in the **technical account** for long-term business and the calculation of the long-term business provision and/or the provision for linked liabilities as appropriate.

Surrenders shall be included within **claims incurred** and recognised either when paid or at the earlier date on which, following notification, the policy ceases to be included within the calculation of the long-term business provision and/or the provision for linked liabilities. **3.6**

Deferred acquisition costs

Except as required by paragraph 3.10, acquisition costs shall be deferred except to the extent that: **3.7**

(a) the costs in question have already been recovered (for example where the design of the policy provides for the recovery of costs as incurred);

(b) the net present value of margins within the **insurance contracts** is not expected to be sufficient to cover **deferred acquisition costs** after providing for contractual liabilities to **policyholders** and expenses; and

(c) the receipt of future premiums or the achievement of future margins is insufficiently certain based on estimates of future expected discontinuance rates or other experience.

Advertising costs shall not be deferred unless they are directly attributable to the acquisition of new business. **3.8**

Deferred acquisition costs that are carried forward shall be amortised over a period no longer than one in which, net of any related **deferred tax** provision, they are expected to be recoverable out of margins on related insurance contracts in force at the **reporting date**, and in a similar profile to those margins. **3.9**

Acquisition costs shall not be deferred for with-profits funds. **3.10**

Measurement of with-profits liabilities and related assets

The established accounting treatment for long-term insurance business is to measure liabilities for policyholder benefits under the **modified statutory solvency basis (MSSB)**. This FRS requires with-profits funds to use the **realistic value of liabilities** as the basis for the estimated value of the liabilities to be included in the **financial statements**. **3.11**

For with-profits funds: **3.12**

(a) liabilities to policyholders arising from with-profits business shall be stated at the amount of the realistic value of liabilities adjusted to exclude the shareholders' share of projected future **bonuses**;

(b) **reinsurance recoveries** that are recognised shall be measured on a basis that is consistent with the value of the policyholder liabilities to which the reinsurance applies;

(c) an amount may be recognised for the present value of future profits on **non-participating business** written in a with-profits fund if the determination of the realistic value of liabilities in that with-profits fund takes account, directly or indirectly, of this value;

(d) where a with-profits life fund has an interest in a subsidiary or associate and the determination of the realistic value of liabilities to with-profits policyholders takes account of a value of that interest at an amount in excess of the net amounts included in the entity's consolidated accounts, an amount may be recognised representing this excess; and

(e) adjustments to reflect the consequential tax effects of (a) to (d) above shall be made.

Adjustments from the MSSB necessary to meet the above requirements, including the recognition of an amount in accordance with paragraph 3.12(c) or 3.12(d), shall be included in **profit or loss**. An amount equal and opposite to the net amount of these adjustments shall be transferred to or from the **fund for future appropriations (FFA)** and also included in profit or loss.

3.13   In the case of a **mutual**, an FFA or retained surplus account is maintained that represents amounts that have not yet been allocated to specific policyholders. For such entities, the adjustments required by paragraph 3.12 will be offset within profit or loss by a transfer directly to or from this FFA or retained surplus account, with the result that overall profit or loss for the year will be unchanged.

3.14   The realistic value of liabilities shall exclude the amount which represents the shareholders' share of future bonuses. Similar adjustments shall be made if other amounts due to shareholders would otherwise be included in the realistic value of liabilities.

3.15   An entity is permitted to recognise the excess of the market value of a subsidiary over the net amounts included in the consolidated financial statements as a deduction from the sub-total of the FFA and liabilities to policyholders in the same way as the **value of in-force insurance business (VIF)** described in paragraph IG1.3 of the Implementation Guidance.

Value of in-force life assurance business

3.16   Banking and other non-insurance entities with insurance subsidiaries sometimes account for the insurance business in their consolidated financial statements on an **embedded value** or similar basis under which, in addition to the value of the retained surplus in the insurance subsidiary, an asset is recognised for the VIF. This FRS permits the continuation of such a practice only if the valuation policy is amended, if necessary, to exclude from the measurement of the value of the future profit to shareholders any value attributable to future investment margins.

3.17   No value shall be attributed to in-force long-term insurance business other than:

(a)   in accordance with paragraphs 3.12(c), 3.12(d) or 3.16 above; or

(b)   amounts recognised as an **intangible asset** as part of the allocation of **fair values** under acquisition accounting in accordance with paragraph 2.27.

3.18   Where the value attributable to a VIF asset recognised under paragraph 3.16 or paragraph 3.17(b) includes an amount in relation to non-participating business for which the entity also recognises an amount under paragraph 3.12(c) or 3.12(d), the amount recognised under paragraph 3.12(c) or 3.12(d) shall be reduced to exclude the amount that is included in relation to that business under paragraph 3.16 or paragraph 3.17(b).

Section 4 *Disclosure*

Scope of this section

4.1   This section describes the disclosures to be provided by **insurers** in addition to the disclosure requirements of **FRS 102**.

4.2   In accordance with paragraph 8.5 of FRS 102, an entity shall disclose, in the summary of significant **accounting policies**, in relation to both **insurance contracts** and financial instruments that it issues with a **discretionary participation feature**:

(a)   the measurement basis (or bases) used; and

(b)   the other accounting policies used that are relevant to an understanding of the **financial statements**.

Insurers that have **liabilities** arising from **with-profits business** shall also apply Section 5   **4.3**
Disclosure: Additional requirements for with-profits business of this FRS.

Explanation of recognised amounts from insurance contracts

An insurer shall disclose information that identifies and explains the amounts in its   **4.4**
financial statements arising from insurance contracts.

To comply with paragraph 4.4 an insurer shall disclose: **4.5**

(a)   the recognised assets, liabilities, income and expense (and, if it presents its statement
of cash flows using the direct method, cash flows) arising from insurance contracts.
Furthermore, if the insurer is a **cedant**, it shall disclose:

    (i)   gains and losses recognised in **profit or loss** on buying reinsurance; and

    (ii)   if the cedant defers and amortises gains and losses arising on buying reinsurance,
the amortisation for the period and the amounts remaining unamortised at the
beginning and end of the period;

(b)   the process used to determine the assumptions that have the greatest effect on the
measurement of the recognised amounts described in (a). When practicable, an
insurer shall also give quantified disclosure of those assumptions;

(c)   the effect of changes in assumptions used to measure **insurance assets** and **insurance
liabilities**, showing separately the effect of each change that has a material effect on
the financial statements; and

(d)   reconciliations of changes in insurance liabilities, **reinsurance assets** and, if any,
related **deferred acquisition costs**.

Schedule 3 to the **Regulations** requires disclosure of the total amount of commissions for   **4.6**
direct business including acquisition, renewal, collection and portfolio management. For
this purpose, commission shall exclude payments made to employees of the undertaking.

Nature and extent of risks arising from insurance contracts

An insurer shall disclose information that enables users of its financial statements to   **4.7**
evaluate the nature and extent of risks arising from insurance contracts.

To comply with paragraph 4.7, an insurer shall disclose: **4.8**

(a)   its objectives, policies and processes for managing risks arising from insurance
contracts and the methods used to manage those risks;

(b)   information about **insurance risk** (both before and after risk mitigation by
reinsurance), including information about:

    (i)   sensitivity to insurance risk (see paragraph 4.9);

    (ii)   concentrations of insurance risk, including a description of how management
determines concentrations and a description of the shared characteristic that
identifies each concentration (eg type of **insured event**, geographical area, or
currency); and

    (iii)   actual **claims** compared with previous estimates (ie claims development).
The disclosure about claims development shall go back to the period when
the earliest material claim arose for which there is still uncertainty about the
amount and timing of the claims payments, but need not go back more than
ten years. An insurer need not disclose this information for claims for which
uncertainty about the amount and timing of claims payments is typically
resolved within one year;

(c)   information about **credit risk**, **liquidity risk** and **market risk** that, as a **financial institution**, Section 34 *Specialised Activities* of FRS 102 would require if the insurance contracts were within the scope of Sections 11 *Basic Financial Instruments* and 12 *Other Financial Instruments Issues* of FRS 102. However:

   (i)   an insurer need not provide the maturity analyses required by paragraph 34.28 of FRS 102 if it discloses information about the estimated timing of the net cash outflows resulting from recognised insurance liabilities instead. This may take the form of an analysis, by estimated timing, of the amounts recognised in the **statement of financial position**;

   (ii)   if an insurer uses an alternative method to manage sensitivity to market conditions, such as an **embedded value** analysis, it may use that sensitivity analysis to meet the requirement in paragraph 34.29 of FRS 102. Such an insurer shall also provide the disclosures required by paragraph 34.30 of FRS 102; and

(d)   information about exposures to market risk arising from **embedded derivatives** contained in a host insurance contract if the insurer is not required to, and does not, measure the embedded derivatives at **fair value**.

4.9   To comply with paragraph 4.8(b)(i), an insurer shall disclose either (a) or (b) as follows:

(a)   A sensitivity analysis that shows how profit or loss and **equity** would have been affected if changes in the relevant risk variable that were reasonably possible at the end of the **reporting period** had occurred; the methods and assumptions used in preparing the sensitivity analysis; and any changes from the previous period in the methods and assumptions used. However, if an insurer uses an alternative method to manage sensitivity to market conditions, such as an embedded value analysis, it may meet this requirement by disclosing that alternative sensitivity analysis and the disclosures required by paragraph 34.30 of FRS 102.

(b)   Qualitative information about sensitivity, and information about those terms and conditions of insurance contracts that have a material effect on the amount, timing and uncertainty of the insurer's future cash flows.

Financial instruments, other than insurance contracts, containing discretionary participation features

4.10   An insurer that has financial instruments, other than insurance contracts, that it issues with a discretionary participation feature shall, in relation to those financial instruments, disclose:

(a)   the carrying amount of those financial instruments at the **reporting date**, in total, either in the statement of financial position or in the **notes to the financial statements**; and

(b)   the information required by paragraphs 11.42 and 11.48 of FRS 102.

Section 5 *Disclosure: Additional requirements for with-profits business*

Scope of this section

5.1   This section describes the disclosures to be provided by **insurers** that have liabilities arising from **with-profits business**, in addition to the disclosure requirements of **FRS 102** and Section 4 *Disclosure* of this FRS.

5.2   Where an entity has changed its **accounting policies** in accordance with paragraph 2.3, and its new accounting policies are no longer consistent with policies on which the disclosure requirements of this section are based, the requirements of this section that are no longer consistent with the entity's accounting policies need not be applied.

Disclosure and presentation relating to with-profits business

Amounts recognised under paragraph 3.12(c) or 3.12(d) shall be presented in one of the 5.3 following ways:

(a) Where it is possible to apportion the amount recognised between an amount relating to liabilities to **policyholders** and an amount relating to the **fund for future appropriation (FFA)**, these portions shall be presented in the **statement of financial position** as a deduction in arriving at the amount of liabilities to policyholders and the FFA respectively.

(b) Where it is not possible to make a reasonably approximate apportionment of the amount recognised, the amount shall be presented in the statement of financial position as a separate item deducted from a sub-total of liabilities to policyholders and the FFA.

(c) Where the presentation under paragraph 5.3(a) or 5.3(b) does not comply with statutory requirements for balance sheet presentation applying to the entity, the amount recognised under paragraph 3.12(c) or 3.12(d) shall be recognised as an asset.

The **FFA** shall be disclosed separately in the statement of financial position, and not 5.4 combined with technical provisions or other liabilities. Entities that consolidate interests in an entity carrying on **long-term insurance business** on a basis that combines the FFA and technical provisions into a single amount of liabilities to policyholders are required to show these elements separately.

Where the balance on the FFA of a with-profits life fund is negative, as a result of the 5.5 transfer made in accordance with paragraph 3.12 or otherwise, the entity shall include in the **notes to the financial statements** an explanation of the nature of the negative balance and the circumstances in which it arose, and why no action to eliminate it has been considered necessary.

Section 6 *Transition to this FRS*

Scope of this section

The transitional provisions in paragraphs 6.3 and 6.4 apply to both an entity that is already 6.1 applying **FRS 102** when it first applies this FRS and an entity that applies both FRS 102 and this FRS together for the first time.

Section 35 *Transition to this FRS* of FRS 102 also applies to a first-time adopter of FRS 102. 6.2

Disclosure

In applying paragraph 4.8(b)(iii), an entity need not disclose information about **claims** 6.3 development that occurred earlier than five years before the end of the first financial year in which it applies this FRS. Furthermore, if it is impracticable, when an entity first applies this FRS, to prepare information about claims development that occurred before the beginning of the earliest period for which an entity presents full comparative information that complies with this FRS, the entity shall disclose that fact.

Re-designation of financial assets

If an **insurer** changes its **accounting policies** for **insurance liabilities**, it is permitted, but 6.4 not required, to reclassify some or all of its **financial assets** as a financial asset at **fair value** through **profit or loss** provided those assets meet the criteria in paragraph 11.14(b) of

FRS 102 (or if the entity has made the accounting policy choice under paragraphs 11.2(b) or (c), or paragraphs 12.2(b) or (c) of FRS 102 to apply the **recognition** and measurement provisions of either IAS 39 *Financial Instruments: Recognition and Measurement* or IFRS 9 Financial Instruments, the relevant requirements of IAS 39 or IFRS 9, as applicable) at that date. This reclassification is permitted if an insurer changes accounting policies when it first applies this FRS and if it makes a subsequent policy change permitted by paragraph 2.3. The reclassification is a change in accounting policy and Section 10 *Accounting Policies, Estimates and Errors* of FRS 102 applies.

Approval by the FRC

Financial Reporting Standard 103 *Insurance Contracts* was approved for issue by the Financial Reporting Council on 5 March 2014, following its consideration of the Accounting Council's Advice for this FRS.

The Accounting Council's Advice to the FRC to issue FRS 103

Introduction

This report provides an overview of the main issues that have been considered by the **1** Accounting Council in advising the Financial Reporting Council (FRC) to issue FRS 103 Insurance Contracts. The FRC, in accordance with the *Statutory Auditors (Amendment of Companies Act 2006 and Delegation of Functions etc) Order 2012* (SI 2012/1741), is the prescribed body for issuing accounting standards in the UK. The Foreword to Accounting Standards sets out the application of accounting standards in the Republic of Ireland.

In accordance with the *FRC Codes and Standards: procedures*, any proposal to issue, **2** amend or withdraw a code or standard is put to the FRC Board with the full advice of the relevant Councils and/or the Codes & Standards Committee. Ordinarily, the FRC Board will only reject the advice put to it where:

- it is apparent that a significant group of stakeholders has not been adequately consulted;
- the necessary assessment of the impact of the proposal has not been completed, including an analysis of costs and benefits;
- insufficient consideration has been given to the timing or cost of implementation; or
- the cumulative impact of a number of proposals would make the adoption of an otherwise satisfactory proposal inappropriate.

The FRC has established the Accounting Council as the relevant Council to assist it in the **3** setting of accounting standards.

Advice

When FRS 102 *The Financial Reporting Standard applicable in the UK and Republic of* **4** *Ireland* was issued in March 2013 it referred to the accounting for insurance contracts being addressed by FRS 103 *Insurance Contracts*, which was yet to be completed. A standard on insurance contracts was required to fill a gap in current accounting standards. Respondents agreed with the proposal to develop FRS 103 from IFRS 4 *Insurance Contracts*, in accordance with the FRC's overall objective for the future of UK GAAP.

FRS 103 largely permits insurers to continue with their existing accounting policies for **5** insurance contracts and as a result the incremental costs of implementation, in addition to those that will be incurred in implementing FRS 102, are not significant. Overall the introduction of FRS 103 will have a positive impact on financial reporting.

Therefore, the Accounting Council is advising the FRC to issue FRS 103 *Insurance* **6** *Contracts*.

FRS 100 *Application of Financial Reporting Requirements* and FRS 101 *Reduced* **7** *Disclosure Framework* which were both issued in November 2012 and FRS 102 which was issued in March 2013, are also part of this suite of financial reporting standards. The Accounting Council's advice to the FRC on those standards is contained in those standards.

Background

8   Accounting standards were formerly developed by the Accounting Standards Board (ASB)[3]. The ASB commenced its project to update accounting standards in 2002; the FRC issued FRS 100 and FRS 101 in November 2012 and FRS 102 in March 2013. FRS 103 supplements FRS 102 for entities with insurance contracts.

9   FRS 103 was developed from IFRS 4 *Insurance Contracts*. It also contains much of the requirements of FRS 27 *Life Assurance* (prior to it being withdrawn by this standard) and elements of the Association of British Insurers' *Statement of Recommended Practice on Accounting for Insurance Business* (the ABI SORP) (published in December 2005 and amended in December 2006).

10   The requirements in this FRS take into consideration:

(a)   the findings from the previous consultations on the future of financial reporting in the UK and Republic of Ireland that took place between 2002 and 2012, which includes responses to the Discussion Paper *Insurance Accounting – Mind the UK GAAP* issued in 2012; and

(b)   the responses to FRED 49: Draft FRS 103 *Insurance Contracts* issued in July 2013.

Objective

11   During its consultations on updating accounting standards, the ASB (and subsequently the FRC) gave careful consideration to its objective and the intended effects. In developing the requirements for the future of UK GAAP, including this FRS, the overriding objective is:

> To enable users of accounts to receive high-quality understandable financial reporting proportionate to the size and complexity of the entity and users' information needs.

12   In achieving this objective, the Accounting Council decided (and the FRC subsequently adopted this decision) that it should provide succinct financial reporting standards that:

- have consistency with global accounting standards through the application of an IFRS-based solution unless an alternative clearly better meets the overriding objective;
- reflect up-to-date thinking and developments in the way businesses operate and the transactions they undertake;
- balance consistent principles for accounting by all UK and Republic of Ireland entities with practical solutions, based on size, complexity, public interest and users' information needs;
- promote efficiency within groups; and
- are cost-effective to apply.

Using IFRS 4 *Insurance Contracts* as a basis for FRS 103

13   The recently issued accounting standards have consistency with global accounting standards, where appropriate, with FRS 102 being based upon the IFRS for SMEs. FRS 103 has been developed in accordance with the same overall objective and principles and is applicable to those entities applying FRS 102 that have insurance contracts. It is based upon IFRS 4 and it must be consistent with FRS 102 where relevant. One of the options the Accounting Council previously explored, but rejected, was including a requirement in FRS 102 for entities with insurance contracts to apply IFRS 4.

---

[3] *References in this section are made to the FRC, ASB or Accounting Council, as appropriate in terms of the time period and context of the reference.*

In developing FRS 103 the Accounting Council aimed to provide a financial reporting   **14**
framework for entities with insurance contracts that allows them to generally continue
with their existing accounting policies, whilst consolidating and modernising the relevant
accounting requirements. FRS 103 is also deregulatory in some areas, for example, by
permitting entities to improve their accounting policies and by including best practice
guidance that will allow entities some flexibility in how they comply with the disclosure
principles.

In using IFRS 4 as a basis for FRS 103, however, the Accounting Council noted that   **15**
IFRS 4 does not set specific requirements for the underlying recognition and measurement
of insurance contracts, reflecting the fact that it was an interim standard issued by the
IASB to facilitate harmonisation between jurisdictions pending completion of the second
phase of its insurance contracts project. Therefore the Accounting Council advises that in
developing FRS 103 the text of IFRS 4 should be supplemented by some of the existing
requirements and practice in accounting for insurance contracts in the UK and Republic
of Ireland.

As a result, much of FRS 27, which was issued by the ASB after Lord Penrose's *Report of*   **16**
the Equitable Life Inquiry and is still relevant to entities with long-term insurance business,
has been incorporated into FRS 103 or the accompanying Implementation Guidance,
along with elements of the ABI SORP providing guidance on applying the requirements
of FRS 27 and company law applicable to insurance companies. The Accounting Council
advises that when FRS 103 becomes effective, FRS 27 should be withdrawn.

FRS 103 and the accompanying Implementation Guidance consolidate all relevant,   **17**
existing accounting requirements and guidance applicable to entities with insurance
contracts, other than company law and the requirements of the PRA Handbook. This is
consistent with the FRC's general approach to setting accounting standards and eliminates
unnecessary duplication. The ABI has confirmed that it will withdraw the ABI SORP once
FRS 103 is effective.

The Accounting Council notes the prospective commencement of Solvency II, which at   **18**
the time of giving this advice is currently expected for 1 January 2016, in the light of
which it will review whether or not consequential changes to FRS 103 will be required in
due course.

The Accounting Council also notes that the IASB has a long-running active project to   **19**
revise IFRS 4; the aims of this project are 'to provide a single principle-based Standard to
account for all types of insurance contracts, including reinsurance contracts that an insurer
holds'. Once the IASB has issued its new standard[4] , the Accounting Council advises that
the FRC should review the requirements of FRS 103. The most appropriate timing for this
review cannot be determined at the present time.

The Accounting Council has been mindful of not imposing multiple changes in accounting   **20**
and reporting on insurers, in quick succession, where this can be avoided. It is also
cognisant that, given the complexity and conceptual nature of the issues being addressed
by the IASB's insurance contracts project, the development, at this time, of a UK-specific
accounting basis for insurers was unlikely to be supported.

The respondents to FRED 49 supported the introduction of a standard based on that   **21**
exposure draft, and agreed that the resulting standard should be expected to be an interim
standard that will be reviewed following further industry developments.

---

[4] *An Exposure Draft ED/2013/7 Insurance Contracts was issued in June 2013.*

22   Therefore, following analysis of the options and consideration of the feedback from respondents, the Accounting Council advises the FRC that FRS 103 should be issued, and its requirements should be kept under review in the light of regulatory and accounting changes affecting the insurance industry that are discussed above.

Supplementing IFRS 4 from FRS 27 and the ABI SORP

23   In developing FRS 103 from IFRS 4 the Accounting Council was mindful that UK accounting standards should not be more restrictive than EU-adopted IFRS, unless this was necessary for compliance with company law.

24   In order to supplement IFRS 4, FRS 27 and the ABI SORP were reviewed, with material incorporated as follows:

   (a)   requirements that should be a core part of the standard;
   (b)   material that provided important guidance for applying the requirements of FRS 103 or FRS 102 and should be included as Implementation Guidance; or
   (c)   material that was guidance in nature, but was either repeating other requirements (including the PRA Handbook and Schedule 3 to the Regulations), or concerned matters where diversity in practice was unlikely to arise, which has not been incorporated into FRS 103.

25   Paragraphs that have been sourced from the ABI SORP, and to a lesser extent those from FRS 27, have been revised where they needed updating, for example, to reflect new legislative requirements or for consistency with FRS 102; changes in language for consistency with FRS 102 are not intended to result in a change in meaning. In relation to taxation in entities with long-term insurance business, where a new taxation regime was introduced on 1 January 2013, new guidance has been drafted and incorporated into Section 2 *Guidance for entities with general insurance business or long-term insurance business* of the Implementation Guidance.

Definition of an insurance contract

26   FRS 102 includes a definition of an insurance contract, which will be new to entities applying FRS 102 (and FRS 103) that have not previously applied FRS 26 (IAS 39) *Financial Instruments: Recognition and Measurement*. The definition requires entities to assess whether their contracts meet the definition of insurance (and therefore fall within the scope of FRS 103) or do not meet the definition and therefore fall within Section 11 *Basic Financial Instruments* or Section 12 *Other Financial Instruments Issues* of FRS 102.

27   The definition in FRS 102 is expanded upon in Appendix II: *Definition of an Insurance Contract* of FRS 103. It includes examples of contracts that are, and are not, insurance contracts.

Continuation of existing accounting policies

28   Notwithstanding the need for insurers to make a distinction between insurance and investment contracts, FRS 103 largely permits insurers to continue with their existing accounting policies for insurance contracts. The Accounting Council advises a period of stability in financial reporting for insurance contracts in advance of the expected regulatory changes from Solvency II and the future new accounting standard from the IASB. There are a small number of exceptions to this principle.

Improvement of existing accounting policies

IFRS 4 permits entities to improve their accounting policies for insurance contracts in 29 certain circumstances, providing they continue to comply with any other relevant legal or regulatory requirements. Although the majority of respondents to FRED 49 agreed with this proposal and the rationale for it (ie that FRS 103 should not be more restrictive than EU-adopted IFRS or FRS 101), some did not. Those disagreeing raised concerns about the potential to reduce consistency of reporting between entities in the insurance industry and that it would be easier to change accounting policies for insurance contracts than FRS 102 would permit for other transactions. The Accounting Council considered these concerns and noted that some of the respondents acknowledged that their concerns may not have a significant effect in practice because there is limited evidence of UK entities applying IFRS 4 taking advantage of this option, and therefore it is not clear that it will be widely used by entities applying FRS 103.

Therefore the Accounting Council advises that this option is included in FRS 103 to ensure 30 that entities applying FRS 103 will have the same flexibility as those entities in the UK and Republic of Ireland that are applying EU-adopted IFRS and FRS 101. In addition, Section 3 *Recognition and Measurement: Requirements for entities with long-term insurance business* and Section 5 *Disclosure: Additional requirements for with-profits business* note that entities that have improved their accounting policies will no longer have to comply with the requirements of those sections (which are based on the requirements of FRS 27 and the ABI SORP) where these are no longer consistent with their accounting policies.

New entrants

The Accounting Council noted that any new entrants to the insurance market would 31 not have existing accounting policies for insurance contracts. Therefore to provide new entrants with the same benchmark accounting policies and the same flexibility to make improvements, the Accounting Council advises that new entrants shall first consider the sections of FRS 103 based on the requirements of FRS 27 and the ABI SORP, as a means to establishing current practice before considering whether to 'improve' those benchmark accounting policies.

Entities that are not legally constituted as insurance providers

Some entities that are not legally constituted as insurance providers may be issuing 32 contracts meeting the definition of an insurance contract in FRS 103. Examples include appliance servicing agreements, and some product warranty arrangements. Although such contracts are within the scope of FRS 103 an entity previously applying an accounting policy based on FRS 12 *Provisions, contingent liabilities and contingent assets* or some other method will be able to continue to apply a similar policy based on Section 21 *Provisions and Contingencies* of FRS 102. However, an entity may, alternatively, choose to apply the recognition and measurement requirements of FRS 103.

Although an entity with such contracts should generally be able to continue to apply its 33 previous accounting policies to such contracts on first-time application of FRS 103, it will need to consider other requirements of FRS 103, for example the liability adequacy test and may need to provide additional disclosures to those provided in the past.

Excessive prudence

34   The Accounting Council notes that paragraph 95 of the ABI SORP explained that claims provisions should be set such that there is no adverse run-off deviation. This may lead to provisions containing excessive prudence – an issue acknowledged by paragraph 2.7, which allows the practice to continue, but prevents it being introduced or extended. Excessive prudence is contrary to Section 2 *Concepts and Pervasive Principles* and Section 21 of FRS 102, and as such the Accounting Council recommends that paragraph IG2.10 of the Implementation Guidance prevents excessive prudence being applied where a new accounting policy is being introduced (ie there is no change for existing accounting policies).

Embedded derivatives

35   Entities that are applying FRS 103 will also be applying FRS 102. FRS 102 does not require entities to identify separable embedded derivatives, but instead, as a simplification from full IFRS, a contract with certain non-typical features shall be measured at fair value. The Accounting Council considered whether a similar approach should be applied to insurance contracts, but advises that for insurance contracts more relevant information will be provided to users if separable embedded derivatives are recognised and measured separately from the host contract (unless the embedded derivative is itself an insurance contract).

Insurance contracts denominated in foreign currencies

36   Some respondents to FRED 49 identified a further area where compliance with FRS 102, for entities that had not previously applied FRS 26, would lead to a change from existing accounting policies. This relates to insurance contracts held in a foreign currency, which are not held by an overseas subsidiary. Some of the assets and liabilities recognised in relation to an insurance contract would be monetary items and some would be non-monetary items, and as a result applying the requirements of FRS 102 would lead to some being retranslated at the reporting date, whilst others would not, resulting in accounting mismatches in the income statement.

37   As a result the Accounting Council advises that all assets and liabilities arising from an insurance contract shall be treated as monetary items for the purposes of reporting foreign currency transactions in the functional currency.

Compliance with company law

38   There are a small number of areas where IFRS 4 conflicts with the requirements of Schedule 3 to the Regulations, and therefore in developing FRS 103 amendments have been made to the text from IFRS 4 to ensure compliance with company law. The three principal examples are:

(a)   Equalisation provisions – provisions for future claims arising under insurance contracts that are not in existence at the end of the reporting period are prohibited under IFRS 4, but may be a requirement under a regulatory framework that applies to the entity (for example INSPRU 1.4), with separate presentation required by the Regulations. An amendment has been made in paragraph 2.13(a) to reflect these legal and regulatory requirements. In addition, a consequential amendment to FRS 101 is made to ensure consistent accounting by insurers applying either FRS 101 or FRS 103.

(b)   Equity treatment for discretionary participation features – IFRS 4 gives entities options for the presentation of the discretionary participation feature of a contract, if it is separated. However, the Regulations specifically prevent presentation as part of equity and paragraph 2.30(c) reflects this.

(c)   Discounting – IFRS 4 permits an entity to continue measuring insurance liabilities on an undiscounted basis but does not allow an entity to choose a new policy without discounting. However, the Regulations state when discounting is permitted or prohibited. An amendment has been made in paragraph 2.6 to reflect this legal requirement and would not restrict a new entrant's ability to apply discounting where it is required by the Regulations.

Applicability to insurance contracts and to insurance companies

The Accounting Council acknowledges that there are challenges in bringing the texts   39
of IFRS 4, FRS 27 and the ABI SORP together into FRS 103 and the accompanying Implementation Guidance, as a result of each being written at different times (and therefore potentially using different language) for different purposes:

(a)   IFRS 4 applies to insurance contracts, as defined in the standard;
(b)   FRS 27 applies to all entities that have a life assurance business; and
(c)   the ABI SORP applies to insurance companies and groups that are subject to the requirements of Schedule 3 to the Regulations.

FRS 103 applies to insurance contracts, but where requirements from FRS 27 or the   40
ABI SORP have been incorporated their application has been restricted in the scope of each section, where necessary, to avoid extending those requirements to all entities with insurance contracts unnecessarily.

Disclosure

The disclosure principles set out in FRS 103 require entities to disclose the amounts   41
recognised in the financial statements, and the related risks and uncertainties with those balances. These provisions are complementary to the disclosure requirements of Section 11 and the *Financial Institutions* sub-section of Section 34 *Specialised Activities* of FRS 102.

The Accounting Council noted that, for financial instruments, other than insurance   42
contracts with discretionary participation features, IFRS 4 does not contain disclosure requirements, because they are within the scope of IFRS 7 *Financial Instruments: Disclosures*. Therefore, it advises that for such contracts, FRS 103 requires entities to provide the relevant disclosures from Section 11 of FRS 102. This will maintain consistency with the requirements of EU-adopted IFRS for these instruments, but implemented in a proportionate manner.

FRS 103, consistently with IFRS 4, includes a requirement that entities present claims   43
development information. Disclosure of this information is also required by the Regulations, but FRS 103 goes further than the Regulations in requiring information over a 10-year period. The Accounting Council advises that, as this does not contradict the Regulations and respondents confirmed that the information should generally be available to management, for consistency with global accounting standards the requirement is included in FRS 103.

Captive insurers

44   Some respondents to FRED 49 noted that there were no disclosure exemptions proposed for captive insurers and considered that it might be appropriate to provide some, given that there would often be limited interest outside the relevant group in the financial statements of a captive insurer. A captive insurer is one that provides insurance cover for other entities in the group to which it belongs, and only a small part, if any, of its risk exposure relates to entities outside the group.

45   The Accounting Council considered this issue. It noted that an insurer is a financial institution (as defined in FRS 102) and that in developing FRS 102 (and FRS 101) it had advised that entities that are financial institutions should not be permitted to provide reduced disclosures in relation to financial instruments, because they are a significant part of their business, including in relation to treasury subsidiaries. The Accounting Council considers that this reasoning also holds for captive insurers, especially because it notes that equivalent disclosures will not always be given in the consolidated financial statements; at group level the relevant risks will not be reported as insurance risks. Therefore it is important that the insurance risk taken on by the captive insurer is appropriately disclosed in its individual financial statements. Therefore the Accounting Council advises that no disclosure exemptions should be permitted for captive insurers in relation to insurance contracts (or other financial instruments).

Disclosure: Capital

46   Prior to the application of FRS 102 there were no specific capital disclosure requirements for entities with general insurance business unless they applied FRS 26, in which case some general requirements were contained in FRS 29 (IFRS 7) *Financial Instruments: Disclosure*. For entities with long-term insurance business, there were capital and liability disclosure requirements in FRS 27.

47   FRS 102 requires all financial institutions (including insurance companies) to make the disclosures regarding capital set out in paragraphs 34.31 and 34.32 of FRS 102. In addition, the Implementation Guidance accompanying FRS 103 includes best practice guidance in Section 3: *Guidance on capital disclosures for entities with long-term insurance business* for entities with long-term insurance business on meeting this requirement in relation to life assurance capital and liability. These disclosures were previously required by FRS 27. This may provide entities with some flexibility over how they meet the requirements, but the Accounting Council does not anticipate a reduction in the usefulness of the information disclosed.

48   The Accounting Council considered whether to expand the applicability of the long-term insurance business capital disclosures to all insurers, but this was rejected as being unduly onerous on entities with general insurance business, in the context of an accounting standard that consolidates existing practice, pending future developments relating to the accounting and regulatory environment for insurers. FRED 49 asked for respondents' views on whether the guidance in Section 3 of the Implementation Guidance should be considered best practice for other financial institutions as well. The feedback received was generally that this should be considered in the context of a review of FRS 102, not the development of FRS 103, and that some modification would be necessary in order for this to be applicable to other financial institutions. The Accounting Council notes these views and advises that the first three-yearly review of FRS 102 should consider the effectiveness of its disclosure requirements for financial institutions and whether or not any amendment is required.

The Accounting Council advises the following changes are made to the requirements of **49** FRS 27 when incorporated into FRS 103:

(a)   90% subsidiary exemptions
To maintain the consistency with FRS 101 and FRS 102, the disclosure exemptions for 90% subsidiaries in paragraph 31 of FRS 27 have not been brought into FRS 103, because FRS 102 does not permit qualifying entities that are financial institutions exemptions from disclosures relating to financial instruments. Whilst this will change the level of disclosures needed by subsidiaries, the Accounting Council considers that these disclosures are useful, and that the information will be readily available as a result of the associated regulatory reporting to the PRA.

(b)   Disclosures on requirements and targets

Paragraph 45(a) of FRS 27 gives an option for entities to disclose information on the capital requirements or capital targets set by management. In developing the Implementation Guidance the Accounting Council advises changing 'or' to 'and' so that disclosure of both the requirement and management's targets are best practice. The Accounting Council considers that this is effectively required by paragraph 45(d) of FRS 27, and so is a clarification of an existing requirement.

Implementation Guidance accompanying draft FRS 103

The Implementation Guidance accompanying FRS 103 is not mandatory. Section 2 of **50** the Implementation Guidance contains material originally in the ABI SORP which the Accounting Council considers provides useful guidance on the application of the requirements of FRS 102, FRS 103 and company law.

The Accounting Council also notes that the Technical Actuarial Standards issued by the **51** FRC[5] apply to a wide range of actuarial work and may be relevant when implementing aspects of FRS 103.

Memorandum of Understanding concerning FRS 27 *Life Assurance*

In December 2004 a Memorandum of Understanding concerning FRS 27 *Life Assurance* **52** was entered into by the Accounting Standards Board, the Association of British Insurers and certain entities with life assurance activities concerning the application of the requirements of FRS 27 in financial statements prepared in accordance with EU-adopted IFRS.

As this was relevant only at a particular point in time and FRS 27 is now being withdrawn, **53** the FRC will also withdraw the Memorandum of Understanding once FRS 103 is effective.

Approval of this advice

This advice to the FRC was approved by the nine members of the Accounting Council on **54** 13 February 2014.

---

[5] *In RoI, the guidance issued by the Society of Actuaries in Ireland in ASPLA1 and ASPLA3 may be relevant.*

Appendix I: Glossary

This appendix is an integral part of the FRS.

accounting policies	The specific principles, bases, conventions, rules and practices applied by an entity in preparing and presenting **financial statements**.
acquisition costs	Costs arising from the conclusion of **insurance contracts** including direct costs and indirect costs connected with the processing of proposals and the issuing of policies. Further details are set out in note 6 to the Notes on the Profit and loss Account format in Schedule 3 to the **Regulations**.
Act	The Companies Act 2006
amortised cost (of a financial asset or financial liability)	The amount at which the **financial asset** or **financial liability** is measured at initial **recognition** minus principal repayments, plus or minus the cumulative **amortisation** using the **effective interest method** of any difference between that initial amount and the maturity amount, and minus any reduction (directly or through the use of an allowance account) for impairment or uncollectability.
bonuses	Amounts allocated to **policyholders** under **with-profits** contracts whose existence but not size is specified in the contract. Bonuses may be regular, occasional or terminal.
business combination	The bringing together of separate entities or businesses into one reporting entity.
catastrophe provision	Amount recognised over **reporting periods** between catastrophe events to provide contingency against future catastrophe **claims**.
category of business	Groupings of **general insurance business** with similar characteristics (such as patterns of risk, **claims** incurrence and settlement patterns, and setting of premiums).
cedant	The **policyholder** under a **reinsurance contract**.
claim	The amount payable under an **insurance contract** arising from the occurrence of an **insured event**.
claims incurred	A **claim** is incurred when the event giving rise to the claim occurs. Claims incurred include paid claims and movements in outstanding claims.

claims outstanding	In relation to **general insurance business**: The amounts provided to cover the estimated ultimate cost of settling **claims** arising out of events which have occurred by the **reporting date**, including incurred but not reported (IBNR) claims and claims handling expenses, less amounts already paid in respect of those claims. In relation to **long-term insurance business**: The amounts provided to cover the estimated ultimate cost of settling claims arising out of events, which have been notified by the reporting date being the sums due to beneficiaries together with claims handling expenses, less amounts already paid in respect of those claims.
credit risk	The risk that one party to a **financial instrument** will cause a financial loss for the other party by failing to discharge an obligation.
deferred acquisition costs	Costs arising from the conclusion of **insurance contracts** that are incurred during a **reporting period** but which relate to a subsequent reporting period and are carried forward to subsequent reporting periods. In relation to **general insurance business**: Costs relating to the unexpired period of risk of contracts in force at the **reporting date**. In relation to **long-term insurance business**: Costs relating to contracts in-force at the reporting date in the expectation that they will be recoverable out of future margins within **insurance contracts** after providing for contractual liabilities.
deferred tax	Income tax payable (recoverable) in respect of the taxable profit (tax loss) for future **reporting periods** as a result of past transactions or events.
delegated authority	Agreement for another entity (eg a broker) to underwrite business in the entity's own name.
deposit component	A contractual component that is not accounted for as a **derivative** under Sections 11 and 12 of **FRS 102** and would be within the scope of FRS 102 if it were a separate instrument.
derivative	A **financial instrument** or other contract with all three of the following characteristics: (a) its value changes in response to the change in a specified interest rate, financial instrument price, commodity price, foreign exchange rate, index of prices or rates, credit rating or credit index, or other variable (sometimes called the 'underlying'), provided in the case of a non-financial variable that the variable is not specific to a party to the contract; (b) it requires no initial net investment or an initial net investment that is smaller than would be required for other types of contracts that would be expected to have a similar response to changes in market factors; and (c) it is settled at a future date.

deterministic approach	A method which calculates the value of a policy under a defined scenario and a single set of assumptions.
direct insurance contract	An **insurance contract** that is not a **reinsurance contract**.
discontinued operation	A component of an entity that has been disposed of and: (a) represented a separate major line of business or geographical area of operations; (b) was part of a single co-ordinated plan to dispose of a separate major line of business or geographical area of operations; or (c) was a subsidiary acquired exclusively with a view to resale.
discounting	The reduction to **present value** at a given date of future cash flows at an assumed date by the application of an appropriate discount factor reflecting the time value of money.
discretionary participation feature	A contractual right to receive, as a supplement to **guaranteed benefits**, additional benefits: (a) that are likely to be a significant portion of the total contractual benefits; (b) whose amount or timing is contractually at the discretion of the issuer; and (c) that are contractually based on: (i) the performance of a specified pool of contracts or a specified type of contract; (ii) realised and/or unrealised **investment returns** on a specified pool of assets held by the issuer; or (iii) the **profit or loss** of the company, fund or other entity that issues the contract.
earned premium	For **general insurance business**, earned premium is the proportion of **written premiums** (including where relevant those of previous **reporting periods**) attributable to the risks borne by the **insurer** during the **reporting period**.
effective interest method	A method of calculating the **amortised cost** of a **financial asset** or a **financial liability** (or a group of **financial assets** or **financial liabilities**) and of allocating the interest income or interest expense over the relevant period.
embedded derivative	A component of a hybrid (combined) instrument that also includes a non-derivative host contract—with the effect that some of the cash flows of the combined instrument vary in a way similar to a stand-alone **derivative**. A **derivative** that is attached to a **financial instrument** but is contractually transferable independently of that instrument, or has a different counterparty from that instrument, is not an embedded derivative, but a separate **financial instrument**.

embedded value	A measure of the consolidated value of shareholder's interests in the business, calculated as free surplus plus required capital plus the **value of in-force life assurance business (VIF)**. Different approaches are adopted in terms of methodology and valuation basis, with most entities tending to adopt either the CFO Forum's EEV or MCEV principles.
equalisation provisions	As defined in the relevant regulatory framework.
equity	The residual interest in the assets of the entity after deducting all its **liabilities**.
EU-adopted IFRS	**IFRS** that have been adopted in the European Union in accordance with EU Regulation 1606/2002
existing accounting policies	The **accounting policies** adopted by a reporting entity in its last annual **financial statements** before adoption of this FRS.
fair value	The amount for which an asset could be exchanged, or a **liability** settled, between knowledgeable, willing parties in an arm's length transaction. In the absence of any specific guidance provided in the relevant section of this FRS, the guidance in paragraphs 11.27 to 11.32 of **FRS 102** shall be used in determining fair value.
financial asset	Any asset that is: (a) cash; (b) an equity instrument of another entity; (c) a contractual right: (i) to receive cash or another financial asset from another entity; or (ii) to exchange financial assets or **financial liabilities** with another entity under conditions that are potentially favourable to the entity; or (d) a contract that will or may be settled in the entity's own equity instruments and: (i) under which the entity is or may be obliged to receive a variable number of the entity's own equity instruments; or (ii) that will or may be settled other than by the exchange of a fixed amount of cash or another financial asset for a fixed number of the entity's own equity instruments. For this purpose the entity's own equity instruments do not include instruments that are themselves contracts for the future receipt or delivery of the entity's own equity instruments.
financial guarantee contract	A contract that requires the issuer to make specified payments to reimburse the holder for a loss it incurs because a specified debtor fails to make payment when due in accordance with the original or modified terms of a debt instrument.

financial institution	Any of the following:
	(a) a bank which is:
	(i) a firm with a Part 4A permission[6] which includes accepting deposits and:
	(a) which is a credit institution; or
	(b) whose Part 4A permission includes a requirement that it complies with the rules in the General Prudential sourcebook and the Prudential sourcebook for Banks, Building Societies and Investment Firms relating to banks, but which is not a building society, a friendly society or a credit union;
	(ii) an EEA bank which is a full credit institution;
	(b) a building society which is defined in section 119(1) of the Building Societies Act 1986 as a building society incorporated (or deemed to be incorporated) under that Act;
	(c) a credit union, being a body corporate registered under the Industrial and Provident Societies Act 1965 as a credit union in accordance with the Credit Unions Act 1979, which is an authorised person;
	(d) custodian bank, broker-dealer or stockbroker;
	(e) an entity that undertakes the business of effecting or carrying out **insurance contracts**, including general and life assurance entities;
	(f) an incorporated friendly society incorporated under the Friendly Societies Act 1992 or a registered friendly society registered under section 7(1)(a) of the Friendly Societies Act 1974 or any enactment which it replaced, including any registered branches;
	(g) an investment trust, Irish Investment Company[7], venture capital trust, mutual fund, exchange traded fund, unit trust, open-ended investment company (OEIC);
	(h) a retirement benefit plan; or
	(i) any other entity whose principal activity is to generate wealth or manage risk through **financial instruments**. This is intended to cover entities that have business activities similar to those listed above but are not specifically included in the list above.
	A parent entity whose sole activity is to hold investments in other group entities is not a financial institution.
financial instrument	A contract that gives rise to a **financial asset** of one entity and a **financial liability** or equity instrument of another entity.

[6] *As defined in section 55A of the Financial Services and Markets Act 2000 or references to equivalent provisions of any successor legislation.*

[7] *An Irish Investment Company is a corporate vehicle as defined by section 47(3) of the Companies (Amendment) Act 1983 and paragraph 58 of the Schedule to the Companies (Amendment) Act 1986, and regulated by the Central Bank of Ireland.*

financial liability	Any **liability** that is:
	
	(a) a contractual obligation:
	
	   (i) to deliver cash or another **financial asset** to another entity; or
	
	   (ii) to exchange financial assets or financial liabilities with another entity under conditions that are potentially unfavourable to the entity; or
	
	(b) a contract that will or may be settled in the entity's own equity instruments and:
	
	   (i) under which the entity is or may be obliged to deliver a variable number of the entity's own equity instruments; or
	
	   (ii) will or may be settled other than by the exchange of a fixed amount of cash or another financial asset for a fixed number of the entity's own equity instruments. For this purpose the entity's own equity instruments do not include instruments that are themselves contracts for the future receipt or delivery of the entity's own equity instruments.

financial position	The relationship of the assets, **liabilities** and **equity** of an entity as reported in the **statement of financial position**.
financial reinsurance	Where a **reinsurance contract** is intended, either in whole or in part, to mitigate the requirement to establish prudent provisions, and/or to provide an element of financing, the identifiable elements of the contract which do not transfer **significant insurance risk** are considered to be financial reinsurance.
financial risk	The risk of a possible future change in one or more of a specified interest rate, **financial instrument** price, commodity price, foreign exchange rate, index of prices or rates, credit rating or credit index or other variable, provided in the case of a non-financial variable that the variable is not specific to a party to the contract.
financial statements	Structured representation of the **financial position**, financial performance and cash flows of an entity.
FRS 101	FRS 101 *Reduced Disclosure Framework*
FRS 102	FRS 102 *The Financial Reporting Standard applicable in the UK and Republic of Ireland*
FRS 103	FRS 103 *Insurance Contracts*
fund for future appropriations (FFA)	The balance sheet item required by Schedule 3 to the **Regulations** to comprise all funds the allocation of which, either to **policyholders** or to shareholders, has not been determined by the end of the **reporting period**.
general insurance business	**Insurance contracts** (including reinsurance) falling within one of the classes of insurance specified in Part I of Schedule 1 to the Financial Services and Markets Act 2000 (Regulated Activities) Order 2001 (SI 2001/544).

gross premium method	A form of actuarial valuation of **liabilities** arising under long-term insurance contracts where the premiums brought into account are the full amounts receivable under the contract. The method includes explicit estimates of cash flows for: (a) premiums, adjusted for renewals and lapses; (b) expected claims and for **with-profits business** future regular but not occasional or terminal **bonuses**; (c) costs of maintaining contracts; and (d) future renewal expenses. Cash flows are discounted at the valuation interest rate. The methodology may be set out in the relevant regulatory framework. The discount rate is based on the expected return on the assets deemed to back the **liabilities**. This will be adjusted to reflect any further risks although, under this method, most of the key risks will be reflected in the modelling of the cash flows. For **linked business**, allowance may be made for the purchase of future units required by the contract terms and credit is taken for future charges permitted under those terms.
guaranteed benefits	Payments or other benefits to which a particular **policyholder** or investor has an unconditional right that is not subject to the contractual discretion of the issuer.
guaranteed element	An obligation to pay **guaranteed benefits**, included in a contract that contains a **discretionary participation feature**.
IFRS (International Financial Reporting Standards)	Standards and interpretations issued (or adopted) by the International Accounting Standards Board (IASB). They comprise: (a) International Financial Reporting Standards; (b) International Accounting Standards; and (c) Interpretations developed by the IFRS Interpretations Committee (IFRIC) or the former Standing Interpretations Committee (SIC).
income statement	**Financial statement** that presents all items of income and expense recognised in a **reporting period**, excluding the items of other comprehensive income (referred to as the profit and loss account in the **Act**).
INSPRU	See **Prudential sourcebook for insurers (INSPRU)**.
insurance asset	An **insurer's** net contractual rights under an **insurance contract**.
insurance contract	A contract under which one party (the **insurer**) accepts **significant insurance risk** from another party (the **policyholder**) by agreeing to compensate the policyholder if a specified uncertain future event (the **insured event**) adversely affects the policyholder. (See Appendix II for guidance on this definition.)

insurance liability	An **insurer's** net contractual obligations under an **insurance contract**.
insurance risk	Risk, other than **financial risk**, transferred from the holder of a contract to the issuer.
insured event	An uncertain future event that is covered by an **insurance contract** and creates **insurance risk**.
insurer	The party that has an obligation under an **insurance contract** to compensate a **policyholder** if an **insured event** occurs.
intangible asset	An identifiable non-monetary asset without physical substance. Such an asset is identifiable when: (a) it is separable, ie capable of being separated or divided from the entity and sold, transferred, licensed, rented or exchanged, either individually or together with a related contract, asset or **liability**; or (b) it arises from contractual or other legal rights, regardless of whether those rights are transferable or separable from the entity or from other rights and obligations.
investment contract	Contract that has the legal form of an **insurance contract** but does not expose the **insurer** to **significant insurance risk**, for example life insurance contracts in which the insurer bears no significant mortality risk.
investment return	Comprises all investment income, **realised investment gains and losses** and movements in **unrealised investment gains and losses**. It also includes investment expenses and charges and, if appropriate, interest payable.
liability	A present obligation of the entity arising from past events, the settlement of which is expected to result in an outflow from the entity of resources embodying economic benefits.
liability adequacy test	An assessment of whether the carrying amount of an **insurance liability** needs to be increased (or the carrying amount of related **deferred acquisition costs** or related **intangible assets** decreased), based on a review of future cash flows.
linked business	**Long-term insurance business** where the benefits payable to **policyholders** are wholly or partly to be determined by reference to the value of, or the income from, property of any description or by reference to fluctuations in, or in an index of, the value of property of any description.
liquidity risk	The risk that an entity will encounter difficulty in meeting obligations associated with **financial liabilities** that are settled by delivering cash or another **financial asset**.
longer term rate of investment return	An estimate of the long-term trend **investment return** for the relevant category of investments having regard to past performance, current trends and future expectations.
long-term insurance business	**Insurance contracts** (including reinsurance) falling within one of the classes of insurance specified in Part II of Schedule 1 to the Financial Services and Markets Act 2000 (Regulated Activities) Order 2001 (SI 2001/544).

market risk	The risk that the **fair value** or future cash flows of a **financial instrument** will fluctuate because of changes in market prices. Market risk comprises three types of risk: currency risk, interest rate risk and other price risk. Interest rate risk – the risk that the fair value or future cash flows of a financial instrument will fluctuate because of changes in market interest rates. Currency risk – the risk that the fair value or future cash flows of a financial instrument will fluctuate because of changes in foreign exchange rates. Other price risk – the risk that the fair value or future cash flows of a financial instrument will fluctuate because of changes in market prices (other than those arising from interest rate risk or currency risk), whether those changes are caused by factors specific to the financial instrument or its issuer, or factors affecting all similar financial instruments traded in the market.
modified statutory solvency basis (MSSB)	The basis for determining **insurance liabilities** which is the **statutory solvency basis** adjusted for the following items: (a) to defer new business **acquisition costs** incurred where the benefit of such costs will be obtained in subsequent **reporting periods**; and (b) to treat investment, resilience and similar reserves, or reserves held in respect of general contingencies or the specific contingency that the fund will be closed to new business, where such items are held in respect of **long-term insurance business**, as reserves rather than provisions. These are included, as appropriate, within shareholders' capital and reserves or the **fund for future appropriations (FFA)**.
mutual	As defined in the **PRA** Rulebook.
net premium method	An actuarial valuation of **liabilities** arising under **long-term insurance contracts** where the premium brought into account at any valuation date is that which, on the valuation assumptions regarding interest, mortality and disability, will exactly provide for the benefits guaranteed. A variation of the net premium method involves **zillmerisation**. The detailed methodology for UK companies is included in regulations contained in the **PRA** Rulebook as at 31 December 2015.
non-controlling interest	The **equity** in a **subsidiary** not attributable, directly or indirectly, to a **parent**.
non-participating business	**Long-term insurance business** where **policyholders** are not entitled to share in the surplus of the relevant long-term business.
non-technical account	The section of the **income statement** (referred to as the profit and loss account in the **Act**) prescribed by Part 1 of Schedule 3 to the **Regulations** in addition to the **technical accounts** for **general** and **long-term insurance business**.

notes (to financial statements)	Notes contain information in addition to that presented in the **statement of financial position**, statement of comprehensive income, **income statement** (if presented), combined statement of income and retained earnings (if presented), statement of changes in equity and statement of cash flows. Notes provide narrative descriptions or disaggregations of items presented in those statements and information about items that do not qualify for **recognition** in those statements.
options and guarantees	Features of life assurance contracts that: (a) confer potentially valuable guarantees underlying the level or nature of **policyholder** benefits; or (b) are options to change these benefits exercisable at the discretion of the **policyholder**. For the purposes of this FRS, the term is used to refer only to those options and guarantees whose potential value is affected by the behaviour of financial variables.
owners	Holders of instruments classified as **equity**.
pipeline premiums	Premiums written but not reported to the undertaking by the **reporting date**.
policyholder	A party that has a right to compensation under an **insurance contract** if an **insured event** occurs.
portfolio claims	Amounts payable by one **insurer** to another in consideration for a contract whereby the latter agrees to assume responsibility for the unpaid **claims incurred** by the former prior to a date specified in the contract.
portfolio premiums	Amounts payable by one **insurer** to another in consideration for a contract whereby the latter agrees to assume responsibility for the **claims** arising on a portfolio of in-force business written by the former from a future date until the expiry of the policies.
portfolio transfer	The bulk transfer of contracts or risks to another entity.
present value	A current estimate of the present discounted value of the future net cash flows in the normal course of business.
principles and practices of financial management (PPFM)	The statement that the Financial Conduct Authority requires each **with-profits** life fund to make available to its **policyholders** containing, inter alia, a description of the fund's investment management and bonus distribution policies.
profit or loss	The total of income less expenses, excluding the components of other comprehensive income.
Prudential Regulatory Authority (PRA)	The division of the Bank of England responsible for the prudential regulation and supervision of banks, building societies, credit unions, **insurers** and major investment firms in the UK.

Prudential sourcebook for insurers (INSPRU)	The section of the **PRA** Rulebook detailing the prudential rules for **insurers**, including capital requirements, credit, market and **liquidity risk** for periods ending before 1 January 2016.
realised investment gains and losses	(a) For investments included in the **financial statements** at **fair value**, the difference between the net proceeds on disposal and their purchase price. (b) For investments included at **amortised cost**, the difference between the net proceeds on disposal and the latest carrying value (or if acquired after the last **reporting date**, the purchase price).
realistic value of liabilities	That element of the amount defined by rule 1.3.40 of **INSPRU** as at 31 December 2015, excluding current **liabilities** falling within the definition set out in rule 1.3.190 of INSPRU as at 31 December 2015 that are recognised separately in the **statement of financial position**.
recognition	The process of incorporating in the **statement of financial position** or statement of comprehensive income an item that meets the definition of an asset, **liability, equity**, income or expense and satisfies the following criteria: (a) it is probable that any future economic benefit associated with the item will flow to or from the entity; and (b) the item has a cost or value that can be measured with reliability.
Regulations	The Large and Medium-sized Companies and Groups (Accounts and Reports) Regulations 2008 (SI 2008/410)
regulatory capital resources	An entity's capital resources as calculated in accordance with regulatory framework.
reinsurance assets	A **cedant**'s net contractual rights under a **reinsurance contract**.
reinsurance contract	An **insurance contract** issued by one **insurer** (the **reinsurer**) to compensate another **insurer** (the **cedant**) for losses on one or more contracts issued by the **cedant**. Retrocession is the reinsurance outwards of risks previously accepted by an **insurer** as reinsurance inwards. The recipient is known as the retrocessionaire.
reinsurance recovery	The amount recoverable or recovered from a **reinsurer** (or retrocessionaire) under a **reinsurance contract**.
reinsurer	The party that has an obligation under a **reinsurance contract** to compensate a **cedant** if an **insured event** occurs.
reporting date	The end of the latest period covered by **financial statements** or by an interim financial report.
reporting period	The period covered by **financial statements** or by an interim financial report.

restructuring	A restructuring is a programme that is planned and controlled by management and materially changes either: (a) the scope of a business undertaken by an entity; or (b) the manner in which that business is conducted.
run-off deviation	For **general insurance business**, the difference (before any reduction in respect of **discounting**) between: (a) the provisions made at the beginning of the **reporting period** for outstanding **claims incurred** in previous reporting periods; and (b) the payments made during the reporting period on account of claims incurred in previous reporting periods and the claims provision at the end of the reporting period for such outstanding claims.
separable embedded derivative	An **embedded derivative** where: (a) the economic characteristics and risks of the **embedded derivative** are not closely related to the economic characteristics and risks of the host contract; (b) a separate instrument with the same terms as the **embedded derivative** would meet the definition of a **derivative**; and (c) the hybrid (combined) instrument is not measured at **fair value** with changes in **fair value** recognised in **profit or loss**. The guidance in IAS 39 and IFRS 4 shall be used in determining whether an **embedded derivative** is separable.
significant insurance risk	An **insured event** or risk which could cause an **insurer** to pay significant additional benefits in any scenario, excluding scenarios that lack commercial substance.
Solvency II Directive	Directive 2009/138/EC of the European Parliament and of the Council of 25 November 2009 on the taking-up and pursuit of the business of Insurance and Reinsurance (Solvency II), as amended by Directive 2013/58/EU, and as implemented in the United Kingdom and Republic of Ireland.
statement of financial position	**Financial statement** that presents the relationship of an entity's assets, **liabilities** and **equity** as of a specific date (referred to as the balance sheet in the **Act**).
statutory solvency basis	The basis of determination of **insurance liabilities** in accordance with rule 1 of **INSPRU** as at 31 December 2015.
structured settlement	An arrangement by consent between the parties concerned or under a Court Order whereby damages in the form of a lump sum are replaced by a smaller lump sum and a series of periodic payments. These are also referred to as Periodic Payment Orders or PPOs.

surrender	To cease paying premiums such that the **insurance contract** ceases to have effect.
surrender option	The option to **surrender** an **insurance contract** in return for some form of reduced **claim**.
technical account	In relation to **general insurance business**: The section of the **income statement** (referred to as the profit and loss account in the **Act**) for recording insurance business within the classes specified in Part I of Schedule 1 to the Regulated Activities Order which must be prepared in accordance with the format prescribed in Part I of Schedule 3 to the **Regulations**.
	In relation to **long-term insurance business**: The section of the income statement (referred to as the profit and loss account in the Act) for recording insurance business within the classes specified in Part II of Schedule 1 to the Regulated Activities Order, which must be prepared in accordance with the format prescribed in Part I of Schedule 3 to the Regulations.
unbundle	To account for the components of a contract as if they were separate contracts.
unearned premiums provision	For **general insurance business**, the proportion of **written premiums** relating to periods of risk after the **reporting date**, which are deferred to subsequent **reporting periods**.
unexpired risks provision	The excess of the estimated value of **claims** and expenses likely to arise after the end of the **reporting period** from contracts concluded before that date, insofar as their estimated value exceeds the provision for unearned premiums (after deduction of any **acquisition costs** deferred), and any premiums receivable under those contracts.
unrealised investment gains and losses	The difference between the **fair value** at the **reporting date** of investments held on that date and their purchase price. Movements in unrealised investment gains and losses comprise:
	(a) the increase/decrease in the **reporting period** in the value of investments held at the reporting date; and
	(b) the reversal of unrealised investment gains and losses recognised in earlier reporting periods in respect of investment disposals of the current period.
value of in-force life assurance business (VIF)	The net **present value** of the shareholders' interest in the expected after tax cash flows from **long-term insurance business**, on the assumption that all assets backing the business will be distributed over time to in-force **policyholders** and/or shareholders. The calculation of VIF should allow for uncertainties associated with the assessment of future cash flows, as well as for the time value of money. VIF includes both the shareholders' interest which is expected to arise in the form of cash flows over the lifetime of current in-force contracts and the interest in the surplus assets which, in practice, is not expected to be distributed over this period.

with-profits business	Long-term insurance business which provides benefits through eligibility to participate in discretionary distributions based on profits arising from the insurer's business or from a particular part of the insurer's business. A with-profits contract is an example of a contract with a discretionary participation feature.
written premiums	In relation to general insurance business: Premiums, which an insurer is contractually entitled to receive from the insured in relation to contracts of insurance. These are premiums on contracts entered into during the reporting period and adjustments arising in the reporting period to premiums receivable in respect of contracts entered into in previous reporting periods.
	In relation to long-term insurance business: Premiums to which the insurer is contractually entitled becoming due for payment in the reporting period.
zillmerisation	A variation of the net premium method which increases the future premiums valued to take account of acquisition costs incurred.

Appendix II: Definition of an insurance contract

This appendix is an integral part of the FRS.

A2.1   This appendix gives guidance on the definition of an **insurance contract** in Appendix I. It addresses the following issues:

(a)   the term 'uncertain future event' (paragraphs A2.2 to A2.4);

(b)   payments in kind (paragraphs A2.5 to A2.7);

(c)   **insurance risk** and other risks (paragraphs A2.8 to A2.17);

(d)   examples of insurance contracts (paragraphs A2.18 to A2.24);

(e)   **significant insurance risk** (paragraphs A2.25 to A2.31); and

(f)   changes in the level of insurance risk (paragraphs A2.32 and A2.33).

Uncertain future event

A2.2   Uncertainty (or risk) is the essence of an insurance contract. Accordingly, at least one of the following is uncertain at the inception of an insurance contract:

(a)   whether an **insured event** will occur;

(b)   when it will occur; or

(c)   how much the **insurer** will need to pay if it occurs.

A2.3   In some insurance contracts, the insured event is the discovery of a loss during the term of the contract, even if the loss arises from an event that occurred before the inception of the contract. In other insurance contracts, the insured event is an event that occurs during the term of the contract, even if the resulting loss is discovered after the end of the contract term.

A2.4   Some insurance contracts cover events that have already occurred, but whose financial effect is still uncertain. An example is a **reinsurance contract** that covers the direct insurer against adverse development of **claims** already reported by **policyholders**. In such contracts, the insured event is the discovery of the ultimate cost of those claims.

Payments in kind

A2.5   Some insurance contracts require or permit payments to be made in kind. An example is when the insurer replaces a stolen article directly, instead of reimbursing the policyholder. Another example is when an insurer uses its own hospitals and medical staff to provide medical services covered by the contracts.

A2.6   Some fixed-fee service contracts in which the level of service depends on an uncertain event meet the definition of an insurance contract in this FRS but are not regulated as insurance contracts. One example is a maintenance contract in which the service provider agrees to repair specified equipment after a malfunction. The fixed service fee is based on the expected number of malfunctions, but it is uncertain whether a particular machine will break down. The malfunction of the equipment adversely affects its owner and the contract compensates the owner (in kind, rather than cash). Another example is a contract for car breakdown services in which the provider agrees, for a fixed annual fee, to provide roadside assistance or tow the car to a nearby garage. The latter contract could meet the definition of an insurance contract even if the provider does not agree to carry out repairs or replace parts.

Applying the FRS to the contracts described in paragraph A2.6 is likely to be no more burdensome than applying FRS 102 if such contracts were outside the scope of this FRS: **A2.7**

(a)   There are unlikely to be material liabilities for malfunctions and breakdowns that have already occurred.

(b)   If Section 23 *Revenue* of FRS 102 applied, the service provider would recognise revenue by reference to the stage of completion (and subject to other specified criteria). That approach is also acceptable under this FRS, which permits the service provider to continue its **existing accounting policies** for these contracts unless they involve practices prohibited by paragraph 2.13.

(c)   If this FRS did not apply to these contracts, the service provider would apply Section 21 *Provisions and Contingencies* of FRS 102 to determine whether the contracts are onerous.

Distinction between insurance risk and other risks

The definition of an insurance contract refers to insurance risk, which this FRS defines as risk, other than **financial risk**, transferred from the holder of a contract to the issuer. A contract that exposes the issuer to financial risk without significant insurance risk is not an insurance contract. **A2.8**

The definition of financial risk in Appendix I: *Glossary* includes a list of financial and non-financial variables. That list includes non-financial variables that are not specific to a party to the contract, such as an index of earthquake losses in a particular region or an index of temperatures in a particular city. It excludes non-financial variables that are specific to a party to the contract, such as the occurrence or non-occurrence of a fire that damages or destroys an asset of that party. Furthermore, the risk of changes in the **fair value** of a non-financial asset is not a financial risk if the fair value reflects not only changes in market prices for such assets (a financial variable) but also the condition of a specific non-financial asset held by a party to a contract (a non-financial variable). For example, if a guarantee of the residual value of a specific car exposes the guarantor to the risk of changes in the car's physical condition, that risk is insurance risk, not financial risk. **A2.9**

Some contracts expose the issuer to financial risk, in addition to significant insurance risk. For example, many life insurance contracts both guarantee a minimum rate of return to policyholders (creating financial risk) and promise death benefits that at some times significantly exceed the policyholder's account balance (creating insurance risk in the form of mortality risk). Such contracts are insurance contracts. **A2.10**

Under some contracts, an insured event triggers the payment of an amount linked to a price index. Such contracts are insurance contracts, provided the payment that is contingent on the insured event can be significant. For example, a life-contingent annuity linked to a cost-of-living index transfers insurance risk because payment is triggered by an uncertain event—the survival of the annuitant. The link to the price index is an **embedded derivative**, but it also transfers insurance risk. If the resulting transfer of insurance risk is significant, the embedded derivative meets the definition of an insurance contract (which need not be separated and measured at fair value). **A2.11**

The definition of insurance risk refers to risk that the insurer accepts from the policyholder. In other words, insurance risk is a pre-existing risk transferred from the policyholder to the insurer. Thus, a new risk created by the contract is not insurance risk. **A2.12**

The definition of an insurance contract refers to an adverse effect on the policyholder. The definition does not limit the payment by the insurer to an amount equal to the financial impact of the adverse event. For example, the definition does not exclude 'new-for-old' **A2.13** coverage that pays the policyholder sufficient to permit replacement of a damaged old asset by a new asset. Similarly, the definition does not limit payment under a term life insurance contract to the financial loss suffered by the deceased's dependants, nor does it preclude the payment of predetermined amounts to quantify the loss caused by death or an accident.

A2.14   Some contracts require a payment if a specified uncertain event occurs, but do not require an adverse effect on the policyholder as a precondition for payment. Such a contract is not an insurance contract even if the holder uses the contract to mitigate an underlying risk exposure. For example, if the holder uses a **derivative** to hedge an underlying non-financial variable that is correlated with cash flows from an asset of the entity, the derivative is not an insurance contract because payment is not conditional on whether the holder is adversely affected by a reduction in the cash flows from the asset. Conversely, the definition of an insurance contract refers to an uncertain event for which an adverse effect on the policyholder is a contractual precondition for payment. This contractual precondition does not require the insurer to investigate whether the event actually caused an adverse effect, but permits the insurer to deny payment if it is not satisfied that the event caused an adverse effect.

A2.15   Lapse or persistency risk (ie the risk that the counterparty will cancel the contract earlier or later than the issuer had expected in pricing the contract) is not insurance risk because the payment to the counterparty is not contingent on an uncertain future event that adversely affects the counterparty. Similarly, expense risk (ie the risk of unexpected increases in the administrative costs associated with the servicing of a contract, rather than in costs associated with insured events) is not insurance risk because an unexpected increase in expenses does not adversely affect the counterparty.

A2.16   Therefore, a contract that exposes the issuer to lapse risk, persistency risk or expense risk is not an insurance contract unless it also exposes the issuer to insurance risk. However, if the issuer of that contract mitigates that risk by using a second contract to transfer part of that risk to another party, the second contract exposes that other party to insurance risk.

A2.17   An insurer can accept significant insurance risk from the policyholder only if the insurer is an entity separate from the policyholder. In the case of a **mutual** insurer, the mutual accepts risk from each policyholder and pools that risk. Although policyholders bear that pooled risk collectively in their capacity as **owners**, the mutual has still accepted the risk that is the essence of an insurance contract.

Examples of insurance contracts

A2.18   The following are examples of contracts that are insurance contracts, if the transfer of insurance risk is significant:

(a)   insurance against theft or damage to property.

(b)   insurance against product liability, professional liability, civil liability or legal expenses.

(c)   life insurance and prepaid funeral plans (although death is certain, it is uncertain when death will occur or, for some types of life insurance, whether death will occur within the period covered by the insurance).

(d)   life-contingent annuities and pensions (ie contracts that provide compensation for the uncertain future event—the survival of the annuitant or pensioner—to assist the annuitant or pensioner in maintaining a given standard of living, which would otherwise be adversely affected by his or her survival).

(e)   disability and medical cover.

(f)   surety bonds, fidelity bonds, performance bonds and bid bonds (ie contracts that provide compensation if another party fails to perform a contractual obligation, for example an obligation to construct a building).

(g)   credit insurance that provides for specified payments to be made to reimburse the holder for a loss it incurs because a specified debtor fails to make payment when due under the original or modified terms of a debt instrument. These contracts could have various legal forms, such as that of a guarantee, some types of letter of credit, a credit derivative default contract or an insurance contract. However, although these contracts meet the definition of an insurance contract, they also meet the definition of a **financial guarantee contract** in FRS 102 and are within the scope of Section 21 of FRS 102, not this FRS (see paragraph 1.7(d)). Nevertheless, if an issuer of financial guarantee contracts has previously asserted explicitly that it regards such contracts as insurance contracts and has used accounting applicable to insurance contracts, the issuer may elect to apply either Section 21 of FRS 102 or this FRS to such financial guarantee contracts.

(h)   product warranties. Product warranties issued by another party for goods sold by a manufacturer, dealer or retailer are within the scope of this FRS. However, product warranties issued directly by a manufacturer, dealer or retailer are outside its scope, because they are within the scope of Sections 21 and 23 of FRS 102.

(i)   title insurance (ie insurance against the discovery of defects in title to land that were not apparent when the insurance contract was written). In this case, the insured event is the discovery of a defect in the title, not the defect itself.

(j)   travel assistance (ie compensation in cash or in kind to policyholders for losses suffered while they are travelling). Paragraphs A2.6 and A2.7 discuss some contracts of this kind.

(k)   catastrophe bonds that provide for reduced payments of principal, interest or both if a specified event adversely affects the issuer of the bond (unless the specified event does not create significant insurance risk, for example if the event is a change in an interest rate or foreign exchange rate).

(l)   insurance swaps and other contracts that require a payment based on changes in climatic, geological or other physical variables that are specific to a party to the contract.

(m)   reinsurance contracts.

The following are examples of items that are not insurance contracts: **A2.19**

(a)   **investment contracts** that have the legal form of an insurance contract but do not expose the insurer to significant insurance risk, for example life insurance contracts in which the insurer bears no significant mortality risk (such contracts are non-insurance **financial instruments** or service contracts, see paragraphs A2.20 and A2.21).

(b)   contracts that have the legal form of insurance, but pass all significant insurance risk back to the policyholder through non-cancellable and enforceable mechanisms that adjust future payments by the policyholder as a direct result of insured losses, for example some **financial reinsurance** contracts or some group contracts (such contracts are normally non-insurance financial instruments or service contracts, see paragraphs A2.20 and A2.21).

(c)   self-insurance, in other words retaining a risk that could have been covered by insurance (there is no insurance contract because there is no agreement with another party).

(d)   contracts (such as gambling contracts) that require a payment if a specified uncertain future event occurs, but do not require, as a contractual precondition for payment, that the event adversely affects the policyholder. However, this does not preclude the specification of a predetermined payout to quantify the loss caused by a specified event such as death or an accident (see also paragraph A2.13).

(e)   derivatives that expose one party to financial risk but not insurance risk, because they require that party to make payment based solely on changes in one or more of a specified interest rate, financial instrument price, commodity price, foreign exchange rate, index of prices or rates, credit rating or credit index or other variable, provided in the case of a non-financial variable that the variable is not specific to a party to the contract (see FRS 102).

(f)   a credit-related guarantee (or letter of credit, credit derivative default contract or credit insurance contract) that requires payments even if the holder has not incurred a loss on the failure of the debtor to make payments when due.

(g)   contracts that require a payment based on a climatic, geological or other physical variable that is not specific to a party to the contract (commonly described as weather derivatives).

(h)   catastrophe bonds that provide for reduced payments of principal, interest or both, based on a climatic, geological or other physical variable that is not specific to a party to the contract.

A2.20   If the contracts described in paragraph A2.19 create **financial assets** or **financial liabilities**, they are within the scope of Sections 11 *Basic Financial Instruments* and 12 *Other Financial Instruments Issues* of FRS 102. Among other things, this means that the parties to the contract use what is sometimes called deposit accounting, which involves the following:

(a)   one party recognises the consideration received as a financial liability, rather than as revenue; and

(b)   the other party recognises the consideration paid as a financial asset, rather than as an expense.

A2.21   If the contracts described in paragraph A2.19 do not create financial assets or financial liabilities, Section 23 of FRS 102 applies. Under Section 23 of FRS 102, revenue associated with a transaction involving the rendering of services is recognised by reference to the stage of completion of the transaction if the outcome of the transaction can be estimated reliably.

Examples of revenue recognition under the principles in Section 23 of FRS 102

A2.22   Examples 15, 17 and 17A in the appendix to Section 23 of FRS 102 are relevant to the **recognition** of revenue for the types of contract described in paragraph A2.19.

A2.23   Where the consideration for a contract meeting the definition of an investment contract comprises both a fee for the origination and an ongoing charge for the provision of (eg investment management) services, the insurance undertaking shall record the origination fee as revenue on the date on which it becomes entitled to it where it can be demonstrated that the undertaking has no further obligations in respect of the fee.

A2.24   Incremental costs that are directly attributable to securing an investment management contract are recognised as an asset if they can be identified separately and measured reliably and if it is probable that they will be recovered. The asset represents the entity's contractual right to benefit from providing investment management services and is amortised as the entity recognises the related revenue. If the entity has a portfolio of investment management contracts, it may assess their recoverability on a portfolio basis.

Significant insurance risk

A contract is an insurance contract only if it transfers significant insurance risk. Paragraphs A2.8 to A2.21 discuss insurance risk. The following paragraphs discuss the assessment of whether insurance risk is significant.

A2.25

Insurance risk is significant if, and only if, an insured event could cause an insurer to pay significant additional benefits in any scenario, excluding scenarios that lack commercial substance (ie have no discernible effect on the economics of the transaction). If significant additional benefits would be payable in scenarios that have commercial substance, the condition in the previous sentence may be met even if the insured event is extremely unlikely or even if the expected (ie probability-weighted) **present value** of contingent cash flows is a small proportion of the expected present value of all the remaining contractual cash flows.

A2.26

The additional benefits described in paragraph A2.26 refer to amounts that exceed those that would be payable if no insured event occurred (excluding scenarios that lack commercial substance). Those additional amounts include claims handling and claims assessment costs, but exclude:

A2.27

(a)   the loss of the ability to charge the policyholder for future services. For example, in an investment-linked life insurance contract, the death of the policyholder means that the insurer can no longer perform investment management services and collect a fee for doing so. However, this economic loss for the insurer does not reflect insurance risk, just as a mutual fund manager does not take on insurance risk in relation to the possible death of the client. Therefore, the potential loss of future investment management fees is not relevant in assessing how much insurance risk is transferred by a contract;

(b)   waiver on death of charges that would be made on cancellation or **surrender**. Because the contract brought those charges into existence, the waiver of these charges does not compensate the policyholder for a pre-existing risk. Hence, they are not relevant in assessing how much insurance risk is transferred by a contract;

(c)   a payment conditional on an event that does not cause a significant loss to the holder of the contract. For example, consider a contract that requires the issuer to pay one million currency units if an asset suffers physical damage causing an insignificant economic loss of one currency unit to the holder. In this contract, the holder transfers to the insurer the insignificant risk of losing one currency unit. At the same time, the contract creates non-insurance risk that the issuer will need to pay 999,999 currency units if the specified event occurs. Because the issuer does not accept significant insurance risk from the holder, this contract is not an insurance contract;

(d)   possible **reinsurance recoveries**. The insurer accounts for these separately.

An insurer shall assess the significance of insurance risk contract by contract, rather than by reference to materiality to the **financial statements**[8]. Thus, insurance risk may be significant even if there is a minimal probability of material losses for a whole book of contracts. This contract-by-contract assessment makes it easier to classify a contract as an insurance contract. However, if a relatively homogeneous book of small contracts is known to consist of contracts that all transfer insurance risk, an insurer need not examine each contract within that book to identify a few non-derivative contracts that transfer insignificant insurance risk.

A2.28

It follows from paragraphs A2.26 to A2.28 that if a contract pays a death benefit exceeding the amount payable on survival, the contract is an insurance contract unless the additional

A2.29

---

[8] *For this purpose, contracts entered into simultaneously with a single counterparty (or contracts that are otherwise interdependent) form a single contract.*

death benefit is insignificant (judged by reference to the contract rather than to an entire book of contracts). As noted in paragraph A2.27(b), the waiver on death of cancellation or surrender charges is not included in this assessment if this waiver does not compensate the policyholder for a pre-existing risk. Similarly, an annuity contract that pays out regular sums for the rest of a policyholder's life is an insurance contract, unless the aggregate life-contingent payments are insignificant.

A2.30   Paragraph A2.26 refers to additional benefits. These additional benefits could include a requirement to pay benefits earlier if the insured event occurs earlier and the payment is not adjusted for the time value of money. An example is whole life insurance for a fixed amount (in other words, insurance that provides a fixed death benefit whenever the policyholder dies, with no expiry date for the cover). It is certain that the policyholder will die, but the date of death is uncertain. The insurer will suffer a loss on those individual contracts for which policyholders die early, even if there is no overall loss on the whole book of contracts.

A2.31   If an insurance contract is **unbundled** into a **deposit component** and an insurance component, the significance of insurance risk transfer is assessed by reference to the insurance component. The significance of insurance risk transferred by an embedded derivative is assessed by reference to the embedded derivative.

Changes in the level of insurance risk

A2.32   Some contracts do not transfer any insurance risk to the issuer at inception, although they do transfer insurance risk at a later time. For example, consider a contract that provides a specified **investment return** and includes an option for the policyholder to use the proceeds of the investment on maturity to buy a life-contingent annuity at the current annuity rates charged by the insurer to other new annuitants when the policyholder exercises the option. The contract transfers no insurance risk to the issuer until the option is exercised, because the insurer remains free to price the annuity on a basis that reflects the insurance risk transferred to the insurer at that time. However, if the contract specifies the annuity rates (or a basis for setting the annuity rates), the contract transfers insurance risk to the issuer at inception.

A2.33   A contract that qualifies as an insurance contract remains an insurance contract until all rights and obligations are extinguished or expire.

Appendix III: Tables of concordance between FRS 103, FRS 27 and the ABI SORP

This appendix maps the source material in FRS 27 and the ABI SORP into the FRS.

FRS 27

Source paragraph	Location in FRS 103/ IG	Notes
1	Summary (vi)	
2	Appendix I	Integrated into Appendix I: Glossary
3	Not used	Not applicable under FRS 103
4	3.7 and 3.12	
5	5.3	
6	3.11	
7	IG1.1	
8	Not used	
9	Not used	
10	3.14	
11	Not used	
12	Not used	
13	IG1.3	Significant deletions/amendments to the text
14	IG1.5	Significant deletions/amendments to the text
15	IG1.6	
16	3.15	Significant deletions/amendments to the text
17	IG1.10	
18	3.13	
19	IG1.11	
20	IG1.12	
21	IG1.13	Significant deletions/amendments to the text
22	Not used	Covered by the Regulations
23	5.5	
24	5.4	
25	Not used	
26	Not used	
27	3.16	Significant deletions/amendments to the text
28	3.17	
29	3.18	
30	Not used	Covered by paragraph 8.5 of FRS 102
31	Not used	Subsidiary exemption from disclosure no longer applicable

Source paragraph	Location in FRS 103/ IG	Notes
32	IG3.1	
33	IG3.2	
34	IG3.3	
35	IG3.4	
36	Not used	
37	IG3.5	
38	IG3.6	
39	IG3.7	
40	IG3.8	
41	IG3.9	Provides guidance on best practice
42	IG3.10	
43	IG3.11	
44	IG3.12	Significant deletions/amendments to the text
45	IG3.13	
46	Not used	
47	Not used	
48	IG3.14	
49	IG3.16	Significant deletions/amendments to the text
50	IG3.17	
51	IG3.18	Provides guidance on best practice
52	IG3.19	
53	IG3.20	
54	Not used	
55	IG3.21	
56	IG3.22	Provides guidance on best practice
57	Not used	
58	IG3.23	
59	IG3.15	Paragraph moved to before FRS 27.49
60	Not used	

ABI SORP

Source section / paragraph	Paragraphs used	Location in FRS 103/IG
Definitions	Various	Integrated into Appendix I: Glossary
Gross written premiums	83, 84, 85, 87, 88, 89, 90, 91	IG2.1 – IG2.8
Claims	94, 95, 99, 100, 101	IG2.9 – IG2.13
Discounting	105, 106, 107, 108, 110, 112, 113	IG2.14 – IG2.20
Unexpired risks provision	117, 118, 119, 120, 121, 122, 123	IG2.21 – IG2.27
Equalisation reserves	125	IG2.28
Portfolio premiums and claims	127, 128, 129, 130	IG2.29 – IG2.32
Structured settlements	131	IG2.33
Deferred acquisition costs	132, 133, 135	IG2.34 – IG2.36
Measurement of with-profits liabilities and related assets	149, 151, 152, 153, 154	IG1.2, IG1.4 and IG1.7 – IG1.9
Examples of revenue recognition	159, 161	A2.23 – A2.24
Premiums	163, 164	3.3 – 3.4
Claims	166, 167	3.5 – 3.6
Deferred acquisition costs	171, 174, 175*	3.8 – 3.10 * 175 is placed before 171
Technical provisions	178, 180, 182, 183, 184, 185, 186, 187, 188*, 189**, 190, 191	IG2.38 – IG2.49 * 188 is placed after 184 ** 189 is placed after 191
Fund for future appropriations	194, 195	IG2.50 – IG2.51
Reserves relating to long term business	196, 197	IG2.52 – IG2.53
Present value of acquired in-force business	200, 201	IG2.54 – IG2.55
Disaggregated information about single and regular premiums	213*, 214, 216*, 217	IG2.56 – IG2.58 * 213 and 216 are combined, and placed after 214

Source section / paragraph	Paragraphs used	Location in FRS 103/IG
Commission	218	4.6
Exchange gains and losses	219	2.32
Income Statement	225, 226	IG2.59 – IG2.60
Retirement benefits	230, 232*, 234*	2.33 – 2.34 * 232 and 234 are combined
Valuation of reinsurance asset	259, 260	IG2.61 Combined with FRS 27.12
Reinsurance balance	264	IG2.62
Allocation of investment return	290, 291, 292, 293, 295, 296, 297, 298, 305	IG2.63 – IG2.71
The longer term rate of investment return	299, 300, 301, 302, 303, 304	IG2.72 – IG2.77
Investments in unit trusts/OEICs	311	IG2.78

Appendix IV: Note on Legal Requirements

INTRODUCTION

This appendix provides an overview of how the requirements in FRS 103 address United Kingdom company law requirements. It is therefore written from the perspective of a company to which the Companies Act 2006 applies. Appendix V contains the Republic of Ireland legal references. **A4.1**

Many entities that are not constituted as companies apply accounting standards promulgated by the FRC for the purposes of preparing financial statements that present a true and fair view[9]. A brief consideration of the legal framework for some other entities can be found at A4.3. **A4.2**

Entities not subject to company law

Many entities that apply FRS 103 are not companies, but are nevertheless required by their governing legislation, or other regulation or requirement to prepare financial statements that present a true and fair view of the financial performance and financial position of the reporting entity. However, the FRC sets accounting standards within the framework of the Act and therefore it is the company law requirements that the FRC primarily considered when developing FRS 103. Entities preparing financial statements within other legal frameworks will need to satisfy themselves that FRS 103 does not conflict with any relevant legal obligations. **A4.3**

The FRC notes the following:

Legislation	Overview of requirements
Friendly Societies Act 1992	Every society shall prepare a balance sheet and an income and expenditure account for each financial year giving a true and fair view of the affairs of the society and its income and expenditure for the year.
	The Friendly Societies (Accounts and Related Provisions) Regulations 1994 (as amended) make further requirements about the form and content of friendly society accounts, which do not generally appear inconsistent with the requirements of FRS 102 and FRS 103. However, for a non-directive society (as defined in the regulations) the regulations set out a different required format.
Co-operative and Community Benefit Societies Act 2014	The Insurance Accounts Directive (Miscellaneous Insurance Undertakings) Regulations 2008 require every society that is an insurance undertaking to prepare its financial statements substantially as though it were a company registered under the Companies Act 2006.

---

[9] *More information about the 'true and fair' concept can be found on the FRC's website at http://www.frc.org.uk/ Our-Work/Codes-Standards/Accounting-and-Reporting-Policy/True-and-Fair.aspx.*

Legislation	Overview of requirements
Insurance Accounts Directive (Lloyd's Syndicate and Aggregate Accounts) Regulations 2008	In respect of each syndicate managing agents shall prepare accounts on an underwriting year basis that give a true and fair view of the results of that underwriting year.

Appendix V: Republic of Ireland (RoI) Legal References

INTRODUCTION

The table below outlines the provisions of the Companies Acts 1963 to 2013 and related Regulations which implement EC Accounting Directives in Ireland (Irish company law) which correspond to the provisions of UK company law referred to in the FRS. **A5.1**

In an Irish context, the principal legislation of relevance is the European Communities (Insurance Undertakings: Accounts) Regulations 1996 (SI No. 23 of 1996) (Insurance Undertakings Regulations 1996 or IUR 1996). **A5.2**

The following Irish legislation is also referenced in the table below: **A5.3**

- European Communities (Non-life Insurance) Framework Regulations 1994 – SI 359 of 1994;
- European Communities (Life Assurance) Framework Regulations 1994 – SI 360 of 1994;
- The Building Societies Act 1989;
- The Credit Union Acts 1997 and 2012;
- The Central Bank Act 1971;
- The Charities Act 2009; and
- The Friendly Societies Acts 1896 to 1977.

Throughout the FRS, general references are made to 'the Regulations', which are defined in the Glossary as the UK Large and Medium-sized Companies and Groups (Accounts and Reports) Regulations 2008 (SI 2008/410). Schedule 3 and Schedule 6 of those Regulations apply to UK insurance companies preparing Companies Act individual accounts and Companies Act group accounts respectively. General references are also made in this FRS to 'the Act', which is defined in the Glossary as the (UK) 'Companies Act 2006'. Such general references to 'the Regulations' and 'the Act' in the FRS are not included in the table below. In an Irish context, reference should be made to the relevant provisions of the Irish legislation outlined above. **A5.4**

Other notes

The table below is intended to serve as a general reference guide to the corresponding or similar provisions in Irish law and does not purport to be complete. It should be noted that not all of the Irish legal provisions in the table below are equivalent to the corresponding UK legal provisions and reference should be made to the Irish legislation for an understanding of relevant requirements. In some cases reference may need to be made to other parts of Irish legislation. **A5.5**

Furthermore, the table below does not address the regulatory aspects of accounting for insurance contracts. Where this FRS makes reference to the handbook, regulations, rules or guidance of the UK Prudential Regulatory Authority (PRA), reference should be made in an Irish context to the regulatory requirements and guidance of the Central Bank of Ireland as well as legislation applicable to insurance undertakings. Of particular relevance in this regard are SI 359 of 1994 and SI 360 of 1994, as noted above. It should also be noted that there are some differences between the UK and Irish regulatory requirements, for example the 'PRA Realistic Capital Regime' for with-profits insurance business is not relevant in Ireland. **A5.6**

SECTION 1: SCOPE

Paragraph	UK Reference	RoI Reference
1.4	Schedule 3 to the Regulations	Insurance Undertakings Regulations 1996

SECTION 4: DISCLOSURE

Paragraph	UK Reference	RoI Reference
4.6	Schedule 3 to the Regulations	Insurance Undertakings Regulations 1996

ACCOUNTING COUNCIL'S ADVICE TO THE FRC TO ISSUE FRS 103 INSURANCE CONTRACTS

Paragraph	UK Reference	RoI Reference
24, 38, 39	Schedule 3 to the Regulations	Insurance Undertakings Regulations 1996

APPENDIX I: GLOSSARY

Paragraph	UK Reference	RoI Reference
'Acquisition costs'	Note 6 to the Notes on the Profit and Loss Account format in Schedule 3 to the Regulations	Note 6 to the Notes on the profit and loss account format in Section B of Chapter 2 of Part I of the Schedule to the Insurance Undertakings Regulations 1996
'Financial institution' and Footnote 6	Part 4A permission; Section 55A of the Financial Services and Markets Act 2000	There is no equivalent legislation in Ireland to the Financial Services and Markets Act 2000. Banks in Ireland are licensed under Section 9 of the Central Bank Act 1971
'Financial institution'	Section 119(1) of the Building Societies Act 1986	Section 2(1) of the Building Societies Act 1989
'Financial institution'	Industrial and Provident Societies Act 1965 and Credit Unions Act 1979	Credit Union Acts 1997 to 2012
'Financial institution'	Friendly Societies Act 1992; section 7(1)(a) of the Friendly Societies Act 1974	Friendly Societies Acts 1896 to 1977
'Fund for future appropriations (FFA)'	Schedule 3 to the Regulations	Insurance Undertakings Regulations 1996
'General insurance business'	Part I of Schedule 1 to the Financial Services and Markets Act 2000 (Regulated Activities) Order 2001 (SI 2001/544)	Annex 1 of SI 359 of 1994
'Long term insurance business'	Part II of Schedule 1 to the Financial Services and Markets Act 2000 (Regulated Activities) Order 2001 (SI 2001/544)	Annex 1 of SI 360 of 1994

Paragraph	UK Reference	RoI Reference
'Non-technical account'	Part 1 of Schedule 3 to the Regulations	Section B of Chapter 2 of Part 1 of the Schedule to the Insurance Undertakings Regulations 1996
'Technical account'	Part I of Schedule 1 to the Regulated Activities Order	Annex 1 of SI 359 of 1994
'Technical account'	Part II of Schedule 1 to the Regulated Activities Order	Annex 1 of SI 360 of 1994
'Technical account'	Part I of Schedule 3 to the Regulations	Section B of Chapter 2 of Part 1 of the Schedule to the Insurance Undertakings Regulations 1996

APPENDIX IV: NOTE ON LEGAL REQUIREMENTS

Paragraph	UK Reference	RoI Reference
A4.3	Friendly Societies Act 1992	Friendly Societies Acts 1896 to 1977
A4.3	Industrial and Provident Societies Acts 1965	The Industrial and Provident Societies (Amendment) Act 1978
A4.3	Insurance Accounts Directive (Lloyd's Syndicate and Aggregate Accounts) Regulations 2008	There is no equivalent legislation in Ireland.

Amendments to FRS 103:
Insurance Contracts – Solvency II

(May 2016)

Contents

Paragraphs

Summary

Amendments to FRS 103 – Solvency II

Amendments to FRS 103 *Insurance Contracts*
Section 1 Scope   1–3
Section 2 Accounting Policies, Recognition and Measurement   4–5
Section 3 Recognition and Measurement: Requirements for entities
    with long-term insurance business   6–14
Section 4 Disclosure   15–16
Appendix I: Glossary   17–19
Appendix IV: Note on legal requirements   20–21

Amendments to Implementation Guidance to accompany
FRS 103 *Insurance Contracts*
Implementation Guidance – Section 1 Guidance for entities
    with long-term insurance business   22–34
Implementation Guidance – Section 2 Guidance for entities with
    general insurance business or long-term insurance business   35–42

Approval by the FRC

The Corporate Reporting Council's Advice to the FRC to issue
Amendments to FRS 103 – Solvency II
Introduction   1–4
Advice   5–7
Background   8–10
Amendments to FRS 103   11–23
Effective date   24
Future development of FRS 103   25
Approval of this advice   26

Summary

(i)　With effect from 1 January 2015, the Financial Reporting Council (FRC) revised financial reporting standards in the United Kingdom and Republic of Ireland. The revisions fundamentally reformed financial reporting, replacing the extant standards with five Financial Reporting Standards:

    (a)　FRS 100 *Application of Financial Reporting Requirements*;

    (b)　FRS 101 *Reduced Disclosure Framework*;

    (c)　FRS 102 *The Financial Reporting Standard applicable in the UK and Republic of Ireland*;

    (d)　FRS 103 *Insurance Contracts*; and

    (e)　FRS 104 *Interim Financial Reporting*.

The FRC has also issued FRS 105 *The Financial Reporting Standard applicable to the Micro-entities Regime* to support the implementation of the new micro-entities regime. It is effective from 1 January 2016 with early application permitted.

These limited amendments to FRS 103 update it to reflect the implementation, from 1 January 2016, of the Solvency II Directive.

(ii)　The FRC's overriding objective in setting accounting standards is to enable users of accounts to receive high-quality understandable financial reporting proportionate to the size and complexity of the entity and users' information needs.

(iii)　In meeting this objective, the FRC aims to provide succinct financial reporting standards that:

    (a)　have consistency with international accounting standards through the application of an IFRS-based solution unless an alternative clearly better meets the overriding objective;

    (b)　reflect up-to-date thinking and developments in the way entities operate and the transactions they undertake;

    (c)　balance consistent principles for accounting by all UK and Republic of Ireland entities with practical solutions, based on size, complexity, public interest and users' information needs;

    (d)　promote efficiency within groups; and

    (e)　are cost-effective to apply.

Amendments to FRS 103 – Solvency II

(iv)　These amendments to FRS 103 update the terminology and definitions used for changes in the regulatory framework, following the implementation of the Solvency II Directive. Established accounting policies can continue to be applied if an entity so chooses.

Amendments to FRS 103 *Insurance Contracts*

Amendments to Section 1 *Scope*

1　The following paragraphs set out the amendments to Section 1 *Scope* (deleted text is struck through, inserted text is underlined).

2　Paragraph 1.5 is amended as follows:

1.5 Paragraph 2.3 permits entities to change their **accounting policies**, either on adoption of this FRS or subsequently, providing their new accounting policies meet certain criteria. Entities that are setting accounting policies in relation to insurance contracts, or other financial instruments with discretionary participation features, for the first time, shall <u>for long-term insurance business either:</u>

<u>(a)</u> first consider the requirements of Section 3, the Regulations and any relevant parts of FRS 102, ~~as a means of establishing current practice~~ as a benchmark before assessing whether to set accounting policies that differ from those benchmark policies in accordance with paragraph 2.3<u>; or</u>

<u>(b) establish accounting policies that are based on the rules under the</u> **Solvency II Directive** <u>for the recognition and measurement of technical provisions, and any relevant requirements of this FRS, the Regulations and FRS 102. In doing so an entity shall make appropriate adjustments to the Solvency II rules to ensure that the accounting policies result in information that is relevant and reliable.</u>

The Implementation Guidance accompanying this FRS also provides guidance.

Paragraph 1.11A is inserted as follows: 3

<u>1.11A In May 2016 amendments were made to this FRS, to update it for changes in the regulatory framework. An entity shall apply these amendments for accounting periods ending on or after 1 January 2016.</u>

Amendments to Section 2 *Accounting Policies, Recognition and Measurement*

The following paragraph sets out the amendments to Section 2 *Accounting Policies,*   4
Recognition and Measurement (inserted text is underlined).

Paragraph 2.3A is inserted as follows: 5

<u>2.3A One basis for changing accounting policies might be to enable them to be more consistent with the rules under the</u> **Solvency II Directive** <u>for the recognition and measurement of technical provisions. In doing so an entity shall make appropriate adjustments to the Solvency II rules to meet the requirements of paragraph 2.3.</u>

Amendments to Section 3 *Recognition and Measurement: Requirements for entities with long-term insurance business*

The following paragraphs set out the amendments to Section 3 *Recognition and*   6
Measurement: Requirements for entities with long-term insurance business (deleted text is struck through, inserted text is underlined).

Paragraph 3.1 is amended as follows (and 'realistic capital regime' is no longer shown in   7
bold type):

3.1 This section sets out requirements for entities applying this FRS that are carrying out **long-term insurance business**:

(a)   Paragraphs 3.3 to 3.9<u>0</u>~~10~~ and 3.16 to 3.18 apply to all long-term insurance business.

(b)   Paragraphs 3.1<u>0</u>~~1~~ to 3.15 apply to **with-profits business** and with-profits funds, to which the **Prudential Regulatory Authority (PRA)** realistic capital regime <u>(as set out in section 1.3 of</u> **INSPRU** <u>as at 31 December 2015)</u> ~~i~~<u>was</u> being applied, either voluntarily or compulsorily<u>, prior to 1 January 2016.</u>

8   Paragraph 3.1A is inserted as follows:

> 3.1A This section sets out the benchmark for setting **accounting policies** for long-term insurance business as at 1 January 2015. Entities are permitted to change their accounting policies in accordance with paragraph 2.3. Entities that are setting accounting policies for the first time may apply this benchmark in accordance with paragraph 1.5(a) or are permitted to set alternative policies in accordance with paragraph 1.5(b).

9   Paragraph 3.2 is amended as follows:

> 3.2 Where an entity has changed its **accounting policies** in accordance with paragraph 2.3 or adopted accounting policies in accordance with paragraph 1.5(b), and its ~~new~~ accounting policies are ~~no longer~~not consistent with this section, the requirements of this section that are ~~no longer~~not consistent with the entity's accounting policies need not be applied.

10   Paragraph 3.7 is amended as follows, and renumbered as paragraph 3.10:

> 3.~~7~~10 **Acquisition costs** shall not be deferred for with-profits funds ~~to which the PRA realistic capital regime is being applied, either voluntarily or compulsorily~~.

11   Paragraphs 3.8 is amended as follows, and renumbered as paragraph 3.7:

> 3.8~~7~~ Except as required by paragraph 3.10~~7~~, acquisition costs shall be deferred except to the extent that:
>
> (a)   …

12   Paragraphs 3.9 and 3.10 are renumbered as paragraphs 3.8 and 3.9.

13   Paragraph 3.11 is amended as follows:

> 3.11 The established accounting treatment for long-term insurance business is to measure liabilities for policyholder benefits under the **modified statutory solvency basis (MSSB)**. This FRS requires ~~those~~ with-profits funds ~~within the scope of the PRA realistic capital regime~~ to use the **realistic value of liabilities** as the basis for the estimated value of the liabilities to be included in the **financial statements**.

14   Paragraph 3.12 is amended as follows:

> 3.12 For with-profits funds ~~to which the PRA realistic capital regime is being applied, either voluntarily or compulsorily~~:
>
> (a)   liabilities to policyholders arising from with-profits business shall be stated at the amount of the realistic value of liabilities adjusted to exclude the shareholders' share of projected future **bonuses**;
>
> (b)   **reinsurance recoveries** that are recognised shall be measured on a basis that is consistent with the value of the policyholder liabilities to which the reinsurance applies;
>
> (c)   an amount may be recognised for the **present value** of future profits on **non-participating business** written in a with-profits fund if:
>
> > (i)   ~~the non-participating business is measured on a realistic basis for the purposes of the regulatory returns made under the PRA realistic capital regime;~~
> >
> > (ii)   ~~the value is determined in accordance with the PRA regulations; and~~
> >
> > (iii)   the determination of the realistic value of liabilities in that with-profits fund takes account, directly or indirectly, of this value;

(d)   where a with-profits life fund has an interest in a subsidiary or associate and the determination of the realistic value of liabilities to with-profits policyholders takes account of a value of that interest at an amount in excess of the net amounts included in the entity's consolidated accounts, an amount may be recognised representing this excess; and

(e)   adjustments to reflect the consequential tax effects of (a) to (d) above shall be made.

Adjustments from the MSSB necessary to meet the above requirements, including the recognition of an amount in accordance with paragraph 3.12(c) or 3.12(d), shall be included in **profit or loss**. An amount equal and opposite to the net amount of these adjustments shall be transferred to or from the **fund for future appropriations (FFA)** and also included in profit or loss.

Amendments to Section 4 *Disclosure*

The following paragraph sets out the amendments to Section 4 *Disclosure* (deleted text is   **15** struck through, inserted text is underlined).

Paragraph 4.5 is amended as follows: **16**

   4.5 To comply with paragraph 4.4 an insurer shall disclose:

(a)   ...

(b)   the process used to determine the assumptions that have the greatest effect on the measurement of the recognised amounts described in (a̲b). When practicable, an insurer shall also give quantified disclosure of those assumptions;

(c)   ...

Amendments to Appendix I: Glossary

The following glossary terms and definitions, and footnote 8 (subsequent footnotes will be   **17** renumbered sequentially), are deleted:

~~long-term fund~~	~~The fund or funds maintained by an undertaking in respect of its **long-term insurance business** in accordance with the PRA rules.~~
~~realistic capital regime~~	~~As set out in section 1.3 of INSPRU[8].~~

~~[8] References to the PRA's Prudential sourcebook for insurers, and to individual rules therein, are to the rules made on 1 April 2013 by the FCA and PRA Handbook Designation (General Modifications) Instrument 2013.~~

The following glossary term and definition is inserted in alphabetical order: **18**

<u>**Solvency II Directive**</u>	<u>Directive 2009/138/EC of the European Parliament and of the Council of 25 November 2009 on the taking-up and pursuit of the business of Insurance and Reinsurance (Solvency II), as amended by Directive 2013/58/EU, and as implemented in the United Kingdom and Republic of Ireland.</u>

19   The following glossary terms and definitions are amended as follows (deleted text is struck through, inserted text is underlined):

equalisation provisions	As defined in the relevant regulatory framework ~~(eg INSPRU)~~.
gross premium method	A form of actuarial valuation of **liabilities** arising under long-term insurance contracts where the premiums brought into account are the full amounts receivable under the contract. The method includes explicit estimates of cash flows for: (a) premiums, adjusted for renewals and lapses; (b) expected claims and for **with-profits business** future regular but not occasional or terminal **bonuses**; (c) costs of maintaining contracts; and (d) future renewal expenses. Cash flows are discounted at the valuation interest rate. The methodology may be set out in the relevant regulatory framework. ~~For UK companies this is included in the PRA Handbook.~~ The discount rate is based on the expected return on the assets deemed to back the **liabilities** ~~as prescribed by the PRA Handbook. This may be further constrained by a maximum rate set by the PRA.~~ This will be adjusted to reflect any further risks although, under this method, most of the key risks will be reflected in the modelling of the cash flows. For **linked business**, allowance may be made for the purchase of future units required by the contract terms and credit is taken for future charges permitted under those terms.
modified statutory solvency (MSSB)	The basis for determining **insurance liabilities** which is the **statutory solvency basis** adjusted for the following items: (a) to defer new business **acquisition costs** incurred where the benefit of such costs will be obtained in subsequent **reporting periods**; and (b) to treat investment, resilience and similar reserves, or reserves held in respect of general contingencies or the specific contingency that the fund will be closed to new business, where such items are held <u>in respect of **long-term insurance business**</u> ~~within the long-term fund~~, as reserves rather than provisions. These are included, as appropriate, within shareholders' capital and reserves or the **fund for future appropriations (FFA)**.
mutual	As defined in the **PRA** ~~Handbook~~<u>Rulebook</u>.
net premium method	An actuarial valuation of **liabilities** arising under long-term **insurance contracts** where the premium brought into account at any valuation date is that which, on the valuation assumptions regarding interest, mortality and disability, will exactly provide for the benefits guaranteed. A variation of the net premium method involves **zillmerisation**. The detailed methodology for UK companies is included in regulations contained in the **PRA** ~~Handbook~~<u>Rulebook as at 31 December 2015</u>.

non-participating business	**Long-term insurance business** where **policyholders** are not entitled to share in the surplus of the relevant ~~long-term fund~~ long-term business.
principles and practices of financial management (PPFM)	The statement that the **PRA** Financial Conduct Authority requires each **with-profits** life fund to make available to its **policyholders** containing, inter alia, a description of the fund's investment management and bonus distribution policies.
Prudential sourcebook for insurers (INSPRU)	The section of the **PRA** ~~Handbook~~ Rulebook detailing the prudential rules for **insurers**, including capital requirements, credit, market and **liquidity risk** for periods ending before 1 January 2016.
realistic value of liabilities	That element of the amount defined by rule 1.3.40 ~~in~~ of **INSPRU** as at 31 December 2015, excluding current **liabilities** falling within the definition set out in rule 1.3.190 of INSPRU as at 31 December 2015 that are recognised separately in the **statement of financial position**.
regulatory capital resources	An entity's capital resources as calculated in accordance with ~~the capital resources table in INSPRU~~ regulatory framework.
statutory solvency basis	The basis of determination of **insurance liabilities** in accordance with rule 1 of **INSPRU** as at 31 December 2015.
with-profits business	**Long-term insurance business** ~~where policyholders are contractually entitled to share in the surplus of the relevant long-term fund~~ which provides benefits through eligibility to participate in discretionary distributions based on profits arising from the **insurer**'s business or from a particular part of the insurer's business. A with-profits contract is an example of a contract with a **discretionary participation feature**.

Amendments to Appendix IV: Note on legal requirements

The following paragraph sets out the amendments to Appendix IV: *Note on legal requirements* (deleted text is struck through, inserted text is underlined).   **20**

The table in paragraph A4.3 is amended as follows (only the line that is amended is shown here):   **21**

Legislation	Overview of requirements
~~Industrial and Provident Societies Act 1965~~ Co-operative and Community Benefit Societies Act 2014	The Insurance Accounts Directive (Miscellaneous Insurance Undertakings) Regulations 2008 require every society that is an insurance undertaking to prepare its financial statements substantially as though it were a company registered under the Companies Act 2006.

Amendments to Implementation Guidance to accompany FRS 103 *Insurance Contracts*

Amendments to Implementation Guidance – Section 1 *Guidance for entities with long-term insurance business*

22   The following paragraphs set out the amendments to Implementation Guidance – Section 1 *Guidance for entities with long-term insurance business* (deleted text is struck through, inserted text is underlined).

23   Paragraph IG1.1 is amended as follows (footnote 1 is not amended and is not repeated here):

> IG1.1 An entity may, but is not required to, adopt the requirements of paragraph 3.12 of **FRS 103** *Insurance Contracts* for UK[1] **with-profits business** that does not fall within the scope of the PRA realistic capital regime or for which the PRA has granted a full waiver from compliance with this regimeparagraph 3.1(b) of FRS 103. If an entity changes its **accounting policy** for such with-profits business it shall only do so in accordance with paragraph 2.3 of FRS 103.

24   Paragraph IG1.2 is amended as follows:

> IG1.2 The shareholders' share of projected future **bonuses** deducted in accordance with paragraph 3.12(a) of FRS 103 should be calculated as the value of future transfers to shareholders calculated using market consistent financial assumptions, and assuming that transfers take place at a level consistent with those assumptions used to calculate the **realistic value of liabilities**within the PRA realistic balance sheet. Where an explicit assumption is not required in order to calculate the **liabilities** under the PRA's approach then continuation of the current profit sharing arrangements should be assumed unless the firm has plans to change this approach. Non-economic projection assumptions should be consistent with those used in determining the realistic value of liabilitieselsewhere in the realistic balance sheet. The amount deducted in accordance with this paragraph should be taken to the **fund for future appropriations (FFA)**. If shareholders transfers have been included as part of the PRA realistic value of liabilitiesy (or otherwise included in liabilities) then the amount of such transfers should be taken out of liabilities and included in the FFA, together with any related tax liability. If shareholders transfers have not been set up as part of the PRA realistic value of liabilitiesy or elsewhere, no adjustment is required.

25   Paragraph IG1.3 is amended as follows and 'realistic value of liabilities' is no longer shown in bold type:

> IG1.3 Under the PRA realistic capital regimeIn determining the realistic value of liabilities, a with-profits life fund may take account ofincludes within assets the value of future profits expected to arise from any **non-participating business** that forms part of the with-profits fund—sometimes referred to as the **value of in-force life assurance business (VIF)**. Excluding the VIF from the **statement of financial position** whilst recognising the realistic value of liabilities in full, and valuing the non-participating liabilities in the with-profits fund on a statutory basis, would give rise to an inconsistency in the fund's net assets. An entity is therefore permitted to recognise the VIF if that business has been taken into account in measuring the liability, in the circumstances of paragraph 3.12(c) of FRS 103, even though there is not a direct link between the value of the asset and the amount of the liabilities. Where there is not a direct link between the value of the business and the amount of realistic liabilities, but the value is taken into account in determining those liabilities, it is appropriate

to recognise the total value of the business. Although not separately identifiable, any excess value over that included in realistic liabilities will be taken to the FFA.

Paragraph IG1.4 is amended as follows: **26**

IG1.4 Paragraph 3.12(c) of FRS 103 permits an amount to be recognised for VIF on non-participating business written in a with-profits fund when: ~~(i) the non-participating business is measured on this basis for the purposes of the regulatory returns made under the PRA realistic capital regime; (ii) the VIF is calculated on the basis used in the PRA realistic capital regime; and (iii)~~ the determination of the realistic value of liabilities takes account of this value either directly or indirectly. Where with-profits **policyholders** are entitled to a share of the profits on non-participating business it would generally be expected that the determination of the realistic liabilities would take account, directly or indirectly, of the value of future profits on this business.

Paragraph IG1.6 is amended as follows: **27**

IG1.6 The VIF recognised within assets ~~for regulatory purposes~~ as described in paragraph IG1.3~~2~~ is determined as the discounted value of future profits expected to arise from the policies, taking into account liabilities relating to the policies measured on th~~e~~a **statutory solvency basis**. ~~When~~This includes adjustments ~~are~~ made ~~onto~~ a **modified statutory solvency basis (MSSB)** for the purposes of the **financial statements** (for example, to adjust liabilities to exclude certain additional reserves included in the liabilities ~~for regulatory purposes~~when measured on the statutory solvency basis, or where future income included in the VIF covers **deferred acquisition costs** included in the ~~MSSB~~ statement of financial position)~~.~~; ~~A~~a corresponding adjustment to the value of in-force policies will need to be made in order to ensure a consistent valuation.

Paragraph IG1.7 is amended as follows: **28**

IG1.7 Paragraph 3.12 of FRS 103 ~~requires~~permits ~~that~~ the recognition of a VIF asset ~~recognised~~when the ~~should be~~ determin~~ed~~ation ~~in accordance with~~ of the realistic value of liabilities takes account of this value~~capital regime requirements~~. Paragraph IG1.4 explains that the value calculated ~~under the realistic capital regime requirements~~ must be adjusted to ensure consistency where adjustments have been made onto the MSSB measurement basis in relation to non-participating contracts. The measurement of the VIF asset ~~recognised in accordance with the realistic capital regime~~ may take into account the release of capital requirements for non-participating business. It would not be appropriate to recognise this release of capital requirements within the VIF asset presented in the accounts because the MSSB liabilities do not include an allowance for capital. Therefore the amount of the VIF asset ~~determined for the purposes of the PRA realistic capital regime~~should be adjusted accordingly.

Paragraph IG1.8 is amended as follows: **29**

IG1.8 The profit recognition profile for non-participating contracts which do not satisfy FRS 103's definition of an insurance contract or contain a **discretionary participation feature** will be determined by the requirements of Sections 11, 12 and 23 of **FRS 102**. Where these contracts are written in a with-profits fund, paragraph IG1.4 will apply but the VIF recognised for such contracts ~~for the purposes of the PRA's realistic capital regime~~should be adjusted to reflect the difference in the profit recognition bases between the basis used to determine the VIF ~~used in~~taken into account in determining the realistic value of liabilities~~capital regime~~ and the profit recognition profile determined by FRS 102.

30   Paragraph IG1.9 is amended as follows:

IG1.9 Paragraph 3.12(d) of FRS 103 permits that where a with-profits fund has an interest in a subsidiary or associate and the determination of~~that is valued for PRA regulatory purposes~~ the realistic value of liabilities takes account of a value for that interest at an amount in excess of the net amounts that would be included in the entity's consolidated accounts, an amount may be recognised representing this excess ~~if the determination of the realistic value of liabilities to with-profits policyholders takes account of this value~~. As explained in paragraph 3.15 of FRS 103 this situation could arise where the subsidiary or associate writes non-participating business and the value of the subsidiary or associate ~~recognised for PRA reporting purposes~~ incorporates the VIF of non-participating business written in the subsidiary or associate. The value of the subsidiary or associate ~~recognised for PRA reporting purposes~~ is reduced by the subsidiary's or associate's capital requirement as noted in rule 1.3.33(3) of **INSPRU** as at 31 December 2015. When preparing both consolidated and non-consolidated accounts, the excess value that may be recognised should therefore be taken as the excess before deduction of the subsidiary's or associate's capital requirement.

31   Paragraph IG1.10 is amended as follows:

IG1.10 Where the amounts on a 'realistic' basis determined in accordance with paragraph 3.12 of FRS 103 are different from the amounts on ~~the~~a MSSB, a corresponding amount is transferred to or from the FFA, so that there is no effect on **equity**. The potential shareholders' share corresponding to additional bonuses to policyholders that have been included in the policyholders' liability should be accounted for in the FFA. As a result, there will generally be no change in the profit for the **reporting period** except where the adjustments result in a negative balance on the FFA and the entity determines that this negative balance should result in a deduction from equity through **profit or loss**.

32   Paragraph IG1.11 is amended as follows:

IG1.11 Entities with with-profits business within the scope of paragraph 3.1(b) of FRS 103~~the PRA realistic capital regime~~ are required to measure the liability of that business in respect of **options and guarantees** relating to policyholders either at **fair value** or at an amount estimated using a **market-consistent stochastic model** ~~in accordance with PRA regulations~~.

33   Paragraph IG1.12 is amended as follows (footnote 2 is not amended and is not repeated here):

IG1.12 For all entities with **long-term insurance business**, the best basis for measuring policyholders' options and guarantees is one that includes their time value[2]. Any **deterministic approach** to valuation of a policy with a guarantee or optionality feature will generally fail to deal appropriately with the time value of the option. Therefore stochastic modelling techniques to evaluate the range of potential outcomes should be used unless a market value for the option is available. The ~~PRA realistic capital regime~~regulatory framework includes a requirement to value options and guarantees on this basis. For the liabilities of businesses not falling within the scope of the ~~PRA realistic capital regime~~paragraph 3.1(b) of FRS 103, entities are encouraged, but not required, to adopt these valuation techniques. Where options are not valued on this basis, additional disclosures are required; these are set out in paragraph IG3.14(c).

34   Paragraph IG1.13 is amended as follows:

IG1.13 In determining the value of guarantees and options under the ~~PRA realistic capital regime~~regulatory framework, the entity will take into account under each scenario in the market-consistent stochastic modelling management actions it anticipates would be taken in response to variations in market variables (such as changing the balance of the investment portfolio between debt instruments and equity, varying the amount charged to policyholders, or varying its bonus policy) that will affect the amount payable under the guarantee or option. Such actions must be realistically capable of being implemented within the timescale assumed in the scenario analysis, and be consistent with the entity's published **principles and practices of financial managements (PPFM)**.

Amendments to Implementation Guidance – Section 2 *Guidance for entities with general insurance business or long-term insurance business*

The following paragraphs set out the amendments to Implementation Guidance – Section 2 *Guidance for entities with general insurance business or long-term insurance business* (deleted text is struck through, inserted text is underlined). **35**

Paragraph IG2.28 is amended as follows: **36**

IG2.28 Disclosure should be made where an equalisation reserve has been established in accordance with the **PRA** ~~Handbook~~Rulebook. Where equalisation reserves are established, an entity should disclose the following in the notes to the financial statements:

(a)   that the amounts provided are not liabilities because they are in addition to the provisions required to meet the anticipated ultimate cost of settlement of outstanding claims at the reporting date;

(b)   notwithstanding this, they are required by Schedule 3 to the Regulations to be included within technical provisions; and

(c)   the impact of the equalisation reserves on **equity** and the effect of movements in the reserves on the profit or loss for the reporting period.

Paragraph IG2.42 is amended as follows: **37**

IG2.42 The long-term business provision may be calculated on the basis used for regulatory reporting ~~under PRA rules~~ subject to appropriate adjustments including~~:~~

~~(a)~~   ~~reassessment of the provisions and reserves included in the statutory liabilities for solvency purposes to consider the extent to which they should be included in the long-term business provision. This will require the exclusion of the appropriate proportion of reserves (such as investment reserves, reserves to cover general contingencies and reserves to cover the specific contingency of the fund being closed to new business). Any amount in excess of the necessary provision should be disclosed in the financial statements as a reserve or in the **fund for future appropriations (FFA)** as appropriate; and~~

~~(b)~~   the reversal of any reduction in policyholder liabilities ~~in the regulatory returns~~ where these liabilities already implicitly take account of a pension fund surplus through future expense assumptions which reflect lower expected contributions.

Paragraph IG2.48 is amended as follows: **38**

IG2.48 The net assets held to cover linked liabilities at the reporting date may differ from the technical provisions for linked liabilities. The reasons for any significant mismatching should be disclosed.~~In practice this should apply only to overseas companies included in consolidated financial statements because of the requirements of rule 3.1.57 of **INSPRU**.~~

39   In paragraph IG2.50 the first occurrence of 'FFA' is replaced by 'fund for future appropriations (FFA)' in bold type.

40   Paragraph IG2.53 is amended as follows:

> IG2.53 The investment return (which includes movements in realised and **unrealised investment gains and losses**) and related tax charges on assets representing reserves which are held ~~for~~within the relevant **long-term insurance business**~~long-term fund~~ for solvency purposes ~~under the PRA rules~~ should be credited to the technical account for long-term business. Allocations may then be made as appropriate to the **non-technical account** in accordance with paragraphs IG2.65 and IG2.66 or to the FFA. When the regulatory framework does not require the entity to set up a long-term fund for its long-term insurance business, the entity shall make the allocations as appropriate between the technical and non-technical account and disclose the basis of its allocation in the notes to the financial statements.

41   The rubric before paragraph IG2.56 is amended as follows:

> *Paragraphs IG2.56 to IG2.58* ~~provide guidance for applying the requirements of paragraphs 2 and 3 of the instructions for completing Form 47 in the PRA rules. They~~ *are only relevant to long-term insurance business.*

42   Paragraph IG2.60 is amended as follows:

> IG2.60 On consolidation, the profit or loss of any non-insurance entity belonging to the long-term fund (as defined in **INSRPU** as at 31 December 2015) may be included directly in the technical account for long-term business. Where material, more detailed disclosure should be provided in the notes to the financial statements. Where an entity carrying on general insurance business is ~~owned by~~an asset of the long-term ~~fund~~insurance business, the profit or loss of this business should be transferred from the non-technical account to the technical account for long-term business using new lines for this purpose.

Approval by the FRC

Amendments to FRS 103 Insurance Contracts – Solvency II was approved for issue by the Board of the Financial Reporting Council on 19 May 2016, following its consideration of the Corporate Reporting Council's Advice.

The Corporate Reporting Council's Advice to the FRC to issue *Amendments to FRS 103 – Solvency II*

Introduction

1   This report provides an overview of the main issues that have been considered by the Corporate Reporting Council in advising the Financial Reporting Council (FRC) to issue *Amendments to FRS 103 Insurance Contracts – Solvency II*.

2   The FRC, in accordance with the *Statutory Auditors (Amendment of Companies Act 2006 and Delegation of Functions etc) Order 2012* (SI 2012/1741), is a prescribed body for issuing accounting standards in the UK. The *Foreword to Accounting Standards* sets out the application of accounting standards in the Republic of Ireland.

3   In accordance with the *FRC Codes and Standards: procedures*, any proposal to issue, amend or withdraw a code or standard is put to the FRC Board with the full advice of the relevant Councils and/or the Codes & Standards Committee. Ordinarily, the FRC Board will only reject the advice put to it where:

(a)   it is apparent that a significant group of stakeholders has not been adequately consulted;

(b)   the necessary assessment of the impact of the proposal has not been completed, including an analysis of costs and benefits;

(c)   insufficient consideration has been given to the timing or cost of implementation; or

(d)   the cumulative impact of a number of proposals would make the adoption of an otherwise satisfactory proposal inappropriate.

4   The FRC has established the Corporate Reporting Council as the relevant Council to assist it in the setting of accounting standards.

Advice

5   The Corporate Reporting Council is advising the FRC to issue *Amendments to FRS 103 Insurance Contracts – Solvency II*.

6   The Corporate Reporting Council advises that these proposals will update FRS 103 *Insurance Contracts* for changes in the regulatory framework and ensure that established accounting policies can continue to be applied if an entity so chooses.

7   The Accounting Council's Advice[1] to the FRC to issue FRS 103 was set out in that standard. The Corporate Reporting Council's Advice to the FRC in respect of these amendments will be included in the revised FRS 103.

Background

8   When FRS 103 was issued in March 2014 the Accounting Council advised the FRC to review, in due course, whether or not consequential changes to FRS 103 would be required for the commencement of Solvency II.

9   As Solvency II is effective from 1 January 2016 this review has now been carried out and the Corporate Reporting Council advises that limited amendments are made to FRS 103 to reflect the changes in the regulatory regime. The Corporate Reporting Council does not advise making any other changes to FRS 103 at this time.

---

[1] *From 1 April 2016 the Accounting Council was renamed as the Corporate Reporting Council.*

The FRC consulted on the proposals for amendments to FRS 103 in FRED 64 *Draft*   **10**
amendments to FRS 103 – Solvency II. The responses to FRED 64 have been considered
in developing this advice.

Amendments to FRS 103

FRS 103 makes a number of references to the PRA realistic capital regime, which was   **11**
replaced by Solvency II from 1 January 2016. In addition, it refers to the Prudential
sourcebook for insurers (INSPRU), which was replaced from the same date. As these
references are out of date, amendments are required to FRS 103.

In considering the amendments that are required, the Corporate Reporting Council advises   **12**
that entities should be permitted to continue to apply established accounting practices in
their financial statements, if they choose to do so. It notes that FRS 103 already includes
the ability for an insurer to change its accounting policies for insurance contracts if it
judges certain criteria are met, and therefore there is no need to introduce specific new
accounting policies relating to Solvency II.

In response to suggestions from respondents to FRED 64, the Corporate Reporting   **13**
Council advises making it clearer in FRS 103 that one basis for changing accounting
policies might be in order to achieve greater alignment with Solvency II. This is reflected
in paragraph 2.3A.

Scope of Section 3 Recognition and Measurement: Requirements for entities with long-
term insurance business of FRS 103

The Corporate Reporting Council notes that paragraph 3.1(b) of FRS 103 describes the   **14**
circumstances in which the requirements for with-profits liabilities and related assets
apply, which was based on those to which the PRA realistic capital regime applied.
The Corporate Reporting Council considered the following two options for revising the
description of the scope of these requirements:

(a)   describe more fully the current scope; or
(b)   describe the scope by reference to Solvency II.

The Corporate Reporting Council noted that describing the scope by reference to Solvency   **15**
II may extend the application of the relevant requirements of FRS 103 to entities not
previously within their scope. As the Corporate Reporting Council's aim was to limit the
amount of change in accounting policies that would be required, the Corporate Reporting
Council advises effectively retaining the existing definition, but qualifying it to note that
entities are within the scope of the requirements if they applied the realistic capital regime
prior to 1 January 2016.

Revised definitions

Some of the key definitions within FRS 103 were based, either directly or indirectly, on the   **16**
rules of INSPRU. As a result of INSPRU being replaced by Solvency II for many insurers,
these definitions needed revising. In FRED 64 the FRC proposed a revised description for
the 'established method of accounting for long-term insurance business' (to replace the
modified statutory solvency basis) and that both that definition and the definition of the
'realistic value of liabilities' should be principles-based, and consistent with accounting
policies applied in periods ending before 1 January 2016.

17   Respondents noted that the definitions described features that could be attributed to many bases and included the term 'appropriate' without further guidance. Some respondents suggested that retaining the current definitions, but clarifying that the references to INSPRU were to INSPRU as at 31 December 2015, would be a preferable solution. The Corporate Reporting Council noted that, as it did not intend the changes to FRS 103 to result in changes in accounting practice, however the phrases were defined, in practical terms entities would need to refer to INSPRU as at 31 December 2015 in order to continue with their existing accounting policies. Therefore the Corporate Reporting Council advises retaining the existing definitions of the 'modified statutory solvency basis' and the 'realistic value of liabilities', and amending them to refer to INSPRU as at 31 December 2015. The Corporate Reporting Council noted that the PRA Rulebook can be accessed 'as at' a certain date, and therefore this is a practical solution.

New entrants

18   Some of the respondents to FRED 64 noted that paragraph 1.5 of FRS 103 required new entrants establishing accounting policies for insurance contracts for the first time to consider the requirements of Section 3 of FRS 103 as a means of establishing current practice as a benchmark before assessing whether to 'improve' those policies. They noted that this might be unduly burdensome as new entrants would be required to assess their accounting policies against a benchmark which they would not need to consider for regulatory reporting purposes.

19   The Corporate Reporting Council considered the framework that should apply to new entrants, which might include both entirely new entities and new entities established within an existing group or business, as a result of a business reorganisation. Section 3 of FRS 103 was developed from previous UK accounting practice, and does not have an equivalent in IFRS. As a result, some respondents suggested that Section 3 of FRS 103 could be deleted, which would be consistent with IFRS and have little, or no, practical effect on existing entities.

20   The Corporate Reporting Council advises that a benchmark should be retained, in order to maintain a consistent starting point for insurers selecting their accounting policies for insurance contracts for the first time. The Corporate Reporting Council also notes that, although existing entities are not required to change their accounting policies, the change in regulatory regime may be a trigger for some entities to 'improve' their accounting policies, in order to make them more consistent with the new regulatory framework. As a result, 'current practice' may be evolving. Therefore, in light of the fact that the current benchmark is based on the previous regulatory regime, and the possible changes in current practice, the Corporate Reporting Council advises permitting two alternative starting points for new entrants. One is the requirements of Section 3 of FRS 102, and the other is to establish policies that are consistent with the relevant requirements of the Solvency II Directive, subject to any appropriate adjustments.

Accounting policies based on the requirements of Solvency II

21   The Corporate Reporting Council considered whether aspects of the rules under the Solvency II Directive might need amendment for use in measuring liabilities for financial reporting purposes. The Corporate Reporting Council advises that appropriate adjustments may be necessary in order to ensure that the financial statements meet the qualitative characteristics of information in financial statements (as set out in Section 2 *Concepts and Pervasive Principles* of FRS 102). This is reflected in paragraphs 1.5(b) and 2.3A of FRS 103.

The Corporate Reporting Council notes that items to consider, when determining whether   **22**
and to what extent appropriate adjustments are required, might include the following:

(a)   transitional adjustments that may be made for regulatory purposes;
(b)   the volatility adjustment to the discount rate that is made for regulatory purposes;
(c)   the risk margin that is applied for regulatory purposes; and
(d)   'surplus funds' when these reflect contractual obligations of cash flows to
      policyholders.

Regulatory framework

Not all entities applying FRS 103 will be subject to the same regulatory framework.   **23**
In some instances the regulatory framework will set requirements relating to amounts
to be recognised in the financial statements. When FRS 103 refers to a requirement of
the regulatory framework, the Corporate Reporting Council advises that an entity shall
apply the requirements of the regulatory framework that applies to it. This may result
in differences in accounting between some entities. For example, most entities will not
be required by the regulatory framework to recognise an equalisation provision from
1 January 2016.

Effective date

The Corporate Reporting Council advises that these amendments should be effective   **24**
for accounting periods ending on or after 1 January 2016. Early adoption should not be
permitted because this is consistent with the effective date of the new regulatory framework.

Future development of FRS 103

When FRS 103 was issued, the Accounting Council advised that, in addition to reviewing   **25**
FRS 103 when Solvency II was implemented, once the IASB had issued its new insurance
standard the requirements of FRS 103 should be reviewed. This project has not yet been
completed by the IASB, and consequently it is still not possible to determine the appropriate
timing for this further review of FRS 103.

Approval of this advice

This advice to the FRC was approved by the Corporate Reporting Council on 10 May 2016.   **26**

FRS 104
Interim Financial Reporting

(March 2015)

Contents

	Paragraphs
Summary	
FRS 104 Interim Financial Reporting	
Objective	1–1A
Scope	2–4
Content of an interim financial report	5–27
Minimum components of an interim financial report	8–8F
Form and content of interim financial statements	9–14
Significant events and transactions	15–16-18
Other disclosures	16A–16B
Disclosure of compliance with this FRS	19
Periods for which interim financial statements are required to be presented	20–22
Materiality	23–27
Recognition and measurement	28–45
Same accounting policies as annual	28–36
Revenues received seasonally, cyclically, or occasionally	37–38
Costs incurred unevenly during the financial year	39–40
Use of estimates	41–42
Restatement of previously reported interim periods	43–45
Effective date	46–56
Consequential amendments to FRS 100 *Application of Financial Reporting Requirements*	57
Consequential amendments to FRS 102 *The Financial Reporting Standard applicable in the UK and Republic of Ireland*	58
Approval by the FRC	
The Accounting Council's Advice to the FRC to issue FRS 104	
Introduction	1–3
Advice	4
Background	5–7
Objective	8–10
FRS 104 Interim Financial Reporting	11–20
Basis and scope of FRS 104	11–14
Key changes to IAS 34	15–17
Other information included in the interim financial report	18–19
Comparative information	20
Preliminary announcements	21
Effective date	22
Approval of this advice	23

Appendices

I   Glossary

II   Illustrations and examples

III   Significant differences between FRS 104 and IAS 34

IV   Table of comparison between terminology used in the DTRs and FRS 104

V   Note on UK regulatory requirements

VI   Republic of Ireland legal references

FRS 104 is issued by the Financial Reporting Council (FRC). It is the FRC's pronouncement on interim reporting that UK and Irish issuers not using EU-adopted IFRS may apply under the Disclosure and Transparency Rules and the Transparency (Directive 2004/109/EC) Regulations 2007 (as amended by the Transparency (Directive 2004/109/EC) (Amendments) Regulations 2015) respectively.

Summary

In 2012, 2013 and 2014 the Financial Reporting Council (FRC) revised accounting **(i)** standards in the United Kingdom (UK) and Republic of Ireland (RoI). The revisions fundamentally reformed financial reporting, replacing the extant standards with four Financial Reporting Standards:

(a) FRS 100 *Application of Financial Reporting Requirements*;
(b) FRS 101 *Reduced Disclosure Framework*;
(c) FRS 102 *The Financial Reporting Standard applicable in the UK and Republic of Ireland*; and
(d) FRS 103 *Insurance Contracts*.

The FRC's overriding objective in setting financial reporting standards is to enable users **(ii)** of accounts to receive high-quality understandable financial reporting proportionate to the size and complexity of the entity and users' information needs.

In meeting this objective, the FRC aims to provide succinct financial reporting standards **(iii)** that:

(a) have consistency with international accounting standards through the application of an IFRS-based solution unless an alternative clearly better meets the overriding objective;
(b) reflect up-to-date thinking and developments in the way entities operate and the transactions they undertake;
(c) balance consistent principles for accounting by all UK and RoI entities with practical solutions, based on size, complexity, public interest and users' information needs;
(d) promote efficiency within groups; and
(e) are cost-effective to apply.

Financial Reporting Standard 104 *Interim Financial Reporting* replaces the Statement **(iv)** *Half-yearly financial reports* issued by the Accounting Standards Board (ASB) in 2007 (ASB Statement Half-yearly reports). The change from a Statement to a Financial Reporting Standard has no effect on the scope of entities required to prepare an interim financial report nor on the extent to which entities that prepare an interim financial report are required to comply with this standard. The scope of FRS 104 and the extent to which its application is mandatory is explained further below. FRS 104 is not an accounting standard[1].

The FRC also withdraws the Statement *Preliminary announcements* issued by the ASB in **(v)** 1998 (ASB Statement Preliminary announcements).

Reasons for replacing the ASB Statement Half-yearly reports

When FRS 102 was issued, the FRC decided that FRS 102 should not contain interim **(vi)** reporting requirements, but that instead the existing reporting guidance contained in the ASB Statement Half-yearly reports should be reviewed.

The ASB updated the ASB Statement Half-yearly reports in July 2007 for the **(vii)** implementation of the EU Transparency Directive (Directive 2004/109/EC) in the UK and the RoI which resulted in the introduction of the Disclosure and Transparency Rules (DTRs) and the Transparency (Directive 2004/109/EC) Regulations 2007 respectively.

---

[1] *Refer to the Foreword to Accounting Standards issued in March 2015 for more detail on accounting standards.*

Issuers continue to have the same reporting obligations under the DTRs[2] in relation to half-yearly financial reports, but a replacement of the ASB Statement Half-yearly reports is necessary because of the revisions to the annual financial reporting requirements referred to in paragraph (i) above.

(viii)   With the publication of FRS 104 the ASB Statement Half-yearly reports is withdrawn.

Reasons for withdrawing the ASB Statement Preliminary announcements

(ix)   The ASB Statement Preliminary announcements was published in 1998 and has not subsequently been updated to reflect regulatory changes and market practice developments. The guidance contained therein is therefore out of date and the ASB Statement Preliminary announcements is withdrawn with immediate effect. However, the FRC will, as part of a future project, evaluate whether reporting guidance on certain aspects of preliminary announcements would be useful.

FRS 104 *Interim Financial Reporting*

(x)   FRS 104 is based on the interim financial reporting requirements promulgated by the International Accounting Standards Board in IAS 34 *Interim Financial Reporting*. We conducted a two-month consultation on these interim reporting requirements in FRED 56 Draft *FRS 104 Interim Financial Reporting*, which closed in January 2015.

(xi)   FRS 104 does not require any entity to prepare an interim report, nor does it change the extent to which laws or regulations may require the preparation of such a report. Entities should consider whether any such laws or regulations apply to them. For example, paragraph 4.2.2R of the DTRs requires listed entities within the scope of that rule to prepare a half-yearly financial report that must include a condensed set of financial statements, such as the interim financial report described in FRS 104. Similarly, AIM companies are required under the AIM Rules for Companies issued by the London Stock Exchange to prepare a half-yearly report.

(xii)   Where an entity does prepare an interim financial report, FRS 104 does not, in itself, require such reports to be prepared in accordance with FRS 104. However, laws or regulations may contain such a requirement. Paragraph 4.2.10R of the DTRs set out that UK issuers within the scope of that rule which do not apply EU-adopted IFRS in their annual financial statements can prepare their condensed interim financial statements in accordance with IAS 34 or pronouncements on interim reporting issued by the FRC. FRS 104 replaces the ASB Statement Half-yearly reports as the FRC's pronouncement on interim reporting, described in paragraph 4.2.10(4)R of the DTRs.

(xiii)   FRS 104 is intended for use in the preparation of interim reports by entities that apply FRS 102 when preparing their annual financial statements. Entities applying FRS 101 to prepare the annual financial statements may also use FRS 104 as a basis for their interim financial reports.

(xiv)   As explained above, FRS 104 does not impose an obligation on entities to produce interim financial reports nor does it mandate its application by any entity. However, entities that make a statement of compliance with this standard are required to apply all of the provisions of FRS 104.

---

[2] *References to the UK DTRs should also be read as references to the Irish Transparency (Directive 2004/109/EC) Regulations 2007, including any subsequent amendments thereto.*

FRS 104 is effective for interim periods commencing on or after 1 January 2015, with early application being permitted. **(xv)**

Organisation of FRS 104

In order to maintain consistency with the paragraph numbering of IAS 34, when a paragraph in IAS 34 has been deleted and has not been replaced with an alternative paragraph in FRS 104, the phrase [not used] is stated. Some paragraphs have been deleted in IAS 34 and are marked as [deleted]. These paragraphs are also identified as [deleted] in FRS 104. **(xvi)**

Terms defined in the Glossary (Appendix I) are in **bold type** the first time they appear in FRS 104. **(xvii)**

FRS 104 Interim Financial Reporting

Objective

1   **Timely** and **reliable** interim financial reporting can improve the ability of investors, creditors or others to understand an entity's capacity to generate earnings and **cash flows** and its **financial position** and liquidity.

1A   This FRS sets out content, **recognition** and **measurement** principles for **interim financial reports**.

Scope

2   This FRS, in itself, does not require an entity to prepare interim financial reports. Where an entity is required by laws or regulations or voluntarily chooses to prepare interim financial reports it may voluntarily choose to apply this FRS. This FRS does not mandate how frequently or how soon after the end of an **interim period** interim financial reports should be issued.

2A   This FRS is intended for use by entities that prepare annual **financial statements** in accordance with **FRS 102**. If entities that prepare the annual financial statements in accordance with **FRS 101** apply this FRS, references made in this FRS to FRS 102 shall be read as references to the equivalent requirements in **EU-adopted IFRS** as amended by paragraph AG1 of FRS 101.

3   An entity that makes a statement of compliance with this FRS shall comply with all of the provisions of this FRS. This FRS does need not be applied to immaterial items.

3A   UK issuers not using EU-adopted IFRS that, as provided for in DTR 4.2.10(4)R[3], include a statement in their half-yearly financial report that the condensed set of financial statements has been prepared in accordance with pronouncements on interim reporting issued by the FRC, shall apply this FRS.

4   [Not used]

Content of an interim financial report

5   [Not used]

6   In the interest of timeliness and cost and to avoid repetition of information previously reported, an entity may be required to or may elect to provide less information at interim dates as compared with its annual financial statements. This FRS defines the minimum components of an interim financial report as including condensed interim financial statements and selected explanatory notes (see paragraph 8). The interim financial report is intended to provide an update on the most recent complete set of annual financial statements. Accordingly, it focuses on new activities, events, and circumstances and does not duplicate information previously reported.

7   Nothing in this FRS is intended to prohibit or discourage an entity from publishing a complete set of financial statements as described in Section 3 Financial Statement Presentation of FRS 102, instead of the condensed interim financial statements and selected

---

[3] *Irish issuers should read references to the UK DTRs as references to the Irish Transparency (Directive 2004/109/EC) Regulations 2007, including any subsequent amendments thereto.*

explanatory notes described in paragraph 8. A complete set of financial statements shall include all of the disclosures required by this FRS as well as the disclosures required by FRS 102. The recognition and measurement requirements set out in this FRS also apply to a complete set of financial statements.

Minimum components of an interim financial report

An interim financial report shall include, at a minimum, the following components: **8**

(a) a condensed **statement of financial position**;
(b) a single condensed **statement of comprehensive income** or a separate condensed **income statement** and a separate condensed statement of comprehensive income;
(c) a condensed statement of changes in equity;
(d) a condensed **statement of cash flows**; and
(e) selected explanatory notes.

An entity shall present a single condensed statement of comprehensive income or a separate **8A** condensed income statement and a separate condensed statement of comprehensive income (see paragraph 8(b)), consistent with the basis of presentation applied in its most recent annual financial statements.

An entity that has presented a single **statement of income and retained earnings** in **8B** place of the statement of comprehensive income and statement of changes in equity in accordance with paragraph 3.18 of FRS 102 in its most recent annual financial statements, is permitted to present a single condensed statement of income and retained earnings if, during any of the periods for which the interim financial statements are required to be presented in accordance with paragraph 20A, the only changes to **equity** arise from **profit or loss,** payment of dividends, corrections of prior period **errors** or changes in **accounting policies**.

An entity that has presented only an income statement, or a statement of comprehensive **8C** income in which the 'bottom line' is labelled 'profit or loss' in accordance with paragraph 3.19 of FRS 102 in its most recent annual financial statements, is permitted to use the same basis of presentation if there are no items of **other comprehensive income** in any of the periods for which the interim financial statements are required to be presented in accordance with paragraph 20B.

When the presentation of the components of the interim financial statements will be **8D** changed in its next annual financial statements an entity is permitted to present the components of the interim financial statements on that new basis, instead of the basis applied in its most recent annual financial statements as required by paragraphs 8A to 8C.

An entity may use titles for the statements other than those used in this FRS as long as they **8E** are not misleading.

Paragraph 8(d) does not apply to entities that will not present a statement of cash flows in **8F** its next annual financial statements.

Form and content of interim financial statements

If an entity publishes a complete set of financial statements in its interim financial report, **9** the form and content of those statements shall conform to the requirements of Section 3 of FRS 102 for a complete set of financial statements. An entity that will not present a statement of cash flows in its next annual financial statements is not required to include that statement in its interim financial report.

10   The condensed interim financial statements shall include, at a minimum, each of the headings and subtotals that were included in the entity's most recent annual financial statements and the selected explanatory notes as required by this FRS. Additional line items or notes shall be included if their omission would make the condensed interim financial statements misleading.

11   An entity shall present basic and diluted earnings per share for an interim period when the entity has presented earnings per share information in accordance with IAS 33 *Earnings per Share* (as adopted in the EU) in its most recent annual financial statements.

11A   If an entity presents basic and diluted earnings per share, it shall do so in the statement that presents the components of profit or loss (see paragraph 8(b)).

12   [Not used]

13   [Deleted]

14   [Not used]

Significant events and transactions

15   An entity shall include in its interim financial report an explanation of events and transactions that are significant to an understanding of the changes in financial position and **performance** of the entity since the end of the last annual **reporting period**. Information disclosed in relation to those events and transactions shall update the relevant information presented in the most recent annual financial report.

15A   A user of an entity's interim financial report will have access to the most recent annual financial report of that entity. Therefore, it is unnecessary for the interim financial report to provide relatively insignificant updates to the information that was reported in the most recent annual financial report.

15B   The following is a list of events and transactions for which disclosures would be required, if they are significant, either in the notes to the interim financial statements or, if disclosed elsewhere in the interim financial report, cross-referred to the disclosure in the notes to the interim financial statements. Disclosure of this information is required in an entity's interim financial report only if the entity would be required to make the disclosure in its annual financial statements. This list is not exhaustive:

(a)   the write-down of **inventories** to net realisable value and the reversal of such a write-down;

(b)   recognition of a loss from the impairment of **financial assets**, **property, plant and equipment**, **intangible assets**, or other **assets**, and the reversal of such an **impairment loss**;

(c)   the reversal of any **provisions** for the costs of **restructuring**;

(d)   acquisitions and disposals of items of property, plant and equipment;

(e)   commitments for the purchase of property, plant and equipment;

(f)   litigation settlements;

(g)   corrections of prior period errors;

(h)   changes in the business or economic circumstances that affect the **fair value** of the entity's financial assets and **financial liabilities**, where those assets or liabilities are measured at fair value;

(i)   any loan default or breach of a loan agreement that has not been remedied on or before the end of the reporting period;

(j)   **related party transactions**, unless the transaction was entered into between two or more members of a **group**, provided that any **subsidiary** which is party to the transaction is wholly owned by such a member; and

(k)   [not used]

(l)   [not used]

(m)   changes in **contingent liabilities** or **contingent assets**.

Individual sections of FRS 102 provide guidance regarding disclosure requirements for many of the items listed in paragraph 15B. When an event or transaction is significant to an understanding of the changes in an entity's financial position or performance since the last annual reporting period, its interim financial report should provide an explanation of and an update to the relevant information included in the financial statements of the last annual reporting period.   **15C**

[Deleted]   **16-18**

Other disclosures

In addition to disclosing significant events and transactions in accordance with paragraphs 15–15C, an entity shall include the following information, either in the notes to its interim financial statements or, if disclosed elsewhere in the interim financial report, cross-referred to the information in the notes to the interim financial statements (the information shall normally be reported on a financial year-to-date basis):   **16A**

(a)   A statement that the same accounting policies and methods of computation are followed in the interim financial statements as compared with the most recent annual financial statements or, if those policies or methods have been changed, a description of the nature and effect of the change.[4]

(b)   Explanatory comments about the seasonality or cyclicality of interim operations.

(c)   The nature and amount of items affecting assets, **liabilities**, equity, profit or loss or cash flows that are unusual because of their nature, size or incidence.

(d)   The nature and amount of changes in estimates of amounts reported in prior interim periods of the current financial year or changes in estimates of amounts reported in prior financial years.

(e)   Issues, repurchases and repayments of debt and equity securities.

(f)   Dividends paid (aggregate or per share) separately for **ordinary shares** and other shares.

(g)   The following segment information (disclosure of segment information is required in an entity's interim financial report only if the entity has presented segment information in accordance with IFRS 8 *Operating Segments* (as adopted in the EU) in its most recent annual financial statements):

   (i)   **Revenues** from external customers, if included in the measure of segment profit or loss reviewed by the chief operating decision maker or otherwise regularly provided to the chief operating decision maker.

   (ii)   Intersegment revenues, if included in the measure of segment profit or loss reviewed by the chief operating decision maker or otherwise regularly provided to the chief operating decision maker.

   (iii)   A measure of segment profit or loss.

   (iv)   A measure of total assets and liabilities for a particular reportable segment if such amounts are regularly provided to the chief operating decision maker and

---

[4] *Where a company is subject to the UK Corporate Governance Code, provision C.1.3 requires its directors to state, in the annual and half-yearly financial statements, whether they consider it appropriate to adopt the going concern basis of accounting and to identify any material uncertainties to the company's ability to do so for a period of at least twelve months from the date of approval of the financial statements.*

if there has been a **material** change from the amount disclosed in the most recent annual financial statements for that reportable segment.

    (v)   A description of differences from the most recent annual financial statements in the basis of segmentation or in the basis of measurement of segment profit or loss.

    (vi) A reconciliation of the total of the reportable segments' measures of profit or loss to the entity's profit or loss before **tax expense** (tax income) and **discontinued operations**. However, if an entity allocates to reportable segments items such as tax expense (tax income), the entity may reconcile the total of the segments' measures of profit or loss to profit or loss after those items. Material reconciling items shall be separately identified and described in that reconciliation.

(h)   Events after the interim period that have not been reflected in the financial statements for the interim period.

(i)   The effect of changes in the composition of the entity during the interim period, including **business combinations**, obtaining or losing control of subsidiaries and long-term investments, restructurings, and discontinued operations. In the case of business combinations, the entity shall disclose the information required by paragraphs 19.25 and 19.25A of FRS 102 (disclosure of this information is required in an entity's interim financial report only if the entity would be required to make the disclosure in the annual financial statements).

(j)   For **financial instruments** disclosures that help users of interim financial reports to evaluate the significance of financial instruments measured at fair value; the entity shall disclose the information required by paragraphs 11.43, 11.48A(e) and 34.22 of FRS 102 (disclosure of this information is required in an entity's interim financial report only if the entity would be required to make the disclosure in its annual financial statements).

(k)   [Not used]

16B   An interim financial report that covers part of an annual financial reporting period during which an entity transitions from one financial reporting framework to another shall, in order to comply with the disclosure requirements in paragraph 16A(a), disclose the following information:

(a)   a description of the nature of each change in accounting policy;

(b)   a reconciliation of its equity determined in accordance with its previous financial reporting framework to its equity determined in accordance with the new financial reporting framework for the following dates:

    (i)   the **date of transition** to the new financial reporting framework; and

    (ii)   at the end of the comparable year-to-date period of the immediately preceding financial year; and

(c)   a reconciliation of profit or loss determined in accordance with its previous financial reporting framework for the comparable interim period (current and if different year-to-date) of the immediately preceding financial year.

The requirements of paragraph 35.14 of FRS 102 apply in respect of the reconciliations presented.

Disclosure of compliance with this FRS

19   If an entity's interim financial report is in compliance with this FRS, that fact shall be disclosed.

Periods for which interim financial statements are required to be presented

Interim financial reports shall include interim financial statements (condensed or complete) for periods as follows: **20**

(a) A statement of financial position as of the end of the current interim period and a comparative statement of financial position as of the end of the immediately preceding financial year.

(b) A single statement of comprehensive income or separate statements of income and of comprehensive income for the current interim period and, if different, cumulatively for the current financial year to date, with a comparative single statement of comprehensive income or separate statements of income and of comprehensive income for the comparable interim period (current and, if different, year-to-date) of the immediately preceding financial year. Paragraph 8A sets out when an entity shall present a single statement of comprehensive income or separate statements of income and of comprehensive income.

(c) A statement of changes in equity cumulatively for the current financial year to date, with a comparative statement for the comparable year-to-date period of the immediately preceding financial year.

(d) A statement of cash flows cumulatively for the current financial year-to-date, with a comparative statement for the comparable year-to-date period of the immediately preceding financial year. This requirement does not apply to entities that do not present a statement of cash flows in accordance with paragraphs 8F or 9.

An entity that presents a single condensed statement of income and retained earnings in place of the statement of comprehensive income and statement of changes in equity in accordance with paragraph 8B, shall present a single condensed statement of income and retained earnings for the periods set out in paragraph 20(b). **20A**

An entity that presents an income statement, or a statement of comprehensive income in which the 'bottom line' is labelled 'profit or loss' in accordance with paragraph 8C, shall present an income statement, or a statement of comprehensive income on that basis for the periods set out in paragraph 20(b). **20B**

For an entity whose business is highly seasonal, financial information for the 12 months up to the end of the interim period and comparative information for the prior 12-month period may be useful. Accordingly, entities whose business is highly seasonal are encouraged to consider reporting such information in addition to the information called for in paragraps 20 to 20B. **21**

See paragraphs A2.1 and A2.2 of Appendix II *Illustrations and Examples* to this FRS for illustrative examples of the periods that shall be presented by an entity that reports half-yearly and an entity that reports quarterly. **22**

Materiality

In deciding how to recognise, measure, classify, or disclose an item for interim financial reporting purposes, materiality shall be assessed in relation to the interim period financial data. In making assessments of materiality, it shall be recognised that interim measurements may rely on estimates to a greater extent than measurements of annual financial data. **23**

As described in paragraph 2.6 of FRS 102, an item is material if its omission or misstatement could influence the economic decisions of users of the financial statements. **24**

While judgement is always required in assessing materiality, this FRS bases the recognition and disclosure decision on data for the interim period by itself for reasons **25** of understandability of the interim figures. Thus, for example, unusual items, changes in accounting policies or estimates, and errors are recognised and disclosed on the basis of materiality in relation to interim period data to avoid misleading inferences that might result from non-disclosure. The overriding goal is to ensure that an interim financial report includes all information that is **relevant** to understanding an entity's financial position and performance during the interim period.

26-27   [Not used]

Recognition and measurement

Same accounting policies as annual

28   An entity shall apply the same accounting policies in its interim financial statements as are applied in its most recent annual financial statements, except for accounting policy changes made after the date of the most recent annual financial statements that are to be reflected in the next annual financial statements.

28A   The frequency of an entity's reporting (annual, half-yearly or quarterly) shall not affect the measurement of its annual results, with the exception described in paragraph 30(a). To achieve that objective, measurements for interim reporting purposes shall be made on a year-to-date basis.

29   Year-to-date measurements may involve changes in estimates of amounts reported in prior interim periods of the current financial year, but the principles for recognising assets, liabilities, **income**, and **expenses** for interim periods are the same as in annual financial statements.

30   To illustrate:

(a)   The principles for recognising and measuring losses from inventory write-downs, restructurings, or impairments in an interim period are the same as those that an entity would follow if it prepared only annual financial statements. However, if such items are recognised and measured in one interim period and the estimate changes in a subsequent interim period of that financial year, the original estimate is changed in the subsequent interim period either by accrual of an additional amount of loss or by reversal of the previously recognised amount, unless the reversal of a previously recognised impairment is prohibited by FRS 102.

(b)   A cost that does not meet the definition of an asset at the end of an interim period is not deferred in the statement of financial position either to await future information as to whether it has met the definition of an asset or to smooth earnings over interim periods within a financial year.

(c)   **Income tax** expense is recognised in each interim period based on the best estimate of the weighted average annual income tax rate expected for the full financial year, using the tax rates and laws that have been enacted or **substantively enacted** at the end of an interim reporting period. Amounts accrued for income tax expense in one interim period may have to be adjusted in a subsequent interim period of that financial year if the estimate of the annual income tax rate changes.

31   Under Section 2 *Concepts and Pervasive Principles* of FRS 102, recognition is the '...process of incorporating in the statement of financial position or statement of comprehensive income an item that meets the definition of an asset, liability, equity, income or expense and satisfies the ... criteria [for recognition]'. The definitions of assets, liabilities, equity, income, and expenses are fundamental to recognition, at the end of both annual and interim financial reporting periods.

For assets, the same tests of future economic benefits apply at interim dates and at the **32** end of an entity's financial year. Costs that, by their nature, would not qualify as assets at financial year-end would not qualify at interim dates either. Similarly, a liability at the end of an interim reporting period must represent an existing obligation at that date, just as it must at the end of an annual reporting period.

An essential characteristic of income (revenue) and expenses is that the related inflows **33** and outflows of assets and liabilities have already taken place. If those inflows or outflows have taken place, the related revenue and expense are recognised; otherwise they are not recognised. Section 2 of FRS 102 states that 'an entity shall recognise expenses in the statement of comprehensive income (or in the income statement, if presented) when a decrease in future economic benefits related to a decrease in an asset or an increase of a liability has arisen that can be measured reliably'. Section 2 of FRS 102 does not allow the recognition of items in the statement of financial position which do not meet the definition of assets or liabilities.

In measuring the assets, liabilities, equity, income, expenses, and cash flows reported in **34** its financial statements, an entity that reports only annually is able to take into account information that becomes available throughout the financial year. Its measurements are, in effect, on a year-to-date basis.

An entity uses information available when the interim financial report is being prepared. **35** Amounts of income and expenses reported in the current interim period will reflect any changes in estimates of amounts reported in the last published financial statements. The amounts reported in the last published financial statements, whether at the end of a prior interim period or at the end of the prior financial year, are not retrospectively adjusted for a **change in accounting estimate**. Paragraph 16A(d) requires that the nature and amount of any significant changes in estimates are disclosed.

[Not used] **36**

Revenues received seasonally, cyclically, or occasionally

Revenues that are received seasonally, cyclically, or occasionally within a financial year **37** shall not be anticipated or deferred as of an interim date if anticipation or deferral would not be appropriate at the end of the entity's financial year.

Examples include dividend revenue, royalties, and government grants. Additionally, some **38** entities consistently earn more revenues in certain interim periods of a financial year than in other interim periods, for example, seasonal revenues of retailers. Such revenues are recognised when they occur.

Costs incurred unevenly during the financial year

Costs that are incurred unevenly during an entity's financial year shall be anticipated or **39** deferred for interim reporting purposes if, and only if, it is also appropriate to anticipate or defer that type of cost at the end of the financial year.

See paragraphs A2.3 to A2.38 of Appendix II to this FRS for illustrative examples of **40** applying the requirements set out in paragraphs 28 to 39.

Use of estimates

41   The measurement procedures to be followed in an interim financial report shall be designed to ensure that the resulting information is reliable and that all material financial information that is relevant to an understanding of the financial position or performance of the entity is appropriately disclosed. While measurements in both annual and interim financial reports are often based on reasonable estimates, the preparation of interim financial reports generally will require a greater use of estimation methods than annual financial reports.

42   See paragraphs A2.39 to A2.47 of Appendix II to this FRS for illustrative examples of the use of estimates in interim periods.

Restatement of previously reported interim periods

43   A change in accounting policy, other than one for which the transition is specified in FRS 102, shall be reflected by:

(a)   restating the financial statements of prior interim periods of the current financial year and the comparable interim periods of any prior financial years that will be restated in the annual financial statements in accordance with Section 10 *Accounting Policies, Estimates and Errors* of FRS 102; or

(b)   when it is **impracticable** to determine the cumulative effect at the beginning of the financial year of applying a new accounting policy to all prior periods, adjusting the financial statements of prior interim periods of the current financial year, and comparable interim periods of prior financial years to apply the new accounting policy **prospectively** from the earliest date practicable.

44   One objective of the preceding principle is to ensure that a single accounting policy is applied to a particular class of transactions throughout an entire financial year. Under Section 10 of FRS 102, a change in accounting policy is reflected by **retrospective application**, with restatement of prior period financial data as far back as is practicable. However, if the cumulative amount of the adjustment relating to prior financial years is impracticable to determine, then under Section 10 of FRS 102 the new policy is applied prospectively from the earliest date practicable. The effect of the principle in paragraph 43 is to require that within the current financial year any change in accounting policy is applied either retrospectively or, if that is not practicable, prospectively, from no later than the beginning of the financial year.

45   To allow accounting changes to be reflected as of an interim date within the financial year would allow two differing accounting policies to be applied to a particular class of transactions within a single financial year. The result would be interim allocation difficulties, obscured operating results, and complicated analysis and understandability of interim period information.

Effective date

46   This FRS is effective for interim periods beginning on or after 1 January 2015. Early application is permitted if an entity also applies FRS 101 or FRS 102 for an accounting period beginning before 1 January 2015.

47-56   [Not used]

Consequential amendments to FRS 100 *Application of Financial Reporting Requirements*

Paragraph 15 is amended as follows (deleted text is struck through, inserted text is underlined):

57

15 The following statements are also withdrawn:

Statement of Principles for Financial Reporting
Statement of Principles for Financial Reporting – Interpretation for public benefit entities
Reporting Statement: Retirement Benefits – Disclosures~~:~~
Reporting Statement: Preliminary announcements (withdrawn in March 2015)
Reporting Statement: Half-yearly financial reports (withdrawn in March 2015).

Consequential amendments to FRS 102 *The Financial Reporting Standard applicable in the UK and Republic of Ireland*

Paragraph 3.25 and the Glossary are amended as set out below (inserted text is underlined). The new glossary term is inserted in alphabetical order:

58

3.25 This FRS does not address presentation of **interim financial reports**. An entity that prepares such reports shall describe the basis for preparing and presenting the information. **FRS 104** sets out a basis for the preparation and presentation of interim financial reports that an entity may apply.

Appendix I: Glossary

FRS 104	FRS 104 *Interim Financial Reporting*

Approval by the FRC

Financial Reporting Standard FRS 104 *Interim Financial Reporting* was approved for issue by the Financial Reporting Council on 4 March 2015, following its consideration of the Accounting Council's Advice for this FRS.

The Accounting Council's Advice to the FRC to issue FRS 104

Introduction

1   This report provides an overview of the main issues that have been considered by the Accounting Council in advising the Financial Reporting Council (FRC) to issue FRS 104 *Interim Financial Reporting*.

2   In accordance with the *FRC Codes and Standards: procedures*, any proposal to issue, amend or withdraw a code or standard is put to the FRC Board with the full advice of the relevant Councils and/or the Codes & Standards Committee. Ordinarily, the FRC Board will only reject the advice put to it where:

(a)   it is apparent that a significant group of stakeholders has not been adequately consulted;

(b)   the necessary assessment of the impact of the proposal has not been completed, including an analysis of costs and benefits;

(c)   insufficient consideration has been given to the timing or cost of implementation; or

(d)   the cumulative impact of a number of proposals would make the adoption of an otherwise satisfactory proposal inappropriate.

3   The FRC has established the Accounting Council as the relevant Council to assist it in the setting of financial reporting standards.

Advice

4   The Accounting Council is advising the FRC to issue FRS 104 *Interim Financial Reporting* to:

(a)   Replace the existing interim financial reporting guidance in the Reporting Statement *Half-yearly financial reporting* issued by the Accounting Standards Board (ASB) in 2007 (ASB Statement Half-yearly reports). FRS 104 is based on IFRS to ensure that the FRC's revised interim and annual reporting requirements are based on a consistent framework.

(b)   Withdraw the Reporting Statement *Preliminary announcements* issued by the ASB in 1998 (ASB Statement Preliminary announcements) because its content is out of date.

Background

5   The ASB issued the ASB Statement Half-yearly reports in July 2007 in response to the introduction of the Disclosure and Transparency Rules (DTRs)[5] and the more comprehensive half-yearly financial reporting requirements contained therein. When FRS 102 *The Financial Reporting Standard applicable in the UK and Republic of Ireland* was issued, the FRC decided that FRS 102 should not contain interim reporting requirements, but that instead the existing reporting guidance contained in the ASB Statement Half-yearly reports should be reviewed.

6   Since the ASB Statement Preliminary announcements was published in 1998 it has not been updated to reflect regulatory changes and market practice developments.

---

5 *References to the Disclosure and Transparency Rules applicable in the UK should be read to include references to the Transparency (Directive 2004/109/EC) Regulations 2007, including any subsequent amendments thereto, applicable in the Republic of Ireland.*

The FRC consulted on the proposals to replace the ASB Statement Half-yearly reports   7
and withdraw the ASB Statement Preliminary announcements in FRED 56 *Draft FRS 104*
Interim Financial Reporting. The Accounting Council's advice takes into account the
responses to FRED 56.

Objective

The FRC gives careful consideration to its objective and the intended effects when   8
developing new financial reporting standards or requirements for the UK and Republic
of Ireland. In developing financial reporting standards, including FRS 104, the overriding
objective of the FRC is to enable users of accounts to receive high-quality understandable
financial reporting proportionate to the size and complexity of the entity and users'
information needs.

In meeting this objective, the FRC aims to provide succinct financial reporting standards   9
that:

(a)   have consistency with global accounting standards through the application of
      an IFRS-based solution unless an alternative clearly better meets the overriding
      objective;
(b)   reflect up-to-date thinking and developments in the way businesses operate and the
      transactions they undertake;
(c)   balance consistent principles for accounting by all UK and Republic of Ireland
      entities with practical solutions, based on size, complexity, public interest and users'
      information needs;
(d)   promote efficiency within groups; and
(e)   are cost-effective to apply.

The objectives of FRS 104 are to introduce UK and Irish interim reporting requirements   10
that, consistent with the annual reporting requirements, are based on an IFRS-framework
and to promote the publication of useful financial information at an interim date.

FRS 104 Interim Financial Reporting

Basis and scope of FRS 104

The FRC consulted on the introduction of interim financial reporting requirements in   11
FRS 102 in FRED 48 *The Financial Reporting Standard applicable in the UK and Republic*
of Ireland during 2012. The FRC proposed that entities preparing interim financial reports
should apply IAS 34 *Interim Financial Reporting*. Respondents agreed with this proposal.

In line with the proposal in FRED 48, FRED 56 proposed interim reporting requirements   12
based on IAS 34, although with certain adaptations to tailor the reporting requirements
for entities that prepare their annual financial statements in accordance with FRS 102.
Respondents to FRED 56 agreed with this proposal.

FRS 104 has been developed primarily for entities preparing the annual financial   13
statements in accordance with FRS 102. We are mindful, however, that a small number of
entities may prepare the annual financial statements in accordance with FRS 101 *Reduced*
Disclosure Framework. These entities may be required to produce half-yearly financial
reports in accordance with the DTRs because, although being a member of a larger group,
they have issued their own listed debt securities.

14   Considering that only a small minority of entities that use FRS 101 will also produce interim financial reports, it is in the Accounting Council's view not an effective solution to develop a separate set of interim reporting requirements solely for entities that apply FRS 101. Instead, as set out in FRS 104, these entities should apply the same requirements applicable to entities that use FRS 102, except that any reference to a specific requirement in FRS 102 is read as a reference to the equivalent requirement in EU-adopted IFRS, as amended by paragraph AG1 of FRS 101. A majority of respondents to FRED 56 supported this approach.

Key changes to IAS 34

15   The reporting requirements of IAS 34 have been adapted for application by entities that prepare their annual financial statements in accordance with FRS 102. The key changes made to IAS 34 for the purpose of developing FRS 104 include (please refer to Appendix III *Significant differences between FRS 104 and IAS 34* of FRS 104 for more detail):

(a)   Disclosures that are not required by FRS 102 have been deleted. For example certain fair value disclosure requirements that apply under IAS 34 have not been repeated in FRS 104.

(b)   Some disclosure requirements, for example those in relation to fair value measurements and business combinations, apply only if the entity would be required to make the same disclosures in the annual financial statements. This exempts entities that are not financial institutions and entities that report in accordance with FRS 101 from disclosing information in the interim financial report that they are not required to disclose in the annual financial statements.

(c)   Related party disclosures may be omitted for transactions between wholly owned members of a group since FRS 102 exempts such transactions from disclosure in the annual financial statements.

(d)   Disclosure requirements that apply when an entity adopts a new financial reporting framework for the first time have been inserted. Similar disclosures are required under IFRS, although they are not part of IAS 34.

(e)   The annual financial statements disclosure requirements in paragraph 26 of IAS 34 concerning significant changes of estimates reported in an interim period have been deleted because FRS 104 addresses only reporting requirements in interim financial reports.

(f)   FRS 102 permits the presentation of simplified primary financial statements under certain circumstances. These presentation requirements have been included in FRS 104 to ensure consistency of presentation in the annual and interim financial statements.

(g)   Entities that are not required to present a cash flow statement in the annual financial statements are also exempt from this requirement in the interim financial report.

(h)   The principle that the frequency of reporting should not affect the measurement of the annual results has been qualified where FRS 102 would prohibit a reversal of an impairment charge[6]. This is consistent with the requirements in IFRIC 10 *Interim Financial Reporting and Impairment*.

(i)   The preparation requirements in paragraph 14 of IAS 34 pertaining to consolidated interim financial reports have been deleted, because entities that apply FRS 104 will generally prepare entity-only annual financial statements and interim financial reports.

16   Respondents to FRED 56 largely supported these adaptations of IAS 34. In particular they agreed that FRS 104 should not impose disclosure requirements that exceed those applicable to the annual financial statements of an entity.

---

6 *FRS 102 as issued in August 2014 does not prohibit the reversal of impairments. However, as set out in FRED 59 Draft amendments to FRS 102 The Financial Reporting Standard applicable in the UK and Republic of Ireland - Small entities and other minor amendments issued in February 2015, the FRC proposes to amend FRS 102 in respect of the reversal of goodwill impairment charges.*

A number of respondents recommended that the Appendices to IAS 34 should be repeated   17
in FRS 104 as they provide useful guidance for preparers. The Accounting Council agrees
with this feedback and advises that the appendices should be included as non-mandatory
guidance in FRS 104 adapted for use by entities that prepare their annual financial
statements in accordance with FRS 102.

Other information included in the interim financial report

FRS 104 sets out the minimum components of an interim financial report and, consistent   18
with IAS 34, requires only the inclusion of a set of interim financial statements and
explanatory notes. Laws and regulations may, however, set out additional narrative
reporting requirements. For example, the DTRs require entities to prepare an interim
management report.

A minority of respondents to FRED 56 suggested that the FRC should issue separate   19
guidance on narrative reporting in interim financial reports. The Accounting Council
advises that FRS 104 should not include additional narrative reporting requirements
because entities applying FRS 104 would then be subject to reporting requirements that
exceed those of entities that apply IFRS and prepare their interim financial reports in
accordance with IAS 34.

Comparative information

FRS 104 requires entities to present comparative period information and the comparatives   20
have to be presented on the same basis as the current period information. Entities which
adopt FRS 102 for accounting periods beginning on or after 1 January 2015 are therefore
required to restate the comparative period information in accordance with FRS 102.
Additionally, as set out in paragraph 16B of FRS 104, entities should provide explanations
of the effect of the accounting policy changes and reconciliations of equity and profit or
loss. The Accounting Council advises that these disclosures are necessary for users of
interim financial reports to understand the impact of the adoption of FRS 102. Respondents
to FRED 56 supported the Accounting Council's position.

Preliminary announcements

The ASB Statement Preliminary announcements issued in 1998 is out of date. A majority of   21
respondents to FRED 56 therefore supported the proposed withdrawal. A small number of
respondents, however, suggested that the FRC should issue new guidance in this area. The
Accounting Council retains its advice that the ASB Statement Preliminary announcements
should be withdrawn as soon as possible. The FRC should consider whether new guidance
in this area is useful, as part of a future project.

Effective date

The interim financial reporting requirements replacing the ASB Statement Half-yearly   22
reports are effective from the same date as FRS 102 and apply to interim periods beginning
on or after 1 January 2015. Some respondents to FRED 56 suggested that FRS 104 should
be available for application sooner. The Accounting Council advises that early application
should be permitted, provided that an entity applies FRS 101 or FRS 102 to an accounting
period beginning before 1 January 2015.

Approval of this advice

This advice to the FRC was approved by the Accounting Council on 12 February 2015.   23

Appendix I
Glossary

This glossary is an integral part of FRS 104.

accounting policies	The specific principles, bases, conventions, rules and practices applied by an entity in preparing and presenting **financial statements**.
asset	A resource controlled by the entity as a result of past events and from which future economic benefits are expected to flow to the entity.
associate	An entity, including an unincorporated entity such as a partnership, over which the investor has **significant influence** and that is neither a **subsidiary** nor an interest in a **joint venture**.
business	An integrated set of activities and **assets** conducted and managed for the purpose of providing: (a) a return to investors; or (b) lower costs or other economic benefits directly and proportionately to policyholders or participants. A business generally consists of inputs, processes applied to those inputs, and resulting outputs that are, or will be, used to generate **revenues**. If **goodwill** is present in a transferred set of activities and assets, the transferred set shall be presumed to be a business.
business combination	The bringing together of separate entities or **businesses** into one reporting entity.
carrying amount	The amount at which an **asset** or **liability** is recognised in the **statement of financial position**.
cash	Cash on hand and demand deposits.
cash equivalents	Short-term, highly liquid investments that are readily convertible to known amounts of **cash** and that are subject to an insignificant risk of changes in value.
cash flows	Inflows and outflows of **cash** and **cash equivalents**.
cash-generating unit	The smallest identifiable group of **assets** that generates cash inflows that are largely independent of the cash inflows from other assets or groups of assets.
change in accounting estimate	An adjustment of the **carrying amount** of an **asset** or a **liability**, or the amount of the periodic consumption of an asset, that results from the assessment of the present status of, and expected future benefits and obligations associated with, assets and liabilities. Changes in accounting estimates result from new information or new developments and, accordingly, are not corrections of **errors**.
component of an entity	Operations and **cash flows** that can be clearly distinguished, operationally and for financial reporting purposes, from the rest of the entity.

contingent asset	A possible **asset** that arises from past events and whose existence will be confirmed only by the occurrence or non-occurrence of one or more uncertain future events not wholly within the control of the entity.

contingent liability	(a) a possible obligation that arises from past events and whose existence will be confirmed only by the occurrence or non-occurrence of one or more uncertain future events not wholly within the control of the entity; or
	
	(b) a present obligation that arises from past events but is not recognised because:
	
	   (i) it is not probable that an outflow of resources embodying economic benefits will be required to settle the obligation; or
	   (ii) the amount of the obligation cannot be measured with sufficient reliability.

control (of an entity)	The power to govern the financial and operating policies of an entity so as to obtain benefits from its activities.
current tax	The amount of income tax payable (refundable) in respect of the taxable profit (tax loss) for the current period or past **reporting periods**.
date of transition	The beginning of the earliest period for which an entity presents full comparative information in a given standard in its first **financial statements** that comply with that standard.
deferred tax	Income tax payable (recoverable) in respect of the **taxable profit (tax loss)** for future **reporting periods** as a result of past transactions or events.
discontinued operation	A **component of an entity** that has been disposed of and: (a) represented a separate major line of **business** or geographical area of operations; (b) was part of a single co-ordinated plan to dispose of a separate major line of business or geographical area of operations; or (c) was a **subsidiary** acquired exclusively with a view to resale.
DTRs	Disclosure and Transparency Rules issued by the Financial Conduct Authority.
employee benefits	All forms of consideration given by an entity in exchange for service rendered by employees.
equity	The residual interest in the **assets** of the entity after deducting all its **liabilities**.
errors	Omissions from, and misstatements in, the entity's **financial statements** for one or more prior periods arising from a failure to use, or misuse of, reliable information that: (a) was available when financial statements for those periods were authorised for issue; and (b) could reasonably be expected to have been obtained and taken into account in the preparation and presentation of those financial statements.

EU-adopted IFRS	IFRS that have been adopted in the European Union in accordance with EU Regulation 1606/2002.
expenses	Decreases in economic benefits during the **reporting period** in the form of outflows or depletions of **assets** or incurrences of **liabilities** that result in decreases in **equity**, other than those relating to distributions to equity investors.
fair value	The amount for which an **asset** could be exchanged, a **liability** settled, or an equity instrument granted could be exchanged, between knowledgeable, willing parties in an arm's length transaction. The guidance in paragraphs 11.27 to 11.32 of **FRS 102** shall be used in determining fair value.
fair value less costs to sell	The amount obtainable from the sale of an **asset** or **cash-generating unit** in an arm's length transaction between knowledgeable, willing parties, less the costs of disposal.
financial asset	Any **asset** that is: (a) **cash**; (b) an equity instrument of another entity; (c) a contractual right: (i) to receive cash or another financial asset from another entity; or (ii) to exchange financial assets or financial liabilities with another entity under conditions that are potentially favourable to the entity; or (d) a contract that will or may be settled in the entity's own equity instruments and: (i) under which the entity is or may be obliged to receive a variable number of the entity's own equity instruments; or (ii) that will or may be settled other than by the exchange of a fixed amount of cash or another financial asset for a fixed number of the entity's own equity instruments. For this purpose the entity's own equity instruments do not include instruments that are themselves contracts for the future receipt or delivery of the entity's own equity instruments.
financial instrument	A contract that gives rise to a **financial asset** of one entity and a **financial liability** or equity instrument of another entity.

financial liability	Any **liability** that is:
	
	(a) a contractual obligation:
	
	   (i) to deliver **cash** or another **financial asset** to another entity; or
	
	   (ii) to exchange financial assets or financial liabilities with another entity under conditions that are potentially unfavourable to the entity; or
	
	(b) a contract that will or may be settled in the entity's own equity instruments and:
	
	   (i) under which the entity is or may be obliged to deliver a variable number of the entity's own equity instruments; or
	
	   (ii) will or may be settled other than by the exchange of a fixed amount of cash or another financial asset for a fixed number of the entity's own equity instruments. For this purpose the entity's own equity instruments do not include instruments that are themselves contracts for the future receipt or delivery of the entity's own equity instruments.

financial position	The relationship of the **assets**, **liabilities** and **equity** of an entity as reported in the **statement of financial position**.
financial statements	Structured representation of the **financial position**, financial **performance** and **cash flows** of an entity.
financing activities	Activities that result in changes in the size and composition of the contributed **equity** and borrowings of the entity.
FRS 101	FRS 101 *Reduced Disclosure Framework*
FRS 102	FRS 102 *The Financial Reporting Standard applicable in the UK and Republic of Ireland*
goodwill	Future economic benefits arising from **assets** that are not capable of being individually identified and separately recognised.
group	A **parent** and all its **subsidiaries**.
IFRS (International Financial Reporting Standards)	Standards and interpretations issued (or adopted) by the International Accounting Standards Board (IASB). They comprise: (a) International Financial Reporting Standards; (b) International Accounting Standards; and (c) Interpretations developed by the IFRS Interpretations Committee (IFRIC) or the former Standing Interpretations Committee (SIC).
impairment loss	The amount by which the **carrying amount** of an **asset** exceeds: (a) in the case of **inventories**, its selling price less costs to complete and sell; or (b) in the case of other assets, its **recoverable amount**.
impracticable	Applying a requirement is impracticable when the entity cannot apply it after making every reasonable effort to do so.

income	Increases in economic benefits during the **reporting period** in the form of inflows or enhancements of **assets** or decreases of **liabilities** that result in increases in **equity**, other than those relating to contributions from equity investors.
income statement	**Financial statement** that presents all items of **income** and **expense** recognised in a **reporting period**, excluding the items of **other comprehensive income**.
income tax	All domestic and foreign taxes that are based on **taxable profits**. Income tax also includes taxes, such as withholding taxes, that are payable by a **subsidiary**, **associate** or **joint venture** on distributions to the reporting entity.
intangible asset	An identifiable non-monetary asset without physical substance. Such an **asset** is identifiable when: (a) it is separable, ie capable of being separated or divided from the entity and sold, transferred, licensed, rented or exchanged, either individually or together with a related contract, asset or **liability**; or (b) it arises from contractual or other legal rights, regardless of whether those rights are transferable or separable from the entity or from other rights and obligations.
interim financial report	A financial report containing either a complete set of **financial statements** or a set of condensed financial statements for an **interim period**.
interim period	A financial **reporting period** shorter than a full financial year.
inventories	**Assets**: (a) held for sale in the ordinary course of business; (b) in the process of production for such sale; or (c) in the form of materials or supplies to be consumed in the production process or in the rendering of services.
joint control	The contractually agreed sharing of **control** over an economic activity. It exists only when the strategic financial and operating decisions relating to the activity require the unanimous consent of the parties sharing control (the **venturers**).
joint venture	A contractual arrangement whereby two or more parties undertake an economic activity that is subject to **joint control**. Joint ventures can take the form of jointly controlled operations, jointly controlled assets, or **jointly controlled entities**.
jointly controlled entity	A **joint venture** that involves the establishment of a corporation, partnership or other entity in which each **venturer** has an interest. The entity operates in the same way as other entities, except that a contractual arrangement between the venturers establishes **joint control** over the economic activity of the entity.

key management personnel	Those persons having authority and responsibility for planning, directing and controlling the activities of the entity, directly or indirectly, including any director (whether executive or otherwise) of that entity.
liability	A present obligation of the entity arising from past events, the settlement of which is expected to result in an outflow from the entity of resources embodying economic benefits.
material	Omissions or misstatements of items are material if they could, individually or collectively, influence the economic decisions of users taken on the basis of the **financial statements**. Materiality depends on the size and nature of the omission or misstatement judged in the surrounding circumstances. The size or nature of the item, or a combination of both, could be the determining factor.
measurement	The process of determining the monetary amounts at which the elements of the **financial statements** are to be recognised and carried in the **statement of financial position** and **statement of comprehensive income**.
ordinary share	An equity instrument that is subordinate to all other classes of equity instrument.
other comprehensive income	Items of **income** and **expense** (including reclassification adjustments) that are not recognised in **profit or loss** as required or permitted by **FRS 102**.
parent	An entity that has one or more **subsidiaries**.
performance	The relationship of the **income** and **expenses** of an entity, as reported in the **statement of comprehensive income**.
post-employment benefits	**Employee benefits** (other than **termination benefits** and short-term employee benefits) that are payable after the completion of employment.
post-employment benefit plans	Formal or informal arrangements under which an entity provides **post-employment benefits** for one or more employees.
present value	A current estimate of the present discounted value of the future net **cash flows** in the normal course of **business**.
probable	More likely than not.
profit or loss	The total of **income** less **expenses**, excluding the components of **other comprehensive income**.
property, plant and equipment	Tangible **assets** that: (a) are held for use in the production or supply of goods or services, for rental to others, or for administrative purposes; and (b) are expected to be used during more than one period.
prospectively (applying a change in accounting policy)	Applying the new **accounting policy** to transactions, other events and conditions occurring after the date as at which the policy is changed.
provision	A **liability** of uncertain timing or amount.

recognition	The process of incorporating in the **statement of financial position** or **statement of comprehensive income** an item that meets the definition of an **asset, liability, equity, income** or **expense** and satisfies the following criteria: (a) it is **probable** that any future economic benefit associated with the item will flow to or from the entity; and (b) the item has a cost or value that can be measured with **reliability**.
recoverable amount	The higher of an **asset's** (or **cash-generating unit's**) **fair value less costs to sell** and its **value in use**.
related party	A related party is a person or entity that is related to the entity that is preparing its **financial statements** (the reporting entity).

	(a) A person or a close member of that person's family is related to a reporting entity if that person:
	
	    (i) has **control** or **joint control** over the reporting entity;
	
	    (ii) has **significant influence** over the reporting entity; or
	
	    (iii) is a member of the **key management personnel** of the reporting entity or of a **parent** of the reporting entity.
	
	(b) An entity is related to a reporting entity if any of the following conditions apply:
	
	    (i) the entity and the reporting entity are members of the same **group** (which means that each parent, **subsidiary** and fellow subsidiary is related to the others).
	
	    (ii) one entity is an **associate** or **joint venture** of the other entity (or of a member of a group of which the other entity is a member).
	
	    (iii) both entities are joint ventures of the same third entity.
	
	    (iv) one entity is a joint venture of a third entity and the other entity is an associate of the third entity.
	
	    (v) the entity is a **post-employment benefit plan** for the benefit of employees of either the reporting entity or an entity related to the reporting entity. If the reporting entity is itself such a plan, the sponsoring employers are also related to the reporting entity.
	
	    (vi) the entity is controlled or jointly controlled by a person identified in (a).
	
	    (vii) a person identified in (a)(i) has **significant influence** over the entity or is a member of the key management personnel of the entity (or of a parent of the entity).

	(viii) the entity, or any member of a group of which it is a part, provides key management personnel services to the reporting entity or to the parent of the reporting entity.
related party transaction	A transfer of resources, services or obligations between a reporting entity and a **related party**, regardless of whether a price is charged.
relevant or relevance	The quality of information that allows it to influence the economic decisions of users by helping them evaluate past, present or future events or confirming, or correcting, their past evaluations.
reliable or reliability	The quality of information that makes it free from **material error** and bias and represents faithfully that which it either purports to represent or could reasonably be expected to represent.
reporting period	The period covered by **financial statements** or by an **interim financial report**.
restructuring	A restructuring is a programme that is planned and controlled by management and materially changes either: (a) the scope of a business undertaken by an entity; or (b) the manner in which that business is conducted.
retrospective application (of an accounting policy)	Applying a new **accounting policy** to transactions, other events and conditions as if that policy had always been applied.
revenue	The gross inflow of economic benefits during the period arising in the course of the ordinary activities of an entity when those inflows result in increases in **equity**, other than increases relating to contributions from equity participants.
significant influence	Significant influence is the power to participate in the financial and operating policy decisions of the **associate** but is not **control** or **joint control** over those policies.
statement of cash flows	**Financial statement** that provides information about the changes in **cash** and **cash equivalents** of an entity for a period, showing separately changes during the period from operating, investing and **financing activities**.
statement of comprehensive income	**Financial statement** that presents all items of **income** and **expense** recognised in a period, including those items recognised in determining **profit or loss** (which is a subtotal in the statement of comprehensive income) and items of **other comprehensive income**. If an entity chooses to present both an **income statement** and a statement of comprehensive income, the statement of comprehensive income begins with profit or loss and then displays the items of other comprehensive income.
statement of financial position	**Financial statement** that presents the relationship of an entity's **assets**, **liabilities** and **equity** as of a specific date.
statement of income and retained earnings	**Financial statement** that presents the **profit or loss** and changes in retained earnings for a **reporting period**.

subsidiary	An entity, including an unincorporated entity such as a partnership, that is **controlled** by another entity (known as the **parent**).
substantively enacted	Tax rates shall be regarded as substantively enacted when the remaining stages of the enactment process historically have not affected the outcome and are unlikely to do so. A UK tax rate shall be regarded as having been substantively enacted if it is included in either: (a) a Bill that has been passed by the House of Commons and is awaiting only passage through the House of Lords and Royal Assent; or (b) a resolution having statutory effect that has been passed under the Provisional Collection of Taxes Act 1968. (Such a resolution could be used to collect taxes at a new rate before that rate has been enacted. In practice, corporation tax rates are now set a year ahead to avoid having to invoke the Provisional Collection of Taxes Act for the quarterly payment system.) A Republic of Ireland tax rate can be regarded as having been substantively enacted if it is included in a Bill that has been passed by the Dáil.
tax expense	The aggregate amount included in **total comprehensive income** or **equity** for the **reporting period** in respect of **current tax** and **deferred tax**.
taxable profit (tax loss)	The profit (loss) for a **reporting period** upon which income taxes are payable or recoverable, determined in accordance with the rules established by the taxation authorities. Taxable profit equals taxable income less amounts deductible from taxable income.
termination benefits	**Employee benefits** provided in exchange for the termination of an employee's employment as a result of either: (a) an entity's decision to terminate an employee's employment before the normal retirement date; or (b) an employee's decision to accept voluntary redundancy in exchange for those benefits.
timely or timeliness	Providing the information in **financial statements** within the decision time frame.
total comprehensive income	The change in **equity** during a period resulting from transactions and other events, other than those changes resulting from transactions from equity participants (equal to the sum of **profit or loss** and **other comprehensive income**).
value in use	The **present value** of the future **cash flows** expected to be derived from an **asset** or **cash-generating unit**.
venturer	A party to a **joint venture** that has **joint control** over that joint venture.

Appendix II
Illustrations and examples

This appendix accompanies, but is not part of FRS 104. It provides guidance for applying some of the requirements in FRS 104.

Illustration of periods required to be presented

The following examples illustrate the application of the principle in paragraph 20 of FRS 104.

Entity publishes interim financial reports half-yearly

The entity's financial year ends on 31 December (calendar year). The entity will present the following financial statements (condensed or complete) as identified by a tickmark ✓ in its half-yearly interim financial report for the six-month period ending on 30 June 20X1:   **A2.1**

	30 Jun 20X0	31 Dec 20X0	30 Jun 20X1
Statement of financial position as at	✗	✓	✓
Single statement of comprehensive income or separate statements of income and comprehensive income for the six-month period ending on	✓	✗	✓
Statement of changes in equity for the six-month period ending on	✓	✗	✓
Statement of cash flows for the six-month period ending on	✓	✗	✓

Entity publishes interim financial reports quarterly

The entity's financial year ends on 31 December (calendar year). The entity will present the financial statements (condensed or complete) as shown in paragraph A2.1 and the financial statements (condensed or complete) shown below as identified by a tickmark ✓ in its quarterly interim financial report for the six-month period ending on 30 June 20X1:   **A2.2**

	30 Jun 20X0	31 Dec 20X0	30 Jun 20X1
Single statement of comprehensive income or separate statements of income and comprehensive income for the three-month period ending on	✓	✗	✓

Examples of applying the recognition and measurement principles

The following are examples of applying the general recognition and measurement principles set out in paragraphs 28–39 of FRS 104.

Employer payroll taxes and insurance contributions

A2.3   If employer payroll taxes or contributions to government-sponsored insurance funds are assessed on an annual basis, the employer's related expense is recognised in interim periods using an estimated average annual effective payroll tax or contribution rate, even though a large portion of the payments may be made early in the financial year. A common example is an employer payroll tax or insurance contribution that is imposed up to a certain maximum level of earnings per employee. For higher income employees, the maximum income is reached before the end of the financial year, and the employer makes no further payments through the end of the year.

Major planned periodic maintenance or overhaul

A2.4   The cost of a planned major periodic maintenance or overhaul or other seasonal expenditure that is expected to occur late in the year is not anticipated for interim reporting purposes unless an event has caused the entity to have a legal or constructive obligation. The mere intention or necessity to incur expenditure related to the future is not sufficient to give rise to an obligation.

Provisions

A2.5   A provision is recognised when an entity has no realistic alternative but to make a transfer of economic benefits as a result of an event that has created a legal or constructive obligation. The amount of the obligation is adjusted upward or downward, with a corresponding loss or gain recognised in profit or loss, if the entity's best estimate of the amount of the obligation changes.

A2.6   FRS 104 requires that an entity applies the same criteria for recognising and measuring a provision at an interim date as it would at the end of its financial year. The existence or non-existence of an obligation to transfer benefits is not a function of the length of the reporting period. It is a question of fact.

Year-end bonuses

A2.7   The nature of year-end bonuses varies widely. Some are earned simply by continued employment during a time period. Some bonuses are earned based on a monthly, quarterly, or annual measure of operating result. They may be purely discretionary, contractual, or based on years of historical precedent.

A2.8   A bonus is anticipated for interim reporting purposes if, and only if:

(a)   the bonus is a legal obligation or past practice would make the bonus a constructive obligation for which the entity has no realistic alternative but to make the payments; and

(b)   a reliable estimate of the obligation can be made.

Section 28 *Employee Benefits* of FRS 102 provides guidance.

Contingent lease payments

A2.9   Contingent lease payments can be an example of a legal or constructive obligation that is recognised as a liability. If a lease provides for contingent payments based on the lessee achieving a certain level of annual sales, an obligation can arise in the interim periods of the financial year before the required annual level of sales has been achieved, if that required level of sales is expected to be achieved and the entity, therefore, has no realistic alternative but to make the future lease payment.

Intangible assets

An entity will apply the definition and recognition criteria for an intangible asset in the same way in an interim period as in an annual period. Costs incurred before the recognition criteria for an intangible asset are met are recognised as an expense. Costs incurred after the specific point in time at which the criteria are met are recognised as part of the cost of an intangible asset. 'Deferring' costs as assets in an interim statement of financial position in the hope that the recognition criteria will be met later in the financial year is not justified.

A2.10

Pensions

The cost of a defined benefit plan for an interim period is calculated on a year-to-date basis. For the measurement of the defined benefit obligation at an interim reporting date refer to paragraph A2.42.

A2.11

Vacations, holidays, and other short-term compensated absences

Accumulating paid absences are those that are carried forward and can be used in future periods if the current period's entitlement is not used in full. Section 28 of FRS 102 requires that an entity measure the expected cost of an obligation for accumulating paid absences at the amount the entity expects to pay as a result of the unused entitlement that has accumulated at the end of the reporting period. That principle is also applied at the end of interim financial reporting periods. Conversely, an entity recognises no expense or liability for non-accumulating paid absences at the end of an interim reporting period, just as it recognises none at the end of an annual reporting period.

A2.12

Other planned but irregularly occurring costs

An entity's budget may include certain costs expected to be incurred irregularly during the financial year, such as charitable contributions and employee training costs. Those costs generally are discretionary even though they are planned and tend to recur from year to year. Recognising an obligation at the end of an interim financial reporting period for such costs that have not yet been incurred generally is not consistent with the definition of a liability.

A2.13

Measuring interim income tax expense

Interim period income tax expense is accrued using the tax rate that would be applicable to expected total annual earnings; that is, the estimated average annual effective income tax rate applied to the pre-tax income of the interim period.

A2.14

This is consistent with the basic concept set out in paragraph 28 of FRS 104 that the same accounting recognition and measurement principles shall be applied in an interim financial report as are applied in annual financial statements. Income taxes are assessed on an annual basis. Interim period income tax expense is calculated by applying to an interim period's pre-tax income the tax rate that would be applicable to expected total annual earnings; that is, the estimated average annual effective income tax rate. That estimated average annual rate would reflect a blend of the progressive tax rate structure expected to be applicable to the full year's earnings including enacted or substantively enacted

A2.15

changes in the income tax rates scheduled to take effect later in the financial year. The estimated average annual income tax rate would be re-estimated on a year-to-date basis, consistent with paragraph 28 of FRS 104. Paragraph 16A of FRS 104 requires disclosure of a significant change in estimate.

A2.16   To the extent practicable, a separate estimated average annual effective income tax rate is determined for each taxing jurisdiction and applied individually to the interim period pre-tax income of each jurisdiction. Similarly, if different income tax rates apply to different categories of income (such as capital gains or income earned in particular industries), to the extent practicable a separate rate is applied to each individual category of interim period pre-tax income. While that degree of precision is desirable, it may not be achievable in all cases, and a weighted average of rates across jurisdictions or across categories of income is used if it is a reasonable approximation of the effect of using more specific rates.

A2.17   To illustrate the application of the foregoing principle, an entity reporting quarterly expects to earn Currency Units (CU)10,000 pre-tax each quarter and operates in a jurisdiction with a tax rate of 20 per cent on the first CU20,000 of annual earnings and 30 per cent on all additional earnings. Actual earnings match expectations. The following table shows the amount of income tax expense that is reported in each quarter:

	1st Quarter	2nd Quarter	3rd Quarter	4th Quarter	Annual
Tax expense	CU2,500	CU2,500	CU2,500	CU2,500	CU10,000

CU10,000 of tax is expected to be payable for the full year on CU40,000 of pre-tax income.

A2.18   As another illustration, an entity reports quarterly, earns CU15,000 pre-tax profit in the first quarter but expects to incur losses of CU5,000 in each of the three remaining quarters (thus having zero income for the year), and operates in a jurisdiction in which its estimated average annual income tax rate is expected to be 20 per cent. The following table shows the amount of income tax expense that is reported in each quarter:

	1st Quarter	2nd Quarter	3rd Quarter	4th Quarter	Annual
Tax expense	CU3,000	CU(1,000)	CU(1,000)	CU(1,000)	nil

Difference in financial reporting year and tax year

A2.19   If the financial reporting year and the income tax year differ, income tax expense for the interim periods of that financial reporting year is measured using separate weighted average estimated effective tax rates for each of the income tax years applied to the portion of pre-tax income earned in each of those income tax years.

A2.20   To illustrate, an entity's financial reporting year ends on 30 June and it reports quarterly. Its taxable year ends on 31 December. For the financial year that begins 1 July, Year 1 and ends 30 June, Year 2, the entity earns CU10,000 pre-tax each quarter. The estimated average annual income tax rate is 30 per cent in Year 1 and 40 per cent in Year 2.

	Quarter ending 30 Sep Year 1	Quarter ending 31 Dec Year 1	Quarter ending 31 Mar Year 2	Quarter ending 30 Jun Year 2	Year ending 30 Jun Year 2
Tax expense	CU3,000	CU3,000	CU4,000	CU4,000	CU14,000

Tax credits

Some tax jurisdictions give taxpayers credits against the tax payable based on amounts of capital expenditures, exports, research and development expenditures, or other bases. Anticipated tax benefits of this type for the full year are generally reflected in computing the estimated annual effective income tax rate, because those credits are granted and calculated on an annual basis under most tax laws and regulations. On the other hand, tax benefits that relate to a one-off event are recognised in computing income tax expense in that interim period, in the same way that special tax rates applicable to particular categories of income are not blended into a single effective annual tax rate.   **A2.21**

Tax loss and tax credit carrybacks and carryforwards

The benefits of a tax loss carryback are reflected in the interim period in which the related tax loss occurs. Section 29 *Income Tax* of FRS 102 provides that 'an entity shall recognise a current tax asset for the benefit of a tax loss that can be carried back to recover tax paid in a previous period'. A corresponding reduction of tax expense or increase of tax income is also recognised.   **A2.22**

Section 29 of FRS 102 provides that unrelieved tax losses shall only be recognised to the extent that it is probable that they will be recovered against the reversal of deferred tax liabilities or other future taxable profits.   **A2.23**

To illustrate, an entity that reports quarterly has an operating loss carryforward of CU10,000 for income tax purposes at the start of the current financial year for which a deferred tax asset has not been recognised. The entity earns CU10,000 in the first quarter of the current year and expects to earn CU10,000 in each of the three remaining quarters. Excluding the carryforward, the estimated average annual income tax rate is expected to be 40 per cent. Tax expense is as follows: **A2.24**

	1st Quarter	2nd Quarter	3rd Quarter	4th Quarter	Annual
Tax expense	CU3,000	CU3,000	CU3,000	CU3,000	CU12,000

Contractual or anticipated purchase price changes

Volume rebates or discounts and other contractual changes in the prices of raw materials, labour, or other purchased goods and services are anticipated in interim periods, by both the payer and the recipient, if it is probable that they have been earned or will take effect. Thus, contractual rebates and discounts are anticipated but discretionary rebates and discounts are not anticipated because the resulting asset or liability would not satisfy the conditions set out in FRS 102 that an asset must be a resource controlled by the entity as a result of a past event and that a liability must be a present obligation whose settlement is expected to result in an outflow of resources.   **A2.25**

Depreciation and amortisation

Depreciation and amortisation for an interim period is based only on assets owned during that interim period. It does not take into account asset acquisitions or dispositions planned for later in the financial year.   **A2.26**

Inventories

A2.27   Inventories are measured for interim financial reporting by the same principles as at financial year-end. Section 13 *Inventories* of FRS 102 establishes standards for recognising and measuring inventories. Inventories pose particular problems at the end of any financial reporting period because of the need to determine inventory quantities, costs, and net realisable values. Nonetheless, the same measurement principles are applied for inventories at an interim date. To save cost and time, entities often use estimates to measure inventories at interim dates to a greater extent than at the end of annual reporting periods. Following are examples of how to apply the net realisable value test at an interim date and how to treat manufacturing variances at interim dates.

Net realisable value of inventories

A2.28   The net realisable value of inventories is determined by reference to selling prices and related costs to complete and dispose at interim dates. An entity will reverse a write-down to net realisable value in a subsequent interim period only if it would be appropriate to do so at the end of the financial year.

A2.29   [Deleted]

Interim period manufacturing cost variances

A2.30   Price, efficiency, spending, and volume variances of a manufacturing entity are recognised in income at interim reporting dates to the same extent that those variances are recognised in income at financial year-end. Deferral of variances that are expected to be absorbed by year-end is not appropriate because it could result in reporting inventory at the interim date at more or less than its portion of the actual cost of manufacture.

Foreign currency translation gains and losses

A2.31   Foreign currency translation gains and losses are measured for interim financial reporting by the same principles as at financial year-end.

A2.32   Section 30 *Foreign Currency Translation* of FRS 102 specifies how to translate the financial statements for foreign operations into the presentation currency, including guidelines for using average or closing foreign exchange rates and guidelines for recognising the resulting adjustments in profit or loss, or in other comprehensive income. Consistently with Section 30 of FRS 102, the actual average and closing rates for the interim period are used. Entities do not anticipate future changes in foreign exchange rates in the remainder of the current financial year in translating foreign operations at an interim date.

A2.33   If Section 30 of FRS 102 requires translation adjustments to be recognised as income or expense in the period in which they arise, that principle is applied during each interim period. Entities do not defer some foreign currency translation adjustments at an interim date if the adjustment is expected to reverse before the end of the financial year.

Interim financial reporting in hyperinflationary economies

A2.34   Interim financial reports in hyperinflationary economies are prepared by the same principles as at financial year-end.

A2.35   Section 31 *Hyperinflation* of FRS 102 requires that the financial statements of an entity that reports in the currency of a hyperinflationary economy shall be stated in terms of the measuring unit current at the end of the reporting period, and the gain or loss on the net monetary position is included in profit or loss. Also, comparative financial data reported for prior periods are restated to the current measuring unit.

Entities follow those same principles at interim dates, thereby presenting all interim data in the measuring unit as of the end of the interim period, with the resulting gain or loss on the net monetary position included in the interim period's profit or loss. Entities do not annualise the recognition of the gain or loss. Nor do they use an estimated annual inflation rate in preparing an interim financial report in a hyperinflationary economy. **A2.36**

Impairment of assets

Section 27 *Impairment of Assets* of FRS 102 requires that an impairment loss be recognised if the recoverable amount has declined below carrying amount. **A2.37**

FRS 104 requires that an entity shall apply the same impairment testing, recognition, and reversal criteria at an interim date as it would at the end of its financial year. That does not mean, however, that an entity must necessarily make a detailed impairment calculation at the end of each interim period. Rather, an entity will review for indications of significant impairment since the end of the most recent financial year to determine whether such a calculation is needed. **A2.38**

Examples of the use of estimates

The following examples illustrate the application of the principle in paragraph 41 of FRS 104.

Inventories

Full stock-taking and valuation procedures may not be required for inventories at interim dates, although it may be done at financial year-end. It may be sufficient to make estimates at interim dates based on sales margins. **A2.39**

Classifications of assets and liabilities

Entities may do a more thorough investigation for classifying assets as current or fixed assets and liabilities as due within one year or after more than one year (or an equivalent classification between current and non-current assets and liabilities) at annual reporting dates than at interim dates. **A2.40**

Provisions

Determination of the appropriate amount of a provision (such as a provision for warranties, environmental costs, and site restoration costs) may be complex and often costly and time-consuming. Entities sometimes engage outside experts to assist in the annual calculations. Making similar estimates at interim dates often entails updating of the prior annual provision rather than the engaging of outside experts to do a new calculation. **A2.41**

Pensions

A2.42   Section 28 of FRS 102 requires an entity to determine the present value of defined benefit obligations and the fair value of plan assets at the end of each reporting period. FRS 102 does not require an entity to involve a professionally qualified actuary in the measurement of the obligations nor does FRS 102 require an annual comprehensive actuarial valuation. For interim reporting purposes, the defined benefit obligation can often be reliably measured by extrapolation of the latest actuarial valuation adjusted for changes in employee demographics such as number of employees and salary levels.

Income taxes

A2.43   Entities may calculate income tax expense and deferred income tax liability at annual dates by applying the tax rate for each individual jurisdiction to measures of income for each jurisdiction. Paragraph A2.16 acknowledges that while that degree of precision is desirable at interim reporting dates as well, it may not be achievable in all cases, and a weighted average of rates across jurisdictions or across categories of income is used if it is a reasonable approximation of the effect of using more specific rates.

Contingencies

A2.44   The measurement of contingencies may involve the opinions of legal experts or other advisers. Formal reports from independent experts are sometimes obtained with respect to contingencies. Such opinions about litigation, claims, assessments, and other contingencies and uncertainties may or may not also be needed at interim dates.

Revaluations and fair value accounting

A2.45   Section 17 *Property, Plant and Equipment* of FRS 102 allows an entity to choose as its accounting policy the revaluation model whereby items of property, plant and equipment are revalued to fair value. Similarly, Section 16 *Investment Property* of FRS 102 requires an entity to measure the fair value of investment property. For those measurements, an entity that relies on professionally qualified valuers at annual reporting dates is not required to rely on them at interim reporting dates.

A2.46   [Not used]

Specialised industries

A2.47   Because of complexity, costliness, and time, interim period measurements in specialised industries might be less precise than at financial year-end. An example would be calculation of insurance reserves by insurance companies.

Appendix III
Significant differences between FRS 104 and IAS 34

Paragraphs in FRS 104	Changes made to IAS 34
2 to 3A	The scope of FRS 104 has been amended to reflect that FRS 104 is intended for use by entities that prepare annual financial statements in accordance with FRS 102.
	It sets out when entities preparing half-yearly financial reports in accordance with the DTRs shall apply FRS 104.
	FRS 104 does not contain recommendations or requirements as to whether, when or how frequently an entity should prepare interim financial reports.
4 to 5	These paragraphs have been deleted.
	Definitions of terms are included in the Glossary to FRS 104.
	Entities that elect to prepare a complete set of financial statements refer to FRS 102 for the content requirements; these are not repeated in FRS 104.
8A	This paragraph clarifies when an entity presents a single statement of comprehensive income or separate statements of income and comprehensive income in the interim financial report.
8B to 8D	An entity is permitted to apply the exemptions in paragraphs 3.18 and 3.19 of FRS 102 in the interim financial statements under certain conditions.
8E	This new paragraph repeats requirements contained in paragraph 5 of IAS 34.
8F	This paragraph grants entities a conditional exemption from the preparation of a statement of cash flows.
9	A conditional exemption from the preparation of a statement of cash flows is provided to entities consistent with paragraph 8F of FRS 104.
12	This paragraph has been deleted.
14	This paragraph has been deleted.
	The requirements are not relevant for entities that apply FRS 102.
	Entities that prepare interim financial reports in accordance with FRS 104 will generally prepare them on an entity-only basis.
15B	It has been clarified that entities are permitted to include cross-references in the notes from disclosures made elsewhere in the interim financial report.
	Disclosure of the information is only required if the information would be disclosable in the annual financial statements.
	Paragraphs 15B(j), (k) and (l) have been amended or deleted because disclosures required by these paragraphs in IAS 34 are not required in the annual financial statements under FRS 102.

Paragraphs in FRS 104	Changes made to IAS 34
16A	It has been clarified that entities are permitted to include cross-references in the notes from disclosures made elsewhere in the interim financial report.
	Paragraphs 16A(i) and (j) have been amended to limit the disclosure requirements to those required by FRS 102 in annual financial statements. An entity that is not required to make the disclosures in the annual financial statements is exempt from providing the disclosures in the interim financial report.
	Paragraph 16A(k) has been deleted because similar disclosures are not required by FRS 102 in annual financial statements.
19	References to compliance with IFRSs have been deleted as not applicable for entities applying FRS 104.
20A to 20B	The requirements have been clarified in respect of entities that apply any of the presentational options provided for in paragraphs 8B to 8C of FRS 104.
26 to 27	These paragraphs have been deleted.
	FRS 104 does not set out disclosure requirements pertaining to annual financial statements.
35 to 36	The requirements of these paragraphs have been consolidated in paragraph 35 of FRS 104.
	Paragraph 36 has been deleted.
46 to 56	The effective date requirements have been amended in FRS 104.
	Paragraphs 47 to 56 have been deleted as they are not needed in FRS 104.

Appendix IV
Table of comparison between terminology used in the DTRs and FRS 104

The following table compares broadly equivalent terminology used in the Disclosure and Transparency Rules (DTRs) with terminology used in FRS 104.

Terminology used in the DTRs	Terminology used in FRS 104
Balance sheet	Statement of financial position
Condensed set of financial statements	Condensed interim financial statements and selected explanatory notes
Half-yearly financial report	Interim financial report
Profit and loss account	Income statement (under the two-statement approach) Part of the statement of comprehensive income (under the single-statement approach)

Appendix V
Note on UK regulatory requirements

A5.1   This Appendix provides an overview of how the requirements in FRS 104 complement the legal reporting requirements set out in the Disclosure and Transparency Rules (DTRs) of the United Kingdom (UK) Financial Conduct Authority (FCA).

Scope

A5.2   FRS 104 does not specify whether, how frequently or how soon after the end of an interim period an entity should present interim financial reports. The DTRs set out requirements in this regard.

A5.3   Issuers that are required to publish half-yearly financial reports in accordance with the DTRs must include a responsibility statement in the report. In accordance with paragraph 4.2.10R of the DTRs, a person making the responsibility statement will satisfy the requirement to confirm that the condensed set of financial statements gives a true and fair view of the assets, liabilities, financial position and profit or loss of the issuer (or the undertakings included in the consolidation as a whole) by including a statement that the condensed set of financial statements has been prepared in accordance with IAS 34 *Interim Financial Reporting* or, for UK issuers not using EU-adopted IFRS, pronouncements on interim reporting issued by the Financial Reporting Council[7].

A5.4   FRS 104 constitutes the pronouncement on interim reporting for UK issuers not using EU-adopted IFRS as described in the preceding paragraph. The application of FRS 104 is conditional upon the person making the responsibility statement having reasonable grounds to be satisfied that the condensed set of financial statements prepared in accordance with FRS 104 is not misleading.

Content and basis of preparation of the interim financial statements

A5.5   In accordance with the DTRs, an issuer that is required to prepare consolidated accounts must prepare the condensed set of financial statements in accordance with IAS 34 and the requirements set out in FRS 104 do not apply to these issuers.

A5.6   An issuer that is not required to prepare consolidated accounts must, as a minimum, apply the content and preparation requirements set out in paragraph 4.2.5R of the DTRs. The content and preparation requirements of FRS 104 are consistent with those set out in the DTRs, although they are more prescriptive and detailed.

A5.7   As required by the DTRs and FRS 104, the accounting policies and presentation applied to the interim financial statements should be consistent with those of the most recent annual financial statements, unless changes are made in the next annual financial statements. In that case the new accounting policies and presentation must be reflected in the interim financial statements. An interim financial report prepared in the year of adoption of FRS 102 *The Financial Reporting Standard applicable in the UK and Republic of Ireland* must therefore be prepared in accordance with the new FRS 102 compliant accounting

---

[7] *At the time of the publication of FRS 104 the DTRs refer to pronouncements on interim reporting issued by the Accounting Standard Board. Following the publication of FRS 104 the FCA will seek a change to the DTRs so that the DTRs refer to pronouncements on interim reporting issued by the FRC.*

policies and presentation requirements. FRS 104 also requires certain transitional disclosures in the first set of interim financial statements that is prepared in accordance with the new FRS 102 compliant accounting policies.

Cross-referencing to the interim management report

Paragraphs 4.2.7R and 4.2.8R of the DTRs require issuers to publish an interim management report and specify certain minimum disclosures. Where FRS 104 requires disclosure of the same information in the interim financial statements, an issuer is permitted to include a cross-reference to the information disclosed in the interim management report, instead of duplicating the same information in the notes.

A5.8

Appendix VI
Republic of Ireland legal references

A6.1 In the Republic of Ireland (RoI) the Investment Funds Companies and Miscellaneous Provisions Act 2006 provides for, inter alia, the implementation of certain aspects of the EU Transparency Directive (Directive 2004/109/EC). Where entities fall within the scope of the EU Transparency Directive, the half-yearly reporting requirements are set out in Regulation 6(2) of the Transparency (Directive 2004/109/EC) Regulations 2007.

A6.2 FRS 104 includes various references to the requirements of the Disclosure and Transparency Rules (DTRs) of the Financial Conduct Authority as they apply to issuers whose home state is the United Kingdom. The tables below outline the corresponding provisions in the Transparency (Directive 2004/109/EC) Regulations 2007, including subsequent amendments thereto (Transparency Regulations), as they apply to Irish issuers.

A6.3 FRS 104 constitutes the pronouncement on interim reporting for Irish issuers not using EU-adopted IFRS, as provided for in Regulation 8(5)(d)(ii) of the Transparency Regulations.

Summary

Paragraph	DTRs reference	Transparency Regulations reference
xi	Paragraph 4.2.2R	Regulation 6(2)
xii	Paragraphs 4.2.10R and 4.2.10(4)R	Regulations 6(3)(c) and 8(5) (a) to (d)

FRS 104

Paragraph	DTRs reference	Transparency Regulations reference
3A	Paragraph 4.2.10(4)R	Regulations 8(5) (a) to (d)

Appendix I: Glossary

'DTRs'	Equivalent aspects of the EU Transparency Directive are implemented in the Republic of Ireland through the Transparency (Directive 2004/109/EC) Regulations 2007, including subsequent amendments thereto.

Appendix V: Note on UK regulatory requirements

Paragraph	DTRs reference	Transparency Regulations reference
A5.3	Paragraph 4.2.10R	Regulations 6(3)(c) and 8(5)
A5.6	Paragraph 4.2.5R	Regulation 7
A5.9	Paragraphs 4.2.7R and 4.2.8R	Regulations 8(2) and 8(3)

FRS 105
The Financial Reporting Standard applicable
to the Micro-entities Regime

(July 2015)

Contents

		Paragraphs
Summary		

FRS 105 The Financial Reporting Standard applicable to the Micro-entities Regime

Section 1	Scope	1.1–1.5
Section 2	Concepts and Pervasive Principles	2.1–2.37
Section 3	Financial Statement Presentation	3.1–3.14
Section 4	Statement of Financial Position	4.1–4.4
Section 5	Income Statement	5.1–5.4
Section 6	Notes to the Financial Statements	6.1–6A.3
Section 7	Subsidiaries, Associates, Jointly Controlled Entities and Intermediate Payment Arrangements	7.1–7.8
Section 8	Accounting Policies, Estimates and Errors	8.1–8.17
Section 9	Financial Instruments	9.1–9.29
Section 10	Inventories	10.1–10.22
Section 11	Investments in Joint Ventures	11.1–11.9
Section 12	Property, Plant and Equipment and Investment Property	12.1–12.29
Section 13	Intangible Assets other than Goodwill	13.1–13.18
Section 14	Business Combinations and Goodwill	14.1–14.3
Section 15	Leases	15.1–15.33
Section 16	Provisions and Contingencies	16.1–16A.8
Section 17	Liabilities and Equity	17.1–17.15
Section 18	Revenue	18.1–18A.35
Section 19	Government Grants	19.1–19.10
Section 20	Borrowing Costs	20.1–20.2
Section 21	Share-based Payment	21.1–21.10
Section 22	Impairment of Assets	22.1–22.21
Section 23	Employee Benefits	23.1–23.22
Section 24	Income Tax	24.1–24.13
Section 25	Foreign Currency Translation	25.1–25.6
Section 26	Events after the End of the Reporting Period	26.1–26.10
Section 27	Specialised Activities	27.1–27.6
Section 28	Transition to this FRS	28.1–28.12

Approval by the FRC

The Accounting Council's Advice to the FRC to issue FRS 105

Introduction	1–4
Advice	5–6
Background	7–10
Objective	11–12
Consistent recognition and measurement requirements with FRS 102	13–16
Amendments to FRS 102 to align FRS 105 with the legal requirements	17–23
Further simplifications over and above the legal requirements	24–31
Transitional provisions – fair value / revaluation as deemed cost	32–34

Structure and language of FRS 105   35
Residents' management companies   36–37
Effective date   38–39
Approval of this advice   40

Appendices
I   Glossary
II   Table of equivalence for UK Companies Act terminology
III   Note on legal requirements
IV   Republic of Ireland (RoI) legal references

Editor's note: Amendments to this version of the standard, to bring limited liability partnerships and qualifying partnerships within the scope of the micro-entities regime, are set out in the next section of this book.

FRS 105 *The Financial Reporting Standard applicable to the Micro-entities Regime* is an accounting standard. It is issued by the Financial Reporting Council in respect of its application in the United Kingdom and promulgated by the Institute of Chartered Accountants in Ireland in respect of its application in the Republic of Ireland.

Summary

With effect from 1 January 2015 the Financial Reporting Council (FRC) revised financial   **(i)**
reporting standards in the United Kingdom and Republic of Ireland. The revisions
fundamentally reformed financial reporting, replacing the extant standards with five
Financial Reporting Standards:

(a)   FRS 100 *Application of Financial Reporting Requirements*;
(b)   FRS 101 *Reduced Disclosure Framework*;
(c)   FRS 102 *The Financial Reporting Standard applicable in the UK and Republic of Ireland*;
(d)   FRS 103 *Insurance Contracts*; and
(e)   FRS 104 *Interim Financial Reporting*.

The revisions made by the FRC followed a sustained and detailed period of consultation.   **(ii)**
The FRC made these fundamental changes recognising that the introduction of International
Financial Reporting Standards for listed groups in 2002 (with application from 2005)
called into question the need for two sets of financial reporting standards. Evidence from
consultation supported a move towards an international-based framework for financial
reporting, but one that was proportionate to the needs of preparers and users.

The FRC's overriding objective in setting accounting standards is to enable users of   **(iii)**
accounts to receive high-quality understandable financial reporting proportionate to the
size and complexity of the entity and users' information needs.

In meeting this objective, the FRC aims to provide succinct financial reporting standards   **(iv)**
that:

(a)   have consistency with international accounting standards through the application
      of an IFRS-based solution unless an alternative clearly better meets the overriding
      objective;
(b)   reflect up-to-date thinking and developments in the way entities operate and the
      transactions they undertake;
(c)   balance consistent principles for accounting by all UK and Republic of Ireland
      entities with practical solutions, based on size, complexity, public interest and users'
      information needs;
(d)   promote efficiency within groups; and
(e)   are cost-effective to apply.

FRS 105 *The Financial Reporting Standard applicable to the Micro-entities Regime* is   **(v)**
an accounting standard intended for financial statements of companies which qualify for
the micro-entities regime. FRS 105 is effective for accounting periods beginning on or
after 1 January 2016. Early application is permitted. The FRC withdraws the Financial
Reporting Standard for Smaller Entities from the effective date of this FRS.

Development of FRS 105

In November 2013, *The Small Companies (Micro-entities' Accounts) Regulations 2013*   **(vi)**
(SI 2013/3008) were made which amended *The Small Companies and Groups (Accounts
and Directors' Report) Regulations 2008* (SI 2008/409). The amendment introduced a
new optional reporting framework for companies that meet the qualifying criteria of a
micro-entity. In response to this change of UK company law and the revision of financial
reporting standards in the United Kingdom and Republic of Ireland set out in paragraph
(i), the FRC developed FRS 105.

(vii)   In February 2015 the FRC issued Financial Reporting Exposure Draft (FRED) 58 *Draft FRS 105 The Financial Reporting Standard applicable to the Micro-entities Regime* to consult on the new accounting standard for micro-entities. Respondents were generally supportive of the proposed requirements and comments made during the consultation were taken into account when FRS 105 was finalised.

(viii)   FRS 105 is based on FRS 102, but its accounting requirements are adapted to satisfy the legal requirements applicable to micro-entities and to reflect the simpler nature and smaller size of micro-entities.

(ix)   The application of the micro-entities regime is optional, however, a micro-entity that chooses to prepare its financial statements in accordance with the micro-entities regime is required to apply FRS 105. A company that qualifies for this regime, but chooses not to apply it, is required to apply another accounting standard. The possible options are set out in FRS 100 *Application of Financial Reporting Requirements*.

(x)   At the same time as the FRC issues FRS 105, the FRC also makes amendments to FRS 102 to incorporate consequential changes resulting from the *The Companies, Partnerships and Groups (Accounts and Reports) Regulations 2015* (SI 2015/980). FRS 105 takes into account any relevant changes made to FRS 102 in this regard.

Organisation of FRS 105

(xi)   FRS 105 is organised by topic with each topic presented in a separate numbered section. Cross-references to paragraphs are identified by section followed by paragraph number. Paragraph numbers are in the form of xx.yy, where xx is the section number and yy is the sequential paragraph number within that section.

(xii)   In examples that include monetary amounts, the measuring unit is Currency Unit (abbreviated as CU)

(xiii)   All the paragraphs of FRS 105 have equal authority. Some sections include appendices of implementation guidance or examples. Some of these are an integral part of this FRS while others provide guidance concerning its application; each specifies its status.

(xiv)   FRS 105 is set out in Sections 1 to 28 and the Glossary (Appendix I). Terms defined in the glossary are in **bold type** the first time they appear in each section.

(xv)   Where references to other sections or paragraphs are made, these are in reference to FRS 105 unless otherwise stated.

FRS 105 The Financial Reporting Standard applicable to the Micro-entities Regime

Section 1 *Scope*

Scope of this Financial Reporting Standard

1.1   This FRS applies to the **financial statements** of a **micro-entity**. The financial statements of a micro-entity prepared in accordance with this FRS that include the **micro-entity minimum accounting items** are presumed in law to show a true and fair view of the micro-entity's **financial position** and **profit or loss** in accordance with the **micro-entities regime**.

References to a micro-entity in this FRS are to a micro-entity that chooses to apply the **1.2** micro-entities regime.

This FRS permits, but does not require, a micro-entity to include information additional to **1.3** the micro-entity minimum accounting items in its financial statements. If a micro-entity includes additional information it shall have regard to any requirement of Section 1A *Small Entities* of **FRS 102** that relates to that information.

Date from which effective

A micro-entity applying the micro-entities regime shall apply this FRS for accounting **1.4** periods beginning on or after 1 January 2016. Early application is permitted.

In May 2016 amendments were made to this FRS to extend its scope to include **limited** **1.5** **liability partnerships (LLPs)** and **qualifying partnerships** following a change in legislation. An LLP or a qualifying partnership which qualifies as a micro-entity and is applying the micro-entities regime shall apply this FRS for accounting periods beginning on or after 1 January 2016. Early application by a micro-entity that is an LLP or a qualifying partnership is:

(a) permitted for accounting periods beginning on or after 1 January 2015 provided that *The Limited Liability Partnerships, Partnerships and Groups (Accounts and Audit) Regulations 2016* (SI 2016/575) are applied from the same date; and
(b) required if the LLP or qualifying partnership applies *The Limited Liability Partnerships, Partnerships and Groups (Accounts and Audit) Regulations 2016* (SI 2016/575) to a reporting period beginning before 1 January 2016.

Section 2 *Concepts and Pervasive Principles*

Scope of this section

This section sets out the concepts and basic principles that generally underlie the **2.1** **recognition** and **measurement** of transactions of **micro-entities** within the scope of this FRS.

Financial position

The **financial position** of a micro-entity is the relationship of its **assets**, **liabilities** and **2.2** **equity** as of a specific date as presented in the **statement of financial position**. These are defined as follows:

(a) An asset is a resource controlled by the micro-entity as a result of past events and from which future economic benefits are expected to flow to the micro-entity.
(b) A liability is a present obligation of the micro-entity arising from past events, the settlement of which is expected to result in an outflow from the micro-entity of resources embodying economic benefits.
(c) Equity is the residual interest in the assets of the micro-entity after deducting all its liabilities.

Some items that meet the definition of an asset or a liability may not be recognised as **2.3** assets or liabilities in the statement of financial position because they do not satisfy the criteria for recognition in paragraphs 2.22 and 2.24. In particular, the expectation that future economic benefits will flow to or from a micro-entity must be sufficiently certain to meet the probability criterion before an asset or liability is recognised.

Assets

2.4   The future economic benefit of an asset is its potential to contribute, directly or indirectly, to the flow of cash to the micro-entity. Those cash flows may come from using the asset or from disposing of it.

2.5   Many assets, for example **property, plant and equipment**, have a physical form. However, physical form is not essential to the existence of an asset. Some assets are intangible.

2.6   In determining the existence of an asset, the right of ownership is not essential. Thus, for example, property held on a **lease** is an asset if the micro-entity controls the benefits that are expected to flow from the property.

Liabilities

2.7   An essential characteristic of a liability is that the micro-entity has a present obligation to act or perform in a particular way. The obligation may be either a legal obligation or a **constructive obligation**. A legal obligation is legally enforceable as a consequence of a binding contract or statutory requirement. A constructive obligation is an obligation that derives from a micro-entity's actions when:

(a)   by an established pattern of past practice, published policies or a sufficiently specific current statement, the micro-entity has indicated to other parties that it will accept certain responsibilities; and

(b)   as a result, the micro-entity has created a valid expectation on the part of those other parties that it will discharge those responsibilities.

2.8   The settlement of a present obligation usually involves the payment of cash, transfer of other assets, provision of services, the replacement of that obligation with another obligation, or conversion of the obligation to equity. An obligation may also be extinguished by other means, such as a creditor waiving or forfeiting its rights.

Equity

2.9   Equity is the residual interest in the assets of the micro-entity after deducting all its liabilities.

Performance

2.10   **Performance** is the relationship of the **income** and **expenses** of a micro-entity during a **reporting period**. Income and expenses are defined as follows:

(a)   Income is increases in economic benefits during the reporting period in the form of inflows or enhancements of assets or decreases of liabilities that result in increases in equity, other than those relating to contributions from equity investors.

(b)   Expenses are decreases in economic benefits during the reporting period in the form of outflows or depletions of assets or incurrences of liabilities that result in decreases in equity, other than those relating to distributions to equity investors.

2.11   The recognition of income and expenses results directly from the recognition and measurement of assets and liabilities. Criteria for the recognition of income and expenses are discussed in paragraphs 2.26 and 2.27.

Income

The definition of income encompasses both **revenue** and **gains**. 2.12

(a) Revenue is income that arises in the course of the ordinary activities of a micro-entity and is referred to by a variety of names including sales, fees, interest, dividends, royalties and rent.
(b) Gains are other items that meet the definition of income but are not revenue.

Expenses

The definition of expenses encompasses losses as well as those expenses that arise in the 2.13 course of the ordinary activities of the micro-entity.

(a) Expenses that arise in the course of the ordinary activities of the micro-entity include, for example, cost of sales, wages and **depreciation**. They usually take the form of an outflow or depletion of assets such as cash, **inventory**, or property, plant and equipment.
(b) Losses are other items that meet the definition of expenses and may arise in the course of the ordinary activities of the micro-entity.

Recognition of assets, liabilities, income and expenses

Recognition is the process of incorporating in the statement of financial position or **income** 2.14 **statement** an item that meets the definition of an asset, liability, equity, income or expense and satisfies the following criteria:

(a) it is **probable** that any future economic benefit associated with the item will flow to or from the micro-entity; and
(b) the item has a cost or value that can be measured reliably.

The uncertainties that inevitably surround many events and circumstances are 2.15 acknowledged by the exercise of **prudence** in the preparation of the financial statements. Prudence is the inclusion of a degree of caution in the exercise of the judgements needed in making the estimates required under conditions of uncertainty, such that assets or income are not overstated and liabilities or expenses are not understated. However, the exercise of prudence does not allow the deliberate understatement of assets or income, or the deliberate overstatement of liabilities or expenses. In short, prudence does not permit bias.

The probability of future economic benefit

The concept of probability is used in the first recognition criterion to refer to the degree 2.16 of uncertainty that the future economic benefits associated with the item will flow to or from the micro-entity. Assessments of the degree of uncertainty attaching to the flow of future economic benefits are made on the basis of the evidence relating to conditions at the end of the reporting period available when the financial statements are prepared. Those assessments are made individually for individually significant items, and for a group for a large population of individually insignificant items.

Reliability of measurement

The second criterion for the recognition of an item is that it possesses a cost or value that 2.17 can be measured with reliability. In many cases, the cost or value of an item is known. In other cases it must be estimated. The use of reasonable estimates is an essential part of the preparation of financial statements and does not undermine their reliability. When a reasonable estimate cannot be made, the item is not recognised in the financial statements.

2.18   An item that fails to meet the recognition criteria may qualify for recognition at a later date as a result of subsequent circumstances or events.

Measurement of assets, liabilities, income and expenses

2.19   Measurement is the process of determining the monetary amounts at which a micro-entity measures assets, liabilities, income and expenses in its financial statements. Measurement involves the selection of a basis of measurement. This FRS specifies which measurement basis a micro-entity shall use for many types of assets, liabilities, income and expenses.

Pervasive recognition and measurement principles

2.20   In the absence of a requirement in this FRS that applies specifically to a transaction or other event or condition, paragraph 8.4 provides guidance for making a judgement and paragraph 8.5 requires a micro-entity to look to the definitions, recognition criteria and measurement concepts for assets, liabilities, income and expenses and the pervasive principles set out in this section.

Accrual basis

2.21   A micro-entity shall prepare its financial statements using the **accrual basis** of accounting. On the accrual basis, items are recognised as assets, liabilities, equity, income or expenses when they satisfy the definitions and recognition criteria for those items.

Recognition in financial statements

Assets

2.22   A micro-entity shall recognise an asset in the statement of financial position when it is probable that the future economic benefits will flow to the micro-entity and the asset has a cost or value that can be measured reliably. An asset is not recognised in the statement of financial position when expenditure has been incurred for which it is considered not probable that economic benefits will flow to the micro-entity beyond the current reporting period. Instead such a transaction results in the recognition of an expense in the income statement.

2.23   A micro-entity shall not recognise a **contingent asset** as an asset. When the flow of future economic benefits to the micro-entity is virtually certain, then the related asset is not a contingent asset, and its recognition is appropriate.

Liabilities

2.24   A micro-entity shall recognise a liability in the statement of financial position when:

(a)   the micro-entity has an obligation at the end of the reporting period as a result of a past event;

(b)   it is probable that the micro-entity will be required to transfer resources embodying economic benefits in settlement; and

(c)   the settlement amount can be measured reliably.

A **contingent liability** is either a possible but uncertain obligation or a present obligation that is not recognised because it fails to meet one or both of the conditions (b) and (c) in paragraph 2.24.   **2.25**

Income

The recognition of income results directly from the recognition and measurement of assets and liabilities. A micro-entity shall recognise income in the income statement when an increase in future economic benefits related to an increase in an asset or a decrease of a liability has arisen that can be measured reliably.   **2.26**

Expenses

The recognition of expenses results directly from the recognition and measurement of assets and liabilities. A micro-entity shall recognise expenses in the income statement when a decrease in future economic benefits related to a decrease in an asset or an increase of a liability has arisen that can be measured reliably.   **2.27**

Profit or loss

Profit or loss is the arithmetical difference between income and expenses. It is not a separate element of financial statements, and a separate recognition principle is not needed for it.   **2.28**

Generally this FRS does not allow the recognition of items in the statement of financial position that do not meet the definition of assets or of liabilities regardless of whether they result from applying the notion commonly referred to as the 'matching concept' for measuring profit or loss.   **2.29**

Measurement at initial recognition

At initial recognition, a micro-entity shall measure assets and liabilities at cost.   **2.30**

Under limited circumstances this FRS requires a micro-entity to estimate the cost of an asset or liability based on its **fair value**. Where this FRS requires a micro-entity to determine the fair value of an asset or liability, it shall use the following hierarchy to estimate the fair value: **2.31**

(a) The best evidence of fair value is the open market price for an identical asset or liability in an **active market**.

(b) When an open market price is not available, the price of a recent transaction for an identical asset or liability provides evidence of fair value as long as there has not been significant change in economic circumstances or a significant lapse of time since the transaction took place.

(c) If neither (a) nor (b) above are available, the fair value shall be estimated using a valuation technique. The objective of using a valuation technique is to estimate what the price of a recent transaction for an identical asset or liability would have been on the measurement date in an arm's length exchange motivated by normal business considerations.

Subsequent measurement

Financial assets and financial liabilities

2.32   A micro-entity measures **financial assets** and **financial liabilities** as follows:

(a)   Investments in preference shares or **ordinary shares** and investments in **subsidiaries** and **associates** and interests in **jointly controlled entities** shall be measured at cost less impairment.

(b)   **Derivatives** are measured at cost adjusted for amounts recognised in profit or loss over the term of the instruments and any impairment loss.

(c)   **Financial instruments** other than financial instruments covered by paragraphs (a) and (b) are measured at cost adjusted for the allocation of interest, the amortisation of any **transaction costs** included in the cost of the instruments and any impairment loss.

Non-financial assets

2.33   **Property, plant and equipment**, **investment property** and **biological assets** are measured at cost less accumulated depreciation and accumulated **impairment losses**.

2.34   **Inventories** are measured at the lower of cost and selling price less costs to complete and sell.

2.35   Measurement of assets at amounts lower than their initial historical cost is intended to ensure that an asset is not measured at an amount greater than the micro-entity expects to recover from the sale or use of that asset.

Liabilities other than financial liabilities

2.36   Most liabilities other than financial liabilities are measured at the best estimate of the amount that would be required to settle the obligation at the **reporting date**.

Offsetting

2.37   A micro-entity shall not offset assets and liabilities, or income and expenses, unless required or permitted by this FRS.

(a)   Measuring assets net of valuation allowances (for example, allowances for inventory obsolescence and allowances for uncollectible receivables) is not offsetting.

(b)   If a micro-entity's normal **operating activities** do not include buying and selling **fixed assets**, including investments and operating assets, then the micro-entity reports gains and losses on disposal of such assets by deducting from the proceeds on disposal the **carrying amount** of the asset and related selling expenses.

Section 3 *Financial Statement Presentation*

Scope of this section

3.1   This section explains what compliance with this FRS requires and what makes up a complete set of **financial statements** for a **micro-entity**.

Presumed true and fair view

The financial statements of a micro-entity that comply with this FRS are presumed in law **3.2** to give a true and fair view of the **financial position** and **profit or loss** of the micro-entity in accordance with the **micro-entities regime**.

Going concern

When preparing financial statements using this FRS, the management of a micro-entity **3.3** shall make an assessment of whether the going concern basis of accounting is appropriate. The going concern basis of accounting is appropriate unless management either intends to liquidate the micro-entity or to cease trading, or has no realistic alternative but to do so. In assessing whether the going concern basis of accounting is appropriate, management takes into account all available information about the future, which is at least, but is not limited to, 12 months from the date when the financial statements are authorised for issue.

Frequency of reporting

A micro-entity shall present a complete set of financial statements (including comparative **3.4** information as set out in paragraph 3.7) at the end of each **reporting period**.

Consistency of presentation

A micro-entity shall retain the presentation and classification of items in the financial **3.5** statements from one period to the next unless:

(a) it is apparent, following a significant change in the nature of the micro-entity's operations or a review of its financial statements, that another presentation or classification would be more appropriate having regard to the criteria for the selection and application of **accounting policies** in Section 8 *Accounting Policies, Estimates and Errors*; or

(b) this FRS requires a change in presentation.

When the presentation or classification of items in the financial statements is changed, **3.6** a micro-entity shall reclassify comparative amounts unless the reclassification is **impracticable**.

Comparative information

Except when this FRS permits or requires otherwise, a micro-entity shall present **3.7** comparative information in respect of the preceding period for all amounts presented in the current period's financial statements.

Materiality

A micro-entity need not provide a specific disclosure required by this FRS if the **3.8** information is not **material**. This exemption does not apply to the disclosures required by paragraph 6.2(a).

Complete set of financial statements

3.9   A complete set of financial statements of a micro-entity shall include the following:

(a)   a **statement of financial position** as at the **reporting date** with **notes** included at the foot of the statement; and

(b)   an **income statement** for the reporting period.

3.10   Because paragraph 3.7 requires comparative amounts in respect of the previous period for all amounts presented in the financial statements, a complete set of financial statements means that a micro-entity shall present, as a minimum, two of each of the required financial statements and related notes.

3.11   In a complete set of financial statements, a micro-entity shall present each financial statement with equal prominence.

3.12   A micro-entity may use titles for the financial statements other than those used in this FRS as long as they are not misleading.

Identification of the financial statements

3.13   A micro-entity shall clearly identify each of the financial statements and the notes. In addition, a micro-entity shall display the following information prominently, and repeat it when necessary for an understanding of the information presented:

(a)   the name of the reporting entity and any change in its name since the end of the preceding reporting period;

(b)   the date of the end of the reporting period and the period covered by the financial statements;

(c)   the presentation currency; and

(d)   the level of rounding, if any, used in presenting amounts in the financial statements.

Statement of compliance with the micro-entity provisions

3.14   In accordance with section 414(3) of the **Act**[1], financial statements prepared in accordance with the **micro-entity provisions** shall on the **statement of financial position**, in a prominent position above the signature, contain a statement that the financial statements are prepared in accordance with the micro-entity provisions.

Section 4 *Statement of Financial Position*

Scope of this section

4.1   This section sets out the information that is to be presented in a **statement of financial position** and how to present it. The statement of financial position (which is referred to as the balance sheet in the **Act**) presents a **micro-entity's assets, liabilities** and **equity** as of a specific date – the end of the **reporting period**.

4.2   A micro-entity is permitted, but not required, to present information additional to that required by this section. Paragraph 1.3 applies to any additional information presented.

[1] *Or, when relevant, Regulation 12 of the* Limited Liability Partnerships (Accounts and Audit) (Application of Companies Act 2006) Regulations 2008 *(SI 2008/1911).*

Information to be presented in the statement of financial position

A micro-entity shall present a statement of financial position in accordance with one of the formats set out in Section C of Part 1 of Schedule 1 to the **Small Companies Regulations** or Section C of Part 1 of Schedule 1 to the **Small LLP Regulations**[2], as illustrated below:

4.3

Format 1	CU	CU
Called up share capital not paid		X
Fixed assets		X
Current assets	X	
Prepayments and accrued income	X	
Creditors: amounts falling due within one year	(X)	
Net current assets / (liabilities)		X/(X)
Total assets less current liabilities		X
Creditors: amounts falling due after more than one year		(X)
Provisions for liabilities		(X)
Accruals and deferred income		(X)
		X
Capital and reserves		X

Format 2	CU	CU
Assets		
Called up share capital not paid		X
Fixed assets		X
Current assets		X
Prepayments and accrued income		X
		X
Capital, Reserves and Liabilities		
Capital and reserves		X
Provisions for liabilities		X
Creditors		
Amounts falling due within one year	X	
Amounts falling due after one year	X	
		X
Accruals and deferred income		X
		X

Creditors: amounts falling due within one year

A micro-entity shall classify a creditor as due within one year when the micro-entity does not have an unconditional right, at the end of the reporting period, to defer settlement of the creditor for at least 12 months after the **reporting date**.

4.4

---

[2] *LLPs shall describe the items as set out in the Small LLP Regulations. In particular, 'Called up share capital not paid' shall not be used and 'Loans and other debts due to members' and 'Members' other interests' shall be used*

Section 5 *Income Statement*

Scope of this section

5.1   This section requires a **micro-entity** to present its **profit or loss** for a period, ie its financial **performance** for the period. It sets out the information that is to be presented in the **income statement** (which is referred to as the profit and loss account in the **Act**) and how to present it.

5.2   A micro-entity is permitted, but not required, to present information additional to that required by this section. Paragraph 1.3 applies to any additional information presented.

Presentation of profit or loss

5.3   A micro-entity shall present its profit or loss for a period in an income statement in accordance with Section C of Part 1 of Schedule 1 to the **Small Companies Regulations** or Section C of Part 1 of Schedule 1 to the **Small LLP Regulations**, as illustrated below:

	CU
Turnover	X
Other income	X
Cost of raw materials and consumables	(X)
Staff costs	(X)
Depreciation and other amounts written off assets	(X)
Other charges	(X)
Tax	(X)
Profit or loss[3]	X / (X)

5.4   Under this FRS, the effects of corrections of **material errors** and changes in **accounting policies** are presented as retrospective adjustments of prior periods rather than as part of profit or loss in the period in which they arise (see Section 8 *Accounting Policies, Estimates and Errors*).

Section 6 *Notes to the Financial Statements*[3]

Scope of this section

6.1   This section sets out the information that shall be disclosed in the **notes** to the **financial statements** and where. A **micro-entity** is permitted, but not required, to disclose information additional to that required by this section. Paragraph 1.3 applies to any additional information disclosed.

Structure and content of the notes

6.2   In accordance with section 472(1A) of the **Act**, the notes to the financial statements of a micro-entity shall be presented at the foot of the **statement of financial position** and shall include the following information:

---

[3] *LLPs shall describe this item as Profit or loss for the financial year before members' remuneration and profit*

(a)   advances, credit and guarantees granted to directors as required by section 413 of the Act (see paragraph 6A.1 in the Appendix to this Section); and

(b)   financial commitments, guarantees and contingencies as required by regulation 5A of, and paragraph 57 of Part 3 of Schedule 1 to, the **Small Companies Regulations** (see paragraphs 6A.2 and 6A.3 in the Appendix to this Section).

In accordance with Regulation 30 of the *Limited Liability Partnerships (Accounts and Audit) (Application of Companies Act 2006) Regulations 2008* (SI 2008/1911), the notes to the financial statements of an **LLP** which qualifies as a micro-entity shall be presented at the foot of the statement of financial position and shall include financial commitments, guarantees and contingencies as required by paragraph 55 of Part 3 of Schedule 1 to the **Small LLPs Regulations** (see paragraphs 6A.2 and 6A.3 in the Appendix to this Section).   **6.3**

Appendix to Section 6

Company law disclosure requirements

This appendix is an integral part of this FRS.

This appendix sets out the company law disclosure requirements referred to in paragraph 6.2. Other than substituting company law terminology with the equivalent terminology used in this FRS (see Appendix II Table of equivalence for UK Companies Act terminology), the text is as close as possible to that set out in company law.

Where this FRS contains a disclosure requirement related to a company law requirement this has been indicated.

Details of advances and credits granted by a micro-entity to its directors and guarantees   **6A.1**
of any kind entered into by a micro-entity on behalf of its directors must be shown in the notes to the financial statements.

The details required of an advance or credit are:

(a)   *its amount;*

(b)   *an indication of the interest rate;*

(c)   *its main conditions;*

(d)   *any amounts repaid;*

(e)   *any amounts written off; and*

(f)   *any amounts waived.*

There must also be stated in the notes to the financial statements the totals of amounts stated under (a), (d), (e) and (f).

The details required of a guarantee are:

(a)   *its main terms;*

(b)   *the amount of the maximum liability that may be incurred by a micro-entity;*

(c)   *any amount paid and any liability incurred by a micro-entity for the purpose of fulfilling the guarantee (including any loss incurred by reason of enforcement of the guarantee).*

There must also be stated in the notes to the financial statements the totals of amounts stated under (b) and (c). (Section 413 of the Act)

6A.2   *The total amount of any financial commitments, guarantees and contingencies that are not included in the statement of financial position must be stated. (paragraph 57(1) of Schedule 1 to the Small Companies Regulations or paragraph 55(1) of Schedule 1 to the Small LLPs Regulations)*

The total amount of any commitments concerning pensions must be separately disclosed. (paragraph 57(3) of Schedule 1 to the Small Companies Regulations or paragraph 55(3) of Schedule 1 to the Small LLPs Regulations)

The total amount of any commitments which are undertaken on behalf of or for the benefit of:

(a)   *any parent, fellow subsidiary or any subsidiary of a micro-entity; or*

(b)   *any undertaking in which a micro-entity has a participating interest,*

must be separately stated and those within (a) must also be stated separately from those within (b). (paragraph 57(4) of Schedule 1 to the Small Companies Regulations or paragraph 55(4) of Schedule 1 to the Small LLPs Regulations)

The following paragraphs in this FRS address these disclosure requirements within the context of specific transactions:

(a)   Section 9 *Financial Instruments*: paragraph 9.28

(b)   Section 11 *Investments in Joint Ventures*: paragraph 11.9

(c)   Section 12 *Property, Plant and Equipment and Investment Property*: paragraph 12.28

(d)   Section 13 *Intangible Assets other than Goodwill*: paragraph 13.17

(e)   Section 14 *Business Combinations and Goodwill*: paragraph 14.3

(f)   Section 15 *Leases*: paragraphs 15.17 and 15.33.

(g)   Section 16 *Provisions and Contingencies*: paragraph 16.19

(h)   Section 23 *Employee Benefits*: paragraph 23.22.

(i)   Section 27 *Specialised Activities*: paragraph 27.5.

6A.3   *An indication of the nature and form of any valuable security given by the micro-entity in respect of commitments, guarantees and contingencies within paragraph 6A.2. must be given. (paragraph 57(2) of Schedule 1 to the Small Companies Regulations or paragraph 55(2) of Schedule 1 to the Small LLPs Regulations)*

The following paragraphs in this FRS address these disclosure requirements within the context of specific transactions:

(a)   Section 9 *Financial Instruments*: paragraph 9.29.

(b)   Section 10 *Inventories*: paragraph 10.22.

(c)   Section 12 *Property, Plant and Equipment and Investment Property*: paragraph 12.29.

(d)   Section 13 *Intangible Assets other than Goodwill*: paragraph 13.18.

(e)   Section 27 *Specialised Activities*: paragraph 27.6.

Section 7 *Subsidiaries, Associates, Jointly Controlled Entities and Intermediate Payment Arrangements*

Scope of this section

7.1   This section sets out how a **micro-entity** shall account for investments in **subsidiaries** and **associates**, interests in **jointly controlled entities** and intermediate payment arrangements.

Investments in subsidiaries, associates and interests in jointly controlled entities

A micro-entity shall account for any investments in subsidiaries and associates and any interests in jointly controlled entities in accordance with Section 9 *Financial Instruments*.   **7.2**

Consolidated financial statements

An entity that is required or chooses to present **consolidated financial statements** is excluded from the **micro-entities regime** (sections 384A(8) and 384B(2) of the **Act**[4]) and shall not apply this FRS.   **7.3**

Intermediate payment arrangements (eg ESOPs)

Intermediate payment arrangements may take a variety of forms: **7.4**

(a)   The intermediary is usually established by the micro-entity and constituted as a trust, although other arrangements are possible.

(b)   The relationship between the micro-entity and the intermediary may take different forms. For example, when the intermediary is constituted as a trust, the micro-entity will not have a right to direct the intermediary's activities. However, in these and other cases the micro-entity may give advice to the intermediary or may be relied on by the intermediary to provide the information it needs to carry out its activities. Sometimes, the way the intermediary has been set up gives it little discretion in the broad nature of its activities.

(c)   The arrangements are most commonly used to pay employees, although they are sometimes used to compensate suppliers of goods and services other than employee services. Sometimes the micro-entity's employees and other suppliers are not the only beneficiaries of the arrangement. Other beneficiaries may include past employees and their dependants, and the intermediary may be entitled to make charitable donations.

(d)   The precise identity of the persons or entities that will receive payments from the intermediary, and the amounts that they will receive, are not usually agreed at the outset.

(e)   The micro-entity often has the right to appoint or veto the appointment of the intermediary's trustees (or its directors or the equivalent).

(f)   The payments made to the intermediary and the payments made by the intermediary are often cash payments but may involve other transfers of value.

Examples of intermediate payment arrangements are employee share ownership plans (ESOPs) and employee benefit trusts that are used to facilitate employee shareholdings under remuneration schemes. In a typical employee benefit trust arrangement for **share-based payment transactions**, a micro-entity makes payments to a trust or guarantees borrowing by the trust, and the trust uses its funds to accumulate assets to pay the micro-entity's employees for services the employees have rendered to the micro-entity.

Although the trustees of an intermediary must act at all times in accordance with the interests of the beneficiaries of the intermediary, most intermediaries (particularly those established as a means of remunerating employees) are specifically designed so as to serve the purposes of the micro-entity, and to ensure that there will be minimal risk of any conflict arising between the duties of the trustees of the intermediary and the interest of

---

[4] *Or, when relevant, Regulation 5A of the* Limited Liability Partnerships (Accounts and Audit) (Application of Companies Act 2006) Regulations 2008 *(SI 2008/1911).*

the micro-entity, such that there is nothing to encumber implementation of the wishes of the micro-entity in practice. Where this is the case, the micro-entity has de facto **control**.

Accounting for intermediate payment arrangements

7.5   When a micro-entity makes payments (or transfers **assets**) to an intermediary, there is a rebuttable presumption that the entity has exchanged one asset for another and that the payment itself does not represent an immediate **expense**. To rebut this presumption at the time the payment is made to the intermediary, the micro-entity must demonstrate:

(a)   it will not obtain future economic benefit from the amounts transferred; or

(b)   it does not have control of the right or other access to the future economic benefit it is expected to receive.

7.6   Where a payment to an intermediary is an exchange by the micro-entity of one asset for another, any assets that the intermediary acquires in a subsequent exchange transaction will also be under the control of the micro-entity. Accordingly, assets and **liabilities** of the intermediary shall be accounted for by the micro-entity as an extension of its own business and recognised in its **financial statements**. An asset will cease to be recognised as an asset of the micro-entity when, for example, the asset of the intermediary **vests** unconditionally with identified beneficiaries.

7.7   A micro-entity may distribute its own equity instruments, or other equity instruments, to an intermediary in order to facilitate employee shareholdings under a remuneration scheme. Where this is the case and the micro-entity has control, or de facto control, of the assets and liabilities of the intermediary, the commercial effect is that the micro-entity is, for all practical purposes, in the same position as if it had purchased the shares directly.

7.8   Where an intermediary holds the micro-entity's equity instruments, the micro-entity shall account for the equity instruments as if it had purchased them directly. The micro-entity shall account for the assets and liabilities of the intermediary in its financial statements as follows:

(a)   The consideration paid for the equity instruments of the sponsoring entity shall be deducted from equity until such time that the equity instruments vest unconditionally with employees.

(b)   Other assets and liabilities of the intermediary shall be recognised as assets and liabilities of the micro-entity.

(c)   No **gain** or loss shall be recognised in **profit or loss** on the purchase, sale, issue or cancellation of the micro-entity's own equity instruments.

(d)   Finance costs and any administration expenses shall be recognised on an **accruals basis** rather than as funding payments are made to the intermediary.

(e)   Any dividend income arising on the micro-entity's own equity instruments shall be excluded from profit or loss and deducted from the aggregate of dividends paid.

Section 8 *Accounting Policies, Estimates and Errors*

Scope of this section

8.1   This section provides guidance for selecting and applying the **accounting policies** used in preparing **financial statements**. It also covers **changes in accounting estimates** and corrections of **errors** in prior period financial statements.

Selection and application of accounting policies

Accounting policies are the specific principles, bases, conventions, rules and practices applied by a **micro-entity** in preparing and presenting financial statements. **8.2**

If this FRS specifically addresses a transaction, other event or condition, a micro-entity shall apply this FRS. However, the micro-entity need not follow a requirement in this FRS if the effect of doing so would not be **material**. This exemption does not apply to the disclosures required by paragraph 6.2(a). **8.3**

If this FRS does not specifically address a transaction, other event or condition, a micro-entity's management shall use its judgement in developing and applying an accounting policy that results in information that: **8.4**

(a) represents faithfully the transactions, other events or conditions;
(b) reflects the economic substance of the transactions, other events and conditions, and not merely the legal form;
(c) is neutral, ie free from bias; and
(d) is **prudent**.

In making the judgement described in paragraph 8.4, management shall refer to and consider the definitions, **recognition** criteria and **measurement** concepts for **assets**, **liabilities**, **income** and **expenses** and the pervasive principles in Section 2 *Concepts and Pervasive Principles*. A micro-entity is not required to provide any disclosures other than those required by Section 6 *Notes to the Financial Statements* in respect of these transactions or events. **8.5**

Consistency of accounting policies

A micro-entity shall select and apply its accounting policies consistently for similar transactions, other events and conditions. **8.6**

Changes in accounting policies

A micro-entity shall change an accounting policy only if the change: **8.7**

(a) is required by this FRS; or
(b) results in the financial statements providing reliable and more relevant information about the effects of transactions, other events or conditions on the micro-entity's **financial position** and financial **performance**.

The following are not changes in accounting policies: **8.8**

(a) the application of an accounting policy for transactions, other events or conditions that differ in substance from those previously occurring; and
(b) the application of a new accounting policy for transactions, other events or conditions that did not occur previously or were not material.

Applying changes in accounting policies

A micro-entity shall account for changes in accounting policy as follows: **8.9**

(a) a micro-entity shall account for a change in accounting policy resulting from a change in the requirements of this FRS in accordance with the transitional provisions, if any, specified in that amendment; and

(b)   a micro-entity shall account for all other changes in accounting policy retrospectively (see paragraph 8.10).

Retrospective application

8.10   When a change in accounting policy is applied retrospectively in accordance with paragraph 8.9, the micro-entity shall apply the new accounting policy to comparative information for prior periods to the earliest date for which it is practicable, as if the new accounting policy had always been applied. When it is **impracticable** to determine the individual-period effects of a change in accounting policy on comparative information for one or more prior periods presented, the micro-entity shall apply the new accounting policy to the **carrying amounts** of assets and liabilities as at the beginning of the earliest period for which **retrospective application** is practicable, which may be the current period, and shall make a corresponding adjustment to the opening balance of each affected component of **equity** for that period.

Changes in accounting estimates

8.11   A **change in accounting estimate** is an adjustment of the carrying amount of an asset or a liability, or the amount of the periodic consumption of an asset, that results from the assessment of the present status of, and expected future benefits and obligations associated with, assets and liabilities. Changes in accounting estimates result from new information or new developments and, accordingly, are not corrections of errors. When it is difficult to distinguish a change in an accounting policy from a change in an accounting estimate, the change is treated as a change in an accounting estimate.

8.12   A micro-entity shall recognise the effect of a change in an accounting estimate, other than a change to which paragraph 8.13 applies, **prospectively** by including it in **profit or loss** in:

(a)   the period of the change, if the change affects that period only; or

(b)   the period of the change and future periods, if the change affects both.

8.13   To the extent that a change in an accounting estimate gives rise to changes in assets and liabilities, or relates to an item of equity, the micro-entity shall recognise it by adjusting the carrying amount of the related asset, liability or equity item in the period of the change.

Corrections of prior period errors

8.14   Prior period errors are omissions from, and misstatements in, a micro-entity's financial statements for one or more prior periods arising from a failure to use, or misuse of, reliable information that:

(a)   was available when financial statements for those periods were authorised for issue; and

(b)   could reasonably be expected to have been obtained and taken into account in the preparation and presentation of those financial statements.

8.15   Such errors include the effects of mathematical mistakes, mistakes in applying accounting policies, oversights or misinterpretations of facts, and fraud.

8.16   To the extent practicable, a micro-entity shall correct a material prior period error retrospectively in the first financial statements authorised for issue after its discovery by:

(a) restating the comparative amounts for the prior period(s) presented in which the error occurred; or

(b) if the error occurred before the earliest prior period presented, restating the opening balances of assets, liabilities and equity for the earliest prior period presented.

When it is impracticable to determine the period-specific effects of a material error on comparative information for one or more prior periods presented, the micro-entity shall restate the opening balances of assets, liabilities and equity for the earliest period for which retrospective restatement is practicable (which may be the current period). **8.17**

Section 9 *Financial Instruments*

Scope of this section

This section deals with the **recognition, derecognition, measurement** and disclosure of **financial instruments (financial assets** and **financial liabilities).** **9.1**

All financial instruments are accounted for in accordance with this section, unless they are excluded by paragraph 9.3. Examples of financial instruments in the scope of this section include: **9.2**

(a) cash;

(b) accounts receivable and payable (trade debtors and creditors);

(c) commercial paper and commercial bills held;

(d) demand and fixed-term deposits with banks or similar institutions;

(e) bonds, loans and similar instruments;

(f) investments;

(g) options, warrants, futures contracts, forward contracts and interest rate swaps.

This section does not apply to the following financial instruments: **9.3**

(a) Financial instruments that meet the definition of a **micro-entity's** own **equity,** and the equity component of **compound financial instruments** issued by the reporting micro-entity that contain both a liability and an equity component (see Section 17 *Liabilities and Equity*).

(b) **Leases,** to which Section 15 *Leases* applies. However, the derecognition requirements in paragraphs 9.21 to 9.23 and impairment accounting requirements in paragraphs 9.16 to 9.19 apply to derecognition and impairment of receivables recognised by a lessor and the derecognition requirements in paragraphs 9.25 and 9.26 apply to payables recognised by a lessee arising under a **finance lease**.

(c) Employers' rights and obligations under employee benefit plans, to which Section 23 *Employee Benefits* applies.

(d) Financial instruments, contracts and obligations to which Section 21 *Share-based Payment* applies.

(e) Reimbursement assets and **financial guarantee contracts** accounted for in accordance with Section 16 *Provisions and Contingencies*.

(f) Contracts for contingent consideration in a **business combination** (see Section 14 *Business Combinations and Goodwill*). This exemption applies only to the acquirer.

Initial recognition of financial assets and liabilities

A micro-entity shall recognise a financial asset or a financial liability only when the micro-entity becomes a party to the contractual provisions of the instrument. **9.4**

Initial measurement

9.5   A financial asset or financial liability is recognised initially at its cost. The cost is measured at the transaction price.

Examples – Transaction price of a financial asset or liability

1 For a loan the transaction price is the amount borrowed or loaned.

2 For trade receivables or payables (trade debtors or trade creditors) the transaction price equals the invoice price unless payment is deferred beyond normal credit terms (see paragraph 9.6).

3 For an investment the transaction price is the consideration given (eg cash paid to acquire the investment).

4 For an option the transaction price is the premium paid to purchase the option.

9.6   When a micro-entity purchases **inventory, property, plant and equipment, investment property** or sells goods or services with settlement deferred beyond normal credit terms, the transaction price is the cash price available on the date of the transaction (see Sections 10 *Inventories*, 12 *Property, Plant and Equipment* and *Investment Property* and 18 *Revenue* respectively).

Example – Transaction price when payment is deferred

A micro-entity sells goods to a customer for CU100. Customers are usually required to pay within 14 days of the invoice date, but the micro-entity agrees with the customer that payment will be deferred for one year. The micro-entity sells the same item for CU90, if payment is received within the usual credit terms.

The cash price for the goods and thereby the transaction price is CU90.

9.7   **Transaction costs** shall be added to the cost of a financial asset or shall be deducted from the cost of a financial liability, unless they are not **material** in which case they are recognised immediately as an **expense** in **profit or loss**.

Examples – Transaction costs

1 A micro-entity receives a bank loan of CU500. The bank charges CU5 in arrangement fees. The micro-entity determines that the transaction costs are immaterial and recognises them immediately in profit or loss as an expense. The cost of the loan is CU500.

2 A micro-entity is making an investment and buys shares in another entity for CU1,000. The micro-entity incurs legal fees and other transaction costs totalling CU100. The micro-entity determines that the transaction costs are material and includes them in the cost of the investment. The total cost of the investment is CU1,100.

3 A micro-entity takes out a forward foreign currency exchange contract and is charged a fee of CU30. The micro-entity determines that the transaction costs are material. The total cost of the forward foreign currency exchange contract is CU30.

Subsequent measurement

At the end of each **reporting period**, a micro-entity shall measure financial instruments **9.8** as follows, without any deduction for transaction costs the micro-entity may incur on sale or other disposal:

(a) Investments in preference shares or **ordinary shares** and investments in **subsidiaries** and **associates** and interests in **jointly controlled entities** shall be measured at cost less impairment.

(b) **Derivatives** shall be measured as set out in paragraph 9.10.

(c) Financial instruments other than those covered by paragraphs (a) and (b) shall be measured as set out in paragraphs 9.12 to 9.15.

All financial assets must be assessed for impairment or uncollectability. See paragraphs 9.16 to 9.19.

Derivatives

Derivatives include forward foreign currency exchange contracts and interest rate swaps. **9.9** More examples are given in paragraph 9.2(g).

The transaction price of a financial instrument that is a derivative plus any transaction **9.10** costs not immediately recognised in profit or loss (see paragraph 9.7) less any **impairment losses** recognised to date, is allocated to profit or loss over the term of the contract on a straight-line basis, unless another systematic basis of allocation is more appropriate.

Contractual payments

Under a derivative contract a micro-entity may be required to make or may be entitled to **9.11** receive payments. A micro-entity shall recognise amounts payable or receivable as they accrue.

Financial instruments measured in accordance with paragraph 9.8(c)

Financial instruments other than those covered in paragraphs 9.8(a) and 9.8(b) are **9.12** measured as follows:

(a) the transaction price (see paragraph 9.5);

(b) plus, in the case of a financial asset, or minus in the case of a financial liability, transaction costs not yet recognised in profit or loss (see paragraph 9.15);

(c) plus the cumulative interest income or expense recognised in profit or loss to date (see paragraphs 9.13 and 9.14);

(d) minus all repayments of principal and all interest payments or receipts to date;

(e) minus, in the case of a financial asset, any reduction (directly or through the use of an allowance account) for impairment or uncollectability (see paragraphs 9.16 to 9.19).

Allocation of interest income or expense

Total interest income or expense is the difference between the initial transaction price and **9.13** the total amount of the subsequent contractual receipts or payments, excluding transaction costs.

A micro-entity shall allocate total interest income or expense over the term of the contract **9.14** as follows:

(a)   For transactions where settlement is deferred beyond normal credit terms (see paragraph 9.6), total interest income or expense shall be allocated on a straight-line basis over the term of the contract.

(b)   In all other cases, interest income or expense is allocated at a constant rate on the financial asset's or financial liability's **carrying amount** excluding transaction costs not yet recognised in profit or loss (see paragraph 9.12(b)). The applicable rate will normally be the contractual rate of interest and may be a variable or a fixed rate.

Transaction costs

9.15   Transaction costs not immediately recognised in profit or loss in accordance with paragraph 9.7, are recognised in profit or loss on a straight-line basis over the term of the contract.

Example 1: Measurement of a loan liability

A micro-entity receives a loan of CU1,000 on 1 January 20X0. The micro-entity pays loan arrangement fees of CU50. The contractual interest rate is five per cent payable annually in arrears on 31 December. The loan is repayable after two years. The micro-entity's annual reporting period ends on 31 December.

The micro-entity determines that the loan arrangement fees (transaction costs) are material and on 1 January 20X0 recognises the loan at its transaction price of CU1,000 less the transaction costs of CU50. The transactions costs of CU50 are recognised in the profit and loss account on a straight-line basis over two years, ie CU25 each year.

The carrying value of the loan is as follows:

Year	Carrying amount at 1 Jan	Interest at 5%	Transaction costs in profit or loss	Cash payments	Carrying amount at 31 Dec
	CU	CU	CU	CU	CU
20X0	(950)	(50)	(25)	50	(975)
20X1	(975)	(50)	(25)	1,050	0

Example 2: Measurement of a loan asset

A micro-entity makes an interest-free loan of CU900 on 1 January 20X0. The loan is repayable after two years. In 20X1 the micro-entity agrees that the borrower only needs to repay CU450 which is paid on 31 December 20X1. The micro-entity's annual reporting period ends on 31 December.

The loan is recognised at its transaction price of CU900 on 1 January 20X0. In 20X1 an impairment loss for the uncollectability of CU450 is recognised. The carrying amount of the loan is as follows:

Year	Carrying amount at 1 Jan	Impairment	Cash receipts	Carrying amount at 31 Dec
	CU	CU	CU	CU
20X0	900	-	-	900
20X1	900	(450)	(450)	0

Impairment of financial assets

Recognition and measurement

At the end of each reporting period, a micro-entity shall assess whether there is evidence   **9.16**
of impairment of any financial asset.

Evidence that a financial asset could be impaired includes the following events: **9.17**

(a)   significant financial difficulty of the debtor;
(b)   a breach of contract, such as a default or delinquency in interest or principal payments;
(c)   the creditor, for economic or legal reasons relating to the debtor's financial difficulty, granting to the debtor a concession that the creditor would not otherwise consider;
(d)   it has become **probable** that the debtor will enter bankruptcy or other financial reorganisation;
(e)   declining market values of the asset or similar assets;
(f)   significant changes with an adverse effect on the asset that have taken place in the technological, market, economic or legal environment; and
(g)   the contract has become an **onerous contract**.

A micro-entity shall measure an impairment loss for financial assets as set out below. An   **9.18**
impairment loss is immediately recognised in profit or loss.

(a)   An investment in preference shares or ordinary shares and an investment in subsidiaries and associates and an interest in jointly controlled entities is impaired and an impairment loss shall be recognised if the asset's carrying amount exceeds the best estimate of the asset's selling price as at the **reporting date**.
(b)   An asset that is a derivative is impaired and an impairment loss shall be recognised if the asset's carrying value exceeds the asset's **fair value less costs to sell**.
(c)   An asset measured in accordance with paragraph 9.8(c), is impaired and an impairment loss shall be recognised, if the asset's carrying amount exceeds the total of estimated net cash flows that can be generated from the asset. When the effect of the time value of money is material, the amount of the net cash flows shall be the present value of the estimated net cash flows. The discount rate shall be the asset's current contractual interest rate.

Reversal

A micro-entity shall reverse a previously recognised impairment loss if in a subsequent   **9.19**
period the amount of an impairment loss decreases and the decrease can be related to an
event occurring after the impairment was recognised (eg an improvement in the debtor's
credit rating). The micro-entity shall recognise the amount of the reversal in profit or loss
immediately.

Onerous contracts

At each reporting date a micro-entity shall assess whether a derivative constitutes an   **9.20**
onerous contract. A derivative is an onerous contract when the expected unavoidable
payments exceed the economic benefits expected to be received from the derivative. A
derivative which does not mitigate a specific risk or risks of a micro-entity is an onerous
contract when the expected payments exceed the expected cash receipts under the contract.
The present obligation arising from an onerous contract shall be measured in accordance
with Section 16.

Example: Assessment of whether a derivative is onerous

A micro-entity takes out a loan with a variable rate of interest. In order to mitigate the risk of fluctuating interest payments, the micro-entity enters into an interest rate swap. Through the interest rate swap the micro-entity pays a fixed rate of interest and receives a variable rate of interest equal to the interest on the loan.

Scenario 1:

Interest rates are going down and as a result the payments made by the micro-entity under the interest rate swap are higher than the receipts. The interest rate swap is not an onerous contract because the micro-entity continues to benefit from the interest rate swap by effectively paying a fixed rate of interest on the loan.

Scenario 2:

The micro-entity repays the loan early, but the interest rate swap cannot be terminated. The micro-entity expects that the payments due under the interest rate swap exceed the receipts. The interest rate swap is an onerous contract because the micro-entity no longer derives a benefit from it.

Derecognition of a financial asset

9.21   A micro-entity shall derecognise a financial asset only when:

(a)   the contractual rights to the cash flows from the financial asset expire or are settled;

(b)   the micro-entity transfers to another party substantially all of the risks (eg slow or non-payment risk) and rewards of ownership (eg future cash flows from a debtor); or

(c)   when no future economic benefits are expected from holding it or its disposal.

9.22   A micro-entity shall recognise any **gain** or loss on the derecognition of a financial asset in profit or loss when the item is derecognised.

9.23   If a micro-entity received any proceeds from the transfer of a financial asset, but the conditions in paragraph 9.21 are not met, a micro-entity shall continue to recognise the asset in its entirety and shall recognise a financial liability for the consideration received. The asset and liability shall not be offset. In subsequent periods, the micro-entity shall recognise any **income** on the transferred asset and any expense incurred on the financial liability.

Example 1: Debt factoring arrangement that qualifies for derecognition

A micro-entity sells a group of its accounts receivable to a bank at less than their carrying amount. The micro-entity is obliged to remit promptly to the bank all amounts collected, but it has no obligation to the bank for slow payment or non-payment by the debtors.

In this case, the micro-entity has transferred to the bank substantially all of the risks and rewards of ownership of the receivables. Accordingly, it removes the receivables from its statement of financial position (ie derecognises them), and it shows no liability in respect of the proceeds received from the bank. The micro-entity recognises a loss calculated as the difference between the carrying amount of the receivables at the time of sale and the proceeds received from the bank. The micro-entity recognises a liability to the extent that it has collected funds from the debtors but has not yet remitted them to the bank.

Example 2: Debt factoring arrangement that does not qualify for derecognition

The facts are the same as in the preceding example except that the micro-entity has agreed to buy back from the bank any receivables for which the debtor is in arrears as to principal or interest for more than 120 days.

In this case, the micro-entity has retained the risk of slow payment or non-payment by the debtors – a significant risk with respect to receivables. Accordingly, the micro-entity does not treat the receivables as having been sold to the bank, and it does not derecognise them. Instead, it treats the proceeds from the bank as a loan. The micro-entity continues to recognise the receivables as an asset until they are collected or written off as uncollectible.

Transfers of non-cash collateral

When a micro-entity participates in arrangements where it provides or receives financial assets other than cash as collateral (eg a micro-entity pledges commercial papers as security against a loan), the micro-entity shall apply the requirements of paragraphs 11.35(b) to 11.35(d) of **FRS 102**.   **9.24**

Derecognition of a financial liability

A micro-entity shall derecognise a financial liability (or a part of a financial liability) only when it is extinguished – ie when the obligation specified in the contract is discharged, is cancelled or expires.   **9.25**

A micro-entity shall recognise any gain or loss on the derecognition of a financial liability (or a part of a financial liability) in profit or loss when the item is derecognised.   **9.26**

Presentation

A financial asset and a financial liability shall be offset and the net amount presented in the **statement of financial position** when, and only when, a micro-entity: **9.27**

(a) currently has a legally enforceable right to set off the recognised amounts; and
(b) intends either to settle on a net basis, or to realise the asset and settle the liability simultaneously.

Disclosures in the notes

A micro-entity shall determine the amount of any financial commitments, guarantees and contingencies not recognised in the statement of financial position arising from its financial instruments and disclose that amount within the total amount of financial commitments, guarantees and contingencies (see paragraph 6A.2).   **9.28**

A micro-entity shall disclose an indication of the nature and form of any financial asset given as security in respect of its commitments, guarantees and contingencies (see paragraph 6A.3).   **9.29**

Section 10 *Inventories*

Scope of this section

This section sets out the principles for recognising and measuring **inventories**.   **10.1**

10.2   This section applies to all inventories, except:

(a)   work in progress arising under **construction contracts**, including directly related service contracts (see Section 18 *Revenue*); and

(b)   **biological assets** related to **agricultural activity** and **agricultural produce** at the point of harvest (see Section 27 *Specialised Activities*).

Measurement of inventories

10.3   A **micro-entity** shall measure inventories at the lower of cost and estimated selling price less costs to complete and sell.

Cost of inventories

10.4   A micro-entity shall include in the cost of inventories all costs of purchase, costs of conversion and other costs incurred in bringing the inventories to their present location and condition.

10.5   Where inventories are acquired through a **non-exchange transaction**, their cost shall be measured at their **fair value** at the date of acquisition.

Costs of purchase

10.6   The costs of purchase of inventories comprise the purchase price, import duties and other taxes (other than those subsequently recoverable by the micro-entity from the taxing authorities), and transport, handling and other costs directly attributable to the acquisition of finished goods, materials and services. Trade discounts, rebates and other similar items are deducted in determining the costs of purchase.

10.7   If payment is deferred beyond normal credit terms, the purchase price is the cash price available at the date of purchase. Any excess of the deferred payment amount over the cash price available at the date of purchase is recognised as interest and accounted for in accordance with paragraph 9.14(a).

Costs of conversion

10.8   The costs of conversion of inventories include costs directly related to the units of production, such as direct labour. They also include a systematic allocation of fixed and variable production overheads that are incurred in converting materials into finished goods. Fixed production overheads are those indirect costs of production that remain relatively constant regardless of the volume of production, such as **depreciation** and maintenance of factory buildings and equipment, and the cost of factory management and administration. Variable production overheads are those indirect costs of production that vary directly, or nearly directly, with the volume of production, such as indirect materials and indirect labour.

10.9   Production overheads include the costs for obligations (recognised and measured in accordance with Section 16 *Provisions and Contingencies*) for dismantling, removing and restoring a site on which an item of **property, plant and equipment** is located that are incurred during the **reporting period** as a consequence of having used that item of property, plant and equipment to produce inventory during that period.

Allocation of production overheads

A micro-entity shall allocate fixed production overheads to the costs of conversion on the basis of the normal capacity of the production facilities. Normal capacity is the production expected to be achieved on average over a number of periods or seasons under normal circumstances, taking into account the loss of capacity resulting from planned maintenance. The actual level of production may be used if it approximates normal capacity. The amount of fixed overhead allocated to each unit of production is not increased as a consequence of low production or idle plant. Unallocated overheads are recognised as an **expense** in the period in which they are incurred. In periods of abnormally high production, the amount of fixed overhead allocated to each unit of production is decreased so that inventories are not measured above cost. Variable production overheads are allocated to each unit of production on the basis of the actual use of the production facilities. **10.10**

Other costs included in inventories

A micro-entity shall include other costs in the cost of inventories only to the extent that they are incurred in bringing the inventories to their present location and condition. **10.11**

Costs excluded from inventories

Examples of costs excluded from the cost of inventories and recognised as expenses in the period in which they are incurred are: **10.12**

(a) abnormal amounts of wasted materials, labour or other production costs;
(b) storage costs, unless those costs are necessary during the production process before a further production stage;
(c) administrative overheads that do not contribute to bringing inventories to their present location and condition; and
(d) selling costs.

Cost of inventories of a service provider

To the extent that service providers have inventories, they measure them at the costs of their production. These costs consist primarily of the labour and other costs of personnel directly engaged in providing the service, including supervisory personnel, and attributable overheads. Labour and other costs relating to sales and general administrative personnel are not included but are recognised as expenses in the period in which they are incurred. The cost of inventories of a service provider does not include profit margins or non-attributable overheads that are often factored into prices charged by service providers. **10.13**

Cost of agricultural produce harvested from biological assets

Section 27 requires that inventories comprising agricultural produce that a micro-entity has harvested from its biological assets should be measured on initial **recognition**, at the point of harvest, at the lower of cost and estimated selling price less costs to complete and sell. This becomes the cost of the inventories at that date for application of this section. **10.14**

Techniques for measuring cost, such as standard costing, retail method and most recent purchase price

A micro-entity may use techniques such as the standard cost method, the retail method or most recent purchase price for measuring the cost of inventories if the result approximates **10.15** cost. Standard costs take into account normal levels of materials and supplies, labour, efficiency and capacity utilisation. They are regularly reviewed and, if necessary, revised in the light of current conditions. The retail method measures cost by reducing the sales value of the inventory by the appropriate percentage gross margin.

Cost formulas

10.16 A micro-entity shall measure the cost of inventories of items that are not ordinarily interchangeable and goods or services produced and segregated for specific projects by using specific identification of their individual costs.

10.17 A micro-entity shall measure the cost of inventories, other than those dealt with in paragraph 10.16, by using the first-in, first-out (FIFO) or weighted average cost formula. A micro-entity shall use the same cost formula for all inventories having a similar nature and use to the micro-entity. For inventories with a different nature or use, different cost formulas may be justified. The last-in, first-out method (LIFO) is not permitted by this FRS.

Impairment of inventories

10.18 Implicit in the requirement for a micro-entity to measure inventories at the lower of cost and estimated selling price less costs to complete, is a requirement that a micro-entity shall assess at the end of each reporting period whether any inventories are impaired, ie the **carrying amount** is not fully recoverable (eg because of damage, obsolescence or declining selling prices). If an item (or group of items) of inventory is impaired, the micro-entity shall recognise an **impairment loss**.

10.19 When the circumstances that previously caused inventories to be impaired no longer exist or when there is clear evidence of an increase in selling price less costs to complete and sell because of changed economic circumstances, the micro-entity shall reverse the amount of the impairment (ie the reversal is limited to the amount of the original impairment loss).

Recognition as an expense

10.20 When inventories are sold, the micro-entity shall recognise the carrying amount of those inventories as an expense in the period in which the related **revenue** is recognised.

10.21 Some inventories may be allocated to other asset accounts, for example, inventory used as a component of self-constructed property, plant or equipment. Inventories allocated to another **asset** in this way are accounted for subsequently in accordance with the section of this FRS relevant to that type of asset.

Disclosure in the notes

10.22 A micro-entity shall disclose an indication of the nature and form of any items of inventory given as security in respect of its commitments, guarantees and contingencies (see paragraph 6A.3).

Section 11 *Investments in Joint Ventures*

Scope of this section

This section applies to the accounting for investments in **joint ventures** that are **jointly controlled** operations and jointly controlled **assets**. | **11.1**

A **micro-entity** shall refer to Section 7 *Subsidiaries, Associates, Jointly Controlled Entities and Intermediate Payment Arrangements* which sets out the requirements for investments in joint ventures that are **jointly controlled entities**. | **11.2**

Joint ventures defined

Joint control is the contractually agreed sharing of **control** over an economic activity, and exists only when the strategic financial and operating decisions relating to the activity require the unanimous consent of the parties sharing control (the **venturers**). | **11.3**

A joint venture is a contractual arrangement whereby two or more parties undertake an economic activity that is subject to joint control. Joint ventures can take the form of jointly controlled operations, jointly controlled assets, or jointly controlled entities. | **11.4**

Jointly controlled operations

The operation of some joint ventures involves the use of the assets and other resources of the venturers rather than the establishment of a corporation, partnership or other entity, or a financial structure that is separate from the venturers themselves. Each venturer uses its own **property, plant and equipment** and carries its own **inventories**. It also incurs its own **expenses** and **liabilities** and raises its own finance, which represent its own obligations. The joint venture activities may be carried out by the venturer's employees alongside the venturer's similar activities. The joint venture agreement usually provides a means by which the **revenue** from the sale of the joint product and any expenses incurred in common are shared among the venturers. | **11.5**

In respect of its interests in jointly controlled operations, a venturer shall recognise in its **financial statements**: | **11.6**

(a)   the assets that it controls and the liabilities that it incurs; and
(b)   the expenses that it incurs and its share of the **income** that it earns from the sale of goods or services by the joint venture.

Jointly controlled assets

Some joint ventures involve the joint control, and often the joint ownership, by the venturers of one or more assets contributed to, or acquired for the purpose of, the joint venture and dedicated to the purposes of the joint venture. | **11.7**

In respect of its interest in a jointly controlled asset, a venturer shall recognise in its financial statements: | **11.8**

(a)   its share of the jointly controlled assets, classified in accordance with the format adopted set out in Section 4 *Statement of Financial Position*;
(b)   any liabilities that it has incurred;
(c)   its share of any liabilities incurred jointly with the other venturers in relation to the joint venture;

(d)   any income from the sale or use of its share of the output of the joint venture, together with its share of any expenses incurred by the joint venture; and

(e)   any expenses that it has incurred in respect of its interest in the joint venture.

Disclosure in the notes

11.9   A micro-entity shall determine the amount of any financial commitments, guarantees and contingencies not recognised in the **statement of financial position** arising from its jointly controlled operations and jointly controlled assets and disclose that amount within the total amount of financial commitments, guarantees and contingencies (see paragraph 6A.2).

Section 12 *Property, Plant and Equipment and Investment Property*

Scope of this section

12.1   This section applies to the accounting for **property, plant and equipment** and **investment property**.

12.2   Property, plant and equipment does not include **biological assets** related to **agricultural activity** (see Section 27 *Specialised Activities*).

Recognition

12.3   A **micro-entity** shall recognise the cost of an item of property, plant and equipment or investment property as an **asset** if, and only if:

(a)   it is **probable** that future economic benefits associated with the item will flow to the micro-entity; and

(b)   the cost of the item can be measured reliably.

12.4   Spare parts and servicing equipment are usually carried as **inventory** and recognised in **profit or loss** as consumed. However, major spare parts and stand-by equipment are property, plant and equipment when a micro-entity expects to use them during more than one period. Similarly, if the spare parts and servicing equipment can be used only in connection with an item of property, plant and equipment, they are considered property, plant and equipment.

12.5   Parts of some items of property, plant and equipment or investment property may require replacement at regular intervals (eg the roof of a building). A micro-entity shall add to the **carrying amount** of an item of property, plant and equipment or investment property the cost of replacing part of such an item when that cost is incurred if the replacement part is expected to provide incremental future benefits to the micro-entity. The carrying amount of those parts that are replaced is derecognised in accordance with paragraphs 12.26 and 12.27.

12.6   A condition of continuing to operate an item of property, plant and equipment (eg a bus) or investment property may be performing regular major inspections for faults regardless of whether parts of the item are replaced. When each major inspection is performed, its cost is recognised in the carrying amount of the item of property, plant and equipment or investment property as a replacement if the **recognition** criteria are satisfied. Any remaining carrying amount of the cost of the previous major inspection (as distinct from physical parts) is derecognised. This is done regardless of whether the cost of the previous major inspection was identified in the transaction in which the item was acquired or constructed. If necessary, the estimated cost of a future similar inspection may be used as an indication of what the cost of the existing inspection component was when the item was acquired or constructed.

Land and buildings are separable assets, and a micro-entity shall account for them separately, even when they are acquired together.   **12.7**

Measurement at initial recognition

A micro-entity shall measure an item of property, plant and equipment or investment property at initial recognition at its cost.   **12.8**

Elements of cost

The cost of an item of property, plant and equipment or investment property comprises all of the following: **12.9**

(a)   Its purchase price, including legal and brokerage fees, import duties and non-refundable purchase taxes, after deducting trade discounts and rebates.

(b)   Any costs directly attributable to bringing the asset to the location and condition necessary for it to be capable of operating in the manner intended by management. These can include the costs of site preparation, initial delivery and handling, installation and assembly, and testing of functionality.

(c)   The initial estimate of the costs, recognised and measured in accordance with Section 16 *Provisions and Contingencies*, of dismantling and removing the item and restoring the site on which it is located, the obligation for which a micro-entity incurs either when the item is acquired or as a consequence of having used the item during a particular period for purposes other than to produce inventories during that period.

The following costs are not costs of an item of property, plant and equipment or investment property, and a micro-entity shall recognise them as an **expense** when they are incurred: **12.10**

(a)   costs of opening a new facility;

(b)   costs of introducing a new product or service (including costs of advertising and promotional activities);

(c)   costs of conducting business in a new location or with a new class of customer (including costs of staff training); and

(d)   administration and other general overhead costs.

The **income** and related **expenses** of incidental operations during construction or development of an item of property, plant and equipment or investment property are recognised in **profit or loss** if those operations are not necessary to bring the item to its intended location and operating condition.   **12.11**

Measurement of cost

The cost of an item of property, plant and equipment or investment property is the cash price equivalent at the recognition date. If payment is deferred beyond normal credit terms, the cost is the cash price available at the recognition date. Any excess of the deferred payment amount over the cash price available at the recognition date is recognised as interest and accounted for in accordance with paragraph 9.14(a).   **12.12**

Exchanges of assets

12.13   An item of property, plant or equipment or investment property may be acquired in exchange for a non-monetary asset or assets, or a combination of monetary and non-monetary assets. A micro-entity shall measure the cost of the acquired asset at **fair value** unless:

(a)   the exchange transaction lacks commercial substance; or

(b)   the fair value of neither the asset received nor the asset given up is reliably measurable. In that case, the asset's cost is measured at the carrying amount of the asset given up.

Measurement after initial recognition

12.14   A micro-entity shall measure all items of property, plant and equipment and investment property after initial recognition at cost less any accumulated **depreciation** and any accumulated **impairment losses**. A micro-entity shall recognise the costs of day-to-day servicing of an item of property, plant and equipment or investment property in profit or loss in the period in which the costs are incurred.

Depreciation

12.15   If the major components of an item of property, plant and equipment or investment property have significantly different patterns of consumption of economic benefits, a micro-entity shall allocate the initial cost of the asset to its major components and depreciate each such component separately over its **useful life**. Other assets shall be depreciated over their useful lives as a single asset. There are some exceptions, such as land which generally has an unlimited useful life and therefore is not usually depreciated.

12.16   The depreciation charge for each period shall be recognised in profit or loss unless another section of this FRS requires the cost to be recognised as part of the cost of an asset. For example, the depreciation of manufacturing property, plant and equipment is included in the costs of inventories (see Section 10 *Inventories*).

Depreciable amount and depreciation period

12.17   A micro-entity shall allocate the **depreciable amount** of an asset on a systematic basis over its useful life.

12.18   Factors may indicate that the **residual value** or useful life of an asset has changed since the most recent annual **reporting date**. If such indicators are present, a micro-entity shall review its previous estimates and, if current expectations differ, amend the residual value, depreciation method or useful life. The micro-entity shall account for the change in residual value, depreciation method or useful life as a change in an accounting estimate in accordance with paragraphs 8.11 to 8.13.

12.19   Depreciation of an asset begins when it is available for use, ie when it is in the location and condition necessary for it to be capable of operating in the manner intended by management. Depreciation of an asset ceases when the asset is derecognised. Depreciation does not cease when the asset becomes idle or is retired from active use unless the asset is fully depreciated. However, under usage methods of depreciation the depreciation charge can be zero while there is no production.

A micro-entity shall consider all the following factors in determining the useful life of an asset: **12.20**

(a) The expected usage of the asset. Usage is assessed by reference to the asset's expected capacity or physical output.

(b) Expected physical wear and tear, which depends on operational factors such as the number of shifts for which the asset is to be used and the repair and maintenance programme, and the care and maintenance of the asset while idle.

(c) Technical or commercial obsolescence arising from changes or improvements in production, or from a change in the market demand for the product or service output of the asset.

(d) Legal or similar limits on the use of the asset, such as the expiry dates of related **leases**.

Depreciation method

A micro-entity shall select a depreciation method that reflects the pattern in which it expects to consume the asset's future economic benefits. The possible depreciation methods include the straight-line method, the diminishing balance method and a method based on usage such as the units of production method. **12.21**

If there is an indication that there has been a significant change since the last annual reporting date in the pattern by which a micro-entity expects to consume an asset's future economic benefits, the micro-entity shall review its present depreciation method and, if current expectations differ, change the depreciation method to reflect the new pattern. The micro-entity shall account for the change as a change in an accounting estimate in accordance with paragraphs 8.11 to 8.13. **12.22**

Impairment

Recognition and measurement of impairment

At each reporting date, a micro-entity shall apply Section 22 *Impairment of Assets* to determine whether an item or group of items of property, plant and equipment or investment property is impaired and, if so, how to recognise and measure the impairment loss. That section explains when and how a micro-entity reviews the carrying amount of its assets, how it determines the **recoverable amount** of an asset, and when it recognises or reverses an impairment loss. **12.23**

Compensation for impairment

An entity shall include in profit or loss, compensation from third parties for items of property, plant and equipment or investment property that were impaired, lost or given up only when the compensation is virtually certain. **12.24**

Property, plant and equipment or investment property held for sale

Paragraph 22.7(f) states that a plan to dispose of an asset before the previously expected date is an indicator of impairment that triggers the calculation of the asset's recoverable amount for the purpose of determining whether the asset is impaired. **12.25**

Derecognition

12.26   A micro-entity shall **derecognise** an item of property, plant and equipment or investment property:

(a)   on disposal; or

(b)   when no future economic benefits are expected from its use or disposal.

12.27   A micro-entity shall recognise the **gain** or loss on the derecognition of an item of property, plant and equipment or investment property in profit or loss when the item is derecognised (unless Section 15 *Leases* requires otherwise on a sale and leaseback). The micro-entity shall not classify such gains as **turnover** in the **income statement**.

Disclosure in the notes

12.28   A micro-entity shall determine the amount of any financial commitments not recognised in the **statement of financial position** for the acquisition of property, plant and equipment or investment property and disclose that amount within the total amount of financial commitments, guarantees and contingencies (see paragraph 6A.2).

12.29   A micro-entity shall disclose an indication of the nature and form of any items of property, plant and equipment or investment property given as security in respect of its commitments, guarantees and contingencies (see paragraph 6A.3).

Section 13 *Intangible Assets other than Goodwill*

Scope of this section

13.1   This section applies to the accounting for all separately acquired **intangible assets** and internally generated intangible assets, other than intangible assets held by a **micro-entity** for sale in the ordinary course of business (see Section 10 *Inventories* and Section 18 *Revenue*).

13.2   For the accounting of intangible assets acquired as part of a **business combination** including **goodwill** see Section 14 *Business Combinations and Goodwill*.

Recognition

13.3   A micro-entity shall recognise all separately acquired intangible assets.

13.4   An internally generated intangible shall not be recognised as an **asset**. All expenditure incurred shall be recognised as an **expense** immediately in **profit or loss**.

13.5   A micro-entity shall recognise the expenditure on the following items as an expense and shall not recognise such expenditure as intangible assets (the list is not exhaustive):

(a)   Expenditure on **research** and **development** activities.

(b)   Internally generated brands, logos, publishing titles, customer lists and items similar in substance.

(c)   Start-up activities (ie start-up costs), which include establishment costs such as legal and secretarial costs incurred in establishing a legal entity, expenditure to open a new facility or business (ie pre-opening costs) and expenditure for starting new operations or launching new products or processes (ie pre-operating costs).

(d)   Training activities.

(e)   Advertising and promotional activities.

(f)   Relocating or reorganising part or all of a micro-entity.

(g)   Internally generated goodwill.

Initial measurement

A micro-entity shall measure a separately acquired intangible asset initially at cost which comprises: **13.6**

(a)   its purchase price, including import duties and non-refundable purchase taxes, after deducting trade discounts and rebates; and

(b)   any directly attributable cost of preparing the asset for its intended use.

Exchanges of assets

An intangible asset may be acquired in exchange for a non-monetary asset or assets, or a combination of monetary and non-monetary assets. A micro-entity shall measure the cost of such an intangible asset at **fair value** unless: **13.7**

(a)   the exchange transaction lacks commercial substance; or

(b)   the fair value of neither the asset received nor the asset given up is reliably measurable. In that case, the asset's cost is measured at the **carrying amount** of the asset given up.

Measurement after initial recognition

A micro-entity shall measure a separately acquired intangible asset after initial recognition at cost less any accumulated **amortisation** and any accumulated **impairment losses**. The requirements for amortisation are set out in paragraphs 13.9 to 13.14. **13.8**

Amortisation over useful life

Intangible assets shall be considered to have a finite **useful life**. The useful life of an intangible asset that arises from contractual or other legal rights shall not exceed the period of the contractual or other legal rights, but may be shorter depending on the period over which the micro-entity expects to use the asset. If the contractual or other legal rights are conveyed for a limited term that can be renewed, the useful life of the intangible asset shall include the renewal period(s) only if there is evidence to support renewal by the micro-entity without significant cost. **13.9**

If, in exceptional cases, a micro-entity is unable to make a reliable estimate of the useful life of an intangible asset, the life shall not exceed ten years. **13.10**

Amortisation period and amortisation method

A micro-entity shall allocate the **depreciable amount** of an intangible asset on a systematic basis over its useful life. The amortisation charge for each period shall be recognised in profit or loss, unless another section of this FRS requires the cost to be recognised as part of the cost of an asset. For example, the amortisation of an intangible asset may be included in the costs of **inventories** or **property, plant and equipment**. **13.11**

Amortisation begins when the intangible asset is available for use, ie when it is in the location and condition necessary for it to be usable in the manner intended by management. Amortisation ceases when the asset is derecognised. The micro-entity shall choose an **13.12** amortisation method that reflects the pattern in which it expects to consume the asset's future economic benefits. If the micro-entity cannot determine that pattern reliably, it shall use the straight-line method.

Residual value

13.13   A micro-entity shall assume that the **residual value** of an intangible asset is zero unless:

(a)   there is a commitment by a third party to purchase the asset at the end of its useful life; or

(b)   there is an **active market** for the asset and:

    (i)   residual value can be determined by reference to that market; and

    (ii)   it is **probable** that such a market will exist at the end of the asset's useful life.

Review of amortisation period and amortisation method

13.14   Factors may indicate that the residual value or useful life of an intangible asset has changed since the most recent annual **reporting date**. If such indicators are present, a micro-entity shall review its previous estimates and, if current expectations differ, amend the residual value, amortisation method or useful life. The micro-entity shall account for the change in residual value, amortisation method or useful life as a change in an accounting estimate in accordance with paragraphs 8.11 to 8.13.

Recoverability of the carrying amount—impairment losses

13.15   To determine whether a separately acquired intangible asset is impaired, a micro-entity shall apply Section 22 *Impairment of Assets*. That section explains when and how a micro-entity reviews the carrying amount of its assets, how it determines the **recoverable amount** of an asset, and when it recognises or reverses an **impairment loss**.

Retirements and disposals

13.16   A micro-entity shall derecognise a separately acquired intangible asset, and shall recognise a **gain** or loss in profit or loss:

(a)   on disposal; or

(b)   when no future economic benefits are expected from its use or disposal.

Disclosure in the notes

13.17   A micro-entity shall determine the amount of any financial commitments, guarantees and contingencies not recognised in the **statement of financial position** for the acquisition of separately acquired intangible assets and disclose that amount within the total amount of financial commitments, guarantees and contingencies (see paragraph 6A.2).

13.18   A micro-entity shall disclose an indication of the nature and form of any intangible assets given as security in respect of its commitments, guarantees and contingencies (see paragraph 6A.3).

Section 14 *Business Combinations and Goodwill*

Accounting for a trade and asset acquisition

Where a **micro-entity** effects a **business combination** by acquiring the trade and **assets**   **14.1**
of another **business,** it shall apply Section 19 *Business Combinations and Goodwill* of
FRS 102, except for the following:

(a)   a micro-entity shall not separately identify and recognise **intangible assets**;
(b)   a micro-entity shall not recognise a **deferred tax asset** or **liability**;
(c)   a micro-entity shall not apply paragraph 19.23 of FRS 102, but instead apply
      paragraph 14.2 of this FRS;
(d)   a micro-entity shall not recognise and measure a **share-based payment transaction**
      in accordance with Section 28 *Employee Benefit* of FRS 102, but instead apply
      Section 23 *Employee Benefits* of this FRS; and
(e)   a micro-entity is not required to provide any of the disclosures.

Goodwill arising on a trade and asset acquisition

Where a micro-entity has recognised **goodwill** acquired in a trade and asset acquisition   **14.2**
(in accordance with paragraph 19.22 of FRS 102), the micro-entity shall measure that
goodwill at cost less accumulated **amortisation** and accumulated **impairment losses**:

(a)   A micro-entity shall follow the principles in paragraphs 13.9 to 13.14 of this FRS for
      amortisation of goodwill. Goodwill shall be considered to have a finite **useful life**,
      and shall be amortised on a systematic basis over its life. If, in exceptional cases, a
      micro-entity is unable to make a reliable estimate of the useful life of goodwill, the
      life shall not exceed ten years.
(b)   A micro-entity shall follow Section 22 *Impairment of Assets* of this FRS for
      recognising and measuring the impairment of goodwill.

Disclosure in the notes

A micro-entity shall determine the amount of any financial commitments, guarantees and   **14.3**
contingencies not recognised in the **statement of financial position** for trade and asset
acquisitions and disclose that amount within the total amount of financial commitments,
guarantees and contingencies (see paragraph 6A.2).

Section 15 *Leases*

Scope of this section

This section covers accounting for all **leases** other than licensing agreements for such   **15.1**
items as motion picture films, video recordings, plays, manuscripts, patents and copyrights
(see Section 13 *Intangible Assets other than Goodwill*).

This section applies to agreements that transfer the right to use **assets** even though   **15.2**
substantial services by the lessor may be called for in connection with the operation or
maintenance of such assets. This section does not apply to agreements that are contracts for
services that do not transfer the right to use assets from one contracting party to the other.

Some arrangements do not take the legal form of a lease but convey rights to use   **15.3**
assets in return for payments. Examples of such arrangements may include outsourcing
arrangements, telecommunication contracts that provide rights to capacity and take-or-pay
contracts.

15.4   Determining whether an arrangement is, or contains, a lease shall be based on the substance of the arrangement.

Classification of leases

15.5   A lease is classified as a **finance lease** if it transfers substantially all the risks and rewards incidental to ownership. A lease is classified as an **operating lease** if it does not transfer substantially all the risks and rewards incidental to ownership.

15.6   Whether a lease is a finance lease or an operating lease depends on the substance of the transaction rather than the form of the contract. Examples of situations that individually or in combination would normally lead to a lease being classified as a finance lease are:

    (a)   the lease transfers ownership of the asset to the lessee by the end of the **lease term**;

    (b)   the lessee has the option to purchase the asset at a price that is expected to be sufficiently lower than the **fair value** at the date the option becomes exercisable for it to be reasonably certain, at the **inception of the lease**, that the option will be exercised;

    (c)   the lease term is for the major part of the economic life of the asset even if title is not transferred;

    (d)   at the inception of the lease the **present value** of the **minimum lease payments** amounts to at least substantially all of the fair value of the leased asset; and

    (e)   the leased assets are of such a specialised nature that only the lessee can use them without major modifications.

15.7   Indicators of situations that individually or in combination could also lead to a lease being classified as a finance lease are:

    (a)   if the lessee can cancel the lease, the lessor's losses associated with the cancellation are borne by the lessee;

    (b)   **gains** or losses from the fluctuation in the **residual value** of the leased asset accrue to the lessee (eg in the form of a rent rebate equalling most of the sales proceeds at the end of the lease); and

    (c)   the lessee has the ability to continue the lease for a secondary period at a rent that is substantially lower than market rent.

15.8   The examples and indicators in paragraphs 15.6 and 15.7 are not always conclusive. If it is clear from other features that the lease does not transfer substantially all risks and rewards incidental to ownership, the lease is classified as an operating lease. For example, this may be the case if ownership of the asset is transferred to the lessee at the end of the lease for a variable payment equal to the asset's then fair value, or if there are **contingent rents**, as a result of which the lessee does not have substantially all risks and rewards incidental to ownership.

15.9   Lease classification is made at the inception of the lease and is not changed during the term of the lease unless the lessee and the lessor agree to change the provisions of the lease (other than simply by renewing the lease), in which case the lease classification shall be re-evaluated.

Financial statements of lessees: finance leases

Initial recognition

15.10   At the **commencement of the lease term**, a lessee shall recognise its rights of use and obligations under finance leases as assets and **liabilities** in its **statement of financial**

position at amounts equal to the fair value of the leased asset or, if lower, the present value of the minimum lease payments, determined at the inception of the lease. Any initial direct costs of the lessee (incremental costs that are directly attributable to negotiating and arranging a lease) are added to the amount recognised as an asset.

The present value of the minimum lease payments shall be calculated using the **interest rate implicit in the lease**. If this cannot be determined, the **lessee's incremental borrowing rate** shall be used.   **15.11**

Subsequent measurement

A lessee shall apportion minimum lease payments between the finance charge and the reduction of the outstanding liability. The lessee shall allocate the finance charge to each period during the lease term so as to produce a constant periodic rate of interest on the remaining balance of the liability. A lessee shall charge **contingent rents** as **expenses** in the periods in which they are incurred.   **15.12**

A lessee shall depreciate an asset leased under a finance lease in accordance with Section 12 *Property, Plant and Equipment and Investment Property*. If there is no reasonable certainty that the lessee will obtain ownership by the end of the lease term, the asset shall be fully depreciated over the shorter of the lease term and its **useful life**. A lessee shall also assess at each **reporting date** whether an asset leased under a finance lease is impaired (see Section 22 *Impairment of Assets*).   **15.13**

Financial statements of lessees: operating leases

Recognition and measurement

A lessee shall recognise lease payments under operating leases (excluding costs for services such as insurance and maintenance) as an expense over the lease term on a straight-line basis unless another systematic basis is representative of the time pattern of the user's benefit, even if the payments are not on that basis.   **15.14**

A lessee shall recognise the aggregate benefit of **lease incentives** as a reduction to the expense recognised in accordance with paragraph 15.14 over the lease term, on a straight-line basis unless another systematic basis is representative of the time pattern of the lessee's benefit from the use of the leased asset. Any costs incurred by the lessee (for example costs for termination of a pre-existing lease, relocation or leasehold improvements) shall be accounted for in accordance with the applicable section.   **15.15**

Where an operating lease becomes an **onerous contract** a **micro-entity** shall also apply Section 16 *Provisions and Contingencies*.   **15.16**

Disclosure in the notes

A micro-entity shall determine the amount of any financial commitments, guarantees and contingencies not recognised in the statement of financial position arising from operating leases and disclose that amount within the total amount of financial commitments, guarantees and contingencies (see paragraph 6A.2).   **15.17**

Financial statements of lessors: finance leases

Initial recognition and measurement

15.18   A lessor shall recognise assets held under a finance lease in its statement of financial position and present them as a receivable at an amount equal to the **net investment in the lease**. The net investment in a lease is the lessor's **gross investment in the lease** discounted at the interest rate implicit in the lease. The gross investment in the lease is the aggregate of:

(a)   the minimum lease payments receivable by the lessor under a finance lease; and

(b)   any unguaranteed residual value accruing to the lessor.

15.19   For finance leases other than those involving manufacturer or dealer lessors, initial direct costs (costs that are incremental and directly attributable to negotiating and arranging a lease) are included in the initial measurement of the finance lease receivable and reduce the amount of **income** recognised over the lease term.

Subsequent measurement

15.20   The **recognition** of finance income shall be based on a pattern reflecting a constant periodic rate of return on the lessor's net investment in the finance lease. Lease payments relating to the period, excluding costs for services, are applied against the gross investment in the lease to reduce both the principal and the unearned finance income. If there is an indication that the estimated unguaranteed residual value used in computing the lessor's gross investment in the lease has changed significantly, the income allocation over the lease term is revised, and any reduction in respect of amounts accrued is recognised immediately in **profit or loss**.

Manufacturer or dealer lessors

15.21   Manufacturers or dealers often offer to customers the choice of either buying or leasing an asset. A finance lease of an asset by a manufacturer or dealer lessor gives rise to two types of income:

(a)   profit or loss equivalent to the profit or loss resulting from an outright sale of the asset being leased, at normal selling prices, reflecting any applicable volume or trade discounts; and

(b)   finance income over the lease term.

15.22   The sales **revenue** recognised at the commencement of the lease term by a manufacturer or dealer lessor is the fair value of the asset or, if lower, the present value of the minimum lease payments accruing to the lessor, computed at a market rate of interest. The cost of sale recognised at the commencement of the lease term is the cost, or **carrying amount** if different, of the leased asset less the present value of the unguaranteed residual value. The difference between the sales revenue and the cost of sale is the selling profit, which is recognised in accordance with the micro-entity's policy for outright sales.

15.23   If artificially low rates of interest are quoted, selling profit shall be restricted to that which would apply if a market rate of interest were charged. Costs incurred by manufacturer or dealer lessors in connection with negotiating and arranging a lease shall be recognised as an expense when the selling profit is recognised.

Financial statements of lessors: operating leases

Recognition and measurement

A lessor shall recognise lease income from operating leases (excluding amounts for services such as insurance and maintenance) in profit or loss on a straight-line basis over the lease term unless another systematic basis is representative of the time pattern of the lessee's benefit from the leased asset, even if the receipt of payments is not on that basis. **15.24**

A lessor shall recognise the aggregate cost of lease incentives as a reduction to the income recognised in accordance with paragraph 15.24 over the lease term on a straight-line basis, unless another systematic basis is representative of the time pattern over which the lessor's benefit from the leased asset is diminished. **15.25**

A lessor shall recognise as an expense, costs, including **depreciation**, incurred in earning the lease income. The depreciation policy for depreciable leased assets shall be consistent with the lessor's normal depreciation policy for similar assets. **15.26**

A lessor shall add to the carrying amount of the leased asset any initial direct costs it incurs in negotiating and arranging an operating lease and shall recognise such costs as an expense over the lease term on the same basis as the lease income. **15.27**

To determine whether a leased asset has become impaired, a lessor shall apply Section 22. **15.28**

A manufacturer or dealer lessor does not recognise any selling profit on entering into an operating lease because it is not the equivalent of a sale. **15.29**

Sale and leaseback transactions

A sale and leaseback transaction involves the sale of an asset and the leasing back of the same asset. The lease payment and the sale price are usually interdependent because they are negotiated as a package. The accounting treatment of a sale and leaseback transaction depends on the type of lease. **15.30**

Sale and leaseback transaction results in a finance lease

If a sale and leaseback transaction results in a finance lease, the seller-lessee shall not recognise immediately, as income, any excess of sales proceeds over the carrying amount. Instead, the seller-lessee shall defer such excess and amortise it over the lease term. **15.31**

Sale and leaseback transaction results in an operating lease

If a sale and leaseback transaction results in an operating lease, and it is clear that the transaction is established at fair value, the seller-lessee shall recognise any profit or loss immediately. If the sale price is below fair value, the seller-lessee shall recognise any profit or loss immediately unless the loss is compensated for by future lease payments at below market price. In that case the seller-lessee shall defer and amortise such loss in proportion to the lease payments over the period for which the asset is expected to be used. If the sale price is above fair value, the seller-lessee shall defer the excess over fair value and amortise it over the period for which the asset is expected to be used. **15.32**

Disclosure in the notes

15.33 A micro-entity shall determine the amount of any financial commitments, guarantees and contingencies not recognised in the statement of financial position arising from a sale and lease back transaction and disclose that amount within the total amount of financial commitments, guarantees and contingencies (see paragraph 6A.2).

Section 16 *Provisions and Contingencies*

Scope of this section

16.1 This section applies to all **provisions**, **contingent liabilities** and **contingent assets** except those provisions covered by other sections of this FRS. Where those other sections contain no specific requirements to deal with contracts that have become onerous, this section applies to those contracts.

16.2 This section does not apply to **financial instruments** that are within the scope of Section 9 *Financial Instruments* unless the contracts are **onerous contracts** or **financial guarantee contracts**.

16.3 The requirements in this section do not apply to executory contracts unless they are onerous contracts. Executory contracts are contracts under which neither party has performed any of its obligations or both parties have partially performed their obligations to an equal extent.

16.4 The word 'provision' is sometimes used in the context of such items as **depreciation**, impairment of **assets**, and uncollectible receivables. Those are adjustments of the **carrying amounts** of assets, rather than **recognition** of **liabilities**, and therefore are not covered by this section.

Initial recognition

16.5 A **micro-entity** shall recognise a provision only when:

(a)   the micro-entity has an obligation at the **reporting date** as a result of a past event;

(b)   it is **probable** (ie more likely than not) that the micro-entity will be required to transfer economic benefits in settlement; and

(c)   the amount of the obligation can be estimated reliably.

16.6 The micro-entity shall recognise the provision as a liability in the **statement of financial position** and shall recognise the amount of the provision as an **expense**, unless another section of this FRS requires the cost to be recognised as part of the cost of an asset such as **inventories** or **property, plant and equipment**.

16.7 The condition in paragraph 16.5(a) means that the micro-entity has no realistic alternative to settling the obligation. This can happen when the micro-entity has a legal obligation that can be enforced by law or when the micro-entity has a **constructive obligation** because the past event (which may be an action of the micro-entity) has created valid expectations in other parties that the micro-entity will discharge the obligation. Obligations that will arise from the micro-entity's future actions (ie the future conduct of its business) do not satisfy the condition in paragraph 16.5(a), no matter how likely they are to occur and even if they are contractual. To illustrate, because of commercial pressures or legal requirements, a micro-entity may intend or need to carry out expenditure to operate in a particular way in the future (for example, by fitting smoke filters in a particular type of factory). Because the micro-entity can avoid the future expenditure by its future actions, for example by changing its method of operation or selling the factory, it has no present obligation for that future expenditure and no provision is recognised.

Initial measurement

A micro-entity shall measure a provision at the best estimate of the amount required to settle the obligation at the reporting date. The best estimate is the amount a micro-entity would rationally pay to settle the obligation at the end of the **reporting period** or to transfer it to a third party at that time. **16.8**

(a) When the provision involves a large population of items, the estimate of the amount reflects the weighting of all possible outcomes by their associated probabilities. The provision will therefore be different depending on whether the probability of a loss of a given amount is, for example, 60 per cent or 90 per cent. Where there is a continuous range of possible outcomes, and each point in that range is as likely as any other, the mid-point of the range is used.

(b) When the provision arises from a single obligation, the individual most likely outcome may be the best estimate of the amount required to settle the obligation. However, even in such a case, the micro-entity considers other possible outcomes. When other possible outcomes are either mostly higher or mostly lower than the most likely outcome, the best estimate will be a higher or lower amount.

When the effect of the time value of money is **material**, the amount of a provision shall be the **present value** of the amount expected to be required to settle the obligation. The discount rate (or rates) shall be a pre-tax rate (or rates) that reflect(s) current market assessments of the time value of money and risks specific to the liability. The risks specific to the liability shall be reflected either in the discount rate or in the estimation of the amounts required to settle the obligation, but not both.

A micro-entity shall exclude **gains** from the expected disposal of assets from the **measurement** of a provision. **16.9**

When some or all of the amount required to settle a provision may be reimbursed by another party (eg through an insurance claim), the micro-entity shall recognise the reimbursement as a separate asset only when it is virtually certain that the micro-entity will receive the reimbursement on settlement of the obligation. The amount recognised for the reimbursement shall not exceed the amount of the provision. The reimbursement receivable shall be presented in the statement of financial position as an asset and shall not be offset against the provision. In the **income statement** the expense relating to a provision may be presented net of the amount recognised for a reimbursement. **16.10**

Subsequent measurement

A micro-entity shall charge against a provision only those expenditures for which the provision was originally recognised. **16.11**

A micro-entity shall review provisions at each reporting date and adjust them to reflect the current best estimate of the amount that would be required to settle the obligation at that reporting date. Any adjustments to the amounts previously recognised shall be recognised in **profit or loss** unless the provision was originally recognised as part of the cost of an asset (see paragraph 16.6). When a provision is measured at the present value of the amount expected to be required to settle the obligation, the unwinding of the discount shall be recognised as interest expense in profit or loss in the period it arises. **16.12**

Onerous contracts

16.13   If a micro-entity has an onerous contract, the present obligation under the contract shall be recognised and measured as a provision (see Example 2 of the Appendix to this section).

Future operating losses

16.14   Provisions shall not be recognised for future operating losses (see Example 1 of the Appendix to this section).

Restructuring

16.15   A **restructuring** gives rise to a constructive obligation only when a micro-entity:

(a)   has a detailed formal plan for the restructuring identifying at least:

   (i)   the business or part of a business concerned;

   (ii)   the principal locations affected;

   (iii)   the location, function, and approximate number of employees who will be compensated for terminating their services;

   (iv)   the expenditures that will be undertaken; and

   (v)   when the plan will be implemented; and

(b)   has raised a valid expectation in those affected that it will carry out the restructuring by starting to implement that plan or announcing its main features to those affected by it.

16.16   A micro-entity recognises a provision for restructuring costs only when it has a legal or constructive obligation at the reporting date to carry out the restructuring.

Contingent liabilities

16.17   A contingent liability is either a possible but uncertain obligation or a present obligation that is not recognised because it fails to meet one or both of the conditions (b) and (c) in paragraph 16.5. A micro-entity shall not recognise a contingent liability as a liability, except for provisions for contingent liabilities of an acquiree in a trade and asset acquisition (see Section 14 *Business Combinations and Goodwill*). Paragraph 16.19 sets out the disclosure requirements for a contingent liability. When a micro-entity is jointly and severally liable for an obligation, the part of the obligation that is expected to be met by other parties is treated as a contingent liability.

Contingent assets

16.18   A micro-entity shall not recognise a contingent asset as an asset. However, when the flow of future economic benefits to the micro-entity is virtually certain, then the related asset is not a contingent asset, and its recognition is appropriate.

Disclosures in the notes

16.19   A micro-entity shall determine the amount of any financial commitments, guarantees and contingencies not recognised in the statement of financial position and disclose that amount within the total amount of financial commitments, guarantees and contingencies (see paragraph 6A.2). A micro-entity is not required to disclose the amount of a contingent liability where the possibility of an outflow of resources is remote.

Appendix to Section 16

Examples of recognising and measuring provisions

This appendix accompanies, but is not part of, Section 16. It provides guidance for applying the requirements of Section 16 in recognising and measuring provisions.

All of the micro-entities in the examples in this appendix have 31 December as their reporting date. In all cases, it is assumed that a reliable estimate can be made of any outflows expected. In some examples the circumstances described may have resulted in impairment of the assets; this aspect is not dealt with in the examples. References to 'best estimate' are to the present value amount, when the effect of the time value of money is material.

Example 1 Future operating losses

A micro-entity determines that it is probable that it will incur future operating losses for several years.   **16A.1**

Present obligation as a result of a past obligating event: There is no past event that obliges the micro-entity to pay out resources.

Conclusion: The micro-entity does not recognise a provision for future operating losses. Expected future losses do not meet the definition of a liability. The expectation of future operating losses may be an indicator that one or more assets are impaired (see Section 22 *Impairment of Assets* of this FRS).

Example 2 Onerous contracts

An onerous contract is one in which the unavoidable costs of meeting the obligations under the contract exceed the economic benefits expected to be received under it. The unavoidable costs under a contract reflect the least net cost of exiting from the contract, which is the lower of the cost of fulfilling it and any compensation or penalties arising from failure to fulfil it. For example, a micro-entity may be contractually required under an operating lease to make payments to lease an asset for which it no longer has any use.   **16A.2**

Present obligation as a result of a past obligating event: The micro-entity is contractually required to pay out resources for which it will not receive commensurate benefits.

Conclusion: If a micro-entity has a contract that is onerous, the micro-entity recognises and measures the present obligation under the contract as a provision.

Example 3 Warranties

A manufacturer gives warranties at the time of sale to purchasers of its product. Under the terms of the contract for sale, the manufacturer undertakes to make good, by repair or replacement, manufacturing defects that become apparent within three years from the date of sale. On the basis of experience, it is probable (ie more likely than not) that there will be some claims under the warranties.   **16A.3**

Present obligation as a result of a past obligating event: The obligating event is the sale of the product with a warranty, which gives rise to a legal obligation.

An outflow of resources embodying economic benefits in settlement: Probable for the warranties as a whole.

Conclusion: The micro-entity recognises a provision for the best estimate of the costs of making good under the warranty products sold before the reporting date.

Illustration of calculations:

In 20X0, goods are sold for CU100,000. Experience indicates that 90 per cent of products sold require no warranty repairs; six per cent of products sold require minor repairs costing 30 per cent of the sale price; and four per cent of products sold require major repairs or replacement costing 70 per cent of sale price. Therefore estimated warranty costs are:

CU100,000 × 90% × 0 =	CU0
CU100,000 × 6% × 30% =	CU1,800
CU100,000 × 4% × 70% =	CU2,800
Total	CU4,600

The expenditures for warranty repairs and replacements for products sold in 20X0 are expected to be made 60 per cent in 20X1, 30 per cent in 20X2, and ten per cent in 20X3, in each case at the end of the period. Because the estimated cash flows already reflect the probabilities of the cash outflows, and assuming there are no other risks or uncertainties that must be reflected, to determine the present value of those cash flows the micro-entity uses a 'risk-free' discount rate based on government bonds with the same term as the expected cash outflows (six per cent for one-year bonds and seven per cent for two-year and three-year bonds). Calculation of the present value, at the end of 20X0, of the estimated cash flows related to the warranties for products sold in 20X0 is as follows:

Year	Expected cash payments (CU)		Discount rate	Discount factor	Present value (CU)
1	60% × CU4,600	2,760	6%	0.9434 (at 6% for 1 year)	2,604
2	30% × CU4,600	1,380	7%	0.8734 (at 7% for 2 years)	1,205
3	10% × CU4,600	460	7%	0.8163 (at 7% for 3 years)	375
Total					4,184

The micro-entity will recognise a warranty obligation of CU4,184 at the end of 20X0 for products sold in 20X0.

Example 4 Refunds policy

16A.4   A retail store has a policy of refunding purchases by dissatisfied customers, even though it is under no legal obligation to do so. Its policy of making refunds is generally known.

Present obligation as a result of a past obligating event: The obligating event is the sale of the product, which gives rise to a constructive obligation because the conduct of the store has created a valid expectation on the part of its customers that the store will refund purchases.

An outflow of resources embodying economic benefits in settlement: Probable that a proportion of goods will be returned for refund.

Conclusion: The micro-entity recognises a provision for the best estimate of the amount required to settle the refunds.

Example 5 Closure of a division: no implementation before end of reporting period

On 12 December 20X0 the board of a micro-entity decided to close down a division. Before the end of the reporting period (31 December 20X0) the decision was not communicated to any of those affected and no other steps were taken to implement the decision.

16A.5

Present obligation as a result of a past obligating event: There has been no obligating event, and so there is no obligation.

Conclusion: The micro-entity does not recognise a provision.

Example 6 Closure of a division: communication and implementation before end of reporting period

On 12 December 20X0 the board of a micro-entity decided to close a division making a particular product. On 20 December 20X0 a detailed plan for closing the division was agreed by the board, letters were sent to customers warning them to seek an alternative source of supply, and redundancy notices were sent to the staff of the division.

16A.6

Present obligation as a result of a past obligating event: The obligating event is the communication of the decision to the customers and employees, which gives rise to a constructive obligation from that date, because it creates a valid expectation that the division will be closed.

An outflow of resources embodying economic benefits in settlement: Probable.

Conclusion: The micro-entity recognises a provision at 31 December 20X0 for the best estimate of the costs that would be incurred to close the division at the reporting date.

Example 7 Staff retraining as a result of changes in the income tax system

The government introduces changes to the income tax system. As a result of those changes, a micro-entity will need to retrain a large proportion of its administrative and sales workforce in order to ensure continued compliance with tax regulations. At the end of the reporting period, no retraining of staff has taken place.

16A.7

Present obligation as a result of a past obligating event: The tax law change does not impose an obligation on a micro-entity to do any retraining. An obligating event for recognising a provision (the retraining itself) has not taken place.

Conclusion: The micro-entity does not recognise a provision.

Example 8 A court case

16A.8   A customer has sued Micro-entity X, seeking damages for injury the customer allegedly sustained from using a product sold by Micro-entity X. Micro-entity X disputes liability on grounds that the customer did not follow directions in using the product. Up to the date the financial statements for the year to 31 December 20X1 were authorised for issue, the micro-entity's lawyers advise that it is probable that the micro-entity will not be found liable. However, when the micro-entity prepares the financial statements for the year to 31 December 20X2, its lawyers advise that, owing to developments in the case, it is now probable that the micro-entity will be found liable.

(a)   At 31 December 20X1

Present obligation as a result of a past obligating event: On the basis of the evidence available when the financial statements were approved, there is no obligation as a result of past events.

Conclusion: No provision is recognised, but the micro-entity shall make the disclosures required by paragraph 16.19.

(b)   At 31 December 20X2

Present obligation as a result of a past obligating event: On the basis of the evidence available, there is a present obligation. The obligating event is the sale of the product to the customer.

An outflow of resources embodying economic benefits in settlement: Probable.

Conclusion: A provision is recognised at the best estimate of the amount to settle the obligation at 31 December 20X2, and the expense is recognised in profit or loss. It is not a correction of an error in 20X1 because, on the basis of the evidence available when the 20X1 financial statements were approved, a provision should not have been recognised at that time.

Section 17 *Liabilities and Equity*

Scope of this section

17.1   This section establishes principles for classifying **financial instruments** as either **liabilities** or **equity** and deals with the accounting for **compound financial instruments**, such as convertible debt. It also addresses the issue of equity instruments, distributions to individuals or other parties acting in their capacity as investors in equity instruments (ie in their capacity as **owners**) and the accounting for purchases of own equity.

17.2   This section shall be applied to all types of financial instruments except:

(a)   Investments in **subsidiaries** and **associates** and interests in **jointly controlled entities** that are accounted for in accordance with Section 9 *Financial Instruments*.

(b)   Employers' rights and obligations under employee benefit plans to which Section 23 *Employee Benefits* applies.

(c)   Financial instruments, contracts and obligations under **share-based payment transactions** to which Section 21 *Share-based Payment* applies, except that paragraph 17.14 shall be applied to **treasury shares** issued, purchased, sold, transferred or cancelled in connection with employee share option plans, employee share purchase plans, and all other share-based payment arrangements.

(d)   **Financial guarantee contracts** (see Section 16 *Provisions and Contingencies*).

Classification of an instrument as liability or equity

Equity is the residual interest in the **assets** of a **micro-entity** after deducting all its liabilities. **17.3** Equity includes investments by the owners of the micro-entity, plus additions to those investments earned through profitable operations and retained for use in the micro-entity's operations, minus reductions to owners' investments as a result of unprofitable operations and distributions to owners.

A financial instrument is classified as equity where the issuer can be required to settle an **17.4** obligation in cash or by delivery of another **financial asset** (or otherwise to settle it in such a way that it would be a **financial liability**) only in the event of the liquidation of the issuer.

A financial instrument is a financial liability of the issuer where the issuer does not have an **17.5** unconditional right to avoid settling an obligation in cash or by delivery of another financial asset (or otherwise to settle it in such a way that it would be a financial liability), other than for the reason described in paragraph 17.4.

Examples of instruments and their classification as equity or liabilities are set out below: **17.6**

(a) An instrument is classified as equity if the only payment holders of the instruments are entitled to receive is a pro rata share of the net assets of the micro-entity on liquidation.

(b) An instrument is classified as a liability if it obliges the micro-entity to make payments to the holder before liquidation, such as a mandatory dividend.

(c) A preference share that provides for mandatory redemption by the issuer for a fixed or determinable amount at a fixed or determinable future date, or gives the holder the right to require the issuer to redeem the instrument at or after a particular date for a fixed or determinable amount, is a financial liability.

Original issue of shares or other equity instruments

A micro-entity shall recognise the issue of shares or other equity instruments as equity when **17.7** it issues those instruments and another party is obliged to provide cash or other resources to the micro-entity in exchange for the instruments.

(a) If the micro-entity receives the cash or other resources before the equity instruments are issued, and the micro-entity cannot be required to repay the cash or other resources received, the micro-entity shall recognise the corresponding increase in equity to the extent of consideration received.

(b) To the extent that the equity instruments have been subscribed for but not issued (or called up), and the micro-entity has not yet received the cash or other resources, the micro-entity shall not recognise an increase in equity.

A micro-entity shall measure the equity instruments at the **fair value** of the cash or **17.8** other resources received or receivable, net of direct costs of issuing the equity instruments.

A micro-entity shall account for the **transaction costs** of an equity transaction as a **17.9** deduction from equity, net of any related **income tax** benefit.

Exercise of options, rights and warrants

A micro-entity shall apply the principles in paragraphs 17.7 to 17.9 to equity issued by **17.10** means of exercise of options, rights, warrants and similar equity instruments.

Convertible debt and similar compound financial instruments

17.11   On issuing convertible debt, or a similar compound financial instrument, a micro-entity shall allocate the proceeds between the liability component and the equity component of the instrument. To make the allocation, the micro-entity shall first determine the amount of the liability component as the fair value of a similar liability that does not have a conversion feature or similar associated equity component. The micro-entity shall allocate the residual amount as the equity component. Transaction costs shall be allocated between the debt component and the equity component on the basis of their relative fair values.

17.12   The micro-entity shall not revise the allocation in a subsequent period.

17.13   In periods after the instruments were issued, the micro-entity shall account for the liability component as a financial instrument in accordance with Section 9. The example shown in the Appendix to Section 22 *Liabilities and Equity* of **FRS 102** illustrates the accounting for convertible debt by an issuer.

Treasury shares

17.14   Treasury shares are the equity instruments of a micro-entity that have been issued and subsequently reacquired by the micro-entity. A micro-entity shall deduct from equity the fair value of the consideration given for the treasury shares. The micro-entity shall not recognise a **gain** or loss in **profit or loss** on the purchase, sale, transfer or cancellation of treasury shares.

Distributions to owners

17.15   A micro-entity shall reduce its equity reserves for the amount of distributions to its owners (holders of its equity instruments).

Section 18 *Revenue*

Scope of this section

18.1   This section shall be applied in accounting for **revenue** arising from the following transactions and events:

    (a)   the sale of goods (whether produced by the **micro-entity** for the purpose of sale or purchased for resale);

    (b)   the rendering of services;

    (c)   **construction contracts** in which the micro-entity is the contractor; and

    (d)   the use by others of micro-entity **assets** yielding interest, royalties or dividends.

18.2   Revenue or other **income** arising from **lease** agreements is dealt with in Section 15 *Leases*.

Measurement of revenue

18.3   A micro-entity shall measure revenue at the amount receivable, taking into account any trade discounts, prompt settlement discounts and volume rebates allowed by the micro-entity.

18.4   A micro-entity shall include in revenue only the gross inflows of economic benefits received and receivable by the micro-entity on its own account. A micro-entity shall exclude from revenue all amounts collected on behalf of third parties such as sales taxes, goods and services taxes and value added taxes. In an agency relationship, a micro-entity (the **agent**) shall include in revenue only the amount of its commission. The amounts collected on behalf of the **principal** are not revenue of the micro-entity.

Deferred payment

If payment is deferred beyond normal credit terms, the amount of revenue recognised is equal to the cash price available on the transaction date. Any excess of the deferred payment amount over the cash price available on the transaction date is recognised as interest and accounted for in accordance with paragraph 9.14(a).   **18.5**

Exchanges of goods or services

A micro-entity shall not recognise revenue: **18.6**

(a)   when goods or services are exchanged for goods or services that are of a similar nature and value; or
(b)   when goods or services are exchanged for dissimilar goods or services but the transaction lacks commercial substance.

A micro-entity shall recognise revenue when goods are sold or services are exchanged for dissimilar goods or services in a transaction that has commercial substance. In that case, the micro-entity shall measure the transaction: **18.7**

(a)   at the **fair value** of the goods or services received, adjusted by the amount of any cash transferred;
(b)   if the amount under (a) cannot be measured reliably, then at the fair value of the goods or services given up adjusted by the amount of any cash transferred; or
(c)   if the fair value of neither the goods or services received nor the goods or services given up can be measured reliably, then at the **carrying amount** of the goods or services given up adjusted by the amount of any cash transferred.

Identification of the revenue transaction

A micro-entity shall apply the **recognition** criteria to the separately identifiable components of a single transaction when necessary to reflect the substance of the transaction. For example, a micro-entity applies the recognition criteria to the separately identifiable components of a single transaction when the selling price of a product includes an identifiable amount for subsequent servicing. Conversely, a micro-entity applies the recognition criteria to two or more transactions together when they are linked in such a way that the commercial effect cannot be understood without reference to the series of transactions as a whole.   **18.8**

Sale of goods

A micro-entity shall recognise revenue from the sale of goods when all the following conditions are satisfied: **18.9**

(a)   the micro-entity has transferred to the buyer the significant risks and rewards of ownership of the goods;
(b)   the micro-entity retains neither continuing managerial involvement to the degree usually associated with ownership nor effective control over the goods sold;
(c)   the amount of revenue can be measured reliably;
(d)   it is **probable** that the economic benefits associated with the transaction will flow to the micro-entity; and
(e)   the costs incurred or to be incurred in respect of the transaction can be measured reliably.

18.10   The assessment of when a micro-entity has transferred the significant risks and rewards of ownership to the buyer requires an examination of the circumstances of the transaction. In most cases, the transfer of the risks and rewards of ownership coincides with the transfer of the legal title or the passing of possession to the buyer. This is the case for most retail sales. In other cases, the transfer of risks and rewards of ownership occurs at a time different from the transfer of legal title or the passing of possession.

18.11   A micro-entity does not recognise revenue if it retains significant risks and rewards of ownership. Examples of situations in which the micro-entity may retain the significant risks and rewards of ownership are:

(a)   when the micro-entity retains an obligation for unsatisfactory performance not covered by normal warranties;

(b)   when the receipt of the revenue from a particular sale is contingent on the buyer selling the goods;

(c)   when the goods are shipped subject to installation and the installation is a significant part of the contract that has not yet been completed; and

(d)   when the buyer has the right to rescind the purchase for a reason specified in the sales contract, or at the buyer's sole discretion without any reason, and the micro-entity is uncertain about the probability of return.

18.12   If an entity retains only an insignificant risk of ownership, the transaction is a sale and the entity recognises the revenue. For example, a seller recognises revenue when it retains the legal title to the goods solely to protect the collectability of the amount due. Similarly, an entity recognises revenue when it offers a refund if the customer finds the goods faulty or is not satisfied for other reasons, and the entity can estimate the returns reliably. In such cases, the entity recognises a **provision** for returns in accordance with Section 16 *Provisions and Contingencies*.

Rendering of services

18.13   When the outcome of a transaction involving the rendering of services can be estimated reliably, a micro-entity shall recognise revenue associated with the transaction by reference to the stage of completion of the transaction at the end of the **reporting period** (sometimes referred to as the percentage of completion method). The outcome of a transaction can be estimated reliably when all the following conditions are satisfied:

(a)   the amount of revenue can be measured reliably;

(b)   it is probable that the economic benefits associated with the transaction will flow to the micro-entity;

(c)   the stage of completion of the transaction at the end of the reporting period can be measured reliably; and

(d)   the costs incurred for the transaction and the costs to complete the transaction can be measured reliably.

Paragraphs 18.18 to 18.24 provide guidance for applying the percentage of completion method.

18.14   When services are performed by an indeterminate number of acts over a specified period of time, a micro-entity recognises revenue on a straight-line basis over the specified period unless there is evidence that some other method better represents the stage of completion. When a specific act is much more significant than any other act, the micro-entity postpones recognition of revenue until the significant act is executed.

When the outcome of the transaction involving the rendering of services cannot be estimated reliably, a micro-entity shall recognise revenue only to the extent of the **expenses** recognised that are recoverable.   **18.15**

Construction contracts

When the outcome of a construction contract can be estimated reliably, a micro-entity shall recognise contract revenue and contract costs associated with the construction contract as revenue and expenses respectively by reference to the stage of completion of the contract activity at the end of the reporting period (often referred to as the percentage of completion method). Reliable estimation of the outcome requires reliable estimates of the stage of completion, future costs and collectability of billings. Paragraphs 18.18 to 18.24 provide guidance for applying the percentage of completion method.   **18.16**

The requirements of this section are usually applied separately to each construction contract. However, in some circumstances, it is necessary to apply this section to the separately identifiable components of a single contract or to a group of contracts together in order to reflect the substance of a contract or a group of contracts.   **18.17**

Percentage of completion method

This method is used to recognise revenue from rendering services (see paragraphs 18.13 to 18.15) and from construction contracts (see paragraphs 18.16 and 18.17). A micro-entity shall review and, when necessary, revise the estimates of revenue and costs as the service transaction or construction contract progresses.   **18.18**

A micro-entity shall determine the stage of completion of a transaction or contract using the method that measures most reliably the work performed. Possible methods include: **18.19**

(a)   the proportion that costs incurred for work performed to date bear to the estimated total costs. Costs incurred for work performed to date do not include costs relating to future activity, such as for materials or prepayments;

(b)   surveys of work performed; and

(c)   completion of a physical proportion of the contract work or the completion of a proportion of the service contract.

Progress payments and advances received from customers often do not reflect the work performed.

A micro-entity shall recognise costs that relate to future activity on the transaction or contract, such as for materials or prepayments, as an asset if it is probable that the costs will be recovered.   **18.20**

A micro-entity shall recognise as an expense immediately any costs whose recovery is not probable.   **18.21**

When the outcome of a construction contract cannot be estimated reliably: **18.22**

(a)   a micro-entity shall recognise revenue only to the extent of contract costs incurred that it is probable will be recoverable; and

(b)   the micro-entity shall recognise contract costs as an expense in the period in which they are incurred.

When it is probable that total contract costs will exceed total contract revenue on a construction contract, the expected loss shall be recognised as an expense immediately,   **18.23** with a corresponding provision for an **onerous contract** (see Section 16 *Provisions and Contingencies*).

18.24   If the collectability of an amount already recognised as contract revenue is no longer probable, the micro-entity shall recognise the uncollectible amount as an expense rather than as an adjustment of the amount of contract revenue.

Interest, royalties and dividends

18.25   A micro-entity shall recognise revenue arising from the use by others of micro-entity assets yielding interest, royalties and dividends on the bases set out in paragraph 18.26 when:

(a)   it is probable that the economic benefits associated with the transaction will flow to the micro-entity; and

(b)   the amount of the revenue can be measured reliably.

18.26   A micro-entity shall recognise revenue on the following bases:

(a)   Interest income shall be recognised in accordance with Section 9 *Financial Instruments*.

(b)   Royalties shall be recognised on an **accrual basis** in accordance with the substance of the relevant agreement.

(c)   Dividends shall be recognised when the shareholder's right to receive payment is established.

Appendix to Section 18

Examples of revenue recognition under the principles in Section 18

This appendix accompanies, but is not part of, Section 18. It provides guidance for applying the requirements of Section 18 in recognising revenue.

18A.1   The following examples focus on particular aspects of a transaction and are not a comprehensive discussion of all the relevant factors that might influence the recognition of revenue. The examples generally assume that the amount of revenue can be measured reliably, it is probable that the economic benefits will flow to the micro-entity and the costs incurred or to be incurred can be measured reliably.

Sale of goods

18A.2   The law in different countries may cause the recognition criteria in Section 18 to be met at different times. In particular, the law may determine the point in time at which the micro-entity transfers the significant risks and rewards of ownership. Therefore, the examples in this appendix need to be read in the context of the laws relating to the sale of goods in the country in which the transaction takes place.

Example 1 'Bill and hold' sales, in which delivery is delayed at the buyer's request but the buyer takes title and accepts billing

18A.3   The seller recognises revenue when the buyer takes title, provided:

(a)   it is probable that delivery will be made;

(b)   the item is on hand, identified and ready for delivery to the buyer at the time the sale is recognised;

(c)   the buyer specifically acknowledges the deferred delivery instructions; and

(d)   the usual payment terms apply.

Revenue is not recognised when there is simply an intention to acquire or manufacture the goods in time for delivery.

Example 2 Goods shipped subject to conditions: installation and inspection

The seller normally recognises revenue when the buyer accepts delivery, and installation and inspection are complete. However, revenue is recognised immediately upon the buyer's acceptance of delivery when: **18A.4**

(a)   the installation process is simple, for example the installation of a factory-tested television receiver that requires only unpacking and connection of power and antennae; or

(b)   the inspection is performed only for the purposes of final determination of contract prices, for example, shipments of iron ore, sugar or soya beans.

Example 3 Goods shipped subject to conditions: on approval when the buyer has negotiated a limited right of return

If there is uncertainty about the possibility of return, the seller recognises revenue when the shipment has been formally accepted by the buyer or the goods have been delivered and the time period for rejection has elapsed.   **18A.5**

Example 4 Goods shipped subject to conditions: consignment sales under which the recipient (buyer) undertakes to sell the goods on behalf of the shipper (seller)

The shipper recognises revenue when the goods are sold by the recipient to a third party.   **18A.6**

Example 5 Goods shipped subject to conditions: cash on delivery sales

The seller recognises revenue when delivery is made and cash is received by the seller or its agent.   **18A.7**

Example 6 Layaway sales under which the goods are delivered only when the buyer makes the final payment in a series of instalments

The seller recognises revenue from such sales when the goods are delivered. However, when experience indicates that most such sales are consummated, revenue may be recognised when a significant deposit is received, provided the goods are on hand, identified and ready for delivery to the buyer.   **18A.8**

Example 7 Orders when payment (or partial payment) is received in advance of delivery for goods not currently held in inventory, for example, the goods are still to be manufactured or will be delivered direct to the buyer from a third party

The seller recognises revenue when the goods are delivered to the buyer.   **18A.9**

Example 8 Sale and repurchase agreements (other than swap transactions) under which the seller concurrently agrees to repurchase the same goods at a later date, or when the seller has a call option to repurchase, or the buyer has a put option to require the repurchase, by the seller, of the goods

18A.10   For a sale and repurchase agreement on an asset other than a financial asset, the seller must analyse the terms of the agreement to ascertain whether, in substance, the risks and rewards of ownership have been transferred to the buyer. If they have been transferred, the seller recognises revenue. When the seller has retained the risks and rewards of ownership, even though legal title has been transferred, the transaction is a financing arrangement and does not give rise to revenue. For a sale and repurchase agreement on a financial asset, the derecognition provisions of Section 9 apply.

Example 9 Sales to intermediate parties, such as distributors, dealers or others for resale

18A.11   The seller generally recognises revenue from such sales when the risks and rewards of ownership have been transferred. However, when the buyer is acting, in substance, as an agent, the sale is treated as a consignment sale.

Example 10 Subscriptions to publications and similar items

18A.12   When the items involved are of similar value in each time period, the seller recognises revenue on a straight-line basis over the period in which the items are dispatched. When the items vary in value from period to period, the seller recognises revenue on the basis of the sales value of the item dispatched in relation to the total estimated sales value of all items covered by the subscription.

Example 11 Instalment sales, under which the consideration is receivable in instalments

18A.13   The seller recognises revenue based on the cash price a customer would pay at the date of sale. If the total amount paid through instalments is greater than the cash price payable at the date of sale, any excess is recognised as interest and accounted for in accordance with paragraph 9.14(a).

Example 12 Agreements for the construction of real estate

18A.14   A micro-entity that undertakes the construction of real estate, directly or through subcontractors, and enters into an agreement with one or more buyers before construction is complete, shall account for the agreement using the percentage of completion method, only if:

(a)   the buyer is able to specify the major structural elements of the design of the real estate before construction begins and/or specify major structural changes once construction is in progress (whether it exercises that ability or not); or

(b)   the buyer acquires and supplies construction materials and the micro-entity provides only construction services.

18A.15   If the micro-entity is required to provide services together with construction materials in order to perform its contractual obligation to deliver real estate to the buyer, the agreement shall be accounted for as the sale of goods. In this case, the buyer does not obtain control or the significant risks and rewards of ownership of the work in progress in its current state as construction progresses. Rather, the transfer occurs only on delivery of the completed real estate to the buyer.

Example 13 Sale with customer loyalty award

A micro-entity sells product A for CU100. Purchasers of product A get an award credit enabling them to buy product B for CU10. The normal selling price of product B is CU18. The micro-entity estimates that 40 per cent of the purchasers of product A will use their award to buy product B at CU10. The normal selling price of product A, after taking into account discounts that are usually offered but that are not available during this promotion, is CU95.   **18A.16**

The fair value of the award credit is 40 per cent × [CU18 – CU10] = CU3.20. The micro-entity allocates the total revenue of CU100 between product A and the award credit by reference to their relative fair values of CU95 and CU3.20 respectively. Therefore: **18A.17**

(a)   Revenue for product A is CU100 × [CU95 / (CU95 + CU3.20)] = CU96.74
(b)   Revenue for product B is CU100 × [CU3.20 / (CU95 + CU3.20)] = CU3.26

Rendering of services

Example 14 Installation fees

The seller recognises installation fees as revenue by reference to the stage of completion of the installation, unless they are incidental to the sale of a product, in which case they are recognised when the goods are sold.   **18A.18**

Example 15 Servicing fees included in the price of the product

When the selling price of a product includes an identifiable amount for subsequent servicing (eg after sales support and product enhancement on the sale of software), the seller defers that amount and recognises it as revenue over the period during which the service is performed. The amount deferred is that which will cover the expected costs of the services under the agreement, together with a reasonable profit on those services.   **18A.19**

Example 16 Advertising commissions

Media commissions are recognised when the related advertisement or commercial appears before the public. Production commissions are recognised by reference to the stage of completion of the project.   **18A.20**

Example 17 Admission fees

The seller recognises revenue from artistic performances, banquets and other special events when the event takes place. When a subscription to a number of events is sold, the seller allocates the fee to each event on a basis that reflects the extent to which services are performed at each event.   **18A.21**

Example 18 Tuition fees

The seller recognises revenue over the period of instruction.   **18A.22**

Example 19 Initiation, entrance and membership fees

18A.23   Revenue recognition depends on the nature of the services provided. If the fee permits only membership, and all other services or products are paid for separately, or if there is a separate annual subscription, the fee is recognised as revenue when no significant uncertainty about its collectability exists. If the fee entitles the member to services or publications to be provided during the membership period, or to purchase goods or services at prices lower than those charged to non-members, it is recognised on a basis that reflects the timing, nature and value of the benefits provided.

Franchise fees

18A.24   Franchise fees may cover the supply of initial and subsequent services, equipment and other tangible assets, and know-how. Accordingly, franchise fees are recognised as revenue on a basis that reflects the purpose for which the fees were charged. The following methods of franchise fee recognition are appropriate.

Example 20 Franchise fees: Supplies of equipment and other tangible assets

18A.25   The franchisor recognises the fair value of the assets sold as revenue when the items are delivered or title passes.

Example 21 Franchise fees: Supplies of initial and subsequent services

18A.26   The franchisor recognises fees for the provision of continuing services, whether part of the initial fee or a separate fee, as revenue as the services are rendered. When the separate fee does not cover the cost of continuing services together with a reasonable profit, part of the initial fee, sufficient to cover the costs of continuing services and to provide a reasonable profit on those services, is deferred and recognised as revenue as the services are rendered.

18A.27   The franchise agreement may provide for the franchisor to supply equipment, inventories, or other tangible assets at a price lower than that charged to others or a price that does not provide a reasonable profit on those sales. In these circumstances, part of the initial fee, sufficient to cover estimated costs in excess of that price and to provide a reasonable profit on those sales, is deferred and recognised over the period the goods are likely to be sold to the franchisee. The balance of an initial fee is recognised as revenue when performance of all the initial services and other obligations required of the franchisor (such as assistance with site selection, staff training, financing and advertising) has been substantially accomplished.

18A.28   The initial services and other obligations under an area franchise agreement may depend on the number of individual outlets established in the area. In this case, the fees attributable to the initial services are recognised as revenue in proportion to the number of outlets for which the initial services have been substantially completed.

18A.29   If the initial fee is collectible over an extended period and there is a significant uncertainty that it will be collected in full, the fee is recognised as cash instalments are received.

Example 22 Franchise fees: Continuing franchise fees

18A.30   Fees charged for the use of continuing rights granted by the agreement, or for other services provided during the period of the agreement, are recognised as revenue as the services are provided or the rights used.

Example 23 Franchise fees: Agency transactions

Transactions may take place between the franchisor and the franchisee that, in substance, involve the franchisor acting as agent for the franchisee. For example, the franchisor may order supplies and arrange for their delivery to the franchisee at no profit. Such transactions do not give rise to revenue. **18A.31**

Example 24 Fees from the development of customised software

The software developer recognises fees from the development of customised software as revenue by reference to the stage of completion of the development, including completion of services provided for post-delivery service support. **18A.32**

Interest, royalties and dividends

Example 25 Licence fees and royalties

The licensor recognises fees and royalties paid for the use of its assets (such as trademarks, patents, software, music copyright, record masters and motion picture films) in accordance with the substance of the agreement. As a practical matter, this may be on a straight-line basis over the life of the agreement, for example, when a licensee has the right to use specified technology for a specified period of time. **18A.33**

An assignment of rights for a fixed fee or non-refundable guarantee under a non-cancellable contract that permits the licensee to exploit those rights freely and the licensor has no remaining obligations to perform is, in substance, a sale. An example is a licensing agreement for the use of software when the licensor has no obligations after delivery. Another example is the granting of rights to exhibit a motion picture film in markets in which the licensor has no control over the distributor and expects to receive no further revenues from the box office receipts. In such cases, revenue is recognised at the time of sale. **18A.34**

In some cases, whether or not a licence fee or royalty will be received is contingent on the occurrence of a future event. In such cases, revenue is recognised only when it is probable that the fee or royalty will be received, which is normally when the event has occurred. **18A.35**

Section 19 *Government Grants*

Scope of this section

This section specifies the accounting for all **government grants**. **19.1**

Government grants exclude those forms of government assistance that cannot reasonably have a value placed upon them and transactions with government that cannot be distinguished from the normal trading transactions of the **micro-entity**. **19.2**

Recognition and measurement

Government grants, including non-monetary grants, shall not be recognised until there is reasonable assurance that: **19.3**

(a)   the micro-entity will comply with the conditions attaching to them; and
(b)   the grants will be received.

19.4 A micro-entity shall measure grants at the **fair value** of the **asset** received or receivable.

19.5 Where a grant becomes repayable it shall be recognised as a **liability** when the repayment meets the definition of a liability.

19.6 A micro-entity shall classify government grants either as a grant relating to revenue or a grant relating to assets.

19.7 Government grants relating to revenue shall be recognised in income on a systematic basis over the periods in which the micro-entity recognises the related costs for which the grant is intended to compensate.

19.8 A government grant that becomes receivable as compensation for **expenses** or losses already incurred or for the purpose of giving immediate financial support to the entity with no future related costs shall be recognised as **income** in **profit or loss** in the period in which it becomes receivable.

19.9 Government grants relating to assets shall be recognised in income on a systematic basis over the expected **useful life** of the asset.

19.10 Where part of a government grant relating to an asset is deferred it shall be recognised as deferred income and not deducted from the **carrying amount** of the asset.

Section 20 *Borrowing Costs*

Scope of this section

20.1 This section specifies the accounting for **borrowing costs**. Borrowing costs include:

(a) interest expense recognised in accordance with Section 9 *Financial Instruments*;

(b) finance charges in respect of **finance leases** recognised in accordance with Section 15 *Leases*; and

(c) exchange differences arising from foreign currency borrowings to the extent that they are regarded as an adjustment to interest costs.

Recognition

20.2 A **micro-entity** shall recognise all borrowing costs as an **expense** in **profit or loss** in the period in which they are incurred.

Section 21 *Share-based Payment*

Scope of this section

21.1 This section specifies the accounting for all **share-based payment transactions** including:

(a) **equity-settled share-based payment transactions;**

(b) **cash-settled share-based payment transactions;** and

(c) transactions in which the **micro-entity** receives or acquires goods or services and the terms of the arrangement provide either the micro-entity or the supplier of those goods or services with a choice of whether the micro-entity settles the transaction in cash (or other **assets**) or by issuing equity instruments.

Equity-settled share-based payment transactions

A micro-entity shall not account for equity-settled share-based payments transactions until shares are issued, at which point the micro-entity shall apply the requirements of Section 17 *Liabilities and Equity*.   **21.2**

Cash-settled share-based payment transactions

A micro-entity shall recognise the goods or services received or acquired in a cash-settled share-based payment transaction when it obtains the goods or as the services are received and recognise a corresponding **liability**.   **21.3**

If the cash-settled share-based payments granted to employees **vest** immediately, the employee is not required to complete a specified period of service before becoming unconditionally entitled to those cash-settled share-based payments. In the absence of evidence to the contrary, the micro-entity shall presume that services rendered by the employee as consideration for the share-based payments have been received. In this case, on **grant date** the micro-entity shall recognise the services received in full, with a corresponding liability.   **21.4**

If the cash-settled share-based payments do not vest until the employee completes a specified period of service, the micro-entity shall presume that the services to be rendered by the employee as consideration for those cash-settled share-based payments will be received in the future, during the vesting period. The micro-entity shall account for those services as they are rendered by the employee during the vesting period, with a corresponding increase in the liability.   **21.5**

When the goods or services received or acquired in a cash-settled share-based payment transaction do not qualify for **recognition** as assets, the micro-entity shall recognise them as **expenses**.   **21.6**

A micro-entity shall measure the goods and services acquired and the liability incurred in accordance with the measurement requirements for a provision in Section 16 *Provisions and Contingencies*.   **21.7**

Share-based payment transactions with cash alternatives

Some share-based payment transactions give either the micro-entity or the counterparty a choice of settling the transaction in cash (or other assets) or by the transfer of equity instruments.   **21.8**

When the micro-entity has a choice of settlement of the transaction in cash (or other assets) or by the transfer of equity instruments, the micro-entity shall account for the whole transaction as set out in paragraph 21.2 unless: **21.9**

(a)   the choice of settlement in equity instruments has no commercial substance (eg because the micro-entity is legally prohibited from issuing shares); or

(b)   the micro-entity has a past practice or a stated policy of settling in cash, or generally settles in cash whenever the counterparty asks for cash settlement.

In circumstances (a) and (b) the micro-entity shall account for the transaction as a wholly cash-settled transaction in accordance with paragraphs 21.3 to 21.7.

When the counterparty has a choice of settlement of the transaction in cash (or other assets) or by the transfer of equity instruments, the micro-entity shall account for the transaction as   **21.10** a wholly cash-settled share-based payment transaction in accordance with paragraphs 21.3 to 21.7 unless:

(a)   the choice of settlement in cash (or other assets) has no commercial substance because the cash settlement amount (or value of the other assets) bears no relationship to, and is likely to be lower in value than, the **fair value** of the equity instruments.

In circumstance (a) the entity shall account for the whole transaction as set out in paragraph 21.2.

Section 22 *Impairment of Assets*

Objective and scope

22.1   An **impairment loss** occurs when the **carrying amount** of an **asset** exceeds its **recoverable amount**. This section shall be applied in accounting for the impairment of all assets (including **goodwill**), other than the following, for which other sections of this FRS establish impairment requirements:

(a)   assets arising from **construction contracts** (see Section 18 *Revenue*);

(b)   **financial assets** within the scope of Section 9 *Financial Instruments*; and

(c)   **inventories** (see Section 10 *Inventories*).

Impairment of assets

General principles

22.2   If, and only if, the recoverable amount of an asset is less than its carrying amount, the **micro-entity** shall reduce the carrying amount of the asset to its recoverable amount.

22.3   If it is not possible to estimate the recoverable amount of the individual asset, a micro-entity shall estimate the recoverable amount of the **cash-generating unit** to which the asset belongs. This may be the case because measuring the recoverable amount requires forecasting cash flows, and sometimes individual assets do not generate cash flows by themselves. An impairment loss for a cash-generating unit shall be recognised and measured in accordance with the relevant requirements of Section 27 *Impairment of Assets* of **FRS 102**.

22.4   A micro-entity that has goodwill acquired in a **business combination** shall apply the additional impairment requirements applicable to goodwill in paragraphs 27.24 to 27.27 of FRS 102.

22.5   A micro-entity shall recognise an impairment loss immediately in **profit or loss**.

Indicators of impairment

22.6   A micro-entity shall assess at each **reporting date** whether there is any indication that an asset may be impaired. If any such indication exists, the micro-entity shall estimate the recoverable amount of the asset. If there is no indication of impairment, it is not necessary to estimate the recoverable amount.

22.7   In assessing whether there is any indication that an asset may be impaired, a micro-entity shall consider, as a minimum, the following indications:

External sources of information

(a) During the period, an asset's market value has declined significantly more than would be expected as a result of the passage of time or normal use.

(b) Significant changes with an adverse effect on the micro-entity have taken place during the period, or will take place in the near future, in the technological, market, economic or legal environment in which the micro-entity operates or in the market to which an asset is dedicated.

(c) Market interest rates or other market rates of return on investments have increased during the period, and those increases are likely to affect materially the discount rate used in calculating an asset's **value in use** and decrease the asset's **fair value less costs to sell**.

(d) The carrying amount of the net assets of the micro-entity is more than the estimated **fair value** of the micro-entity as a whole (such an estimate may have been made, for example, in relation to the potential sale of part or all of the micro-entity).

Internal sources of information

(e) Evidence is available of obsolescence or physical damage of an asset.

(f) Significant changes with an adverse effect on the micro-entity have taken place during the period, or are expected to take place in the near future, in the extent to which, or manner in which, an asset is used or is expected to be used. These changes include the asset becoming idle, plans to discontinue or restructure the operation to which an asset belongs, plans to dispose of an asset before the previously expected date, and reassessing the **useful life** of an asset as finite rather than indefinite.

(g) Evidence is available from internal reporting that indicates that the economic performance of an asset is, or will be, worse than expected. In this context economic performance includes operating results and cash flows.

If there is an indication that an asset may be impaired, this may indicate that the micro-entity should review the remaining useful life, the **depreciation (amortisation)** method or the **residual value** for the asset and adjust it in accordance with the section of this FRS applicable to the asset (eg Section 12 *Property, Plant and Equipment and Investment Property* and Section 13 *Intangible Assets other than Goodwill*), even if no impairment loss is recognised for the asset.   **22.8**

Measuring recoverable amount

The recoverable amount of an asset is the higher of its fair value less costs to sell and its value in use.   **22.9**

It is not always necessary to determine both an asset's fair value less costs to sell and its value in use. If either of these amounts exceeds the asset's carrying amount, the asset is not impaired and it is not necessary to estimate the other amount.   **22.10**

If there is no reason to believe that an asset's value in use materially exceeds its fair value less costs to sell, the asset's fair value less costs to sell may be used as its recoverable amount. This will often be the case for an asset that is held for disposal.   **22.11**

Fair value less costs to sell

Fair value less costs to sell is the amount obtainable from the sale of an asset in an arm's length transaction between knowledgeable, willing parties, less the costs of disposal. The best evidence of the fair value less costs to sell of an asset is a price in a binding sale agreement in an arm's length transaction or a market price in an **active market**. If there is   **22.12** no binding sale agreement or active market for an asset, fair value less costs to sell is based on the best information available to reflect the amount that a micro-entity could obtain, at the reporting date, from the disposal of the asset in an arm's length transaction between knowledgeable, willing parties, after deducting the costs of disposal. In determining this amount, a micro-entity considers the outcome of recent transactions for similar assets within the same industry.

22.13   When determining an asset's fair value less costs to sell, consideration shall be given to any restrictions imposed on that asset. Costs to sell shall also include the cost of obtaining relaxation of a restriction where necessary in order to enable the asset to be sold. If a restriction would also apply to any potential purchaser of an asset, the fair value of the asset may be lower than that of an asset whose use is not restricted.

Value in use

22.14   Value in use is the **present value** of the future cash flows expected to be derived from an asset. This present value calculation involves the following steps:

(a)   estimating the future cash inflows and outflows to be derived from the continuing use of the asset and from its ultimate disposal; and

(b)   applying the appropriate discount rate to those future cash flows.

22.15   In measuring value in use, estimates of future cash flows shall include:

(a)   projections of cash inflows from the continuing use of the asset;

(b)   projections of cash outflows that are necessarily incurred to generate the cash inflows from continuing use of the asset (including cash outflows to prepare the asset for use) and can be directly attributed, or allocated on a reasonable and consistent basis, to the asset; and

(c)   net cash flows, if any, expected to be received (or paid) for the disposal of the asset at the end of its useful life in an arm's length transaction between knowledgeable, willing parties.

The micro-entity may wish to use any recent financial budgets or forecasts to estimate the cash flows, if available, and extrapolate the projections using a steady or declining growth rate for subsequent years, unless an increasing rate can be justified.

22.16   Estimates of future cash flows shall not include:

(a)   cash inflows or outflows from **financing activities**; or

(b)   income tax receipts or payments.

22.17   Future cash flows shall be estimated for the asset in its current condition. Estimates of future cash flows shall not include estimated future cash inflows or outflows that are expected to arise from:

(a)   a future **restructuring** to which a micro-entity is not yet committed; or

(b)   improving or enhancing the asset's performance.

22.18   The discount rate(s) used in the present value calculation shall be a pre-tax rate(s) that reflect(s) current market assessments of:

(a)   the time value of money; and

(b)   the risks specific to the asset for which the future cash flow estimates have not been adjusted.

The discount rate(s) used to measure an asset's value in use shall not reflect risks for which the future cash flow estimates have been adjusted, to avoid double-counting.

Reversal of an impairment loss

An impairment loss recognised for **goodwill** shall not be reversed in a subsequent period. **22.19**

For all assets other than goodwill, if and only if the reasons for the impairment loss have **22.20** ceased to apply, an impairment loss shall be reversed in a subsequent period. A micro-entity shall assess at each reporting date whether there is any indication that an impairment loss recognised in prior periods may no longer exist or may have decreased. Indications that an impairment loss may have decreased or may no longer exist are generally the opposite of those set out in paragraph 22.7. If any such indication exists, the micro-entity shall determine whether all or part of the prior impairment loss should be reversed.

Reversal where recoverable amount was estimated for an individual impaired asset

When the prior impairment loss was based on the recoverable amount of the individual **22.21** impaired asset, the following requirements apply:

(a) The micro-entity shall estimate the recoverable amount of the asset at the current reporting date.
(b) If the estimated recoverable amount of the asset exceeds its carrying amount, the micro-entity shall increase the carrying amount to recoverable amount, subject to the limitation described in paragraph (c) below. That increase is a reversal of an impairment loss. The micro-entity shall recognise the reversal immediately in profit or loss.
(c) The reversal of an impairment loss shall not increase the carrying amount of the asset above the carrying amount that would have been determined (net of amortisation or depreciation) had no impairment loss been recognised for the asset in prior years.
(d) After a reversal of an impairment loss is recognised, the micro-entity shall adjust the depreciation (amortisation) charge for the asset in future periods to allocate the asset's revised carrying amount, less its residual value (if any), on a systematic basis over its remaining useful life.

Section 23 *Employee Benefits*

Scope of this section

Employee benefits are all forms of consideration given by a **micro-entity** in exchange **23.1** for service rendered by employees, including directors and management. This section applies to all employee benefits, except for **share-based payment transactions**, which are covered by Section 21 *Share-based Payment*. Employee benefits covered by this section will be one of the following four types:

(a) short-term employee benefits, which are employee benefits (other than **termination benefits**) that are expected to be settled wholly before 12 months after the end of the **reporting period** in which the employees render the related service;
(b) **post-employment benefits**, which are employee benefits (other than termination benefits and short-term employee benefits) that are payable after the completion of employment;

(c)   other long-term employee benefits, which are all employee benefits, other than short-term employee benefits, post-employment benefits and termination benefits; or

(d)   termination benefits, which are employee benefits provided in exchange for the termination of an employee's employment as a result of either:

   (i)   a micro-entity's decision to terminate an employee's employment before the normal retirement date; or

   (ii) an employee's decision to accept voluntary redundancy in exchange for those benefits.

General recognition principle for all employee benefits

23.2   A micro-entity shall recognise the cost of all employee benefits to which its employees have become entitled as a result of service rendered to the micro-entity during the reporting period:

(a)   As a **liability**, after deducting amounts that have been paid directly to the employees or as a contribution to an employee benefit fund[5]. If the amount paid exceeds the obligation arising from service before the **reporting date**, a micro-entity shall recognise that excess as an **asset** to the extent that the prepayment will lead to a reduction in future payments or a cash refund.

(b)   As an **expense**, unless another section of this FRS requires the cost to be recognised as part of the cost of an asset such as **inventories** (for example in accordance with paragraph 10.8) or **property, plant and equipment** (in accordance with paragraph 12.9).

Short-term employee benefits

Examples

23.3   Short-term employee benefits include items such as the following, if expected to be settled wholly before 12 months after the end of the annual reporting period in which the employees render the related service:

(a)   wages, salaries and social security contributions;

(b)   paid annual leave and paid sick leave;

(c)   profit-sharing and bonuses; and

(d)   non-monetary benefits (such as medical care, housing, cars and free or subsidised goods or services) for current employees.

Measurement of short-term benefits generally

23.4   When an employee has rendered service to a micro-entity during the reporting period, the micro-entity shall measure the amounts recognised in accordance with paragraph 23.2 at the undiscounted amount of short-term employee benefits expected to be paid in exchange for that service.

---

[5] *Contributions to an employee benefit fund that is an intermediate payment arrangement shall be accounted for in accordance with Section 7 Subsidiaries, Associates, Jointly Controlled Entities and Intermediate Payment Arrangements, and as a result if the employer is a sponsoring micro-entity the assets and liabilities of the intermediary will be accounted for by the sponsoring micro-entity as an extension of its own business. In which case the payment to the employee benefit fund does not extinguish the liability of the employer.*

Recognition and measurement: Short-term compensated absences

23.5 A micro-entity may compensate employees for absence for various reasons including annual leave and sick leave. Some short-term compensated absences accumulatethey can be carried forward and used in future periods if the employee does not use the current period's entitlement in full. Examples include annual leave and sick leave. A micro-entity shall recognise the expected cost of **accumulating compensated absences** when the employees render service that increases their entitlement to future compensated absences. The micro-entity shall measure the expected cost of accumulating compensated absences at the undiscounted additional amount that the micro-entity expects to pay as a result of the unused entitlement that has accumulated at the end of the reporting period. The micro-entity shall present this amount as falling due within one year at the reporting date.

23.6 A micro-entity shall recognise the cost of other (non-accumulating) compensated absences when the absences occur. The micro-entity shall measure the cost of non-accumulating compensated absences at the undiscounted amount of salaries and wages paid or payable for the period of absence.

Recognition: Profit-sharing and bonus plans

23.7 A micro-entity shall recognise the expected cost of profit-sharing and bonus payments only when:

(a)   the micro-entity has a present legal or **constructive obligation** to make such payments as a result of past events (this means that the micro-entity has no realistic alternative but to make the payments); and

(b)   a reliable estimate of the obligation can be made.

Post-employment benefits: Distinction between defined contribution plans and defined benefit plans

23.8 Post-employment benefits include, for example:

(a)   retirement benefits, such as pensions; and

(b)   other post-employment benefits, such as post-employment life insurance and post-employment medical care.

Arrangements whereby a micro-entity provides post-employment benefits are **post-employment benefit plans**. A micro-entity shall apply this section to all such arrangements whether or not they involve the establishment of a separate entity to receive contributions and to pay benefits. In some cases, these arrangements are imposed by law rather than by action of the micro-entity. In some cases, these arrangements arise from actions of the micro-entity even in the absence of a formal, documented plan.

23.9 Post-employment benefit plans are classified as either **defined contribution plans** or **defined benefit plans**, depending on their principal terms and conditions:

(a)   Defined contribution plans are post-employment benefit plans under which a micro-entity pays fixed contributions into a separate entity (a fund) and has no legal or constructive obligation to pay further contributions or to make direct benefit payments to employees if the fund does not hold sufficient assets to pay all employee benefits relating to employee service in the current and prior periods. The amount of the post-employment benefits received by the employee is determined by the amount of contributions paid by a micro-entity (and perhaps also the employee) to a post-employment benefit plan or to an insurer, together with investment returns arising from the contributions.

(b)   Defined benefit plans are post-employment benefit plans other than defined contribution plans. Under defined benefit plans, the micro-entity's obligation is to provide the agreed benefits to current and former employees, and actuarial risk (that benefits will cost more or less than expected) and investment risk (that returns on assets set aside to fund the benefits will differ from expectations) are borne, in substance, by the micro-entity. If actuarial or investment experience is worse than expected, the micro-entity's obligation may be increased, and vice versa if actuarial or investment experience is better than expected.

Post-employment benefit plans

Recognition and measurement – requirements applicable to all plans

23.10   When contributions to a defined contribution or defined benefit plan are not expected to be settled wholly within 12 months after the end of the reporting period in which the employees render the related service, the liability recognised in accordance with paragraph 23.2(a) shall be measured at the **present value** of the contributions payable using the methodology for selecting a discount rate specified in paragraph 23.11. The unwinding of the discount shall be recognised as interest expense in **profit or loss** in the period in which it arises.

23.11   A micro-entity shall determine the rate used to discount the future payments by reference to market yields at the reporting date on high quality corporate bonds. In countries with no deep market in such bonds, the micro-entity shall use the market yields (at the reporting date) on government bonds. The currency and term of the corporate bonds or government bonds shall be consistent with the currency and estimated period of the future payments.

Recognition and measurement – requirements applicable to defined benefit plans

23.12   When a micro-entity participates in a defined benefit plan (which may include a **multi-employer plan** or **state plan**) and has entered into an agreement with the plan that determines how the micro-entity will fund a deficit (such as a schedule of contributions), the micro-entity shall recognise a liability for the contributions payable that arise from the agreement (to the extent that they relate to the deficit) and the resulting expense in profit or loss in accordance with paragraphs 23.2 and 23.10.

23.13   Where a micro-entity participates in a defined benefit plan that shares risks between entities under common control it shall recognise a cost equal to its contribution payable for the period. If a micro-entity is legally responsible for the plan and has entered into an agreement with the plan that determines how a deficit will be funded, the micro-entity shall recognise a liability for the contributions payable that arise from the agreement (to the extent that they relate to the deficit) and the resulting expense in profit or loss in accordance with paragraphs 23.2 and 23.10.

Other long-term employee benefits

23.14   Other long-term employee benefits include items such as the following, if not expected to be settled wholly before 12 months after the end of the annual reporting period in which the employees render the related service:

(a)   long-term paid absences such as long-service or sabbatical leave;

(b)   other long-service benefits;

(c)   long-term disability benefits;
(d)   profit-sharing and bonuses; and
(e)   deferred remuneration.

A micro-entity shall recognise a liability for other long-term employee benefits measured at the present value of the benefit obligation at the reporting date calculated using the methodology for selecting a discount rate in paragraph 23.11. The unwinding of the discount shall be recognised as interest expense in profit or loss in the period in which it arises.	**23.15**

Termination benefits

A micro-entity may be committed, by legislation, by contractual or other agreements with employees or their representatives or by a constructive obligation based on business practice, custom or a desire to act equitably, to make payments (or provide other benefits) to employees when it terminates their employment. Such payments are termination benefits.	**23.16**

Recognition

Because termination benefits do not provide a micro-entity with future economic benefits, a micro-entity shall recognise them as an expense in profit or loss immediately.	**23.17**

A micro-entity shall recognise termination benefits as a liability and an expense only when the micro-entity is demonstrably committed either: **23.18**

(a)   to terminate the employment of an employee or group of employees before the normal retirement date; or
(b)   to provide termination benefits as a result of an offer made in order to encourage voluntary redundancy.

A micro-entity is demonstrably committed to a termination only when the micro-entity has a detailed formal plan for the termination[6] and is without realistic possibility of withdrawal from the plan.	**23.19**

Measurement

A micro-entity shall measure termination benefits at the best estimate of the expenditure that would be required to settle the obligation at the reporting date. In the case of an offer made to encourage voluntary redundancy, the measurement of termination benefits shall be based on the number of employees expected to accept the offer.	**23.20**

When termination benefits are due more than 12 months after the end of the reporting period, they shall be measured at their discounted present value using the methodology for selecting a discount rate specified in paragraph 23.11.	**23.21**

Disclosures in the notes

A micro entity shall disclose any commitment not recognised in the statement of financial position concerning pensions separately from other financial commitments, guarantees and contingencies (see paragraph 6A.2).	**23.22**

---

[6] *An example of the features of a detailed formal plan for restructuring, which may include termination benefits, is given in paragraph 16.15.*

Section 24 *Income Tax*

Scope of this section

24.1   For the purpose of this FRS, **income tax** includes all domestic and foreign taxes that are based on **taxable profit**.

24.2   This section covers accounting for income tax. It requires a **micro-entity** to recognise the **current tax** consequences of transactions and other events that have been recognised in the **financial statements**. Current tax is tax payable (refundable) in respect of the taxable profit (tax loss) for the current period or past **reporting periods**. This section prohibits the recognition of **deferred tax** which represents the future tax consequences of transactions and events recognised in the financial statements of the current and previous periods.

24.3   This section also covers accounting for value added tax (VAT) and other similar sales taxes, which are not income taxes.

Current tax

24.4   A micro-entity shall recognise a current tax **liability** for tax payable on taxable profit for the current and past periods. If the amount of tax paid for the current and past periods exceeds the amount of tax payable for those periods, the micro-entity shall recognise the excess as a current tax **asset**.

24.5   A micro-entity shall recognise a current tax asset for the benefit of a tax loss that can be carried back to recover tax paid in a previous period.

24.6   A micro-entity shall measure a current tax liability (asset) at the amount of tax it expects to pay (recover) using the tax rates and laws that have been enacted or **substantively enacted** by the **reporting date**.

Deferred tax

24.7   A micro-entity shall not recognise deferred tax.

Measurement of current tax

24.8   A micro-entity shall not discount current tax assets and liabilities.

Withholding tax on dividends

24.9   When a micro-entity pays dividends to its shareholders, it may be required to pay a portion of the dividends to taxation authorities on behalf of shareholders. Outgoing dividends and similar amounts payable shall be recognised at an amount that includes any withholding tax but excludes other taxes, such as attributable tax credits.

24.10   Incoming dividends and similar income receivable shall be recognised at an amount that includes any withholding tax but excludes other taxes, such as attributable tax credits. Any withholding tax suffered shall be shown as part of the tax charge.

Value Added Tax and other similar sales taxes

Turnover included in **profit or loss** shall exclude VAT and other similar sales taxes on taxable outputs and VAT imputed under the flat rate VAT scheme. **Expenses** shall exclude recoverable VAT and other similar recoverable sales taxes. Irrecoverable VAT allocable to **fixed assets** and to other items separately recognised shall be included in their cost where practicable and **material**.

24.11

Presentation

Allocation in profit or loss

A micro-entity shall present changes in a current tax liability (asset) as **tax expense** (income).

24.12

Offsetting

A micro-entity shall offset current tax assets and current tax liabilities, if and only if, it has a legally enforceable right to set off the amounts and it intends either to settle on a net basis or to realise the asset and settle the liability simultaneously.

24.13

Section 25 *Foreign Currency Translation*

Scope of this section

A **micro-entity** may have transactions in foreign currencies. This section prescribes how to include foreign currency transactions in the financial statements of a micro-entity. Where a micro-entity has a foreign branch, the micro-entity should refer to the requirements of Section 30 *Foreign Currency Translation* of **FRS 102** to determine if the foreign branch has a different functional currency, and if so, should apply the requirements of Section 30 of FRS 102 to those transactions undertaken by the foreign branch.

25.1

Reporting foreign currency transactions

Initial recognition

A foreign currency transaction is a transaction that is denominated or requires settlement in a foreign currency, including transactions arising when a micro-entity:

25.2

(a) buys or sells goods or services whose price is denominated in a foreign currency;
(b) borrows or lends funds when the amounts payable or receivable are denominated in a foreign currency; or
(c) otherwise acquires or disposes of **assets**, or incurs or settles **liabilities**, denominated in a foreign currency.

A micro-entity shall record a foreign currency transaction by applying to the foreign currency amount the spot exchange rate at the date of the transaction unless:

25.3

(a) the transaction is to be settled at a contracted rate, in which case that rate shall be used; or
(b) where a trading transaction is covered by a related or matching forward contract, in which case the rate of exchange specified in that contract shall be used.

25.4   The date of a transaction is the date on which the transaction first qualifies for **recognition** in accordance with this FRS. For practical reasons, a rate that approximates the actual rate at the date of the transaction is often used, for example, an average rate for a week or a month might be used for all transactions in each foreign currency occurring during that period. However, if exchange rates fluctuate significantly, the use of the average rate for a period is inappropriate.

Reporting at the end of the subsequent reporting periods

25.5   At the end of each **reporting period**, unless it is applying a contracted rate in accordance with paragraph 25.3 a micro-entity shall:

(a)   translate foreign currency **monetary items** using the **closing rate**; and

(b)   translate non-monetary items that are measured in terms of historical cost in a foreign currency using the exchange rate at the date of the transaction.

25.6   A micro-entity shall recognise, in **profit or loss** in the period in which they arise, exchange differences arising on the settlement of monetary items or on translating monetary items at rates different from those at which they were translated on initial recognition during the period or in previous periods.

Section 26 *Events after the End of the Reporting Period*

Scope of this section

26.1   This section defines events after the end of the **reporting period** and sets out principles for recognising and measuring those events.

Events after the end of the reporting period defined

26.2   Events after the end of the reporting period are those events, favourable and unfavourable, that occur between the end of the reporting period and the date when the financial statements are authorised for issue. There are two types of events:

(a)   those that provide evidence of conditions that existed at the end of the reporting period (adjusting events after the end of the reporting period); and

(b)   those that are indicative of conditions that arose after the end of the reporting period (non-adjusting events after the end of the reporting period).

26.3   Events after the end of the reporting period include all events up to the date when the **financial statements** are authorised for issue, even if those events occur after the public announcement of **profit or loss** or other selected financial information.

Recognition and measurement

Adjusting events after the end of the reporting period

26.4   A **micro-entity** shall adjust the amounts recognised in its **financial statements** to reflect adjusting events after the end of the reporting period.

26.5   The following are examples of adjusting events after the end of the reporting period that require a micro-entity to adjust the amounts recognised in its financial statements, or to recognise items that were not previously recognised:

(a) The settlement after the end of the reporting period of a court case that confirms that the micro-entity had a present obligation at the end of the reporting period. The micro-entity adjusts any previously recognised **provision** related to this court case in accordance with Section 16 *Provisions and Contingencies* or recognises a new provision. The micro-entity does not merely disclose a **contingent liability**. Rather, the settlement provides additional evidence to be considered in determining the provision that should be recognised at the end of the reporting period in accordance with Section 16.

(b) The receipt of information after the end of the reporting period indicating that an **asset** was impaired at the end of the reporting period, or that the amount of a previously recognised **impairment loss** for that asset needs to be adjusted. For example:

   (i) the bankruptcy of a customer that occurs after the end of the reporting period usually confirms that a loss existed at the end of the reporting period on a trade receivable and that the micro-entity needs to adjust the **carrying amount** of the trade receivable; and

   (ii) the sale of **inventories** after the end of the reporting period may give evidence about their selling price at the end of the reporting period for the purpose of assessing impairment at that date.

(c) The determination after the end of the reporting period of the cost of assets purchased, or the proceeds from assets sold, before the end of the reporting period.

(d) The determination after the end of the reporting period of the amount of profit-sharing or bonus payments, if the micro-entity had a legal or **constructive obligation** at the end of the reporting period to make such payments as a result of events before that date (see Section 23 *Employee Benefits*).

(e) The discovery of fraud or **errors** that show that the financial statements are incorrect.

Non-adjusting events after the end of the reporting period

A micro-entity shall not adjust the amounts recognised in its financial statements to reflect non-adjusting events after the end of the reporting period. **26.6**

Examples of non-adjusting events after the end of the reporting period include: **26.7**

(a) A decline in market value of investments between the end of the reporting period and the date when the financial statements are authorised for issue. The decline in market value does not normally relate to the condition of the investments at the end of the reporting period, but reflects circumstances that have arisen subsequently. Therefore, a micro-entity does not adjust the amounts recognised in its financial statements for the investments.

(b) An amount that becomes receivable as a result of a favourable judgement or settlement of a court case after the **reporting date** but before the financial statements are authorised for issue. This would be a **contingent asset** at the reporting date (see paragraph 16.18). However, agreement on the amount of damages for a judgement that was reached before the reporting date, but was not previously recognised because the amount could not be measured reliably, may constitute an adjusting event.

Going concern

A micro-entity shall not prepare its financial statements on a going concern basis if **26.8** management determines after the end of the reporting period that it either intends to liquidate the micro-entity or to cease trading, or that it has no realistic alternative but to do so.

26.9   Deterioration in operating results and **financial position** after the reporting period may lead management to determine that they intend to liquidate the micro-entity or to cease trading or that they have no realistic alternative but to do so. If the going concern basis of accounting is no longer appropriate, the effect is so pervasive that this section requires a fundamental change in the basis of accounting.

Dividends

26.10   If a micro-entity declares dividends to holders of its equity instruments after the end of the reporting period, the micro-entity shall not recognise those dividends as a **liability** at the end of the reporting period because no obligation exists at that time.

Section 27 *Specialised Activities*

Scope of this section

27.1   This section sets out the financial reporting requirements for **micro-entities** involved in agriculture.

Agriculture

Recognition

27.2   A micro-entity that is engaged in **agricultural activity** shall recognise a **biological asset** or an item of **agricultural produce** when, and only when:

(a)   the micro-entity controls the **asset** as a result of past events;

(b)   it is **probable** that future economic benefits associated with the asset will flow to the micro-entity; and

(c)   the cost of the **asset** can be measured reliably.

Measurement

27.3   A micro-entity shall measure biological assets at cost less any accumulated **depreciation** and any accumulated **impairment losses**.

27.4   Agricultural produce harvested from a micro-entity's biological assets shall be measured at the point of harvest at the lower of cost and estimated selling price less costs to complete and sell.

Such measurement is the cost at that date when applying Section 10 *Inventories* or another applicable section of this FRS.

Disclosure in the notes

27.5   A micro-entity shall determine the amount of any financial commitments, guarantees and contingencies not recognised in the **statement of financial position** for the acquisition of a biological asset and disclose that amount within the total amount of financial commitments, guarantees and contingencies (see paragraph 6A.2).

27.6   A micro-entity shall disclose an indication of the nature and form of any biological asset or item of agricultural produce given as security in respect of its commitments, guarantees and contingencies (see paragraph 6A.3).

Section 28 *Transition to this FRS*

Scope of this section

This section applies to a **first-time adopter of this FRS**, regardless of its previous accounting framework.   **28.1**

Notwithstanding the requirements in paragraphs 28.3 and 28.4, a **micro-entity** that has applied this FRS in a previous **reporting period**, but whose most recent previous annual **financial statements** were prepared in accordance with a different accounting framework, must either apply this section or else apply this FRS retrospectively in accordance with Section 8 *Accounting Policies, Changes in Estimates and Errors* as if the micro-entity had never stopped applying this FRS.   **28.2**

First-time adoption

A first-time adopter of this FRS shall apply this section in its first financial statements that conform to this FRS.   **28.3**

A micro-entity's first financial statements that conform to this FRS are the first financial statements prepared in accordance with this FRS if, for example, the micro-entity: **28.4**

(a)   did not present financial statements for previous periods; or
(b)   presented its most recent previous financial statements under previous UK and Republic of Ireland requirements or **FRS 102** and that are therefore not consistent with this FRS in all respects.

Paragraph 3.9 defines a complete set of financial statements for a micro-entity.   **28.5**

Paragraph 3.10 requires a micro-entity to disclose, in a complete set of financial statements, comparative information in respect of the preceding period for all amounts presented in the financial statements. Therefore, a micro-entity's **date of transition** to this FRS is the beginning of the earliest period for which the micro-entity presents full comparative information in accordance with this FRS in its first financial statements that comply with this FRS.   **28.6**

Procedures for preparing financial statements at the date of transition

Except as provided in paragraphs 28.9 to 28.11, a micro-entity shall, in its opening **statement of financial position** as of its date of transition to this FRS (ie the beginning of the earliest period presented):   **28.7**

(a)   recognise all **assets** and **liabilities** whose **recognition** is required by this FRS;
(b)   not recognise items as assets or liabilities if this FRS does not permit such recognition;
(c)   reclassify items that it recognised under its previous financial reporting framework as one type of asset, liability or component of **equity**, but are a different type of asset, liability or component of equity under this FRS; and
(d)   apply this FRS in **measuring** all recognised assets and liabilities.

This section does not require the opening statement of financial position to be presented.

The **accounting policies** that a micro-entity uses in its opening statement of financial position under this FRS may differ from those that it used for the same date using its previous financial reporting framework. The resulting adjustments arise from transactions, other events or conditions before the date of transition to this FRS. Therefore, a micro-entity   **28.8** shall recognise those adjustments directly in equity reserves at the date of transition to this FRS.

28.9   On first-time adoption of this FRS, a micro-entity shall not retrospectively change the accounting that it followed under its previous financial reporting framework for any of the following transactions:

(a)   *Derecognition of financial assets and financial liabilities*
Financial assets and **financial liabilities** derecognised under a micro-entity's previous accounting framework before the date of transition shall not be recognised upon adoption of this FRS. Conversely, for financial assets and liabilities that would have been derecognised under this FRS in a transaction that took place before the date of transition, but that were not derecognised under a micro-entity's previous accounting framework, a micro-entity may choose:

(i)   to derecognise them on adoption of this FRS; or
(ii)   to continue to recognise them until disposed of or settled.

(b)   *Accounting estimates.*

28.10   A micro-entity may use one or more of the following exemptions in preparing its first financial statements that conform to this FRS:

(a)   *Business combinations and goodwill*
A first-time adopter is not required to apply Section 14 *Business Combinations and Goodwill* to **business combinations** that were effected before the date of transition to this FRS. However, if a first-time adopter restates any business combination to comply with Section 14, it shall restate all later business combinations. If a first-time adopter does not apply Section 14 retrospectively, the first-time adopter shall recognise and measure all its assets and liabilities acquired or assumed in a past business combination at the date of transition to this FRS in accordance with paragraphs 28.7 to 28.9 or, if applicable, with paragraphs 28.10(b) to (h) except that no adjustment shall be made to the **carrying amount** of **goodwill**.

(b)   *Share-based payment transactions*
A first-time adopter is not required to apply Section 21 *Share-based Payment* to obligations arising from **share-based payment transactions** that were settled before the date of transition to this FRS.

(c)   *Investment properties*
A first-time adopter is not required to retrospectively apply paragraph 12.15 to determine the depreciated cost of each of the major components of an **investment property** at the date of transition to this FRS. If this exemption is applied, a first-time adopter shall:

(i)   Determine the total cost of the investment property including all of its components. Where no **depreciation** had been charged under the micro-entity's previous financial reporting framework, this can be calculated by reversing any revaluation **gains** or losses previously recorded in equity reserves.

(ii)   The cost of land, if any, shall be separated from buildings.

(iii)   Estimate the total depreciated cost of the investment property (excluding land) at the date of transition to this FRS, by recognising accumulated depreciation since the date of initial acquisition calculated on the basis of the **useful life** of the most significant component of the item of investment property (eg the main structural elements of the building).

(iv)   A portion of the estimated total depreciated cost calculated in paragraph (iii) shall then be allocated to each of the other major components (ie excluding the most significant component identified above) to determine their depreciated cost. The allocation should be made on a reasonable and consistent basis. For example, a possible basis of allocation is to multiply the current cost to replace the component by the ratio of its remaining useful life to the expected useful life of a replacement component.

(v) Any amount of the total depreciated cost not allocated under paragraph (iv) shall be allocated to the most significant component of the investment property.

(d) *Compound financial instruments*

Paragraph 17.11 requires a micro-entity to split a **compound financial instrument** into its liability and equity components at the date of issue. A first-time adopter need not separate those two components if the liability component is not outstanding at the date of transition to this FRS.

(e) *Arrangements containing a lease*

A first-time adopter may elect to determine whether an arrangement existing at the date of transition to this FRS contains a **lease** (see paragraph 15.4) on the basis of facts and circumstances existing at that date, rather than when the arrangement was entered into.

(f) *Decommissioning liabilities included in the cost of property, plant and equipment or investment property*

Paragraph 12.9(c) states that the cost of an item of **property, plant and equipment** or **investment property** includes the initial estimate of the costs of dismantling and removing the item and restoring the site on which it is located, the obligation for which a micro-entity incurs either when the item is acquired or as a consequence of having used the item during a particular period for purposes other than to produce **inventories** during that period. A first-time adopter may elect to measure this component of the cost of an item of property, plant and equipment or investment property at the date of transition to this FRS, rather than on the date(s) when the obligation initially arose.

(g) *Dormant companies*

A company within the **Act's** definition of a dormant company may elect to retain its accounting policies for reported assets, liabilities and equity at the date of transition to this FRS until there is any change to those balances or the company undertakes any new transactions.

(h) *Lease incentives*

A first-time adopter is not required to apply paragraphs 15.15 and 15.25 to **lease incentives** provided the term of the lease commenced before the date of transition to this FRS. The first-time adopter shall continue to recognise any residual benefit or cost associated with these lease incentives on the same basis as that applied at the date of transition to this FRS.

If it is **impracticable** for a micro-entity to restate the opening statement of financial position at the date of transition for one or more of the adjustments required by paragraph 28.7, the micro-entity shall apply paragraphs 28.7 to 28.10 for such adjustments in the earliest period for which it is practicable to do so.   **28.11**

Where applicable to the transactions, events or arrangements affected by applying these exemptions, a micro-entity may continue to use the exemptions that are applied at the date of transition to this FRS when preparing subsequent financial statements, until such time when the assets and liabilities associated with those transactions, events or arrangements are derecognised.   **28.12**

Approval by the FRC

Financial Reporting Standard 105 *The Financial Reporting Standard applicable to the Micro-entities Regime* was approved for issue by the Financial Reporting Council on 1 July 2015, following its consideration of the Accounting Council's Advice for this FRS.

The Accounting Council's Advice to the FRC to issue FRS 105

Introduction

1   This report provides an overview of the main issues that have been considered by the Accounting Council in advising the Financial Reporting Council (FRC) to issue FRS 105 *The Financial Reporting Standard applicable to the Micro-entities Regime*, incorporating the Council's advice following the publication of Financial Reporting Exposure Draft (FRED) 58 *Draft FRS 105 The Financial Reporting Standard applicable to the Micro-entities Regime* and FRED 50 *Draft FRC Abstract 1 Residential Management Companies' Financial Statements and Consequential Amendments to the FRSSE.*

2   The FRC, in accordance with the *Statutory Auditors (Amendment of Companies Act 2006 and Delegation of Functions etc) Order 2012* (SI 2012/1741), is a prescribed body for issuing accounting standards in the UK. The *Foreword to Accounting Standards* sets out the application of accounting standards in the Republic of Ireland.

3   In accordance with the *FRC Codes and Standards: procedures*, any proposal to issue, amend or withdraw a code or standard is put to the FRC Board with the full advice of the relevant Councils and/or the Codes & Standards Committee. Ordinarily, the FRC Board will only reject the advice put to it where:

(a)   it is apparent that a significant group of stakeholders has not been adequately consulted;

(b)   the necessary assessment of the impact of the proposal has not been completed, including an analysis of costs and benefits;

(c)   insufficient consideration has been given to the timing or cost of implementation; or

(d)   the cumulative impact of a number of proposals would make the adoption of an otherwise satisfactory proposal inappropriate.

4   The FRC has established the Accounting Council as the relevant Council to assist it in the setting of accounting standards.

Advice

5   The Accounting Council is advising the FRC to issue FRS 105 *The Financial Reporting Standard applicable to the Micro-entities Regime* to facilitate the effective adoption of the micro-entities regime introduced by company law. FRS 105 has been developed from the recognition and measurement requirements of FRS 102 *The Financial Reporting Standard applicable in the UK and Republic of Ireland*, adapted for compliance with the specific company law requirements applicable to the micro-entities regime and other appropriate simplifications.

6   The Accounting Council's Advice on FRS 102 is contained in that standard.

Background

7   The micro-entities regime was introduced in UK company law in 2013 with significantly reduced financial statements presentation and disclosure requirements. In order to reflect the legal requirements of the new micro-entities regime, the FRC amended the *Financial Reporting Standard for Smaller Entities* (FRSSE) in April 2014, but this was intended to be a temporary solution until the FRC developed a new standard for entities that prepare financial statements under the micro-entities regime.

In February 2015, the FRC published FRED 58 to consult on a new accounting standard **8** for micro-entities.

In August 2013, the FRC issued FRED 50, a consultation on residential management **9** companies' financial statements which is relevant in the context of the reporting by micro-entities.

The Accounting Council has considered the responses to FREDs 50 and 58 and took them **10** into account when issuing its advice.

Objective

The FRC gives careful consideration to its objective and the intended effects when **11** developing new accounting standards or requirements for the UK and Republic of Ireland. In developing accounting standards, including FRS 105, the overriding objective of the FRC is to enable users of accounts to receive high-quality understandable financial reporting proportionate to the size and complexity of the entity and users' information needs.

In meeting this objective, the FRC aims to provide succinct financial reporting standards **12** that:

(a) have consistency with global accounting standards through the application of an IFRS-based solution unless an alternative clearly better meets the overriding objective;
(b) reflect up-to-date thinking and developments in the way businesses operate and the transactions they undertake;
(c) balance consistent principles for accounting by all UK and Republic of Ireland entities with practical solutions, based on size, complexity, public interest and users' information needs;
(d) promote efficiency within groups; and
(e) are cost-effective to apply.

Consistent recognition and measurement requirements with FRS 102

The Accounting Council is of the view that the reporting requirements for all small entities **13** (including micro-entities) should be based on FRS 102 because it improves consistency across the financial reporting framework in the UK and Republic of Ireland.

To that end, FRED 58 proposed that FRS 105 applies the recognition and measurement **14** requirements of FRS 102, adapted where necessary to reflect the legal requirements of the micro-entities regime and simplified further to reflect the size and nature of micro-entities.

Respondents to the consultation supported that FRS 105 should be developed from **15** FRS 102 and the standard has been finalised on that basis.

The Accounting Council notes that it would not otherwise have recommended some of **16** the simplifications made in FRS 105, including the omission of some of the disclosures required by FRS 102, if they had not been necessary to ensure legal compliance with the micro-entities regime. For example, the Accounting Council continues to believe that investment property should always, where practicable, be measured at fair value as this provides more relevant information to users of the financial statements on an investment property company's financial position and performance. However, company law prohibits the revaluation of any asset by micro-entities and instead requires that fixed assets are measured at cost less depreciation and impairment.

Amendments to FRS 102 to align FRS 105 with the legal requirements

Scope

17   FRS 105 is an accounting standard applicable to the preparation of the financial statements of a micro-entity which are presumed in law to give a true and fair view in accordance with the micro-entities regime.

18   During its deliberations, the Accounting Council was requested to consider whether FRS 105 could be applied to financial statements prepared for the purpose of submission to the tax authorities by unincorporated businesses and individuals that, if they were companies, would be eligible to apply the micro-entities regime.

19   The Accounting Council notes that the form and content of financial statements prepared for tax purposes is a matter for the relevant tax authorities to determine and believes it is therefore not possible for the FRC to explicitly permit or prohibit the application of FRS 105 for such purpose. The Accounting Council notes that compliance with FRS 105 by businesses incorporated as companies that meet the conditions to apply the micros-entities regime will result in financial statements that in law are presumed to give a true and fair view.

20   The availability of the micro-entities regime is restricted to the smallest of companies and some types of entities are excluded. For example, charities and financial institutions are ineligible to report under this regime. For that reason, in contrast to FRS 102, FRS 105 does not contain any specific requirements that only apply to these entities.

21   The micro-entities regime is not available to entities that are required or choose to prepare consolidated financial statements. FRS 105 therefore does not contain accounting requirements that are relevant for the preparation of consolidated financial statements.

Presentation and disclosure

22   The micro-entities regime specifies certain minimum presentation and disclosure requirements. Financial statements which include the prescribed minimum accounting items are presumed in law to give a true and fair view and no further disclosures need to be made. FRS 105 has been adapted to reflect the legal minimum presentation and disclosure requirements.

Recognition and measurement

23   The micro-entities regime prohibits the use of the Alternative Accounting Rules or the Fair Value Rules set out in company law and therefore micro-entities are not permitted to revalue or subsequently measure assets or liabilities at fair value. To take account of the legal restrictions on fair value measurement, FRS 105 does not allow the subsequent measurement of any asset or liability at fair value. This affects in particular financial instruments and investment properties which a micro-entity has to measure at depreciated cost.

Further simplifications over and above the legal requirements

24   The micro-entities regime is intended to be deregulatory and the Accounting Council believes it is appropriate to simplify some of the accounting requirements applicable under FRS 102. The Accounting Council considers that simplifications would be appropriate if:

(a) the benefits of applying the accounting treatment in FRS 102 do not outweigh the burden for micro-entities and an alternative, more straightforward, treatment could be identified;

(b) the lack of detail in the formats of the financial statements and/or supporting disclosures would limit the understanding of the financial information presented; and/or

(c) transactions occur infrequently amongst micro-entities.

The Accounting Council notes that permitting accounting policy choices in FRS 105 **25** would add complexity for preparers of a micro-entity's financial statements and could cause confusion to users due to the lack of detail in the formats of the financial statements and lack of supporting disclosures to explain the policy choice taken. As a result, the Accounting Council advises that FRS 105 should not contain accounting policy options, except on first-time adoption of FRS 105.

The Accounting Council advises that first-time adopters of FRS 105 should be given a **26** choice on whether they apply the requirements of FRS 105 fully retrospectively or whether they apply one or more of the transitional exemptions. Although this introduces a degree of complexity for preparers and users, the Accounting Council believes transitional exemptions are important for a smooth transition and not allowing a choice would disadvantage micro-entities unnecessarily over entities that transition to FRS 102.

In all other cases where accounting policy options are provided in FRS 102 they should be **27** removed in FRS 105. The Accounting Council advises that FRS 105 should mandate the most straightforward and easy to apply option.

The key areas where simplifications have been made are: **28**

(a) Prohibition of accounting for deferred taxation on the basis that this is a complex area of accounting and the lack of disclosure in a micro-entity's financial statements make it impossible to distinguish between current and deferred tax.

(b) Prohibition of accounting for equity-settled share-based payments prior to the issue of the shares, because of the prohibition to use fair value measurements and lack of supporting disclosure in the financial statements.

(c) A requirement that the contributions payable to any post-employment benefit plans are accounted for as an expense, subject to a requirement for defined benefit plans to recognise a liability for a schedule of contributions to the extent that it relates to the deficit. The simplification was made on the basis that very few micro-entities will have defined benefit pension schemes.

(d) The distinction between functional and presentation currency is removed as it will be very rare for micro-entities to have a different functional and presentational currency.

(e) Requirement to use contracted rates to translate foreign currency denominated assets and liabilities rather than spot rates. This will simplify the accounting when micro-entities enter into foreign currency forward contracts.

(f) All borrowing and development costs must be expensed, because this is considered the simplest option of accounting for these costs.

(g) Mandating the application of the accrual model to account for government grants because this is considered the simplest method of accounting for these transactions.

(h) Simplifications in relation to the accounting for financial instruments as far as the allocation of interest and transaction costs is concerned. The effective interest rate method is considered too onerous to apply by micro-entities.

(i) Removal of the requirement to impute a market-rate of interest in lending arrangements conducted at non-market rates because considering the nature and size of micro-entities the costs of mandating this requirement would exceed the benefits.

(j) Simplified requirements for classifying financial instruments as equity or debt because most micro-entities will issue simple equity instruments.

(k)   Prohibition of the recognition of separately identifiable intangible assets in a trade and asset acquisition because these are not required items in the financial statements formats.

(l)   Removal of the requirements concerning accounting for hyperinflation because this is unlikely to be an issue for micro-entities.

(m)   Removal of accounting requirements relating to specialised activities including extractive activities, service concessions, heritage assets and funding commitments because micro-entities will not typically enter into these transactions.

Feedback on the proposed simplification from respondents to FRED 58

29   Most respondents supported the proposed simplifications and the principles applied by the Accounting Council to assess whether a simplification is appropriate. It was noted that some stakeholders are of the view that the recognition of deferred tax should be permitted or required in FRS 105. However, after having considered these comments the Accounting Council retains its view that without additional disclosure the benefits of requiring micro-entities to account for deferred tax do not exceed the costs.

30   FRED 58 proposed that government grants should be accounted for using the performance model. The views of respondents on whether FRS 105 should require the performance or accrual model were divided. The evidence provided by respondents suggests that the accrual model may in practice be easier to apply than the performance model and the Accounting Council therefore advises that FRS 105 should mandate the accrual model.

Determining accounting policies where FRS 105 does not contain requirements

31   A micro-entity that enters into a transaction that is not specifically covered in FRS 105 is required to refer to the concepts and pervasive principles set out in Section 2 *Concepts and Pervasive Principles* of FRS 105 in determining its accounting policies. The Accounting Council notes that micro-entities are not required to refer to other accounting standards or authoritative guidance because these requirements may be inconsistent with the legal requirements of the micro-entities regime.

Transitional provisions – fair value / revaluation as deemed cost

32   The micro-entities regime requires micro-entities to apply the historical cost accounting rules, which require fixed assets to be included at purchase price or production cost. Therefore the Accounting Council advises that it would be inconsistent with the legal framework for micro-entities to provide in FRS 105 a transitional exemption to allow micro-entities to carry forward previous revaluations of property, plant and equipment or the fair value of investment properties or investments in shares as deemed cost.

33   FRS 105 provides a transitional exemption in respect of the determination of the depreciated historical cost of investment properties. Under the transitional exemption a micro-entity is permitted, for the purpose of estimating accumulated depreciation at the date of transition, to treat an investment property as if it were a single asset with a useful economic life equal to that of its most significant component, which is likely to be comprised of its main structural elements such as foundations, walls etc. This exempts a micro-entity from having to determine the historical cost of each component that has been replaced in the past and the depreciation that would have been charged since their initial recognition.

The Accounting Council notes that the micro-entities regime is optional and that if a **34** micro-entity wishes to retain revalued amounts in its financial statement it could continue to apply the small company regime, rather than moving to the micro-entities regime.

Structure and language of FRS 105

FRS 105 should be as easily accessible and understandable as possible. A number of **35** respondents to FRED 58 suggested that the accessibility of FRS 105 could be enhanced by departing from the section and paragraph numbering of FRS 102. The Accounting Council agrees and advises that FRS 105 should where possible maintain consistency with the language and terminology used in FRS 102, but use its own structure (ie section and paragraph numbering).

Residents' management companies

In considering the feedback received from the FRC's previous consultations, the Accounting **36** Council noted that no clear consensus existed amongst respondents on the appropriate basis of accounting in the statutory financial statements of residents' management companies[7] where service charge monies are held on trust in accordance with section 42 of the Landlord and Tenant Act 1987. However, there was general agreement that no change should be made to FRS 105, or any other relevant financial reporting standard (including FRS 102), to address such a narrow and sector-specific issue.

The Accounting Council considered this issue carefully. It assessed the case for further **37** intervention by reference to the FRC's published *Principles for the development of Codes, Standards and Guidance*[8] and, in particular, the extent to which the anticipated benefits from any changes to current practices would outweigh the costs incurred by the entities involved. It agreed with respondents that this matter does not merit a change in accounting standards, and therefore advises that no changes are made to FRS 105 (or FRS 102) that are specific to residents' management companies.

Effective date

FRS 105 is effective for accounting periods commencing on or after 1 January 2016, in line **38** with the mandatory effective date of the consequential amendments to FRS 102 resulting from the UK's new small companies regime. Early application of FRS 105 is permitted.

See Appendix IV *Republic of Ireland (RoI) legal references* of FRS 105 for information on **39** the applicability of the micro-entities regime in the Republic of Ireland.

Approval of this advice

This advice to the FRC was approved by the Accounting Council on 16 June 2015. **40**

---

[7] *An organisation which may be referred to in the lease, which is responsible for the provision of services, and manages and arranges maintenance of the property, but which does not necessarily have any legal interest in the property.*

[8] *This can be found on the FRC's website at www.frc.org.uk/FRC-Documents/FRC/About-the-FRC/Principles-for-the-development-of-Codes.pdf.*

Appendix I: Glossary

This glossary is an integral part of this FRS.

accounting policies	The specific principles, bases, conventions, rules and practices applied by an entity in preparing and presenting **financial statements**.
accrual basis (of accounting)	The effects of transactions and other events are recognised when they occur (and not as cash or its equivalent is received or paid) and they are recorded in the accounting records and reported in the **financial statements** of the periods to which they relate.
accumulating compensated absences	Compensated absences that are carried forward and can be used in future periods if the current period's entitlement is not used in full.
Act	The Companies Act 2006
active market	A market in which all the following conditions exist: (a) the items traded in the market are homogeneous; (b) willing buyers and sellers can normally be found at any time; and (c) prices are available to the public.
agent	An entity is acting as an agent when it does not have exposure to the significant risks and rewards associated with the sale of goods or the rendering of services. One feature indicating that an entity is acting as an agent is that the amount the entity earns is predetermined, being either a fixed fee per transaction or a stated percentage of the amount billed to the customer.
agricultural activity	The management by an entity of the biological transformation of **biological assets** for sale, into **agricultural produce** or into additional biological assets.
agricultural produce	The harvested product of the entity's **biological assets**.
amortisation	The systematic allocation of the **depreciable amount** of an **asset** over its **useful life**.
asset	A resource controlled by the entity as a result of past events and from which future economic benefits are expected to flow to the entity.

associate	An entity, including an unincorporated entity such as a partnership, over which the investor has **significant influence** and that is neither a **subsidiary** nor an interest in a **joint venture**.
biological asset	A living animal or plant.
borrowing costs	Interest and other costs incurred by an entity in connection with the borrowing of funds.
business	An integrated set of activities and **assets** conducted and managed for the purpose of providing: (a) a return to investors; or (b) lower costs or other economic benefits directly and proportionately to policyholders or participants. A business generally consists of inputs, processes applied to those inputs, and resulting outputs that are, or will be, used to generate **revenues**. If **goodwill** is present in a transferred set of activities and assets, the transferred set shall be presumed to be a business.
business combination	The bringing together of separate entities or **businesses** into one reporting entity.
carrying amount	The amount at which an **asset** or **liability** is recognised in the **statement of financial position**.
cash-generating unit	The smallest identifiable group of **assets** that generates cash inflows that are largely independent of the cash inflows from other assets or groups of assets.
cash-settled share-based payment transaction	A **share-based payment transaction** in which the entity acquires goods or services by incurring a **liability** to transfer cash or other **assets** to the supplier of those goods or services for amounts that are based on the price (or value) of the entity's shares or other equity instruments of the entity or another group entity.
change in accounting estimate	An adjustment of the **carrying amount** of an **asset** or a **liability**, or the amount of the periodic consumption of an asset, that results from the assessment of the present status of, and expected future benefits and obligations associated with, assets and liabilities. Changes in accounting estimates result from new information or new developments and, accordingly, are not corrections of **errors**.

closing rate	The spot exchange rate at the end of the **reporting period**.
commencement of lease term	The date from which the lessee is entitled to exercise its right to use the leased asset. It is the date of initial **recognition** of the **lease** (ie the recognition of the **assets**, **liabilities**, **income** or **expenses** resulting from the lease, as appropriate).
compound financial instrument	A **financial instrument** that, from the issuer's perspective, contains both a **liability** and an **equity** element.
consolidated financial statements	The **financial statements** of a **parent** and its **subsidiaries** presented as those of a single economic entity.
construction contract	A contract specifically negotiated for the construction of an **asset** or a combination of assets that are closely interrelated or interdependent in terms of their design, technology and function or their ultimate purpose or use.
constructive obligation	An obligation that derives from an entity's actions where: (a) by an established pattern of past practice, published policies or a sufficiently specific current statement, the entity has indicated to other parties that it will accept certain responsibilities; and (b as a result, the entity has created a valid expectation on the part of those other parties that it will discharge those responsibilities
contingent asset	A possible **asset** that arises from past events and whose existence will be confirmed only by the occurrence or non-occurrence of one or more uncertain future events not wholly within the control of the entity.

contingent liability	(a) a possible obligation that arises from past events and whose existence will be confirmed only by the occurrence or non-occurrence of one or more uncertain future events not wholly within the control of the entity; or
	(b) a present obligation that arises from past events but is not recognised because:
	(i) it is not **probable** that an outflow of resources embodying economic benefits will be required to settle the obligation; or
	(ii) the amount of the obligation cannot be measured with sufficient reliability.
contingent rent	That portion of the lease payments that is not fixed in amount but is based on the future amount of a factor that changes other than with the passage of time (eg percentage of future sales, amount of future use, future price indices, and future market rates of interest).
control (of an entity)	The power to govern the financial and operating policies of an entity so as to obtain benefits from its activities.
current tax	The amount of **income tax** payable (refundable) in respect of the **taxable profit (tax loss)** for the current period or past **reporting periods**.
date of transition	The beginning of the earliest period for which an entity presents full comparative information in a given standard in its first financial statements that comply with that standard.
deferred tax	Income tax payable (recoverable) in respect of the **taxable profit (tax loss)** for future **reporting periods** as a result of past transactions or events.
defined benefit plans	**Post-employment benefit plans** other than **defined contribution plans**.
defined contribution plans	**Post-employment benefit plans** under which an entity pays fixed contributions into a separate entity (a fund) and has no legal or **constructive obligation** to pay further contributions or to make direct benefit payments to employees if the fund does not hold sufficient **assets** to pay all **employee benefits** relating to employee service in the current and prior periods.
depreciable amount	The cost of an **asset**, or other amount substituted for cost (in the **financial statements**), less its **residual value**.

depreciation	The systematic allocation of the **depreciable amount** of an **asset** over its **useful life**.
derecognition	The removal of a previously recognised **asset** or **liability** from an entity's **statement of financial position**.
derivative	Is a **financial instrument** with the following three characteristics: (a) its value changes in response to the change in a specified interest rate, financial instrument price, commodity price, foreign exchange rate, index of prices or rates, credit rating or credit index, or other variable (sometimes called the 'underlying'), provided in the case of a non-financial variable that the variable is not specific to a party to the contract; (b) it requires no initial net investment or an initial net investment that is smaller than would be required for other types of contracts that would be expected to have a similar response to changes in market factors; and (c) it is settled at a future date.
development	The application of **research** findings or other knowledge to a plan or design for the production of new or substantially improved materials, devices, products, processes, systems or services before the start of commercial production or use.
employee benefits	All forms of consideration given by an entity in exchange for service rendered by employees.
equity	The residual interest in the **assets** of the entity after deducting all its **liabilities**.
equity-settled share-based payment transaction	A **share-based payment transaction** in which the entity: (a) receives goods or services as consideration for its own equity instruments (including shares or **share options**); or (b) receives goods or services but has no obligation to settle the transaction with the supplier.

errors	Omissions from, and misstatements in, the entity's **financial statements** for one or more prior periods arising from a failure to use, or misuse of, reliable information that:
	(a) was available when financial statements for those periods were authorised for issue; and
	(b) could reasonably be expected to have been obtained and taken into account in the preparation and presentation of those financial statements.
expenses	Decreases in economic benefits during the **reporting period** in the form of outflows or depletions of **assets** or incurrences of **liabilities** that result in decreases in **equity**, other than those relating to distributions to equity investors.
fair value	The amount for which an **asset** could be exchanged, a **liability** settled, or an equity instrument granted could be exchanged, between knowledgeable, willing parties in an arm's length transaction. In the absence of any specific guidance provided in the relevant section of this FRS, the guidance in paragraph 2.31 shall be used in determining fair value.
fair value less costs to sell	The amount obtainable from the sale of an **asset** in an arm's length transaction between knowledgeable, willing parties, less the costs of disposal.
finance lease	A **lease** that transfers substantially all the risks and rewards incidental to ownership of an **asset**. Title may or may not eventually be transferred. A lease that is not a finance lease is an **operating lease**.

financial asset	Any **asset** that is:
	(a) cash;
	(b) an equity instrument of another entity;
	(c) a contractual right:
	    (i) to receive cash or another financial asset from another entity; or
	    (ii) to exchange financial assets or **financial liabilities** with another entity under conditions that are potentially favourable to the entity; or
	(d) a contract that will or may be settled in the entity's own equity instruments and:
	    (i) under which the entity is or may be obliged to receive a variable number of the entity's own equity instruments; or
	    (ii) that will or may be settled other than by the exchange of a fixed amount of cash or another financial asset for a fixed number of the entity's own equity instruments. For this purpose the entity's own equity instruments do not include instruments that are themselves contracts for the future receipt or delivery of the entity's own equity instruments.

financial guarantee contract	A contract that requires the issuer to make specified payments to reimburse the holder for a loss it incurs because a specified debtor fails to make payments when due in accordance with the original or modified terms of a debt instrument.
financial instrument	A contract that gives rise to a **financial asset** of one entity and a **financial liability** or equity instrument of another entity.

financial liability	Any **liability** that is:
	(a) a contractual obligation:
	(i) to deliver cash or another **financial asset** to another entity; or
	(ii) to exchange financial assets or financial liabilities with another entity under conditions that are potentially unfavourable to the entity, or
	(b) a contract that will or may be settled in the entity's own equity instruments and:
	(i) under which the entity is or may be obliged to deliver a variable number of the entity's own equity instruments; or
	(ii) will or may be settled other than by the exchange of a fixed amount of cash or another financial asset for a fixed number of the entity's own equity instruments. For this purpose the entity's own equity instruments do not include instruments that are themselves contracts for the future receipt or delivery of the entity's own equity instruments.
financial position	The relationship of the **assets, liabilities** and **equity** of an entity as reported in the **statement of financial position**.
financial statements	A structured presentation of the **financial position** and financial **performance** of an entity.
financing activities	Activities that result in changes in the size and composition of the contributed **equity** and borrowings of the entity.
first-time adopter of this FRS	An entity that presents its first annual **financial statements** that conform to this FRS, regardless of its previous accounting framework.
fixed assets	**Assets** of an entity which are intended for use on a continuing basis in the entity's activities.
FRS 102	FRS 102 *The Financial Reporting Standard applicable in the UK and Republic of Ireland*
gains	Increases in economic benefits that meet the definition of **income** but are not **revenue**.

goodwill	Future economic benefits arising from **assets** that are not capable of being individually identified and separately recognised.
government grant	Assistance by government in the form of a transfer of resources to an entity in return for past or future compliance with specified conditions relating to the **operating activities** of the entity. Government refers to government, government agencies and similar bodies whether local, national or international.
grant date	The date at which the entity and another party (including an employee) agree to a share-based payment arrangement, being when the entity and the counterparty have a shared understanding of the terms and conditions of the arrangement. At grant date the entity confers on the counterparty the right to cash, other **assets**, or equity instruments of the entity, provided the specified vesting conditions, if any, are met. If that agreement is subject to an approval process (for example, by shareholders), grant date is the date when that approval is obtained.
gross investment in a lease	The aggregate of: (a) the **minimum lease payments** receivable by the lessor under a **finance lease**; and (b) any unguaranteed **residual value** accruing to the lessor.
impairment loss	The amount by which the **carrying amount** of an **asset** exceeds: (a) in the case of **inventories**, its selling price less costs to complete and sell; (b) in the case of **financial assets** the amounts as set out in paragraph 9.18; or (c) in the case of any other asset, its **recoverable amount**.
impracticable	Applying a requirement is impracticable when the entity cannot apply it after making every reasonable effort to do so.
inception of the lease	The earlier of the date of the lease agreement and the date of commitment by the parties to the principal provisions of the **lease**.

income	Increases in economic benefits during the **reporting period** in the form of inflows or enhancements of **assets** or decreases of **liabilities** that result in increases in **equity**, other than those relating to contributions from equity investors.
income statement	**Financial statement** that presents all items of **income** and **expense** recognised in a **reporting period** (referred to as the profit and loss account in the **Act**).
income tax	All domestic and foreign taxes that are based on **taxable profits**. Income tax also includes taxes, such as withholding taxes, that are payable by a **subsidiary**, **associate** or **joint venture** on distributions to the reporting entity.
intangible asset	An identifiable non-monetary asset without physical substance. Such an **asset** is identifiable when: (a) it is separable, ie capable of being separated or divided from the entity and sold, transferred, licensed, rented or exchanged, either individually or together with a related contract, asset or **liability**; or (b) it arises from contractual or other legal rights, regardless of whether those rights are transferable or separable from the entity or from other rights and obligations.
interest rate implicit in the lease	The discount rate that, at the **inception of the lease**, causes the aggregate **present value** of: (a) the **minimum lease payments**; and (b) the unguaranteed **residual value** to be equal to the sum of: (i) the **fair value** of the leased **asset**; and (ii) any initial direct costs of the lessor.
inventories	**Assets**: (a) held for sale in the ordinary course of business; (b) in the process of production for such sale; or (c) in the form of materials or supplies to be consumed in the production process or in the rendering of services.

investment property	Property (land or a building, or part of a building, or both) held by the owner or by the lessee under a **finance lease** to earn rentals or for capital appreciation or both, rather than for: (a) use in the production or supply of goods or services or for administrative purposes; or (b) sale in the ordinary course of business.
joint control	The contractually agreed sharing of **control** over an economic activity. It exists only when the strategic financial and operating decisions relating to the activity require the unanimous consent of the parties sharing control (the **venturers**).
joint venture	A contractual arrangement whereby two or more parties undertake an economic activity that is subject to **joint control**. Joint ventures can take the form of jointly controlled operations, jointly controlled **assets**, or **jointly controlled entities**.
jointly controlled entity	A **joint venture** that involves the establishment of a corporation, partnership or other entity in which each **venturer** has an interest. The entity operates in the same way as other entities, except that a contractual arrangement between the venturers establishes **joint control** over the economic activity of the entity.
lease	An agreement whereby the lessor conveys to the lessee in return for a payment or series of payments the right to use an **asset** for an agreed period of time.
lease incentives	Incentives provided by the lessor to the lessee to enter into a new or renew an **operating lease**. Examples of such incentives include up-front cash payments to the lessee, the reimbursement or assumption by the lessor of costs of the lessee (such as relocation costs, leasehold improvements and costs associated with pre-existing lease commitments of the lessee), or initial periods of the **lease** provided by the lessor rent-free or at a reduced rent.

lease term	The non-cancellable period for which the lessee has contracted to **lease** the **asset** together with any further terms for which the lessee has the option to continue to lease the asset, with or without further payment, when at the **inception of the lease** it is reasonably certain that the lessee will exercise the option.
lessee's incremental borrowing rate (of interest)	The rate of interest the lessee would have to pay on a similar **lease** or, if that is not determinable, the rate that, at the **inception of the lease**, the lessee would incur to borrow over a similar term, and with a similar security, the funds necessary to purchase the **asset**.
liability	A present obligation of the entity arising from past events, the settlement of which is expected to result in an outflow from the entity of resources embodying economic benefits.
limited liability partnership (LLP)	A limited liability partnership formed under the Limited Liability Partnerships Act 2000 or the Limited Liability Partnerships Act (Northern Ireland) 2002.
material	Omissions or misstatements of items are material if they could, individually or collectively, influence the economic decisions of users taken on the basis of the **financial statements**. Materiality depends on the size and nature of the omission or misstatement judged in the surrounding circumstances. The size or nature of the item, or a combination of both, could be the determining factor.
measurement	The process of determining the monetary amounts at which the elements of the **financial statements** are to be recognised and carried in the **statement of financial position** and **income statement**.

micro-entity	(a) A company meeting the definition of a micro-entity as set out in section 384A of the **Act**, and not prevented from applying the micro-entity provisions by section 384B of the Act;
	(b) an **LLP** which qualifies as a micro-entity and is not prevented from applying the micro-entity provisions in accordance with Regulation 5A of the *Limited Liability Partnerships (Accounts and Audit) (Application of Companies Act 2006) Regulations 2008* (SI 2008/1911); or
	(c) a **qualifying partnership** that would meet the definition of a micro-entity as set out in section 384A of the Act, and not be prevented from applying the micro-entity provisions by section 384B of the Act, if the partnership were a company.
micro-entity minimum accounting items	The item of information required under the **micro-entities regime** to be contained in the **financial statements** of a **micro-entity**. These are set out in Sections 4 *Statement of Financial Position*, 5 *Income Statement* and 6 *Notes to the Financial Statements* of this FRS.
micro-entity provisions	(a) Any provisions of Part 15, Part 16 or regulations made under Part 15 of the **Act**; or
	(b) any provisions of the **Small LLP Regulations**, relating specifically to the individual accounts of an entity which qualifies as a **micro-entity**.
micro-entities regime	The legal requirements and exemptions relating to the preparation of the **financial statements** of **micro-entities** as set out in the **Act**, the **Small Companies Regulations** and the **Small LLP Regulations**.

minimum lease payments	The payments over the **lease term** that the lessee is or can be required to make, excluding **contingent rent**, costs for services and taxes to be paid by and reimbursed to the lessor, together with:
	
	(a) for a lessee, any amounts guaranteed by the lessee or by a party related to the lessee; or
	
	(b) for a lessor, any **residual value** guaranteed to the lessor by:
	
	   (i) the lessee;
	
	   (ii) a party related to the lessee; or
	
	   (iii) a third party unrelated to the lessor that is financially capable of discharging the obligations under the guarantee.
	
	However, if the lessee has an option to purchase the **asset** at a price that is expected to be sufficiently lower than **fair value** at the date the option becomes exercisable for it to be reasonably certain, at the **inception of the lease**, that the option will be exercised, the minimum lease payments comprise the minimum payments payable over the lease term to the expected date of exercise of this purchase option and the payment required to exercise it.

monetary items	Units of currency held and **assets** and **liabilities** to be received or paid in a fixed or determinable number of units of currency.
multi-employer (benefit) plans	**Defined contribution plans** (other than **state plans**) or **defined benefit plans** (other than state plans) that: (a) pool the **assets** contributed by various entities that are not under common control; and (b) use those assets to provide benefits to employees of more than one entity, on the basis that contribution and benefit levels are determined without regard to the identity of the entity that employs the employees concerned.
net investment in a lease	The **gross investment in a lease** discounted at the **interest rate implicit in the lease**.

non-exchange transaction	A transaction whereby an entity receives value from another entity without directly giving approximately equal value in exchange, or gives value to another entity without directly receiving approximately equal value in exchange.
notes (to the financial statements prepared under this FRS)	Notes contain information in addition to that presented in the **statement of financial position** and **income statement**. Notes are required to be presented at the foot of the statement of financial position.
onerous contract	A contract in which the unavoidable costs of meeting the obligations under the contract exceed the economic benefits expected to be received under it.
operating activities	The principal revenue-producing activities of the entity and other activities that are not investing or **financing activities**.
operating lease	A **lease** that does not transfer substantially all the risks and rewards incidental to ownership. A lease that is not an operating lease is a **finance lease**.
ordinary share	An equity instrument that is subordinate to all other classes of equity instrument.
owners	Holders of instruments classified as **equity**.
parent	An entity that has one or more **subsidiaries**.
performance	The relationship of the **income** and **expenses** of a **micro-entity**, as reported in the **income statement**.
post-employment benefits	**Employee benefits** (other than **termination benefits** and short-term employee benefits) that are payable after the completion of employment.
post-employment benefit plans	Formal or informal arrangements under which an entity provides **post-employment benefits** for one or more employees.
present value	A current estimate of the present discounted value of the future net **cash flows** in the normal course of business.

principal	An entity is acting as a principal when it has exposure to the significant risks and rewards associated with the sale of goods or the rendering of services. Features that indicate that an entity is acting as a principal include: (a) the entity has the primary responsibility for providing the goods or services to the customer or for fulfilling the order, for example by being responsible for the acceptability of the products or services ordered or purchased by the customer; (b) the entity has **inventory** risk before or after the customer order, during shipping or on return; (c) the entity has latitude in establishing prices, either directly or indirectly, for example by providing additional goods or services; and (d) the entity bears the customer's credit risk for the amount receivable from the customer.
probable	More likely than not.
profit or loss	The total of **income** less **expenses**.
property, plant and equipment	Tangible assets that: are held for use in the production or supply of goods or services, for rental to others, or for administrative purposes; and are expected to be used during more than one period.
prospectively (applying a change in accounting policy)	Applying the new **accounting policy** to transactions, other events and conditions occurring after the date as at which the policy is changed.
provision	A **liability** of uncertain timing or amount.
prudence	The inclusion of a degree of caution in the exercise of the judgements needed in making the estimates required under conditions of uncertainty, such that **assets** or **income** are not overstated and **liabilities** or **expenses** are not understated.
qualifying partnership	A partnership meeting the definition of a qualifying partnership as set out in the Partnerships (Accounts) Regulations 2008 (SI 2008/569).

recognition	The process of incorporating in the **statement of financial position** or **income statement** an item that meets the definition of an **asset**, **liability**, **equity**, **income** or **expense** and satisfies the following criteria:
	(a) it is **probable** that any future economic benefit associated with the item will flow to or from the **entity**; and
	(b) the item has a cost or value that can be measured with reliability.
recoverable amount	The higher of an **asset's** (or **cash-generating unit's**) **fair value less costs to sell** and its **value in use**.
reporting date	The end of the latest period covered by **financial statements**.
reporting period	The period covered by **financial statements**.
research	Original and planned investigation undertaken with the prospect of gaining new scientific or technical knowledge and understanding.
residual value (of an asset)	The estimated amount that an entity would currently obtain from disposal of an **asset**, after deducting the estimated costs of disposal, if the asset were already of the age and in the condition expected at the end of its **useful life**.
restructuring	A restructuring is a programme that is planned and controlled by management and materially changes either:
	(a) the scope of a business undertaken by an entity; or
	(b) the manner in which that business is conducted.
retrospective application (of an accounting policy)	Applying a new **accounting policy** to transactions, other events and conditions as if that policy had always been applied.
revenue	The gross inflow of economic benefits during the period arising in the course of the ordinary activities of an entity when those inflows result in increases in **equity**, other than increases relating to contributions from equity participants.

share-based payment transaction	A transaction in which the entity: (a) receives goods or services (including employee services) as consideration for its own equity instruments (including shares or **share options**); or (b) receives goods or services but has no obligation to settle the transaction with supplier; or (c) acquires goods or services by incurring **liabilities** to the supplier of those goods or services for amounts that are based on the price (or value) of the entity's shares or other equity instruments of the entity or another group entity.
share option	A contract that gives the holder the right, but not the obligation, to subscribe to the entity's shares at a fixed or determinable price for a specific period of time.
significant influence	Is the power to participate in the financial and operating policy decisions of the **associate** but is not **control** or **joint control** over those policies.
Small Companies Regulations	The Small Companies and Groups (Accounts and Directors' Report) Regulations 2008 (SI 2008/409)
Small LLP Regulations	The Small Limited Liability Partnership (Accounts) Regulations 2008 (SI 2008/1912)
state (employee benefit) plan	Employee benefit plans established by legislation to cover all entities (or all entities in a particular category, for example a specific industry) and operated by national or local government or by another body (for example an autonomous agency created specifically for this purpose) which is not subject to control or influence by the reporting entity.
statement of financial position	**Financial statement** that presents the relationship of an entity's **assets**, **liabilities** and **equity** as of a specific date (referred to as the balance sheet in the **Act**).
subsidiary	An entity, including an unincorporated entity such as a partnership, that is **controlled** by another entity (known as the **parent**).

substantively enacted	Tax rates shall be regarded as substantively enacted when the remaining stages of the enactment process historically have not affected the outcome and are unlikely to do so.
	A UK tax rate shall be regarded as having been substantively enacted if it is included in either:
	(a) a Bill that has been passed by the House of Commons and is awaiting only passage through the House of Lords and Royal Assent; or
	(b) a resolution having statutory effect that has been passed under the Provisional Collection of Taxes Act 1968. (Such a resolution could be used to collect taxes at a new rate before that rate has been enacted. In practice, corporation tax rates are now set a year ahead to avoid having to invoke the Provisional Collection of Taxes Act for the quarterly payment system.)
	A Republic of Ireland tax rate can be regarded as having been substantively enacted if it is included in a Bill that has been passed by the Dail.
tax expense	The aggregate amount included in **profit or loss** or **equity** for the **reporting period** in respect of **current tax**.
taxable profit (tax loss)	The profit (loss) for a **reporting period** upon which **income taxes** are payable or recoverable, determined in accordance with the rules established by the taxation authorities. Taxable profit equals taxable income less amounts deductible from taxable **income**.
termination benefits	**Employee benefits** provided in exchange for the termination of an employee's employment as a result of either:
	(a) an entity's decision to terminate an employee's employment before the normal retirement date; or
	(b) an employee's decision to accept voluntary redundancy in exchange for those benefits.

transaction costs (financial instruments)	Incremental costs that are directly attributable to the acquisition, issue or disposal of a **financial asset** or **financial liability**, or the issue or reacquisition of an entity's own equity instrument. An incremental cost is one that would not have been incurred if the entity had not acquired, issued or disposed of the financial asset or financial liability, or had not issued or reacquired its own equity instrument.
treasury shares	An entity's own equity instruments that are held by the entity.
turnover	The amounts derived from the provision of goods and services after deduction of: (a) trade discounts; (b) value added tax; and (c) any other taxes based on the amounts so derived.
useful life	The period over which an **asset** is expected to be available for use by an entity or the number of production or similar units expected to be obtained from the asset by an entity.
value in use	The **present value** of the future cash flows expected to be derived from an **asset** or **cash-generating unit**.
venturer	A party to a **joint venture** that has **joint control** over that joint venture.
vest	Become an entitlement. Under a share-based payment arrangement, a counterparty's right to receive cash, other **assets** or equity instruments of the entity vests when the counterparty's entitlement is no longer conditional on the satisfaction of any vesting conditions.

Appendix II:
Table of equivalence for UK Companies Act terminology

The following table compares company law terminology with broadly equivalent terminology used in this FRS. In some cases there are minor differences between the broadly equivalent definitions, which are also summarised below.

Company law terminology	FRS 105 terminology
Accounting reference date	Reporting date
Accounts	Financial statements
Balance sheet	Statement of financial position
Capital and reserves	Equity
Cash at bank and in hand	Cash
Debtors	Trade receivables
Diminution in value [of assets]	Impairment
Financial year	Reporting period
Net realisable value [of any current asset]	Estimated selling price less costs to complete and sell
Profit and loss account	Income statement
Stocks	Inventories
Tangible assets	Includes: property, plant and equipment and investment property
Trade creditors	Trade payables

Appendix III:
Note on legal requirements

INTRODUCTION

This appendix provides an overview of how the requirements of FRS 105 address UK **A3.1**
company law requirements. It is therefore written from the perspective of a company
to which *The Small Companies and Groups (Accounts and Directors' Report)
Regulations 2008* (SI 2008/409) amended by *The Small Companies (Micro-Entities'
Accounts) Regulations 2013* (SI 2013/3008) and *The Companies, Partnerships and Groups
(Accounts and Reports) Regulations 2015* (SI 2015/980) apply. The same provisions
generally apply to limited liability partnerships (LLPs) and qualifying partnerships following
amendments to legislation made in *The Limited Liability Partnerships, Partnerships and
Groups (Accounts and Audit) Regulations 2016* (SI 2016/575) (see paragraph A3.6).

The Small Companies (Micro-Entities' Accounts) Regulations 2013 were made in **A3.2**
November 2013 and apply to the financial statements of micro-entities for accounting
periods ending on or after 30 September 2013 for companies filing their accounts on or
after 1 December 2013.

The definition of a micro-entity is contained in sections 384A and 384B of the Companies **A3.3**
Act 2006 (Act). The qualifying conditions are met by a company in a year in which it does
not exceed two or more of the following criteria:

(a) Turnover	£632,000
(b) Balance sheet total	£316,000
(c) Number of employees	10

For any company, other than a newly incorporated company, to qualify as a micro-entity, **A3.4**
the qualifying conditions must be met for two consecutive years. A company will cease to
qualify as a micro-entity if it fails to meet the qualifying conditions for two consecutive
years. However, if a company which qualified as a micro-entity in one period no longer
meets the criteria for a micro-entity in the next period, the company may continue to claim
the exemptions available in the next period. If that company then reverts back to being a
micro-entity by meeting the criteria, the exemptions will continue uninterrupted.

Certain companies are excluded by section 384B of the Act from being treated as micro- **A3.5**
entities, including those excluded from the small companies regime for reasons of public
interest (as set out in section 384), certain financial institutions, charities, those voluntarily
preparing group accounts and those included in group accounts. The Act should be referred
to for a full list of excluded companies.

The Limited Liability Partnerships, Partnerships and Groups (Accounts and Audit) **A3.6**
Regulations 2016 (SI 2016/575) were made in May 2016 and extend the micro-entities
regime to LLPs and qualifying partnerships for accounting periods beginning on or after
1 January 2016 with early application permitted for accounting periods beginning on or
after 1 January 2015. LLPs and qualifying partnerships are eligible to apply the micro-
entities regime, provided they meet the relevant conditions, which mirror the requirements
of sections 384A and 384B of the Act for companies. Entities that are not companies,
LLPs, or qualifying partnerships do not meet the definition of a micro-entity.

Applicable accounting framework

A3.7   Accounts prepared in accordance with FRS 105 are classified as 'Companies Act individual accounts' for the purposes of section 395 of the Act and are therefore required to comply with the applicable provisions of Parts 15 and 16 of the Act and with the Regulations referred to in paragraph A3.1.

Fair value at initial recognition

A3.8   *The Small Companies (Micro-Entities' Accounts) Regulations 2013* state that micro-entities are not permitted to apply the Alternative Accounting Rules or the Fair Value Rules as set out in company law. Therefore micro-entities are only permitted to apply the Historical Cost Accounting Rules.

A3.9   FRS 105 states that certain types of assets and liabilities must be measured at fair value at initial recognition, for example inventories acquired through a non-exchange transaction. This does not breach the prohibition against fair value accounting as the use of a fair value is a method of estimating cost at initial recognition.

True and fair view

A3.10   FRS 105 is an accounting standard and all accounting standards issued by the Financial Reporting Council are applicable to the preparation of financial statements that are intended to give a true and fair view. Financial statements of a micro-entity that include the minimum accounting items specified by *The Small Companies (Micro-Entities' Accounts) Regulations 2013* are presumed in law to give a true and fair view.

Distributable profits

A3.11   The determination of profits available for distribution is a complex area where accounting and company law interface. In determining profits available for distribution any entity may refer to Technical Release 02/10 *Guidance on realised and distributable profits under the Companies Act 2006* issued by the Institute of Chartered Accountants in England and Wales and the Institute of Chartered Accountants of Scotland, or any successor document, to determine profits available for distribution.

Appendix IV:
Republic of Ireland (RoI) legal references

At the time of issuing FRS 105, the micro-entities legislation is not available for application in the Republic of Ireland. However, the Irish Department of Jobs, Enterprise and Innovation has consulted on the possible enactment of this legislation in its *Consultation on the transposition of the EU Accounting Directive 2013/34/EU.* **A4.1**

If legislation giving effect to the micro-entities option is enacted in Ireland, FRS 105 will be available for application in line with the effective date of the relevant legislation and will be updated to include Republic of Ireland legal references. **A4.2**

Amendments to FRS 105: The Financial Reporting Standard applicable to the Micro-entities Regime – Limited Liability Partnerships and Qualifying Partnerships

(May 2016)

Contents

Paragraphs

Summary

Amendments to FRS 105 *The Financial Reporting Standard applicable to the*
   Micro-entities Regime
   Amendments to Section 1   Scope   1–2
   Amendments to Section 3   Financial Statement Presentation   3–4
   Amendments to Section 4   Statement of Financial Position   5–6
   Amendments to Section 5   Income Statement   7–8
   Amendments to Section 6   Notes to the Financial Statements   9–11
   Amendments to Section 7   Subsidiaries, Associates, Jointly Controlled
      Entities and Intermediate Payment Arrangements   12–13
   Amendments to Section 22   Impairment of Assets   14–15
   Amendments to Appendix I: Glossary   16–18
   Amendments to Appendix III: Note on legal requirements   19–21

Approval by the FRC

The Corporate Reporting Council's Advice to the FRC to issue *Amendments to*
FRS 105 – Limited Liability Partnerships and Qualifying Partnerships
   Introduction   1–4
   Advice   5–7
   Background   8–9
   Amendments to FRS 105   10–14
   Effective date   15
   Approval of this Advice   16

Amendments to FRS 105 The Financial Reporting Standard applicable to the Micro-entities Regime – Limited Liability Partnerships and Qualifying Partnerships amends an accounting standard. It is issued by the Financial Reporting Council in respect of its application in the United Kingdom and promulgated by the Institute of Chartered Accountants in Ireland in respect of its application in the Republic of Ireland.

Summary

(i) With effect from 1 January 2015 the Financial Reporting Council (FRC) revised financial reporting standards in the United Kingdom and Republic of Ireland. The revisions fundamentally reformed financial reporting, replacing the extant standards with five Financial Reporting Standards:

   (a) FRS 100 *Application of Financial Reporting Requirements*;
   (b) FRS 101 *Reduced Disclosure Framework*;
   (c) FRS 102 *The Financial Reporting Standard applicable in the UK and Republic of Ireland*;
   (d) FRS 103 *Insurance Contracts*; and
   (e) FRS 104 *Interim Financial Reporting*.

The FRC has also issued FRS 105 *The Financial Reporting Standard applicable to the Micro-entities Regime* to support the implementation of the new micro-entities regime. It is effective from 1 January 2016 with early application permitted.

These limited amendments to FRS 105 extend its scope to include eligible limited liability partnerships (LLPs) and qualifying partnerships, following a change in legislation. For LLPs and qualifying partnerships early application is permitted only for accounting periods beginning on or after 1 January 2015.

(ii) The FRC's overriding objective in setting accounting standards is to enable users of accounts to receive high-quality understandable financial reporting proportionate to the size and complexity of the entity and users' information needs.

(iii) In meeting this objective, the FRC aims to provide succinct financial reporting standards that:

   (a) have consistency with international accounting standards through the application of an IFRS-based solution unless an alternative clearly better meets the overriding objective;
   (b) reflect up-to-date thinking and developments in the way entities operate and the transactions they undertake;
   (c) balance consistent principles for accounting by all UK and Republic of Ireland entities with practical solutions, based on size, complexity, public interest and users' information needs;
   (d) promote efficiency within groups; and
   (e) are cost-effective to apply.

Amendments to FRS 105 – Limited Liability Partnerships and Qualifying Partnerships

(iv) In November 2013 the Government introduced an optional new reporting framework for companies that meet the qualifying criteria of a micro-entity. In response the FRC developed FRS 105 which may be used by eligible companies.

(v) These amendments to FRS 105 extend its scope to include eligible LLPs and qualifying partnerships following a change in legislation. The use of the micro-entities regime remains optional.

(vi) These amendments are applicable to accounting periods beginning on or after 1 January 2016. Early application is permitted for accounting periods beginning on or after 1 January 2015.

Amendments to FRS 105 *The Financial Reporting Standard applicable to the Micro-entities Regime*

Amendments to Section 1 *Scope*

The following paragraph sets out the amendments to Section 1 *Scope* (inserted text is underlined).   1

Paragraph 1.5 is inserted as follows: 2

1.5 In May 2016 amendments were made to this FRS to extend its scope to include **limited liability partnerships (LLPs)** and **qualifying partnerships** following a change in legislation. An LLP or a qualifying partnership which qualifies as a micro-entity and is applying the micro-entities regime shall apply this FRS for accounting periods beginning on or after 1 January 2016. Early application by a micro-entity that is an LLP or a qualifying partnership is:

(a)   permitted for accounting periods beginning on or after 1 January 2015 provided that *The Limited Liability Partnerships, Partnerships and Groups (Accounts and Audit) Regulations 2016* (SI 2016/575) are applied from the same date; and

(b)   required if the LLP or qualifying partnership applies *The Limited Liability Partnerships, Partnerships and Groups (Accounts and Audit) Regulations 2016* (SI 2016/575) to a reporting period beginning before 1 January 2016.

Amendments to Section 3 *Financial Statement Presentation*

The following paragraph sets out the amendments to Section 3 *Financial Statement Presentation* (inserted text is underlined).   3

A new footnote (to be sequentially numbered) is inserted after the word 'Act' in paragraph 3.14 (subsequent footnotes are renumbered sequentially) as follows: 4

footnote Or, when relevant, Regulation 12 of the *Limited Liability Partnerships (Accounts and Audit) (Application of Companies Act 2006) Regulations 2008* (SI 2008/1911).

Amendments to Section 4 *Statement of Financial Position*

The following paragraph sets out the amendments to Section 4 *Statement of Financial Position* (deleted text is struck through, inserted text is underlined).   5

Paragraph 4.3 is amended and a new footnote (to be sequentially numbered) is inserted (subsequent footnotes are renumbered sequentially) as follows: 6

4.3 A micro-entity shall present a statement of financial position in accordance with one of the formats set out in Section C of Part 1 of Schedule 1 to the **Small Companies Regulations** or Section C of Part 1 of Schedule 1 to the **Small LLP Regulations**footnote, as followsillustrated below:

Format 1	CU	CU
Called up share capital not paid		X
Fixed assets		X
Current assets	X	
Prepayments and accrued income	X	
Creditors: amounts falling due within one year	(X)	
Net current assets / (liabilities)		X/(X)

Total assets less current liabilities		X
Creditors: amounts falling due after more than one year		(X)
Provisions for liabilities		(X)
Accruals and deferred income		(X)
		X
Capital and reserves		X

Format 2	CU	CU
Assets		
Called up share capital not paid		X
Fixed assets		X
Current assets		X
Prepayments and accrued income		X
		X
Capital, Reserves and Liabilities		
Capital and reserves		X
Provisions for liabilities		X
Creditors		
Amounts falling due within one year	X	
Amounts falling due after one year	X	
		X
Accruals and deferred income		X
		X

footnote LLPs shall describe the items as set out in the Small LLP Regulations. In particular, 'Called up share capital not paid' shall not be used and 'Loans and other debts due to members' and 'Members' other interests' shall be used instead of 'Capital and reserves'.

Amendments to Section 5 *Income Statement*

7 The following paragraph sets out the amendments to Section 5 *Income Statement* (deleted text is struck through, inserted text is underlined).

8 Paragraph 5.3 is amended and a new footnote (to be sequentially numbered) is inserted (subsequent footnotes are renumbered sequentially) as follows:

5.3 A micro-entity shall present its profit or loss for a period in an income statement in accordance with Section C of Part 1 of Schedule 1 to the **Small Companies Regulations** or Section C of Part 1 of Schedule 1 to the **Small LLP Regulations**, as followsillustrated below:

	CU
Turnover	X
Other income	X
Cost of raw materials and consumables	(X)
Staff costs	(X)
Depreciation and other amounts written off assets	(X)
Other charges	(X)
Tax	(X)
Profit or loss footnote	X / (X)

footnote LLPs shall describe this item as 'Profit or loss for the financial year before members' remuneration and profit shares'.

Amendments to Section 6 *Notes to the Financial Statements*

The following paragraphs set out the amendments to Section 6 *Notes to the Financial Statements* (deleted text is struck through, inserted text is underlined).   **9**

Paragraph 6.3 is inserted as follows: **10**

6.3 In accordance with Regulation 30 of the *Limited Liability Partnerships (Accounts and Audit) (Application of Companies Act 2006) Regulations 2008* (SI 2008/1911), the notes to the financial statements of an **LLP** which qualifies as a micro-entity shall be presented at the foot of the statement of financial position and shall include financial commitments, guarantees and contingencies as required by paragraph 55 of Part 3 of Schedule 1 to the **Small LLPs Regulations** (see paragraphs 6A.2 and 6A.3 in the Appendix to this Section).

Paragraphs 6A.2 and 6A.3 are amended as follows: **11**

6A.2 *The total amount of any financial commitments, guarantees and contingencies that are not included in the statement of financial position must be stated.* (~~Schedule 1,~~ *paragraph 57(1)* of Schedule 1 to the Small Companies Regulations or paragraph 55(1) of Schedule 1 to the Small LLPs Regulations)

The total amount of any commitments concerning pensions must be separately disclosed. (~~Schedule 1,~~ *paragraph 57(3)* of Schedule 1 to the Small Companies Regulations or paragraph 55(3) of Schedule 1 to the Small LLPs Regulations)

The total amount of any commitments which are undertaken on behalf of or for the benefit of:

(a)   *any parent, fellow subsidiary or any subsidiary of a micro-entity; or*
(b)   *any undertaking in which a micro-entity has a participating interest,*

must be separately stated and those within (a) must also be stated separately from those within (b). (~~Schedule 1,~~ *paragraph 57(4)* of Schedule 1 to the Small Companies Regulations or paragraph 55(4) of Schedule 1 to the Small LLPs Regulations)

The following paragraphs …

6A.3 *An indication of the nature and form of any valuable security given by the micro-entity in respect of commitments, guarantees and contingencies within paragraph 6A.2 must be given.* (~~Schedule 1,~~ *paragraph 57(2)* of Schedule 1 to the Small Companies Regulations or paragraph 55(2) of Schedule 1 to the Small LLPs Regulations)

The following paragraphs …

Amendments to Section 7 *Subsidiaries, Associates, Jointly Controlled Entities and Intermediate Payment Arrangements*

The following paragraph sets out the amendment to Section 7 *Subsidiaries, Associates, Jointly Controlled Entities and Intermediate Payment Arrangements* (inserted text is underlined).   **12**

13   A new footnote (to be sequentially numbered) is inserted after the word 'Act' in paragraph 7.3 (subsequent footnotes are renumbered sequentially) as follows:

^{footnote} Or, when relevant, Regulation 5A of the *Limited Liability Partnerships (Accounts and Audit) (Application of Companies Act 2006) Regulations 2008* (SI 2008/1911).

Amendments to Section 22 *Impairment of Assets*

14   The following paragraph sets out the amendments to Section 22 *Impairment of Assets.*

15   Footnote 1 in paragraph 22.19 is deleted (subsequent footnotes are renumbered sequentially).

Amendments to Appendix I: Glossary

16   The following paragraphs set out the amendments to Appendix I: *Glossary* (deleted text is struck through, inserted text is underlined).

17   The following glossary terms and definitions are inserted in alphabetical order:

limited liability partnership (LLP)	A limited liability partnership formed under the Limited Liability Partnerships Act 2000 or the Limited Liability Partnerships Act (Northern Ireland) 2002.
qualifying partnership	A partnership meeting the definition of a qualifying partnership as set out in the Partnerships (Accounts) Regulations 2008 (SI 2008/569).
Small LLP Regulations	The Small Limited Liability Partnership (Accounts) Regulations 2008 (SI 2008/1912)

18   The following glossary terms and definitions are amended as follows:

micro-entity	Is an entity that meets all of the following conditions: (a) it is a company established under company law; (b) it qualifies as a micro-entity in accordance with section 384A of the Act; and (c) it is not excluded from being treated as a micro-entity under section 384B of the Act. Micro-entities are a subset of small companies as defined in the Act. (a) A company meeting the definition of a micro-entity as set out in section 384A of the **Act**, and not prevented from applying the micro-entity provisions by section 384B of the Act;

	(b) an **LLP** which qualifies as a micro-entity and is not prevented from applying the micro-entity provisions in accordance with Regulation 5A of the *Limited Liability Partnerships (Accounts and Audit) (Application of Companies Act 2006) Regulations 2008* (SI 2008/1911); or
	(c) a **qualifying partnership** that would meet the definition of a micro-entity as set out in section 384A of the Act, and not be prevented from applying the micro-entity provisions by section 384B of the Act, if the partnership were a company.
micro-entity provisions	~~Means a~~(a) Any provisions of Part 15, Part 16 or regulations made under Part 15 of the **Act**; or (b) any provisions of the **Small LLP Regulations,** relating specifically to the individual accounts of an entity which qualifies as a **micro-entity**.
micro-entities regime	The legal requirements and exemptions relating to the preparation of the **financial statements** of **micro-entities** as set out in the **Act**, the ~~and~~ **Small Companies Regulations** and the **Small LLP Regulations**.

Amendments to Appendix III: Note on legal requirements

The following paragraphs set out the amendments to Appendix III: *Note on legal requirements* (deleted text is struck through, inserted text is underlined).   **19**

Paragraph A3.1 is amended as follows: **20**

A3.1 This appendix provides an overview of how the requirements of FRS 105 address UK company law requirements. It is therefore written from the perspective of a company to which *The Small Companies and Groups (Accounts and Directors' Report) Regulations 2008* (SI 2008/409) amended by *The Small Companies (Micro-Entities' Accounts) Regulations 2013* (SI 2013/3008) and *The Companies, Partnerships and Groups (Accounts and Reports) Regulations 2015* (SI 2015/980) apply. The same provisions generally apply to limited liability partnerships (LLPs) and qualifying partnerships following amendments to legislation made in *The Limited Liability Partnerships, Partnerships and Groups (Accounts and Audit) Regulations 2016* (SI 2016/575) (see paragraph A3.6).

Paragraph A3.6 is amended as follows: **21**

A3.6 *The Limited Liability Partnerships, Partnerships and Groups (Accounts and Audit) Regulations 2016* (SI 2016/575) were made in May 2016 and extend the micro-entities regime to LLPs and qualifying partnerships for accounting periods beginning on or after 1 January 2016 with early application permitted for accounting periods beginning on or after 1 January 2015. LLPs and qualifying partnerships are eligible to apply the micro-entities regime, provided they meet the relevant conditions, which mirror the requirements of sections 384A and 384B of the Act for companies. Entities that are not companies, ~~such as limited liability partnerships (LLPs),~~ or qualifying partnerships do not meet the definition of a micro-entity.

Approval by the FRC

Amendments to *FRS 105 The Financial Reporting Standard applicable to the Micro-entities Regime – Limited Liability Partnerships and Qualifying Partnerships* was approved by the Board of the Financial Reporting Council for issue on 17 May 2016, following its consideration of the Corporate Reporting Council's Advice.

The Corporate Reporting Council's Advice to the FRC to issue *Amendments to FRS 105 – Limited Liability Partnerships and Qualifying Partnerships*

Introduction

This report provides an overview of the main issues that have been considered by the Corporate Reporting Council in advising the Financial Reporting Council (FRC) to issue *Amendments to FRS 105 The Financial Reporting Standard applicable to the Micro-entities Regime – Limited Liability Partnerships and Qualifying Partnerships*.   **1**

The FRC, in accordance with the *Statutory Auditors (Amendment of Companies Act 2006 and Delegation of Functions etc) Order 2012* (SI 2012/1741), is a prescribed body for issuing accounting standards in the UK. The *Foreword to Accounting Standards* sets out the application of accounting standards in the Republic of Ireland.   **2**

In accordance with the *FRC Codes and Standards: procedures*, any proposal to issue, amend or withdraw a code or standard is put to the FRC Board with the full advice of the relevant Councils and/or the Codes & Standards Committee. Ordinarily, the FRC Board will only reject the advice put to it where: **3**

(a)   it is apparent that a significant group of stakeholders has not been adequately consulted;

(b)   the necessary assessment of the impact of the proposal has not been completed, including an analysis of costs and benefits;

(c)   insufficient consideration has been given to the timing or cost of implementation; or

(d)   the cumulative impact of a number of proposals would make the adoption of an otherwise satisfactory proposal inappropriate.

The FRC has established the Corporate Reporting Council as the relevant Council to assist it in the setting of accounting standards.   **4**

Advice

The Corporate Reporting Council is advising the FRC to issue *Amendments to FRS 105 The Financial Reporting Standard applicable to the Micro-entities Regime – Limited Liability Partnerships and Qualifying Partnerships*.   **5**

The amendments update FRS 105 *The Financial Reporting Standard applicable to the Micro-entities Regime* in line with changes in UK legislation which have extended the micro-entities regime to limited liability partnerships (LLPs) and qualifying partnerships.   **6**

The Accounting Council's Advice[1] to the FRC to issue FRS 105 *The Financial Reporting Standard applicable to the Micro-entities Regime* was set out in that standard. The Corporate Reporting Council's Advice to the FRC in respect of these amendments will be included in the revised FRS 105.   **7**

Background

When FRS 105 was issued, UK company law restricted the availability of the new micro-entities regime to eligible companies. FRS 105 reflected this legal restriction. In   **8**

---

[1] *From 1 April 2016 the Accounting Council was renamed as the Corporate Reporting Council.*

May 2016 Regulations were made which extended the micro-entities regime to LLPs and qualifying partnerships.

9   In accordance with the FRC's *Framework for developing Standards, Statements of Practice, Codes and Guidance*, these amendments have been assessed as not requiring a formal consultation. FRS 105 was developed to support the existing micro-entities regime for companies, which as a result of a change in legislation has been extended to LLPs and qualifying partnerships, and these amendments simply extend the scope of FRS 105 (with some consequential amendments) consistently with the change in legislation.

Amendments to FRS 105

10   In developing its advice to the FRC, the Corporate Reporting Council was guided by the overriding objective to enable users of accounts to receive high-quality understandable financial reporting proportionate to the size and complexity of the entity and users' information needs.

11   In meeting this objective, the FRC aims to provide succinct financial reporting standards that:

(a)   have consistency with international accounting standards through the application of an IFRS-based solution unless an alternative clearly better meets the overriding objective;

(b)   reflect up-to-date thinking and developments in the way entities operate and the transactions they undertake;

(c)   balance consistent principles for accounting by all UK and Republic of Ireland entities with practical solutions, based on size, complexity, public interest and users' information needs;

(d)   promote efficiency within groups; and

(e)   are cost-effective to apply.

12   The Corporate Reporting Council advises that, as the micro-entities regime is now available to LLPs and qualifying partnerships, FRS 105 should be updated to reflect the extent to which the micro-entities regime is available in law. In order to achieve this the definition of a micro-entity and other related glossary terms have been updated.

13   The presentation and disclosure requirements applicable to the financial statements of LLPs and qualifying partnerships that adopt the micro-entities regime are almost identical to those applicable to the financial statements of companies that are micro-entities. Where there are differences these have been reflected in the amendments to FRS 105.

14   The Corporate Reporting Council advises that the current recognition and measurement requirements of FRS 105 are also suitable for LLPs and qualifying partnerships applying the micro-entities regime and therefore no amendments have been made to the recognition and measurement requirements of FRS 105.

Effective date

15   The Corporate Reporting Council advises that in line with the effective date of the changes in legislation, the amendments to FRS 105 should be effective for accounting periods beginning on or after 1 January 2016 with early adoption permitted for accounting periods beginning on or after 1 January 2015.

Approval of this Advice

16   This advice to the FRC was approved by the Corporate Reporting Council on 14 April 2016.

Part Two

Company Law

Part Two

Company Law

Large and Medium-sized Companies and Groups (Accounts and Reports) Regulations 2008 (SI 2008/410)

Part 1   Introduction

Part 2   Form and content of accounts

Part 3   Directors' report

Part 4   Directors' remuneration report

Part 5   Interpretation

Schedule 1 – Companies Act individual accounts: companies which are not banking or insurance companies

Schedule 2 – Banking companies: Companies Act individual accounts

Schedule 3 – Insurance companies: Companies Act individual accounts

Schedule 4 – Information on related undertakings required whether preparing Companies Act or IAS accounts

Schedule 5 – Information about benefits of directors

Schedule 6 – Companies Act group accounts

Schedule 7 – Matters to be dealt with in Directors' Report

Schedule 8 – Quoted companies: Directors' Remuneration Report

Schedule 9 – Interpretation of term "provisions"

Schedule 10 – General interpretation

Large and Medium-Sized Companies and Groups (Accounts and Reports) Regulations 2008 (SI 2008/410)

(SI 2008/410 as amended by SI 2015/980 The Companies, Partnerships and Groups (Accounts and Reports) Regulations 2015 and SI 2015/1672 Companies, Partnerships and Groups (Accounts and Reports) (No. 2) Regulations 2015)

Made on 19 February 2008 by the Secretary of State, in exercise of the powers conferred by s. 396(3), 404(3), 409(1) to (3), 412(1) to (3), 416(4), 421(1) and (2), 445(3)(a) and (b), 677(3)(a), 712(2)(b)(i), 831(3)(a), 832(4)(a), 836(1)(b)(i) and 1292(1)(a) and (c) of the Companies Act 2006. In accordance with s. 473(3) and 1290 of the Companies Act 2006 a draft of this instrument was laid before Parliament and approved by a resolution of each House of Parliament. Operative from 6 April 2008.

PART 1 – INTRODUCTION
CITATION AND INTERPRETATION

1(1) These Regulations may be cited as the Large and Medium-sized Companies and Groups (Accounts and Reports) Regulations 2008.

1(2) In these Regulations **"the 2006 Act"** means the Companies Act 2006.

Commencement and application

2(1) These Regulations come into force on 6th April 2008.

2(2) Subject to paragraph (3), they apply in relation to financial years beginning on or after 6th April 2008.

2(3) The requirement for disclosure in paragraph 4 of Schedule 8 to these Regulations (directors' remuneration report: disclosure relating to consideration of conditions in company and group) applies in relation to financial years beginning on or after 6th April 2009.

2(4) These Regulations apply to companies other than those which are subject to the small companies regime under Part 15 of the 2006 Act.

PART 2 – FORM AND CONTENT OF ACCOUNTS

Companies Act individual accounts (companies other than banking and insurance companies)

3(1) Subject to regulation 4, the directors of a company–

    (a)   for which they are preparing Companies Act individual accounts under section 396 of the 2006 Act (Companies Act: individual accounts), and

    (b)   which is not a banking company or an insurance company, must comply with the provisions of Schedule 1 to these Regulations as to the form and content of the balance sheet and profit and loss account, and additional information to be provided by way of notes to the accounts.

3(2)   The profit and loss account of a company that falls within section 408 of the 2006 Act (individual profit and loss account where group accounts prepared) need not contain the information specified in paragraphs 65 to 69 of Schedule 1 to these Regulations (information supplementing the profit and loss account).

Medium-sized companies: exemptions for Companies Act individual accounts

4(1)   This regulation applies to a company–

- (a)   which qualifies as medium-sized in relation to a financial year under section 465 of the 2006 Act, and
- (b)   the directors of which are preparing Companies Act individual accounts under section 396 of that Act for that year.

4(2A)   The individual accounts for the year need not comply with paragraph 45 (disclosure with respect to compliance with accounting standards) of Schedule 1 to these Regulations.

4(2B)   Paragraph 72 (related party transactions) applies with the modification that only particulars of transactions which have not been concluded under normal market conditions with the following must be disclosed–

- (a)   owners holding a participating interest in the company;
- (b)   companies in which the company itself has a participating interest; and
- (c)   the company's directors.

4(3)   [Omitted by SI 2015/980, reg. 26(3).]

History – Reg. 4(2A) and (2B) substituted for reg. 4(2) by SI 2015/980, reg. 26(2), with effect in relation to–
- (a)   financial years beginning on or after 1 January 2016, and
- (b)   a financial year of a company beginning on or after 1 January 2015, but before 1 January 2016, if the directors of the company so decide.

Reg. 4(3) omitted by SI 2015/980, reg. 26(3), with effect in relation to–
- (a)   financial years beginning on or after 1 January 2016, and
- (b)   a financial year of a company beginning on or after 1 January 2015, but before 1 January 2016, if the directors of the company so decide.

Former reg. 4(3) read as follows:
"**4(3)**   The directors of the company may deliver to the registrar of companies a copy of the accounts for the year–
- (a)   which includes a profit and loss account in which the following items listed in the profit and loss account formats set out in Schedule 1 are combined as one item – items 2, 3 and 6 in format 1; items 2 to 5 in format 2; items A.1 and B.2 in format 3; items A.1, A.2 and B.2 to B.4 in format 4;
- (b)   which does not contain the information required by paragraph 68 of Schedule 1 (particulars of turnover)."

Companies Act individual accounts: banking companies

5(1)   The directors of a company–

- (a)   for which they are preparing Companies Act individual accounts under section 396 of the 2006 Act, and
- (b)   which is a banking company, must comply with the provisions of Schedule 2 to these Regulations as to the form and content of the balance sheet and profit

and loss account, and additional information to be provided by way of notes to the accounts.

5(2)   The profit and loss account of a banking company that falls within section 408 of the 2006 Act (individual profit and loss account where group accounts prepared) need not contain the information specified in paragraphs 85 to 91 of Schedule 2 to these Regulations (information supplementing the profit and loss account).

5(3)   Accounts prepared in accordance with this regulation must contain a statement that they are prepared in accordance with the provisions of these Regulations relating to banking companies.

Companies Act individual accounts: insurance companies

6(1)   The directors of a company–

  (a)   for which they are preparing Companies Act individual accounts under section 396 of the 2006 Act, and

  (b)   which is an insurance company, must comply with the provisions of Schedule 3 to these Regulations as to the form and content of the balance sheet and profit and loss account, and additional information to be provided by way of notes to the accounts.

6(2)   The profit and loss account of a company that falls within section 408 of the 2006 Act (individual profit and loss account where group accounts prepared) (a) need not contain the information specified in paragraphs 83 to 89 of Schedule 3 to these Regulations (information supplementing the profit and loss account).

6(3)   Accounts prepared in accordance with this regulation must contain a statement that they are prepared in accordance with the provisions of these Regulations relating to insurance companies.

Information about related undertakings (Companies Act or IAS individual or group accounts)

7(1)   Companies Act or IAS individual or group accounts must comply with the provisions of Schedule 4 to these Regulations as to information about related undertakings to be given in notes to the company's accounts.

7(2)   In Schedule 4–

Part 1 contains provisions applying to all companies

Part 2 contains provisions applying only to companies not required to prepare group accounts

Part 3 contains provisions applying only to companies required to prepare group accounts

Part 4 contains additional disclosures for banking companies and groups

Part 5 contains interpretative provisions.

7(3)   Information otherwise required to be given by Schedule 4 need not be disclosed with respect to an undertaking that–

    (a)   is established under the law of a country outside the United Kingdom, or

    (b)   carries on business outside the United Kingdom,

if the conditions specified in section 409(4) of the 2006 Act are met (see section 409(5) of the 2006 Act for disclosure required where advantage taken of this exemption).

  This paragraph does not apply in relation to the information otherwise required by paragraph 3, 7 or 21 of Schedule 4.

Information about directors' benefits: remuneration (Companies Act or IAS individual or group accounts: quoted and unquoted companies)

  8(1)   Companies Act or IAS individual or group accounts must comply with the provisions of Schedule 5 to these Regulations as to information about directors' remuneration to be given in notes to the company's accounts.

  8(2)   In Schedule 5–

    Part 1 contains provisions applying to quoted and unquoted companies,

    Part 2 contains provisions applying only to unquoted companies, and

    Part 3 contains supplementary provisions.

Companies Act group accounts

  9(1)   Subject to paragraphs (2) and (3), where the directors of a parent company prepare Companies Act group accounts under section 403 of the 2006 Act (group accounts: applicable accounting framework), those accounts must comply with the provisions of Part 1 of Schedule 6 to these Regulations as to the form and content of the consolidated balance sheet and consolidated profit and loss account, and additional information to be provided by way of notes to the accounts.

  9(2)   The directors of the parent company of a banking group preparing Companies Act group accounts must do so in accordance with the provisions of Part 1 of Schedule 6 as modified by Part 2 of that Schedule.

  9(3)   The directors of the parent company of an insurance group preparing Companies Act group accounts must do so in accordance with the provisions of Part 1 of Schedule 6 as modified by Part 3 of that Schedule.

  9(4)   Accounts prepared in accordance with paragraph (2) or (3) must contain a statement that they are prepared in accordance with the provisions of these Regulations relating to banking groups or to insurance groups, as the case may be.

PART 3 – DIRECTORS' REPORT
DIRECTORS' REPORT

  10(1)   The report which the directors of a company are required to prepare under section 415 of the 2006 Act (duty to prepare directors' report) must disclose the matters specified in Schedule 7 to these Regulations.

10(2)   In Schedule 7–

Part 1 relates to matters of a general nature including political donations and expenditure,

Part 2 relates to the acquisition by a company of its own shares or a charge on them,

Part 3 relates to the employment, training and advancement of disabled persons,

Part 4 relates to the involvement of employees in the affairs, policy and performance of the company,

Part 6 relates to certain disclosures required by publicly traded companies, and

Part 7 relates to disclosures in relation to greenhouse gas emissions.

History – Reg. 10(2) substituted by SI 2013/1970, reg. 7(1) and (2), with effect from 1 October 2013 in respect of financial years ending on or after 30 September 2013.

This version of reg. 10 applies to financial years ending on or after 30 September 2013. The version applying to financial years ending before 30 September 2013 read as follows:

"**10(1)**   The report which the directors of a company are required to prepare under section 415 of the 2006 Act (duty to prepare directors' report) must disclose the matters specified in Schedule 7 to these Regulations.

10(2)   In Schedule 7–

Part 1 relates to matters of a general nature, including changes in asset values and contributions for political and charitable purposes,

Part 2 relates to the acquisition by a company of its own shares or a charge on them,

Part 3 relates to the employment, training and advancement of disabled persons,

Part 4 relates to the involvement of employees in the affairs, policy and performance of the company, and

Part 5 relates to the company's policy and practice on the payment of creditors."

PART 4 – DIRECTORS' REMUNERATION REPORT

DIRECTORS' REMUNERATION REPORT (QUOTED COMPANIES)

11(1)   The remuneration report which the directors of a quoted company are required to prepare under section 420 of the 2006 Act (duty to prepare directors' remuneration report) must contain the information specified in Schedule 8 to these Regulations, and must comply with any requirement of that Schedule as to how information is to be set out in the report.

11(1A)   The document setting out a revised directors' remuneration policy in accordance with section 422A of the 2006 Act must contain the information specified in Schedule 8 to these Regulations, and must comply with any requirements in that Schedule as to how that information is to be set out.

11(2)   [Revoked.]

11(3)   For the purposes of section 497 in Part 16 of the 2006 Act (auditor's report on auditable part of directors' remuneration report), "the auditable part" of a directors' remuneration report is the information set out in the report as identified in Part 5 of Schedule 8 to these Regulations.

History – Reg. 11(1A) inserted, 11(2) revoked and, in 11(3), "the information set out in the report as identified in Part 5" substituted for "the part containing the information required by Part 3" by SI 2013/1981, reg. 2, with effect from 1 October 2013 in relation to a company's financial year ending on or after 30 September 2013.

This version of reg. 11 applies to financial years ending on or after 30 September 2013. The version applying to financial years ending before 30 September 2013 read as follows:

"**11(1)** The remuneration report which the directors of a quoted company are required to prepare under section 420 of the 2006 Act (duty to prepare directors' remuneration report) must contain the information specified in Schedule 8 to these Regulations, and must comply with any requirement of that Schedule as to how information is to be set out in the report.

11(2) In Schedule 8–

Part 1 is introductory,

Part 2 relates to information about remuneration committees, performance related remuneration, consideration of conditions elsewhere in company and group and liabilities in respect of directors' contracts,

Part 3 relates to detailed information about directors' remuneration (information included under Part 3 is required to be reported on by the auditor (see subsection (3)), and

Part 4 contains interpretative and supplementary provisions.

11(3) For the purposes of section 497 in Part 16 of the 2006 Act (auditor's report on auditable part of directors' remuneration report), "**the auditable part**" of a directors' remuneration report is the part containing the information required by Part 3 of Schedule 8 to these Regulations."

PART 5 – INTERPRETATION
DEFINITION OF "PROVISIONS"

12 Schedule 9 to these Regulations defines "**provisions**" for the purposes of these Regulations and for the purposes of–

(a)   section 677(3)(a) (Companies Act accounts: relevant provisions for purposes of financial assistance) in Part 18 of the 2006 Act,

(b)   section 712(2)(b)(i) (Companies Act accounts: relevant provisions to determine available profits for redemption or purchase by private company out of capital) in that Part,

(c)   sections 831(3)(a) (Companies Act accounts: net asset restriction on public company distributions), 832(4)(a) (Companies Act accounts: investment companies distributions) and 836(1)(b)(i) (Companies Act accounts: relevant provisions for distribution purposes) in Part 23 of that Act, and

(d)   section 841(2)(a) (Companies Act accounts: provisions to be treated as realised losses) in that Part.

Notes – Para. (d) inserted by SI 2009/1581 reg 12(1) and (2): 27 June 2009 applying in relation to financial years beginning on or after 6 April 2008 which have not ended before 27 June 2009

General interpretation

13 Schedule 10 to these Regulations contains general definitions for the purposes of these Regulations.

SCHEDULES

SCHEDULE 1   Regulation 3(1)

COMPANIES ACT INDIVIDUAL ACCOUNTS: COMPANIES WHICH ARE NOT BANKING OR INSURANCE COMPANIES

PART 1 – GENERAL RULES AND FORMATS
SECTION A – GENERAL RULES

1(1) Subject to the following provisions of this Schedule–

  (a) every balance sheet of a company must show the items listed in either of the balance sheet formats in Section B of this Part, and

  (b) every profit and loss account must show the items listed in either of the profit and loss account formats in Section B.

1(2) References in this Schedule to the items listed in any of the formats in Section B are to those items read together with any of the notes following the formats which apply to those items.

1(3) Subject to paragraph 1A, the items must be shown in the order and under the headings and sub-headings given in the particular format used, but–

  (a) the notes to the formats may permit alternative positions for any particular items, and

  (b) the heading or sub-heading for any item does not have to be distinguished by any letter or number assigned to that item in the format used.

History – In para. 1(1)(b), the word "either" substituted for the words "any one" by SI 2015/980, reg. 27(2)(a), with effect in relation to–

  (a) financial years beginning on or after 1 January 2016, and

  (b) a financial year of a company beginning on or after 1 January 2015, but before 1 January 2016, if the directors of the company so decide.

In para. 1(3), the words "Subject to paragraph 1A," inserted by SI 2015/980, reg. 27(2)(b), with effect in relation to–

  (a) financial years beginning on or after 1 January 2016, and

  (b) a financial year of a company beginning on or after 1 January 2015, but before 1 January 2016, if the directors of the company so decide.

1A(1) The company's directors may adapt one of the balance sheet formats in Section B so to distinguish between current and non-current items in a different way, provided that–

  (a) the information given is at least equivalent to that which would have been required by the use of such format had it not been thus adapted, and

  (b) the presentation of those items is in accordance with generally accepted accounting principles or practice.

1A(2) The company's directors may adapt one of the profit and loss account formats in Section B, provided that–

(a)   the information given is at least equivalent to that which would have been required by the use of such format had it not been thus adapted, and

(b)   the presentation is in accordance with generally accepted accounting principles or practice.

1A(3)   So far as is practicable, the following provisions of Section A of this Part of this Schedule apply to the balance sheet or profit or loss account of a company notwithstanding any such adaptation pursuant to this paragraph.

History – Para. 1A inserted by SI 2015/980, reg. 27(2)(c), with effect in relation to–
(a)   financial years beginning on or after 1 January 2016, and
(b)   a financial year of a company beginning on or after 1 January 2015, but before 1 January 2016, if the directors of the company so decide.

2(1)   Where in accordance with paragraph 1 a company's balance sheet or profit and loss account for any financial year has been prepared by reference to one of the formats in Section B, the company's directors must use the same format in preparing Companies Act individual accounts for subsequent financial years, unless in their opinion there are special reasons for a change.

2(2)   Particulars of any such change must be given in a note to the accounts in which the new format is first used, and the reasons for the change must be explained.

3(1)   Any item required to be shown in a company's balance sheet or profit and loss account may be shown in greater detail than required by the particular format used.

3(2)   The balance sheet or profit and loss account may include an item representing or covering the amount of any asset or liability, income or expenditure not otherwise covered by any of the items listed in the format used, save that none of the following may be treated as assets in any balance sheet–

(a)   preliminary expenses,

(b)   expenses of, and commission on, any issue of shares or debentures, and

(c)   costs of research.

4(1)   Where the special nature of the company's business requires it, the company's directors must adapt the arrangement, headings and sub-headings otherwise required in respect of items given an Arabic number in the balance sheet or profit and loss account format used.

4(2)   The directors may combine items to which Arabic numbers are given in any of the formats in Section B if–

(a)   their individual amounts are not material to assessing the state of affairs or profit or loss of the company for the financial year in question, or

(b)   the combination facilitates that assessment.

4(3)   Where sub-paragraph (2)(b) applies, the individual amounts of any items which have been combined must be disclosed in a note to the accounts.

5(1)   Subject to sub-paragraph (2), the directors must not include a heading or sub-heading corresponding to an item in the balance sheet or profit and loss account format used if there is no amount to be shown for that item for the financial year to which the balance sheet or profit and loss account relates.

5(2) Where an amount can be shown for the item in question for the immediately preceding financial year that amount must be shown under the heading or sub-heading required by the format for that item.

6 Every profit and loss account must show the amount of a company's profit or loss before taxation.

History – In para. 6, the words "on ordinary activities" omitted by SI 2015/980, reg. 27(2)(d), with effect in relation to–

    (a)   financial years beginning on or after 1 January 2016, and

    (b)   a financial year of a company beginning on or after 1 January 2015, but before 1 January 2016, if the directors of the company so decide.

7(1) For every item shown in the balance sheet or profit and loss account the corresponding amount for the immediately preceding financial year must also be shown.

7(2) Where that corresponding amount is not comparable with the amount to be shown for the item in question in respect of the financial year to which the balance sheet or profit and loss account relates, the former amount may be adjusted, and particulars of the non-comparability and of any adjustment must be disclosed in a note to the accounts.

8 Amounts in respect of items representing assets or income may not be set off against amounts in respect of items representing liabilities or expenditure (as the case may be), or vice versa.

9 The company's directors must, in determining how amounts are presented within items in the profit and loss account and balance sheet, have regard to the substance of the reported transaction or arrangement, in accordance with generally accepted accounting principles or practice.

9A Where an asset or liability relates to more than one item in the balance sheet, the relationship of such asset or liability to the relevant items must be disclosed either under those items or in the notes to the accounts.

History – Para. 9A inserted by SI 2015/980, reg. 27(2)(e), with effect in relation to–

    (a)   financial years beginning on or after 1 January 2016, and

    (b)   a financial year of a company beginning on or after 1 January 2015, but before 1 January 2016, if the directors of the company so decide.

SECTION B – THE REQUIRED FORMATS FOR ACCOUNTS
Balance sheet formats – Format 1

A.   Called up share capital not paid *(1)*

B.   Fixed assets

    I.   Intangible assets

        1.   Development costs

        2.   Concessions, patents, licences, trade marks and similar rights and assets *(2)*

        3.   Goodwill *(3)*

        4.   Payments on account

II.   Tangible assets

    1.   Land and buildings
    2.   Plant and machinery
    3.   Fixtures, fittings, tools and equipment
    4.   Payments on account and assets in course of construction

III.   Investments

    1.   Shares in group undertakings
    2.   Loans to group undertakings
    3.   Participating interests
    4.   Loans to undertakings in which the company has a participating interest
    5.   Other investments other than loans
    6.   Other loans
    7.   Own shares *(4)*

C.   Current assets

I.   Stocks

    1.   Raw materials and consumables
    2.   Work in progress
    3.   Finished goods and goods for resale
    4.   Payments on account

II.   Debtors *(5)*

    1.   Trade debtors
    2.   Amounts owed by group undertakings
    3.   Amounts owed by undertakings in which the company has a participating interest
    4.   Other debtors
    5.   Called up share capital not paid *(1)*
    6.   Prepayments and accrued income *(6)*

III.   Investments

    1.   Shares in group undertakings
    2.   Own shares *(4)*
    3.   Other investments

IV.   Cash at bank and in hand

D.   Prepayments and accrued income *(6)*

E.   Creditors: amounts falling due within one year

    1.   Debenture loans *(7)*
    2.   Bank loans and overdrafts
    3.   Payments received on account *(8)*
    4.   Trade creditors

5.   Bills of exchange payable
6.   Amounts owed to group undertakings
7.   Amounts owed to undertakings in which the company has a participating interest
8.   Other creditors including taxation and social security *(9)*
9.   Accruals and deferred income *(10)*

F.   Net current assets (liabilities) *(11)*

G.   Total assets less current liabilities

H.   Creditors: amounts falling due after more than one year

1.   Debenture loans *(7)*
2.   Bank loans and overdrafts
3.   Payments received on account *(8)*
4.   Trade creditors
5.   Bills of exchange payable
6.   Amounts owed to group undertakings
7.   Amounts owed to undertakings in which the company has a participating interest
8.   Other creditors including taxation and social security *(9)*
9.   Accruals and deferred income *(10)*

I.   Provisions for liabilities

1.   Pensions and similar obligations
2.   Taxation, including deferred taxation
3.   Other provisions

J.   Accruals and deferred income *(10)*

K.   Capital and reserves

I.   Called up share capital *(12)*
II.   Share premium account
III. Revaluation reserve
IV. Other reserves

1.   Capital redemption reserve
2.   Reserve for own shares
3.   Reserves provided for by the articles of association
4.   Other reserves, including the fair value reserve

V.   Profit and loss account

Balance sheet formats – Format 2

ASSETS

A.   Called up share capital not paid *(1)*

B.   Fixed assets

I.   Intangible assets

    1.   Development costs

    2.   Concessions, patents, licences, trade marks and similar rights and assets *(2)*

    3.   Goodwill *(3)*

    4.   Payments on account

II.   Tangible assets

    1.   Land and buildings

    2.   Plant and machinery

    3.   Fixtures, fittings, tools and equipment

    4.   Payments on account and assets in course of construction

III.   Investments

    1.   Shares in group undertakings

    2.   Loans to group undertakings

    3.   Participating interests

    4.   Loans to undertakings in which the company has a participating interest

    5.   Other investments other than loans

    6.   Other loans

    7.   Own shares *(4)*

C.   Current assets

    I.   Stocks

        1.   Raw materials and consumables

        2.   Work in progress

        3.   Finished goods and goods for resale

        4.   Payments on account

    II.   Debtors *(5)*

        1.   Trade debtors

        2.   Amounts owed by group undertakings

        3.   Amounts owed by undertakings in which the company has a participating interest

        4.   Other debtors

        5.   Called up share capital not paid *(1)*

        6.   Prepayments and accrued income *(6)*

    III.   Investments

        1.   Shares in group undertakings

        2.   Own shares *(4)*

        3.   Other investments

    IV.   Cash at bank and in hand

D.   Prepayments and accrued income *(6)*

CAPITAL, RESERVES AND LIABILITIES

A. Capital and reserves

    I.   Called up share capital *(12)*

    II.   Share premium account

    III. Revaluation reserve

    IV. Other reserves

        1.   Capital redemption reserve

        2.   Reserve for own shares

        3.   Reserves provided for by the articles of association

        4.   Other reserves, including the fair value reserve

    V.   Profit and loss account

B. Provisions for liabilities

        1.   Pensions and similar obligations

        2.   Taxation, including deferred taxation

        3.   Other provisions

C. Creditors *(13)*

        1.   Debenture loans *(7)*

        2.   Bank loans and overdrafts

        3.   Payments received on account *(8)*

        4.   Trade creditors

        5.   Bills of exchange payable

        6.   Amounts owed to group undertakings

        7.   Amounts owed to undertakings in which the company has a participating interest

        8.   Other creditors including taxation and social security *(9)*

        9.   Accruals and deferred income *(10)*

D. Accruals and deferred income *(10)*

Notes on the balance sheet formats

(1) Called up share capital not paid

(Formats 1 and 2, items A and C.II.5.)
This item may be shown in either of the two positions given in formats 1 and 2.

(2) Concessions, patents, licences, trade marks and similar rights and assets

(Formats 1 and 2, item B.I.2.)
Amounts in respect of assets are only to be included in a company's balance sheet under this item if either–

    (a)   the assets were acquired for valuable consideration and are not required to be shown under goodwill, or

    (b)   the assets in question were created by the company itself.

(3)   Goodwill

(Formats 1 and 2, item B.I.3.)
Amounts representing goodwill are only to be included to the extent that the goodwill was acquired for valuable consideration.

(4)   Own shares

(Formats 1 and 2, items B.III.7 and C.III.2.)
The nominal value of the shares held must be shown separately.

(5)   Debtors

(Formats 1 and 2, items C.II.1 to 6.)
The amount falling due after more than one year must be shown separately for each item included under debtors.

(6)   Prepayments and accrued income

(Formats 1 and 2, items C.II.6 and D.)
This item may be shown in either of the two positions given in formats 1 and 2.

(7)   Debenture loans

(Format 1, items E.1 and H.1 and format 2, item C.1.)
The amount of any convertible loans must be shown separately.

(8)   Payments received on account

(Format 1, items E.3 and H.3 and format 2, item C.3.)
Payments received on account of orders must be shown for each of these items in so far as they are not shown as deductions from stocks.

(9)   Other creditors including taxation and social security

(Format 1, items E.8 and H.8 and format 2, item C.8.)
The amount for creditors in respect of taxation and social security must be shown separately from the amount for other creditors.

(10) Accruals and deferred income

(Format 1, items E.9, H.9 and J and format 2, items C.9 and D.)
The two positions given for this item in format 1 at E.9 and H.9 are an alternative to the position at J, but if the item is not shown in a position corresponding to that at J it may be shown in either or both of the other two positions (as the case may require).
The two positions given for this item in format 2 are alternatives.

(11) Net current assets (liabilities)

(Format 1, item F.)
In determining the amount to be shown for this item any amounts shown under "prepayments and accrued income" must be taken into account wherever shown.

(12) Called up share capital

(Format 1, item K.I and format 2, item A.I.)
The amount of allotted share capital and the amount of called up share capital which has been paid up must be shown separately.

(13) Creditors

(Format 2, items C.1 to 9.)
Amounts falling due within one year and after one year must be shown separately for each of these items and for the aggregate of all of these items.

Profit and loss account formats – Format 1

(see note (17) below)

1. Turnover

2. Cost of sales *(14)*

3. Gross profit or loss

4. Distribution costs *(14)*

5. Administrative expenses *(14)*

6. Other operating income

7. Income from shares in group undertakings

8. Income from participating interests

9. Income from other fixed asset investments *(15)*

10. Other interest receivable and similar income *(15)*

11. Amounts written off investments

12. Interest payable and similar expenses *(16)*

13. Tax on profit or loss

14. Profit or loss after taxation

15. Omitted

16. Omitted

17. Omitted

18. Omitted

19. Other taxes not shown under the above items

20. Profit or loss for the financial year

Profit and loss account formats – Format 2

1. Turnover

2. Change in stocks of finished goods and in work in progress

3. Own work capitalised

4. Other operating income

5. (a) Raw materials and consumables

    (b) Other external expenses

6. Staff costs

    (a) wages and salaries

    (b) social security costs

    (c) other pension costs

7. (a) Depreciation and other amounts written off tangible and intangible fixed assets

    (b) Amounts written off current assets, to the extent that they exceed write-offs which are normal in the undertaking concerned

8. Other operating expenses

9. Income from shares in group undertakings

10. Income from participating interests

11. Income from other fixed asset investments *(15)*

12. Other interest receivable and similar income *(15)*

13. Amounts written off investments

14. Interest payable and similar expenses *(16)*

15. Tax on profit or loss

16. Profit or loss after taxation

17. Omitted

18. Omitted

19. Omitted

20. Omitted

21. Other taxes not shown under the above items

22. Profit or loss for the financial year

Notes on the profit and loss account formats

(14) Cost of sales: distribution costs: administrative expenses

(Format 1, items 2, 4 and 5.)

These items must be stated after taking into account any necessary provisions for depreciation or diminution in value of assets.

(15) Income from other fixed asset investments: other interest receivable and similar income

(Format 1, items 9 and 10; format 2, items 11 and 12.)

Income and interest derived from group undertakings must be shown separately from income and interest derived from other sources.

(16) Interest payable and similar expenses

(Format 1, item 12; format 2, item 14.)

The amount payable to group undertakings must be shown separately.

(17) Format 1

The amount of any provisions for depreciation and diminution in value of tangible and intangible fixed assets falling to be shown under item 7(a) in format 2 must be disclosed in a note to the accounts in any case where the profit and loss account is prepared using format 1.

History – In section B, the following amendments were made by SI 2015/980, reg. 27(3), with effect in relation to– (a) financial years beginning on or after 1 January 2016, and (b) a financial year of a company beginning on or after 1 January 2015, but before 1 January 2016, if the directors of the company so decide:

- in balance sheet format 1, item "4 Other reserves, including the fair value reserve" substitute for "4 Other reserves".
- the heading "CAPITAL, RESERVES AND LIABILITIES" substituted for the word "LIABILITIES".
- in balance sheet format 2, item "4 Other reserves, including the fair value reserve" substitute for "4 Other reserves".
- in profit and loss account format 1–
  - at item 12, the word "expenses" substitute for "charges";
  - at item 13, the words "on ordinary activities" omitted;
  - at item 14, the words "on ordinary activities" omitted;
  - items 15–18 omit.
- in profit and loss account format 2–
  - at item 5(b), the word "expenses" substitute for "charges";
  - item 7(b) substituted;
  - at item 8, the word "expenses" substitute for "charges";
  - at item 14, the word "expenses" substitute for "charges";
  - at item 15, the words "on ordinary activities" omitted;
  - at item 16, the words "on ordinary activities" omitted;
  - items 17–20 omitted.
- profit and loss account format 3 omitted.
- profit and loss account format 4 omitted.
- in note (14) of "Notes on the profit and loss account formats", the words "and format 3, items A.1, 2 and 3" omitted.
- in note (15), the words "format 3, items B.5 and 6 and format 4, items B.7 and 8" omitted.
- in note (16) title, the word "expenses" substitute for "charges"; and the words "format 3, item A.5 and format 4, item A.7" omitted.
- note (17) title, "Format 1" substituted; the words "item 7(a) in format 2" substitute for "items 7(a) and A.4(a) respectively in formats 2 and 4"; and the words "or format 3" omitted.

PART 2 – ACCOUNTING PRINCIPLES AND RULES
SECTION A – ACCOUNTING PRINCIPLES

Preliminary

10(1) The amounts to be included in respect of all items shown in a company's accounts must be determined in accordance with the principles set out in this Section.

10(2) But if it appears to the company's directors that there are special reasons for departing from any of those principles in preparing the company's accounts in respect of any financial year they may do so, in which case particulars of the departure, the reasons for it and its effect must be given in a note to the accounts.

Accounting principles

11 The company is presumed to be carrying on business as a going concern.

12 Accounting policies and measurement bases must be applied consistently within the same accounts and from one financial year to the next.

History – In para. 12, the words "and measurement bases" inserted by SI 2015/980, reg. 28(2)(a), with effect in relation to–
- (a) financial years beginning on or after 1 January 2016, and
- (b) a financial year of a company beginning on or after 1 January 2015, but before 1 January 2016, if the directors of the company so decide.

13 The amount of any item must be determined on a prudent basis, and in particular–

- (a) only profits realised at the balance sheet date are to be included in the profit and loss account,
- (b) all liabilities which have arisen in respect of the financial year to which the accounts relate or a previous financial year must be taken into account, including those which only become apparent between the balance sheet date and the date on which it is signed on behalf of the board of directors in accordance with Section 414 of the 2006 Act (approval and signing of accounts) and
- (c) all provisions for diminution of value must be recognised, whether the result of the financial year is a profit or a loss.

History – Para. 13(c), (and the word "and" preceding it) inserted; the word "and" in para. (a) omitted by SI 2015/980, reg. 28(2)(b), with effect in relation to–
- (a) financial years beginning on or after 1 January 2016, and
- (b) a financial year of a company beginning on or after 1 January 2015, but before 1 January 2016, if the directors of the company so decide.

14 All income and charges relating to the financial year to which the accounts relate must be taken into account, without regard to the date of receipt or payment.

15 In determining the aggregate amount of any item, the amount of each individual asset or liability that falls to be taken into account must be determined separately.

15A The opening balance sheet for each financial year shall correspond to the closing balance sheet for the preceding financial year.

History – Para. 15A inserted by SI 2015/980, reg. 28(2)(c), with effect in relation to–
    (a)   financial years beginning on or after 1 January 2016, and
    (b)   a financial year of a company beginning on or after 1 January 2015, but before
        1 January 2016, if the directors of the company so decide.

SECTION B – HISTORICAL COST ACCOUNTING RULES

Preliminary

16 Subject to Sections C and D of this Part of this Schedule, the amounts to be included in respect of all items shown in a company's accounts must be determined in accordance with the rules set out in this Section.

Fixed assets

General rules

17(1) The amount to be included in respect of any fixed asset must be its purchase price or production cost.

17(2) This is subject to any provision for depreciation or diminution in value made in accordance with paragraphs 18 to 20.

Rules for depreciation and diminution in value

18 In the case of any fixed asset which has a limited useful economic life, the amount of–
    (a)   its purchase price or production cost, or
    (b)   where it is estimated that any such asset will have a residual value at the end of
        the period of its useful economic life, its purchase price or production cost less
        that estimated residual value, must be reduced by provisions for depreciation
        calculated to write off that amount systematically over the period of the asset's
        useful economic life.

19(1) Where a fixed asset investment falling to be included under item B.III of either of the balance sheet formats set out in Part 1 of this Schedule has diminished in value, provisions for diminution in value may be made in respect of it and the amount to be included in respect of it may be reduced accordingly.

19(2) Provisions for diminution in value must be made in respect of any fixed asset which has diminished in value if the reduction in its value is expected to be permanent (whether its useful economic life is limited or not), and the amount to be included in respect of it must be reduced accordingly.

19(3) Provisions made under sub-paragraph (1) or (2) must be charged to the profit and loss account and disclosed separately in a note to the accounts if not shown separately in the profit and loss account.

History – Para. 19(3) substituted by SI 2015/980, reg. 28(3)(a), with effect in relation to–
    (a)   financial years beginning on or after 1 January 2016, and
    (b)   a financial year of a company beginning on or after 1 January 2015, but before
        1 January 2016, if the directors of the company so decide.

Former para. 19(3) read as follows:

"**19(3)**   Any provisions made under sub-paragraph (1) or (2) which are not shown in the profit and loss account must be disclosed (either separately or in aggregate) in a note to the accounts."

20(1)   Where the reasons for which any provision was made in accordance with paragraph 19 have ceased to apply to any extent, that provision must be written back to the extent that it is no longer necessary.

20(1A)   But provision made in accordance with paragraph 19(2) in respect of goodwill must not be written back to any extent.

20(2)   Any amounts written back under sub-paragraph (1) must be recognised in the profit and loss account and disclosed separately in a note to the accounts if not shown separately in the profit and loss account.

History – Para. 20(1A) inserted by SI 2015/1672, reg. 4(2), with effect in relation to–
- (a)   financial years beginning on or after 1 January 2016, and
- (b)   a financial year of a company beginning on or after 1 January 2015 but before 1 January 2016, if the directors of the company have decided.

Para. 20(2) substituted by SI 2015/980, reg. 28(3)(b), with effect in relation to–
- (a)   financial years beginning on or after 1 January 2016, and
- (b)   a financial year of a company beginning on or after 1 January 2015, but before 1 January 2016, if the directors of the company so decide.

Former para. 20(2) read as follows:

"**20(2)**   Any amounts written back in accordance with sub-paragraph (1) which are not shown in the profit and loss account must be disclosed (either separately or in aggregate) in a note to the accounts."

Intangible Assets

21(1)   Where this is in accordance with generally accepted accounting principles or practice, development costs may be included in "other intangible assets" under "fixed assets" in the balance sheet formats set out in Section B of Part 1 of this Schedule.

21(2)   If any amount is included in a company's balance sheet in respect of development costs, the note on accounting policies (see paragraph 44 of this Schedule) must include the following information–
- (a)   the period over which the amount of those costs originally capitalised is being or is to be written off, and
- (b)   the reasons for capitalising the development costs in question.

History – Para. 21 and the heading preceding it substituted by SI 2015/980, reg. 28(3)(c), with effect in relation to–
- (a)   financial years beginning on or after 1 January 2016, and
- (b)   a financial year of a company beginning on or after 1 January 2015, but before 1 January 2016, if the directors of the company so decide.

Former para. 21 read as follows:

"Development costs

21(1)   Notwithstanding that an item in respect of **"development costs"** is included under **"fixed assets"** in the balance sheet formats set out in Part 1 of this Schedule, an amount may only be included in a company's balance sheet in respect of development costs in special circumstances.

21(2)   If any amount is included in a company's balance sheet in respect of development costs the following information must be given in a note to the accounts–

(a)   the period over which the amount of those costs originally capitalised is being or is to be written off, and

(b)   the reasons for capitalising the development costs in question."

22(1)   Intangible assets must be written off over the useful economic life of the intangible asset.

22(2)   Where in exceptional cases the useful life of intangible assets cannot be reliably estimated, such assets must be written off over a period chosen by the directors of the company.

22(3)   The period referred to in sub-paragraph (2) must not exceed ten years.

22(4)   There must be disclosed in a note to the accounts the period referred to in sub-paragraph (2) and the reasons for choosing that period.

History – Para. 22 substituted by SI 2015/980, reg. 28(3)(c), with effect in relation to–
(a)   financial years beginning on or after 1 January 2016, and
(b)   a financial year of a company beginning on or after 1 January 2015, but before 1 January 2016, if the directors of the company so decide.

Former para. 22 read as follows:

"**22(1)**   The application of paragraphs 17 to 20 in relation to goodwill (in any case where goodwill is treated as an asset) is subject to the following.

22(2)   Subject to sub-paragraph (3), the amount of the consideration for any goodwill acquired by a company must be reduced by provisions for depreciation calculated to write off that amount systematically over a period chosen by the directors of the company.

22(3)   The period chosen must not exceed the useful economic life of the goodwill in question.

22(4)   In any case where any goodwill acquired by a company is shown or included as an asset in the company's balance sheet there must be disclosed in a note to the accounts–
(a)   the period chosen for writing off the consideration for that goodwill, and
(b)   the reasons for choosing that period."

Current assets

23   Subject to paragraph 24, the amount to be included in respect of any current asset must be its purchase price or production cost.

24(1)   If the net realisable value of any current asset is lower than its purchase price or production cost, the amount to be included in respect of that asset must be the net realisable value.

24(2)   Where the reasons for which any provision for diminution in value was made in accordance with sub-paragraph (1) have ceased to apply to any extent, that provision must be written back to the extent that it is no longer necessary.

Miscellaneous and supplementary provisions

Excess of money owed over value received as an asset item

25(1)   Where the amount repayable on any debt owed by a company is greater than the value of the consideration received in the transaction giving rise to the debt, the amount of the difference may be treated as an asset.

25(2)   Where any such amount is so treated–

(a)   it must be written off by reasonable amounts each year and must be completely written off before repayment of the debt, and

(b)   if the current amount is not shown as a separate item in the company's balance sheet, it must be disclosed in a note to the accounts.

Assets included at a fixed amount

26(1)   Subject to sub-paragraph (2), assets which fall to be included–

(a)   amongst the fixed assets of a company under the item "tangible assets", or

(b)   amongst the current assets of a company under the item "raw materials and consumables", may be included at a fixed quantity and value.

26(2)   Sub-paragraph (1) applies to assets of a kind which are constantly being replaced where–

(a)   their overall value is not material to assessing the company's state of affairs, and

(b)   their quantity, value and composition are not subject to material variation.

Determination of purchase price or production cost

27(1)   The purchase price of an asset is to be determined by adding to the actual price paid any expenses incidental to its acquisition and then subtracting any incidental reductions in the cost of acquisition.

27(2)   The production cost of an asset is to be determined by adding to the purchase price of the raw materials and consumables used the amount of the costs incurred by the company which are directly attributable to the production of that asset.

27(3)   In addition, there may be included in the production cost of an asset–

(a)   a reasonable proportion of the costs incurred by the company which are only indirectly attributable to the production of that asset, but only to the extent that they relate to the period of production, and

(b)   interest on capital borrowed to finance the production of that asset, to the extent that it accrues in respect of the period of production, provided, however, in a case within paragraph (b), that the inclusion of the interest in determining the cost of that asset and the amount of the interest so included is disclosed in a note to the accounts.

27(4)   In the case of current assets distribution costs may not be included in production costs.

History – In para. 27(1), the words "and then subtracting any incidental reductions in the cost of acquisition" inserted by SI 2015/980, reg. 28(3)(d), with effect in relation to–

(a)   financial years beginning on or after 1 January 2016, and

(b)   a financial year of a company beginning on or after 1 January 2015, but before 1 January 2016, if the directors of the company so decide.

28(1)   The purchase price or production cost of–

    (a)   any assets which fall to be included under any item shown in a company's balance sheet under the general item "stocks", and

    (b)   any assets which are fungible assets (including investments), may be determined by the application of any of the methods mentioned in sub-paragraph (2) in relation to any such assets of the same class, provided that the method chosen is one which appears to the directors to be appropriate in the circumstances of the company.

28(2)   Those methods are–

    (a)   the method known as "first in, first out" (FIFO),

    (b)   the method known as "last in, first out" (LIFO),

    (c)   a weighted average price, and

    (d)   any other method reflecting generally accepted best practice.

28(3)   Where in the case of any company–

    (a)   the purchase price or production cost of assets falling to be included under any item shown in the company's balance sheet has been determined by the application of any method permitted by this paragraph, and

    (b)   the amount shown in respect of that item differs materially from the relevant alternative amount given below in this paragraph, the amount of that difference must be disclosed in a note to the accounts.

28(4)   Subject to sub-paragraph (5), for the purposes of sub-paragraph (3)(b), the relevant alternative amount, in relation to any item shown in a company's balance sheet, is the amount which would have been shown in respect of that item if assets of any class included under that item at an amount determined by any method permitted by this paragraph had instead been included at their replacement cost as at the balance sheet date.

28(5)   The relevant alternative amount may be determined by reference to the most recent actual purchase price or production cost before the balance sheet date of assets of any class included under the item in question instead of by reference to their replacement cost as at that date, but only if the former appears to the directors of the company to constitute the more appropriate standard of comparison in the case of assets of that class.

History – In para. 28(2)(d), the words "reflecting generally accepted best practice" substituted for the words "similar to any of the methods mentioned above" by SI 2015/980, reg. 28(3)(e), with effect in relation to–

    (a)   financial years beginning on or after 1 January 2016, and

    (b)   a financial year of a company beginning on or after 1 January 2015, but before 1 January 2016, if the directors of the company so decide.

Substitution of original stated amount where price or cost unknown

29(1)   This paragraph applies where–

    (a)   there is no record of the purchase price or production cost of any asset of a company or of any price, expenses or costs relevant for determining its purchase price or production cost in accordance with paragraph 27, or

    (b)   any such record cannot be obtained without unreasonable expense or delay.

29(2)   In such a case, the purchase price or production cost of the asset must be taken, for the purposes of paragraphs 17 to 24, to be the value ascribed to it in the earliest available record of its value made on or after its acquisition or production by the company.

Equity method in respect of participating interests

29A(1) Participating interests may be accounted for using the equity method.

29A(2) If participating interests are accounted for using the equity method–

(a) the proportion of profit or loss attributable to a participating interest and recognised in the profit and loss account may be that proportion which corresponds to the amount of any dividends, and

(b) where the profit attributable to a participating interest and recognised in the profit and loss account exceeds the amount of any dividends, the difference must be placed in a reserve which cannot be distributed to shareholders.

29A(3) The reference to **"dividends"** in sub-paragraph (2) includes dividends already paid and those whose payment can be claimed.

History – Para. 29A and the heading preceding it inserted by SI 2015/980, reg. 28(3)(f), with effect in relation to–

(a) financial years beginning on or after 1 January 2016, and

(b) a financial year of a company beginning on or after 1 January 2015, but before 1 January 2016, if the directors of the company so decide.

SECTION C – ALTERNATIVE ACCOUNTING RULES

Preliminary

30(1) The rules set out in Section B are referred to below in this Schedule as the historical cost accounting rules.

30(2) Those rules, with the omission of paragraphs 16, 22 and 26 to 29, are referred to below in this Part of this Schedule as the depreciation rules; and references below in this Schedule to the historical cost accounting rules do not include the depreciation rules as they apply by virtue of paragraph 33.

31 Subject to paragraphs 33 to 35, the amounts to be included in respect of assets of any description mentioned in paragraph 32 may be determined on any basis so mentioned.

Alternative accounting rules

32(1) Intangible fixed assets, other than goodwill, may be included at their current cost.

32(2) Tangible fixed assets may be included at a market value determined as at the date of their last valuation or at their current cost.

32(3) Investments of any description falling to be included under item B III of either of the balance sheet formats set out in Part 1 of this Schedule may be included either–

(a) at a market value determined as at the date of their last valuation, or

(b) at a value determined on any basis which appears to the directors to be appropriate in the circumstances of the company.

But in the latter case particulars of the method of valuation adopted and of the reasons for adopting it must be disclosed in a note to the accounts.

32(4)   [Omitted by SI 2015/980, reg. 17(4)(a).]

32(5)   [Omitted by SI 2015/980, reg. 17(4)(a).]

History – Para. 32(4) and (5) omitted by SI 2015/980, reg. 28(4)(a), with effect in relation to–
(a)   financial years beginning on or after 1 January 2016, and
(b)   a financial year of a company beginning on or after 1 January 2015, but before 1 January 2016, if the directors of the company so decide.
Former reg. 32(4) and (5) read as follows:
  "**32(4)**   Investments of any description falling to be included under item C III of either of the balance sheet formats set out in Part 1 of this Schedule may be included at their current cost.
  32(5)   Stocks may be included at their current cost."

Application of the depreciation rules

33(1)   Where the value of any asset of a company is determined on any basis mentioned in paragraph 32, that value must be, or (as the case may require) be the starting point for determining, the amount to be included in respect of that asset in the company's accounts, instead of its purchase price or production cost or any value previously so determined for that asset.

The depreciation rules apply accordingly in relation to any such asset with the substitution for any reference to its purchase price or production cost of a reference to the value most recently determined for that asset on any basis mentioned in paragraph 32.

33(2)   The amount of any provision for depreciation required in the case of any fixed asset by paragraphs 18 to 20 as they apply by virtue of sub-paragraph (1) is referred to below in this paragraph as the adjusted amount, and the amount of any provision which would be required by any of those paragraphs in the case of that asset according to the historical cost accounting rules is referred to as the historical cost amount.

33(3)   Where sub-paragraph (1) applies in the case of any fixed asset the amount of any provision for depreciation in respect of that asset–

(a)   included in any item shown in the profit and loss account in respect of amounts written off assets of the description in question, or
(b)   taken into account in stating any item so shown which is required by note (14) of the notes on the profit and loss account formats set out in Part 1 of this Schedule to be stated after taking into account any necessary provision for depreciation or diminution in value of assets included under it,

may be the historical cost amount instead of the adjusted amount, provided that the amount of any difference between the two is shown separately in the profit and loss account or in a note to the accounts.

Additional information to be provided in case of departure from historical cost accounting rules

34(1)   This paragraph applies where the amounts to be included in respect of assets covered by any items shown in a company's accounts have been determined on any basis mentioned in paragraph 32.

34(2)   The items affected and the basis of valuation adopted in determining the amounts of the assets in question in the case of each such item must be disclosed in the note on accounting policies (see paragraph 44 of this Schedule).

34(3)   In the case of each balance sheet item affected, the comparable amounts determined according to the historical cost accounting rules must be shown in a note to the accounts.

34(4)   In sub-paragraph (3), references in relation to any item to the comparable amounts determined as there mentioned are references to–

(a)   the aggregate amount which would be required to be shown in respect of that item if the amounts to be included in respect of all the assets covered by that item were determined according to the historical cost accounting rules, and

(b)   the aggregate amount of the cumulative provisions for depreciation or diminution in value which would be permitted or required in determining those amounts according to those rules.

History – In para. 34(2), the words "the note on accounting policies (see paragraph 44 of this Schedule)" substituted for the words "a note to the accounts" by SI 2015/980, reg. 28(4)(b), with effect in relation to–

(a)   financial years beginning on or after 1 January 2016, and

(b)   a financial year of a company beginning on or after 1 January 2015, but before 1 January 2016, if the directors of the company so decide.

Para. 34(3) substituted by SI 2015/980, reg. 28(4)(c), with effect in relation to–

(a)   financial years beginning on or after 1 January 2016, and

(b)   a financial year of a company beginning on or after 1 January 2015, but before 1 January 2016, if the directors of the company so decide.

Former para. 34(3) read as follows:

"**34(3)**   In the case of each balance sheet item affected (except stocks) either–

(a)   the comparable amounts determined according to the historical cost accounting rules, or

(b)   the differences between those amounts and the corresponding amounts actually shown in the balance sheet in respect of that item, must be shown separately in the balance sheet or in a note to the accounts."

Revaluation reserve

35(1)   With respect to any determination of the value of an asset of a company on any basis mentioned in paragraph 32, the amount of any profit or loss arising from that determination (after allowing, where appropriate, for any provisions for depreciation or diminution in value made otherwise than by reference to the value so determined and any adjustments of any such provisions made in the light of that determination) must be credited or (as the case may be) debited to a separate reserve ("the revaluation reserve").

35(2)   The amount of the revaluation reserve must be shown in the company's balance sheet under a separate sub-heading in the position given for the item "revaluation reserve" under "Capital and reserves" in format 1 or 2 of the balance sheet formats set out in Part 1 of this Schedule.

35(3) An amount may be transferred–

(a)   from the revaluation reserve–

(i)   to the profit and loss account, if the amount was previously charged to that account or represents realised profit, or

(ii)   on capitalisation,

(b)   to or from the revaluation reserve in respect of the taxation relating to any profit or loss credited or debited to the reserve.

The revaluation reserve must be reduced to the extent that the amounts transferred to it are no longer necessary for the purposes of the valuation method used.

35(4) In sub-paragraph (3)(a)(ii) **"capitalisation"**, in relation to an amount standing to the credit of the revaluation reserve, means applying it in wholly or partly paying up unissued shares in the company to be allotted to members of the company as fully or partly paid shares.

35(5) The revaluation reserve must not be reduced except as mentioned in this paragraph.

35(6) The treatment for taxation purposes of amounts credited or debited to the revaluation reserve must be disclosed in a note to the accounts.

History – In para. 35(2), the words "under "Capital and reserves"" inserted; and the words "but need not be shown under that name" omitted by SI 2015/980, reg. 28(4)(d), with effect in relation to–

(a)   financial years beginning on or after 1 January 2016, and

(b)   a financial year of a company beginning on or after 1 January 2015, but before 1 January 2016, if the directors of the company so decide.

SECTION D – FAIR VALUE ACCOUNTING

Inclusion of financial instruments at fair value

36(1) Subject to sub-paragraphs (2) to (5), financial instruments (including derivatives) may be included at fair value.

36(2) Sub-paragraph (1) does not apply to financial instruments that constitute liabilities unless–

(a)   they are held as Part of a trading portfolio,

(b)   they are derivatives, or

(c)   they are financial instruments falling within sub-paragraph (4).

36(3) Unless they are financial instruments falling within sub-paragraph (4), sub-paragraph (1) does not apply to–

(a)   financial instruments (other than derivatives) held to maturity,

(b)   loans and receivables originated by the company and not held for trading purposes,

(c)   interests in subsidiary undertakings, associated undertakings and joint ventures,

(d)   equity instruments issued by the company,

(e)   contracts for contingent consideration in a business combination, or

(f)   other financial instruments with such special characteristics that the instruments, according to generally accepted accounting principles or practice, should be accounted for differently from other financial instruments.

36(4)   Financial instruments which under international accounting standards may be included in accounts at fair value, may be so included, provided that the disclosures required by such accounting standards are made.

36(5)   If the fair value of a financial instrument cannot be determined reliably in accordance with paragraph 37, sub-paragraph (1) does not apply to that financial instrument.

36(6)   In this paragraph–
"associated undertaking" has the meaning given by paragraph 19 of Schedule 6 to these Regulations;
"joint venture" has the meaning given by paragraph 18 of that Schedule.

History – Para. 36(4) substituted by SI 2015/980, reg. 28(5)(a), with effect in relation to–
(a)   financial years beginning on or after 1 January 2016, and
(b)   a financial year of a company beginning on or after 1 January 2015, but before 1 January 2016, if the directors of the company so decide.
Former para. 36(4) read as follows:
"**36(4)**   Financial instruments that, under international accounting standards adopted by the European Commission on or before 5th September 2006 in accordance with the IAS Regulation, may be included in accounts at fair value, may be so included, provided that the disclosures required by such accounting standards are made."

Determination of fair value

37(1)   The fair value of a financial instrument is its value determined in accordance with this paragraph.

37(2)   If a reliable market can readily be identified for the financial instrument, its fair value is determined by reference to its market value.

37(3)   If a reliable market cannot readily be identified for the financial instrument but can be identified for its components or for a similar instrument, its fair value is determined by reference to the market value of its components or of the similar instrument.

37(4)   If neither sub-paragraph (2) nor (3) applies, the fair value of the financial instrument is a value resulting from generally accepted valuation models and techniques.

37(5)   Any valuation models and techniques used for the purposes of sub-paragraph (4) must ensure a reasonable approximation of the market value.

Hedged items

38   A company may include any assets and liabilities, or identified portions of such assets or liabilities, that qualify as hedged items under a fair value hedge accounting system at the amount required under that system.

Other assets that may be included at fair value

39(1) This paragraph applies to–

(a) stocks,

(b) investment property, and

(c) living animals and plants.

39(2) Such stocks, investment property, and living animals and plants may be included at fair value, provided that, as the case may be, all such stocks, investment property, and living animals and plants are so included where their fair value can reliably be determined.

39(3) In this paragraph, **"fair value"** means fair value determined in accordance with generally accepted accounting principles or practice.

History – Para. 39 substituted by SI 2015/980, reg. 28(5)(b), with effect in relation to–

(a) financial years beginning on or after 1 January 2016, and

(b) a financial year of a company beginning on or after 1 January 2015, but before 1 January 2016, if the directors of the company so decide.

Former para. 39 read as follows:

"**39(1)** This paragraph applies to–

(a) investment property, and

(b) living animals and plants, that, under international accounting standards, may be included in accounts at fair value.

39(2) Such investment property and such living animals and plants may be included at fair value, provided that all such investment property or, as the case may be, all such living animals and plants are so included where their fair value can reliably be determined.

39(3) In this paragraph, **"fair value"** means fair value determined in accordance with relevant international accounting standards."

Accounting for changes in value

40(1) This paragraph applies where a financial instrument is valued in accordance with paragraph 36 or 38 or an asset is valued in accordance with paragraph 39.

40(2) Notwithstanding paragraph 13 in this Part of this Schedule, and subject to sub-paragraphs (3) and (4), a change in the value of the financial instrument or of the investment property or living animal or plant must be included in the profit and loss account.

40(3) Where–

(a) the financial instrument accounted for is a hedging instrument under a hedge accounting system that allows some or all of the change in value not to be shown in the profit and loss account, or

(b) the change in value relates to an exchange difference arising on a monetary item that forms Part of a company's net investment in a foreign entity, the amount of the change in value must be credited to or (as the case may be) debited from a separate reserve ("the fair value reserve").

40(4) Where the instrument accounted for–

(a) is an available for sale financial asset, and

(b) is not a derivative, the change in value may be credited to or (as the case may be) debited from the fair value reserve.

The fair value reserve

41(1) The fair value reserve must be adjusted to the extent that the amounts shown in it are no longer necessary for the purposes of paragraph 40(3) or (4).

41(2) The treatment for taxation purposes of amounts credited or debited to the fair value reserve must be disclosed in a note to the accounts.

PART 3 – NOTES TO THE ACCOUNTS

Preliminary

42(1) Any information required in the case of a company by the following provisions of this Part of this Schedule must be given by way of a note to the accounts.

42(2) These notes must be presented in the order in which, where relevant, the items to which they relate are presented in the balance sheet and in the profit and loss account.

History – Para. 42 substituted by SI 2015/980, reg. 29(2), with effect in relation to–
- (a) financial years beginning on or after 1 January 2016, and
- (b) a financial year of a company beginning on or after 1 January 2015, but before 1 January 2016, if the directors of the company so decide.

Former para. 42 read as follows:

"**42** Any information required in the case of any company by the following provisions of this Part of this Schedule must (if not given in the company's accounts) be given by way of a note to the accounts."

General

Reserves and dividends

43 There must be stated–
- (a) any amount set aside or proposed to be set aside to, or withdrawn or proposed to be withdrawn from, reserves,
- (b) the aggregate amount of dividends paid in the financial year (other than those for which a liability existed at the immediately preceding balance sheet date),
- (c) the aggregate amount of dividends that the company is liable to pay at the balance sheet date, and
- (d) the aggregate amount of dividends that are proposed before the date of approval of the accounts, and not otherwise disclosed under sub-paragraph (b) or (c).

Disclosure of accounting policies

44 The accounting policies adopted by the company in determining the amounts to be included in respect of items shown in the balance sheet and in determining the profit or loss of the company must be stated (including such policies with respect to the depreciation and diminution in value of assets).

45   It must be stated whether the accounts have been prepared in accordance with applicable accounting standards and particulars of any material departure from those standards and the reasons for it must be given (see regulation 4(2) for exemption for medium-sized companies).

Information supplementing the balance sheet

46   Paragraphs 47 to 64 require information which either supplements the information given with respect to any particular items shown in the balance sheet or is otherwise relevant to assessing the company's state of affairs in the light of the information so given.

Share capital and debentures

47(1)   The following information must be given with respect to the company's share capital–

    (a)   where shares of more than one class have been allotted, the number and aggregate nominal value of shares of each class allotted, and

    (b)   where shares are held as treasury shares, the number and aggregate nominal value of the treasury shares and, where shares of more than one class have been allotted, the number and aggregate nominal value of the shares of each class held as treasury shares.

47(2)   In the case of any Part of the allotted share capital that consists of redeemable shares, the following information must be given–

    (a)   the earliest and latest dates on which the company has power to redeem those shares,

    (b)   whether those shares must be redeemed in any event or are liable to be redeemed at the option of the company or of the shareholder, and

    (c)   whether any (and, if so, what) premium is payable on redemption.

48   If the company has allotted any shares during the financial year, the following information must be given–

    (a)   the classes of shares allotted, and

    (b)   as respects each class of shares, the number allotted, their aggregate nominal value, and the consideration received by the company for the allotment.

49(1)   With respect to any contingent right to the allotment of shares in the company the following particulars must be given–

    (a)   the number, description and amount of the shares in relation to which the right is exercisable,

    (b)   the period during which it is exercisable, and

    (c)   the price to be paid for the shares allotted.

49(2)   In sub-paragraph (1) **"contingent right to the allotment of shares"** means any option to subscribe for shares and any other right to require the allotment of shares to any person whether arising on the conversion into shares of securities of any other description or otherwise.

50(1)   If the company has issued any debentures during the financial year to which the accounts relate, the following information must be given–

(a)   the classes of debentures issued, and

(b)   as respects each class of debentures, the amount issued and the consideration received by the company for the issue.

50(2)   Where any of the company's debentures are held by a nominee of or trustee for the company, the nominal amount of the debentures and the amount at which they are stated in the accounting records kept by the company in accordance with Section 386 of the 2006 Act (duty to keep accounting records) must be stated.

Fixed assets

51(1)   In respect of each item which is or would but for paragraph 4(2)(b) be shown under the general item "fixed assets" in the company's balance sheet the following information must be given–

(a)   the appropriate amounts in respect of that item as at the date of the beginning of the financial year and as at the balance sheet date respectively,

(b)   the effect on any amount shown in the balance sheet in respect of that item of–

(i)   any revision of the amount in respect of any assets included under that item made during that year on any basis mentioned in paragraph 32,

(ii)   acquisitions during that year of any assets,

(iii)   disposals during that year of any assets, and

(iv)   any transfers of assets of the company to and from that item during that year.

51(2)   The reference in sub-paragraph (1)(a) to the appropriate amounts in respect of any item as at any date there mentioned is a reference to amounts representing the aggregate amounts determined, as at that date, in respect of assets falling to be included under that item on either of the following bases, that is to say–

(a)   on the basis of purchase price or production cost (determined in accordance with paragraphs 27 and 28), or

(b)   on any basis mentioned in paragraph 32, (leaving out of account in either case any provisions for depreciation or diminution in value).

51(3)   In respect of each item within sub-paragraph (1) there must also be stated–

(a)   the cumulative amount of provisions for depreciation or diminution in value of assets included under that item as at each date mentioned in sub-paragraph (1) (a),

(b)   the amount of any such provisions made in respect of the financial year,

(c)   the amount of any adjustments made in respect of any such provisions during that year in consequence of the disposal of any assets, and

(d)   the amount of any other adjustments made in respect of any such provisions during that year.

52   Where any fixed assets of the company (other than listed investments) are included under any item shown in the company's balance sheet at an amount determined on any basis mentioned in paragraph 32, the following information must be given–

(a)   the years (so far as they are known to the directors) in which the assets were severally valued and the several values, and

(b)   in the case of assets that have been valued during the financial year, the names of the persons who valued them or particulars of their qualifications for doing so and (whichever is stated) the bases of valuation used by them.

53   In relation to any amount which is or would but for paragraph 4(2)(b) be shown in respect of the item "land and buildings" in the company's balance sheet there must be stated–

    (a)   how much of that amount is ascribable to land of freehold tenure and how much to land of leasehold tenure, and

    (b)   how much of the amount ascribable to land of leasehold tenure is ascribable to land held on long lease and how much to land held on short lease.

Investments

54(1)   In respect of the amount of each item which is or would but for paragraph 4(2)(b) be shown in the company's balance sheet under the general item "investments" (whether as fixed assets or as current assets) there must be stated how much of that amount is ascribable to listed investments.

54(2)   Where the amount of any listed investments is stated for any item in accordance with subparagraph (1), the following amounts must also be stated–

    (a)   the aggregate market value of those investments where it differs from the amount so stated, and

    (b)   both the market value and the stock exchange value of any investments of which the former value is, for the purposes of the accounts, taken as being higher than the latter.

Information about fair value of assets and liabilities

55(1)   This paragraph applies where financial instruments or other assets have been valued in accordance with, as appropriate, paragraph 36, 38 or 39.

55(2)   There must be stated–

    (a)   the significant assumptions underlying the valuation models and techniques used to determine the fair value of the instruments or other assets,

    (b)   for each category of financial instrument or other asset, the fair value of the assets in that category and the changes in value–

        (i)   included directly in the profit and loss account, or

        (ii)   credited to or (as the case may be) debited from the fair value reserve, in respect of those assets, and

    (c)   for each class of derivatives, the extent and nature of the instruments, including significant terms and conditions that may affect the amount, timing and certainty of future cash flows.

55(3)   Where any amount is transferred to or from the fair value reserve during the financial year, there must be stated in tabular form–

    (a)   the amount of the reserve as at the date of the beginning of the financial year and as at the balance sheet date respectively,

    (b)   the amount transferred to or from the reserve during the year, and

    (c)   the source and application respectively of the amounts so transferred.

History – Para. 55 substituted by SI 2015/980, reg. 29(3), with effect in relation to–

    (a)   financial years beginning on or after 1 January 2016, and

    (b)   a financial year of a company beginning on or after 1 January 2015, but before 1 January 2016, if the directors of the company so decide.

Former para. 55 read as follows:

"**55(1)** This paragraph applies where financial instruments have been valued in accordance with paragraph 36 or 38.

55(2) There must be stated–

(a) the significant assumptions underlying the valuation models and techniques used where the fair value of the instruments has been determined in accordance with paragraph 37(4),

(b) for each category of financial instrument, the fair value of the instruments in that category and the changes in value–

   (i) included in the profit and loss account, or

   (ii) credited to or (as the case may be) debited from the fair value reserve, in respect of those instruments, and

(c) for each class of derivatives, the extent and nature of the instruments, including significant terms and conditions that may affect the amount, timing and certainty of future cash flows.

55(3) Where any amount is transferred to or from the fair value reserve during the financial year, there must be stated in tabular form–

(a) the amount of the reserve as at the date of the beginning of the financial year and as at the balance sheet date respectively,

(b) the amount transferred to or from the reserve during that year, and

(c) the source and application respectively of the amounts so transferred."

56 Where the company has derivatives that it has not included at fair value, there must be stated for each class of such derivatives–

(a) the fair value of the derivatives in that class, if such a value can be determined in accordance with paragraph 37, and

(b) the extent and nature of the derivatives.

57(1) This paragraph applies if–

(a) the company has financial fixed assets that could be included at fair value by virtue of paragraph 36,

(b) the amount at which those items are included under any item in the company's accounts is in excess of their fair value, and

(c) the company has not made provision for diminution in value of those assets in accordance with paragraph 19(1) of this Schedule.

57(2) There must be stated–

(a) the amount at which either the individual assets or appropriate groupings of those individual assets are included in the company's accounts,

(b) the fair value of those assets or groupings, and

(c) the reasons for not making a provision for diminution in value of those assets, including the nature of the evidence that provides the basis for the belief that the amount at which they are stated in the accounts will be recovered.

Information where investment property and living animals and plants included at fair value

58(1) This paragraph applies where the amounts to be included in a company's accounts in respect of stocks, investment property or living animals and plants have been determined in accordance with paragraph 39.

58(2) The balance sheet items affected and the basis of valuation adopted in determining the amounts of the assets in question in the case of each such item must be disclosed in a note to the accounts.

58(3) In the case of investment property, for each balance sheet item affected there must be shown, either separately in the balance sheet or in a note to the accounts–

(a) the comparable amounts determined according to the historical cost accounting rules, or

(b) the differences between those amounts and the corresponding amounts actually shown in the balance sheet in respect of that item.

58(4) In sub-paragraph (3), references in relation to any item to the comparable amounts determined in accordance with that sub-paragraph are to–

(a) the aggregate amount which would be required to be shown in respect of that item if the amounts to be included in respect of all the assets covered by that item were determined according to the historical cost accounting rules, and

(b) the aggregate amount of the cumulative provisions for depreciation or diminution in value which would be permitted or required in determining those amounts according to those rules.

History – In para. 58(1), the word "stocks," inserted by SI 2015/980, reg. 29(4), with effect in relation to–

(a) financial years beginning on or after 1 January 2016, and

(b) a financial year of a company beginning on or after 1 January 2015, but before 1 January 2016, if the directors of the company so decide.

Reserves and provisions

59(1) This paragraph applies where any amount is transferred–

(a) to or from any reserves, or

(b) to any provision for liabilities, or

(c) from any provision for liabilities otherwise than for the purpose for which the provision was established, and the reserves or provisions are or would but for paragraph 4(2)(b) be shown as separate items in the company's balance sheet.

59(2) The following information must be given in respect of the aggregate of reserves or provisions included in the same item in tabular form–

(a) the amount of the reserves or provisions as at the date of the beginning of the financial year and as at the balance sheet date respectively,

(b) any amounts transferred to or from the reserves or provisions during that year, and

(c) the source and application respectively of any amounts so transferred.

59(3) Particulars must be given of each provision included in the item "other provisions" in the company's balance sheet in any case where the amount of that provision is material.

History – In para. 59(2), the words "in tabular form" inserted by SI 2015/980, reg. 29(5), with effect in relation to–

(a) financial years beginning on or after 1 January 2016, and

(b) a financial year of a company beginning on or after 1 January 2015, but before 1 January 2016, if the directors of the company so decide.

Provision for taxation

60   The amount of any provision for deferred taxation must be stated separately from the amount of any provision for other taxation.

Details of indebtedness

61(1)   For the aggregate of all items shown under "creditors" in the company's balance sheet there must be stated the aggregate of the following amounts–

(a)   the amount of any debts included under "creditors" which are payable or repayable otherwise than by instalments and fall due for payment or repayment after the end of the period of five years beginning with the day next following the end of the financial year, and

(b)   in the case of any debts so included which are payable or repayable by instalments, the amount of any instalments which fall due for payment after the end of that period.

61(2)   Subject to sub-paragraph (3), in relation to each debt falling to be taken into account under sub-paragraph (1), the terms of payment or repayment and the rate of any interest payable on the debt must be stated.

61(3)   If the number of debts is such that, in the opinion of the directors, compliance with subparagraph (2) would result in a statement of excessive length, it is sufficient to give a general indication of the terms of payment or repayment and the rates of any interest payable on the debts.

61(4)   In respect of each item shown under "creditors" in the company's balance sheet there must be stated–

(a)   the aggregate amount of any debts included under that item in respect of which any security has been given by the company, and

(b)   an indication of the nature and form of the securities so given.

61(5)   References above in this paragraph to an item shown under "creditors" in the company's balance sheet include references, where amounts falling due to creditors within one year and after more than one year are distinguished in the balance sheet–

(a)   in a case within sub-paragraph (1), to an item shown under the latter of those categories, and

(b)   in a case within sub-paragraph (4), to an item shown under either of those categories. References to items shown under "creditors" include references to items which would but for paragraph 4(2)(b) be shown under that heading.

History – In para. 61(4)(b), the words "and form" inserted by SI 2015/980, reg. 29(6), with effect in relation to–

(a)   financial years beginning on or after 1 January 2016, and

(b)   a financial year of a company beginning on or after 1 January 2015, but before 1 January 2016, if the directors of the company so decide.

62   If any fixed cumulative dividends on the company's shares are in arrear, there must be stated–

(a)   the amount of the arrears, and

(b)   the period for which the dividends or, if there is more than one class, each class of them are in arrear.

Guarantees and other financial commitments

63(1) Particulars must be given of any charge on the assets of the company to secure the liabilities of any other person including the amount secured.

63(2) Particulars and the total amount of any financial commitments, guarantees and contingencies that are not included in the balance sheet must be disclosed.

63(3) An indication of the nature and form of any valuable security given by the company in respect of commitments, guarantees and contingencies within sub-paragraph (2) must be given.

63(4) The total amount of any commitments within sub-paragraph (2) concerning pensions must be separately disclosed.

63(5) Particulars must be given of pension commitments which are included in the balance sheet.

63(6) Where any commitment within sub-paragraph (4) or (5) relates wholly or partly to pensions payable to past directors of the company separate particulars must be given of that commitment.

63(7) The total amount of any commitments, guarantees and contingencies within sub-paragraph (2) which are undertaken on behalf of or for the benefit of–

    (a)   any parent undertaking or fellow subsidiary undertaking of the company,

    (b)   any subsidiary undertaking of the company, or

    (c)   any undertaking in which the company has a participating interest

must be separately stated and those within each of paragraphs (a), (b) and (c) must also be stated separately from those within any other of those paragraphs.

History – Para. 63 substituted by SI 2015/980, reg. 29(7), with effect in relation to–
    (a)   financial years beginning on or after 1 January 2016, and
    (b)   a financial year of a company beginning on or after 1 January 2015, but before 1 January 2016, if the directors of the company so decide.
Former para. 63 read as follows:

"Guarantees and other financial commitments

63(1) Particulars must be given of any charge on the assets of the company to secure the liabilities of any other person, including, where practicable, the amount secured.

63(2) The following information must be given with respect to any other contingent liability not provided for–
    (a)   the amount or estimated amount of that liability,
    (b)   its legal nature, and
    (c)   whether any valuable security has been provided by the company in connection with that liability and if so, what.

63(3) There must be stated, where practicable, the aggregate amount or estimated amount of contracts for capital expenditure, so far as not provided for.

63(4) Particulars must be given of–
    (a)   any pension commitments included under any provision shown in the company's balance sheet, and
    (b)   any such commitments for which no provision has been made, and where any such commitment relates wholly or partly to pensions payable to past directors of the company separate particulars must be given of that commitment so far as it relates to such pensions.

63(5) Particulars must also be given of any other financial commitments that–

    (a)   have not been provided for, and

    (b)   are relevant to assessing the company's state of affairs."

Miscellaneous matters

64(1) Particulars must be given of any case where the purchase price or production cost of any asset is for the first time determined under paragraph 29.

64(2) Where any outstanding loans made under the authority of Section 682(2)(b), (c) or (d) of the 2006 Act (various cases of financial assistance by a company for purchase of its own shares) are included under any item shown in the company's balance sheet, the aggregate amount of those loans must be disclosed for each item in question.

Information supplementing the profit and loss account

65 Paragraphs 66 to 69 require information which either supplements the information given with respect to any particular items shown in the profit and loss account or otherwise provides particulars of income or expenditure of the company or of circumstances affecting the items shown in the profit and loss account (see regulation 3(2) for exemption for companies falling within Section 408 of the 2006 Act (individual profit and loss account where group accounts prepared)).

Separate statement of certain items of income and expenditure

66(1) Subject to sub-paragraph (2), there must be stated the amount of the interest on or any similar charges in respect of bank loans and overdrafts, and loans of any other kind made to the company.

66(2) Sub-paragraph (1) does not apply to interest or charges on loans to the company from group undertakings, but, with that exception, it applies to interest or charges on all loans, whether made on the security of debentures or not.

Particulars of tax

67(1) Particulars must be given of any special circumstances which affect liability in respect of taxation of profits, income or capital gains for the financial year or liability in respect of taxation of profits, income or capital gains for succeeding financial years.

67(2) The following amounts must be stated–

    (a)   the amount of the charge for United Kingdom corporation tax,

    (b)   if that amount would have been greater but for relief from double taxation, the amount which it would have been but for such relief,

    (c)   the amount of the charge for United Kingdom income tax, and

    (d)   the amount of the charge for taxation imposed outside the United Kingdom of profits, income and (so far as charged to revenue) capital gains.

These amounts must be stated separately in respect of each of the amounts which is or would but for paragraph 4(2)(b) be shown under the item "tax on profit or loss" in the profit and loss account.

History – In para. 67(2), the words "These amounts must be stated separately in respect of each of the amounts which is or would but for paragraph 4(2)(b) be shown under the item "tax on profit or loss" in the profit and loss account." substituted for the words "These amounts must be stated separately in respect of each of the amounts which is or would but for paragraph 4(2)(b) be shown under the items "tax on profit or loss on ordinary activities" and "tax in extraordinary profit or loss" in the profit and loss account." by SI 2015/980, reg. 29(8), with effect in relation to–

    (a)   financial years beginning on or after 1 January 2016, and

    (b)   a financial year of a company beginning on or after 1 January 2015, but before 1 January 2016, if the directors of the company so decide.

Particulars of turnover

68(1) If in the course of the financial year the company has carried on business of two or more classes that, in the opinion of the directors, differ substantially from each other, the amount of the turnover attributable to each class must be stated and the class described (see regulation 4(3)(b) for exemption for medium-sized companies in accounts delivered to registrar).

68(2) If in the course of the financial year the company has supplied markets that, in the opinion of the directors, differ substantially from each other, the amount of the turnover attributable to each such market must also be stated.

In this paragraph **"market"** means a market delimited by geographical bounds.

68(3) In analysing for the purposes of this paragraph the source (in terms of business or in terms of market) of turnover, the directors of the company must have regard to the manner in which the company's activities are organised.

68(4) For the purposes of this paragraph–

    (a)   classes of business which, in the opinion of the directors, do not differ substantially from each other must be treated as one class, and

    (b)   markets which, in the opinion of the directors, do not differ substantially from each other must be treated as one market, and any amounts properly attributable to one class of business or (as the case may be) to one market which are not material may be included in the amount stated in respect of another.

68(5) Where in the opinion of the directors the disclosure of any information required by this paragraph would be seriously prejudicial to the interests of the company, that information need not be disclosed, but the fact that any such information has not been disclosed must be stated.

Miscellaneous matters

69(1) Where any amount relating to any preceding financial year is included in any item in the profit and loss account, the effect must be stated.

69(2) The amount, nature and effect of any individual items of income or expenditure which are of exceptional size or incidence must be stated.

History – Para. 69(2) substituted for para. 69(2) and (3) by SI 2015/980, reg. 29(9), with effect in relation to–
    (a)   financial years beginning on or after 1 January 2016, and
    (b)   a financial year of a company beginning on or after 1 January 2015, but before 1 January 2016, if the directors of the company so decide.

Sums denominated in foreign currencies

70   Where any sums originally denominated in foreign currencies have been brought into account under any items shown in the balance sheet format or profit and loss account formats, the basis on which those sums have been translated into sterling (or the currency in which the accounts are drawn up) must be stated.

Dormant companies acting as agents

71   Where the directors of a company take advantage of the exemption conferred by Section 480 of the 2006 Act (dormant companies: exemption from audit), and the company has during the financial year in question acted as an agent for any person, the fact that it has so acted must be stated.

Related party transactions

72(1)   Particulars may be given of transactions which the company has entered into with related parties, and must be given if such transactions are material and have not been concluded under normal market conditions (see regulation 4(2B) for a modification for medium-sized companies).

72(2)   The particulars of transactions required to be disclosed by sub-paragraph (1) must include–

    (a)   the amount of such transactions,
    (b)   the nature of the related party relationship, and
    (c)   other information about the transactions necessary for an understanding of the financial position of the company.

72(3)   Information about individual transactions may be aggregated according to their nature, except where separate information is necessary for an understanding of the effects of related party transactions on the financial position of the company.

72(4)   Particulars need not be given of transactions entered into between two or more members of a group, provided that any subsidiary undertaking which is a party to the transaction is whollyowned by such a member.

72(5)   In this paragraph, **"related party"** has the same meaning as in international accounting standards.

History – In para. 72(1), the words "regulation 4(2B) for a modification" substituted for the words "regulation 4(2) for exemption" by SI 2015/980, reg. 29(10), with effect in relation to–
    (a)   financial years beginning on or after 1 January 2016, and
    (b)   a financial year of a company beginning on or after 1 January 2015, but before 1 January 2016, if the directors of the company so decide.

Post balance sheet events

72A   The nature and financial effect of material events arising after the balance sheet date which are not reflected in the profit and loss account or balance sheet must be stated.

History – Para. 72A and the heading preceding it inserted by SI 2015/980, reg. 29(11), with effect in relation to–
- (a)   financial years beginning on or after 1 January 2016, and
- (b)   a financial year of a company beginning on or after 1 January 2015, but before 1 January 2016, if the directors of the company so decide.

Appropriations

72B   Particulars must be given of the proposed appropriation of profit or treatment of loss or, where applicable, particulars of the actual appropriation of the profits or treatment of the losses.

History – Para. 72B and the heading preceding it inserted by SI 2015/980, reg. 29(11), with effect in relation to–
- (a)   financial years beginning on or after 1 January 2016, and
- (b)   a financial year of a company beginning on or after 1 January 2015, but before 1 January 2016, if the directors of the company so decide.

PART 4 – SPECIAL PROVISION WHERE COMPANY IS A PARENT COMPANY OR SUBSIDIARY UNDERTAKING

COMPANY'S OWN ACCOUNTS: GUARANTEES AND OTHER FINANCIAL COMMITMENTS IN FAVOUR OF GROUP UNDERTAKINGS

73   [Omitted by SI 2015/980, reg. 30.]

History – Para. 73 omitted by SI 2015/980, reg. 30, with effect in relation to–
- (a)   financial years beginning on or after 1 January 2016, and
- (b)   a financial year of a company beginning on or after 1 January 2015, but before 1 January 2016, if the directors of the company so decide.

Former para. 73 read as follows:

"**73**   Commitments within any of sub-paragraphs (1) to (5) of paragraph 63 (guarantees and other financial commitments) which are undertaken on behalf of or for the benefit of–
- (a)   any parent undertaking or fellow subsidiary undertaking, or
- (b)   any subsidiary undertaking of the company, must be stated separately from the other commitments within that paragraph, and commitments within paragraph
- (a)   must also be stated separately from those within paragraph (b)."

PART 5 – SPECIAL PROVISIONS WHERE THE COMPANY IS AN INVESTMENT COMPANY

74(1)   Paragraph 35 does not apply to the amount of any profit or loss arising from a determination of the value of any investments of an investment company on any basis mentioned in paragraph 32(3).

74(2) Any provisions made by virtue of paragraph 19(1) or (2) in the case of an investment company in respect of any fixed asset investments need not be charged to the company's profit and loss account provided they are either–

(a)   charged against any reserve account to which any amount excluded by sub-paragraph (1) from the requirements of paragraph 35 has been credited, or

(b)   shown as a separate item in the company's balance sheet under the sub-heading "other reserves".

74(3) For the purposes of this paragraph, as it applies in relation to any company, **"fixed asset investment"** means any asset falling to be included under any item shown in the company's balance sheet under the subdivision "investments" under the general item "fixed assets".

75(1) Any distribution made by an investment company which reduces the amount of its net assets to less than the aggregate of its called-up share capital and undistributable reserves shall be disclosed in a note to the company's accounts.

75(2) For purposes of this paragraph, a company's net assets are the aggregate of its assets less the aggregate of its liabilities (including any provision for liabilities within paragraph 2 of Schedule 9 to these Regulations that is made in Companies Act accounts and any provision that is made in IAS accounts); and **"undistributable reserves"** has the meaning given by Section 831(4) of the 2006 Act.

75(3) A company shall be treated as an investment company for the purposes of this Part of this Schedule in relation to any financial year of the company if–

(a)   during the whole of that year it was an investment company as defined by Section 833 of the 2006 Act, and

(b)   it was not at any time during that year prohibited from making a distribution by virtue of Section 832 of the 2006 Act due to either or both of the conditions specified in Section 832(4)(a) or (b) (no distribution where capital profits have been distributed etc) not being met.

SCHEDULE 2   Regulation 5(1)

BANKING COMPANIES: COMPANIES ACT INDIVIDUAL ACCOUNTS

PART 1 – GENERAL RULES AND FORMATS
SECTION A – GENERAL RULES

1   Subject to the following provisions of this Part of this Schedule–

(a)   every balance sheet of a company must show the items listed in the balance sheet format set out in Section B of this Part, and

(b)   every profit and loss account must show the items listed in either of the profit and loss account formats in Section B.

2(1) References in this Part of this Schedule to the items listed in any of the formats set out in Section B, are to those items read together with any of the notes following the formats which apply to those items.

2(2) The items must be shown in the order and under the headings and sub-headings given in the particular format used, but–

(a)   the notes to the formats may permit alternative positions for any particular items,

(b)   the heading or sub-heading for any item does not have to be distinguished by any letter or number assigned to that item in the format used, and

(c)   where the heading of an item in the format used contains any wording in square brackets, that wording may be omitted if not applicable to the company.

3(1) Where in accordance with paragraph 1 a company's profit and loss account for any financial year has been prepared by reference to one of the formats in Section B, the company's directors must use the same format in preparing the profit and loss account for subsequent financial years, unless in their opinion there are special reasons for a change.

3(2) Particulars of any change must be given in a note to the accounts in which the new format is first used, and the reasons for the change must be explained.

4(1) Any item required to be shown in a company's balance sheet or profit and loss account may be shown in greater detail than required by the particular format used.

4(2) The balance sheet or profit and loss account may include an item representing or covering the amount of any asset or liability, income or expenditure not specifically covered by any of the items listed in the format used, save that none of the following may be treated as assets in any balance sheet–

(a)   preliminary expenses,

(b)   expenses of, and commission on, any issue of shares or debentures, and

(c)   costs of research.

5(1) Items to which lower case letters are assigned in any of the formats in Section B may be combined in a company's accounts for any financial year if–

(a)   their individual amounts are not material for the purpose of giving a true and fair view, or

(b)   the combination facilitates the assessment of the state of affairs or profit or loss of the company for that year.

5(2) Where sub-paragraph (1)(b) applies, the individual amounts of any items so combined must be disclosed in a note to the accounts and any notes required by this Schedule to the items so combined must, notwithstanding the combination, be given.

6(1) Subject to sub-paragraph (2), the directors must not include a heading or sub-heading corresponding to an item in the balance sheet or profit and loss account format used if there is no amount to be shown for that item for the financial year to which the balance sheet or profit and loss account relates.

6(2) Where an amount can be shown for the item in question for the immediately preceding financial year, that amount must be shown under the heading or sub-heading required by the format for that item.

7(1) For every item shown in the balance sheet or profit and loss account the corresponding amount for the immediately preceding financial year must also be shown.

7(2)   Where that corresponding amount is not comparable with the amount to be shown for the item in question in respect of the financial year to which the balance sheet or profit and loss account relates, the former amount may be adjusted, and particulars of the non-comparability and of any adjustment must be disclosed in a note to the accounts.

8(1)   Subject to the following provisions of this paragraph and without prejudice to note (6) to the balance sheet format, amounts in respect of items representing assets or income may not be set off against amounts in respect of items representing liabilities or expenditure (as the case may be), or vice versa.

8(2)   Charges required to be included in profit and loss account format 1, items 11(a) and 11(b) or format 2, items A7(a) and A7(b) may be set off against income required to be included in format 1, items 12(a) and 12(b) or format 2, items B5(a) and B5(b) and the resulting figure shown as a single item (in format 2 at position A7 if negative and at position B5 if positive).

8(3)   Charges required to be included in profit and loss account format 1, item 13 or format 2, item A8 may also be set off against income required to be included in format 1, item 14 or format 2, item B6 and the resulting figure shown as a single item (in format 2 at position A8 if negative and at position B6 if positive).

9(1)   Assets must be shown under the relevant balance sheet headings even where the company has pledged them as security for its own liabilities or for those of third parties or has otherwise assigned them as security to third parties.

9(2)   A company may not include in its balance sheet assets pledged or otherwise assigned to it as security unless such assets are in the form of cash in the hands of the company.

9(3)   Assets acquired in the name of and on behalf of third parties must not be shown in the balance sheet.

10   The company's directors must, in determining how amounts are presented within items in the profit and loss account and balance sheet, have regard to the substance of the reported transaction or arrangement, in accordance with generally accepted accounting principles or practice.

10A   Where an asset or liability relates to more than one item in the balance sheet, the relationship of such asset or liability to the relevant items must be disclosed either under those items or in the notes to the accounts.

History – Para. 10A inserted by SI 2015/980, reg. 31(2), with effect in relation to–
   (a)   financial years beginning on or after 1 January 2016, and
   (b)   a financial year of a company beginning on or after 1 January 2015, but before 1 January 2016, if the directors of the company so decide.

SECTION B – THE REQUIRED FORMATS

Balance sheet format
ASSETS

1.   Cash and balances at central [or post office] banks *(1)*
2.   Treasury bills and other eligible bills *(20)*

    (a) Treasury bills and similar securities *(2)*

    (b) Other eligible bills *(3)*

3. Loans and advances to banks *(4)*, *(20)*

    (a) Repayable on demand

    (b) Other loans and advances

4. Loans and advances to customers *(5)*, *(20)*

5. Debt securities [and other fixed-income securities] *(6)*, *(20)*

    (a) Issued by public bodies

    (b) Issued by other issuers

6. Equity shares [and other variable-yield securities]

7. Participating interests

8. Shares in group undertakings

9. Intangible fixed assets *(7)*

10. Tangible fixed assets *(8)*

11. Called up capital not paid *(9)*

12. Own shares *(10)*

13. Other assets

14. Called up capital not paid *(9)*

15. Prepayments and accrued income

Total assets

LIABILITIES

1. Deposits by banks *(11)*, *(20)*

    (a) Repayable on demand

    (b) With agreed maturity dates or periods of notice

2. Customer accounts *(12)*, *(20)*

    (a) Repayable on demand

    (b) With agreed maturity dates or periods of notice

3. Debt securities in issue *(13)*, *(20)*

    (a) Bonds and medium term notes

    (b) Others

4. Other liabilities

5. Accruals and deferred income

6. Provisions for liabilities

    (a)   Provisions for pensions and similar obligations

    (b)   Provisions for tax

    (c)   Other provisions

7.   Subordinated liabilities *(14), (20)*

8.   Called up share capital *(15)*

9.   Share premium account

10. Reserves

    (a)   Capital redemption reserve

    (b)   Reserve for own shares

    (c)   Reserves provided for by the articles of association

    (d)   Other reserves

11. Revaluation reserve

12. Profit and loss account

Total liabilities

MEMORANDUM ITEMS

1.   Contingent liabilities *(16)*

    (1)   Acceptances and endorsements

    (2)   Guarantees and assets pledged as collateral security *(17)*

    (3)   Other contingent liabilities

2.   Commitments *(18)*

    (1)   Commitments arising out of sale and option to resell transactions *(19)*

    (2)   Other commitments

Notes on the balance sheet format and memorandum items

(1)   Cash and balances at central [or post office] banks

(Assets item 1.)

Cash is to comprise all currency including foreign notes and coins.

Only those balances which may be withdrawn without notice and which are deposited with central or post office banks of the country or countries in which the company is established may be included in this item. All other claims on central or post office banks must be shown under assets items 3 or 4.

(2)   Treasury bills and other eligible bills: Treasury bills and similar securities

(Assets item 2.(a).)

Treasury bills and similar securities are to comprise treasury bills and similar debt instruments issued by public bodies which are eligible for refinancing with central banks of the country or countries in which the company is established. Any treasury bills or similar debt instruments not so eligible must be included under assets item 5(a).

(3)   Treasury bills and other eligible bills: Other eligible bills

(Assets item 2.(b).)

Other eligible bills are to comprise all bills purchased to the extent that they are eligible, under national law, for refinancing with the central banks of the country or countries in which the company is established.

(4)   Loans and advances to banks

(Assets item 3.)

Loans and advances to banks are to comprise all loans and advances to domestic or foreign credit institutions made by the company arising out of banking transactions. However loans and advances to credit institutions represented by debt securities or other fixed-income securities must be included under assets item 5 and not this item.

(5)   Loans and advances to customers

(Assets item 4.)

Loans and advances to customers are to comprise all types of assets in the form of claims on domestic and foreign customers other than credit institutions. However loans and advances represented by debt securities or other fixed-income securities must be included under assets item 5 and not this item.

(6)   Debt securities [and other fixed-income securities]

(Assets item 5.)

This item is to comprise transferable debt securities and any other transferable fixed-income securities issued by credit institutions, other undertakings or public bodies. Debt securities and other fixed-income securities issued by public bodies are, however, only to be included in this item if they may not be shown under assets item 2.

Where a company holds its own debt securities these must not be included under this item but must be deducted from liabilities item 3.(a) or (b), as appropriate.

Securities bearing interest rates that vary in accordance with specific factors, for example the interest rate on the inter-bank market or on the Euromarket, are also to be regarded as fixed-income securities to be included under this item.

(7)   Intangible fixed assets

(Assets item 9.)

This item is to comprise–

(a)   development costs,
(b)   concessions, patents, licences, trade marks and similar rights and assets,

    (c)   goodwill, and

    (d)   payments on account.

Amounts are, however, to be included in respect of (b) only if the assets were acquired for valuable consideration or the assets in question were created by the company itself.

Amounts representing goodwill are only to be included to the extent that the goodwill was acquired for valuable consideration.

The amount of any goodwill included in this item must be disclosed in a note to the accounts.

(8)   Tangible fixed assets

(Assets item 10.)

This item is to comprise–

    (a)   land and buildings,

    (b)   plant and machinery,

    (c)   fixtures and fittings, tools and equipment, and

    (d)   payments on account and assets in the course of construction.

The amount included in this item with respect to land and buildings occupied by the company for its own activities must be disclosed in a note to the accounts.

(9)   Called up capital not paid

(Assets items 11 and 14.)

The two positions shown for this item are alternatives.

(10) Own shares

(Assets item 12.)

The nominal value of the shares held must be shown separately under this item.

(11) Deposits by banks

(Liabilities item 1.)

Deposits by banks are to comprise all amounts arising out of banking transactions owed to other domestic or foreign credit institutions by the company. However liabilities in the form of debt securities and any liabilities for which transferable certificates have been issued must be included under liabilities item 3 and not this item.

(12) Customer accounts

(Liabilities item 2.)

This item is to comprise all amounts owed to creditors that are not credit institutions. However liabilities in the form of debt securities and any liabilities for which transferable certificates have been issued must be shown under liabilities item 3 and not this item.

(13) Debt securities in issue

(Liabilities item 3.)

This item is to include both debt securities and debts for which transferable certificates have been issued, including liabilities arising out of own acceptances and promissory notes. (Only acceptances which a company has issued for its own refinancing and in respect of which it is the first party liable are to be treated as own acceptances.)

(14) Subordinated liabilities

(Liabilities item 7.)

This item is to comprise all liabilities in respect of which there is a contractual obligation that, in the event of winding up or bankruptcy, they are to be repaid only after the claims of other creditors have been met.

This item must include all subordinated liabilities, whether or not a ranking has been agreed between the subordinated creditors concerned.

(15) Called up share capital

(Liabilities item 8.)

The amount of allotted share capital and the amount of called up share capital which has been paid up must be shown separately.

(16) Contingent liabilities

(Memorandum item 1.)

This item is to include all transactions whereby the company has underwritten the obligations of a third party.

Liabilities arising out of the endorsement of rediscounted bills must be included in this item. Acceptances other than own acceptances must also be included.

(17) Contingent liabilities: Guarantees and assets pledged as collateral security

(Memorandum item 1(2).)

This item is to include all guarantee obligations incurred and assets pledged as collateral security on behalf of third parties, particularly in respect of sureties and irrevocable letters of credit.

(18) Commitments

(Memorandum item 2.)

This item is to include every irrevocable commitment which could give rise to a credit risk.

(19) Commitments: Commitments arising out of sale and option to resell transactions

(Memorandum item 2(1).)

This item is to comprise commitments entered into by the company in the context of sale and option to resell transactions.

(20) Claims on, and liabilities to, undertakings in which a participating interest is held or group undertakings

(Assets items 2 to 5, liabilities items 1 to 3 and 7.)

The following information must be given either by way of subdivision of the relevant items or by way of notes to the accounts.

The amount of the following must be shown for each of assets items 2 to 5–

(a)   claims on group undertakings included therein, and

(b)   claims on undertakings in which the company has a participating interest included therein.

The amount of the following must be shown for each of liabilities items 1, 2, 3 and 7–

(i)   liabilities to group undertakings included therein, and

(ii)   liabilities to undertakings in which the company has a participating interest included therein.

Special rules

Subordinated assets

11(1) The amount of any assets that are subordinated must be shown either as a subdivision of any relevant asset item or in the notes to the accounts; in the latter case disclosure must be by reference to the relevant asset item or items in which the assets are included.

11(2) In the case of assets items 2 to 5 in the balance sheet format, the amounts required to be shown by note (20) to the format as sub-items of those items must be further subdivided so as to show the amount of any claims included therein that are subordinated.

11(3) For this purpose, assets are subordinated if there is a contractual obligation to the effect that, in the event of winding up or bankruptcy, they are to be repaid only after the claims of other creditors have been met, whether or not a ranking has been agreed between the subordinated creditors concerned.

Syndicated loans

12(1) Where a company is a party to a syndicated loan transaction the company must include only that part of the total loan which it itself has funded.

12(2) Where a company is a party to a syndicated loan transaction and has agreed to reimburse (in whole or in part) any other party to the syndicate any funds advanced by that party or any interest thereon upon the occurrence of any event, including the default of the borrower, any additional liability by reason of such a guarantee must be included as a contingent liability in Memorandum item 1(2).

Sale and repurchase transactions

13(1) The following rules apply where a company is a party to a sale and repurchase transaction.

13(2) Where the company is the transferor of the assets under the transaction–

    (a)   the assets transferred must, notwithstanding the transfer, be included in its balance sheet,

    (b)   the purchase price received by it must be included in its balance sheet as an amount owed to the transferee, and

    (c)   the value of the assets transferred must be disclosed in a note to its accounts.

13(3) Where the company is the transferee of the assets under the transaction, it must not include the assets transferred in its balance sheet but the purchase price paid by it to the transferor must be so included as an amount owed by the transferor.

Sale and option to resell transactions

14(1) The following rules apply where a company is a party to a sale and option to resell transaction.

14(2) Where the company is the transferor of the assets under the transaction, it must not include in its balance sheet the assets transferred but it must enter under Memorandum item 2 an amount equal to the price agreed in the event of repurchase.

14(3) Where the company is the transferee of the assets under the transaction it must include those assets in its balance sheet.

Managed funds

15(1) For the purposes of this paragraph, "managed funds" are funds which the company administers in its own name but on behalf of others and to which it has legal title.

15(2) The company must, in any case where claims and obligations arising in respect of managed funds fall to be treated as claims and obligations of the company, adopt the following accounting treatment.

15(3) Claims and obligations representing managed funds are to be included in the company's balance sheet, with the notes to the accounts disclosing the total amount included with respect to such assets and liabilities in the balance sheet and showing the amount included under each relevant balance sheet item in respect of such assets or (as the case may be) liabilities.

Profit and loss account formats – Format 1: Vertical layout

1. Interest receivable *(1)*

    (1)   Interest receivable and similar income arising from debt securities [and other fixed-income securities]
    (2)   Other interest receivable and similar income

2. Interest payable *(2)*

3. Dividend income

    (a)   Income from equity shares [and other variable-yield securities]
    (b)   Income from participating interests
    (c)   Income from shares in group undertakings

4. Fees and commissions receivable *(3)*

5. Fees and commissions payable *(4)*

6. Dealing [profits] [losses] *(5)*

7. Other operating income

8. Administrative expenses

    (a)   Staff costs

        (i)   Wages and salaries
        (ii)   Social security costs
        (iii) Other pension costs

    (b)   Other administrative expenses

9. Depreciation and amortisation *(6)*

10. Other operating charges

11. Provisions

    (a)   Provisions for bad and doubtful debts *(7)*
    (b)   Provisions for contingent liabilities and commitments *(8)*

12. Adjustments to provisions

    (a)   Adjustments to provisions for bad and doubtful debts *(9)*
    (b)   Adjustments to provisions for contingent liabilities and commitments *(10)*

13. Amounts written off fixed asset investments *(11)*

14. Adjustments to amounts written off fixed asset investments *(12)*

15. [Profit] [loss] on ordinary activities before tax

16. Tax on [profit] [loss] on ordinary activities

17. [Profit] [loss] on ordinary activities after tax

18. Extraordinary income

19. Extraordinary charges

20. Extraordinary [profit] [loss]

21. Tax on extraordinary [profit] [loss]

22. Extraordinary [profit] [loss] after tax

23. Other taxes not shown under the preceding items

24. [Profit] [loss] for the financial year

Profit and loss account formats – Format 2: Horizontal layout

A. Charges

1.   Interest payable *(2)*

2.   Fees and commissions payable *(4)*

3.   Dealing losses *(5)*

4.   Administrative expenses

    (a) Staff costs

       (i)   Wages and salaries

       (ii) Social security costs

       (iii) Other pension costs

    (b) Other administrative expenses

5.   Depreciation and amortisation *(6)*

6.   Other operating charges

7.   Provisions

    (a) Provisions for bad and doubtful debts *(7)*

    (b) Provisions for contingent liabilities and commitments *(8)*

8.   Amounts written off fixed asset investments *(11)*

9.   Profit on ordinary activities before tax

10. Tax on [profit] [loss] on ordinary activities

11. Profit on ordinary activities after tax

12. Extraordinary charges

13. Tax on extraordinary [profit] [loss]

14. Extraordinary loss after tax

15. Other taxes not shown under the preceding items

16. Profit for the financial year

B.   Income

1.   Interest receivable *(1)*

    (1) Interest receivable and similar income arising from debt securities [and other fixed-income securities]

    (2) Other interest receivable and similar income

2.   Dividend income

    (a) Income from equity shares [and other variable-yield securities]
    (b) Income from participating interests
    (c) Income from shares in group undertakings

3.   Fees and commissions receivable *(3)*

4.   Dealing profits *(5)*

5.   Adjustments to provisions

    (a) Adjustments to provisions for bad and doubtful debts *(9)*
    (b) Adjustments to provisions for contingent liabilities and commitments *(10)*

6.   Adjustments to amounts written off fixed asset investments *(12)*

7.   Other operating income

8.   Loss on ordinary activities before tax

9.   Loss on ordinary activities after tax

10. Extraordinary income

11. Extraordinary profit after tax

12. Loss for the financial year

Notes on the profit and loss account formats

(1)   Interest receivable

(Format 1, item 1; format 2, item B1.)

This item is to include all income arising out of banking activities, including–

    (a) income from assets included in assets items 1 to 5 in the balance sheet format, however calculated,

    (b) income resulting from covered forward contracts spread over the actual duration of the contract and similar in nature to interest, and

    (c) fees and commissions receivable similar in nature to interest and calculated on a time basis or by reference to the amount of the claim (but not other fees and commissions receivable).

(2)   Interest payable

(Format 1, item 2; format 2, item A1.)

This item is to include all expenditure arising out of banking activities, including–

(a)   charges arising out of liabilities included in liabilities items 1, 2, 3 and 7 in the balance sheet format, however calculated,

(b)   charges resulting from covered forward contracts, spread over the actual duration of the contract and similar in nature to interest, and

(c)   fees and commissions payable similar in nature to interest and calculated on a time basis or by reference to the amount of the liability (but not other fees and commissions payable).

(3)   Fees and commissions receivable

(Format 1, item 4; format 2, item B3.)

Fees and commissions receivable are to comprise income in respect of all services supplied by the company to third parties, but not fees or commissions required to be included under interest receivable (format 1, item 1; format 2, item B1).

In particular the following fees and commissions receivable must be included (unless required to be included under interest receivable)–

(a)   fees and commissions for guarantees, loan administration on behalf of other lenders and securities transactions,

(b)   fees, commissions and other income in respect of payment transactions, account administration charges and commissions for the safe custody and administration of securities,

(c)   fees and commissions for foreign currency transactions and for the sale and purchase of coin and precious metals, and

(d)   fees and commissions charged for brokerage services in connection with savings and insurance contracts and loans.

(4)   Fees and commissions payable

(Format 1, item 5; format 2, item A2.)

Fees and commissions payable are to comprise charges for all services rendered to the company by third parties but not fees or commissions required to be included under interest payable (format 1, item 2; format 2, item A1).

In particular the following fees and commissions payable must be included (unless required to be included under interest payable)–

(a)   fees and commissions for guarantees, loan administration and securities transactions;

(b)   fees, commissions and other charges in respect of payment transactions, account administration charges and commissions for the safe custody and administration of securities;

(c)   fees and commissions for foreign currency transactions and for the sale and purchase of coin and precious metals; and

(d)   fees and commissions for brokerage services in connection with savings and insurance contracts and loans.

(5)   Dealing [profits] [losses]

(Format 1, item 6; format 2, items B4 and A3.)

This item is to comprise–

(a)   the net profit or net loss on transactions in securities which are not held as financial fixed assets together with amounts written off or written back with respect to such securities, including amounts written off or written back as a result of the application of paragraph 33(1),

(b)   the net profit or loss on exchange activities, save in so far as the profit or loss is included in interest receivable or interest payable (format 1, items 1 or 2; format 2, items B1 or A1), and

(c)   the net profits and losses on other dealing operations involving financial instruments, including precious metals.

(6)   Depreciation and amortisation

(Format 1, item 9; format 2, item A5.)

This item is to comprise depreciation and other amounts written off in respect of balance sheet assets items 9 and 10.

(7)   Provisions: Provisions for bad and doubtful debts

(Format 1, item 11(a); format 2, item A7(a).)

Provisions for bad and doubtful debts are to comprise charges for amounts written off and for provisions made in respect of loans and advances shown under balance sheet assets items 3 and 4.

(8)   Provisions: Provisions for contingent liabilities and commitments

(Format 1, item 11(b); format 2, item A7(b).)

This item is to comprise charges for provisions for contingent liabilities and commitments of a type which would, if not provided for, be shown under Memorandum items 1 and 2.

(9)   Adjustments to provisions: Adjustments to provisions for bad and doubtful debts

(Format 1, item 12(a); format 2, item B5(a).)

This item is to include credits from the recovery of loans that have been written off, from other advances written back following earlier write offs and from the reduction of provisions previously made with respect to loans and advances.

(10) Adjustments to provisions: Adjustments to provisions for contingent liabilities and commitments

(Format 1, item 12(b); format 2, item B5(b).)

This item comprises credits from the reduction of provisions previously made with respect to contingent liabilities and commitments.

(11) Amounts written off fixed asset investments

(Format 1, item 13; format 2, item A8.)

Amounts written off fixed asset investments are to comprise amounts written off in respect of assets which are transferable securities held as financial fixed assets, participating interests and shares in group undertakings and which are included in assets items 5 to 8 in the balance sheet format.

(12) Adjustments to amounts written off fixed asset investments

(Format 1, item 14; format 2, item B6.)

Adjustments to amounts written off fixed asset investments are to include amounts written back following earlier write offs and provisions in respect of assets which are transferable securities held as financial fixed assets, participating interests and group undertakings and which are included in assets items 5 to 8 in the balance sheet format.

PART 2 – ACCOUNTING PRINCIPLES AND RULES
SECTION A – ACCOUNTING PRINCIPLES

Preliminary

16(1) The amounts to be included in respect of all items shown in a company's accounts must be determined in accordance with the principles set out in this Section.

16(2) But if it appears to the company's directors that there are special reasons for departing from any of those principles in preparing the company's accounts in respect of any financial year they may do so, in which case particulars of the departure, the reasons for it and its effect must be given in a note to the accounts.

Accounting principles

17 The company is presumed to be carrying on business as a going concern.

18 Accounting policies and measurement bases must be applied consistently within the same accounts and from one financial year to the next.

History – In para. 18, the words "and measurement bases" inserted by SI 2015/980, reg. 32(2)(a), with effect in relation to–
   (a) financial years beginning on or after 1 January 2016, and
   (b) a financial year of a company beginning on or after 1 January 2015, but before 1 January 2016, if the directors of the company so decide.

19 The amount of any item must be determined on a prudent basis, and in particular–

    (a)   only profits realised at the balance sheet date are to be included in the profit and loss account,

    (b)   all liabilities which have arisen in respect of the financial year to which the accounts relate or a previous financial year must be taken into account, including those which only become apparent between the balance sheet date and the date on which it is signed on behalf of the board of directors in accordance with section 414 of the 2006 Act (approval and signing of accounts) and

    (c)   all provisions for diminution of value must be recognised, whether the result of the financial year is a profit or a loss.

History – Para. 19(c), (and the word "and" preceding it) inserted; the word "and" in para. (a) omitted by SI 2015/980, reg. 32(2)(b), with effect in relation to–

    (a)   financial years beginning on or after 1 January 2016, and

    (b)   a financial year of a company beginning on or after 1 January 2015, but before 1 January 2016, if the directors of the company so decide.

20 All income and charges relating to the financial year to which the accounts relate must be taken into account, without regard to the date of receipt or payment.

21 In determining the aggregate amount of any item, the amount of each individual asset or liability that falls to be taken into account must be determined separately.

21A The opening balance sheet for each financial year shall correspond to the closing balance sheet for the preceding financial year.

History – Para. 21A inserted by SI 2015/980, reg. 32(2)(c), with effect in relation to–

    (a)   financial years beginning on or after 1 January 2016, and

    (b)   a financial year of a company beginning on or after 1 January 2015, but before 1 January 2016, if the directors of the company so decide.

SECTION B – HISTORICAL COST ACCOUNTING RULES

Preliminary

22 Subject to Sections C and D of this Part of this Schedule, the amounts to be included in respect of all items shown in a company's accounts must be determined in accordance with the rules set out in this Section.

Fixed assets

General rules

23(1) The amount to be included in respect of any fixed asset is its cost.

23(2) This is subject to any provision for depreciation or diminution in value made in accordance with paragraphs 24 to 26.

Rules for depreciation and diminution in value

24   In the case of any fixed asset which has a limited useful economic life, the amount of–

    (a) its cost, or

    (b) where it is estimated that any such asset will have a residual value at the end of the period of its useful economic life, its cost less that estimated residual value, must be reduced by provisions for depreciation calculated to write off that amount systematically over the period of the asset's useful economic life.

25(1)   Where a fixed asset investment to which sub-paragraph (2) applies has diminished in value, provisions for diminution in value may be made in respect of it and the amount to be included in respect of it may be reduced accordingly.

25(2)   This sub-paragraph applies to fixed asset investments of a description falling to be included under assets item 7 (participating interests) or 8 (shares in group undertakings) in the balance sheet format, or any other holding of securities held as a financial fixed asset.

25(3)   Provisions for diminution in value must be made in respect of any fixed asset which has diminished in value if the reduction in its value is expected to be permanent (whether its useful economic life is limited or not), and the amount to be included in respect of it must be reduced accordingly.

25(4)   Provisions made under this paragraph must be charged to the profit and loss account and disclosed separately in a note to the accounts if they have not been shown separately in the profit and loss account.

History – Para. 25(4) substituted by SI 2015/980, reg. 32(3)(a), with effect in relation to–

    (a)   financial years beginning on or after 1 January 2016, and

    (b)   a financial year of a company beginning on or after 1 January 2015, but before 1 January 2016, if the directors of the company so decide.

Former para. 25(4) read as follows:

"**25(4)**   Any provisions made under this paragraph which are not shown in the profit and loss account must be disclosed (either separately or in aggregate) in a note to the accounts."

26(1)   Where the reasons for which any provision was made in accordance with paragraph 25 have ceased to apply to any extent, that provision must be written back to the extent that it is no longer necessary.

26(1A)   But provision made in accordance with paragraph 25(3) in respect of goodwill must not be written back to any extent.

26(2)   Any amounts written back under sub-paragraph (1) must be recognised in the profit and loss account and disclosed separately in a note to the accounts if not shown separately in the profit and loss account.

History – Para. 26(1A) inserted by SI 2015/1672, reg. 4(4), with effect in relation to–

    (a)   financial years beginning on or after 1 January 2016, and

    (b)   a financial year of a company beginning on or after 1 January 2015 but before 1 January 2016, if the directors of the company have decided.

Para. 26(2) substituted by SI 2015/980, reg. 32(3)(b), with effect in relation to–
  (a)   financial years beginning on or after 1 January 2016, and
  (b)   a financial year of a company beginning on or after 1 January 2015, but before
        1 January 2016, if the directors of the company so decide.
Former para. 26(2) read as follows:

  "**26(2)**   Any amounts written back in accordance with sub-paragraph (1) which are not shown
in the profit and loss account must be disclosed (either separately or in aggregate) in a note to
the accounts."

Intangible assets

  27(1)   Where this is in accordance with generally accepted accounting principles or
practice, development costs may be included under assets item 9 in the balance sheet
format.

  27(2)   If any amount is included in a company's balance sheet in respect of development
costs, the note on accounting policies (see paragraph 53 of this Schedule) must include
the following information–

  (a)   the period over which the amount of those costs originally capitalised is being
        or is to be written off, and
  (b)   the reasons for capitalising the development costs in question.

History – Para. 27 and the heading preceding it substituted by SI 2015/980, reg. 32(3)(c), with
effect in relation to–
  (a)   financial years beginning on or after 1 January 2016, and
  (b)   a financial year of a company beginning on or after 1 January 2015, but before
        1 January 2016, if the directors of the company so decide.
Former para. 27 read as follows:

"Development costs

  27(1)   Notwithstanding that amounts representing "development costs" may be included under
assets item 9 in the balance sheet format, an amount may only be included in a company's balance
sheet in respect of development costs in special circumstances.

  27(2)   If any amount is included in a company's balance sheet in respect of development costs
the following information must be given in a note to the accounts–
  (a)   the period over which the amount of those costs originally capitalised is being or is
          to be written off, and
  (b)   the reasons for capitalising the development costs in question."

Goodwill

  28(1)   Intangible assets must be written off over the useful economic life of the
intangible asset.

  28(2)   Where in exceptional cases the useful life of intangible assets cannot be reliably
estimated, such assets must be written off over a period chosen by the directors of the
company.

  28(3)   The period referred to in sub-paragraph (2) must not exceed ten years.

  28(4)   There must be disclosed in a note to the accounts the period referred to in sub-
paragraph (2) and the reasons for choosing that period.

History – Para. 28 substituted by SI 2015/980, reg. 32(3)(c), with effect in relation to–
    (a)   financial years beginning on or after 1 January 2016, and
    (b)   a financial year of a company beginning on or after 1 January 2015, but before
        1 January 2016, if the directors of the company so decide.

Former para. 28 read as follows:

"**28(1)** The application of paragraphs 23 to 26 in relation to goodwill (in any case where goodwill is treated as an asset) is subject to the following.

28(2) Subject to sub-paragraph (3), the amount of the consideration for any goodwill acquired by a company must be reduced by provisions for depreciation calculated to write off that amount systematically over a period chosen by the directors of the company.

28(3) The period chosen must not exceed the useful economic life of the goodwill in question.

28(4) In any case where any goodwill acquired by a company is included as an asset in the company's balance sheet there must be disclosed in a note to the accounts–
    (a)   the period chosen for writing off the consideration for that goodwill, and
    (b)   the reasons for choosing that period."

Treatment of fixed assets

29(1) Assets included in assets items 9 (intangible fixed assets) and 10 (tangible fixed assets) in the balance sheet format must be valued as fixed assets.

29(2) Other assets falling to be included in the balance sheet must be valued as fixed assets where they are intended for use on a continuing basis in the company's activities.

Financial fixed assets

30(1) Debt securities, including fixed-income securities, held as financial fixed assets must be included in the balance sheet at an amount equal to their maturity value plus any premium, or less any discount, on their purchase, subject to the following provisions of this paragraph.

30(2) The amount included in the balance sheet with respect to such securities purchased at a premium must be reduced each financial year on a systematic basis so as to write the premium off over the period to the maturity date of the security and the amounts so written off must be charged to the profit and loss account for the relevant financial years.

30(3) The amount included in the balance sheet with respect to such securities purchased at a discount must be increased each financial year on a systematic basis so as to extinguish the discount over the period to the maturity date of the security and the amounts by which the amount is increased must be credited to the profit and loss account for the relevant years.

30(4) The notes to the accounts must disclose the amount of any unamortized premium or discount not extinguished which is included in the balance sheet by virtue of sub-paragraph (1).

30(5) For the purposes of this paragraph **"premium"** means any excess of the amount paid for a security over its maturity value and **"discount"** means any deficit of the amount paid for a security over its maturity value.

Current assets

31   The amount to be included in respect of loans and advances, debt or other fixed-income securities and equity shares or other variable yield securities not held as financial fixed assets must be their cost, subject to paragraphs 32 and 33.

32(1)   If the net realisable value of any asset referred to in paragraph 31 is lower than its cost, the amount to be included in respect of that asset is the net realisable value.

32(2)   Where the reasons for which any provision for diminution in value was made in accordance with sub-paragraph (1) have ceased to apply to any extent, that provision must be written back to the extent that it is no longer necessary.

33(1)   Subject to paragraph 32, the amount to be included in the balance sheet in respect of transferable securities not held as financial fixed assets may be the higher of their cost or their market value at the balance sheet date.

33(2)   The difference between the cost of any securities included in the balance sheet at a valuation under sub-paragraph (1) and their market value must be shown (in aggregate) in the notes to the accounts.

Miscellaneous and supplementary provisions

Excess of money owed over value received as an asset item

34(1)   Where the amount repayable on any debt owed by a company is greater than the value of the consideration received in the transaction giving rise to the debt, the amount of the difference may be treated as an asset.

34(2)   Where any such amount is so treated–

   (a)   it must be written off by reasonable amounts each year and must be completely written off before repayment of the debt, and

   (b)   if the current amount is not shown as a separate item in the company's balance sheet, it must be disclosed in a note to the accounts.

Determination of cost

35(1)   The cost of an asset that has been acquired by the company is to be determined by adding to the actual price paid any expenses incidental to its acquisition and then subtracting any incidental reductions in the cost of acquisition.

35(2)   The cost of an asset constructed by the company is to be determined by adding to the purchase price of the raw materials and consumables used the amount of the costs incurred by the company which are directly attributable to the construction of that asset.

35(3)   In addition, there may be included in the cost of an asset constructed by the company–

   (a)   a reasonable proportion of the costs incurred by the company which are only indirectly attributable to the construction of that asset, but only to the extent that they relate to the period of construction, and

(b)   interest on capital borrowed to finance the construction of that asset, to the extent that it accrues in respect of the period of construction, provided, however, in a case within paragraph (b), that the inclusion of the interest in determining the cost of that asset and the amount of the interest so included is disclosed in a note to the accounts.

History – In para. 35(1), the words "and then subtracting any incidental reductions in the cost of acquisition" inserted by SI 2015/980, reg. 32(3)(d), with effect in relation to–
(a)   financial years beginning on or after 1 January 2016, and
(b)   a financial year of a company beginning on or after 1 January 2015, but before 1 January 2016, if the directors of the company so decide.

36(1)   The cost of any assets which are fungible assets (including investments), may be determined by the application of any of the methods mentioned in sub-paragraph (2) in relation to any such assets of the same class, provided that the method chosen is one which appears to the directors to be appropriate in the circumstances of the company.

36(2)   Those methods are–

(a)   the method known as "first in, first out" (FIFO),
(b)   the method known as "last in, first out" (LIFO),
(c)   a weighted average price, and
(d)   any other method reflecting generally accepted best practice.

36(3)   Where in the case of any company–

(a)   the cost of assets falling to be included under any item shown in the company's balance sheet has been determined by the application of any method permitted by this paragraph, and
(b)   the amount shown in respect of that item differs materially from the relevant alternative amount given below in this paragraph, the amount of that difference must be disclosed in a note to the accounts.

36(4)   Subject to sub-paragraph (5), for the purposes of sub-paragraph (3)(b), the relevant alternative amount, in relation to any item shown in a company's balance sheet, is the amount which would have been shown in respect of that item if assets of any class included under that item at an amount determined by any method permitted by this paragraph had instead been included at their replacement cost as at the balance sheet date.

36(5)   The relevant alternative amount may be determined by reference to the most recent actual purchase price before the balance sheet date of assets of any class included under the item in question instead of by reference to their replacement cost as at that date, but only if the former appears to the directors of the company to constitute the more appropriate standard of comparison in the case of assets of that class.

History – In para. 36(2)(d), the words "reflecting generally accepted best practice" substituted for the words "similar to any of the methods mentioned above" by SI 2015/980, reg. 32(3)(e), with effect in relation to–
(a)   financial years beginning on or after 1 January 2016, and
(b)   a financial year of a company beginning on or after 1 January 2015, but before 1 January 2016, if the directors of the company so decide.

Substitution of original stated amount where price or cost unknown

37(1) This paragraph applies where–

(a) there is no record of the purchase price of any asset acquired by a company or of any price, expenses or costs relevant for determining its cost in accordance with paragraph 35, or

(b) any such record cannot be obtained without unreasonable expense or delay.

37(2) In such a case, its cost is to be taken, for the purposes of paragraphs 23 to 33, to be the value ascribed to it in the earliest available record of its value made on or after its acquisition by the company.

SECTION C – ALTERNATIVE ACCOUNTING RULES

Preliminary

38(1) The rules set out in Section B are referred to below in this Schedule as the historical cost accounting rules.

38(2) Paragraphs 23 to 26 and 30 to 34 are referred to below in this Section as the depreciation rules; and references below in this Schedule to the historical cost accounting rules do not include the depreciation rules as they apply by virtue of paragraph 41.

39 Subject to paragraphs 41 to 43, the amounts to be included in respect of assets of any description mentioned in paragraph 40 may be determined on any basis so mentioned.

Alternative accounting rules

40(1) Intangible fixed assets, other than goodwill, may be included at their current cost.

40(2) Tangible fixed assets may be included at a market value determined as at the date of their last valuation or at their current cost.

40(3) Investments of any description falling to be included under assets items 7 (participating interests) or 8 (shares in group undertakings) of the balance sheet format and any other securities held as financial fixed assets may be included either–

(a) at a market value determined as at the date of their last valuation, or

(b) at a value determined on any basis which appears to the directors to be appropriate in the circumstances of the company.

But in the latter case particulars of the method of valuation adopted and of the reasons for adopting it must be disclosed in a note to the accounts.

40(4) [Omitted by SI 2015/980, reg. 32(4)]

History – Para. 40(4) omitted by SI 2015/980, reg. 32(4)(a), with effect in relation to–

(a) financial years beginning on or after 1 January 2016, and

(b) a financial year of a company beginning on or after 1 January 2015, but before 1 January 2016, if the directors of the company so decide.

Former para. 40(4) read as follows:

"**40(4)**   Securities of any description not held as financial fixed assets (if not valued in accordance with paragraph 33) may be included at their current cost."

Application of the depreciation rules

41(1)   Where the value of any asset of a company is determined in accordance with paragraph 40, that value must be, or (as the case may require) be the starting point for determining, the amount to be included in respect of that asset in the company's accounts, instead of its cost or any value previously so determined for that asset.

The depreciation rules apply accordingly in relation to any such asset with the substitution for any reference to its cost of a reference to the value most recently determined for that asset in accordance with paragraph 40.

41(2)   The amount of any provision for depreciation required in the case of any fixed asset by paragraphs 24 to 26 as they apply by virtue of sub-paragraph (1) is referred to below in this paragraph as the adjusted amount, and the amount of any provision which would be required by any of those paragraphs in the case of that asset according to the historical cost accounting rules is referred to as the historical cost amount.

41(3)   Where sub-paragraph (1) applies in the case of any fixed asset the amount of any provision for depreciation in respect of that asset included in any item shown in the profit and loss account in respect of amounts written off assets of the description in question may be the historical cost amount instead of the adjusted amount, provided that the amount of any difference between the two is shown separately in the profit and loss account or in a note to the accounts.

Additional information to be provided in case of departure from historical cost accounting rules

42(1)   This paragraph applies where the amounts to be included in respect of assets covered by any items shown in a company's accounts have been determined in accordance with paragraph 40.

42(2)   The items affected and the basis of valuation adopted in determining the amounts of the assets in question in the case of each such item must be disclosed in the note on accounting policies (see paragraph 53 of this Schedule).

42(3)   In the case of each balance sheet item affected, the comparable amounts determined according to the historical cost accounting rules must be shown in a note to the accounts.

42(4)   In sub-paragraph (3), references in relation to any item to the comparable amounts determined as there mentioned are references to—

    (a)   the aggregate amount which would be required to be shown in respect of that item if the amounts to be included in respect of all the assets covered by that item were determined according to the historical cost accounting rules, and

    (b)   the aggregate amount of the cumulative provisions for depreciation or diminution in value which would be permitted or required in determining those amounts according to those rules.

History – In para. 42(2), the words "the note on accounting policies (see paragraph 53 of this Schedule)" substituted for the words "a note to the accounts" by SI 2015/980, reg. 32(4)(b), with effect in relation to–

(a)   financial years beginning on or after 1 January 2016, and

(b)   a financial year of a company beginning on or after 1 January 2015, but before 1 January 2016, if the directors of the company so decide.

Para. 42(3) substituted by SI 2015/980, reg. 32(4)(c), with effect in relation to–

(a)   financial years beginning on or after 1 January 2016, and

(b)   a financial year of a company beginning on or after 1 January 2015, but before 1 January 2016, if the directors of the company so decide.

Former para. 42(3) read as follows:

"**42(3)**   In the case of each balance sheet item affected either–

(a)   the comparable amounts determined according to the historical cost accounting rules, or

(b)   the differences between those amounts and the corresponding amounts actually shown in the balance sheet in respect of that item, must be shown separately in the balance sheet or in a note to the accounts."

Revaluation reserve

43(1)   With respect to any determination of the value of an asset of a company in accordance with paragraph 40, the amount of any profit or loss arising from that determination (after allowing, where appropriate, for any provisions for depreciation or diminution in value made otherwise than by reference to the value so determined and any adjustments of any such provisions made in the light of that determination) must be credited or (as the case may be) debited to a separate reserve ("the revaluation reserve").

43(2)   The amount of the revaluation reserve must be shown in the company's balance sheet under liabilities item 11 in the balance sheet format.

43(3)   An amount may be transferred–

(a)   from the revaluation reserve–

(i)   to the profit and loss account, if the amount was previously charged to that account or represents realised profit, or

(ii)   on capitalisation,

(b)   to or from the revaluation reserve in respect of the taxation relating to any profit or loss credited or debited to the reserve.

The revaluation reserve must be reduced to the extent that the amounts transferred to it are no longer necessary for the purposes of the valuation method used.

43(4)   In sub-paragraph (3)(a)(ii) **"capitalisation"**, in relation to an amount standing to the credit of the revaluation reserve, means applying it in wholly or partly paying up unissued shares in the company to be allotted to members of the company as fully or partly paid shares.

43(5)   The revaluation reserve must not be reduced except as mentioned in this paragraph.

43(6)   The treatment for taxation purposes of amounts credited or debited to the revaluation reserve must be disclosed in a note to the accounts.

History – In para. 43(2), the words "but need not be shown under that name" omitted by SI 2015/980, reg. 32(4)(d), with effect in relation to–
  (a)   financial years beginning on or after 1 January 2016, and
  (b)   a financial year of a company beginning on or after 1 January 2015, but before 1 January 2016, if the directors of the company so decide.

SECTION D – FAIR VALUE ACCOUNTING

Inclusion of financial instruments at fair value

44(1) Subject to sub-paragraphs (2) to (5), financial instruments (including derivatives) may be included at fair value.

44(2) Sub-paragraph (1) does not apply to financial instruments that constitute liabilities unless–
  (a)   they are held as part of a trading portfolio,
  (b)   they are derivatives, or
  (c)   they are financial instruments falling within sub-paragraph (4).

44(3) Unless they are financial instruments falling within sub-paragraph (4), sub-paragraph (1) does not apply to–
  (a)   financial instruments (other than derivatives) held to maturity,
  (b)   loans and receivables originated by the company and not held for trading purposes,
  (c)   interests in subsidiary undertakings, associated undertakings and joint ventures,
  (d)   equity instruments issued by the company,
  (e)   contracts for contingent consideration in a business combination, or
  (f)   other financial instruments with such special characteristics that the instruments, according to generally accepted accounting principles or practice, should be accounted for differently from other financial instruments.

44(4) Financial instruments which under international accounting standards may be included in accounts at fair value, may be so included, provided that the disclosures required by such accounting standards are made.

44(5) If the fair value of a financial instrument cannot be determined reliably in accordance with paragraph 45, sub-paragraph (1) does not apply to that financial instrument.

44(6) In this paragraph–

"associated undertaking" has the meaning given by paragraph 19 of Schedule 6 to these Regulations;
"joint venture" has the meaning given by paragraph 18 of that Schedule.

History – Para. 44(4) substituted by SI 2015/980, reg. 32(5)(a), with effect in relation to–
  (a)   financial years beginning on or after 1 January 2016, and
  (b)   a financial year of a company beginning on or after 1 January 2015, but before 1 January 2016, if the directors of the company so decide.
Former para. 44(4) read as follows:
"**44(4)** Financial instruments that, under international accounting standards adopted by the European Commission on or before 5th September 2006 in accordance with the IAS Regulation,

may be included in accounts at fair value, may be so included, provided that the disclosures required by such accounting standards are made."

Determination of fair value

45(1) The fair value of a financial instrument is its value determined in accordance with this paragraph.

45(2) If a reliable market can readily be identified for the financial instrument, its fair value is determined by reference to its market value.

45(3) If a reliable market cannot readily be identified for the financial instrument but can be identified for its components or for a similar instrument, its fair value is determined by reference to the market value of its components or of the similar instrument.

45(4) If neither sub-paragraph (2) nor (3) applies, the fair value of the financial instrument is a value resulting from generally accepted valuation models and techniques.

45(5) Any valuation models and techniques used for the purposes of sub-paragraph (4) must ensure a reasonable approximation of the market value.

Hedged items

46 A company may include any assets and liabilities, or identified portions of such assets or liabilities, that qualify as hedged items under a fair value hedge accounting system at the amount required under that system.

Other assets that may be included at fair value

47(1) This paragraph applies to–

    (a)   investment property, and
    (b)   living animals and plants.

47(2) Such investment property and living animals and plants may be included at fair value, provided that, as the case may be, all such investment property or living animals and plants are so included where their fair value can be reliably determined.

47(3) In this paragraph, **"fair value"** means fair value determined in accordance with generally accepted accounting principles or practice.

History – Para. 47 substituted by SI 2015/980, reg. 32(5)(b), with effect in relation to–
    (a)   financial years beginning on or after 1 January 2016, and
    (b)   a financial year of a company beginning on or after 1 January 2015, but before 1 January 2016, if the directors of the company so decide.
Former para. 47 read as follows:
    "**47(1)** This paragraph applies to–
      (a)   investment property, and
      (b)   living animals and plants, that, under international accounting standards, may be included in accounts at fair value.

47(2) Such investment property and such living animals and plants may be included at fair value, provided that all such investment property or, as the case may be, all such living animals and plants are so included where their fair value can reliably be determined.

47(3) In this paragraph, **"fair value"** means fair value determined in accordance with relevant international accounting standards."

Accounting for changes in value

48(1) This paragraph applies where a financial instrument is valued in accordance with paragraph 44 or 46 or an asset is valued in accordance with paragraph 47.

48(2) Notwithstanding paragraph 19 in this Part of this Schedule, and subject to sub-paragraphs (3) and (4), a change in the value of the financial instrument or of the investment property or living animal or plant must be included in the profit and loss account.

48(3) Where—

    (a)   the financial instrument accounted for is a hedging instrument under a hedge accounting system that allows some or all of the change in value not to be shown in the profit and loss account, or

    (b)   the change in value relates to an exchange difference arising on a monetary item that forms part of a company's net investment in a foreign entity, the amount of the change in value must be credited to or (as the case may be) debited from a separate reserve ("the fair value reserve").

48(4) Where the instrument accounted for—

    (a)   is an available for sale financial asset, and

    (b)   is not a derivative, the change in value may be credited to or (as the case may be) debited from the fair value reserve.

The fair value reserve

49(1) The fair value reserve must be adjusted to the extent that the amounts shown in it are no longer necessary for the purposes of paragraph 48(3) or (4).

49(2) The treatment for taxation purposes of amounts credited or debited to the fair value reserve must be disclosed in a note to the accounts.

Assets and liabilities denominated in foreign currencies

50(1) Subject to the following sub-paragraphs, amounts to be included in respect of assets and liabilities denominated in foreign currencies must be in sterling (or the currency in which the accounts are drawn up) after translation at an appropriate spot rate of exchange prevailing at the balance sheet date.

50(2) An appropriate rate of exchange prevailing on the date of purchase may however be used for assets held as financial fixed assets and assets to be included under assets items 9 (intangible fixed assets) and 10 (tangible fixed assets) in the balance sheet format, if they are not covered or not specifically covered in either the spot or forward currency markets.

50(3) An appropriate spot rate of exchange prevailing at the balance sheet date must be used for translating uncompleted spot exchange transactions.

50(4) An appropriate forward rate of exchange prevailing at the balance sheet date must be used for translating uncompleted forward exchange transactions.

50(5) This paragraph does not apply to any assets or liabilities held, or any transactions entered into, for hedging purposes or to any assets or liabilities which are themselves hedged.

51(1) Subject to sub-paragraph (2), any difference between the amount to be included in respect of an asset or liability under paragraph 50 and the book value, after translation into sterling (or the currency in which the accounts are drawn up) at an appropriate rate, of that asset or liability must be credited or, as the case may be, debited to the profit and loss account.

51(2) In the case, however, of assets held as financial fixed assets, of assets to be included under assets items 9 (intangible fixed assets) and 10 (tangible fixed assets) in the balance sheet format and of transactions undertaken to cover such assets, any such difference may be deducted from or credited to any non-distributable reserve available for the purpose.

PART 3 – NOTES TO THE ACCOUNTS

Preliminary

52(1) Any information required in the case of a company by the following provisions of this Part of this Schedule must be given by way of a note to the accounts.

52(2) These notes must be presented in the order in which, where relevant, the items to which they relate are presented in the balance sheet and in the profit and loss account.

History – Para. 52 substituted by SI 2015/980, reg. 33(2), with effect in relation to–
 (a) financial years beginning on or after 1 January 2016, and
 (b) a financial year of a company beginning on or after 1 January 2015, but before
      1 January 2016, if the directors of the company so decide.
Former para. 52 read as follows:
 "**52** Any information required in the case of any company by the following provisions of this Part of this Schedule must (if not given in the company's accounts) be given by way of a note to the accounts."

General

Disclosure of accounting policies

53 The accounting policies adopted by the company in determining the amounts to be included in respect of items shown in the balance sheet and in determining the profit or loss of the company must be stated (including such policies with respect to the depreciation and diminution in value of assets).

54   It must be stated whether the accounts have been prepared in accordance with applicable accounting standards and particulars of any material departure from those standards and the reasons for it must be given.

Sums denominated in foreign currencies

55   Where any sums originally denominated in foreign currencies have been brought into account under any items shown in the balance sheet format or profit and loss account formats, the basis on which those sums have been translated into sterling (or the currency in which the accounts are drawn up) must be stated.

Reserves and dividends

56   There must be stated–

   (a)   any amount set aside or proposed to be set aside to, or withdrawn or proposed to be withdrawn from, reserves,

   (b)   the aggregate amount of dividends paid in the financial year (other than those for which a liability existed at the immediately preceding balance sheet date),

   (c)   the aggregate amount of dividends that the company is liable to pay at the balance sheet date, and

   (d)   the aggregate amount of dividends that are proposed before the date of approval of the accounts, and not otherwise disclosed under sub-paragraph (b) or (c).

Information supplementing the balance sheet

57   Paragraphs 58 to 84 require information which either supplements the information given with respect to any particular items shown in the balance sheet or is otherwise relevant to assessing the company's state of affairs in the light of the information so given.

Share capital and debentures

58(1)   Where shares of more than one class have been allotted, the number and aggregate nominal value of shares of each class allotted must be given.

58(2)   In the case of any part of the allotted share capital that consists of redeemable shares, the following information must be given–

   (a)   the earliest and latest dates on which the company has power to redeem those shares,

   (b)   whether those shares must be redeemed in any event or are liable to be redeemed at the option of the company or of the shareholder, and

   (c)   whether any (and, if so, what) premium is payable on redemption.

59   If the company has allotted any shares during the financial year, the following information must be given–

   (a)   the classes of shares allotted, and

   (b)   as respects each class of shares, the number allotted, their aggregate nominal value and the consideration received by the company for the allotment.

60(1)   With respect to any contingent right to the allotment of shares in the company the following particulars must be given–

   (a)   the number, description and amount of the shares in relation to which the right is exercisable,

   (b)   the period during which it is exercisable, and

   (c)   the price to be paid for the shares allotted.

60(2)   In sub-paragraph (1) **"contingent right to the allotment of shares"** means any option to subscribe for shares and any other right to require the allotment of shares to any person whether arising on the conversion into shares of securities of any other description or otherwise.

61(1)   If the company has issued any debentures during the financial year to which the accounts relate, the following information must be given–

   (a)   the classes of debentures issued, and

   (b)   as respects each class of debentures, the amount issued and the consideration received by the company for the issue.

61(2)   Where any of the company's debentures are held by a nominee of or trustee for the company, the nominal amount of the debentures and the amount at which they are stated in the accounting records kept by the company in accordance with section 386 of the 2006 Act (duty to keep accounting records) must be stated.

Fixed assets

62(1)   In respect of any fixed assets of the company included in any assets item in the company's balance sheet the following information must be given by reference to each such item–

   (a)   the appropriate amounts in respect of those assets included in the item as at the date of the beginning of the financial year and as at the balance sheet date respectively,

   (b)   the effect on any amount shown included in the item in respect of those assets of–

      (i)   any determination during that year of the value to be ascribed to any of those assets in accordance with paragraph 40,

      (ii)   acquisitions during that year of any fixed assets,

      (iii)   disposals during that year of any fixed assets, and

      (iv)   any transfers of fixed assets of the company to and from that item during that year.

62(2)   The reference in sub-paragraph (1)(a) to the appropriate amounts in respect of any fixed assets (included in an assets item) as at any date there mentioned is a reference to amounts representing the aggregate amounts determined, as at that date, in respect of fixed assets falling to be included under the item on either of the following bases–

   (a)   on the basis of cost (determined in accordance with paragraphs 35 and 36), or

   (b)   on any basis permitted by paragraph 40, (leaving out of account in either case any provisions for depreciation or diminution in value).

62(3)   In addition, in respect of any fixed assets of the company included in any assets item in the company's balance sheet, there must be stated (by reference to each such item)–

(a)   the cumulative amount of provisions for depreciation or diminution in value of those assets included under that item as at each date mentioned in sub-paragraph (1)(a),

(b)   the amount of any such provisions made in respect of the financial year,

(c)   the amount of any adjustments made in respect of any such provisions during that year in consequence of the disposal of any of those assets, and

(d)   the amount of any other adjustments made in respect of any such provisions during that year.

62(4)   The requirements of this paragraph need not be complied with to the extent that a company takes advantage of the option of setting off charges and income afforded by paragraph 8(3) in Part 1 of this Schedule.

63   Where any fixed assets of the company (other than listed investments) are included under any item shown in the company's balance sheet at an amount determined in accordance with paragraph 40, the following information must be given–

(a)   the years (so far as they are known to the directors) in which the assets were severally valued and the several values, and

(b)   in the case of assets that have been valued during the financial year, the names of the persons who valued them or particulars of their qualifications for doing so and (whichever is stated) the bases of valuation used by them.

64   In relation to any amount which is included under assets item 10 in the balance sheet format (tangible fixed assets) with respect to land and buildings there must be stated–

(a)   how much of that amount is ascribable to land of freehold tenure and how much to land of leasehold tenure, and

(b)   how much of the amount ascribable to land of leasehold tenure is ascribable to land held on long lease and how much to land held on short lease.

65   There must be disclosed separately the amount of–

(a)   any participating interests, and

(b)   any shares in group undertakings that are held in credit institutions.

Information about fair value of assets and liabilities

66(1)   This paragraph applies where financial instruments or other assets have been valued in accordance with, as appropriate, paragraph 44, 46 or 47.

66(2)   There must be stated–

(a)   the significant assumptions underlying the valuation models and techniques used to determine the fair value of the financial instruments or other assets,

(b)   for each category of financial instrument or other asset, the fair value of the assets in that category and the changes in value–

(i)   included directly in the profit and loss account, or

(ii)   credited to or (as the case may be) debited from the fair value reserve, in respect of those assets, and

(c)   for each class of derivatives, the extent and nature of the instruments, including significant terms and conditions that may affect the amount, timing and certainty of future cash flows.

66(3) Where any amount is transferred to or from the fair value reserve during the financial year, there must be stated in tabular form–

(a) the amount of the reserve as at the date of the beginning of the financial year and as at the balance sheet date respectively,

(b) the amount transferred to or from the reserve during the year, and

(c) the source and application respectively of the amounts so transferred.

History – Para. 66 substituted by SI 2015/980, reg. 33(3), with effect in relation to–

(a) financial years beginning on or after 1 January 2016, and

(b) a financial year of a company beginning on or after 1 January 2015, but before 1 January 2016, if the directors of the company so decide.

Former para. 66 read as follows:

"**66(1)** This paragraph applies where financial instruments have been valued in accordance with paragraph 44 or 46.

66(2) There must be stated–

(a) the significant assumptions underlying the valuation models and techniques used where the fair value of the instruments has been determined in accordance with paragraph 45(4),

(b) for each category of financial instrument, the fair value of the instruments in that category and the changes in value–

(i) included in the profit and loss account, or

(ii) credited to or (as the case may be) debited from the fair value reserve, in respect of those instruments, and

(c) for each class of derivatives, the extent and nature of the instruments, including significant terms and conditions that may affect the amount, timing and certainty of future cash flows.

66(3) Where any amount is transferred to or from the fair value reserve during the financial year, there must be stated in tabular form–

(a) the amount of the reserve as at the date of the beginning of the financial year and as at the balance sheet date respectively,

(b) the amount transferred to or from the reserve during that year, and

(c) the source and application respectively of the amounts so transferred."

67 Where the company has derivatives that it has not included at fair value, there must be stated for each class of such derivatives–

(a) the fair value of the derivatives in that class, if such a value can be determined in accordance with paragraph 45, and

(b) the extent and nature of the derivatives.

68(1) This paragraph applies if–

(a) the company has financial fixed assets that could be included at fair value by virtue of paragraph 44,

(b) the amount at which those items are included under any item in the company's accounts is in excess of their fair value, and

(c) the company has not made provision for diminution in value of those assets in accordance with paragraph 25(1) in Part 2 of this Schedule.

68(2) There must be stated–

(a) the amount at which either the individual assets or appropriate groupings of those individual assets are included in the company's accounts,

(b) the fair value of those assets or groupings, and

(c) the reasons for not making a provision for diminution in value of those assets, including the nature of the evidence that provides the basis for the belief that the amount at which they are stated in the accounts will be recovered.

Information where investment property and living animals and plants included at fair value

69(1) This paragraph applies where the amounts to be included in a company's accounts in respect of investment property or living animals and plants have been determined in accordance with paragraph 47.

69(2) The balance sheet items affected and the basis of valuation adopted in determining the amounts of the assets in question in the case of each such item must be disclosed in a note to the accounts.

69(3) In the case of investment property, for each balance sheet item affected there must be shown, either separately in the balance sheet or in a note to the accounts–

(a)   the comparable amounts determined according to the historical cost accounting rules, or

(b)   the differences between those amounts and the corresponding amounts actually shown in the balance sheet in respect of that item.

69(4) In sub-paragraph (3), references in relation to any item to the comparable amounts determined in accordance with that sub-paragraph are to–

(a)   the aggregate amount which would be required to be shown in respect of that item if the amounts to be included in respect of all the assets covered by that item were determined according to the historical cost accounting rules, and

(b)   the aggregate amount of the cumulative provisions for depreciation or diminution in value which would be permitted or required in determining those amounts according to those rules.

Reserves and provisions

70(1) This paragraph applies where any amount is transferred–

(a)   to or from any reserves, or

(b)   to any provision for liabilities, or

(c)   from any provision for liabilities otherwise than for the purpose for which the provision was established, and the reserves or provisions are or would but for paragraph 5(1) in Part 1 of this Schedule be shown as separate items in the company's balance sheet.

70(2) The following information must be given in respect of the aggregate of reserves or provisions included in the same item in tabular form–

(a)   the amount of the reserves or provisions as at the date of the beginning of the financial year and as at the balance sheet date respectively,

(b)   any amounts transferred to or from the reserves or provisions during that year, and

(c)   the source and application respectively of any amounts so transferred.

70(3) Particulars must be given of each provision included in liabilities item 6.(c) (other provisions) in the company's balance sheet in any case where the amount of that provision is material.

History – In para. 70(2), the words "in tabular form" inserted by SI 2015/980, reg. 33(4), with effect in relation to–

(a) financial years beginning on or after 1 January 2016, and

(b) a financial year of a company beginning on or after 1 January 2015, but before 1 January 2016, if the directors of the company so decide.

Provision for taxation

71 The amount of any provision for deferred taxation must be stated separately from the amount of any provision for other taxation.

Maturity analysis

72(1) A company must disclose separately for each of assets items 3.(b) and 4 and liabilities items 1.(b), 2.(b) and 3.(b) the aggregate amount of the loans and advances and liabilities included in those items broken down into the following categories–

(a) those repayable in not more than three months,

(b) those repayable in more than three months but not more than one year,

(c) those repayable in more than one year but not more than five years,

(d) those repayable in more than five years, from the balance sheet date.

72(2) A company must also disclose the aggregate amounts of all loans and advances falling within assets item 4 (loans and advances to customers) which are–

(a) repayable on demand, or

(b) are for an indeterminate period, being repayable upon short notice.

72(3) For the purposes of sub-paragraph (1), where a loan or advance or liability is repayable by instalments, each such instalment is to be treated as a separate loan or advance or liability.

Debt and other fixed-income securities

73 A company must disclose the amount of debt and fixed-income securities included in assets item 5 (debt securities [and other fixed-income securities]) and the amount of such securities included in liabilities item 3.(a) (bonds and medium term notes) that (in each case) will become due within one year of the balance sheet date.

Subordinated liabilities

74(1) The following information must be disclosed in relation to any borrowing included in liabilities item 7 (subordinated liabilities) that exceeds 10% of the total for that item–

(a) its amount,

(b) the currency in which it is denominated,

(c) the rate of interest and the maturity date (or the fact that it is perpetual),

(d) the circumstances in which early repayment may be demanded,

(e) the terms of the subordination, and

(f) the existence of any provisions whereby it may be converted into capital or some other form of liability and the terms of any such provisions.

74(2) The general terms of any other borrowings included in liabilities item 7 must also be stated.

Fixed cumulative dividends

75   If any fixed cumulative dividends on the company's shares are in arrear, there must be stated–

    (a)   the amount of the arrears, and

    (b)   the period for which the dividends or, if there is more than one class, each class of them are in arrear.

Details of assets charged

76(1)   There must be disclosed, in relation to each liabilities and memorandum item of the balance sheet format–

    (a)   the aggregate amount of any assets of the company which have been charged to secure any liability or potential liability included under that item,

    (b)   the aggregate amount of the liabilities or potential liabilities so secured, and

    (c)   an indication of the nature of the security given.

76(2)   Particulars must also be given of any other charge on the assets of the company to secure the liabilities of any other person, including, where practicable, the amount secured.

Guarantees and other financial commitments

77(1)   Particulars and the total amount of any financial commitments, guarantees and contingencies that are not included in the balance sheet must be disclosed.

77(2)   An indication of the nature and form of any valuable security given by the company in respect of commitments, guarantees and contingencies within sub-paragraph (1) must be given.

77(3)   The total amount of any commitments within sub-paragraph (1) concerning pensions must be separately disclosed.

77(4)   Particulars must be given of pension commitments which are included in the balance sheet.

77(5)   Where any commitment within sub-paragraph (3) or (4) relates wholly or partly to pensions payable to past directors of the company separate particulars must be given of that commitment.

77(6)   The total amount of any commitments, guarantees and contingencies within sub-paragraph (1) which are undertaken on behalf of or for the benefit of–

    (a)   any parent undertaking or fellow subsidiary undertaking of the company,

    (b)   any subsidiary undertaking of the company, or

    (c)   any undertaking in which the company has a participating interest

must be separately stated and those within each of paragraphs (a), (b) and (c) must also be stated separately from those within any other of those paragraphs.

77(7) There must be disclosed the nature and amount of any contingent liabilities and commitments included in Memorandum items 1 and 2 which are material in relation to the company's activities

History – Para. 77 substituted by SI 2015/980, reg. 33(5), with effect in relation to–
- (a) financial years beginning on or after 1 January 2016, and
- (b) a financial year of a company beginning on or after 1 January 2015, but before 1 January 2016, if the directors of the company so decide.

Former para. 77 read as follows:

"**77(1)** There must be stated, where practicable, the aggregate amount or estimated amount of contracts for capital expenditure, so far as not provided for.

77(2) Particulars must be given of–
- (a) any pension commitments included under any provision shown in the company's balance sheet, and
- (b) any such commitments for which no provision has been made, and where any such commitment relates wholly or partly to pensions payable to past directors of the company separate particulars must be given of that commitment so far as it relates to such pensions.

77(3) Particulars must also be given of any other financial commitments, including any contingent liabilities, that–
- (a) have not been provided for,
- (b) have not been included in the memorandum items in the balance sheet format, and
- (c) are relevant to assessing the company's state of affairs.

77(4) Commitments within any of the preceding sub-paragraphs undertaken on behalf of or for the benefit of–
- (a) any parent company or fellow subsidiary undertaking of the company, or
- (b) any subsidiary undertaking of the company, must be stated separately from the other commitments within that sub-paragraph (and commitments within paragraph(a) must be stated separately from those within paragraph (b)).

77(5) There must be disclosed the nature and amount of any contingent liabilities and commitments included in Memorandum items 1 and 2 which are material in relation to the company's activities."

Memorandum items: Group undertakings

78(1) With respect to contingent liabilities required to be included under Memorandum item 1 in the balance sheet format, there must be stated in a note to the accounts the amount of such contingent liabilities incurred on behalf of or for the benefit of–
- (a) any parent undertaking or fellow subsidiary undertaking, or
- (b) any subsidiary undertaking,

of the company; in addition the amount incurred in respect of the undertakings referred to in paragraph (a) must be stated separately from the amount incurred in respect in respect of the undertakings referred to in paragraph (b).

78(2) With respect to commitments required to be included under Memorandum item 2 in the balance sheet format, there must be stated in a note to the accounts the amount of such commitments undertaken on behalf of or for the benefit of–
- (a) any parent undertaking or fellow subsidiary undertaking, or
- (b) any subsidiary undertaking, of the company; in addition the amount incurred in respect of the undertakings referred to in paragraph
- (a) must be stated separately from the amount incurred in respect of the undertakings referred to in paragraph (b).

Transferable securities

79(1)   There must be disclosed for each of assets items 5 to 8 in the balance sheet format the amount of transferable securities included under those items that are listed and the amount of those that are unlisted.

79(2)   In the case of each amount shown in respect of listed securities under sub-paragraph (1), there must also be disclosed the aggregate market value of those securities, if different from the amount shown.

79(3)   There must also be disclosed for each of assets items 5 and 6 the amount of transferable securities included under those items that are held as financial fixed assets and the amount of those that are not so held, together with the criterion used by the directors to distinguish those held as financial fixed assets.

Leasing transactions

80   The aggregate amount of all property (other than land) leased by the company to other persons must be disclosed, broken down so as to show the aggregate amount included in each relevant balance sheet item.

Assets and liabilities denominated in a currency other than sterling (or the currency in which the accounts are drawn up)

81(1)   The aggregate amount, in sterling (or the currency in which the accounts are drawn up), of all assets denominated in a currency other than sterling (or the currency used) together with the aggregate amount, in sterling (or the currency used), of all liabilities so denominated, is to be disclosed.

81(2)   For the purposes of this paragraph an appropriate rate of exchange prevailing at the balance sheet date must be used to determine the amounts concerned.

Sundry assets and liabilities

82   Where any amount shown under either of the following items is material, particulars must be given of each type of asset or liability included in that item, including an explanation of the nature of the asset or liability and the amount included with respect to assets or liabilities of that type–

> (a)   assets item 13 (other assets),
> (b)   liabilities item 4 (other liabilities).

Unmatured forward transactions

83(1)   The following must be disclosed with respect to unmatured forward transactions outstanding at the balance sheet date–

> (a)   the categories of such transactions, by reference to an appropriate system of classification,
> (b)   whether, in the case of each such category, they have been made, to any material extent, for the purpose of hedging the effects of fluctuations in interest rates,

exchange rates and market prices or whether they have been made, to any material extent, for dealing purposes.

83(2) Transactions falling within sub-paragraph (1) must include all those in relation to which income or expenditure is to be included in–

(a)   format 1, item 6 or format 2, items B4 or A3 (dealing [profits][losses]),

(b)   format 1, items 1 or 2, or format 2, items B1 or A1, by virtue of notes (1)(b) and (2)(b) to the profit and loss account formats (forward contracts, spread over the actual duration of the contract and similar in nature to interest).

Miscellaneous matters

84(1)   Particulars must be given of any case where the cost of any asset is for the first time determined under paragraph 37 in Part 2 of this Schedule.

84(2)   Where any outstanding loans made under the authority of section 682(2)(b), (c) or (d) of the 2006 Act (various cases of financial assistance by a company for purchase of its own shares) are included under any item shown in the company's balance sheet, the aggregate amount of those loans must be disclosed for each item in question.

Information supplementing the profit and loss account

85   Paragraphs 86 to 91 require information which either supplements the information given with respect to any particular items shown in the profit and loss account or otherwise provides particulars of income or expenditure of the company or of circumstances affecting the items shown in the profit and loss account (see regulation 5(2) for exemption for companies falling within section 408 of the 2006 Act (individual profit and loss account where group accounts prepared)).

Particulars of tax

86(1)   Particulars must be given of any special circumstances which affect liability in respect of taxation of profits, income or capital gains for the financial year or liability in respect of taxation of profits, income or capital gains for succeeding financial years.

86(2)   The following amounts must be stated–

(a)   the amount of the charge for United Kingdom corporation tax,

(b)   if that amount would have been greater but for relief from double taxation, the amount which it would have been but for such relief,

(c)   the amount of the charge for United Kingdom income tax, and

(d)   the amount of the charge for taxation imposed outside the United Kingdom of profits, income and (so far as charged to revenue) capital gains.

These amounts must be stated separately in respect of each of the amounts which is shown under the following items in the profit and loss account, that is to say format 1 item 16, format 2 item A10 (tax on [profit][loss] on ordinary activities) and format 1 item 21, format 2 item A13 (tax on extraordinary [profit][loss]).

Particulars of income

87(1) A company must disclose, with respect to income included in the following items in the profit and loss account formats, the amount of that income attributable to each of the geographical markets in which the company has operated during the financial year—

    (a)   format 1 item 1, format 2 item B1 (interest receivable),

    (b)   format 1 item 3, format 2 item B2 (dividend income),

    (c)   format 1 item 4, format 2 item B3 (fees and commissions receivable),

    (d)   format 1 item 6, format 2 item B4 (dealing profits), and

    (e)   format 1 item 7, format 2 item B7 (other operating income).

87(2) In analysing for the purposes of this paragraph the source of any income, the directors must have regard to the manner in which the company's activities are organised.

87(3) For the purposes of this paragraph, markets which do not differ substantially from each other shall be treated as one market.

87(4) Where in the opinion of the directors the disclosure of any information required by this paragraph would be seriously prejudicial to the interests of the company, that information need not be disclosed, but the fact that any such information has not been disclosed must be stated.

Management and agency services

88 A company providing any management and agency services to customers must disclose that fact, if the scale of such services provided is material in the context of its business as a whole.

Subordinated liabilities

89 Any amounts charged to the profit and loss account representing charges incurred during the year with respect to subordinated liabilities must be disclosed.

Sundry income and charges

90 Where any amount to be included in any of the following items is material, particulars must be given of each individual component of the figure, including an explanation of their nature and amount—

    (a)   in format 1—

        (i)   items 7 and 10 (other operating income and charges),

        (ii) items 18 and 19 (extraordinary income and charges);

    (b)   in format 2—

        (i)   items A6 and B7 (other operating charges and income),

        (ii) items A12 and B10 (extraordinary charges and income).

Miscellaneous matters

91(1) Where any amount relating to any preceding financial year is included in any item in the profit and loss account, the effect must be stated.

91(2) The amount, nature and effect of any individual items of income or expenditure which are of exceptional size or incidence must be stated.

History – Para. 91(2) substituted by SI 2015/980, reg. 33(6), with effect in relation to–
    (a)   financial years beginning on or after 1 January 2016, and
    (b)   a financial year of a company beginning on or after 1 January 2015, but before 1 January 2016, if the directors of the company so decide.
Former para. 91(2) read as follows:
    "**91(2)**   The effect must be stated of any transactions that are exceptional by virtue of size or incidence though they fall within the ordinary activities of the company."

Related party transactions

92(1) Particulars may be given of transactions which the company has entered into with related parties, and must be given if such transactions are material and have not been concluded under normal market conditions.

92(2) The particulars of transactions required to be disclosed by sub-paragraph (1) must include–

    (a)   the amount of such transactions,
    (b)   the nature of the related party relationship, and
    (c)   other information about the transactions necessary for an understanding of the financial position of the company.

92(3) Information about individual transactions may be aggregated according to their nature, except where separate information is necessary for an understanding of the effects of related party transactions on the financial position of the company.

92(4) Particulars need not be given of transactions entered into between two or more members of a group, provided that any subsidiary undertaking which is a party to the transaction is whollyowned by such a member.

92(5) In this paragraph, "**related party**" has the same meaning as in international accounting standards.

Post balance sheet events

92A The nature and financial effect of material events arising after the balance sheet date which are not reflected in the profit and loss account of balance sheet must be stated.

History – Para. 92A and the heading preceding it inserted by SI 2015/980, reg. 33(7), with effect in relation to–
    (a)   financial years beginning on or after 1 January 2016, and
    (b)   a financial year of a company beginning on or after 1 January 2015, but before 1 January 2016, if the directors of the company so decide.

Appropriations

92B   Particulars must be given of the proposed appropriation of profit or treatment of loss or, where applicable, particulars of the actual appropriation of the profits or treatment of the losses.

History – Para. 92B and the heading preceding it inserted by SI 2015/980, reg. 33(7), with effect in relation to–

    (a)   financial years beginning on or after 1 January 2016, and

    (b)   a financial year of a company beginning on or after 1 January 2015, but before 1 January 2016, if the directors of the company so decide.

PART 4 – INTERPRETATION OF THIS SCHEDULE
DEFINITIONS FOR THIS SCHEDULE

93   The following definitions apply for the purposes of this Schedule.

Financial fixed assets

94   **"Financial fixed assets"** means loans and advances and securities held as fixed assets; participating interests and shareholdings in group undertakings are to be regarded as financial fixed assets.

Financial instruments

95   For the purposes of this Schedule, references to "derivatives" include commodity-based contracts that give either contracting party the right to settle in cash or in some other financial instrument, except when such contracts–

    (a)   were entered into for the purpose of, and continue to meet, the company's expected purchase, sale or usage requirements,

    (b)   were designated for such purpose at their inception, and

    (c)   are expected to be settled by delivery of the commodity.

96(1)   The expressions listed in sub-paragraph (2) have the same meaning in paragraphs 44 to 49, 66 to 68 and 95 of this Schedule as they have in Council Directives 2013/34/EU on the annual financial statements etc of certain types of undertaking and 86/635/EEC on the annual accounts and consolidated accounts of banks and other financial institutions.

96(2)   Those expressions are "available for sale financial asset", "business combination", "commodity-based contracts", "derivative", "equity instrument", "exchange difference", "fair value hedge accounting system", "financial fixed asset", "financial instrument", "foreign entity", "hedge accounting", "hedge accounting system", "hedged items", "hedging instrument", "held for trading purposes", "held to maturity", "monetary item", "receivables", "reliable market" and "trading portfolio".

History – In para. 96(1), the words "2013/34/EU on the annual financial statements etc of certain types of undertaking" substituted for the words "78/660/EEC on the annual accounts of certain types of companies" by SI 2015/980, reg. 33(8), with effect in relation to–

    (a)   financial years beginning on or after 1 January 2016, and

    (b)   a financial year of a company beginning on or after 1 January 2015, but before 1 January 2016, if the directors of the company so decide.

Repayable on demand

97 **"Repayable on demand"**, in connection with deposits, loans or advances, means that they can at any time be withdrawn or demanded without notice or that a maturity or period of notice of not more than 24 hours or one working day has been agreed for them.

Sale and repurchase transaction

98(1) **"Sale and repurchase transaction"** means a transaction which involves the transfer by a credit institution or customer ("the transferor") to another credit institution or customer ("the transferee") of assets subject to an agreement that the same assets, or (in the case of fungible assets) equivalent assets, will subsequently be transferred back to the transferor at a specified price on a date specified or to be specified by the transferor.

98(2) The following are not to be regarded as sale and repurchase transactions for the purposes of sub-paragraph (1)–

    (a)   forward exchange transactions,

    (b)   options,

    (c)   transactions involving the issue of debt securities with a commitment to repurchase all or part of the issue before maturity, or

    (d)   any similar transactions.

Sale and option to resell transaction

99 **"Sale and option to resell transaction"** means a transaction which involves the transfer by a credit institution or customer ("the transferor") to another credit institution or customer ("the transferee") of assets subject to an agreement that the transferee is entitled to require the subsequent transfer of the same assets, or (in the case of fungible assets) equivalent assets, back to the transferor at the purchase price or another price agreed in advance on a date specified or to be specified.

SCHEDULE 3
Regulation 6(1)

INSURANCE COMPANIES: COMPANIES ACT INDIVIDUAL ACCOUNTS

PART 1 – GENERAL RULES AND FORMATS
SECTION A – GENERAL RULES

1(1) Subject to the following provisions of this Schedule–

    (a)   every balance sheet of a company must show the items listed in the balance sheet format in Section B of this Part, and

    (b)   every profit and loss account must show the items listed in the profit and loss account format in Section B.

1(2) References in this Schedule to the items listed in any of the formats in Section B are to those items read together with any of the notes following the formats which apply to those items.

1(3) The items must be shown in the order and under the headings and sub-headings given in the particular format, but–

- (a) the notes to the formats may permit alternative positions for any particular items, and
- (b) the heading or sub-heading for any item does not have to be distinguished by any letter or number assigned to that item in the format used.

2(1) Any item required to be shown in a company's balance sheet or profit and loss account may be shown in greater detail than required by the particular format.

2(2) The balance sheet or profit and loss account may include an item representing or covering the amount of any asset or liability, income or expenditure not specifically covered by any of the items listed in the formats set out in Section B, save that none of the following may be treated as assets in any balance sheet–

- (a) preliminary expenses,
- (b) expenses of, and commission on, any issue of shares or debentures, and
- (c) costs of research.

3(1) The directors may combine items to which Arabic numbers are given in the balance sheet format set out in Section B (except for items concerning technical provisions and the reinsurers' share of technical provisions), and items to which lower case letters in parentheses are given in the profit and loss account format so set out (except for items within items I.1 and 4 and II.1, 5 and 6) if–

- (a) their individual amounts are not material for the purpose of giving a true and fair view, or
- (b) the combination facilitates the assessment of the state of affairs or profit or loss of the company for the financial year in question.

3(2) Where sub-paragraph (1)(b) applies–

- (a) the individual amounts of any items which have been combined must be disclosed in a note to the accounts, and
- (b) any notes required by this Schedule to the items so combined must, notwithstanding the combination, be given.

4(1) Subject to sub-paragraph (2), the directors must not include a heading or sub-heading corresponding to an item in the balance sheet or profit and loss account format used if there is no amount to be shown for that item for the financial year to which the balance sheet or profit and loss account relates.

4(2) Where an amount can be shown for the item in question for the immediately preceding financial year that amount must be shown under the heading or sub-heading required by the format for that item.

5(1) For every item shown in the balance sheet or profit and loss account the corresponding amount for the immediately preceding financial year must also be shown.

5(2) Where that corresponding amount is not comparable with the amount to be shown for the item in question in respect of the financial year to which the balance sheet or profit and loss account relates, the former amount may be adjusted, and particulars of the non-comparability and of any adjustment must be disclosed in a note to the accounts.

6 Subject to the provisions of this Schedule, amounts in respect of items representing assets or income may not be set off against amounts in respect of items representing liabilities or expenditure (as the case may be), or vice versa.

7(1)   The provisions of this Schedule which relate to long-term business apply, with necessary modifications, to business which consists of effecting or carrying out relevant contracts of general insurance which–

(a)   is transacted exclusively or principally according to the technical principles of long-term business, and

(b)   is a significant amount of the business of the company.

7(2)   For the purposes of paragraph (1), a contract of general insurance is a relevant contract if the risk insured against relates to–

(a)   accident, or

(b)   sickness.

7(3)   Sub-paragraph (2) must be read with–

(a)   section 22 of the Financial Services and Markets Act 2000,

(b)   the Financial Services and Markets Act 2000 (Regulated Activities) Order 2001, and

(c)   Schedule 2 to that Act.

8   The company's directors must, in determining how amounts are presented within items in the profit and loss account and balance sheet, have regard to the substance of the reported transaction or arrangement, in accordance with generally accepted accounting principles or practice.

8A   Where an asset or liability relates to more than one item in the balance sheet, the relationship of such asset or liability to the relevant items must be disclosed either under those items or in the notes to the accounts.

History – Para. 8A inserted by SI 2015/980, reg. 34(2), with effect in relation to–

(a)   financial years beginning on or after 1 January 2016, and

(b)   a financial year of a company beginning on or after 1 January 2015, but before 1 January 2016, if the directors of the company so decide.

SECTION B – THE REQUIRED FORMATS

Preliminary

9(1)   Where in respect of any item to which an Arabic number is assigned in the balance sheet or profit and loss account format, the gross amount and reinsurance amount or reinsurers' share are required to be shown, a sub-total of those amounts must also be given.

9(2)   Where in respect of any item to which an Arabic number is assigned in the profit and loss account format, separate items are required to be shown, then a separate sub-total of those items must also be given in addition to any sub-total required by sub-paragraph (1).

10(1)   In the profit and loss account format set out below–

(a)   the heading "Technical account – General business" is for business which consists of effecting or carrying out contracts of general business; and

(b)   the heading "Technical account – Long-term business" is for business which consists of effecting or carrying out contracts of long-term insurance.

10(2) In sub-paragraph (1), references to–

   (a)   contracts of general or long-term insurance, and

   (b)   the effecting or carrying out of such contracts, must be read with section 22 of the Financial Services and Markets Act 2000, the Financial Services and Markets Act 2000 (Regulated Activities) Order 2001, and Schedule 2 to that Act.

Balance sheet format

ASSETS

A. Called up share capital not paid *(1)*

B. Intangible assets

    1. Development costs

    2. Concessions, patents, licences, trade marks and similar rights and assets *(2)*

    3. Goodwill *(3)*

    4. Payments on account

C. Investments

    I.   Land and buildings *(4)*

    II. Investments in group undertakings and participating interests

        1. Shares in group undertakings

        2. Debt securities issued by, and loans to, group undertakings

        3. Participating interests

        4. Debt securities issued by, and loans to, undertakings in which the company has a participating interest

    III. Other financial investments

        1. Shares and other variable-yield securities and units in unit trusts

        2. Debt securities and other fixed-income securities *(5)*

        3. Participation in investment pools *(6)*

        4. Loans secured by mortgages *(7)*

        5. Other loans *(7)*

        6. Deposits with credit institutions *(8)*

        7. Other *(9)*

    IV. Deposits with ceding undertakings *(10)*

D. Assets held to cover linked liabilities *(11)*

Da. Reinsurers' share of technical provisions *(12)*

    1. Provision for unearned premiums

    2. Long-term business provision

    3. Claims outstanding

    4. Provisions for bonuses and rebates

    5. Other technical provisions

    6. Technical provisions for unit-linked liabilities

E.   Debtors *(13)*

    I.   Debtors arising out of direct insurance operations

        1.   Policyholders
        2.   Intermediaries

    II.   Debtors arising out of reinsurance operations

    III.   Other debtors

    IV.   Called up share capital not paid *(1)*

F.   Other assets

    I.   Tangible assets

        1.   Plant and machinery
        2.   Fixtures, fittings, tools and equipment
        3.   Payments on account (other than deposits paid on land and buildings) and assets (other than buildings) in course of construction

    II.   Stocks

        1.   Raw materials and consumables
        2.   Work in progress
        3.   Finished goods and goods for resale
        4.   Payments on account

    III.   Cash at bank and in hand
    IV.   Own shares *(14)*
    V.   Other *(15)*

G.   Prepayments and accrued income

    I.   Accrued interest and rent *(16)*
    II.   Deferred acquisition costs *(17)*
    III.   Other prepayments and accrued income

LIABILITIES

A.   Capital and reserves

    I.   Called up share capital or equivalent funds
    II.   Share premium account
    III.   Revaluation reserve
    IV.   Reserves

        1.   Capital redemption reserve
        2.   Reserve for own shares

       3.   Reserves provided for by the articles of association

       4.   Other reserves

    V.   Profit and loss account

B. Subordinated liabilities *(18)*

Ba. Fund for future appropriations *(19)*

C. Technical provisions

    1.   Provision for unearned premiums *(20)*

       (a) gross amount
       (b) reinsurance amount *(12)*

    2.   Long-term business provision *(20) (21) (26)*

       (a) gross amount
       (b) reinsurance amount *(12)*

    3.   Claims outstanding *(22)*

       (a) gross amount
       (b) reinsurance amount *(12)*

    4.   Provision for bonuses and rebates *(23)*

       (a) gross amount
       (b) reinsurance amount *(12)*

    5.   Equalisation provision *(24)*

    6.   Other technical provisions *(25)*

       (a) gross amount
       (b) reinsurance amount *(12)*

D. Technical provisions for linked liabilities *(26)*

       (a) gross amount
       (b) reinsurance amount *(12)*

E. Provisions for other risks

    1.   Provisions for pensions and similar obligations
    2.   Provisions for taxation
    3.   Other provisions

F. Deposits received from reinsurers *(27)*

G. Creditors *(28)*

    I.   Creditors arising out of direct insurance operations

    II. Creditors arising out of reinsurance operations

    III. Debenture loans *(29)*

    IV. Amounts owed to credit institutions

    V. Other creditors including taxation and social security

H.   Accruals and deferred income

Notes on the balance sheet format

History – In note (24), "made by the Financial Conduct Authority or the Prudential Regulation Authority" substituted for "in section 1.4 of the Prudential Sourcebook for Insurers made by the Financial Services Authority" by SI 2013/472, Sch. 2, para. 135(a), with effect from 1 April 2013.

(1)   Called up share capital not paid

(Assets items A and E.IV.)

  This item may be shown in either of the positions given in the format.

(2)   Concessions, patents, licences, trade marks and similar rights and assets

(Assets item B.2.)

  Amounts in respect of assets are only to be included in a company's balance sheet under this item if either–

   (a)   the assets were acquired for valuable consideration and are not required to be shown under goodwill, or

   (b)   the assets in question were created by the company itself.

(3)   Goodwill

(Assets item B.3.)

  Amounts representing goodwill are only to be included to the extent that the goodwill was acquired for valuable consideration.

(4)   Land and buildings

(Assets item C.I.)

  The amount of any land and buildings occupied by the company for its own activities must be shown separately in the notes to the accounts.

(5)   Debt securities and other fixed-income securities

(Assets item C.III.2.)

  This item is to comprise transferable debt securities and any other transferable fixed-income securities issued by credit institutions, other undertakings or public bodies, in so far as they are not covered by assets item C.II.2 or C.II.4.

Securities bearing interest rates that vary in accordance with specific factors, for example the interest rate on the inter-bank market or on the Euromarket, are also to be regarded as debt securities and other fixed-income securities and so be included under this item.

(6)   Participation in investment pools

(Assets item C.III.3.)

This item is to comprise shares held by the company in joint investments constituted by several undertakings or pension funds, the management of which has been entrusted to one of those undertakings or to one of those pension funds.

(7)   Loans secured by mortgages and other loans

(Assets items C.III.4 and C.III.5.)

Loans to policyholders for which the policy is the main security are to be included under "Other loans" and their amount must be disclosed in the notes to the accounts. Loans secured by mortgage are to be shown as such even where they are also secured by insurance policies. Where the amount of "Other loans" not secured by policies is material, an appropriate breakdown must be given in the notes to the accounts.

(8)   Deposits with credit institutions

(Assets item C.III.6.)

This item is to comprise sums the withdrawal of which is subject to a time restriction. Sums deposited with no such restriction must be shown under assets item F.III even if they bear interest.

(9)   Other

(Assets item C.III.7.)

This item is to comprise those investments which are not covered by assets items C.III.1 to 6. Where the amount of such investments is significant, they must be disclosed in the notes to the accounts.

(10) Deposits with ceding undertakings

(Assets item C.IV.)

Where the company accepts reinsurance this item is to comprise amounts, owed by the ceding undertakings and corresponding to guarantees, which are deposited with those ceding undertakings or with third parties or which are retained by those undertakings.

These amounts may not be combined with other amounts owed by the ceding insurer to the reinsurer or set off against amounts owed by the reinsurer to the ceding insurer.

Securities deposited with ceding undertakings or third parties which remain the property of the company must be entered in the company's accounts as an investment, under the appropriate item.

(11) Assets held to cover linked liabilities

(Assets item D.)

In respect of long-term business, this item is to comprise investments made pursuant to long-term policies under which the benefits payable to the policyholder are wholly or partly to be determined by reference to the value of, or the income from, property of any description (whether or not specified in the contract) or by reference to fluctuations in, or in an index of, the value of property of any description (whether or not so specified).

This item is also to comprise investments which are held on behalf of the members of a tontine and are intended for distribution among them.

(12) Reinsurance amounts

(Assets item Da: liabilities items C.1.(b), 2.(b), 3.(b), 4.(b) and 6.(b) and D.(b).)

The reinsurance amounts may be shown either under assets item Da or under liabilities items C.1.(b), 2.(b), 3.(b), 4.(b) and 6.(b) and D.(b).

The reinsurance amounts are to comprise the actual or estimated amounts which, under contractual reinsurance arrangements, are deducted from the gross amounts of technical provisions.

As regards the provision for unearned premiums, the reinsurance amounts must be calculated according to the methods referred to in paragraph 50 below or in accordance with the terms of the reinsurance policy.

(13) Debtors

(Assets item E.)

Amounts owed by group undertakings and undertakings in which the company has a participating interest must be shown separately as sub-items of assets items E.I, II and III.

(14) Own shares

(Assets item F.IV.)

The nominal value of the shares must be shown separately under this item.

(15) Other

(Assets item F.V.)

This item is to comprise those assets which are not covered by assets items F.I to IV. Where such assets are material they must be disclosed in the notes to the accounts.

(16) Accrued interest and rent

(Assets item G.I.)

This item is to comprise those items that represent interest and rent that have been earned up to the balance-sheet date but have not yet become receivable.

(17) Deferred acquisition costs

(Assets item G.II.)

This item is to comprise the costs of acquiring insurance policies which are incurred during a financial year but relate to a subsequent financial year ("deferred acquisition costs"), except in so far as–

    (a)   allowance has been made in the computation of the long-term business provision made under paragraph 52 below and shown under liabilities item C2 or D in the balance sheet, for–

        (i)   the explicit recognition of such costs, or

        (ii) the implicit recognition of such costs by virtue of the anticipation of future income from which such costs may prudently be expected to be recovered, or

    (b)   allowance has been made for such costs in respect of general business policies by a deduction from the provision for unearned premiums made under paragraph 50 below and shown under liabilities item C.I in the balance sheet.

Deferred acquisition costs arising in general business must be distinguished from those arising in long-term business.

In the case of general business, the amount of any deferred acquisition costs must be established on a basis compatible with that used for unearned premiums.

There must be disclosed in the notes to the accounts–

    (c)   how the deferral of acquisition costs has been treated (unless otherwise expressly stated in the accounts), and

    (d)   where such costs are included as a deduction from the provisions at liabilities item C.I, the amount of such deduction, or

    (e)   where the actuarial method used in the calculation of the provisions at liabilities item C.2 or D has made allowance for the explicit recognition of such costs, the amount of the costs so recognised.

(18) Subordinated liabilities

(Liabilities item B.)

This item is to comprise all liabilities in respect of which there is a contractual obligation that, in the event of winding up or of bankruptcy, they are to be repaid only after the claims of all other creditors have been met (whether or not they are represented by certificates).

(19) Fund for future appropriations

(Liabilities item Ba.)

This item is to comprise all funds the allocation of which either to policyholders or to shareholders has not been determined by the end of the financial year.

Transfers to and from this item must be shown in item II.12a in the profit and loss account.

(20) Provision for unearned premiums

(Liabilities item C.1.)

In the case of long-term business the provision for unearned premiums may be included in liabilities item C.2 rather than in this item.

The provision for unearned premiums is to comprise the amount representing that part of gross premiums written which is estimated to be earned in the following financial year or to subsequent financial years.

(21) Long-term business provision

(Liabilities item C.2.)

This item is to comprise the actuarially estimated value of the company's liabilities (excluding technical provisions included in liabilities item D), including bonuses already declared and after deducting the actuarial value of future premiums.

This item is also to comprise claims incurred but not reported, plus the estimated costs of settling such claims.

(22) Claims outstanding

(Liabilities item C.3.)

This item is to comprise the total estimated ultimate cost to the company of settling all claims arising from events which have occurred up to the end of the financial year (including, in the case of general business, claims incurred but not reported) less amounts already paid in respect of such claims.

(23) Provision for bonuses and rebates

(Liabilities item C.4.)

This item is to comprise amounts intended for policyholders or contract beneficiaries by way of bonuses and rebates as defined in Note *(5)* on the profit and loss account format to the extent that such amounts have not been credited to policyholders or contract beneficiaries or included in liabilities item Ba or in liabilities item C.2.

(24) Equalisation provision

(Liabilities item C.5.)

This item is to comprise the amount of any equalisation reserve maintained in respect of general business by the company, in accordance with the rules made by the Financial Conduct Authority or the Prudential Regulation Authority under Part 10 of the Financial Services and Markets Act 2000.

This item is also to comprise any amounts which, in accordance with Council Directive 87/343/EEC of 22nd June 1987, are required to be set aside by a company to equalise fluctuations in loss ratios in future years or to provide for special risks.

A company which otherwise constitutes reserves to equalise fluctuations in loss ratios in future years or to provide for special risks must disclose that fact in the notes to the accounts.

(25) Other technical provisions

(Liabilities item C.6.)

This item is to comprise, inter alia, the provision for unexpired risks as defined in paragraph 91 below. Where the amount of the provision for unexpired risks is significant, it must be disclosed separately either in the balance sheet or in the notes to the accounts.

(26) Technical provisions for linked liabilities

(Liabilities item D.)

This item is to comprise technical provisions constituted to cover liabilities relating to investment in the context of long-term policies under which the benefits payable to policyholders are wholly or partly to be determined by reference to the value of, or the income from, property of any description (whether or not specified in the contract) or by reference to fluctuations in, or in an index of, the value of property of any description (whether or not so specified).

Any additional technical provisions constituted to cover death risks, operating expenses or other risks (such as benefits payable at the maturity date or guaranteed surrender values) must be included under liabilities item C.2.

This item must also comprise technical provisions representing the obligations of a tontine's organiser in relation to its members.

(27) Deposits received from reinsurers

(Liabilities item F.)

Where the company cedes reinsurance, this item is to comprise amounts deposited by or withheld from other insurance undertakings under reinsurance contracts. These amounts may not be merged with other amounts owed to or by those other undertakings.

Where the company cedes reinsurance and has received as a deposit securities which have been transferred to its ownership, this item is to comprise the amount owed by the company by virtue of the deposit.

(28) Creditors

(Liabilities item G.)

Amounts owed to group undertakings and undertakings in which the company has a participating interest must be shown separately as sub-items.

(29) Debenture loans

(Liabilities item G.III.)

The amount of any convertible loans must be shown separately.

Special rules for balance sheet format

Additional items

11(1) Every balance sheet of a company which carries on long-term business must show separately as an additional item the aggregate of any amounts included in liabilities item A (capital and reserves) which are required not to be treated as realised profits under section 843 of the 2006 Act.

11(2) A company which carries on long-term business must show separately, in the balance sheet or in the notes to the accounts, the total amount of assets representing the long-term fund valued in accordance with the provisions of this Schedule.

Managed funds

12(1) For the purposes of this paragraph "managed funds" are funds of a group pension fund–

(a)   the management of which constitutes long-term insurance business, and
(b)   which the company administers in its own name but on behalf of others, and
(c)   to which it has legal title.

12(2) The company must, in any case where assets and liabilities arising in respect of managed funds fall to be treated as assets and liabilities of the company, adopt the following accounting treatment: assets and liabilities representing managed funds are to be included in the company's balance sheet, with the notes to the accounts disclosing the total amount included with respect to such assets and liabilities in the balance sheet and showing the amount included under each relevant balance sheet item in respect of such assets or (as the case may be) liabilities.

Deferred acquisition costs

13 The costs of acquiring insurance policies which are incurred during a financial year but which relate to a subsequent financial year must be deferred in a manner specified in Note *(17)* on the balance sheet format.

Profit and loss account format

I.   Technical account – General business

    1.   Earned premiums, net of reinsurance

        (a)   gross premiums written *(1)*
        (b)   outward reinsurance premiums *(2)*
        (c)   change in the gross provision for unearned premiums
        (d)   change in the provision for unearned premiums, reinsurers' share

2. Allocated investment return transferred from the non-technical account (item III.6) *(10)*

2a. Investment income *(8) (10)*

    (a) income from participating interests, with a separate indication of that derived from group undertakings

    (b) income from other investments, with a separate indication of that derived from group undertakings (aa) income from land and buildings (bb) income from other investments

    (c) value re-adjustments on investments

    (d) gains on the realisation of investments

3. Other technical income, net of reinsurance

4. Claims incurred, net of reinsurance *(4)*

    (a) claims paid

        (aa) gross amount

        (bb) reinsurers' share

    (b) change in the provision for claims

        (aa) gross amount

        (bb) reinsurers' share

5. Changes in other technical provisions, net of reinsurance, not shown under other headings

6. Bonuses and rebates, net of reinsurance *(5)*

7. Net operating expenses

    (a) acquisition costs *(6)*

    (b) change in deferred acquisition costs

    (c) administrative expenses *(7)*

    (d) reinsurance commissions and profit participation

8. Other technical charges, net of reinsurance

8a. Investment expenses and charges *(8)*

    (a) investment management expenses, including interest

    (b) value adjustments on investments

    (c) losses on the realisation of investments

9. Change in the equalisation provision

10. Sub-total (balance on the technical account for general business) (item III.1)

II.   Technical account – Long-term business

   1.   Earned premiums, net of reinsurance

      (a)   gross premiums written *(1)*

      (b)   outward reinsurance premiums *(2)*

      (c)   change in the provision for unearned premiums, net of reinsurance *(3)*

   2.   Investment income *(8) (10)*

      (a)   income from participating interests, with a separate indication of that derived from group undertakings

      (b)   income from other investments, with a separate indication of that derived from group undertakings (aa) income from land and buildings (bb) income from other investments

      (c)   value re-adjustments on investments

      (d)   gains on the realisation of investments

   3.   Unrealised gains on investments *(9)*

   4.   Other technical income, net of reinsurance

   5.   Claims incurred, net of reinsurance *(4)*

      (a)   claims paid

         (aa) gross amount

         (bb) reinsurers' share

      (b)   change in the provision for claims

         (aa) gross amount

         (bb) reinsurers' share

   6.   Change in other technical provisions, net of reinsurance, not shown under other headings

      (a)   Long-term business provision, net of reinsurance *(3)*

         (aa) gross amount

         (bb) reinsurers' share

      (b)   other technical provisions, net of reinsurance

   7.   Bonuses and rebates, net of reinsurance *(5)*

   8.   Net operating expenses

      (a)   acquisition costs *(6)*

      (b)   change in deferred acquisition costs

      (c)   administrative expenses *(7)*

      (d)   reinsurance commissions and profit participation

9. Investment expenses and charges *(8)*

    (a) investment management expenses, including interest
    (b) value adjustments on investments
    (c) losses on the realisation of investments

10. Unrealised losses on investments *(9)*

11. Other technical charges, net of reinsurance

11a. Tax attributable to the long-term business

12. Allocated investment return transferred to the non-technical account (item III.4)

12a. Transfers to or from the fund for future appropriations

13. Sub-total (balance on the technical account – long-term business) (item III.2)

III. Non-technical account

1. Balance on the general business technical account (item I.10)

2. Balance on the long-term business technical account (item II.13)

2a. Tax credit attributable to balance on the long-term business technical account

3. Investment income *(8)*

    (a) income from participating interests, with a separate indication of that derived from group undertakings
    (b) income from other investments, with a separate indication of that derived from group undertakings (aa) income from land and buildings (bb) income from other investments
    (c) value re-adjustments on investments
    (d) gains on the realisation of investments

3a. Unrealised gains on investments *(9)*

4. Allocated investment return transferred from the long-term business technical account (item II.12) *(10)*

5. Investment expenses and charges *(8)*

    (a) investment management expenses, including interest

    (b) value adjustments on investments

    (c) losses on the realisation of investments

5a. Unrealised losses on investments *(9)*

6. Allocated investment return transferred to the general business technical account (item I.2) *(10)*

7.   Other income

8.   Other charges, including value adjustments

8a. Profit or loss on ordinary activities before tax

9.   Tax on profit or loss on ordinary activities

10. Profit or loss on ordinary activities after tax

11. Extraordinary income

12. Extraordinary charges

13. Extraordinary profit or loss

14. Tax on extraordinary profit or loss

15. Other taxes not shown under the preceding items

16. Profit or loss for the financial year

Notes on the profit and loss account format

(1)   Gross premiums written

(General business technical account: item I.1.(a).

Long-term business technical account: item II.1.(a).)

This item is to comprise all amounts due during the financial year in respect of insurance contracts entered into regardless of the fact that such amounts may relate in whole or in part to a later financial year, and must include inter alia–

(i)   premiums yet to be determined, where the premium calculation can be done only at the end of the year;

(ii)   single premiums, including annuity premiums, and, in long-term business, single premiums resulting from bonus and rebate provisions in so far as they must be considered as premiums under the terms of the contract;

(iii) additional premiums in the case of half-yearly, quarterly or monthly payments and additional payments from policyholders for expenses borne by the company;

(iv)   in the case of co-insurance, the company's portion of total premiums;

(v)   reinsurance premiums due from ceding and retroceding insurance undertakings, including portfolio entries, after deduction of cancellations and portfolio withdrawals credited to ceding and retroceding insurance undertakings.

The above amounts must not include the amounts of taxes or duties levied with premiums.

(2)   Outward reinsurance premiums

(General business technical account: item I.1.(b).

Long-term business technical account: item II.1.(b).)

This item is to comprise all premiums paid or payable in respect of outward reinsurance contracts entered into by the company. Portfolio entries payable on the conclusion or amendment of outward reinsurance contracts must be added; portfolio withdrawals receivable must be deducted.

(3)   Change in the provision for unearned premiums, net of reinsurance

(Long-term business technical account: items II.1.(c) and II.6.(a).)

In the case of long-term business, the change in unearned premiums may be included either in item II.1.(c) or in item II.6.(a) of the long-term business technical account.

(4)   Claims incurred, net of reinsurance

(General business technical account: item I.4.

Long-term business technical account: item II.5.)

This item is to comprise all payments made in respect of the financial year with the addition of the provision for claims (but after deducting the provision for claims for the preceding financial year).

These amounts must include annuities, surrenders, entries and withdrawals of loss provisions to and from ceding insurance undertakings and reinsurers and external and internal claims management costs and charges for claims incurred but not reported such as are referred to in paragraphs 53(2) and 55 below.

Sums recoverable on the basis of subrogation and salvage (within the meaning of paragraph 53 below) must be deducted.

Where the difference between–

(a)   the loss provision made at the beginning of the year for outstanding claims incurred in previous years, and

(b)   the payments made during the year on account of claims incurred in previous years and the loss provision shown at the end of the year for such outstanding claims, is material, it must be shown in the notes to the accounts, broken down by category and amount.

(5)   Bonuses and rebates, net of reinsurance

(General business technical account: item I.6.

Long-term business technical account: item II.7.)

Bonuses are to comprise all amounts chargeable for the financial year which are paid or payable to policyholders and other insured parties or provided for their benefit, including amounts used to increase technical provisions or applied to the reduction of future premiums, to the extent that such amounts represent an allocation of surplus or profit arising on business as a whole or a section of business, after deduction of amounts provided in previous years which are no longer required.

Rebates are to comprise such amounts to the extent that they represent a partial refund of premiums resulting from the experience of individual contracts.

Where material, the amount charged for bonuses and that charged for rebates must be disclosed separately in the notes to the accounts.

(6)   Acquisition costs

(General business technical account: item I.7.(a).

Long-term business technical account: item II.8.(a).)

This item is to comprise the costs arising from the conclusion of insurance contracts. They must cover both direct costs, such as acquisition commissions or the cost of drawing up the insurance document or including the insurance contract in the portfolio, and indirect costs, such as advertising costs or the administrative expenses connected with the processing of proposals and the issuing of policies.

In the case of long-term business, policy renewal commissions must be included under item II.8.(c) in the long-term business technical account.

(7)   Administrative expenses

(General business technical account: item I.7.(c).

Long-term business technical account: item II.8.(c).)

This item must include the costs arising from premium collection, portfolio administration, handling of bonuses and rebates, and inward and outward reinsurance. They must in particular include staff costs and depreciation provisions in respect of office furniture and equipment in so far as these need not be shown under acquisition costs, claims incurred or investment charges.

Item II.8.(c) must also include policy renewal commissions.

(8)   Investment income, expenses and charges

(General business technical account: items I.2a and 8a.

Long-term business technical account: items II.2 and 9.

Non-technical account: items III.3 and 5.)

Investment income, expenses and charges must, to the extent that they arise in the long-term fund, be disclosed in the long-term business technical account. Other investment income, expenses and charges must either be disclosed in the non-technical account or attributed between the appropriate technical and non-technical accounts. Where the company makes such an attribution it must disclose the basis for it in the notes to the accounts.

(9)   Unrealised gains and losses on investments

(Long-term business technical account: items II.3 and 10.

    Non-technical account: items III.3a and 5a.)

In the case of investments attributed to the long-term fund, the difference between the valuation of the investments and their purchase price or, if they have previously been valued, their valuation as at the last balance sheet date, may be disclosed (in whole or in part) in item II.3 or II.10 (as the case may be) of the long-term business technical account, and in the case of investments shown as assets under assets item D (assets held to cover linked liabilities) must be so disclosed.

In the case of other investments, the difference between the valuation of the investments and their purchase price or, if they have previously been valued, their valuation as at the last balance sheet date, may be disclosed (in whole or in part) in item III.3a or III.5a (as the case may require) of the non-technical account.

(10)   Allocated investment return

(General business technical account: item I.2.

    Long-term business technical account: item II.2.

    Non-technical account: items III.4 and 6.)

The allocated return may be transferred from one part of the profit and loss account to another.

Where part of the investment return is transferred to the general business technical account, the transfer from the non-technical account must be deducted from item III.6 and added to item I.2.

Where part of the investment return disclosed in the long-term business technical account is transferred to the non-technical account, the transfer to the non-technical account shall be deducted from item II.12 and added to item III.4.

The reasons for such transfers (which may consist of a reference to any relevant statutory requirement) and the bases on which they are made must be disclosed in the notes to the accounts.

PART 2 – ACCOUNTING PRINCIPLES AND RULES
SECTION A – ACCOUNTING PRINCIPLES

Preliminary

14   The amounts to be included in respect of all items shown in a company's accounts must be determined in accordance with the principles set out in this Section.

15   But if it appears to the company's directors that there are special reasons for departing from any of those principles in preparing the company's accounts in respect of any financial year they may do so, in which case particulars of the departure, the reasons for it and its effect must be given in a note to the accounts.

Accounting principles

16   The company is presumed to be carrying on business as a going concern.

17   Accounting policies and measurement bases must be applied consistently within the same accounts and from one financial year to the next.

History – In para. 17, the words "and measurement bases" inserted by SI 2015/980, reg. 35(2)(a), with effect in relation to–
- (a)   financial years beginning on or after 1 January 2016, and
- (b)   a financial year of a company beginning on or after 1 January 2015, but before 1 January 2016, if the directors of the company so decide.

18   The amount of any item must be determined on a prudent basis, and in particular–
- (a)   subject to note (9) on the profit and loss account format, only profits realised at the balance sheet date are to be included in the profit and loss account
- (b)   all liabilities which have arisen in respect of the financial year to which the accounts relate or a previous financial year must be taken into account, including those which only become apparent between the balance sheet date and the date on which it is signed on behalf of the board of directors in accordance with section 414 of the 2006 Act (approval and signing of accounts) and
- (c)   all provisions for diminution of value must be recognised, whether the result of the financial year is a profit or a loss.

History – Para. 18(c), (and the word "and" preceding it) inserted; the word "and" in para. (a) omitted by SI 2015/980, reg. 35(2)(b), with effect in relation to–
- (a)   financial years beginning on or after 1 January 2016, and
- (b)   a financial year of a company beginning on or after 1 January 2015, but before 1 January 2016, if the directors of the company so decide.

19   All income and charges relating to the financial year to which the accounts relate are to be taken into account, without regard to the date of receipt or payment.

20   In determining the aggregate amount of any item, the amount of each individual asset or liability that falls to be taken into account must be determined separately.

20A   The opening balance sheet for each financial year shall correspond to the closing balance sheet for the preceding financial year.

History – Para. 20A inserted by SI 2015/980, reg. 35(2)(c), with effect in relation to–
- (a)   financial years beginning on or after 1 January 2016, and
- (b)   a financial year of a company beginning on or after 1 January 2015, but before 1 January 2016, if the directors of the company so decide.

Valuation

21(1)   The amounts to be included in respect of assets of any description mentioned in paragraph 22 (valuation of assets: general) must be determined either–

(a)   in accordance with that paragraph and paragraph 24 (but subject to paragraphs 27 to 29), or

(b)   so far as applicable to an asset of that description, in accordance with Section C (valuation at fair value).

21(2)   The amounts to be included in respect of assets of any description mentioned in paragraph 24 (alternative valuation of fixed-income securities) may be determined–

(a)   in accordance with that paragraph (but subject to paragraphs 27 to 29), or

(b)   so far as applicable to an asset of that description, in accordance with Section C.

21(3)   The amounts to be included in respect of assets which–

(a)   are not assets of a description mentioned in paragraph 22 or 23, but

(b)   are assets of a description to which Section C is applicable, may be determined in accordance with that Section.

21(4)   Subject to sub-paragraphs (1) to (3), the amounts to be included in respect of all items shown in a company's accounts are determined in accordance with Section C.

SECTION B – CURRENT VALUE ACCOUNTING RULES

Valuation of assets: general

22(1)   Subject to paragraph 24, investments falling to be included under assets item C (investments) must be included at their current value calculated in accordance with paragraphs 25 and 26.

22(2)   Investments falling to be included under assets item D (assets held to cover linked liabilities) must be shown at their current value calculated in accordance with paragraphs 25 and 26.

23(1)   Intangible assets other than goodwill may be shown at their current cost.

23(2)   Assets falling to be included under assets items F.I (tangible assets) and F.IV (own shares) in the balance sheet format may be shown at their current value calculated in accordance with paragraphs 25 and 26 or at their current cost.

23(3)   Assets falling to be included under assets item F.II (stocks) may be shown at current cost.

Alternative valuation of fixed-income securities

24(1)   This paragraph applies to debt securities and other fixed-income securities shown as assets under assets items C.II (investments in group undertakings and participating interests) and C.III (other financial investments).

24(2)   Securities to which this paragraph applies may either be valued in accordance with paragraph 22 or their amortised value may be shown in the balance sheet, in which case the provisions of this paragraph apply.

24(3) Subject to sub-paragraph (4), where the purchase price of securities to which this paragraph applies exceeds the amount repayable at maturity, the amount of the difference–

(a)   must be charged to the profit and loss account, and

(b)   must be shown separately in the balance sheet or in the notes to the accounts.

24(4) The amount of the difference referred to in sub-paragraph (3) may be written off in instalments so that it is completely written off when the securities are repaid, in which case there must be shown separately in the balance sheet or in the notes to the accounts the difference between the purchase price (less the aggregate amount written off) and the amount repayable at maturity.

24(5) Where the purchase price of securities to which this paragraph applies is less than the amount repayable at maturity, the amount of the difference must be released to income in instalments over the period remaining until repayment, in which case there must be shown separately in the balance sheet or in the notes to the accounts the difference between the purchase price (plus the aggregate amount released to income) and the amount repayable at maturity.

24(6) Both the purchase price and the current value of securities valued in accordance with this paragraph must be disclosed in the notes to the accounts.

24(7) Where securities to which this paragraph applies which are not valued in accordance with paragraph 22 are sold before maturity, and the proceeds are used to purchase other securities to which this paragraph applies, the difference between the proceeds of sale and their book value may be spread uniformly over the period remaining until the maturity of the original investment.

Meaning of "current value"

25(1) Subject to sub-paragraph (5), in the case of investments other than land and buildings, **"current value"** means market value determined in accordance with this paragraph.

25(2) In the case of listed investments, **"market value"** means the value on the balance sheet date or, when the balance sheet date is not a stock exchange trading day, on the last stock exchange trading day before that date.

25(3) Where a market exists for unlisted investments, **"market value"** means the average price at which such investments were traded on the balance sheet date or, when the balance sheet date is not a trading day, on the last trading day before that date.

25(4) Where, on the date on which the accounts are drawn up, listed or unlisted investments have been sold or are to be sold within the short term, the market value must be reduced by the actual or estimated realisation costs.

25(5) Except where the equity method of accounting is applied, all investments other than those referred to in sub-paragraphs (2) and (3) must be valued on a basis which has prudent regard to the likely realisable value.

26(1) In the case of land and buildings, **"current value"** means the market value on the date of valuation, where relevant reduced as provided in sub-paragraphs (4) and (5).

26(2) **"Market value"** means the price at which land and buildings could be sold under private contract between a willing seller and an arm's length buyer on the date of valuation, it being assumed that the property is publicly exposed to the market, that market conditions permit orderly disposal and that a normal period, having regard to the nature of the property, is available for the negotiation of the sale.

26(3) The market value must be determined through the separate valuation of each land and buildings item, carried out at least every five years in accordance with generally recognised methods of valuation.

26(4) Where the value of any land and buildings item has diminished since the preceding valuation under sub-paragraph (3), an appropriate value adjustment must be made.

26(5) The lower value arrived at under sub-paragraph (4) must not be increased in subsequent balance sheets unless such increase results from a new determination of market value arrived at in accordance with sub-paragraphs (2) and (3).

26(6) Where, on the date on which the accounts are drawn up, land and buildings have been sold or are to be sold within the short term, the value arrived at in accordance with sub-paragraphs (2) and (4) must be reduced by the actual or estimated realisation costs.

26(7) Where it is impossible to determine the market value of a land and buildings item, the value arrived at on the basis of the principle of purchase price or production cost is deemed to be its current value.

Application of the depreciation rules

27(1) Where–

  (a)   the value of any asset of a company is determined in accordance with paragraph 22 or 23, and

  (b)   in the case of a determination under paragraph 22, the asset falls to be included under assets item C.I, that value must be, or (as the case may require) must be the starting point for determining, the amount to be included in respect of that asset in the company's accounts, instead of its cost or any value previously so determined for that asset.

Paragraphs 36 to 41 and 43 apply accordingly in relation to any such asset with the substitution for any reference to its cost of a reference to the value most recently determined for that asset in accordance with paragraph 22 or 23 (as the case may be).

27(2) The amount of any provision for depreciation required in the case of any asset by paragraph 37 or 38 as it applies by virtue of sub-paragraph (1) is referred to below in this paragraph as the adjusted amount, and the amount of any provision which would be required by that paragraph in the case of that asset according to the historical cost accounting rules is referred to as the historical cost amount.

27(3) Where sub-paragraph (1) applies in the case of any asset the amount of any provision for depreciation in respect of that asset included in any item shown in the profit and loss account in respect of amounts written off assets of the description in question may be the historical cost amount instead of the adjusted amount, provided that the amount of any difference between the two is shown separately in the profit and loss account or in a note to the accounts.

Additional information to be provided

28(1) This paragraph applies where the amounts to be included in respect of assets covered by any items shown in a company's accounts have been determined in accordance with paragraph 22 or 23.

28(2) The items affected and the basis of valuation adopted in determining the amounts of the assets in question in the case of each such item must be disclosed in a note to the accounts.

28(3) The purchase price of investments valued in accordance with paragraph 22 must be disclosed in the notes to the accounts.

28(4) In the case of each balance sheet item valued in accordance with paragraph 23 either–

    (a)   the comparable amounts determined according to the historical cost accounting rules (without any provision for depreciation or diminution in value), or

    (b)   the differences between those amounts and the corresponding amounts actually shown in the balance sheet in respect of that item, must be shown separately in the balance sheet or in a note to the accounts.

28(5) In sub-paragraph (4), references in relation to any item to the comparable amounts determined as there mentioned are references to–

    (a)   the aggregate amount which would be required to be shown in respect of that item if the amounts to be included in respect of all the assets covered by that item were determined according to the historical cost accounting rules, and

    (b)   the aggregate amount of the cumulative provisions for depreciation or diminution in value which would be permitted or required in determining those amounts according to those rules.

Revaluation reserve

29(1) Subject to sub-paragraph (7), with respect to any determination of the value of an asset of a company in accordance with paragraph 22 or 23, the amount of any profit or loss arising from that determination (after allowing, where appropriate, for any provisions for depreciation or diminution in value made otherwise than by reference to the value so determined and any adjustments of any such provisions made in the light of that determination) must be credited or (as the case may be) debited to a separate reserve ("the revaluation reserve").

29(2) The amount of the revaluation reserve must be shown in the company's balance sheet under liabilities item A.III, but need not be shown under the name "revaluation reserve".

29(3) An amount may be transferred–

    (a)   from the revaluation reserve–

        (i)   to the profit and loss account, if the amount was previously charged to that account or represents realised profit, or

        (ii)   on capitalisation,

    (b)   to or from the revaluation reserve in respect of the taxation relating to any profit or loss credited or debited to the reserve.

The revaluation reserve must be reduced to the extent that the amounts transferred to it are no longer necessary for the purposes of the valuation method used.

29(4) In sub-paragraph (3)(a)(ii) **"capitalisation"**, in relation to an amount standing to the credit of the revaluation reserve, means applying it in wholly or partly paying up unissued shares in the company to be allotted to members of the company as fully or partly paid shares.

29(5) The revaluation reserve must not be reduced except as mentioned in this paragraph.

29(6) The treatment for taxation purposes of amounts credited or debited to the revaluation reserve must be disclosed in a note to the accounts.

29(7) This paragraph does not apply to the difference between the valuation of investments and their purchase price or previous valuation shown in the long-term business technical account or the non-technical account in accordance with note (9) on the profit and loss account format.

SECTION C – VALUATION AT FAIR VALUE

Inclusion of financial instruments at fair value

30(1) Subject to sub-paragraphs (2) to (5), financial instruments (including derivatives) may be included at fair value.

30(2) Sub-paragraph (1) does not apply to financial instruments that constitute liabilities unless–

    (a)   they are held as part of a trading portfolio,

    (b)   they are derivatives, or

    (c)   they are financial instruments falling within paragraph (4).

30(3) Except where they fall within paragraph (4), or fall to be included under assets item D (assets held to cover linked liabilities), sub-paragraph (1) does not apply to–

    (a)   financial instruments (other than derivatives) held to maturity,

    (b)   loans and receivables originated by the company and not held for trading purposes,

    (c)   interests in subsidiary undertakings, associated undertakings and joint ventures,

    (d)   equity instruments issued by the company,

    (e)   contracts for contingent consideration in a business combination, or

    (f)   other financial instruments with such special characteristics that the instruments, according to generally accepted accounting principles or practice, should be accounted for differently from other financial instruments.

30(4) Financial instruments which under international accounting standards may be included in accounts at fair value, may be so included, provided that the disclosures required by such accounting standards are made.

30(5) If the fair value of a financial instrument cannot be determined reliably in accordance with paragraph 31, sub-paragraph (1) does not apply to that financial instrument.

30(6)   In this paragraph–

"**associated undertaking**" has the meaning given by paragraph 19 of Schedule 6 to these Regulations; and

"**joint venture**" has the meaning given by paragraph 18 of that Schedule.

History – Para. 30(4) substituted by SI 2015/980, reg. 35(3)(a), with effect in relation to–
- (a)   financial years beginning on or after 1 January 2016, and
- (b)   a financial year of a company beginning on or after 1 January 2015, but before 1 January 2016, if the directors of the company so decide.

Former para. 30(4) read as follows:

"**30(4)**   Financial instruments that, under international accounting standards adopted by the European Commission on or before 5th September 2006 in accordance with the IAS Regulation, may be included in accounts at fair value, may be so included, provided that the disclosures required by such accounting standards are made."

Determination of fair value

31(1)   The fair value of a financial instrument is its value determined in accordance with this paragraph.

31(2)   If a reliable market can readily be identified for the financial instrument, its fair value is determined by reference to its market value.

31(3)   If a reliable market cannot readily be identified for the financial instrument but can be identified for its components or for a similar instrument, its fair value is determined by reference to the market value of its components or of the similar instrument.

31(4)   If neither sub-paragraph (2) nor (3) applies, the fair value of the financial instrument is a value resulting from generally accepted valuation models and techniques.

31(5)   Any valuation models and techniques used for the purposes of sub-paragraph (4) must ensure a reasonable approximation of the market value.

Hedged items

32   A company may include any assets and liabilities, or identified portions of such assets or liabilities, that qualify as hedged items under a fair value hedge accounting system at the amount required under that system.

Other assets that may be included at fair value

33(1)   This paragraph applies to–
- (a)   investment property, and
- (b)   living animals and plants.

33(2)   Such investment property and living animals and plants may be included at fair value provided that, as the case may be, all such investment property or living animals and plants are so included where their fair value can be reliably determined.

33(3)   In this paragraph, "**fair value**" means fair value determined in accordance with generally accepted accounting principles or practice.

History – Para. 33 substituted by SI 2015/980, reg. 35(3)(b), with effect in relation to–

    (a)   financial years beginning on or after 1 January 2016, and

    (b)   a financial year of a company beginning on or after 1 January 2015, but before 1 January 2016, if the directors of the company so decide.

Former para. 33 read as follows:

"**33(1)** This paragraph applies to–

    (a)   investment property, and

    (b)   living animals and plants, that, under international accounting standards, may be included in accounts at fair value.

33(2) Such investment property and such living animals and plants may be included at fair value, provided that all such investment property or, as the case may be, all such living animals and plants are so included where their fair value can reliably be determined.

33(3) In this paragraph, "**fair value**" means fair value determined in accordance with relevant international accounting standards."

Accounting for changes in value

34(1) This paragraph applies where a financial instrument is valued in accordance with paragraph 30 or 32 or an asset is valued in accordance with paragraph 33.

34(2) Notwithstanding paragraph 18 in this Part of this Schedule, and subject to sub-paragraphs (3) and (4), a change in the value of the financial instrument or of the investment property or living animal or plant must be included in the profit and loss account.

34(3) Where–

    (a)   the financial instrument accounted for is a hedging instrument under a hedge accounting system that allows some or all of the change in value not to be shown in the profit and loss account, or

    (b)   the change in value relates to an exchange difference arising on a monetary item that forms part of a company's net investment in a foreign entity, the amount of the change in value must be credited to or (as the case may be) debited from a separate reserve ("the fair value reserve").

34(4) Where the instrument accounted for–

    (a)   is an available for sale financial asset, and

    (b)   is not a derivative, the change in value may be credited to or (as the case may be) debited from the fair value reserve.

The fair value reserve

35(1) The fair value reserve must be adjusted to the extent that the amounts shown in it are no longer necessary for the purposes of paragraph 34(3) or (4).

35(2) The treatment for taxation purposes of amounts credited or debited to the fair value reserve must be disclosed in a note to the accounts.

SECTION D – HISTORICAL COST ACCOUNTING RULES

Valuation of assets

General rules

36(1) The rules in this Section are "the historical cost accounting rules".

36(2) Subject to any provision for depreciation or diminution in value made in accordance with paragraph 37 or 38, the amount to be included in respect of any asset in the balance sheet format is its cost.

37 In the case of any asset included under assets item B (intangible assets), C.I (land and buildings), F.I (tangible assets) or F.II (stocks) which has a limited useful economic life, the amount of–

    (a)   its cost, or

    (b)   where it is estimated that any such asset will have a residual value at the end of the period of its useful economic life, its cost less that estimated residual value, must be reduced by provisions for depreciation calculated to write off that amount systematically over the period of the asset's useful economic life.

38(1) This paragraph applies to any asset included under assets item B (intangible assets), C (investments), F.I (tangible assets) or F.IV (own shares).

38(2) Where an asset to which this paragraph applies has diminished in value, provisions for diminution in value may be made in respect of it and the amount to be included in respect of it may be reduced accordingly.

38(3) Provisions for diminution in value must be made in respect of any asset to which this paragraph applies if the reduction in its value is expected to be permanent (whether its useful economic life is limited or not), and the amount to be included in respect of it must be reduced accordingly.

38(4) Any provisions made under sub-paragraph (2) or (3) which are not shown in the profit and loss account must be disclosed (either separately or in aggregate) in a note to the accounts.

39(1) Where the reasons for which any provision was made in accordance with paragraph 38 have ceased to apply to any extent, that provision must be written back to the extent that it is no longer necessary.

39(1A) But provision made in accordance with paragraph 38(2) or (3) in respect of goodwill must not be written back to any extent.

39(2) Any amounts written back in accordance with sub-paragraph (1) which are not shown in the profit and loss account must be disclosed (either separately or in aggregate) in a note to the accounts.

History – Para. 39(1A) inserted by SI 2015/1672, reg. 4(6), with effect in relation to–
    (a)   financial years beginning on or after 1 January 2016, and
    (b)   a financial year of a company beginning on or after 1 January 2015 but before 1 January 2016, if the directors of the company have decided.

40(1) This paragraph applies to assets included under assets items E.I, II and III (debtors) and F.III (cash at bank and in hand) in the balance sheet.

40(2) If the net realisable value of an asset to which this paragraph applies is lower than its cost the amount to be included in respect of that asset is the net realisable value.

40(3) Where the reasons for which any provision for diminution in value was made in accordance with sub-paragraph (2) have ceased to apply to any extent, that provision must be written back to the extent that it is no longer necessary.

Intangible assets

41(1) Where this is in accordance with generally accepted accounting principles or practice, development costs may be included under assets item B (intangible assets) in the balance sheet format.

41(2) If any amount is included in a company's balance sheet in respect of development costs, the note on accounting policies (see paragraph 61 of this Schedule) must include the following information–

    (a)   the period over which the amount of those costs originally capitalised is being or is to be written off, and

    (b)   the reasons for capitalising the development costs in question.

History – Para. 41 and the heading preceding it substituted by SI 2015/980, reg. 35(4)(a), with effect in relation to–

    (a)   financial years beginning on or after 1 January 2016, and

    (b)   a financial year of a company beginning on or after 1 January 2015, but before 1 January 2016, if the directors of the company so decide.

Former para. 41 read as follows:

"Development costs

41(1) Notwithstanding that amounts representing "development costs" may be included under assets item B (intangible assets) in the balance sheet format, an amount may only be included in a company's balance sheet in respect of development costs in special circumstances.

41(2) If any amount is included in a company's balance sheet in respect of development costs the following information must be given in a note to the accounts–

    (a)   the period over which the amount of those costs originally capitalised is being or is to be written off, and

    (b)   the reasons for capitalising the development costs in question."

Goodwill

42(1) Intangible assets must be written off over the useful economic life of the intangible asset.

42(2) Where in exceptional cases the useful life of intangible assets cannot be reliably estimated, such assets must be written off over a period chosen by the directors of the company.

42(3) The period referred to in sub-paragraph (2) must not exceed ten years.

42(4) There must be disclosed in a note to the accounts the period referred to in sub-paragraph (2) and the reasons for choosing that period.

History – Para. 42 substituted by SI 2015/980, reg. 35(4)(a), with effect in relation to–

    (a)   financial years beginning on or after 1 January 2016, and

    (b)   a financial year of a company beginning on or after 1 January 2015, but before 1 January 2016, if the directors of the company so decide.

Former para. 42 read as follows:

"**42(1)** The application of paragraphs 36 to 39 in relation to goodwill (in any case where goodwill is treated as an asset) is subject to the following.

42(2) Subject to sub-paragraph (3), the amount of the consideration for any goodwill acquired by a company must be reduced by provisions for depreciation calculated to write off that amount systematically over a period chosen by the directors of the company.

42(3) The period chosen must not exceed the useful economic life of the goodwill in question.

42(4) In any case where any goodwill acquired by a company is included as an asset in the company's balance sheet, there must be disclosed in a note to the accounts–

    (a)   the period chosen for writing off the consideration for that goodwill, and

    (b)   the reasons for choosing that period."

Miscellaneous and supplementary provisions

Excess of money owed over value received as an asset item

43(1) Where the amount repayable on any debt owed by a company is greater than the value of the consideration received in the transaction giving rise to the debt, the amount of the difference may be treated as an asset.

43(2) Where any such amount is so treated–

    (a)   it must be written off by reasonable amounts each year and must be completely written off before repayment of the debt, and

    (b)   if the current amount is not shown as a separate item in the company's balance sheet, it must be disclosed in a note to the accounts.

Assets included at a fixed amount

44(1) Subject to sub-paragraph (2), assets which fall to be included under assets item F.I (tangible assets) in the balance sheet format may be included at a fixed quantity and value.

44(2) Sub-paragraph (1) applies to assets of a kind which are constantly being replaced where–

    (a)   their overall value is not material to assessing the company's state of affairs, and

    (b)   their quantity, value and composition are not subject to material variation.

Determination of cost

45(1) The cost of an asset that has been acquired by the company is to be determined by adding to the actual price paid any expenses incidental to its acquisition and then subtracting any incidental reductions in the cost of acquisition.

45(2) The cost of an asset constructed by the company is to be determined by adding to the purchase price of the raw materials and consumables used the amount of the costs incurred by the company which are directly attributable to the construction of that asset.

45(3) In addition, there may be included in the cost of an asset constructed by the company–

    (a)   a reasonable proportion of the costs incurred by the company which are only indirectly attributable to the construction of that asset, but only to the extent that they relate to the period of construction, and

    (b)   interest on capital borrowed to finance the construction of that asset, to the extent that it accrues in respect of the period of construction, provided, however, in a case within paragraph (b), that the inclusion of the interest in determining the cost of that asset and the amount of the interest so included is disclosed in a note to the accounts.

History – In para. 45(1), the words "and then subtracting any incidental reductions in the cost of acquisition" inserted by SI 2015/980, reg. 35(4)(b), with effect in relation to–

    (a)   financial years beginning on or after 1 January 2016, and

    (b)   a financial year of a company beginning on or after 1 January 2015, but before 1 January 2016, if the directors of the company so decide.

46(1) The cost of any assets which are fungible assets may be determined by the application of any of the methods mentioned in sub-paragraph (2) in relation to any such assets of the same class, provided that the method chosen is one which appears to the directors to be appropriate in the circumstances of the company.

46(2) Those methods are–

    (a)   the method known as "first in, first out" (FIFO),

    (b)   the method known as "last in, first out" (LIFO),

    (c)   a weighted average price, and

    (d)   any other method reflecting generally accepted best practice.

46(3) Where in the case of any company–

    (a)   the cost of assets falling to be included under any item shown in the company's balance sheet has been determined by the application of any method permitted by this paragraph, and

    (b)   the amount shown in respect of that item differs materially from the relevant alternative amount given below in this paragraph, the amount of that difference must be disclosed in a note to the accounts.

46(4) Subject to sub-paragraph (5), for the purposes of sub-paragraph (3)(b), the relevant alternative amount, in relation to any item shown in a company's balance sheet, is the amount which would have been shown in respect of that item if assets of any class included under that item at an amount determined by any method permitted by this paragraph had instead been included at their replacement cost as at the balance sheet date.

46(5) The relevant alternative amount may be determined by reference to the most recent actual purchase price before the balance sheet date of assets of any class included under the item in question instead of by reference to their replacement cost as at that date, but only if the former appears to the directors of the company to constitute the more appropriate standard of comparison in the case of assets of that class.

History – In para. 46(2)(d), the words "reflecting generally accepted best practice" substituted for the words "similar to any of the methods mentioned above" by SI 2015/980, reg. 35(4)(c), with effect in relation to–

    (a)   financial years beginning on or after 1 January 2016, and

    (b)   a financial year of a company beginning on or after 1 January 2015, but before 1 January 2016, if the directors of the company so decide.

Substitution of original amount where price or cost unknown

47(1)   This paragraph applies where–

(a)   there is no record of the purchase price of any asset acquired by a company or of any price, expenses or costs relevant for determining its cost in accordance with paragraph 45, or

(b)   any such record cannot be obtained without unreasonable expense or delay.

47(2)   In such a case, the cost of the asset must be taken, for the purposes of paragraphs 36 to 42, to be the value ascribed to it in the earliest available record of its value made on or after its acquisition by the company.

SECTION E – RULES FOR DETERMINING PROVISIONS

Preliminary

48   Provisions which are to be shown in a company's accounts are to be determined in accordance with this Section.

Technical provisions

49   The amount of technical provisions must at all times be sufficient to cover any liabilities arising out of insurance contracts as far as can reasonably be foreseen.

Provision for unearned premiums

50(1)   The provision for unearned premiums must in principle be computed separately for each insurance contract, save that statistical methods (and in particular proportional and flat rate methods) may be used where they may be expected to give approximately the same results as individual calculations.

50(2)   Where the pattern of risk varies over the life of a contract, this must be taken into account in the calculation methods.

Provision for unexpired risks

51   The provision for unexpired risks (as defined in paragraph 91) must be computed on the basis of claims and administrative expenses likely to arise after the end of the financial year from contracts concluded before that date, in so far as their estimated value exceeds the provision for unearned premiums and any premiums receivable under those contracts.

Long-term business provision

52(1)   The long-term business provision must in principle be computed separately for each long-term contract, save that statistical or mathematical methods may be used where they may be expected to give approximately the same results as individual calculations.

52(2) A summary of the principal assumptions in making the provision under sub-paragraph (1) must be given in the notes to the accounts.

52(3) The computation must be made annually by a Fellow of the Institute or Faculty of Actuaries on the basis of recognised actuarial methods, with due regard to the actuarial principles laid down in Directive 2002/83/EC of the European Parliament and of the Council of 5th November 2002 concerning life assurance.

Prospective amendments – In Sch. 3, para. 52(3), the words "Directive 2009/138/EC of the European Parliament and of the Council of 25 November 2009 on the taking-up and pursuit of the business of Insurance and Reinsurance (Solvency II)" substituted for the words "Directive 2002/83/EC of the European Parliament and of the Council of 5th November 2002 concerning life assurance" by SI 2015/575, Sch. 2, para. 26, with effect from 1 January 2016.

Provisions for claims outstanding

General business

53(1) A provision must in principle be computed separately for each claim on the basis of the costs still expected to arise, save that statistical methods may be used if they result in an adequate provision having regard to the nature of the risks.

53(2) This provision must also allow for claims incurred but not reported by the balance sheet date, the amount of the allowance being determined having regard to past experience as to the number and magnitude of claims reported after previous balance sheet dates.

53(3) All claims settlement costs (whether direct or indirect) must be included in the calculation of the provision.

53(4) Recoverable amounts arising out of subrogation or salvage must be estimated on a prudent basis and either deducted from the provision for claims outstanding (in which case if the amounts are material they must be shown in the notes to the accounts) or shown as assets.

53(5) In sub-paragraph (4), **"subrogation"** means the acquisition of the rights of policy holders with respect to third parties, and **"salvage"** means the acquisition of the legal ownership of insured property.

53(6) Where benefits resulting from a claim must be paid in the form of annuity, the amounts to be set aside for that purpose must be calculated by recognised actuarial methods, and paragraph 54 does not apply to such calculations.

53(7) Implicit discounting or deductions, whether resulting from the placing of a current value on a provision for an outstanding claim which is expected to be settled later at a higher figure or otherwise effected, is prohibited.

54(1) Explicit discounting or deductions to take account of investment income is permitted, subject to the following conditions–

   (a) the expected average interval between the date for the settlement of claims being discounted and the accounting date must be at least four years;

   (b) the discounting or deductions must be effected on a recognised prudential basis;

(c)   when calculating the total cost of settling claims, the company must take account of all factors that could cause increases in that cost;

(d)   the company must have adequate data at its disposal to construct a reliable model of the rate of claims settlements;

(e)   the rate of interest used for the calculation of present values must not exceed a rate prudently estimated to be earned by assets of the company which are appropriate in magnitude and nature to cover the provisions for claims being discounted during the period necessary for the payment of such claims, and must not exceed either–

    (i)   a rate justified by the performance of such assets over the preceding five years, or

    (ii)   a rate justified by the performance of such assets during the year preceding the balance sheet date.

54(2)   When discounting or effecting deductions, the company must, in the notes to the accounts, disclose–

(a)   the total amount of provisions before discounting or deductions,

(b)   the categories of claims which are discounted or from which deductions have been made,

(c)   for each category of claims, the methods used, in particular the rates used for the estimates referred to in sub-paragraph (1)(d) and (e), and the criteria adopted for estimating the period that will elapse before the claims are settled.

Long-term business

55   The amount of the provision for claims must be equal to the sums due to beneficiaries, plus the costs of settling claims.

Equalisation reserves

56   The amount of any equalisation reserve maintained in respect of general business by the company, in accordance with the rules made by the Financial Conduct Authority or the Prudential Regulation Authority under Part 10 of the Financial Services and Markets Act 2000, must be determined in accordance with such rules.

History – The words "made by the Financial Conduct Authority or the Prudential Regulation Authority" substituted for "in section 1.4 of the Prudential Sourcebook for Insurers made by the Financial Services Authority" by SI 2013/472, Sch. 2, para. 135(b), with effect from 1 April 2013.

Accounting on a non-annual basis

57(1)   Either of the methods described in paragraphs 58 and 59 may be applied where, because of the nature of the class or type of insurance in question, information about premiums receivable or claims payable (or both) for the underwriting years is insufficient when the accounts are drawn up for reliable estimates to be made.

57(2)   The use of either of the methods referred to in sub-paragraph (1) must be disclosed in the notes to the accounts together with the reasons for adopting it.

57(3) Where one of the methods referred to in sub-paragraph (1) is adopted, it must be applied systematically in successive years unless circumstances justify a change.

57(4) In the event of a change in the method applied, the effect on the assets, liabilities, financial position and profit or loss must be stated in the notes to the accounts.

57(5) For the purposes of this paragraph and paragraph 58, **"underwriting year"** means the financial year in which the insurance contracts in the class or type of insurance in question commenced.

58(1) The excess of the premiums written over the claims and expenses paid in respect of contracts commencing in the underwriting year shall form a technical provision included in the technical provision for claims outstanding shown in the balance sheet under liabilities item C.3.

58(2) The provision may also be computed on the basis of a given percentage of the premiums written where such a method is appropriate for the type of risk insured.

58(3) If necessary, the amount of this technical provision must be increased to make it sufficient to meet present and future obligations.

58(4) The technical provision constituted under this paragraph must be replaced by a provision for claims outstanding estimated in accordance with paragraph 53 as soon as sufficient information has been gathered and not later than the end of the third year following the underwriting year.

58(5) The length of time that elapses before a provision for claims outstanding is constituted in accordance with sub-paragraph (4) must be disclosed in the notes to the accounts.

59(1) The figures shown in the technical account or in certain items within it must relate to a year which wholly or partly precedes the financial year (but by no more than 12 months).

59(2) The amounts of the technical provisions shown in the accounts must if necessary be increased to make them sufficient to meet present and future obligations.

59(3) The length of time by which the earlier year to which the figures relate precedes the financial year and the magnitude of the transactions concerned must be disclosed in the notes to the accounts.

PART 3 – NOTES TO THE ACCOUNTS
PRELIMINARY

60(1) Any information required in the case of a company by the following provisions of this Part of this Schedule must be given by way of a note to the accounts.

60(2) These notes must be presented in the order in which, where relevant, the items to which they relate are presented in the balance sheet and in the profit and loss account.

History – Para. 60 substituted by SI 2015/980, reg. 36(2), with effect in relation to–
    (a)   financial years beginning on or after 1 January 2016, and
    (b)   a financial year of a company beginning on or after 1 January 2015, but before 1 January 2016, if the directors of the company so decide.

Former para. 60 read as follows:

"**60** Any information required in the case of any company by the following provisions of this Part of this Schedule must (if not given in the company's accounts) be given by way of a note to the accounts."

General

Disclosure of accounting policies

61 The accounting policies adopted by the company in determining the amounts to be included in respect of items shown in the balance sheet and in determining the profit or loss of the company must be stated (including such policies with respect to the depreciation and diminution in value of assets).

62 It must be stated whether the accounts have been prepared in accordance with applicable accounting standards and particulars of any material departure from those standards and the reasons for it must be given.

Sums denominated in foreign currencies

63 Where any sums originally denominated in foreign currencies have been brought into account under any items shown in the balance sheet or profit and loss account format, the basis on which those sums have been translated into sterling (or the currency in which the accounts are drawn up) must be stated.

Reserves and dividends

64 There must be stated–
    (a)   any amount set aside or proposed to be set aside to, or withdrawn or proposed to be withdrawn from, reserves,
    (b)   the aggregate amount of dividends paid in the financial year (other than those for which a liability existed at the immediately preceding balance sheet date),
    (c)   the aggregate amount of dividends that the company is liable to pay at the balance sheet date, and
    (d)   the aggregate amount of dividends that are proposed before the date of approval of the accounts, and not otherwise disclosed under sub-paragraph (b) or (c).

Information supplementing the balance sheet

Share capital and debentures

65(1) Where shares of more than one class have been allotted, the number and aggregate nominal value of shares of each class allotted must be given.

65(2) In the case of any part of the allotted share capital that consists of redeemable shares, the following information must be given–

    (a)   the earliest and latest dates on which the company has power to redeem those shares,

    (b)   whether those shares must be redeemed in any event or are liable to be redeemed at the option of the company or of the shareholder, and

    (c)   whether any (and, if so, what) premium is payable on redemption.

66 If the company has allotted any shares during the financial year, the following information must be given–

    (a)   the classes of shares allotted, and

    (b)   as respects each class of shares, the number allotted, their aggregate nominal value and the consideration received by the company for the allotment.

67(1) With respect to any contingent right to the allotment of shares in the company the following particulars must be given–

    (a)   the number, description and amount of the shares in relation to which the right is exercisable,

    (b)   the period during which it is exercisable, and

    (c)   the price to be paid for the shares allotted.

67(2) In sub-paragraph (1) **"contingent right to the allotment of shares"** means any option to subscribe for shares and any other right to require the allotment of shares to any person whether arising on the conversion into shares of securities of any other description or otherwise.

68(1) If the company has issued any debentures during the financial year to which the accounts relate, the following information must be given–

    (a)   the classes of debentures issued, and

    (b)   as respects each class of debentures, the amount issued and the consideration received by the company for the issue.

68(2) Where any of the company's debentures are held by a nominee of or trustee for the company, the nominal amount of the debentures and the amount at which they are stated in the accounting records kept by the company in accordance with section 386 of the 2006 Act (duty to keep accounting records) must be stated.

Assets

69(1) In respect of any assets of the company included in assets items B (intangible assets), C.I (land and buildings) and C.II (investments in group undertakings and participating interests) in the company's balance sheet the following information must be given by reference to each such item–

    (a)   the appropriate amounts in respect of those assets included in the item as at the date of the beginning of the financial year and as at the balance sheet date respectively,

    (b)   the effect on any amount included in assets item B in respect of those assets of–

        (i)   any determination during that year of the value to be ascribed to any of those assets in accordance with paragraph 23,

        (ii)   acquisitions during that year of any assets,

(iii) disposals during that year of any assets, and

(iv) any transfers of assets of the company to and from the item during that year.

69(2) The reference in sub-paragraph (1)(a) to the appropriate amounts in respect of any assets (included in an assets item) as at any date there mentioned is a reference to amounts representing the aggregate amounts determined, as at that date, in respect of assets falling to be included under the item on either of the following bases–

(a) on the basis of cost (determined in accordance with paragraphs 45 and 46), or

(b) on any basis permitted by paragraph 22 or 23, (leaving out of account in either case any provisions for depreciation or diminution in value).

69(3) In addition, in respect of any assets of the company included in any assets item in the company's balance sheet, there must be stated (by reference to each such item)–

(a) the cumulative amount of provisions for depreciation or diminution in value of those assets included under the item as at each date mentioned in sub-paragraph (1)(a),

(b) the amount of any such provisions made in respect of the financial year,

(c) the amount of any adjustments made in respect of any such provisions during that year in consequence of the disposal of any of those assets, and

(d) the amount of any other adjustments made in respect of any such provisions during that year.

70 Where any assets of the company (other than listed investments) are included under any item shown in the company's balance sheet at an amount determined on any basis mentioned in paragraph 22 or 23, the following information must be given–

(a) the years (so far as they are known to the directors) in which the assets were severally valued and the several values, and

(b) in the case of assets that have been valued during the financial year, the names of the persons who valued them or particulars of their qualifications for doing so and (whichever is stated) the bases of valuation used by them.

71 In relation to any amount which is included under assets item C.I (land and buildings) there must be stated–

(a) how much of that amount is ascribable to land of freehold tenure and how much to land of leasehold tenure, and

(b) how much of the amount ascribable to land of leasehold tenure is ascribable to land held on long lease and how much to land held on short lease.

Investments

72 In respect of the amount of each item which is shown in the company's balance sheet under assets item C (investments) there must be stated how much of that amount is ascribable to listed investments.

Information about fair value of assets and liabilities

73(1) This paragraph applies where financial instruments or other assets have been valued in accordance with, as appropriate, paragraph 30, 32 or 33.

73(2)   There must be stated–

    (a)   the significant assumptions underlying the valuation models and techniques used to determine the fair value of the financial instruments or other assets,

    (b)   in the case of financial instruments, their purchase price, the items affected and the basis of valuation,

    (c)   for each category of financial instrument or other asset, the fair value of the assets in that category and the changes in value–

        (i)   included directly in the profit and loss account, or

        (ii)   credited to or (as the case may be) debited from the fair value reserve, in respect of those assets, and

    (c)   for each class of derivatives, the extent and nature of the instruments, including significant terms and conditions that may affect the amount, timing and certainty of future cash flows.

73(3)   Where any amount is transferred to or from the fair value reserve during the financial year, there must be stated in tabular form–

    (a)   the amount of the reserve as at the date of the beginning of the financial year and as at the balance sheet date respectively,

    (b)   the amount transferred to or from the reserve during the year, and

    (c)   the source and application respectively of the amounts so transferred.

History – Para. 73 substituted by SI 2015/980, reg. 36(3), with effect in relation to–

    (a)   financial years beginning on or after 1 January 2016, and

    (b)   a financial year of a company beginning on or after 1 January 2015, but before 1 January 2016, if the directors of the company so decide.

Former para. 73 read as follows:

"**73(1)**   This paragraph applies where financial instruments have been valued in accordance with paragraph 30 or 32.

73(2)   The items affected and the basis of valuation adopted in determining the amounts of the financial instruments must be disclosed.

73(3)   The purchase price of the financial instruments must be disclosed.

73(4)   There must be stated–

    (a)   the significant assumptions underlying the valuation models and techniques used, where the fair value of the instruments has been determined in accordance with paragraph 31(4),

    (b)   for each category of financial instrument, the fair value of the instruments in that category and the changes in value–

        (i)   included in the profit and loss account, or

        (ii)   credited to or (as the case may be) debited from the fair value reserve, in respect of those instruments, and

    (c)   for each class of derivatives, the extent and nature of the instruments, including significant terms and conditions that may affect the amount, timing and certainty of future cash flows.

73(5)   Where any amount is transferred to or from the fair value reserve during the financial year, there must be stated in tabular form–

    (a)   the amount of the reserve as at the date of the beginning of the financial year and as at the balance sheet date respectively,

    (b)   the amount transferred to or from the reserve during that year, and

    (c)   the source and application respectively of the amounts so transferred."

74   Where the company has derivatives that it has not included at fair value, there must be stated for each class of such derivatives–

(a)   the fair value of the derivatives in that class, if such a value can be determined in accordance with paragraph 31, and

(b)   the extent and nature of the derivatives.

75(1)   This paragraph applies if–

(a)   the company has financial fixed assets that could be included at fair value by virtue of paragraph 30,

(b)   the amount at which those assets are included under any item in the company's accounts is in excess of their fair value, and

(c)   the company has not made provision for diminution in value of those assets in accordance with paragraph 38(2) of this Schedule.

75(2)   There must be stated–

(a)   the amount at which either the individual assets or appropriate groupings of those individual assets are included in the company's accounts,

(b)   the fair value of those assets or groupings, and

(c)   the reasons for not making a provision for diminution in value of those assets, including the nature of the evidence that provides the basis for the belief that the amount at which they are stated in the accounts will be recovered.

Information where investment property and living animals and plants included at fair value

76(1)   This paragraph applies where the amounts to be included in a company's accounts in respect of investment property or living animals and plants have been determined in accordance with paragraph 33.

76(2)   The balance sheet items affected and the basis of valuation adopted in determining the amounts of the assets in question in the case of each such item must be disclosed in a note to the accounts.

76(3)   In the case of investment property, for each balance sheet item affected there must be shown, either separately in the balance sheet or in a note to the accounts–

(a)   the comparable amounts determined according to the historical cost accounting rules, or

(b)   the differences between those amounts and the corresponding amounts actually shown in the balance sheet in respect of that item.

76(4)   In sub-paragraph (3), references in relation to any item to the comparable amounts determined in accordance with that sub-paragraph are to–

(a)   the aggregate amount which would be required to be shown in respect of that item if the amounts to be included in respect of all the assets covered by that item were determined according to the historical cost accounting rules, and

(b)   the aggregate amount of the cumulative provisions for depreciation or diminution in value which would be permitted or required in determining those amounts according to those rules.

Reserves and provisions

77(1) This paragraph applies where any amount is transferred–

(a)   to or from any reserves,

(b)   to any provisions for other risks, or

(c)   from any provisions for other risks otherwise than for the purpose for which the provision was established, and the reserves or provisions are or would but for paragraph 3(1) be shown as separate items in the company's balance sheet.

77(2) The following information must be given in respect of the aggregate of reserves or provisions included in the same item–

(a)   the amount of the reserves or provisions as at the date of the beginning of the financial year and as at the balance sheet date respectively,

(b)   any amounts transferred to or from the reserves or provisions during that year, and

(c)   the source and application respectively of any amounts so transferred.

77(3) Particulars must be given of each provision included in liabilities item E.3 (other provisions) in the company's balance sheet in any case where the amount of that provision is material.

Provision for taxation

78   The amount of any provision for deferred taxation must be stated separately from the amount of any provision for other taxation.

Details of indebtedness

79(1) In respect of each item shown under "creditors" in the company's balance sheet there must be stated the aggregate of the following amounts–

(a)   the amount of any debts included under that item which are payable or repayable otherwise than by instalments and fall due for payment or repayment after the end of the period of five years beginning with the day next following the end of the financial year, and

(b)   in the case of any debts so included which are payable or repayable by instalments, the amount of any instalments which fall due for payment after the end of that period.

79(2) Subject to sub-paragraph (3), in relation to each debt falling to be taken into account under sub-paragraph (1), the terms of payment or repayment and the rate of any interest payable on the debt must be stated.

79(3) If the number of debts is such that, in the opinion of the directors, compliance with subparagraph (2) would result in a statement of excessive length, it is sufficient to give a general indication of the terms of payment or repayment and the rates of any interest payable on the debts.

79(4) In respect of each item shown under "creditors" in the company's balance sheet there must be stated–

(a) the aggregate amount of any debts included under that item in respect of which any security has been given by the company, and

(b) an indication of the nature of the securities so given.

79(5) References above in this paragraph to an item shown under "creditors" in the company's balance sheet include references, where amounts falling due to creditors within one year and after more than one year are distinguished in the balance sheet–

(a) in a case within sub-paragraph (1), to an item shown under the latter of those categories, and

(b) in a case within sub-paragraph (4), to an item shown under either of those categories. References to items shown under "creditors" include references to items which would but for paragraph 3(1)(b) be shown under that heading.

80 If any fixed cumulative dividends on the company's shares are in arrear, there must be stated–

(a) the amount of the arrears, and

(b) the period for which the dividends or, if there is more than one class, each class of them are in arrear.

Guarantees and other financial commitments

81(1) Particulars must be given of any charge on the assets of the company to secure the liabilities of any other person including the amount secured.

81(2) Particulars and the total amount of any financial commitments, guarantees and contingencies (excluding those which arise out of insurance contracts) that are not included in the balance sheet must be disclosed.

81(3) An indication of the nature and form of any valuable security given by the company in respect of commitments, guarantees and contingencies within sub-paragraph (2) must be given.

81(4) The total amount of any commitments within sub-paragraph (2) concerning pensions must be separately disclosed.

81(5) Particulars must be given of pension commitments which are included in the balance sheet.

81(6) Where any commitment within sub-paragraph (4) or (5) relates wholly or partly to pensions payable to past directors of the company separate particulars must be given of that commitment.

81(7) The total amount of any commitments, guarantees and contingencies within sub-paragraph (2) which are undertaken on behalf of or for the benefit of–

(a) any parent undertaking or fellow subsidiary undertaking of the company,

(b) any subsidiary undertaking of the company, or

(c) any undertaking in which the company has a participating interest

must be separately stated and those within each of paragraphs (a), (b) and (c) must also be stated separately from those within any other of those paragraphs.

History – Para. 81 substituted by SI 2015/980, reg. 36(4), with effect in relation to–

    (a)   financial years beginning on or after 1 January 2016, and

    (b)   a financial year of a company beginning on or after 1 January 2015, but before 1 January 2016, if the directors of the company so decide.

Former para. 81 read as follows:

"**81(1)** Particulars must be given of any charge on the assets of the company to secure the liabilities of any other person, including, where practicable, the amount secured.

81(2) The following information must be given with respect to any other contingent liability not provided for (other than a contingent liability arising out of an insurance contract)–

    (a)   the amount or estimated amount of that liability,

    (b)   its legal nature, and

    (c)   whether any valuable security has been provided by the company in connection with that liability and if so, what.

81(3) There must be stated, where practicable, the aggregate amount or estimated amount of contracts for capital expenditure, so far as not provided for.

81(4) Particulars must be given of–

    (a)   any pension commitments included under any provision shown in the company's balance sheet, and

    (b)   any such commitments for which no provision has been made, and where any such commitment relates wholly or partly to pensions payable to past directors of the company separate particulars must be given of that commitment so far as it relates to such pensions.

81(5) Particulars must also be given of any other financial commitments, other than commitments arising out of insurance contracts, that–

    (a)   have not been provided for, and

    (b)   are relevant to assessing the company's state of affairs.

81(6) Commitments within any of the preceding sub-paragraphs undertaken on behalf of or for the benefit of–

    (a)   any parent undertaking or fellow subsidiary undertaking, or

    (b)   any subsidiary undertaking of the company, must be stated separately from the other commitments within that sub-paragraph, and commitments within paragraph

    (a)   must also be stated separately from those within paragraph (b)."

Miscellaneous matters

82(1) Particulars must be given of any case where the cost of any asset is for the first time determined under paragraph 47.

82(2) Where any outstanding loans made under the authority of section 682(2)(b)), (c) or (d) of the 2006 Act (various cases of financial assistance by a company for purchase of its own shares) are included under any item shown in the company's balance sheet, the aggregate amount of those loans must be disclosed for each item in question.

Information supplementing the profit and loss account

Separate statement of certain items of income and expenditure

83(1) Subject to sub-paragraph (2), there must be stated the amount of the interest on or any similar charges in respect of–

    (a)   bank loans and overdrafts, and

    (b)   loans of any other kind made to the company.

83(2) Sub-paragraph (1) does not apply to interest or charges on loans to the company from group undertakings, but, with that exception, it applies to interest or charges on all loans, whether made on the security of debentures or not.

Particulars of tax

84(1) Particulars must be given of any special circumstances which affect liability in respect of taxation of profits, income or capital gains for the financial year or liability in respect of taxation of profits, income or capital gains for succeeding financial years.

84(2) The following amounts must be stated–

    (a)   the amount of the charge for United Kingdom corporation tax,

    (b)   if that amount would have been greater but for relief from double taxation, the amount which it would have been but for such relief,

    (c)   the amount of the charge for United Kingdom income tax, and

    (d)   the amount of the charge for taxation imposed outside the United Kingdom of profits, income and (so far as charged to revenue) capital gains.

Those amounts must be stated separately in respect of each of the amounts which is shown under the following items in the profit and loss account, that is to say item III.9 (tax on profit or loss on ordinary activities) and item III.14 (tax on extraordinary profit or loss).

Particulars of business

85(1) As regards general business a company must disclose–

    (a)   gross premiums written,

    (b)   gross premiums earned,

    (c)   gross claims incurred,

    (d)   gross operating expenses, and

    (e)   the reinsurance balance.

85(2) The amounts required to be disclosed by sub-paragraph (1) must be broken down between direct insurance and reinsurance acceptances, if reinsurance acceptances amount to 10 per cent or more of gross premiums written.

85(3) Subject to sub-paragraph (4), the amounts required to be disclosed by sub-paragraphs (1) and (2) with respect to direct insurance must be further broken down into the following groups of classes–

    (a)   accident and health,

    (b)   motor (third party liability),

    (c)   motor (other classes),

    (d)   marine, aviation and transport,

    (e)   fire and other damage to property,

    (f)   third-party liability,

    (g)   credit and suretyship,

    (h)   legal expenses,

    (i)   assistance, and

    (j)   miscellaneous, where the amount of the gross premiums written in direct insurance for each such group exceeds 10 million Euros.

85(4) The company must in any event disclose the amounts relating to the three largest groups of classes in its business.

86(1) As regards long-term business, the company must disclose–

    (a)   gross premiums written, and

    (b)   the reinsurance balance.

86(2) Subject to sub-paragraph (3)–

    (a)   gross premiums written must be broken down between those written by way of direct insurance and those written by way of reinsurance, and

    (b)   gross premiums written by way of direct insurance must be broken down–

        (i)   between individual premiums and premiums under group contracts,

        (ii)   between periodic premiums and single premiums, and

        (iii)   between premiums from non-participating contracts, premiums from participating contracts and premiums from contracts where the investment risk is borne by policyholders.

86(3) Disclosure of any amount referred to in sub-paragraph (2)(a) or (2)(b)(i), (ii) or (iii) is not required if it does not exceed 10 per cent of the gross premiums written or (as the case may be) of the gross premiums written by way of direct insurance.

87(1) Subject to sub-paragraph (2), there must be disclosed as regards both general and long-term business the total gross direct insurance premiums resulting from contracts concluded by the company–

    (a)   in the member State of its head office,

    (b)   in the other member States, and

    (c)   in other countries.

87(2) Disclosure of any amount referred to in sub-paragraph (1) is not required if it does not exceed 5 per cent of total gross premiums.

Commissions

88 There must be disclosed the total amount of commissions for direct insurance business accounted for in the financial year, including acquisition, renewal, collection and portfolio management commissions.

Miscellaneous matters

89(1) Where any amount relating to any preceding financial year is included in any item in the profit and loss account, the effect must be stated.

89(2) The amount, nature and effect of any individual items of income or expenditure which are of exceptional size or incidence must be stated.

History – Para. 89(2) substituted for para. 89(2) and (3) by SI 2015/980, reg. 36(5), with effect in relation to–

    (a)   financial years beginning on or after 1 January 2016, and

    (b)   a financial year of a company beginning on or after 1 January 2015, but before 1 January 2016, if the directors of the company so decide.

Related party transactions

90(1) Particulars may be given of transactions which the company has entered into with related parties, and must be given if such transactions are material and have not been concluded under normal market conditions.

90(2) The particulars of transactions required to be disclosed by sub-paragraph (1) must include–

    (a)   the amount of such transactions,

    (b)   the nature of the related party relationship, and

    (c)   other information about the transactions necessary for an understanding of the financial position of the company.

90(3) Information about individual transactions may be aggregated according to their nature, except where separate information is necessary for an understanding of the effects of related party transactions on the financial position of the company.

90(4) Particulars need not be given of transactions entered into between two or more members of a group, provided that any subsidiary undertaking which is a party to the transaction is whollyowned by such a member.

90(5) In this paragraph, **"related party"** has the same meaning as in international accounting standards.

Post balance sheet events

90A The nature and financial effect of material events arising after the balance sheet date which are not reflected in the profit and loss account of balance sheet must be stated.

History – Para. 90A and the heading preceding it inserted by SI 2015/980, reg. 36(6), with effect in relation to–

    (a)   financial years beginning on or after 1 January 2016, and

    (b)   a financial year of a company beginning on or after 1 January 2015, but before 1 January 2016, if the directors of the company so decide.

Appropriations

90B Particulars must be given of the proposed appropriation of profit or treatment of loss or, where applicable, particulars of the actual appropriation of the profits or treatment of the losses.

History – Para. 90B and the heading preceding it inserted by SI 2015/980, reg. 36(6), with effect in relation to–

    (a)   financial years beginning on or after 1 January 2016, and

    (b)   a financial year of a company beginning on or after 1 January 2015, but before 1 January 2016, if the directors of the company so decide.

PART 4 – INTERPRETATION OF THIS SCHEDULE

Definitions for this schedule

91   The following definitions apply for the purposes of this Schedule and its interpretation–

"**general business**" means business which consists of effecting or carrying out contracts of general insurance;

"**long-term business**" means business which consists of effecting or carrying out contracts of long-term insurance;

"**long-term fund**" means the fund or funds maintained by a company in respect of its long-term business in accordance with rules made by the Financial Conduct Authority or the Prudential Regulation Authority under Part 10 of the Financial Services and Markets Act 2000;

"**policyholder**" has the meaning given by article 3 of the Financial Services and Markets Act 2000 (Meaning of "Policy" and "Policyholder") Order 2001;

"**provision for unexpired risks**" means the amount set aside in addition to unearned premiums in respect of risks to be borne by the company after the end of the financial year, in order to provide for all claims and expenses in connection with insurance contracts in force in excess of the related unearned premiums and any premiums receivable on those contracts.

History – In the definition of "long-term fund", "rules made by the Financial Conduct Authority or the Prudential Regulation Authority" substituted for "rule 1.5.22 in the Prudential Sourcebook for Insurers made by the Financial Services Authority" by SI 2013/472, Sch. 2, para. 135(c), with effect from 1 April 2013.

SCHEDULE 4   Regulation 7

INFORMATION ON RELATED UNDERTAKINGS REQUIRED WHETHER PREPARING COMPANIES ACT OR IAS ACCOUNTS

PART 1 – PROVISIONS APPLYING TO ALL COMPANIES

Subsidiary undertakings

1(1)   The following information must be given where at the end of the financial year the company has subsidiary undertakings.

1(2)   The name of each subsidiary undertaking must be stated.

1(3)   There must be stated with respect to each subsidiary undertaking–
  (a)   the address of the undertaking's registered office (whether in or outside the United Kingdom),
  (b)   if it is unincorporated, the address of its principal place of business.

History – Para. 1(3)(a) substituted by SI 2015/980, reg. 37(2), with effect in relation to–
    (a)   financial years beginning on or after 1 January 2016, and
    (b)   a financial year of a company beginning on or after 1 January 2015, but before
        1 January 2016, if the directors of the company so decide.

Financial information about subsidiary undertakings

2(1) There must be disclosed with respect to each subsidiary undertaking not included in consolidated accounts by the company–

    (a)   the aggregate amount of its capital and reserves as at the end of its relevant financial year, and

    (b)   its profit or loss for that year.

2(2) That information need not be given if the company is exempt by virtue of section 400 or 401 of the 2006 Act from the requirement to prepare group accounts (parent company included in accounts of larger group).

2(3) That information need not be given if the company's investment in the subsidiary undertaking is included in the company's accounts by way of the equity method of valuation.

2(4) That information need not be given if–

    (a)   the subsidiary undertaking is not required by any provision of the 2006 Act to deliver a copy of its balance sheet for its relevant financial year and does not otherwise publish that balance sheet in the United Kingdom or elsewhere, and

    (b)   the company's holding is less than 50% of the nominal value of the shares in the undertaking.

2(5) Information otherwise required by this paragraph need not be given if it is not material.

2(6) For the purposes of this paragraph the **"relevant financial year"** of a subsidiary undertaking is–

    (a)   if its financial year ends with that of the company, that year, and

    (b)   if not, its financial year ending last before the end of the company's financial year.

Shares and debentures of company held by subsidiary undertakings

3(1) The number, description and amount of the shares in the company held by or on behalf of its subsidiary undertakings must be disclosed.

3(2) Sub-paragraph (1) does not apply in relation to shares in the case of which the subsidiary undertaking is concerned as personal representative or, subject as follows, as trustee.

3(3) The exception for shares in relation to which the subsidiary undertaking is concerned as trustee does not apply if the company, or any of its subsidiary undertakings, is beneficially interested under the trust, otherwise than by way of security only for the purposes of a transaction entered into by it in the ordinary course of a business which includes the lending of money.

3(4)   Part 5 of this Schedule has effect for the interpretation of the reference in sub-paragraph (3) to a beneficial interest under a trust.

Significant holdings in undertakings other than subsidiary undertakings

4(1)   The information required by paragraphs 5 and 6 must be given where at the end of the financial year the company has a significant holding in an undertaking which is not a subsidiary undertaking of the company, and which does not fall within paragraph 18 (joint ventures) or 19 (associated undertakings).

4(2)   A holding is significant for this purpose if–

    (a)   it amounts to 20% or more of the nominal value of any class of shares in the undertaking, or

    (b)   the amount of the holding (as stated or included in the company's individual accounts) exceeds one-fifth of the amount (as so stated) of the company's assets.

5(1)   The name of the undertaking must be stated.

5(2)   There must be stated–

    (a)   the address of the undertaking's registered office (whether in or outside the United Kingdom),

    (b)   if it is unincorporated, the address of its principal place of business.

5(3)   There must also be stated–

    (a)   the identity of each class of shares in the undertaking held by the company, and

    (b)   the proportion of the nominal value of the shares of that class represented by those shares.

History – Para. 5(2)(a) substituted by SI 2015/980, reg. 37(3), with effect in relation to–

    (a)   financial years beginning on or after 1 January 2016, and

    (b)   a financial year of a company beginning on or after 1 January 2015, but before 1 January 2016, if the directors of the company so decide.

6(1)   Subject to paragraph 14, there must also be stated–

    (a)   the aggregate amount of the capital and reserves of the undertaking as at the end of its relevant financial year, and

    (b)   its profit or loss for that year.

6(2)   That information need not be given in respect of an undertaking if–

    (a)   the undertaking is not required by any provision of the 2006 Act to deliver a copy of its balance sheet for its relevant financial year and does not otherwise publish that balance sheet in the United Kingdom or elsewhere, and

    (b)   the company's holding is less than 50% of the nominal value of the shares in the undertaking.

6(3)   Information otherwise required by this paragraph need not be given if it is not material.

6(4)   For the purposes of this paragraph the **"relevant financial year"** of an undertaking is–

(a)   if its financial year ends with that of the company, that year, and
(b)   if not, its financial year ending last before the end of the company's financial year.

Membership of certain undertakings

7(1) The information required by this paragraph must be given where at the end of the financial year the company is a member of an undertaking having unlimited liability.

7(2) There must be stated–

(a)   the name and legal form of the undertaking, and
(b)   the address of the undertaking's registered office (whether in or outside the United Kingdom) or, if it does not have such an office, its head office (whether in or outside the United Kingdom).

7(3) Where the undertaking is a qualifying partnership there must also be stated either–

(a)   that a copy of the latest accounts of the undertaking has been or is to be appended to the copy of the company's accounts sent to the registrar under section 444 of the 2006 Act, or
(b)   the name of at least one body corporate (which may be the company) in whose group accounts the undertaking has been or is to be dealt with on a consolidated basis.

7(4) Information otherwise required by sub-paragraph (2) need not be given if it is not material.

7(5) Information otherwise required by sub-paragraph (3)(b) need not be given if the notes to the company's accounts disclose that advantage has been taken of the exemption conferred by regulation 7 of the Partnerships (Accounts) Regulations 2008.

7(6) [Omitted by SI 2015/980, reg. 37(4)(b).]

7(7) In this paragraph–

"dealt with on a consolidated basis" and **"qualifying partnership"** have the same meanings as in the Partnerships (Accounts) Regulations 2008;

7(8) [Omitted by SI 2015/980, reg. 37(4)(d).]

7(9) [Omitted by SI 2015/980, reg. 37(4)(e).]

7(10) [Omitted by SI 2015/980, reg. 37(4)(f).]

History – In sub-para. (5), "Partnerships (Accounts) Regulations 2008" substituted for "Partnerships and Unlimited Companies (Accounts) Regulations 1993" by SI 2008/569, reg. 17(2), with effect from 6 April 2008.

Sub-paragraph (6) substituted and sub-para. (7)–(10) inserted by SI 2013/2005, reg. 6, with effect from 1 September 2013 applying in relation to a financial year of a company beginning on or after 1 October 2013.

This version of para. 7 applies to financial years beginning on or after 1 October 2013. The version applying to financial years beginning before 1 October 2013 read as follows:

"**7(1)**   The information required by this paragraph must be given where at the end of the financial year the company is a member of a qualifying undertaking.

7(2)   There must be stated–

(a)   the name and legal form of the undertaking, and

(b)   the address of the undertaking's registered office (whether in or outside the United (Kingdom) or, if it does not have such an office, its head office (whether in or outside the United Kingdom).

7(3)   Where the undertaking is a qualifying partnership there must also be stated either–

(a)   that a copy of the latest accounts of the undertaking has been or is to be appended to the copy of the company's accounts sent to the registrar under section 444 of the 2006 Act, or

(b)   the name of at least one body corporate (which may be the company) in whose group accounts the undertaking has been or is to be dealt with on a consolidated basis.

7(4)   Information otherwise required by sub-paragraph (2) need not be given if it is not material.

7(5)   Information otherwise required by sub-paragraph (3)(b) need not be given if the notes to the company's accounts disclose that advantage has been taken of the exemption conferred by regulation 7 of the Partnerships (Accounts) Regulations 2008.

7(6)   In this paragraph–

"dealt with on a consolidated basis", **"member"** and **"qualifying partnership"** have the same meanings as in the Partnerships (Accounts) Regulations 2008;

"qualifying undertaking" means–

(a)   a qualifying partnership, or

(b)   an unlimited company each of whose members is–

(i)   a limited company,

(ii)   another unlimited company each of whose members is a limited company, or

(iii)   a Scottish partnership each of whose members is a limited company, and references in this paragraph to a limited company, another unlimited company or a Scottish partnership include a comparable undertaking incorporated in or formed under the law of a country or territory outside the United Kingdom."

In para. 7(1), the words "an undertaking having unlimited liability" substituted for the words "a qualifying undertaking" by SI 2015/980, reg. 37(4)(a), with effect in relation to–

(a)   financial years beginning on or after 1 January 2016, and

(b)   a financial year of a company beginning on or after 1 January 2015, but before 1 January 2016, if the directors of the company so decide.

Para. 7(6) omitted by SI 2015/980, reg. 37(4)(b), with effect in relation to–

(a)   financial years beginning on or after 1 January 2016, and

(b)   a financial year of a company beginning on or after 1 January 2015, but before 1 January 2016, if the directors of the company so decide.

Former para. 7(6) read as follows:

"**7(6)**   In sub-paragraph (1) **"member"**, in relation to a qualifying undertaking which is a qualifying partnership, has the same meaning as in the Partnerships (Accounts) Regulations 2008."

In para. 7(7), the definition of "qualifying undertaking" omitted by SI 2015/980, reg. 37(4)(c), with effect in relation to–

(a)   financial years beginning on or after 1 January 2016, and

(b)   a financial year of a company beginning on or after 1 January 2015, but before 1 January 2016, if the directors of the company so decide.

Para. 7(8)–(10) omitted by SI 2015/980, reg. 37(4)(d)–(f), with effect in relation to–

(a)   financial years beginning on or after 1 January 2016, and

(b)   a financial year of a company beginning on or after 1 January 2015, but before 1 January 2016, if the directors of the company so decide.

Former para. 7(8)–(10) read as follows:

"**7(8)**   In sub-paragraph (7) the references to a limited company, another unlimited company, a Scottish partnership which is not a limited partnership or a Scottish partnership which is a limited partnership include a comparable undertaking incorporated in or formed under the law of a country or territory outside the United Kingdom.

7(9)   In sub-paragraph (7) **"general partner"** means–

(a)   in relation to a Scottish partnership which is a limited partnership, a person who is a general partner within the meaning of the Limited Partnerships Act 1907, and

(b)   in relation to an undertaking incorporated in or formed under the law of any country or territory outside the United Kingdom and which is comparable to a Scottish partnership which is a limited partnership, a person comparable to such a general partner.

7(10)   In sub-paragraphs (7), (8) and (9) **"limited partnership"** means a partnership registered under the Limited Partnerships Act 1907."

Parent undertaking drawing up accounts for larger group

8(1)   Where the company is a subsidiary undertaking, the following information must be given with respect to the parent undertaking of–

(a)   the largest group of undertakings for which group accounts are drawn up and of which the company is a member, and

(b)   the smallest such group of undertakings.

8(2)   The name of the parent undertaking must be stated.

8(3)   There must be stated–

(a)   the address of the undertaking's registered office (whether in or outside the United Kingdom),

(b)   if it is unincorporated, the address of its principal place of business.

8(4)   If copies of the group accounts referred to in sub-paragraph (1) are available to the public, there must also be stated the addresses from which copies of the accounts can be obtained.

History – Para. 8(3)(a) substituted by SI 2015/980, reg. 37(5), with effect in relation to–

(a)   financial years beginning on or after 1 January 2016, and

(b)   a financial year of a company beginning on or after 1 January 2015, but before 1 January 2016, if the directors of the company so decide.

Identification of ultimate parent company

9(1)   Where the company is a subsidiary undertaking, the following information must be given with respect to the company (if any) regarded by the directors as being the company's ultimate parent company.

9(2)   The name of that company must be stated.

9(3)   If that company is incorporated outside the United Kingdom, the country in which it is incorporated must be stated (if known to the directors).

9(4)   In this paragraph **"company"** includes any body corporate.

PART 2 – COMPANIES NOT REQUIRED TO PREPARE GROUP ACCOUNTS

REASON FOR NOT PREPARING GROUP ACCOUNTS

10(1) The reason why the company is not required to prepare group accounts must be stated.

10(2) If the reason is that all the subsidiary undertakings of the company fall within the exclusions provided for in section 405 of the 2006 Act (Companies Act group accounts: subsidiary undertakings included in the consolidation), it must be stated with respect to each subsidiary undertaking which of those exclusions applies.

Holdings in subsidiary undertakings

11(1) There must be stated in relation to shares of each class held by the company in a subsidiary undertaking–

    (a)   the identity of the class, and

    (b)   the proportion of the nominal value of the shares of that class represented by those shares.

11(2) The shares held by or on behalf of the company itself must be distinguished from those attributed to the company which are held by or on behalf of a subsidiary undertaking.

Financial years of subsidiary undertakings

12 Where–

    (a)   disclosure is made under paragraph 2(1) with respect to a subsidiary undertaking, and

    (b)   that undertaking's financial year does not end with that of the company, there must be stated in relation to that undertaking the date on which its last financial year ended (last before the end of the company's financial year).

Exemption from giving information about significant holdings in non-subsidiary undertakings

13(1) The information otherwise required by paragraph 6 (significant holdings in undertakings other than subsidiary undertaking) need not be given if–

    (a)   the company is exempt by virtue of section 400 or 401 of the 2006 Act from the requirement to prepare group accounts (parent company included in accounts of larger group), and

    (b)   the investment of the company in all undertakings in which it has such a holding as is mentioned in sub-paragraph (1) is shown, in aggregate, in the notes to the accounts by way of the equity method of valuation.

Construction of references to shares held by company

14(1) References in Parts 1 and 2 of this Schedule to shares held by a company are to be construed as follows.

14(2) For the purposes of paragraphs 2, 11 and 12 (information about subsidiary undertakings)–

(a) there must be attributed to the company any shares held by a subsidiary undertaking, or by a person acting on behalf of the company or a subsidiary undertaking; but

(b) there must be treated as not held by the company any shares held on behalf of a person other than the company or a subsidiary undertaking.

14(3) For the purposes of paragraphs 4 to 6 (information about undertakings other than subsidiary undertakings)–

(a) there must be attributed to the company shares held on its behalf by any person; but

(b) there must be treated as not held by a company shares held on behalf of a person other than the company.

14(4) For the purposes of any of those provisions, shares held by way of security must be treated as held by the person providing the security–

(a) where apart from the right to exercise them for the purpose of preserving the value of the security, or of realising it, the rights attached to the shares are exercisable only in accordance with that person's instructions, and

(b) where the shares are held in connection with the granting of loans as part of normal business activities and apart from the right to exercise them for the purpose of preserving the value of the security, or of realising it, the rights attached to the shares are exercisable only in that person's interests.

PART 3 – COMPANIES REQUIRED TO PREPARE GROUP ACCOUNTS

Introductory

15 In this Part of this Schedule **"the group"** means the group consisting of the parent company and its subsidiary undertakings.

Subsidiary undertakings

16(1) In addition to the information required by paragraph 2, the following information must also be given with respect to the undertakings which are subsidiary undertakings of the parent company at the end of the financial year.

16(2) It must be stated whether the subsidiary undertaking is included in the consolidation and, if it is not, the reasons for excluding it from consolidation must be given.

16(3) It must be stated with respect to each subsidiary undertaking by virtue of which of the conditions specified in section 1162(2) or (4) of the 2006 Act it is a subsidiary undertaking of its immediate parent undertaking.

That information need not be given if the relevant condition is that specified in subsection (2)(a) of that section (holding of a majority of the voting rights) and the immediate parent undertaking holds the same proportion of the shares in the undertaking as it holds voting rights.

Holdings in subsidiary undertakings

17(1) The following information must be given with respect to the shares of a subsidiary undertaking held–

    (a)   by the parent company, and

    (b)   by the group, and the information under paragraphs

    (a)   and

    (b)   must (if different) be shown separately.

17(2) There must be stated–

    (a)   the identity of each class of shares held, and

    (b)   the proportion of the nominal value of the shares of that class represented by those shares.

Joint ventures

18(1) The following information must be given where an undertaking is dealt with in the consolidated accounts by the method of proportional consolidation in accordance with paragraph 18 of Schedule 6 to these Regulations (joint ventures)–

    (a)   the address of the undertaking's registered office (whether in or outside the United Kingdom),

    (b)   the address of the principal place of business of the undertaking,

    (c)   the factors on which joint management of the undertaking is based, and

    (d)   the proportion of the capital of the undertaking held by undertakings included in the consolidation.

18(2) Where the financial year of the undertaking did not end with that of the company, there must be stated the date on which a financial year of the undertaking last ended before that date.

History – Para. 18(1)(a) substituted by SI 2015/980, reg. 38(2), with effect in relation to–

    (a)   financial years beginning on or after 1 January 2016, and

    (b)   a financial year of a company beginning on or after 1 January 2015, but before 1 January 2016, if the directors of the company so decide.

Associated undertakings

19(1) The following information must be given where an undertaking included in the consolidation has an interest in an associated undertaking.

19(2) The name of the associated undertaking must be stated.

19(3) There must be stated–

    (a)   if the undertaking is incorporated outside the United Kingdom, the country in which it is incorporated,

    (b)   the address of the undertaking's registered office (whether in or outside the United Kingdom),

19(4) The following information must be given with respect to the shares of the undertaking held–

(a)   by the parent company, and

(b)   by the group, and the information under paragraphs (a) and (b) must be shown separately.

19(5)   There must be stated–

(a)   the identity of each class of shares held, and

(b)   the proportion of the nominal value of the shares of that class represented by those shares.

19(6)   In this paragraph **"associated undertaking"** has the meaning given by paragraph 19 of Schedule 6 to these Regulations; and the information required by this paragraph must be given notwithstanding that paragraph 21(3) of that Schedule (materiality) applies in relation to the accounts themselves.

History – Para. 19(3)(b) substituted by SI 2015/980, reg. 38(3), with effect in relation to–

(a)   financial years beginning on or after 1 January 2016, and

(b)   a financial year of a company beginning on or after 1 January 2015, but before 1 January 2016, if the directors of the company so decide.

Requirement to give information about other significant holdings of parent company or group

20(1)   The information required by paragraphs 5 and 6 must also be given where at the end of the financial year the group has a significant holding in an undertaking which is not a subsidiary undertaking of the parent company and does not fall within paragraph 18 (joint ventures) or 19 (associated undertakings), as though the references to the company in those paragraphs were a reference to the group.

20(2)   A holding is significant for this purpose if–

(a)   it amounts to 20% or more of the nominal value of any class of shares in the undertaking, or

(b)   the amount of the holding (as stated or included in the group accounts) exceeds one-fifth of the amount of the group's assets (as so stated).

20(3)   For the purposes of those paragraphs as applied to a group the **"relevant financial year"** of an outside undertaking is–

(a)   if its financial year ends with that of the parent company, that year, and

(b)   if not, its financial year ending last before the end of the parent company's financial year.

Group's membership of certain undertakings

21   The information required by paragraph 7 must also be given where at the end of the financial year the group is a member of an undertaking having unlimited liability.

History – In para. 21, the words "an undertaking having unlimited liability" substituted for the words "a qualifying undertaking" by SI 2015/980, reg. 38(4), with effect in relation to–

(a)   financial years beginning on or after 1 January 2016, and

(b)   a financial year of a company beginning on or after 1 January 2015, but before 1 January 2016, if the directors of the company so decide.

Construction of references to shares held by parent company or group

22(1) References in Parts 1 and 3 of this Schedule to shares held by that parent company or group are to be construed as follows.

22(2) For the purposes of paragraphs 4 to 6, 17, 19(4) and (5) and 12 (information about holdings in subsidiary and other undertakings)–

(a) there must be attributed to the parent company shares held on its behalf by any person; but

(b) there must be treated as not held by the parent company shares held on behalf of a person other than the company.

22(3) References to shares held by the group are to any shares held by or on behalf of the parent company or any of its subsidiary undertakings; but any shares held on behalf of a person other than the parent company or any of its subsidiary undertakings are not to be treated as held by the group.

22(4) Shares held by way of security must be treated as held by the person providing the security–

(a) where apart from the right to exercise them for the purpose of preserving the value of the security, or of realising it, the rights attached to the shares are exercisable only in accordance with his instructions, and

(b) where the shares are held in connection with the granting of loans as part of normal business activities and apart from the right to exercise them for the purpose of preserving the value of the security, or of realising it, the rights attached to the shares are exercisable only in his interests.

PART 4 – ADDITIONAL DISCLOSURES FOR BANKING COMPANIES AND GROUPS

23(1) This paragraph applies where accounts are prepared in accordance with the special provisions of Schedules 2 and 6 relating to banking companies or groups.

23(2) The information required by paragraph 5 of this Schedule, modified where applicable by paragraph 20 (information about significant holdings of the company or group in undertakings other than subsidiary undertakings) need only be given in respect of undertakings (otherwise falling within the class of undertakings in respect of which disclosure is required) in which the company or group has a significant holding amounting to 20% or more of the nominal value of the shares in the undertaking.

In addition any information required by those paragraphs may be omitted if it is not material.

23(3) Paragraphs 14(3) and (4) and 22(3) and (4) of this Schedule apply with necessary modifications for the purposes of this paragraph.

PART 5 – INTERPRETATION OF REFERENCES TO "BENEFICIAL INTEREST"

Residual interests under pension and employees' share schemes

24(1) Where shares in an undertaking are held on trust for the purposes of a pension scheme or an employees' share scheme, there must be disregarded any residual interest which has not vested in possession, being an interest of the undertaking or any of its subsidiary undertakings.

24(2) In this paragraph a **"residual interest"** means a right of the undertaking in question (the "residual beneficiary") to receive any of the trust property in the event of–

    (a)   all the liabilities arising under the scheme having been satisfied or provided for, or

    (b)   the residual beneficiary ceasing to participate in the scheme, or

    (c)   the trust property at any time exceeding what is necessary for satisfying the liabilities arising or expected to arise under the scheme.

24(3) In sub-paragraph (2) references to a right include a right dependent on the exercise of a discretion vested by the scheme in the trustee or any other person; and references to liabilities arising under a scheme include liabilities that have resulted or may result from the exercise of any such discretion.

24(4) For the purposes of this paragraph a residual interest vests in possession–

    (a)   in a case within sub-paragraph (2)(a), on the occurrence of the event there mentioned, whether or not the amount of the property receivable pursuant to the right mentioned in that sub-paragraph is then ascertained,

    (b)   in a case within sub-paragraph (2)(b) or (c), when the residual beneficiary becomes entitled to require the trustee to transfer to that beneficiary any of the property receivable pursuant to that right.

Employer's charges and other rights of recovery

25(1) Where shares in an undertaking are held on trust there must be disregarded–

    (a)   if the trust is for the purposes of a pension scheme, any such rights as are mentioned in sub-paragraph (2),

    (b)   if the trust is for the purposes of an employees' share scheme, any such rights as are mentioned in paragraph (a) of that sub-paragraph, being rights of the undertaking or any of its subsidiary undertakings.

25(2) The rights referred to are–

    (a)   any charge or lien on, or set-off against, any benefit or other right or interest under the scheme for the purpose of enabling the employer or former employer of a member of the scheme to obtain the discharge of a monetary obligation due to him from the member, and

    (b)   any right to receive from the trustee of the scheme, or as trustee of the scheme to retain, an amount that can be recovered or retained under section 61 of the Pension Schemes Act 1993 or section 57 of the Pension Schemes (Northern Ireland) Act 1993 (deduction of contributions equivalent premium from refund of scheme contributions) or otherwise as reimbursement or partial reimbursement for any contributions equivalent premium paid in connection with the scheme under Chapter 3 of Part 3 of that Act.

Trustee's right to expenses, remuneration, indemnity etc.

26   Where an undertaking is a trustee, there must be disregarded any rights which the undertaking has in its capacity as trustee including, in particular, any right to recover its expenses or be remunerated out of the trust property and any right to be indemnified out of that property for any liability incurred by reason of any act or omission of the undertaking in the performance of its duties as trustee.

Supplementary

27(1)   This Schedule applies in relation to debentures as it applies in relation to shares.

27(2)   **"Pension scheme"** means any scheme for the provision of benefits consisting of or including relevant benefits for or in respect of employees or former employees; and **"relevant benefits"** means any pension, lump sum, gratuity or other like benefit given or to be given on retirement or on death or in anticipation of retirement or, in connection with past service, after retirement or death.

27(3)   In sub-paragraph (2) of this paragraph and in paragraph 25(2) **"employee"** and **"employer"** are to be read as if a director of an undertaking were employed by it.

SCHEDULE 5

Regulation 8

INFORMATION ABOUT BENEFITS OF DIRECTORS

PART 1 – PROVISIONS APPLYING TO QUOTED AND UNQUOTED COMPANIES

Total amount of directors' remuneration etc.

1(1)   There must be shown–

(a)   the aggregate amount of remuneration paid to or receivable by directors in respect of qualifying services;

(b)   the aggregate of the amount of gains made by directors on the exercise of share options;

(c)   the aggregate of the amount of money paid to or receivable by directors, and the net value of assets (other than money and share options) received or receivable by directors, under long term incentive schemes in respect of qualifying services; and

(d)   the aggregate value of any company contributions–

(i)   paid, or treated as paid, to a pension scheme in respect of directors' qualifying services, and

(ii)   by reference to which the rate or amount of any money purchase benefits that may become payable will be calculated.

1(2)   There must be shown the number of directors (if any) to whom retirement benefits are accruing in respect of qualifying services–

(a)   under money purchase schemes, and

(b)   under defined benefit schemes.

1(3)   In the case of a company which is not a quoted company and whose equity share capital is not listed on the market known as AIM–

    (a) sub-paragraph (1) has effect as if paragraph (b) were omitted and, in paragraph (c), "assets" did not include shares; and

    (b) the number of each of the following (if any) must be shown, namely–

        (i) the directors who exercised share options, and

        (ii) the directors in respect of whose qualifying services shares were received or receivable under long term incentive schemes.

PART 2 – PROVISIONS APPLYING ONLY TO UNQUOTED COMPANIES

Details of highest paid director's emoluments etc.

2(1)   Where the aggregates shown under paragraph 1(1)(a), (b) and (c) total £200,000 or more, there must be shown–

    (a) so much of the total of those aggregates as is attributable to the highest paid director, and

    (b) so much of the aggregate mentioned in paragraph 1(1)(d) as is so attributable.

2(2)   Where sub-paragraph (1) applies and the highest paid director has performed qualifying services during the financial year by reference to which the rate or amount of any defined benefits that may become payable will be calculated, there must also be shown–

    (a) the amount at the end of the year of his accrued pension, and

    (b) where applicable, the amount at the end of the year of his accrued lump sum.

2(3)   Subject to sub-paragraph (4), where sub-paragraph (1) applies in the case of a company which is not a listed company, there must also be shown–

    (a) whether the highest paid director exercised any share options, and

    (b) whether any shares were received or receivable by that director in respect of qualifying services under a long term incentive scheme.

2(4)   Where the highest paid director has not been involved in any of the transactions specified in sub-paragraph (3), that fact need not be stated.

Excess retirement benefits of directors and past directors

3(1)   Subject to sub-paragraph (2), there must be shown the aggregate amount of–

    (a) so much of retirement benefits paid to or receivable by directors under pension schemes, and

    (b) so much of retirement benefits paid to or receivable by past directors under such schemes, as (in each case) is in excess of the retirement benefits to which they were respectively entitled on the date on which the benefits first became payable or 31st March 1997, whichever is the later.

3(2)   Amounts paid or receivable under a pension scheme need not be included in the aggregate amount if–

(a) the funding of the scheme was such that the amounts were or, as the case may be, could have been paid without recourse to additional contributions, and

(b) amounts were paid to or receivable by all pensioner members of the scheme on the same basis.

3(3) In sub-paragraph (2), **"pensioner member"**, in relation to a pension scheme, means any person who is entitled to the present payment of retirement benefits under the scheme.

3(4) In this paragraph–

(a) references to retirement benefits include benefits otherwise than in cash, and

(b) in relation to so much of retirement benefits as consists of a benefit otherwise than in cash, references to their amount are to the estimated money value of the benefit, and the nature of any such benefit must also be disclosed.

Compensation to directors for loss of office

4(1) There must be shown the aggregate amount of any compensation to directors or past directors in respect of loss of office.

4(2) This includes compensation received or receivable by a director or past director–

(a) for loss of office as director of the company, or

(b) for loss, while director of the company or on or in connection with his ceasing to be a director of it, of–

    (i) any other office in connection with the management of the company's affairs, or

    (ii) any office as director or otherwise in connection with the management of the affairs of any subsidiary undertaking of the company.

4(3) In this paragraph references to compensation for loss of office include–

(a) compensation in consideration for, or in connection with, a person's retirement from office, and

(b) where such a retirement is occasioned by a breach of the person's contract with the company or with a subsidiary undertaking of the company–

    (i) payments made by way of damages for the breach, or

    (ii) payments made by way of settlement or compromise of any claim in respect of the breach.

4(4) In this paragraph–

(a) references to compensation include benefits otherwise than in cash, and

(b) in relation to such compensation references to its amount are to the estimated money value of the benefit.

The nature of any such compensation must be disclosed.

Sums paid to third parties in respect of directors' services

5(1) There must be shown the aggregate amount of any consideration paid to or receivable by third parties for making available the services of any person–

(a)   as a director of the company, or
(b)   while director of the company–

    (i)   as director of any of its subsidiary undertakings, or
    (ii)   otherwise in connection with the management of the affairs of the company or any of its subsidiary undertakings.

5(2) In sub-paragraph (1)–

(a)   the reference to consideration includes benefits otherwise than in cash, and
(b)   in relation to such consideration the reference to its amount is to the estimated money value of the benefit.

The nature of any such consideration must be disclosed.

5(3) For the purposes of this paragraph a **"third party"** means a person other than–

(a)   the director himself or a person connected with him or a body corporate controlled by him, or
(b)   the company or any of its subsidiary undertakings.

PART 3 – SUPPLEMENTARY PROVISIONS

General nature of obligations

6(1) This Schedule requires information to be given only so far as it is contained in the company's books and papers or the company has the right to obtain it from the persons concerned.

6(2) For the purposes of this Schedule any information is treated as shown if it is capable of being readily ascertained from other information which is shown.

Provisions as to amounts to be shown

7(1) The following provisions apply with respect to the amounts to be shown under this Schedule.

7(2) The amount in each case includes all relevant sums, whether paid by or receivable from the company, any of the company's subsidiary undertakings or any other person.

7(3) References to amounts paid to or receivable by a person include amounts paid to or receivable by a person connected with him or a body corporate controlled by him (but not so as to require an amount to be counted twice).

7(4) Except as otherwise provided, the amounts to be shown for any financial year are–

(a)   the sums receivable in respect of that year (whenever paid), or
(b)   in the case of sums not receivable in respect of a period, the sums paid during that year.

7(5) Sums paid by way of expenses allowance that are charged to United Kingdom income tax after the end of the relevant financial year must be shown in a note to the first accounts in which it is practicable to show them and must be distinguished from the amounts to be shown apart from this provision.

7(6) Where it is necessary to do so for the purpose of making any distinction required in complying with this Schedule, the directors may apportion payments between the matters in respect of which they have been paid or are receivable in such manner as they think appropriate.

Exclusion of sums liable to be accounted for to company etc.

8(1) The amounts to be shown under this Schedule do not include any sums that are to be accounted for–

    (a)   to the company or any of its subsidiary undertakings, or

    (b)   by virtue of sections 219 and 222(3) of the 2006 Act (payments in connection with share transfers: duty to account) to persons who sold their shares as a result of the offer made.

8(2) Where–

    (a)   any such sums are not shown in a note to the accounts for the relevant financial year on the ground that the person receiving them is liable to account for them, and

    (b)   the liability is afterwards wholly or partly released or is not enforced within a period of two years, those sums, to the extent to which the liability is released or not enforced, must be shown in a note to the first accounts in which it is practicable to show them and must be distinguished from the amounts to be shown apart from this provision.

Meaning of "remuneration"

9(1) In this Schedule **"remuneration"** of a director includes–

    (a)   salary, fees and bonuses, sums paid by way of expenses allowance (so far as they are chargeable to United Kingdom income tax), and

    (b)   subject to sub-paragraph (2), the estimated money value of any other benefits received by the director otherwise than in cash.

9(2) The expression does not include–

    (a)   the value of any share options granted to the director or the amount of any gains made on the exercise of any such options,

    (b)   any company contributions paid, or treated as paid, under any pension scheme or any benefits to which the director is entitled under any such scheme, or

    (c)   any money or other assets paid to or received or receivable by the director under any long term incentive scheme.

Meaning of "highest paid director"

10 In this Schedule, **"the highest paid director"** means the director to whom is attributable the greatest part of the total of the aggregates shown under paragraph 1(1)(a), (b) and (c).

Meaning of "long term incentive scheme"

11(1) In this Schedule **"long term incentive scheme"** means an agreement or arrangement–

    (a)   under which money or other assets may become receivable by a director, and

    (b)   which includes one or more qualifying conditions with respect to service or performance which cannot be fulfilled within a single financial year.

11(2) For this purpose the following must be disregarded–

    (a)   bonuses the amount of which falls to be determined by reference to service or performance within a single financial year;

    (b)   compensation for loss of office, payments for breach of contract and other termination payments; and

    (c)   retirement benefits.

Meaning of "shares" and "share option" and related expressions

12   In this Schedule–

    (a)   **"shares"** means shares (whether allotted or not) in the company, or any undertaking which is a group undertaking in relation to the company, and includes a share warrant as defined by section 779(1) of the 2006 Act; and

    (b)   **"share option"** means a right to acquire shares.

Meaning of "pension scheme" and related expressions

13(1) In this Schedule–

"pension scheme" means a retirement benefits scheme as defined by section 611 of the Income and Corporation Taxes Act 1988; and

"retirement benefits" has the meaning given by section 612(1) of that Act.

13(2) In this Schedule **"accrued pension"** and **"accrued lump sum"**, in relation to any pension scheme and any director, mean respectively the amount of the annual pension, and the amount of the lump sum, which would be payable under the scheme on his attaining normal pension age if–

    (a)   he had left the company's service at the end of the financial year,

    (b)   there was no increase in the general level of prices in the United Kingdom during the period beginning with the end of that year and ending with his attaining that age,

    (c)   no question arose of any commutation of the pension or inverse commutation of the lump sum, and

    (d)   any amounts attributable to voluntary contributions paid by the director to the scheme, and any money purchase benefits which would be payable under the scheme, were disregarded.

13(3) In this Schedule, **"company contributions"**, in relation to a pension scheme and a director, means any payments (including insurance premiums) made, or treated as made, to the scheme in respect of the director by a person other than the director.

13(4) In this Schedule, in relation to a director–

"defined benefits" means retirement benefits payable under a pension scheme that are not money purchase benefits;

"defined benefit scheme" means a pension scheme that is not a money purchase scheme;

"money purchase benefits" means retirement benefits payable under a pension scheme the rate or amount of which is calculated by reference to payments made, or treated as made, by the director or by any other person in respect of the director and which are not average salary benefits; and

"money purchase scheme" means a pension scheme under which all of the benefits that may become payable to or in respect of the director are money purchase benefits.

13(5) In this Schedule, **"normal pension age"**, in relation to any pension scheme and any director, means the age at which the director will first become entitled to receive a full pension on retirement of an amount determined without reduction to take account of its payment before a later age (but disregarding any entitlement to pension upon retirement in the event of illness, incapacity or redundancy).

13(6) Where a pension scheme provides for any benefits that may become payable to or in respect of any director to be whichever are the greater of–

(a) money purchase benefits as determined by or under the scheme; and

(b) defined benefits as so determined, the company may assume for the purposes of this paragraph that those benefits will be money purchase benefits, or defined benefits, according to whichever appears more likely at the end of the financial year.

13(7) For the purpose of determining whether a pension scheme is a money purchase or defined benefit scheme, any death in service benefits provided for by the scheme are to be disregarded.

References to subsidiary undertakings

14(1) Any reference in this Schedule to a subsidiary undertaking of the company, in relation to a person who is or was, while a director of the company, a director also, by virtue of the company's nomination (direct or indirect) of any other undertaking, includes that undertaking, whether or not it is or was in fact a subsidiary undertaking of the company.

14(2) Any reference to a subsidiary undertaking of the company–

(a) for the purposes of paragraph 1 (remuneration etc.) is to an undertaking which is a subsidiary undertaking at the time the services were rendered, and

(b) for the purposes of paragraph 4 (compensation for loss of office) is to a subsidiary undertaking immediately before the loss of office as director.

Other minor definitions

15(1) In this Schedule–

"net value", in relation to any assets received or receivable by a director, means value after deducting any money paid or other value given by the director in respect of those assets;

"qualifying services", in relation to any person, means his services as a director of the company, and his services while director of the company–

(a) as director of any of its subsidiary undertakings; or

(b) otherwise in connection with the management of the affairs of the company or any of its subsidiary undertakings.

15(2) References in this Schedule to a person being "connected" with a director, and to a director "controlling" a body corporate, are to be construed in accordance with sections 252 to 255 of the 2006 Act.

15(3) For the purposes of this Schedule, remuneration paid or receivable or share options granted in respect of a person's accepting office as a director are treated as emoluments paid or receivable or share options granted in respect of his services as a director.

SCHEDULE 6 Regulation 9

COMPANIES ACT GROUP ACCOUNTS

PART 1 – GENERAL RULES

General rules

1(1) Group accounts must comply so far as practicable with the provisions of Schedule 1 to these Regulations as if the undertakings included in the consolidation ("the group") were a single company (see Parts 2 and 3 of this Schedule for modifications for banking and insurance groups).

1(2) Where the parent company is treated as an investment company for the purposes of Part 5 of Schedule 1 (special provisions for investment companies) the group must be similarly treated.

2(1) The consolidated balance sheet and profit and loss account must incorporate in full the information contained in the individual accounts of the undertakings included in the consolidation, subject to the adjustments authorised or required by the following provisions of this Schedule and to such other adjustments (if any) as may be appropriate in accordance with generally accepted accounting principles or practice.

2(1A) Group accounts must be drawn up as at the same date as the accounts of the parent company.

2(2) If the financial year of a subsidiary undertaking included in the consolidation does not end with that of the parent company, the group accounts must be made up–

(a) from the accounts of the subsidiary undertaking for its financial year last ending before the end of the parent company's financial year, provided that year ended no more than three months before that of the parent company, or

(b) from interim accounts prepared by the subsidiary undertaking as at the end of the parent company's financial year.

History – Para. 2(1A) inserted by SI 2015/980, reg. 39(2), with effect in relation to–

    (a)   financial years beginning on or after 1 January 2016, and

    (b)   a financial year of a company beginning on or after 1 January 2015, but before 1 January 2016, if the directors of the company so decide.

3(1)   Where assets and liabilities to be included in the group accounts have been valued or otherwise determined by undertakings according to accounting rules differing from those used for the group accounts, the values or amounts must be adjusted so as to accord with the rules used for the group accounts.

3(2)   If it appears to the directors of the parent company that there are special reasons for departing from sub-paragraph (1) they may do so, but particulars of any such departure, the reasons for it and its effect must be given in a note to the accounts.

3(3)   The adjustments referred to in this paragraph need not be made if they are not material for the purpose of giving a true and fair view.

4   Any differences of accounting rules as between a parent company's individual accounts for a financial year and its group accounts must be disclosed in a note to the latter accounts and the reasons for the difference given.

5   Amounts that in the particular context of any provision of this Schedule are not material may be disregarded for the purposes of that provision.

Elimination of group transactions

6(1)   Debts and claims between undertakings included in the consolidation, and income and expenditure relating to transactions between such undertakings, must be eliminated in preparing the group accounts.

6(2)   Where profits and losses resulting from transactions between undertakings included in the consolidation are included in the book value of assets, they must be eliminated in preparing the group accounts.

6(3)   The elimination required by sub-paragraph (2) may be effected in proportion to the group's interest in the shares of the undertakings.

6(4)   Sub-paragraphs (1) and (2) need not be complied with if the amounts concerned are not material for the purpose of giving a true and fair view.

Acquisition and merger accounting

7(1)   The following provisions apply where an undertaking becomes a subsidiary undertaking of the parent company.

7(2)   That event is referred to in those provisions as an "acquisition", and references to the "undertaking acquired" are to be construed accordingly.

8   An acquisition must be accounted for by the acquisition method of accounting unless the conditions for accounting for it as a merger are met and the merger method of accounting is adopted.

9(1)   The acquisition method of accounting is as follows.

9(2)   The identifiable assets and liabilities of the undertaking acquired must be included in the consolidated balance sheet at their fair values as at the date of acquisition.

9(3)   The income and expenditure of the undertaking acquired must be brought into the group accounts only as from the date of the acquisition.

9(4)   There must be set off against the acquisition cost of the interest in the shares of the undertaking held by the parent company and its subsidiary undertakings the interest of the parent company and its subsidiary undertakings in the adjusted capital and reserves of the undertaking acquired.

9(5)   The resulting amount if positive must be treated as goodwill, and if negative as a negative consolidation difference.

9(6)   Negative goodwill may be transferred to the consolidated profit and loss account where such a treatment is in accordance with the principles and rules of Part 2 of Schedule 1 to these Regulations.

History – Para. 9(6) inserted by SI 2015/980, reg. 39(3), with effect in relation to–
  (a)   financial years beginning on or after 1 January 2016, and
  (b)   a financial year of a company beginning on or after 1 January 2015, but before
       1 January 2016, if the directors of the company so decide.

10   The conditions for accounting for an acquisition as a merger are–

  (a)   that the undertaking whose shares are acquired is ultimately controlled by the
        same party both before and after the acquisition,
  (b)   that the control referred to in paragraph (a) is not transitory, and
  (c)   that adoption of the merger method accords with generally accepted accounting
        principles or practice.

History – Para. 10 substituted by SI 2015/980, reg. 39(4), with effect in relation to–
  (a)   financial years beginning on or after 1 January 2016, and
  (b)   a financial year of a company beginning on or after 1 January 2015, but before
       1 January 2016, if the directors of the company so decide.
Former para. 10 read as follows:
  "**10(1)**   The conditions for accounting for an acquisition as a merger are–
  (a)   that at least 90% of the nominal value of the relevant shares in the undertaking
         acquired (excluding any shares in the undertaking held as treasury shares) is held
         by or on behalf of the parent company and its subsidiary undertakings,
  (b)   that the proportion referred to in paragraph (a) was attained pursuant to an
         arrangement providing for the issue of equity shares by the parent company or one
         or more of its subsidiary undertakings,
  (c)   that the fair value of any consideration other than the issue of equity shares given
         pursuant to the arrangement by the parent company and its subsidiary undertakings
         did not exceed 10% of the nominal value of the equity shares issued, and
  (d)   that adoption of the merger method of accounting accords with generally accepted
         accounting principles or practice.
  10(2)   The reference in sub-paragraph (1)(a) to the **"relevant shares"** in an undertaking acquired is to those carrying unrestricted rights to participate both in distributions and in the assets of the undertaking upon liquidation."

11(1) The merger method of accounting is as follows.

11(2) The assets and liabilities of the undertaking acquired must be brought into the group accounts at the figures at which they stand in the undertaking's accounts, subject to any adjustment authorised or required by this Schedule.

11(3) The income and expenditure of the undertaking acquired must be included in the group accounts for the entire financial year, including the period before the acquisition.

11(4) The group accounts must show corresponding amounts relating to the previous financial year as if the undertaking acquired had been included in the consolidation throughout that year.

11(5) There must be set off against the aggregate of–

    (a)   the appropriate amount in respect of qualifying shares issued by the parent company or its subsidiary undertakings in consideration for the acquisition of shares in the undertaking acquired, and

    (b)   the fair value of any other consideration for the acquisition of shares in the undertaking acquired, determined as at the date when those shares were acquired, the nominal value of the issued share capital of the undertaking acquired held by the parent company and its subsidiary undertakings.

11(6) The resulting amount must be shown as an adjustment to the consolidated reserves.

11(7) In sub-paragraph (5)(a) **"qualifying shares"** means–

    (a)   in relation to which any of the following provisions applies (merger relief), and in respect of which the appropriate amount is the nominal value–

        (i)   section 131 of the Companies Act 1985,

        (ii)   Article 141 of the Companies (Northern Ireland) Order 1986, or

        (iii)   section 612 of the 2006 Act, or

    (b)   shares in relation to which any of the following provisions applies (group reconstruction relief), and in respect of which the appropriate amount is the nominal value together with any minimum premium value within the meaning of that section–

        (i)   section 132 of the Companies Act 1985,

        (ii)   Article 142 of the Companies (Northern Ireland) Order 1986, or

        (iii)   section 611 of the 2006 Act.

12(1) Where a group is acquired, paragraphs 9 to 11 apply with the following adaptations.

12(2) References to shares of the undertaking acquired are to be construed as references to shares of the parent undertaking of the group.

12(3) Other references to the undertaking acquired are to be construed as references to the group; and references to the assets and liabilities, income and expenditure and capital and reserves of the undertaking acquired must be construed as references to the assets and liabilities, income and expenditure and capital and reserves of the group after making the set-offs and other adjustments required by this Schedule in the case of group accounts.

13(1)   The following information with respect to acquisitions taking place in the financial year must be given in a note to the accounts.

13(2)   There must be stated–

(a)   the name of the undertaking acquired or, where a group was acquired, the name of the parent undertaking of that group, and

(b)   whether the acquisition has been accounted for by the acquisition or the merger method of accounting; and in relation to an acquisition which significantly affects the figures shown in the group accounts, the following further information must be given.

13(3)   The composition and fair value of the consideration for the acquisition given by the parent company and its subsidiary undertakings must be stated.

13(4)   Where the acquisition method of accounting has been adopted, the book values immediately prior to the acquisition, and the fair values at the date of acquisition, of each class of assets and liabilities of the undertaking or group acquired must be stated in tabular form, including a statement of the amount of any goodwill or negative consolidation difference arising on the acquisition, together with an explanation of any significant adjustments made.

13(5)   In ascertaining for the purposes of sub-paragraph (4) the profit or loss of a group, the book values and fair values of assets and liabilities of a group or the amount of the assets and liabilities of a group, the set-offs and other adjustments required by this Schedule in the case of group accounts must be made.

14(1)   There must also be stated in a note to the accounts the cumulative amount of goodwill resulting from acquisitions in that and earlier financial years which has been written off otherwise than in the consolidated profit and loss account for that or any earlier financial year.

14(2)   That figure must be shown net of any goodwill attributable to subsidiary undertakings or businesses disposed of prior to the balance sheet date.

15   Where during the financial year there has been a disposal of an undertaking or group which significantly affects the figure shown in the group accounts, there must be stated in a note to the accounts–

(a)   the name of that undertaking or, as the case may be, of the parent undertaking of that group, and

(b)   the extent to which the profit or loss shown in the group accounts is attributable to profit or loss of that undertaking or group.

16   The information required by paragraph 13, 14 or 15 need not be disclosed with respect to an undertaking which–

(a)   is established under the law of a country outside the United Kingdom, or

(b)   carries on business outside the United Kingdom, if in the opinion of the directors of the parent company the disclosure would be seriously prejudicial to the business of that undertaking or to the business of the parent company or any of its subsidiary undertakings and the Secretary of State agrees that the information should not be disclosed.

16A   Where an acquisition has taken place in the financial year and the merger method of accounting has been adopted, the notes to the accounts must also disclose–

(a) the address of the registered office of the undertaking acquired (whether in or outside the United Kingdom),

(b) the name of the party referred to in paragraph 10(a),

(c) the address of the registered office of that party (whether in or outside the United Kingdom), and

(d) the information referred to in paragraph 11(6).

History – Para. 16A inserted by SI 2015/980, reg. 39(5), with effect in relation to–

(a) financial years beginning on or after 1 January 2016, and

(b) a financial year of a company beginning on or after 1 January 2015, but before 1 January 2016, if the directors of the company so decide.

Non-controlling interests

17(1) The formats set out in Schedule 1 to these Regulations have effect in relation to group accounts with the following additions.

17(2) In the balance sheet formats there must be shown, as a separate item and under the heading "non-controlling interests", the amount of capital and reserves attributable to shares in subsidiary undertakings included in the consolidation held by or on behalf of persons other than the parent company and its subsidiary undertakings.

17(3) In the profit and loss account formats there must be shown, as a separate item and under the heading "non-controlling interests", the amount of any profit or loss attributable to shares in subsidiary undertakings included in the consolidation held by or on behalf of persons other than the parent company and its subsidiary undertakings.

17(4) For the purposes of paragraph 4(1) and (2) of Schedule 1 (power to adapt or combine items)–

(a) the additional item required by sub-paragraph (2) above is treated as one to which a letter is assigned, and

(b) the additional item required by sub-paragraph (3) above is treated as one to which an Arabic number is assigned.

History – Para. 17 and the heading preceding it substituted by SI 2015/980, reg. 39(6), with effect in relation to–

(a) financial years beginning on or after 1 January 2016, and

(b) a financial year of a company beginning on or after 1 January 2015, but before 1 January 2016, if the directors of the company so decide.

Former para. 17 read as follows:

"Minority interests

17(1) The formats set out in Schedule 1 to these Regulations have effect in relation to group accounts with the following additions.

17(2) In the balance sheet formats there must be shown, as a separate item and under an appropriate heading, the amount of capital and reserves attributable to shares in subsidiary undertakings included in the consolidation held by or on behalf of persons other than the parent company and its subsidiary undertakings.

17(3) In the profit and loss account formats there must be shown, as a separate item and under an appropriate heading–

(a) the amount of any profit or loss on ordinary activities, and

(b) the amount of any profit or loss on extraordinary activities, attributable to shares in subsidiary undertakings included in the consolidation held by or on behalf of persons other than the parent company and its subsidiary undertakings.

17(4) For the purposes of paragraph 4(1) and (2) of Schedule 1 (power to adapt or combine items)–

    (a)   the additional item required by sub-paragraph (2) above is treated as one to which a letter is assigned, and

    (b)   the additional items required by sub-paragraph (3)(a) and (b) above are treated as ones to which an Arabic number is assigned."

Joint ventures

18(1) Where an undertaking included in the consolidation manages another undertaking jointly with one or more undertakings not included in the consolidation, that other undertaking ("the joint venture") may, if it is not–

    (a)   a body corporate, or

    (b)   a subsidiary undertaking of the parent company, be dealt with in the group accounts by the method of proportional consolidation.

18(2) The provisions of this Schedule relating to the preparation of consolidated accounts and sections 402 and 405 of the 2006 Act apply, with any necessary modifications, to proportional consolidation under this paragraph.

18(3) In addition to the disclosure of the average number of employees employed during the financial year (see section 411(7) of the 2006 Act), there must be a separate disclosure in the notes to the accounts of the average number of employees employed by undertakings that are proportionately consolidated.

History – In para. 18(2), the words "and sections 402 and 405 of the 2006 Act" inserted by SI 2015/980, reg. 39(7), with effect in relation to–

    (a)   financial years beginning on or after 1 January 2016, and

    (b)   a financial year of a company beginning on or after 1 January 2015, but before 1 January 2016, if the directors of the company so decide.

Para. 18(3) inserted by SI 2015/980, reg. 39(8), with effect in relation to–

    (a)   financial years beginning on or after 1 January 2016, and

    (b)   a financial year of a company beginning on or after 1 January 2015, but before 1 January 2016, if the directors of the company so decide.

Associated undertakings

19(1) An **"associated undertaking"** means an undertaking in which an undertaking included in the consolidation has a participating interest and over whose operating and financial policy it exercises a significant influence, and which is not–

    (a)   a subsidiary undertaking of the parent company, or

    (b)   a joint venture dealt with in accordance with paragraph 18.

19(2) Where an undertaking holds 20% or more of the voting rights in another undertaking, it is presumed to exercise such an influence over it unless the contrary is shown.

19(3) The voting rights in an undertaking means the rights conferred on shareholders in respect of their shares or, in the case of an undertaking not having a share capital, on members, to vote at general meetings of the undertaking on all, or substantially all, matters.

19(4)   The provisions of paragraphs 5 to 11 of Schedule 7 to the 2006 Act (parent and subsidiary undertakings: rights to be taken into account and attribution of rights) apply in determining for the purposes of this paragraph whether an undertaking holds 20% or more of the voting rights in another undertaking.

20(1)   The formats set out in Schedule 1 to these Regulations have effect in relation to group accounts with the following modifications.

20(2)   In the balance sheet formats replace the items headed "Participating interests", that is–

(a)   in format 1, item B.III.3, and

(b)   in format 2, item B.III.3 under the heading "ASSETS", by two items: "Interests in associated undertakings" and "Other participating interests".

20(3)   In the profit and loss account formats replace the items headed "Income from participating interests", that is–

(a)   in format 1, item 8, and

(b)   in format 2, item 10.

History – Para. 20(3)(c) and (d) omitted; and the word "and" in para. (a) inserted by SI 2015/980, reg. 39(9), with effect in relation to–

(a)   financial years beginning on or after 1 January 2016, and

(b)   a financial year of a company beginning on or after 1 January 2015, but before 1 January 2016, if the directors of the company so decide.

21(1)   The interest of an undertaking in an associated undertaking, and the amount of profit or loss attributable to such an interest, must be shown by the equity method of accounting (including dealing with any goodwill arising in accordance with paragraphs 17 to 20 and 22 of Schedule 1 to these Regulations).

21(2)   Where the associated undertaking is itself a parent undertaking, the net assets and profits or losses to be taken into account are those of the parent and its subsidiary undertakings (after making any consolidation adjustments).

21(3)   The equity method of accounting need not be applied if the amounts in question are not material for the purpose of giving a true and fair view.

Related party transactions

22   Paragraph 72 of Schedule 1 to these Regulations applies to transactions which the parent company, or other undertakings included in the consolidation, have entered into with related parties, unless they are intra group transactions.

Total amount of directors' remuneration etc

22A   Paragraph 1 of Schedule 5 to these Regulations applies to group accounts with the modification that only the amounts and values referred to in that paragraph received or receivable by the directors of the parent company from the parent company and any of its subsidiary undertakings must be disclosed in the notes to the accounts.

History – Para. 22A inserted by SI 2015/980, reg. 39(10), with effect in relation to–

    (a)   financial years beginning on or after 1 January 2016, and

    (b)   a financial year of a company beginning on or after 1 January 2015, but before 1 January 2016, if the directors of the company so decide.

Deferred tax balances

22B   Deferred tax balances must be recognised on consolidation where it is probable that a charge to tax will arise within the foreseeable future for one of the undertakings included in the consolidation.

History – Para. 22B inserted by SI 2015/980, reg. 39(10), with effect in relation to–

    (a)   financial years beginning on or after 1 January 2016, and

    (b)   a financial year of a company beginning on or after 1 January 2015, but before 1 January 2016, if the directors of the company so decide.

PART 2 – MODIFICATIONS FOR BANKING GROUPS

GENERAL APPLICATION OF PROVISIONS APPLICABLE TO INDIVIDUAL ACCOUNTS

23   In its application to banking groups, Part 1 of this Schedule has effect with the following modifications.

24   In paragraph 1 of this Schedule–

    (a)   the reference in sub-paragraph (1) to the provisions of Schedule 1 to these Regulations is to be construed as a reference to the provisions of Schedule 2 to these Regulations, and

    (b)   sub-paragraph (2) is to be omitted.

24A   In paragraph 9 of this Schedule, the reference in sub-paragraph (6) to Schedule 1 is to these Regulations is to be construed as a reference to Schedule 2.

History – Para. 24A inserted by SI 2015/980, reg. 39(11), with effect in relation to–

    (a)   financial years beginning on or after 1 January 2016, and

    (b)   a financial year of a company beginning on or after 1 January 2015, but before 1 January 2016, if the directors of the company so decide.

Non-controlling interests and associated undertakings

History – In heading, the words "NON-CONTROLLING INTERESTS AND ASSOCIATED UNDERTAKINGS" substituted for the words "MINORITY INTERESTS AND ASSOCIATED UNDERTAKINGS" by SI 2015/980, reg. 39(12), with effect in relation to–

    (a)   financial years beginning on or after 1 January 2016, and

    (b)   a financial year of a company beginning on or after 1 January 2015, but before 1 January 2016, if the directors of the company so decide.

25(1)   This paragraph adapts paragraphs 17 and 20 (which require items in respect of "non-controlling interests" and associated undertakings to be added to the formats set out in Schedule 1 to these Regulations) to the formats prescribed by Schedule 2 to these Regulations.

25(2) In paragraph 17–

    (a)   in sub-paragraph (1), for the reference to Schedule 1 to these Regulations, substitute a reference to Schedule 2,

    (b)   sub-paragraph (3) is to apply as if the reference to **"a separate item"** were a reference to **"separate items"** and the reference to **"the amount of any profit or loss"** were a reference to the following–

        (i)   the amount of any profit or loss on ordinary activities, and

        (ii) the amount of any profit or loss on extraordinary activities, and

    (c)   sub-paragraph (4) is not to apply, but for the purposes of paragraph 5(1) of Part 1 of Schedule 2 to these Regulations (power to combine items) the additional items required by the foregoing provisions of this paragraph are to be treated as items to which a letter is assigned.

25(3) Paragraph 20(2) is to apply with respect to a balance sheet prepared under Schedule 2 to these Regulations as if it required assets item 7 (participating interests) in the balance sheet format to be replaced by the two replacement items referred to in that paragraph.

25(4) Paragraph 20(3) is not to apply, but the following items in the profit and loss account formats–

    (a)   format 1 item 3(b) (income from participating interests),

    (b)   format 2 item B2(b) (income from participating interests),

are replaced by the following–

        (i)   "Income from participating interests other than associated undertakings", to be shown at position 3(b) in format 1 and position B2(b) in format 2, and

        (ii) "Income from associated undertakings", to be shown at an appropriate position.

History – Para. 25 substituted by SI 2015/980, reg. 39(12), with effect in relation to–

    (a)   financial years beginning on or after 1 January 2016, and

    (b)   a financial year of a company beginning on or after 1 January 2015, but before 1 January 2016, if the directors of the company so decide.

Former para. 25 read as follows:

"**25(1)** This paragraph adapts paragraphs 17 and 20 (which require items in respect of "Minority interests" and associated undertakings to be added to the formats set out in Schedule 1 to these Regulations) to the formats prescribed by Schedule 2 to these Regulations.

  25(2) In paragraph 17–

    (a)   in sub-paragraph (1), for the reference to Schedule 1 to these Regulations, substitute a reference to Schedule 2, and

    (b)   paragraph 17(4) is not to apply, but for the purposes of paragraph 5(1) of Part I of Schedule 2 to these Regulations (power to combine items) the additional items required by the foregoing provisions of this paragraph are to be treated as items to which a letter is assigned.

  25(3) Paragraph 20(2) is to apply with respect to a balance sheet prepared under Schedule 2 to these Regulations as if it required assets item 7 (participating interests) in the balance sheet format to be replaced by the two replacement items referred to in that paragraph.

  25(4) Paragraph 20(3) is not to apply, but the following items in the profit and loss account formats–

    (a)   format 1 item 3(b) (income from participating interests),

    (b)   format 2 item B2(b) (income from participating interests), are replaced by the following–

(i) "Income from participating interests other than associated undertakings", to be shown at position 3(b) in format 1 and position B2(b) in format 2, and

(ii) "Income from associated undertakings", to be shown at an appropriate position."

26 In paragraph 21(1) of this Schedule, for the references to paragraphs 17 to 20 and 22 of Schedule 1 to these Regulations substitute references to paragraphs 23 to 26 and 28 of Schedule 2 to these Regulations.

Related party transactions

27 In paragraph 22 of this Schedule, for the reference to paragraph 72 of Schedule 1 to these Regulations substitute a reference to paragraph 92 of Schedule 2 to these Regulations.

Foreign currency translation

28 Any difference between–

(a) the amount included in the consolidated accounts for the previous financial year with respect to any undertaking included in the consolidation or the group's interest in any associated undertaking, together with the amount of any transactions undertaken to cover any such interest, and

(b) the opening amount for the financial year in respect of those undertakings and in respect of any such transactions, arising as a result of the application of paragraph 50 of Schedule 2 to these Regulations may be credited to (where (a) is less than (b)), or deducted from (where (a) is greater than (b)), (as the case may be) consolidated reserves.

29 Any income and expenditure of undertakings included in the consolidation and associated undertakings in a foreign currency may be translated for the purposes of the consolidated accounts at the average rates of exchange prevailing during the financial year.

Information as to undertaking in which shares held as a result of financial assistance operation

30(1) The following provisions apply where the parent company of a banking group has a subsidiary undertaking which–

(a) is a credit institution of which shares are held as a result of a financial assistance operation with a view to its reorganisation or rescue, and

(b) is excluded from consolidation under section 405(3)(c) of the 2006 Act (interest held with a view to resale).

30(2) Information as to the nature and terms of the operations must be given in a note to the group accounts, and there must be appended to the copy of the group accounts delivered to the registrar in accordance with section 441 of the 2006 Act a copy of the undertaking's latest individual accounts and, if it is a parent undertaking, its latest group accounts.

If the accounts appended are required by law to be audited, a copy of the auditor's report must also be appended.

30(3) Any requirement of Part 35 of the 2006 Act as to the delivery to the registrar of a certified translation into English must be met in relation to any document required to be appended by subparagraph (2).

30(4) The above requirements are subject to the following qualifications–

(a)   an undertaking is not required to prepare for the purposes of this paragraph accounts which would not otherwise be prepared, and if no accounts satisfying the above requirements are prepared none need be appended;

(b)   the accounts of an undertaking need not be appended if they would not otherwise be required to be published, or made available for public inspection, anywhere in the world, but in that case the reason for not appending the accounts must be stated in a note to the consolidated accounts.

30(5) Where a copy of an undertaking's accounts is required to be appended to the copy of the group accounts delivered to the registrar, that fact must be stated in a note to the group accounts.

PART 3 – MODIFICATIONS FOR INSURANCE GROUPS
GENERAL APPLICATION OF PROVISIONS APPLICABLE TO INDIVIDUAL ACCOUNTS

31   In its application to insurance groups, Part 1 of this Schedule has effect with the following modifications.

32   In paragraph 1 of this Schedule–

(a)   the reference in sub-paragraph (1) to the provisions of Schedule 1 to these Regulations is to be construed as a reference to the provisions of Schedule 3 to these Regulations, and

(b)   sub-paragraph (2) is to be omitted.

Financial years of subsidiary undertakings

33   In paragraph 2(2)(a), for "three months" substitute "six months".

Assets and liabilities to be included in group accounts

34   In paragraph 3, after sub-paragraph (1) insert–

"**3(1A)**   Sub-paragraph (1) is not to apply to those liabilities items the valuation of which by the undertakings included in a consolidation is based on the application of provisions applying only to insurance undertakings, nor to those assets items changes in the values of which also affect or establish policyholders' rights.

3(1B)   Where sub-paragraph (1A) applies, that fact must be disclosed in the notes to the consolidated accounts.".

Elimination of group transactions

35   For sub-paragraph (4) of paragraph 6 substitute–

"**6(4)** Sub-paragraphs (1) and (2) need not be complied with–

(a) where a transaction has been concluded according to normal market conditions and a policyholder has rights in respect of the transaction, or

(b) if the amounts concerned are not material for the purpose of giving a true and fair view.

6(5) Where advantage is taken of sub-paragraph (4)(a) that fact must be disclosed in the notes to the accounts, and where the transaction in question has a material effect on the assets, liabilities, financial position and profit or loss of all the undertakings included in the consolidation that fact must also be so disclosed.".

35A In paragraph 9 of this Schedule, the reference in sub-paragraph (6) to Schedule 1 to these Regulations is to be construed as a reference to Schedule 3 to these Regulations.

History – Para. 35A inserted by SI 2015/980, reg. 39(13), with effect in relation to–
(a) financial years beginning on or after 1 January 2016, and
(b) a financial year of a company beginning on or after 1 January 2015, but before 1 January 2016, if the directors of the company so decide.

Non-controlling interests

36 In paragraph 17–

(a) in sub-paragraph (1), for the reference to Schedule 1 to these Regulations, substitute a reference to Schedule 3,

(b) sub-paragraph (3) is to apply as if the reference to **"a separate item"** were a reference to **"separate items"** and as if the reference to **"the amount of any profit or loss"** were a reference to the following–

(i) the amount of any profit or loss on ordinary activities, and
(ii) the amount of any profit or loss on extraordinary activities, and

(c) for sub-paragraph (4), substitute–

"**17(4)** Paragraph 3(1) of Schedule 3 to these Regulations (power to combine items) does not apply in relation to the additional items required by the above provisions of this paragraph."

History – Para. 36 and the heading preceding it substituted by SI 2015/980, reg. 39(14), with effect in relation to–
(a) financial years beginning on or after 1 January 2016, and
(b) a financial year of a company beginning on or after 1 January 2015, but before 1 January 2016, if the directors of the company so decide.
Former para. 36 read as follows:

"**Minority interests**

36 In paragraph 17–
(a) in sub-paragraph (1), for the reference to Schedule 1 to these Regulations, substitute a reference to Schedule 3, and
(b) for sub-paragraph (4) substitute–
"**17(4)** Paragraph 3(1) of Schedule 3 to these Regulations (power to combine items) does not apply in relation to the additional items required by the above provisions of this paragraph."."."

Associated undertakings

37   In paragraph 20–

    (a)   in sub-paragraph (1), for the reference to Schedule 1 to these Regulations substitute a reference to Schedule 3 to these Regulations, and

    (b)   for sub-paragraphs (2) and (3) substitute–

"**20(2)**   In the balance sheet format, replace asset item C.II.3 (participating interests) with two items, "Interests in associated undertakings" and "Other participating interests".

20(3)   In the profit and loss account format, replace items II.2.(a) and III.3.(a) (income from participating interests, with a separate indication of that derived from group undertakings) with–

    (a)   "Income from participating interests other than associated undertakings, with a separate indication of that derived from group undertakings", to be shown as items II.2.(a) and III.3.(a), and

    (b)   "Income from associated undertakings", to be shown as items II.2.(aa) and III.3.(aa).".

38   In paragraph 21(1) of this Schedule, for the references to paragraphs 17 to 20 and 22 of Schedule 1 to these Regulations, substitute references to paragraphs 36 to 39 and 42 of Schedule 3 to these Regulations.

Related party transactions

39   In paragraph 22 of this Schedule, for the reference to paragraph 72 of Schedule 1 to these Regulations substitute a reference to paragraph 90 of Schedule 3 to these Regulations.

Modifications of schedule 3 to these regulations for purposes of paragraph 31

40(1)   For the purposes of paragraph 31 of this Schedule, Schedule 3 to these Regulations is to be modified as follows.

40(2)   The information required by paragraph 11 (additional items) need not be given.

40(3)   In the case of general business, investment income, expenses and charges may be disclosed in the non-technical account rather than in the technical account.

40(4)   In the case of subsidiary undertakings which are not authorised to carry on long-term business in the United Kingdom, notes (8) and (9) to the profit and loss account format have effect as if references to investment income, expenses and charges arising in the long-term fund or to investments attributed to the long-term fund were references to investment income, expenses and charges or (as the case may be) investments relating to long-term business.

40(5)   In the case of subsidiary undertakings which do not have a head office in the United Kingdom, the computation required by paragraph 52 must be made annually by an actuary or other specialist in the field on the basis of recognised actuarial methods.

40(6)   The information required by paragraphs 85 to 88 need not be shown.

SCHEDULE 7

Regulation 10

MATTERS TO BE DEALT WITH IN DIRECTORS' REPORT

PART 1 – MATTERS OF A GENERAL NATURE

Introduction

1 In addition to the information required by section 416 of the 2006 Act, the directors' report must contain the following information.

1A Where a company has chosen in accordance with section 414C(11) to set out in the company's strategic report information required by this Schedule to be contained in the directors' report it shall state in the directors' report that it has done so and in respect of which information it has done so.

History – Para. 1A inserted by SI 2013/1970, reg. 7(1) and (3)(a), with effect from 1 October 2013 in respect of financial years ending on or after 30 September 2013.

Asset values

2 [Repealed.]

History – Para. 2 repealed by SI 2013/1970, reg. 7(1) and (3)(b), with effect from 1 October 2013 in respect of financial years ending on or after 30 September 2013. Prior to repeal, para. 2 read as follows:

"**2(1)** If, in the case of such of the fixed assets of the company as consist in interests in land, their market value (as at the end of the financial year) differs substantially from the amount at which they are included in the balance sheet, and the difference is, in the directors' opinion, of such significance as to require that the attention of members of the company or of holders of its debentures should be drawn to it, the report must indicate the difference with such degree of precision as is practicable.

2(2) In relation to a group directors' report sub-paragraph (1) has effect as if the reference to the fixed assets of the company was a reference to the fixed assets of the company and of its subsidiary undertakings included in the consolidation."

Political donations and expenditure

3(1) If–

    (a) the company (not being the wholly-owned subsidiary of a company incorporated in the United Kingdom) has in the financial year–

        (i) made any political donation to any political party or other political organisation,

        (ii) made any political donation to any independent election candidate, or

        (iii) incurred any political expenditure, and

    (b) the amount of the donation or expenditure, or (as the case may be) the aggregate amount of all donations and expenditure falling within paragraph (a), exceeded £2000, the directors' report for the year must contain the following particulars.

3(2) Those particulars are–

(a)   as respects donations falling within sub-paragraph (1)(a)(i) or (ii)–

    (i)   the name of each political party, other political organisation or independent election candidate to whom any such donation has been made, and

    (ii)   the total amount given to that party, organisation or candidate by way of such donations in the financial year; and

(b)   as respects expenditure falling within sub-paragraph (1)(a)(iii), the total amount incurred by way of such expenditure in the financial year.

3(3) If–

(a)   at the end of the financial year the company has subsidiaries which have, in that year, made any donations or incurred any such expenditure as is mentioned in sub-paragraph (1)(a), and

(b)   it is not itself the wholly-owned subsidiary of a company incorporated in the United Kingdom, the directors' report for the year is not, by virtue of sub-paragraph (1), required to contain the particulars specified in sub-paragraph (2).

But, if the total amount of any such donations or expenditure (or both) made or incurred in that year by the company and the subsidiaries between them exceeds £2000, the directors' report for the year must contain those particulars in relation to each body by whom any such donation or expenditure has been made or incurred.

3(4) Any expression used in this paragraph which is also used in Part 14 of the 2006 Act (control of political donations and expenditure) has the same meaning as in that Part.

4(1) If the company (not being the wholly-owned subsidiary of a company incorporated in the United Kingdom) has in the financial year made any contribution to a non-EU political party, the directors' report for the year must contain–

(a)   a statement of the amount of the contribution, or

(b)   (if it has made two or more such contributions in the year) a statement of the total amount of the contributions.

4(2) If–

(a)   at the end of the financial year the company has subsidiaries which have, in that year, made any such contributions as are mentioned in sub-paragraph (1), and

(b)   it is not itself the wholly-owned subsidiary of a company incorporated in the United Kingdom, the directors' report for the year is not, by virtue of sub-paragraph (1), required to contain any such statement as is there mentioned, but it must instead contain a statement of the total amount of the contributions made in the year by the company and the subsidiaries between them.

4(3) In this paragraph, **"contribution"**, in relation to an organisation, means–

(a)   any gift of money to the organisation (whether made directly or indirectly);

(b)   any subscription or other fee paid for affiliation to, or membership of, the organisation; or

(c)   any money spent (otherwise than by the organisation or a person acting on its behalf) in paying any expenses incurred directly or indirectly by the organisation.

4(4)   In this paragraph, **"non-EU political party"** means any political party which carries on, or proposes to carry on, its activities wholly outside the member States.

Charitable donations

5   [Repealed.]

History – Para. 5 repealed by SI 2013/1970, reg. 7(1) and (3)(b), with effect from 1 October 2013 in respect of financial years ending on or after 30 September 2013. Prior to repeal, para. 5 read as follows:

"**5(1)**   If–
(a)   the company (not being the wholly-owned subsidiary of a company incorporated in the United Kingdom) has in the financial year given money for charitable purposes, and
(b)   the money given exceeded £2000 in amount, the directors' report for the year must contain, in the case of each of the purposes for which money has been given, a statement of the amount of money given for that purpose.

5(2)   If–
(a)   at the end of the financial year the company has subsidiaries which have, in that year, given money for charitable purposes, and
(b)   it is not itself the wholly owned subsidiary of a company incorporated in the United Kingdom, sub-paragraph (1) does not apply to the company. But, if the amount given in that year for charitable purposes by the company and the subsidiaries between them exceeds £2000, the directors' report for the year must contain, in the case of each of the purposes for which money has been given by the company and the subsidiaries between them, a statement of the amount of money given for that purpose.

5(3)   Money given for charitable purposes to a person who, when it was given, was ordinarily resident outside the United Kingdom is to be left out of account for the purposes of this paragraph.

5(4)   For the purposes of this paragraph, **"charitable purposes"** means purposes which are exclusively charitable, and as respects Scotland a purpose is charitable if it is listed in section 7(2) of the Charities and Trustee Investment (Scotland) Act 2005."

Financial instruments

6(1)   In relation to the use of financial instruments by a company, the directors' report must contain an indication of–
(a)   the financial risk management objectives and policies of the company, including the policy for hedging each major type of forecasted transaction for which hedge accounting is used, and
(b)   the exposure of the company to price risk, credit risk, liquidity risk and cash flow risk, unless such information is not material for the assessment of the assets, liabilities, financial position and profit or loss of the company.

6(2)   In relation to a group directors' report sub-paragraph (1) has effect as if the references to the company were references to the company and its subsidiary undertakings included in the consolidation.

6(3)   In sub-paragraph (1) the expressions **"hedge accounting"**, **"price risk"**, **"credit risk"**, **"liquidity risk"** and **"cash flow risk"** have the same meaning as they have in Council Directive 78/660/EEC on the annual accounts of certain types of companies, and in Council Directive 83/349/EEC on consolidated accounts.

Miscellaneous

7(1)   The directors' report must contain–

    (a)   particulars of any important events affecting the company which have occurred since the end of the financial year,

    (b)   an indication of likely future developments in the business of the company,

    (c)   an indication of the activities (if any) of the company in the field of research and development, and

    (d)   (unless the company is an unlimited company) an indication of the existence of branches (as defined in section 1046(3) of the 2006 Act) of the company outside the United Kingdom.

7(2)   In relation to a group directors' report paragraphs (a), (b) and (c) of sub-paragraph (1) have effect as if the references to the company were references to the company and its subsidiary undertakings included in the consolidation.

PART 2 – DISCLOSURE REQUIRED BY COMPANY ACQUIRING ITS OWN SHARES ETC.

8   This Part of this Schedule applies where shares in a public company–

    (a)   are purchased by the company or are acquired by it by forfeiture or surrender in lieu of forfeiture, or in pursuance of any of the following provisions (acquisition of own shares by company limited by shares)–

        (i)   section 143(3) of the Companies Act 1985,

        (ii)   Article 153(3) of the Companies (Northern Ireland) Order 1986, or

        (iii)   section 659 of the 2006 Act, or

    (b)   are acquired by another person in circumstances where paragraph (c) or (d) of any of the following provisions applies (acquisition by company's nominee, or by another with company financial assistance, the company having a beneficial interest)–

        (i)   section 146(1) of the Companies Act 1985,

        (ii)   Article 156(1) of the Companies (Northern Ireland) Order 1986, or

        (iii)   section 662(1) of the 2006 Act applies, or

    (c)   are made subject to a lien or other charge taken (whether expressly or otherwise) by the company and permitted by any of the following provisions (exceptions from general rule against a company having a lien or charge on its own shares)–

        (i)   section 150(2) or (4) of the Companies Act 1985,

        (ii)   Article 160(2) or (4) of the Companies (Northern Ireland) Order 1986, or

        (iii)   section 670(2) or (4) of the 2006 Act.

History – In the opening words, "public" inserted by SI 2013/1970, reg. 7(1) and (3)(c), with effect from 1 October 2013 in respect of financial years ending on or after 30 September 2013.

9   The directors' report for a financial year must state–

(a)   the number and nominal value of the shares so purchased, the aggregate amount of the consideration paid by the company for such shares and the reasons for their purchase;

(b)   the number and nominal value of the shares so acquired by the company, acquired by another person in such circumstances and so charged respectively during the financial year;

(c)   the maximum number and nominal value of shares which, having been so acquired by the company, acquired by another person in such circumstances or so charged (whether or not during that year) are held at any time by the company or that other person during that year;

(d)   the number and nominal value of the shares so acquired by the company, acquired by another person in such circumstances or so charged (whether or not during that year) which are disposed of by the company or that other person or cancelled by the company during that year;

(e)   where the number and nominal value of the shares of any particular description are stated in pursuance of any of the preceding sub-paragraphs, the percentage of the called-up share capital which shares of that description represent;

(f)   where any of the shares have been so charged the amount of the charge in each case; and

(g)   where any of the shares have been disposed of by the company or the person who acquired them in such circumstances for money or money's worth the amount or value of the consideration in each case.

PART 3 – DISCLOSURE CONCERNING EMPLOYMENT ETC. OF DISABLED PERSONS

10(1)   This Part of this Schedule applies to the directors' report where the average number of persons employed by the company in each week during the financial year exceeded 250.

10(2)   That average number is the quotient derived by dividing, by the number of weeks in the financial year, the number derived by ascertaining, in relation to each of those weeks, the number of persons who, under contracts of service, were employed in the week (whether throughout it or not) by the company, and adding up the numbers ascertained.

10(3)   The directors' report must in that case contain a statement describing such policy as the company has applied during the financial year–

(a)   for giving full and fair consideration to applications for employment by the company made by disabled persons, having regard to their particular aptitudes and abilities,

(b)   for continuing the employment of, and for arranging appropriate training for, employees of the company who have become disabled persons during the period when they were employed by the company, and

(c)   otherwise for the training, career development and promotion of disabled persons employed by the company.

10(4)   In this Part–

(a) **"employment"** means employment other than employment to work wholly or mainly outside the United Kingdom, and "employed" and "employee" are to be construed accordingly; and

(b) **"disabled person"** means the same as in the Disability Discrimination Act 1995.

PART 4 – EMPLOYEE INVOLVEMENT

11(1) This Part of this Schedule applies to the directors' report where the average number of persons employed by the company in each week during the financial year exceeded 250.

11(2) That average number is the quotient derived by dividing, by the number of weeks in the financial year, the number derived by ascertaining, in relation to each of those weeks, the number of persons who, under contracts of service, were employed in the week (whether throughout it or not) by the company, and adding up the numbers ascertained.

11(3) The directors' report must in that case contain a statement describing the action that has been taken during the financial year to introduce, maintain or develop arrangements aimed at–

(a) providing employees systematically with information on matters of concern to them as employees,

(b) consulting employees or their representatives on a regular basis so that the views of employees can be taken into account in making decisions which are likely to affect their interests,

(c) encouraging the involvement of employees in the company's performance through an employees' share scheme or by some other means,

(d) achieving a common awareness on the part of all employees of the financial and economic factors affecting the performance of the company.

11(4) In sub-paragraph (3) **"employee"** does not include a person employed to work wholly or mainly outside the United Kingdom; and for the purposes of sub-paragraph (2) no regard is to be had to such a person.

PART 5 – POLICY AND PRACTICE ON PAYMENT OF CREDITORS

12 [Repealed.]

History – Para. 12 repealed by SI 2013/1970, reg. 7(1) and (3)(d), with effect from 1 October 2013 in respect of financial years ending on or after 30 September 2013. Prior to repeal, para. 12 read as follows:

"**12(1)** This Part of this Schedule applies to the directors' report for a financial year if–
   (a) the company was at any time within the year a public company, or
   (b) the company did not qualify as small or medium-sized in relation to the year by virtue of section 382 or 465 of the 2006 Act and was at any time within the year a member of a group of which the parent company was a public company.

12(2) The report must state, with respect to the next following financial year–
   (a) whether in respect of some or all of its suppliers it is the company's policy to follow any code or standard on payment practice and, if so, the name of the code or standard and the place where information about, and copies of, the code or standard can be obtained,
   (b) whether in respect of some or all of its suppliers it is the company's policy–

      (i)   to settle the terms of payment with those suppliers when agreeing the terms of each transaction,

      (ii)   to ensure that those suppliers are made aware of the terms of payment, and

      (iii) to abide by the terms of payment,

(c)   where the company's policy is not as mentioned in paragraph (a) or (b) in respect of some or all of its suppliers, what its policy is with respect to the payment of those suppliers; and if the company's policy is different for different suppliers or classes of suppliers, the report must identify the suppliers to which the different policies apply.

In this sub-paragraph references to the company's suppliers are references to persons who are or may become its suppliers.

12(3) The report must also state the number of days which bears to the number of days in the financial year the same proportion as X bears to Y where–

X = the aggregate of the amounts which were owed to trade creditors at the end of the year; and

Y = the aggregate of the amounts in which the company was invoiced by suppliers during the year.

12(4) For the purposes of sub-paragraphs (2) and (3) a person is a supplier of the company at any time if–

(a)   at that time, he is owed an amount in respect of goods or services supplied, and

(b)   that amount would be included under the heading corresponding to item E.4 (trade creditors) in format 1 if–

      (i)   the company's accounts fell to be prepared as at that time,

      (ii)   those accounts were prepared in accordance with Schedule 1 to these Regulations, and

      (iii) that format were adopted.

12(5) For the purpose of sub-paragraph (3), the aggregate of the amounts which at the end of the financial year were owed to trade creditors is taken to be–

(a)   where in the company's accounts format 1 of the balance sheet formats set out in Part 1 of Schedule 1 to these Regulations is adopted, the amount shown under the heading corresponding to item E.4 (trade creditors) in that format,

(b)   where format 2 is adopted, the amount which, under the heading corresponding to item C.4 (trade creditors) in that format, is shown as falling due within one year, and

(c)   where the company's accounts are prepared in accordance with Schedule 2 or 3 to these Regulations or the company's accounts are IAS accounts, the amount which would be shown under the heading corresponding to item E.4 (trade creditors) in format 1 if the company's accounts were prepared in accordance with Schedule 1 and that format were adopted."

PART 6 – DISCLOSURE REQUIRED BY CERTAIN PUBLICLY-TRADED COMPANIES

13(1) This Part of this Schedule applies to the directors' report for a financial year if the company had securities carrying voting rights admitted to trading on a regulated market at the end of that year.

13(2) The report must contain detailed information, by reference to the end of that year, on the following matters–

(a)   the structure of the company's capital, including in particular–

      (i)   the rights and obligations attaching to the shares or, as the case may be, to each class of shares in the company, and

      (ii)   where there are two or more such classes, the percentage of the total share capital represented by each class;

(b)   any restrictions on the transfer of securities in the company, including in particular–

  (i)   limitations on the holding of securities, and

  (ii)   requirements to obtain the approval of the company, or of other holders of securities in the company, for a transfer of securities;

(c)   in the case of each person with a significant direct or indirect holding of securities in the company, such details as are known to the company of–

  (i)   the identity of the person,

  (ii)   the size of the holding, and

  (iii)   the nature of the holding;

(d)   in the case of each person who holds securities carrying special rights with regard to control of the company–

  (i)   the identity of the person, and

  (ii)   the nature of the rights;

(e)   where–

  (i)   the company has an employees' share scheme, and

  (ii)   shares to which the scheme relates have rights with regard to control of the company that are not exercisable directly by the employees, how those rights are exercisable;

(f)   any restrictions on voting rights, including in particular–

  (i)   limitations on voting rights of holders of a given percentage or number of votes,

  (ii)   deadlines for exercising voting rights, and

  (iii)   arrangements by which, with the company's co-operation, financial rights carried by securities are held by a person other than the holder of the securities;

(g)   any agreements between holders of securities that are known to the company and may result in restrictions on the transfer of securities or on voting rights;

(h)   any rules that the company has about–

  (i)   appointment and replacement of directors, or

  (ii)   amendment of the company's articles of association;

(i)   the powers of the company's directors, including in particular any powers in relation to the issuing or buying back by the company of its shares;

(j)   any significant agreements to which the company is a party that take effect, alter or terminate upon a change of control of the company following a takeover bid, and the effects of any such agreements;

(k)   any agreements between the company and its directors or employees providing for compensation for loss of office or employment (whether through resignation, purported redundancy or otherwise) that occurs because of a takeover bid.

13(3)   For the purposes of sub-paragraph (2)(a) a company's capital includes any securities in the company that are not admitted to trading on a regulated market.

13(4)   For the purposes of sub-paragraph (2)(c) a person has an indirect holding of securities if–

(a)   they are held on his behalf, or

(b)   he is able to secure that rights carried by the securities are exercised in accordance with his wishes.

13(5) Sub-paragraph (2)(j) does not apply to an agreement if–

(a)   disclosure of the agreement would be seriously prejudicial to the company, and

(b)   the company is not under any other obligation to disclose it.

13(6) In this paragraph–

"securities" means shares or debentures;

"takeover bid" has the same meaning as in the Takeovers Directive;

"the Takeovers Directive" means Directive 2004/25/EC of the European Parliament and of the Council;

"voting rights" means rights to vote at general meetings of the company in question, including rights that arise only in certain circumstances.

14   The directors' report must also contain any necessary explanatory material with regard to information that is required to be included in the report by this Part.

PART 7 – DISCLOSURES CONCERNING GREENHOUSE GAS EMISSIONS

15(1) This Part of this Schedule applies to the directors' report for a financial year if the company is a quoted company.

15(2) The report must state the annual quantity of emissions in tonnes of carbon dioxide equivalent from activities for which that company is responsible including–

(a)   the combustion of fuel; and

(b)   the operation of any facility.

15(3) The report must state the annual quantity of emissions in tonnes of carbon dioxide equivalent resulting from the purchase of electricity, heat, steam or cooling by the company for its own use.

15(4) Sub-paragraphs (2) and (3) apply only to the extent that it is practical for the company to obtain the information in question; but where it is not practical for the company to obtain some or all of that information, the report must state what information is not included and why.

16   The directors' report must state the methodologies used to calculate the information disclosed under paragraph 15(2) and (3).

17   The directors' report must state at least one ratio which expresses the quoted company's annual emissions in relation to a quantifiable factor associated with the company's activities.

18   With the exception of the first year for which the directors' report contains the information required by paragraphs 15(2) and (3) and 17, the report must state not only the information required by paragraphs 15(2) and (3) and 17, but also that information as disclosed in the report for the preceding financial year.

19   The directors' report must state if the period for which it is reporting the information required by paragraph 15(2) and (3) is different to the period in respect of which the directors' report is prepared.

20   The following definitions apply for the purposes of this Part of this Schedule–

"emissions" means emissions into the atmosphere of a greenhouse gas as defined in "**tonne of carbon dioxide equivalent**" has the meaning given in section 93(2) of the Climate Change Act 2008.

History – Pt. 7 inserted by SI 2013/1970, reg. 7(1) and (3)(e), with effect from 1 October 2013 in respect of financial years ending on or after 30 September 2013.

SCHEDULE 8

Regulation 11

QUOTED COMPANIES: DIRECTORS' REMUNERATION REPORT

PART 1 – INTRODUCTORY

1(1) In the directors' remuneration report for a financial year ("the relevant financial year") there must be shown, subject to sub-paragraph (2), the information specified in Parts 2, 3, and 4.

1(2) The directors' remuneration policy as specified in Part 4, may, subject to subparagraph (3), be omitted from the directors' remuneration report for a financial year, if the company does not intend, at the accounts meeting at which the report is to be laid, to move a resolution to approve the directors' remuneration policy in accordance with section 439A of the 2006 Act.

1(3) Where the directors' remuneration policy is omitted from the report in accordance with sub-paragraph (2), there must be set out in the report the following information–

    (a) the date of the last general meeting of the company at which a resolution was moved by the company in respect of that directors' remuneration policy and at which that policy was approved; and

    (b) where, on the company's website or at some other place, a copy of that directors' remuneration policy may be inspected by the members of the company.

2(1) Information required to be shown in the report for or in respect of a particular person must be shown in the report in a manner that links the information to that person identified by name.

2(2) Nothing in this Schedule prevents the directors setting out in the report any such additional information as they think fit, and any item required to be shown in the report may be shown in greater detail than required by the provisions of this Schedule.

2(3) Where the requirements of this Schedule make reference to a "director" those requirements may be complied with in such manner as to distinguish between directors who perform executive functions and those who do not.

2(4) Any requirement of this Schedule to provide information in respect of a director may, in respect of those directors who do not perform executive functions, be omitted or otherwise modified where that requirement is not applicable to such a director and in such a case, particulars of, and the reasons for, the omission or modification must be given in the report.

2(5) Any requirement of this Schedule to provide information in respect of performance measures or targets does not require the disclosure of information which, in the opinion of the directors, is commercially sensitive in respect of the company.

2(6) Where information that would otherwise be required to be in the report is not included in reliance on sub-paragraph (5), particulars of, and the reasons for, the omission must be given in the report and an indication given of when (if at all) the information is to be reported to the members of the company.

2(7) Where any provision of this Schedule requires a sum or figure to be given in respect of any financial year preceding the relevant financial year, in the first directors' remuneration report prepared in accordance with this Schedule, that sum or figure may, where the sum or figure is not readily available from the reports and accounts of the company prepared for those years, be given as an estimate and a note of explanation provided in the report.

PART 2 – ANNUAL STATEMENT

3 The directors' remuneration report must contain a statement by the director who fulfils the role of chair of the remuneration committee (or, where there is no such person, by a director nominated by the directors to make the statement) summarising for the relevant financial year–

    (a)   the major decisions on directors' remuneration;

    (b)   any substantial changes relating to directors' remuneration made during the year; and

    (c)   the context in which those changes occurred and decisions have been taken.

PART 3 – ANNUAL REPORT ON REMUNERATION

Single total figure of remuneration for each director

4(1) The directors' remuneration report must, for the relevant financial year, for each person who has served as a director of the company at any time during that year, set out in a table in the form set out in paragraph 5 ("the single total figure table") the information prescribed by paragraphs 6 and 7 below.

4(2) The report may set out in separate tables the information to be supplied in respect of directors who perform executive functions and those who do not.

4(3) Unless otherwise indicated the sums set out in the table are those in respect of the relevant financial year and relate to the director's performance of, or agreement to perform, qualifying services.

5(1) The form of the table required by paragraph 4 is–

	Single	**Total**	**Figure**	**Table**		
	a	b	c	d	e	**Total**
Director 1	xxx	xxx	xxx	xxx	xxx	xxx
Director 1	xxx	xxx	xxx	xxx	xxx	xxx

5(2) The directors may choose to display the table using an alternative orientation, in which case references in this Schedule to columns are to be read as references to rows.

6(1) In addition to the columns described in paragraph 7, columns–

    (a)   must be included to set out any other items in the nature of remuneration (other than items required to be disclosed under paragraph 15) which are not set out in the columns headed "(a)" to "(e)"; and

    (b)   may be included if there are any sub-totals or other items which the directors consider necessary in order to assist the understanding of the table.

6(2) Any additional columns must be inserted before the column marked "Total".

7(1) Subject to paragraph 9, in the single total figure table, the sums that are required to be set out in the columns are–

    (a)   in the column headed "a", the total amount of salary and fees;

    (b)   in the column headed "b", all taxable benefits;

    (c)   in the column headed "c", money or other assets received or receivable for the relevant financial year as a result of the achievement of performance measures and targets relating to a period ending in that financial year other than–

        (i)   those which result from awards made in a previous financial year and where final vesting is determined as a result of the achievement of performance measures or targets relating to a period ending in the relevant financial year; or

        (ii)   those receivable subject to the achievement of performance measures or targets in a future financial year;

    (d)   in the column headed "d", money or other assets received or receivable for periods of more than one financial year where final vesting–

        (i)   is determined as a result of the achievement of performance measures or targets relating to a period ending in the relevant financial year; and

        (ii)   is not subject to the achievement of performance measures or targets in a future financial year;

    (e)   in the column headed "e", all pension related benefits including–

        (i)   payments (whether in cash or otherwise) in lieu of retirement benefits;

        (ii)   all benefits in year from participating in pension schemes;

    (f)   in the column headed "Total", the total amount of the sums set out in the previous columns.

7(2) Where it is necessary to assist the understanding of the table by the creation of subtotals the columns headed "a" to "e" may be set out in an order other than the one set out in paragraph 5.

8(1) In respect of any items in paragraph 7(1)(c) or (d) where the performance measures or targets are substantially (but not fully) completed by the end of the relevant financial year–

    (a)   the sum given in the table may include sums which relate to the following financial year; but

    (b)   where such sums are included, those sums must not be included in the corresponding column of the single total figure table prepared for that following financial year; and

    (c)   a note to the table must explain the basis of the calculation.

8(2) Where any money or other assets reported in the single total figure table in the directors' remuneration report prepared in respect of any previous financial year are the subject of a recovery of sums paid or the withholding of any sum for any reason in the relevant financial year–

(a)   the recovery or withholding so attributable must be shown in a separate column in the table as a negative value and deducted from the column headed "Total"; and

(b)   an explanation for the recovery or withholding and the basis of the calculation must be given in a note to the table.

8(3) Where the calculations in accordance with paragraph 10 (other than in respect of a recovery or withholding) result in a negative value, the result must be expressed as zero in the relevant column in the table.

9(1) Each column in the single total figure table must contain, in such manner as to permit comparison, two sums as follows–

(a)   the sum set out in the corresponding column in the report prepared in respect of the financial year preceding the relevant financial year; and

(b)   the sum for the relevant financial year.

9(2) When, in the single total figure table, a sum is given in the column which relates to the preceding financial year and that sum, when set out in the report for that preceding year was given as an estimated sum, then in the relevant financial year–

(a)   it must be given as an actual sum;

(b)   the amount representing the difference between the estimate and the actual must not be included in the column relating to the relevant financial year; and

(c)   details of the calculation of the revised sum must be given in a note to the table.

10(1) The methods to be used to calculate the sums required to be set out in the single total figure table are–

(a)   for the column headed "a", cash paid to or receivable by the person in respect of the relevant financial year;

(b)   for the column headed "b", the gross value before payment of tax;

(c)   for column "c", the total cash equivalent including any amount deferred, other than where the deferral is subject to the achievement of further performance measures or targets in a future financial year;

(d)   for column "d"–

  (i)   the cash value of any monetary award;

  (ii)   the value of any shares or share options awarded, calculated by–

    (aa)   multiplying the original number of shares granted by the proportion that vest (or an estimate);

    (bb)   multiplying the total arrived at in (aa) by the market price of shares at the date on which the shares vest; and

  (iii)   the value of any additional cash or shares receivable in respect of dividends accrued (actually or notionally);

(e)   for the column headed "e",–

  (i)   for the item in paragraph 7(1)(e)(i), the cash value;

  (ii)   for the item in paragraph 7(1)(e)(ii), what the aggregate pension input amount would be across all the pension schemes of the company or group in which the director accrues benefits, calculated using the method set out in section 229 of the Finance Act 2004 where–

    (aa)   references to **"pension input period"** are to be read as references to the company's financial year, or where a person becomes a director during the financial year, the period starting on the date the person became a director and ending at the end of the financial year;

(bb)   all pension schemes of the company or group which provide relevant benefits to the director are deemed to be registered schemes;

(cc)   all pension contributions paid by the director during the pension input period are deducted from the pension input amount;

(dd)   in the application of section 234 of that Act, the figure 20 is substituted for the figure 16 each time it appears;

(ee)   subsections 229(3) and (4) do not apply; and

(ff)   section 277 of that Act is read as follows–

"277   Valuation assumptions

277   For the purposes of this Part the valuation assumptions in relation to a person, benefits and a date are–

(a)   if the person has not left the employment to which the arrangement relates on or before the date, that the person left that employment on the date with a prospective right to benefits under the arrangement,

(b)   if the person has not reached such age (if any) as must have been reached to avoid any reduction in the benefits on account of age, that on the date the person is entitled to receive the benefits without any reduction on account of age, and

(c)   that the person's right to receive the benefits had not been occasioned by physical or mental impairment.".

10(2)   For the item in paragraph 7(1)(e)(ii) where there has not been a company contribution to the pension scheme in respect of the director, but if such a contribution had been made it would have been measured for pension input purposes under section 233(1)(b) of the Finance Act 2004, when calculating the pension input amount for the purposes of subparagraph (1)(e)(ii) it should be calculated as if the cash value of any contribution notionally allocated to the scheme in respect of the person by or on behalf of the company including any adjustment made for any notional investment return achieved during the relevant financial year were a contribution paid by the employer in respect of the individual for the purposes of section 233(1)(b) of the Finance Act 2004.

10(3)   For the purposes of the calculation in sub-paragraph (1)(d)(ii)–

(a)   where the market price of shares at the date on which the shares vest is not ascertainable by the date on which the remuneration report is approved by the directors, an estimate of the market price of the shares shall be calculated on the basis of an average market value over the last quarter of the relevant financial year; and

(b)   where the award was an award of shares or share options, the cash amount the individual was or will be required to pay to acquire the share must be deducted from the total.

Definitions applicable to the single total figure table

11(1)   In paragraph 7(1)(b) **"taxable benefits"** includes–

(a)   sums paid by way of expenses allowance that are–

(i)   chargeable to United Kingdom income tax (or would be if the person were an individual, or would be if the person were resident in the United Kingdom for tax purposes), and

(ii)   paid to or receivable by the person in respect of qualifying services; and

(b)   any benefits received by the person, other than salary, (whether or not in cash) that–

(i)   are emoluments of the person, and

(ii)   are received by the person in respect of qualifying services.

11(2)   A payment or other benefit received in advance of a director commencing qualifying services, but in anticipation of performing qualifying services, is to be treated as if received on the first day of performance of the qualifying services.

Additional requirements in respect of the single total figure table

12(1)   In respect of the sum required to be set out by paragraph 7(1)(b), there must be set out after the table a summary identifying–

(a)   the types of benefits the value of which is included in the sum set out in the column headed "b"; and

(b)   the value (where significant).

12(2)   For every component the value of which is included in the sums required to be set out in the columns headed "c" and "d" of the table by paragraphs 7(1)(c) and (d), there must be set out after the table the relevant details.

12(3)   In sub-paragraph (2) **"the relevant details"** means–

(a)   details of any performance measures and the relative weighting of each;

(b)   within each performance measure, the performance targets set at the beginning of the performance period and corresponding value of the award achievable;

(c)   for each performance measure, details of actual performance relative to the targets set and measured over the relevant reporting period, and the resulting level of award; and

(d)   where any discretion has been exercised in respect of the award, particulars must be given of how the discretion was exercised and how the resulting level of award was determined.

12(4)   For each component the value of which is included in the sum set out in the column headed "c" of the table, the report must state if any amount was deferred, the percentage deferred, whether it was deferred in cash or shares, if relevant, and whether the deferral was subject to any conditions other than performance measures.

12(5)   Where additional columns are included in accordance with paragraph 6(1)(a), there must be set out in a note to the table the basis on which the sums in the column were calculated, and other such details as are necessary for an understanding of the sums set out in the column, including any performance measures relating to that component of remuneration or if there are none, an explanation of why not.

Total pension entitlements

13(1)   The directors' remuneration report must, for each person who has served as a director of the company at any time during the relevant financial year, and who has a prospective entitlement to defined benefits or cash balance benefits (or to benefits under a hybrid arrangement which includes such benefits) in respect of qualifying services, contain the following information in respect of pensions–

    (a)   details of those rights as at the end of that year, including the person's normal retirement date;

    (b)   a description of any additional benefit that will become receivable by a director in the event that that director retires early; and

    (c)   where a person has rights under more than one type of pension benefit identified in column headed "e" of the single total figure table, separate details relating to each type of pension benefit.

13(2) For the purposes of this paragraph, "defined benefits", "cash balance benefits" and "hybrid arrangement" have the same meaning as in section 152 of the Finance Act 2004.

13(3) **"Normal retirement date"** means an age specified in the pension scheme rules (or otherwise determined) as the earliest age at which, while the individual continues to accrue benefits under the pension scheme, entitlement to a benefit arises–

    (a)   without consent (whether of an employer, the trustees or managers of the scheme or otherwise), and

    (b)   without an actuarial reduction,

but disregarding any special provision as to early repayment on grounds of ill health, redundancy or dismissal.

Scheme interests awarded during the financial year

14(1) The directors' remuneration report must for each person who has served as a director of the company at any time during the relevant financial year contain a table setting out–

    (a)   details of the scheme interests awarded to the person during the relevant financial year; and

    (b)   for each scheme interest–

        (i)   a description of the type of interest awarded;

        (ii)   a description of the basis on which the award is made;

        (iii)   the face value of the award;

        (iv)   the percentage of scheme interests that would be receivable if the minimum performance was achieved;

        (v)   for a scheme interest that is a share option, an explanation of any difference between the exercise price per share and the price specified under paragraph 14(3);

        (vi)   the end of the period over which the performance measures and targets for that interest have to be achieved (or if there are different periods for different measures and targets, the end of whichever of those periods ends last); and

        (vii)   a summary of the performance measures and targets if not set out elsewhere in the report.

14(2) In respect of a scheme interest relating to shares or share options, **"face value"** means the maximum number of shares that would vest if all performance measures and targets are met multiplied by either–

(a)   the share price at date of grant or

(b)   the average share price used to determine the number of shares awarded.

14(3) Where the report sets out the face value of an award in respect of a scheme interest relating to shares or share options, the report must specify–

(a)   whether the face value has been calculated using the share price at date of grant or the average share price;

(b)   where the share price at date of grant is used, the amount of that share price and the date of grant;

(c)   where the average share price is used, what that price was and the period used for calculating the average.

Payments to past directors

15   The directors' remuneration report must, for the relevant financial year, contain details of any payments of money or other assets to any person who was not a director of the company at the time the payment was made, but who had been a director of the company before that time, excluding–

(a)   any payments falling within paragraph 16;

(b)   any payments which are shown in the single total figure table;

(c)   any payments which have been disclosed in a previous directors' remuneration report of the company;

(d)   any payments which are below a *de minimis* threshold set by the company and stated in the report;

(e)   payments by way of regular pension benefits commenced in a previous year or dividend payments in respect of scheme interests retained after leaving office; and

(f)   payments in respect of employment with or any other contractual service performed for the company other than as a director.

Payments for loss of office

16 The directors' remuneration report must for the relevant financial year set out, for each person who has served as a director of the company at any time during that year, or any previous year, excluding payments which are below a *de minimis* threshold set by the company and stated in the report–

(a)   the total amount of any payment for loss of office paid to or receivable by the person in respect of that financial year, broken down into each component comprised in that payment and the value of each component;

(b)   an explanation of how each component was calculated;

(c)   any other payments paid to or receivable by the person in connection with the termination of qualifying services, whether by way of compensation for loss of office or otherwise, including the treatment of outstanding incentive awards that vest on or following termination; and

(d)   where any discretion was exercised in respect of the payment, an explanation of how it was exercised.

Statement of directors' shareholding and share interests

17   The directors' remuneration report for the relevant financial year must contain, for each person who has served as a director of the company at any time during that year–

(a)   a statement of any requirements or guidelines for the director to own shares in the company and state whether or not those requirements or guidelines have been met;

(b)   in tabular form or forms–

(i)   the total number of interests in shares in the company of the director including interests of connected persons (as defined for the purposes of section 96B(2) of the Financial Services and Markets Act 2000);

(ii)   total number of scheme interests differentiating between–

(aa)   shares and share options; and

(bb)   those with or without performance measures;

(iii)   details of those scheme interests (which may exclude any details included elsewhere in the report); and

(iv)   details of share options which are–

(aa)   vested but unexercised; and

(bb)   exercised in the relevant financial year.

Performance graph and table

18(1)   The directors' remuneration report must–

(a)   contain a line graph that shows for each of–

(i)   a holding of shares of that class of the company's equity share capital whose listing, or admission to dealing, has resulted in the company falling within the definition of "quoted company", and

(ii)   a hypothetical holding of shares made up of shares of the same kinds and number as those by reference to which a broad equity market index is calculated, a line drawn by joining up points plotted to represent, for each of the financial years in the relevant period, the total shareholder return on that holding; and

(b)   state the name of the index selected for the purposes of the graph and set out the reasons for selecting that index.

18(2)   The report must also set out in tabular form the following information for each of the financial years in the relevant period in respect of the director undertaking the role of chief executive officer–

(a)   total remuneration as set out in the single total figure table;

(b)   the sum set out in the table in column headed "c" in the single total figure table expressed as a percentage of the maximum that could have been paid in respect of that component in the financial year; and

(c)   the sum set out in column headed "d" in the single total figure table restated as a percentage of the number of shares vesting against the maximum number of shares that could have been received, or, where paid in money and other assets, as a percentage of the maximum that could have been paid in respect of that component in the financial year.

18(3) For the purposes of sub-paragraphs (1), (2) and (6), **"relevant period"** means the specified period of financial years of which the last is the relevant financial year.

18(4) Where the relevant financial year–

(a) is the company's first financial year for which the performance graph is prepared in accordance with this paragraph, **"specified"** in sub-paragraph (3) means "five";

(b) is the company's "second", "third", "fourth", "fifth" financial year in which the report is prepared in accordance with this Schedule, **"specified"** in sub-paragraph (3) means "six", "seven", "eight", "nine" as the case may be; and

(c) is any financial year after the fifth financial year in which the report is prepared in accordance with this Schedule, **"specified"** means "ten".

18(5) Sub-paragraph (2) may be complied with by use of either–

(a) a sum based on the information supplied in the directors' remuneration reports for those previous years, or,

(b) where no such report has been compiled, a suitable corresponding sum.

18(6) For the purposes of sub-paragraph (1), the "total shareholder return" for a relevant period on a holding of shares must be calculated using a fair method that–

(a) takes as its starting point the percentage change over the period in the market price of the holding;

(b) involves making–

(i) the assumptions specified in sub-paragraph (7) as to reinvestment of income, and

(ii) the assumption specified in sub-paragraph (9) as to the funding of liabilities; and

(c) makes provision for any replacement of shares in the holding by shares of a different description;

and the same method must be used for each of the holdings mentioned in sub-paragraph (1).

18(7) The assumptions as to reinvestment of income are–

(a) that any benefit in the form of shares of the same kind as those in the holding is added to the holding at the time the benefit becomes receivable; and

(b) that any benefit in cash, and an amount equal to the value of any benefit not in cash and not falling within paragraph (a), is applied at the time the benefit becomes receivable in the purchase at their market price of shares of the same kind as those in the holding and that the shares purchased are added to the holding at that time.

18(8) In sub-paragraph (7) **"benefit"** means any benefit (including, in particular, any dividend) receivable in respect of any shares in the holding by the holder from the company of whose share capital the shares form part.

18(9)   The assumption as to the funding of liabilities is that, where the holder has a liability to the company of whose capital the shares in the holding form part, shares are sold from the holding–

    (a)   immediately before the time by which the liability is due to be satisfied, and

    (b)   in such numbers that, at the time of the sale, the market price of the shares sold equals the amount of the liability in respect of the shares in the holding that are not being sold.

18(10)   In sub-paragraph (9) **"liability"** means a liability arising in respect of any shares in the holding or from the exercise of a right attached to any of those shares.

Percentage change in remuneration of director undertaking the role of chief executive officer

19(1)   The directors' remuneration report must set out (in a manner which permits comparison) in relation to each of the kinds of remuneration required to be set out in each of the columns headed "a", "b" and "c" of the single total figure table the following information–

    (a)   the percentage change from the financial year preceding the relevant financial year in respect of the director undertaking the role of the chief executive officer; and

    (b)   the average percentage change from the financial year preceding the relevant financial year in respect of the employees of the company taken as a whole.

19(2)   Where for the purposes of sub-paragraph (1)(b), a comparator group comprising the employees taken as a whole is considered by the company as an inappropriate comparator group of employees, the company may use such other comparator group of employees as the company identifies, provided the report contains a statement setting out why that group was chosen.

19(3)   Where the company is a parent company, the statement must relate to the group and not the company, and the director reported on is the director undertaking the role of chief executive officer of the parent company, and the employees are the employees of the group.

Relative importance of spend on pay

20(1)   The directors' remuneration report must set out in a graphical or tabular form that shows in respect of the relevant financial year and the immediately preceding financial year the actual expenditure of the company, and the difference in spend between those years, on–

    (a)   remuneration paid to or receivable by all employees of the group;

    (b)   distributions to shareholders by way of dividend and share buyback; and

    (c)   any other significant distributions and payments or other uses of profit or cashflow deemed by the directors to assist in understanding the relative importance of spend on pay.

20(2)   There must be set out in a note to the report an explanation in respect of subparagraph (1)(c) why the particular matters were chosen by the directors and how the amounts were calculated.

20(3)   Where the matters chosen for the report in respect of sub-paragraph (1)(c) in the relevant financial year are not the same as the other items set out in the report for previous years, an explanation for that change must be given.

Statement of implementation of remuneration policy in the following financial year

21(1)   The directors' remuneration report must contain a statement describing how the company intends to implement the approved directors' remuneration policy in the financial year following the relevant financial year.

21(2)   The statement must include, where applicable, the–

   (a)   performance measures and relative weightings for each; and

   (b)   performance targets determined for the performance measures and how awards will be calculated.

21(3)   Where this is not the first year of the approved remuneration policy, the statement should detail any significant changes in the way that the remuneration policy will be implemented in the next financial year compared to how it was implemented in the relevant financial year.

21(4)   This statement need not include information that is elsewhere in the report, including any disclosed in the directors' remuneration policy.

Consideration by the directors of matters relating to directors' remuneration

22(1)   If a committee of the company's directors has considered matters relating to the directors' remuneration for the relevant financial year, the directors' remuneration report must–

   (a)   name each director who was a member of the committee at any time when the committee was considering any such matter;

   (b)   state whether any person provided to the committee advice, or services, that materially assisted the committee in their consideration of any such matter and name any person that has done so;

   (c)   in the case of any person named under paragraph (b), who is not a director of the company (other than a person who provided legal advice on compliance with any relevant legislation), state–

      (i)   the nature of any other services that that person has provided to the company during the relevant financial year;

      (ii)   by whom that person was appointed, whether or not by the committee and how they were selected;

      (iii)   whether and how the remuneration committee has satisfied itself that the advice received was objective and independent; and

      (iv)   the amount of fee or other charge paid by the company to that person for the provision of the advice or services referred to in paragraph (b) and the basis on which it was charged.

22(2)   In sub-paragraph (1)(b) **"person"** includes (in particular) any director of the company who does not fall within sub-paragraph (1)(a).

22(3)   Sub-paragraph (1)(c) does not apply where the person was, at the time of the provision of the advice or service, an employee of the company.

22(4)   This paragraph also applies to a committee which considers remuneration issues during the consideration of an individual's nomination as a director.

Statement of voting at general meeting

23   The directors' remuneration report must contain a statement setting out in respect of the last general meeting at which a resolution of the following kind was moved by the company–

(a)   in respect of a resolution to approve the directors' remuneration report, the percentage of votes cast for and against and the number of votes withheld;

(b)   in respect of a resolution to approve the directors' remuneration policy, the percentage of votes cast for and against and the number of votes withheld; and,

(c)   where there was a significant percentage of votes against either such resolution, a summary of the reasons for those votes, as far as known to the directors, and any actions taken by the directors in response to those concerns.

PART 4 – DIRECTORS' REMUNERATION POLICY

Introductory

24(1)   The information required to be included in the directors' remuneration report by the provisions of this Part must be set out in a separate part of the report and constitutes the directors' remuneration policy of the company.

24(2)   Where a company intends to move a resolution at a meeting of the company to approve a directors' remuneration policy and it is intended that some or all of the provisions of the last approved directors' remuneration policy are to continue to apply after the resolution is approved, this fact must be stated in the policy which is the subject of the resolution and it must be made clear which provisions of the last approved policy are to continue to apply and for what period of time it is intended that they shall apply.

24(3)   Notwithstanding the requirements of this Part, the directors' remuneration policy part of the report must set out all those matters for which the company requires approval for the purposes of Chapter 4A of Part 10 of the 2006 Act.

24(4)   Where any provision of the directors' remuneration policy provides for the exercise by the directors of a discretion on any aspect of the policy, the policy must clearly set out the extent of that discretion in respect of any such variation, change or amendment.

24(5)   The directors' remuneration policy (or revised directors' remuneration policy) of a company in respect of which a company moves a resolution for approval in accordance with section 439A of the 2006 Act must, on the first occasion that such a resolution is moved after 1st October 2013 set out the date from which it is intended by the company that that policy is to take effect.

Future policy table

25(1) The directors' remuneration report must contain in tabular form a description of each of the components of the remuneration package for the directors of the company which are comprised in the directors' remuneration policy of the company.

25(2) Where the report complies with sub-paragraph (1) by reference to provisions which apply generally to all directors, the table must also include any particular arrangements which are specific to any director individually.

25(3) References in this Part to **"component parts of the remuneration package"** include, but are not limited to, all those items which are relevant for the purposes of the single total figure table.

26 In respect of each of the components described in the table there must be set out the following information–

- (a) how that component supports the short and long-term strategic objectives of the company (or, where the company is a parent company, the group);
- (b) an explanation of how that component of the remuneration package operates;
- (c) the maximum that may be paid in respect of that component (which may be expressed in monetary terms, or otherwise);
- (d) where applicable, a description of the framework used to assess performance including–
  - (i) a description of any performance measures which apply and, where more than one performance measure applies, an indication of the weighting of the performance measure or group of performance measures;
  - (ii) details of any performance period; and
  - (iii) the amount (which may be expressed in monetary terms or otherwise) that may be paid in respect of–
    - (aa) the minimum level of performance that results in any payment under the policy, and
    - (bb) any further levels of performance set in accordance with the policy;
- (e) an explanation as to whether there are any provisions for the recovery of sums paid or the withholding of the payment of any sum.

27 There must accompany the table notes which set out–

- (a) in respect of any component falling within paragraph 26(d)(i)–(iii), an explanation of why any performance measures were chosen and how any performance targets are set;
- (b) in respect of any component (other than salary, fees, benefits or pension) which is not subject to performance measures, an explanation of why there are no such measures;
- (c) if any component did not form part of the remuneration package in the last approved directors' remuneration policy, why that component is now contained in the remuneration package;
- (d) in respect of any component which did form a part of such a package, what changes have been made to it and why; and
- (e) an explanation of the differences (if any) in the company's policy on the remuneration of directors from the policy on the remuneration of employees generally (within the company, or where the company is a parent company, the group).

28   The information required by paragraph 25 may, in respect of directors not performing an executive function, be set out in a separate table and there must be set out in that table the approach of the company to the determination of–

    (a)   the fee payable to such directors;

    (b)   any additional fees payable for any other duties to the company;

    (c)   such other items as are to be considered in the nature of remuneration.

Approach to recruitment remuneration

29(1)   The directors' remuneration policy must contain a statement of the principles which would be applied by the company when agreeing the components of a remuneration package for the appointment of directors.

29(2)   The statement must set out the various components which would be considered for inclusion in that package and the approach to be adopted by the company in respect of each component.

29(3)   The statement must, subject to sub-paragraph (4), set out the maximum level of variable remuneration which may be granted (which can be expressed in monetary terms or otherwise).

29(4)   Remuneration which constitutes compensation for the forfeit of any award under variable remuneration arrangements entered into with a previous employer is not included within sub-paragraph (3) of this paragraph, but is subject to the requirements of subparagraphs (1) and (2).

Service contracts

30   The directors' remuneration policy must contain a description of any obligation on the company which–

    (a)   is contained in all directors' service contracts;

    (b)   is contained in the service contracts of any one or more existing directors (not being covered by paragraph (a)); or

    (c)   it is proposed would be contained in directors' service contracts to be entered into by the company

and which could give rise to, or impact on, remuneration payments or payments for loss of office but which is not disclosed elsewhere in this report.

31   Where the directors' service contracts are not kept available for inspection at the company's registered office, the report must give details of where the contracts are kept, and if the contracts are available on a website, a link to that website.

32   The provisions of paragraphs 30 and 31 relating to directors' service contracts apply in like manner to the terms of letters of appointment of directors.

Illustrations of application of remuneration policy

33   The directors' remuneration report must, in respect of each person who is a director (other than a director who is not performing an executive function), set out in the form of a bar chart an indication of the level of remuneration that would be received by the director in accordance with the directors' remuneration policy in the first year to which the policy applies.

34(1)   The bar chart must contain separate bars representing–

(a)   minimum remuneration receivable, that is to say, including, but not limited to, salary, fees, benefits and pension;

(b)   the remuneration receivable if the director was, in respect of any performance measures or targets, performing in line with the company's expectation;

(c)   maximum remuneration receivable (not allowing for any share price appreciation).

34(2)   Each bar of the chart must contain separate parts which represent–

(a)   salary, fees, benefits, pension and any other item falling within sub-paragraph 34(1)(a);

(b)   remuneration where performance measures or targets relate to one financial year;

(c)   remuneration where performance measures or targets relate to more than one financial year.

34(3)   Each bar must show–

(a)   percentage of the total comprised by each of the parts; and

(b)   total value of remuneration expected for each bar.

35(1)   A narrative description of the basis of calculation and assumptions used to compile the bar chart must be set out to enable an understanding of the charts presented.

35(2)   In complying with sub-paragraph (1) it is not necessary for any matter to be included in the narrative description which has been set out in the future policy table required by paragraph 25.

Policy on payment for loss of office

36   The directors' remuneration policy must set out the company's policy on the setting of notice periods under directors' service contracts.

37   The directors' remuneration policy must also set out the principles on which the determination of payments for loss of office will be approached including–

(a)   an indication of how each component of the payment will be calculated;

(b)   whether, and if so how, the circumstances of the director's loss of office and performance during the period of qualifying service are relevant to any exercise of discretion; and

(c)   any contractual provision agreed prior to 27th June 2012 that could impact on the quantum of the payment.

Statement of consideration of employment conditions elsewhere in company

38   The directors' remuneration policy must contain a statement of how pay and employment conditions of employees (other than directors) of the company and, where the company is a parent company, of the group of other undertakings within the same group as the company, were taken into account when setting the policy for directors' remuneration.

39   The statement must also set out–

   (a)   whether, and if so, how, the company consulted with employees when drawing up the directors' remuneration policy set out in this part of the report;

   (b)   whether any remuneration comparison measurements were used and if so, what they were, and how that information was taken into account.

Statement of consideration of shareholder views

40   The directors' remuneration policy must contain a statement of whether, and if so how, any views in respect of directors' remuneration expressed to the company by shareholders (whether at a general meeting or otherwise) have been taken into account in the formulation of the directors' remuneration policy.

PART 5 – PROVISIONS OF THE DIRECTORS' REMUNERATION REPORT WHICH ARE SUBJECT TO AUDIT

41   The information contained in the directors' remuneration report which is subject to audit is the information required by paragraphs 4 to 17 (inclusive) of Part 3 of this Schedule.

PART 6 – REVISED DIRECTORS' REMUNERATION POLICY

42   A revised directors' remuneration policy prepared in accordance with section 422A of the 2006 Act must contain all those matters required by Part 4 of this Schedule to be in the directors' remuneration policy.

43   A revised directors' remuneration policy must be set out in the same manner as required by Part 4 of this Schedule in respect of that part of the directors' remuneration report.

PART 7 – INTERPRETATION AND SUPPLEMENTARY

44(1)   In this Schedule–

"amount", in relation to a gain made on the exercise of a share option, means the difference between–

   (a)   the market price of the shares on the day on which the option was exercised; and

   (b)   the price actually paid for the shares;

"**company contributions**", in relation to a pension scheme and a person, means any payments (including insurance premiums) made, or treated as made, to the scheme in respect of the person by anyone other than the person;

"**emoluments**" f a person–

(a) include salary, fees and bonuses, sums paid by way of expenses allowance (so far as they are chargeable to United Kingdom income tax or would be if the person were an individual or would be if the person were resident in the United Kingdom for tax purposes), but

(b) do not include any of the following, namely–

  (i) the value of any share options granted to him or the amount of any gains made on the exercise of any such options;

  (ii) any company contributions paid, or treated as paid, in respect of him under any pension scheme or any benefits to which he is entitled under any such scheme; or

  (iii) any money or other assets paid to or received or receivable by him under any scheme;

"**pension scheme**" means a retirement benefits scheme within the meaning given by section 150(1) of the Finance Act 2004 which is–

(a) one in which the company participates or

(b) one to which the company paid a contribution during the financial year;

"**performance measure**" is the measure by which performance is to be assessed, but does not include any condition relating to service:

"**performance target**" is the specific level of performance to be attained in respect of that performance measure;

"**qualifying services**", in relation to any person, means his services as a director of the company, and his services at any time while he is a director of the company–

(a) as a director of an undertaking that is a subsidiary undertaking of the company at that time;

(b) as a director of any other undertaking of which he is a director by virtue of the company's nomination (direct or indirect); or

(c) otherwise in connection with the management of the affairs of the company or any such subsidiary undertaking or any such other undertaking;

"**remuneration committee**" means a committee of directors of the company having responsibility for considering matters related to the remuneration of directors;

"**retirement benefits**" means relevant benefits within the meaning given by section 393B of the Income Tax (Earnings and Pensions) Act 2003 read as if subsection (2) were omitted;

"**scheme**" (other than a pension scheme) means any agreement or arrangement under which money or other assets may become receivable by a person and which includes one or more qualifying conditions with respect to service or performance that cannot be fulfilled within a single financial year, and for this purpose the following must be disregarded, namely–

(a) any payment the amount of which falls to be determined by reference to service or performance within a single financial year;

(b) compensation in respect of loss of office, payments for breach of contract and other termination payments; and

(c) retirement benefits;

"**scheme interest**" means an interest under a scheme;

"**shares**" means shares (whether allotted or not) in the company, or any undertaking which is a group undertaking in relation to the company, and includes a share warrant as defined by section 779(1) of the 2006 Act;

"**share option**" means a right to acquire shares;

"**value**" in relation to shares received or receivable on any day by a person who is or has been a director of a company, means the market price of the shares on that day.

44(2) In this Schedule "**compensation in respect of loss of office**" includes compensation received or receivable by a person for–

(a)   loss of office as director of the company, or

(b)   loss, while director of the company or on or in connection with his ceasing to be a director of it, of–

    (i)   any other office in connection with the management of the company' affairs; or

    (ii)   any office as director or otherwise in connection with the management of the affairs of any undertaking that, immediately before the loss, is a subsidiary undertaking of the company or an undertaking of which he is a director by virtue of the company's nomination (direct or indirect);

(c)   compensation in consideration for, or in connection with, a person's retirement from office; and

(d)   where such a retirement is occasioned by a breach of the person's contract with the company or with an undertaking that, immediately before the breach, is a subsidiary undertaking of the company or an undertaking of which he is a director by virtue of the company's nomination (direct or indirect)–

    (i)   payments made by way of damages for the breach; or

    (ii)   payments made by way of settlement or compromise of any claim in respect of the breach.

44(3)   References in this Schedule to compensation include benefits otherwise than in cash; and in relation to such compensation references in this Schedule to its amounts are to the estimated money value of the benefit.

44(4)   References in this Schedule to a person being "**connected**" with a director, and to a director "**controlling**" a body corporate, are to be construed in accordance with sections 252 to 255 of the 2006 Act.

45   For the purposes of this Schedule emoluments paid or receivable or share options granted in respect of a person's accepting office as a director are to be treated as emoluments paid or receivable or share options granted in respect of his services as a director.

46(1)   The following applies with respect to the amounts to be shown under this Schedule.

46(2)   The amount in each case includes all relevant sums paid by or receivable from–

(a)   ) the company; and

(b)   the company's subsidiary undertakings; and

(c)   any other person,

except sums to be accounted for to the company or any of its subsidiary undertakings or any other undertaking of which any person has been a director while director of the company, by virtue of section 219 of the 2006 Act (payment in connection with share transfer: requirement of members' approval), to past or present members of the company or any of its subsidiaries or any class of those members.

46(3)   Reference to amounts paid to or receivable by a person include amounts paid to or receivable by a person connected with the person or a body corporate controlled by the person (but not so as to require an amount to be counted twice).

47(1)   The amounts to be shown for any financial year under Part 3 of this Schedule are the sums receivable in respect of that year (whenever paid) or, in the case of sums not receivable in respect of a period, the sums paid during that year.

47(2)   But where–

   (a)   any sums are not shown in the directors' remuneration report for the relevant financial year on the ground that the person receiving them is liable to account for them as mentioned in paragraph 46(2), but the liability is thereafter wholly or partly released or is not enforced within a period of 2 years; or

   (b)   any sums paid by way of expenses allowance are charged to United Kingdom income tax after the end of the relevant financial year or, in the case of any such sums paid otherwise than to an individual, it does not become clear until the end of the relevant financial year that those sums would be charged to such tax were the person an individual,

those sums must, to the extent to which the liability is released or not enforced or they are charged as mentioned above (as the case may be), be shown in the first directors' remuneration report in which it is practicable to show them and must be distinguished from the amounts to be shown apart from this provision.

48   Where it is necessary to do so for the purpose of making any distinction required by the preceding paragraphs in an amount to be shown in compliance with this Schedule, the directors may apportion any payments between the matters in respect of which these have been paid or are receivable in such manner as they think appropriate.

49   The Schedule requires information to be given only so far as it is contained in the company's books and papers, available to members of the public or the company has the right to obtain it.

History – Sch. 8 substituted by SI 2013/1981, reg. 3 and Sch., with with effect from 1 October 2013. The following transitional provision is made by SI 2013/1981, reg. 4:

"**4(1)**   The amendments made by these Regulations to the 2008 Regulations do not apply to a company in respect of a financial year ending before 30th September 2013.

4(2)   The provisions of the 2008 Regulations as they stood immediately before 1st October 2013 continue to apply in respect of a financial year ending before 30th September 2013.

4(3)   The provisions of Part 6 of Schedule 8 apply to a revised directors' remuneration policy set out in a document in accordance with section 422A(3) of the Companies Act 2006 on or after 1st October 2013."

Prior to substitution, Sch. 8 read as follows:

QUOTED COMPANIES: DIRECTORS' REMUNERATION REPORT

Part 1 – Introductory

1(1) In the directors' remuneration report for a financial year ("the relevant financial year") there must be shown the information specified in Parts 2 and 3.

1(2) Information required to be shown in the report for or in respect of a particular person must be shown in the report in a manner that links the information to that person identified by name.

Part 2 – Information not subject to audit

Consideration by the directors of matters relating to directors' remuneration

2(1) If a committee of the company's directors has considered matters relating to the directors' remuneration for the relevant financial year, the directors' remuneration report must–

    (a)   name each director who was a member of the committee at any time when the committee was considering any such matter;

    (b)   name any person who provided to the committee advice, or services, that materially assisted the committee in their consideration of any such matter;

    (c)   in the case of any person named under paragraph (b), who is not a director of the company, state–

        (i)   the nature of any other services that that person has provided to the company during the relevant financial year; and

        (ii)   whether that person was appointed by the committee.

2(2) In sub-paragraph (1)(b) **"person"** includes (in particular) any director of the company who does not fall within sub-paragraph (1)(a).

Statement of company's policy on directors' remuneration

3(1) The directors' remuneration report must contain a statement of the company's policy on directors' remuneration for the following financial year and for financial years subsequent to that.

3(2) The policy statement must include–

    (a)   for each director, a detailed summary of any performance conditions to which any entitlement of the director–

        (i)   to share options, or

        (ii)   under a long term incentive scheme, is subject;

    (b)   an explanation as to why any such performance conditions were chosen;

    (c)   a summary of the methods to be used in assessing whether any such performance conditions are met and an explanation as to why those methods were chosen;

    (d)   if any such performance condition involves any comparison with factors external to the company–

        (i)   a summary of the factors to be used in making each such comparison, and

        (ii)   if any of the factors relates to the performance of another company, of two or more other companies or of an index on which the securities of a company or companies are listed, the identity of that company, of each of those companies or of the index;

    (e)   a description of, and an explanation for, any significant amendment proposed to be made to the terms and conditions of any entitlement of a director to share options or under a long term incentive scheme; and

    (f)   if any entitlement of a director to share options, or under a long term incentive scheme, is not subject to performance conditions, an explanation as to why that is the case.

3(3) The policy statement must, in respect of each director's terms and conditions relating to remuneration, explain the relative importance of those elements which are, and those which are not, related to performance.

3(4) The policy statement must summarise, and explain, the company's policy on–

    (a)   the duration of contracts with directors, and

    (b)   notice periods, and termination payments, under such contracts.

3(5) In sub-paragraphs (2) and (3), references to a director are to any person who serves as a director of the company at any time in the period beginning with the end of the relevant financial year and ending with the date on which the directors' remuneration report is laid before the company in general meeting.

Statement of consideration of conditions elsewhere in company and group

4 The directors' remuneration report must contain a statement of how pay and employment conditions of employees of the company and of other undertakings within the same group as the company were taken into account when determining directors' remuneration for the relevant financial year.

Performance graph

5(1) The directors' remuneration report must–

    (a)   contain a line graph that shows for each of–

        (i)   a holding of shares of that class of the company's equity share capital whose listing, or admission to dealing, has resulted in the company falling within the definition of **"quoted company"**, and

        (ii)   a hypothetical holding of shares made up of shares of the same kinds and number as those by reference to which a broad equity market index is calculated, a line drawn by joining up points plotted to represent, for each of the financial years in the relevant period, the total shareholder return on that holding; and

    (b)   state the name of the index selected for the purposes of the graph and set out the reasons for selecting that index.

5(2) For the purposes of sub-paragraphs (1) and (4), **"relevant period"** means the five financial years of which the last is the relevant financial year.

5(3) Where the relevant financial year–

    (a)   is the company's second, third or fourth financial year, sub-paragraph (2) has effect with the substitution of "two", "three" or "four" (as the case may be) for "five"; and

    (b)   is the company's first financial year, **"relevant period"**, for the purposes of subparagraphs (1) and (4), means the relevant financial year.

5(4) For the purposes of sub-paragraph (1), the **"total shareholder return"** for a relevant period on a holding of shares must be calculated using a fair method that–

    (a)   takes as its starting point the percentage change over the period in the market price of the holding;

    (b)   involves making–

        (i)   the assumptions specified in sub-paragraph (5) as to reinvestment of income, and

        (ii)   the assumption specified in sub-paragraph (7) as to the funding of liabilities, and

    (c)   makes provision for any replacement of shares in the holding by shares of a different description; and the same method must be used for each of the holdings mentioned in sub-paragraph (1).

5(5) The assumptions as to reinvestment of income are–

    (a)   that any benefit in the form of shares of the same kind as those in the holding is added to the holding at the time the benefit becomes receivable; and

    (b)   that any benefit in cash, and an amount equal to the value of any benefit not in cash and not falling within paragraph (a), is applied at the time the benefit becomes receivable in the purchase at their market price of shares of the same kind as those in the holding and that the shares purchased are added to the holding at that time.

5(6) In sub-paragraph (5) **"benefit"** means any benefit (including, in particular, any dividend) receivable in respect of any shares in the holding by the holder from the company of whose share capital the shares form part.

5(7) The assumption as to the funding of liabilities is that, where the holder has a liability to the company of whose capital the shares in the holding form part, shares are sold from the holding–

    (a)   immediately before the time by which the liability is due to be satisfied, and

(b)   in such numbers that, at the time of the sale, the market price of the shares sold equals the amount of the liability in respect of the shares in the holding that are not being sold.

5(8)   In sub-paragraph (7) **"liability"** means a liability arising in respect of any shares in the holding or from the exercise of a right attached to any of those shares.

Service contracts

6(1)   The directors' remuneration report must contain, in respect of the contract of service or contract for services of each person who has served as a director of the company at any time during the relevant financial year, the following information–

(a)   the date of the contract, the unexpired term and the details of any notice periods;

(b)   any provision for compensation payable upon early termination of the contract; and

(c)   such details of other provisions in the contract as are necessary to enable members of the company to estimate the liability of the company in the event of early termination of the contract.

6(2)   The directors' remuneration report must contain an explanation for any significant award made to a person in the circumstances described in paragraph 15.

Part 3 – Information subject to audit

Amount of each director's emoluments and compensation in the relevant financial year

7(1)   The directors' remuneration report must for the relevant financial year show, for each person who has served as a director of the company at any time during that year, each of the following–

(a)   the total amount of salary and fees paid to or receivable by the person in respect of qualifying services;

(b)   the total amount of bonuses so paid or receivable;

(c)   the total amount of sums paid by way of expenses allowance that are–

(i)   chargeable to United Kingdom income tax (or would be if the person were an individual), and

(ii)   paid to or receivable by the person in respect of qualifying services;

(d)   the total amount of–

(i)   any compensation for loss of office paid to or receivable by the person, and

(ii)   any other payments paid to or receivable by the person in connection with the termination of qualifying services;

(e)   the total estimated value of any benefits received by the person otherwise than in cash that–

(i)   do not fall within any of paragraphs (a) to (d) or paragraphs 8 to 12,

(ii)   are emoluments of the person, and

(iii)   are received by the person in respect of qualifying services; and

(f)   the amount that is the total of the sums mentioned in paragraphs (a) to (e).

7(2)   The directors' remuneration report must show, for each person who has served as a director of the company at any time during the relevant financial year, the amount that for the financial year preceding the relevant financial year is the total of the sums mentioned in paragraphs (a) to (e) of sub-paragraph (1).

7(3)   The directors' remuneration report must also state the nature of any element of a remuneration package which is not cash.

7(4)   The information required by sub-paragraphs (1) and (2) must be presented in tabular form.

Share options

8(1)   The directors' remuneration report must contain, in respect of each person who has served as a director of the company at any time in the relevant financial year, the information specified in paragraph 9.

8(2)   Sub-paragraph (1) is subject to paragraph 10 (aggregation of information to avoid excessively lengthy reports).

8(3)   The information specified in sub-paragraphs (a) to (c) of paragraph 9 must be presented in tabular form in the report.

8(4)   In paragraph 9 **"share option"**, in relation to a person, means a share option granted in respect of qualifying services of the person.

9   The information required by sub-paragraph (1) of paragraph 8 in respect of such a person as is mentioned in that sub-paragraph is–

- (a)   the number of shares that are subject to a share option–
    - (i)   at the beginning of the relevant financial year or, if later, on the date of the appointment of the person as a director of the company, and
    - (ii)   at the end of the relevant financial year or, if earlier, on the cessation of the person's appointment as a director of the company, in each case differentiating between share options having different terms and conditions;
- (b)   information identifying those share options that have been awarded in the relevant financial year, those that have been exercised in that year, those that in that year have expired unexercised and those whose terms and conditions have been varied in that year;
- (c)   for each share option that is unexpired at any time in the relevant financial year–
    - (i)   the price paid, if any, for its award,
    - (ii)   the exercise price,
    - (iii)   the date from which the option may be exercised, and
    - (iv)   the date on which the option expires;
- (d)   a description of any variation made in the relevant financial year in the terms and conditions of a share option;
- (e)   a summary of any performance criteria upon which the award or exercise of a share option is conditional, including a description of any variation made in such performance criteria during the relevant financial year;
- (f)   for each share option that has been exercised during the relevant financial year, the market price of the shares, in relation to which it is exercised, at the time of exercise; and
- (g)   for each share option that is unexpired at the end of the relevant financial year–
    - (i)   the market price at the end of that year, and
    - (ii)   the highest and lowest market prices during that year, of each share that is subject to the option.

10(1)   If, in the opinion of the directors of the company, disclosure in accordance with paragraphs 8 and 9 would result in a disclosure of excessive length then, (subject to subparagraphs (2) and (3))–

- (a)   information disclosed for a person under paragraph 9(a) need not differentiate between share options having different terms and conditions;
- (b)   for the purposes of disclosure in respect of a person under paragraph 9(c)(i) and (ii) and (g), share options may be aggregated and (instead of disclosing prices for each share option) disclosure may be made of weighted average prices of aggregations of share options;
- (c)   for the purposes of disclosure in respect of a person under paragraph 9(c)(iii) and (iv), share options may be aggregated and (instead of disclosing dates for each share option) disclosure may be made of ranges of dates for aggregation of share options.

10(2)   Sub-paragraph (1)(b) and (c) does not permit the aggregation of–

- (a)   share options in respect of shares whose market price at the end of the relevant financial year is below the option exercise price, with
- (b)   share options in respect of shares whose market price at the end of the relevant financial year is equal to, or exceeds, the option exercise price.

10(3)   Sub-paragraph (1) does not apply (and accordingly, full disclosure must be made in accordance with paragraphs 8 and 9) in respect of share options that during the relevant financial year have been awarded or exercised or had their terms and conditions varied.

Long term incentive schemes

11(1)   The directors' remuneration report must contain, in respect of each person who has served as a director of the company at any time in the relevant financial year, the information specified in paragraph 12.

11(2)   Sub-paragraph (1) does not require the report to contain share option details that are contained in the report in compliance with paragraphs 8 to 10.

11(3)   The information specified in paragraph 12 must be presented in tabular form in the report.

11(4) For the purposes of paragraph 12–

    (a)   **"scheme interest"**, in relation to a person, means an interest under a long term incentive scheme that is an interest in respect of which assets may become receivable under the scheme in respect of qualifying services of the person; and

    (b)   such an interest **"vests"** at the earliest time when–

        (i)   it has been ascertained that the qualifying conditions have been fulfilled, and

        (ii)   the nature and quantity of the assets receivable under the scheme in respect of the interest have been ascertained.

11(5) In this Schedule **"long term incentive scheme"** means any agreement or arrangement under which money or other assets may become receivable by a person and which includes one or more qualifying conditions with respect to service or performance that cannot be fulfilled within a single financial year, and for this purpose the following must be disregarded, namely–

    (a)   any bonus the amount of which falls to be determined by reference to service or performance within a single financial year;

    (b)   compensation in respect of loss of office, payments for breach of contract and other termination payments; and

    (c)   retirement benefits.

12(1) The information required by sub-paragraph (1) of paragraph 11 in respect of such a person as is mentioned in that sub-paragraph is–

    (a)   details of the scheme interests that the person has at the beginning of the relevant financial year or if later on the date of the appointment of the person as a director of the company;

    (b)   details of the scheme interests awarded to the person during the relevant financial year;

    (c)   details of the scheme interests that the person has at the end of the relevant financial year or if earlier on the cessation of the person's appointment as a director of the company;

    (d)   for each scheme interest within paragraphs (a) to (c)–

        (i)   the end of the period over which the qualifying conditions for that interest have to be fulfilled (or if there are different periods for different conditions, the end of whichever of those periods ends last); and

        (ii)   a description of any variation made in the terms and conditions of the scheme interests during the relevant financial year; and

    (e)   for each scheme interest that has vested in the relevant financial year–

        (i)   the relevant details (see sub-paragraph (3)) of any shares,

        (ii)   the amount of any money, and

        (iii)   the value of any other assets, that have become receivable in respect of the interest.

12(2) The details that sub-paragraph (1)(b) requires of a scheme interest awarded during the relevant financial year include, if shares may become receivable in respect of the interest, the following–

    (a)   the number of those shares;

    (b)   the market price of each of those shares when the scheme interest was awarded; and

    (c)   details of qualifying conditions that are conditions with respect to performance.

12(3) In sub-paragraph (1)(e)(i) **"the relevant details"**, in relation to any shares that have become receivable in respect of a scheme interest, means–

    (a) the number of those shares;

    (b) the date on which the scheme interest was awarded;

    (c) the market price of each of those shares when the scheme interest was awarded;

    (d) the market price of each of those shares when the scheme interest vested; and

    (e) details of qualifying conditions that were conditions with respect to performance.

Pensions

13(1) The directors' remuneration report must, for each person who has served as a director of the company at any time during the relevant financial year, contain the information in respect of pensions that is specified in sub-paragraphs (2) and (3).

13(2) Where the person has rights under a pension scheme that is a defined benefit scheme in relation to the person and any of those rights are rights to which he has become entitled in respect of qualifying services of his–

(a) details–

    (i) of any changes during the relevant financial year in the person's accrued benefits under the scheme, and

    (ii) of the person's accrued benefits under the scheme as at the end of that year;

    [version of sub-paragraph (b) applying in relation to financial years beginning on or after 6 April 2008 and ending before 26 June 2009]

(b) the transfer value, calculated in a manner consistent with "Retirement Benefit Schemes – Transfer Values (GN 11)" published by the Institute of Actuaries and the Faculty of Actuaries and dated 6th April 2001, of the person's accrued benefits under the scheme at the end of the relevant financial year;

    [version of sub-paragraph (b) applying in relation to financial years beginning on or after 6 April 2008 and not ending before 26 June 2009]

(b) the transfer value, calculated in accordance with regulations 7 to 7E of the Occupational Pension Schemes (Transfer Values) Regulations 1996, of the person's accrued benefits under the scheme at the end of the relevant financial year;

(c) the transfer value of the person's accrued benefits under the scheme that in compliance with paragraph (b) was contained in the directors' remuneration report for the previous financial year or, if there was no such report or no such value was contained in that report, the transfer value, calculated in such a manner as is mentioned in paragraph (b), of the person's accrued benefits under the scheme at the beginning of the relevant financial year;

(d) the amount obtained by subtracting–

    (i) the transfer value of the person's accrued benefits under the scheme that is required to be contained in the report by paragraph (c), from

    (ii) the transfer value of those benefits that is required to be contained in the report by paragraph (b), and then subtracting from the result of that calculation the amount of any contributions made to the scheme by the person in the relevant financial year.

13(3) Where–

(a) the person has rights under a pension scheme that is a money purchase scheme in relation to the person, and

(b) any of those rights are rights to which he has become entitled in respect of qualifying services of his, details of any contribution to the scheme in respect of the person that is paid or payable by the company for the relevant financial year or paid by the company in that year for another financial year.

Notes – Paragraph (2)(b) substituted by SI 2009/1581 reg 12(1) and (3): 27 June 2009 applying in relation to financial years beginning on or after 6 April 2008 which have not ended before 27 June 2009

Excess retirement benefits of directors and past directors

14(1) Subject to sub-paragraph (3), the directors' remuneration report must show in respect of each person who has served as a director of the company–

(a) at any time during the relevant financial year, or

(b) at any time before the beginning of that year, the amount of so much of retirement benefits paid to or receivable by the person under pension schemes as is in excess of the retirement benefits to which he was entitled on the date on which the benefits first became payable or 31st March 1997, whichever is the later.

14(2) In subsection (1) **"retirement benefits"** means retirement benefits to which the person became entitled in respect of qualifying services of his.

14(3) Amounts paid or receivable under a pension scheme need not be included in an amount required to be shown under sub-paragraph (1) if–

(a) the funding of the scheme was such that the amounts were or, as the case may be, could have been paid without recourse to additional contributions; and

(b)   amounts were paid to or receivable by all pensioner members of the scheme on the same basis; and in this sub-paragraph **"pensioner member"**, in relation to a pension scheme, means any person who is entitled to the present payment of retirement benefits under the scheme.

14(4)   In this paragraph–

(a)   references to retirement benefits include benefits otherwise than in cash; and

(b)   in relation to so much of retirement benefits as consists of a benefit otherwise than in cash, references to their amount are to the estimated money value of the benefit, and the nature of any such benefit must also be shown in the report.

Compensation for past directors

15   The directors' remuneration report must contain details of any significant award made in the relevant financial year to any person who was not a director of the company at the time the award was made but had previously been a director of the company, including (in particular) compensation in respect of loss of office and pensions but excluding any sums which have already been shown in the report under paragraph 7(1)(d).

Sums paid to third parties in respect of a director's services

16(1)   The directors' remuneration report must show, in respect of each person who served as a director of the company at any time during the relevant financial year, the aggregate amount of any consideration paid to or receivable by third parties for making available the services of the person–

(a)   as a director of the company, or

(b)   while director of the company–

    (i)   as director of any of its subsidiary undertakings, or

    (ii)   as director of any other undertaking of which he was (while director of the company) a director by virtue of the company's nomination (direct or indirect), or

    (iii)   otherwise in connection with the management of the affairs of the company or any such other undertaking.

16(2)   The reference to consideration includes benefits otherwise than in cash; and in relation to such consideration the reference to its amount is to the estimated money value of the benefit. The nature of any such consideration must be shown in the report.

16(3)   The reference to third parties is to persons other than–

(a)   the person himself or a person connected with him or a body corporate controlled by him, and

(b)   the company or any such other undertaking as is mentioned in sub-paragraph (1)(b)(ii).

PART 4 – INTERPRETATION AND SUPPLEMENTARY

17(1)   In this Schedule–

"amount", in relation to a gain made on the exercise of a share option, means the difference between–

(a)   the market price of the shares on the day on which the option was exercised; and

(b)   the price actually paid for the shares;

"company contributions", in relation to a pension scheme and a person, means any payments (including insurance premiums) made, or treated as made, to the scheme in respect of the person by anyone other than the person;

"defined benefit scheme", in relation to a person, means a pension scheme which is not a money purchase scheme in relation to the person;

"emoluments" of a person–

(a)   includes salary, fees and bonuses, sums paid by way of expenses allowance (so far as they are chargeable to United Kingdom income tax or would be if the person were an individual), but

(b)   does not include any of the following, namely–

    (i)   the value of any share options granted to him or the amount of any gains made on the exercise of any such options;

    (ii)   any company contributions paid, or treated as paid, in respect of him under any pension scheme or any benefits to which he is entitled under any such scheme; or

      (iii)   any money or other assets paid to or received or receivable by him under any long term incentive scheme;

"long term incentive scheme" has the meaning given by paragraph 11(5); **"money purchase benefits"**, in relation to a person, means retirement benefits the rate or amount of which is calculated by reference to payments made, or treated as made, by the person or by any other person in respect of that person and which are not average salary benefits;

"money purchase scheme", in relation to a person, means a pension scheme under which all of the benefits that may become payable to or in respect of the person are money purchase benefits in relation to the person;

"pension scheme" means a retirement benefits scheme within the meaning given by section 611 of the Income and Corporation Taxes Act 1988;

"qualifying services", in relation to any person, means his services as a director of the company, and his services at any time while he is a director of the company–

(a)   as a director of an undertaking that is a subsidiary undertaking of the company at that time;

(b)   as a director of any other undertaking of which he is a director by virtue of the company's nomination (direct or indirect); or

(c)   otherwise in connection with the management of the affairs of the company or any such subsidiary undertaking or any such other undertaking;

"retirement benefits" means relevant benefits within the meaning given by section 612(1) of the Income and Corporation Taxes Act 1988;

"shares" means shares (whether allotted or not) in the company, or any undertaking which is a group undertaking in relation to the company, and includes a share warrant as defined by section 779(1) of the 2006 Act;

"share option" means a right to acquire shares;

"value", in relation to shares received or receivable on any day by a person who is or has been a director of the company, means the market price of the shares on that day.

17(2) In this Schedule **"compensation in respect of loss of office"** includes compensation received or receivable by a person for–

(a)   loss of office as director of the company, or

(b)   loss, while director of the company or on or in connection with his ceasing to be a director of it, of–

    (i)   any other office in connection with the management of the company's affairs, or

    (ii)   any office as director or otherwise in connection with the management of the affairs of any undertaking that, immediately before the loss, is a subsidiary undertaking of the company or an undertaking of which he is a director by virtue of the company's nomination (direct or indirect);

(c)   compensation in consideration for, or in connection with, a person's retirement from office; and

(d)   where such a retirement is occasioned by a breach of the person's contract with the company or with an undertaking that, immediately before the breach, is a subsidiary undertaking of the company or an undertaking of which he is a director by virtue of the company's nomination (direct or indirect)–

    (i)   payments made by way of damages for the breach; or

    (ii)   payments made by way of settlement or compromise of any claim in respect of the breach.

17(3) References in this Schedule to compensation include benefits otherwise than in cash; and in relation to such compensation references in this Schedule to its amounts are to the estimated money value of the benefit.

17(4) References in this Schedule to a person being "connected" with a director, and to a director "controlling" a body corporate, are to be construed in accordance with sections 252 to 255 of the 2006 Act.

18(1) For the purposes of this Schedule emoluments paid or receivable or share options granted in respect of a person's accepting office as a director are to be treated as emoluments paid or receivable or share options granted in respect of his services as a director.

18(2) Where a pension scheme provides for any benefits that may become payable to or in respect of a person to be whichever are the greater of–

    (a)   such benefits determined by or under the scheme as are money purchase benefits in relation to the person; and

    (b)   such retirement benefits determined by or under the scheme to be payable to or in respect of the person as are not money purchase benefits in relation to the person, the company may assume for the purposes of this Schedule that those benefits will be money purchase benefits in relation to the person, or not, according to whichever appears more likely at the end of the relevant financial year.

18(3) In determining for the purposes of this Schedule whether a pension scheme is a money purchase scheme in relation to a person or a defined benefit scheme in relation to a person, any death in service benefits provided for by the scheme are to be disregarded.

19(1) The following applies with respect to the amounts to be shown under this Schedule.

19(2) The amount in each case includes all relevant sums paid by or receivable from–

    (a)   the company; and

    (b)   the company's subsidiary undertakings; and

    (c)   any other person, except sums to be accounted for to the company or any of its subsidiary undertakings or any other undertaking of which any person has been a director while director of the company, by virtue of section 219 of the 2006 Act (payment in connection with share transfer: requirement of members' approval), to past or present members of the company or any of its subsidiaries or any class of those members.

19(3) Reference to amounts paid to or receivable by a person include amounts paid to or receivable by a person connected with him or a body corporate controlled by him (but not so as to require an amount to be counted twice).

20(1) The amounts to be shown for any financial year under Part 3 of this Schedule are the sums receivable in respect of that year (whenever paid) or, in the case of sums not receivable in respect of a period, the sums paid during that year.

20(2) But where–

    (a)   any sums are not shown in the directors' remuneration report for the relevant financial year on the ground that the person receiving them is liable to account for them as mentioned in paragraph 19(2), but the liability is thereafter wholly or partly released or is not enforced within a period of 2 years; or

    (b)   any sums paid by way of expenses allowance are charged to United Kingdom income tax after the end of the relevant financial year or, in the case of any such sums paid otherwise than to an individual, it does not become clear until the end of the relevant financial year that those sums would be charged to such tax were the person an individual, those sums must, to the extent to which the liability is released or not enforced or they are charged as mentioned above (as the case may be), be shown in the first directors' remuneration report in which it is practicable to show them and must be distinguished from the amounts to be shown apart from this provision.

21 Where it is necessary to do so for the purpose of making any distinction required by the preceding paragraphs in an amount to be shown in compliance with this Part of this Schedule, the directors may apportion any payments between the matters in respect of which these have been paid or are receivable in such manner as they think appropriate.

22 The Schedule requires information to be given only so far as it is contained in the company's books and papers, available to members of the public or the company has the right to obtain it."

SCHEDULE 9

Regulation 12

INTERPRETATION OF TERM "PROVISIONS"

PART 1 – MEANING FOR PURPOSES OF THESE REGULATIONS

Definition of "provisions"

1(1) In these Regulations, references to provisions for depreciation or diminution in value of assets are to any amount written off by way of providing for depreciation or diminution in value of assets.

1(2) Any reference in the profit and loss account formats or the notes to them set out in Schedule 1, 2 or 3 to these Regulations to the depreciation of, or amounts written off, assets of any description is to any provision for depreciation or diminution in value of assets of that description.

2 References in these Regulations to provisions for liabilities or, in the case of insurance companies, to provisions for other risks are to any amount retained as reasonably necessary for the purpose of providing for any liability the nature of which is clearly defined and which is either likely to be incurred, or certain to be incurred but uncertain as to amount or as to the date on which it will arise.

2A At the balance sheet date, a provision must represent the best estimate of the expenses likely to be incurred or, in the case of a liability, of the amount required to meet that liability.

History – Para. 2A inserted by SI 2015/980, reg. 40, with effect in relation to–
   (a)   financial years beginning on or after 1 January 2016, and
   (b)   a financial year of a company beginning on or after 1 January 2015, but before 1 January 2016, if the directors of the company so decide.

2B Provisions must not be used to adjust the value of assets.

History – Para. 2B inserted by SI 2015/980, reg. 40, with effect in relation to–
   (a)   financial years beginning on or after 1 January 2016, and
   (b)   a financial year of a company beginning on or after 1 January 2015, but before 1 January 2016, if the directors of the company so decide.

PART 2 – MEANING FOR PURPOSES OF PARTS 18 AND 23 OF THE 2006 ACT

Financial assistance for purchase of own shares

3 The specified provisions for the purposes of section 677(3)(a) of the 2006 Act (Companies Act accounts: relevant provisions for purposes of financial assistance) are provisions within paragraph 2 of this Schedule.

Redemption or purchase by private company out of capital

4   The specified provisions for the purposes of section 712(2)(b)(i) of the 2006 Act (Companies Act accounts: relevant provisions to determine available profits for redemption or purchase out of capital) are provisions of any of the kinds mentioned in paragraphs 1 and 2 of this Schedule.

Net asset restriction on public companies distributions

5   The specified provisions for the purposes of section 831(3)(a) of the 2006 Act (Companies Act accounts: net asset restriction on public company distributions) are–
  (a)   provisions within paragraph 2 of this Schedule, and
  (b)   in the case of an insurance company, any amount included under liabilities items Ba (fund for future appropriations), C (technical provisions) and D (technical provisions for linked liabilities) in a balance sheet drawn up in accordance with Schedule 3 to these Regulations.

Distributions by investment companies

6   The specified provisions for the purposes of section 832(4)(a) of the 2006 Act (Companies Act accounts: investment companies distributions) are provisions within paragraph 2 of this Schedule.

Justification of distribution by references to accounts

7   The specified provisions for the purposes of section 836(1)(b)(i) of the 2006 Act (Companies Act accounts: relevant provisions for distribution purposes)–
  (a)   are provisions of any of the kinds mentioned in paragraphs 1 and 2 of this Schedule, and
  (b)   in the case of an insurance company, any amount included under liabilities items Ba (fund for future appropriations), C (technical provisions) and D (technical provisions for linked liabilities) in a balance sheet drawn up in accordance with Schedule 3 to these Regulations.

Realised losses

8   The specified provisions for the purposes of section 841(2)(a) of the 2006 Act (Companies Act accounts: treatment of provisions as realised losses) are provisions of any of the kinds mentioned in paragraphs 1 and 2 of this Schedule.

Notes – Para. 8 inserted by SI 2009/1581 reg 12(1) and (4): 27 June 2009 applying in relation to financial years beginning on or after 6 April 2008 which have not ended before 27 June 2009

SCHEDULE 10

Regulation 13

GENERAL INTERPRETATION

Capitalisation

1   **"Capitalisation"**, in relation to work or costs, means treating that work or those costs as a fixed asset.

Financial instruments

2   Save in Schedule 2 to these Regulations, references to **"derivatives"** include commodity-based contracts that give either contracting party the right to settle in cash or in some other financial instrument, except where such contracts–

    (a)   were entered into for the purpose of, and continue to meet, the company's expected purchase, sale or usage requirements,

    (b)   were designated for such purpose at their inception, and

    (c)   are expected to be settled by delivery of the commodity (for banking companies, see the definition in paragraph 94 of Schedule 2 to these Regulations).

3(1)   Save in Schedule 2 to these Regulations, the expressions listed in sub-paragraph (2) have the same meaning as they have in Directive 2013/34/EC of the European Parliament and of the Council of 26 June 2013 on the annual financial statements etc of certain types of undertakings and Council Directive 91/674/EEC of 19 December 1991 on the annual accounts and consolidated accounts of insurance undertakings (for banking companies, see the definition in paragraph 96 of Schedule 2 to these Regulations).

3(2)   Those expressions are "available for sale financial asset", "business combination", "commodity-based contracts", "derivative", "equity instrument", "exchange difference", "fair value hedge accounting system", "financial fixed asset", "financial instrument", "foreign entity", "hedge accounting", "hedge accounting system", "hedged items", "hedging instrument", "held for trading purposes", "held to maturity", "monetary item", "receivables", "reliable market" and "trading portfolio".

History – Para. 3(1) substituted by SI 2015/980, reg. 41, with effect in relation to–

    (a)   financial years beginning on or after 1 January 2016, and

    (b)   a financial year of a company beginning on or after 1 January 2015, but before 1 January 2016, if the directors of the company so decide.

Former para. 3(1) read as follows:

"**3(1)**   Save in Schedule 2 to these Regulations, the expressions listed in sub-paragraph (2) have the same meaning as they have in Council Directive 78/660/EEC on the annual accounts of certain types of companies(a) and 91/674/EEC on the annual accounts and consolidated accounts of insurance undertakings(b) (for banking companies, see the definition in paragraph 96 of Schedule 2 to these Regulations)."

Fixed and current assets

4   **"Fixed assets"** means assets of a company which are intended for use on a continuing basis in the company's activities, and **"current assets"** means assets not intended for such use.

Fungible assets

5 **"Fungible assets"** means assets of any description which are substantially indistinguishable one from another.

Historical cost accounting rules

6 References to the historical cost accounting rules are to be read in accordance with paragraph 30 of Schedule 1, paragraph 38 of Schedule 2 and paragraph 36(1) of Schedule 3 to these Regulations.

Leases

7(1) **"Long lease"** means a lease in the case of which the portion of the term for which it was granted remaining unexpired at the end of the financial year is not less than 50 years.

7(2) **"Short lease"** means a lease which is not a long lease.

7(3) **"Lease"** includes an agreement for a lease.

Listed investments

8(1) **"Listed investment"** means an investment as respects which there has been granted a listing on–

    (a) a recognised investment exchange other than an overseas investment exchange, or

    (b) a stock exchange of repute outside the United Kingdom.

8(2) **"Recognised investment exchange"** and **"overseas investment exchange"** have the meaning given in Part 18 of the Financial Services and Markets Act 2000(a).

Loans

9 A loan or advance (including a liability comprising a loan or advance) is treated as falling due for repayment, and an instalment of a loan or advance is treated as falling due for payment, on the earliest date on which the lender could require repayment or (as the case may be) payment, if he exercised all options and rights available to him.

Materiality

10 Amounts which in the particular context of any provision of Schedules 1, 2 or 3 to these Regulations are not material may be disregarded for the purposes of that provision.

Participating interests

11(1) A **"participating interest"** means an interest held by an undertaking in the shares of another undertaking which it holds on a long-term basis for the purpose of securing a contribution to its activities by the exercise of control or influence arising from or related to that interest.

11(2) A holding of 20% or more of the shares of the undertaking is to be presumed to be a participating interest unless the contrary is shown.

11(3) The reference in sub-paragraph (1) to an interest in shares includes–

(a)   an interest which is convertible into an interest in shares, and

(b)   an option to acquire shares or any such interest, and an interest or option falls within paragraph (a) or (b) notwithstanding that the shares to which it relates are, until the conversion or the exercise of the option, unissued.

11(4) For the purposes of this regulation an interest held on behalf of an undertaking is to be treated as held by it.

11(5) In the balance sheet and profit and loss formats set out in Schedules 1, 2 and 3 to these Regulations, "participating interest" does not include an interest in a group undertaking.

11(6) For the purpose of this regulation as it applies in relation to the expression "participating interest"–

(a)   in those formats as they apply in relation to group accounts, and

(b)   in paragraph 19 of Schedule 6 (group accounts: undertakings to be accounted for as associated undertakings),

the references in sub-paragraphs (1) to (4) to the interest held by, and the purposes and activities of, the undertaking concerned are to be construed as references to the interest held by, and the purposes and activities of, the group (within the meaning of paragraph 1 of that Schedule).

Purchase price

12   **"Purchase price"**, in relation to an asset of a company or any raw materials or consumables used in the production of such an asset, includes any consideration (whether in cash or otherwise) given by the company in respect of that asset or those materials or consumables, as the case may be.

Realised profits and realised losses

13   **"Realised profits"** and **"realised losses"** have the same meaning as in section 853(4) and (5) of the 2006 Act.

Staff costs

14(1) **"Social security costs"** means any contributions by the company to any state social security or pension scheme, fund or arrangement.

14(2) **"Pension costs"** includes–

(a) any costs incurred by the company in respect of any pension scheme established for the purpose of providing pensions for persons currently or formerly employed by the company,

(b) any sums set aside for the future payment of pensions directly by the company to current or former employees, and

(c) any pensions paid directly to such persons without having first been set aside.

14(3) Any amount stated in respect of the item **"social security costs"** or in respect of the item **"wages and salaries"** in the company's profit and loss account must be determined by reference to payments made or costs incurred in respect of all persons employed by the company during the financial year under contracts of service.

Scots land tenure

15 In the application of these Regulations to Scotland, **"land of freehold tenure"** means land in respect of which the company is the owner; **"land of leasehold tenure"** means land of which the company is the tenant under a lease.

Companies Act 2006 – Extracts from Part 15 Accounts and Reports

(Sections 380–474)

Contents

	Page
Chapter 1 – Introduction	**901**
General	**901**
380 Scheme of this Part	
Companies subject to the small companies regime	**901**
381 Companies subject to the small companies regime	
382 Companies qualifying as small: general	
383 Companies qualifying as small: parent companies	
384 Companies excluded from the small companies regime	
384A Companies qualifying as micro-entities	
384B Companies excluded from being treated as micro-entities	
Quoted and unquoted companies	**908**
385 Quoted and unquoted companies	
Chapter 2 – Accounting Records	**908**
386 Duty to keep accounting records	
387 Duty to keep accounting records: offence	
388 Where and for how long records to be kept	
389 Where and for how long records to be kept: offences	
Chapter 3 – A Company's Financial Year	**911**
390 A company's financial year	
391 Accounting reference periods and accounting reference date	
392 Alteration of accounting reference date	
Chapter 4 – Annual Accounts	**913**
General	**913**
393 Accounts to give true and fair view	
Individual accounts	**914**
394 Duty to prepare individual accounts	
394A Individual accounts: exemption for dormant subsidiaries	
394B Companies excluded from the dormant subsidiaries exemption	
394C Dormant subsidiaries exemption: parent undertaking declaration of guarantee	
395 Individual accounts: applicable accounting framework	
396 Companies Act individual accounts	
397 IAS individual accounts	
Group accounts: Small companies	**920**
398 Option to prepare group accounts	
Group accounts: Other companies	**920**
399 Duty to prepare group accounts	
400 Exemption for company included in EEA group accounts of larger group	

401   Exemption for company included in non-EEA group
       accounts of larger group
402   Exemption if no subsidiary undertakings need be
       included in the consolidation

Group accounts: General   925
403   Group accounts: applicable accounting framework
404   Companies Act group accounts
405   Companies Act group accounts: subsidiary undertakings
       included in the consolidation
406   IAS group accounts
407   Consistency of financial reporting within group
408   Individual profit and loss account where group accounts prepared

Information to be given in notes to the accounts   930
409   Information about related undertakings
410   Information about related undertakings: alternative compliance
410A   Information about off-balance sheet arrangements
411   Information about employee numbers and costs
412   Information about directors' benefits: remuneration
413   Information about directors' benefits: advances, credit and guarantees

Approval and signing of accounts   936
414   Approval and signing of accounts

Chapter 4A – Strategic report   937
414A   Duty to prepare strategic report
414B   Strategic report: small companies exemption
414C   Contents of strategic report
414D   Approval and signing of strategic report

Chapter 5 – Directors' Report   939
415   Duty to prepare directors' report
415A   Directors' report: small companies exemption
416   Contents of directors' report: general
417   Contents of directors' report: business review
418   Contents of directors' report: statement as to disclosure to auditors
419   Approval and signing of directors' report
419A   Approval and signing of separate corporate governance statement

Chapter 6 – Quoted Companies: Directors' Remuneration Report   945
420   Duty to prepare directors' remuneration report
421   Contents of directors' remuneration report
422   Approval and signing of directors' remuneration report
422A   Revisions to directors' remuneration policy

Chapter 7 – Publication of Accounts and Reports   947

Duty to circulate copies of accounts and reports   947
423   Duty to circulate copies of annual accounts and reports
424   Time allowed for sending out copies of accounts and reports
425   Default in sending out copies of accounts and reports: offences

Option to provide strategic report with supplementary material   948
426   Option to provide summary financial statement
426A   Supplementary material
427   Form and contents of summary financial statement: unquoted companies
428   Form and contents of summary financial statement: quoted companies
429   Summary financial statements: offences [applying to financial years ending
       before 30 September 2013]

Quoted companies: requirements as to website publication   952
430   Quoted companies: annual accounts and reports to be
        made available on website

Right of member or debenture holder to demand copies of
accounts and reports   953
431   Right of member or debenture holder to copies of accounts
        and reports: unquoted companies
432   Right of member or debenture holder to copies of accounts
        and reports: quoted companies

Requirements in connection with publication of accounts and reports   955
433   Name of signatory to be stated in published copies of accounts and reports
434   Requirements in connection with publication of statutory accounts
435   Requirements in connection with publication of non-statutory accounts
436   Meaning of "publication" in relation to accounts and reports

Chapter 8 – Public Companies: Laying of Accounts and Reports
        Before General Meeting   958
437   Public companies: laying of accounts and reports before general meeting
438   Public companies: offence of failure to lay accounts and reports

Chapter 9 – Quoted Companies: Members' Approval of Directors'
        Remuneration Report   959
439   Quoted companies: members' approval of directors' remuneration report
439A   Quoted companies: members' approval of directors' remuneration policy
440   Quoted companies: offences in connection with procedure for approval

Chapter 10 – Filing of Accounts and Reports   961

Duty to file accounts and reports   961
441   Duty to file accounts and reports with the registrar
442   Period allowed for filing accounts
443   Calculation of period allowed

Filing obligations of different descriptions of company   963
444   Filing obligations of companies subject to small companies regime
444A   Filing obligations of companies entitled to small companies exemption
        in relation to directors' report
445   Filing obligations of medium-sized companies
446   Filing obligations of unquoted companies
447   Filing obligations of quoted companies
448   Unlimited companies exempt from obligation to file accounts
448A   Dormant subsidiaries exempt from obligation to file accounts
448B   Companies excluded from the dormant subsidiaries exemption
448C   Dormant subsidiaries filing exemption: parent undertaking
        declaration of guarantee

Requirements where abbreviated accounts delivered   975
449   Special auditor's report where abbreviated accounts delivered
450   Approval and signing of abbreviated accounts

Failure to file accounts and reports   977
451   Default in filing accounts and reports: offences
452   Default in filing accounts and reports: court order
453   Civil penalty for failure to file accounts and reports

Chapter 11 – Revision of Defective Accounts and Reports   978

Voluntary revision   978
454   Voluntary revision of accounts etc

Secretary of state's notice   **980**
455   Secretary of State's notice in respect of accounts or reports

Application to court   **981**
456   Application to court in respect of defective accounts or reports
         [version applying to financial years ending on or after 30 September 2013]
457   Other persons authorised to apply to the court
458   Disclosure of information by tax authorities

Power of authorised person to require documents etc   **985**
459   Power of authorised person to require documents, information
         and explanations
460   Restrictions on disclosure of information obtained under compulsory powers
461   Permitted disclosure of information obtained under compulsory powers
462   Power to amend categories of permitted disclosure

Chapter 12 – Supplementary Provisions   **989**

Liability for false or misleading statements in reports   **989**
463   Liability for false or misleading statements in reports

Accounting and reporting standards   **990**
464   Accounting standards

Companies qualifying as medium-sized   **990**
465   Companies qualifying as medium-sized: general
466   Companies qualifying as medium-sized: parent companies
467   Companies excluded from being treated as medium-sized

General power to make further provision about accounts and reports   **994**
468   General power to make further provision about accounts and reports

Other supplementary provisions   **995**
469   Preparation and filing of accounts in euros
470   Power to apply provisions to banking partnerships
471   Meaning of "annual accounts" and related expressions
472   Notes to the accounts
472A   Meaning of "corporate governance statement" etc
473   Parliamentary procedure for certain regulations under this Part
474   Minor definitions

Chapter 1 – Introduction

General

380 Scheme of this Part

380(1) The requirements of this Part as to accounts and reports apply in relation to each financial year of a company.

380(2) In certain respects different provisions apply to different kinds of company.

380(3) [Omitted by SI 2015/980, reg. 4(2).]

380(4) [Omitted by SI 2015/980, reg. 4(2).]

Commencement Date – 6 April 2008 applying to accounts and reports for financial years beginning on or after 6 April 2008

Editorial note: this section is modified in its application to LLPs by Part 1 *General Introductory Provisions* of SI 2008 No 1911 The Limited Liability Partnerships (Accounts and Audit) (Application of Companies Act 2006) Regulations 2008

History – S. 380(3) and (4) omitted by SI 2015/980, reg. 4(2), with effect in relation to–

 (a) financial years beginning on or after 1 January 2016, and

 (b) a financial year of a company beginning on or after 1 January 2015, but before 1 January 2016, if the directors of the company so decide.

Former s. 380(3) and (4) read as follows:

 "**380(3)** The main distinctions for this purpose are–

 (a) between companies subject to the small companies regime (see section 381) and companies that are not subject to that regime; and

 (b) between quoted companies (see section 385) and companies that are not quoted.

 380(4) In this Part, where provisions do not apply to all kinds of company–

 (a) provisions applying to companies subject to the small companies regime appear before the provisions applying to other companies,

 (b) provisions applying to private companies appear before the provisions applying to public companies, and

 (c) provisions applying to quoted companies appear after the provisions applying to other companies."

Companies subject to the small companies regime

381 Companies subject to the small companies regime

The small companies regime applies to a company for a financial year in relation to which the company–

 (a) qualifies as small (see sections 382 and 383), and

 (b) is not excluded from the regime (see section 384).

Commencement Date – 6 April 2008 applying to accounts and reports for financial years beginning on or after 6 April 2008

Amended by SI 2008/393 reg 6(1): 6 April 2008

Editorial note: this section is modified in its application to LLPs by Part 2 LLPs Qualifying As Small LLPs Subject To The Small LLPs Regime of SI 2008 No 1911 The Limited Liability Partnerships (Accounts and Audit) (Application of Companies Act 2006) Regulations 2008

382 Companies qualifying as small: general

382(1) A company qualifies as small in relation to its first financial year if the qualifying conditions are met in that year.

382(1A) Subject to subsection (2), a company qualifies as small in relation to a subsequent financial year if the qualifying conditions are met in that year.

382(2) In relation to a subsequent financial year, where on its balance sheet date, a company meets or ceases to meet the qualifying conditions, that affects its qualification as a small company only if it occurs in two consecutive financial years.

382(3) The qualifying conditions are met by a company in a year in which it satisfies two or more of the following requirements–

1.	Turnover	Not more than £10.2 million
2.	Balance sheet total	Not more than 5.1 million
3.	Number of employees	Not more than 50

382(4) For a period that is a company's financial year but not in fact a year the maximum figures for turnover must be proportionately adjusted.

382(5) The balance sheet total means the aggregate of the amounts shown as assets in the company's balance sheet.

382(6) The number of employees means the average number of persons employed by the company in the year, determined as follows–

    (a)   find for each month in the financial year the number of persons employed under contracts of service by the company in that month (whether throughout the month or not),

    (b)   add together the monthly totals, and

    (c)   divide by the number of months in the financial year.

382(7) This section is subject to section 383 (companies qualifying as small: parent companies).

Commencement Date – 6 April 2008 applying to accounts and reports for financial years beginning on or after 6 April 2008. Any question whether for the purposes of s. 382 a company qualified as small in a financial year beginning before 6 April 2008 is to be determined by reference to the corresponding provisions of the Companies Act 1985 or SI 1986/1032 (NI 6) (SI 2007/3495, Sch. 4, para. 7).

History – S. 382(1A) inserted and 382(2) substituted by SI 2013/3008, reg. 4(1) and (2), with effect from 1 December 2013 in respect of (a) financial years ending on or after 30 September 2013; and (b) companies, which deliver the accounts required by section 444 to the registrar on or after 1 December 2013. Before substitution, s. 382(2) read:

    "**382(2)** A company qualifies as small in relation to a subsequent financial year–

    (a)   if the qualifying conditions are met in that year and the preceding financial year;

    (b)   if the qualifying conditions are met in that year and the company qualified as small in relation to the preceding financial year;

    (c)   if the qualifying conditions were met in the preceding financial year and the company qualified as small in relation to that year."

This is subject to the following provisions of SI 2013/3008, reg. 3:

"Disapplication of these regulations to entities to which provisions of the 2006 Act or the 2008 regulations have been applied

3(1) The amendments made by these Regulations [SI 2013/3008] to any provision of the 2006 Act [CA 2006] or the 2008 Regulations [SI 2008/409] do not have effect in relation to the application of any such provision–

    (a)   to qualifying partnerships by regulations 4(1) and 9(1) of and Part 1 of the Schedule to the Partnerships (Accounts) Regulations 2008 (SI 2008/569);

    (b)   to qualifying partnerships by regulations 4(1) and 9(1) of and Part 1 of the Schedule to the Partnerships (Accounts) Regulations 2008 (SI 2008/569);

    (c)   to limited liability partnerships by the Small Limited Liability Partnerships (Accounts) Regulations 2008 (SI 2008/1912);

    (d)   to overseas companies by Chapter 3 of Part 5 or Chapter 3 of Part 6 of the Overseas Companies Regulations 2009 (SI 2009/1801);

(e)   to unregistered companies by regulation 3 of and Schedule 1 to the Unregistered Companies Regulations 2009 (SI 2009/2436); or

(f)   to companies registered pursuant to section 1040 of the 2006 Act by regulation 18 of the Companies (Companies Authorised to Register) Regulations 2009 (SI 2009/2437).

3(2)   Any new provision of the 2006 Act or the 2008 Regulations inserted by these Regulations is not, by virtue of any provision mentioned in sub-paragraphs (a) to (f) of paragraph (1), applied to the entities mentioned in those sub-paragraphs."

S. 382(3) amended by SI 2008/393, reg. 3(1): 6 April 2008 applying in relation to financial years beginning on or after 6 April 2008. In determining whether a company qualifies as small under s. 382(2) (qualification in relation to subsequent financial year by reference to circumstances in preceding financial years) in relation to a financial year ending on or after 6 April 2008, the company shall be treated as having qualified as small in any previous financial year in which it would have so qualified if amendments to the same effect as those made by SI 2008/393 had been in force (SI 2008/393, reg. 2(3)).

In s. 382(3), in the table, in item 1, the words "Not more than £10.2 million" substituted for "Not more than £6.5 million" by SI 2015/980, reg. (4)(3)(a), with effect in relation to–

(a)   financial years beginning on or after 1 January 2016, and

(b)   a financial year of a company beginning on or after 1 January 2015, but before 1 January 2016, if the directors of the company so decide.

In s. 382(3), in the table, in item 2, the words "Not more than 5.1 million" substituted for "Not more than £3.26 million" by SI 2015/980, reg. (4)(3)(b), with effect in relation to–

(a)   financial years beginning on or after 1 January 2016, and

(b)   a financial year of a company beginning on or after 1 January 2015, but before 1 January 2016, if the directors of the company so decide.

Notes – This section is modified in its application to LLPs by Part 2 LLPs Qualifying As Small LLPs Subject To The Small LLPs Regime of SI 2008/1911 the Limited Liability Partnerships (Accounts and Audit) (Application of Companies Act 2006) Regulations 2008.

383   Companies qualifying as small: parent companies

383(1)   A parent company qualifies as a small company in relation to a financial year only if the group headed by it qualifies as a small group.

383(2)   A group qualifies as small in relation to the parent company's first financial year if the qualifying conditions are met in that year.

383(2A)   Subject to subsection (3), a group qualifies as small in relation to a subsequent financial year of the parent company if the qualifying conditions are met in that year.

383(3)   In relation to a subsequent financial year of the parent company, where on the parent company's balance sheet date the group meets or ceases to meet the qualifying conditions, that affects the group's qualification as a small group only if it occurs in two consecutive financial years.

383(4)   The qualifying conditions are met by a group in a year in which it satisfies two or more of the following requirements–

1. Aggregate turnover	Not more than £10.2 million net (or £12.2 million gross
2. Aggregate balance sheet total	Not more than £5.1 million net (or £6.1 million gross
3. Aggregate number of employees	Not more than 50

383(5)   The aggregate figures are ascertained by aggregating the relevant figures determined in accordance with section 382 for each member of the group.

383(6)   In relation to the aggregate figures for turnover and balance sheet total–

"**net**" means after any set-offs and other adjustments made to eliminate group transactions–

    (a)   in the case of Companies Act accounts, in accordance with regulations under section 404,

    (b)   in the case of IAS accounts, in accordance with international accounting standards; and

"gross" means without those set-offs and other adjustments. A company may satisfy any relevant requirement on the basis of either the net or the gross figure.

383(7) The figures for each subsidiary undertaking shall be those included in its individual accounts for the relevant financial year, that is–

    (a)   if its financial year ends with that of the parent company, that financial year, and

    (b)   if not, its financial year ending last before the end of the financial year of the parent company. If those figures cannot be obtained without disproportionate expense or undue delay, the latest available figures shall be taken.

Commencement Date – 6 April 2008 applying to accounts and reports for financial years beginning on or after 6 April 2008. Any question whether for the purposes of s. 383 a company or group qualified as small in a financial year beginning before 6 April 2008 is to be determined by reference to the corresponding provisions of the Companies Act 1985 or SI 1986/1032(NI 6) (SI 2007/3495, Sch. 4, para. 7).

History – S. 383(2A) inserted and 383(3) substituted by SI 2013/3008, reg. 4(1) and (3), with effect from 1 December 2013 in respect of (a) financial years ending on or after 30 September 2013; and (b) companies, which deliver the accounts required by section 444 to the registrar on or after 1 December 2013. Before substitution, s. 383(3) read:

"**383(3)**   A group qualifies as small in relation to a subsequent financial year of the parent company–

    (a)   if the qualifying conditions are met in that year and the preceding financial year;

    (b)   if the qualifying conditions are met in that year and the group qualified as small in relation to the preceding financial year;

    (c)   if the qualifying conditions were met in the preceding financial year and the group qualified as small in relation to that year.

This is subject to the following provisions of SI 2013/3008, reg. 3:

"Disapplication of these regulations to entities to which provisions of the 2006 Act or the 2008 regulations have been applied

    3(1)   The amendments made by these Regulations [SI 2013/3008] to any provision of the 2006 Act [CA 2006] or the 2008 Regulations [SI 2008/409] do not have effect in relation to the application of any such provision–

    (a)   to qualifying partnerships by regulations 4(1) and 9(1) of and Part 1 of the Schedule to the Partnerships (Accounts) Regulations 2008 (SI 2008/569);

    (b)   to qualifying partnerships by regulations 4(1) and 9(1) of and Part 1 of the Schedule to the Partnerships (Accounts) Regulations 2008 (SI 2008/569);

    (c)   to limited liability partnerships by the Small Limited Liability Partnerships (Accounts) Regulations 2008 (SI 2008/1912);

    (d)   to overseas companies by Chapter 3 of Part 5 or Chapter 3 of Part 6 of the Overseas Companies Regulations 2009 (SI 2009/1801);

    (e)   to unregistered companies by regulation 3 of and Schedule 1 to the Unregistered Companies Regulations 2009 (SI 2009/2436); or

    (f)   to companies registered pursuant to section 1040 of the 2006 Act by regulation 18 of the Companies (Companies Authorised to Register) Regulations 2009 (SI 2009/2437).

    3(2)   Any new provision of the 2006 Act or the 2008 Regulations inserted by these Regulations is not, by virtue of any provision mentioned in sub-paragraphs (a) to (f) of paragraph (1), applied to the entities mentioned in those sub-paragraphs.""

S. 383(4) amended by SI 2008/393, reg. 3(2): 6 April 2008 applying in relation to financial years beginning on or after 6 April 2008. In determining whether a company or group qualifies as small under s. 383(3) (qualification in relation to subsequent financial year by reference to circumstances in preceding financial years) in relation to a financial year ending on or after 6 April 2008, the company or group shall be treated as having qualified as small in any previous financial year in which it would have so qualified if amendments to the same effect as those made by SI 2008/393 had been in force (SI 2008/393, reg. 2(3)).

In s. 383(4), in the table, in item 1, the words "Not more than £10.2 million net (or £12.2 million gross)" substituted for "Not more than £6.5 million net (or £7.8 million gross)" by SI 2015/980, reg. (4)(4)(a), with effect in relation to–
- (a)   financial years beginning on or after 1 January 2016, and
- (b)   a financial year of a company beginning on or after 1 January 2015, but before 1 January 2016, if the directors of the company so decide.

In s. 383(4), in the table, in item 2, the words "Not more than £5.1 million net (or £6.1 million gross)" substituted for "Not more than £3.26 million net (or £3.9 million gross)" by SI 2015/980, reg. (4)(4)(b), with effect in relation to–
- (a)   financial years beginning on or after 1 January 2016, and
- (b)   a financial year of a company beginning on or after 1 January 2015, but before 1 January 2016, if the directors of the company so decide.

Notes – This section is modified in its application to LLPs by Part 2 LLPs Qualifying As Small LLPs Subject To The Small LLPs Regime of SI 2008/1911 the Limited Liability Partnerships (Accounts and Audit) (Application of Companies Act 2006) Regulations 2008.

This section is modified in its application to unregistered companies by SI 2009/2436 the Unregistered Companies Regulations 2009.

384   Companies excluded from the small companies regime

384(1)   The small companies regime does not apply to a company that was at any time within the financial year to which the accounts relate–
- (a)   a public company,
- (b)   a company that–
  - (i)   is an authorised insurance company, a banking company, an e-money issuer, a MiFID investment firm or a UCITS management company, or
  - (ii)   carries on insurance market activity, or
- (c)   a member of an ineligible group.

384(2)   A group is ineligible if any of its members is–
- (a)   a traded company,
- (b)   a body corporate (other than a company) whose shares are admitted to trading on a regulated market in an EEA State,
- (c)   a person (other than a small company) who has permission under Part 4A of the Financial Services and Markets Act 2000 (c. 8) to carry on a regulated activity,
- (ca)   an e-money issuer,
- (d)   a small company that is an authorised insurance company, a banking company, a MiFID investment firm or a UCITS management company, or
- (e)   a person who carries on insurance market activity.

384(3)   A company is a small company for the purposes of subsection (2) if it qualified as small in relation to its last financial year ending on or before the end of the financial year to which the accounts relate.

Commencement Date – 6 April 2008 applying to accounts and reports for financial years beginning on or after 6 April 2008. Any question whether for the purposes of s 384(3) a company qualified as small in a financial year beginning before 6 April 2008 is to be determined by reference to the corresponding provisions of the Companies Act 1985 or SI 1986/1032 (NI 6) (SI 2007/3495, Sch. 4, para. 7).

History – S. 384(1) and (2) amended by SI 2007/2932, reg. 3(1) and (2): 1 November 2007.

The version of s. 384(2) above applies in relation to a financial year of a company beginning on or after 1 October 2013. The version applying in relation to a financial year of a company beginning before 1 October 2013 read as follows:

"**384(2)**   A group is ineligible if any of its members is–
- (a)   a public company,

(b)   a body corporate (other than a company) whose shares are admitted to trading on a regulated market in an EEA State,

(c)   a person (other than a small company) who has permission under Part 4A of the Financial Services and Markets Act 2000 (c. 8) to carry on a regulated activity,

(d)   a small company that is an authorised insurance company, a banking company, an e-money issuer, a MiFID investment firm or a UCITS management company, or

(e)   a person who carries on insurance market activity."

In s. 384(2)(c), "Part 4A" substituted for "Part 4" by Financial Services Act 2012, Sch. 18, para. 110 and 111, with effect from 1 April 2013.

S. 384(2)(ca) inserted and, in s. 384(2)(d), "an e-money issuer,", repealed by SI 2013/2005, reg. 2(1) and (2), with effect from 1 September 2013 applying in relation to a financial year of a company beginning on or after 1 October 2013.

In s. 384(1), the words "is, or" omitted by SI 2015/980, reg. (4)(5)(a), with effect in relation to–

(a)   financial years beginning on or after 1 January 2016, and

(b)   a financial year of a company beginning on or after 1 January 2015, but before 1 January 2016, if the directors of the company so decide.

S. 384(2)(a) substituted by SI 2015/980, reg. (4)(5)(b), with effect in relation to–

(a)   financial years beginning on or after 1 January 2016, and

(b)   a financial year of a company beginning on or after 1 January 2015, but before 1 January 2016, if the directors of the company so decide.

Notes – This section is modified in its application to LLPs by the Limited Liability Partnerships (Accounts and Audit) (Application of Companies Act 2006) Regulations 2008 (SI 2008/1911), Pt. 2.

384A   Companies qualifying as micro-entities

384A(1)   A company qualifies as a micro-entity in relation to its first financial year if the qualifying conditions are met in that year.

384A(2)   Subject to subsection (3), a company qualifies as a micro-entity in relation to a subsequent financial year if the qualifying conditions are met in that year.

384A(3)   In relation to a subsequent financial year, where on its balance sheet date a company meets or ceases to meet the qualifying conditions, that affects its qualification as a micro-entity only if it occurs in two consecutive financial years.

384A(4)   The qualifying conditions are met by a company in a year in which it satisfies two or more of the following requirements–

1.	Turnover	Not more than £632,000
2.	Balance sheet total	Not more than £316,000
3.	Number of employees	Not more than 10

384A(5)   For a period that is a company's financial year but not in fact a year the maximum figures for turnover must be proportionately adjusted.

384A(6)   The balance sheet total means the aggregate of the amounts shown as assets in the company's balance sheet.

384A(7)   The number of employees means the average number of persons employed by the company in the year, determined as follows–

(a)   find for each month in the financial year the number of persons employed under contracts of service by the company in that month (whether throughout the month or not),

(b)   add together the monthly totals, and

(c)   divide by the number of months in the financial year.

384A(8)   In the case of a company which is a parent company, the company qualifies as a micro-entity in relation to a financial year only if–

(a)   the company qualifies as a micro-entity in relation to that year, as determined by subsections (1) to (7), and

(b)   the group headed by the company qualifies as a small group, as determined by section 383(2) to (7).

History – S. 384A inserted by SI 2013/3008, reg. 4(1) and (4), with effect from 1 December 2013 in respect of (a) financial years ending on or after 30 September 2013; and (b) companies, which deliver the accounts required by section 444 to the registrar on or after 1 December 2013.

This is subject to the following provisions of SI 2013/3008, reg. 3:

"Disapplication of these regulations to entities to which provisions of the 2006 Act or the 2008 regulations have been applied

3(1)   The amendments made by these Regulations [SI 2013/3008] to any provision of the 2006 Act [CA 2006] or the 2008 Regulations [SI 2008/409] do not have effect in relation to the application of any such provision–

(a)   to qualifying partnerships by regulations 4(1) and 9(1) of and Part 1 of the Schedule to the Partnerships (Accounts) Regulations 2008 (SI 2008/569);

(b)   to limited liability partnerships by the Limited Liability Partnerships (Accounts and Audit) (Application of Companies Act 2006) Regulations 2008 (SI 2008/1911);

(c)   to limited liability partnerships by the Small Limited Liability Partnerships (Accounts) Regulations 2008 (SI 2008/1912);

(d)   to overseas companies by Chapter 3 of Part 5 or Chapter 3 of Part 6 of the Overseas Companies Regulations 2009 (SI 2009/1801);

(e)   to unregistered companies by regulation 3 of and Schedule 1 to the Unregistered Companies Regulations 2009 (SI 2009/2436); or

(f)   to companies registered pursuant to section 1040 of the 2006 Act by regulation 18 of the Companies (Companies Authorised to Register) Regulations 2009 (SI 2009/2437).

3(2)   Any new provision of the 2006 Act or the 2008 Regulations inserted by these Regulations is not, by virtue of any provision mentioned in sub-paragraphs (a) to (f) of paragraph (1), applied to the entities mentioned in those sub-paragraphs."

384B   Companies excluded from being treated as micro-entities

384B(1)   The micro-entity provisions do not apply in relation to a company's accounts for a particular financial year if the company was at any time within that year–

(a)   a company excluded from the small companies regime by virtue of section 384,

(b)   an investment undertaking as defined in Article 2(14) of Directive 2013/34/EU of 26 June 2013 on the annual financial statements etc. of certain types of undertakings,

(c)   a financial holding undertaking as defined in Article 2(15) of that Directive,

(d)   a credit institution as defined in Article 4 of Directive 2006/48/EC of the European Parliament and of the Council of 14 June 2006 relating to the taking up and pursuit of the business of credit institutions, other than one referred to in Article 2 of that Directive,

(e)   an insurance undertaking as defined in Article 2(1) of Council Directive 91/674/EEC of 19 December 1991 on the annual accounts of insurance undertakings, or

(f)   a charity.

384B(2)   The micro-entity provisions also do not apply in relation to a company's accounts for a financial year if–

(a)   the company is a parent company which prepares group accounts for that year as permitted by section 398, or

(b)   the company is not a parent company but its accounts are included in consolidated group accounts for that year.

History – S. 384B inserted by SI 2013/3008, reg. 4(1) and (4), with effect from 1 December 2013 in respect of (a) financial years ending on or after 30 September 2013; and (b) companies, which deliver the accounts required by section 444 to the registrar on or after 1 December 2013.

This is subject to the following provisions of SI 2013/3008 reg. 3:

"Disapplication of these regulations to entities to which provisions of the 2006 Act or the 2008 regulations have been applied

384B(1) The amendments made by these Regulations [SI 2013/3008] to any provision of the 2006 Act [CA 2006] or the 2008 Regulations [SI 2008/409] do not have effect in relation to the application of any such provision–

(a)   to qualifying partnerships by regulations 4(1) and 9(1) of and Part 1 of the Schedule to the Partnerships (Accounts) Regulations 2008 (SI 2008/569);

(b)   to limited liability partnerships by the Limited Liability Partnerships (Accounts and Audit) (Application of Companies Act 2006) Regulations 2008 (SI 2008/1911);

(c)   to limited liability partnerships by the Small Limited Liability Partnerships (Accounts) Regulations 2008 (SI 2008/1912);

(d)   to overseas companies by Chapter 3 of Part 5 or Chapter 3 of Part 6 of the Overseas Companies Regulations 2009 (SI 2009/1801);

(e)   to unregistered companies by regulation 3 of and Schedule 1 to the Unregistered Companies Regulations 2009 (SI 2009/2436); or

(f)   to companies registered pursuant to section 1040 of the 2006 Act by regulation 18 of the Companies (Companies Authorised to Register) Regulations 2009 (SI 2009/2437).

384B(2) Any new provision of the 2006 Act or the 2008 Regulations inserted by these Regulations is not, by virtue of any provision mentioned in sub-paragraphs (a) to (f) of paragraph (1), applied to the entities mentioned in those sub-paragraphs."

Quoted and unquoted companies

385 Quoted and unquoted companies

385(1) For the purposes of this Part a company is a quoted company in relation to a financial year if it is a quoted company immediately before the end of the accounting reference period by reference to which that financial year was determined.

385(2) A **"quoted company"** means a company whose equity share capital–

(a)   has been included in the official list in accordance with the provisions of Part 6 of the Financial Services and Markets Act 2000 (c. 8), or

(b)   is officially listed in an EEA State, or

(c)   is admitted to dealing on either the New York Stock Exchange or the exchange known as Nasdaq. In paragraph (a) **"the official list"** has the meaning given by section 103(1) of the Financial Services and Markets Act 2000.

385(3) An **"unquoted company"** means a company that is not a quoted company.

385(4) The Secretary of State may by regulations amend or replace the provisions of subsections (1) to (2) so as to limit or extend the application of some or all of the provisions of this Part that are expressed to apply to quoted companies.

385(5) Regulations under this section extending the application of any such provision of this Part are subject to affirmative resolution procedure.

385(6) Any other regulations under this section are subject to negative resolution procedure.

Commencement Date – 6 April 2008 applying to accounts and reports for financial years beginning on or after 6 April 2008

Chapter 2 – Accounting Records

386 Duty to keep accounting records

386(1) Every company must keep adequate accounting records.

386(2) **"Adequate accounting records"** means records that are sufficient–

(a)   to show and explain the company's transactions,

(b) to disclose with reasonable accuracy, at any time, the financial position of the company at that time, and

(c) to enable the directors to ensure that any accounts required to be prepared comply with the requirements of this Act (and, where applicable, of Article 4 of the IAS Regulation).

386(3) Accounting records must, in particular, contain–

(a) entries from day to day of all sums of money received and expended by the company and the matters in respect of which the receipt and expenditure takes place, and

(b) a record of the assets and liabilities of the company.

386(4) If the company's business involves dealing in goods, the accounting records must contain–

(a) statements of stock held by the company at the end of each financial year of the company,

(b) all statements of stocktakings from which any statement of stock as is mentioned in paragraph (a) has been or is to be prepared, and

(c) except in the case of goods sold by way of ordinary retail trade, statements of all goods sold and purchased, showing the goods and the buyers and sellers in sufficient detail to enable all these to be identified.

386(5) A parent company that has a subsidiary undertaking in relation to which the above requirements do not apply must take reasonable steps to secure that the undertaking keeps such accounting records as to enable the directors of the parent company to ensure that any accounts required to be prepared under this Part comply with the requirements of this Act (and, where applicable, of Article 4 of the IAS Regulation).

Commencement Date – 6 April 2008 applying to accounts and reports for financial years beginning on or after 6 April 2008

Editorial note: this section is modified in its application to LLPs by Part 3 *Accounting Records* of SI 2008 No 1911 The Limited Liability Partnerships (Accounts and Audit) (Application of Companies Act 2006) Regulations 2008

387 Duty to keep accounting records: offence

387(1) If a company fails to comply with any provision of section 386 (duty to keep accounting records), an offence is committed by every officer of the company who is in default.

387(2) It is a defence for a person charged with such an offence to show that he acted honestly and that in the circumstances in which the company's business was carried on the default was excusable.

387(3) A person guilty of an offence under this section is liable–

(a) on conviction on indictment, to imprisonment for a term not exceeding two years or a fine (or both);

(b) on summary conviction–

(i) in England and Wales, to imprisonment for a term not exceeding twelve months or to a fine not exceeding the statutory maximum (or both);

(ii) in Scotland or Northern Ireland, to imprisonment for a term not exceeding six months, or to a fine not exceeding the statutory maximum (or both).

Commencement Date – 6 April 2008 applying to accounts and reports for financial years beginning on or after 6 April 2008

Editorial note: this section is modified in its application to LLPs by Part 3 *Accounting Records* of SI 2008 No 1911 The Limited Liability Partnerships (Accounts and Audit) (Application of Companies Act 2006) Regulations 2008

388 Where and for how long records to be kept

388(1) A company's accounting records–

(a)   must be kept at its registered office or such other place as the directors think fit, and

(b)   must at all times be open to inspection by the company's officers.

388(2) If accounting records are kept at a place outside the United Kingdom, accounts and returns with respect to the business dealt with in the accounting records so kept must be sent to, and kept at, a place in the United Kingdom, and must at all times be open to such inspection.

388(3) The accounts and returns to be sent to the United Kingdom must be such as to–

(a)   disclose with reasonable accuracy the financial position of the business in question at intervals of not more than six months, and

(b)   enable the directors to ensure that the accounts required to be prepared under this Part comply with the requirements of this Act (and, where applicable, of Article 4 of the IAS Regulation).

388(4) Accounting records that a company is required by section 386 to keep must be preserved by it–

(a)   in the case of a private company, for three years from the date on which they are made;

(b)   in the case of a public company, for six years from the date on which they are made.

388(5) Subsection (4) is subject to any provision contained in rules made under section 411 of the Insolvency Act 1986 (c. 45) (company insolvency rules) or Article 359 of the Insolvency (Northern Ireland) Order 1989 (S.I. 1989/2405 (N.I. 19)).

Commencement Date – 6 April 2008 applying to accounts and reports for financial years beginning on or after 6 April 2008

Editorial note: this section is modified in its application to LLPs by Part 3 Accounting Records of SI 2008 No 1911 The Limited Liability Partnerships (Accounts and Audit) (Application of Companies Act 2006) Regulations 2008

389 Where and for how long records to be kept: offences

389(1) If a company fails to comply with any provision of subsections (1) to (3) of section 388 (requirements as to keeping of accounting records), an offence is committed by every officer of the company who is in default.

389(2) It is a defence for a person charged with such an offence to show that he acted honestly and that in the circumstances in which the company's business was carried on the default was excusable.

389(3) An officer of a company commits an offence if he–

(a)   fails to take all reasonable steps for securing compliance by the company with subsection (4) of that section (period for which records to be preserved), or

(b)   intentionally causes any default by the company under that subsection.

389(4) A person guilty of an offence under this section is liable–

(a)   on conviction on indictment, to imprisonment for a term not exceeding two years or a fine (or both);

(b)   on summary conviction–

(i)   in England and Wales, to imprisonment for a term not exceeding twelve months or to a fine not exceeding the statutory maximum (or both);

(ii) in Scotland or Northern Ireland, to imprisonment for a term not exceeding six months, or to a fine not exceeding the statutory maximum (or both).

Commencement Date – 6 April 2008 applying to accounts and reports for financial years beginning on or after 6 April 2008

Editorial note: this section is modified in its application to LLPs by Part 3 Accounting Records of SI 2008 No 1911 The Limited Liability Partnerships (Accounts and Audit) (Application of Companies Act 2006) Regulations 2008

Chapter 3 – A Company's Financial Year

390 A company's financial year

390(1) A company's financial year is determined as follows.

390(2) Its first financial year–

(a) begins with the first day of its first accounting reference period, and

(b) ends with the last day of that period or such other date, not more than seven days before or after the end of that period, as the directors may determine.

390(3) Subsequent financial years–

(a) begin with the day immediately following the end of the company's previous financial year, and

(b) end with the last day of its next accounting reference period or such other date, not more than seven days before or after the end of that period, as the directors may determine.

390(4) In relation to an undertaking that is not a company, references in this Act to its financial year are to any period in respect of which a profit and loss account of the undertaking is required to be made up (by its constitution or by the law under which it is established), whether that period is a year or not.

390(5) The directors of a parent company must secure that, except where in their opinion there are good reasons against it, the financial year of each of its subsidiary undertakings coincides with the company's own financial year.

Commencement Date – 6 April 2008

Editorial note: this section is modified in its application to Overseas Companies by Part 5 Delivery Of Accounting Documents: general and Part 6 Delivery Of Accounting Documents: credit or financial institutions of SI 2009 No 1801 The Overseas Companies Regulations 2009.

Editorial note: this section is modified in its application to LLPs by Part 4 Financial Years of SI 2008 No 1911 The Limited Liability Partnerships (Accounts and Audit) (Application of Companies Act 2006) Regulations 2008

391 Accounting reference periods and accounting reference date

391(1) A company's accounting reference periods are determined according to its accounting reference date in each calendar year.

391(2) The accounting reference date of a company incorporated in Great Britain before 1st April 1996 is–

(a) the date specified by notice to the registrar in accordance with section 224(2) of the Companies Act 1985 (c. 6) (notice specifying accounting reference date given within nine months of incorporation), or

(b) failing such notice–

(i) in the case of a company incorporated before 1st April 1990, 31st March, and

(ii) in the case of a company incorporated on or after 1st April 1990, the last day of the month in which the anniversary of its incorporation falls.

391(3) The accounting reference date of a company incorporated in Northern Ireland before 22nd August 1997 is–

(a) the date specified by notice to the registrar in accordance with article 232(2) of the Companies (Northern Ireland) Order 1986 (S.I. 1986/1032 (N.I. 6)) (notice specifying accounting reference date given within nine months of incorporation), or

(b) failing such notice–

(i) in the case of a company incorporated before the coming into operation of Article 5 of the Companies (Northern Ireland) Order 1990 (S.I. 1990/593 (N.I. 5)), 31st March, and

(ii) in the case of a company incorporated after the coming into operation of that Article, the last day of the month in which the anniversary of its incorporation falls.

391(4) The accounting reference date of a company incorporated–

(a) in Great Britain on or after 1st April 1996 and before the commencement of this Act,

(b) in Northern Ireland on or after 22nd August 1997 and before the commencement of this Act, or

(c) after the commencement of this Act, is the last day of the month in which the anniversary of its incorporation falls.

391(5) A company's first accounting reference period is the period of more than six months, but not more than 18 months, beginning with the date of its incorporation and ending with its accounting reference date.

391(6) Its subsequent accounting reference periods are successive periods of twelve months beginning immediately after the end of the previous accounting reference period and ending with its accounting reference date.

391(7) This section has effect subject to the provisions of section 392 (alteration of accounting reference date).

Commencement Date – 6 April 2008

Editorial note: this section is modified in its application to Overseas Companies by Part 5 *Delivery Of Accounting Documents: general* and Part 6 *Delivery Of Accounting Documents: credit or financial institutions* of SI 2009 No 1801 The Overseas Companies Regulations 2009.

Editorial note: this section is modified in its application to LLPs by Part 4 *Financial Years* of SI 2008 No 1911 The Limited Liability Partnerships (Accounts and Audit) (Application of Companies Act 2006) Regulations 2008

392 Alteration of accounting reference date

392(1) A company may by notice given to the registrar specify a new accounting reference date having effect in relation to–

(a) the company's current accounting reference period and subsequent periods, or

(b) the company's previous accounting reference period and subsequent periods. A company's **"previous accounting reference period"** means the one immediately preceding its current accounting reference period.

392(2) The notice must state whether the current or previous accounting reference period–

(a) is to be shortened, so as to come to an end on the first occasion on which the new accounting reference date falls or fell after the beginning of the period, or

(b) is to be extended, so as to come to an end on the second occasion on which that date falls or fell after the beginning of the period.

392(3) A notice extending a company's current or previous accounting reference period is not effective if given less than five years after the end of an earlier accounting reference period of the company that was extended under this section. This does not apply–

(a) to a notice given by a company that is a subsidiary undertaking or parent undertaking of another EEA undertaking if the new accounting reference date coincides with that of the other EEA undertaking or, where that undertaking is not a company, with the last day of its financial year, or

(b) where the company is in administration under Part 2 of the Insolvency Act 1986 (c. 45) or Part 3 of the Insolvency (Northern Ireland) Order 1989 (S.I. 1989/2405 (N.I. 19)), or

(c) where the Secretary of State directs that it should not apply, which he may do with respect to a notice that has been given or that may be given.

392(4) A notice under this section may not be given in respect of a previous accounting reference period if the period for filing accounts and reports for the financial year determined by reference to that accounting reference period has already expired.

392(5) An accounting reference period may not be extended so as to exceed 18 months and a notice under this section is ineffective if the current or previous accounting reference period as extended in accordance with the notice would exceed that limit. This does not apply where the company is in administration under Part 2 of the Insolvency Act 1986 (c. 45) or Part 3 of the Insolvency (Northern Ireland) Order 1989 (S.I. 1989/2405 (N.I. 19)).

392(6) In this section **"EEA undertaking"** means an undertaking established under the law of any part of the United Kingdom or the law of any other EEA State.

Commencement Date – 6 April 2008. Until s 1068(1) comes into force, the notice referred to in s 392 (notice of alteration of accounting reference date) must be given in the form prescribed for the purposes of the Companies Act 1985 s 225(1) or SI 1986/1032 (NI 6) art 233(1) (SI 2007/3495 Sch 4 para 8).

Editorial note: this section is modified in its application to Overseas Companies by Part 5 *Delivery Of Accounting Documents: general* and Part 6 *Delivery Of Accounting Documents: credit or financial institutions* of SI 2009 No 1801 The Overseas Companies Regulations 2009.

Editorial note: this section is modified in its application to LLPs by Part 4 *Financial Years* of SI 2008 No 1911 The Limited Liability Partnerships (Accounts and Audit) (Application of Companies Act 2006) Regulations 2008

Chapter 4 – Annual Accounts

General

393 Accounts to give true and fair view

393(1) The directors of a company must not approve accounts for the purposes of this Chapter unless they are satisfied that they give a true and fair view of the assets, liabilities, financial position and profit or loss–

(a) in the case of the company's individual accounts, of the company;

(b) in the case of the company's group accounts, of the undertakings included in the consolidation as a whole, so far as concerns members of the company.

393(1A) The following provisions apply to the directors of a company which qualifies as a micro-entity in relation to a financial year (see sections 384A and 384B) in their consideration of whether the Companies Act individual accounts of the company for that year give a true and fair view as required by subsection (1)(a)–

(a) where the accounts comprise only micro-entity minimum accounting items, the directors must disregard any provision of an accounting standard which would require the accounts to contain information additional to those items,

(b) in relation to a micro-entity minimum accounting item contained in the accounts, the directors must disregard any provision of an accounting standard which would require the accounts to contain further information in relation to that item, and

(c) where the accounts contain an item of information additional to the micro-entity minimum accounting items, the directors must have regard to any provision of an accounting standard which relates to that item.

393(2) The auditor of a company in carrying out his functions under this Act in relation to the company's annual accounts must have regard to the directors' duty under subsection (1).

Commencement Date – 6 April 2008 applying to accounts and reports for financial years beginning on or after 6 April 2008.

History – S. 393(1A) inserted by SI 2013/3008, reg. 5(1) and (2), with effect from 1 December 2013 in respect of (a) financial years ending on or after 30 September 2013; and (b) companies, which deliver the accounts required by section 444 to the registrar on or after 1 December 2013.

This is subject to the following provisions of SI 2013/3008, reg. 3:

"Disapplication of these regulations to entities to which provisions of the 2006 Act or the 2008 regulations have been applied

3(1) The amendments made by these Regulations [SI 2013/3008] to any provision of the 2006 Act [CA 2006] or the 2008 Regulations [SI 2008/409] do not have effect in relation to the application of any such provision–

(a) to qualifying partnerships by regulations 4(1) and 9(1) of and Part 1 of the Schedule to the Partnerships (Accounts) Regulations 2008 (SI 2008/569);

(b) to limited liability partnerships by the Limited Liability Partnerships (Accounts and Audit) (Application of Companies Act 2006) Regulations 2008 (SI 2008/1911);

(c) to limited liability partnerships by the Small Limited Liability Partnerships (Accounts) Regulations 2008 (SI 2008/1912);

(d) to overseas companies by Chapter 3 of Part 5 or Chapter 3 of Part 6 of the Overseas Companies Regulations 2009 (SI 2009/1801);

(e) to unregistered companies by regulation 3 of and Schedule 1 to the Unregistered Companies Regulations 2009 (SI 2009/2436); or

(f) to companies registered pursuant to section 1040 of the 2006 Act by regulation 18 of the Companies (Companies Authorised to Register) Regulations 2009 (SI 2009/2437).

3(2) Any new provision of the 2006 Act or the 2008 Regulations inserted by these Regulations is not, by virtue of any provision mentioned in sub-paragraphs (a) to (f) of paragraph (1), applied to the entities mentioned in those sub-paragraphs."

Notes – This section is modified in its application to LLPs by Part 5 Annual Accounts of SI 2008/1911 the Limited Liability Partnerships (Accounts and Audit) (Application of Companies Act 2006) Regulations 2008.

Individual accounts

394 Duty to prepare individual accounts

The directors of every company must prepare accounts for the company for each of its financial years unless the company is exempt from that requirement under section 394A. Those accounts are referred to as the company's **"individual accounts"**.

Commencement Date – 6 April 2008 applying to accounts and reports for financial years beginning on or after 6 April 2008

History – Words "unless the company is exempt from that requirement under section 394A" inserted by SI 2012/2301, reg. 8, with effect from 1 October 2012.

Notes – This section is modified in its application to Overseas Companies by Pt. 5 *Delivery Of Accounting Documents: general* and Pt. 6 *Delivery Of Accounting Documents: credit or financial institutions* of the Overseas Companies Regulations 2009 (SI 2009/1801).

This section is modified in its application to LLPs by Pt. 5 *Annual Accounts* of the Limited Liability Partnerships (Accounts and Audit) (Application of Companies Act 2006) Regulations 2008 (SI 2008/1911).

394A Individual accounts: exemption for dormant subsidiaries

394A(1) A company is exempt from the requirement to prepare individual accounts for a financial year if–

(a)   it is itself a subsidiary undertaking,

(b)   it has been dormant throughout the whole of that year, and

(c)   its parent undertaking is established under the law of an EEA State.

394A(2) Exemption is conditional upon compliance with all of the following conditions–

(a)   all members of the company must agree to the exemption in respect of the financial year in question,

(b)   the parent undertaking must give a guarantee under section 394C in respect of that year,

(c)   the company must be included in the consolidated accounts drawn up for that year or to an earlier date in that year by the parent undertaking in accordance with–

    (i) the provisions of Directive 2013/34/EU of the European Parliament and of the Council on the annual financial statements, consolidated financial statements and related reports of certain types of undertakings, or

    (ii) international accounting standards,

(d)   the parent undertaking must disclose in the notes to the consolidated accounts that the company is exempt from the requirement to prepare individual accounts by virtue of this section, and

(e)   the directors of the company must deliver to the registrar within the period for filing the company's accounts and reports for that year–

    (i) a written notice of the agreement referred to in subsection (2)(a),

    (ii) the statement referred to in section 394C(1),

    (iii) a copy of the consolidated accounts referred to in subsection (2)(c),

    (iv) a copy of the auditor's report on those accounts, and

    (v) a copy of the consolidated annual report drawn up by the parent undertaking.

History – S. 394A inserted by SI 2012/2301, reg. 9, with effect from 1 October 2012 and applying to accounts for financial years ending on or after 1 October 2012.
S. 394A(2)(c)(i) substituted by SI 2015/980, reg. 5(2), with effect in relation to–

(a)   financial years beginning on or after 1 January 2016, and

(b)   a financial year of a company beginning on or after 1 January 2015, but before 1 January 2016, if the directors of the company so decide.

394B Companies excluded from the dormant subsidiaries exemption

A company is not entitled to the exemption conferred by section 394A (dormant subsidiaries) if it was at any time within the financial year in question–

(a)   a traded company,

(b)   a company that–

    (i) is an authorised insurance company, a banking company, an e-money issuer, a MiFID investment firm or a UCITS management company, or

    (ii) carries on insurance market activity, or

(c)   a special register body as defined in section 117(1) of the Trade Union and Labour Relations (Consolidation) Act 1992 (c 52) or an employers' association as defined in section 122 of that Act or Article 4 of the Industrial Relations (Northern Ireland) Order 1992 (S.I. 1992/807) (NI 5).

History – S. 394B inserted by SI 2012/2301, reg. 9, with effect from 1 October 2012 and applying to accounts for financial years ending on or after 1 October 2012.

S. 394B(a) substituted by SI 2015/980, reg. 5(3), with effect in relation to–

(a)   financial years beginning on or after 1 January 2016, and

(b)   a financial year of a company beginning on or after 1 January 2015, but before 1 January 2016, if the directors of the company so decide.

394C   Dormant subsidiaries exemption: parent undertaking declaration of guarantee

394C(1)   A guarantee is given by a parent undertaking under this section when the directors of the subsidiary company deliver to the registrar a statement by the parent undertaking that it guarantees the subsidiary company under this section.

394C(2)   The statement under subsection (1) must be authenticated by the parent undertaking and must specify–

(a)   the name of the parent undertaking,

(b)   if the parent undertaking is incorporated in the United Kingdom, its registered number (if any),

(c)   if the parent undertaking is incorporated outside the United Kingdom and registered in the country in which it is incorporated, the identity of the register on which it is registered and the number with which it is so registered,

(d)   the name and registered number of the subsidiary company in respect of which the guarantee is being given,

(e)   the date of the statement, and

(f)   the financial year to which the guarantee relates.

394C(3)   A guarantee given under this section has the effect that–

(a)   the parent undertaking guarantees all outstanding liabilities to which the subsidiary company is subject at the end of the financial year to which the guarantee relates, until they are satisfied in full, and

(b)   the guarantee is enforceable against the parent undertaking by any person to whom the subsidiary company is liable in respect of those liabilities.

History – S. 394C inserted by SI 2012/2301, reg. 9, with effect from 1 October 2012 and applying to accounts for financial years ending on or after 1 October 2012.

395   Individual accounts: applicable accounting framework

395(1)   A company's individual accounts may be prepared–

(a)   in accordance with section 396 ("Companies Act individual accounts"), or

(b)   in accordance with international accounting standards ("IAS individual accounts"). This is subject to the following provisions of this section and to section 407 (consistency of financial reporting within group).

395(2)   The individual accounts of a company that is a charity must be Companies Act individual accounts.

395(3)   After the first financial year in which the directors of a company prepare IAS individual accounts ("the first IAS year"), all subsequent individual accounts of the company must be prepared in accordance with international accounting standards unless there is a relevant change of circumstance.

This is subject to subsection (4A).

395(4) There is a relevant change of circumstance if, at any time during or after the first IAS year–

(a)   the company becomes a subsidiary undertaking of another undertaking that does not prepare IAS individual accounts,

(aa)   the company ceases to be a subsidiary undertaking,

(b)   the company ceases to be a company with securities admitted to trading on a regulated market in an EEA State, or

(c)   a parent undertaking of the company ceases to be an undertaking with securities admitted to trading on a regulated market in an EEA State.

395(4A) After a financial year in which the directors of a company prepare IAS individual accounts for the company, the directors may change to preparing Companies Act individual accounts for a reason other than a relevant change of circumstance provided they have not changed to Companies Act individual accounts in the period of five years preceding the first day of that financial year.

395(4B) In calculating the five year period for the purpose of subsection (4A), no account should be taken of a change due to a relevant change of circumstance.

395(5) If, having changed to preparing Companies Act individual accounts, the directors again prepare IAS individual accounts for the company, subsections (3) and (4) apply again as if the first financial year for which such accounts are again prepared were the first IAS year.

Commencement Date – 6 April 2008 applying to accounts and reports for financial years beginning on or after 6 April 2008.

History – In s. 395(3), the words "This is subject to subsection (4A)." inserted by SI 2012/2301, reg. 12, with effect from 1 October 2012.

S. 395(4) amended by SI 2008/393, reg. 9: 6 April 2008 applying in relation to financial years beginning on or after 6 April 2008.

S. 395(4A) and (4B) inserted by SI 2012/2301, reg. 13, with effect from 1 October 2012 and applying to accounts for financial years ending on or after 1 October 2012.

In s. 395(5), after "Companies Act individual accounts", the words "following a relevant change of circumstance" repealed by SI 2012/2301, reg. 14, with effect from 1 October 2012 and applying to accounts for financial years ending on or after 1 October 2012.

Version of s. 395 applying to financial years ending before 1 October 2012 reads as follows:

"**395(1)** A company's individual accounts may be prepared–

(a)   in accordance with section 396 ("Companies Act individual accounts"), or

(b)   in accordance with international accounting standards ("IAS individual accounts"). This is subject to the following provisions of this section and to section 407 (consistency of financial reporting within group).

395(2) The individual accounts of a company that is a charity must be Companies Act individual accounts.

395(3) After the first financial year in which the directors of a company prepare IAS individual accounts ("the first IAS year"), all subsequent individual accounts of the company must be prepared in accordance with international accounting standards unless there is a relevant change of circumstance.

395(4) There is a relevant change of circumstance if, at any time during or after the first IAS year–

(a)   the company becomes a subsidiary undertaking of another undertaking that does not prepare IAS individual accounts,

(aa)   the company ceases to be a subsidiary undertaking,

(b)   the company ceases to be a company with securities admitted to trading on a regulated market in an EEA State, or

(c)   a parent undertaking of the company ceases to be an undertaking with securities admitted to trading on a regulated market in an EEA State.

395(5) If, having changed to preparing Companies Act individual accounts following a relevant change of circumstance, the directors again prepare IAS individual accounts for the company, subsections (3) and (4) apply again as if the first financial year for which such accounts are again prepared were the first IAS year."

Notes – This section is modified in its application to Overseas Companies by Pt. 5 *Delivery Of Accounting Documents: general* and Pt. 6 *Delivery Of Accounting Documents: credit or financial institutions* of the Overseas Companies Regulations 2009 (SI 2009/1801).

This section is modified in its application to LLPs by Pt. 5 *Annual Accounts* of the Limited Liability Partnerships (Accounts and Audit) (Application of Companies Act 2006) Regulations 2008 (SI 2008/1911).

396 Companies Act individual accounts

396(A1) Companies Act individual accounts must state–

(a)   the part of the United Kingdom in which the company is registered,

(b)   the company's registered number,

(c)   whether the company is a public or a private company and whether it is limited by shares or by guarantee,

(d)   the address of the company's registered office, and

(e)   where appropriate, the fact that the company is being wound-up.

396(1) Companies Act individual accounts must comprise–

(a)   a balance sheet as at the last day of the financial year, and

(b)   a profit and loss account.

396(2) The accounts must–

(a)   in the case of the balance sheet, give a true and fair view of the state of affairs of the company as at the end of the financial year, and

(b)   in the case of the profit and loss account, give a true and fair view of the profit or loss of the company for the financial year.

396(2A) In the case of the individual accounts of a company which qualifies as a micro-entity in relation to the financial year (see sections 384A and 384B), the micro-entity minimum accounting items included in the company's accounts for the year are presumed to give the true and fair view required by subsection (2).

396(3) The accounts must comply with provision made by the Secretary of State by regulations as to–

(a)   the form and content of the balance sheet and profit and loss account, and

(b)   additional information to be provided by way of notes to the accounts.

396(4) If compliance with the regulations, and any other provision made by or under this Act as to the matters to be included in a company's individual accounts or in notes to those accounts, would not be sufficient to give a true and fair view, the necessary additional information must be given in the accounts or in a note to them.

396(5) If in special circumstances compliance with any of those provisions is inconsistent with the requirement to give a true and fair view, the directors must depart from that provision to the extent necessary to give a true and fair view. Particulars of any such departure, the reasons for it and its effect must be given in a note to the accounts.

396(6) Subsections (4) and (5) do not apply in relation to the micro-entity minimum accounting items included in the individual accounts of a company for a financial year in relation to which the company qualifies as a micro-entity.

Commencement Date – 6 April 2008 applying to accounts and reports for financial years beginning on or after 6 April 2008.

History – S. 396(2A) and (6) inserted by SI 2013/3008, reg. 5(1) and (3), with effect from 1 December 2013 in respect of (a) financial years ending on or after 30 September 2013; and (b) companies, which deliver the accounts required by s. 444 to the registrar on or after 1 December 2013.

S. 396(A1) inserted by SI 2015/980, reg. 5(4), with effect in relation to–

(a)   financial years beginning on or after 1 January 2016, and

(b)   a financial year of a company beginning on or after 1 January 2015, but before 1 January 2016, if the directors of the company so decide.

Statutory instruments – For regulations under this section see the Small Companies and Groups (Accounts and Directors' Report) Regulations 2008 (SI 2008/409) and the Large and Medium-sized Companies and Groups (Accounts and Reports) Regulations 2008 (SI 2008/410).

Notes – This section is modified in its application to Overseas Companies by Pt. 5 *Delivery Of Accounting Documents: general* and Pt. 6 *Delivery Of Accounting Documents: credit or financial institutions* of the Overseas Companies Regulations 2009 (SI 2009/1801).

This section is modified in its application to LLPs by Pt. 5 *Annual Accounts* of the Limited Liability Partnerships (Accounts and Audit) (Application of Companies Act 2006) Regulations 2008 (SI 2008/1911).

This section is modified in its application to unregistered companies by the Unregistered Companies Regulations 2009 (SI 2009/2436).

This is subject to the following provisions of SI 2013/3008, reg. 3:

"Disapplication of these regulations to entities to which provisions of the 2006 Act or the 2008 regulations have been applied

3(1) The amendments made by these Regulations [SI 2013/3008] to any provision of the 2006 Act [CA 2006] or the 2008 Regulations [SI 2008/409] do not have effect in relation to the application of any such provision–

- (a) to qualifying partnerships by regulations 4(1) and 9(1) of and Part 1 of the Schedule to the Partnerships (Accounts) Regulations 2008 (SI 2008/569);
- (b) to limited liability partnerships by the Limited Liability Partnerships (Accounts and Audit) (Application of Companies Act 2006) Regulations 2008 (SI 2008/1911);
- (c) to limited liability partnerships by the Small Limited Liability Partnerships (Accounts) Regulations 2008 (SI 2008/1912);
- (d) to overseas companies by Chapter 3 of Part 5 or Chapter 3 of Part 6 of the Overseas Companies Regulations 2009 (SI 2009/1801);
- (e) to unregistered companies by regulation 3 of and Schedule 1 to the Unregistered Companies Regulations 2009 (SI 2009/2436); or
- (f) to companies registered pursuant to section 1040 of the 2006 Act by regulation 18 of the Companies (Companies Authorised to Register) Regulations 2009 (SI 2009/2437).

3(2) Any new provision of the 2006 Act or the 2008 Regulations inserted by these Regulations is not, by virtue of any provision mentioned in sub-paragraphs (a) to (f) of paragraph (1), applied to the entities mentioned in those sub-paragraphs."

397 IAS individual accounts

397(1) IAS individual accounts must state–

- (a) the part of the United Kingdom in which the company is registered,
- (b) the company's registered number,
- (c) whether the company is a public or a private company and whether it is limited by shares or by guarantee,
- (d) the address of the company's registered office, and
- (e) where appropriate, the fact that the company is being wound-up.

397(2) The notes to the accounts must state that the accounts have been prepared in accordance with international accounting standards.

History – S. 397 substituted by SI 2015/980, reg. 5(5), with effect in relation to–

- (a) financial years beginning on or after 1 January 2016, and
- (b) a financial year of a company beginning on or after 1 January 2015, but before 1 January 2016, if the directors of the company so decide.

Former s. 397 read as follows:

"397 IAS individual accounts

397 Where the directors of a company prepare IAS individual accounts, they must state in the notes to the accounts that the accounts have been prepared in accordance with international accounting standards.

Commencement Date – 6 April 2008 applying to accounts and reports for financial years beginning on or after 6 April 2008

Notes – This section is modified in its application to Overseas Companies by Pt. 5 *Delivery Of Accounting Documents: general* and Pt. 6 *Delivery Of Accounting Documents: credit or financial institutions* of the Overseas Companies Regulations 2009 (SI 2009/1801).

This section is modified in its application to LLPs by Pt. 5 *Annual Accounts* of the Limited Liability Partnerships (Accounts and Audit) (Application of Companies Act 2006) Regulations 2008 (SI 2008/1911)."

Group accounts: small companies

398 Option to prepare group accounts

If at the end of a financial year a company subject to the small companies regime is a parent company the directors, as well as preparing individual accounts for the year, may prepare group accounts for the year.

Commencement Date – 6 April 2008 applying to accounts and reports for financial years beginning on or after 6 April 2008

Notes – This section is modified in its application to LLPs by Pt. 5 *Annual Accounts* of the Limited Liability Partnerships (Accounts and Audit) (Application of Companies Act 2006) Regulations 2008 (SI 2008/1911).

Group accounts: Other companies

399 Duty to prepare group accounts

399(1) This section applies to companies that are not subject to the small companies regime.

399(2) If at the end of a financial year the company is a parent company the directors, as well as preparing individual accounts for the year, must prepare group accounts for the year unless the company is exempt from that requirement.

399(2A) A company is exempt from the requirement to prepare group accounts if–

(a)   it would be subject to the small companies regime but for being a public company, and

(b)   it is not a traded company.

399(3) There are further exemptions under–

section 400 (company included in EEA accounts of larger group),

section 401 (company included in non-EEA accounts of larger group), and

section 402 (company none of whose subsidiary undertakings need be included in the consolidation).

399(4) A company to which this section applies but which is exempt from the requirement to prepare group accounts, may do so.

Commencement Date – 6 April 2008 applying to accounts and reports for financial years beginning on or after 6 April 2008.

History – S. 399(2A) inserted by SI 2015/980, reg. 5(6)(a), with effect in relation to–

(a)   financial years beginning on or after 1 January 2016, and

(b)   a financial year of a company beginning on or after 1 January 2015, but before 1 January 2016, if the directors of the company so decide.

In s. 399(3), the word "further" inserted by SI 2015/980, reg. 5(6)(b), with effect in relation to–

(a)   financial years beginning on or after 1 January 2016, and

(b)   a financial year of a company beginning on or after 1 January 2015, but before 1 January 2016, if the directors of the company so decide.

Notes – This section is modified in its application to Overseas Companies by Pt. 5 *Delivery Of Accounting Documents: general* and Pt. 6 *Delivery Of Accounting Documents: credit or financial institutions* of the Overseas Companies Regulations 2009 (SI 2009/1801).
This section is modified in its application to LLPs by Pt. 5 *Annual Accounts* of the Limited Liability Partnerships (Accounts and Audit) (Application of Companies Act 2006) Regulations 2008 (SI 2008/1911).

400 Exemption for company included in EEA group accounts of larger group

400(1) A company is exempt from the requirement to prepare group accounts if it is itself a subsidiary undertaking and its immediate parent undertaking is established under the law of an EEA State, in the following cases–

(a) where the company is a wholly-owned subsidiary of that parent undertaking;

(b) where that parent undertaking holds 90% or more of the allotted shares in the company and the remaining shareholders have approved the exemption;

(c) where that parent undertaking holds more than 50% (but less than 90%) of the allotted shares in the company and notice requesting the preparation of group accounts has not been served on the company by the shareholders holding in aggregate at least 5% of the allotted shares in the company.

Such notice must be served at least six months before the end of the financial year to which it relates.

400(2) Exemption is conditional upon compliance with all of the following conditions–

(a) the company must be included in consolidated accounts for a larger group drawn up to the same date, or to an earlier date in the same financial year, by a parent undertaking established under the law of an EEA State;

(b) those accounts must be drawn up and audited, and that parent undertaking's annual report must be drawn up, according to that law–

(i) in accordance with the provisions of Directive 2013/34/EU of the European Parliament and of the Council on the annual financial statements, consolidated financial statements and related reports of certain types of undertakings, or

(ii) in accordance with international accounting standards;

(c) the company must disclose in the notes to its individual accounts that it is exempt from the obligation to prepare and deliver group accounts;

(d) the company must state in its individual accounts the name of the parent undertaking that draws up the group accounts referred to above and–

(i) the address of the undertaking's registered office (whether in or outside the United Kingdom), or

(ii) if it is unincorporated, the address of its principal place of business;

(e) the company must deliver to the registrar, within the period for filing its accounts and reports for the financial year in question, copies of–

(i) those group accounts, and

(ii) the parent undertaking's annual report, together with the auditor's report on them;

(f) any requirement of Part 35 of this Act as to the delivery to the registrar of a certified translation into English must be met in relation to any document comprised in the accounts and reports delivered in accordance with paragraph (e).

400(3) For the purposes of subsection (1)(b) and (c) shares held by a wholly-owned subsidiary of the parent undertaking, or held on behalf of the parent undertaking or a wholly-owned subsidiary, shall be attributed to the parent undertaking.

400(4) The exemption does not apply to a company which is a traded company.

400(5) Shares held by directors of a company for the purpose of complying with any share qualification requirement shall be disregarded in determining for the purposes of this section whether the company is a wholly-owned subsidiary.

400(6) [Omitted by SI 2015/980, reg. 5(7)(e).]

Commencement Date – 6 April 2008 applying to accounts and reports for financial years beginning on or after 6 April 2008.

History – S. 400(1)(b) substituted by SI 2015/980, reg. 5(7)(a), with effect in relation to–
  (a) financial years beginning on or after 1 January 2016, and
  (b) a financial year of a company beginning on or after 1 January 2015, but before 1 January 2016, if the directors of the company so decide.

S. 400(2)(b)(i) substituted by SI 2015/980, reg. 5(7)(b)(i), with effect in relation to–
  (a) financial years beginning on or after 1 January 2016, and
  (b) a financial year of a company beginning on or after 1 January 2015, but before 1 January 2016, if the directors of the company so decide.

In s. 400(2)(c), the words "the notes to" inserted by SI 2015/980, reg. 5(7)(b)(ii), with effect in relation to–
  (a) financial years beginning on or after 1 January 2016, and
  (b) a financial year of a company beginning on or after 1 January 2015, but before 1 January 2016, if the directors of the company so decide.

S. 400(2)(d)(i) substituted by SI 2015/980, reg. 5(7)(b)(iii), with effect in relation to–
  (a) financial years beginning on or after 1 January 2016, and
  (b) a financial year of a company beginning on or after 1 January 2015, but before 1 January 2016, if the directors of the company so decide.

In s. 400(3), the words "and (c)" inserted by SI 2015/980, reg. 5(7)(c), with effect in relation to–
  (a) financial years beginning on or after 1 January 2016, and
  (b) a financial year of a company beginning on or after 1 January 2015, but before 1 January 2016, if the directors of the company so decide.

In s. 400(4), the words "which is a traded company" substituted for the words "any of whose securities are admitted to trading on a regulated market in an EEA State" by SI 2015/980, reg. 5(7)(d), with effect in relation to–
  (a) financial years beginning on or after 1 January 2016, and
  (b) a financial year of a company beginning on or after 1 January 2015, but before 1 January 2016, if the directors of the company so decide.

S. 400(6) omitted by SI 2015/980, reg. 5(7)(e), with effect in relation to–
  (a) financial years beginning on or after 1 January 2016, and
  (b) a financial year of a company beginning on or after 1 January 2015, but before 1 January 2016, if the directors of the company so decide.

Former s. 400(6) read as follows:
  "**400(6)** In subsection (4) **"securities"** includes–
  (a) shares and stock,
  (b) debentures, including debenture stock, loan stock, bonds, certificates of deposit and other instruments creating or acknowledging indebtedness,
  (c) warrants or other instruments entitling the holder to subscribe for securities falling within paragraph (a) or (b), and
  (d) certificates or other instruments that confer–
      (i) property rights in respect of a security falling within paragraph (a), (b) or (c),
      (ii) any right to acquire, dispose of, underwrite or convert a security, being a right to which the holder would be entitled if he held any such security to which the certificate or other instrument relates, or
      (iii) a contractual right (other than an option) to acquire any such security otherwise than by subscription."

Notes – This section is modified in its application to LLPs by Pt. 5 *Annual Accounts* of the Limited Liability Partnerships (Accounts and Audit) (Application of Companies Act 2006) Regulations 2008 (SI 2008/1911).

401   Exemption for company included in non-EEA group accounts of larger group

401(1)   A company is exempt from the requirement to prepare group accounts if it is itself a subsidiary undertaking and its parent undertaking is not established under the law of an EEA State, in the following cases–

(a)   where the company is a wholly-owned subsidiary of that parent undertaking;

(b)   where that parent undertaking holds 90% or more of the allotted shares in the company and the remaining shareholders have approved the exemption; or

(c)   where that parent undertaking holds more than 50% (but less than 90%) of the allotted shares in the company and notice requesting the preparation of group accounts has not been served on the company by the shareholders holding in aggregate at least 5% of the allotted shares in the company.

Such notice must be served at least six months before the end of the financial year to which it relates.

401(2)   Exemption is conditional upon compliance with all of the following conditions–

(a)   the company and all of its subsidiary undertakings must be included in consolidated accounts for a larger group drawn up to the same date, or to an earlier date in the same financial year, by a parent undertaking;

(b)   those accounts and, where appropriate, the group's annual report, must be drawn up–

(i)   in accordance with the provisions of Directive 2013/34/EU of the European Parliament and of the Council of 26 June 2013 on the annual financial statements, consolidated financial statements and related reports of certain types of undertakings,

(ii)   in a manner equivalent to consolidated accounts and consolidated reports so drawn up,

(iii)   in accordance with international accounting standards adopted pursuant to the IAS Regulation, or

(iv)   in accordance with accounting standards which are equivalent to such international accounting standards, as determined pursuant to Commission Regulation (EC) No. 1569/2007(6) of 21 December 2007 establishing a mechanism for the determination of equivalence of accounting standards applied by third country issuers of securities pursuant to Directives 2003/71/EC and 2004/109/EC of the European Parliament and of the Council;

(c)   the group accounts must be audited by one or more persons authorised to audit accounts under the law under which the parent undertaking which draws them up is established;

(d)   the company must disclose in its individual accounts that it is exempt from the obligation to prepare and deliver group accounts;

(e)   the company must state in its individual accounts the name of the parent undertaking which draws up the group accounts referred to above and–

(i)   the address of the undertaking's registered office (whether in or outside the United Kingdom), or;

(ii)   if it is unincorporated, the address of its principal place of business;

(f)   the company must deliver to the registrar, within the period for filing its accounts and reports for the financial year in question, copies of–

(i)   the group accounts, and

      (ii)   where appropriate, the consolidated annual report, together with the auditor's report on them;

(g)   any requirement of Part 35 of this Act as to the delivery to the registrar of a certified translation into English must be met in relation to any document comprised in the accounts and reports delivered in accordance with paragraph (f).

401(3) For the purposes of subsection (1)(b) and (c), shares held by a wholly-owned subsidiary of the parent undertaking, or held on behalf of the parent undertaking or a wholly-owned subsidiary, are attributed to the parent undertaking.

401(4) The exemption does not apply to a company which is a traded company.

401(5) Shares held by directors of a company for the purpose of complying with any share qualification requirement shall be disregarded in determining for the purposes of this section whether the company is a wholly-owned subsidiary.

401(6) [Omitted by SI 2015/980, reg. 5(8)(f).]

Commencement Date – 6 April 2008 applying to accounts and reports for financial years beginning on or after 6 April 2008.

History – S. 401(1)(b) substituted by SI 2015/980, reg. 5(8)(a), with effect in relation to–
    (a)   financial years beginning on or after 1 January 2016, and
    (b)   a financial year of a company beginning on or after 1 January 2015, but before 1 January 2016, if the directors of the company so decide.

S. 401(2)(b) substituted by SI 2015/980, reg. 5(8)(b), with effect in relation to–
    (a)   financial years beginning on or after 1 January 2016, and
    (b)   a financial year of a company beginning on or after 1 January 2015, but before 1 January 2016, if the directors of the company so decide.

S. 401(2)(e)(i) substituted by SI 2015/980, reg. 5(8)(c), with effect in relation to–
    (a)   financial years beginning on or after 1 January 2016, and
    (b)   a financial year of a company beginning on or after 1 January 2015, but before 1 January 2016, if the directors of the company so decide.

In s. 401(3), the words "and (c)" inserted by SI 2015/980, reg. 5(8)(d), with effect in relation to–
    (a)   financial years beginning on or after 1 January 2016, and
    (b)   a financial year of a company beginning on or after 1 January 2015, but before 1 January 2016, if the directors of the company so decide.

In s. 401(4), the words "which is a traded company" substituted for the words "any of whose securities are admitted to trading on a regulated market in an EEA State" by SI 2015/980, reg. 5(8)(e), with effect in relation to–
    (a)   financial years beginning on or after 1 January 2016, and
    (b)   a financial year of a company beginning on or after 1 January 2015, but before 1 January 2016, if the directors of the company so decide.

S. 401(6) omitted by SI 2015/980, reg. 5(8)(f), with effect in relation to–
    (a)   financial years beginning on or after 1 January 2016, and
    (b)   a financial year of a company beginning on or after 1 January 2015, but before 1 January 2016, if the directors of the company so decide.

Former s. 401(6) read as follows:

    "**401(6)** In subsection (4) **"securities"** includes–
    (a)   shares and stock,
    (b)   debentures, including debenture stock, loan stock, bonds, certificates of deposit and other instruments creating or acknowledging indebtedness,
    (c)   warrants or other instruments entitling the holder to subscribe for securities falling within paragraph (a) or (b), and
    (d)   certificates or other instruments that confer–
        (i)   property rights in respect of a security falling within paragraph (a), (b) or (c),
        (ii)   any right to acquire, dispose of, underwrite or convert a security, being a right to which the holder would be entitled if he held any such security to which the certificate or other instrument relates, or
        (iii) a contractual right (other than an option) to acquire any such security otherwise than by subscription."

Notes – This section is modified in its application to LLPs by Pt. 5 *Annual Accounts* of the Limited Liability Partnerships (Accounts and Audit) (Application of Companies Act 2006) Regulations 2008 (SI 2008/1911).

402 Exemption if no subsidiary undertakings need be included in the consolidation

A parent company is exempt from the requirement to prepare group accounts if under section 405 all of its subsidiary undertakings could be excluded from consolidation in Companies Act group accounts.

Commencement Date – 6 April 2008 applying to accounts and reports for financial years beginning on or after 6 April 2008.

Notes – This section is modified in its application to Overseas Companies by Pt. 5 *Delivery Of Accounting Documents: general* and Pt. 6 *Delivery Of Accounting Documents: credit or financial institutions* of the Overseas Companies Regulations 2009 (SI 2009/1801).
This section is modified in its application to LLPs by Pt. 5 *Annual Accounts* of the Limited Liability Partnerships (Accounts and Audit) (Application of Companies Act 2006) Regulations 2008 (SI 2008/1911).

Group accounts: General

403 Group accounts: applicable accounting framework

403(1) The group accounts of certain parent companies are required by Article 4 of the IAS Regulation to be prepared in accordance with international accounting standards ("IAS group accounts").

403(2) The group accounts of other companies may be prepared–

(a)   in accordance with section 404 ("Companies Act group accounts"), or

(b)   in accordance with international accounting standards ("IAS group accounts"). This is subject to the following provisions of this section.

403(3) The group accounts of a parent company that is a charity must be Companies Act group accounts.

403(4) After the first financial year in which the directors of a parent company prepare IAS group accounts ("the first IAS year"), all subsequent group accounts of the company must be prepared in accordance with international accounting standards unless there is a relevant change of circumstance.

This is subject to subsection (5A).

403(5) There is a relevant change of circumstance if, at any time during or after the first IAS year–

(a)   the company becomes a subsidiary undertaking of another undertaking that does not prepare IAS group accounts,

(b)   the company ceases to be a company with securities admitted to trading on a regulated market in an EEA State, or

(c)   a parent undertaking of the company ceases to be an undertaking with securities admitted to trading on a regulated market in an EEA State.

403(5A) After a financial year in which the directors of a parent company prepare IAS group accounts for the company, the directors may change to preparing Companies Act group accounts for the company for a reason other than a relevant change of circumstance provided they have not changed to Companies Act group accounts in the period of five years preceding the first day of that financial year.

403(5B) In calculating the five year period for the purpose of subsection (5A), no account should be taken of a change due to a relevant change of circumstance.

403(6) If, having changed to preparing Companies Act group accounts following a relevant change of circumstance, the directors again prepare IAS group accounts for the company, subsections (4) and (5) apply again as if the first financial year for which such accounts are again prepared were the first IAS year.

Commencement Date – 6 April 2008 applying to accounts and reports for financial years beginning on or after 6 April 2008.

History – In s. 403(4), the words "This is subject to subsection (5A)." inserted by SI 2012/2301, reg. 15, with effect from 1 October 2012.

S. 403(5A) and (5B) inserted by SI 2012/2301, reg. 16, with effect from 1 October 2012 and applying to accounts for financial years ending on or after 1 October 2012.

In s. 403(6), the words "following a relevant change of circumstance" repealed by SI 2012/2301, reg. 17, with effect from 1 October 2012 and applying to accounts for financial years ending on or after 1 October 2012.

Version of s. 403 applying to financial years ending before 1 October 2012 read as follows:

"**403(1)**   The group accounts of certain parent companies are required by Article 4 of the IAS Regulation to be prepared in accordance with international accounting standards ("IAS group accounts").

403(2)   The group accounts of other companies may be prepared–

(a)   in accordance with section 404 ("Companies Act group accounts"), or

(b)   in accordance with international accounting standards ("IAS group accounts"). This is subject to the following provisions of this section.

403(3)   The group accounts of a parent company that is a charity must be Companies Act group accounts.

403(4)   After the first financial year in which the directors of a parent company prepare IAS group accounts ("the first IAS year"), all subsequent group accounts of the company must be prepared in accordance with international accounting standards unless there is a relevant change of circumstance.

403(5)   There is a relevant change of circumstance if, at any time during or after the first IAS year–

(a)   the company becomes a subsidiary undertaking of another undertaking that does not prepare IAS group accounts,

(b)   the company ceases to be a company with securities admitted to trading on a regulated market in an EEA State, or

(c)   a parent undertaking of the company ceases to be an undertaking with securities admitted to trading on a regulated market in an EEA State.

403(6)   If, having changed to preparing Companies Act group accounts following a relevant change of circumstance, the directors again prepare IAS group accounts for the company, subsections (4) and (5) apply again as if the first financial year for which such accounts are again prepared were the first IAS year."

Notes – This section is modified in its application to Overseas Companies by Pt. 5 *Delivery Of Accounting Documents: general* and Pt. 6 *Delivery Of Accounting Documents: credit or financial institutions* of the Overseas Companies Regulations 2009 (SI 2009/1801).

This section is modified in its application to LLPs by Pt. 5 *Annual Accounts* of the Limited Liability Partnerships (Accounts and Audit) (Application of Companies Act 2006) Regulations 2008 (SI 2008/1911).

404   Companies Act group accounts

404(A1)   Companies Act group accounts must state, in respect of the parent company–

(a)   the part of the United Kingdom in which the company is registered,

(b)   the company's registered number,

(c)   whether the company is a public or a private company and whether it is limited by shares or by guarantee,

(d)   the address of the company's registered office, and

(e)   where appropriate, the fact that the company is being wound-up.

404(1)   Companies Act group accounts must comprise–

(a)   a consolidated balance sheet dealing with the state of affairs of the parent company and its subsidiary undertakings, and

(b)   a consolidated profit and loss account dealing with the profit or loss of the parent company and its subsidiary undertakings.

404(2)   The accounts must give a true and fair view of the state of affairs as at the end of the financial year, and the profit or loss for the financial year, of the undertakings included in the consolidation as a whole, so far as concerns members of the company.

404(3)   The accounts must comply with provision made by the Secretary of State by regulations as to–

(a)   the form and content of the consolidated balance sheet and consolidated profit and loss account, and

(b)   additional information to be provided by way of notes to the accounts.

404(4)   If compliance with the regulations, and any other provision made by or under this Act as to the matters to be included in a company's group accounts or in notes to those accounts, would not be sufficient to give a true and fair view, the necessary additional information must be given in the accounts or in a note to them.

404(5)   If in special circumstances compliance with any of those provisions is inconsistent with the requirement to give a true and fair view, the directors must depart from that provision to the extent necessary to give a true and fair view.

Particulars of any such departure, the reasons for it and its effect must be given in a note to the accounts.

Commencement Date – 6 April 2008 applying to accounts and reports for financial years beginning on or after 6 April 2008.

History – S. 404(A1) inserted by SI 2015/980, reg. 5(9), with effect in relation to–

(a)   financial years beginning on or after 1 January 2016, and

(b)   a financial year of a company beginning on or after 1 January 2015, but before 1 January 2016, if the directors of the company so decide.

Statutory instruments – For regulations under this section see the Small Companies and Groups (Accounts and Directors' Report) Regulations 2008 (SI 2008/409) and the Large and Medium-sized Companies and Groups (Accounts and Reports) Regulations 2008 (SI 2008/410).

Notes – This section is modified in its application to Overseas Companies by Pt. 5 *Delivery Of Accounting Documents: general* and Pt. 6 *Delivery Of Accounting Documents: credit or financial institutions* of the Overseas Companies Regulations 2009 (SI 2009/1801).

This section is modified in its application to LLPs by Pt. 5 *Annual Accounts* of the Limited Liability Partnerships (Accounts and Audit) (Application of Companies Act 2006) Regulations 2008 (SI 2008/1911).

This section is modified in its application to unregistered companies by the Unregistered Companies Regulations 2009 (SI 2009/2436).

405   Companies Act group accounts: subsidiary undertakings included in the consolidation

405(1)   Where a parent company prepares Companies Act group accounts, all the subsidiary undertakings of the company must be included in the consolidation, subject to the following exceptions.

405(2)   A subsidiary undertaking may be excluded from consolidation if its inclusion is not material for the purpose of giving a true and fair view (but two or more undertakings may be excluded only if they are not material taken together).

405(3)   A subsidiary undertaking may be excluded from consolidation where–

(a)   severe long-term restrictions substantially hinder the exercise of the rights of the parent company over the assets or management of that undertaking, or

    (b)   extremely rare circumstances mean that the information necessary for the preparation of group accounts cannot be obtained without disproportionate expense or undue delay, or

    (c)   the interest of the parent company is held exclusively with a view to subsequent resale.

405(4) The reference in subsection (3)(a) to the rights of the parent company and the reference in subsection (3)(c) to the interest of the parent company are, respectively, to rights and interests held by or attributed to the company for the purposes of the definition of "parent undertaking" (see section 1162) in the absence of which it would not be the parent company.

Commencement Date – 6 April 2008 applying to accounts and reports for financial years beginning on or after 6 April 2008.

History – In s. 405(3)(b), the words "extremely rare circumstances mean that" inserted by SI 2015/980, reg. 5(10), with effect in relation to–

    (a)   financial years beginning on or after 1 January 2016, and

    (b)   a financial year of a company beginning on or after 1 January 2015, but before 1 January 2016, if the directors of the company so decide.

Notes – This section is modified in its application to Overseas Companies by Pt. 5 *Delivery Of Accounting Documents: general* and Pt. 6 *Delivery Of Accounting Documents: credit or financial institutions* of the Overseas Companies Regulations 2009 (SI 2009/1801).

This section is modified in its application to LLPs by Pt. 5 *Annual Accounts* of the Limited Liability Partnerships (Accounts and Audit) (Application of Companies Act 2006) Regulations 2008 (SI 2008/1911).

406   IAS group accounts

406(1) IAS group accounts must state–

    (a)   the part of the United Kingdom in which the company is registered,

    (b)   the company's registered number,

    (c)   whether the company is a public or a private company and whether it is limited by shares or by guarantee,

    (d)   the address of the company's registered office, and

    (e)   where appropriate, the fact that the company is being wound-up.

406(2) The notes to the accounts must state that the accounts have been prepared in accordance with international accounting standards.

History – S. 406 substituted by SI 2015/980, reg. 5(11), with effect in relation to–

    (a)   financial years beginning on or after 1 January 2016, and

    (b)   a financial year of a company beginning on or after 1 January 2015, but before 1 January 2016, if the directors of the company so decide.

Former s. 406 read as follows:

"406   IAS group accounts

    406 Where the directors of a company prepare IAS group accounts, they must state in the notes to those accounts that the accounts have been prepared in accordance with international accounting standards.

Commencement Date – 6 April 2008 applying to accounts and reports for financial years beginning on or after 6 April 2008.

Notes – This section is modified in its application to Overseas Companies by Pt. 5 *Delivery Of Accounting Documents: general* and Pt. 6 *Delivery Of Accounting Documents: credit or financial institutions* of the Overseas Companies Regulations 2009 (SI 2009/1801).

This section is modified in its application to LLPs by Pt. 5 *Annual Accounts* of the Limited Liability Partnerships (Accounts and Audit) (Application of Companies Act 2006) Regulations 2008 (SI 2008/1911)."

407   Consistency of financial reporting within group

407(1)   The directors of a parent company must secure that the individual accounts of–

(a)   the parent company, and

(b)   each of its subsidiary undertakings, are all prepared using the same financial reporting framework, except to the extent that in their opinion there are good reasons for not doing so.

407(2)   Subsection (1) does not apply if the directors do not prepare group accounts for the parent company.

407(3)   Subsection (1) only applies to accounts of subsidiary undertakings that are required to be prepared under this Part.

407(4)   Subsection (1) does not require accounts of undertakings that are charities to be prepared using the same financial reporting framework as accounts of undertakings which are not charities.

407(5)   Subsection (1)(a) does not apply where the directors of a parent company prepare IAS group accounts and IAS individual accounts.

Commencement Date – 6 April 2008 applying to accounts and reports for financial years beginning on or after 6 April 2008.

Notes – This section is modified in its application to LLPs by Pt. 5 *Annual Accounts* of the Limited Liability Partnerships (Accounts and Audit) (Application of Companies Act 2006) Regulations 2008 (SI 2008/1911).

408   Individual profit and loss account where group accounts prepared

408(1)   This section applies where–

(a)   a company prepares group accounts in accordance with this Act, and

(b)   the company's individual balance sheet shows the company's profit and loss for the financial year determined in accordance with this Act.

408(2)   [Omitted by SI 2015/980, reg. 5(12)(b).]

408(3)   The company's individual profit and loss account must be approved in accordance with section 414(1) (approval by directors) but may be omitted from the company's annual accounts for the purposes of the other provisions of the Companies Acts.

408(4)   The exemption conferred by this section is conditional upon its being disclosed in the company's annual accounts that the exemption applies.

Commencement Date – 6 April 2008 applying to accounts and reports for financial years beginning on or after 6 April 2008.

History – Subsection (2) amended by SI 2008/393, reg. 10: 6 April 2008 applying in relation to financial years beginning on or after 6 April 2008.
S. 408(1)(b) substituted by SI 2015/980, reg. 5(12)(a), with effect in relation to–

(a)   financial years beginning on or after 1 January 2016, and

(b)   a financial year of a company beginning on or after 1 January 2015, but before 1 January 2016, if the directors of the company so decide.

S. 408(2) omitted by SI 2015/980, reg. 5(12)(b), with effect in relation to–

(a)   financial years beginning on or after 1 January 2016, and

(b)   a financial year of a company beginning on or after 1 January 2015, but before 1 January 2016, if the directors of the company so decide.

Former s. 408(2) read as follows:

"**408(2)**   The company's individual profit and loss account need not contain the information specified in section 411 (information about employee numbers and costs)."

Notes – This section is modified in its application to LLPs by Pt. 5 *Annual Accounts* of the Limited Liability Partnerships (Accounts and Audit) (Application of Companies Act 2006) Regulations 2008 (SI 2008/1911).

Information to be given in notes to the accounts

409 Information about related undertakings

409(1) The Secretary of State may make provision by regulations requiring information about related undertakings to be given in notes to a company's annual accounts.

409(2) The regulations–

    (a)   may make different provision according to whether or not the company prepares group accounts, and

    (b)   may specify the descriptions of undertaking in relation to which they apply, and make different provision in relation to different descriptions of related undertaking.

409(3) The regulations may provide that information need not be disclosed with respect to an undertaking that–

    (a)   is established under the law of a country outside the United Kingdom, or

    (b)   carries on business outside the United Kingdom, if the following conditions are met.

409(4) The conditions are–

    (a)   that in the opinion of the directors of the company the disclosure would be seriously prejudicial to the business of–

        (i)   that undertaking,

        (ii) the company,

        (iii) any of the company's subsidiary undertakings, or

        (iv) any other undertaking which is included in the consolidation;

    (b)   that the Secretary of State agrees that the information need not be disclosed.

409(5) Where advantage is taken of any such exemption, that fact must be stated in a note to the company's annual accounts.

Commencement Date – 6 April 2008 applying to accounts and reports for financial years beginning on or after 6 April 2008.

Statutory instruments – For regulations under this section see the Small Companies and Groups (Accounts and Directors' Report) Regulations 2008 (SI 2008/409) and the Large and Medium-sized Companies and Groups (Accounts and Reports) Regulations 2008 (SI 2008/410).

Notes – This section is modified in its application to LLPs by Pt. 5 *Annual Accounts* of the Limited Liability Partnerships (Accounts and Audit) (Application of Companies Act 2006) Regulations 2008 (SI 2008/1911).

This section is modified in its application to unregistered companies by the Unregistered Companies Regulations 2009 (SI 2009/2436).

410 Information about related undertakings: alternative compliance

Omitted by SI 2015/980, reg. 5(13).

History – S. 410 omitted by SI 2015/980, reg. 5(13), with effect in relation to–

    (a)   financial years beginning on or after 1 January 2016, and

    (b)   a financial year of a company beginning on or after 1 January 2015, but before 1 January 2016, if the directors of the company so decide.

Former s. 410 read as follows:

"410 Information about related undertakings: alternative compliance

410(1) This section applies where the directors of a company are of the opinion that the number of undertakings in respect of which the company is required to disclose information under any provision of regulations under section 409 (related undertakings) is such that compliance with that provision would result in information of excessive length being given in notes to the company's annual accounts.

410(2) The information need only be given in respect of–
(a) the undertakings whose results or financial position, in the opinion of the directors, principally affected the figures shown in the company's annual accounts, and
(b) where the company prepares group accounts, undertakings excluded from consolidation under section 405(3) (undertakings excluded on grounds other than materiality).

410(3) If advantage is taken of subsection (2)–
(a) there must be included in the notes to the company's annual accounts a statement that the information is given only with respect to such undertakings as are mentioned in that subsection, and
(b) the full information (both that which is disclosed in the notes to the accounts and that which is not) must be annexed to the company's next annual return. For this purpose the **"next annual return"** means that next delivered to the registrar after the accounts in question have been approved under section 414.

410(4) If a company fails to comply with subsection (3)(b), an offence is committed by–
(a) the company, and
(b) every officer of the company who is in default.

410(5) A person guilty of an offence under subsection (4) is liable on summary conviction to a fine not exceeding level 3 on the standard scale and, for continued contravention, a daily default fine not exceeding one-tenth of level 3 on the standard scale.

Commencement Date – 6 April 2008 applying to accounts and reports for financial years beginning on or after 6 April 2008.

Notes – This section is modified in its application to LLPs by Pt. 5 *Annual Accounts* of the Limited Liability Partnerships (Accounts and Audit) (Application of Companies Act 2006) Regulations 2008 (SI 2008/1911)."

410A Information about off-balance sheet arrangements

410A(1) If in any financial year–
(a) a company is or has been party to arrangements that are not reflected in its balance sheet, and
(b) at the balance sheet date the risks or benefits arising from those arrangements are material,
the information required by this section must be given in the notes to the company's annual accounts.

410A(2) The information required is–
(a) the nature and business purpose of the arrangements, and
(b) the financial impact of the arrangements on the company.

410A(3) The information need only be given to the extent necessary for enabling the financial position of the company to be assessed.

410A(4) If the company is subject to the small companies regime in relation to the financial year (see section 381), it need not comply with subsection (2)(b).

410A(5) This section applies in relation to group accounts as if the undertakings included in the consolidation were a single company.

Commencement Date – Section 410A inserted by SI 2008/393 reg 8: 6 April 2008 applying in relation to financial years beginning on or after 6 April 2008.

History – S. 410A(1) substituted by SI 2015/980, reg. 5(14)(a), with effect in relation to–
(a) financial years beginning on or after 1 January 2016, and
(b) a financial year of a company beginning on or after 1 January 2015, but before 1 January 2016, if the directors of the company so decide.
Former s. 410A(1) read as follows:
"**410A(1)** In the case of a company that is not subject to the small companies regime, if in any financial year–
(a) the company is or has been party to arrangements that are not reflected in its balance sheet, and

(b)   at the balance sheet date the risks or benefits arising from those arrangements are material,

the information required by this section must be given in notes to the company's annual accounts."

S. 410A(4) substituted by SI 2015/980, reg. 5(14)(b), with effect in relation to–

(a)   financial years beginning on or after 1 January 2016, and

(b)   a financial year of a company beginning on or after 1 January 2015, but before 1 January 2016, if the directors of the company so decide.

Former s. 410A(4) read as follows:

"**410A(4)** If the company qualifies as medium-sized in relation to the financial year (see sections 465 to 467) it need not comply with subsection (2)(b)."

Notes – This section is modified in its application to LLPs by Pt. 5 *Annual Accounts* of the Limited Liability Partnerships (Accounts and Audit) (Application of Companies Act 2006) Regulations 2008 (SI 2008/1911).

411 Information about employee numbers and costs

411(1) The notes to a company's annual accounts must disclose the average number of persons employed by the company in the financial year.

411(1A) In the case of a company not subject to the small companies regime, the notes to the company's accounts must also disclose the average number of persons within each category of persons so employed.

411(2) The categories by reference to which the number required to be disclosed by subsection (1A) is to be determined must be such as the directors may select having regard to the manner in which the company's activities are organised.

411(3) The average number required by subsection (1) or (1A) is determined by dividing the relevant annual number by the number of months in the financial year.

411(4) The relevant annual number is determined by ascertaining for each month in the financial year–

(a)   for the purposes of subsection (1), the number of persons employed under contracts of service by the company in that month (whether throughout the month or not);

(b)   for the purposes of subsection (1A), the number of persons in the category in question of persons so employed; and adding together all the monthly numbers.

411(5) Except in the case of a company subject to the small companies regime, the notes to the company's annual accounts or the profit and loss account must disclose, with reference to all persons employed by the company during the financial year, the total staff costs of the company relating to the financial year broken down between–

(a)   wages and salaries paid or payable in respect of that year to those persons,

(b)   social security costs incurred by the company on their behalf, and

(c)   other pension costs so incurred.

411(6) In subsection (5)–

"pension costs" includes any costs incurred by the company in respect of–

(a)   any pension scheme established for the purpose of providing pensions for persons currently or formerly employed by the company,

(b)   any sums set aside for the future payment of pensions directly by the company to current or former employees, and

(c)   any pensions paid directly to such persons without having first been set aside;

"social security costs" means any contributions by the company to any state social security or pension scheme, fund or arrangement.

411(7) This section applies in relation to group accounts as if the undertakings included in the consolidation were a single company.

Commencement Date – 6 April 2008 applying to accounts and reports for financial years beginning on or after 6 April 2008.

History – S. 411(1) and (1A) substituted by SI 2015/980, reg. 5(15)(a), with effect in relation to–
    (a)   financial years beginning on or after 1 January 2016, and
    (b)   a financial year of a company beginning on or after 1 January 2015, but before 1 January 2016, if the directors of the company so decide.
Former s. 411(1) read as follows:

    "**411(1)**   In the case of a company not subject to the small companies regime, the following information with respect to the employees of the company must be given in notes to the company's annual accounts–
    (a)   the average number of persons employed by the company in the financial year, and
    (b)   the average number of persons so employed within each category of persons employed by the company."

S. 411(2), the words "subsection (1A)" substituted for the words "subsection (1)(b)" by SI 2015/980, reg. 5(15)(b), with effect in relation to–
    (a)   financial years beginning on or after 1 January 2016, and
    (b)   a financial year of a company beginning on or after 1 January 2015, but before 1 January 2016, if the directors of the company so decide.
S. 411(3), the words "subsection (1) or (1A)" substituted for "subsection (1)(a) or (b)" by SI 2015/980, reg. 5(15)(c), with effect in relation to–
    (a)   financial years beginning on or after 1 January 2016, and
    (b)   a financial year of a company beginning on or after 1 January 2015, but before 1 January 2016, if the directors of the company so decide.
S. 411(4)(a), the words "subsection (1)" substituted for the words "subsection (1)(a)" by SI 2015/980, reg. 5(15)(d)(i), with effect in relation to–
    (a)   financial years beginning on or after 1 January 2016, and
    (b)   a financial year of a company beginning on or after 1 January 2015, but before 1 January 2016, if the directors of the company so decide.
S. 411(4)(b), the words "subsection (1A)" substituted for the words "subsection (1)(b)" by SI 2015/980, reg. 5(15)(d)(ii), with effect in relation to–
    (a)   financial years beginning on or after 1 January 2016, and
    (b)   a financial year of a company beginning on or after 1 January 2015, but before 1 January 2016, if the directors of the company so decide.
S. 411(5) substituted by SI 2015/980, reg. 5(15)(e), with effect in relation to–
    (a)   financial years beginning on or after 1 January 2016, and
    (b)   a financial year of a company beginning on or after 1 January 2015, but before 1 January 2016, if the directors of the company so decide.
Former s. 411(5) read as follows:

    "**411(5)**   In respect of all persons employed by the company during the financial year who are taken into account in determining the relevant annual number for the purposes of subsection (1)(a) there must also be stated the aggregate amounts respectively of–
    (a)   wages and salaries paid or payable in respect of that year to those persons;
    (b)   social security costs incurred by the company on their behalf; and
    (c)   other pension costs so incurred. This does not apply in so far as those amounts, or any of them, are stated elsewhere in the company's accounts."

Subsection (7) substituted by SI 2008/393, reg. 11: 6 April 2008 applying in relation to financial years beginning on or after 6 April 2008.

Notes – This section is modified in its application to LLPs by Pt. 5 *Annual Accounts* of the Limited Liability Partnerships (Accounts and Audit) (Application of Companies Act 2006) Regulations 2008 (SI 2008/1911).

412 Information about directors' benefits: remuneration

    412(1)   The Secretary of State may make provision by regulations requiring information to be given in notes to a company's annual accounts about directors' remuneration.

    412(2)   The matters about which information may be required include–
    (a)   gains made by directors on the exercise of share options;

(b)   benefits received or receivable by directors under long-term incentive schemes;

(c)   payments for loss of office (as defined in section 215);

(d)   benefits receivable, and contributions for the purpose of providing benefits, in respect of past services of a person as director or in any other capacity while director;

(e)   consideration paid to or receivable by third parties for making available the services of a person as director or in any other capacity while director.

412(3)   Without prejudice to the generality of subsection (1), regulations under this section may make any such provision as was made immediately before the commencement of this Part by Part 1 of Schedule 6 to the Companies Act 1985 (c. 6).

412(4)   For the purposes of this section, and regulations made under it, amounts paid to or receivable by–

(a)   a person connected with a director, or

(b)   a body corporate controlled by a director, are treated as paid to or receivable by the director. The expressions **"connected with"** and **"controlled by"** in this subsection have the same meaning as in Part 10 (company directors).

412(5)   It is the duty of–

(a)   any director of a company, and

(b)   any person who is or has at any time in the preceding five years been a director of the company, to give notice to the company of such matters relating to himself as may be necessary for the purposes of regulations under this section.

412(6)   A person who makes default in complying with subsection (5) commits an offence and is liable on summary conviction to a fine not exceeding level 3 on the standard scale.

Commencement Date – 6 April 2008 applying to accounts and reports for financial years beginning on or after 6 April 2008.

Statutory instruments – For regulations under this section see the Small Companies and Groups (Accounts and Directors' Report) Regulations 2008 (SI 2008/409) and the Large and Medium-sized Companies and Groups (Accounts and Reports) Regulations 2008 (SI 2008/410).

Notes – This section is modified in its application to unregistered companies by the Unregistered Companies Regulations 2009 (SI 2009/2436).

413   Information about directors' benefits: advances, credit and guarantees

413(1)   In the case of a company that does not prepare group accounts, details of–

(a)   advances and credits granted by the company to its directors, and

(b)   guarantees of any kind entered into by the company on behalf of its directors, must be shown in the notes to its individual accounts.

413(2)   In the case of a parent company that prepares group accounts, details of–

(a)   advances and credits granted to the directors of the parent company, by that company or by any of its subsidiary undertakings, and

(b)   guarantees of any kind entered into on behalf of the directors of the parent company, by that company or by any of its subsidiary undertakings, must be shown in the notes to the group accounts.

413(3)   The details required of an advance or credit are–

(a)   its amount,

(b)   an indication of the interest rate,

(c)   its main conditions,

(d)   any amounts repaid,

(e)   any amounts written off, and

(f)   any amounts waived.

413(4) The details required of a guarantee are–

(a)   its main terms,

(b)   the amount of the maximum liability that may be incurred by the company (or its subsidiary), and

(c)   any amount paid and any liability incurred by the company (or its subsidiary) for the purpose of fulfilling the guarantee (including any loss incurred by reason of enforcement of the guarantee).

413(5) There must also be stated in the notes to the accounts the totals–

(a)   of amounts stated under subsection (3)(a),

(b)   of amounts stated under subsection (3)(d),

(ba)   of amounts stated under subsection 3(e),

(bb)   of amounts stated under subsection 3(f),

(c)   of amounts stated under subsection (4)(b), and

(d)   of amounts stated under subsection (4)(c).

413(6) References in this section to the directors of a company are to the persons who were directors at any time in the financial year to which the accounts relate.

413(7) The requirements of this section apply in relation to every advance, credit or guarantee subsisting at any time in the financial year to which the accounts relate–

(a)   whenever it was entered into,

(b)   whether or not the person concerned was a director of the company in question at the time it was entered into, and

(c)   in the case of an advance, credit or guarantee involving a subsidiary undertaking of that company, whether or not that undertaking was such a subsidiary undertaking at the time it was entered into.

[version of subsection (8) applying to financial years ending before 23 December 2009]

413(8) Banking companies and the holding companies of credit institutions need only state the details required by subsections (3)(a) and (4)(b).

[version of subsection (8) applying to financial years ending on or after 23 December 2009]

413(8) Banking companies and the holding companies of credit institutions need only state the details required by subsections (5)(a) and (c).

Commencement Date – 6 April 2008 applying to accounts and reports for financial years beginning on or after 6 April 2008.

History – S. 413(3)(e) and (f) inserted; and the word "and" in para. (c) omitted by SI 2015/980, reg. 5(16)(a), with effect in relation to–

(a)   financial years beginning on or after 1 January 2016, and

(b)   a financial year of a company beginning on or after 1 January 2015, but before 1 January 2016, if the directors of the company so decide.

S. 413(5)(ba) and (bb) inserted by SI 2015/980, reg. 5(16)(b), with effect in relation to–

(a)   financial years beginning on or after 1 January 2016, and

(b)   a financial year of a company beginning on or after 1 January 2015, but before 1 January 2016, if the directors of the company so decide.

S. 413(6), the word "directors" substituted for the words "a director" by SI 2015/980, reg. 5(16)(c), with effect in relation to–

(a)   financial years beginning on or after 1 January 2016, and

(b)   a financial year of a company beginning on or after 1 January 2015, but before 1 January 2016, if the directors of the company so decide.

Subsection (8) amended by SI 2009/3022: 23 December 2009 applying to financial years which end on or after 23 December 2009.

Approval and signing of accounts

414 Approval and signing of accounts

414(1) A company's annual accounts must be approved by the board of directors and signed on behalf of the board by a director of the company.

414(2) The signature must be on the company's balance sheet.

414(3) If the accounts are prepared in accordance with the small companies regime, the balance sheet must contain, in a prominent position above the signature–

(a)   in the case of individual accounts prepared in accordance with the micro-entity provisions, a statement to that effect, or

(b)   in the case of accounts not prepared as mentioned in paragraph (a), a statement to the effect that the accounts have been prepared in accordance with the provisions applicable to companies subject to the small companies regime.

414(4) If annual accounts are approved that do not comply with the requirements of this Act (and, where applicable, of Article 4 of the IAS Regulation), every director of the company who–

(a)   knew that they did not comply, or was reckless as to whether they complied, and

(b)   failed to take reasonable steps to secure compliance with those requirements or, as the case may be, to prevent the accounts from being approved, commits an offence.

414(5) A person guilty of an offence under this section is liable–

(a)   on conviction on indictment, to a fine;

(b)   on summary conviction, to a fine not exceeding the statutory maximum.

Commencement Date – 6 April 2008 applying to accounts and reports for financial years beginning on or after 6 April 2008.

History – S. 414(3) substituted by SI 2013/3008, reg. 5(1) and (4), with effect from 1 December 2013 in respect of (a) financial years ending on or after 30 September 2013; and (b) companies, which deliver the accounts required by section 444 to the registrar on or after 1 December 2013. Before substitution, subsection (3) read:

"**414(3)** If the accounts are prepared in accordance with the provisions applicable to companies subject to the small companies regime, the balance sheet must contain a statement to that effect in a prominent position above the signature."

Notes – This section is modified in its application to Overseas Companies by Pt. 5 *Delivery Of Accounting Documents: general* and Pt. 6 *Delivery Of Accounting Documents: credit or financial institutions* of the Overseas Companies Regulations 2009 (SI 2009/1801).

This section is modified in its application to LLPs by Pt. 5 *Annual Accounts* of the Limited Liability Partnerships (Accounts and Audit) (Application of Companies Act 2006) Regulations 2008 (SI 2008/1911).

This is subject to the following provisions of SI 2013/3008, reg. 3:

"Disapplication of these regulations to entities to which provisions of the 2006 Act or the 2008 regulations have been applied

3(1) The amendments made by these Regulations [SI 2013/3008] to any provision of the 2006 Act [CA 2006] or the 2008 Regulations [SI 2008/409] do not have effect in relation to the application of any such provision–

(a)   to qualifying partnerships by regulations 4(1) and 9(1) of and Part 1 of the Schedule to the Partnerships (Accounts) Regulations 2008 (SI 2008/569);

(b)   to limited liability partnerships by the Limited Liability Partnerships (Accounts and Audit) (Application of Companies Act 2006) Regulations 2008 (SI 2008/1911);

(c)   to limited liability partnerships by the Small Limited Liability Partnerships (Accounts) Regulations 2008 (SI 2008/1912);

(d)   to overseas companies by Chapter 3 of Part 5 or Chapter 3 of Part 6 of the Overseas Companies Regulations 2009 (SI 2009/1801);

(e)   to unregistered companies by regulation 3 of and Schedule 1 to the Unregistered Companies Regulations 2009 (SI 2009/2436); or

(f)   to companies registered pursuant to section 1040 of the 2006 Act by regulation 18 of the Companies (Companies Authorised to Register) Regulations 2009 (SI 2009/2437).

3(2) Any new provision of the 2006 Act or the 2008 Regulations inserted by these Regulations is not, by virtue of any provision mentioned in sub-paragraphs (a) to (f) of paragraph (1), applied to the entities mentioned in those sub-paragraphs."

Chapter 4A – Strategic report

414A Duty to prepare strategic report

414A(1) The directors of a company must prepare a strategic report for each financial year of the company.

414A(2) Subsection (1) does not apply if the company is entitled to the small companies exemption.

414A(3) For a financial year in which–

(a)   the company is a parent company, and

(b)   the directors of the company prepare group accounts,

the strategic report must be a consolidated report (a "group strategic report") relating to the undertakings included in the consolidation.

414A(4) A group strategic report may, where appropriate, give greater emphasis to the matters that are significant to the undertakings included in the consolidation, taken as a whole.

414A(5) In the case of failure to comply with the requirement to prepare a strategic report, an offence is committed by every person who–

(a)   was a director of the company immediately before the end of the period for filing accounts and reports for the financial year in question, and

(b)   failed to take all reasonable steps for securing compliance with that requirement.

414A(6) A person guilty of an offence under this section is liable–

(a)   on conviction on indictment, to a fine;

(b)   on summary conviction, to a fine not exceeding the statutory maximum.

History – S. 414A inserted by SI 2013/1970, reg. 2 and 3, with effect from 1 October 2013 in respect of financial years ending on or after 30 September 2013.

414B Strategic report: small companies exemption

A company is entitled to the small companies exemption in relation to the strategic report for a financial year if–

(a)   it is entitled to prepare accounts for the year in accordance with the small companies regime, or

(b)   it would be so entitled but for being or having been a member of an ineligible group.

History – S. 414B inserted by SI 2013/1970, reg. 2 and 3, with effect from 1 October 2013 in respect of financial years ending on or after 30 September 2013.
In s. 414B, the word "the" inserted by SI 2015/980, reg. 6, with effect in relation to–

(a)   financial years beginning on or after 1 January 2016, and

(b)   a financial year of a company beginning on or after 1 January 2015, but before 1 January 2016, if the directors of the company so decide.

414C Contents of strategic report

414C(1)   The purpose of the strategic report is to inform members of the company and help them assess how the directors have performed their duty under section 172 (duty to promote the success of the company).

414C(2)   The strategic report must contain–

(a)   a fair review of the company's business, and

(b)   a description of the principal risks and uncertainties facing the company.

414C(3)   The review required is a balanced and comprehensive analysis of—

(a)   the development and performance of the company's business during the financial year, and

(b)   the position of the company's business at the end of that year, consistent with the size and complexity of the business.

414C(4)   The review must, to the extent necessary for an understanding of the development, performance or position of the company's business, include–

(a)   analysis using financial key performance indicators, and

(b)   where appropriate, analysis using other key performance indicators, including information relating to environmental matters and employee matters.

414C(5)   In subsection (4), **"key performance indicators"** means factors by reference to which the development, performance or position of the company's business can be measured effectively.

414C(6)   Where a company qualifies as medium-sized in relation to a financial year (see sections 465 to 467), the review for the year need not comply with the requirements of subsection (4) so far as they relate to non-financial information.

414C(7)   In the case of a quoted company the strategic report must, to the extent necessary for an understanding of the development, performance or position of the company's business, include–

(a)   the main trends and factors likely to affect the future development, performance and position of the company's business, and

(b)   information about–

(i)   environmental matters (including the impact of the company's business on the environment),

(ii)   the company's employees, and

(iii) social, community and human rights issues, including information about any policies of the company in relation to those matters and the effectiveness of those policies.

If the report does not contain information of each kind mentioned in paragraphs (b)(i), (ii) and (iii), it must state which of those kinds of information it does not contain.

414C(8)   In the case of a quoted company the strategic report must include–

(a)   a description of the company's strategy,

(b)   a description of the company's business model,

(c)   a breakdown showing at the end of the financial year–

(i)   the number of persons of each sex who were directors of the company;

(ii)   the number of persons of each sex who were senior managers of the company (other than persons falling within sub-paragraph (i)); and

(iii) the number of persons of each sex who were employees of the company.

414C(9)   In subsection (8), **"senior manager"** means a person who–

(a)   has responsibility for planning, directing or controlling the activities of the company, or a strategically significant part of the company, and

(b)   is an employee of the company.

414C(10) In relation to a group strategic report–

(a) the reference to the company in subsection (8)(c)(i) is to the parent company; and

(b) the breakdown required by subsection (8)(c)(ii) must include the number of persons of each sex who were the directors of the undertakings included in the consolidation.

414C(11) The strategic report may also contain such of the matters otherwise required by regulations made under section 416(4) to be disclosed in the directors' report as the directors consider are of strategic importance to the company.

414C(12) The report must, where appropriate, include references to, and additional explanations of, amounts included in the company's annual accounts.

414C(13) Subject to paragraph (10), in relation to a group strategic report this section has effect as if the references to the company were references to the undertakings included in the consolidation.

414C(14) Nothing in this section requires the disclosure of information about impending developments or matters in the course of negotiation if the disclosure would, in the opinion of the directors, be seriously prejudicial to the interests of the company.

History – S. 414C inserted by SI 2013/1970, reg. 2 and 3, with effect from 1 October 2013 in respect of financial years ending on or after 30 September 2013.

414D Approval and signing of strategic report

414D(1) The strategic report must be approved by the board of directors and signed on behalf of the board by a director or the secretary of the company.

414D(2) If a strategic report is approved that does not comply with the requirements of this Act, every director of the company who–

(a) knew that it did not comply, or was reckless as to whether it complied, and

(b) failed to take reasonable steps to secure compliance with those requirements or, as the case may be, to prevent the report from being approved, commits an offence.

414D(3) A person guilty of an offence under this section is liable–

(a) on conviction on indictment, to a fine;

(b) on summary conviction, to a fine not exceeding the statutory maximum.

History – S. 414D inserted by SI 2013/1970, reg. 2 and 3, with effect from 1 October 2013 in respect of financial years ending on or after 30 September 2013.

Chapter 5 – Directors' Report

415 Duty to prepare directors' report

415(1) The directors of a company must prepare a directors' report for each financial year of the company.

415(1A) Subsection (1) does not apply if the company qualifies as a micro-entity (see sections 384A and 384B).

415(2) For a financial year in which–

(a) the company is a parent company, and

(b) the directors of the company prepare group accounts, the directors' report must be a consolidated report (a "group directors' report") relating to the undertakings included in the consolidation.

415(3) A group directors' report may, where appropriate, give greater emphasis to the matters that are significant to the undertakings included in the consolidation, taken as a whole.

415(4) In the case of failure to comply with the requirement to prepare a directors' report, an offence is committed by every person who–

(a)   was a director of the company immediately before the end of the period for filing accounts and reports for the financial year in question, and

(b)   failed to take all reasonable steps for securing compliance with that requirement.

415(5) A person guilty of an offence under this section is liable–

(a)   on conviction on indictment, to a fine;

(b)   on summary conviction, to a fine not exceeding the statutory maximum.

Commencement Date – 6 April 2008 applying to accounts and reports for financial years beginning on or after 6 April 2008.

History – S. 415(1A) inserted by SI 2015/980, reg. 7, with effect in relation to–

(a)   financial years beginning on or after 1 January 2016, and

(b)   a financial year of a company beginning on or after 1 January 2015, but before 1 January 2016, if the directors of the company so decide.

415A Directors' report: small companies exemption

415A(1) A company is entitled to small companies exemption in relation to the directors' report for a financial year if–

(a)   it is entitled to prepare accounts for the year in accordance with the small companies regime, or

(b)   it would be so entitled but for being or having been a member of an ineligible group.

415A(2) The exemption is relevant to–

section 416(3) (contents of report: statement of amount recommended by way of dividend), and

sections 444 to 446 (filing obligations of different descriptions of company).

History – This version of s. 415A applies to financial years ending on or after 30 September 2013. The version applying to financial years ending before 30 September 2013 reads as follows:

"415A Directors' report: small companies exemption

415A(1) A company is entitled to small companies exemption in relation to the directors' report for a financial year if–

(a)   it is entitled to prepare accounts for the year in accordance with the small companies regime, or

(b)   it would be so entitled but for being or having been a member of an ineligible group.

415A(2) The exemption is relevant to–

section 416(3) (contents of report: statement of amount recommended by way of dividend),

section 417 (contents of report: business review), and

sections 444 to 446 (filing obligations of different descriptions of company).

Notes – Section 415A inserted by SI 2008/393, reg. 6(2): 6 April 2008 applying in relation to financial years beginning on or after 6 April 2008."

S. 415A inserted by SI 2008/393, reg. 6(2): 6 April 2008 applying in relation to financial years beginning on or after 6 April 2008.

In s. 415A(2), "and" inserted after "dividend","and "section 417 (contents of report: business review), and" repealed by SI 2013/1970, reg. 2 and 4, with effect from 1 October 2013 in respect of financial years ending on or after 30 September 2013.

416 Contents of directors' report: general

416(1) The directors' report for a financial year must state–

(a)   the names of the persons who, at any time during the financial year, were directors of the company,

(b)   [repealed].

416(2) [Repealed].

416(3) Except in the case of a company entitled to the small companies exemption, the report must state the amount (if any) that the directors recommend should be paid by way of dividend.

416(4) The Secretary of State may make provision by regulations as to other matters that must be disclosed in a directors' report. Without prejudice to the generality of this power, the regulations may make any such provision as was formerly made by Schedule 7 to the Companies Act 1985.

Commencement Date – 6 April 2008 applying to accounts and reports for financial years beginning on or after 6 April 2008.

History – This version of s. 416 applies to financial years ending on or after 30 September 2013. The version applying to financial years ending before 30 September 2013 reads as follows:

"416 Contents of directors' report: general

416(1) The directors' report for a financial year must state–

(a)   the names of the persons who, at any time during the financial year, were directors of the company, and

(b)   the principal activities of the company in the course of the year.

416(2) In relation to a group directors' report subsection (1)(b) has effect as if the reference to the company was to the undertakings included in the consolidation.

416(3) Except in the case of a company entitled to the small companies exemption, the report must state the amount (if any) that the directors recommend should be paid by way of dividend.

416(4) The Secretary of State may make provision by regulations as to other matters that must be disclosed in a directors' report. Without prejudice to the generality of this power, the regulations may make any such provision as was formerly made by Schedule 7 to the Companies Act 1985.

Commencement Date – 6 April 2008 applying to accounts and reports for financial years beginning on or after 6 April 2008."

S. 416(3) amended by SI 2008/393, reg. 6(3): 6 April 2008 applying in relation to financial years beginning on or after 6 April 2008.

S. 416(1)(b) and (2) repealed by SI 2013/1970, reg. 2 and 6, with effect from 1 October 2013 in respect of financial years ending on or after 30 September 2013.

Statutory instruments – For regulations under this section see the Small Companies and Groups (Accounts and Directors' Report) Regulations 2008 (SI 2008/409) and the Large and Medium-sized Companies and Groups (Accounts and Reports) Regulations 2008 (SI 2008/410).

Notes – This section is modified in its application to unregistered companies by the Unregistered Companies Regulations 2009 (SI 2009/2436).

417 Contents of directors' report: business review

417 [S. 417 repealed by SI 2013/1970, reg. 2 and 5, with effect from 1 October 2013 in respect of financial years ending on or after 30 September 2013.]

Commencement Date – 1 October 2007 applying to directors' reports for financial years beginning on or after 1 October 2007.

History – Current version came in to force on 6 April 2008.

S. 417(1) amended by SI 2008/393, reg. 6(4): 6 April 2008 applying in relation to financial years beginning on or after 6 April 2008.

S. 417 repealed by SI 2013/1970, reg. 2 and 5, with effect from 1 October 2013 in respect of financial years ending on or after 30 September 2013. S. 417 previously read as follows:

"417   Contents of directors' report: business review

417(1)   Unless the company is entitled to the small companies' exemption, the directors' report must contain a business review.

417(2)   The purpose of the business review is to inform members of the company and help them assess how the directors have performed their duty under section 172 (duty to promote the success of the company).

417(3)   The business review must contain–
(a)   a fair review of the company's business, and
(b)   a description of the principal risks and uncertainties facing the company.

417(4)   The review required is a balanced and comprehensive analysis of–
(a)   the development and performance of the company's business during the financial year, and
(b)   the position of the company's business at the end of that year, consistent with the size and complexity of the business.

417(5)   In the case of a quoted company the business review must, to the extent necessary for an understanding of the development, performance or position of the company's business, include–
(a)   the main trends and factors likely to affect the future development, performance and position of the company's business; and
(b)   information about–
   (i)   environmental matters (including the impact of the company's business on the environment),
   (ii)   the company's employees, and
   (iii)   social and community issues, including information about any policies of the company in relation to those matters and the effectiveness of those policies; and
(c)   subject to subsection (11), information about persons with whom the company has contractual or other arrangements which are essential to the business of the company. If the review does not contain information of each kind mentioned in paragraphs (b)(i), (ii) and (iii) and (c), it must state which of those kinds of information it does not contain.

417(6)   The review must, to the extent necessary for an understanding of the development, performance or position of the company's business, include–
(a)   analysis using financial key performance indicators, and
(b)   where appropriate, analysis using other key performance indicators, including information relating to environmental matters and employee matters.
"Key performance indicators" means factors by reference to which the development, performance or position of the company's business can be measured effectively.

417(7)   Where a company qualifies as medium-sized in relation to a financial year (see sections 465 to 467), the directors' report for the year need not comply with the requirements of subsection (6) so far as they relate to non-financial information.

417(8)   The review must, where appropriate, include references to, and additional explanations of, amounts included in the company's annual accounts.

417(9)   In relation to a group directors' report this section has effect as if the references to the company were references to the undertakings included in the consolidation.

417(10)   Nothing in this section requires the disclosure of information about impending developments or matters in the course of negotiation if the disclosure would, in the opinion of the directors, be seriously prejudicial to the interests of the company.

417(11)   Nothing in subsection (5)(c) requires the disclosure of information about a person if the disclosure would, in the opinion of the directors, be seriously prejudicial to that person and contrary to the public interest.

Commencement Date – 1 October 2007 applying to directors' reports for financial years beginning on or after 1 October 2007.

History – Current version came in to force on 6 April 2008.
S. 417(1) amended by SI 2008/393, reg. 6(4): 6 April 2008 applying in relation to financial years beginning on or after 6 April 2008."

Transitional – Version in force transitionally from 1 October 2007 to 5 April 2008:

"417   Contents of directors' report: business review

417(1)   Unless the company is entitled to small companies exemption in relation to the directors' report, the report must contain a business review.

417(1A)   A company is entitled to small companies exemption in relation to the directors' report for a financial year if it–

(a)   qualifies as small in relation to that year under Part 7 of the Companies Act 1985 or Part 8 of the Companies (Northern Ireland) Order 1986, and

(b)   is not, and was not at any time within that year, an ineligible company as defined in section 247A(1B) of that Act or Article 255A(1B) of that Order.

417(2)   The purpose of the business review is to inform members of the company and help them assess how the directors have performed their duty under section 172 (duty to promote the success of the company).

417(3)   The business review must contain–

(a)   a fair review of the company's business, and

(b)   a description of the principal risks and uncertainties facing the company.

417(4)   The review required is a balanced and comprehensive analysis of–

(a)   the development and performance of the company's business during the financial year, and

(b)   the position of the company's business at the end of that year, consistent with the size and complexity of the business.

417(5)   In the case of a quoted company the business review must, to the extent necessary for an understanding of the development, performance or position of the company's business, include–

(a)   the main trends and factors likely to affect the future development, performance and position of the company's business; and

(b)   information about–

> (i)   environmental matters (including the impact of the company's business on the environment),
>
> (ii)   the company's employees, and
>
> (iii)   social and community issues, including information about any policies of the company in relation to those matters and the effectiveness of those policies; and

(c)   subject to subsection (11), information about persons with whom the company has contractual or other arrangements which are essential to the business of the company. If the review does not contain information of each kind mentioned in paragraphs (b)(i), (ii) and (iii) and (c), it must state which of those kinds of information it does not contain.

417(6)   The review must, to the extent necessary for an understanding of the development, performance or position of the company's business, include–

(a)   analysis using financial key performance indicators, and

(b)   where appropriate, analysis using other key performance indicators, including information relating to environmental matters and employee matters.

"Key performance indicators" means factors by reference to which the development, performance or position of the company's business can be measured effectively.

417(7)   Where a company–

(a)   qualifies as medium-sized in relation to a financial year under Part 7 of the Companies Act 1985 or Part 8 of the Companies (Northern Ireland) Order 1986, and

(b)   is not, and was not at any time within that year, an ineligible company as defined in section 247A(1B) of that Act or Article 255A(1B) of that Order,

the directors' report for the year need not comply with the requirements of subsection (6) so far as they relate to non-financial information.

417(8)   The review must, where appropriate, include references to, and additional explanations of, amounts included in the company's annual accounts.

417(9)   In relation to a group directors' report this section has effect as if the references to the company were references to the undertakings included in the consolidation.

417(10)   Nothing in this section requires the disclosure of information about impending developments or matters in the course of negotiation if the disclosure would, in the opinion of the directors, be seriously prejudicial to the interests of the company.

417(11)   Nothing in subsection (5)(c) requires the disclosure of information about a person if the disclosure would, in the opinion of the directors, be seriously prejudicial to that person and contrary to the public interest.

Commencement Date – 1 October 2007 applying to directors' reports for financial years beginning on or after 1 October 2007

Transitional adaptations made by SI 2007/2194 Sch 1 para 16 and revoked by SI 2007/3495 art 10(1)(b) as from 6 April 2008"

418 Contents of directors' report: statement as to disclosure to auditors

418(1) This section applies to a company unless–

(a)   it is exempt for the financial year in question from the requirements of Part 16 as to audit of accounts, and

(b)   the directors take advantage of that exemption.

418(2) The directors' report must contain a statement to the effect that, in the case of each of the persons who are directors at the time the report is approved–

(a)   so far as the director is aware, there is no relevant audit information of which the company's auditor is unaware, and

(b)   he has taken all the steps that he ought to have taken as a director in order to make himself aware of any relevant audit information and to establish that the company's auditor is aware of that information.

418(3) **"Relevant audit information"** means information needed by the company's auditor in connection with preparing his report.

418(4) A director is regarded as having taken all the steps that he ought to have taken as a director in order to do the things mentioned in subsection (2)(b) if he has–

(a)   made such enquiries of his fellow directors and of the company's auditors for that purpose, and

(b)   taken such other steps (if any) for that purpose, as are required by his duty as a director of the company to exercise reasonable care, skill and diligence.

418(5) Where a directors' report containing the statement required by this section is approved but the statement is false, every director of the company who–

(a)   knew that the statement was false, or was reckless as to whether it was false, and

(b)   failed to take reasonable steps to prevent the report from being approved, commits an offence.

418(6) A person guilty of an offence under subsection (5) is liable–

(a)   on conviction on indictment, to imprisonment for a term not exceeding two years or a fine (or both);

(b)   on summary conviction–

(i) in England and Wales, to imprisonment for a term not exceeding twelve months or to a fine not exceeding the statutory maximum (or both);

(ii) in Scotland or Northern Ireland, to imprisonment for a term not exceeding six months, or to a fine not exceeding the statutory maximum (or both).

Commencement Date – 6 April 2008 applying to accounts and reports for financial years beginning on or after 6 April 2008.

419 Approval and signing of directors' report

419(1) The directors' report must be approved by the board of directors and signed on behalf of the board by a director or the secretary of the company.

419(2) If in preparing the report advantage is taken of the small companies exemption, it must contain a statement to that effect in a prominent position above the signature.

419(3) If a directors' report is approved that does not comply with the requirements of this Act, every director of the company who–

(a)   knew that it did not comply, or was reckless as to whether it complied, and

(b)   failed to take reasonable steps to secure compliance with those requirements or, as the case may be, to prevent the report from being approved, commits an offence.

419(4) A person guilty of an offence under this section is liable–

(a) on conviction on indictment, to a fine;

(b) on summary conviction, to a fine not exceeding the statutory maximum.

Commencement Date – 6 April 2008 applying to accounts and reports for financial years beginning on or after 6 April 2008

History – S. 419(2) amended by SI 2008/393, reg. 6(5): 6 April 2008 applying in relation to financial years beginning on or after 6 April 2008.

419A Approval and signing of separate corporate governance statement

Any separate corporate governance statement must be approved by the board of directors and signed on behalf of the board by a director or the secretary of the company.

History – S. 419A inserted by SI 2009/1581, reg. 2: 27 June 2009 applying in relation to financial years beginning on or after 29 June 2008 which have not ended before 27 June 2009.

Chapter 6 – Quoted Companies: Directors' Remuneration Report

420 Duty to prepare directors' remuneration report

420(1) The directors of a quoted company must prepare a directors' remuneration report for each financial year of the company.

420(2) In the case of failure to comply with the requirement to prepare a directors' remuneration report, every person who–

(a) was a director of the company immediately before the end of the period for filing accounts and reports for the financial year in question, and

(b) failed to take all reasonable steps for securing compliance with that requirement, commits an offence.

420(3) A person guilty of an offence under this section is liable–

(a) on conviction on indictment, to a fine;

(b) on summary conviction, to a fine not exceeding the statutory maximum.

Commencement Date – 6 April 2008 applying to accounts and reports for financial years beginning on or after 6 April 2008.

421 Contents of directors' remuneration report

421(1) The Secretary of State may make provision by regulations as to–

(a) the information that must be contained in a directors' remuneration report,

(b) how information is to be set out in the report, and

(c) what is to be the auditable part of the report.

421(2) Without prejudice to the generality of this power, the regulations may make any such provision as was made, immediately before the commencement of this Part, by Schedule 7A to the Companies Act 1985 (c. 6).

421(2A) The regulations must provide that any information required to be included in the report as to the policy of the company with respect to the making of remuneration payments and payments for loss of office (within the meaning of Chapter 4A of Part 10) is to be set out in a separate part of the report.

421(3) It is the duty of–

(a) any director of a company, and

(b) any person who is or has at any time in the preceding five years been a director of the company, to give notice to the company of such matters relating to himself as may be necessary for the purposes of regulations under this section.

421(4) A person who makes default in complying with subsection (3) commits an offence and is liable on summary conviction to a fine not exceeding level 3 on the standard scale.

Commencement Date – 6 April 2008 applying to accounts and reports for financial years beginning on or after 6 April 2008.

History – S. 421(2A) inserted by the Enterprise and Regulatory Reform Act 2013, s. 79(1), with effect from 25 April 2013.

Statutory instruments – For regulations under this section see the Large and Medium-sized Companies and Groups (Accounts and Reports) Regulations 2008 (SI 2008/410).

Notes – This section is modified in its application to unregistered companies by the Unregistered Companies Regulations 2009 (SI 2009/2436).

422 Approval and signing of directors' remuneration report

422(1) The directors' remuneration report must be approved by the board of directors and signed on behalf of the board by a director or the secretary of the company.

422(2) If a directors' remuneration report is approved that does not comply with the requirements of this Act, every director of the company who–

(a) knew that it did not comply, or was reckless as to whether it complied, and

(b) failed to take reasonable steps to secure compliance with those requirements or, as the case may be, to prevent the report from being approved, commits an offence.

422(3) A person guilty of an offence under this section is liable–

(a) on conviction on indictment, to a fine;

(b) on summary conviction, to a fine not exceeding the statutory maximum.

Commencement Date – 6 April 2008 applying to accounts and reports for financial years beginning on or after 6 April 2008.

422A Revisions to directors' remuneration policy

422A(1) The directors' remuneration policy contained in a company's directors' remuneration report may be revised.

422A(2) Any such revision must be approved by the board of directors.

422A(3) The policy as so revised must be set out in a document signed on behalf of the board by a director or the secretary of the company.

422A(4) Regulations under section 421(1) may make provision as to–

(a) the information that must be contained in a document setting out a revised directors' remuneration policy, and

(b) how information is to be set out in the document.

422A(5) Sections 422(2) and (3), 454, 456 and 463 apply in relation to such a document as they apply in relation to a directors' remuneration report.

422A(6) In this section, **"directors' remuneration policy"** means the policy of a company with respect to the matters mentioned in section 421(2A).

History – S. 422A inserted by the Enterprise and Regulatory Reform Act 2013, s. 79(2), with effect from a day to be appointed by the Secretary of State.

Chapter 7 – Publication of Accounts and Reports

Duty to circulate copies of accounts and reports

423   Duty to circulate copies of annual accounts and reports

423(1)   Every company must send a copy of its annual accounts and reports for each financial year to–

(a)   every member of the company,

(b)   every holder of the company's debentures, and

(c)   every person who is entitled to receive notice of general meetings.

423(2)   Copies need not be sent to a person for whom the company does not have a current address.

423(3)   A company has a "**current address**" for a person if–

(a)   an address has been notified to the company by the person as one at which documents may be sent to him, and

(b)   the company has no reason to believe that documents sent to him at that address will not reach him.

423(4)   In the case of a company not having a share capital, copies need not be sent to anyone who is not entitled to receive notices of general meetings of the company.

423(5)   Where copies are sent out over a period of days, references in the Companies Acts to the day on which copies are sent out shall be read as references to the last day of that period.

423(6)   This section has effect subject to section 426 (option to provide strategic report with supplementary material).

Commencement Date – 6 April 2008 applying to accounts and reports for financial years beginning on or after 6 April 2008.

History – This version of s. 423 applies to financial years ending on or after 30 September 2013. The version applying to financial years ending before 30 September 2013 reads as follows:

"423   Duty to circulate copies of annual accounts and reports

423(1)   Every company must send a copy of its annual accounts and reports for each financial year to–

(a)   every member of the company,

(b)   every holder of the company's debentures, and

(c)   every person who is entitled to receive notice of general meetings.

423(2)   Copies need not be sent to a person for whom the company does not have a current address.

423(3)   A company has a "**current address**" for a person if–

(a)   an address has been notified to the company by the person as one at which documents may be sent to him, and

(b)   the company has no reason to believe that documents sent to him at that address will not reach him.

423(4)   In the case of a company not having a share capital, copies need not be sent to anyone who is not entitled to receive notices of general meetings of the company.

423(5)   Where copies are sent out over a period of days, references in the Companies Acts to the day on which copies are sent out shall be read as references to the last day of that period.

423(6)   This section has effect subject to section 426 (option to provide summary financial statement)."

In s. 423(6), "strategic report with supplementary material" substituted for "summary financial statement" by SI 2013/1970, Sch., para. 1 and 3, with effect from 1 October 2013 in respect of financial years ending on or after 30 September 2013.

Notes – This section is modified in its application to LLPs by Pt. 6 *Publication Of Accounts And Auditor's Report* of the Limited Liability Partnerships (Accounts and Audit) (Application of Companies Act 2006) Regulations 2008 (SI 2008/1911).

424 Time allowed for sending out copies of accounts and reports

424(1) The time allowed for sending out copies of the company's annual accounts and reports is as follows.

424(2) A private company must comply with section 423 not later than–

    (a)   the end of the period for filing accounts and reports, or

    (b)   if earlier, the date on which it actually delivers its accounts and reports to the registrar.

424(3) A public company must comply with section 423 at least 21 days before the date of the relevant accounts meeting.

424(4) If in the case of a public company copies are sent out later than is required by subsection (3), they shall, despite that, be deemed to have been duly sent if it is so agreed by all the members entitled to attend and vote at the relevant accounts meeting.

424(5) Whether the time allowed is that for a private company or a public company is determined by reference to the company's status immediately before the end of the accounting reference period by reference to which the financial year for the accounts in question was determined.

424(6) In this section the **"relevant accounts meeting"** means the accounts meeting of the company at which the accounts and reports in question are to be laid.

Commencement Date – 6 April 2008 applying to accounts and reports for financial years beginning on or after 6 April 2008.

425 Default in sending out copies of accounts and reports: offences

425(1) If default is made in complying with section 423 or 424, an offence is committed by–

    (a)   the company, and

    (b)   every officer of the company who is in default.

425(2) A person guilty of an offence under this section is liable–

    (a)   on conviction on indictment, to a fine;

    (b)   on summary conviction, to a fine not exceeding the statutory maximum.

Commencement Date – 6 April 2008 applying to accounts and reports for financial years beginning on or after 6 April 2008.

Notes – This section is modified in its application to LLPs by Pt. 6 *Publication Of Accounts And Auditor's Report* of the Limited Liability Partnerships (Accounts and Audit) (Application of Companies Act 2006) Regulations 2008 (SI 2008/1911).

Option to provide strategic report with supplementary material

History – In the heading, the words "strategic report with supplementary material" substituted for "summary financial statements" by SI 2013/1970, para. 10(2).

426 Option to provide summary financial statement

426(1) A company may–

    (a)   in such cases as may be specified by regulations made by the Secretary of State, and

(b)   provided any conditions so specified are complied with, provide a copy of the strategic report together with the supplementary material described in section 426A instead of copies of the accounts and reports required to be sent out in accordance with section 423.

426(2)   Copies of those accounts and reports must, however, be sent to any person entitled to be sent them in accordance with that section and who wishes to receive them.

426(3)   The Secretary of State may make provision by regulations as to the manner in which it is to be ascertained, whether before or after a person becomes entitled to be sent a copy of those accounts and reports, whether he wishes to receive them.

426(4)   [Repealed.]

426(5)   This section applies to copies of accounts and reports required to be sent out by virtue of section 146 to a person nominated to enjoy information rights as it applies to copies of accounts and reports required to be sent out in accordance with section 423 to a member of the company.

426(6)   Regulations under this section are subject to negative resolution procedure.

Commencement Date – 6 April 2008 applying to accounts and reports for financial years beginning on or after 6 April 2008.

History – This version of s. 426 applies in relation to financial years ending on or after 30 September 2013. The version applying for financial years ending before 30 September 2013 reads as follows:

"426   Option to provide summary financial statement

426(1)   A company may–
(a)   in such cases as may be specified by regulations made by the Secretary of State, and
(b)   provided any conditions so specified are complied with, provide a summary financial statement instead of copies of the accounts and reports required to be sent out in accordance with section 423.

426(2)   Copies of those accounts and reports must, however, be sent to any person entitled to be sent them in accordance with that section and who wishes to receive them.

426(3)   The Secretary of State may make provision by regulations as to the manner in which it is to be ascertained, whether before or after a person becomes entitled to be sent a copy of those accounts and reports, whether he wishes to receive them.

426(4)   A summary financial statement must comply with the requirements of–
section 427 (form and contents of summary financial statement: unquoted companies), or
section 428 (form and contents of summary financial statement: quoted companies).

426(5)   This section applies to copies of accounts and reports required to be sent out by virtue of section 146 to a person nominated to enjoy information rights as it applies to copies of accounts and reports required to be sent out in accordance with section 423 to a member of the company.

426(6)   Regulations under this section are subject to negative resolution procedure."

The following amendments were made by SI 2013/1970, reg. 9 and 10, with effect from 6 August 2013 for the purposes of the exercise of the powers to make regulations in the amended section and, for all other purposes, with effect from 1 October 2013 in respect of financial years ending on or after 30 September 2013:

- in the cross-heading before the section and in the heading to the section for "summary financial statement" substitute "strategic report with supplementary material";
- in subsection (1) for "summary financial statement" substitute "copy of the strategic report together with the supplementary material described in section 426A";
- omit subsection (4).

Statutory instruments – For regulations under this section see the Companies (Summary Financial Statement) Regulations 2008 (SI 2008/374).

Notes – This section is modified in its application to unregistered companies by the Unregistered Companies Regulations 2009 (SI 2009/2436).

426A Supplementary material

426A(1) The supplementary material referred to in section 426 must be prepared in accordance with this section.

426A(2) The supplementary material must—

(a)   contain a statement that the strategic report is only part of the company's annual accounts and reports;

(b)   state how a person entitled to them can obtain a full copy of the company's annual accounts and reports;

(c)   state whether the auditor's report on the annual accounts was unqualified or qualified and, if it was qualified, set out the report in full together with any further material needed to understand the qualification;

(d)   state whether, in that report, the auditor's statement under section 496 (whether strategic report and directors' report consistent with the accounts) was unqualified or qualified and, if it was qualified, set out the qualified statement in full together with any further material needed to understand the qualification;

(e)   in the case of a quoted company, contain a copy of that part of the directors' remuneration report which sets out the single total figure table in respect of the company's directors' remuneration in accordance with the requirements of Schedule 8 to the Large and Medium-sized Companies (Accounts and Reports) Regulations 2008 (S.I. 2008/410).

History – S. 426A inserted by SI 2013/1970, reg. 9 and 12, with effect from 1 October 2013 in respect of financial years ending on or after 30 September 2013.

427 Form and contents of summary financial statement: unquoted companies

427 [Section 427 repealed by SI 2013/1970, reg. 9 and 11, with effect from 1 October 2013 in respect of financial years ending on or after 30 September 2013.]

Commencement Date – 6 April 2008 applying to accounts and reports for financial years beginning on or after 6 April 2008.

History – S. 427 is repealed by SI 2013/1970, reg. 9 and 11, with effect from 1 October 2013 in respect of financial years ending on or after 30 September 2013. S. 427 previously read as follows:

"427 Form and contents of summary financial statement: unquoted companies

427(1) A summary financial statement by a company that is not a quoted company must—

(a)   be derived from the company's annual accounts, and

(b)   be prepared in accordance with this section and regulations made under it.

427(2) The summary financial statement must be in such form, and contain such information, as the Secretary of State may specify by regulations. The regulations may require the statement to include information derived from the directors' report.

427(3) Nothing in this section or regulations made under it prevents a company from including in a summary financial statement additional information derived from the company's annual accounts or the directors' report.

427(4) The summary financial statement must—

(a)   state that it is only a summary of information derived from the company's annual accounts;

(b)   state whether it contains additional information derived from the directors' report and, if so, that it does not contain the full text of that report;

(c)   state how a person entitled to them can obtain a full copy of the company's annual accounts and the directors' report;

(d)   contain a statement by the company's auditor of his opinion as to whether the summary financial statement—

      (i) is consistent with the company's annual accounts and, where information derived from the directors' report is included in the statement, with that report, and

      (ii) complies with the requirements of this section and regulations made under it;

(e)   state whether the auditor's report on the annual accounts was unqualified or qualified and, if it was qualified, set out the report in full together with any further material needed to understand the qualification;

(f)   state whether, in that report, the auditor's statement under section 496 (whether directors' report consistent with accounts) was qualified or unqualified and, if it was qualified, set out the qualified statement in full together with any further material needed to understand the qualification;

(g)   state whether that auditor's report contained a statement under–

      (i) section 498(2)(a) or (b) (accounting records or returns inadequate or accounts not agreeing with records and returns), or

      (ii) section 498(3) (failure to obtain necessary information and explanations), and if so, set out the statement in full.

427(5) Regulations under this section may provide that any specified material may, instead of being included in the summary financial statement, be sent separately at the same time as the statement.

427(6) Regulations under this section are subject to negative resolution procedure."

Statutory instruments – For regulations under this section see the Companies (Summary Financial Statement) Regulations 2008 (SI 2008/374).

Notes – This section is modified in its application to unregistered companies by the Unregistered Companies Regulations 2009 (SI 2009/2436).

428 Form and contents of summary financial statement: quoted companies

428 [Section 428 repealed by SI 2013/1970, reg. 9 and 11, with effect from 1 October 2013 in respect of financial years ending on or after 30 September 2013.]

Commencement Date – 6 April 2008 applying to accounts and reports for financial years beginning on or after 6 April 2008.

History – S. 428 is repealed by SI 2013/1970, reg. 9 and 11, with effect from 1 October 2013 in respect of financial years ending on or after 30 September 2013. S. 428 previously read as follows:

"428 Form and contents of summary financial statement: quoted companies

428(1) A summary financial statement by a quoted company must–

(a)   be derived from the company's annual accounts and the directors' remuneration report, and

(b)   be prepared in accordance with this section and regulations made under it.

428(2) The summary financial statement must be in such form, and contain such information, as the Secretary of State may specify by regulations. The regulations may require the statement to include information derived from the directors' report.

428(3) Nothing in this section or regulations made under it prevents a company from including in a summary financial statement additional information derived from the company's annual accounts, the directors' remuneration report or the directors' report.

428(4) The summary financial statement must–

(a)   state that it is only a summary of information derived from the company's annual accounts and the directors' remuneration report;

(b)   state whether it contains additional information derived from the directors' report and, if so, that it does not contain the full text of that report;

(c)   state how a person entitled to them can obtain a full copy of the company's annual accounts, the directors' remuneration report or the directors' report;

(d)   contain a statement by the company's auditor of his opinion as to whether the summary financial statement–

      (i) is consistent with the company's annual accounts and the directors' remuneration report and, where information derived from the directors' report is included in the statement, with that report, and

      (ii) complies with the requirements of this section and regulations made under it;

(e)   state whether the auditor's report on the annual accounts and the auditable part of the directors' remuneration report was unqualified or qualified and, if it was qualified, set out the report in full together with any further material needed to understand the qualification;

(f)   state whether that auditor's report contained a statement under–

(i)   section 498(2) (accounting records or returns inadequate or accounts or directors' remuneration report not agreeing with records and returns), or

(ii)   section 498(3) (failure to obtain necessary information and explanations), and if so, set out the statement in full;

(g)   state whether, in that report, the auditor's statement under section 496 (whether directors' report consistent with accounts) was qualified or unqualified and, if it was qualified, set out the qualified statement in full together with any further material needed to understand the qualification.

428(5)   Regulations under this section may provide that any specified material may, instead of being included in the summary financial statement, be sent separately at the same time as the statement.

428(6)   Regulations under this section are subject to negative resolution procedure."

Statutory instruments – For regulations under this section see the Companies (Summary Financial Statement) Regulations 2008 (SI 2008/374).

Notes – This section is modified in its application to unregistered companies by the Unregistered Companies Regulations 2009 (SI 2009/2436).

429   Summary financial statements: offences [applying to financial years ending before 30 September 2013]

429   [Section 429 repealed by SI 2013/1970, reg. 9 and 13, with effect from 1 October 2013 in respect of financial years ending on or after 30 September 2013.]

Commencement Date – 6 April 2008 applying to accounts and reports for financial years beginning on or after 6 April 2008.

History – Section 429 is repealed by SI 2013/1970, reg. 9 and 13, with effect from 1 October 2013 in respect of financial years ending on or after 30 September 2013. S. 429 previously read as follows:

"429   Summary financial statements: offences

429(1)   If default is made in complying with any provision of section 426, 427 or 428, or of regulations under any of those sections, an offence is committed by–

(a)   the company, and

(b)   every officer of the company who is in default.

429(2)   A person guilty of an offence under this section is liable on summary conviction to a fine not exceeding level 3 on the standard scale."

Quoted companies: requirements as to website publication

430   Quoted companies: annual accounts and reports to be made available on website

430(1)   A quoted company must ensure that its annual accounts and reports–

(a)   are made available on a website, and

(b)   remain so available until the annual accounts and reports for the company's next financial year are made available in accordance with this section.

430(2)   The annual accounts and reports must be made available on a website that–

(a)   is maintained by or on behalf of the company, and

(b)   identifies the company in question.

430(3)   Access to the annual accounts and reports on the website, and the ability to obtain a hard copy of the annual accounts and reports from the website, must not be–

(a)   conditional on the payment of a fee, or

(b)   otherwise restricted, except so far as necessary to comply with any enactment or regulatory requirement (in the United Kingdom or elsewhere).

430(4) The annual accounts and reports–

(a)   must be made available as soon as reasonably practicable, and

(b)   must be kept available throughout the period specified in subsection (1)(b).

430(5) A failure to make the annual accounts and reports available on a website throughout that period is disregarded if–

(a)   the annual accounts and reports are made available on the website for part of that period, and

(b)   the failure is wholly attributable to circumstances that it would not be reasonable to have expected the company to prevent or avoid.

430(6) In the event of default in complying with this section, an offence is committed by every officer of the company who is in default.

430(7) A person guilty of an offence under subsection (6) is liable on summary conviction to a fine not exceeding level 3 on the standard scale.

Commencement Date – 6 April 2008 applying to accounts and reports for financial years beginning on or after 6 April 2008.

Prospective amendments – The following amendments are made by the Enterprise and Regulatory Reform Act 2013, s. 81(1) and (6)–(9), with effect from a day to be appointed by the Secretary of State:

•   After s. 430(2), insert:

"**430(2A)** If the directors' remuneration policy of a quoted company is revised in accordance with section 422A, the company must ensure that the revised policy is made available on the website on which its annual accounts and reports are made available.

430(2B) If a person ceases to be a director of a quoted company, the company must ensure that the following information is made available on the website on which its annual accounts and reports are made available–

(a)   the name of the person concerned,

(b)   particulars of any remuneration payment (within the meaning of Chapter 4A of Part 10) made or to be made to the person after ceasing to be a director, including its amount and how it was calculated, and

(c)   particulars of any payment for loss of office (within the meaning of that Chapter) made or to be made to the person, including its amount and how it was calculated."

•   In s. 430(3), the words "the material made available on the website under subsections (1) to (2B)" substituted for "the annual accounts and reports on the website" and "such material from" substituted for "the annual accounts and reports from" .

•   After s. 430(4), insert:

"**430(4A)** Where subsection (2A) or (2B) applies, the material in question–

(a)   must be made available as soon as reasonably practicable, and

(b)   must be kept available until the next directors' remuneration report of the company is made available on the website."

•   In s. 430(5), in the words before para (a), for the words "material available on a website throughout the period mentioned in subsection (4) or (as the case may be) (4A)" substituted for the words from "the annual accounts and reports" to "that period".

•   In s. 430(5)(a), the words "the material is" substituted for "the annual accounts and reports are".

Right of member or debenture holder to demand copies of accounts and reports

431 Right of member or debenture holder to copies of accounts and reports: unquoted companies

431(1) A member of, or holder of debentures of, an unquoted company is entitled to be provided, on demand and without charge, with a copy of–

(a)   the company's last annual accounts,

(aa)   the strategic report (if any) for the last financial year,

(b)   the last directors' report, and

(c)   the auditor's report on those accounts (including the statement on that report and (where applicable) on the strategic report).

431(2) The entitlement under this section is to a single copy of those documents, but that is in addition to any copy to which a person may be entitled under section 423.

431(3) If a demand made under this section is not complied with within seven days of receipt by the company, an offence is committed by–

(a)   the company, and

(b)   every officer of the company who is in default.

431(4) A person guilty of an offence under this section is liable on summary conviction to a fine not exceeding level 3 on the standard scale and, for continued contravention, a daily default fine not exceeding one-tenth of level 3 on the standard scale.

Commencement Date – 6 April 2008 applying to accounts and reports for financial years beginning on or after 6 April 2008.

History – In s. 431(1), para. (aa) inserted and, in para. (c), "and (where applicable) on the strategic report" inserted by SI 2013/1970, Sch., para. 1 and 4, with effect from 1 October 2013 in respect of financial years ending on or after 30 September 2013.

Notes – This section is modified in its application to LLPs by Pt. 6 *Publication Of Accounts And Auditor's Report* of the Limited Liability Partnerships (Accounts and Audit) (Application of Companies Act 2006) Regulations 2008 (SI 2008/1911)

432   Right of member or debenture holder to copies of accounts and reports: quoted companies

432(1) A member of, or holder of debentures of, a quoted company is entitled to be provided, on demand and without charge, with a copy of–

(a)   the company's last annual accounts,

(b)   the last directors' remuneration report,

(ba)   the strategic report (if any) for the last financial year,

(c)   the last directors' report, and

(d)   the auditor's report on those accounts (including the report on the directors' remuneration report, on the strategic report (where this is covered by the auditor's report) and on the directors' report).

432(2) The entitlement under this section is to a single copy of those documents, but that is in addition to any copy to which a person may be entitled under section 423.

432(3) If a demand made under this section is not complied with within seven days of receipt by the company, an offence is committed by–

(a)   the company, and

(b)   every officer of the company who is in default.

432(4) A person guilty of an offence under this section is liable on summary conviction to a fine not exceeding level 3 on the standard scale and, for continued contravention, a daily default fine not exceeding one-tenth of level 3 on the standard scale.

Commencement Date – 6 April 2008 applying to accounts and reports for financial years beginning on or after 6 April 2008.

History – In s. 432(1), para. (ba) inserted and, in para. (d), ", on the strategic report (where this is covered by the auditor's report)" inserted by SI 2013/1970, Sch., para. 1 and 5, with effect from 1 October 2013 in respect of financial years ending on or after 30 September 2013.

Requirements in connection with publication of accounts and reports

433 Name of signatory to be stated in published copies of accounts and reports

433(1) Every copy of a document to which this section applies that is published by or on behalf of the company must state the name of the person who signed it on behalf of the board.

433(2) In the case of an unquoted company, this section applies to copies of–

(a) the company's balance sheet,

(aa) the strategic report, and

(b) the directors' report.

433(3) In the case of a quoted company, this section applies to copies of–

(a) the company's balance sheet,

(b) the directors' remuneration report,

(ba) the strategic report, and

(c) the directors' report.

433(4) If a copy is published without the required statement of the signatory's name, an offence is committed by–

(a) the company, and

(b) every officer of the company who is in default.

433(5) A person guilty of an offence under this section is liable on summary conviction to a fine not exceeding level 3 on the standard scale.

Commencement Date – 6 April 2008 applying to accounts and reports for financial years beginning on or after 6 April 2008.

History – This version of s. 433 applies for financial years ending on or after 30 September 2013. The text applying to financial years ending before 30 September 2013 read as follows:

> **"433 Name of signatory to be stated in published copies of accounts and reports**
>
> **433(1)** Every copy of a document to which this section applies that is published by or on behalf of the company must state the name of the person who signed it on behalf of the board.
> **433(2)** In the case of an unquoted company, this section applies to copies of–
> (a) the company's balance sheet, and
> (b) the directors' report.
> **433(3)** In the case of a quoted company, this section applies to copies of–
> (a) the company's balance sheet,
> (b) the directors' remuneration report, and
> (c) the directors' report.
> **433(4)** If a copy is published without the required statement of the signatory's name, an offence is committed by–
> (a) the company, and
> (b) every officer of the company who is in default.
> **433(5)** A person guilty of an offence under this section is liable on summary conviction to a fine not exceeding level 3 on the standard scale."

Subsections (2)(aa) and (3)(ba) inserted by SI 2013/1970, Sch., para. 1 and 6, with effect from 1 October 2013 in respect of financial years ending on or after 30 September 2013.

Notes – This section is modified in its application to LLPs by Pt. 6 *Publication Of Accounts And Auditor's Report* of the Limited Liability Partnerships (Accounts and Audit) (Application of Companies Act 2006) Regulations 2008 (SI 2008/1911).

434   Requirements in connection with publication of statutory accounts

434(1)   If a company publishes any of its statutory accounts, they must be accompanied by the auditor's report on those accounts (unless the company is exempt from audit and the directors have taken advantage of that exemption).

434(2)   A company that prepares statutory group accounts for a financial year must not publish its statutory individual accounts for that year without also publishing with them its statutory group accounts.

434(3)   A company's **"statutory accounts"** are its accounts for a financial year as required to be delivered to the registrar under section 441.

434(4)   If a company contravenes any provision of this section, an offence is committed by –

(a)   the company, and

(b)   every officer of the company who is in default.

434(5)   A person guilty of an offence under this section is liable on summary conviction to a fine not exceeding level 3 on the standard scale.

434(6)   [Repealed]

Commencement Date – 6 April 2008 applying to accounts and reports for financial years beginning on or after 6 April 2008.

History – This version of s. 434 applies to financial years ending on or after 30 September 2013. The version applying to financial years ending before 30 September 2013 read as follows:

"434   Requirements in connection with publication of statutory accounts

434(1)   If a company publishes any of its statutory accounts, they must be accompanied by the auditor's report on those accounts (unless the company is exempt from audit and the directors have taken advantage of that exemption).

434(2)   A company that prepares statutory group accounts for a financial year must not publish its statutory individual accounts for that year without also publishing with them its statutory group accounts.

434(3)   A company's **"statutory accounts"** are its accounts for a financial year as required to be delivered to the registrar under section 441.

434(4)   If a company contravenes any provision of this section, an offence is committed by–

(a)   the company, and

(b)   every officer of the company who is in default.

434(5)   A person guilty of an offence under this section is liable on summary conviction to a fine not exceeding level 3 on the standard scale.

434(6)   This section does not apply in relation to the provision by a company of a summary financial statement (see section 426)."

S. 434(6) repealed by SI 2013/1970, Sch., para. 1 and 7, with effect from 1 October 2013 in respect of financial years ending on or after 30 September 2013.

Notes – This section is modified in its application to LLPs by Pt. 6 *Publication Of Accounts And Auditor's Report* of the Limited Liability Partnerships (Accounts and Audit) (Application of Companies Act 2006) Regulations 2008 (SI 2008/1911)

435   Requirements in connection with publication of non-statutory accounts

435(1)   If a company publishes non-statutory accounts, it must publish with them a statement indicating –

(a)   that they are not the company's statutory accounts,

(b)   whether statutory accounts dealing with any financial year with which the non-statutory accounts purport to deal have been delivered to the registrar, and

    (c)   whether an auditor's report has been made on the company's statutory accounts for any such financial year, and if so whether the report–

        (i)   was qualified or unqualified, or included a reference to any matters to which the auditor drew attention by way of emphasis without qualifying the report, or

        (ii)   contained a statement under section 498(2) (accounting records or returns inadequate or accounts or directors' remuneration report not agreeing with records and returns), or section 498(3) (failure to obtain necessary information and explanations).

435(2) The company must not publish with non-statutory accounts the auditor's report on the company's statutory accounts.

435(3) References in this section to the publication by a company of 'non-statutory accounts' are to the publication of–

    (a)   any balance sheet or profit and loss account relating to, or purporting to deal with, a financial year of the company, or

    (b)   an account in any form purporting to be a balance sheet or profit and loss account for a group headed by the company relating to, or purporting to deal with, a financial year of the company, otherwise than as part of the company's statutory accounts.

435(4) In subsection (3)(b) "a group headed by the company" means a group consisting of the company and any other undertaking (regardless of whether it is a subsidiary undertaking of the company) other than a parent undertaking of the company.

435(5) If a company contravenes any provision of this section, an offence is committed by –

    (a)   the company, and

    (b)   every officer of the company who is in default.

435(6) A person guilty of an offence under this section is liable on summary conviction to a fine not exceeding level 3 on the standard scale.

435(7) [Repealed]

Commencement Date – 6 April 2008 applying to accounts and reports for financial years beginning on or after 6 April 2008.

History – This version of s. 435 applies to financial years ending on or after 30 September 2013. The version applying to financial years ending before 30 September 2013 read as follows:

"435 Requirements in connection with publication of non-statutory accounts

435(1) If a company publishes non-statutory accounts, it must publish with them a statement indicating–

    (a)   that they are not the company's statutory accounts,

    (b)   whether statutory accounts dealing with any financial year with which the non-statutory accounts purport to deal have been delivered to the registrar, and

    (c)   whether an auditor's report has been made on the company's statutory accounts for any such financial year, and if so whether the report–

        (i)   was qualified or unqualified, or included a reference to any matters to which the auditor drew attention by way of emphasis without qualifying the report, or

        (ii)   contained a statement under section 498(2) (accounting records or returns inadequate or accounts or directors' remuneration report not agreeing with records and returns), or section 498(3) (failure to obtain necessary information and explanations).

435(2) The company must not publish with non-statutory accounts the auditor's report on the company's statutory accounts.

435(3) References in this section to the publication by a company of **"non-statutory accounts"** are to the publication of–

    (a)   any balance sheet or profit and loss account relating to, or purporting to deal with, a financial year of the company, or

(b)   an account in any form purporting to be a balance sheet or profit and loss account for a group headed by the company relating to, or purporting to deal with, a financial year of the company, otherwise than as part of the company's statutory accounts.

435(4)   In subsection (3)(b) **"a group headed by the company"** means a group consisting of the company and any other undertaking (regardless of whether it is a subsidiary undertaking of the company) other than a parent undertaking of the company.

435(5)   If a company contravenes any provision of this section, an offence is committed by–

(a)   the company, and

(b)   every officer of the company who is in default.

435(6)   A person guilty of an offence under this section is liable on summary conviction to a fine not exceeding level 3 on the standard scale.

435(7)   This section does not apply in relation to the provision by a company of a summary financial statement (see section 426)."

Subsection (7) repealed by SI 2013/1970, Sch., para. 1 and 8, with effect from 1 October 2013 in respect of financial years ending on or after 30 September 2013.

Notes – This section is modified in its application to LLPs by Pt. 6 *Publication Of Accounts And Auditor's Report* of the Limited Liability Partnerships (Accounts and Audit) (Application of Companies Act 2006) Regulations 2008 (SI 2008/1911)

436   Meaning of "publication" in relation to accounts and reports

436(1)   This section has effect for the purposes of–

section 433 (name of signatory to be stated in published copies of accounts and reports),

section 434 (requirements in connection with publication of statutory accounts), and

section 435 (requirements in connection with publication of non-statutory accounts).

436(2)   For the purposes of those sections a company is regarded as publishing a document if it publishes, issues or circulates it or otherwise makes it available for public inspection in a manner calculated to invite members of the public generally, or any class of members of the public, to read it.

Commencement Date – 6 April 2008 applying to accounts and reports for financial years beginning on or after 6 April 2008.

Notes – This section is modified in its application to LLPs by Pt. 6 *Publication Of Accounts And Auditor's Report* of the Limited Liability Partnerships (Accounts and Audit) (Application of Companies Act 2006) Regulations 2008 (SI 2008/1911)

Chapter 8 – Public Companies: Laying of Accounts and Reports Before General Meeting

437   Public companies: laying of accounts and reports before general meeting

437(1)   The directors of a public company must lay before the company in general meeting copies of its annual accounts and reports.

437(2)   This section must be complied with not later than the end of the period for filing the accounts and reports in question.

437(3)   In the Companies Acts **"accounts meeting"**, in relation to a public company, means a general meeting of the company at which the company's annual accounts and reports are (or are to be) laid in accordance with this section.

Commencement Date – 6 April 2008 applying to accounts and reports for financial years beginning on or after 6 April 2008.

438 Public companies: offence of failure to lay accounts and reports

438(1) If the requirements of section 437 (public companies: laying of accounts and reports before general meeting) are not complied with before the end of the period allowed, every person who immediately before the end of that period was a director of the company commits an offence.

438(2) It is a defence for a person charged with such an offence to prove that he took all reasonable steps for securing that those requirements would be complied with before the end of that period.

438(3) It is not a defence to prove that the documents in question were not in fact prepared as required by this Part.

438(4) A person guilty of an offence under this section is liable on summary conviction to a fine not exceeding level 5 on the standard scale and, for continued contravention, a daily default fine not exceeding one-tenth of the greater of £5,000 or level 4 on the standard scale.

Commencement Date – 6 April 2008 applying to accounts and reports for financial years beginning on or after 6 April 2008.

History – In s. 438(4), the words "one-tenth of the greater of £5,000 or level 4 on the standard scale" substituted for the words "one-tenth of level 5 on the standard scale" by SI 2015/664, Sch. 3, Pt. 1, para. 9(12), with effect from 12 March 2015.

Chapter 9 – Quoted Companies: Members' Approval of Directors' Remuneration Report

439 Quoted companies: members' approval of directors' remuneration report

439(1) A quoted company must, prior to the accounts meeting, give to the members of the company entitled to be sent notice of the meeting notice of the intention to move at the meeting, as an ordinary resolution, a resolution approving the directors' remuneration report for the financial year.

439(2) The notice may be given in any manner permitted for the service on the member of notice of the meeting.

439(3) The business that may be dealt with at the accounts meeting includes the resolution. This is so notwithstanding any default in complying with subsection (1) or (2).

439(4) The existing directors must ensure that the resolution is put to the vote of the meeting.

439(5) No entitlement of a person to remuneration is made conditional on the resolution being passed by reason only of the provision made by this section.

439(6) In this section–

"**the accounts meeting**" means the general meeting of the company before which the company's annual accounts for the financial year are to be laid; and

"**existing director**" means a person who is a director of the company immediately before that meeting.

Commencement Date – 6 April 2008 applying to accounts and reports for financial years beginning on or after 6 April 2008.

Prospective amendments – The following amendment is made by the Enterprise and Regulatory Reform Act 2013, s. 79(3), with effect from a day to be appointed by the Secretary of State:

- In s. 439(1), at the end insert "other than the part containing the directors' remuneration policy (as to which see section 439A)".

439A   Quoted companies: members' approval of directors' remuneration policy

439A(1)   A quoted company must give notice of the intention to move, as an ordinary resolution, a resolution approving the relevant directors' remuneration policy–

    (a)   at the accounts meeting held in the first financial year which begins on or after the day on which the company becomes a quoted company, and

    (b)   at an accounts or other general meeting held no later than the end of the period of three financial years beginning with the first financial year after the last accounts or other general meeting in relation to which notice is given under this subsection.

439A(2)   A quoted company must give notice of the intention to move at an accounts meeting, as an ordinary resolution, a resolution approving the relevant directors' remuneration policy if–

    (a)   a resolution required to be put to the vote under section 439 was not passed at the last accounts meeting of the company, and

    (b)   no notice under this section was given in relation to that meeting or any other general meeting held before the next accounts meeting.

439A(3)   Subsection (2) does not apply in relation to a quoted company before the first meeting in relation to which it gives notice under subsection (1).

439A(4)   A notice given under subsection (2) is to be treated as given under subsection (1) for the purpose of determining the period within which the next notice under subsection (1) must be given.

439A(5)   Notice of the intention to move a resolution to which this section applies must be given, prior to the meeting in question, to the members of the company entitled to be sent notice of the meeting.

439A(6)   Subsections (2) to (4) of section 439 apply for the purposes of a resolution to which this section applies as they apply for the purposes of a resolution to which section 439 applies, with the modification that, for the purposes of a resolution relating to a general meeting other than an accounts meeting, subsection (3) applies as if for "accounts meeting" there were substituted "general meeting".

439A(7)   For the purposes of this section, the relevant directors' remuneration policy is –

    (a)   in a case where notice is given in relation to an accounts meeting, the remuneration policy contained in the directors' remuneration report in respect of which a resolution under section 439 is required to be put to the vote at that accounts meeting;

    (b)   in a case where notice is given in relation to a general meeting other than an accounts meeting–

        (i)   the remuneration policy contained in the directors' remuneration report in respect of which such a resolution was required to be put to the vote at the last accounts meeting to be held before that other general meeting, or

        (ii)   where that policy has been revised in accordance with section 422A, the policy as so revised.

439A(8)   In this section–

    (a)   **"accounts meeting"** means a general meeting of the company before which the company's annual accounts for a financial year are to be laid;

    (b)   **"directors' remuneration policy"** means the policy of the company with respect to the matters mentioned in section 421(2A).

History – Section 439A inserted by the Enterprise and Regulatory Reform Act 2013, s 79(4), with effect from a day to be appointed by the Secretary of State. The following transitional provisions are made by the Enterprise and Regulatory Reform Act 2013, s. 82(1) and (2):

"**82(1)** In relation to a company that is a quoted company immediately before the day on which section 79 of this Act comes into force, section 439A(1)(a) of the Companies Act 2006 (as inserted by section 79(4) of this Act) applies as if–

(a)   the reference to the day on which the company becomes a quoted company were a reference to the day on which section 79 of this Act comes into force, and

(b)   at the end of the paragraph (but before the ", and") there were inserted "or at an earlier general meeting"

82(2) In relation to a company that is a quoted company immediately before the day on which section 79 of this Act comes into force, the Companies Act 2006, s. 226D(6)(a) (as inserted by section 80 of this Act) applies as if the reference to the day on which the company becomes a quoted company were a reference to the day on which section 79 of this Act comes into force."

440 Quoted companies: offences in connection with procedure for approval

440(1) In the event of default in complying with section 439(1) (notice to be given of resolution for approval of directors' remuneration report), an offence is committed by every officer of the company who is in default.

440(2) If the resolution is not put to the vote of the accounts meeting, an offence is committed by each existing director.

440(3) It is a defence for a person charged with an offence under subsection (2) to prove that he took all reasonable steps for securing that the resolution was put to the vote of the meeting.

440(4) A person guilty of an offence under this section is liable on summary conviction to a fine not exceeding level 3 on the standard scale.

440(5) In this section–

"**the accounts meeting**" means the general meeting of the company before which the company's annual accounts for the financial year are to be laid; and

"**existing director**" means a person who is a director of the company immediately before that meeting.

Commencement Date – 6 April 2008 applying to accounts and reports for financial years beginning on or after 6 April 2008.

Prospective amendments – The following amendments are made by the Enterprise and Regulatory Reform Act 2013, s. 81(1) and (10), with effect from a day to be appointed by the Secretary of State:

- In s. 440(1), after "section 439(1)" insert "or 439A(1) or (2)";
- In s. 440(1), in the words in brackets, after "report" insert "or policy";
- In s. 440(2), the words "the meeting to which it relates" substituted for "the accounts meeting";
- In s. 440(5), omit the definition of "the accounts meeting".

Chapter 10 – Filing of Accounts and Reports

Duty to file accounts and reports

441 Duty to file accounts and reports with the registrar

441(1) The directors of a company must deliver to the registrar for each financial year the accounts and reports required by–

section 444 (filing obligations of companies subject to small companies regime),

section 444A (filing obligations of companies entitled to small companies exemption in relation to directors' report),

section 445 (filing obligations of medium-sized companies),

section 446 (filing obligations of unquoted companies), or

section 447 (filing obligations of quoted companies).

441(2) This is subject to–

section 448 (unlimited companies exempt from filing obligations), and

section 448A (dormant subsidiaries exempt from filing obligations).

Commencement Date – 6 April 2008 applying to accounts and reports for financial years beginning on or after 6 April 2008.

History – S. 441(2) substituted by SI 2012/2301, reg. 10, with effect from 1 October 2012. Before this substitution, the subsection read:

"**441(2)** This is subject to section 448 (unlimited companies exempt from filing obligations)."

S. 441(4) amended by SI 2008/393, reg. 6(6): 6 April 2008 applying in relation to financial years beginning on or after 6 April 2008.

Notes – This section is modified where a company ceases to be exempt from audit by the Companies (Revision of Defective Accounts and Reports) Regulations 2008 (SI 2008/373).

This section is modified in its application to Overseas Companies by Pt. 5 Delivery Of Accounting Documents: general and Pt. 6 Delivery Of Accounting Documents: credit or financial institutions of the Overseas Companies Regulations 2009 (SI 2009/1801).

This section is modified in its application to LLPs by Pt. 7 Filing Of Accounts And Auditor's Report of the Limited Liability Partnerships (Accounts and Audit) (Application of Companies Act 2006) Regulations 2008 (SI 2008/1911).

442 Period allowed for filing accounts

442(1) This section specifies the period allowed for the directors of a company to comply with their obligation under section 441 to deliver accounts and reports for a financial year to the registrar. This is referred to in the Companies Acts as the "period for filing" those accounts and reports.

442(2) The period is–

(a)   for a private company, nine months after the end of the relevant accounting reference period, and

(b)   for a public company, six months after the end of that period. This is subject to the following provisions of this section.

442(3) If the relevant accounting reference period is the company's first and is a period of more than twelve months, the period is–

(a)   nine months or six months, as the case may be, from the first anniversary of the incorporation of the company, or

(b)   three months after the end of the accounting reference period, whichever last expires.

442(4) If the relevant accounting reference period is treated as shortened by virtue of a notice given by the company under section 392 (alteration of accounting reference date), the period is–

(a)   that applicable in accordance with the above provisions, or

(b)   three months from the date of the notice under that section, whichever last expires.

442(5) Subject to subsection (5A), if for any special reason the Secretary of State thinks fit he may, on an application made before the expiry of the period otherwise allowed, by notice in writing to a company extend that period by such further period as may be specified in the notice.

442(5A) Any such extension must not have the effect of extending the period for filing to more than twelve months after the end of the relevant accounting reference period.

442(6) Whether the period allowed is that for a private company or a public company is determined by reference to the company's status immediately before the end of the relevant accounting reference period.

442(7) In this section **"the relevant accounting reference period"** means the accounting reference period by reference to which the financial year for the accounts in question was determined.

Commencement Date – 6 April 2008 applying to accounts and reports for financial years beginning on or after 6 April 2008.

History – In s. 442(5), the words "Subject to subsection (5A)," inserted by SI 2015/980, reg. 8(2)(a), with effect in relation to–

    (a)   financial years beginning on or after 1 January 2016, and

    (b)   a financial year of a company beginning on or after 1 January 2015, but before 1 January 2016, if the directors of the company so decide.

S. 442(5A) inserted by SI 2015/980, reg. 8(2)(b), with effect in relation to–

    (a)   financial years beginning on or after 1 January 2016, and

    (b)   a financial year of a company beginning on or after 1 January 2015, but before 1 January 2016, if the directors of the company so decide.

Notes – This section is modified in its application to Overseas Companies by Pt. 5 *Delivery Of Accounting Documents: general* and Pt. 6 *Delivery Of Accounting Documents: credit or financial institutions* of the Overseas Companies Regulations 2009 (SI 2009/1801).

This section is modified in its application to LLPs by Pt. 7 *Filing Of Accounts And Auditor's Report* of the Limited Liability Partnerships (Accounts and Audit) (Application of Companies Act 2006) Regulations 2008 (SI 2008/1911).

443 Calculation of period allowed

443(1) This section applies for the purposes of calculating the period for filing a company's accounts and reports which is expressed as a specified number of months from a specified date or after the end of a specified previous period.

443(2) Subject to the following provisions, the period ends with the date in the appropriate month corresponding to the specified date or the last day of the specified previous period.

443(3) If the specified date, or the last day of the specified previous period, is the last day of a month, the period ends with the last day of the appropriate month (whether or not that is the corresponding date).

443(4) If–

    (a)   the specified date, or the last day of the specified previous period, is not the last day of a month but is the 29th or 30th, and

    (b)   the appropriate month is February, the period ends with the last day of February.

443(5) **"The appropriate month"** means the month that is the specified number of months after the month in which the specified date, or the end of the specified previous period, falls.

Commencement Date – 6 April 2008 applying to accounts and reports for financial years beginning on or after 6 April 2008.

Notes – This section is modified in its application to LLPs by Pt. 7 *Filing Of Accounts And Auditor's Report* of the Limited Liability Partnerships (Accounts and Audit) (Application of Companies Act 2006) Regulations 2008 (SI 2008/1911).

Filing obligations of different descriptions of company

444 Filing obligations of companies subject to small companies regime

444(1) The directors of a company subject to the small companies regime–

    (a)   must deliver to the registrar for each financial year a copy of the balance sheet drawn up as at the last day of that year, and

(b)   may also deliver to the registrar–

   (i)   a copy of the company's profit and loss account for that year, and

   (ii)   a copy of the directors' report for that year.

444(2)   Where the directors deliver to the registrar a copy of the company's profit and loss account under subsection (1)(b)(i), the directors must also deliver to the registrar a copy of the auditor's report on the accounts (and any directors' report) that it delivers. This does not apply if the company is exempt from audit and the directors have taken advantage of that exemption.

444(2A)   Where the balance sheet or profit and loss account is abridged pursuant to paragraph 1A of Schedule 1 to the Small Companies and Groups (Accounts and Directors' Report) Regulations (S.I. 2008/409)(11), the directors must also deliver to the registrar a statement by the company that all the members of the company have consented to the abridgement.

444(3)   The copies of accounts and reports delivered to the registrar must be copies of the company's annual accounts and reports.

444(3A)   [Omitted by SI 2015/980, reg. 8(3)(e).]

444(3B)   [Omitted by SI 2015/980, reg. 8(3)(e).]

444(4)   [Omitted by SI 2015/980, reg. 8(3)(e).]

444(5)   Where the directors of a company subject to the small companies regime–

   (a)   do not deliver to the registrar a copy of the company's profit and loss account, or

   (b)   do not deliver to the registrar a copy of the directors' report, the copy of the balance sheet delivered to the registrar must contain in a prominent position a statement that the company's annual accounts and reports have been delivered in accordance with the provisions applicable to companies subject to the small companies regime.

[subsections (6) and (7) as in force from 1 October 2009]

444(5A)   Subject to subsection (5C), where the directors of a company subject to the small companies regime do not deliver to the registrar a copy of the company's profit and loss account–

   (a)   the copy of the balance sheet delivered to the registrar must disclose that fact, and

   (b)   unless the company is exempt from audit and the directors have taken advantage of that exemption, the notes to the balance sheet delivered must satisfy the requirements in subsection (5B).

444(5B)   Those requirements are that the notes to the balance sheet must–

   (a)   state whether the auditor's report was qualified or unqualified,

   (b)   where that report was qualified, disclose the basis of the qualification (reproducing any statement under section 498(2)(a) or (b) or section 498(3), if applicable),

   (c)   where that report was unqualified, include a reference to any matters to which the auditor drew attention by way of emphasis, and

   (d)   state–

      (i)   the name of the auditor and (where the auditor is a firm) the name of the person who signed the auditor's report as senior statutory auditor, or

      (ii)   if the conditions in section 506 (circumstances in which names may be omitted) are met, that a resolution has been passed and notified to the Secretary of State in accordance with that section.

444(5C)   Subsection (5A) does not apply in relation to a company if–

   (a)   the company qualifies as a micro-entity (see sections 384A and 384B) in relation to a financial year, and

(b)   the company's accounts are prepared for that year in accordance with any of the micro-entity provisions.

444(6)   The copies of the balance sheet and any directors' report delivered to the registrar under this section must state the name of the person who signed it on behalf of the board.

444(7)   The copy of the auditor's report delivered to the registrar under this section must–

(a)   state the name of the auditor and (where the auditor is a firm) the name of the person who signed it as senior statutory auditor, or

(b)   if the conditions in section 506 (circumstances in which names may be omitted) are met, state that a resolution has been passed and notified to the Secretary of State in accordance with that section.

Commencement Date – 6 April 2008 applying to accounts and reports for financial years beginning on or after 6 April 2008.

History – In s. 444(1)(a), the words "the balance sheet" substituted for the words "a balance sheet" by SI 2015/980, reg. 8(3)(a), with effect in relation to–

(a)   financial years beginning on or after 1 January 2016, and

(b)   a financial year of a company beginning on or after 1 January 2015, but before 1 January 2016, if the directors of the company so decide.

In s. 444(2), the words "Where the directors deliver to the registrar a copy of the company's profit and loss account under subsection (1)(b)(i)," inserted by SI 2015/980, reg. 8(3)(b), with effect in relation to–

(a)   financial years beginning on or after 1 January 2016, and

(b)   a financial year of a company beginning on or after 1 January 2015, but before 1 January 2016, if the directors of the company so decide.

S. 444(2A) inserted by SI 2015/980, reg. 8(3)(c), with effect in relation to–

(a)   financial years beginning on or after 1 January 2016, and

(b)   a financial year of a company beginning on or after 1 January 2015, but before 1 January 2016, if the directors of the company so decide.

S. 444(3), the words "Subject to subsection (3A)," omitted by SI 2015/980, reg. 8(3)(d), with effect in relation to–

(a)   financial years beginning on or after 1 January 2016, and

(b)   a financial year of a company beginning on or after 1 January 2015, but before 1 January 2016, if the directors of the company so decide.

S. 444(3A)–(4) omitted by SI 2015/980, reg. 8(3)(e), with effect in relation to–

(a)   financial years beginning on or after 1 January 2016, and

(b)   a financial year of a company beginning on or after 1 January 2015, but before 1 January 2016, if the directors of the company so decide.

Former s. 444(3A)–(4) read as follows:

"**444(3A)**   Except where subsection (3B) applies, where a company prepares Companies Act accounts–

(a)   the directors may deliver to the registrar a copy of a balance sheet drawn up in accordance with regulations made by the Secretary of State, and

(b)   there may be omitted from the copy profit and loss account delivered to the registrar such items as may be specified by the regulations.

These are referred to in this Part as "**abbreviated accounts**".

444(3B)   This subsection applies in relation to the Companies Act individual accounts of a company if–

(a)   the company qualifies as a micro-entity (see sections 384A and 384B) in relation to a financial year, and

(b)   those accounts are prepared for that year in accordance with any of the micro-entity provisions.

444(4)   If abbreviated accounts are delivered to the registrar the obligation to deliver a copy of the auditor's report on the accounts is to deliver a copy of the special auditor's report required by section 449."

S. 444(5), the words "deliver to the registrar IAS accounts, or Companies Act accounts that are not abbreviated accounts, and in accordance with this section" omitted by SI 2015/980, reg. 8(3)(f), with effect in relation to–

(a)   financial years beginning on or after 1 January 2016, and

(b)   a financial year of a company beginning on or after 1 January 2015, but before 1 January 2016, if the directors of the company so decide.

S. 444(5A)–(5C) inserted by SI 2015/980, reg. 8(3)(g), with effect in relation to–

(a)   financial years beginning on or after 1 January 2016, and

(b)   a financial year of a company beginning on or after 1 January 2015, but before 1 January 2016, if the directors of the company so decide.

S. 444(2) amended by SI 2008/393, reg. 12: 6 April 2008 applying in relation to financial years beginning on or after 6 April 2008.

S. 444(3) substituted and (3A) and (3B) inserted by SI 2013/3008, reg. 6, with effect from 1 December 2013 in respect of (a) financial years ending on or after 30 September 2013; and (b) companies, which deliver the accounts required by section 444 to the registrar on or after 1 December 2013. Before substitution, subsection (3) read:

"**444(3)**   The copies of accounts and reports delivered to the registrar must be copies of the company's annual accounts and reports, except that where the company prepares Companies Act accounts–

(a)   the directors may deliver to the registrar a copy of a balance sheet drawn up in accordance with regulations made by the Secretary of State, and

(b)   there may be omitted from the copy profit and loss account delivered to the registrar such items as may be specified by the regulations. These are referred to in this Part as "abbreviated accounts"."

Transitional – Transitional adaptations made by SI 2007/3495, Sch. 1, para. 6. S. 444(6), (6A) and (7) as transitionally substituted for s. 444(6) and (7) from 6 April 2008 to 30 September 2009 read as follows:

"**444(6)**   The copy of the balance sheet delivered to the registrar under this section must–

(a)   state the name of the person who signed it on behalf of the board under section 414, and

(b)   be signed on behalf of the board by a director of the company.

444(6A)   The copy of the directors' report delivered to the registrar under this section must–

(a)   state the name of the person who signed it on behalf of the board under section 419, and

(b)   be signed on behalf of the board by a director or the secretary of the company.

444(7)   The copy of the auditor's report delivered to the registrar under this section must–

(a)   state the name of the auditor and (where the auditor is a firm) the name of the person who signed it as senior statutory auditor, and

(b)   be signed by the auditor or (where the auditor is a firm) in the name of the firm by a person authorised to sign on its behalf,

or, if the conditions in section 506 (circumstances in which names may be omitted) are met, state that a resolution has been passed and notified to the Secretary of State in accordance with that section."

Statutory instruments – For regulations under s. 444(3) see the Small Companies and Groups (Accounts and Directors' Report) Regulations 2008 (SI 2008/409).

Notes – This section is modified in its application to LLPs by Pt. 7 *Filing Of Accounts And Auditor's Report* of the Limited Liability Partnerships (Accounts and Audit) (Application of Companies Act 2006) Regulations 2008 (SI 2008/1911).

This section is modified in its application to unregistered companies by the Unregistered Companies Regulations 2009 (SI 2009/2436).

This is subject to the following provisions of SI 2013/3008, reg. 3:

"Disapplication of these regulations to entities to which provisions of the 2006 Act or the 2008 regulations have been applied

3(1)   The amendments made by these Regulations [SI 2013/3008] to any provision of the 2006 Act [CA 2006] or the 2008 Regulations [SI 2008/409] do not have effect in relation to the application of any such provision–

(a)   to qualifying partnerships by regulations 4(1) and 9(1) of and Part 1 of the Schedule to the Partnerships (Accounts) Regulations 2008 (SI 2008/569);

(b)   to limited liability partnerships by the Limited Liability Partnerships (Accounts and Audit) (Application of Companies Act 2006) Regulations 2008 (SI 2008/1911);

(c)   to limited liability partnerships by the Small Limited Liability Partnerships (Accounts) Regulations 2008 (SI 2008/1912);

(d)   to overseas companies by Chapter 3 of Part 5 or Chapter 3 of Part 6 of the Overseas Companies Regulations 2009 (SI 2009/1801);

    (e)   to unregistered companies by regulation 3 of and Schedule 1 to the Unregistered Companies Regulations 2009 (SI 2009/2436); or

    (f)   to companies registered pursuant to section 1040 of the 2006 Act by regulation 18 of the Companies (Companies Authorised to Register) Regulations 2009 (SI 2009/2437).

    3(2) Any new provision of the 2006 Act or the 2008 Regulations inserted by these Regulations is not, by virtue of any provision mentioned in sub-paragraphs (a) to (f) of paragraph (1), applied to the entities mentioned in those sub-paragraphs."

444A Filing obligations of companies entitled to small companies exemption in relation to directors' report

    444A(1) The directors of a company that is entitled to small companies exemption in relation to the directors' report for a financial year–

    (a)   must deliver to the registrar a copy of the company's annual accounts for that year, and

    (b)   may also deliver to the registrar a copy of the directors' report.

    444A(2) The directors must also deliver to the registrar a copy of the auditor's report on the accounts (and any directors' report) that it delivers.

This does not apply if the company is exempt from audit and the directors have taken advantage of that exception.

    444A(3) The copies of the balance sheet and directors' report delivered to the registrar under this section must state the name of the person who signed it on behalf of the board.

    444A(4) The copy of the auditor's report delivered to the registrar under this section must–

    (a)   state the name of the auditor and (where the auditor is a firm) the name of the person who signed it as senior statutory auditor, or

    (b)   if the conditions in section 506 (circumstances in which names may be omitted) are met, state that a resolution has been passed and notified to the Secretary of State in accordance with that section.

    444A(5) This section does not apply to companies within section 444 (filing obligations of companies subject to the small companies regime).

History – S. 444A inserted by SI 2008/393, reg. 6(7): 6 April 2008 applying in relation to financial years beginning on or after 6 April 2008.

S. 444A(4) substituted by SI 2009/1581, reg. 10: 1 October 2009. Previously read as follows:

    "**444A(4)** The copy of the auditor's report delivered to the registrar under this section must–

    (a)   state the name of the auditor and (where the auditor is a firm) the name of the person who signed it as senior statutory auditor, and

    (b)   be signed by the auditor or (where the auditor is a firm) in the name of the firm by a person authorised to sign on its behalf,

or, if the conditions in section 506 (circumstances in which names may be omitted) are met, state that a resolution has been passed and notified to the Secretary of State in accordance with that section."

445 Filing obligations of medium-sized companies

    445(1) The directors of a company that qualifies as a medium-sized company in relation to a financial year (see sections 465 to 467) must deliver to the registrar a copy of–

    (a)   the company's annual accounts,

    (aa)   the strategic report, and

    (b)   the directors' report.

    445(2) They must also deliver to the registrar a copy of the auditor's report on those accounts (and on the strategic report and the directors' report). This does not apply if the company is exempt from audit and the directors have taken advantage of that exemption.

445(3)   [Omitted by SI 2015/980, reg. 8(4).]

445(4)   [Omitted by SI 2015/980, reg. 8(5).]

445(5)   The copies of the balance sheet, strategic report and directors' report delivered to the registrar under this section must state the name of the person who signed it on behalf of the board.

445(6)   The copy of the auditor's report delivered to the registrar under this section must–

(a)   state the name of the auditor and (where the auditor is a firm) the name of the person who signed it as senior statutory auditor, or

(b)   if the conditions in section 506 (circumstances in which names may be omitted) are met, state that a resolution has been passed and notified to the Secretary of State in accordance with that section.

445(7)   This section does not apply to companies within–

(a)   section 444 (filing obligations of companies subject to the small companies regime), or

(b)   section 444A (filing obligations of companies entitled to small companies exemption in relation to directors' report).

Commencement Date – 6 April 2008 applying to accounts and reports for financial years beginning on or after 6 April 2008.

History – S. 445(3) omitted by SI 2015/980, reg. 8(4), with effect in relation to–

(a)   financial years beginning on or after 1 January 2016, and

(b)   a financial year of a company beginning on or after 1 January 2015, but before 1 January 2016, if the directors of the company so decide.

Former s. 445(3) read as follows:

"**445(3)**   Where the company prepares Companies Act accounts, the directors may deliver to the registrar a copy of the company's annual accounts for the financial year–

(a)   that includes a profit and loss account in which items are combined in accordance with regulations made by the Secretary of State, and

(b)   that does not contain items whose omission is authorised by the regulations. These are referred to in this Part as "abbreviated accounts""

S. 445(4) omitted by SI 2015/980, reg. 8(5), with effect in relation to–

(a)   financial years beginning on or after 1 January 2016, and

(b)   a financial year of a company beginning on or after 1 January 2015, but before 1 January 2016, if the directors of the company so decide.

Former s. 445(4) read as follows:

"**445(4)**   If abbreviated accounts are delivered to the registrar the obligation to deliver a copy of the auditor's report on the accounts is to deliver a copy of the special auditor's report required by section 449."

This version of s. 445 applies to financial years ending on or after 30 September 2013. The text of the version applying to financial years ending before 30 September 2013 read as follows:

"445   Filing obligations of medium-sized companies

445(1)   The directors of a company that qualifies as a medium-sized company in relation to a financial year (see sections 465 to 467) must deliver to the registrar a copy of–

(a)   the company's annual accounts, and

(b)   the directors' report.

445(2)   They must also deliver to the registrar a copy of the auditor's report on those accounts (and on the directors' report). This does not apply if the company is exempt from audit and the directors have taken advantage of that exemption.

445(3)   Where the company prepares Companies Act accounts, the directors may deliver to the registrar a copy of the company's annual accounts for the financial year–

(a)   that includes a profit and loss account in which items are combined in accordance with regulations made by the Secretary of State, and

(b)   that does not contain items whose omission is authorised by the regulations. These are referred to in this Part as "abbreviated accounts".

445(4)   If abbreviated accounts are delivered to the registrar the obligation to deliver a copy of the auditor's report on the accounts is to deliver a copy of the special auditor's report required by section 449.

445(5)   The copies of the balance sheet and directors' report delivered to the registrar under this section must state the name of the person who signed it on behalf of the board.

445(6)   The copy of the auditor's report delivered to the registrar under this section must–

(a)   state the name of the auditor and (where the auditor is a firm) the name of the person who signed it as senior statutory auditor, or

(b)   if the conditions in section 506 (circumstances in which names may be omitted) are met, state that a resolution has been passed and notified to the Secretary of State in accordance with that section.

445(7)   This section does not apply to companies within–

(a)   section 444 (filing obligations of companies subject to the small companies regime), or

(b)   section 444A (filing obligations of companies entitled to small companies exemption in relation to directors' report)."

S. 445(7) substituted by SI 2008/393, reg. 6(8): 6 April 2008 applying in relation to financial years beginning on or after 6 April 2008.

Subsection (1)(aa) inserted, "the strategic report and" inserted in subsection (2) and ", strategic report" inserted in subsection (5) by SI 2013/1970, Sch., para. 1 and 9, with effect from 1 October 2013 in respect of financial years ending on or after 30 September 2013.

Statutory instruments – For regulations under this section see the Large and Medium-sized Companies and Groups (Accounts and Reports) Regulations 2008 (SI 2008/410).

Notes – This section is modified in its application to LLPs by Pt. 7 Filing Of Accounts And Auditor's Report of the Limited Liability Partnerships (Accounts and Audit) (Application of Companies Act 2006) Regulations 2008 (SI 2008/1911).

This section is modified in its application to unregistered companies by the Unregistered Companies Regulations 2009 (SI 2009/2436).

446   Filing obligations of unquoted companies

446(1)   The directors of an unquoted company must deliver to the registrar for each financial year of the company a copy of–

(a)   the company's annual accounts,

(aa)   the strategic report,

(b)   the directors' report, and

(c)   any separate corporate governance statement.

446(2)   The directors must also deliver to the registrar a copy of the auditor's report on those accounts (and the strategic report (where this is covered by the auditor's report), the directors' report and any separate corporate governance statement). This does not apply if the company is exempt from audit and the directors have taken advantage of that exemption.

446(3)   The copies of the balance sheet, [strategic report,] directors' report and any separate corporate governance statement delivered to the registrar under this section must state the name of the person who signed it on behalf of the board.

446(4)   The copy of the auditor's report delivered to the registrar under this section must–

(a)   state the name of the auditor and (where the auditor is a firm) the name of the person who signed it as senior statutory auditor, or

(b)   if the conditions in section 506 (circumstances in which names may be omitted) are met, state that a resolution has been passed and notified to the Secretary of State in accordance with that section.

446(5)   This section does not apply to companies within–

(a)   section 444 (filing obligations of companies subject to the small companies regime),

(aa)   section 444A (filing obligations of companies entitled to small companies exemption in relation to directors' report), or

(b)   section 445 (filing obligations of medium-sized companies).

Commencement Date – 6 April 2008 applying to accounts and reports for financial years beginning on or after 6 April 2008.

History – This version of s. 446 applies to financial years ending on or after 30 September 2013. The version applying to financial years ending before 30 September 2013 read as follows:

"446   Filing obligations of unquoted companies

446(1)   The directors of an unquoted company must deliver to the registrar for each financial year of the company a copy of–

(a)   the company's annual accounts,

(b)   the directors' report, and

(c)   any separate corporate governance statement

446(2)   The directors must also deliver to the registrar a copy of the auditor's report on those accounts (and the directors' report and any separate corporate governance statement). This does not apply if the company is exempt from audit and the directors have taken advantage of that exemption.

446(3)   The copies of the balance sheet, directors' report and any separate corporate governance statement delivered to the registrar under this section must state the name of the person who signed it on behalf of the board.

446(4)   The copy of the auditor's report delivered to the registrar under this section must–

(a)   state the name of the auditor and (where the auditor is a firm) the name of the person who signed it as senior statutory auditor, or

(b)   if the conditions in section 506 (circumstances in which names may be omitted) are met, state that a resolution has been passed and notified to the Secretary of State in accordance with that section.

446(5)   This section does not apply to companies within–

(a)   section 444 (filing obligations of companies subject to the small companies regime),

(aa)   section 444A (filing obligations of companies entitled to small companies exemption in relation to directors' report), or

(b)   section 445 (filing obligations of medium-sized companies)."

S. 446(1), (2) and (3) amended by SI 2009/1581, reg. 3: 27 June 2009 applying in relation to financial years beginning on or after 29 June 2008 which have not ended before 27 June 2009.

S. 446(5) amended by SI 2008/393, reg. 6(9): 6 April 2008 applying in relation to financial years beginning on or after 6 April 2008.

Subsection (1)(aa) inserted, "the strategic report (where this is covered by the auditor's report)," inserted in subsection (2) and ", strategic report" inserted in subsection (3) (the punctuation of this insertion has been corrected editorially) by SI 2013/1970, Sch., para. 1 and 10, with effect from 1 October 2013 in respect of financial years ending on or after 30 September 2013.

Transitional – Transitional adaptations made by SI 2007/3495, Sch. 1, para. 8 and SI 2009/1581, reg. 3(4) and (5). S. 446(3), (3A) and (4) as transitionally substituted for s. 446(3) and (4) from 6 April 2008 to 30 September 2009 and s. 446(3B) as transitionally inserted from 27 June 2009 to 30 September 2009 read as follows:

"446(3)   The copy of the balance sheet delivered to the registrar under this section must–

(a)   state the name of the person who signed it on behalf of the board under section 414, and

(b)   be signed on behalf of the board by a director of the company.

446(3A)   The copy of the directors' report delivered to the registrar under this section must–

(a)   state the name of the person who signed it on behalf of the board under section 419, and

(b)   be signed on behalf of the board by a director or the secretary of the company.

446(3B)   The copy of any separate corporate governance statement delivered to the registrar under this section must–

(a)   state the name of the person who signed it on behalf of the board under section 419A, and

(b)   be signed on behalf of the board by a director or the secretary of the company.

446(4) The copy of the auditor's report delivered to the registrar under this section must–

(a) state the name of the auditor and (where the auditor is a firm) the name of the person who signed it as senior statutory auditor, and

(b) be signed by the auditor or (where the auditor is a firm) in the name of the firm by a person authorised to sign on its behalf,

or, if the conditions in section 506 (circumstances in which names may be omitted) are met, state that a resolution has been passed and notified to the Secretary of State in accordance with that section."

Notes – This section is modified in its application to LLPs by Pt. 7 Filing Of Accounts And Auditor's Report of the Limited Liability Partnerships (Accounts and Audit) (Application of Companies Act 2006) Regulations 2008 (SI 2008/1911).

447 Filing obligations of quoted companies

447(1) The directors of a quoted company must deliver to the registrar for each financial year of the company a copy of–

(a) the company's annual accounts,

(b) the directors' remuneration report,

(ba) the strategic report,

(c) the directors' report, and

(d) any separate corporate governance statement.

447(2) They must also deliver a copy of the auditor's report on those accounts (and on the directors' remuneration report, the strategic report (where this is covered by the auditor's report), the directors' report and any separate corporate governance statement).

447(3) The copies of the balance sheet, the directors' remuneration report, [the strategic report,] the directors' report and any separate corporate governance statement delivered to the registrar under this section must state the name of the person who signed it on behalf of the board.

447(4) The copy of the auditor's report delivered to the registrar under this section must –

(a) state the name of the auditor and (where the auditor is a firm) the name of the person who signed it as senior statutory auditor, or

(b) if the conditions in section 506 (circumstances in which names may be omitted) are met, state that a resolution has been passed and notified to the Secretary of State in accordance with that section.

Commencement Date – 6 April 2008 applying to accounts and reports for financial years beginning on or after 6 April 2008.

History – This version of s. 447 applies to financial years ending on or after 30 September 2013. The version applying to financial years ending before 30 September 2013 read as follows:

"447 Filing obligations of quoted companies

447(1) The directors of a quoted company must deliver to the registrar for each financial year of the company a copy of–

(a) the company's annual accounts,

(b) the directors' remuneration report,

(c) the directors' report, and

(d) any separate corporate governance statement.

447(2) They must also deliver a copy of the auditor's report on those accounts (and on the directors' remuneration report, the directors' report and any separate corporate governance statement).

447(3) The copies of the balance sheet, the directors' remuneration report, the directors' report and any separate corporate governance statement delivered to the registrar under this section must state the name of the person who signed it on behalf of the board.

447(4) The copy of the auditor's report delivered to the registrar under this section must–

(a)   state the name of the auditor and (where the auditor is a firm) the name of the person who signed it as senior statutory auditor, or

(b)   if the conditions in section 506 (circumstances in which names may be omitted) are met, state that a resolution has been passed and notified to the Secretary of State in accordance with that section."

S. 447(1), (2) and (3) amended by SI 2009/1581, reg. 4: 27 June 2009 applying in relation to financial years beginning on or after 29 June 2008 which have not ended before 27 June 2009.
S. 447(1)(ba) inserted, "the strategic report (where this is covered by the auditor's report)," inserted in subsection (2) and ", strategic report" inserted in subsection (3) (the punctuation of this insertion has been corrected editorially) by SI 2013/1970, Sch., para. 1 and 11, with effect from 1 October 2013 in respect of financial years ending on or after 30 September 2013.

Transitional – Transitional adaptations made by SI 2007/3495, Sch. 1, para. 9 and SI 2009/1581, reg. 4(4) and (5). S. 447(3), (3A), (3B) and (4) as transitionally substituted for subsections (3) and (4) from 6 April 2008 to 30 September 2009, and s. 447(3C) as transitionally inserted from 27 June 2009 to 30 September 2009, read as follows:

"**447(3)** The copy of the balance sheet delivered to the registrar under this section must–

(a)   state the name of the person who signed it on behalf of the board under section 414, and

(b)   be signed on behalf of the board by a director of the company.

447(3A) The copy of the directors' remuneration report delivered to the registrar under this section must–

(a)   state the name of the person who signed it on behalf of the board under section 422, and

(b)   be signed on behalf of the board by a director or the secretary of the company.

447(3B) The copy of the directors' report delivered to the registrar under this section must–

(a)   state the name of the person who signed it on behalf of the board under section 419, and

(b)   be signed on behalf of the board by a director or the secretary of the company.

447(3C) The copy of any separate corporate governance statement delivered to the registrar under this section must–

(a)   state the name of the person who signed it on behalf of the board under section 419A, and

(b)   be signed on behalf of the board by a director or the secretary of the company.

447(4) The copy of the auditor's report delivered to the registrar under this section must–

(a)   state the name of the auditor and (where the auditor is a firm) the name of the person who signed it as senior statutory auditor, and

(b)   be signed by the auditor or (where the auditor is a firm) in the name of the firm by a person authorised to sign on its behalf,

or, if the conditions in section 506 (circumstances in which names may be omitted) are met, state that a resolution has been passed and notified to the Secretary of State in accordance with that section."

448 Unlimited companies exempt from obligation to file accounts

448(1) The directors of an unlimited company are not required to deliver accounts and reports to the registrar in respect of a financial year if the following conditions are met.

448(2) The conditions are that at no time during the relevant accounting reference period–

(a)   has the company been, to its knowledge, a subsidiary undertaking of an undertaking which was then limited, or

(b)   have there been, to its knowledge, exercisable by or on behalf of two or more undertakings which were then limited, rights which if exercisable by one of them would have made the company a subsidiary undertaking of it, or

(c)   has the company been a parent company of an undertaking which was then limited. The references above to an undertaking being limited at a particular time are to an undertaking (under whatever law established) the liability of whose members is at that time limited.

448(3) The exemption conferred by this section does not apply if–

(a)   the company is a banking or insurance company or the parent company of a banking or insurance group, or

(b)   each of the members of the company is–
   (i) a limited company,
   (ii) another unlimited company each of whose members is a limited company,
   (iii) a Scottish partnership which is not a limited partnership, each of whose members is a limited company, or
   (iv) a Scottish partnership which is a limited partnership, each of whose general partners is a limited company.

The references in paragraph (b) to a limited company, another unlimited company, a Scottish partnership which is not a limited partnership or a Scottish partnership which is a limited partnership include a comparable undertaking incorporated in or formed under the law of a country or territory outside the United Kingdom.

448(4) Where a company is exempt by virtue of this section from the obligation to deliver accounts–

(a)   section 434(3) (requirements in connection with publication of statutory accounts: meaning of **"statutory accounts"**) has effect with the substitution for the words "as required to be delivered to the registrar under section 441" of the words "as prepared in accordance with this Part and approved by the board of directors"; and

(b)   section 435(1)(b) (requirements in connection with publication of nonstatutory accounts: statement whether statutory accounts delivered) has effect with the substitution for the words from "whether statutory accounts" to "have been delivered to the registrar" of the words "that the company is exempt from the requirement to deliver statutory accounts".

448(5) In this section–

"general partner" means–

(a)   in relation to a Scottish partnership which is a limited partnership, a person who is a general partner within the meaning of the *Limited Partnerships Act 1907*; and

(b)   in relation to an undertaking incorporated in or formed under the law of any country or territory outside the United Kingdom and which is comparable to a Scottish partnership which is a limited partnership, a person comparable to such a general partner;

"limited partnership" means a partnership registered under the Limited Partnerships Act 1907; and

the **"relevant accounting reference period"**, in relation to a financial year, means the accounting reference period by reference to which that financial year was determined.

Commencement Date – 6 April 2008 applying to accounts and reports for financial years beginning on or after 6 April 2008.

History – S. 448(3) amended by SI 2008/393, reg. 13: 6 April 2008 applying in relation to financial years beginning on or after 6 April 2008.

S. 448(3) amended by SI 2013/2005, reg. 2(1) and (3)–(6). Subsection (3) as it applied in relation to a financial year of a company beginning before 1 October 2013, read as follows:

"**448(3)** The exemption conferred by this section does not apply if–
(a)   the company is a banking or insurance company or the parent company of a banking or insurance group, or
(b)   each of the members of the company is–
   (i) a limited company,
   (ii) another unlimited company each of whose members is a limited company, or
   (iii) a Scottish partnership each of whose members is a limited company.

The references in paragraph (b) to a limited company, another unlimited company or a Scottish partnership include a comparable undertaking incorporated in or formed under the law of a country or territory outside the United Kingdom."

S. 448(5) amended by SI 2013/2005, reg. 2(1) and (3)–(6). Subsection (5) as it applied in relation to a financial year of a company beginning before 1 October 2013, read as follows:

"**448(5)**   In this section the **"relevant accounting reference period"**, in relation to a financial year, means the accounting reference period by reference to which that financial year was determined."

448A   Dormant subsidiaries exempt from obligation to file accounts

448A(1)   The directors of a company are not required to deliver a copy of the company's individual accounts to the registrar in respect of a financial year if–

(a)   the company is a subsidiary undertaking,

(b)   it has been dormant throughout the whole of that year, and

(c)   its parent undertaking is established under the law of an EEA State.

448A(2)   Exemption is conditional upon compliance with all of the following conditions–

(a)   all members of the company must agree to the exemption in respect of the financial year in question,

(b)   the parent undertaking must give a guarantee under section 448C in respect of that year,

(c)   the company must be included in the consolidated accounts drawn up for that year or to an earlier date in that year by the parent undertaking in accordance with–

(i)   the provisions of Directive 2013/34/EU of the European Parliament and of the Council on the annual financial statements, consolidated financial statements and related reports of certain types of undertakings, or

(ii)   international accounting standards,

(d)   the parent undertaking must disclose in the notes to the consolidated accounts that the directors of the company are exempt from the requirement to deliver a copy of the company's individual accounts to the registrar by virtue of this section, and

(e)   the directors of the company must deliver to the registrar within the period for filing the company's accounts and reports for that year–

(i)   a written notice of the agreement referred to in subsection (2)(a),

(ii)   the statement referred to in section 448C(1),

(iii)   copy of the consolidated accounts referred to in subsection (2)(c),

(iv)   a copy of the auditor's report on those accounts, and

(v)   a copy of the consolidated annual report drawn up by the parent undertaking.

History – S. 448A inserted by SI 2012/2301, reg. 11, with effect from 1 October 2012 and applying to accounts for financial years ending on or after 1 October 2012.

S. 448A(2)(c)(i) substituted by SI 2015/980, reg. 8(6), with effect in relation to–

(a)   financial years beginning on or after 1 January 2016, and

(b)   a financial year of a company beginning on or after 1 January 2015, but before 1 January 2016, if the directors of the company so decide.

448B   Companies excluded from the dormant subsidiaries exemption

The directors of a company are not entitled to the exemption conferred by section 448A (dormant subsidiaries) if the company was at any time within the financial year in question–

(a)   a traded company,

(b)   a company that–

(i) is an authorised insurance company, a banking company, an e-Money issuer, a MiFID investment firm or a UCITS management company, or

(ii) carries on insurance market activity, or

(c) a special register body as defined in section 117(1) of the Trade Union and Labour Relations (Consolidation) Act 1992 (c 52) or an employers' association as defined in section 122 of that Act or Article 4 of the Industrial Relations (Northern Ireland) Order 1992 (S.I. 1992/807) (NI 5).

History – S. 448B inserted by SI 2012/2301, reg. 11, with effect from 1 October 2012 and applying to accounts for financial years ending on or after 1 October 2012.
S. 448B(a) substituted by SI 2015/980, reg. 8(7), with effect in relation to–
(a)   financial years beginning on or after 1 January 2016, and
(b)   a financial year of a company beginning on or after 1 January 2015, but before 1 January 2016, if the directors of the company so decide.

448C Dormant subsidiaries filing exemption: parent undertaking declaration of guarantee

448C(1) A guarantee is given by a parent undertaking under this section when the directors of the subsidiary company deliver to the registrar a statement by the parent undertaking that it guarantees the subsidiary company under this section.

448C(2) The statement under subsection (1) must be authenticated by the parent undertaking and must specify–

(a)   the name of the parent undertaking,

(b)   if the parent undertaking is incorporated in the United Kingdom, its registered number (if any),

(c)   if the parent undertaking is incorporated outside the United Kingdom and registered in the country in which it is incorporated, the identity of the register on which it is registered and the number with which it is so registered,

(d)   the name and registered number of the subsidiary company in respect of which the guarantee is being given,

(e)   the date of the statement, and

(f)   the financial year to which the guarantee relates.

448C(3) A guarantee given under this section has the effect that–

(a)   the parent undertaking guarantees all outstanding liabilities to which the subsidiary company is subject at the end of the financial year to which the guarantee relates, until they are satisfied in full, and

(b)   the guarantee is enforceable against the parent undertaking by any person to whom the subsidiary company is liable in respect of those liabilities.

History – S. 448C inserted by SI 2012/2301, reg. 11, with effect from 1 October 2012 and applying to accounts for financial years ending on or after 1 October 2012.

Requirements where abbreviated accounts delivered

449 Special auditor's report where abbreviated accounts delivered

449 [Omitted by SI 2015/980, reg. 8(8).]

History – S. 449 omitted by SI 2015/980, reg. 8(8), with effect in relation to–
(a)   financial years beginning on or after 1 January 2016, and
(b)   a financial year of a company beginning on or after 1 January 2015, but before 1 January 2016, if the directors of the company so decide.
Former s. 449 read as follows:

"449   Special auditor's report where abbreviated accounts delivered

449(1)   This section applies where–
(a)   the directors of a company deliver abbreviated accounts to the registrar, and
(b)   the company is not exempt from audit (or the directors have not taken advantage of any such exemption).

449(2)   The directors must also deliver to the registrar a copy of a special report of the company's auditor stating that in his opinion–
(a)   the company is entitled to deliver abbreviated accounts in accordance with the section in question, and
(b)   the abbreviated accounts to be delivered are properly prepared in accordance with regulations under that section.

449(3)   The auditor's report on the company's annual accounts need not be delivered, but–
(a)   if that report was qualified, the special report must set out that report in full together with any further material necessary to understand the qualification, and
(b)   if that report contained a statement under–
(i)   section 498(2)(a) or (b) (accounts, records or returns inadequate or accounts not agreeing with records and returns), or
(ii)   section 498(3) (failure to obtain necessary information and explanations), the special report must set out that statement in full.

449(4)   The provisions of–
sections 503 to 506 (signature of auditor's report),
and sections 507 to 509 (offences in connection with auditor's report),
apply to a special report under this section as they apply to an auditor's report on the company's annual accounts prepared under Part 16.

449(4A)   The copy of the special report delivered to the registrar under this section must–
(a)   be signed by the auditor or (where the auditor is a firm) in the name of the firm by a person authorised to sign on its behalf, or
(b)   if the conditions in section 506 (circumstances in which names may be omitted) are met, state that a resolution has been passed and notified to the Secretary of State in accordance with that section.

449(5)   If abbreviated accounts are delivered to the registrar, the references in section 434 or 435 (requirements in connection with publication of accounts) to the auditor's report on the company's annual accounts shall be read as references to the special auditor's report required by this section.

Commencement Date – 6 April 2008 applying to accounts and reports for financial years beginning on or after 6 April 2008.

Transitional – S. 449(4A) inserted transitionally by SI 2007/3495, Sch. 1, para. 10.

Notes – This section is modified in its application to LLPs by Pt. 7 *Filing Of Accounts And Auditor's Report* of the Limited Liability Partnerships (Accounts and Audit) (Application of Companies Act 2006) Regulations 2008 (SI 2008/1911).
This section is modified in its application to unregistered companies by the Unregistered Companies Regulations 2009 (SI 2009/2436)."

450   Approval and signing of abbreviated accounts

450   [Omitted by SI 2015/980, reg. 8(9).]

History – S. 450 omitted by SI 2015/980, reg. 8(9), with effect in relation to–
(a)   financial years beginning on or after 1 January 2016, and
(b)   a financial year of a company beginning on or after 1 January 2015, but before 1 January 2016, if the directors of the company so decide.

Former s. 450 read as follows:

"450   Approval and signing of abbreviated accounts

450(1)   Abbreviated accounts must be approved by the board of directors and signed on behalf of the board by a director of the company.
450(2)   The signature must be on the balance sheet.
450(3)   The balance sheet must contain in a prominent position above the signature a statement to the effect that it is prepared in accordance with the special provisions of this Act

relating (as the case may be) to companies subject to the small companies regime or to medium-sized companies.

450(4) If abbreviated accounts are approved that do not comply with the requirements of regulations under the relevant section, every director of the company who–

(a)   knew that they did not comply, or was reckless as to whether they complied, and

(b)   failed to take reasonable steps to prevent them from being approved, commits an offence.

450(5) A person guilty of an offence under subsection (4) is liable–

(a)   on conviction on indictment, to a fine;

(b)   on summary conviction, to a fine not exceeding the statutory maximum.

Commencement Date –   6 April 2008 applying to accounts and reports for financial years beginning on or after 6 April 2008.

Notes – This section is modified in its application to LLPs by Pt. 7 *Filing Of Accounts And Auditor's Report* of the Limited Liability Partnerships (Accounts and Audit) (Application of Companies Act 2006) Regulations 2008 (SI 2008/1911).

This section is modified in its application to unregistered companies by the Unregistered Companies Regulations 2009 (SI 2009/2436)."

Failure to file accounts and reports

451   Default in filing accounts and reports: offences

451(1) If the requirements of section 441 (duty to file accounts and reports) are not complied with in relation to a company's accounts and reports for a financial year before the end of the period for filing those accounts and reports, every person who immediately before the end of that period was a director of the company commits an offence.

451(2) It is a defence for a person charged with such an offence to prove that he took all reasonable steps for securing that those requirements would be complied with before the end of that period.

451(3) It is not a defence to prove that the documents in question were not in fact prepared as required by this Part.

451(4) A person guilty of an offence under this section is liable on summary conviction to a fine not exceeding level 5 on the standard scale and, for continued contravention, a daily default fine not exceeding one-tenth of the greater of £5,000 or level 4 on the standard scale.

Commencement Date – 6 April 2008 applying to accounts and reports for financial years beginning on or after 6 April 2008.

History – In s. 451(4), the words "one-tenth of the greater of £5,000 or level 4 on the standard scale" substituted for the words "one-tenth of level 5 on the standard scale" by SI 2015/664, Sch. 3, Pt. 1, para. 9(13), with effect from 12 March 2015.

Notes – This section is modified in its application to Overseas Companies by Pt. 5 *Delivery Of Accounting Documents: general* and Pt. 6 *Delivery Of Accounting Documents: credit or financial institutions* of the Overseas Companies Regulations 2009 (SI 2009/1801).

This section is modified in its application to LLPs by Pt. 7 *Filing Of Accounts And Auditor's Report* of the Limited Liability Partnerships (Accounts and Audit) (Application of Companies Act 2006) Regulations 2008 (SI 2008/1911).

452   Default in filing accounts and reports: court order

452(1) If–

(a)   the requirements of section 441 (duty to file accounts and reports) are not complied with in relation to a company's accounts and reports for a financial year before the end of the period for filing those accounts and reports, and

(b)   the directors of the company fail to make good the default within 14 days after the service of a notice on them requiring compliance, the court may, on the application of any member or creditor of the company or of the registrar, make an order directing the directors (or any of them) to make good the default within such time as may be specified in the order.

452(2) The court's order may provide that all costs (in Scotland, expenses) of and incidental to the application are to be borne by the directors.

Commencement Date – 6 April 2008 applying to accounts and reports for financial years beginning on or after 6 April 2008.

Notes – This section is modified in its application to LLPs by Pt. 7 *Filing Of Accounts And Auditor's Report* of the Limited Liability Partnerships (Accounts and Audit) (Application of Companies Act 2006) Regulations 2008 (SI 2008/1911).

453 Civil penalty for failure to file accounts and reports

453(1) Where the requirements of section 441 are not complied with in relation to a company's accounts and reports for a financial year before the end of the period for filing those accounts and reports, the company is liable to a civil penalty. This is in addition to any liability of the directors under section 451.

453(2) The amount of the penalty shall be determined in accordance with regulations made by the Secretary of State by reference to–

    (a)   the length of the period between the end of the period for filing the accounts and reports in question and the day on which the requirements are complied with, and

    (b)   whether the company is a private or public company.

453(3) The penalty may be recovered by the registrar and is to be paid into the Consolidated Fund.

453(4) It is not a defence in proceedings under this section to prove that the documents in question were not in fact prepared as required by this Part.

453(5) Regulations under this section having the effect of increasing the penalty payable in any case are subject to affirmative resolution procedure. Otherwise, the regulations are subject to negative resolution procedure.

Commencement Date – 6 April 2008 applying to accounts and reports for financial years beginning on or after 6 April 2008.

Statutory instruments – For regulations made under this provision see the Companies (Late Filing Penalties) and Limited Liability Partnerships (Filing Periods and Late Filing Penalties) Regulations 2008 (SI 2008/497).

Notes – This section is modified in its application to LLPs by Pt. 7 *Filing Of Accounts And Auditor's Report* of the Limited Liability Partnerships (Accounts and Audit) (Application of Companies Act 2006) Regulations 2008 (SI 2008/1911).

This section is modified in its application to unregistered companies by the Unregistered Companies Regulations 2009 (SI 2009/2436).

Chapter 11 – Revision of Defective Accounts and Reports

Voluntary revision

454 Voluntary revision of accounts etc

454(1) If it appears to the directors of a company that–

    (a)   the company's annual accounts,

    (b)   the directors' remuneration report or the directors' report, or

    (c)   a strategic report of the company,

did not comply with the requirements of this Act (or, where applicable, of Article 4 of the IAS Regulation), they may prepare revised accounts or a revised report or statement.

454(2) Where copies of the previous accounts or report have been sent out to members, delivered to the registrar or (in the case of a public company) laid before the company in general meeting, the revisions must be confined to–

(a) the correction of those respects in which the previous accounts or report did not comply with the requirements of this Act (or, where applicable, of Article 4 of the IAS Regulation), and

(b) the making of any necessary consequential alterations.

454(3) The Secretary of State may make provision by regulations as to the application of the provisions of this Act in relation to–

(a) revised annual accounts,

(b) a revised directors' remuneration report or directors' report, or

(c) a revised strategic report of the company.

454(4) The regulations may, in particular–

(a) make different provision according to whether the previous accounts or report are replaced or are supplemented by a document indicating the corrections to be made;

(b) make provision with respect to the functions of the company's auditor in relation to the revised accounts or report;

(c) require the directors to take such steps as may be specified in the regulations where the previous accounts or report have been–

(i) sent out to members and others under section 423,

(ii) laid before the company in general meeting, or

(iii) delivered to the registrar,

or where a strategic report and supplementary material containing information derived from the previous accounts or report have been sent to members under section 426;

(d) apply the provisions of this Act (including those creating criminal offences) subject to such additions, exceptions and modifications as are specified in the regulations.

454(5) Regulations under this section are subject to negative resolution procedure.

Commencement Date – 6 April 2008 applying to accounts and reports for financial years beginning on or after 6 April 2008.

History – S. 454(1)(c) was substituted by SI 2013/1970, Sch., para. 1 and 12(a), with effect from 1 October 2013 in respect of financial years ending on or after 30 September 2013. Former subs. (1)(c) read as follows:

"(c) a summary financial statement of the company, did not comply with the requirements of this Act (or, where applicable, of Article 4 of the IAS Regulation), they may prepare revised accounts or a revised report or statement."

The following amendments were made by SI 2013/1970, Sch., para. 1 and 12(b) and (c), with effect from 6 August 2013 for the purposes of the exercise of the powers to make regulations in the amended section and, for all other purposes, with effect from 1 October 2013 in respect of financial years ending on or after 30 September 2013:

- subs. (3)(c) substituted; before substitution, para. (c) read::

"(c) a revised summary financial statement."

- in subsection (4)(a), the words "or report" substituted for ", report or statement";
- in subsection (4)(b), the words "or report" substituted for ", report or statement";
- in the closing words of subsection (4)(c), the words "strategic report and supplementary material" substituted for "summary financial statement" and "have" substituted for "has".

Statutory instruments – For regulations under this section see the Companies (Revision of Defective Accounts and Reports) Regulations 2008 (SI 2008/373).

Notes – This section is modified in its application to LLPs by Pt. 8 Revision Of Defective Accounts of the Limited Liability Partnerships (Accounts and Audit) (Application of Companies Act 2006) Regulations 2008 (SI 2008/1911).

This section is modified in its application to unregistered companies by the Unregistered Companies Regulations 2009 (SI 2009/2436).

Secretary of state's notice

455   Secretary of State's notice in respect of accounts or reports

455(1)   This section applies where–

(a)   copies of a company's annual accounts, strategic report or directors' report have been sent out under section 423, or

(b)   a copy of a company's annual accounts, strategic report or directors' report has been delivered to the registrar or (in the case of a public company) laid before the company in general meeting, and it appears to the Secretary of State that there is, or may be, a question whether the accounts or report comply with the requirements of this Act (or, where applicable, of Article 4 of the IAS Regulation).

455(2)   The Secretary of State may give notice to the directors of the company indicating the respects in which it appears that such a question arises or may arise.

455(3)   The notice must specify a period of not less than one month for the directors to give an explanation of the accounts or report or prepare revised accounts or a revised report.

455(4)   If at the end of the specified period, or such longer period as the Secretary of State may allow, it appears to the Secretary of State that the directors have not–

(a)   given a satisfactory explanation of the accounts or report, or

(b)   revised the accounts or report so as to comply with the requirements of this Act (or, where applicable, of Article 4 of the IAS Regulation), the Secretary of State may apply to the court.

455(5)   The provisions of this section apply equally to revised annual accounts, revised strategic reports and revised directors' reports, in which case they have effect as if the references to revised accounts or reports were references to further revised accounts or reports.

Commencement Date – 6 April 2008 applying to accounts and reports for financial years beginning on or after 6 April 2008.

History – This version of s. 455 applies to financial years ending on or after 30 September 2013. The version applying to financial years ending before 30 September 2013 read as follows:

"455   Secretary of State's notice in respect of accounts or reports

455(1)   This section applies where–

(a)   copies of a company's annual accounts or directors' report have been sent out under section 423, or

(b)   a copy of a company's annual accounts or directors' report has been delivered to the registrar or (in the case of a public company) laid before the company in general meeting, and it appears to the Secretary of State that there is, or may be, a question whether the accounts or report comply with the requirements of this Act (or, where applicable, of Article 4 of the IAS Regulation).

455(2)   The Secretary of State may give notice to the directors of the company indicating the respects in which it appears that such a question arises or may arise.

455(3)   The notice must specify a period of not less than one month for the directors to give an explanation of the accounts or report or prepare revised accounts or a revised report.

455(4)   If at the end of the specified period, or such longer period as the Secretary of State may allow, it appears to the Secretary of State that the directors have not–

(a) given a satisfactory explanation of the accounts or report, or

(b) revised the accounts or report so as to comply with the requirements of this Act (or, where applicable, of Article 4 of the IAS Regulation), the Secretary of State may apply to the court.

455(5) The provisions of this section apply equally to revised annual accounts and revised directors' reports, in which case they have effect as if the references to revised accounts or reports were references to further revised accounts or reports."

In s. 455(1)(a) and (b), ", strategic report" inserted and in subsection (5), ", revised strategic reports" inserted by SI 2013/1970, Sch., para. 1 and 13, with effect from 1 October 2013 in respect of financial years ending on or after 30 September 2013.

Notes – This section is modified in its application to LLPs by Pt. 8 Revision Of Defective Accounts of the Limited Liability Partnerships (Accounts and Audit) (Application of Companies Act 2006) Regulations 2008 (SI 2008/1911).

Application to court

456 Application to court in respect of defective accounts or reports [version applying to financial years ending on or after 30 September 2013]

456(1) An application may be made to the court–

(a) by the Secretary of State, after having complied with section 455, or

(b) by a person authorised by the Secretary of State for the purposes of this section, for a declaration (in Scotland, a declarator) that the annual accounts of a company do not comply, or a strategic report or a directors' report does not comply, with the requirements of this Act (or, where applicable, of Article 4 of the IAS Regulation) and for an order requiring the directors of the company to prepare revised accounts or a revised report.

456(2) Notice of the application, together with a general statement of the matters at issue in the proceedings, shall be given by the applicant to the registrar for registration.

456(3) If the court orders the preparation of revised accounts, it may give directions as to–

(a) the auditing of the accounts,

(b) the revision of any directors' remuneration report, strategic report and supplementary material or, directors' report, and

(c) the taking of steps by the directors to bring the making of the order to the notice of persons likely to rely on the previous accounts, and such other matters as the court thinks fit.

456(4) If the court orders the preparation of a revised strategic report or directors' report it may give directions as to–

(a) the review of the report by the auditors,

(b) [repealed]

(c) the taking of steps by the directors to bring the making of the order to the notice of persons likely to rely on the previous report, and

(d) such other matters as the court thinks fit.

456(5) If the court finds that the accounts or report did not comply with the requirements of this Act (or, where applicable, of Article 4 of the IAS Regulation) it may order that all or part of–

(a) the costs (in Scotland, expenses) of and incidental to the application, and

(b) any reasonable expenses incurred by the company in connection with or in consequence of the preparation of revised accounts or a revised report, are to be borne by such of the directors as were party to the approval of the defective accounts or report. For this purpose every director of the company at the time of the approval of the accounts or report shall be taken to have been a party to the approval unless he shows that he took all reasonable steps to prevent that approval.

456(6)   Where the court makes an order under subsection (5) it shall have regard to whether the directors party to the approval of the defective accounts or report knew or ought to have known that the accounts or report did not comply with the requirements of this Act (or, where applicable, of Article 4 of the IAS Regulation), and it may exclude one or more directors from the order or order the payment of different amounts by different directors.

456(7)   On the conclusion of proceedings on an application under this section, the applicant must send to the registrar for registration a copy of the court order or, as the case may be, give notice to the registrar that the application has failed or been withdrawn.

456(8)   The provisions of this section apply equally to revised annual accounts, revised strategic reports and revised directors' reports, in which case they have effect as if the references to revised accounts or reports were references to further revised accounts or reports.

Commencement Date – 6 April 2008 applying to accounts and reports for financial years beginning on or after 6 April 2008.

History – This version of s. 456 applies to financial years ending on or after 30 September 2013. The following amendments were made by SI 2013/1970, Sch., para. 1 and 14, with effect from 1 October 2013 in respect of financial years ending on or after 30 September 2013:

- in the closing words of subsection (1), the words "or a strategic report" inserted before "or a directors' report";
- in subsection (3)(b), the words "strategic report and supplementary material or," inserted after "remuneration report," and "or summary financial statement" omitted;
- in subsection (4), the words "strategic report or" inserted before "directors' report";
- subsection (4)(b) omitted ;
- in subsection (8), the words ", revised strategic reports and revised directors' reports" substituted for "and revised directors' reports".

The version applying to financial years ending before 30 September 2013 read as follows:

"456   Application to court in respect of defective accounts or reports

456(1)   An application may be made to the court–

(a)   by the Secretary of State, after having complied with section 455, or

(b)   by a person authorised by the Secretary of State for the purposes of this section, for a declaration (in Scotland, a declarator) that the annual accounts of a company do not comply, or a directors' report does not comply, with the requirements of this Act (or, where applicable, of Article 4 of the IAS Regulation) and for an order requiring the directors of the company to prepare revised accounts or a revised report.

456(2)   Notice of the application, together with a general statement of the matters at issue in the proceedings, shall be given by the applicant to the registrar for registration.

456(3)   If the court orders the preparation of revised accounts, it may give directions as to–

(a)   the auditing of the accounts,

(b)   the revision of any directors' remuneration report, directors' report or summary financial statement, and

(c)   the taking of steps by the directors to bring the making of the order to the notice of persons likely to rely on the previous accounts, and such other matters as the court thinks fit.

456(4)   If the court orders the preparation of a revised directors' report it may give directions as to–

(a)   the review of the report by the auditors,

(b)   the revision of any summary financial statement,

(c)   the taking of steps by the directors to bring the making of the order to the notice of persons likely to rely on the previous report, and

(d)   such other matters as the court thinks fit.

456(5)   If the court finds that the accounts or report did not comply with the requirements of this Act (or, where applicable, of Article 4 of the IAS Regulation) it may order that all or part of–

(a)   the costs (in Scotland, expenses) of and incidental to the application, and

(b)   any reasonable expenses incurred by the company in connection with or in consequence of the preparation of revised accounts or a revised report, are to be borne by such of the directors as were party to the approval of the defective accounts or report. For this purpose every director of the company at the time of the approval of the accounts or report shall be taken to have been a party to the approval unless he shows that he took all reasonable steps to prevent that approval.

456(6) Where the court makes an order under subsection (5) it shall have regard to whether the directors party to the approval of the defective accounts or report knew or ought to have known that the accounts or report did not comply with the requirements of this Act (or, where applicable, of Article 4 of the IAS Regulation), and it may exclude one or more directors from the order or order the payment of different amounts by different directors.

456(7) On the conclusion of proceedings on an application under this section, the applicant must send to the registrar for registration a copy of the court order or, as the case may be, give notice to the registrar that the application has failed or been withdrawn.

456(8) The provisions of this section apply equally to revised annual accounts and revised directors' reports, in which case they have effect as if the references to revised accounts or reports were references to further revised accounts or reports."

Notes – This section is modified in its application to LLPs by Pt. 8 Revision Of Defective Accounts of the Limited Liability Partnerships (Accounts and Audit) (Application of Companies Act 2006) Regulations 2008 (SI 2008/1911).

457 Other persons authorised to apply to the court

457(1) The Secretary of State may by order (an "authorisation order") authorise for the purposes of section 456 any person appearing to him–

(a)   to have an interest in, and to have satisfactory procedures directed to securing, compliance by companies with the requirements of this Act (or, where applicable, of Article 4 of the IAS Regulation) relating to accounts, strategic reports and directors' reports,

(b)   to have satisfactory procedures for receiving and investigating complaints about companies' annual accounts, strategic reports and directors' reports, and

(c)   otherwise to be a fit and proper person to be authorised.

457(2) A person may be authorised generally or in respect of particular classes of case, and different persons may be authorised in respect of different classes of case.

457(3) The Secretary of State may refuse to authorise a person if he considers that his authorisation is unnecessary having regard to the fact that there are one or more other persons who have been or are likely to be authorised.

457(4) If the authorised person is an unincorporated association, proceedings brought in, or in connection with, the exercise of any function by the association as an authorised person may be brought by or against the association in the name of a body corporate whose constitution provides for the establishment of the association.

457(5) An authorisation order may contain such requirements or other provisions relating to the exercise of functions by the authorised person as appear to the Secretary of State to be appropriate. No such order is to be made unless it appears to the Secretary of State that the person would, if authorised, exercise his functions as an authorised person in accordance with the provisions proposed.

457(6) Where authorisation is revoked, the revoking order may make such provision as the Secretary of State thinks fit with respect to pending proceedings.

457(7) An order under this section is subject to negative resolution procedure.

Commencement Date – 6 April 2008 applying to accounts and reports for financial years beginning on or after 6 April 2008.

History – This version of s. 457 applies to financial years ending on or after 30 September 2013. The version applying to financial years ending before 30 September 2013 read as follows:

"457 Other persons authorised to apply to the court

457(1) The Secretary of State may by order (an "authorisation order") authorise for the purposes of section 456 any person appearing to him–

(a)   to have an interest in, and to have satisfactory procedures directed to securing, compliance by companies with the requirements of this Act (or, where applicable, of Article 4 of the IAS Regulation) relating to accounts and directors' reports,

(b)   to have satisfactory procedures for receiving and investigating complaints about companies' annual accounts and directors' reports, and

(c)   otherwise to be a fit and proper person to be authorised.

457(2) A person may be authorised generally or in respect of particular classes of case, and different persons may be authorised in respect of different classes of case.

457(3) The Secretary of State may refuse to authorise a person if he considers that his authorisation is unnecessary having regard to the fact that there are one or more other persons who have been or are likely to be authorised.

457(4) If the authorised person is an unincorporated association, proceedings brought in, or in connection with, the exercise of any function by the association as an authorised person may be brought by or against the association in the name of a body corporate whose constitution provides for the establishment of the association.

457(5) An authorisation order may contain such requirements or other provisions relating to the exercise of functions by the authorised person as appear to the Secretary of State to be appropriate. No such order is to be made unless it appears to the Secretary of State that the person would, if authorised, exercise his functions as an authorised person in accordance with the provisions proposed.

457(6) Where authorisation is revoked, the revoking order may make such provision as the Secretary of State thinks fit with respect to pending proceedings.

457(7) An order under this section is subject to negative resolution procedure."

In subs. (1)(a) and (b) ", strategic reports" inserted by SI 2013/1970, Sch., para. 1 and 15, with effect from 1 October 2013 in respect of financial years ending on or after 30 September 2013.

Notes – This section is modified in its application to unregistered companies by the Unregistered Companies Regulations 2009 (SI 2009/2436).

458 Disclosure of information by tax authorities

458(1) The Commissioners for Her Majesty's Revenue and Customs may disclose information to a person authorised under section 457 for the purpose of facilitating–

(a)   the taking of steps by that person to discover whether there are grounds for an application to the court under section 456 (application in respect of defective accounts etc), or

(b)   a decision by the authorised person whether to make such an application.

458(2) This section applies despite any statutory or other restriction on the disclosure of information. Provided that, in the case of personal data within the meaning of the Data Protection Act 1998 (c. 29), information is not to be disclosed in contravention of that Act.

458(3) Information disclosed to an authorised person under this section–

(a)   may not be used except in or in connection with–

(i)   taking steps to discover whether there are grounds for an application to the court under section 456, or

(ii)   deciding whether or not to make such an application, or in, or in connection with, proceedings on such an application; and

(b)   must not be further disclosed except–

(i)   to the person to whom the information relates, or

(ii)   in, or in connection with, proceedings on any such application to the court.

458(4) A person who contravenes subsection (3) commits an offence unless–

(a) he did not know, and had no reason to suspect, that the information had been disclosed under this section, or

(b) he took all reasonable steps and exercised all due diligence to avoid the commission of the offence.

458(5) A person guilty of an offence under subsection (4) is liable–

(a) on conviction on indictment, to imprisonment for a term not exceeding two years or a fine (or both);

(b) on summary conviction–

(i) in England and Wales, to imprisonment for a term not exceeding twelve months or to a fine not exceeding the statutory maximum (or both);

(ii) in Scotland or Northern Ireland, to imprisonment for a term not exceeding six months, or to a fine not exceeding the statutory maximum (or both).

458(6) Where an offence under this section is committed by a body corporate, every officer of the body who is in default also commits the offence.

For this purpose–

(a) any person who purports to act as director, manager or secretary of the body is treated as an officer of the body, and

(b) if the body is a company, any shadow director is treated as an officer of the company.

Commencement Date – 6 April 2008 applying to accounts and reports for financial years beginning on or after 6 April 2008.

History – S. 458(6) inserted by SI 2008/948, Sch. 1, para. 244: 6 April 2008.

Notes – This section is modified in its application to LLPs by Pt. 8 *Revision Of Defective Accounts* of the Limited Liability Partnerships (Accounts and Audit) (Application of Companies Act 2006) Regulations 2008 (SI 2008/1911).

Power of authorised person to require documents etc

459 Power of authorised person to require documents, information and explanations

459(1) This section applies where it appears to a person who is authorised under section 457 that there is, or may be, a question whether a company's annual accounts, strategic report or directors' report complies with the requirements of this Act (or, where applicable, of Article 4 of the IAS Regulation).

459(2) The authorised person may require any of the persons mentioned in subsection

459(3) to produce any document, or to provide him with any information or explanations, that he may reasonably require for the purpose of–

(a) discovering whether there are grounds for an application to the court under section 456, or

(b) deciding whether to make such an application.

459(3) Those persons are–

(a) the company;

(b) any officer, employee, or auditor of the company;

(c) any persons who fell within paragraph (b) at a time to which the document or information required by the authorised person relates.

459(4) If a person fails to comply with such a requirement, the authorised person may apply to the court.

459(5)   If it appears to the court that the person has failed to comply with a requirement under subsection (2), it may order the person to take such steps as it directs for securing that the documents are produced or the information or explanations are provided.

459(6)   A statement made by a person in response to a requirement under subsection

459(2)   or an order under subsection (5) may not be used in evidence against him in any criminal proceedings.

459(7)   Nothing in this section compels any person to disclose documents or information in respect of which a claim to legal professional privilege (in Scotland, to confidentiality of communications) could be maintained in legal proceedings.

459(8)   In this section **"document"** includes information recorded in any form.

Commencement Date – 6 April 2008 applying to accounts and reports for financial years beginning on or after 6 April 2008.

History – In subsection (1), ", strategic report or directors' report complies" substituted for "or directors' report comply" by SI 2013/1970, Sch., para. 1 and 16, with effect from 1 October 2013 in respect of financial years ending on or after 30 September 2013.

Notes – This section is modified in its application to LLPs by Pt. 8 *Revision Of Defective Accounts* of the Limited Liability Partnerships (Accounts and Audit) (Application of Companies Act 2006) Regulations 2008 (SI 2008/1911).

460 Restrictions on disclosure of information obtained under compulsory powers

460(1)   This section applies to information (in whatever form) obtained in pursuance of a requirement or order under section 459 (power of authorised person to require documents etc) that relates to the private affairs of an individual or to any particular business.

460(2)   No such information may, during the lifetime of that individual or so long as that business continues to be carried on, be disclosed without the consent of that individual or the person for the time being carrying on that business.

460(3)   This does not apply–

(a)   to disclosure permitted by section 461 (permitted disclosure of information obtained under compulsory powers), or

(b)   to the disclosure of information that is or has been available to the public from another source.

460(4)   A person who discloses information in contravention of this section commits an offence, unless–

(a)   he did not know, and had no reason to suspect, that the information had been disclosed under section 459, or

(b)   he took all reasonable steps and exercised all due diligence to avoid the commission of the offence.

460(5)   A person guilty of an offence under this section is liable–

(a)   on conviction on indictment, to imprisonment for a term not exceeding two years or a fine (or both);

(b)   on summary conviction–

(i)   in England and Wales, to imprisonment for a term not exceeding twelve months or to a fine not exceeding the statutory maximum (or both);

(ii)   in Scotland or Northern Ireland, to imprisonment for a term not exceeding six months, or to a fine not exceeding the statutory maximum (or both).

460(6)   Where an offence under this section is committed by a body corporate, every officer of the body who is in default also commits the offence.

For this purpose–

462 Power to amend categories of permitted disclosure

462(1) The Secretary of State may by order amend section 461(3), (4) and (5).

462(2) An order under this section must not–

(a) amend subsection (3) of that section (UK public authorities) by specifying a person unless the person exercises functions of a public nature (whether or not he exercises any other function);

(b) amend subsection (4) of that section (purposes for which disclosure permitted) by adding or modifying a description of disclosure unless the purpose for which the disclosure is permitted is likely to facilitate the exercise of a function of a public nature;

(c) amend subsection (5) of that section (overseas regulatory authorities) so as to have the effect of permitting disclosures to be made to a body other than one that exercises functions of a public nature in a country or territory outside the United Kingdom.

462(3) An order under this section is subject to negative resolution procedure.

Commencement Date – 6 April 2008 applying to accounts and reports for financial years beginning on or after 6 April 2008.

Chapter 12 – Supplementary Provisions

Liability for false or misleading statements in reports

463 Liability for false or misleading statements in reports

463(1) The reports to which this section applies are–

(a) the strategic report,

(b) the directors' report,

(c) the directors' remuneration report,

(d) [repealed].

463(2) A director of a company is liable to compensate the company for any loss suffered by it as a result of–

(a) any untrue or misleading statement in a report to which this section applies, or

(b) the omission from a report to which this section applies of anything required to be included in it.

463(3) He is so liable only if–

(a) he knew the statement to be untrue or misleading or was reckless as to whether it was untrue or misleading, or

(b) he knew the omission to be dishonest concealment of a material fact.

463(4) No person shall be subject to any liability to a person other than the company resulting from reliance, by that person or another, on information in a report to which this section applies.

463(5) The reference in subsection (4) to a person being subject to a liability includes a reference to another person being entitled as against him to be granted any civil remedy or to rescind or repudiate an agreement.

463(6) This section does not affect–

(a) liability for a civil penalty, or

(b) liability for a criminal offence.

Commencement Date – 20 January 2007.

History – This version of s. 463 applies to financial years ending on or after 30 September 2013. The version applying to financial years ending before 30 September 2013 read as follows:

"463   Liability for false or misleading statements in reports

463(1)   The reports to which this section applies are–
(a)   the directors' report,
(b)   the directors' remuneration report, and
(c)   a summary financial statement so far as it is derived from either of those reports.

463(2)   A director of a company is liable to compensate the company for any loss suffered by it as a result of–
(a)   any untrue or misleading statement in a report to which this section applies, or
(b)   the omission from a report to which this section applies of anything required to be included in it.

463(3)   He is so liable only if–
(a)   he knew the statement to be untrue or misleading or was reckless as to whether it was untrue or misleading, or
(b)   he knew the omission to be dishonest concealment of a material fact.

463(4)   No person shall be subject to any liability to a person other than the company resulting from reliance, by that person or another, on information in a report to which this section applies.

463(5)   The reference in subsection (4) to a person being subject to a liability includes a reference to another person being entitled as against him to be granted any civil remedy or to rescind or repudiate an agreement.

463(6)   This section does not affect–
(a)   liability for a civil penalty, or
(b)   liability for a criminal offence."

Subsection (1)(za) inserted and (1)(c) repealed by SI 2013/1970, Sch., para. 1 and 17, with effect from 1 October 2013 in respect of financial years ending on or after 30 September 2013.

Accounting and reporting standards

464   Accounting standards

464(1)   In this Part **"accounting standards"** means statements of standard accounting practice issued by such body or bodies as may be prescribed by regulations.

464(2)   References in this Part to accounting standards applicable to a company's annual accounts are to such standards as are, in accordance with their terms, relevant to the company's circumstances and to the accounts.

464(3)   Regulations under this section may contain such transitional and other supplementary and incidental provisions as appear to the Secretary of State to be appropriate.

Commencement Date – 6 April 2008 applying to accounts and reports for financial years beginning on or after 6 April 2008.

Notes – This section is modified in its application to LLPs by Pt. 9 *Accounts: Supplementary Provisions* of the Limited Liability Partnerships (Accounts and Audit) (Application of Companies Act 2006) Regulations 2008 (SI 2008/1911).

This section is modified in its application to unregistered companies by the Unregistered Companies Regulations 2009 (SI 2009/2436).

Companies qualifying as medium-sized

465   Companies qualifying as medium-sized: general

465(1)   A company qualifies as medium-sized in relation to its first financial year if the qualifying conditions are met in that year.

465(2)   A company qualifies as medium-sized in relation to a subsequent financial year–

(a)   if the qualifying conditions are met in that year and the preceding financial year;

(b)   if the qualifying conditions are met in that year and the company qualified as medium-sized in relation to the preceding financial year;

(c)   if the qualifying conditions were met in the preceding financial year and the company qualified as medium-sized in relation to that year.

465(3)   The qualifying conditions are met by a company in a year in which it satisfies two or more of the following requirements–

1.	Turnover	Not more than £36 million
2.	Balance sheet total	Not more than £18 million
3.	Number of employees	Not more than 250

465(4)   For a period that is a company's financial year but not in fact a year the maximum figures for turnover must be proportionately adjusted.

465(5)   The balance sheet total means the aggregate of the amounts shown as assets in the company's balance sheet.

465(6)   **"The number of employees"** means the average number of persons employed by the company in the year, determined as follows–

(a)   find for each month in the financial year the number of persons employed under contracts of service by the company in that month (whether throughout the month or not),

(b)   add together the monthly totals, and

(c)   divide by the number of months in the financial year.

465(7)   This section is subject to section 466 (companies qualifying as medium-sized: parent companies).

Commencement Date – 6 April 2008 applying to accounts and reports for financial years beginning on or after 6 April 2008

Any question whether for the purposes of s 465 a company qualified as medium-sized in a financial year beginning before 6 April 2008 is to be determined by reference to the corresponding provisions of the Companies Act 1985 or SI 1986/1032 (NI 6) (SI 2007/3495, Sch. 4, para. 7).

History – S. 465(3) amended by SI 2008/393, reg. 4(1): 6 April 2008 applying in relation to financial years beginning on or after 6 April 2008. In determining whether a company qualifies as medium-sized under s. 465(2) (qualification in relation to subsequent financial year by reference to circumstances in preceding financial years) in relation to a financial year ending on or after 6 April 2008, the company shall be treated as having qualified as medium-sized in any previous financial year in which it would have so qualified if amendments to the same effect as those made by SI 2008/393 had been in force (SI 2008/393, reg. 2(3)).

In s. 465(3), in the table, in item 1, the words "Not more than £36 million" substituted for the words "Not more than £25.9 million" by SI 2015/980, reg. 9(2)(a), with effect in relation to–

(a)   financial years beginning on or after 1 January 2016, and

(b)   a financial year of a company beginning on or after 1 January 2015, but before 1 January 2016, if the directors of the company so decide.

In s. 465(3), in the table, in item 2, the words "Not more than £18 million" substituted for the words "Not more than £12.9 million" by SI 2015/980, reg. 9(2)(b), with effect in relation to–

(a)   financial years beginning on or after 1 January 2016, and

(b)   a financial year of a company beginning on or after 1 January 2015, but before 1 January 2016, if the directors of the company so decide.

Cross references – Any question whether for the purposes of s. 465 a company qualified as medium-sized in a financial year beginning before 6 April 2008 is to be determined by reference to the corresponding provisions of the Companies Act 1985 or SI 1986/1032 (NI 6) (SI 2007/3495, Sch. 4, para. 7).

Notes – This section is modified in its application to LLPs by Pt. 9 *Accounts: Supplementary Provisions* of the Limited Liability Partnerships (Accounts and Audit) (Application of Companies Act 2006) Regulations 2008 (SI 2008/1911).

466   Companies qualifying as medium-sized: parent companies

466(1)   A parent company qualifies as a medium-sized company in relation to a financial year only if the group headed by it qualifies as a medium-sized group.

466(2)   A group qualifies as medium-sized in relation to the parent company's first financial year if the qualifying conditions are met in that year.

466(3)   A group qualifies as medium-sized in relation to a subsequent financial year of the parent company–

(a)   if the qualifying conditions are met in that year and the preceding financial year;

(b)   if the qualifying conditions are met in that year and the group qualified as medium-sized in relation to the preceding financial year;

(c)   if the qualifying conditions were met in the preceding financial year and the group qualified as medium-sized in relation to that year.

466(4)   The qualifying conditions are met by a group in a year in which it satisfies two or more of the following requirements–

1.	Aggregate turnover	Not more than £36 million net (or £43.2 million gross)
2.	Aggregate balance sheet total	Not more than £18 million net (or £21.6 million gross)
3.	Aggregate number of employees	Not more than 250

466(5)   The aggregate figures are ascertained by aggregating the relevant figures determined in accordance with section 465 for each member of the group.

466(6)   In relation to the aggregate figures for turnover and balance sheet total–

"net" means after any set-offs and other adjustments made to eliminate group transactions–

(a)   in the case of Companies Act accounts, in accordance with regulations under section 404,

(b)   in the case of IAS accounts, in accordance with international accounting standards; and

"gross" means without those set-offs and other adjustments. A company may satisfy any relevant requirement on the basis of either the net or the gross figure.

466(7)   The figures for each subsidiary undertaking shall be those included in its individual accounts for the relevant financial year, that is–

(a)   if its financial year ends with that of the parent company, that financial year, and

(b)   if not, its financial year ending last before the end of the financial year of the parent company. If those figures cannot be obtained without disproportionate expense or undue delay, the latest available figures shall be taken.

Commencement Date – 6 April 2008 applying to accounts and reports for financial years beginning on or after 6 April 2008.

History – S. 466(4) amended by SI 2008/393, reg. 4(2): 6 April 2008 applying in relation to financial years beginning on or after 6 April 2008. In determining whether a company or group qualifies as medium-sized under s. 466(3) (qualification in relation to subsequent financial year by reference to circumstances in preceding financial years) in relation to a financial year ending on or after 6 April 2008, the company or group shall be treated as having qualified as medium-sized in any previous financial year in which it would have so qualified if amendments to the same effect as those made by SI 2008/393 had been in force (SI 2008/393, reg. 2(3)).

In s. 466(4), in the table, in item 1, the words "Not more than £36 million net (or £43.2 million gross)" substituted for the words "Not more than £25.9 million net (or £31.1 million gross)" by SI 2015/980, reg. 9(3)(a), with effect in relation to–

    (a)   financial years beginning on or after 1 January 2016, and

    (b)   a financial year of a company beginning on or after 1 January 2015, but before 1 January 2016, if the directors of the company so decide.

In s. 466(4), in the table, in item 2, the words "Not more than £18 million net (or £21.6 million gross)" substituted for the words "Not more than £12.9 million net (or £15.5 million gross)" by SI 2015/980, reg. 9(3)(b), with effect in relation to–

    (a)   financial years beginning on or after 1 January 2016, and

    (b)   a financial year of a company beginning on or after 1 January 2015, but before 1 January 2016, if the directors of the company so decide.

Cross references – Any question whether for the purposes of s. 466 a company or group qualified as medium-sized in a financial year beginning before 6 April 2008 is to be determined by reference to the corresponding provisions of the Companies Act 1985 or SI 1986/1032 (NI 6) (SI 2007/3495, Sch. 4, para. 7).

Notes – This section is modified in its application to LLPs by Pt. 9 *Accounts: Supplementary Provisions* of the Limited Liability Partnerships (Accounts and Audit) (Application of Companies Act 2006) Regulations 2008 (SI 2008/1911).

467 Companies excluded from being treated as medium-sized

467(1) A company is not entitled to take advantage of any of the provisions of this Part relating to companies qualifying as medium-sized if it was at any time within the financial year in question–

    (a)   a public company,

    (b)   a company that–

        (i) has permission under Part 4A of the Financial Services and Markets Act 2000 (c. 8) to carry on a regulated activity, or

        (ii) carries on insurance market activity,

    (ba)   an e-money issuer, or

    (c)   a member of an ineligible group.

467(2) A group is ineligible if any of its members is–

    (a)   a traded company,

    (b)   a body corporate (other than a company) whose shares are admitted to trading on a regulated market,

    (c)   a person (other than a small company) who has permission under Part 4A of the Financial Services and Markets Act 2000 to carry on a regulated activity,

    (ca)   an e-money issuer,

    (d)   a small company that is an authorised insurance company, a banking company, an MiFID investment firm or a UCITS management company, or

    (e)   a person who carries on insurance market activity.

467(3) A company is a small company for the purposes of subsection (2) if it qualified as small in relation to its last financial year ending on or before the end of the financial year in question.

467(4) This section does not prevent a company from taking advantage of section 417(7) (business review: non-financial information) by reason only of its having been a member of an ineligible group at any time within the financial year in question.

Commencement Date – 6 April 2008 applying to accounts and reports for financial years beginning on or after 6 April 2008.

History – S. 467(1) substituted by SI 2013/2005, reg. 2(1) and (7), with effect from 1 September 2013 applying in relation to a financial year of a company beginning on or after 1 October 2013. The text applying in relation to a financial year of a company beginning before 1 October 2013 was as follows:

> "**467(1)**   A company is not entitled to take advantage of any of the provisions of this Part relating to companies qualifying as medium-sized if it was at any time within the financial year in question–
>
> (a)   a public company,
>
> (b)   a company that–
>
> > (i)   has permission under Part 4A of the Financial Services and Markets Act 2000 (c. 8) to carry on a regulated activity, or
> >
> > (ii)   carries on insurance market activity, or
>
> (c)   a member of an ineligible group."

In s. 467(1)(i) and (2)(c), "Part 4A" substituted for "Part 4" by Financial Services Act 2012, Sch. 18, para. 110 and 113, with effect from 1 April 2013.

S. 467(2)(a) substituted by SI 2015/980, reg. 9(4), with effect in relation to–

(a)   financial years beginning on or after 1 January 2016, and

(b)   a financial year of a company beginning on or after 1 January 2015, but before 1 January 2016, if the directors of the company so decide.

S. 467(2)(ca) inserted and, in s. 467(2)(d), "an e-money issuer," repealed by SI 2013/2005, reg. 2(1) and (7), with effect from 1 September 2013 applying in relation to a financial year of a company beginning on or after 1 October 2013. S. 467(2) applying in relation to a financial year of a company beginning before 1 October 2013, read as follows:

> "**467(2)**   A group is ineligible if any of its members is–
>
> (a)   a public company,
>
> (b)   a body corporate (other than a company) whose shares are admitted to trading on a regulated market,
>
> (c)   a person (other than a small company) who has permission under Part 4A of the Financial Services and Markets Act 2000 to carry on a regulated activity,
>
> (d)   a small company that is an authorised insurance company, a banking company, an e-money issuer, an MiFID investment firm or a UCITS management company, or
>
> (e)   a person who carries on insurance market activity."

S. 467(2) amended by SI 2007/2932, reg. 3(1) and (3): 1 November 2007.

S. 467(4) inserted by SI 2008/393, reg. 7: 6 April 2008 applying in relation to financial years beginning on or after 6 April 2008.

Cross references – Any question whether for the purposes of s. 467(3) a company qualified as small in a financial year beginning before 6 April 2008 is to be determined by reference to the corresponding provisions of the Companies Act 1985 or SI 1986/1032 (NI 6) (SI 2007/3495, Sch. 4, para. 7).

Notes – This section is modified in its application to LLPs by Pt. 9 *Accounts: Supplementary Provisions* of the Limited Liability Partnerships (Accounts and Audit) (Application of Companies Act 2006) Regulations 2008 (SI 2008/1911).

General power to make further provision about accounts and reports

468   General power to make further provision about accounts and reports

468(1)   The Secretary of State may make provision by regulations about–

(a)   the accounts and reports that companies are required to prepare;

(b)   the categories of companies required to prepare accounts and reports of any description;

(c)   the form and content of the accounts and reports that companies are required to prepare;

(d)   the obligations of companies and others as regards–

> (i)   the approval of accounts and reports,
>
> (ii)   the sending of accounts and reports to members and others,

>   (iii) the laying of accounts and reports before the company in general meeting,
>
>   (iv) the delivery of copies of accounts and reports to the registrar, and
>
>   (v) the publication of accounts and reports.

468(2) The regulations may amend this Part by adding, altering or repealing provisions.

468(3) But they must not amend (other than consequentially)–

    (a)   section 393 (accounts to give true and fair view), or

    (b)   the provisions of Chapter 11 (revision of defective accounts and reports).

468(4) The regulations may create criminal offences in cases corresponding to those in which an offence is created by an existing provision of this Part. The maximum penalty for any such offence may not be greater than is provided in relation to an offence under the existing provision.

468(5) The regulations may provide for civil penalties in circumstances corresponding to those within section 453(1) (civil penalty for failure to file accounts and reports). The provisions of section 453(2) to (5) apply in relation to any such penalty.

Commencement Date – 20 January 2007 (power to make regulations), 6 April 2008 applying to accounts and reports for financial years beginning on or after 6 April 2008.

Notes – This section is modified in its application to LLPs by Pt. 9 *Accounts: Supplementary Provisions* of the Limited Liability Partnerships (Accounts and Audit) (Application of Companies Act 2006) Regulations 2008 (SI 2008/1911).

Other supplementary provisions

469 Preparation and filing of accounts in euros

469(1) The amounts set out in the annual accounts of a company may also be shown in the same accounts translated into euros.

469(2) When complying with section 441 (duty to file accounts and reports), the directors of a company may deliver to the registrar an additional copy of the company's annual accounts in which the amounts have been translated into euros.

469(3) In both cases–

    (a)   the amounts must have been translated at the exchange rate prevailing on the date to which the balance sheet is made up, and

    (b)   that rate must be disclosed in the notes to the accounts.

469(3A) Subsection (3)(b) does not apply to the Companies Act individual accounts of a company for a financial year in which the company qualifies as a micro-entity (see sections 384A and 384B).

469(4) For the purposes of sections 434 and 435 (requirements in connection with published accounts) any additional copy of the company's annual accounts delivered to the registrar under subsection (2) above shall be treated as statutory accounts of the company. In the case of such a copy, references in those sections to the auditor's report on the company's annual accounts shall be read as references to the auditor's report on the annual accounts of which it is a copy.

Commencement Date – 6 April 2008 applying to accounts and reports for financial years beginning on or after 6 April 2008.

History – Subsection (3A) inserted by SI 2013/3008, reg. 7(1) and (2), with effect from 1 December 2013 in respect of (a) financial years ending on or after 30 September 2013; and (b) companies, which deliver the accounts required by section 444 to the registrar on or after 1 December 2013.

Notes – This section is modified in its application to LLPs by Pt. 9 *Accounts: Supplementary Provisions* of the Limited Liability Partnerships (Accounts and Audit) (Application of Companies Act 2006) Regulations 2008 (SI 2008/1911).
This is subject to the following provisions of SI 2013/3008, reg. 3:

"DISAPPLICATION OF THESE REGULATIONS TO ENTITIES TO WHICH PROVISIONS OF THE 2006 Act OR THE 2008 REGULATIONS HAVE BEEN APPLIED

3(1) The amendments made by these Regulations [SI 2013/3008] to any provision of the 2006 Act [CA 2006] or the 2008 Regulations [SI 2008/409] do not have effect in relation to the application of any such provision–

(a)   to qualifying partnerships by regulations 4(1) and 9(1) of and Part 1 of the Schedule to the Partnerships (Accounts) Regulations 2008 (SI 2008/569);

(b)   to limited liability partnerships by the Limited Liability Partnerships (Accounts and Audit) (Application of Companies Act 2006) Regulations 2008 (SI 2008/1911);

(c)   to limited liability partnerships by the Small Limited Liability Partnerships (Accounts) Regulations 2008 (SI 2008/1912);

(d)   to overseas companies by Chapter 3 of Part 5 or Chapter 3 of Part 6 of the Overseas Companies Regulations 2009 (SI 2009/1801);

(e)   to unregistered companies by regulation 3 of and Schedule 1 to the Unregistered Companies Regulations 2009 (SI 2009/2436); or

(f)   to companies registered pursuant to section 1040 of the 2006 Act by regulation 18 of the Companies (Companies Authorised to Register) Regulations 2009 (SI 2009/2437).

3(2) Any new provision of the 2006 Act or the 2008 Regulations inserted by these Regulations is not, by virtue of any provision mentioned in sub-paragraphs (a) to (f) of paragraph (1), applied to the entities mentioned in those sub-paragraphs."

470 Power to apply provisions to banking partnerships

470(1) The Secretary of State may by regulations apply to banking partnerships, subject to such exceptions, adaptations and modifications as he considers appropriate, the provisions of this Part (and of regulations made under this Part) applying to banking companies.

470(2) A **"banking partnership"** means a partnership which has permission under Part 4A of the Financial Services and Markets Act 2000 (c. 8). But a partnership is not a banking partnership if it has permission to accept deposits only for the purpose of carrying on another regulated activity in accordance with that permission.

470(3) Expressions used in this section that are also used in the provisions regulating activities under the Financial Services and Markets Act 2000 have the same meaning here as they do in those provisions.

See section 22 of that Act, orders made under that section and Schedule 2 to that Act.

470(4) Regulations under this section are subject to affirmative resolution procedure.

Commencement Date – 20 January 2007 (power to make regulations), 6 April 2008 applying to accounts and reports for financial years beginning on or after 6 April 2008.

History – In s. 470(2), "Part 4A" substituted for "Part 4" by Financial Services Act 2012, Sch. 18, para. 110 and 114, with effect from 1 April 2013.

471 Meaning of "annual accounts" and related expressions

471(1) In this Part a company's **"annual accounts"**, in relation to a financial year, means–

(a)   any individual accounts prepared by the company for that year (see section 394), and

(b)   any group accounts prepared by the company for that year (see sections 398 and 399).

This is subject to section 408 (option to omit individual profit and loss account from annual accounts where information notes to the individual balance sheet).

471(2) In the case of an unquoted company, its **"annual accounts and reports"** for a financial year are–

(a) its annual accounts,

(aa) the strategic report (if any),

(b) the directors' report, and

(c) the auditor's report on those accounts, the strategic report (where this is covered by the auditor's report) and the directors' report (unless the company is exempt from audit).

471(3) In the case of a quoted company, its **"annual accounts and reports"** for a financial year are–

(a) its annual accounts,

(b) the directors' remuneration report,

(ba) the strategic report (if any),

(c) the directors' report, and

(d) the auditor's report on those accounts, on the auditable part of the directors' remuneration report, on the strategic report (where this is covered by the auditor's report) and on the directors' report.

Commencement Date – 6 April 2008 applying to accounts and reports for financial years beginning on or after 6 April 2008.

History – S. 471(1)(a) substituted by SI 2012/2301, reg. 18, with effect from 1 October 2012. For financial years ending before 1 October 2012, s. 471(1)(a) read as follows:
"(a)   the company's individual accounts for that year (see section 394), and"

Subsections (2)(aa) and (3)(ba) inserted, in subsection (2)(c), ", the strategic report (where this is covered by the auditor's report)" inserted and, in subsection (3)(d), ", on the strategic report (where this is covered by the auditor's report)" inserted by SI 2013/1970, Sch., para. 1 and 18, with effect from 1 October 2013 in respect of financial years ending on or after 30 September 2013.

In subsection (1), "notes to the individual balance sheet" substituted for "group accounts" by SI 2013/3008, reg. 7(1) and (3), with effect from 1 December 2013 in respect of (a) financial years ending on or after 30 September 2013; and (b) companies, which deliver the accounts required by section 444 to the registrar on or after 1 December 2013.S. 1230(2) substituted by SI 2007/3494, reg. 10, with effect from 6 April 2008.

Notes – This section is modified in its application to Overseas Companies by Pt. 5 *Delivery Of Accounting Documents: general* and Pt. 6 *Delivery Of Accounting Documents: credit or financial institutions* of the Overseas Companies Regulations 2009 (SI 2009/1801).

This section is modified in its application to LLPs by Pt. 9 *Accounts: Supplementary Provisions* of the Limited Liability Partnerships (Accounts and Audit) (Application of Companies Act 2006) Regulations 2008 (SI 2008/1911).

This is subject to the following provisions of SI 2013/3008, reg. 3:

"Disapplication of these regulations to entities to which provisions of the 2006 Act or the 2008 regulations have been applied

3(1) The amendments made by these Regulations [SI 2013/3008] to any provision of the 2006 Act [CA 2006] or the 2008 Regulations [SI 2008/409] do not have effect in relation to the application of any such provision–

(a) to qualifying partnerships by regulations 4(1) and 9(1) of and Part 1 of the Schedule to the Partnerships (Accounts) Regulations 2008 (SI 2008/569);

(b) to limited liability partnerships by the Limited Liability Partnerships (Accounts and Audit) (Application of Companies Act 2006) Regulations 2008 (SI 2008/1911);

(c) to limited liability partnerships by the Small Limited Liability Partnerships (Accounts) Regulations 2008 (SI 2008/1912);

(d) to overseas companies by Chapter 3 of Part 5 or Chapter 3 of Part 6 of the Overseas Companies Regulations 2009 (SI 2009/1801);

(e) to unregistered companies by regulation 3 of and Schedule 1 to the Unregistered Companies Regulations 2009 (SI 2009/2436); or

(f) to companies registered pursuant to section 1040 of the 2006 Act by regulation 18 of the Companies (Companies Authorised to Register) Regulations 2009 (SI 2009/2437).

3(2) Any new provision of the 2006 Act or the 2008 Regulations inserted by these Regulations is not, by virtue of any provision mentioned in sub-paragraphs (a) to (f) of paragraph (1), applied to the entities mentioned in those sub-paragraphs."

472 Notes to the accounts

472(1)   [Omitted by SI 2015/980, reg. 9(5)(a).]

472(1A)   In the case of a company which qualifies as a micro-entity in relation to a financial year (see sections 384A and 384B), the notes to the accounts for that year required by section 413 of this Act and regulation 5A of, and paragraph 57 of Part 3 of Schedule 1 to, the Small Companies and Groups (Accounts and Directors' Report) Regulations 2008 (S.I. 2008/409) must be included at the foot of the balance sheet.

472(2)   References in this Part to a company's annual accounts, or to a balance sheet or profit and loss account, include notes to the accounts giving information which is required by any provision of this Act or international accounting standards, and required or allowed by any such provision to be given in a note to company accounts.

Commencement Date – 6 April 2008 applying to accounts and reports for financial years beginning on or after 6 April 2008.

History – S. 472(1) omitted by SI 2015/980, reg. 9(5)(a), with effect in relation to–
    (a)   financial years beginning on or after 1 January 2016, and
    (b)   a financial year of a company beginning on or after 1 January 2015, but before 1 January 2016, if the directors of the company so decide.

Former s. 472(1) read as follows:
    "**472(1)**   Information required by this Part to be given in notes to a company's annual accounts may be contained in the accounts or in a separate document annexed to the accounts."

S. 472(1A), the word "But" omitted by SI 2015/980, reg. 9(5)(b), with effect in relation to–
    (a)   financial years beginning on or after 1 January 2016, and
    (b)   a financial year of a company beginning on or after 1 January 2015, but before 1 January 2016, if the directors of the company so decide.

S. 472(1A) inserted by SI 2013/3008, reg. 7(1) and (4), with effect from 1 December 2013 in respect of (a) financial years ending on or after 30 September 2013; and (b) companies, which deliver the accounts required by section 444 to the registrar on or after 1 December 2013.

Notes – This section is modified in its application to Overseas Companies by Pt. 5 *Delivery Of Accounting Documents: general* and Pt. 6 *Delivery Of Accounting Documents: credit or financial institutions* of the Overseas Companies Regulations 2009 (SI 2009/1801).

This section is modified in its application to LLPs by Pt. 9 *Accounts: Supplementary Provisions* of the Limited Liability Partnerships (Accounts and Audit) (Application of Companies Act 2006) Regulations 2008 (SI 2008/1911).

This is subject to the following provisions of SI 2013/3008, reg. 3:

"Disapplication of these regulations to entities to which provisions of the 2006 Act or the 2008 regulations have been applied

3(1)   The amendments made by these Regulations [SI 2013/3008] to any provision of the 2006 Act [CA 2006] or the 2008 Regulations [SI 2008/409] do not have effect in relation to the application of any such provision–
    (a)   to qualifying partnerships by regulations 4(1) and 9(1) of and Part 1 of the Schedule to the Partnerships (Accounts) Regulations 2008 (SI 2008/569);
    (b)   to limited liability partnerships by the Limited Liability Partnerships (Accounts and Audit) (Application of Companies Act 2006) Regulations 2008 (SI 2008/1911);
    (c)   to limited liability partnerships by the Small Limited Liability Partnerships (Accounts) Regulations 2008 (SI 2008/1912);
    (d)   to overseas companies by Chapter 3 of Part 5 or Chapter 3 of Part 6 of the Overseas Companies Regulations 2009 (SI 2009/1801);
    (e)   to unregistered companies by regulation 3 of and Schedule 1 to the Unregistered Companies Regulations 2009 (SI 2009/2436); or
    (f)   to companies registered pursuant to section 1040 of the 2006 Act by regulation 18 of the Companies (Companies Authorised to Register) Regulations 2009 (SI 2009/2437).

3(2) Any new provision of the 2006 Act or the 2008 Regulations inserted by these Regulations is not, by virtue of any provision mentioned in sub-paragraphs (a) to (f) of paragraph (1), applied to the entities mentioned in those sub-paragraphs."

472A Meaning of "corporate governance statement" etc

472A(1) In this Part **"corporate governance statement"** means the statement required by rules 7.2.1 to 7.2.11 in the Disclosure Rules and Transparency Rules sourcebook made by the Financial Conduct Authority.

472A(2) Those rules were inserted by Annex C of the Disclosure Rules and Transparency Rules Sourcebook (Corporate Governance Rules) Instrument 2008 made by the Authority on 26th June 2008 (FSA 2008/32).

472A(3) A **"separate"** corporate governance statement means one that is not included in the directors' report.

History – S. 472A inserted by SI 2009/1581, reg. 5: 27 June 2009 applying in relation to financial years beginning on or after 29 June 2008 which have not ended before 27 June 2009.
In subsection (1), "made by the Financial Conduct Authority" substituted for "issued by the Financial Services Authority" by SI 2013/636, Sch., para. 9(1) and (2), with effect from 1 April 2013.

473 Parliamentary procedure for certain regulations under this Part

473(1) This section applies to regulations under the following provisions of this Part–
section 396 (Companies Act individual accounts),
section 404 (Companies Act group accounts),
section 409 (information about related undertakings),
section 412 (information about directors' benefits: remuneration, pensions and compensation for loss of office),
section 416 (contents of directors' report: general),
section 421 (contents of directors' remuneration report),
section 444 (filing obligations of companies subject to small companies regime),
section 445 (filing obligations of medium-sized companies),
section 468 (general power to make further provision about accounts and reports).

473(2) Any such regulations may make consequential amendments or repeals in other provisions of this Act, or in other enactments.

473(3) Regulations that–
(a) restrict the classes of company which have the benefit of any exemption, exception or special provision,
(b) require additional matter to be included in a document of any class, or
(c) otherwise render the requirements of this Part more onerous, are subject to affirmative resolution procedure.

473(4) Otherwise, the regulations are subject to negative resolution procedure.

Commencement Date – 20 January 2007 (power to make regulations), 6 April 2008 applying to accounts and reports for financial years beginning on or after 6 April 2008.

Notes – This section is modified in its application to LLPs by Pt. 9 *Accounts: Supplementary Provisions* of the Limited Liability Partnerships (Accounts and Audit) (Application of Companies Act 2006) Regulations 2008 (SI 2008/1911).

474 Minor definitions

474(1) In this Part–

"e-money issuer" means–

(a)   an electronic money institution, within the meaning of the Electronic Money Regulations 2011 (SI 2011/99), or

(b)   a person who has permission under Part 4A of the Financial Services and Markets Act 2000 (c. 8) to carry on the activity of issuing electronic money within the meaning of article 9B of the Financial Services and Markets Act 2000 (Regulated Activities) Order 2001 (SI 2001/544);

"group" means a parent undertaking and its subsidiary undertakings;

"IAS Regulation" means EC Regulation No. 1606/2002 of the European Parliament and of the Council of 19 July 2002 on the application of international accounting standards;

"included in the consolidation", in relation to group accounts, or

"included in consolidated group accounts", means that the undertaking is included in the accounts by the method of full (and not proportional) consolidation, and references to an undertaking excluded from consolidation shall be construed accordingly;

"international accounting standards" means the international accounting standards, within the meaning of the IAS Regulation, adopted from time to time by the European Commission in accordance with that Regulation;

"micro-entity minimum accounting item" means an item of information required by this Part or by regulations under this Part to be contained in the Companies Act individual accounts of a company for a financial year in relation to which it qualifies as a micro-entity (see sections 384A and 384B);

"micro-entity provisions" means any provisions of this Part, Part 16 or regulations under this Part relating specifically to the individual accounts of a company which qualifies as a micro-entity;

"MiFID investment firm" means an investment firm within the meaning of Article 4.1.1 of Directive 2004/39/EC of the European Parliament and of the Council of 21 April 2004 on markets in financial instruments, other than–

(a)   a company to which that Directive does not apply by virtue of Article 2 of that Directive,

(b)   a company which is an exempt investment firm within the meaning of regulation 4A(3) of the Financial Services and Markets Act 2000 (Markets in Financial Instruments) Regulations 2007, and

(c)   any other company which fulfils all the requirements set out in regulation 4C(3) of those Regulations;

"profit and loss account", in relation to a company that prepares IAS accounts, includes an income statement or other equivalent financial statement required to be prepared by international accounting standards;

"qualified", in relation to an auditor's report, means that the report does not state the auditor's unqualified opinion that the accounts have been properly prepared in accordance with this Act;

"regulated activity" has the meaning given in section 22 of the Financial Services and Markets Act 2000, except that it does not include activities of the kind specified in any of the following provisions of the Financial Services and Markets Act 2000 (Regulated Activities) Order 2001 (S.I. 2001/544)–

(a)   article 25A (arranging regulated mortgage contracts),

(b)   article 25B (arranging regulated home reversion plans),

    (c)   article 25C (arranging regulated home purchase plans),

    (d)   article 25E (arranging regulated sale and rent back agreements),

    (e)   article 39A (assisting administration and performance of a contract of insurance),

    (f)   article 53A (advising on regulated mortgage contracts),

    (g)   article 53B (advising on regulated home reversion plans),

    (h)   article 53C (advising on regulated home purchase plans),

    (i)   article 53D (advising on regulated sale and rent back agreements),

    (j)   article 21 (dealing as agent), article 25 (arranging deals in investments) or article 53 (advising on investments) where the activity concerns relevant investments that are not contractually based investments (within the meaning of article 3 of that Order), or

    (k)   article 64 (agreeing to carry on a regulated activity of the kind mentioned in paragraphs (a) to (h));

"traded company" means a company any of whose transferable securities are admitted to trading on a regulated market;

"turnover", in relation to a company, means the amounts derived from the provision of goods, after deduction of–

    (a)   trade discounts,

    (b)   value added tax, and

    (c)   any other taxes based on the amounts so derived;

"UCITS management company" has the meaning given by the Glossary forming part of the Handbook made by the Financial Conduct Authority under the Financial Services and Markets Act 2000 (c. 8).

    474(2) In the case of an undertaking not trading for profit, any reference in this Part to a profit and loss account is to an income and expenditure account. References to profit and loss and, in relation to group accounts, to a consolidated profit and loss account shall be construed accordingly.

Commencement Date – 6 April 2008 applying to accounts and reports for financial years beginning on or after 6 April 2008.

History – In s. 474(1), the definition of "e-money issuer" substituted by SI 2013/2005, reg. 2(1) and (8), with effect from 1 September 2013 applying in relation to a financial year of a company beginning on or after 1 October 2013. The definition applying in relation to a financial year of a company beginning before 1 October 2013 previously read as follows: "**"e-money issuer"** means a person who has permission under Part 4A of the Financial Services and Markets Act 2000 (c. 8) to carry on the activity of issuing electronic money within the meaning of article 9B of the Financial Services and Markets Act 2000 (Regulated Activities) Order 2001 (S.I. 2001/544);"

S. 474(1) amended by SI 2007/2932, reg. 3(1) and (4): 1 November 2007.

S. 474(1) amended by SI 2009/1342, art. 26: 1 July 2009.

In s. 474(1), in the definition of "e-money issuer", "Part 4A" substituted for "Part 4" by Financial Services Act 2012, Sch. 18, para. 110 and 115, with effect from 1 April 2013.

In s. 474(1) in the definition of "UCITS management company", "Financial Conduct Authority" substituted for "Financial Services Authority" by SI 2013/636, Sch., para. 9(1) and (3), with effect from 1 April 2013.

In s. 474(1), definitions of "micro-entity minimum accounting item" and "micro-entity provisions" inserted by SI 2013/3008, reg. 7(1) and (5), with effect from 1 December 2013 in respect of (a) financial years ending on or after 30 September 2013; and (b) companies, which deliver the accounts required by section 444 to the registrar on or after 1 December 2013.

S. 474(1), the definitions of "qualified" and "traded company" inserted by SI 2015/980, reg. 9(6)(a), with effect in relation to–

    (a)   financial years beginning on or after 1 January 2016, and

    (b)   a financial year of a company beginning on or after 1 January 2015, but before 1 January 2016, if the directors of the company so decide.

In s. 474(1), in the definition of "turnover", the words "falling within the company's ordinary activities" omitted by SI 2015/980, reg. 9(6)(b), with effect in relation to–
   (a)   financial years beginning on or after 1 January 2016, and
   (b)   a financial year of a company beginning on or after 1 January 2015, but before 1 January 2016, if the directors of the company so decide.

Notes – This section is modified in its application to Overseas Companies by Pt. 5 *Delivery Of Accounting Documents: general* and Pt. 6 *Delivery Of Accounting Documents: credit or financial institutions* of the Overseas Companies Regulations 2009 (SI 2009/1801).
This section is modified in its application to LLPs by Pt. 9 *Accounts: Supplementary Provisions* of the Limited Liability Partnerships (Accounts and Audit) (Application of Companies Act 2006) Regulations 2008 (SI 2008/1911).
This is subject to the following provisions of SI 2013/3008, reg. 3:

"Disapplication of these regulations to entities to which provisions of the 2006 Act or the 2008 regulations have been applied

3(1) The amendments made by these Regulations [SI 2013/3008] to any provision of the 2006 Act [CA 2006] or the 2008 Regulations [SI 2008/409] do not have effect in relation to the application of any such provision–
   (a)   to qualifying partnerships by regulations 4(1) and 9(1) of and Part 1 of the Schedule to the Partnerships (Accounts) Regulations 2008 (SI 2008/569);
   (b)   to limited liability partnerships by the Limited Liability Partnerships (Accounts and Audit) (Application of Companies Act 2006) Regulations 2008 (SI 2008/1911);
   (c)   to limited liability partnerships by the Small Limited Liability Partnerships (Accounts) Regulations 2008 (SI 2008/1912);
   (d)   to overseas companies by Chapter 3 of Part 5 or Chapter 3 of Part 6 of the Overseas Companies Regulations 2009 (SI 2009/1801);
   (e)   to unregistered companies by regulation 3 of and Schedule 1 to the Unregistered Companies Regulations 2009 (SI 2009/2436); or
   (f)   to companies registered pursuant to section 1040 of the 2006 Act by regulation 18 of the Companies (Companies Authorised to Register) Regulations 2009 (SI 2009/2437).

3(2) Any new provision of the 2006 Act or the 2008 Regulations inserted by these Regulations is not, by virtue of any provision mentioned in sub-paragraphs (a) to (f) of paragraph (1), applied to the entities mentioned in those sub-paragraphs."